# Translated Texts for Historians

300–800 AD is the time of late antiquity and the early middle ages: the transformation of the classical world, the beginnings of Europe and of Islam, and the evolution of Byzantium. TTH makes available sources from a range of languages, including Greek, Latin, Syriac, Coptic, Arabic, Georgian, Gothic, Armenian, Middle Persian and Mandaic. Each volume provides an expert scholarly translation, with an introduction setting texts and authors in context, and with notes on content, interpretation and debates.

*Editorial Committee*
Phil Booth, St Peter's College, Oxford
Sebastian Brock, Faculty of Asian and Middle Eastern Studies,
    University of Oxford
Averil Cameron, Keble College, Oxford
Marios Costambeys, University of Liverpool
Carlotta Dionisotti, King's College, London
Peter Heather, King's College, London
Julia Hillner, Universität Bonn
Robert Hoyland, Institute for Study of the Ancient World,
    New York University
William E. Klingshirn, The Catholic University of America
Rosalind Love, University of Cambridge
Neil McLynn, Corpus Christi College, Oxford
Richard Price, Royal Holloway, University of London
Claudia Rapp, Institut für Byzantinistik und Neogräzistik,
    Universität Wien
Judith Ryder, University of Oxford
Raymond Van Dam, University of Michigan
Yuhan Sohrab-Dinshaw Vevaina, Faculty of Asian and Middle Eastern
    Studies, University of Oxford
Michael Whitby, University of Birmingham
Ian Wood, University of Leeds

*General Editors*
Gillian Clark, University of Bristol
Mark Humphries, Swansea University
Mary Whitby, University of Oxford

A full list of published titles in the **Translated Texts for Historians** series is available on request. The most recently published are shown below.

**The Canons of the Quinisext Council (691/2)**
Translated with an introduction and notes by RICHARD PRICE
Volume 74, 224pp., ISBN 978-1-78962-236-2 cased ISBN 978-1-78962-813-5 limp

**Jordanes: *Romana* and *Getica***
Translated with an introduction and notes by PETER VAN NUFFELEN and LIEVE VAN HOOF
Volume 75, 480pp., ISBN 978-1-78962-810-4 cased

**Sidonius Apollinaris Complete Poems**
Translated with commentary by RICHARD GREEN
Volume 76, 320pp., ISBN 978-1-800-34859-2 cased

**Codex Epistolaris Carolinus: Letters from the popes to the Frankish rulers, 739–791**
Translated with an introduction and notes by ROSAMOND MCKITTERICK, DORINE VAN ESPELO, RICHARD POLLARD and RICHARD PRICE
Volume 77, 544pp., ISBN 978-1-80034-871-4 cased

**Themistius and Valens: Orations 6–13**
Translated, annotated and introduced by SIMON SWAIN
Volume 78, 414pp., ISBN 978-1-80085-677-6 cased

**The Acts of the Council of Constantinople of 869–70**
Translated by RICHARD PRICE with an introduction and notes by FEDERICO MONTINARO
Volume 79, 520pp., ISBN 978-1-80085-684-4 cased

**Yaḥyā Sām bar Sarwān: The Book of Kings and the Explanations of This World: A Universal History from the Late Sasanian Empire**
Translated with introduction and commentary by CHARLES G. HÄBERL
Volume 80, 320pp., ISBN 978-1-80085-627-1 cased

**The Festal Letters of Athanasius of Alexandria, with the Festal Index and the Historia Acephala**
Translated with commentary by DAVID BRAKKE and DAVID M. GWYNN
Volume 81, 360pp., ISBN 978-1-80207-682-0 cased

**The Letters of Libanius from the Age of Theodosius**
Translated with commentary by SCOTT BRADBURY and DAVID MONCUR
Volume 82, 480pp., ISBN 978-1-80207-683-7 cased

**The Definitive Zoroastrian Critique of Islam: Chapters 11–12 of the *Škand Gumānīg-Wizār* by Mardānfarrox son of Ohrmazddād**
Translated with commentary by CHRISTIAN C. SAHNER
Volume 83, 248pp., ISBN 978-1-80207-852-7 cased

For full details of **Translated Texts for Historians**, including prices and ordering information, please contact: Liverpool University Press, 4 Cambridge Street, Liverpool, L69 7ZU, UK (Tel +44-[0]151-794 2233. Email janet.mcdermott@liverpool.ac.uk, http://www.liverpooluniversitypress.co.uk).

Translated Texts for Historians
Volume 85

# Bede: *Commentary on the Gospel of Luke*

Translated with introduction and notes by
CALVIN B. KENDALL and FAITH WALLIS

Liverpool
University
Press

First published 2023
Liverpool University Press
4 Cambridge Street
Liverpool, L69 7ZU

Copyright © 2023 Calvin B. Kendall and Faith Wallis

Calvin B. Kendall and Faith Wallis have asserted the right to be identified as the authors of this book in accordance with the Copyright, Designs and Patents Act 1988.

All rights reserved. No part of this book may be reproduced stored in a retrieval system, or transmitted, in any form or by any means, electronic, mechanical, photocopying, recording, or otherwise, without the prior written permission of the publisher.

British Library Cataloguing-in-Publication Data
A British Library CIP Record is available.

ISBN 978-1-83764-504-6 (hardback)

Typeset by Carnegie Book Production, Lancaster

# CONTENTS

| | |
|---|---|
| Acknowledgements | vi |
| Abbreviations | vii |
| Introduction | 1 |
| 1  Why did Bede compose a Commentary on Luke? | 1 |
| 2  The structure of *On Luke* | 13 |
| 3  Bede's expository strategies | 23 |
| 4  Key themes in *On Luke* | 56 |
| 5  Bede's style and vocabulary | 71 |
| 6  The manuscripts and the transmission of the text | 72 |
| 7  List of full manuscripts and manuscripts of extracts of Bede's *Commentary on Luke* | 75 |
| 8  Editions of Bede's *Commentary on Luke* | 91 |
| 9  Principles governing the present translation | 92 |
| Bede: *Commentary on the Gospel of Luke* | 93 |
| Prologue | 95 |
| The Chapters of the Gospel According To Luke | 105 |
| Book I | 115 |
| Book II | 221 |
| Book III | 307 |
| Book IV | 393 |
| Book V | 479 |
| Book VI | 569 |
| Appendix 1. Emendations to text of CCSL 120 | 649 |
| Appendix 2. Chapter numbers and Eusebian canon section numbers | 653 |
| Appendix 3. Luke canon section and table numbers with equivalent canon section numbers and modern chapter/verse parallels in Matthew, Mark, and John | 669 |
| Bibliography | 681 |
| Index of Sources | 697 |
| General Index | 725 |

# ACKNOWLEDGEMENTS

Much of the work on this translation was carried out during the global COVID-19 pandemic, when libraries were shut and spirits were low. Thanks, however, to the endless patience and encouragement of Dr Mary Whitby and the editorial board of Translated Texts for Historians, we set our face against both these challenges – against the first by relying on the resources and ingenuity of our respective university libraries, which found ways to make materials available to us electronically when their doors were closed, and against the second by committing ourselves to a steady routine of volleying our drafts back and forth through e-mail, until at last the task was complete. The translation proper is the work of Calvin B. Kendall; the introduction is largely from the pen of Faith Wallis, save for the sections on the structure of the commentary, Bede's style, his debt to the Codex Amiatinus, and the manuscripts of *In Lucam*, which fell to Calvin Kendall's lot. That being said, both of us read, revised, queried, and performed stylistic surgery on every word of the present volume – our third and most ambitious collaborative project for this series. We owe special debts to Dr Peter Darby of the University of Nottingham for his valuable comments on our draft Introduction, and to Dr Michael Lapidge, who read the entire typescript with scrupulous care, and proposed many improvements. Faith Wallis thanks her dear husband Kendall Wallis for his priceless services as in-house research assistant, personal reference librarian, brewer, and 'therapy human'.

# ABBREVIATIONS

| | |
|---|---|
| Ambrose, *Expos. Lucam* | *Expositio Euangelii secundum Lucam* |
| ASE | Anglo-Saxon England |
| Augustine, *Contra aduers.* | *Contra aduersarium legis et prophetarum* |
| —, *De consensu euang.* | *De consensu euangelistarum* |
| —, *In Iohannis euang.* | *In Iohannis euangelium tractatus CXXIV* |
| —, *Quaestiones euang.* | *Quaestiones euangeliorum* |
| —, *Quaestiones xui in Matt.* | *Quaestiones xui in Matthaeum* |
| BAV | Biblioteca Apostolica Vaticana |
| Bede, *DTR* | *De temporum ratione* |
| BLB | Badische Landesbibliothek |
| BN | Bibliothèque nationale |
| BNP | Biblioteca Nacional de Portugal |
| BOH | *Baedae Opera Historica* |
| BOT | *Bedae Opera De Temporibus* |
| BVMM | Bibliothèque virtuelle des manuscrits médiévaux |
| CCSL | Corpus Christianorum series latina |
| CLA | Codices Latini Antiquiores |
| CSEL | Corpus Scriptorum Ecclesiasticorum Latinorum |
| CSS | Cistercian Studies Series |
| D/R | Douay-Rheims translation of the Bible |
| DMLBS | *Dictionary of Medieval Latin from British Sources* |
| DVL | Digital Vatican Library |
| Eusebius, *Hist. eccl.* | *Historia ecclesiastica* |
| GCS | Griechischen christlichen Schriftsteller |
| Isidore, *Etym.* | *Etymologiae* |
| iuxta LXX | According to the Old Latin translation of the Septuagint (the Greek Old Testament); see also below, under Books of the Bible: Psalms |

viii     BEDE: *COMMENTARY ON THE GOSPEL OF LUKE*

| | |
|---|---|
| Gregory, *Hom. in Euang.* | *Homeliae in Euangelia* |
| —, *Hom. in Hiezech.* | *Homeliae in Hiezechielem prophetam* |
| Jerome, *De situ et nom.* | *De situ et nominibus locorum Hebraicorum* |
| —, *Hebr. nom.* | *Liber interpretationis Hebraicorum nominum* |
| KJV | King James Version |
| LCL | Loeb Classical Library |
| MDZ | Münchener Digitalisierungszentrum |
| NRSV | New Revised Standard Version |
| OLD | *Oxford Latin Dictionary* |
| PG | Patrologia Graeca |
| PL | Patrologia Latina |
| SC | Sources chrétiennes |
| TTH | Translated Texts for Historians |
| UB-Graz | Graz, Universitätsbibliothek |
| WDB | Wolfenbüttel, Herzog-August-Bibliothek Digitale Bibliothek |
| Weber/Gryson | *Biblia Sacra Vulgata*, ed. Weber and Gryson |

## BOOKS OF THE BIBLE

N.B.: the four books that are customarily referred to either as 1–4 Kings (D/R), or as 1–2 Samuel and 1–2 Kings (KJV, NRSV), we cite according to the hybrid system used in the running titles of the Weber/Gryson edition of the Vulgate: that is, the first two books will be referred to as 1–2 Samuel and the third and fourth books as 3–4 Kings.

| | |
|---|---|
| Gen. | Genesis |
| Exod. | Exodus |
| Lev. | Leviticus |
| Num. | Numbers |
| Deut. | Deuteronomy |
| Jos. | Joshua |
| Judg. | Judges |
| Ruth | Ruth |
| 1–2 Sam. | 1–2 Samuel |

# ABBREVIATIONS

| | |
|---|---|
| 3–4 Kings | 3–4 Kings |
| 1–2 Chron. | 1–2 Chronicles |
| Job | Job |
| Ps. | Psalms (Bede quotes from *iuxta LXX*, unless otherwise indicated; where the numbering of NRSV differs from the Vulgate numbering, NRSV numbers are given in parentheses) |
| Prov. | Proverbs |
| Eccles. | Ecclesiastes |
| Song | Song of Solomon / Song of Songs |
| Wisd. | Wisdom of Solomon |
| Ecclus. | Ecclesiasticus |
| Isa. | Isaiah |
| Jer. | Jeremiah |
| Lam. | Lamentations |
| Ezek. | Ezekiel |
| Dan. | Daniel |
| Hosea | Hosea |
| Joel | Joel |
| Amos | Amos |
| Micah | Micah |
| Hab. | Habakkuk |
| Hagg. | Haggai |
| Zech. | Zechariah |
| Mal. | Malachi |
| 1–2 Macc. | 1–2 Maccabees |

**New Testament**

| | |
|---|---|
| Matt. | Matthew |
| Mark | Mark |
| Luke | Luke |
| John | John |
| Acts | Acts of the Apostles |
| Rom. | Romans |
| 1–2 Cor. | 1–2 Corinthians |
| Gal. | Galatians |
| Eph. | Ephesians |
| Phil. | Philippians |

| | |
|---|---|
| Col. | Colossians |
| 1–2 Thess. | 1–2 Thessalonians |
| 1–2 Tim. | 1–2 Timothy |
| Titus | Titus |
| Philm. | Philemon |
| Hebr. | Hebrews |
| James | James |
| 1–2 Pet. | 1–2 Peter |
| 1–3 John | 1–3 John |
| Jude | Jude |
| Rev. | Revelation/Apocalypse |

# INTRODUCTION

## 1. WHY DID BEDE COMPOSE A COMMENTARY ON LUKE?

### 1.1 A commission from Acca

In his autobiographical notice at the close of the *Ecclesiastical History*, Bede prefaced the list of his biblical commentaries with the modest claim that they were composed 'for my own benefit and that of my brothers', and that they consisted of 'brief extracts from the works of the venerable fathers' along with 'notes of my own to clarify their sense and interpretation'. Concealed behind this explanation is Bede's originality as an exponent of Scripture.[1] There is no question that he leaned heavily on the works of the Fathers, but only when he could and when he wished to, and he did so on his own terms. Patristic authority was not always available: his very first commentary, on *Revelation*, is a case in point.[2] Even when prior exegesis was abundant (one thinks of *On Genesis*), Bede was both selective and capable of modifying his sources. Moreover, his 'notes' were often substantial passages of original exposition. And, despite his stated intention to 'clarify' the Bible for the sake of his brethren, Bede's commentaries are not necessarily easy reading in terms either of content or of style.[3]

The *Commentary on Luke* was composed sometime after 710, and before 716, because it is mentioned in Bede's prologue to *On First Samuel*, which he was writing when Ceolfrith left Wearmouth-Jarrow for Rome

---

1 Bede's originality as an exegete is now broadly appreciated: it was initially signalled by Jenkins, 'Bede as Exegete and Theologian', 152–200, and more recently by de Margerie, 'Bède le Vénérable', 188, 195; Ray, 'What Do We Know about Bede's Commentaries?', 1–20; Ray, 'Who did Bede Think He Was?', 11–35; and Holder, 'Bede and the New Testament', 142–55.
2 Wallis, trans., *Bede: Commentary on Revelation*, Introduction, 1–38.
3 On the complexities of Bede's style in the commentary on Luke, see below, 71–72, and in his commentaries in general, Sharpe, 'The Varieties of Bede's Prose', 339–55.

that year.⁴ It therefore falls into the early stage of Bede's career, after *On Revelation* (c. 708), around the same time as the first book of *On Genesis*, and certainly after *On Acts* (c. 710) and the commentary on 1 John that became part of *On the Seven Catholic Epistles*. *On Luke*, *On Acts*, *On Genesis*, *On First Samuel*, and *On Ezra and Nehemiah* form a suite of commentaries prefaced by dedicatory letters to Bishop Acca of Hexham. After a long hiatus, one final work was addressed to Acca, *On the Temple* – apparently to console him in his exile (732).⁵ Bede also composed two letter-treatises to Acca explaining Isaiah 24:22 (and refuting the notion of universal salvation) and on the *mansiones* or resting-places, *i.e.*, camps of the Israelites on their journey from Egypt to the promised land.⁶ In addition, his poem on the day of Judgement (*De die iudicii*) was almost certainly composed for Acca.⁷ However, only one other exegetical work by Bede contains a dedication, and that is *On Revelation*, whose preface addresses his fellow monk Hwætberht.

The answer to the question 'why did Bede compose a commentary on Luke?' would thus appear to be answered by Bede himself: he was asked to do so by his diocesan bishop, and asked repeatedly. In an unusual move, Bede includes a letter from Acca as part of his preface, and addresses its content in his own dedicatory epistle.⁸ So behind our initial question lies a second question: why did Acca desire a commentary on Luke? Acca's letter furnishes an apparently straightforward explanation, but Bede's

---

4 Brown, *A Companion to Bede*, 14: 709×716; Brown and Biggs, *Bede*, 2:86: 'around 711'; O'Brien, *Bede's Temple*, xix: 710×716. See also *In Sam*. Prologus 10, line 40; trans. DeGregorio and Love, 103.

5 *On the Temple* was composed to console Acca after he was driven from his see in 731, as recorded in the Moore Continuation of the *Ecclesiastical History*: O'Brien, *Bede's Temple*, 165.

6 *On the Resting Places of the Children of Israel* (*De mansionibus filiorum Israel*) and *On What Isaiah Says* (*De eo quod ait Isaias*) date to about 716: Brown, *Companion to Bede*, 45, 55; both works are translated by Trent Foley and Arthur G. Holder, *Bede: A Biblical Miscellany*. These are epistolary essays in response to queries from Acca, not full commentaries. Bede is also said to have composed verses for a church at Hexham, which referred to Acca: Lapidge, 'Some Remnants of Bede's Lost *Liber epigrammatum*', 804.

7 Ed. and trans. Lapidge, *Bede's Latin Poetry*, 155–79; see also Lapidge's introduction, esp. 35. For an analysis of this poem and its context, see Darby, 'Apocalypse and Reform in Bede's *De die iudicii*'.

8 The letter from Acca has the distinction of being the only surviving text not written by Bede himself to witness that he was noticed by name by any of his contemporaries: Higham, *(Re-)Reading Bede*, 6. To be sure, we owe the letter's survival to Bede's decision to include it in the commentary on Luke, but it stands out for being in the author's own words.

emotional response suggests that the context of Acca's request has to be excavated from between its lines. Moreover, this letter forms part of a longer correspondence.[9]

Acca succeeded Wilfrid as bishop of Hexham in 710,[10] but he and Bede probably knew one another well before this. As a member of Wilfred's inner circle, Acca probably witnessed the moment in 708 when someone accused Bede, apparently in the bishop's presence, of being a heretic. What provoked this charge was the world-chronicle in Bede's *On Times* (c. 703), where Bede broke with the tradition of Eusebius and Jerome by preferring the Vulgate chronology of Old Testament history to the one found in the Septuagint. The Septuagint appeared to date the birth of Christ to *annus mundi* 5199. This date more or less agreed with the established notion that world history unfolded in six ages, the last of which began with the Incarnation, while simultaneously harmonizing with the more controversial but popular idea that each of these six ages was 1,000 years long. That each single age lasted for 1,000 years seemed to be supported by Psalm 89:4, which was quoted in I Peter 3:8. Bede, influenced by Irish scholars as well as the special reverence for the Vulgate in Wearmouth-Jarrow,[11] preferred the chronology of what he called the *hebraica ueritas*. This chronology resulted in a date for the Incarnation of *annus mundi* 3592, which challenged the concept of a world-age equalling 1,000 years, since the Incarnation inaugurated the Sixth Age. At a public assembly and with Bishop Wilfred apparently present, someone accused Bede of claiming that Christ did not become incarnate at the beginning of the Sixth Age. This was equated with heresy and though Wilfrid did not approve of the charge neither did he dismiss it.

When Bede heard about it a mere two days later, he composed an incandescent letter of rebuttal addressed to another member of Wilfrid's entourage named Plegwine.[12] He not only defended his chronology but he

---

9 The analysis presented here is indebted to the study by Stancliffe, 'Bede and Bishop Acca', 171–94, and particularly to her discussion of the preface of the Luke commentary, 178–81.

10 The date of Wilfrid's death (24 April 710) was demonstrated by Levison, *England and the Continent*, 278–79, and recently reaffirmed by Stancliffe, 'Dating Wilfrid's Death'.

11 Irish influence: McCarthy, 'Bede's Primary Source', 157–79; Stancliffe, 'Bede and Bishop Acca', 177; Darby, *Bede and the End of Time*, 21–57. On the Vulgate in Wearmouth, see Stancliffe, 'Bede and Bishop Acca', 183, and literature on the Codex Amiatinus cited below, n. 46.

12 See the analysis of Darby, 'Heresy and Authority in Bede's *Letter to Plegwine*', 145–67; Darby, *Bede and the End of Time*, 35–57; Palmer, *The Apocalypse in the Early Middle Ages*,

4     BEDE: *COMMENTARY ON THE GOSPEL OF LUKE*

turned the tables by accusing his accuser of heresy:[13] if every age were literally 1,000 years long, then everyone would know exactly when the Last Judgement would come – something that Christ denied that anyone, even he, could know.[14] He asked Plegwine to pass his letter 'to our religious and very learned brother David' and ask him to read it before Bishop Wilfred.[15] 'David' may have been Acca, whom Bede praises in *Ecclesiastical History* 5.30 for his musical accomplishments.[16]

Furthermore, in explaining the Vulgate's figures for the lengths of each generation of the Old Testament patriarchs, Bede observes that one entire generation (that of Cainan [Gen. 11:13]) was erroneously inserted into the Second Age by the Seventy Translators. This was corrected by Eusebius, and by Jerome in his Vulgate translation of Genesis. Bede then adds that Luke also followed the Seventy in his genealogy of Christ (Luke 3:34–36), and untactfully remarks that Eusebius's and Jerome's revision 'called into doubt both the Gospel of Luke and the Seventy Translators'.[17] This unfortunate expression must have compounded Bede's troubles, for if the evangelists were inspired by the Holy Spirit, how could Luke be mistaken about Christ's ancestors? Both Eusebius and Jerome had corrected the

---

98–105; Wallis, 'Why Did Bede Write a Commentary on Revelation?', 26–32; Chazelle, 'Debating the End Times with Bede'; Hilliard, 'The Venerable Bede as Scholar, Gentile and Preacher', esp. 103–05 (who sees the heresy episode as informing Bede's self-conscious assertions of orthodoxy in his exegetical works). O'Brien, *Bede's Temple*, argues that the heresy charge was not serious, and that Bede's reaction to it has been exaggerated (142): however, Bede was still defending himself in 725, when he composed the preface to *The Reckoning of Time* (ed. Jones 263–64; trans. Wallis 3–4). Bede also singles out this letter 'on the Six Ages of the World' in his catalogue of his writings (Colgrave and Mynors, eds, *Bede's Ecclesiastical History*, 568–69).

13  This rhetorical and legal strategy of *remotio criminis* has been linked to Bede's indirect or direct exposure to Cicero: Ray, 'Bede and Cicero', 10–11; Darby, 'Heresy and Authority', 154.

14  Bede, *Epistola ad Pleguinam* 14, ed. Jones, 623–4, trans. Wallis, *Bede: The Reckoning of Time*, 412–13.

15  Bede, *Epistola ad Pleguinam* 17, ed. Jones, 627, trans. Wallis, *Bede: The Reckoning of Time*, 415.

16  'Bishop Acca was himself a musician of great experience (*cantator ... peritissimus*) as well as a very learned theologican, untainted in his confession of the catholic faith and thoroughly expert in canon law': Colgrave and Mynors, eds, *Bede's Ecclesiastical History*, 530–31; Stancliffe, 'Bede and Bishop Acca', regards this identification as 'speculative', but agrees that Acca was present as all this was happening at Wilfrid's court (178).

17  Bede, *Epistola ad Pleguinam* 5–6, ed. Jones, 619–20, trans. Wallis, *Bede: The Reckoning of Time*, 408.

INTRODUCTION 5

Septuagint chronology discreetly, and without referring to Luke, so Bede's apparent attack on Luke was not supported by patristic authority. Instead, Bede calls as his witness Augustine's *City of God* 15.11–14, which states that numerals are often incorrectly copied and that, when the Septuagint and Hebrew text diverge, the version in the original language should be preferred. But even here he is skating on thin ice. Elsewhere in *City of God*, Augustine claims that the Holy Spirit inspired the Seventy Translators, and that any discrepancies should be ascribed to the Spirit's decision. He also questioned the value of Jerome's project to translate the Old Testament from the Hebrew, instead of revising the existing Latin translation from the Septuagint.[18] Bede's claim that the chronology of the *hebraica ueritas* was 'recorded by Origen, published by Jerome, praised by Augustine, confirmed by Josephus'[19] is thus somewhat exaggerated.

Whether Plegwine and 'David' complied with Bede's wishes is not known, but if the cloud of heresy continued to hang over Bede, the letter to Plegwine would have poured oil on the fire.

Some at Wearmouth-Jarrow[20] may also have felt that the orthodoxy and learning of their young scholar–monk needed to be clarified in the minds of the episcopal leadership. Shortly after Acca's consecration, and at the prompting of his fellow monk Hwætberht (Eusebius), Bede arranged for a copy of his commentary on Revelation to be sent to the bishop.[21] This commentary insistently refutes any notion that Revelation provides a time-line for the future, and was possibly composed in the immediate aftermath of the episode at Wilfrid's court.[22] But Acca was not satisfied with Revelation; he made it clear from the outset that what he wanted from Bede was a commentary on Luke's Gospel. Again Bede tried to dodge the order, sending the bishop instead his *On the Acts of the Apostles* hastily assembled 'not many days ago' from the author's drafts. Bede's dedicatory letter to this work also reveals that Acca had contacted him several times,

---

18 Stancliffe, 'Bede and Bishop Acca', 182; on the Vulgate, see *De ciuitate Dei* 18.43.
19 Bede, *Epistola ad Pleguinam* 16, ed. Jones, 625, trans. Wallis, *Bede: The Reckoning of Time*, 414.
20 The site commonly referred to in scholarly literature as Wearmouth is now known as Monkwearmouth, a division of modern Sunderland. We have retained the name 'Wearmouth' as more familiar to readers of scholarship on Anglo-Saxon England.
21 Where Abbot Ceolfrith stood on this potentially explosive matter is not known, and he may have deliberately chosen to let others appear to take the initiative.
22 Wallis, trans., *Bede: Commentary on Revelation*, Introduction, 39–51; Wallis, 'Why Did Bede Write a Commentary on Revelation?', 23–45.

admonishing him not to 'dawdle and doze' (an echo of Pope Damasus's rebuke to Jerome when he seemed not to be applying himself to exegesis)[23] but to produce a commentary on Luke. Bede excuses himself for failing to obey, saying that he was 'terrified (*perterritus*)' by the immensity of the task; furthermore, he had been held back by 'troublesome circumstances of which you are very much aware (*obstrepentium causarum, quas tu melius nosti*)'.[24]

The prefatory letter to *On the Acts of the Apostles* proceeds to introduce the author, the evangelist Luke, citing Jerome's statement that he was more familiar with Greek materials than Hebrew sources. But then it brings up the issue of Luke's genealogy of Christ in his Gospel, even though it was not relevant to the Acts.

> It happens accordingly that I am very much amazed, and, struck with overpowering astonishment because of the slowness of my understanding, do not know how to search for an explanation of why, when in the Hebrew Truth (*Hebraica ueritate*) there are found ten generations from the flood down to Abraham, Luke himself (who, being controlled like a pen by the Holy Spirit, could by no means write anything false) chose to put down in his gospel eleven generations, having added Cainan in accordance with the Septuagint.[25]

Bede then drops this subject, and turns to the context in which Luke composed the Acts.

He further attempts to pacify Acca by enclosing his exposition of the first Epistle of John. Acca was not to be put off, though, and his letter to Bede, which Bede included in the preface of *On Luke*, provides some insight into Bede's 'terror' as well as the 'troublesome circumstances'. Apparently Acca had visited Bede personally to encourage him. His letter dismisses Bede's 'terror' at undertaking to comment on a work that already had a patristic

---

23 Stancliffe, 'Bede and Bishop Acca', 183–4; Bede's decision to include both Acca's letter and his own reply may have been inspired by Jerome's *Ep*. 35.1.1 and 36, the latter of which was certainly known to Bede: Lapidge, *The Anglo-Saxon Library*, 217. Acca's questioning of Bede on the interpretation of difficult biblical passages is also reminiscent of Damasus's queries to Jerome.
24 Bede, *Expositio Actuum Apostolorum et Retractatio*, ed. Laistner, CCSL 121:3.11–12 (trans. Wallis); see Wallis, 'Why Did Bede Write a Commentary on Revelation?', 26–27. The reader should be aware that the CCSL edition reprints Laistner's 1939 edition (Cambridge, MA: The Mediaeval Academy of America) but omits Laistner's introduction, which discusses *inter alia* the manuscript tradition of this work.
25 Bede, *Expositio Actuum Apostolorum*, ed. Laistner, CCSL 121:4.7–12; trans. Martin, *The Venerable Bede: Commentary on the Acts of the Apostle*, 4 (slightly modified).

interpreter, Ambrose, particularly if this exposed him to new accusations of 'producing novelties by finding fault with the efforts of men of old'. If Bede wants to 'follow the footsteps of the Fathers' he should look to the examples of Gregory and Augustine, both of whom revisited and revised the works of their predecessors. Augustine himself said that diversity of expression does not amount to divergence of faith. Ambrose may have already composed a commentary, but its style was too demanding for the ordinary reader; even Augustine shared this view. If Bede was concerned about criticism, he should preface his work with Acca's letter to show that he undertook it as an act of obedience. Acca closes by adding an additional reason, almost as an afterthought: Ambrose's commentary omitted certain matters that Bede's profound study of scripture would enable him to address, and Bede owed it to the Church to do so. Though Acca does not enter into specifics, the question of the generations in Luke's genealogy of Christ is undoubtedly what he meant, as Ambrose provided no commentary on this issue. As if to drive the point home, Acca then comments that 'some people' were querying why Bede's *On Revelation* presented a 'novel interpretation' of the four animals of Ezekiel's vision – making the lion a symbol of Matthew and the man the symbol of Mark. In short, Bede was under attack for introducing 'novelties', and had to respond.[26]

It is not easy to discern Bede's relationship to Acca. As a loyal ally of and successor to Wilfrid, was Acca one of the 'Wilfridians' who criticized Bede? Or was he the 'David' whom Bede relied on to plead his case at Wilfrid's court? Acca seems to defy the sharp division that some would make between Wilfrid's style of church government and the traditions of Lindisfarne, as celebrated in Wearmouth-Jarrow by Bede in his lives of Cuthbert and, later, his *Ecclesiastical History*.[27] Clare Stancliffe points out that Bede's account of Acca in the *Ecclesiastical History* credits many of Wilfrid's achievements in architecture, liturgy, and law to Acca, but is silent on Acca's character as a pastor, perhaps even slipping in some veiled contrasts with Aidan and Cuthbert. On the other hand, as Laistner observed, Acca's accomplishments almost exactly replicate those Bede ascribed to Benedict Biscop, in which case the *Ecclesiastical History* account would be highly complimentary.[28] Acca may have hoped to recruit

---

26 Stancliffe, 'Bede and Bishop Acca', 179–80.
27 Hilliard, 'Acca of Hexham through the Eyes of the Venerable Bede', 440–61. He does not discuss the commentary on Luke.
28 Laistner, 'The Library of the Venerable Bede', 238.

Bede as a scholar–theologian, playing Pope Damasus to Bede's Jerome. Hilliard suggests that Bede and Acca shared a vision of Christian education as the engine of Church reform – 'renewal through text'.[29] Hence the bishop 'should probably be seen as a critical, but friendly mediator between Bede and his challenger(s) at Hexham. The eventual appearance of Bede's commentary on Luke justified his faith, and probably won Bede general recognition as a valuable interpreter of Scripture.'[30] In sum, Bede owes his breakthrough as a mature and confident exegete to Acca's prodding.

Bede's reply to Acca, also included in the prologue to *On Luke*, expresses gratitude for Acca's encouragement and implicit promise of protection. He explains his methodology in detail: first, he researched what all the principal Fathers had said about Luke's gospel, taking notes and making extracts on slips of parchment. To avoid constantly repeating their names in the course of the commentary, he devised a system of marginal source marks to indicate which author was being cited, and where the quotation began and ended. 'Where it seemed proper' he added comments of his own. Bede then points out that his identification of the lion with Matthew and the man with Mark in *On Revelation* is in fact taken from Augustine's *On the Harmony of the Gospels*, which he quotes at length 'to repel the false accusations of the complainants you mention in your letter above'. The device of the marginal source-marks was evidently designed to protect him from future charges of 'novelty'.[31]

When Bede comes to confront the question of Luke's chronology in his commentary, he does so with deliberate care and advance preparation. First, he notes the differences between Christ's genealogy as recorded by Matthew and as set out by Luke. Not only do the two evangelists differ on

---

29 Hilliard, 'Acca of Hexham through the Eyes of the Venerable Bede', 452. The notion of renewal through text is deeply embedded in Bede's and Acca's shared monastic identity: see DeGregorio, '*Interpretatio monastica*', 38–53, esp. 52.

30 Stancliffe, 'Bede and Bishop Acca', 185. Bede's relationship with Acca may have suffered strain after 720, when Acca moved to demote Lindisfarne and promote Oswald as the premier Northumbrian saint. It was at this time that Bede accepted a commission from Lindisfarne to rewrite the *vita* of Cuthbert, in a manner calculated to refute Wilfridian criticisms of the saint: Stancliffe, 'Disputed Episcopacy', 7–29.

31 Stansbury, 'Source Marks in Bede's Biblical Commentaries', 383; 'Early-Medieval Commentaries', 70–73. The use of marginal 'quotation marks' and indexing signs is ancient; Bede would have been familiar with some of them from Cassiodorus's *Expositio Psalmorum*: see discussion in Stansbury, 'Source Marks', 386, and 'Early-Medieval Commentaries', 50–58, 63–4, as well as Halporn, 'Methods of Reference in Cassiodorus', 71–91. Source marks are discussed at greater length below, 22–23.

the name of Joseph's father, but Matthew records thirty-eight generations and Luke forty-two. Interestingly, Bede summons the chronographer Julius Africanus (*via* Eusebius) to provide a suitable explanation for the first and quotes Augustine's *Harmony of the Gospels* to resolve the second. Finally he arrives at the generation of Cainan:

> [Luke 3:35–36] **Who was of Shelah, who was of Cainan, who was of Arphaxad,** ... The name and generation of Cainan according to the Hebrew truth [*i.e.*, Vulgate] is found neither in Genesis, nor in Chronicles; but Arphaxad is said to have begotten a son Shelah, or Sale, with no one in between. For, accordingly, you have: *And Arphaxad lived thirty-five years, and begot Sale* [Gen.11:12]. And likewise in Chronicles: *And Arphaxad begot Sale, and Sale begot Heber* [I Chron. 1:18]. You should know, therefore, that the blessed Luke took this genealogy from the edition of the Seventy Interpreters, where it is written that Arphaxad at the age of 135 years begot Cainan, and Cainan himself, when he was 130 years of age, begot Shelah. But which of these is closer to the truth, or whether both can be true, God alone knows. I am simply warning the reader that there is such a great discrepancy in the sequence of time between the two books that from the Flood to the birth of Abraham, 292 years are found to have been reported in the Hebrew Truth, but 1077 years in the translation of the Seventy Interpreters. And now certain chronographers, stepping in as intermediaries, by removing the generation of Cainan alone, and without emending the other years according to the Hebraic exemplar, report this same age as consisting of 942 years.

It seems that Bede has climbed down from the position he took in the *Letter to Plegwine*: he is content to state the facts and resigned to not knowing which account is true. Instead of blaming his own incapacity, however, he states that no human reader can resolve this question, as the answer is known to God alone. By referring to the Vulgate as the Hebrew Truth, however, Bede has tipped his hand.[32] Moreover, this is not the only point of chronological disagreement: the second Age, from the Flood to the birth of Abraham, is longer in the Septuagint by no less than 785 years. Eusebius' elimination of the generation of Cainin only reduces this gap to 650 years. While he did not spell out all the differences between the Vulgate and Septuagint that produced this discrepancy here, or indeed in *On Times*, Bede would laboriously catalogue them all in ch. 66 of *The Reckoning of Time*. So, while the reason why the inspired Evangelist included the generation of Cainan is known to God alone, Bede stands by

---

32  Darby, *Bede and the End of Time*, 46.

his preference for the Vulgate chronology. For good measure, he repeats his opposition to calculating the time of the Second Coming in his exegesis of Luke 17:22–23.[33]

On Luke, then, was conceived in controversy and born in self-defence. And yet it stands out as a milestone in Bede's career. It is, as far as we know, the first work openly addressed to a reading public beyond the walls of Wearmouth-Jarrow (the *Letter to Plegwine* excepted).[34] Compared with the commentaries on Revelation and Acts, *On Luke* is lengthy and discursive, incorporating many substantial extracts from the Fathers: indeed, it is the longest of Bede's commentaries. It is also important to recall that in the early medieval period exegesis was the locus of theology and the principal form of intellectual discourse.[35] The Gospels are the heart of the Christian Bible and their message illuminates all the rest of Scripture, so Bede was committing himself to a singularly ambitious project. Christ's nature as God Incarnate made his every word and deed heavy with hermeneutic weight, as it gave meaning to all that had come before. That nature and those words and deeds were also the core of theological doctrine and the substantial message of all Christian preaching and instruction. A Gospel commentary was therefore a key to all of Scripture and the evidence for the truth of the faith. Even without potential detractors in the wings, Bede had reason to feel 'terrified'.

How he carried out his task can be analysed along two lines: strategic and thematic. Bede deployed the strategies of an exegete to unlock the meaning of the Gospel, but also to make it accessible for use by preachers and teachers.[36] He also made use of some strategies that reflected his personal interests as a historian and as a student of the natural world and the reckoning of time. Secondly, Bede shows a particular interest in certain themes. Some of these, such as the theme of the Temple, he announces; others, such as heresy, or the role of preachers, he weaves into the fabric of the commentary less obviously, but no less insistently.

---

33 See Darby, *Bede and the End of Time*, 83–86, who argues that Bede's insistence on this point here and in other commentaries dedicated to Acca is a distant echo of the Plegwine episode.
34 Darby, 'Heresy and Authority', 148–49.
35 O'Brien, *Bede's Temple*, 2.
36 Holder, 'Bede and the New Testament', 147, 150–52; O'Brien, *Bede's Temple*: Bede's commentaries were directed not only to monks but to 'a clerical audience with pastoral duties to whom Bede provided necessary materials; hence the moral emphasis of Bede's exegesis: the focus on spiritual means which require realization in action' (33).

## 1.2 Author, amanuensis, and scribe

Before considering Bede's literary strategies, however, we should pay attention to what he tells us about the material and physical conditions of authorship under which he worked. In his prefatory letter, Bede claims that he would have fulfilled Acca's commission sooner had he not been obliged to act not only as 'author' but as 'amanuensis, and scribe'.[37] We are reminded here of the economy of literary production in the classical and medieval world. An author might make notes on wax tablets, but the text itself was the product of dictation to a secretary, who would then produce a draft for the author's correction. Once this was done, it could be handed to a scribe to produce a fair copy for distribution. For example, in the prefatory letter to the commentary on Acts, Bede notes that the text of this commentary was prepared for Acca 'not many days ago' and was completed 'as quickly as time permitted in corrected form *from little parchments*' (*emendatum membranulis indideram*).[38] In short, Bede had rushed to review and revise the draft taken down by the *notarius*, which had been written out on scraps of parchment (waste material from the production of formal codices) so that a presentation copy for the bishop could be prepared by the *scriptor*. It was Bede's normal practice (as indeed it was the practice of Cicero and St Paul) to compose aloud to a secretary, who might double as a scribe: even on his deathbed, he composed in this way, and the account of his last days by Cuthbert does not suggest it was exceptional.[39]

Evidently, then, it was unusual for Bede to have to perform all three roles – author, amanuensis, scribe – which is why he could proffer such an excuse for tardiness to Acca, particularly in view of the length of the Luke commentary. Was the normal distribution of labour at Jarrow disrupted for

---

37 His terms are *dictator, notarius*, and *librarius*, which Plummer, 'Bede's Life and Works', interpreted as 'amanuensis, shorthand writer, and copyist' (*BOH* 1: xx). Brown, *A Companion to Bede*, translates variously: 'dictator, stenographer and copyist' (11) or 'author, secretary, and publisher' (60). Both of Brown's suggestions are more correct than Plummer's.

38 Bede, *Expositio Actuum Apostolorum*, ed. Laistner, CCSL 121:3.16–17; trans. Martin, 3 (slightly modified).

39 *Epistola de obitu Bedae*, in Colgrave and Mynors, eds, *Bede's Ecclesiastical History*, 582–84. This passage from the Luke prologue has been interpreted, however, to suggest that Bede himself worked habitually as a scribe, and even worked on the Codex Amiatinus and its sister volumes: see Brown, 'Bede's Life in Context', 11–12. Richard Marsden argues that Bede may have inserted emendations into Amiatinus, but does not identify him as a scribe: '*Manus Bedae*', 65–85.

some reason (perhaps the work on the Codex Amiatinus)?[40] Or was Bede not taking any chances with this particular commentary, because of what was at stake? Was he particularly concerned to supervise every word of this work, from the gathering of research materials to the final copy? This latter explanation finds support in Bede's circumstantial description of his working methods in his reply to Acca, which forms part of the Prologue to *On Luke* – working methods that Acca apparently endorsed, and even prescribed:

> First I gathered together from here and there the most illustrious (so to speak) works of the Fathers and the ones most worthy of so great a task. Then I applied myself conscientiously to examining what the blessed Ambrose, what Augustine, and then what the ever-vigilant Gregory (living up to his name), the apostle of our nation, what Jerome, the expounder of sacred history, and what the other Fathers understood in the words of Luke, and what they said. These I consigned to slips of parchment as you wished (*schedulis ut iussisti*), either verbatim or, for the sake of being concise, in my own words, as I saw fit.

The word *schedula* – a small piece of writing material and, by extension, any (short) document or note committed to such a piece of writing material – is related to the verb *scindere* (to break or cut into pieces, cf. Greek σχίδη), and denotes the trimmings of parchment left over when it is cut to prepare the pages of books. It is tempting to imagine Bede using these *schedulae* as index cards (as indeed they were so employed in the later medieval period, e.g., by the thirteenth-century Dominican Giovanni Balbi in the preparation of the first fully alphabetized Latin dictionary, the *Catholicon*).[41] And it is not impossible that Bede scanned the volumes of the Fathers and made extracts onto *schedulae* of suitable materials that he would later sort into the order of the *lemmata* of Luke's Gospel, much as he gathered extracts from Augustine's works that referred to the Pauline epistles and from Gregory to compose the sixth book of his commentary on

---

40 This is a hypothesis offered by O'Brien, *Bede's Temple*, 202.

41 In medieval usage, the term *scheda/schedula* denoted a single-page document of some kind: see *Dictionary of Medieval Latin from British Sources*, s.v. sceda, schedula. Balbi's definition of *schedula* in the *Catholicon* makes it clear that, physically, *schedulae* were offcuts from the thicker and coarser neck or leg end of the animal skin, which left a rectangular sheet behind. His manipulation of over 14,000 entries of varying lengths into absolute alphabetical order argues strongly for his use of *scedulae* as index cards: see Wallis, *Communis et universalis: The Catholicon of Giovanni Balbi of Genoa, o.p.*, and Flanders, *A Place for Everything*, 167–68.

INTRODUCTION 13

the Song of Songs.[42] However, his insistence that Acca himself prescribed this method seems to point to a different motive, namely ensuring that patristic passages were duly identified and correctly ascribed. Bede goes on:

> Since it was tedious to insert their names individually one at a time and to show in detail what was said by which author, I took the opportunity to inscribe the first letters of their names in the side margin, and by means of these to make known in each case where the words of each of the Fathers which I transcribed begin and where they end, for I am anxious above all that I not be said to steal the statements of my elders, to set them down as if they were my own.

In sum, Bede's meticulous description of his working methods, as well as his unusual adoption of the roles of secretary and scribe as well as author, seem closely connected to the troubled circumstances in which the commentary on Luke was produced. It is also a salutary reminder that medieval authors, as much or more than modern ones, were highly vulnerable to the vagaries of the publication process.

## 2. THE STRUCTURE OF *ON LUKE*

Bede was an educator.[43] He structured *On Luke* not just as a repository of orthodox teachings for the guidance of preachers but as a tool that could lead his readers to patristically endorsed truths of the Bible. He shaped it to this end by surrounding his verse-by-verse commentary with mutually supporting structural devices – a tripartite division of the text of his commentary into books, chapters, and canon sections. The divisions are independent of each other and serve different purposes.

### 2.1 The six-book division of *On Luke*

Bede does not explain what governed his decision to divide *On Luke* into six books. Books 2–6 are all about the same length (between sixty-four and sixty-eight pages in the CCSL edition); Book 1, at eighty pages, is almost one-quarter longer again. In antiquity, when the scroll was the normal

---

42 On extracting and note-taking in classical, patristic, and Late Antique composition, see Stansbury, 'Early-Medieval Commentaries', 51–58; on Bede's practice, 73–75.
43 See Brown, *A Companion to Bede*, 17–32; Kendall, 'Bede and Education', 99–112.

support for a written text, the length of a book was to some degree calibrated to the optimal or maximum size of a scroll, though of course works of literature measured themes and narratives to fit into the framework of 'books'. At the end of Book 1 Bede invokes the traditional trope of closing a book when he feels the reader needs refreshment. However, when the codex replaced the scroll, the 'book' became a purely literary unit, so Bede was in principle free to make as many books as he wished out of Luke (Ambrose, for example, had made ten) and to begin and end them where he wished.

Bede never begins or ends his books in the middle of one of the 'chapters', but, apart from that, he seems to have his own ideas of how the Gospel was structured. Book 1 begins perforce at the beginning, with the conception of John the Baptist, and ends with the Temptation in the Wilderness; in short, it deals with events prior to the beginning of Christ's ministry. Luke surpasses the other evangelists in his attention to this preparatory narrative, and the opening chapters of his Gospel are also filled with rich passages of theological poetry, from the Song of Zechariah to the Song of Simeon. This invites the detailed exposition that makes Bede's Book 1 more extensive than the others. But we should also factor in Bede's personal interest in passages such as the genealogy of Christ (Luke 3:23–38).

With the opening of Book 2, Bede starts to inform his readers of the rationale behind his structure. Book 2 covers the beginning of Jesus's ministry up to the mission of the disciples, but the opening paragraph explains that these parameters were chosen to reflect Luke's special contribution to the history of Christ, in that the other evangelists said relatively less about the beginning of his ministry. Book 3 turns to the events of the Passion, starting with the dinner in the house of Simon the Pharisee and building up to Christ's teaching of the Lord's Prayer and the parable of the man who roused his neighbour at midnight. Bede explains in his opening remarks that this apparent turning point in the narrative is in fact woven into the end of the second book. At the outset of Book 4, Bede's preface changes tone to become less expository and more homiletic, bridging the intensifying narrative of the Passion to the final episode of Book 3, with its message of 'Ask and you will receive'. Book 4 starts with the Pharisees accusing Jesus of casting out demons by the power of Beelzebub and, like Book 3, closes with a parable, in this case the parable of the Prodigal Son. Book 5 also begins with a parable, namely that of the Unjust Steward, and Bede's proem underscores the theme of judgement and repentance. It leads up to Jesus's triumphal entry into Jerusalem, and the scenes in the Temple

INTRODUCTION 15

and Bede's opening paragraphs in Book 6, a disquisition on Solomon's construction of the Temple, mark the Temple as the critical theme of this section of the Commentary. Book 6 is in fact largely taken up with Jesus's encounters and pronouncements in the Temple. By contrast, he moves quite swiftly though the events of the Passion and Resurrection to the Ascension.

In sum, Bede's six-book structure is far from mechanical. Book 1 might be titled 'Preparation, Incarnation and Epiphany'; Book 2 'The Ministry and the Message'; Book 3 'The Message leads to Conflict'; Book 4 'Conflict and Parable; Book 5 'From Parables to the Temple', and Book 6 'The Temple of His Body'.

## 2.2 Bede and the Codex Amiatinus

For a full understanding of the structural devices of *On Luke* – what Bede borrowed and what he invented – it is also necessary to consider the Codex Amiatinus, one of a remarkable trio of Bibles produced at Wearmouth-Jarrow at the time when Bede was working on the Luke commentary. In about 680 Ceolfrith, the prior of Wearmouth, who had accompanied Benedict Biscop to Rome, returned to Northumbria bearing the Codex Grandior, a *Vetus Latina*, or 'Old Latin' translation of the complete Bible, which he had acquired there.[44] Two years later, Ceolfrith was sent to form a new establishment at Jarrow and was appointed abbot. Bede, who at the time of the foundation would have been a boy of about nine, was among the group of monks and novices from Wearmouth that came with him.

In 689 Ceolfrith became abbot of the double monastery. In time, Ceolfrith ordered three 'copies' of the pandect to be made, but with the Latin text of Jerome's Vulgate substituted for the Old Latin.[45] Two of these are almost though not entirely lost, but one, the Codex Amiatinus, survives intact. It is the oldest complete Latin Bible that is still extant, and Bede was certainly familiar with it.[46]

---

44 On Ceolfrith and the Codex Grandior, see Meyvaert, 'Bede, Cassiodorus, and the Codex Amiatinus', 832–39.

45 See Bede, *The Lives of the Abbots* 15 and *The Anonymous History of Abbot Ceolfrith* 20 (in Grocock and Wood, ed. and trans., *Abbots of Wearmouth and Jarrow*, 56–60 and 98).

46 The most recent and authoritative account of the Codex Amiatinus is Chazelle, *The Codex Amiatinus and its 'Sister' Bibles*. See also Richard Gameson's 2017 Jarrow Lecture, *Codex Amiatinus: Making and Meaning*. In preparing this translation we consulted the digital facsimile of the Codex Amiatinus available through the Library of Congress at https://www.loc.gov/item/2021668243.

16     BEDE: *COMMENTARY ON THE GOSPEL OF LUKE*

The Amiatinus divided all of the books of Bible, except Ruth, Chronicles, Psalms, the Song of Songs, Malachi, Tobit, Esther, Ezra, Nehemiah, and Revelation, into numbered chapters and preceded the books with summaries (*capitula*) of their chapters' contents. We know that Bede composed chapter summaries for three of the books for which they are lacking in the Amiatinus: Chronicles, the Song of Songs, and Revelation. Bede also informs us that he composed summaries for the Pentateuch, Joshua, Judges, Kings, Job, Proverbs, Ecclesiastes, and Isaiah; and for all of the books of the New Testament except the Gospels.[47] Paul Meyvaert has shown that the summaries in the Amiatinus from Exodus to Judges are probably the ones composed by Bede.[48]

## 2.3 Chapter numbers and summaries

The Codex Amiatinus concretely exemplifies the Vulgate's multilayered structure. Jerome arranged many of the books of both Testaments *per cola et commata*, 'by verses and phrases': that is, by short, grammatically coherent units of speech.[49] These fundamental units, when laid out line by line, visually punctuate the text, facilitate oral delivery, and reduce the chances of error in copying. But a text arranged, as the Amiatinus is, *per cola et commata* is not economical of space. In surviving manuscripts the successive verses of Luke that Bede comments on are strung out like prose, though their boundaries correspond to boundaries established *per cola et commata*.

Modern editions of the Bible divide the text of each book into a binomial system of chapters and verses. Thus, the Gospel of Luke is divided into twenty-four chapters and each chapter into a numbered set of verses. This system goes back only to around the beginning of the thirteenth century.[50] In Bede's time other systems of division were in use. As Paul Meyvaert observes:

> the number of 'chapters' in a given Book of Scripture could vary considerably. Different sets of summaries were created to correspond to these divisions. The

---

47 Colgrave and Mynors, eds, *Bede's Ecclesiastical History*, 568–69.
48 Meyvaert, 'Bede's *Capitula Lectionum*', 366–69.
49 See Jerome, Prologue to Isaiah, ed. Weber/Gryson, 1096; Jerome, Prologue to Ezekiel, ed. Weber/Gryson, 1266; and Cassiodorus, *Institutions* 1.9, trans. Halporn, 109, and n. 8.
50 Gorman, 'Source Marks and Chapter Divisions', 270.

INTRODUCTION                                                                  17

summaries placed at the opening of a given Biblical book were numbered, and corresponding numbers were inserted at the appropriate place in the text.[51]

The Wearmouth-Jarrow editors of the Codex Amiatinus organized the verses of the Gospel of Luke into ninety-four chapters and prefaced it with ninety-four chapter summaries. The same sequence of ninety-four summaries is found in other Northumbrian gospel texts, including the Lindisfarne Gospels.[52] The system may have reached Northumbria 'from the South Italian (Neapolitan?) exemplar' used for these gospel texts.[53] Bede borrowed this system for *On Luke*. He must have copied the ninety-four chapter summaries from one or more of the texts of the Vulgate at his disposal. A comparison of the summaries in the Amiatinus with those in Bede's text reveals only inconsequential discrepancies between the two, with one exception – a phrase Bede apparently added to the summary for chap. 7 (see note on the text of summary 7 below). The groups or 'chapters' of verses of the Vulgate in the Amiatinus that correspond to the ninety-four summaries are numbered in the margin of the text from 1 to 94,[54] and an examination of six of the earliest manuscripts of *On Luke*[55] confirms that Bede did the same, with, of course, the significant difference that his 'chapters' included his commentaries on the verses.

The Codex Amiatinus itself was probably not Bede's model. The pandect prepared for use at Wearmouth-Jarrow and/or the texts of the Vulgate used for its preparation are more likely to be what he consulted. How and where they differed from the Amiatinus cannot be definitively known. A sequence of errors in the Amiatinus concerning the verses numbered as chaps 21–24 is instructive. In the Amiatinus the text of Luke 6:20–30 is numbered as chap. 21, 6:31–36 as chap. 22, 6:37–49 as chap. 23, and 7:1–10 as chap. 24. For the most part the chapter summaries are detailed enough to indicate where chapter divisions with their numbers

---

51  Meyvaert, 'Bede's *Capitula Lectionum*', 350. See also Wallis, trans., *Bede: Commentary on Revelation*, Introduction, 60–66.
52  Meyvaert, 'Bede's *Capitula Lectionum*', 349 and n. 5; Chazelle, *The Codex Amiatinus and its 'Sister' Bibles*, 150.
53  Meyvaert, 'Bede's *Capitula Lectionum*', 351.
54  Regrettably, Hurst failed to add chapter numbers to the text of *On Luke* in CCSL 120, although he printed the summaries. In the text of Luke in Codex Amiatinus, ch. 14 is misnumbered as ch. 13, and no number is provided in the text for ch. 81. Neither error turns up in the early manuscripts of Bede (see following note).
55  See Appendix 2.

should be placed. Two mistakes are immediately evident in the Amiatinus. The summary for chap. 21,

> Upon passing the whole night in prayer [6:12], he names the twelve apostles [6:13]. The sick are cured by touching him [6:19],

corresponds to Luke 6:12–19, which the Amiatinus does not mark as a separate chapter, not to Luke 6:20–30. Evidently, it was Luke 6:12–19 that should have been labelled chap. 21, as it is in the early manuscripts of Bede's commentary. The summary for chap. 22,

> He calls blessed those that are poor [6:20], those that hunger [6:21], those that weep [6:21], those that suffer persecution [6:22], and calls down woe upon those that are rich [6:24] and to those that laugh [6:25]. He even orders that enemies be loved [6:27] and that resistance should not be offered to one who strikes or who strips another bare [6:29],

accurately describes Luke 6:20–30, the beginning of the Sermon on the Mount. Again, what is labelled as chap. 21 in the Amiatinus ought to have been labelled chap. 22, as it is in four of the six early Bede manuscripts.

However, recognizing these two obvious mistakes in the Amiatinus reveals a new problem. Both the Amiatinus and five of the six manuscripts of Bede agree that chap. 25 begins at Luke 7:11. This leaves room for two chapters between Luke 6:31 and 7:11. Where do (or should) these chapters begin, and what verses do they include? The Amiatinus inserts three chapters into this space: chap. 22 (Luke 6:31–36), chap. 23 (Luke 6:37–49), and chap. 24 (Luke 7:1–10). Only two chapter summaries (summaries 23 and 24) are available to describe them. The summary for chap. 24,

> He heals the slave of a centurion, when the elders and his friends entreat on the centurion's behalf,

specifically describes Luke 7:2–10, and the Amiatinus, therefore, seems to be correct in labelling these verses as chap. 24. No summary exists that would support Luke 6:31–36 as a separate chapter. Either the chapter division at Luke 6:31 or the division at 6:37 must be an error.

The summary for chap. 23,

> He tells the parable [6:39] of the mote and the beam [6:41] as well as of the good and the evil tree [6:43], and of how a house ought to be built [6:49],

applies, strictly speaking, only to Luke 6:39–49. However, the parables mentioned in summary 23 conclude the Sermon on the Mount and reinforce the lessons that come before them. Summary 23, therefore, could arguably extend back to cover either Luke 6:31–49 or 6:37–49, just as by the same logic summary 22 could extend forward to cover Luke 6:20–37.

That Bede did not follow the Amiatinus numbering for these chapters is certain, but what he finally intended remains problematic. The conflicting solutions found in the early manuscripts suggest that he may have made a revision after the first publication of the treatise. All six witnesses agree in marking the beginning of chap. 21 at Luke 6:12. After that they differ in the following ways:

(1) Paris 11681 (**B**) does not provide numbers for chaps 22–24.

(2) Karlsruhe 64 (**K**) and St Gall 85 (**G**) put chap. 22 at Luke 6:20; chap. 23 at Luke 6:31; and chap. 24 at Luke 6:37.[56]

(3) Paris 12281 (**D**) exhibits the same chapter divisions as **K** and **G**, but adopts the numbering of the Amiatinus at Luke 6:31(chap. 22) and 6:37 (chap. 23; it does not have a chap. 24).

(4) Wolfenbüttel 20 (**W**) agrees with **K**, **G**, and **D** in putting chap. 22 at Luke 6:20, but then goes to Luke 6:41 for chap. 23, and Luke 7:2 for chap. 24. Luke 6:41 would be a more logical starting point than Luke 6:37 for a chapter described by summary 23, and Luke 7:2 would be a good starting point for a chapter described by summary 24.

(5) Paris 17451 (**E**), like the Amiatinus, puts a chapter numbered 22 at Luke 6:31 and at Luke 6:37, where the Amiatinus places chap. 23, a chapter number is erased. There are also erasures at Luke 6:41 and 7:2, where **W** begins chapters 23 and 24.

Bede cannot have meant to label Luke 6:37–7:10 as chap. 24, because 6:37–49 is described by chapter summary 23, and only 7:1–10 by summary 24. Despite the fact that none of the six manuscripts begins a chapter at Luke 7:1, there can be no doubt that he would have intended, like the Amiatinus, to begin chap. 24 there (or at Luke 7:2, as attested by **W** and possibly **E**). Whether he finally took Luke 6:20–30 as chap. 22 and Luke 6:31–49 as chap. 23, or Luke 6:20–36 as chap. 22 and Luke 6:37–49 as chap. 23, remains an open question. We call attention to these alternative solutions by labelling the chapter division at Luke 6:31 as chap. 23(a) and the one at Luke 6:37 as chap. 23(b).

---

56 Gorman, 'Source Marks and Chapter Divisions', Appendix 3, records the same divisions as **K** and **G**. He does not say on what basis he reached this conclusion.

One final problem arises from the fact that the Codex Amiatinus erroneously begins chap. 51 at Luke 11:45. Chapter summary 50 demonstrates that Luke 11:45–54 belongs to chap. 50:

> When he was invited to dine with a Pharisee [11:37], he notices that the Pharisee is thinking of the Jewish ritual of washing [11:38], and saying 'woe' six times [11:42, 43, 44, 46, 47, 52] to the Pharisees, he exposes their many sins.

None of the six early Bede manuscripts enters a number for chap. 51. However, chapter summary 51,

> He commands his disciples both to beware of the leaven of hypocrisy [12:1] and not to fear those who kill the body; and not to think what they will say in a time of persecution,

clearly establishes that chap. 51 should begin at Luke 12:1.

How these discrepancies, if they existed in the text or texts of the Vulgate that he was using, could have escaped Bede's notice, or how they could have entered into the manuscript tradition of *On Luke*, remains a puzzle. Later copyists were certainly confused by omissions as well as misplacements of marginal numbers.

### 2.4 Eusebian canon sections and numbers

An independent system of division which Jerome incorporated in the Vulgate is what is known as the Eusebian canons. This was a system developed by Eusebius of Caesarea for cross-referencing parallel events in the Gospels.[57] Each Gospel was divided into consecutively numbered sections. Matthew was assigned 355 sections, Mark, 232, Luke, 342, and John, 232. The section numbers of parallel events were set side by side in canon tables. There were ten tables in all. Canon table 1 recorded incidents found in all four Gospels. Canon tables 2, 3, and 4 compared incidents found in three of the four evangelists (there was no table for Mark/Luke/John). Incidents common to two Gospels were given in canon tables 5, 6, 7, 8, and 9 (there was no table for Mark/John). Canon table 10 (actually four tables, one for each of the gospels) displayed the numbered sections in each successive gospel that were unique to that gospel. The Eusebian

---

57 See Chazelle, *The Codex Amiatinus and its 'Sister Bibles'*, 182–86, for a detailed account of the development of the system and the arcaded canon tables that were designed to frame the numbered sections of each Gospel in parallel columns.

canons enabled exegetes to identify and comment on, or 'harmonize', events in Jesus's life that were reported by all, or some, or only one of the evangelists.[58]

On the evidence of six early manuscripts of *On Luke*, as Appendix 2 demonstrates, Bede intended canon section numbers to be inserted in his text. Other early manuscripts with section numbers include Milan D 23 inf., a manuscript written in the second quarter of the ninth century in central France,[59] and the fragments New Haven 441, from the second half of the eight century, written in Anglo-Saxon minuscule,[60] Munich 29440(1, written during the first half of the ninth century at Polling Abbey in Bavaria, and Munich 29440(2, also of the ninth-century and Bavarian.

In the Codex Amiatinus, the ten canon tables, sandwiched between Jerome's two prefaces to the Gospels, are arranged vertically within arcades that mimic architecture.[61] Columns resting on solid bases and topped by plain capitals support both small semi-circular arches and larger arches above them that form double or triple arcades. Within the arcades and in each canon table the canon section numbers for the respective gospels are arranged vertically in side-by-side columns. The section numbers in the left-most column are always in numerical order. All this information – the section number, the canon table number, and the corresponding section numbers of the other gospels – is also inserted in the margin beside the gospel text.

There are no canon tables in *On Luke*, and Bede probably did not add table numbers to the section numbers.[62] But he must have expected readers of *On Luke* to have access to such tables. Accordingly, we insert canon

---

58 For a comprehensive overview of the canons and their reception, see Crawford, *The Eusebian Canon Tables*.

59 See Gorman, 'Source Marks and Chapter Divisions', plate 7.

60 New Haven 441 puts canon section number 60 in the margin at Luke 6:43; section number 61, at Luke 6:44b; and section number 63, at Luke 6:46. The online digital image does not reveal whether there is a section number 62 at Luke 6:45.

61 See Neuman de Vegvar, 'Remembering Jerusalem', *passim*.

62 A Roman numeral 5 accompanies canon numbers 54 and 60 in Paris 12281 (**D**), fols 56v and 58v. Both canons are found in canon table 5. Canon section number 10 with canon table number 5 and a cross reference to Matthew section number 12 appear in Munich 29440(2). A puzzling Roman numeral 10 capped with a w-shaped squiggle that appears above canon number 117 in Paris 11681, fol. 100v (see Gorman, 'Source Marks and Chapter Divisions', plate 4), should probably not be interpreted as a table number (even though canon 117 is found in table 10), because similarly capped Roman numerals 11 and 12, which cannot be table numbers and are not adjacent to canon numbers, follow sequentially on fol. 101r.

## 22  BEDE: *COMMENTARY ON THE GOSPEL OF LUKE*

section numbers and, for the convenience of the reader, table numbers in their appropriate places in this translation, and provide cross references to their equivalents in Matthew, Mark, and John in Appendix 3.[63]

### 2.5 Source marks

As we mentioned above, a substantial portion of *On Luke* is made up of verbatim quotations from the works of four Latin Fathers of the fourth and fifth centuries – Ambrose, Augustine, Jerome, and Gregory. Bede adapted a method for identifying these passages and their authors by source references placed in the margins. In his reply to Acca, quoted above, he describes the system of source marks[64] that he introduced into his text. Bede's system anticipates the modern employment of quotation marks to mark the beginning and end of borrowed passages and the use of footnotes or an *apparatus fontium* to identify their authorship and the extent of the passage quoted. In the earliest manuscripts of *On Luke*, quotations from the four named authorities are signified by the first two letters (or in the case of Jerome by the first two consonants) of their names: AM = Ambrose; AV = Augustine, GR = Gregory, and HR = Jerome (Hieronymus). The first letter is set in the margin next to the beginning of the quotation, and the second letter next to its end. Bede subsequently employed this same device in his commentary on the Gospel of Mark, but not in his other biblical commentaries. And although his words suggest that other authorities might be treated in the same way, neither he nor later copyists chose to do so. Partly on the basis of his use of this device in his two gospel commentaries, Bede is credited with establishing Ambrose, Augustine, Gregory, and Jerome as the four Latin Doctors of the Church.[65]

Years later, in the preface to his commentary on Mark, Bede appealed to his readers to preserve this system:[66]

> And I humbly pray the reader that, if he should deem these works of ours worthy of copying, he should also carefully preserve in the transcribing the

---

63  Complete canon tables may be found in Weber/Gryson, 1516–26.

64  See Laistner, 'Source-Marks in Bede Manuscripts', 350–54, and Gorman, 'Source Marks and Chapter Divisions', 258–61.

65  Kaczynski, 'Bede's Commentaries on Luke and Mark', 17–26; Gorman, 'Source Marks and Chapter Divisions', 261; Brown, *A Companion to Bede*, 33 and 60, and the references therein.

66  Bede did not invent marginal references; they were used and described by Cassiodorus in his commentary on the Psalms. However, he *did* improve the system to indicate the beginning and end of the cited passage, and created the two-letter abbreviations for the major Church Fathers: see Gorman, 'Source Marks and Chapter Divisions', 260.

INTRODUCTION                                                                                         23

notation of those names which have been placed above in the margin, just as was admittedly done for the commentary on St Luke that we, with the help of God's grace, composed many years ago.[67]

Despite his plea, scribes evidently failed to understand Bede's intentions, and source marks and chapter and canon section numbers faded from the manuscript record.[68]

Since Bede's objective was to inform his readers of the authorship and extent of all quotations from Ambrose, Augustine, Gregory, and Jerome, we feel that the critical apparatus – the combination of the use of italics and footnotes – of the present translation can reasonably substitute for the placement of the initials A/M, A/V, G/R, and H/R in the margins on the basis of imperfect and fragmentary manuscript evidence. We have, however, inserted these initials in the Bibliography of Primary Works after the titles of works whose authorship is identified by source marks in one or more manuscripts.

## 3. BEDE'S EXPOSITORY STRATEGIES

### 3.1 'First I gathered together from here and there the most illustrious works of the Fathers ...'

As Bede explains to Acca, his first step as an exegete was to find out what the Fathers said about Luke so that he could incorporate their words, or at least their ideas, into his own exposition. For the reasons by now evident, Bede had become more sensitive to the process of creating a commentary from a mosaic of quotations than he had been when he composed his earlier works.[69] He now felt obliged to identify his sources, but also to proclaim their impeccable orthodoxy and authority.

In the context of his description of his working methods, the four source marks which Bede placed in the margins of his quotations from Ambrose, Augustine, Gregory, and Jerome produce the impression that

---

67  Bede, *In Marci Euangelium exposition*, ed. Hurst (CCSL 120:432.45–51); trans. Laistner, 'Source-Marks', 350.

68  Bede's sources marks inspired Hrabanus Maurus to adopt the same system in the ninth century and, while the manuscripts of Hrabanus's works also show sporadic transmission of the source marks, they signal an important stage in the evolution of later medieval reference systems, notably in the *Glossa Ordinaria*: see Smith, *The Glossa Ordinaria*, 61.

69  See Wallis, trans., *Bede: Commentary on Revelation*, Introduction, 25–28.

Bede used mainly these four authors, and that they constituted authorities of particular dignity. The marginal notes played a significant role, for they pointed 'to the authority of the person who wrote, not the authority of the written work'.[70] Bede even suggests that *On Luke* is a kind of index to the thinking of the great Fathers. Commenting on Luke 16:18, he says:

> If anyone wishes to find out more about the exposition of this testimony, he should examine not my writings, but those of our elders. Indeed, the blessed Fathers, first of all Augustine in his book of the Lord's Sermon on the Mount, Jerome and Ambrose in their commentaries on the evangelists Matthew and Luke, but also how very many others, have each said enough and more about it in their works.

But these four are not the only authorities Bede called upon. Ironically, the less well-known authors of quotations (Paulinus, Josephus ...) are named explicitly within the text,[71] while vast swaths of Augustine or Jerome depend on the marginal flags for identification. Bede evidently hoped that these flags would be so striking and visible that his overwhelming dependence on the four Fathers would be in no doubt.[72] But, as we shall see, not every borrowing from the four is acknowledged, and neither are all Bede's debts to other authors.[73]

The flagged quotations from the four Fathers are passages quoted *in extenso*. Ambrose is represented exclusively by his own commentary on Luke, which (*pace* Acca) Bede readily exploits.[74] Jerome's principal contribution is his commentary on Matthew; overlapping material between the two synoptic evangelists allows this work to function as a shadow commentary on Luke. The same is true for Augustine's *Questions on Matthew* and *On the Lord's Sermon* – indeed, the latter is the substance of most of

---

70 Kaczynski, 'Bede's Commentaries on Luke and Mark', 20, 24.

71 An exception is Sedulius, who is merely referred to as 'someone' in the quotation from the *Carmen paschale* at the end of the commentary on Luke 11:27, though he is identified by name in Luke 23:33.

72 Kaczynski, 'Bede's Commentaries on Luke and Mark', 24.

73 James Siemens has argued that Bede may have used the *Laterculus Malalianus* associated with Theodore of Tarsus/Canterbury to supplement the rather jejune patristic sources on the Lucan Nativity narrative; however, the parallels, as Siemens admits, are fairly indistinct, and certainly not verbal: 'Another Book for Jarrow's Library?', 15–34.

74 Ambrose's writings did not enjoy wide diffusion in Anglo-Saxon England. The commentary on Luke in particular circulated mainly in the form of extracts, so Bede's commentary may have been the principal vehicle for this work: Bankert *et al.*, *Ambrose in Anglo-Saxon England*, 32–34.

INTRODUCTION                                                                 25

Bede's exposition of the Sermon on the Mount (especially Luke 6:28–42). Augustine is also represented by his *Harmony of the Gospels*, which proved an invaluable resource for handling apparent discrepancies between Luke and other writers, and by the *Enchiridion*, a treasury of moral doctrine (e.g., the meaning of 'alms' in Luke 11:41–42). Many of Gregory's *Homilies on the Gospels* were on Lucan pericopes. They provide Bede with most of his material on the preaching of John the Baptist, on Christ's praise of the Baptist (Luke 7:23–27), on the dinner in the house of Simon the Pharisee (Luke 7:36 *sqq*.), and on most of the parables in Luke 14–16, to cite only a few examples. Sermon-like passages such as the exegesis of Luke 9:23–27 (Christ's charge to his disciples) are lifted from the *Homilies*, as are Christ's mission instructions to the seventy-two disciples (Luke 10:4–7b) and the parable-injunction to keep constant watch (Luke 12:36–40). But Gregory's *Homilies on Ezekiel* and his *Moralia on Job* are also cited frequently.

That being said, Bede is not merely 'cutting and pasting' whole pages of patristic commentary;[75] rather, he also fashions readings from smaller patristic borrowings, layering them to produce a composite explanation. For example, in expounding Luke 12:22–29 (on not being anxious about material needs), Bede interweaves sentences from Jerome on Matthew with segments of Augustine on the Sermon on the Mount, one upon another; his explanation of Luke 16:13c ('You cannot serve God and mammon') performs a similar feat using these two sources, but adding in Augustine's *Questions on the Gospels*. Bede's use of his patristic sources could be very allusive and subtle, and even sometimes manipulative. For example, in his discussion of the Transfiguration, Bede is not quoting from any source *in extenso* and yet his exposition is shot through and through with verbal allusions to Ambrose on Luke and Jerome on Matthew. Ambrose is clearly visible in only two places, but there are echoes throughout 'as if Ambrose's terms were still in Bede's mind, even though he had gone on to write on a different topic'.[76] Joan Hart-Hasler points to Bede's treatment of Luke 9:32: 'But Peter and those who were with him were heavy with sleep. And waking, they saw his majesty, and the two men who stood with him', as a case in point.[77] Ambrose's comment on this verse is:

> Peter saw this grace, and they who were with him also saw it, even though they were heavy with sleep. For the incomprehensible splendor of divinity

---

75  This charge was laid by Sharpe, 'The Varieties of Bede's Prose', 342.
76  Hart-Hasler, 'Bede's Use of Patristic Sources', 199.
77  Hart-Hasler, 'Bede's Use of Patristic Sources', 199–200.

overwhelms the senses of our body. Indeed, if the bodily keenness of our eyes can not endure a ray of sunlight when they look directly into it, how will the corruption of human limbs bear the glory of God? And for that purpose, the substance of the body is made more pure and refined in the resurrection when the accretion of vices has been removed. And perhaps they were heavy with sleep *so that they might see the appearance of the resurrection after resting* [*ut resurrectionis speciem uiderent post quietem*]. And so, when they awoke, *they saw His Majesty* [*uiderunt maiestatem eius*]; for no one sees the glory of Christ unless awake.[78]

Bede's comment on the same verse is:

The disciples were heavy with sleep not by chance, but for an allegorical reason,[79] namely that *they should see the appearance of the resurrection after the* body's *rest* [*ut resurrectionis speciem uiderent post* corporis *quietem*]. The saints, when they are raised up in glory, will *see the majesty* of the Lord [*maiestatem* domini *uide*bunt] the more truly, because they will also rejoice in the immortality of his flesh through which they had conquered death.

Bede draws on Ambrose, but also alters the sense of Ambrose's exegesis. Ambrose states that the glory of the godhead is too great for human eyes to bear, and adds that only the wakened will see the resurrection. Bede passes over the first point and shifts the force of the second to an anagogical reading: the sleeping disciples are the saints who are in heaven after death (the Seventh Age) and who will rise at the end of time to behold his glory in the Eighth Age.[80] This tactic of borrowing Ambrose's phrases but shifting their meaning can also be found in Bede's comment on Luke 9:28, and this time the result is to replace Ambrose's sense with a moral reading.[81] Jerome's commentary on Matthew is handled in much the same way in Bede's reflections on Luke 9:24 and 9:34.[82] In sum, Bede's memory is indeed steeped in the Fathers, even their very words; yet he charts his own interpretative course, one that can depart from the Fathers' express meaning.

---

78 Ambrose, *Expos. Lucam* 7.17 (ed. Adriaen, CCSL 14:220.187–97); trans. Hart-Hasler, 'Bede's Use of Patristic Sources', 200.

79 Literally, 'by reason of a mystery' (*mysterii ratione*). Bede uses *mysterium* as a general term for any of the spiritual/allegorical meanings hidden in the text of the Bible, and more specifically for reference to the truths of salvation and the sacraments of the Church. See Kendall, 'The Responsibility of *Auctoritas*', 106–07.

80 Hart-Hasler, 'Bede's Use of Patristic Sources', 200.

81 Hart-Hasler, 'Bede's Use of Patristic Sources', 200–01.

82 Hart-Hasler, 'Bede's Use of Patristic Sources', 201–02.

INTRODUCTION                                                     27

Hart-Hasler suggests Bede did not make use of Gregory's or Augustine's readings of the Transfiguration because they were not saying anything substantially different from Ambrose or Jerome.[83] But Bede can also decide not to use an available patristic source on critical grounds. For example, the exposition of the parable of the Sower (Luke 8:4–5) opens with a quotation from Gregory's homily on this passage, but then Bede takes off on his own, picking up Gregory again only at Luke 8:14. At Luke 8:15 he gives his own reading first place ('The good ground, as I said above ... '), and consigns Gregory's to 'another interpretation'.[84] Commenting on Luke 10:10–11 ('But into whatever city you enter, and they receive you not, going forth into its streets, say: Even the dust of the city that clings to us, we wipe off against you'), he puts Augustine's rather prosaic explanation in first position, followed by 'another interpretation' by Bede himself, bringing to the fore his favourite theme of the duties and difficulties of teachers. Sometimes Bede is following one author for the bulk of an episode, but feels impelled to include 'another interpretation' from a different author. For example, most of his exposition of Christ's dispute with the Jewish leaders about casting out demons comes from Augustine, *Sermones* 71. However, when it comes to Luke 11:19 ('Now if I cast out devils by Beelzebub, by whom do your children cast them out?'), he seems hesitant about Augustine's interpretation of 'your children' as the disciples, so he adds 'another interpretation' from Jerome's commentary on Matthew, to the effect that 'your children' are Jewish exorcists. In the next sentence (Luke 11:20) he inverts the order, putting in first place Jerome's explanation of the 'finger of God' as the Holy Spirit, with the Son as the 'hand and arm of God'; even though the parts differ, they are all members of one body. He follows this with 'another interpretation' from Augustine's *Questions on the Gospels*. The finger of God is the Holy Spirit, because the Spirit is the source of diverse gifts, and 'in none of our limbs does division appear more than in our fingers'. Jerome and Augustine are saying the same thing – the finger of God is the Holy Spirit – but it leads them in apparently opposite directions – unity in the case of Jerome, diversity in the case of Augustine. Yet both are authoritative readings, diverse but not divergent.

There is at least one substantial borrowing from an author whom Bede does not acknowledge: Origen. At Luke 21:5–6, Bede's argument that the

---

83 Hart-Hasler, 'Bede's Use of Patristic Sources', 203.
84 See also the similar instance at Luke 12:20.

## 28   BEDE: COMMENTARY ON THE GOSPEL OF LUKE

Jerusalem Temple had to be destroyed lest its rituals seduce future believers comes from Origen's tenth *Homily on Leviticus* in the Latin translation of Rufinus.[85] It is the earliest verbatim quotation from Origen in any work by Bede. Later, Bede would acknowledge Origen's contribution to his exposition of Noah's ark in *On Genesis*, but in the Luke commentary this quotation is silent.[86]

Finally, it is quite possible that Bede made use of Hiberno-Latin exegetical works, and notably the *Expositio euangeliorum* erroneously ascribed to Jerome.[87] This commentary, or, more exactly, set of exegetical notes, was very influential not only in Insular circles but on the continent: more than forty early medieval manuscripts survive.[88] Some otherwise untraceable interpretations in Bede's commentary have parallels in the *Expositio* and in at least one case the parallel is verbally quite close. Commenting on the woman who had been crippled for eighteen years (Luke 13:10–11), Bede says:

> It is fitting that she had been bent over for eighteen years, a number which is formed by three multiplied by six, because it shows (*ostendit*) that she was faint through infirm works (*per infirma opera*) in the testimony of the Law, in the prediction of prophecy, and in the revelation of grace (*in testimonio legis in uiticinio prophetiae et in reuelatione gratiae*).

This echoes ps.-Jerome: '*per tres senos, ostendit, quod infirma fuit ante legem, sub lege, sub gratia*'. Both Bede and ps.-Jerome might be drawing on a lost or unidentified common source, but the numerous other parallels signalled in our footnotes to the translation increase the likelihood that Bede had access to this work.

However, Bede's concern to represent patristic tradition in his commentary went well beyond assembling, aligning, and editing extracts.

---

85  See below, Book 6, n. 9.

86  O'Brien, 'A Quotation from Origen's *Homilies on Leviticus*', 185. Bede, *In Genesim* 2, ed. Jones (CCSL 118A:111.1341–46); trans. Kendall, *Bede: On Genesis*, 181, names Origen as the source of one explication of the function of the lower and upper storeys of the ark. Bede made explicit and more ample use of Origen in his later exegesis, e.g., on I Samuel (DeGregorio and Love, eds, *Bede: On First Samuel*, Introduction, 17).

87  PL 30.531–588; Bischoff, 'Turning-Points in the History of Latin Exegesis', in McNamara, ed., *Biblical Studies: The Medieval Irish Contribution*, cat. 11A, 108–09; C.D. Wright, 'Hiberno-Latin and Irish-Influenced Biblical Commentaries'. Not listed in Lapidge, *The Anglo-Saxon Library*. On the notable presence of Irish scholarship in Bede's milieu, see Love, 'The Library of the Venerable Bede', 607, 610–12.

88  O'Reilly, 'Patristic and Insular Iconography', 85.

INTRODUCTION                                                                29

The Fathers' approach to exegesis was profoundly shaped by a particularly Christian intertextuality – the conviction that the Bible was a unity, and that its every word referred to a single subject matter (*hypothesis*), namely Christ; hence the Bible was always talking to itself and interpreting itself.[89] This intertextuality shaped Bede's approach to his exegetical task in commenting on Luke, and merits closer examination.

## 3.2 Intertextual exegesis

In his Old Testament commentaries Bede's preferred method of interpretation was allegorical. After explicating the surface content (the literal level), he might go on to show how it foreshadows a corresponding reference in the New Testament (the typological level), how it offers a moral lesson for the individual Christian (the tropological level), or how it reveals the joys of the promised heavenly kingdom (the anagogical level).[90] Although allegory remains an integral component of Bede's interpretative procedure in *On Luke*,[91] as will become abundantly clear in the remarks that follow, it is ancillary to several interpretative methods more or less common to his patristic sources that might be collectively described as 'intertextual exegesis'. Intertextual exegesis is grounded on the assumption that the language of the Bible was divinely inspired. Bede, like his predecessors, of course knew that the Latin Vulgate had been translated from Hebrew and Greek originals, but, as Augustine argued with respect to the Septuagint, inspiration extended to translation. The words of the texts of both Testaments called up other texts or related compounds, their meanings harmonized, their etymologies signified, their interrelationships enriched the whole. As Arthur Holder observes:

> Bede employed all the exegetical techniques he had learned from the Church Fathers: the etymology of words (especially from the Hebrew and Greek), number symbolism, the interpretation of images drawn from nature and history, and elucidation according to the principal of 'concordance' by which a particular verse is linked to other biblical verses.[92]

---

89 On the patristic roots of intertextual exegesis, and its debt to ancient literary criticism, see Young, *Biblical Exegesis and the Formation of Christian Culture*.
90 See Kendall, *Bede: On Genesis*, Introduction, 4–14.
91 See Holder, 'Bede and the New Testament', 143–44.
92 Holder, 'Bede and the New Testament', 148. Our preferred term 'intertextual exegesis' aims to encompass both what other scholars call 'exegesis by concordance' (a phrase in the Scriptural texts 'triggers' recollection of that phrase in another Scriptural text, suggesting a

Gregory was adept at intertextual exegesis. Bede frequently chooses to pass on Gregory's analysis without adding anything of his own. So, his commentary on Luke 7:27 ('This is he of whom it is written: Behold, I send my angel before your face, who will prepare your way before you') is drawn from Gregory's Homilies on the Gospels:

> What is called 'angel' [*angelus*] in Greek, is called 'messenger' [*nuntius*] in Latin. Rightly, therefore, he who is sent to announce [*nuntiare*] the divine judgement is called an angel so that he might maintain in name the grandeur which he fulfils in the work.

Having introduced the bilingual pairing of *angelus/nuntius*, Gregory proceeds to enrich his lesson by recalling the words of an Old Testament prophet about the angelic nature of the priesthood and by ringing the changes on compounds of the Latin *nuntius*:

> [A]ll who are enrolled under the name of the priesthood are called 'angels', as witnesses the prophet, who says [Mal. 2:7]: 'The lips of the priest will keep knowledge, and they will seek the law at his mouth, because he is the angel of the Lord of hosts'. And likewise each one of the faithful is successful insofar as he receives the grace of divine inspiration, for if he takes care to encourage good works, if he proclaims [*denuntiat*] the eternal kingdom and punishment to the one straying, when he distributes words of holy prophecy [*adnuntiationis*], then truly an angel appears.

The biblical text generates the vocabulary for its explication.

Meaningful wordplay is a fundamental component of intertextual exegesis. Among the significant types of wordplay in the Christian Latin rhetoric of the early Middle Ages may be classed the metaphorical, the allegorical, and the etymological.[93] A striking example of metaphorical wordplay, which exhibits Bede's sensitivity to root meanings, occurs in his paraphrase of Christ's direction to his disciples at Luke 9:44c: 'Lay up in your hearts these words'. 'Lay up' implies, Bede says: 'store away in your minds also the *euentum* [the e-vent, the out-come, the *spilling out*] of my precious blood'. The everyday meaning of *euentum*, in Latin as in its English

---

line of interpretation – in other words 'scripture interprets scripture') and other features such as wordplay, number symbolism, and etymology. See, importantly, the remarks of Joyce Hill on 'the intertextual complexity of Bede's commentaries on Luke and Mark' within a 'dense intertextual tradition': 'Carolingian Perspectives', 246–48. On 'exegesis by concordance' see DeGregorio and Love, eds, *Bede: On First Samuel*, Introduction, 24–26.

93 See Kendall, 'Let Us Now Praise a Famous City', 512–16. For an introduction to various types of wordplay in Bede, see Major, 'Words, Wit, and Wordplay', 185–219.

INTRODUCTION 31

derivative, is a metaphoric extension of its buried, literal root meaning. The event is the spilling out of the blood. Bede's usage here appears to be unique. Sometimes Bede employs a word in two senses. In his commentary on Luke 2:41 the related compounds *refert*, 'refers to', and *transfert*, 'transfers', link the births of John the Baptist and Jesus: 'He [Luke] refers to the birth of the Baptist there, and immediately turns his attention to the Lord and transfers him there after his nativity with a sacrifice'. *Transfert* is used in a double sense: (a) Luke transfers/turns his attention from John to Jesus, and (b) in his narrative transfers Jesus from Bethlehem to Jerusalem.

Two senses may arise out of etymological wordplay, as with *transgressio*, which Bede in his commentary on Luke 3:38 uses in its root sense of 'a passing beyond' when he states: 'eleven signifies the transgression of ten' (= eleven is one more than ten), and then in its metaphorical Christian–Latin sense of 'sin' or 'fault' when he proclaims: 'the transgression of ten signifies the sin of desiring out of pride to have something more'.

The verbal richness of intertextual exegesis is always at risk of being lost in translation. The key word that triggers Bede's commentary on Luke 4:18–19 is the Latin verb *mitto, mittere, misi, missus*, 'to send'. In these verses Luke is quoting the prophet Isaiah:

> The Spirit of the Lord is upon me, because he has anointed me to preach the gospel to the poor, he has sent [*misit*] me to preach deliverance to the captives, and sight to the blind, to release into forgiveness those who are broken, to preach the acceptable year of the Lord, and the day of reward.

The verb is followed almost immediately by a noun compounded from it: 'he has sent me to preach deliverance [*remissionem*] to the captives'. And the same noun, as well as another verb compounded from *mitto*, is repeated: 'To release [*dimittere*] into forgiveness [*remissionem*] those who are broken'. In English we are tempted to translate *remissio* in two different ways: concretely with respect to captives and metaphorically with respect to the humble. For Bede, reading the Vulgate Latin, both senses (and perhaps others) hover about the word. And so he comments:

> And for that reason, he says that he was sent [*missum*] and anointed to heal those broken or bruised of heart …. And indeed he came *to release* [*dimittere*] *into forgiveness* [*remissionem*] those who had been depressed by the heavy and insupportable weight of the Law, and to admit [*admittere*] them into the forgiveness [*remissionem*] of spiritual grace.

Bede then goes on to take up 'the acceptable year of the Lord', which he understands to be the year of jubilee as defined in Leviticus 25:10. With the exception of the last sentence in which it is repeated that the Lord says he is sent [*missum*], there are no further occurrences of the key word in any of its forms. But this is what Bede found in the Vulgate text of Leviticus: 'And you shall sanctify the fiftieth year, and proclaim liberty [*remissionem*] to all the inhabitants of your land; for it is the year of jubilee.' The echo may have led Bede to make the connection.

In another instance, Bede employs intertextual exegesis to resolve a theological dilemma that seemingly arises in one of Jesus's parables, in which, to the man asking [Luke 13:23], 'are they few that are saved?', Jesus replies [Luke 13:25b]:

> 'But when the master of the house goes in and shuts the door, you will begin to stand outside and knock at the door, saying: Lord, open to us. And he answering will say to you: I do not know [*nescio*] you where you are from'.

In his commentary on these verses Bede affirms that 'the master of the house' is Christ. How can it be that there is anything that Christ does not 'know'? Gregory points the way forward. He observes that there are two senses of the verb 'to know': it can mean either 'to know thoroughly' [*cognoscere*], or 'to approve' [*approbare*]. Bede takes Gregory's proposed solution and runs with it:

> How is it that he does not know [*nescit*] where they are from, when the Psalm says: 'The Lord knows [(*g*)*nouit*] the thoughts of men, that they are vain' [Ps. 93:11], and elsewhere it is written: 'He knows [(*g*)*nouit*] the deceiver, and him who is deceived' [Job 12:16], unless [quoting from Gregory's *Moralia in Iob*] 'God is said to know [*scire*], sometimes in the sense of "to know thoroughly" [*cognoscere*], and sometimes in the sense of "to approve" [*approbare*]'. 'For the Lord knows [(*g*)*nouit*] the way of the just' [Ps. 1:6], 'but *he who* does not know [*ignorant*] will not be known [*ignorabitur*]' [1 Cor. 14:38]. And therefore he knows [*scit*] the reprobates [*reprobos*] whom he judges by knowing them thoroughly [*cognoscendo*], for he would not have judged those whom he did not know thoroughly [*cognosceret*] at all, and nevertheless in a certain way he does not know [*nescit*] where they are from, in the sense that he does not approve [*approbat*] the character of their faith and love for himself.

These verbal echoes allow Bede to weave in apparently unrelated texts from both Testaments in support of his argument.

In his explication of Luke 4:22b: 'And they said: Is not this the son of Joseph?' we might have expected Bede to confront head-on and at length the controversial theological issue that the Nazarenes' question raises. But he seems to brush it aside with a remark about the Nazarenes' 'blindness',

INTRODUCTION 33

and takes up instead for discussion the fact that Matthew and Mark call Jesus 'a *faber*' or 'the son of a *faber*'. This odd deflection from the text of Luke is justified only, but crucially, by the underlying verbal formula, 'Jesus is the son of X', which is common to the three synoptic Gospels. The Latin word *faber* is the term that Bede found in the Vulgate text of the Bible. It (or the Greek term that lies behind it) is routinely Englished as 'carpenter' (e.g., D/R, KJV, NRSV). But, according to *OLD, faber* is the word for (1a) 'a craftsman, workman, artisan', and specifically (1b) 'a metal worker, smith', or (1c) 'a builder, building worker' (*faber* is the basis for such English words as 'fabric', 'fabrication', 'fabricate', 'fabricator', etc.). The range of meanings outlined by *OLD* proves to be precisely how Bede understands the word. He may have seen Isidore of Seville's statement that Joseph was a smith (*faber ferrarius*).[94]

That the dominant sense of *faber* in the passage is 'a metal worker, smith' (1b) becomes apparent as we read through it. But, first, its general sense (1a) inspires Bede to see in Jesus and Joseph's occupation and (quasi-) father–son relationship a reflection of Christ's divine status as the Son of the God 'who was the maker (*fabricator*) of everything', in accordance with Genesis 1:1: 'In the beginning God created heaven and earth'. As maker, Bede declares, God works with fire and the Spirit (*Spiritus*), which brings the sense 'smith' to the fore. *Spiritus* of course is the word for the Holy Spirit, the third person of the Trinity, but it is also in origin the Latin word for 'breath' or 'wind' or 'air'. A smith works with fire and air blown with bellows. Hence when John the Baptist says that Christ 'will baptize you in the Holy Spirit and fire' he is making, Bede suggests, an unconscious allusion to Jesus's occupation.

The allegorically charged notion of the smith and the smithy controls the remainder of the passage, eliciting another complementary text from the Old Testament. Like a smith, the Lord 'forges' (*fabricat*) vessels, and converts 'vessels of wrath' (Rom. 9:22) to 'vessels of mercy' (Rom. 9:23) 'by the softening fire of the spirit' ('spirit' operating in several senses), which thought reminds Bede of the verse from Malachi 3:3: 'And he will sit smelting and purifying the silver, and he will purify the sons of Levi, and he will smelt them like gold and like silver'. The Latin verb, which we have translated as 'smelt', is *conflare*, literally 'to blow air on'. Fire and air (spirit) again. That Jesus was a smith or the son of a smith is shown to be anagogically appropriate to his divine mission, but this spiritual understanding is

94 Isidore, *Regula monachorum* (PL 83: 873).

precisely what the Nazarenes fail to grasp when they utter their version of the bridging formula, 'Is not this the son of Joseph?'.

The allegorical imagery of the smith that informs Bede's analysis of Luke 4:22 hovers between the typical and the anagogical, between figure and fulfilment. The anagogical sense crops up again in Bede's comment on Luke 3:21:

> *Jesus being baptized and praying, heaven*, it says, *was opened*, since when the Lord entered the waters of the Jordan with the humility of his body, he opened the gates of heaven to us by the power of his divinity. And when his innocent flesh is bathed in frigid waters, the flaming sword set as a barrier is quenched by the water that was once so injurious.

Bede's thought is more than usually compressed. The innocent flesh is Christ's; the waters are both the river Jordan and the waters of baptism; the flaming sword is the sword that blocks the way back to the tree of life in the garden of Eden. The waters were once injurious (you could drown in the Jordan), but are now life-giving (the power of baptismal waters), and they are frigid for the sake of the submerged metaphor of the smith's technique of tempering iron (this probably tells us more about Bede's experience of the waters of the Tyne than it does about the likely temperatures of the Jordan). The act of tempering anagogically opens the gates of heaven.

In Bede's hands, allegory is flexible and multi-faceted. In regard to Mary's visit to Elizabeth, Luke remarks (Luke 1:38b–39): 'And the angel departed from her. And Mary, rising up in those days, went into the hill country with haste into a city of Juda.' Bede's comment is:

> Having received the Virgin's consent, the angel went directly back to heaven and Mary went into the hill country. She hastens to visit Elizabeth ... . At the same time she provides a typological example [*typicum exemplum*] to show that every soul that has conceived the word of God in his mind may immediately ascend the loftiest peaks of the virtues with the steps of love to enter the city of Juda, that is, of confession and praise, to penetrate the citadel, and to abide in it, as it were, for three months, right up to the perfection of faith, hope, and love.

Bede's words suggest perhaps that Mary is on the borderline between figure and example. She is both before and after Christ. She has not yet conceived, yet with the angel's promise of a son (Luke 1:31) she points forward in time and is in some sense a type of Christ, who will be the pattern for all later saints to imitate and to become in turn examples for others to imitate. Bede makes this point about Christ explicitly in his later comment on Luke 4:20,

INTRODUCTION                                                             35

when he says that Christ offers 'allegorically a model [*exemplum mystice*] for imitation, that each preacher of the word be also a doer of the same'.[95]

Mary going into the hill country (*montana*) prefigures the potential of the soul to ascend to the peaks of the virtues. With an unacknowledged assist from Jerome,[96] Bede explains that etymologically speaking the city of Juda is the citadel of confession and praise. Mary will remain in Juda with Elizabeth for three months (Luke 1:56). Bede interprets the three months as a numerical allegory for the three supreme virtues of faith, hope, and love (1 Cor. 13:13).

Above all, Bede leans towards tropological, or moral (even moralizing), interpretations. For instance, at Luke 10:17–18, when the disciples return from their mission and report that they cast out demons in Jesus's name, Bede claims they are boasting of their own powers, and Christ's response ('I saw Satan like lightning falling from heaven') is not an exclamation of triumph but a rebuke to their pride.

### 3.3 '... *notes of my own to clarify their sense and interpretation*'

Some parts of the commentary on Luke are more 'original' than others, e.g., the first four chapters of Book 2, encompassing Luke 4:14 to 5:12, which have relatively few extended quotations. Even when he is writing in his own voice, though, Bede is constantly mindful of patristic exegetical practice and seeks to model his own work on this practice. One recurrent tactic, comparable in a sense to intertextual exegesis, is the use of biblical *testimonia* to back up his opinions, a move typical of Gregory:[97] for example, commenting on Luke 12:33 (the injunction to sell all one possesses and give alms), Bede says:

> For when one has scorned all possessions for the Lord's sake, it is appropriate that one nevertheless afterwards labour with the work of one's hands so as to be able both to support oneself and to give alms. Hence the Apostle boasts, saying: *I have not coveted any man's silver, or gold, or apparel, as you yourselves know. For such things as were needful for me and those who are with me, these hands have furnished. I have showed you all things, how that so labouring you ought to support the weak.* [Acts 20:33–35]

Bede's account of Christ stilling the storm on the lake (Luke 8:22 *sqq.*) is a highly original allegory, where the sea is 'the dark and bitter commotion of

---
95  See Kendall, 'Imitation and the Venerable Bede's *Historia Ecclesiastica*', 166–68.
96  Cf. Jerome, *Hebr. nom.* (CCSL 72:67.19).
97  Hart-Hasler, 'Bede's Use of Patristic Sources', 202.

the present age' and the ship is the cross, on which Christ 'slept' in death and 'awoke' at the Resurrection. Bede adds a short 'literal level' interpretation at the end (from Jerome) that the Creator of the world commands all his creation. He then indulges in a lengthy series of parallels from other seaside episodes such as the miraculous draught of fish.

Earlier, we discussed how Bede structured his commentary into six books to reflect his understanding of the architecture of Luke's Gospel. Within this framework, however, Bede varies his exegetical strategies along lines dictated by the rhythm of the Gospel. Book 1 is dominated by historical narration, beginning with the annunciation of John the Baptist's birth to his father Zechariah, so Bede's exposition focuses on explaining the details of that narrative.[98] There is opportunity for doctrinal exposition, notably on the nature of the Incarnation and Virgin Birth or the theology of circumcision. But the text does not give him many opportunities to address moral exhortations; an interesting exception is the address to 'shepherds of the Church' in his discussion of the annunciation to the shepherds. And only at the end of Book 1 does he launch into an extended moral disquisition.

Beginning with Book 2, however, Luke's Gospel shifts from a temporally sequential narrative to a more episodic mode of exposition. Accounts of miracles are layered between records of sermons and parables, dialogues with disciples and other individuals, and confrontations with those who refuse to accept Christ's message. Each type of episode prompts a different exegetical strategy. When the text recounts Christ's hostile encounters with the Pharisees and others, the exposition amplifies the theme of Jewish pride and stubbornness.

Christ's miracles stimulate a rather distinctive response. On many occasions, Bede displays concern that the wording of the Gospel text might suggest that Christ was not omnipotent or omniscient, or that Luke himself was not divinely inspired. For example, in the account of the healing of the centurion's slave (Luke 7:2), Bede is anxious that an alert reader could be troubled by the evangelist's statement that the slave was going to die, when in fact the slave did not die. He evades this problem by claiming that Luke knew that the slave would die if Christ did not heal him, or that he would eventually die someday, just as the prophet Isaiah told King Hezekiah that he was about to die, even though the king received a reprieve. At Luke 7:6 Bede faces another problem: why did Christ actually

---

98 See above, section 2.2.

go to the centurion's house, when he could have healed the slave with a word? 'Surely', says Bede,

> he did this so that his powers would not be thought impotent because he travelled physically, but rather, for the sake of an example of humility. On another occasion he did not wish to come to cure the son of the ruler (John 4:46–50) lest he seem to honour wealth. Here, he consented to go immediately to the slave of the centurion, lest he seem to despise the servile condition.

When Jesus 'marvels' at the faith of the centurion (Luke 7:9) Bede rushes to assure the reader, in the words of Augustine (*De Genesi contra Manicheos*), that this is not a sign of mental confusion, but a lesson to us that *we* should be awe-struck. Examples of this anxiety to preserve Christ's divine powers against even the smallest doubt could be multiplied. Sometimes the explanation seems strained (e.g., Christ did not have to ask the demon expelled from the Gerasene man what his name was, but he did so to enhance the audience's appreciation of his power). Elsewhere Bede deflects anticipated criticism that Christ seems to lose his temper (Luke 9:41), or that the disciples are stupid (Luke 9:45, 18:34).

These instances related to miracles are part of a larger pattern of 'asides' in which Bede addresses questions from a hypothetical reader, prefacing his remarks with 'perhaps someone will ask ...' or a similar turn of phrase. Sometimes the issues are semantic (for example, on the different meanings of 'adore' in Luke 4:8) or historical (is the woman with the alabaster jar [Luke 7:36–37] identical with the one who anoints Christ in Bethany in John's Gospel?), but at other times they impinge on Christ's identity and nature. 'If anyone is bothered' that Christ commanded the leper whom he had cured to obey the Mosaic law (Luke 5:14), Augustine can clear up the problem. At Luke 5:15 he enlists Gregory to explain why Christ commanded the leper not to reveal who healed him, when he surely knew that the leper would disobey (lest we conclude that Christ desired something he could not attain). Did Christ break a commandment by refusing to obey the summons of his mother (Luke 8:19)? Did he ignore his own teaching about not casting pearls before swine (20:34)? And why are the Jews only responsible for the martyrdom of the righteous from Abel to Zechariah (Luke 11:51)? One imagines Bede's brethren, or indeed Bede himself, puzzling over this one and, without a patristic source to assist, Bede ventures an explanation of his own:

> Why from the blood of Abel, who first suffered martyrdom, is not to be wondered at, but it must be asked, why up to the blood of Zechariah, when

not only are there many who were killed after him up to the birth of Christ, but also immediately after Christ's birth the innocent children in Bethlehem were killed by this generation. Perhaps because Abel was a shepherd of sheep, and Zechariah a priest, and the one was slain in the field, and the other in the courtyard of the temple, he wanted to make known under their name martyrs of both kinds, that is to say, both the laity and those dedicated to the office of the altar.

Returning to the treatment of miracles, we find Bede is also interested in drawing out the symbolism of the condition that Christ repairs through the miracle. For example, his raising of the dead man, the only son of his mother, who was being carried to his funeral through the city gates (Luke 7:11–18), prompts this elaborate allegory, which closes with a homiletic apostrophe:

> This dead man, who was carried out of the gate of the city in the sight of many, signifies that man is rendered senseless by the deadly destruction of his offences, and in addition that he is not hiding the death of his spirit upon the bed of the heart, but disclosing it by word and deed to the sight of many, as it were through the gates of his own city. He is well said to have been the only son of his mother, because, although formed from many persons, mother Church is one perfect and immaculate virgin, and yet all the faithful very properly confess themselves to be sons of the universal Church. For any of the elect, when instructed in the faith, is a son; when he instructs others, he is a mother ... . I think that the gate of the city, where the dead man was carried out, stands for any one of the corporeal senses. For he who sows discord among brothers, who speaks injustice on high, is carried dead through the gate of the mouth. *Whoever will look at a woman to lust after her* [Matt. 5:19], reveals the signs of his death through the gate of his eyes. Whoever willingly opens his ear to idle tales and lewd songs or slanders, makes this gate of the soul the gate of his death, and whoever does not guard his other senses, himself surrenders the gates of death to himself. I pray, Lord Jesus, that you make all the gates of my city *gates of justice*, that *I* may *go in to them and give praise* to your name [Ps. 117:19/118:19], and that the stench of the corpse carried in not reach your majesty, who frequently visits it with your celestial ministers, but that salvation may take possession of its walls, and praise, its gates.

Here Bede seems to be modelling his exposition on the point-by-point allegoresis of Augustine on the miracle of the Gerasene swine (Luke 8:32–36, 38–39: references in the translation below).

Bede also ties each of the three miracles of resurrection from the dead (the widow's son, the daughter of Jairus, and Lazarus) together with a moral interpretation (Luke 8:55b):

INTRODUCTION 39

For according to the moral sense, those three dead people whom the Saviour raised up in their bodies signify three kinds of resurrection of souls. For some by giving consent to wicked delight but concealing the thought of sin inflict death upon themselves. But the Saviour shows that he restores such people to life by reviving the daughter of the ruler of the synagogue, who had not yet been carried outside, but was dead inside the house, hiding vice as it were in her secret heart. Others, not only by consenting to wicked delight, but also by performing the evil they took delight in, bring on their own death outside the gates. And showing that he brings these to life again, if they repent, he raises up the young son of the widow who had been brought outside the gates, and restored him to his mother, because he restored the soul recovering from the darkness of sin to the unity of the Church, as we have previously taught. But some, not only by thinking or doing illicit things, but also by the very habit of sinning, corrupt themselves by burying themselves as it were. And truly the power and grace of the Saviour is not diminished in raising these people up, even though anxious thoughts are present, which keep watch over their salvation like sisters devoted to Christ. For to proclaim this, he raised Lazarus from the dead, who *had been four days already in the grave* [John 11:17], and whose sister attested that he was already stinking [John 11:39], because the worst infamy is accustomed to accompany wicked deeds.[99]

The more grievous the level of sin symbolized by the dead person, the more words Jesus uses to effect the miracle and the larger the crowd of witnesses.

Finally, Bede supplements Luke by bringing in material from the other gospels. He views Luke as a historian both of the life of Christ and of the primitive Church,[100] and implies that he was using the other evangelists as sources: e.g., Luke 7:10, 'But it is the custom of the blessed Luke to abridge things that he saw were fully expounded by the other evangelists, or even deliberately to omit them. On the other hand, things that he knew were omitted by them, or touched on briefly, he usually elucidates very skilfully'. Bede therefore feels free to use Matthew and Mark to flesh out Jesus's explanation of the parable of the Sower (Luke 8:12) or to supply from Matthew the explanation of the parable of the expulsion of the demon (Luke 11:26b) missing from Luke. Comparison with the other gospels

---

99 A reference to the three resurrections in Luke's Gospel and the significance of their respective locations (although without Bede's moral interpretation) is also found in the 7th c. Hiberno-Insular *Expositio euangeliorum* (PL 30. 571C): see above, 28.

100 Bede stands out in this respect, as well as in his sensitivity to the evangelist's methods: Kelly, 'Bede's Exegesis of Luke's Infancy Narrative', 68.

## 40 BEDE: COMMENTARY ON THE GOSPEL OF LUKE

raises the issue of their occasional discrepancy. A casual reader of Luke's narrative (Luke 3:22b) would probably assume that John the Baptist was already in prison and that Jesus was alone when he heard the voice of God. But Matthew and Mark put the story of John's imprisonment well after this, which takes place in John's presence. The number of petitions in the Lord's Prayer differs among the synoptics (Luke 11:2–4): Bede uses Augustine's *Enchiridion* to reconcile them. The disagreement of the three synoptics over the disease afflicting the demoniac boy (Luke 9:39) is subsumed by allegory of Bede's own devising: the disease is foolishness, and fools are never consistent. Bede's scrupulous efforts to iron out these differences (ably assisted in many instances by Augustine's *Harmony of the Gospels*) is spurred by his memories of recent controversies, 'for it was impossible for any evangelist to write a falsehood' (Luke 6:2).

### 3.4 A preacher's strategies

Sometime in the 720s Bede assembled a volume of fifty homilies on the Gospels. Fourteen of these homilies are on passages from Luke and of these all but two (Luke 2:20 on the Nativity of John the Baptist and Luke 2:25 for the dedication of a church) share material with the commentary on Luke. These sermons are difficult to date, and hence it is not possible to determine whether in any particular case the homily was reworked for the commentary or the commentary for the homily. In some cases, the similarity is very striking: Bede's sermon for the Purification (1.18) contains a section that matches the commentary almost verbatim; on the other hand, the sermon 1.19 for the post-Epiphany period takes Luke 2:42–52 as its pericope, but shares only phrases and verbal echoes with the commentary. We have signalled these parallels in our notes.[101]

Del Giacco's detailed comparison of the commentary and the corresponding homilies shows that, even when Bede is using much the same material in both texts, he is alert to the fact that they each have a distinctive purpose and perhaps a different audience. Following the example of Augustine and other fathers, Bede adopts a more animated and less literary style when he is composing a sermon.[102] He also avoids discussing discrepancies between the gospels, and edits his extracts from the Fathers

---

101 In identifying and analysing these parallels we lean heavily on the work of Del Giacco, 'Exegesis and Sermon', 9–29.
102 Del Giacco, 'Exegesis and Sermon', 13.

INTRODUCTION                                                    41

to eliminate recondite material.¹⁰³ Bede seems to avoid complex theological explanations when he is writing a sermon. For example, when treating the 'overshadowing' of Mary by the power of God (1:35), Bede offers the same interpretation in both his homily and his commentary: like a tree or a cloud that shades a person from the blazing sun, Christ's humanity shaded the temporal womb of Mary so that it could contain Christ's divinity. However, the commentary stresses Christ's dual nature in a rather abstract discussion, while the homily shifts the balance to the human side.¹⁰⁴

Was Bede writing a commentary for a restricted audience of monks and a sermon for a broader and less homogeneous one? In the *Ecclesiastical History* autobiography discussed above, Bede says that he wrote his commentaries for his brethren. But Conor O'Brien argues that the commentaries were directed not only to monks but to a clerical audience with pastoral duties to whom Bede would furnish both materials for preaching and moral encouragement to action. Small details in the Luke commentary show how conscious Bede was of a wider readership. For example, he comments on Luke 18:40–41 by reproducing a passage from Gregory's *Homilies on the Gospels*, but drops Gregory's apostrophe to his 'dearest brothers', which identifies the audience as monks.¹⁰⁵ On the other hand, Bede cannot resist following Ambrose's lead in singling out virgins as the particular audience of comments on the virtues of the Virgin Mary (Luke 1:40).¹⁰⁶ In a similar vein, the commentary's lengthy allegory of the 'turtledove or two young pigeons' offered at Christ's circumcision (Luke 2:24) focuses on the distinction between the contemplative and active lives (a suitable theme for monks), while the corresponding treatment in Homily 1.18 gives a moral reading: the turtledove symbolizes chastity; the pigeon, simplicity.¹⁰⁷ And, in his commentary on Luke 17:34b, Bede identifies the one who will be 'left

---

103 Del Giacco, 'Exegesis and Sermon', 14–16; for examples, see our notes on Luke 1:26–7, 24:36 below.

104 Del Giacco, 'Exegesis and Sermon', 20.

105 O'Brien, *Bede's Temple*, 33. This view is also held by McClure, 'Bede's *Notes on Genesis*', 17–30. DeGregorio, 'The Venerable Bede and Gregory the Great', 43–60, contrasts Gregory's predilection for mystical interpretation with Bede's more tropological bent. See also Holder, 'Bede and the Tradition of Patristic Exegesis', 399–411.

106 Ambrose addresses virgins (plural) and Bede a singular 'virgin', but Bede was probably not thinking of a particular individual.

107 Hom. 1.18, in Bede, *Opera homiletica*, ed. Hurst (CCSL 122:129.52–130.65); trans. Martin and Hurst, *Bede the Venerable: Homilies on the Gospels* 1:181. See Martin, 'Bede and Preaching', 166–67.

behind' at the Second Coming as the person who disrupts 'monastic life'. This would support Del Giacco's position that Bede's commentary was directed to dedicated religious, while his sermons envisaged an audience more engaged in the world. For example, Bede's sermon 1.6 on the Nativity and the corresponding section of the commentary (Luke 2:8 *sqq.*) both link the shepherds to teachers and preachers, but treat contemplation differently.

> While both digress upon 'The Word made flesh', it is the commentary which holds up for admiration the fact that the shepherds wish to see not the child, but rather the Word itself. This focus upon the Word is heightened in the commentary where it speaks of a vision of the divine achieved through long contemplation. In like manner, the ecclesiastical pastors of the commentary, through divine revelation, are lifted to a state of contemplation. For the homily audience this contemplation is more a gift delayed: they should hurry to see and embrace the words of the angels, with love and faith, that they may in the future (that is, after death and resurrection) comprehend with a vision of perfect recognition.[108]

It should be noted that only the commentary (2:18) compares the shepherds to Moses seeing God in the Burning Bush.[109]

Support for this view comes from Bede's comment on Luke 5:16: 'And [Jesus] retired into the desert and prayed'. Bede begins with a passage from Gregory's *Moralia* that argues for a balance between action and contemplation: to love God should not hinder love of neighbour, or *vice versa*. But he follows this with his own remarks that give unequivocal priority to contemplation:

> Indeed, to leave behind the preoccupations of disabling thoughts and to pray on the mountain with one's whole heart, is to hasten to the eternal joys of divine contemplation. To retire into the desert and pray is to repress the turmoil, surging up from within, of earthly desires, and to seek for oneself something hidden with the Lord, where one may speak with him silently about one's inner longings, with all external uproar hushed.

In evaluating the audience of the commentary, it is important to recall that this was (to the best of our knowledge) the first work that Bede composed for an audience of any kind outside Wearmouth-Jarrow. As his career unfolded and his thinking about the role of *spirituales magistri* and *sancti praedicatores* evolved, so his views about the audience for

---

108 Del Giacco, 'Exegesis and Sermon', 17.
109 Del Giacco, 'Exegesis and Sermon', 19.

INTRODUCTION 43

his commentaries may have evolved; moreover, we need not take his claims about his audience in the *Ecclesiastical History* entirely literally. In the Luke commentary, however, he still seems to be imagining a monastic reader as his principal audience. Hence when he composed a sermon on the same theme (whether he did so before or after completing the commentary), he edited out the more expressly monastic references and emphasized the more pastoral themes suggestive of a mixed clerical audience.[110]

It is also important to recall that the commentary on Luke draws a significant amount of its patristic material from homiletic sources, especially Ambrose's commentary (initially delivered as sermons), Gregory's homilies on the Gospel and on Ezekiel, but also his homiletically structured *Moralia*, and Augustine's sermons. The commentary is particularly apt to read like a homily in passages from Luke where Christ himself is pronouncing a sermon. For example, much of Bede's exposition of the Sermon on the Mount is derived from Augustine's *On the Lord's Sermon* (which itself is homiletic in character). When Bede speaks in his own voice, though, he occasionally employs second-person forms of address that are suggestive of a sermon. Commenting on Luke 6:39 ('Can the blind lead the blind?'), Bede says:

> If, it says, anger has blinded you against someone who has committed violence and avarice against someone who asks, will you be able to tend to his defect, when your mind is defective? Or is only he who did the wrong to be considered guilty, and not you also who were unable to bear it? But if his wickedness finds you mild and of a peaceful spirit, not only will he be stirred to repentance, but you will be presented with the reward of patience, because with a seeing eye, that is, with a serene heart, you took care to lead one who was blind to the light.

In sum, the boundary between commentary and sermon is highly porous.

### 3.5 A historian's strategies

So also is the boundary between history and commentary. In *On the Temple* Bede speaks of reading the Bible 'in the historical sense' [*iuxta historicum sensum*] and then defines this as the sense that displays

---

110 See, for example, the discussion of the reason for the persistence of the stigmata (Luke 24:40) and the corresponding homily, which is more hortatory and insistent that the resurrection be preached and that neglect to do so will be punished: Del Giacco, 'Exegesis and Sermon', 17–18.

'for our imitation the actions of the righteous' [*iustorum nobis actus in exemplum*].[111] The prologue to the *Ecclesiastical History* famously defines the mission of history-writing as providing good examples for the reader to imitate.[112] That being said, there are aspects of the commentary that relate specifically to Bede's understanding of the scope and methods of the historian.

The first of these is proclaimed in his comment on Luke 1:1–4. Bede is persuaded that the four Gospels are actually one single account; Luke was aware of what the other evangelists had written, and chose on occasion to abbreviate or exclude material the others had 'already' dealt with (e.g., the explanation of the parable of the Sower discussed above). This commits Bede to addressing and resolving differences between their accounts: *consensus evangeliorum* is, in short, a historical method.[113] Bede is following the Fathers here. We have already mentioned how he uses Jerome's commentary on Matthew as a surrogate commentary on Luke; but Jerome himself sometimes used Luke to gloss Matthew. For instance, in the quotation from Luke 8:24–25, Jerome's commentary on Matthew 8:26 speaks of Jesus commanding and *rebuking* the storm on the Lake of Galilee. Matthew does not speak of 'rebuking', but Luke does, so Jerome is gesturing towards the third Gospel in his commentary on the first.

The second is conveyed in a famous passage where Bede comments on Luke 2:33: 'And his father and mother were wondering at those things which were spoken concerning him'.

> He calls Joseph the father of the Saviour, not because he truly was his father, as the Photinians would have it, but because he was held by all to be his father to preserve Mary's reputation. Neither was the evangelist forgetful, since he reported that she had conceived from the Holy Spirit and had given birth as a virgin, but, expressing the belief of the common people, which is the true law of history, he calls Joseph the father of Christ.

'The true law of history' is a phrase that reappears in the preface to the *Ecclesiastical History*. There Bede is discussing his source material and, in particular, the personal testimonies and memories on which he was obliged to rely when written documents were absent or scanty. He chose

---

111 Bede, *De templo* 2, ed. Hurst (CCSL 119A:229.1470, 1487); trans. Connolly, *Bede: On the Temple*, 112; see O'Brien, *Bede's Temple*, 171.
112 Colgrave and Mynors, eds, *Bede's Ecclesiastical History*, 2–3.
113 Ray, 'Bede, the Exegete, as Historian', 128–32.

his material 'not from any one source but from the faithful testimony' of 'innumerable' and 'reliable' witnesses.

> So I humbly beg the reader, if he finds anything other than the truth set down in what I have written, not to impute it to me. For, in accordance with the principles of true history (*quae uera historiae lex est*) I have simply sought to commit to writing what I have collected from common report, for the instruction of posterity.[114]

As usual, Bede is following the footsteps of the fathers here: in this case, Jerome's *Against Helvetius*. The issue Jerome is addressing is precisely this passage in Luke 2:33: Jerome avers that when the evangelists refer to Joseph as the father of Jesus they are simply relating common opinion.[115] A number of scholars have interpreted *uera lex historiae* to mean that, in matters of human history, what is commonly understood as true can be accepted as true regardless of strict factuality, if the author's intention is either to make a moral point or to avoid distracting or irritating the reader with pedantic details or unresolvable questions.[116] In an important article Roger Ray refined this view, arguing that *uera lex historiae* for Jerome was not a core principle of historiography but a rhetorical exception, 'a brief strategic departure from the normal goal of factual truth' in the interests of a greater good – in this case, the Virgin Mary's public reputation, particularly within the narrative context of Luke 2:33.[117] In the *Ecclesiastical History* Bede uses the phrase in a rather different way, but with a similar rhetorical purpose, namely to excuse any lapses from factuality on the grounds that he was obliged to use sources he could not always verify. In neither case, though, is it *the* true law of history, but at best only *a* true law of history.[118] Walter Goffart critiqued Ray's interpretation, arguing that Bede's *uera lex historiae* is indeed a historiographical issue, and that it refers to the deficiencies of human history in the light of theological truth. The 'true law' in fact marked 'the inherent limitation of historical discourse' to grasp

---

114 Colgrave and Mynors, eds, *Bede's Ecclesiastical History*, 6–7.
115 See Jones, *Saints' Lives and Chronicles*, 83.
116 E.g., Brown, *A Companion to Bede*, 105. For example, in his commentary on Acts, Bede excuses Stephen's historical errors in his defence before the Council on the grounds that he was relating what his accusers believed, and did not wish to distract from his main point: *Expositio actuum apostolorum*, ed. Laistner (CCSL 121:32.31–33.2); trans. Martin, *Bede: Commentary on the Acts of the Apostles*, 71–72.
117 Ray, 'Bede's *Vera Lex Historiae*', 5; see 'Bede, the Exegete', 130.
118 Ray, 'Bede's *Vera Lex Historiae*', 2; see Holder, 'Bede and the New Testament', 154; Thacker, 'Bede and History', 175.

revealed truth, 'the limitation that made the Evangelist speak of the son of Joseph and keep the immaculate conception to himself'.[119]

We would propose that closer inspection of the Luke commentary suggests a different approach to this problem. Bede follows the passage cited above by a quotation from Augustine's *Harmony of the Gospels*. And here Augustine argues that Luke was not at all mistaken, let alone telling a lie, by calling Joseph the father of Jesus. Joseph is just as much Jesus's father as he is Mary's husband. He did not have intercourse with Mary, but the two were truly man and wife, indeed more truly than they would have been if they had been married in the more conventional way; likewise, Joseph was not the biological father of Jesus, but has every right to be called his father because he adopted Jesus as his son. In sum, there is no gap between 'the true law of history' and theological truth, nor does this 'true law' condone relating falsehoods or errors. What is an error on the surface of the text is a fact to those who read with spiritual knowledge; moreover, 'common belief' can, albeit unwittingly, convey theological meaning. Commenting on Luke 1:1–4, Bede says that the authors of pseudo-gospels merely 'set forth a narration in order' and did not convey 'the truth of history' (*historiae ueritatem*): that is, its theological meaning –one might say its identity with theological verity.

Bede's commentary on Luke also reveals his interest in the data of history. He is particularly invested in the historical context in Judaea and the Roman Empire, e.g., filling in the background on King Herod (Luke 1:5), or quoting Josephus on the biography of Quirinius, governor of Syria (Luke 2:23), or the taxation arrangements in the province (20:20). Bede's interest in the history, architecture, rites, and priestly hierarchy of the Jerusalem Temple is pervasive, and plays the role of a guiding theme in the commentary; hence we will discuss it separately below. In addressing discrepancies between Luke and the other evangelists, Bede shows a distinctive focus on questions of chronology. His preface to Book 2 is especially telling. John the Evangelist, says Bede, was the last to compose a gospel. For when he read the synoptics, he realized that they all began Christ's mission after John the Baptist had been thrown into prison. John the Evangelist therefore set out to fill in details about Christ's activities before this event. Bede signals this lapse of time as follows:

> At the beginning of this, that is, my second book on Luke, I have given advance warning by means of this historical record [*his memoratae historiae dictis*],

---

119 Goffart, 'Bede's *uera lex historiae* Explained', 115.

INTRODUCTION 47

in order that readers should not think that what is going to be explained in what follows happened immediately after the fasting of forty days; rather they should understand that the miracles performed by the Lord, whether in Judea or in Galilee, followed sometime later.

Bede's close attention to chronology also surfaces in an off-hand remark in his discussion of Christ's circumcision (Luke 2:21). Bede asks why Moses did not carry out circumcision on any of the Israelites in the desert, 'neglecting for forty uninterrupted years a manifestly divinely ordained practice which had been observed for four hundred and six years'. This chronological detail is offered without comment (it is not pertinent to the question he is addressing), but raises an interesting question. How did Bede arrive at the figure of 406 years between the birth of Isaac when Abraham was 100 years old, and the Exodus when Moses was eighty? In the brief Chronicle in *On Times* Bede states that Isaac was sixty when he begat Jacob; that Jacob was ninety when he begat Joseph; that Joseph lived for 110 years; and that the servitude of the Hebrews in Egypt lasted 147 years for a total of 407 years.[120] Later in his Greater Chronicle in *The Reckoning of Time* 66 (composed in 725) Bede puts the birth of Isaac at A.M. 2048 and the departure from Egypt at A.M. 2453, a period of 405 years.[121] However these slight discrepancies might be explained (407 years in *On Times*; 406 in *On Luke*; 405 in *The Reckoning of Time*), they clearly indicate Bede's abiding interest in chronology.[122] Certainly Bede's response to the question of why Moses did not circumcise the Israelites would not have suffered had this detail been omitted.

### 3.6 A scholar's and scientist's strategies

Bede also brings to his project of commenting on Luke's gospel a distinctive array of erudition that can, with all due qualification, be called scientific. The core of Bede's science was *computus* – the body of data, precept and mathematical procedure required to maintain the Christian calendar, notably in relation to determining the date of Easter. The data were, on

---

120 Bede, *De temporibus* 19; trans. Kendall and Wallis, *On Times*, 120.
121 Bede, *DTR* 66; trans. Wallis, *The Reckoning of Time*, 165–66.
122 If Bede were counting inclusively in *The Reckoning of Time*, the period from A.M. 2048 to 2453 could be said to equal 406 years. But he explains that the period of 430 years mentioned in Exod. 12:40–41 and Gal. 3:17 extends from A.M. 2023 to 2453, where he is certainly counting exclusively.

the one hand, historical and biblical and, on the other, astronomical and cosmological. This determined the structure and contents of Bede's early treatises *On the Nature of Things* and *On Times*, which he later merged and greatly enlarged as *The Reckoning of Time*.[123]

Bede's intense interest in time reckoning leaks into his commentary on numerous occasions. For example, he draws attention to the relationship between the dates of the conception and birth of John the Baptist and of Jesus. John the Baptist was conceived on 24 September (nine months before the feast of his nativity on 24 June), at the autumnal equinox. Hence John the Baptist says of Christ, 'He must increase but I must decrease (John 3:30)': that is, John's conception coincides with the point in the solar year when the night begins to be longer than the day. But Bede is concerned that 24 September is not, in fact, the astronomically correct date of the autumnal equinox. It was the traditional date in the Roman calendar, but by the fourth century astronomers and some computists in the eastern church had corrected the date of the vernal equinox – a critical marker for Easter – to 21 March. By implication, the date of the autumnal equinox should also be set at 21 September, and the solstices at the 21st day of December and June. This, however, would upset the symbolism of the dates of the conception and birth of Jesus and John. Commenting on Gabriel's annunciation to the Virgin Mary 'in the sixth month' (Luke 1:26), Bede finesses the issue:

> You should understand that the sixth month is March, on the twenty-fifth day of which our Lord is said both to have been conceived and to have suffered, just as he was born on the twenty-fifth day of the month of December. If we believe both that the vernal equinox occurred on the former day, as many think, and that the winter solstice occurred on the latter, it is fitting that the one who *enlightens every man that comes into this world* [John 1:9] be conceived and born with an increase of light. But if anyone should prove that light either increases or overcomes the dark before the time of the Lord's birth and conception, we still say both that *John* was then preaching, *before his coming*, the kingdom of heaven [Acts 13:24], and also that the command is now given to preachers: *Make a way for him who ascends upon the west*.[124] And the reason why John was conceived around [*circa*] the autumnal equinox and born around the summer solstice, he himself teaches, who speaks either of himself or of the Old Testament (as many believe): *He must increase, but I must decrease*.

---

123 See Wallis, '*Si Naturam Quaeras*', 61–94 and 'Bede and Science', 113–26.
124 Ps. 67:5 (68:4).

INTRODUCTION 49

It makes no difference to the spiritual meaning of the passage whether one believes that the vernal equinox is on 25 March 'as many think' or not; for, even if it falls before that date, the theological significance is retained. Note as well that John is said to be conceived 'around' the equinox.[125]

Perhaps the most striking computistical passage is one announced by Bede himself (Luke 19:48b): 'Meanwhile I should like to notice briefly how beautifully the shadow of the Paschal feast of the Law agrees with our true Paschal feast in which Christ is sacrificed ... '. Bede then unpacks the Old Testament regulations for timing the choice and slaughter of the Passover lamb, to show how every detail of the ritual matches an event in the passion narrative. The day on which the lamb is brought into the house was the day of Christ's triumphal entry into Jerusalem:

> And five days before the Paschal feast, that is, from the tenth day of the moon to the fourteenth day, they kept the lamb or goat they were going to sacrifice, because although even then they thirsted for his blood, nevertheless *no man laid hands on him, because his hour had not yet come* (John 7:30; 8:20) ... . But at the end of the fourteenth day, that is, when the day had declined into evening, after he delivered to his disciples the sacraments to be celebrated of his body and blood, with those coming to bind him after he had been seized, what follows began to be fulfilled: *And the whole multitude of the children of Israel will sacrifice it in the evening* (Exodus 12:6). For not only the impious who mocked his death, but also the saints who mourned, stood by the cross of Jesus. I wanted to go over these matters briefly, in order to teach the reader that everything which follows in succession up to the passion of the Lord relates to the figure of the lamb kept in the house and prepared for slaughter.

In fact, what we see here is a preliminary sketch of what would become chapters 62 and 63 in *The Reckoning of Time*, on the allegorical meaning of the Paschal computus in relation to the Jewish laws concerning Passover and the Feast of Unleavened Bread.[126]

Closely connected to Bede's concern with the symbolism of astronomy and cosmology is his deep fascination with number symbolism, and with manipulating that symbolism through arithmetical operations. In this he is drawing inspiration particularly from Augustine, but also from Irish

---

125 Del Giacco, 'Exegesis and Sermon', 16, remarks on the similarity of this passage in the commentary to *The Reckoning of Time*, notably chapter 30 (ed. Jones, 371–76; trans. Wallis, 86–89).
126 Ed. Jones, 454–9; trans. Wallis, 149–55, and commentary, 349–52.

exegetes and computists.[127] For example, much of the elaborate passage on the symbolism of forty-two, seventy-seven, and thirty (Jesus's age at his baptism) in Bede's commentary on Luke 3:38b comes from Augustine's *Harmony of the Gospels*.

But Bede's interest in measurement *tout court* and in mathematical operations as a form of exegesis seems to go beyond patristic models. Bede is interested in all kinds of measurement, including money and coinage. On Luke 12:6 he remarks that 'The tuppence for which five sparrows are sold ... is a kind of very lightweight coin made up of two pennies.' The mechanics of Roman finger-reckoning come up repeatedly, particularly in relation to the 'perfection' of the number 100, where the calculator shifts from his left hand to his right (e.g., Luke 2:21).[128]

Bede also practises what might be called 'exegetical arithmetic' – the use of mathematical operations upon symbolic numbers to draw out their spiritual meaning. Here he is following in Augustine's footsteps, or at least learning from his example. Commenting on Luke 3:38b, Bede begins with a long quotation from Augustine on the significance of Luke's count of seventy-seven generations between Adam and Christ, starting from the observation that seventy-seven is the product of eleven and seven. Eleven is the number of sin (excess over the perfection of ten) and seven the number of humanity (the four parts of the body and the three powers of the soul). Bede then follows this up with his own exegetical arithmetic of the number of generations in Matthew, namely forty-two.

Elsewhere, Bede is more independent. Speaking of the age of the prophetess Anna (Luke 2:35–36), he observes that her eighty-four years are the product of seven (which was the number of years she was married) and twelve:

> Seven pertains to the course of this world, which stretches out over seven days; but twelve to the perfection of apostolic teaching. Therefore, either the universal Church or the individual faithful soul which has a care to give over the whole span of its life to apostolic teachings is praised for multiplying as it were seven by twelve and for serving the Lord for eighty-four figurative years.

---

127 In his computistical writing, Bede never lets number symbolism hijack his commitment to exact data; however, he will seize the opportunity afforded by the symbolism of a number when it arises to dilate on theological meanings: see Wallis, '"Number Mystique" in Early Medieval Computus Texts', 181–99.

128 Bede describes this system of finger-calculation in *The Reckoning of Time* 1; see also Wallis's commentary on this chapter, *The Reckoning of Time*, 254–63.

INTRODUCTION 51

Christ's visit to the Temple at the age of twelve (Luke 2:42–43) is handled in a similar way:

> We can say this, because just as the number seven can signify the complete number or perfection, either of things or of times, so also can the number twelve, which consists of the parts of seven multiplied by themselves [*i.e.*, 7 = 3 + 4, 12 = 3 x 4]. Accordingly, where it is fitting that all places and times be filled, the beginning may dawn from the number twelve.

A special application of exegetical arithmetic is *gematria*. *Gematria* is based on the fact that letters in the Greek alphabet also function as numbers. It involves calculating the numerical value of the letters in a name and then providing a symbolic interpretation of the result. In his *Commentary on Revelation*, Bede expressed scepticism at Primasius's gematrical interpretation of the name of the beast '666',[129] but in his own exegesis of Luke 2:21, on the naming of Jesus, he is more enthusiastic:

> Not only the etymology of this sacred name, but also the very number that it contains in its letters is redolent of the mysteries of our eternal salvation. In fact, among the Greeks it is written IHCOYC with six letters, namely I and H and C and O and Y and C, the numerical values of which are ten, eight, two hundred, seventy, four hundred, and two hundred which together add up to eight hundred eighty-eight .... So we can also say that the name of the Saviour is made up of the perfect number eight, because he exhibited in himself the model of resurrection for mortals by rising again on the eighth day. It is made up also of eight multiplied by ten, because the Ten Commandments of the Law instructed us and likewise aided us to know how the number eight ought to be completed in a symbol of his resurrection.

He reinforces this in his remarks on the eighteen people killed by the collapse of the tower at Siloam (13:4–5):

> The number eighteen [in Latin 'ten and eight'] is not an accident. Among the Greeks the number is expressed by I [iota = 10] and H [eta = 8], that is, by the same letters with which the name Jesus begins. They indicate that the Jews especially deserved to be damned, because, having heard the name of the Saviour, they preferred to reject it rather than to accept it.

Bede goes so far as to argue that 'exegetical arithmetic' is justified, even commanded, by Scripture itself. Commenting on the fact that Jesus was baptized at the age of thirty (Luke 3:23), he claims that this number

---

129 Ed. Gryson, 416–17; trans. Wallis, 205–06. Bede explains Greek letter-numerals and alludes to their usefulness as a code in *The Reckoning of Time* 1, trans. Wallis, 12, and commentary, 261–63.

can reveal the symbolism of our baptism in accordance with the faith of the holy Trinity and the workings of the Decalogue of the Law. Of course, the Decalogue is understood the more sublimely and fulfilled the more devotedly by the revelation of the grace of faith. For he who said: Go, *teach all nations, baptizing them in the name of the Father, and of the Son, and of the Holy Spirit*, taught that those who are going to be baptized have as it were a certain consecrated period of three years. It is as if he ordered this same time of three years to be multiplied by ten when he added: *Teaching them to observe all things whatsoever I have commanded you.*

### 3.7 Bede's 'monastic encyclopedia'

Exegesis and computus were facets of a single programme of Christian erudition that might be termed the 'monastic encyclopedia'. Its framework was laid out by Augustine, notably in *On Christian Learning*, but 'operationalized' by monastic practices of instruction, reading, and meditation. It is not a discrete body of knowledge, 'but a web of reference points in Scripture, liturgy, doctrine, and discipline, onto which elements of profane learning ... could be hung'.[130]

The threads of this web visible in Bede's commentary on Luke include philology in the form of interpretation of Hebrew names for people and places (Jerome's works being heavily mined here), but also details about the Hebrew language itself – e.g., 'Boanerges' should be 'Banereem' (Luke 6:14b–15) and Hebrew has no letter 'P'. It broadens out to include geographical details: for example, Bede cites Isidore's account of the character and dimensions of the sea of Galilee (Luke 5:1), even though he does not allegorize either. The *realia* of the Bible also triggered curiosity in, for example, the nature of alabaster (Luke 7:36–37) or the eagle-stone (Luke 17:36–37), for which Bede consulted Pliny, or biblical weights and measures (Luke 16:5–7, 19:13), for which he turned to Isidore.

The point of the monastic encyclopedia, though, was not the display of learning or lore but the derivation of religious teaching from natural similitudes. A striking example is provided by Bede's exegesis of Luke 8:1, where Christ's preaching tour in the company of his disciples is likened to an eagle's training of its young:

> *Just like,* [Moses] says, *the eagle enticing her chicks to fly, and hovering over them, he spread his wings, and has taken him and carried him on his shoulders*

---

130 Wallis, 'Caedmon's Created World and the Monastic Encyclopedia', 99–100.

[Deut. 32:11]. For just as chicks recently hatched cannot conquer the air by flying until they are fledged, so each and every one of the faithful, in order to be capable of flying to heaven, must first clothe themselves with the plumage of the virtues in the nest of faith. So, the teachers of the faithful, the apostles, inasmuch as they can also be set over others to instruct them, themselves ascend step by step to the heights. Indeed, the Lord at first teaches in synagogues, performs miracles, spreads his fame everywhere, receives the multitudes coming together to him, heals, and instructs. After this he appoints disciples, provides for them in the wedding of the bridegroom, leads them through the crops, and defends them from the false accusations of the Pharisees, as the eagle defends her tender chicks from snakebites by introducing [into the nest] a precious eagle-stone.

Bede's audience surely could intuitively grasp the analogy of eagle chicks learning to fly and the disciples learning to preach. The reference to the eagle-stone (*aetitis*) is more obscure, and Bede provides no explanation; it seems to be a case where the 'web' of references set trembling by the idea of 'eagle' turned up an element that Bede immediately recognized, but possibly might have escaped his readers. In this respect, the monastic encyclopedia is an adjunct to intertextual exegesis.

Finally, Bede's monastic encyclopedia made considerable space for medical learning.[131] Commenting on Christ's statement that faith the size of a mustard seed could uproot a mulberry tree (Luke 17:6), he inserts a remedy (probably from Marcellus Empiricus) for 'purging' the head with a gargle made of mustard seed and honey. He allegorizes not only the ingredients but also the process of preparing the recipe:

> Thus certainly faith which is put to the test by the pestle of temptations, skimmed by the sieve of discretion from all superficiality of trivial thoughts, and sweetened with the honey of perfect love, not only empties all the filthy waters of sins from the heart, which is the head of our inner man, in the present, but also prevents them from being able to congregate together again in the future.

In his commentary on Luke 11:27 Bede offers a theory of human reproduction to support the dogma of the two natures – human and divine

---

131 This is a subject that merits further research. Apart from the sources discussed here, one could point to Bede's use of Cassius Felix's *De medicina* in his *Retractio in Actus Apostolorum* (ed. Laistner, 145, lines 15–25); his accounts of the miracle of John of Beverley in the *Historia Ecclesiastica* 5.3 indicate a familiarity with technical literature on bloodletting: see Wallis, *Medieval Medicine: A Reader*, 59–62.

– of Christ. The cue is the outburst of the woman in the crowd: 'Blessed is the womb that bore you, and the breasts that you have sucked'. Bede sees her as inspired by insight into the nature of the Incarnation, for if Christ had not derived his human flesh from the Virgin Mary there would be no point to blessing her womb or her breasts. For, according to natural philosophers (*phisicos*), both seminal fluid and breast milk derive from same source; hence if Mary did not furnish the material for Christ's body, neither could she feed him from her breasts.[132]

Behind this statement lies a rather tangled ancient debate about male and female contributions to conception. Bede is clearly arguing, on the authority of the 'philosophers', that Mary must have provided her own female seminal fluid to make Christ's human body. Embryological texts derived from the Hippocratic tradition held that both men and women produce seed, and the union of these seeds results in conception. This view was readily accessible to Bede through Isidore of Seville, *Etymologies* 11.1.77. Isidore does not, however, claim that female seminal fluid and breast milk are connected, let alone that they derive from the same source. Rather, '[milk] becomes what it is through the transformation of *blood*, for after birth, if any blood is not consumed as nourishment in the womb, it flows along a natural passageway to the breasts and, whitened due to their special property, it takes on the quality of milk'.[133] The missing link that needs to be established is between female seed, blood, and breast milk.

The key figure here is Aristotle, who disputed the Hippocratic two-seed model of embryogenesis. Aristotle argued that only the male produced seed, which was the vehicle of form. The female could not produce seed, as she lacked the requisite vital heat; instead she provided the corresponding matter in the form of menstrual blood, the residue of undigested nutriment. Falling upon this menstrual blood, the semen consolidated it the way rennet consolidates milk into curd, thus initiating the organization of the foetal body (*Generation of Animals* 1.19–20). It is this menstrual blood, the material

---

132 Bede also invokes the views of 'writers on natural history' [*naturalium scriptores*] concerning embryology in his homily on John 2:18–21, where he draws on Augustine's *De diversis quaestionibus octaginta tribus* to demonstrate that the forty-two years that it took to construct the temple (John 2:20) correspond to the forty-two days required to form the fetus in the uterus. Interestingly, milk appears here as well, but only as an analogy for the initial appearance of the conceptus: 'During the first six days after conception <the conceptus> has a likeness to milk ... ' (*Hom.* 2.1, ed. Hurst, 189; trans. Martin and Hurst, *Homilies on the Gospels* 2:8).

133 Isidore, *Etym.* 11.1.77; trans. Barney *et al.*, 236 (emphasis added).

INTRODUCTION 55

from which the infant body is formed, that Isidore is alluding to as the source of breast milk. But Isidore does not specify that the blood in question is menstrual blood, not does he link this blood with the female seed.

One text that does is the *Gynaecia* of Helvidius Vindicianus Afer. Vindicianus was a fourth-century North African well known to St Augustine, and the author of short summaries of medical theory. One of these, the *Letter to Pentadium*, was definitely available to Bede, as he cites it in chapter 35 of *The Reckoning of Time*.[134] The *Gynaecia* is an introduction to anatomy combined with a short account of embryology, and it enjoyed considerable popularity in the early medieval period. The surviving manuscripts date from the eighth to the eleventh century, and some show evidence of interpolations from Isidore – a sure indication of active reading and use.[135] In ch. 18, Vindicianus starts by explaining the origin of *male* seed in the brain. It descends through the spinal marrow and 'congeals in the form of semen in the kidneys'. It is then ejaculated into the female 'with a certain degree of heat of the internal organs and the menstrual blood and from the phlegm which resides in the kidneys, *and from this condition blood evolves and becomes (female) seed*'.[136] Vindicianus is explicit that women have 'testes' (*i.e.*, ovaries).[137] Finally, in ch. 24 he clearly states that the fetus is formed by a mixture of 'paternal and maternal seed', which explains inherited characteristics.[138]

In sum, we feel confident in proposing that Bede stitched together his argument that Luke 11:27 supports the doctrine that Christ's humanity derived from the flesh of his mother Mary from two *fisici*, namely Isidore of Seville (the two-seed theory; the production of breast milk from blood) and Vindicianus (the two-seed theory; the formation of the foetus from menstrual blood that is the female seed). In Christ's case, the Holy Spirit substituted for the paternal seed, and thus Christ inherited both natures.

---

134 Ed. Jones, 373; trans. Wallis, 101.
135 Cilliers, 'Vindicianus's *Gynaecia*', 153–236; see particularly her comments on the manuscripts and text tradition, 154–60. On interpolation as an index of active engagement with medical texts, see Wallis, 'The Experience of the Book', 101–26.
136 Trans. Cilliers, 178–79 (emphasis added). As Cilliers observes (216–17, 221), this passage is quite confused and problematic. It conflates two ancient theories about the origin of sperm, namely the encephalogenic model (seed originates in the brain of the male) and the haematogenous theory (*male* seed evolves in the blood), as explained by Aristotle (*Generation of Animals* 726b1–15).
137 Vindicianus (ed. Cilliers), 178–79.
138 Vindicianus (ed. Cilliers), 184–85.

## 4. KEY THEMES IN *ON LUKE*

### 4.1 The temple

Bede himself tells his readers that the temple is a dominant theme in *On Luke*. The gospel opens in the temple, where the priest Zechariah receives the angel's message about the impending birth of John the Baptist, and its final verse relates how, after Jesus's ascension, the disciples returned to Jerusalem and 'were always in the temple, praising and blessing God' (Luke 24:52–53). Bede comments:

> Among the four heavenly animals, the evangelist Luke is understood as symbolized by the calf, by the sacrifice of which those who were chosen for the priesthood were ordered to be consecrated, because more than the others, he undertook to expound the priesthood of Christ. In a beautiful manner he began his gospel with the service of the temple by the priesthood of Zechariah, and he completed it with the consecration of the temple, when he showed that in that place the apostles were going to be the ministers, so to speak, of the new priesthood, not with the blood of sacrificial victims, but with the praise and blessing of God.

These words resonate with the prologue-letter to Acca, where Bede quotes Augustine's *Harmony of the Gospels*:

> *Moreover, that Luke was symbolized by the calf on account of the greatest Victim of the priest neither side has doubted. For there the account of the narrator begins with the priest Zechariah, there the kinship of Mary and Elizabeth is mentioned, there the sacred mysteries of the first priesthood are said to have been fulfilled in the infant Christ, and various other things can be carefully observed, by which it becomes apparent that Luke's purpose had to do with the role of the priest.*

The immediate aim of this quotation from Augustine is to prove that Bede was not 'introducing novelties' in his commentary on Revelation when he identified Matthew with the lion and Mark with the man; hence Bede's closing words of the commentary serve to cement his claim to orthodoxy.

But there is much more at stake here. *On Luke* marks the first full articulation of what would become a core theme in Bede's theology: what Conor O'Brien calls the 'temple image'. This temple image 'combined the static architecture of the temple with the dynamic ritual of its priests, thus allowing Bede to speak about both the eternal reality of the Church and the lived experience of its members through a single divinely sanctioned building'.[139] It would bear fruit later in Bede's career in two very original works, *On the Temple* and *On the Tabernacle* (the historical predecessor and allegorical counterpart of the temple), and in his ambitious commentary on Ezra and Nehemiah. But its seed was planted in the Luke commentary[140] and fertilized by the Codex Amiatinus that was being completed at Wearmouth-Jarrow even as Bede was writing. As we discussed above, the Codex Amiatinus prefaces the Old Testament with a schematic representation of the Mosaic Tabernacle, and the New Testament with a *maiestas Domini* – an image of Christ in glory, surrounded by the four evangelists and their animal symbols, a visual echo of both Ezekiel's vision of the Lord enthroned on his chariot and the Heavenly Court of Revelation 4. Both images are linked to the temple as symbol of the created cosmos, of the Church of the Jews and the Gentiles, and most significantly, of Christ himself. O'Brien argues that this imagery deeply shaped Bede's evolving thought as he composed the commentary on Luke.[141]

The image of the temple pervades *On Luke* to an almost intrusive degree. In his exegesis of Luke 2:31, Bede even shifts the scenes of the Visitation and the birth of John the Baptist to the precincts of the temple:

> You see that it is not without reason that this evangelist is compared to the calf among the four animals. In his narrative, being as it were the animal destined for sacrifices, he dwells particularly on the Temple and on Jerusalem. For he starts with a priest praying at the altar, and the multitude of the people in the courtyard of the temple, and sends Mary to Jerusalem immediately after the Lord has been conceived, and puts her into the house of the chief-priest. He refers to the birth of the Baptist there, and immediately turns his attention to the Lord and transfers him there after his nativity with a sacrifice. He brings him to that place with his parents year after year, and situates him at the age of twelve in the temple with a group of doctors … . And after other such things, he closes at the end of his Gospel with the disciples praising God in the temple.

His rather spare treatment of the baptism of Christ ignites a lengthy meditation on the symbolism of the 'bronze sea', the monumental vessel for purifying visitors to the temple. The link is the number three:

---

139 O'Brien, *Bede's Temple*, 5. See also the thoughtful analysis of the 'conceptual temple' in Jennifer O'Reilly, 'Introduction', in Connolly, *Bede: On the Temple*.

140 It can be said that the seed was being readied even earlier, since Bede uses the temple as a 'case study' of allegory in *De schematibus et tropis* 2.12, ed. Kendall (CCSL 123A:168.262–169.273); trans. Kendall, *The Figures of Rhetoric*, 207.

141 O'Brien, *Bede's Temple*, *passim*, esp. 7, 92–97, 183–84.

It is said to be enclosed with a thin cord of thirty cubits on the outside, and to be able to contain three thousand measures, since *with the heart we believe for the sake of justice, but with the mouth confession is made for the sake of salvation* ... . And since the bronze sea comes to mind, it is agreeable as well to inquire how it is suited in other ways to the measure of baptism. *From brim to brim*, it says, *of ten cubits*, because we must not be constricted by earthly anxiety, but expanded by the expectation of the heavenly denarius. *Its brim was like the brim of a cup or the leaf of a crisped lily*, of which the cup of the Lord's passion is represented by the first, and the unveiled splendour of his resurrection by the other ... . Its *thickness of three inches* is in order that all the power of those who baptize may be strengthened by the perfection of faith, hope, and love. It was five cubits in height, because whatever thing is offended by sight, hearing, taste, smell, or touch is washed wholly clean by the water of regeneration. The [twelve cast bronze] oxen that support [the 'sea'] look by threes towards the separate quarters of the sky, in order that the entire world may be baptized in the faith of the holy Trinity. And the bronze sea stood on the right side of the sanctuary of the priests *over against the east southward*, because when the grace of the New Testament breathed forth, it was given by *the Orient from on high, (who) has visited us*.

Almost any detail in the gospel seems to trigger a reference to the temple in Bede's mind: for example, the number of people miraculously fed by Christ on two occasions, namely 5,000 and 4,000 (Luke 9:14):

I think for the sake of signifying mystically the difference that five gilded columns indeed were ordered in the entrance of the tabernacle, but four were ordered before the sanctuary, that is, the holy of holies [cf. Exod. 26:32–37]. Because, of course, beginners are restrained from sinning by the Law, but the perfected are admonished by grace to live more devoutly in God.

Christ's reference to 'preaching from the housetops' (Luke 12:3) prompts Bede to explain that Palestinian houses have flat roofs, not 'peaked roofs after our fashion':

Hence the Law ordered that whoever built a new house should put a wall for the roof around the entire edge, lest innocent blood be shed there by anyone slipping and falling headlong [cf. Deut. 22:8]. And in the construction of the temple we read: *And he covered the house with roofs of cedar. And he built a floor over all the house five cubits in height* [3 Kings 6:9–10].

Bede is particularly captivated by the details of temple worship and by the organization of the priesthood. Interestingly, he cites Origen's claim (Luke 21:5–6) that a principal reason why the temple had to be destroyed was

INTRODUCTION 59

> *lest perchance anyone still a suckling infant in the faith, if he saw those things enduring, should be snatched away by the very sight of the various forms while dazzled in amazement at the ritual of sacrifice and at the arrangement of the services. But God, foreseeing our weakness and wishing his Church to be multiplied, caused all those things to be overthrown and completely removed, so that when those things had beyond any doubt ceased to exist, we might believe these things to which those types had pointed the way to be true.*

Bede felt the seductive pull of the temple and its liturgy at a deep level.[142] Against the backdrop of this almost obsessive fascination, O'Brien argues that Bede's use of the temple image follows several interpretative pathways, two of which are represented in *On Luke*. First, the temple is not only a historical structure but a figure of history itself: 'Thinking about the temple image forced Bede to consider the relationship between the Jewish past and the Christian present, and even, when the temple was read as symbolic (rather than simply a part) of history, the relationship between the past, present, and future'.[143] The 'present Church' of the Sixth Age is in continuity with the worship of the temple; at the same time, the eternal Church of the world to come would see the generations of the faithful from among the Jews and the Gentiles form a heavenly temple, which is Christ himself.[144] For example, when Christ instructs the leper whom he has just healed to show himself to the priest and offer the sacrifice demanded in the Law (Luke 5:14b), Bede feels impelled to address those who object to the Lord approving the very sacrifices which the Church rejects. First, he calls on Augustine to explain that, prior to Christ's passion, the sacrifices of the Old Law remained in effect. Then Bede adds his own comment:

> Indeed, because this man signifies allegorically the human race enfeebled by sins ... . And those who were despised and long cut off from the stronghold of the people of God, now at last may be able to return to the temple and to be offered to the priest, namely to him to whom it is truly said: *You are a priest forever* [Ps. 109:4 (110:4)], and to hear from the Apostle: *For the temple of God is holy, which you are* [I Cor. 3:17]. And they may make an offering for their

---

142 O'Brien, *Bede's Temple*, 56; Jennifer O'Reilly comments that Bede is reluctant to provide details about the architecture and liturgy of papal Rome, and that in rewriting Adomnán's *De locis sanctis* he removed the first-person narrations of the pilgrim Arculf, perhaps reflecting his concern with the dangers of pious material curiosity: 'Bede on Seeing the God of Gods in Zion', 3–29, esp. 3–6.
143 O'Brien, *Bede's Temple*, 47.
144 O'Brien, *Bede's Temple*, 70.

cleansing as Moses commanded, that is, that they present their *bodies a living sacrifice, holy, pleasing to God* [Rom. 12:1].

In sum, the rites of the temple remain valid and good, but in the present age are enacted on a spiritual level.

Perhaps the most striking expression of this theme is the prologue to Book Six, which covers the Passion and Resurrection. Bede emphasizes that these events constitute the hinge of human history, the great turning point when all that had been foreshadowed in the Old Testament would be fulfilled and superseded by the new dispensation. He does so by invoking the image of Solomon's temple, 'built ... as an image of Christ and the Church', drawing attention to the passage in 3 Kings 7:45–46 that describes how the bronze vessels were made using casts of clay models, which were afterwards discarded.

> Therefore, it is as though the sacred rites of the Law come first like a clay mould, so that the gifts of gospel truth may follow like vessels of fine brass. Let the common earthenware pot fashioned for the occasion wear away, so that the splendour of the permanent ornamental vessel which lay hidden may be exposed to view ... . With the passage of time, when the sea of brass in whose vivifying wave all those about to enter the Church would be baptized, and when the twin columns of the Law bearing lilies on their capitals [cf. 3 Kings 7:19] would strengthen on this side and that the gate of the sheep devoted to Christ, and when the twice-five hand-basins of our works were prepared for the cleansing of the sacrificial victims [cf. 3 Kings 7:38–39], the earthenware which concealed these things for a long time in the plains is broken apart so that thereafter countless thousands of vessels of election might be brought to the Temple mount. That is, with the impending proclamation of the Lord's passion, by which the sacraments of the Church were revealed which were formerly hidden by the covering of the letter, the clay earth little by little is loosened, and that shadow that concealed heavenly secrets now begins to be destroyed.

Not all of the interpretative motifs that would later coalesce in *On the Temple* are present in *On Luke*, but O'Brien argues that the connection of the bronze 'sea' to baptism (both here and in the passage discussed above) is distinctive and original.[145]

---

145 O'Brien, *Bede's Temple*, 183–84. It also appears in Bede's commentary on the *Song of Songs*, *In Cantica canticorum*, ed. Hurst (CCSL 119B:322.285–92), which Arthur Holder argues was also composed prior to 716: 'The Anti-Pelagian Character of Bede's Commentary on the Song of Songs', 91–103.

INTRODUCTION 61

Secondly, the temple is Christ himself. This is a note that Bede strikes early on, when he compares the womb of the Virgin Mary to the temple as it appeared in the vision of Ezekiel (Luke 2:23). But it features most prominently in the account of the passion, where Bede uses the unconventional phrase 'the altar of the cross' (Luke 22:15, 23:38). Commenting on the denouement of the parable of the vineyard, where the tenants expel the son of the owner from the vineyard and kill him (Luke 20:15), Bede draws the obvious parallel with the Crucifixion, but uses the detail of the expulsion to tie it to the tabernacle/temple:

> In a prefiguration of this Moses put the altar of holocaust on which the blood of victims was poured out, not within the tabernacle, but at its entry, teaching allegorically not only that the altar of the Lord's cross should be placed outside the gate of Jerusalem, but also that Christ himself, the true sacrifice of the Father, should not be received by the inmost heart of the house of the Jews, which he had approached in order to sanctify it, but that he should be bathed in his own blood out of doors.

In sum, the image of the temple is present at every turn in *On Luke*, and proclaimed by Bede himself as a key to the meaning of the text – Christ himself, and God's plan for salvation.

### 4.2 Heretics and Jews

In the introduction to Book One, Bede claims that Luke wrote primarily to 'to refute the audacity of those who wrote falsehoods about [Jesus]', lest 'the weak be exposed to error'. The first sentence of the commentary proper reinforces Bede's conviction that Luke's principal aim was 'in order that there not be an opportunity for false evangelists to preach falsehoods'. These 'false evangelists' have attempted 'to bring forth heresies'. This sets the stage for a commentary that will focus almost obsessively on heresy.

The tendency to find an argument against heresy beneath every verse of the gospel is certainly abetted by Bede's sources. His quotations from Jerome's commentary on Matthew in relation to Luke 6:1 and Luke 8:2 include that Father's swipes at the Ebionites and the Manicheans; in his reflections on Luke 11:47 he is paraphrasing Ambrose: 'And if the same wisdom of God sent the prophets which sent the apostles, let the heretics cease to attribute Christ's origins to the Virgin,[146] let them leave

---

146 Cf. Ambrose, *Expos. Lucam* 1.25 (CCSL 14:19.391–92).

off preaching that there is one God of the Law and the prophets, and another God of the New Testament ... '.[147] But Bede seems to be intent on displaying his detailed knowledge of and contempt for particular heresies and their doctrines: the Arians (e.g. Luke 1:16–17, 1:76; 2:50–51 5:13, 5:21 etc.), Cerinthians (14:15), Marcionites (Luke 18:31–33), Nestorians (Luke 1:32, 1:35b; etc.), Manicheans (Luke 1:16–17; 2:52; 11:40 etc.), Novatians (e.g. Luke 7:13), Apollinarians (Luke 2:52), Pelagians (Luke 8:46; 15:19), Photinians (Luke 2:22–24 etc.), 'Marcion and ... Tatian, the leader of the Encratites' (Luke 17.27), and the followers of Helvidius (Luke 2:6–7).[148] His tone is distinctly combative and defiant, often articulating his opposition as a challenge to the heretics to abjure their error: 'But if Christ is, or rather, because Christ is the Lord God of Israel, let the Arians cease to deny that Christ is the Lord God; let the Photinians blush to attribute Christ's origins to the Virgin, let the Manicheans stop believing that there is one God of the people of Israel and another of the Christians'.[149] The heretic is imagined as an individual whom Bede taunts: 'What do you say here, O Nestorian, you who strive to impugn the obvious truth, denying that the blessed Mary is the mother of God?' (Luke 1:35b).

Bede's fixation with heresy is curious, for, as many scholars have noted, heresy – even Pelagianism – was not a serious problem in eighth-century Britain. He clearly derived his knowledge of particular heresies from his patristic reading. So what explains his concern? Arthur G. Holder argues that Bede's obsession with heresy is more characteristic of his writings before 716, including *On Luke* and *On the Song of Songs*. This was the period prior to the conversion of Iona and its *familia* to the Roman style of Easter reckoning, and for Bede the resistance of Iona represented the stubbornness and separatism that is characteristic of heresy. Indeed, in the *Ecclesiastical History* and in *The Reckoning of Time* Bede identifies the errant *computus* with Pelagianism. Once the Paschal controversy was resolved, Bede's references to heresy declined.[150] Alan Thacker broadly accepts Holder's thesis, but adds that heresy did not cease to trouble Bede after 716; rather, his concerns shifted from doctrinal error to the moral

---

147 Cf. Ambrose, *Expos. Lucam* 1.2 (CCSL 14:7.30–31). Bede also quotes Ambrose against the Manicheans at Luke 5:13.
148 See also Brown, *A Companion to Bede*, 61, n. 126.
149 Luke 1:16–17; see also, e.g., Luke 1:32, 1:76 etc.
150 Holder, 'Hunting Snakes in the Grass', 104–14; 'The Anti-Pelagian Character of Bede's Commentary on the Song of Songs', esp. 101–03.

dimensions of heresy, notably faithlessness (*perfidia*) and sowing of discord.[151] Recent research on Bede's commentary on Proverbs notes that heresy in this work is linked to an internal problem within the church, namely intellectual vanity and exclusivity.[152] By the time he completed *On Genesis* (c. 722–725), as Kendall has shown, Bede had conflated heresy and the Jews with the Saracens and developed an elaborate schema tracing the peoples of the world to the three sons of Noah – Shem, Ham, and Japheth – and, allegorically, tracing the heirs of the Old Covenant – the Jews and the Saracens – to Abraham's elder son, Ishmael, and the heirs of the New Covenant – the Christians – to Abraham's younger son, Isaac.[153] But there is no hint of this in *On Luke*. It is not surprising that Saracens are not mentioned in it. Saracens were just beginning to enter Bede's awareness in the second decade of the eighth century, and to the end of his life he never conceived of Saracens as 'Muslims', or as bearers of a new faith.[154] But it is perhaps surprising that there is also no reference to Shem, or Ham, or Japheth, or Ishmael. It reminds us how tightly focused Bede is on the New Testament in *On Luke*, and how much his attention to the books of the Old Testament enriched his later thought.

*On Luke* is a pivotal work, composed at a time when the Paschal controversy was still simmering; but it picks up on the themes of treachery signalled by Thacker and of exclusivity noted by Wallis. Both 'treachery' and 'exclusivity' encourage Bede to 'telescope' Jews with heretics, even when he contrasts their specific views.[155] For example, commenting on how the demons possessing the Gerasene man recognized Jesus (Luke 8:28), Bede proclaims:

> How great was the madness of Arius to believe Jesus a created being and not God, whom the demons believe to be the Son of the most high God, and tremble! What sacrilege of the Jews to say that he cast out *demons by the*

---

151 Thacker, 'Why Did Heresy Matter to Bede?', 47–66.
152 Wallis, '*Rectores* at Risk', 129–44. Monotheletism constitutes something of a special case, in that it was a 'novel' heresy in Bede's day, not one the Fathers addressed. Bede treats it fully in *Ecclesiastical History* 4.17–18 and 5.19. Interestingly, though Bede recycled a good deal of his Luke commentary when he composed his commentary on Mark (c. 725–731), he expanded his criticism of Eutyches to 'telescope' Monotheletism and Monophysitism. There is one reference to Eutyches in *On Luke* (Luke 11:27). See O'Reilly, 'Bede and Monotheletism', 105–28.
153 Kendall, *Bede: On Genesis*, Introduction, 21–27.
154 See Kendall, 'Bede and Islam', 93–114.
155 Thacker, 'Bede and the Ordering of Understanding', 55–56.

*prince of the demons* [Matt. 9:34], whom the demons themselves claim to have nothing in common with!

And later (Luke 11:27):

> For just as the Jews, by blaspheming the works of the Holy Spirit, denied that the Son of God was the true God and consubstantial with the Father at that time, so in after times heretics, by denying that Mary, ever virgin, had furnished the material of her own flesh for the only-begotten God who was to be born from human limbs by the operative power of the Holy Spirit, said that the Son of man ought not to claim to be both the true God and consubstantial with his mother.

The Jews as they are represented in the gospel are, inevitably, criticized for stubbornly refusing to recognize Christ as the Messiah. Bede reproduces all the Patristic tropes about blindness and carnality, and couches them in occasionally quite offensive language. He says of Luke 5:39 [And no man drinking old wine has immediately a desire for new; for he says, 'The old is better']: 'This signifies the Jews, tainted by the spittle of the old life, who deemed the precepts of the new grace unworthy; besmirched by the traditions of their elders, they were entirely unable to perceive the sweet taste of spiritual words'. But what brings the Jews closer to the image of heretical *perfidia* is the theme of Jewish envy of Gentiles and desire to persecute the Church. Christ would work no miracles in Nazareth (Luke 4:27) not because he lacked the power to do so

> but on account of their envy, and by this final example that the whole race had been forsaken by him, not because it was not loved, but because it did not love that it was loved, with its teachers, of course, scattered from thence over the whole world for the salvation of the Gentiles.

Envy of the Gentiles reappears in the account of the calling of Matthew (5:30):

> Because if the faith of the Gentiles is signified by the choice of Matthew, who formerly longed for the wealth of the world, but now refreshes the body of Christ with zealous devotion, certainly the arrogance of the Pharisees hints at the envy of the Jews which turns them away from the salvation of the Gentiles.

Elsewhere (Luke 19:7), Bede is even more blunt: 'It is clear that the Jews always hated the salvation of the Gentiles.' This image of the Jews as 'dogs in the manger' who refuse to allow non-Jews to partake of their spiritual blessings recalls Bede's hostile attitude towards the Britons, who withheld the Gospel from the English incomers. The Britons were 'false brethren', guilty of *perfidia*, and to be classed with Jews and heretics.[156] Even worse, the Jews would actively attack and persecute the Church. The barren fig-tree (Luke 13:8) represents 'the nation, which lost its land together with its kingdom by a just judgement, [and which] did not fear to persecute the citizens of heaven because they loved heaven, and to kill the very king of heaven and earth ... '. The pitting of mother against daughter and mother-in-law against daughter-in-law at the End Times (Luke 12:53b–c) represents the Synagogue as 'persecutor of the faith', 'because the carnal Synagogue does not cease to persecute the believers both circumcised and uncircumcised'. The Jews (Luke 19:14) 'not only hated [Jesus] in person up to his death on the cross, but also after his resurrection they inflicted persecution on his apostles and scorned the preaching of the heavenly kingdom'.

Like the 'unchosen' Britons, destined by God to be replaced by the English, the Jews were doomed to be replaced as God's people by the Church. Bede quotes Ambrose (Luke 4:33) that 'the devil had entered in[to the synagogue] when Christ had gone out'. The Jewish priesthood at the time of Christ's birth was ignorant, and the faith was corrupted by the Pharisees, just as the kingdom had passed into the hands of a 'low-born foreigner', Herod (Luke 1:24b–25). He cites Gregory's view that the naming of a single Roman governor and multiple Jewish priests signifies the unity of the emerging Gentile Church and the scattering of the Jews because of their faithlessness (Luke 3:2).

However, the commentary on Luke also reveals Bede working through a significant theological issue in connection with the Jews, one that takes us back to his image of the temple. Just as the Church is the continuation as well as the successor of the Jewish temple, so the Church is the union of Jews and Gentiles. In expounding the parable of the two debtors (Luke 7:50), Bede argues that the two men

> signify both peoples, namely the people of the Jews and the people of the Gentiles, who owed to one creditor, that is, to their Creator, not material money, but the coin of their own salvation. For indeed our Creator created them in his own image and likeness, as if he promoted them with a denarius lent for their salvation ... . But the people to whom the Ten Commandments of the Law were given by the servant owe less. And the people to whom the grace of eternal life was entrusted by the Son owe more ... . But because neither of us, Jew

---

156 Thacker, 'Bede, the Britons and the Book of Samuel', 129–47; 'Bede and the Ordering of Understanding', 57; Murray, 'Bede and the Unchosen Race', 52–67.

or Gentile, is saved by our efforts, but by his grace through faith … . Because whether you take this to mean the advantages of perfecting the knowledge which we have received or of avoiding the folly which we have met up with, surely much more is given to the Church than to the Synagogue. The Church was also once corrupted by the fouler filth of idolatry, seeing that no teacher forbade it, but *where sin abounded, grace abounded more* [Rom. 5:20], and now it is uplifted by the greater proclamation of the perfection of the Gospel.[157]

The symmetry of Jew and Gentile is also represented by the ox and ass of Luke 13:15. Moreover, the Jews were destined to be converted at the end of time (Luke 8:40, 13:10–11).[158]

There seems to be two Bedes: the one who hated the Jews, and the one who loved them, and there is no hint in *On Luke* that he saw this as contradictory.[159] His 'discriminate understanding of the Jews' (in Andrew Scheil's phrase) allowed him to have it both ways: the Jews who opposed Christ were reprehensible, but Jews and Christians formed a single edifice, united by the 'corner stone' of Christ.[160] Bede's overwhelming concern with unity lent particular power to this architectural image, which will culminate in *On the Tabernacle* and *On the Temple*. Moreover, Bede's more hostile expressions about the Jews may also reflect his own intense awareness of himself and his people as Gentiles: being Gentile was, as Paul Hilliard argues, an important element in Bede's Christian identity.[161] Finally, as Conor O'Brien observes, it is important to remember that Bede's thinking evolved throughout his career, and that *On Luke* was a relatively early work. O'Brien argues that Bede became more positive towards the material Temple and to Jewish worship as time passed, more interested in parallels between Temple and Church than replacement theories.[162]

---

157 Bede reiterates (Luke 8:40) that, though the Synagogue may reject Christ, at least it is free from idolatry. Cf. his quotation from Augustine's *Quaestiones euang.* in the exposition of the parable of the Prodigal Son (Luke 15:29), where the elder son represents Jews who did not become Christians, but who nonetheless reject idolatry.

158 On the importance of this theme in Bede's evolving understanding of salvation history see Darby, *Bede and the End of Time*, 105–09.

159 See Scheil, *The Footsteps of Israel*, esp. ch. 1, 'Bede and Hate', and ch. 2, 'Bede and Love'. Scheil does not discuss *On Luke* specifically.

160 Scheil discusses the use of the 'biblical cornerstone' as a metaphor: *The Footsteps of Israel*, 77–78.

161 Hilliard, 'The Venerable Bede as Scholar', 106–07.

162 'It seems unlikely that Bede's interest in emphasizing the election of his own people declined in the second half of his career; rather he found that continuity instead of rupture could be turned to this purpose. Something seems to have changed between Bede beginning

The temple image carried with it an ecclesiology that stressed continuity between the Jews of the old dispensation and the Church of the new. But it is also interesting to note in this context that *On Luke* was the last commentary on a New Testament work that Bede would compose. Even as he was completing *On Luke* in the early years of the second decade of the eighth century, he was turning towards the Old Testament – *On the Song of Songs, On First Samuel, On Genesis*. While he would later write a commentary on Mark's Gospel this was in significant measure a repackaging of the Luke commentary, while the *Retractations* is an *addenda et corrigenda* to his commentary on Acts. In short, after finishing *On Luke*, Bede read his theology through the Jewish scriptures. In consequence, the balance shifted towards love, so that he could imagine that his own people – the Christian people and the English people – 'have been admitted among the descendants of the Israelites, since, although according to the flesh we have our origin from other nations, nevertheless by the faith of truth and by purity of the body and mind, we follow in the footsteps of Israel'.[163]

### 4.3 Preachers and teachers

*On Luke* may indeed be a relatively early work, but Bede's later concerns with reforming the clergy and church of Northumbria are already present. The key figure was the individual he called *rector, praedicator, doctor*[164]

---

Book Six of *On Luke* with an overwhelming emphasis on the temple as a fleeting figure to be destroyed when replaced and his completion of *On the Temple*, which, while entirely devoted to exploring the image's figural meaning, only makes one vague comment about the necessity of the temple's destruction'. O'Brien, *Bede's Temple*, 59; see also his 'Bede on the Jewish Church', 63–73, esp. 70–71.

163 *Hom.* 1.17, ed. Hurst CCSL 122:124.177–80; trans. Martin and Hurst, *Homilies on the Gospels* 1:172; cf. Scheil, *The Footsteps of Israel*, 96.

164 'For Bede, the *doctor* was essentially the initiate who had penetrated beyond the veil of the literal sense of Scripture to the *arcana* beneath. He (or indeed she) had to combine the active pursuit of learning with contemplative prayer and exemplary living in order to infuse the active pastorate not just with basic understanding but with right doctrine and true ideals. The *doctores* formed, so to speak, the intellectual powerhouse which inspired and instructed the practical preachers (*praedicatores*) who were to carry out the evangelizing work on the ground': Thacker, 'Bede and the Ordering of Understanding', 43. Thacker notes sixty-three references to *doctores* in *On Luke* (54, n. 59). However, the term 'doctor' is ambiguous: it can denote the Jewish leaders (e.g., Luke 2:46, 8:50) and even 'doctors of secular laws' (Luke 8:43b), but is also coupled with 'pastors' (Luke 11:33). The fishermen called as apostles are the 'doctors of the Church' (Luke 5:2b).

or *magister* – the one who instructs the faithful in word, but also models right behaviour in deed and shows pastoral leadership. In the first instance, these would be bishops and other ordained clergy, but Bede seems to have envisioned monks and clerics of lower rank engaged in this crucial work. Christ in the synagogue (Luke 4:32) or expounding a parable to his disciples (Luke 12:42) is the model for teachers, but so are the Nativity shepherds (Luke 2:15 *sqq.*). To teach is an exalted calling (Luke 12:33–34):

> The difference between the rewards given to good pupils and those given to good teachers is as great as the difference of their merits. For when the Lord at his coming finds the former keeping watch, he will make them sit down to eat, and 'coming by' will minister to them. But when the Lord finds the latter faithfully and wisely dispensing the nourishment of Scripture to a household devoted to himself, he will set them over all he possesses, that is, over all the joys of the heavenly kingdom, not, of course, in order that they may have sole possession of them, but so that they may enjoy eternal possession of them more abundantly than other holy people. *For those who are learned will shine like the brightness of the firmament, and those who instruct many to justice, like stars for all eternity* (Dan. 12:3). And the Apostle says: *Let the priests who rule well be esteemed worthy of double honour, especially those who labour in word and doctrine* (I Tim. 5:17).

Opposed to good teachers are 'wicked prelates' (Luke 12:45), or those whose deeds belie their words (Luke 4:32), or one who shrinks from the task for carnal reasons (Luke 8:16). The parable of the talents expressly targets teachers, and

> the servant, who had been commanded to trade, but who laid up in a handkerchief the Lord's money which he received, represents those who are capable of preaching, but when the Lord prescribes the duty of preaching by the Church, either refuse to undertake it, or if they do undertake it, fail to do so in a worthy fashion. (Luke 19:21–22)

He is consequently an 'evil Catholic' (Luke 19:27).

This concern with teachers who refused to teach would remain constant throughout Bede's career, though other abuses, such as episcopal indolence and a more pervasive sense of decline and danger, would come to dominate his exegetical works.[165]

---

[165] Bede's shifting concerns about reform are analyzed by DeGregorio, "'Nostrorum socordiam temporum'", 107–22 ; see especially 113–14 on the Luke commentary's focus on sloth and ignorance.

INTRODUCTION 69

## 4.4 An anomalous episode: exorcism, the incubus, and 'sacramental healing'

In the midst of this edifice of recurring themes, Bede's account of contemporary exorcism rituals stands out as an anomaly. The passage in question is Luke 8:30, where Jesus asks the demon tormenting the Gadarene man, 'What is your name? But he said: Legion, because many demons had entered into him'. As is his wont, Bede hastens to assure the reader that Christ already knew the demon's name; he only posed to the question to enhance the revelation of his power. But then Bede continues:

> But even the priests of our time, who know how to drive out demons by the grace of exorcism, are accustomed to say that sufferers cannot be healed unless they reveal openly by confession, as far as they can know, all that they suffered, waking or sleeping, from the unclean spirits through sight, hearing, taste, touch, or whatever other sense of body or soul. And especially when, appearing either to men in the shape of a woman or to women in the guise of a man, by an abominable miracle, incorporeal spirits, *demons whom the Gauls call Dusii*,[166] pretend that they desire and perform sexual intercourse with the human body. And the priests order that the name of the demon by which he said he was called be made known as well as the terms of the oath by which they concluded either contract of love.

The reference to the *Dusii* ultimately comes from Augustine's *City of God* 15.23, but it is more likely that Bede was using Isidore here, because he neglects to mention Augustine's other examples of demons who copulate with human women (e.g., the classical Silvani and Pans). Moreover, Augustine is convinced that sexual intercourse really takes place, but Bede is a little bit more cautious: the demons 'pretend' desire and even coitus, and their victim is made to enter into a contract. Unlike Augustine (whose focus is the factuality of the passage from Genesis 6:2 on the coupling of angels with human women), Bede is concerned with the necessity for full disclosure on the part of the victim for exorcism to be successful.[167] He recounts, with a show of reluctance, a remarkable local occurrence:

> An affair very like a fable, but still true, and which is very well known by the testimony of many, is that a certain priest close to me reported that he began

---

166 Augustine, *De ciuitate Dei* 15.23 (CCSL 48:489.18–19) (= Isidore, *Etym.* 8.11.103).
167 In his own commentary on Genesis 6:2 (ed. Jones, 100–01; trans. Kendall, 170–71), Bede avoids any reference to incubi, and prefers the Vulgate 'sons of God' to the Septuagint 'angels'.

to heal a nun from a demon, but that as long as the matter was concealed, he was able to make no progress with her. However, he said that once she had acknowledged the apparition by which she was molested, he immediately put it to flight with the necessary prayers and other kinds of purifications, and that he had healed the body of the same woman of the ulcers she had contracted from the touch of the demon by means of blessed medicinal salt which he applied with care. But he said that when he could not by any means close one of the ulcers which he found had pierced the upper part of her side without it immediately opening, he received the advice by which she was healed from the very woman that he wanted to heal. 'If', she said, 'you sprinkle the holy oil for the sick as the same remedy, and so anoint me, I will immediately be restored. For in the spirit, I once saw a girl in a certain faraway city, which I never saw with my own eyes, labouring under the same adversity, and she was healed in this way by a priest'. He did as she had suggested, and immediately the ulcer consented to accept the remedy, which it had before rejected.

Bede seems a little embarrassed at this digression, and says: 'I have taken care to explain these things briefly in opposition to the deceits of the demons, in order for you to understand how purposefully the Lord asked the name of the spirit he was going to expel'. But this passage cannot fail to stand out: it would seem to belong more in the *Ecclesiastical History* or one of Bede's saints' lives, or even in a homily, than in this commentary, which is so firmly focused on teaching teachers to teach. The thread that links it to Luke 8:30 is highly tenuous: from the need to make the demon speak his name in the Bible text, Bede has shifted to the need from those seeking exorcism or spiritual healing to reveal the nature of their relationship with the demon.

Intriguingly, women are the protagonists in both the incubus passage and the account of the sacramental healing, and it is precisely this that gave this unusual aside a significant after-life. Bede's commentaries were copied and studied on the continent in the Carolingian period, notably by Hincmar, archbishop of Reims (806–882). Hincmar's *On the Divorce of King Lothar and Queen Theutberga* (860) makes particularly heavy use of Bede's *On Luke*, including the anomalous passage discussed above. The issue at stake was the effort by Lothar II to repudiate his queen, Theutberga, so that he could marry his mistress. The queen was accused and condemned by a synod in Aachen, but Hincmar argued that the process was flawed on legal and theological grounds. In particular, he raised the possibility that the king's mistress may have used magic to deceive him and bring about the queen's downfall. It is at this juncture that Hincmar quotes the entire passage discussed above as an example of women's ambivalent vulnerability to demonic magic.[168]

## 5. BEDE'S STYLE AND VOCABULARY

Bede was thoroughly acquainted with patristic Christian authors who deployed a variety of Latin prose styles from plain to highly sophisticated, depending on their audience. Bertram Colgrave has noted, with respect to the *Ecclesiastical History*, that '[m]any scholars have praised Bede's Latin style for its straightforwardness and simplicity ... '.[169] This generalization is misleading, as Colgrave shows. Bede selected from a range of styles to suit the needs or prejudices of his audience. *On Luke* is hardly straightforward or simple.

The exchange of letters between Bishop Acca and Bede that constitutes the Prologue of *On Luke* is carried on in a self-consciously artificial high style. The two men exchange greetings with lofty verbal gestures. Acca addresses 'his most reverend brother in Christ and fellow priest, the presbyter Bede', and Bede replies, doubling the superlatives, to 'his most blessed and exceedingly best beloved Acca'. Acca invokes the modesty *topos* on Bede's behalf and trots out an elegiac couplet, proclaiming his familiarity with classical rhetoric and poetics.

Acca's chief argument in support of Bede's writing a new commentary on Luke, although Ambrose had previously composed one, is that

> there are certain things in the blessed Ambrose's commentary on Luke at once so florid and lofty ... that they can only be understood by learned men. They are considered to be, so to speak, too lofty to be investigated or too bold to be scrutinized by those readers who are ignorant and hard to please (you will find many such in the present age) because it is difficult to understand flowery language or to grasp profundities.

Bede, therefore, should write on Luke 'in order that those who because of the weakness of their faculties are unable to grasp profound or difficult things intellectually may comprehend them more easily when they are explained in a simpler style'. This is just what Bede does not do. Either

---

168 Nelson, 'Hincmar of Reims meets Bede', 334–36.
169 Colgrave and Mynors, eds, *Bede's Ecclesiastical History*, xxxvi. For a study of the rhetoric of the *Ecclesiastical History*, see Kendall, 'Bede's *Historia ecclesiastica*: The Rhetoric of Faith', esp. 147–63.

he quotes Ambrose (and Jerome, Gregory, and Augustine) verbatim, or he adds new interpretations in a style that is at least as elevated as, and if anything more hypotactic than, anything in the prose of the four patristic Fathers.

Bede's vocabulary, apart from his sources, is extensive and remarkably classical. Very occasionally he resorts to what appears to be a rare word or a neologism. We note that he employs the word *parabolatim*, 'allegorically', three times in *On Luke* (CCSL 120: 29.418, 172.259, and 326.1222) and nowhere else in his writings. Othlo of St Emmeram (eleventh century) is the only author we have found who uses the word independently of Bede. It may be Bede's coinage. *Consideratu*, 'in respect of' (CCSL 120: 362.2660) seems to be a neologism that Bede might have come upon in Julian of Eclano. *Nectura* (CCSL 120: 166.3), 'thread', is a rare word that Bede probably encountered in the Codex Amiatinus or one of its companion volumes (re: Ecclus. 6:31). The word *informositas* (CCSL 120: 248.678), 'disfigurement', in place of Augustine's *informitas*, is apparently Bede's coinage, and one that did not catch on.

Bede's preface to Book 6 exhibits an unexpected cluster of neologisms: *umbratice* (CCSL 120: 363.4–5), 'in a shadowy manner'; *incomparandi* (CCSL 120: 363.7–8), 'incomparable'; *permansibilis* (CCSL 120: 363.24), 'permanent'; and *occultatrix* (CCSL 120: 364.36), 'that concealed'. Bede must have been aware of what he was doing, but it is difficult to imagine what effect he intended. Could he have meant the newly minted forms to highlight the momentous shift from the wavering shadows of the Old Testament to the revealed truths of the New?

## 6. THE MANUSCRIPTS AND THE TRANSMISSION OF THE TEXT

Bede's works were in demand from an early date.[170] They were sent forth from the scriptorium at Jarrow to other scriptoria in England, like Hexham in the north and Canterbury in the south, to be copied. Anglo-Saxon missionaries to Germany added to the demand. Pre-Conquest English manuscripts have almost entirely disappeared; they are known at second hand from evidence found in Bede's writings, and from other letters, catalogues, and inferences from continental manuscripts.

---

170 See Laistner, *Hand-List*, 1–14.

# INTRODUCTION

The earliest extant manuscripts of *On Luke*, which date from the second half of the eighth century, suggest the main lines of continental diffusion – one stream flowing to Germany, the other south and east through France. Hannover 3983a+New Haven 441, which survives only in fragments, is written in Anglo-Saxon minuscule, and could have been copied in England or in an Anglo-Saxon centre in Germany. Two other late eighth-century manuscripts, Paris 11681 and Brussels 8654–8672+St-Omer 72, were produced in scriptoria in northern France, Paris 11681 at the abbey of Corbie, and Brussels+St-Omer at the abbey of St-Bertin. St-Bertin was located near the present township of St-Omer not far from the narrowest point of the English Channel directly across from Canterbury. Corbie was a short distance south of St-Bertin. It is reasonable to conjecture that their exemplars were copied at, or passed through, Canterbury, and that from and through northern French abbeys like these *On Luke* spread south and east in the ninth century to monastic centres in France. Within about a century from the time of Bede's death, if not sooner, it had crossed the Pyrenees into Catalunya (San Felix 146).

As we noted above, *On Luke* was widely read in the Carolingian and post-Carolingian period, both on the continent[171] and in the Insular sphere. For the latter, a detailed survey of extracts, quotations, and references in booklists is furnished by the editors of the Bede volumes of *Sources of Anglo-Saxon Literary Culture*.[172] As their work demonstrated, extracts from the commentary were incorporated as *lectiones* into liturgical manuscripts, but the single most significant vehicle for disseminating *On Luke* was the abundant extracts in the Homiliary of Paul the Deacon. This was the source from which Ælfric derived many, but not all of his borrowings. *On Luke* is echoed in works as diverse as the *Old English Orosius* and Byrhtferth's *Vita Ecgwini*, and, on the continent, turns up in the sermons and commentaries of Hrabanus Maurus, Smaragdus, and Haymo of Auxerre.

Of the thirty-four manuscripts of *On Luke* that date from the ninth century, twenty-one were certainly or probably produced in France, and seven in Germany. Italy proves to be a key intermediary in the transmission of *On Luke* to the high Middle Ages. This may in part be owing to the fact that Paul the Deacon, whom Charlemagne commissioned to prepare a

---

171 More Carolingian manuscripts of the Commentary on Luke survive than of any of Bede's other works: see Westgard, 'Bede and the Continent in the Carolingian Age and Beyond', 207.
172 Brown and Biggs, *Bede* 2:84–127.

homiliary for use in the churches of his kingdom, was a monk from Monte Cassino. Paul drew extensively from *On Luke* as well as Bede's other commentaries and homilies.[173] *On Luke* was copied there early in the ninth century (Monte Cassino 37) and more copies survive from the eleventh century. Even more suggestive is the number of manuscripts of extracts from *On Luke* for homiliary use that were made at Monte Cassino or its dependent houses.[174]

By the turn of the millennium there was a considerable bank of material extracted from *On Luke* available in other formats. But Bede's commentary continued to be copied and read as a whole, notably by the creators of the *Glossa ordinaria*, whose gloss on Luke leans heavily on Bede.[175] After a falloff in the chaotic tenth century, interest in *On Luke* as measured by the number of surviving manuscripts begins to pick up in the eleventh, particularly in Italy. In the British Isles access to Bede was crucially dependent on the reimportation of his works after the devastations of the Viking incursions. This reimportation is witnessed by Oxford, Bodley 218, and in the second half of the eleventh century by Cambridge, Pembroke College 83.[176] The highpoint of interest in the commentary is reached in the twelfth century, from which period thirty-seven manuscripts have come down to us. As many as ten of these may have been produced in England, witnessing both the general reinvigoration of intellectual life there as elsewhere in western Europe in the twelfth century, and specifically Bede's renown as a scriptural scholar.[177]

---

173 See Smetana, 'Paul the Deacon's Patristic Anthology', 76, 79–80; Hill, 'Carolingian Perspectives', 231–32.

174 See below, Introduction 7(B), Extracts.

175 Smith, *The Glossa Ordinaria*, esp. 43, 52, and 55; on how the compilers of the *Glossa* edited Bede for brevity and clarity, see 80–83.

176 Lapidge, *The Anglo-Saxon Library*, 168, 171; Westgard, 'Bede and the Continent', 209–10.

177 See Westgard, 'Bede and the Continent', Table 1 (p. 211), for an overview of the '[s]urviving manuscripts of Bede's works, by date of origin'. Additional manuscripts of various of these works, including *On Luke*, have come to light since the table was compiled, but the relative figures remain suggestive.

INTRODUCTION    75

## 7. LIST OF (A) FULL MANUSCRIPTS AND (B) MANUSCRIPTS OF EXTRACTS OF BEDE'S *COMMENTARY ON LUKE*

The list of MSS is based on Laistner, *Hand-List*, 44–50 [= Laistner]; updated by Hurst, ed., CCSL 120:v–vii [= Hurst]; and Gorman, 'Source Marks', Appendix 4 [= Gorman]; supplemented and corrected by information drawn from other sources as specified. Documentation provided by Laistner, Hurst, and Gorman is not repeated here.

Pressmarks of MSS also containing Bede's *Commentary on Mark* are flagged with a dagger, thus: †AVRANCHES, Bibliothèque municipale 107; or, if containing only extracts from both works, with a double-dagger, thus: ‡VATICAN CITY, BAV, Vat. lat. 4222.

### (A) Manuscripts

1. ADMONT, Stiftsbibliothek 109, 150 fols, s. xii.
   Laistner; Manuscripta.at.
2. ALENÇON, Bibliothèque municipale 7, s. xii, St Évroult.
   Laistner; BVMM.
3. AMIENS, Bibliothèque municipale 75, fols 1–142v, s. xii, Corbie.
   Laistner.
4. ANGERS, Bibliothèque municipale 63, 209 fols, s. ix, St-Aubin. The Letter from Acca to Bede is missing. *Domino beatissimo ... quo eis benediceret* (CCSL 120:6.79–424.2422).
   Laistner; Hurst. Hurst's **A**.
5. ARRAS, Bibliothèque municipale, Médiathèque 879 (698), fols 2–145, 147, s. ix$^{2/4}$, St-Vaast.
   Laistner; Gorman; Bischoff, *Katalog* 1:92; Mirabile.
6. †AVRANCHES, Bibliothèque municipale 107, s. xi$^{med}$, Mont-St-Michel(?); prov. Mont-St-Michel.
   Laistner; BVMM; Mirabile.
7. BAMBERG, Staatsbibliothek 115 (B.IV.2), fols 1r–111v, s. ix$^{2/4}$, central France; prov. Bamberg Cathedral. From preface of Book 4 through Book 6 (a few lines missing at end).
   Laistner; Gorman; Bischoff, *Katalog* 1:197; Mirabile. Online: MDZ.
8. BAMBERG, Staatsbibliothek 116 (B.IV.1), fols 1r–182v, 1123/1140, Michelsberg; prov. Michelsberg.
   Laistner; Mirabile.

9. BRUSSELS, Bibliothèque Royale 8654–8672 + ST OMER, Bibliothèque municipale 72 (frag.), 3 bifolios, s. viii²/ix¹, St-Bertin.
CLA 10:1542; CLA Suppl.:1542. Bischoff, *Katalog* 1:156.
10. CAMBRAI, Médiathèque (Bibliothèque) municipale 295 (277), fols 7r–171^bis r, before 817, Cambrai.
Laistner; Gorman; Bischoff, *Katalog* 1:778; Mirabile. Hurst's **C**.
11. CAMBRIDGE, Pembroke College 83, fols 2r–229v, s. ix¹, St-Denis; prov. Bury St Edmunds, s. xi².
Laistner; Gorman; Bischoff, *Katalog* 1:831; Lapidge, *The Anglo-Saxon Library*, 168; Mirabile.
12. CAMBRIDGE, Trinity College 46, fols 1r–237v, s. xii, Christ Church, Canterbury.
Laistner.
13. CAMBRIDGE, University Library Dd i 29, 179 fols, s. xii, Louth Park.
Laistner.
14. CAMBRIDGE, University Library, Addit. 3108, fols 6r–166v, s. xii^ex, England(?).
Hurst; Mirabile.
15. CAMBRIDGE (Mass.), Harvard University, Ms. Typ. 202H (formerly Phillipps 1092; London, Chester Beatty 31; New York, Philip Hofer 19), fols 1v–182r, s. xii^2/4, Germany(?); prov. St Vitus, Gladbach.
Laistner; Hurst; Mirabile.
16. CAMBRIDGE (Mass.), Harvard University, Houghton Library, Riant 36, 31 fols, s. xii, France. A patristic miscellany.
Schoenberg Database.
17. CHARLEVILLE, Bibliothèque municipale 169, s. xii, Signy.
Laistner.
18. *CHARTRES, Bibliothèque municipale 83, s. xii, St Père. Destroyed in World War II.
19. CHELTENHAM (?), Phillipps 467, s. xii.
Hurst.
20. COIMBRA, Monasterium S. Crucis LVIII, Est. 15, Caixa 18, fol. 140 ff. Fragment: ending lost after ... *sua luce fruerentur* (CCSL 120:406.1719).
Laistner.
21. DIJON, Bibliothèque municipale 76, 142 fols, s. x, St-Bénigne.
Laistner.
22. DIJON, Bibliothèque municipale 77, fols 4r–207v, s. xii, from a Cistercian monastery.
Laistner; Hurst. Online: Gallica.

INTRODUCTION 77

23. DOUAI, Bibliothèque municipale 331, s. xv$^{ex}$, English College.
Laistner.
24. DÜSSELDORF, Universitäts- und Landesbibliothek B. 18, s. xii$^{2/4}$,
Altenberg.
Mirabile.
25. DÜSSELDORF, Universitäts- und Landesbibliothek B. 18, 1511,
Düsseldorf.
Mirabile.
26. ETON, Coll. 196, 7 fols, s. xii$^{ex}$.
Hurst.
27. ÉVREUX, Bibliothèque municipale 90, fols 6v–192v, s. xii.
Laistner.
28. FLORENCE, Biblioteca Medicea Laurenziana, Conv. Soppr. 266,
prov. S. Maria (Vallombrosa).
Mirabile.
29. FLORENCE, Biblioteca Medicea Laurenziana, Plut. 16.06,
fols 1r–262v, s. xv.
Laistner. Online: *Biblioteca Firenze*.
30. †FLORENCE, Biblioteca Medicea Laurenziana, Plut. 16.10,
fols 64r–198v, s. xi, Moscheta. The text is unbroken, but in two
hands on different parchment. First hand, to ... *et amato gaudio*
(CCSL 120:382.772): 64r–178v; second hand (on whiter parchment):
179r–198v.
Laistner. Online: *Biblioteca Firenze*.
31. FULDA, Landesbibliothek Aa 13, fols 121v–298v, s. x$^{in}$, St Gall.
Laistner; Gorman; Bischoff, *Katalog* 1:1323; Mirabile.
32. GERONA, Sancti Felicis 146.
Hurst.
33. GHENT, Bibliothèque de l'université 175, 175 fols, s. ix$^{3/3}$, near Reims.
Source marks.
Laistner; Gorman; Bischoff, *Katalog* 1:1360.
34. †GOTHA, Öffentliche Bibliothek 80 (Mbr. I, 44).
Laistner.
35. HANNOVER, Kestner-Museum Nr. 3983a (Cul. I 72–393)/Nr. 3983b
(Cul. I 71–394), s. viii$^{ex}$, England, or Anglo-Saxon centre in Germany.
Fragment: see New Haven, Beinecke 441.
36. HEILIGENKREUZ, Zisterzienserstift 169, fols 1ra–154vb, s. xii$^{med}$,
Heiligenkreuz.
Laistner; Manuscripta.at.

37. IPSWICH, Central Library 2, s. xii and xiii.
Laistner.
38. KARLSRUHE, Badische Landesbibliothek, Augiensis 64, fols 1r–298v, s. ix$^{1/3}$, St-Denis; prov. Reichenau. Source marks. Chapter numbers; canon section numbers.
Laistner; Gorman; Bischoff, *Katalog* 1:1606; Mirabile. Online: BLB.
39. KARLSRUHE, Landesbibliothek, Aug. 237, fols 104v–144v, s. ix/x, Reichenau. An abbreviated version of the *Commentary on Luke* combined with glosses.
Laistner.
40. KLOSTERNEUBURG, Bibliothek des Augustiner Chorherrenstiftes 242, fols 1ra–159va, s. xii$^2$, Klosterneuburg.
Laistner; Mirabile.
41. LISBON, Biblioteca Nacional, Alc. 53, s. xiii.
Laistner.
42. LISBON, Biblioteca Nacional, Alc. 423, fols 1r–199v, s. xii$^{ex}$.
Online: BNP.
43. LONDON, British Library, Addit. 10947, s. xv.
Laistner.
44. LONDON, British Library, Addit. 17980, fols 1r–52v, s. ix$^{med}$, Lorsch. Less than a quarter of the commentary remains. No source marks; no canon section numbers.
Laistner; Gorman; Bischoff, *Katalog* 2:2375. Online: *Virtual Monastic Library of Lorsch*.
45. LONDON, British Library, Addit. 22767, fol. 64b, s. xii and xv.
Thompson, *Index to the Catalogue of Additions*, 146.
46. LONDON, British Library, Addit. 26715, s. xii.
Laistner.
47. LONDON, British Library, Egerton 2204, fols 2r–184r, s. xii$^{2/4 \text{ or } 3/4}$, southern England; prov. Abbey of St Mary in Reading.
Laistner. Online: The British Library MS Viewer.
48. LONDON, Kensington Palace 47, s. xv. Untraced.
Laistner.
49. LONS-LE-SAUNIER, Archives départementales du Jura 1 (12 F 1), fols 2v–230v, 804–815, St-Oyen (St-Claude, Jura, in the abbacy of Authelmus [804–815], Lindsay).
Laistner; Gorman; Lindsay, *Notae Latinae* 462; Bischoff, *Katalog* 2:2509; Mirabile.

INTRODUCTION 79

50. LUCCA, Biblioteca Statale 1376 (L 88), fols 1r–103v, s. xii.
Laistner; Mirabile.
51. MADRID, Biblioteca Nacional 492 (A 77), s. xii.
Laistner.
52. MADRID, Biblioteca Nacional 522 (A 75), fols 2r–218v, s. xii, prov.
Messina.
Laistner; *Inventario General* 2:25; Mirabile.
53. *METZ, Bibliothèque municipale 39, s. x, St Arnulf. Destroyed in World War II.
54. MILAN, Biblioteca Ambrosiana C 127 inf., fols 116r–240v, ca. 825, near St-Denis; prov. Bobbio. Copied for Dungal. Source marks. Gorman, 'Source Marks', Appendix 1, includes five references to Hilary of Poitiers' *De trinitate* among his list of source marks in this manuscript. He does not say what letters constitute the source marks, nor does he attempt to explain this anomaly. See Bede's commentary on Luke 22:43b–22:46. These are Bede's only quotations from Hilary in *On Luke*.
Laistner; Gorman; Vezin, 'Observations sur l'origine des manuscrits légués par Dungal à Bobbio', 134–35; Bischoff, *Manuscripts and Libraries*, 110, n. 89; Bischoff, *Katalog* 2:2608.
55. MILAN, Biblioteca Ambrosiana D 23 inf., s. ix$^{2/4}$, Central France. Partly by a scribe from Auxerre. Canon section numbers.
Laistner; Gorman; Bischoff, *Katalog* 2:2614.
56. MONTE CASSINO, Archivio dell'Abbazia 36, s. xi.
Laistner; Hurst.
57. MONTE CASSINO, Archivio dell'Abbazia 37, pp. 1–180, s. ix$^{in}$, Monte Cassino.
Laistner; Hurst; Gorman; Mirabile.
58. MONTE CASSINO, Archivio dell'Abbazia 98, pp. 521–32, c. 1071–1087, Monte Cassino.
Mirabile.
59. MONTE CASSINO, Archivio dell'Abbazia 111/1, c. 1060, Monte Cassino.
Mirabile.
60. MONTE CASSINO, Archivio dell'Abbazia 271, s. xi$^{med}$, Cesamo.
Mirabile.
61. MUNICH, Bayerische Staatsbibliothek CLM 18088, s.xv$^{4/4}$ (1478), Tegernsee.
Laistner.

62. MUNICH, Bayerische Staatsbibliothek CLM 29440(1 (29162), fols 1r–4v, s. ix[1], Polling Abbey. Fragments. 1r–v: *uirtutibus turbae deum laudant ... undique et ad terram* (CCSL 120:345.1970–347.2042); 2r–v: *[tradi]tionum et obseruationum ... fratribus condescendat* (CCSL 120:358.2479–359.2547 (with gaps)); 3r–v: *deserant [am]monentur ... saluatur in perpetuum et apud d[ominum]* (CCSL 120:365.88–367.157); 4r–v: *et omnis populus manicabat ... non seditio[nem]* (CCSL 120:372.378–374.440 (with gaps)). Source marks; canon section numbers.
Hurst; Hauke, *Katalog* 2:419–20. Online: MDZ.

63. MUNICH, Bayerische Staatsbibliothek CLM 29440(2 (29055a), fol. 1r–v, s. ix, St Emmeram. Fragment: *ueniret quid igitur inter homines ... secernuntur et ita in agro* (CCSL 120:80.2410–82.2487). Source mark; canon section number (xi), with canon table number (v) and cross reference to Matthew section number (xii).
Hauke, *Katalog* 2:420. Online: MDZ.

64. MUNICH, Universitätsbibliothek, fragment.
Hurst.

65. NEW HAVEN, Yale University, Beinecke 441 (Wilfred Merton Collection 42), 1 fol., s. viii[ex], England or Anglo-Saxon centre in Germany. Fragment: *Non est enim arbor* [CCSL 120:149.1933] ... *Ac si aliis uerbis ita dicere[t]* [CCSL 120:151.2000]. Canon section number *lx* in margin at Luke 6:43; section number *lxi*, at Luke 6:44b; section number *lxiii*, at Luke 6:46 (the online digital image does not reveal whether there is a section number 62 at Luke 6:45). Anglo-Saxon minuscule; biblical lemmata in red. Another fragment from same MS is Hannover Kestner-Museum Nr. 3983a.
Laistner; Hurst; CLA 2.220; Shailor. Online: Beinecke Medieval MSS.

66. NEW YORK CITY, Columbia University, Plimpton 56, 1 fol., s. x, French? Fragment from a binding.
Laistner.

67. ORLÉANS, Médiathèque 72, pp. 1–463, s. ix[1], Orléans; prov. Fleury. Sewardus, scribe.
Laistner; Gorman; Bischoff, *Katalog* 2.3678; Mirabile.

68. OSNABRÜCK, Gymnasium Carolinum 11, fol. I, s. xvi[in].
Mirabile.

69. OXFORD, Bodleian Library, Bodl. 218, fols 1r–166v, c. 820, Tours; prov. English (s. x).
Laistner; Gorman; Bischoff, *Katalog* 2.3783; Michael Lapidge, *The Anglo-Saxon Library*, 171; Mirabile. Hurst's **J**.

70. †OXFORD, Bodleian Library, Bodl. 729, fols 3–76, s. xii², Missenden and Windsor.
Laistner; Madan and Craster, *A Summary Catalogue of Western Manuscripts* 2.1:505.
71. †OXFORD, Bodleian Library, Bodl. 732, s. xii², French.
Laistner.
72. OXFORD, Bodleian Library, Lat. theol. c.20, 2 fols, s. x, Germany; prov. C.L. Ricketts, Chicago. Containing Bede on Luke 24:40–52.
Laistner; Schoenberg Database; Bodley Checklist.
73. OXFORD, Merton College K.3.3, s. xv.
Laistner.
74. OXFORD, Merton College 176 (O.3.4), fols 180r–353r, s. xiii$^{in}$.
Laistner; Mirabile.
75. †OXFORD, University College 168, s. xv.
Laistner.
76. †PARIS, Bibliothèque de l'Arsenal 294, s. xii, Fontenay. Source marks.
Laistner.
77. †PARIS, Bibliothèque de l'Arsenal 320, s. xi. Source marks.
Laistner.
78. PARIS, Bibliothèque nationale, Baluze 270, fols 124–31, s. ix$^{2/4}$, north-eastern France(?).
Hurst; Mirabile.
79. PARIS, BN lat. 1744, s. xiii. Apparently, only Acca's letter to Bede and Bede's reply.
Laistner; Hurst.
80. PARIS, BN lat. 2354, 203 fols, s. ix.
Laistner; Hurst; Schoenberg Database.
81. PARIS, BN lat. 2355, 240 fols, s. ix¹, north-eastern France(?); prov. St-Denis.
Laistner; Hurst; Gorman; Bischoff, *Katalog* 3:4173; Mirabile.
82. †PARIS, BN lat. 2356, s. xii, Carmelites.
Laistner; Hurst.
83. PARIS, BN lat. 2357, s. xii$^{ex}$.
Laistner; Hurst.
84. PARIS, BN lat. 2358, 193 fols, s. xii/xiii, prov. La Noe Abbey.
Hurst; Schoenberg Database.
85. †PARIS, BN lat. 2371, s. xiii/xiv, S. French.
Laistner.

86. PARIS, BN lat. 5288, fols 34v–41v, s. ix$^{2/4}$. Fragment: all lost after ... *cuius nimirum gratia geritur* (CCSL 120:20.52). No source marks; no canon section numbers.
Laistner; Bischoff, *Katalog* 3:4357; Mirabile. Online: Gallica.
87. PARIS, BN lat. 6113/1, fols 1, 2, s. ix$^{1/2}$, France. Ch. 5.30–34; 6.6–10. Bischoff, *Katalog* 3:4395; Mirabile.
88. PARIS, BN lat. 9571, fols 1r–259v, s. ix$^{3/4}$, West Germany. Source marks; no canon section numbers.
Laistner; Gorman; Bischoff, *Katalog* 3:4607; Mirabile. Online: Gallica.
89. PARIS, BN lat. 9572, fols 2r–180v, s. xi; prov. St-Martial, Limoges. Omits Acca's letter to Bede. Renumbers *capitula* by books.
Laistner. Online: Gallica.
90. PARIS, BN lat. 11681, fols 4r–196v, s. viii$^2$, Corbie. Written in the Corbie ab script. The oldest ms of Bede's Commentary on Luke. Source marks; chapter numbers; canon section numbers.
Laistner; Hurst; Gorman; Bischoff, *Katalog* 3:4701a; Mirabile. Online: Gallica. Hurst's **B**.
91. PARIS, BN lat. 12281, fols 1r–163v, s. ix$^1$, Burgundy; prov. St-Germain. A composite text, incomplete at beginning and end. Text 1 (fols 1r–94v): *Sic ergo incipit ... dicit gratiae praedicator* (CCSL 120:19.10–243.480); text 2 (fols 95r–163v): *Verum tamen quod ... domus oboedientiae dicitur* (CCSL 120:241.419–423.2401). The exemplar of these texts was probably in Insular script. Source marks; chapter numbers; canon section numbers.
Laistner; Hurst; Gorman; Bischoff, *Katalog* 3:4815; Mirabile. Online: Gallica. Hurst's **D**.
92. PARIS, BN lat. 12282, 183 fols, s. ix$^{2/4}$, Paris; prov. St-Germain. Fols. 1–14 and 180–183 are in a twelfth-century hand. Source marks.
Laistner; Gorman; Bischoff, *Katalog* 3:4816; Mirabile.
93. PARIS, BN lat. 17451, fols 9r–200v, s. ix$^1$, Corbie; prov. Compiègne. Text (beginning and ending missing): *a beato Augustino ... ad praesidem accedere* (CCSL 120:8.127–408.1799). Source marks; chapter numbers; canon section numbers.
Laistner; Hurst; Gorman; Bischoff, *Katalog* 3:5020. Online: Gallica. Hurst's **E**.
94. PARIS, BN, n.a. lat. 2388, fols 4–5, s. ix$^{3/4}$, western Germany(?). Fragment.
Bischoff *Katalog* 3:5129; Mirabile.

95. †PERUGIA, Bibliothèque Capitolare di San Lorenzo 41, fols 244r–339v; 244ra–339vb [??], s. xi², Perugia. Mirabile.
96. PORTO, Biblioteca Pública Municipal, Santa Cruz de Coimbra 58 (836), s. xii² (1139?), Avignon; prov. Coimbra. Mirabile.
97. ROME, Biblioteca Casanatense 1880, fols 1r–142v, s. xi, prov. Siena. Mirabile.
98. ST GALL, Stiftsbibliothek 85, pp. 1–471, c. 820/840, St Gall. Finely written by the monk Wolfcoz with few abbreviations. Biblical citations usually in capitals. Chapter numbers in red beginning with chap. 3 (chap. 9 omitted). Source marks; canon section numbers in black beginning with section 6. Laistner; Gorman. Online: *e-codices*. Hurst's **G**.
99. ST OMER, Bibliothèque municipale 17, fols 1v–177r, s. xii⁴, Clairmarais. Renumbers *capitula* by books. No source marks; no canon section numbers. Laistner. Online: Gallica.
100. ST OMER, Bibliothèque municipale 72: see BRUSSELS, Bibliothèque Royale 8654–8672.
101. SALISBURY, Chapter library 37, fols 5–164, s. xi/xii. Laistner.
102. SALZBURG, St Peter A X 3, s. ix, St-Amand(?). Source marks. Laistner; Gorman; Bischoff, *Katalog* 3:5439; Mirabile.
103. SAN FELIX, Condado de Orgello [Urgell] 146, before 839. Laistner; Rudolf Beer, *Handschriftenschätze Spaniens*, p. 227 (referencing a testament, dated 839, of Sisebut II, bishop of Urgell (833–840), stating that he gave Bede on Luke to the monastery).
104. SÉES [Sagiensis, Hurst]. Hurst.
105. SIENA, Private library, 'Domenico Maffei', frag. 4, s. xii, Italy. Mirabile.
106. SOPRON, Állami Levéltára, R317 (Madas 239), fols 1vb, 2ra, s. xiv$^{med}$. Fragments. Mirabile.
107. SOPRON, Evangélikus Egyházközség, Le 87 (Madas 216), fol. 1r–v. Fragment. Mirabile.

84  BEDE: *COMMENTARY ON THE GOSPEL OF LUKE*

108. STUTTGART, Württembergische Landesbibliothek, HB I.163, s. xii/xiii, prov. Ottobeuren.
Mirabile.

109. SUBIACO, Biblioteca del Monumento Nazionale del Monastero di Santa Scolastica 16, XV, s. xi.
Hurst; Mirabile.

110. TOULOUSE, Bibliothèque municipale 188, fols 2r–207r, 1298, Toulouse. Complete text to ... *et eritis mihi testes* (CCSL 120:423.2381). These words are followed by: *Hunc librum fecit scribi dns B de castaneto dei gta eps albiensis. Anno dni MCCXCVIII*, indicating that the manuscript was commissioned in the year 1298 by Bernard de Castanet, bishop of Albi (1276–1308). The chapter summaries for each book are separately numbered and placed before the book they refer to. No source marks; no canon section numbers.
Laistner. Online: Gallica.

111. TRIER, Stadtbibliothek 187/1208 4°, fols 1–184, s. xv², Trier; prov. Eberhardsklausen.
Laistner; Mirabile.

112. TROYES, Bibliothèque municipale 230, s. xii², Clairvaux.
Laistner.

113. TURIN, Biblioteca nazionale 215.
Laistner.

114. UPPSALA, Universitetsbibliotek (Carolina), C 397, s. xiv, Szczecin (Stettin); prov. Szczecin (Stettin).
Mirabile.

115. UTRECHT, Universiteitsbibliotheek 75, 1468, Carthusians near Utrecht. Note on fol. 176v reads: *scriptum et completum per manus fratris Campi Karthusiensis anno domini 1468 domus Traiecti inferioris*.
Laistner.

116. †VALENCIENNES, Bibliothèque municipale 77, fols 1–129v, s. xii, St-Amand; prov. St-Amand.
Laistner; Mirabile.

117. VATICAN CITY, BAV, Pal. lat. 608, s. xv. The prefatory letters only.
Laistner.

118. VATICAN CITY, BAV, Rossi 611, s. xii$^{ex}$/xiii$^{in}$, central Italy.
Mirabile.

119. VATICAN CITY, BAV, Regin. lat. 307, fols (double columns [a/b]) 3rb–3va, 4rb–4va, 4(bis)ra; 5va, 6rb–6va, 7rb–7va, 8rb–8va,

9rab–9vab, 10rb–10va, 11rb–11va, 12rab–12vab, 13rab–13vab, 14rb–14va, 15rb–15va, 16rab–16vab, 17rb–17va, 18rab–18vab, 19rb–19va, 20rb–20va, 21rab–21vab, 22rb–22va, 23rab–23va(b is blank), 24rab–24vab, 25ra(b is blank), 26rb–26va, 27va, 28rb–28va, 29rab–29vab, 30rb–30va, 31rab–31vab, 32rb–32va, 33rb–33va, 34rab–34vab, 35rb–35va, 36rab–36vab, 37rb–37va, 38rb–38va, 40rb–40va, 41rb–41va, 42rb–42va, 43rb–43va, 44rab–44vab, 45rb–45va, 46rab–46vab, 47rb–47va, 48rb–48va, 49rab–49vab, 50rab–50vab, 51rb–51va, 52rb–52va, 53rb–53va, 54rab–54vab, 55rb–55va, 56rab–56vab, 57rab–57vab, 58va, 59rb–59va, 60rb–60va, 61rab–61vab, 62rb–62va, 63rab–63vab, 64rab–64vab, 65rb–65va, 66rb–66va, 67rab–67vab, 68rb–68va, 69rab–69vab, 70rb–70va, 71rab–71vab, 72rab–72vab, 73rb–73va, 74rb–74va, 75rb–75va, 76rb–76va, 77rab–77vab, 78rab–78vab, 79rb–79va, 80rab–80vab, 81rb–81va, 82rb–82va, 83rb–83va, 84rab–84vab, 85rab–85vab, 86rb–86va, 87rb–87va, 88rb–88va, 89rab–89vab, 90rb–90va, 91rb–91va, 92rab–92vab, 93rb–93va, 94rab–94vab, 95rb–95va, 96rb–96va, s. ix$^{in}$.

An abridgement of Bede's commentary accompanied on facing columns by the text of Luke, which begins on fol. 7ra (a synopsis [*elenchus*] of the contents of Luke precedes it). Despite being abridged, the commentary still far exceeds Luke in length; accordingly, both columns on recto and verso are sometimes given over to Bede. Very occasionally, however, Luke fills both columns. When Luke and Bede appear on facing columns, the format is always the same: recto Luke column a, Bede column b; verso Bede column a, Luke column b. Hurst. Online: DVL.

120. VATICAN CITY, BAV, Urb. lat. 102, s. xv.
    Laistner.
121. VATICAN CITY, BAV, Vat. lat. 378, s. x.
122. VATICAN CITY, BAV, Vat. lat. 638, fols 1r–171r, s. xi.
    Laistner. Online: DVL.
123. VERCELLI, Biblioteca Capitolare Eusebiana 95 (119), s. ix$^2$.
    Hurst; Mirabile.
124. VIENNA, Nationalbibliothek 657, 188 fols, 800–820, northern France(?); prov. Paris.
    Laistner; Manuscripta.at.
125. VIENNA, Nationalbibliothek 915, 164 fols, s. xiii$^2$, Krain(?).
    Laistner; Manuscripta.at.

126. †WOLFENBÜTTEL, Herzogliche Bibliothek, Gud. Lat. 2° 102, fols 86–133v, s. xiv².
Laistner.

127. WOLFENBÜTTEL, Herzogliche Bibliothek, Guelf. 20-Weiss., fols 2r–208v, s. ix¹, Weissenburg. Source marks; chapter numbers; canon section numbers.
Online: WDB.

128. ZÜRICH, Zentralbibliothek XIV 26, s. x/xi. Fragments from different works. Frag. 9 is from a codex of Bede on Luke.
Laistner.

**(B) Extracts**

1. ‡AUGSBURG, Staats- und Stadtbibliothek 2° Cod. 186, s. xv²ᐟ³.
Homiliary: extracts.
Spilling, *Die Handschriftenkataloge* 3:136–39.

2. AVRANCHES, Bibliothèque municipale 106, s. xiii, Mont-St-Michel(?). Extracts.
Laistner.

3. BENEVENTO, Biblioteca Capitolare 6/1, fols 91r–93r; 101r–105v, s. x/xi, Benevento(?). Homiliary: extracts, fols 91r–93r; 101r–105v.
Mirabile.

4. BENEVENTO, Biblioteca Capitolare 8, s. xᵉˣ, Benevento(?). Homiliary: extracts, fols 114v–116r; 123r–124r; 124r–126r; 146v–147v.
Mirabile.

5. BENEVENTO, Biblioteca Capitolare 10, s. x/xi, Benevento(?). Homiliary: extracts, fols 190r–192v; 104v–107r; 136r–138r; 222r–224v.
Mirabile.

6. BENEVENTO, Biblioteca Capitolare 11, s. x/xi, Benevento(?). Homiliary: extracts, fols 31r–33r; 157v–172v.
Mirabile.

7. BENEVENTO, Biblioteca Capitolare 12, s. xiiⁱⁿ. Homiliary: extracts, fols 165r–176r; 54r–57r; 57r–59v; 69v–71r; 104v–106v.
Mirabile.

8. BENEVENTO, Biblioteca Capitolare 13, s. x/xi, Benevento(?). Homiliary: extract, fols 77v–81v.
Mirabile.

INTRODUCTION 87

9. BENEVENTO, Biblioteca Capitolare 18, s. x/xi and xii, Benevento(?).
Homiliary: extracts, fols 169r–171r; 203r–203v.
Mirabile.
10. CIVIDALE DEL FRIULI, Museo Archeologico Nazionale, Biblioteca
Capitolare 11, s. xiv, prov. Cividale del Friuli. Homiliary: extract,
fols 8v–10v.
Mirabile.
11. CIVIDALE DEL FRIULI, Museo Archeologico Nazionale, Biblioteca
Capitolare 13, s. $xiv^{2/4}$, prov. Cividale del Friuli. Homiliary: extract,
fols 16r–17r.
Mirabile.
12. ‡CIVIDALE DEL FRIULI, Museo Archeologico Nazionale,
Biblioteca Capitolare 62, s. xiii. Homiliary: extracts, fols 68ra–70rb;
122va–127va; 127va–131ra; 133vb–136ra.
Mirabile.
13. ‡CIVIDALE DEL FRIULI, Museo Archeologico Nazionale,
Biblioteca Capitolare 63, s. xiii. Homiliary: extracts, fols 15va–18vb;
140ra–142vb; 142vb–144vb; 185rb–187vb; 187vb–191ra; 212vb–215ra.
Mirabile.
14. ‡CIVIDALE DEL FRIULI, Museo Archeologico Nazionale,
Biblioteca Capitolare 64, s. xiii/xiv. Homiliary: extracts, fols 2vb–3vb;
30ra–32ra; 33vb–36va; 180va–183rb; 233va–235ra; 31ra–33vb;
172va–177ra; 3vb–4va; 12vb–16ra; 22va–25va; 77va–79rb; 16ra–18vb;
29va–30ra; 63va–64vb.
Mirabile.
15. ‡CIVIDALE DEL FRIULI, Museo Archeologico Nazionale,
Biblioteca Capitolare 65, s. xiii. Homiliary: extracts, fols 35ra–37va;
44ra–46va; 155vb–158rb; 14va–15vb; 22vb–25vb; 28va–30rb;
34vb–39vb; 141va–142va; 25va–28rb; 28rb–28va; 92va–93vb;
181rb–183va.
Mirabile.
16. ‡CIVIDALE DEL FRIULI, Museo Archeologico Nazionale,
Biblioteca Capitolare 66, s. $xiii^{in}$. Homiliary: extracts,
fols 110rb–112va; 152va–155vb.
Mirabile.
17. ‡CIVIDALE DEL FRIULI, Museo Archeologico Nazionale,
Biblioteca Capitolare 67, s. $xii^{med}$. Homiliary: extracts, fols 68ra–74vb;
76ra–81vb.
Mirabile.

18. GRAZ, Universitätsbibliothek 697, s. xi$^2$, Millstatt. Homiliary, prepared by Paul the Deacon by order of Charlemagne: extracts, fols 25v–29v (3.11), 84r–85r (2.5), 138r–139v (2.5), 160r–v (5.18), 161r–162v (3.10), 227v–228r (5.20), and 228v–231v (3.8).
UB-Graz – Handschriftenkatalog.

19. GREIFSWALD, Bibliothek des Geistlichen Ministeriums XXVI.E.103, fols 213va–214ra, s. xv$^{in}$, Greifswald. Extract: Book IV.xi.33.
Mirabile.

20. ‡MADRID, Biblioteca Nacional 194, s. x, Monte Cassino. Homiliary: extracts, fols 278r–v; 185r–186v; 204r–205r; 209v–210v; 187r–188r; 85r–86v; 89r–90v.
Mirabile.

21. MONTE CASSINO, Archivio dell'Abbazia 100, s. xi$^{in}$. Homiliary, extracts, pp. 7–12; 159–62; 162–68; 288–90; 168–71; 262–65; 279–82; 290–93; 230–33; 248–53; 262–65; 265–79; 279–82; 234–38; 314–19.
Mirabile.

22. MONTE CASSINO, Archivio dell'Abbazia 102, s. xi$^{in}$. Homiliary, extracts, pp. 37–42; 199–203; 212–15; 235–38; 330–33; 338–43; 431–36; 448–52; 475–77; 488–92; 525–33; 665–67.
Mirabile.

23. ‡MONTE CASSINO, Archivio dell'Abbazia 103, s. xi$^{in}$. Homiliary, extract, pp. 347–60.
Mirabile.

24. MONTE CASSINO, Archivio dell'Abbazia 104, c. 1035–1071, Monte Cassino. Homiliary: extracts, pp. 285–89; 254–57; Grimoaldus Casinensis, scribe.
Mirabile.

25. ‡MONTE CASSINO, Archivio dell'Abbazia 105/1, c. 1071–1087. Homiliary: extracts, pp. 257–66; 371–76; 497–531.
Mirabile.

26. ‡MONTE CASSINO, Archivio dell'Abbazia 106/2, c. 1058–1071, Monte Cassino. Homiliary: extract, pp. 612–17; Grimoaldus Casinensis, scribe.
Mirabile.

27. ‡MONTE CASSINO, Archivio dell'Abbazia 107, post 1080, Monte Cassino. Homiliary: extract, pp. 207–11.
Mirabile.

28. MONTE CASSINO, Archivio dell'Abbazia 108, c. 1070, Monte Cassino. Homiliary: extract, pp. 47–59.
   Mirabile.
29. MONTE CASSINO, Archivio dell'Abbazia 109/1, s. xi, Monte Cassino. Homiliary: extracts, pp. 325–29; 140–43; 27–31; 383–89; 338–40; 349–52; 288–92; 318–20; Grimoaldus Casinensis, scribe.
   Mirabile.
30. MONTE CASSINO, Archivio dell'Abbazia 112, c. 1087–1105, Monte Cassino. Homiliary: extracts, pp. 138–51; 210–13; 320–29.
   Mirabile.
31. MONTE CASSINO, Archivio dell'Abbazia 113, s. xi$^{in}$, Monte Cassino. Homiliary: extracts, pp. 160–64; 154–60; 423–39.
   Mirabile.
32. ‡MONTE CASSINO, Archivio dell'Abbazia 114, s. xi$^{ex}$, Monte Cassino. Homiliary: extract, pp. 223–24.
   Mirabile.
33. MONTE CASSINO, Archivio dell'Abbazia 305, c. 1025–1055, Albaneta. Homiliary: extracts, pp. 225–29; 238–42; 295–299; 481–85; 505–08; 519–22; 551–58.
   Mirabile.
34. MONTE CASSINO, Archivio dell'Abbazia 310, s. xi$^2$, Albaneta. Homiliary: extracts, pp. 161–66; 417–20.
   Mirabile.
35. MONTE CASSINO, Archivio dell'Abbazia 462. Homiliary: extract, pp. 181–85.
   Mirabile.
36. ‡MONTE CASSINO, Archivio dell'Abbazia 534, post 1058, Monte Cassino. Homiliary: extracts, pp. 318–22; 358–60; 392–96.
   Mirabile.
37. MONTE CASSINO, Archivio dell'Abbazia 543, s. xi$^{in}$, prov. Cesamo. Extract, pp. 428–31, Iohannes, scribe.
   Mirabile.
38. MUNICH, Bayerische Staatsbibliothek CLM 4533, s. ix–x/xi, southern Germany; prov. Benediktbeurn. Homiliary: extract, fols 198r–201v.
   Mirabile.
39. ‡MUNICH, Bayerische Staatsbibliothek CLM 4534, s. ix/x, prov. Benediktbeurn. Homiliary: extracts, fols 99v–101r; 142r–143v;

154v–156v; 156v–157v; 203v–204v; 164r–v; 175v–176v; 169r–171r; 176v–178r; 181v–183r; 246r–247v; 232r–233r; 276v–278r; 178v–180v; 186v–187v; 146v–149r.
Mirabile.
40. NEW HAVEN, Yale University, Beinecke 481.25, fol. 16, s. xi$^2$, southern Germany. Homiliary: extract: CCSL 120:231.31ff.
Mirabile; Orbis.
41. OXFORD, Bodleian Library, Lat. theol. d.20, s. xi$^{ex}$, Normandy(?). Extract, fols 163v–164r.
Mirabile; Bodley Checklist.
42. PARIS, BN lat. 103. Extracts?
43. PARIS, BN lat. 3719. Extracts?
44. ‡ROME, Biblioteca Vallicelliana A.7, s. xi. Homiliary: extracts, fols 9r–10r; 12r–v; 13r–v; 15r–17r; 10r–v; 137v–139r; 148v–150v; 150v–152v; 209r–211v; 5v–7v; 242v–244r; 263r–264r; 115r–118r; 257r–260v.
Mirabile.
45. ‡ROME, Biblioteca Vallicelliana A.10, s. xii. Homiliary: extract, fols 209r–211v.
Mirabile.
46. ‡ROME, Biblioteca Vallicelliana A.16, s. xi$^{ex}$. Homiliary: extracts, fols 5v–7v; 242v–244v; 263r–264r; 115r–118r; 257r–260v.
Mirabile.
47. SALERNO, Museo del Duomo, s.n. 'Homeliarium'. Homiliary: extract, fols 142v–144v.
Mirabile.
48. VATICAN CITY, BAV, Pal. lat. 563, fol. 44ra–b, s. xii. Extract: CCSL 120:380.682–706.
BAV: Manuscripts Catalogue
49. ‡VATICAN CITY, BAV, Vat. lat. 4222, s. xi. Homiliary: extracts, fols 5r–5v; 106v–107v; 122r; 123v–124v.
Mirabile.

**Excluded: MSS Listed or Mentioned by Laistner, Hurst, or Others**

CHICAGO, Library of C.L. Ricketts 23: see OXFORD, Bodleian Library, Lat. theol. c.20.
LONDON, Library of Chester Beatty 31: see CAMBRIDGE (Mass.), Harvard University, Ms. Typ. 202H.

INTRODUCTION 91

LONDON, Wilfred Merton Collection 42: see NEW HAVEN, Yale
University, Beinecke 441.
MELK, Stiftsbibliothek. Mentioned by Laistner as 'doubtful'. Laistner,
*Hand-List*, 49, states that the 'catalogue of 1483 records this work
with the press-mark B 78 23'. The MS now at Melk with a former
pressmark 'B 78' contains works of Raimundus de Pennaforte.
Not listed in Melk catalogues of 1889 (Vinzenz Staufer) and 2000
(Christine Glaßner).
MUNICH, Bayerische Staatsbibliothek CLM 19901. Fragment: Gregory,
*Homiliae in Evangelia*, Homily 39 on Luke 19:42–47, PL 76:1294.
Bischoff, *Die südostdeutschen Schreibschulen und Bibliotheken* 1:165;
CLA 9.1323 (Lowe's attribution, 'Bedae in Lucam Commentarii
Abbreviato', is mistaken).
NEW YORK CITY, Library of Philip Hofer 19 = CAMBRIDGE (Mass.),
Harvard University, Ms. Typ. 202H.
VIENNA, Nationalbibliothek 997.
Does not contain Bede on Luke. Bischoff, 'Wendepunkte', 245,
263–64.

## 8. EDITIONS OF BEDE'S *COMMENTARY ON LUKE*

BADE (Paris, 1521). The *edition princeps*, in vol. 2 of a projected
three-volume collection of Bede's biblical commentaries, published
by Josse Bade (Iodocus Badius Ascensius) under the title *Secundus
Operum Venerablilis Bedae Presbyteri Tomus ... in Euangelium
Lucae Lib. VI* ... .[178]
DE ROIGNY (Paris, 1544–1545). A reprint of the three vols of Bade's
collection.
HERVAGIUS (Basel, 1563; repr. Cologne, 1612, 1688). The first collection
of the complete works of Bede, in eight volumes, under the title
*Opera Bedae Venerabilis presbyteri, Anglosaxonis: viri in divinis
atque humanis literis exercitatissimi*, edited by Ioannes Hervagius
(Johann Herwagen, the Younger). In vol. 5, columns 175–515. In a
marginal note (col. 178) to Bede's Prologue, Hervagius expresses his
disappointment in not finding source marks even in the oldest of the
manuscripts he examined.

---

178 Gorman, 'Source Marks and Chapter Divisions', plate 1.

Online: MDZ.
GILES (London, 1844). *The Complete Works of Venerable Bede*, in 12 vols (1843–1844), ed. J.A. Giles. *In Lucae Evangelium Expositio* appears (with Bede's Commentary on Mark) in vols 10–11 (1844). A reprint, with corrections, of Hervagius.
MIGNE (Paris, 1862). In PL 92, ed. J.-P. Migne. A reprint of Hervagius.
HURST (Turnhout, 1960). In CCSL 120:1–425.

## 9. PRINCIPLES GOVERNING THE PRESENT TRANSLATION

Our translation, the first into English, is based on the Latin text edited in 1960 for the Corpus Christianorum by David Hurst (page references to the Latin text are inserted into the translation between virgules). Hurst's text is not wholly satisfactory, and we have not hesitated to let alternative readings, which seem to give better sense, inform our translation. See Appendix 1. We base our translations of biblical texts for the most part on the Douay-Rheims translation of the Vulgate, as revised by Bishop Challoner. However, in addition to eliminating archaisms, we have not hesitated to depart from Douay-Rheims to bring our translation into line with Bede's text and to clarify his meaning.

Although Bede refers on a number of occasions in *On Luke* to the 'laws' or 'rules' of allegory, he never spells out what these might be. The specifics of 'fourfold allegory' that he describes in *The Figures of Rhetoric* perhaps came to seem more useful when he moved on to composing commentaries on books of the Old Testament. Still, in this work, in addition to *allegorice* ('allegorically'), he deploys a variety of adverbs and adverbial phrases, such as *typice, mystice, tropice, parabolatim, per significationem*, etc., to introduce spiritual/allegorical interpretations of the literal text, but he does not use them in any consistent or technical sense. Accordingly, we translate any one of these terms simply as 'allegorical(ly)' (or, occasionally, 'mystical(ly)').

# BEDE: *COMMENTARY ON THE GOSPEL OF LUKE*

# PROLOGUE

[LETTER FROM ACCA TO BEDE]

Acca, to his most reverend[1] brother in Christ and fellow priest,[2] the presbyter Bede, eternal salvation in the Lord.

I have often suggested to your fraternal Holiness,[3] both in writing when apart from you and in conversation when with you, that you should, following on your commentary on the Acts of the Apostles, write a commentary on the Gospel of Luke. Hitherto you have preferred to put this off out of modesty, claiming that you have been deterred from attempting this task chiefly for two reasons: that the task itself is difficult, and that it has already been done by the saintly and learned Ambrose. You claim as well that you did not dare to take on a task that exceeded your strength; on the contrary, a work that has been superbly completed by a person of the greatest skill should not be done over again by another. When so great a man has written so powerfully, it is a waste of effort to want to say the same things in a different way like a plagiarist, or to substitute feebler words like one who is ignorant. And finally, you are very afraid of producing novelties by finding fault with the efforts of men of old, and that that old proverb may be said of you:
Why put fish into the sea, why water into rivers?
Instead pour abundant gifts into needy places.[4]

---

1 *reuerendissimo*: note that in his reply Bede uses a similar superlative term, and also in later letters to Acca; Darby, *Northumbrian Letters in the Age of Bede* (forthcoming) notes that '[t]he respectful repetition of each other's choices across their correspondence allowed Bede and Acca to indicate to each other that they had scrutinized each other's letters attentively'. We thank Dr Darby for allowing us to consult his draft text.

2 Acca literally comes down to Bede's level here, not asserting his superior position as bishop: an indication of his friendly intentions. The phrase *fratri et consacerdoti* is borrowed from Augustine's letters, which also omit reference to his episcopal authority: Darby (see note 1 above).

3 Literally, 'holy brotherhood': Acca's honorific title for Bede.

4 The source of this distich has not been traced. Cf. Bieler, 'Corpus Christianorum', 330, n. 9. See also Babcock, 'The "proverbium antiquum"', 53–55. It is also listed in Walther's *Proverbia sententiaeque medii aevi*, 11830, but Walther was unaware of its appearance in

But to this objection of yours I briefly reply that, in the words of the comic playwright: *Nothing has been written which has not been written before;*[5] and that: *love endures all things;*[6] and that among the saints it was never the custom either to look askance at or to dispute with one another,[7] but that everyone has offered what he could for the adornment of the house of the Lord in accordance with his powers. For the blessed pope Gregory was not afraid that he was offending the Father when in his homilies he revised so many of the interpretations of the Gospels which they had expounded; nor did Augustine, or any other of the Fathers, while having regard to earlier treatises, refrain out of fear from explaining the Psalms or other matters when he was asked to do so, or of writing whatever things seemed good to him. But rather, as Augustine himself says, *it is necessary therefore that many books be made from many others diverse in style but not diverse in faith,*[8] and also when it comes to these same questions, that the substance itself should be made known to many, in this way for some, in that way for others.[9]

Moreover, there are certain things in the blessed Ambrose's commentary on Luke at once so florid and lofty (which I do not doubt that your Holiness has also seen) that they can only be understood by learned men. They are considered to be, so to speak, too lofty to be investigated or too bold to be scrutinized by those readers who are ignorant and hard to please (you will find many such in the present age) because it is difficult to understand flowery language or to grasp profundities. Augustine, that most learned Father, gave considerable support to this view when he wrote to Paulina, the servant of God, about seeing God.[10] /6/ He did not think that he ought to use other testimonies than those from this little book of the blessed Ambrose, and at the same time he judged that these things should not only be expressed in plain language, but also explained. The result was that, by

---

Acca's letter, which may have been the source of the thirteenth-century manuscript witnesses he cites. The distich also appears in a 9th-century *vita* of St Agnes, and in Heriger of Lobbes's *Gesta Episcoporum Leodiensium* (10th century): both probably derived it from Acca's letter.

5 Terence, *Eunuchus*, prol. 41: cited by Jerome, *Commentarius in Ecclesiasten* (CCSL 72:257.230–32).
6 1 Cor. 13:4 & 7. See below n. 18.
7 Cf. Gal. 5:26.
8 Augustine, *De trinitate* 1.3 (CCSL 50:33.25–26).
9 Cf. I Cor. 7:7.
10 Cf. Augustine, *Epistolae* 147, '*De uidendo Dei liber*' (CSEL 44:274–331).

PROLOGUE 97

revising, he compiled quite a sizeable volume from the short sentences of the aforesaid treatise.

I decided therefore that this should be pointed out so that both your fraternal Holiness and likewise your readers might be aware of it. For when with the help of God you have completed the work I am asking for, I want this letter to be included with it, at the beginning, stating that you were asked to write on Luke strictly out of consideration for your brotherly affability, in order that those who because of the weakness of their faculties are unable to grasp profound or difficult things intellectually may comprehend them more easily when they are explained in a simpler style. Come, therefore, dearly beloved, press on assiduously with this work, and expound the blessed Luke with your luminous discourse. And since the blessed Ambrose omitted from his discussion some matters which seemed to him (being a person of, one might say, exceptional erudition) obvious and not worth pursuing, take care to explain very diligently these things as well, based on an examination of the works of the other Fathers, either in your words or in theirs. I believe moreover that the author of light will also reveal to your ever-vigilant zeal for learning – you who spend sleepless days and nights in meditating on the Law of God[11] – what ought to be understood in those numerous passages which the Fathers overlooked. For it is quite right and proper and a matter of divine piety and righteousness that you, who have wholly neglected the business of the world in order to pursue the eternal and true light of wisdom with an unwearied mind, may not only pursue here the fruit of a purer understanding, but also in the future may contemplate with a pure heart the very *king in his glory*,[12] *in whom are hid all the treasures of wisdom and knowledge.*[13]

I also suggest that your Holiness explain something that troubles some people. In your Commentary on Revelation, when discussing the four animals, why did you say, in a novel interpretation, that Matthew was signified by the lion and Mark by the man,[14] since some on the contrary

---

11 Cf. Ps. 1:2.
12 Isa. 33:17. This verse was a particular favourite of Bede's, which he cited in many works and paraphrased on his deathbed: see Cuthbert's *Epistola in obitu Bedae* (ed. and trans. Colgrave and Mynors, 584–86), and O'Reilly, 'Bede on Seeing the God of Gods in Zion', 83. See also below, Book 3, n. 317. If Bede's predilection for Isa. 33:17 was known to Acca, he may have included this reference to encourage and stimulate him.
13 Col. 2:3.
14 Cf. Bede, *Expositio Apocalypseos* 1.5 (Rev. 4:7), ed. Gryson (CCSL 121A:281.62–79); trans. Wallis, 134–35, and n. 181.

assign Matthew to the man, because he begins as it were to write of the Lord, and Mark, in whom is heard the voice of one roaring in the desert, to the lion? And I ask you to make known more fully in this work what seems to you more reasonable concerning these matters. May *the God of love and peace*[15] deign to keep your fraternal Holiness mindful of us, and always to inspire in you the careful consideration of the wonders of his Law.[16]

---

15  2 Cor. 13:11.
16  Cf. Ps. 118:18 (119:18).

# PROLOGUE

[REPLY FROM BEDE TO ACCA]

Bede, a humble priest, to his most blessed and exceedingly best beloved[17] bishop Acca, salvation in the eternal Lord.

Truly wonderful and wondrously true is the precept of the illustrious teacher, that *love believes all things and hopes all things.*[18] In your letters, /7/ you state that you are asking me to write something for you, and before you have even received my reply consenting to this request, you sketch out a preface for these little commentaries you have just requested, as if they were already completed and put into their definitive form. Although the foundation has not yet been laid, and the building materials have not even been acquired, you yourself arrange the keys with which the entrance is secured as if the building were already completed at great expenditure of labour. Hence friendly confidence is ashamed not to undertake quickly a work that ought to be undertaken quickly, and trusts to complete it more quickly. The confidence of a mutual love that is beyond any doubt does these things indeed, which are done, as was said, by a loving heart. It believes all things, at least as far as they can be done, and hopes all things.

And therefore, after reading the brief remarks of your dearest Holiness, I immediately submitted myself to the toil of the work enjoined upon me, in which (to say nothing of the innumerable obligations of monastic service) I would be myself at once author, amanuensis, and scribe.[19] First I gathered together from here and there the most illustrious (so to speak) works of the Fathers and the ones most worthy of so great a task. Then I applied myself conscientiously to examining what the blessed Ambrose, what Augustine, and then what the ever-vigilant Gregory (living

---

17 A formula drawn *verbatim* from Dionysius Exiguus's letter on Easter reckoning, addressed to Bishop Petronius: ed. Krusch, *Studien zur christlich-mittelalterlichen Chronologie* [v. 2], 62; this text was well known to Bede, who cites it in chs 11, 16, 30, 38, and 47 of *The Reckoning of Time*.
18 1 Cor. 13:4 & 7. Bede is picking up on the quotation from 1 Cor. 13 in Acca's letter (see above, n. 6). Darby (forthcoming) notes that this '[gives] the effect of Bede completing the sentence that his bishop had begun' – an example of 'communication by concordance'.
19 See Introduction, 11–13.

up to his name),[20] the apostle of our nation, what Jerome, the expounder of sacred history, and what the other Fathers understood in the words of Luke, and what they said. These I consigned to slips of parchment as you wished, either verbatim or, for the sake of being concise, in my own words, as I saw fit. Since it was tedious to insert their names individually one at a time and to show in detail what was said by which author, I took the opportunity to inscribe the first letters of their names in the side margin, and by means of these to make known in each case where the words of each of the Fathers which I transcribed begin and where they end, for I am anxious above all that I not be said to steal the statements of my elders, to set them down as if they were my own. And I earnestly beg and implore readers in the name of the Lord, that, if by chance any should consider any whatever of these works of mine to be worth transcribing, they should remember also to affix these afore-mentioned symbols of the names, just as they find them in my original. Where it seemed proper, I have even added discoveries due to my own toil, which (to speak in the words of your Holiness) the author of light revealed to me. And I, although it is not enough for me to spend (as you put it) sleepless days and nights in meditation on the divine Law, nevertheless do not doubt that I have devoted no little study to the Scriptures, and that I was able to see – that is, to discern correctly by reasoning – only those things which the author of light deigned to open to me, not only in this work, but truly in every text.

As for what you say troubles certain persons – why in the Apocalypse in a new interpretation I assigned Matthew to the lion and Mark to the man – whoever they are who are troubled by this ought to consider that I said that what I was conveying was not a new interpretation but the previous interpretation /**8**/ of the Fathers. For I pointed out that it was not interpreted by myself as it seemed to me, but as it had been interpreted by the blessed Augustine, and I even added in a few words why he affirmed this. Also, it is not irrelevant if, by setting down his very words, I should make known what he thought about the evangelists or their animal types, for by these words that work of mine will not only be saved from baseless censure, but also confirmed by the pre-eminent authority of so great a teacher. Therefore, although he set down beautifully and skilfully many things at the beginning about the evangelists in his book, *On the Harmony of the Gospels*, he adds among other things: *And although each of them*

---

20 The name 'Gregory' derives, as Bede seems to know, from the Greek *gregorios*, 'watchful', 'alert'.

*individually may appear to have maintained a certain order of narration of his own, nevertheless no one of them is found to have been willing to write as if in ignorance of a predecessor, or to have omitted things unknown which another is discovered to have written, but as each was inspired, so he did not add unnecessary duplications of his own toil. For Matthew is understood to have taken up the Incarnation of the Lord with respect to his royal lineage and many of his deeds and words with respect to the present life of mankind. Mark, who followed Matthew closely, seems like his servant and epitomizer. For he said nothing in conjunction with John alone, very few things by himself alone, even fewer with Luke alone, but he said very many things in conjunction with Matthew, and very nearly the same number of things in Matthew's very words whether in conjunction with him alone or with the others as well. Luke, however, appears to have been more concerned with the priestly lineage and role of the Lord. For not only did he go back to David himself, not having traced the family tree of the kings, but he traced his lineage through those who were not kings to Nathan, the son of David, who was not himself a king.*[21] *In this he was unlike Matthew, who, starting from King Solomon, followed the other kings also in order, preserving in these the mystical number,*[22] *of which we will speak later.*[23]

*For the Lord Jesus Christ, the one true King and the one true Priest, the former to rule us, the latter to atone for us, made known that his own nature performed these two roles, which were put before us separately by the Fathers.*[24]

And a little below, he says: *For indeed Christ was made King and Priest as a man, to whom 'God' gave 'the throne of his father David',*[25] *in order that 'of his kingdom' there should be 'no end',*[26] *and that 'the man Christ Jesus be the mediator of God and men'*[27] *'to intercede for us'.*[28] *But Luke did not have an epitomizer, so to speak, associated with him, as Matthew had in Mark. And this fact is possibly not without a certain sacramental mystery, since it is characteristic of kings that they are not without the*

---

21 Cf. Luke 3:23–31.
22 Cf. Matt. 1:1–17.
23 Augustine, *De consensu euang.* 1.2 (CSEL 43:4.4–23).
24 Augustine, *De consensu euang.* 1.3 (CSEL 43:4.25–5.3).
25 Luke 1:32.
26 Luke 1:33.
27 1 Tim. 2:5.
28 Rom. 8:34; Hebr. 7:25 (a blend).

*allegiance of attendants. Hence, Matthew, who had undertaken the task of narrating the royal role of Christ, had, as it were, an attendant attached to himself, who was in a way to follow in his footsteps. But since the priest /9/ used to enter into the holy of holies alone,*[29] *for that reason Luke, whose purpose was centred on the priesthood of Christ, did not have any kind of attending companion, to summarize his narrative in some way.*[30]

*Nevertheless, these three evangelists dwelt chiefly on those things which Christ did in the flesh during his time on earth. But, on the other hand, John turned his attention chiefly to the very divinity of the Lord, whereby he is equal to the Father, and he took particular care to commend it in his Gospel, as much as he believed it to be necessary among men. Accordingly, he is borne higher, a long way from those three, so that you see how they lived with Christ the man on earth, but you see that [John] rose above the cloud, with which the whole earth is covered,*[31] *and came to the heavenly water, from whence with the most acute and powerful vision of his mind's eye he could see that in the beginning the Word was God and with God,*[32] *through which all things were made,*[33] *and he could recognize that it was made flesh in order to dwell among us.*[34]

And likewise, somewhat further down, he says: *Hence, among those who have interpreted the four animals of the Apocalypse as symbolizing the four evangelists,*[35] *the ones who have understood the lion as Matthew, the man as Mark, the calf as Luke, and the eagle as John, seem to me to have paid somewhat more careful heed than those who assigned the man to Matthew, the eagle to Mark, and the lion to John. For the latter wanted to take some inference from the beginnings of the books, instead of from the overall intention of the evangelists, which ought rather to have been thoroughly scrutinised. For he who chiefly brought to our attention the royal role of Christ is far more suitably taken as having been symbolised by the lion. Hence also, in the Apocalypse the lion was mentioned with the royal tribe itself, when it was said: 'the lion of the tribe of Juda has prevailed'.*[36] *For, according to Matthew, not only are the Magi said to have come from*

---

29 Cf. Lev. 16:17.
30 Augustine, *De consensu euang.* 1.3 (CSEL 43:6.3–15).
31 Cf. Eccles. 24:6.
32 Cf. John 1:1.
33 Cf. John 1:3.
34 Augustine, *De consensu euang.* 1.4 (CSEL 43:6.16–7.3); cf. John 1:14.
35 Rev. 4:6–7.
36 Rev. 5:5.

*the east to seek and adore the King whose birth was revealed to them by a star, but also King Herod himself fears the infant King Christ and in order that he may be able to kill him slays many young children.*[37] *Moreover, that Luke was symbolised by the calf on account of the greatest Victim of the priest neither side has doubted. For there the account of the narrator begins with the priest Zechariah, there the kinship of Mary and Elizabeth is mentioned, there the sacred mysteries of the first priesthood are said to have been fulfilled in the infant Christ, and various other things can be carefully observed, by which it becomes apparent that Luke's purpose had to do with the role of the priest.*[38] *But Mark, who did not want to narrate either the royal or priestly lineage, or the kinship or the consecration, and nevertheless is shown to have concerned himself with those things which the man Christ did, seems to have signified only the figure of the man among those four animals. Moreover, these three animals, whether the lion or the man or the calf,* /10/ *walk on earth. Hence, the three evangelists were especially concerned with the things which Christ did in the flesh and what precepts for carrying on mortal life he handed down to those bearing flesh. But truly, John soars like an eagle above the clouds of human weakness and looks upon the light of immutable truth with the sharpest and strongest eyes of the heart.*[39]

I have inserted these few testimonies of the blessed Augustine, excerpted from many, to repel the false accusations of the complainants you mention in your letter above. These testimonies should furnish a safeguard to defend my earlier work, as was said, and affix a not ignoble seal to the present one. May the grace of the heavenly Helper deign to preserve your holy Fatherhood as you pray for us, and to strengthen you always for the defence of his holy Church. /11/

---

37 Cf. Matt. 2:1–16.
38 Cf. Luke 1:5 ff.
39 Augustine, *De consensu euang.* 1.6 (CSEL 43:9.3–10.14).

# THE CHAPTERS
# OF THE GOSPEL ACCORDING TO LUKE[1]

Chap. 1. *In a preface Luke indicates to Theophilus that he will narrate the Gospel in chronological order.* [Luke 1:1–4]

Chap. 2. *The priesthood of the just man Zechariah is recounted and the vision in the temple, in which an angel discloses that a son yet to be born is promised to him, and his conception is also recounted.* [Luke 1:5–25]

Chap. 3. *The angel sent to Mary speaks of the Saviour yet to be born. Soon after the Saviour is conceived, Mary is saluted by Elizabeth as John leapt in her womb. Then, after three months, she returned to her own house.* [Luke 1:26–56]

Chap. 4. *After the birth of John, the power of speech is immediately returned to his mute father and he prophesies. The child is in the wilderness until the day of his manifestation to Israel.* [Luke 1:57–80]

Chap. 5. *The edict of Caesar is related. The birth of Christ is announced to the shepherds by an angel with whom a multitude of the heavenly army sings: Glory to God in the highest.* [Luke 2:1–14]

Chap. 6. *After the departure of the angels, the shepherds set forth and found the Saviour lying in the manger, and they praise God for all the things which they saw.* [Luke 2:15–20]

Chap. 7. *Luke tells of the eighth day of Christ's circumcision,* and the thirty-third of Mary's purification, together with[2] *the prophesy of the just*

---

1 Bede copied the chapter numbers and their summaries from one or more of the texts of the Vulgate at his disposal (see Introduction, 16–20). A comparison of the summaries in the Codex Amiatinus with Bede's text reveals only inconsequential discrepancies between the two, with one exception (see note on ch. 7 below).

2 The number of days of a woman's purification after the birth of a male child, which is not mentioned in Luke, is given in Lev. 12:4, which Bede quotes in the course of his commentary on Luke 2:22 in chapter 7. The phrase is not found in the Codex Amiatinus.

man Simeon, who was present [in the temple], and of Anna the prophetess. [Luke 2:21–41]

Chap. 8. *At the age of twelve, Jesus himself remained in the temple away from his parents. To his mother who was seeking him he says: I must be about my Father's business.* [Luke 2:42–52]

Chap. 9. *In the fifteenth year of the reign of Tiberius Caesar, John is said to have begun to preach. He exhorts all to penance and says he is not worthy to untie the shoes of the Lord.* [Luke 3:1–18]

Chap. 10. *Herod imprisons John. And when the Lord is baptised at the age of thirty years, the divine mystery of the Trinity is revealed at his baptism. The sequence of seventy-seven generations[3] from Christ back to God is compiled.* [Luke 3:19–38]

Chap. 11. *Luke recounts Jesus's fast of forty days, and how he overcame the Devil who tempted him three times.* [Luke 4:1–13] **/12/**

Chap. 12. *Luke tells of Christ's fame after he returned to Galilee. Taking up the book of Isaiah, he said that its prophecy was fulfilled in him, and that a prophet has no honour in his own country. After recounting the episode of the widow of Zarephath and the cleansing of the leper, Naaman of Syria, he tells how Jesus passed through the midst of those who wanted to cast him down headlong.* [Luke 4:14–30]

Chap. 13. *In the synagogue Jesus expels a demon from a man who confesses.* [Luke 4:31–37]

Chap. 14. *Simon Peter's wife's mother and a crowd of many infirm people are made well. The demons are forbidden to confess.* [Luke 4:38–44]

Chap. 15. *Luke recounts how Peter trembled and his companions were afraid after two ships are suddenly filled by the draught of the fish through the word of the Lord.* [Luke 5:1–11]

Chap. 16. *A leper is cleansed and many infirm are cured by the power of the Lord.* [Luke 5:12–16]

Chap. 17. *He cures a palsied man, who was lowered down to him through a hole in the roof, both from his sins and his palsy.* [Luke 5:17–26]

---

3 Counting inclusively (i.e., including both Christ and God in the numbering).

# THE CHAPTERS OF THE GOSPEL ACCORDING TO LUKE

Chap. 18. *Levi also known as Matthew*[4] *is called from the custom-house. Jesus confutes those murmuring about how he dines with the tax collectors and about fasting with the parables of the bridegroom and the garment and the new wine.* [Luke 5:27–39]

Chap. 19. *He refutes those questioning the plucking of ears of wheat on the Sabbath by relating the example of David.* [Luke 6:1–5]

Chap. 20. *In the synagogue he cures a withered hand, and the Pharisees are filled with madness.* [Luke 6:6–11]

Chap. 21. *Upon passing the whole night in prayer, he names the twelve apostles in the morning. The sick are cured by touching him.* [Luke 6:12–19]

Chap. 22. *He calls blessed those that are poor, those that hunger, those that weep, those that suffer persecution, and calls down woe upon those that are rich and to those that laugh. He even orders that enemies be loved and that resistance should not be offered to one who strikes or who strips another bare.* [Luke 6:20–30 or 6:20–36]

Chap. 23.[5] *He tells the parable of the mote and the beam as well as of the good and the evil tree, and of how a house ought to be built.* [Luke 6:31–49 or 6:37–49]

Chap. 24. *He heals the slave of a centurion, when the elders and his friends entreat on the centurion's behalf.* [Luke 7:1–10]

Chap. 25. *A dead man, the only son of a widowed mother, is brought back to life on his bier as he is carried out of the city.* [Luke 7:11–18]

Chap. 26. *After the return of John's messengers, he says many things about John's greatness, and he compares the present generation of the Jews to children sitting in the marketplace.* [Luke 7:19–35]

Chap. 27. *The woman washes the feet of the Lord with her tears as he was reclining at table, and the thought of the Pharisee is reproved by the parable of the two debtors.* [Luke 7:36–50] /**13**/

---

4 Cf. Matt. 9:9.
5 In the text we mark Luke 6:31–49 as ch. 23 (a) and Luke 6:37–49 as ch. 23 (b). See Introduction, 19.

Chap. 28. *The women are said to have ministered of their substance to the Lord and his disciples while he was evangelizing. He also propounds and explains the parable of the sower and the fruits.* [Luke 8:1–15]

Chap. 29. *He says that a candle ought not to be put under a vessel, and that they should be called his mother and his brothers who have done the will of the Father.* [Luke 8:16–21]

Chap. 30. *Sleeping on a ship, he is aroused by those in danger and curbs the power of the sea by a word.* [Luke 8:22–25]

Chap. 31. *He healed a man from a legion of demons, and allowed them to go into swine.* [Luke 8:26–39]

Chap. 32. *On his way to the daughter of Jairus, he heals a woman who has to be restored from an issue of blood; he orders the girl when she is restored to be given something to eat.* [Luke 8:40–56]

Chap. 33. *He sends out the twelve preachers, conferring powers upon them and teaching them the precepts of salvation.* [Luke 9:1–6]

Chap. 34. *Herod is reported to have heard of his fame, and the apostles to have related the things they had done.* [Luke 9:7–11]

Chap. 35. *He feeds five thousand people with five loaves and two fish.* [Luke 9:12–17]

Chap. 36. *When he asks the disciples whom men say he is, Peter answers, the Christ of God; but Jesus foretells that he will suffer.* [Luke 9:18–22]

Chap. 37. *He teaches that anyone who would follow him should deny himself, and he says that some will not see death until they see the kingdom of God. Immediately following this is an account of his transfiguration on a mountain.* [Luke 9:23–36]

Chap. 38. *He healed the son of a certain man from an evil spirit, after rebuking the faithlessness of a generation.* [Luke 9:37–43]

Chap. 39. *Again, he says that he is going to suffer, and, having set a child in their midst, opposing their thoughts of primacy, he teaches the disciples humility, and that one who performs miracles in his name is not to be forbidden.* [Luke 9:44–50]

Chap. 40. *He rebukes the disciples who wish to demand fire from heaven upon those who despise him, and to one who says, I will follow you, he declares that the foxes have holes, and to a youth following him, that he should abandon the dead, and that one holding the plough should not look back.* [Luke 9:51–62]

Chap. 41. *After appointing another seventy-two, he gives them precepts by which they should preach; then he rebukes the faithless cities. When the seventy-two return, rejoicing, he commands* /14/ *that they rejoice not over the subjection of the evil spirits but that their names are written in heaven.* [Luke 10:1–20]

Chap. 42. *The Lord's joyful confession of praise to the Father is related. Afterwards he states that just men in times past have not seen what the disciples see.* [Luke 10:21–24]

Chap. 43. *When a lawyer enquires about eternal life and asks who his neighbour is, he tells a parable of a wounded man; he teaches that the mercy shown him by the Samaritan should be imitated.* [Luke 10:25–37]

Chap. 44. *He curbs the complaint of Martha, who is serving, that her sister is not helping her by saying that Mary has chosen the best part.* [Luke 10:38–42]

Chap. 45. *At their request, he teaches his disciples a form of prayer with five petitions.* [Luke 11:1–4]

Chap. 46. *Telling the parable of the friend who asked for three loaves at midnight, he urges us to ask, to seek, and to knock.* [Luke 11:5–13]

Chap. 47. *He heals a mute man possessed by an evil spirit and restores his speech, and by telling about the armed man who is overcome by a stronger, and about an unclean spirit coming back to a man as much as seven times again, he refutes those who say that he is able to do such things through Beelzebub.* [Luke 11:14–26]

Chap. 48. *To the woman crying out that the womb is blessed that bore him he replies that he is blessed who keeps the word of God; and he speaks of the sign of Jonah, and refers to the queen of the south.* [Luke 11:27–32]

Chap. 49. *Saying that a lamp should not be put under a bushel, he teaches that the eye ought to be single.* [Luke 11:33–36]

Chap. 50. *When he was invited to dine with a Pharisee, he notices that the Pharisee is thinking of the Jewish ritual of washing, and saying 'woe' six times to the Pharisees, he exposes their many sins.* [Luke 11:37–54]

Chap. 51. *He commands his disciples both to beware of the leaven of hypocrisy and not to fear those who kill the body; and not to think what they will say in a time of persecution.* [Luke 12:1–12]

Chap. 52. *When a man asks for his inheritance to be divided between himself and his brother, Jesus delivers a parable of the avaricious rich man, and then he commands his disciples to avoid being solicitous for food and clothing for the birds lack [such solicitousness].* [Luke 12:13–31]

Chap. 53. *Promising a kingdom to his little flock, he orders that things they will possess or do possess are to be sold for alms, and that their loins are to be girded and their lamps burning;* /15/ *also, commanding vigilance, after telling of the good and the bad slave, he declares that the slave who knows the will of his lord will be beaten with many stripes, but the slave who does not know will be beaten with few stripes.* [Luke 12:32–48]

Chap. 54. *He says that he will cast fire on the earth, and divide families, and he declares that those who scrutinize the sky should know that the time has arrived, and settle with his adversary on the way.* [Luke 12:49–59]

Chap. 55. *When it is reported that some people had been killed by Pilate, he says that all except those who do penance will likewise perish, just like the eighteen crushed by the fall of the tower. Also, he teaches about penance by telling the parable about the sterile fig tree. Straightening up the woman who has been bent over for eighteen years, he refutes those disputing and murmuring about healing on the Sabbath with the example of leading an ox to water. And the people rejoice over his glorious miracles.* [Luke 13:1–17]

Chap. 56. *He compares the kingdom of heaven to a grain of mustard seed and to leaven; speaking also of the difficult way of life of the poor, he says that the first will be last and the last will be first.* [Luke 13:18–30]

Chap. 57. *He calls Herod a fox, and he chides Jerusalem for refusing to be protected under his wings.* [Luke 13:31–35]

Chap. 58. *Healing the man with the dropsy on the Sabbath day as if freeing him from a well, he confounds the murmuring Pharisees by [posing a question about] drawing out an ass or an ox after it has fallen into a well [on the Sabbath]. Likewise, he teaches that humility ought to be pursued, and he commands that one not seek the place of honour at a feast, and that not the rich but the poor, who are unable to make recompense, are to be fed.* [Luke 14:1–15]

# THE CHAPTERS OF THE GOSPEL ACCORDING TO LUKE 111

Chap. 59. *He delivers a parable about the invited guests who want to excuse themselves, saying that they were unworthy of the feast.* [Luke 14:16–24]

Chap. 60. *To those who will hate their relatives and their own life besides, and to those who will take up the cross and follow him, he expounds the parable of building the tower and of the war between two kings. And let not anyone be like salt that has lost its savour, but let him have ears to hear.* [Luke 14:25–35]

Chap. 61. *To those murmuring about how he eats with sinners he delivers a parable about the sheep and about the coin that was found, commending the joy to come over the salvation of sinners.* [Luke 15:1–10]

Chap. 62. *Delivering a parable of the frugal and the wasteful son, he teaches the salvation of penitents through the return of the prodigal to his father.* [Luke 15:11–32] /16/

Chap. 63. *He sets forth a parable of what should not be imitated concerning an unjust steward, who diminished the debt owed to his lord by a rather clever ruse.* [Luke 16:1–12]

Chap. 64. *He rebukes the covetous Pharisees, saying that no one can serve God and mammon, and that the Law and the prophets were in effect until John the Baptist, and that anyone putting away his wife commits adultery.* [Luke 16:13–18]

Chap. 65. *Setting forth a parable of the pitiless rich man clothed in purple and the poor man Lazarus, he shows what kind of things the rapacious will suffer, if they deserve punishment for their avarice.* [Luke 16:19–31]

Chap. 66. *He says, woe to him who causes stumbling; but he orders that the brother who repents seven times should be forgiven seven times.* [Luke 17:1–4]

Chap. 67. *The apostles pray that their faith may be increased and they hear about the power to transplant a tree. Through the simile of the slave ploughing or feeding cattle, he teaches that they should say they are worthless [slaves] even when they do everything they have been commanded.* [Luke 17:5–10]

Chap. 68. *After ten lepers are made clean, one only, and he a stranger, returns to give thanks.* [Luke 17:11–19]

Chap. 69. *When asked about the time of the kingdom of God, he answered that it would not come with advance notice, and compares it to lightning. He says that people are going to go about their business like those who lived in the days of Noah and Lot, and if two are in a bed, in a mill, and in a field, that one will be taken and one will be left behind.* [Luke 17:20–37]

Chap. 70. *He tells a parable that we ought always to pray, concerning a widow who demanded vengeance against her adversary from an unjust judge.* [Luke 18:1–8]

Chap. 71. *Through the prayer of the Pharisee and the tax collector in the temple, he teaches that we should not boast of our merits, but confess our sins.* [Luke 18:9–14]

Chap. 72. *He stops the little children from being turned away from his presence, and he signifies under their designation ['children'] that humility is to be obtained.* [Luke 18:15–17]

Chap. 73. *A rich man who asks about obtaining eternal life goes away sad after Jesus's second reply; and the Lord promises eternal things to those who give up temporal things in his name.* [Luke 18:18–30]

Chap. 74. *He foretells that he is to be delivered up in Jerusalem and that he will suffer.* [Luke 18:31–34]

Chap. 75. *Near Jericho he restores sight instantaneously to a blind beggar.* [Luke 18:35–43] /17/

Chap. 76. *As he walks through Jericho, he who came to save what was lost absolves Zacchaeus the tax collector.* [Luke 19:1–10]

Chap. 77. *He tells a parable about the slaves who received ten pounds from their lord with which to engage in business, and he declares that the enemies of his kingdom will perish.* [Luke 19:11–28]

Chap. 78. *He sits on the colt of an ass, and everyone says: Peace in heaven and glory on high. And to those who rebuke his disciples he says: If these shall hold their peace, the stones will cry out.* [Luke 19:29–40]

Chap. 79. *Seeing the city, he wept over it, declaring that it is to be overturned. He cast out of the temple those that were engaged in selling. While the scribes are plotting against him, he is willingly heard by the people.* [Luke 19:41–48]

# THE CHAPTERS OF THE GOSPEL ACCORDING TO LUKE

Chap. 80. *Those enquiring about his power are confuted when he asks in turn about John the Baptist.* [Luke 20:1–8]

Chap. 81. *He speaks a parable about the husbandmen of the vineyard who killed both the slaves and the son of their lord.* [Luke 20:9–18]

Chap. 82. *He confutes those tempting him about the tribute to be rendered to Caesar with the inscription on the denarius.* [Luke 20:19–26]

Chap. 83. *When the Sadducees ask about the wife of the seven brothers, he also supports the resurrection with the testimony of Moses.* [Luke 20:27–40]

Chap. 84. *He asks how Christ may be the son of David when he was called Lord by him in the hundred and ninth Psalm. Also, he reproves the pride of the scribes. He affirms that the widow casting two copper coins into the treasury had cast more than all the others.* [Luke 20:41–21:4]

Chap. 85. *To those praising the construction of the Temple he foretells that it will soon be destroyed, and to those asking about the end he replies that very many evils will come before, and that those who are handed over should not premeditate what they will reply, but that they should possess their souls in patience.* [Luke 21:5–19]

Chap. 86. *He foretells that Jerusalem is to be compassed about with an army, and the woe to those that are with child, and he also prophesies the sword and the captivity, and the signs of heaven that are to be, and that he will come in a cloud with great power and majesty.* [Luke 21:20–27]

Chap. 87. *Look up, he says, because your redemption is at hand. And he orders them to watch and pray, refraining from drunkenness and the cares of this life.* [Luke 21:28–22:2] /**18**/

Chap. 88. *Judas bargains for a price; the disciples prepare the Passover; the mystery of the Lord's Supper is celebrated.* [Luke 22:3–23]

Chap. 89. *He does away with the strife of the disciples, affirming that he himself is their servant; promising them the kingdom, he says to Peter after some other things: Strengthen your brethren.* [Luke 22:24–32]

Chap. 90. *The events of the Passion are narrated, when among other things he even restored with the touch of his hand the ear which Peter had cut off.* [Luke 22:33–23:33]

Chap. 91. *Begging forgiveness from the Father for the men being crucified, he also absolves one of the crucified robbers, who confesses.* [Luke 23:34–56]

Chap. 92. *The women learn by a vision of angels that he has been resurrected; and Peter, running to the sepulchre and seeing what had come to pass, is filled with wonder.* [Luke 24:1–12]

Chap. 93. *After a long conversation he is recognized at the breaking of the bread by two men, that is, Cleophas and his companion whose name is passed over in silence, who were going to a town which was then called Emmaus.* [Luke 24:13–35]

Chap. 94. *Standing in the midst of the disciples who were talking together, he says: Peace be to you; and as they are still frightened and think him a spirit, he strengthens [their faith] by showing his pierced hands and feet. Eating a piece of broiled fish and a honeycomb before them, he gives instructions. Saying that he will send them what the Father has promised, he ascends into heaven.* [Luke 24:36–53] /**19**/

# I

## [Luke 1:1–4:13]

Here begins Book One of the Commentary on Luke.

The blessed evangelist Luke as he set out to write about *all that Jesus did and taught, until the day on which he was taken up*[1] first took care to refute the audacity of those who wrote falsehoods about him: that is to say, silently warning the reader that he should know not only that what Jesus preaches must be obeyed, but that those things these people expressed to the contrary must be utterly detested; and, lest by chance the weak be exposed to error, that reading authors who carelessly write superfluous things must be absolutely avoided. For it is not about everyone in general, but about certain persons gifted with the virtue of special faith or knowledge that it could be said: *And if they drink any deadly thing, it will not hurt them.*[2] Accordingly, therefore, Luke begins:

### Chapter 1

1/10   [Luke 1:1–4] **Inasmuch as many have attempted to set forth in order a narration of the things that have been accomplished among us, according as they, who from the beginning were eyewitnesses and ministers of the word, delivered them to us, it seemed good to me also, having diligently attained to all things from the beginning, to write to you in order, most excellent Theophilus, that you may know the truth of those words in which you have been instructed.** With this preface Luke very clearly signifies that the chief reason he wrote the Gospel was in order that there not be an opportunity for false evangelists to preach falsehoods. As their written works attest, these people, under the name of

---

1  Acts 1:1–2.
2  Mark 16:18.

the apostles, attempted to bring forth heretical sects. Consequently, some are found to have falsely prefaced their writings with the name of Thomas, others with the name of Bartholomew, some with Matthias, and still others with the names of the twelve apostles. But also, Basilides and Apelles left gospels in their name which stink with error, the first declaring as dogma that there are three hundred and sixty-five heavens, and the other that there are two gods who oppose each other. Among these, it should be noted that what is called the Gospel according to the Hebrews[3] should be reckoned not with apocryphal writings, but with ecclesiastical histories. For not only did it seem right to Jerome, the translator of holy Scripture, to make use of many testimonies from it, /20/ but he also translated the work itself into the Latin and Greek language. But Luke quickly refutes false gospels at the beginning of his preface. *Inasmuch as many*, he says, *have attempted to set forth in order a narration*, referring to them as many, that is to say, not so much on account of their number as from the diversity of their multifarious heresies. These people, not endowed with the gift of the Holy Spirit, but striving with futile labour, presented a narrative instead of guarding the truth of history. And for that reason, they left the work on which they laboured in vain to be finished by others – by those, of course, who, although they are four, brought forth not so much four Gospels as one Gospel in four books that harmonize with a variety that is exceptionally lovely. For they set out those things *according as they, who from the beginning were eyewitnesses and ministers of the word, delivered them* to them. This statement applies not only to Luke and Mark, who never saw the Lord in person in the flesh and therefore were obliged to learn what they wrote from oral tradition, but also to the apostles Matthew and John. For they too, in many things that they wrote, needed to hear from those who had been able to know about his infancy, childhood, and genealogy, and to witness his deeds.[4]

Moreover, Luke says it seemed good to him to write, not because he came to that conclusion on his own, but at the instigation of the Holy Spirit, in accordance with what the Apostles say in their epistle: *For it seemed*

---

3 Jerome apparently had access to an Aramaic version of the Gospels, which was written in the Hebrew alphabet. Cf. Jerome, *Dialogus contra Pelagianos* (PL 23:570).

4 For this paragraph, cf. Ambrose, *Expos. Lucam* 1.1–2 (CCSL 14:7.13–27); Jerome, *Commentarii in Matheum* Praefatio (CCSL 77:1.1–40). On the singular weight given to the fact that there were four Gospels (distinct and yet harmonious) and to the association of any addition to the canon of four with heresy in patristic and early medieval Insular exegesis see O'Reilly, 'Patristic and Insular Traditions of the Evangelists', 54–55.

*good to the Holy Spirit, and to us.*[5] By the grace of the Spirit it comes about that what is good seems good to us as well. Indeed, *he says that he comprehended not a few things, but all things.* But, *after having comprehended all things, it seemed good to him to write not all things, but* about *all things*[6] which he believed suitable for strengthening the faith of his readers, because *if all things were written, the world itself would not be able to contain them all.*[7] Hence, *he also deliberately omitted* many things *which were reported by others, so that* manifold *grace might glisten in the Gospels, and so that the individual books might be distinguished by certain miracles of sacraments and deeds of their own.*[8]

'Theophilus' signifies 'loving God' or 'loved by God'.[9] Therefore, whoever loves God or wishes to be loved by God should consider the Gospel to have been written for himself, and as a gift given to himself, and should preserve it as a pledge entrusted to himself, lest either the worm of heretical laceration or the corrosion of filthy avarice waste the wealth of the Word which has been received. But what is promised to this same Theophilus is not that the purpose of some new and as it were unknown words is to be revealed. Rather, it is that the truth of those words about which he has been instructed is to be expressed, doubtless so that he could know in what order anything was /21/ either done or said about the Lord or by the Lord. For he who wishes to be perfect must not only believe in Christ, but also experience the faith of eternal divinity and the order of its temporal dispensation.

## Chapter 2

[Luke 1:5] **There was in the days of King Herod of Judea, a priest named Zechariah, of the priestly family of Abijah, and his wife was descended from the daughters of Aaron, and her name was Elizabeth.** The holy and renowned nobility of the Lord's forerunner derived not only from his parents but also from his ancestors, since his coming proclaimed a faith

---

5 Acts 15:28. For the 'epistle', cf. Acts 15:23–31.
6 Ambrose, *Expos. Lucam* 1.11 (CCSL 14:12.186–88).
7 John 21:25.
8 Ambrose, *Expos. Lucam* 1.11 (CCSL 14:12.191–94).
9 Cf., for 'loved by God', Ambrose, *Expos. Lucam* 1.12 (CCSL 14:12.196–97); Jerome, *Hebr. nom.* (CCSL 72:149.5–6).

not conceived by sudden inspiration, but rather willingly received from ancestral tradition. And since indeed the greatness of Aaron the first high priest of the Law is known to all, something ought to be said briefly about Abijah. David, the king and prophet, sought with great devotion to devise a tabernacle to the God of Jacob,[10] but the Lord decreed that this was to be done by Solomon instead. David, therefore, provided for the same Solomon everything that pertained to the expenses of the house,[11] and he also gave in detail the measurements and description of that house,[12] so that, as the standing of external religious observance increased, he might also enhance the eminence of interior devotion. Nevertheless, he distributed the priestly and Levitical ranks across all the duties of the house of the Lord.[13] *For there were chief men of the sanctuary and chief men of God*, that is, high priests, drawn from *both the sons of Eleazar and the sons of Ithamar.*[14] From these he assigned divisions according to their ministries[15] by twenty-four lots *to enter into the house*[16] of God. Of these the eighth lot fell to the family of Abijah, from which Zechariah came. For *he divided both families amongst themselves by lot:*[17] *one house, that of Eleazar, was over the rest, and another house, that of Ithamar, had the rest under it.*[18] Read Chronicles, but also book seven of the *Antiquities* of Josephus, where it sets forth the law that each generation according to the order of the casting of lots should serve God for eight days from Sabbath to Sabbath; and where it also asserts that the tribe of the Levites was divided into twenty-four sections, so that, chosen by lot in the same fashion, they should serve according to the custom of priests for eight days at a time.[19] Moreover, it is significant that the first herald of the New Testament arrived in the course of the eighth lot,[20] for just as the Old Testament is often expressed by the number seven on account of the Sabbath, so the New Testament is sometimes expressed

---

10 Cf. 2 Sam. 7:1–17.
11 Cf. 3 Kings 5:2–18; 1 Chron. 22.
12 Cf. 3 Kings 6 for the measurements and description. Bede seems to assume that these came from David, which might be implied by 1 Chron. 22.
13 Cf. 1 Chron. 23–27.
14 1 Chron. 24:5.
15 Cf. 1 Chron. 24:3.
16 1 Chron. 24:19.
17 1 Chron. 24:5.
18 1 Chron. 24:6.
19 Cf. Josephus, *Antiquitates* 7.14.7.
20 I.e., John the Baptist came from the house of Abijah.

BOOK ONE                                                         119

by the number eight on account of the sacrament either of the Lord's or of our resurrection. Hence, since /22/ the court of the heavenly kingdom is not entered otherwise than by the observance of each Testament, it is said with good reason that in the Temple of Solomon there was a mystic flight of fifteen steps. And he who is heard crying to the Lord in tribulation is led by the Psalms of the same number of steps to divine things, where at last, placed *in the courts of the house of God*,[21] he can hear: *May the Lord out of Zion bless you.*[22]

And the time of the foreigner Herod, that is, the king, bears witness to the advent of the Lord. For it had been foretold that *the prince shall not depart from Juda, nor a ruler from his thigh, until he comes who is to be sent.*[23] From the time the patriarchs left Egypt up to the time of the prophet Samuel, the Jews were ruled by the judges of their nation; and then they were ruled by kings up to the transmigration to Babylon. But, after the return from Babylon, supreme power was exercised by high priests up to the time of Hyrcanus, at once king and high priest, who was plagued by the envy of his brother with many calamities, and was at last killed deceitfully by Herod, whose father was a low-born foreigner, that is, of Idumean stock,[24] who had been ennobled and made a citizen. The kingdom of Judea was handed over by order of Caesar Augustus to be governed by this Herod, in whose thirty-first year, in accordance with the above-mentioned prophecy, he who was destined to be sent, came.

[Luke 1:6] **And they were both just before God, walking in all the commandments and justifications of the Lord without blame.** *It is well said, 'just before God', for not everyone who is just before man is just before God. Men see in one way, God sees in another; men look at external appearance, God at the heart. And therefore, it can happen that someone with feigned popular virtue may seem just to me, but not be just before God, if justice is not fashioned from simplicity of mind, but is simulated by fawning flattery.* But *blessed is the one who is just in the sight of God. Blessed is the one about whom the Lord deigns to say: 'Behold an Israelite,*

---

21  Ps. 133:1 (134:1).
22  Ps. 133:3 (134:1). The fifteen psalms from numbers 119 to 133 (NRSV numbers 120 to 134) are referred to as 'the gradual psalms', or 'Songs of Ascents'. Bede understands their number (fifteen) as a reference to the number of steps leading up into the temple of Solomon (cf. Ezek. 40:26 & 31) and also as the sum of seven (= Old Testament) plus eight (= New Testament).
23  Gen. 49:10.
24  The Idumeans were from southern Palestine: cf. 2 Macc. 10:15–16.

*in whom there is no guile.'*[25] *For he is a true Israelite who sees God, and knows that he is seen by the Lord, and shows him the secrets of his heart.*[26]

*'Walking'* it says, *'in all the commandments and justifications of the Lord.'* First is the commandment, second the justification. For *when we are obedient to the divine commandments, we are walking in the justifications of the Lord. When we judge, and judge rightly, we are seen to uphold the justifications of the Lord. Full praise, therefore, includes nation, morals, duty, deed, and judgement; nation in ancestors, morals in equity, duty in the priesthood, deed in commandment, and /23/ judgement in justification.*[27] And what it added, *'without blame'*, is just what the Apostle says: *Providing good things, not only in the sight of God, but also in the sight of men.*[28] And Ecclesiastes: *Be not*, it says, *over just*,[29] because *very often too harsh justice provokes men's blame.*[30] But what is moderated, thanks to its sweetness, is precisely what also avoids the complaints of jealousy.

[Luke 1:7] **And they had no son, for Elizabeth was barren, and they were both well advanced in years.** It was arranged by divine providence that John should be born of parents who were advanced in age and had been deprived for a long time of the fruit of marriage. Not only did the unanticipated birth of a child make the gift more appreciated, but the wonder of the miracle prepared others to listen receptively to the future prophet. And then: *All who had heard them laid them up in their heart, saying: What do you think this child will be?*[31]

[Luke 1:8–9] **And it happened, when he executed the priestly function in the order of his term before God, according to the custom of the priesthood,** ... Through Moses, the Lord instituted a single high priest and decreed that another should succeed him in order on his death,[32] and this custom was preserved up to the time of David. Guided, as I said, by the Lord, David decreed that more high priests be appointed who would serve in turn,[33] and that each should in the time of his term strive

---

25 John 1:47.
26 Ambrose, *Expos. Lucam* 1.18 (CCSL 14:15.286–98).
27 Ambrose, *Expos. Lucam* 1.20–21 (CCSL 14:16.327–35).
28 Rom. 12:17. Ambrose here quotes Proverbs 3:4, which is the source of Paul's comment. Bede's preference for Paul's wording is clearly intentional.
29 Eccles. 7:17.
30 Ambrose, *Expos. Lucam* 1.19 (CCSL 14:16.325).
31 Luke 1:66.
32 Cf. Exod. 29:1–9.
33 Cf. 1 Chron. 24:1–3.

BOOK ONE                                121

for purity, and not defile his house at all. Hence now Zechariah shows that he has executed the priestly function in the order of his term.

[Luke 1:9b–10] **It was his lot to offer incense, going into the temple of the Lord. And all the multitude of the people was praying outside, at the hour of incense.** He was not chosen by a new lot when the time of his officiating began, but he was selected by the ancient lot when he first succeeded in the order of his office of high priest in the house of Abijah. And it was decreed that incense be brought by the high priest into the Holy of Holies on the tenth day of the seventh month with all the people waiting expectantly on the outside of the temple. This day was to be called the day of expiation or atonement, which among us,[34] on account of the varied course of the moon from which the Hebrews reckon the months, sometimes falls in September and sometimes in October. This is because the month in which Passover is celebrated marks the beginning of the year both according to the order of creation and by the edict of the Law, as the Lord says to Moses: *This month shall be to you the beginning of months; it shall be the first in the months of the year.*[35] *On the tenth day of this month let every man take a lamb,*[36] and so forth. And the Apostle writing to the Hebrews about this day speaks of it thus: *Into the first tabernacle the priests indeed always entered, accomplishing the offices of sacrifices. But into the second, the high priest alone, once a year, not without blood, which he offers,*[37] and /24/ so forth. Explaining to them the mystery of this day, he shows that Jesus is the true high priest, who, after accomplishing the days of his office, that is, when the dispensation of the flesh was fulfilled in his own blood, entered the mysteries of heaven that he might make the Father look kindly on us and also intercede for the sins of those who still wait in prayer before the doors, and who cherish his advent. Therefore, his descent is beautifully announced by the angel on that day on which his ascension was prefigured by the Law, because *He who descended is the same also who ascended,*[38] and, as the Psalmist says, *His going out is from the height of heaven, and his circuit to its height.*[39]

---

34  I.e., for users of the Roman solar calendar.
35  Exod. 12:2.
36  Exod. 12:3.
37  Hebr. 9:6–7.
38  Eph. 4:10.
39  Ps. 18:7 (19:6).

[Luke 1:11] **And there appeared to him an angel of the Lord, standing on the right side of the altar of incense.** It is with good reason that the angel appears in the temple and next to the altar and on the right side, because he foretells the advent of the true priest and the mystery of the universal sacrifice and the joy of the heavenly gift. For just as things in the present world are foretold by the left side, so good things are often foretold by the right, in accordance with what is sung in praise of wisdom: *Length of days is in her right hand, and in her left hand riches and glory.*[40]

[Luke 1:12–13] **And Zechariah seeing him was troubled, and fear fell upon him. But the angel said to him: Fear not, Zechariah, for your prayer is heard.** The angel comforts the trembling Zechariah, because just as it is characteristic of human frailty to be troubled by the sight of a spiritual creature, so it is characteristic of angelic kindness to solace mortals who tremble at its appearance by immediately soothing them. But, on the other hand, it is characteristic of demonic ferocity to shake violently those whom it perceives are terrified by its presence in the world with even greater horror. The best way to overcome this ferocity is with unshaken faith.

[Luke 1:13b] **And your wife Elizabeth will bear you a son, and you will call his name John.** Saying that his prayer has been heard, the angel immediately promises that his wife will give birth. Not that Zechariah, who had entered the sanctuary to make the offering on behalf of the people, *neglecting the common prayers, could have prayed to beget children, especially since no one prays for what he has no hope of obtaining.* But already mindful of his age and the infertility of his wife, he had no hope that sons would be born to him, *so that he would not believe the angel who promised this.* But when the angel says, 'your prayer is heard', he means *'for the redemption of the people'*.[41] And when he adds, 'and your wife Elizabeth will bear you a son', he makes clear the order of redemption, namely that a son born of Zechariah is to prepare the way to herald the Redeemer of that people.

Whenever God /25/ gives a name to someone, or changes it, it is a mark of particular merit. Thus Abram, because he was going to be *the father of many nations*, was called Abraham.[42] So Jacob deserved to be called Israel, because he saw God. So King Josiah, on account of the loftiness

---

40 Prov. 3:16.
41 Augustine, *Quaestiones euang.* 2.1 (CCSL 44B:41.8–11; 13).
42 Gen. 17:5.

of his outstanding virtue, was named by God long before he was born.[43] Accordingly, *John* is interpreted to mean *in whom is grace or the grace of the Lord.*[44] By this name it was made known that grace was granted in the first place to his parents to whom in their old age a son was born; and then, to John himself, who was going to be great in the presence of the Lord and would be enriched with the gift of the Holy Spirit while still in his mother's womb; and finally, to the children of Israel, whom he was going to turn toward the Lord their God.

[Luke 1:14] **And you will have joy and gladness, and many will rejoice in his nativity.** The father rejoices with good reason that he will receive a son, not only born in his old age, but one of such grace. And others rejoice, to whom he will bring good tidings of a gateway as yet unheard of into the kingdom of heaven. It should be observed that many rejoice in the precursor's birth, but when the Lord is born the angel proclaims *good tidings of great joy that will be to all people,*[45] because the former came to announce the gospel of salvation to many, but the latter to offer it to all who would have it.

[Luke 1:15] **For he will be great in the presence of the Lord, and he will not drink wine and strong drink, and he will be filled with the Holy Spirit even from his mother's womb.** It is a great virtue in the presence of the Lord that one who preaches the joys of heaven in the desert completely spurned earthly delights. But it is also evident that he is great in the presence of the Lord, although it appears that he was despised among men, because he, than whom *no one is greater among those who are born of women,*[46] was beheaded on account of the game of a wanton girl. The same angel who declared how great he was, elaborating further, says, *and he will not drink wine and strong drink [sicera]. Sicera* means '*drunkenness*', by which word the Hebrews signify *every beverage which can cause drunkenness,*[47] whether made from fruits, or from grains, or from some other substance. It was a peculiarity of the law of the Nazarenes to abstain from wine and strong drink at the time of consecration.[48] Hence, John, Samson, and Jeremiah, and others like them always make an effort to

---

43 Cf. 3 Kings 13:2.
44 Jerome, *Hebr. nom.* (CCSL 72:146.16–17).
45 Luke 2:10.
46 Luke 7:28.
47 Jerome, *Hebr. nom.* (CCSL 72:141.24–25).
48 Cf. Num. 6:2–3.

abstain from these in order to be able always to remain Nazarenes, that is, 'holy'.[49] For it is fitting that a vessel that is consecrated to heavenly grace hold back from the enticements of the world, and that he who desires to *be filled with* the new wine of the Holy *Spirit* not *be drunk with the wine in which is luxury.*[50] /26/ Hence, he from whom intoxication with wine is taken away is rightly filled with the grace of the Spirit. He showed then that he himself was filled with grace, as had been foretold, when *on the entrance* of the blessed *Mary he leapt in* his mother's *womb,*[51] and knowing the duty of his office as precursor, he proclaimed the good tidings of the advent of the Lord in the way he could at that point in time.

[Luke 1:16–17] **And he will turn many of the children of Israel to the Lord their God. And he will go before him in the spirit and power of Elijah,** ... Since John, as he was testifying concerning Christ and baptizing peoples in his faith, is said to have converted the children of Israel '*to the Lord their God*', it is perfectly clear that Christ is the Lord God of Israel. But if Christ is, or rather, because Christ is the Lord God of Israel, let the Arians cease to deny that Christ is the Lord God; let the Photinians blush to attribute Christ's origins to the Virgin;[52] let the Manicheans stop believing that there is one God of the people of Israel and another of the Christians.[53] And since John is said to go before him, let them see that God, who was eternal before the ages, was afterwards born in the world as a man, and therefore that his forerunner sometimes referred to him as a man who would come after him and sometimes as the Son of God. He is well said to go before in the spirit and power of Elijah, because just as Elijah was to come as the herald of the Judge,[54] so John was made the herald of the Redeemer. Both men sought out desert wastes with an exactly similar way of life, frugal of nourishment, uncouth in clothing, and both were despised for their belts.[55] Both endure the madness of a king and queen.[56] *Elijah divided the Jordan* before going up to heaven,[57] *John turned the Jordan into*

---

49 Cf. Jerome, *Hebr. nom.* (CCSL 72:147.12).
50 Eph. 5:18.
51 Luke 1:40–41.
52 Cf. Ambrose, *Expos. Lucam* 1.25 (CCSL 14:19.391–92).
53 Cf. Ambrose, *Expos. Lucam* 1.2 (CCSL 14:7.30–31).
54 Cf. Mal. 4:5.
55 Cf. 4 Kings 1:8; Matt. 3:4. Both wore leather belts.
56 Bede makes a similar comparison of the habits and experience of the two prophets in his homily on the beheading of John the Baptist (*Hom.* 2.23: CCSL 122:350.37–41).
57 Cf. 4 Kings 2:8–11.

*a bath of salvation* by which heaven may be sought. *John abides on earth with the Lord, Elijah appears with him in glory.*[58]

[Luke 1:17b] **That he may turn the hearts of the fathers to the children, and the incredulous to the wisdom of the just, to prepare for the Lord a perfect people.** To turn the hearts of the fathers to the children is to impart the spiritual knowledge of the holy elders by preaching to the people. Assuredly, the wisdom of the just is not to take for granted the justice of the works of the Law, but to seek salvation from faith, so that, although those placed under the Law may accomplish to perfection the commandments of the Law, they nevertheless understand that they are to be saved by the grace of God through Christ. For *the just person lives by faith.*[59] And Peter speaks of the yoke of the Law: *which neither our fathers nor we have been able to bear, but we believe we will be saved by the grace of the Lord Jesus, just as they will be also.*[60] Since for a long time the incredulous were imbued with this wisdom both by John, and by Elijah, this statement,[61] which /27/ the angel makes about John, was made earlier in nearly the same words by Malachi about Elijah.[62] 'To prepare for the Lord a perfect people', the angel says. Since he had said that Zechariah's prayer for the people was heard, he teaches in what way the same people ought to be saved and perfected, namely by repenting and believing in Christ in accordance with the prophecy of John.

[Luke 1:18] **And Zechariah said to the angel: How will I know this? For I am an old man, and my wife is advanced in years.** Hesitating on account of the loftiness of the promises, he for whom the vision or words alone of the angel ought to have sufficed in place of a sign, asks for a sign by which he might believe. Hence, he is deservedly punished for his lack of faith by falling dumb, dumbness being both the sign of faith which he sought and the punishment which he deserved for his lack of faith.

[Luke 1:19–20] **And the angel, answering, said to him: I am Gabriel, who stands in the presence of God; and I am sent to speak to you and to bring you these good tidings. And behold, you will be dumb, and you will not be able to speak until the day wherein these things will come to pass, because you have not believed my words, which will be fulfilled**

---

58 Ambrose, *Expos. Lucam* 1.36 (CCSL 14:24.546–48).
59 Rom. 1:17.
60 Acts 15:10–11.
61 I.e., 'That he may turn the hearts of the fathers to the children'.
62 Cf. Mal. 4:6: 'And he will turn the heart of the fathers to the children'.

in their time. Luke wants it to be understood that if a man promised such things, it would be permissible to demand a sign with impunity, but when an angel promises, he should surely not be doubted. And he gives a sign because he is asked, in order that he who spoke in disbelief may learn to believe now in speechlessness. Here it should be noted that the angel not only stands in the presence of God, but also says that he was sent to bring Zechariah these good tidings. *Because even when* angels *come to us, they are carrying out their duty externally in such a way that they nonetheless never fail to do their duty internally in contemplation. And therefore they are sent and at the same time they stand in attendance, because even if an angelic spirit is bound by limitations, nevertheless the highest spirit, which is God himself, is not. And so, even when angels are sent out, they are before him, since to whatever place they come when they are sent, they are running in his presence.*[63]

[Luke 1:21–23] **And the people were waiting for Zechariah, and they wondered that he tarried so long in the temple. And when he came out, he could not speak to them, and they understood that he had seen a vision in the temple. And he made signs to them and remained dumb. And after the days of his office were accomplished, he departed to his own house.** This is what I said, that the chief priests during the time of their term, having dedicated themselves entirely to the offices of the temple, abstained not only from the embrace of their wives, but also from even entering their own houses. In contrast, the priests of our time take orders to serve always at the altar, and therefore offer an example of perpetual chastity. Then, because the priestly succession was sought from the lineage of Aaron, it was necessary to arrange a time for substituting /28/ another descendant. But since now not carnal succession but spiritual perfection is sought, the consequence is that priests are bidden always to keep from wives and to preserve their chastity in order that they may always be able to assist at the altar.

[Luke 1:24] **And after those days, Elizabeth his wife conceived.** That is, after Zechariah's days of office were completed. John, bishop of the city of Constantinople, referring to this hallowed conception, says: *These things took place in the month of September, on the eighth calends of October [24 September], at the beginning of the eleventh day of the moon, when it was proper for the Jews to celebrate the fast of the feast*

---

63 Gregory, *Hom. in Euang.* 2.34.13 (CCSL 141:313.369–75).

*of Tabernacles.*[64] The equinox takes place on that very day of the eighth calends of October, when darkness begins to be longer than daylight. For, he says, *He must increase, but I must decrease.*[65] And indeed, light had diminished in favour of darkness on the day when John was conceived, when the Jews used to offer sacrifices to God in accordance with the Law and the prophets. For these are the sacrifices that were offered hitherto for the sins of the people, and which now had to cease, when John, that is, the Baptist, was conceived. And therefore, his father Zechariah, the priest of the Jews, became dumb, because their sacrifices that used to be offered for the sins of the people now had to cease and fall silent. For the unique priest was coming who would offer from the slaughter of his own special Lamb a sacrifice to God for the sins of all. With these words of the blessed John, we are taught that at that time, on the first day immediately after the day of Atonement, the changing of the priestly term was celebrated, and therefore that the conception of the precursor of the Lord took place on that day. It is significant that these things were foretold by the angel on this day of fasting and mortification, because through John the mortification of penitence was to be preached to mankind.

[Luke 1:24b–25] **And she hid herself five months, saying: Thus has the Lord dealt with me in the days when he had the consideration to take away my reproach among men.** Elizabeth demonstrates how concerned the saints are not to commit any shameful act for which they would have to blush, when she feels ashamed even about the very gifts that she wished to receive. Although she rejoices that the reproach of barrenness has been removed, nonetheless she is ashamed of childbirth in old age. But a mother's labour is cause for shame, as long as the worth of the offspring is concealed. She who hid herself because she had conceived a son soon exulted in a loud voice on the entrance of the mother of God, because she was going to bear a prophet.[66]

---

64 Hurst ascribes this to John Chrysostom, *Homilia in diem natalem* (PG 49:357–58), but, as Rosalind Love has demonstrated, it is in fact from an anonymous fifth-century Latin treatise entitled *De solstitia et aequinoctia* [sic] *conceptionis et nativitatis Domini nostri Jesu Christi et Iohannis Baptistae* (Dekkers, *Clavis patrum latinorum* 3rd ed. no. 2277) printed in PL Supplementum 1:557–67 at 61. Like the anonymous *De duobus filiis* used by Bede in his exegesis of the parable of the Prodigal Son (see below, Book 4, n. 417), this tract was part of a collection of thirty-eight sermons all ascribed to John Chrysostom, though only fourteen are authentic: see Love, 'Bede and John Chrysostom', 76–78.
65 John 3:30. The speaker is John the Baptist.
66 Cf. Luke 1:40–44.

Allegorically, the priesthood of the Jews can be signified by Zechariah, and the Law itself by Elizabeth, which, having been exercised and supported as it were by the manly help of the teaching of the priests, ought to have borne spiritual sons to God, but was entirely unable to do so because of /29/ the damage inflicted by barrenness – not because few, either before the Law or under the Law, led a very righteous life, but because *the Law brought* no one *to perfection*,[67] since it could not lay open the kingdom of heaven unless Christ led the way.

It is well said that *they were both just before God*,[68] because just as the Law is good, *and the commandment holy and just and good*,[69] so likewise the priesthood of the Law is also holy, just, and good for the dispensation of that time. And what follows, that *they were both well advanced in years*,[70] can be explained in this way, that the adolescence or youth, so to speak, of devotion to the Law flourished in the time of Moses himself and thereafter. But when the advent of the Saviour was at hand, grim old age bent it over, and when the order of the priesthood was disrupted by the ambitions and contentions of the chief priests, and the Law itself rent by the teachings of the Pharisees, it was less apt to beget children for God. Therefore, Zechariah goes into the temple, because it is the duty of priests to enter the sanctuary of God and gain an understanding of the latest and greatest of the heavenly mysteries.[71] The multitude is praying outside, because those who cannot enter deeply into all secret and mystical matters must necessarily give their attention humbly to the admonitions of the more learned. Now Zechariah realizes that John is going to be born at the moment when he puts the incense on the altar, because when teachers are kindled with the more ample flame of divine Scripture, they learn that the grace of God will come through Jesus Christ and will bear fruit from the inner kernel of Scripture, as if from the womb of Elizabeth. It is well that this is done by an angel, because the Law is also *ordained by angels in the hand of a mediator*.[72] But the one who fails to believe what is heard is punished with the penalty of silence, because he is dumb who does not understand the spiritual meaning present in Scripture. Such a one does not know how

---

67 Hebr. 7:19.
68 Luke 6:1.
69 Rom. 7:12.
70 Luke 1:7.
71 Cf. Ps. 72:17 (73:17).
72 Gal. 3:19.

BOOK ONE                                                                  129

to give words to the people like a teacher, but devoid as it were of speech and reason, he gives hints with silent nods so to speak. This is what the priesthood of the Jews was like at that time, which did not take the trouble to learn either the rationale of the sacrifices or the words of the prophets. Therefore, while Zechariah remains dumb, Elizabeth conceives John, for although the chief priests do not understand the distinction of the faith, and the Pharisees and scribes lose *the key of knowledge,* so that they themselves neither enter nor permit their pupils to enter,[73] the interior parts of the Law nonetheless abound with the sacraments of Christ. And it is appropriate that Elizabeth conceals her conception for five months either because the lawgiver Moses himself signifies the mysteries of Christ allegorically in five books or because the whole sequence of the Old Testament prefigures the same dispensation of Christ in the five ages of the world through the deeds and words of the saints. /30/ Therefore, since the incarnation of Christ was to be in the sixth age of the world and was to be of spiritual benefit for the fulfilment of the Law, the angel, rightly sent in the sixth month of John's conception, announces to Mary that the Saviour is about to be born, as the following passage in turn demonstrates.

### Chapter 3

[Luke 1:26] **And in the sixth month, the angel Gabriel was sent from God into a city of Galilee, called Nazareth,** ... The angels *are known by individual names for the purpose of signifying by their names what they are able to do in their work. And for that reason, personal names are not assigned in the holy city which is made perfect by the full knowledge of the vision of almighty God – as if their characters cannot be known without their names! – but when they come in order to administer something to us, they also take on names derived from their services among us.*[74]

Therefore *Gabriel, whose name means 'the strength of God',* is sent *to* the Virgin *Mary. Indeed, he came to announce the one who deigned to appear humble in order to vanquish the powers of the air, about whom the Psalmist says: 'The Lord strong and mighty, the Lord mighty in battle', and again, 'the Lord of heavenly armies, he is the King of Glory'.*[75] *He,*

---

73 Cf. Luke 11:52–53.
74 Gregory, *Hom. in Euang.* 2.34.8 (CCSL 141:306.192–98).
75 Ps. 23:8 & 10 (24:8 & 10).

the Lord of heavenly armies and mighty in battle, who was coming to war against the powers of the air, had to be announced, therefore, by the strength of God.[76]

You should understand that the sixth month is March, on the twenty-fifth day of which our Lord is said both to have been conceived and to have suffered, just as he was born on the twenty-fifth day of the month of December. If we believe both that the vernal equinox occurred on the former day, as many think, and that the winter solstice occurred on the latter, it is fitting that the one who *enlightens every man that comes into this world*[77] be conceived and born with an increase of light. But if anyone should prove that light either increases or overcomes the dark before the time of the Lord's birth and conception, we still say both that *John* was then preaching, *before his coming, the kingdom of heaven,*[78] and also that the command is now given to preachers: *Make a way for him who ascends upon the west.*[79] And the reason why John was conceived around the autumnal equinox and born around the summer solstice, he himself teaches, who speaks either of himself or of the Old Testament (as many assert): *He must increase, but I must decrease.*[80]

[Luke 1:27] **To a virgin espoused to a man whose name was Joseph, of the house of David, and the virgin's name was Mary.** For many reasons the Saviour wished to be born not of a simple virgin, but of one who was betrothed. First, of course, so that Mary's lineage might come to be known through the genealogy of Joseph, whose kinswoman Mary was, since /31/ it is not customary in Scripture to construct the genealogy of women. For what is said of the house of David can be understood as applying to both persons. Second, the Saviour wished it, so that she might not be stoned by the Jews as an adulteress, *prefer*ring *that some persons be in doubt about her origins rather than about* his *mother's purity,*[81] and at the same time taking away an opportunity for shameless virgins, lest they should say that

---

76 Gregory, *Hom. in Euang.* 2.34.9 (CCSL 141:307.213–21). Bede paraphrases this in his *Hom.* 1.3 (ed. Hurst [CCSL 122:14.20–15.28]; trans. Martin and Hurst, *Homilies on the Gospels* 1:20), but omits Gregory's discussion of the status of names in heaven: Del Giacco, 'Exegesis and Sermon', 16.
77 John 1:9.
78 Acts 13:24.
79 Ps. 67:5 (68:4).
80 John 3:30.
81 Ambrose, *Expos. Lucam* 2.1 (CCSL 14:30.15–16).

the mother of the Saviour had been disgraced by false suspicions. Third, he wished it, so that while fleeing into Egypt and returning she might have the comfort of a husband who would be at once the guardian and the witness of her most unblemished virginity. Fourth, he wished it, so that Christ's birth not be exposed to the devil, who, if he knew that he was born of a virgin, perhaps might fear to betray him to death because he was more eminent that other men.[82]

Mary means 'the star of the sea' in Hebrew, but 'mistress' in Syriac;[83] and properly so because she was worthy of giving birth both to the Lord of the whole world and to the eternal light for the ages.

[Luke 1:28] **And the angel having come in, said to her: Hail, full of grace, the Lord is with you. Blessed are you among women.** *Rightly is she called 'full of grace', who without a doubt obtains a grace which no other woman ever merited, in that she will conceive and bear the very author of grace.*[84]

[Luke 1:29] **But when she had heard, she was troubled at his saying, and pondered what kind of salutation this might be.** *Learn to know the Virgin by her character, her modesty, her prophetic utterance; learn from the mystery. It is proper for virgins to tremble, and to be terrified at every entrance of a man, to be afraid every time a man speaks to them. Let women learn to copy this example of propriety. She, whom no man might see, is alone in an inner room, where only an angel might find her; alone without a companion, alone without a witness, and lest she be corrupted by any ignoble address, she is saluted by an angel. Learn, virgin, to shun the wantonness of words. Mary even feared the salutation of the angel. But, 'she was pondering', it says, 'what kind of salutation this might be', and therefore she responded with modesty because she was terrified, and with prudence, because she marvelled at the new formula of benediction, which was never before read or experienced.*[85]

[Luke 1:30] **And the angel said to her: Fear not, Mary, for you have found grace with God.** When he saw that she was troubled by this unusual salutation, he calls her by name as if she were intimately known, and bids her not to fear, which is only natural given that he alone had custody over

---

82 For this paragraph, cf. Jerome, *Commentarii in Matheum* 1 (CCSL 77:10.73–79).
83 Isidore, *Etym.* 7.10.1; Jerome, *Hebr. nom.* (CCSL 72:137.16–20).
84 Ambrose, *Expos. Lucam* 2.9 (CCSL 14:34.123–25).
85 Ambrose, *Expos. Lucam* 2.8–9 (CCSL 14:33.111–22).

her. And because he had said she was full of grace, he both affirms that same grace more fully and explains it more copiously, saying:

[Luke 1:31] **Behold you will conceive in your womb, and you will bring forth a son, and you will call his /32/ name Jesus.** *Jesus means 'saviour' or 'salvific'.*[86] The angel who was speaking to Joseph explained the mystery of his name, saying: *For he will save his people from their sins.*[87] He does not say 'the people of Israel' but 'his people', that is, a people called both from foreskin and from circumcision into the unity of faith, so that after they have been gathered together from different sides there might *be one sheepfold and one shepherd.*[88]

[Luke 1:32] **He will be great, and he will be called the Son of the Most High, and the Lord God will give to him the throne of David his father.** It is also said of John that *he will be great*,[89] but he will be great like a man, and Jesus will be great like God. For John will be great in the presence of the Lord, but Jesus *will be great*, the angel says, *and he will be called the Son of the Most High*. Therefore, the Son of the Most High who was conceived and born in a virginal womb is simultaneously one who was created in time as a man from a mother, and was born as God before the ages from the Father. But if he is a man who is likewise God, let Nestorius cease to say that he was only a man born from a virgin, and that this man was admitted by the word of God not into the unity of a single person, but into an inseparable partnership. Moreover, Nestorius is clearly shown to assert that Christ is not one – true God and man – but two, which is a sinful claim, and accordingly he preaches a quaternity, and not the Trinity. But the orthodox faith rightly confesses that just as every individual human being is flesh and spirit, so the one Christ is man and Word, according to what the angel's words also signify when they assert that *the throne of David his father* would be given *to him*. For the angel, who proclaims that he who is going to *be called the Son of the Most High* has that same father David, demonstrates without doubt the one person of Christ in two natures. And he received the throne of David, in order that he himself would call the people, for whom David and his sons once provided the governance of a temporal kingdom, to the eternal kingdom, which was prepared for them from the beginning of the world.[90]

---

86 Isidore, *Etym.* 7.2.7.
87 Matt. 1:21.
88 John 10:16.
89 Luke 1:15.
90 Cf. Matt. 25:34.

BOOK ONE                                                            133

[Luke 1:32b–33] **And he will reign in the house of Jacob forever. And of his kingdom there will be no end.** And Isaiah says: *His empire will be multiplied, and there will be no end of peace upon the throne of David and upon his kingdom, to establish it and strengthen it with judgement and justice.*[91] He did not say 'by acquiring glory and earthly treasures', not 'by victory over many nations and the conquest of proud cities', but *with judgement and justice.* For with these the kingdom of Christ is multiplied and strengthened in each and every one of the faithful and in the universal Church throughout the world as well. For indeed the house of Jacob means the whole Church, which either was born from a good root, or although it was a wild olive shoot was deservedly grafted into the good olive tree of faith.[92] After the triumph of his passion, the Saviour addresses the Church and /33/ says: *You who fear the Lord, praise him; you the universal seed of Jacob, exalt him.*[93] But although the angel's verbs were in the future tense it does not then mean that Jesus was *going* to be great, that he was *going* to be called 'of the Most High', that he was *going* to receive the sceptre of David, and that he was *going* to reign in the house of Jacob. This is what heretics think, straying far from the truth, namely, that Christ did not exist before Mary, but that, taken up as a man to God, he was glorified with the glory which the Word of God had with the Father before the world was,[94] that is, so that the man full of grace and truth with God might receive that same name of the Son, that same person of Christ.

[Luke 1:34] **And Mary said to the angel: How will this be done, because I know not man?** Reverently did she reveal her mind's intention, namely that she had determined to lead the life of a virgin. And because, most excellent of women, she endeavoured to subject herself to so great a virtue, she deserved by a unique right to surpass other women in blessedness. *How will this be done?* she asks. She does not say: *How will I know this?*[95] but, *how will it be done, because I know not man?* inquiring, that is to say, about the kind of obedience to which she may be subjected, but not

---

91  Isa. 9:7.
92  Rom. 11:24. Bede's expression is elliptical; he takes for granted his audience's understanding that Israel is metaphorically a good olive tree (Jer. 11:16–17; Hosea 14:6–7), which when some branches are broken off is restored by a graft (= the Gentiles) from a wild olive tree (Rom. 11:17–24).
93  Ps. 21:24 (22:23).
94  Cf. John 17:5 ('now glorify me, Father, with yourself, with the glory which I had, before the world was, with you').
95  Luke 1:18.

demanding a sign in which she may believe. For it was not fitting for a virgin chosen to give birth to God to be doubtful from lack of faith but wary out of prudence, because man could not easily know a mystery that remained hidden from the world in God. Therefore, since she had read: *Behold a virgin will conceive in her womb, and bear a son*,[96] but had not heard how this could be done, rightly trusting in the things she had read, she inquires of the angel what she did not find in the prophet.[97]

2/5 [Luke 1:35] **And the angel answering, said to her: The Holy Spirit will come upon you, and the power of the Most High will overshadow you.** You will conceive, he says, not from the seed of a man, because you do not have carnal knowledge, but by the action of the Holy Spirit with whom you are filled. You will experience conception, but not sexual desire. Where the Holy Spirit makes a shadow, you will not experience the heat of lust. Truly in what he says, *and the power of the Most High will overshadow you*, each of the two natures of the incarnate Saviour can also be denoted. A shadow, of course, is customarily formed by a light and by a body. And anyone who is overshadowed is certainly restored as much as need be by the light and heat of the sun, but the very heat of the sun is tempered when a small diaphanous cloud or some other body intervenes, so that it can be endured. And such was the case with the blessed Virgin: since no human, no matter how pure, was able to receive *all the fullness of divinity bodily*,[98] the power of the Most High overshadowed her, that is, the incorporeal light of divinity begat in her a human body.[99] On /34/ this subject, the prophet says it well: *Behold, the Lord will ascend upon a swift cloud, and will enter into Egypt*,[100] which is to say: Behold, the Word of God, coeternal with the Father, and the light born of light before the ages, will take flesh and the breath of life at the end of the ages with no burden of sin, and from the womb of a virgin he will *come out of his bride chamber like a bridegroom* into the world.[101]

[Luke 1:35b] **And therefore the holy thing which will be born of you will be called the Son of God.** In contrast to our holiness, Jesus uniquely

---

96 Isa. 7:14.
97 Cf. Ambrose, *Expos. Lucam* 2.18 (CCSL 14:39.276–80).
98 Col. 2:9.
99 This explanation of 'overshadow' is substantially reproduced in Bede's *Hom.* 1.3 (ed. Hurst [CCSL 122:18.137–77]; trans. Martin and Hurst, *Homilies of the Gospels* 2:25). See Del Giacco, 'Exegesis and Sermon', 14 and Introduction, 41.
100 Isa. 19:1.
101 Ps. 18:6 (19:5).

is asserted to be going to be born holy. *Indeed, even if we become holy, we are nevertheless not born so, because we are bound by the very condition of corruptible nature, so that deservedly each one of us may say, lamenting with the prophet: 'For behold, I was conceived in iniquities, and in sins did my mother conceive me'.*[102] *For he alone is truly holy, who was not conceived from the mingling of carnal copulation in order that he might overcome the very condition of corruptible nature.*[103] *The holy thing*, he says, *will be called the Son of God*. What do you say here, O Nestorian, you who strive to impugn the obvious truth, denying that the blessed Mary is the mother of God? Behold, he said that God will come, that the Son of God will be born. How, therefore, is the Son of God not God, or how can she who begat God not be *theotocos*, that is, the mother of God?

**3**/10   [Luke 1:36–37] **And behold your cousin Elizabeth, she also has conceived a son in her old age; and this is the sixth month with her who is called barren. For no word will be impossible with God.** Lest the virgin despair of being able to give birth, she receives the example of a barren old woman about to give birth, in order that she may learn that all things are possible to God, even those that seem contrary to the course of nature. But if it bothers anyone that he calls Elizabeth the cousin of the blessed Mary, when the latter traced her lineage from the house of David, while the former took it from the daughters of Aaron, he should note that their ancestors were able to unite both tribes by means of children given one another in marriage. If perchance this explanation does not satisfy someone who stubbornly insists that this could not have been done, since it is contrary to the edict of the Law,[104] let him read Exodus, where it is written: *And Aaron took to wife Elizabeth the daughter of Aminadab, sister of Nahason, who bore him Nadab, and Abiu, and Eleazar, and Ithamar.*[105] And let him see that prior to the edict of the Law the priestly line of descent had already been joined by divine providence to the royal, so that clearly the Lord Jesus Christ, who was going to be true King and priest according to the flesh, would take his very flesh as well from both, that is to say, from David and from Aaron. And hence in both of these two tribes the mystical /**35**/ chrism was celebrated according to the Law,[106] surely as a

---

102  Ps. 50:7 (51:5) (not *iuxta LXX*).
103  Gregory, *Moralia* 18.52 (CCSL 143A:948.25–31).
104  Cf. Lev. 18:6–18, where rules prohibiting kinship marriages are laid down.
105  Exod. 6:23.
106  Cf., e.g., Exod. 29:29, Lev. 16:32 (high-priest); 1 Sam. 9:16, 3 Kings 1:34 (king).

token equally of the name 'Christ' and of his lineage. And David himself, entering into the house of God, took the holy bread and sword as if king and priest,[107] clearly prefiguring the one who would come from his seed, both to fight for our freedom with the justice of a king and to offer the bread of his flesh for our deliverance.

[Luke 1:38] **And Mary said: Behold, the handmaid of the Lord; let it be done to me according to your word.** How great with devotion was the humility which both desires that the angel's promise be fulfilled, and calls herself, who is chosen as mother, a handmaid, thus making known in the clearest manner that she claims no merit for herself for being obedient to the commands of the Lord. Let it be done, she says; let the one conceived in a virgin without the seed of a man be born of the Holy Spirit with spotless flesh; let the Holy which is born of a human mother without a human father be called the Son of God.

[Luke 1:38b–39] **And the angel departed from her. And Mary, rising up in those days, went into the hill country with haste into a city of Juda.** Having received the Virgin's consent, the angel went directly back to heaven and Mary went into the hill country. She hastens to visit Elizabeth, *not as though she is incredulous about the prophecy*, or dubious *about the precedent*,[108] *but joyful for the sake of the promise and scrupulous in doing her duty.*[109] At the same time she provides a typological example to show that every soul that has conceived the word of God in his mind may immediately ascend the loftiest peaks of the virtues with the steps of love to enter the city of Juda, that is, of confession and praise,[110] to penetrate the citadel, and to abide in it, as it were, for three months, right up to the perfection of faith, hope, and love.

[Luke 1:40] **And she entered into the house of Zechariah and saluted Elizabeth.** Learn, O virgin, *the humility of Mary*, so that you may be able to be chaste in body and devout in spirit. *The younger* visits *the older* and the virgin salutes the wife. *For it is fitting that* the *more chaste the virgin,* the *humbler she is*,[111] and that, by deferring to elders, she graces the state of chastity with the commendation of humility. In another interpretation:

---

107 Cf. 1 Sam. 21:1–9.
108 As Ambrose makes clear, Elizabeth's pregnancy in her old age is a reassuring example to Mary of the fact that God can do whatever he pleases; Bede then goes on to find another meaning in the example.
109 Ambrose, *Expos. Lucam* 2.19 (CCSL 14:39.288–90).
110 Cf. Jerome, *Hebr. nom.* (CCSL 72:67.19).
111 Ambrose, *Expos. Lucam* 2.22 (CCSL 14:40.305–09).

*Mary comes to Elizabeth, and the Lord comes to John*[112] – Elizabeth to be filled with the Holy Spirit, and John that his baptism may be consecrated. And the humbling of those who are greater is assuredly the exaltation of those who are less. Then follows:

[Luke 1:41] **And when Elizabeth heard the salutation of Mary, the infant leaped in her womb. And Elizabeth was filled with the Holy Spirit.** *Notice the distinction and proper meanings of each word. Elizabeth heard Mary's voice first, but John perceived the grace first. She heard according to the order of nature, he leaped by reason of the mystery. She perceived the advent of Mary, he the advent of the Lord. The women* /36/ *speak of grace, the children bring it into effect inwardly, and undertake the mystery of mercy for their mothers' benefit, and in a double miracle the mothers prophesy by the spirit of children. The infant leaped and the mother was filled. The mother was not filled before the son, but after the son had been filled with the Holy Spirit, he filled the mother as well.*[113]

[Luke 1:42] **And she cried out with a loud voice, and said: Blessed are you among women, and blessed is the fruit of your womb.** It should be observed that *the prophecy* made about Christ *is fulfilled not* only *by miracles of deeds, but* also *by the proper signification of words.*[114] For this is the fruit which is promised on oath to the patriarch David: *Of the fruit of your womb I will set upon my throne.*[115] And likewise it should be observed that Mary is blessed by Elizabeth with the same phrase by which she was blessed by Gabriel, in order to show that she is to be venerated both by angels and by men, and deservedly favoured above all women.

[Luke 1:43] **And for what reason has it happened to me, that the mother of my Lord should come to me?** She asks not as though she is ignorant, because, of course, she recognizes that this is owing to the Holy Spirit, namely, that she is saluted by the mother of the Lord in regard to the fulfilment of the pledge [to David], but daunted by the uniqueness of the miracle, she acknowledges that it is not because of her merit but of a divine gift.

[Luke 1:44] **For behold as soon as the voice of your salutation sounded in my ears, the infant in my womb leaped for joy.** As long as she did not know the mystery of religion, Elizabeth blushed *at the burden*

---

112  Ambrose, *Expos. Lucam* 2.22 (CCSL 14:40.312–13).
113  Ambrose, *Expos. Lucam* 2.23 (CCSL 14:40.318–27).
114  Ambrose, *Expos. Lucam* 2.24 (CCSL 14:41.336–37).
115  Ps. 131:11 (132:11) (not *iuxta LXX*).

*of motherhood.* But she *who hid herself because she had conceived a son, began to exult that she was begetting a prophet, and she who blushed before, blesses, and she who was doubtful before, is reassured. 'For behold', she says, 'as soon as the voice of your salutation sounded in my ears, the infant in my womb leaped for joy'. And so she cried out with a loud voice when she sensed the advent of the Lord, because she believed that her offspring was holy. For there was no cause for disgrace when the birth of the prophet attests that the act of generation was imposed, not desired.*[116]

[Luke 1:45] **And blessed is she who believed, because those things will be accomplished that were spoken to her by the Lord.** *You see that Mary did not doubt, but believed, and therefore that she obtained the reward of her faith. 'Blessed', she says, 'is she who believed'.*[117] And truly blessed is the Virgin who, being far superior to the priest, corrected his error after he said no.[118] Nor is it extraordinary that the Lord, who was going to redeem the world, began his work by his mother, so that the same woman through whom salvation for all was prepared might first draw the reward of salvation from her offspring. And likewise, it should be observed how much, /37/ thanks to Mary's entrance, grace enriched Elizabeth's mind, which it illuminated *at once about the past, the present, and the future by the spirit of prophecy. For by saying, 'blessed are you who believed', she clearly indicates that she knew the words of the angel that had been said by the Spirit to Mary, and by adding, 'those things will be accomplished that were spoken to you by the Lord', she indicates that she foresaw also those things that would follow her in the future. Indeed, by calling her the mother* of her Lord, *she indicates that she understood that she was carrying the Redeemer of the human race in her womb.*[119]

[Luke 1:46–47] **And Mary said: My soul magnifies the Lord. And my spirit has rejoiced in God my Saviour, ...** The Lord, she says, has exalted me so greatly and by such an unprecedented gift that it cannot be explained by means of language, but can scarcely be comprehended by that sympathy of the innermost heart, and therefore I am bestowing all the strength of my soul in offering praise

---

116 Ambrose, *Expos. Lucam* 1.45–46 (CCSL 14:29.703–12).
117 Ambrose, *Expos. Lucam* 2.26 (CCSL 14:42.359–60).
118 An elliptical reference to Zechariah's inability to believe, followed by Mary's willingness to do so.
119 Gregory, *Hom. in Hiezech.* 1.1.8 (CCSL 142:9.154–62).

for his favours. I live, I feel, I choose, I carry out joyfully everything whatever for the sake of contemplating the greatness of him for whom there is no end, because my spirit also rejoices in the eternal divinity of the same Jesus, that is, the Saviour, by whose temporal conception my flesh is impregnated. Similar to this is that verse of the Psalmist: *But my soul will rejoice in the Lord, and will be delighted in his salvation.*[120] For he too worshipped the Father and the Son with equal love.

[Luke 1:48] **Because he has looked with favour on the humility of his handmaid. For behold from henceforth all generations will call me blessed.** Since her humility is looked on with favour, she rightly rejoices to be called blessed by all, just as on the contrary she, whose despicable pride is condemned by the name of Eve, that is, 'woe' or 'calamity',[121] having been punished, dwindles. For it is fitting that just as death entered the world by the pride of our first mother, so the entryway to life would again be opened by the humility of Mary.

[Luke 1:49] **Because he who is mighty has done great things to me, and holy is his name.** She looks back to the beginning of the song, where it is said: *My soul magnifies the Lord.*[122] Indeed, that soul alone to whom the Lord deigned to do great things is able to magnify him to those worthy of the proclamation, and to say in exhortation to those who share that same vow and way of life: *Magnify the Lord with me, and let us extol his name in turn.*[123] For he who disdains to magnify to the best of his ability the Lord whom he knows, and to sanctify his name, *will be called the least in the kingdom of heaven.*[124] And his name is said to be 'holy', because by the height of his unique power he surpasses every creature and is far beyond all that he made. This is better understood in the Greek expression, in which the word /38/ itself, which is pronounced *agion*, signifies that he is, as it were, outside of the earth.[125] In imitation of which we also are admonished according to our capacity to be separated from all things that are not holy or dedicated to God when the Lord says: *Be holy because I am holy.*[126] Whoever will consecrate himself will justly seem outside of the

---

120 Ps. 34:9 (35:9).
121 Cf. Jerome, *Hebr. nom.* (CCSL 72:65.16–17).
122 The 'song' (Luke 1:46–55) is the hymn or canticle known as the Magnificat.
123 Ps. 33:4 (34:3) (not *iuxta LXX*).
124 Matt. 5:19.
125 Bede plausibly, but erroneously, derives the Greek *(h)agios*, 'holy', from *a*, 'without', 'not', + *gaia*, 'earth'.
126 Lev. 11:44.

earth and beyond the world. For such a one will be able to say: walking upon the earth, we have our way of life in heaven.[127]

[Luke 1:50] **And his mercy is unto generations and generations, to them that fear him.** Turning from the gifts specific to herself to the judgements of God applicable to all, she describes in successive verses the condition of the whole human race, and explains what the proud and the humble deserve, what the sons of Adam are by their free will, and what the sons of God are by grace. Therefore, she says, he who is mighty has not done great things to me alone, *but* also *in every nation* and generation *he who fears him and works justice is acceptable to him*.[128]

[Luke 1:51] **He has shown strength in his arm, he has scattered the proud in the thought of their heart.** 'In his arm' signifies 'in the Son of God himself'. *Not that God the Father is limited by the shape of human flesh and that the Son is attached to him like the limb of a body, but since 'all things were made by him'*,[129] *he is therefore called the arm of God. For just as it is your arm by which you work, so his Word is called the arm of God, because he wrought the world by the Word. For why does a man stretch out his arm to work something, if not that what he said does not happen immediately? But if he should be endowed with such great power that what he said happened without any motion of his body, his word would be his arm.*[130] When, therefore, we have heard that the arm of God the Father is God the Son, let the carnal usage not trouble us, but let us reflect, as much as he grants us power to do so, upon the virtue and wisdom of God, through which all things are done.

[Luke 1:52–53] **He has brought down the mighty from their throne, and exalted the humble. He has filled the hungry with good things, and sent the rich away empty.** What Mary said, *in his arm*, and what she promised, *unto generations and generations*, in separate phrases, should be connected to these verses also *apo coinu*,[131] because throughout all the generations of historic time the proud never cease to perish, and the humble to be exalted, by the righteous and just dispensation of divine power.

---

127 Cf. Phil. 3:20.
128 Acts 10:35.
129 John 1:3.
130 Augustine, *In Iohannis euang.* 53.2 (CCSL 36:452.7–16).
131 The Greek phrase, literally 'in common', signifies a construction that unites clauses that share an unrepeated word or phrase.

BOOK ONE                                      141

[Luke 1:54] **He has protected his child Israel, being mindful of his mercy, ...** In a lovely manner, Mary calls Israel the 'child of the Lord', who, being obedient and humble, was protected by him for salvation, according to what Hosea says: *Because Israel was a child, and I loved him.*[132] For /39/ he who refuses to be humble assuredly cannot be saved, nor say with the prophet: *For behold God is my helper, and the Lord is the protector of my soul,*[133] and *Whoever will humble himself like this little child, he is the greater in the kingdom of heaven.*[134]

[Luke 1:55] **As he spoke to our fathers, to Abraham and to his seed forever.** 'Seed' signifies not the carnal but the spiritual seed of Abraham, that is, not only his progeny in the flesh, but those who followed his footsteps through faith, either in circumcision or in uncircumcision.[135] For Abraham also, while in a state of uncircumcision, *believed, and it was imputed to him as righteousness.*[136] And he received circumcision as the sign of that faith so that he might become the father of both peoples in faith, as the Apostle explained very thoroughly to the Romans.[137] The advent of the Saviour, therefore, was promised to Abraham and to his seed forever, that is, to the children of promise to whom is said: *And if you are Christ's, then you are the seed of Abraham, heirs according to the promise.*[138] And well do the mothers approach one another with prophecy before the birth both of the Lord and of John, so that just as sin began from women, so also good things may begin from women, and the eternal life which was destroyed by the error of one woman may be restored to the world by two women who eagerly proclaim it.

[Luke 1:56] **And Mary remained with her about three months and returned to her own house.** Mary remained until the time of Elizabeth's giving birth was complete so that she might see the nativity of the forerunner of her Lord, which was the principal reason why she had come. And it was stated above[139] that every chaste soul which has conceived a spiritual desire for the Word necessarily submits soon after to the exalted yoke of heavenly meditation; and having tarried there for about three months, the

---

132 Hosea 11:1.
133 Ps. 53:6 (54:4).
134 Matt. 18:4.
135 Cf. Rom. 2:25–29.
136 Gen. 15:6.
137 Cf. Rom. 4:1–12.
138 Gal. 3:29.
139 See Bede's comment on Luke 1:38b–39.

soul does not cease to persevere until it is irradiated with the perfect light of the principal virtues. The Apostle is evidently describing these months of consummate radiance when he says: *And now there remain faith, hope, and love, these three; but the greatest of these is love.*[140]

## Chapter 4

[Luke 1:57] **Now Elizabeth's time of giving birth was fulfilled, and she brought forth a son.** Holy Scripture is accustomed to employ the word 'fulfilment' only /40/ for the origin, character, or action of good persons, and it signifies that their life has the fullness of perfection. Accordingly: *Elizabeth's time of giving birth was fulfilled*; Mary's *days were fulfilled that she should give birth*;[141] Solomon brought to fulfilment *the building of the house of the Lord.*[142] Abraham and another of the patriarchs died *old and full of days.*[143] And when *the fullness of the time had come, God sent his son.*[144] But on the contrary the days of the wicked are empty and void. For *bloody and deceitful men will not live out half their days.*[145]

[Luke 1:58] **And her neighbours and relatives heard that the Lord had magnified his mercy towards her, and they rejoiced with her.** *The birth of saints holds joy for many, because what is good is common to all. For justice is a virtue held in common. And therefore, the birth of a just man presents a sign of the life to come, and the grace of the virtue that will follow is signified by the prefiguring joy of the neighbours.*[146]

[Luke 1:59–60] **And on the eighth day they came to circumcise the child, and they called him by his father's name Zechariah. And his mother answering said: Not so; but he will be called John.** *In a wonderful manner, the holy evangelist thought that it deserved to be mentioned that many thought the child should be called by his father's name Zechariah, so that you may perceive that the mother was not displeased by the name of someone ignoble, but rather that what had been foretold previously by the angel to Zechariah had been imparted to her by the Holy Spirit. And*

---

140 1 Cor. 13:13.
141 Luke 2:6.
142 2 Chron. 3:1; cf. 2 Chron. 7:11.
143 Gen. 35:29 (the reference is to Isaac).
144 Gal. 4:4.
145 Ps. 54:24 (55:23).
146 Ambrose, *Expos. Lucam* 2.30 (CCSL 14:43.410–14).

*indeed, because he was mute, he was unable to make known the name of his son to his wife, but Elizabeth learned through prophecy what she had not learned from her husband.*[147]

[Luke 1:61–63] **And they said to her: There is no one in your kindred that is called by this name. And they made signs to his father, what he wanted him to be called. And demanding a writing tablet, he wrote, saying: His name is John. And they all wondered.** *'His name', he says, 'is John': that is, we do not give a name to one who has already received a name from God. He has his own name which we have learned, not one which we have chosen. Nor should you wonder that the wife declared the name which she did not hear, for the Holy Spirit who had confided it to the angel revealed it to her, nor could she, who had foretold the Christ, be ignorant of the forerunner of the Lord. And it is properly added that no one in his kindred is called by this name, so that you may understand that the name does not belong to a family, but to a prophet.*[148]

[Luke 1:64–65] **And immediately his mouth was opened and his tongue freed, and he spoke, blessing God. And fear came over all their neighbours.** Because *the voice of one crying out in the wilderness*[149] was born, the tongue of the parent was deservedly freed. For it was not fitting for the father who rejoiced that the herald of the Word had been born to him to be silenced from giving praise. Indeed, his lips, which /41/ incredulity had sealed, faith now freed. In truth, if anyone should wish to examine it thoroughly, this celebrated nativity of John is also an allegory of the incipient sublimity of the grace of the New Testament. The neighbours and relatives preferred to give him the name of his father instead of 'John', because the Jews, who were connected to him through marriage, as it were, wished to pursue by the observance of the Law the righteousness which is from the Law, rather than to receive the grace of faith. But his mother in words and his father in writing took the trouble to make known the name of John, that is, 'the grace of God',[150] because not only the Law itself and the Psalms and the prophets preach in words whose meaning is clearly the grace of Christ, but that ancient priesthood testifies to the same grace in the figurative shadows of sacred rites and sacrifices. That Zechariah speaks on the eighth day of his child's nativity is a beautiful touch, because the

---

147 Ambrose, *Expos. Lucam* 2.31 (CCSL 14:44.429–35).
148 Ambrose, *Expos. Lucam* 2.31–32 (CCSL 14:44.435–38; 445–50).
149 John 1:23.
150 Cf. Jerome, *Hebr. nom.* (CCSL 72:146.16–17; 155.19).

secret mysteries of the priesthood of the Law were revealed by the Lord's resurrection on the eighth day (that is, after the seventh day of the Sabbath), and the tongue of the high-priests of the Jews, which the chains of lack of faith had tied, was freed by a voice of rational understanding.

[Luke 1:65b–66] **And all these things were made known over all the hill country of Judea. And all who had heard them laid them up in their heart, saying: What do you think this child will be? For the hand of the Lord was with him.** *Great are the works of the Lord, sought out according to all that he wills.*[151] For behold, the singular muteness of Zechariah is not only beneficial to himself as punishment of unbelief and as a sign of believing, but it also stupefies all his neighbours with wonder and fear when it is removed. The report of the prophet's birth spreads through all the hill country round about; it stimulates all who were able to hear to inquire more diligently about the circumstance and standing of the child who was born, so that the future prophet of Christ may be commended by these signs and others of this kind, and that antecedent signs may show the way, so to speak, to the forerunner of the truth.

[Luke 1:67–68] **And Zechariah his father was filled with the Holy Spirit, and he prophesied, saying: Blessed be the Lord God of Israel, because he visited and worked the redemption of his people.** How great is the munificence of the heavenly gift, if piety be prompt for the reception of our faith! Here speech, which alone was taken from the unbeliever, was restored with the spirit of prophecy to the believer. And the Lord visited his people, who were languishing, as it were, with a long illness, and redeemed them with the blood of his only Son, when being in the power of sin, they had been, so to speak, sold. Since the blessed Zechariah knew that this was going to happen very soon, he narrates it in prophetic fashion as if it had already happened. And it should be observed that God is said to have visited and redeemed his people, not, of course, because /42/ he found them to be his own when he came, but because he made them his own by visiting them. Similar to this is what is sung at the end of Proverbs about this same people: *Who will find a valiant woman?*[152] For he did not find that woman, namely the Church, valiant (that is, devout in faith), but by betrothing her to himself he rendered her valiant, because he made her perfect in the sublimity of her faith.[153]

---

151 Ps. 110:2 (111:2).
152 Prov. 31:10.
153 In his commentary on Proverbs, Bede also interprets the Valiant Woman as a symbol of

[Luke 1:69] **And he has raised up a horn of salvation for us in the house of David his servant, ...** *Horn of salvation* means the enduring loftiness of salvation. While all bones are covered in flesh, a horn rises up above the flesh, and therefore the kingdom of the Saviour Christ is called a horn of salvation, and by this, its spiritual height, which rises above the joys of the flesh, it is proclaimed to the world. Under this symbol, oils are consecrated to the glory of the kingdom in the horn of David and Solomon.[154]

[Luke 1:70] **As he spoke by the mouth of his holy prophets from of old, ...** *From of old*, Zechariah says, because the prophecy of Christ preceded all the writings of the Old Testament. Not only did Jeremiah, Daniel, and Isaiah, and others like them, who are also specifically called prophets, clearly speak about his advent, but father Adam himself, Abel, and Enoch, and others of the fathers, all give testimony by their own deeds to God's divine plan. Hence the Lord himself, refuting the hardness of heart of the Jews, says: *If you believed in Moses, perhaps you would also believe in me. For he wrote of me.*[155]

[Luke 1:71] **Salvation from our enemies, and from the hand of all who hate us, ...** This must be taken with the above verse, *he has raised up for us*, that is, he has raised up for us salvation from our enemies. For although he had first set forth briefly: *And he has raised up a horn of salvation for us*, immediately explaining as it were what he had said, he goes on: *salvation from our enemies, and from the hand of all who hate us*. And *all who hate us* signifies both evil men and unclean spirits, from whose hand for the present *we are saved by hope*,[156] and in the future by the fact of salvation itself.

[Luke 1:72–74] **To perform mercy to our fathers, and to remember his holy covenant, the oath, which he swore to Abraham our father, that he would grant to us that, being delivered from the hand of our enemies, we may serve him without fear, ...** He had said the Lord was going to be born in the house of David in accordance with the declarations of the prophets; he says the same Lord was going to free us in fulfilment of the covenant that he settled upon Abraham, because, of course, both the gathering in of Gentiles and the incarnation of Christ were promised

---

the Church. The date of this work is uncertain, but it may have been composed shortly after the Luke commentary (Wallis, '*Rectores* at Risk', 131).
154  Cf. 1 Sam. 16:13; 3 Kings 1:39.
155  John 5:46.
156  Rom. 8:24.

especially to these patriarchs of Abraham's seed. Matthew also desired to make this known concisely, by commencing the opening of his gospel in this way: *The book of the generation /43/ of Jesus Christ, the son of David, the son of Abraham.*[157] It should be noted here that in each of the two evangelists David is put before Abraham, because even though David is the later in order of time, nevertheless he is the greater in the gift of promise. For indeed Abraham, who forsook his own country,[158] knew God, and merited the testimony of faith while still placed in the state of uncircumcision, was promised only to this extent the faith of the Gentiles and the sacred assembly of the Church, when the Lord says to him: *And in you all the kindred of the earth will be blessed.*[159] But in a more sublime prophecy that Christ was going to be born in the flesh from himself, David heard, as it says: *And when you have ended your days to go to your fathers, I will raise up your seed after you, which will be of your sons; and I will establish his kingdom. He will build a house for me, and I will establish his throne forever. I will be a father to him, and he will be a son to me.*[160]

[Luke 1:75] **In holiness and righteousness before him all our days.** Clearly and succinctly, Luke makes known how the Lord should be served, namely not only *in holiness and righteousness* but *before him* and *all our days.* For he who either leaves his service before death or stains the purity of his own faith by any impurity or unrighteousness whatever, or strives to stay holy and righteous only before men and not also before the Lord, does not yet serve the Lord perfectly, freed from the hand of spiritual enemies, but in the manner of the ancient Samaritans, tries to serve both the gods of the pagans and the Lord.[161]

[Luke 1:76] **And you, child, will be called the prophet of the Highest. For you will go before the face of the Lord to prepare his ways,** ... While he was speaking *in a lovely manner about the Lord, he* suddenly *directed his speech to the prophet John to point out that this too was a favour of the Lord.*[162] Doubtless the question is asked, how *he can address the child who is eight days old?* But why would the son, *who while still shut in the womb heard the salutation of Mary,* not *hear the voice of his father?*[163] Unless

---

157 Matt. 1:1.
158 Cf. Gen. 12:1.
159 Gen. 12:3.
160 1 Chron. 17:11–13.
161 Cf. 4 Kings 17:41.
162 Ambrose, *Expos. Lucam* 2.34 (CCSL 14:45.472–74).
163 Ambrose, *Expos. Lucam* 2.34 (CCSL 14:45.477–80).

perchance one can imagine that Zechariah wanted to preach as soon as he was able to speak for the sake of instructing those who were present about the future gifts of his son, which he had learned just a short time ago from the angel. Indeed, let the Arians hear and blush, *let the meek hear and rejoice*,[164] that Zechariah calls Christ the Lord most High, whom John preceded, prophesying. And according to what the Psalmist, praising God and the perfect man together in one person, says: *Mother Zion will say this man and that man was born in her, and* /44/ *the Highest himself founded her.*[165] He who founded the man who was born is the same man whom the Psalmist calls the Highest.

[Luke 1:77] **To give knowledge of salvation to his people by the remission of their sins, ...** Desiring, as it were, to set forth and commend more diligently the name of Jesus, that is, the Saviour, Zechariah mentions salvation once again when he reminds us of the horn of salvation that is to be raised up, the future salvation from enemies, and the knowledge of salvation that is to be given to the people. But lest you think a temporal and carnal salvation is promised, he says: *by the remission of their sins*. Indeed, the Jews for that reason prefer not to accept Jesus Christ, but to await the Antichrist, because they wish to be saved not inwardly but outwardly, to be freed not from the dominion of sin, but from the yoke of human servitude.

[Luke 1:78] **Through the bowels of the mercy of our God, in which the Orient from on high has visited us, ...** And the prophet, speaking of the Lord, says: *Behold a man, the Orient is his name.*[166] He is rightly called the Orient, because, by disclosing the rising of the true light to us, he made the children of night and darkness into the children of light, in accordance with what the blessed Zechariah explains next, saying:

[Luke 1:79] **To enlighten those who sit in darkness and in the shadow of death, to direct our feet into the way of peace.** It is for the Lord to enlighten those sitting in darkness and in the shadow of death and those who have lived in sin and the blindness of ignorance, and to shed the rays of knowledge of him and of his love. Concerning this the Apostle says: *You were once darkness, but now light in the Lord.*[167] And our feet are directed into the way of peace, when the path of our actions accords in all things with the grace of our Redeemer and Enlightener. In the appropriate order,

---

164  Ps. 33:3 (34:2).
165  Ps. 86:5 (87:5) (not *iuxta LXX*).
166  Zech. 6:12.
167  Eph. 5:8.

he demonstrates that hearts are first to be enlightened and works are to be directed afterwards, since no one can work peace unless he first learns of it. Hence the Psalmist rightly says: *Seek after peace and pursue it.*[168] Which is to say: May you who were sitting in darkness be enlightened,[169] and may you enter the way of peace from which you were exiled long ago.

[Luke 1:80] **And the child grew and was strengthened in spirit, and was in the wilderness until the day of his manifestation to Israel.** It is fitting and proper for the future preacher of penitence to seek out harsh places of solitude; and by this means as a young man, spending his youth all unkempt in the wilderness, to lift up his listeners from the allurements of the world by his teaching.

## Chapter 5

[Luke 2:1] **And in those days there went out a decree from Caesar Augustus that the whole world should be enrolled.** Just as the Son of God who was about to be born in the flesh chose the parents for himself whom he wanted, and the place of birth which he wished, and conveyed them to that very place /45/ before he was born in the way he wished, so also, he entered the world to save it at the time which he wanted, or rather at the time which he himself together with the Father and the Holy Spirit had determined from ages past and had prophesied through the mouths of the prophets. For by the way in which he was born from a virgin mother, he showed that the glory of virginity and the angelic virtue of chastity were very pleasing to him; so also having been begotten when the world was very much at peace, he taught that he sought and loved peace above all, and he indicated that he always deemed followers of peace and love worthy of being visited. This is in accordance with what he promised to the faithful when he said: *For where there are two or three gathered together in my name, there am I in the midst of them.*[170] For what, as far as men are concerned, could be a greater indicator of an utterly quiet realm and a very beautiful peace, than that the whole world be included in one registration, and that all the countries of the world far and wide be assessed with the same coin of tribute? According to trustworthy historical accounts,

---

168 Ps. 33:15 (34:14).
169 Cf. Isa. 9:2.
170 Matt. 18:20.

BOOK ONE                                                                 149

Augustus, who instigated and directed this registration, ruled for twelve years around the time of Christ's birth in such great peace that the spiritual foreshadowing of the prophet is seen to have been fulfilled literally, with foreign as well as civil wars brought to an end. This is that prophet who foretold in mystical language the divine providence of Christ, saying: *And in the last days the mountain of the house of the Lord shall be prepared on the top of mountains, and it shall be exalted above the hills, and all nations shall flow into it.*[171] After a few words he again attempted to describe the condition of that hallowed time: *And*, he says, *they shall melt down their swords into ploughshares, and their spears into sickles. Nation shall not lift up sword against nation, neither shall they be trained any more for war. O house of Jacob, come, and let us walk in the light of the Lord.*[172]

This new registration of the world bore witness to the advent of that supreme King who enrolled his elect gathered together from all the regions of the world on the register of eternal blessedness. It also aided the leaders of this heavenly kingdom with the quiet peace of its government, because with all nations restrained from the storm of battles, it shielded from the raging heat of violent civil discords the disciples of Christ who were determined to preach wherever they wished to go for the sake of the Word, and protected this period of time by the formidable shadow, as I might call it, of the Roman name. Therefore, *there went out a decree from Caesar Augustus* to proclaim a census of the whole world, because the decree of Christ the King, by which he would obtain the salvation of the whole world, was near at hand. And complementing the name of **Aug**ustus very perfectly, namely both desiring that his people be **aug**mented and himself sufficing to **aug**ment them, he ordered that his followers declare themselves to the critics of belief in him not by the withholding of money /**46**/ but by the offering of faith, saying: *Go into the whole world and preach the gospel to every creature. He who believes and is baptized will be saved.*[173]

[Luke 2:2–3] **This enrolling was first made by Quirinius, the governor of Syria. And all went to be enrolled, every one into his own city.** Josephus, the famous historian of the Jews, also records this census held in the time of Quirinius *in the eighteenth book of his Antiquities in this way*: *'And a certain Quirinius with the consent of the Roman senate, rising through each of the civil offices up to the rank of consul, and honourable in*

---

171  Isa. 2:2.
172  Isa. 2:4–5.
173  Mark 16:15–16.

*other respects as well, came to Syria with a few men, having been sent by Caesar to administer the peoples, and at the same time to become censor of the Roman patrimony.*'[174] Accordingly, when it says: *This enrolling was first made by Quirinius, the governor of Syria*, it signifies that this registration was either the first of those which included the whole world, since most parts of the world were found to have been registered on numerous occasions already, or indeed that it first began at the time when Quirinius was sent to Syria. And just as *all went to be enrolled* in the census, *every one into his own city*, in the reign of Augustus and the administration of Quirinius, so now, when Christ rules, or rather urges and offers rewards, through the governors of the Church, that is, the teachers, let us all go, and let no one be exempted from the tribute of justice.[175] Let us come to him, we who labour and are burdened, and he will refresh us.[176] Let us take up his yoke upon us, and let us learn from it that he is meek and humble of heart, and we will find rest for our souls.[177] For this is our city and our fatherland, the blessed and heavenly rest of our souls, for which we were created in the beginning of the new-born world by the God Christ, and for which we are created anew at the end of the world by the man Christ. Truly, to go to that city of peace and rest and to carry treasures promised to our King, is to observe with daily increasing advances of virtue and faith what the eternal joys of the heavenly light are, and to condemn the good things of the world together with the evils for the sake of acquiring these joys, and after acquiring them, to offer *ourselves* cleansed *of all defilement of the flesh and of the spirit*,[178] a gift more precious than gold to God.

And if we examine more carefully the kind of coin which was paid to Caesar, we will give sufficient demonstration of devotion on our part, and also cleanse the coin of sin. For we cannot seek and find from anywhere better than from that very Gospel, where the Lord says to those tempting him about rendering tribute to Caesar: *Show me the coin of the census. And they offered him*, it says, *a denarius. And Jesus says to them: Whose*

---

174 Eusebius, *Hist. eccl.* 1.5.4 (GCS 9.1:47.6–9) (cf. Josephus, *Antiquitates* 18.1.1).

175 Kelly, 'Bede's Exegesis of Luke's Infancy Narrative', finds the allegory of Augustus and Quirinus as teachers 'not convincing ... although it does follow a Lucan principle, that is, of finding good things to say about the Romans' (62). The ensuing digression on the Tribute Money would seem to support this, though Bede is willing to take any opportunity to stress the role of teachers: see Introduction, 67–68.

176 Cf. Matt. 11:28.

177 Cf. Matt. 11:29.

178 2 Cor. 7:1.

BOOK ONE 151

*image and inscription is this? And they say to him: Caesar's. Then he says* /47/ *to them: Render therefore to Caesar the things that are Caesar's, and to God, the things that are God's.*[179] Here it should be noted first that the denarius, which was valued at ten pennies, was paid to Caesar, because, marked with his image and inscription, it even appears with his name. It should be concluded that, since the Lord commands that the things that are Caesar's are to be rendered to Caesar and the things that are God's to God, the royal denarius also subtly teaches us by analogy that the Decalogue of the Law is to be offered to God our King, that is, the love of God and the love of neighbour, one of which comprises three commandments, the other, seven, and that it is to be kept with our whole heart.[180] Clearly, whoever knows how to pay attention will find the name and face of the eternal King – that is, knowledge of the divine will – in this denarius of holy Scripture, adorned with ten heavenly commandments as if with that number of golden pennies. This is what each person who believes, hopes, and loves, writes with a stylus of zealous castigation. And we carry the denarius with us on our journey hither, as if enclosed in a purse, knowing when to say with the Psalmist: *The light of your countenance, Lord, is signed upon us; you have given gladness in my heart.*[181] Nevertheless, hitherto we keep this sign of faith and delight of hope and love concealed in the secret meditation of our conscience, with God as our witness. But when we reach the fatherland of our King, whose sight we thirst for, and whose beauty we hasten to behold with all our might and with the utmost exertion of our mind,[182] we will offer the gifts of our good way of life, which had lain concealed on earth but are to be crowned in heaven. Then *what* we *said in the dark* will be *said in the light, and what* we *spoke in the ear in the chambers will be preached on the rooftops.*[183]

[Luke 2:4–5] **And Joseph also went up from Galilee, out of the city of Nazareth into Judea, to the city of David, which is called Bethlehem, because he was of the house and family of David, to be enrolled with Mary his espoused wife, who was with child.** By divine dispensation the

---

179 Matt. 22:19–21; cf. Mark 12:15–17; Luke 20:23–25.
180 The reference here seems ultimately to be to the two stone tablets (Deut. 4:13) onto which God wrote the Ten Commandments. In the Catholic tradition, stemming from Augustine, the one tablet contained duties to God in three commandments; the other, duties to our neighbour in seven commandments.
181 Ps. 4:7 (4:6–7).
182 Cf. Isa. 33:17.
183 Luke 12:3, with alteration of voice; cf. Matt. 10:27.

registration for the tax was so decreed that everyone was commanded to go to his own fatherland, not only for the sake of the mystery of which we have spoken, but also so that the Lord, who was conceived in one place and born in another, should the more easily elude the fury of Herod, who was laying traps for him. If he were born to parents who were from Bethlehem, a crafty investigator would have noted their sudden flight as suspicious, especially since everyone knew that they traced their origin from the stock of David, from which the Christ was going to come. David himself furnishes testimony to this by his name, his fatherland, and his office. The name 'David' means *strong in hand or desirable*.[184] /48/ Indeed, he acquired that name because he not only overthrew the giant with great force[185] but was *also beautiful to behold and of a comely face*.[186] But in a deeper mystery, the name also prefigured the one who was going to be born of his house and family, who, *beautiful in form above the sons of men*,[187] would vanquish the prince of the world on this own. And he was both born in Bethlehem and was the shepherd of sheep capable of understanding, that is, he was the teacher of simple souls. Such great and merciful humility of the one who deigned not only to be made flesh for us, but also to be made flesh at the time when he would be enrolled immediately afterwards for Caesar's tax, and for the sake of our liberation would himself be subjected to servitude, is not to be regarded lightly. Likewise, Peter makes known to us what the path of Christ's humility is, for he came not to change conditions but to change souls, saying: *Be subject therefore to every human creature for God's sake, whether it be to the king as being supreme, or to governors as sent by him*.[188] But also his fellow apostle Paul says: *Render therefore to all men their dues: tribute to whom tribute is due, taxes to whom taxes are due, reverence to whom reverence is due, honour to whom honour is due. Owe no man anything, except to love one another*.[189]

[Luke 2:6–7] **And when they were there her days were fulfilled for her to give birth. And she gave birth to her firstborn son.** It was appropriate for the Lord to be born in Bethlehem, both on account of his royal lineage, and because of the mystery of its name. For *Bethlehem means the house*

---

184 Jerome, *Hebr. nom.* (CCSL 72:103.11).
185 Cf. 1 Sam. 17:49.
186 1 Sam. 16:12.
187 Ps. 44:3 (45:2).
188 1 Pet. 2:13–14.
189 Rom. 13:7–8.

BOOK ONE                                                    153

*of bread. For he himself is the one who says: 'I am the living bread that came down from heaven.'*[190] *Therefore the place where the Lord was born was previously called the house of bread, because it was certain that he would appear there in the substance of the flesh to refresh the hearts of the elect with inward abundance.*[191] But to this day and until the end of the world the Lord does not cease to be conceived in Nazareth and to be born in Bethlehem, because whoever listens to him, after taking in the flower of the word makes himself a house of eternal bread. He is conceived daily by faith and born daily by baptism in the virginal womb, that is, in the heart of believers.[192] Daily the mother of God, the Church, accompanying her teacher, going up from the wheel of the worldly way of life (which is what Galilee signifies)[193] into the city of *Judah* (that is, of *confession* and praise),[194] pays the tribute of her devotion to the eternal King. Following the pattern of the blessed Mary ever virgin, at once *married* and *immaculate, she conceives us as a virgin from the Spirit and as a virgin she gives birth to us without a groan,* and as it were espoused indeed *to one,* but impregnated *by another,* she is visibly joined by the separate parts of herself which make one universal Church /49/ to the high priest set over her, but she is perfected by the invisible power of the Holy Spirit.[195]

Hence, also, *Joseph* means '*augmenting*',[196] a name which doubtless indicates that the urgency of a teacher when he speaks is of no avail, if he has not received an augmentation of divine aid in order to be heard with approval. That Mary is described as having given birth to her firstborn son is not to be taken to mean that she also brought forth other sons, as the Helvidian heretics claim,[197] as if Christ could not be called 'firstborn'

---

190  John 6:51.
191  Gregory, *Hom. in Euang.* 1.8.1 (CCSL 141:54.8–13).
192  On Bede's concern to coordinate the Annunciation and the Nativity as a single theology of Incarnation, see MacCarron, *Bede and Time*, ch. 5: 'Nativity and Incarnation in Bede's Theology of Time', esp. 122–24.
193  Jerome interprets Galilee as 'revolving' (*uolubilis*) or 'able to be revolved' (*uolutabilis*): *Hebr. nom.* (CCSL 72:131.2; 140.25), which may have suggested the wheel image to Bede.
194  Jerome, *Hebr. nom.* (CCSL 72:67.19).
195  Ambrose, *Expos. Lucam* 2.7 (CCSL 14:33.103–08).
196  Jerome, *Hebr. nom.* (CCSL 72:146.17).
197  Helvidius was a fourth-century Roman who denied the perpetual virginity of the Virgin Mary. Jerome wrote a refutation, *Aduersus Heluidium*, which Bede knew (cf. Laistner, 'The Library of the Venerable Bede', 239, 264; Lapidge, *The Anglo-Saxon Library*, 215, 313), and from which he derived his phrase 'true law of history': see Introduction, 44–46. Bede quotes from Jerome's refutation in his commentary on Mark, ed. Hurst (CCSL 120:502.529–37).

unless he had brothers, in the same way that one is not customarily called 'only-begotten', unless he lacks brothers. The reason is that both the testimony of the Law and plain reason declare that all only-begotten children are also firstborns, but not that all firstborns can also be called only-begotten. That is, not only is one after whom others come forth from the womb a firstborn, but everyone before whom no one has come forth from the womb is a firstborn. Finally, it is commanded *that every male that opens the womb* be *called holy to the Lord*,[198] whether brothers follow or not. Because he is born first from the womb, he must be consecrated by the law governing the firstborn. But there is a deeper reason why the Son of God appearing in the flesh is both only-begotten of the Father according to the perfection of divinity and firstborn of all creation in accordance with brotherly fellowship. About the latter it is said: *For those whom he foreknew he also predestined to be made conformable to the image of his Son, in order that he might be the firstborn among many brothers*;[199] and about the former: *And we saw his glory, the glory as it were of the only-begotten of the Father.*[200] He is, therefore, only-begotten in the substance of divinity, and firstborn in accepting humanity; firstborn in grace, and only-begotten in nature. Hence it is that he is called brother and Lord: brother because he is firstborn, and Lord because he is only-begotten.

[Luke 2:7b] **And she wrapped him up in swaddling clothes, and laid him in a manger, because there was no place for them in the inn.** *What shall I render to the Lord, for all the things that he has rendered to me?*[201] He who is above all praise is *a child is born to us*,[202] in order that we men may be able to be made righteous.[203] He, who clothes the whole world with varied adornment, is wrapped up in cheap swaddling clothes, in order that we may receive an elegant garment. He, *by* whom *all things were made*,[204] is bound up hands and feet in a cradle, in order that our hands may be stretched out in good work, and our *feet* directed *into the way of peace.*[205] He, for whom there is a throne in heaven, is held in by the narrow confines of a

---

198 Luke 2:23 blended with Ex. 13:2. The passage in Exodus specifically states: 'every *firstborn* that opens the womb'.
199 Rom. 8:29.
200 John 1:14.
201 Ps. 115:12 (116:12).
202 Isa. 9:6.
203 Cf. Ambrose, *Expos. Lucam* 2.41 (CCSL 14:49.580).
204 John 1:3.
205 Luke 1:79.

BOOK ONE 155

rough manger, in order that he may enlarge us with the joys of the heavenly kingdom. He, who is the bread of angels, is laid in a manger, in order that he may refresh us – holy animals as it were – with the grain of his flesh. He, who sits on the right hand of the Father, lacks a place in the inn, in order that he may prepare /50/ *many dwelling places* for us *in the house of* his *Father*.[206] However, the fact that *he is born not in the house of his parents*, but in an inn and *on the way*,[207] can be more profoundly understood allegorically. For he himself says: *I am the way and the truth and the life*.[208] So he who remains eternally the truth and the life by the essence of divinity, by the mystery of the incarnation became the way by which he could lead us to the fatherland where we might enjoy the truth and the life.

[Luke 2:8–9] **And there were in the same country shepherds keeping watch, and watching over their flock in the vigils of the night. And behold an angel of the Lord stood by them, and the brightness of God shone round about them.** There is a beautiful reason why shepherds are keeping watch when the Lord is born, and protecting their flock from nocturnal poaching by watchfulness. It is so that it can be shown that the time is come that the true and only good Shepherd once promised, saying: *Behold I myself will seek my sheep and will visit them, as the shepherd visits his flock, and I will deliver them out of all the places where they have been scattered in the cloudy and dark day.*[209] And a little further on: *And I will set up one shepherd over them, my servant David, to feed them,*[210] *and I will make the evil beasts disappear out of the land,*[211] and so forth. We see that the things which are miraculously said by the prophet are fulfilled more miraculously by the Lord. The prophet Micah is mindful of this place and time, saying: *And you, O cloudy tower of the flock, to you the daughters of Zion will come, and the first power will come, the kingdom of the daughter of Zion.*[212] Indeed, the tower of the flock, which is called in Hebrew the tower of Eder,[213] prophetically

---

206 John 14:2; cf. Ambrose, *Expos. Lucam* 2.41 (CCSL 14:49.583–84).
207 Gregory, *Hom. in Euang.* 1.8.1 (CCSL 141:54.13–14).
208 John 14:6.
209 Ezek. 34:11–12.
210 Ezek. 34:23.
211 Ezek. 34:25.
212 Micah 4:8. Bede interprets this passage from Micah differently from the way it is interpreted by the Douay-Rheims translators and in NRSV.
213 The tower of the flock is mentioned in Gen. 35:21. Jerome, *Hebr. nom.* (CCSL 72:61.7 and 88.29), glosses *Eder* as 'flock'.

156    BEDE: *COMMENTARY ON THE GOSPEL OF LUKE*

indicated these shepherds long ago by its name. It is separated by about a mile to the east from the city of Bethlehem. When they appeared to the shepherds, the daughters of Zion – that is, the angelic powers – came to this tower.[214] Therefore, let the shepherds keep watch over the flock of their sheep at the Lord's birth, and after his providential dispensation has been made clear, let them signify that shepherds of pure souls will keep watch in the Church. Let it be said to them: *Feed the flock of God which is among you.*[215] And this is well said: *An angel appears to the shepherds keeping watch, and the brightness of God shines round about them,* because *those who know how to superintend carefully flocks that are faithful deserve more than others to see sublime things, and while they themselves religiously keep watch over their flock, heavenly grace flashes more abundantly above them.*[216] In another way it is said: *An angel* instructs *Mary, an angel* instructs *Joseph, and an angel* instructs *the shepherds.*[217] The citizens of heaven bear witness that the Lord is going to be conceived, and is conceived, and is born, in order both to give adequate instruction to mortals and to devote their own /51/ service without cease to the Creator. For in times to come as well, when Christ was tempted, when he was about to suffer, as he rose again, and as he ascended to heaven, they are always said to be present.

[Luke 2:9b–10] **And they feared with a great fear. And the angel said to them: Fear not, for behold I bring you good news of great joy that will be to all the people.** The good news of great and eternal joy is not brought to the whole Jewish people, many of whom were rebels, but to the

---

214 Bede is the first western exegete to link Micah 4:8 with its reference to the 'tower of the flock' to the account of Jesus's birth. He knew about the 'real' Tower of the Flock, housing the tombs of three of the Nativity shepherds, from Adomnán's *De locis sanctis* 2.6. The Tower of the Flock is also discussed in Bede's *Hom.* 1.7 (ed. Hurst [CCSL 122:50.143–49]; trans. Martin and Hurst, *Homilies of the Gospels* 1:70). But the two texts are orientated to different audiences: 'Here the essential frameworks of the commentary and homily texts are similar: the Tower of the Flock is situated a mile east of Bethlehem; heavenly creatures appeared there to the shepherds. The reader of the commentary, however, learns the Hebrew name for the Tower of the Flock while the homily audience hears something more mundane: this is the place where the sheep were gathered. The homily then continues with something equally concrete: there is a milestone east of Bethlehem where even the eighth-century pilgrim can now go to see the church which contains the sepulchres ... of three of those very shepherds' (Del Giacco, 'Exegesis and Sermon, 19–20).
215  1 Pet. 5:2.
216  Gregory, *Hom. in Euang.* 1.8.1 (CCSL 141:55.26–30).
217  Ambrose, *Expos. Lucam* 2.51 (CCSL 14:53.704).

people of the faithful of all tribes, nations, and tongues, gathered together into the one Church of Christ.

[Luke 2:11] **For this day is born to you a Saviour, who is Christ the Lord, in the city of David.** This is the supreme power, this is the kingdom of the daughter of Zion, which the testimony of the prophet mentioned above promised would come to the tower of the flock. Here it should be noted that the angel who addresses the shepherds in the vigils of the night actually does not say: 'this night', but *this day is born to you a Saviour*, for no other reason evidently but that he was coming to bring good news of great joy. For when any unhappy things are referred to that were or are to be done during the nocturnal hours, then often either night is specifically added or even mentioned exclusively, as this: *All you will be offended by me this night*,[218] and elsewhere: *Truly I say to you, today, even in this night, before the cock crows twice, you will deny me thrice.*[219] And it is significant that the angel appeared surrounded with so great a light that the brightness of God was said to have shone round the shepherds, that is, rays of light were scattered all around them. This is never added in the Old Testament, in which angels so often appear. But it allegorically foreshadows what the Apostle afterwards openly taught, saying: *The night has passed, and the day is at hand. Let us therefore cast off the works of darkness and put on the armour of light. Let us walk honestly as in the day.*[220]

[Luke 2:12] **And this will be a sign to you. You will find the infant wrapped in swaddling clothes and laid in a manger.** The Saviour's infancy is repeatedly impressed upon us by the messages of the angels and of the testimony of the evangelists, so that what was done for us may be firmly fixed more deeply in our hearts. Because certainly *he was wounded for our iniquities and he was enfeebled for our sins*.[221] And it should be observed that the sign of the Saviour's birth is given with great ingenuity, namely that the infant was not indicated by purple cloth of Tyre, but wrapped in rough swaddling clothes, and that he was to be found not on a bed ornamented with gold, but amongst mangers. That is, that he assumed not only the state of humility and of mortality, but also of poverty for our sakes. He, *being rich, became poor* /**52**/ *for our sakes, that through his*

---

218 Matt. 26:31.
219 Mark 14:30.
220 Rom. 13:12–13.
221 Isa. 53:5.

*poverty we might be rich.*²²² He was the Lord of heaven, but he became poor on earth, that he might teach those who dwell on earth how to acquire the kingdom of heaven through poverty of spirit.

[Luke 2:13–14] **And suddenly there was with the angel a multitude of the heavenly host, praising God and saying: Glory to God in the highest, and on earth peace to men of good will.** As one messenger proclaims the good news that God is born in the flesh, immediately a multitude of the heavenly army arrives and bursts out in unison in praise of the Creator to display the zeal of their perpetual obedience to Christ. At the same time they teach us by their example both how often any brother should resound with words of sacred instruction and how often we ourselves should recall to mind things read or heard that pertain to religious devotion – praises that ought to be rendered immediately to God by word, heart, and deed. It is fitting that the choir of angels which arrived should be called the heavenly army, for it not only humbly obeys that leader *strong in battle,*²²³ who appeared *to vanquish the aerial powers,*²²⁴ but valiantly repulses these opposing powers, so that they cannot tempt mortals as much as they wish. Just as an entire region is defended against hostile attack by an armed force through the foresight of an outstanding commander, so also, because impure spirits are everywhere engaged in destroying peace, God has constituted for our protection an army of angels, by whose presence the wicked daring of the demons may be frustrated and we be afforded the grace of peace. Assuredly, since [Christ] is born God and man, it is right that peace to men and glory to God is sung. The angels glorify God who is born in the flesh for our redemption, because when they see that we are accepted, they rejoice that their number is being replenished. They desire peace to men, because now that the Lord is born in the flesh, they honour as companions those whom they before had looked down upon as weak and worthless. And when they seek peace to men, they offer it specifically to men of good will, that is, to those who acknowledge that the Christ is born, but not to Herod, the high-priests and Pharisees, and other antichrists, who were upset at the news of his nativity, and pursued him as far as they were able with swords. For *there is no peace to the wicked, says the Lord.*²²⁵ But *much peace have they that love your name, and to them*

---

222 2 Cor. 8:9, with second person plural verbs changed to first person plural.
223 Ps. 23:8 (24:8).
224 Gregory, *Hom. in Euang.* 2.34.9 (CCSL 141:307.214–15).
225 Isa. 48:22.

*there is no stumbling block.*²²⁶ And what follows agrees very suitably with these: *I looked for your salvation, Lord,*²²⁷ that is, I sighed for the advent of the Christ to come with a lengthy vigil of expectant prayers. /53/

## Chapter 6

[Luke 2:15] **And after the angels departed from them into heaven, the shepherds said to one another: Let us go over to Bethlehem, and let us see this Word that has happened, which the Lord made and showed to us.** Consider carefully how reasonable the words of the shepherds are and how suitable for the shepherds of the Church. For keeping watch as it were, they rightly did not say: Let us see the child, let us see what is said, but: *Let us see the Word that has happened. In the beginning was the Word,*²²⁸ *and the Word was made flesh.*²²⁹ Let us see how the Word, which always was, was made for us, *which the Lord made and showed to us.* He made himself this Word, since indeed this Word is the Lord. Let us see, therefore, how he himself made this Word, that is, the Lord, and how he manifested his flesh to us. For what we could not see as long as it was the Word, we may see because it is made flesh. It is like what John says: *That which was from the beginning, which we have heard, which we have seen with our eyes, which we have looked upon, and our hands have handled, of the Word of life: for the life was manifested, and we have seen and do bear witness, and declare to you the eternal life, which was with the Father, and has appeared to us.*²³⁰

[Luke 2:16–17] **And they came with haste, and they found Mary and Joseph, and the infant lying in the manger. And seeing, they came to understand about the word that had been spoken to them concerning this child.** The shepherds hasten; they desire to see with all the fervour of their intellect the advent of the Christ whom they have understood. For the presence of Christ is not to be idly inquired after. And for that reason, perhaps some who inquire after it do not deserve to find it, because they seek Christ indolently.²³¹ Therefore these shepherds

---

226 Ps. 118:165 (119:165) (not *iuxta LXX*).
227 Ps. 118:166 (119:166).
228 John 1:1.
229 John 1:14.
230 1 John 1:1–2.
231 Cf. Ambrose, *Expos. Lucam* 2.53 (CCSL 14:54.720).

found him immediately, because they ran with unfeigned faith to him, to whom to go in haste is not to quicken the steps of the feet, but to make constant progress in faith and virtue. *They found*, Luke says, *Mary and Joseph, and the infant lying in the manger*. But the more frequently and delightedly amid the darkness of this life the shepherds of the Lord's flock are exalted by the divine prophecy, the more fervently they enter into the lofty life of the fathers before them by contemplating so to speak the gates of Bethlehem, in which the bread of life both is preserved and restores always. In this they find at first sight nothing other than the virginal beauty of the universal Church – Mary as it were – and the virile company of spiritual teachers – Joseph as it were – and the humble advent *of the mediator of God and men, the man Jesus Christ*,[232] inserted into the pages of holy Scripture – the infant as it were lying in the manger, the Christ. In this manger /54/ of holy Scripture that excellent animal most suited for sacred sacrifices was fed, which in exultation cried out: *The Lord pastures me, and I shall not want, he has set me in a place of pasture.*[233] And a little further on: *You have prepared a table before me against them that afflict me.*[234] *And seeing*, it says, *they came to understand about the word that had been spoken to them concerning this child*, because it surely pertains to the just order of things that when the incarnation of the Word has been known, loved, and celebrated with worthy honour, a mind made more expansive by long meditation may arrive from time to time at a vision of the glory of the Word.[235]

[Luke 2:18] **And all who heard, wondered also at those things that were told them by the shepherds.** The people are urged by the shepherds to revere God. *Do not let this model of faith seem insignificant to you, nor the shepherds' way of life seem base. Indeed, the more base it seems to practical wisdom, the more precious it is to faith.*[236] The Lord chose as his heralds not wise but simple men, who did not know how to embellish the things they heard; he appointed not rhetoricians but fishermen to preach

---

232 1 Tim. 2:5.
233 Ps. 22:1–2 (23:1–2) (not *iuxta LXX*).
234 Ps. 22:5 (23:5).
235 On the subtle differences between this passage, where Bede understands the vision of the divine as the result of contemplation, and the corresponding *Hom*. 1.7 (ed. Hurst [CCSL 122:48.78–49.97]; trans. Martin and Hurst, *Homilies on the Gospels*, 68), where the vision is the reward of a life on evangelization, see Del Giacco, 'Exegesis and Sermon', 17 and Introduction.
236 Ambrose, *Expos. Lucam* 2.53 (CCSL 14:54.725–27).

the gospel. And in the Old Testament, each of the special messengers of his dispensation he chose from amongst the shepherds. The first martyr Abel, who consecrated the innocent way of life of the pastoral office with his own blood, and whose blood calls out from the earth in a prefiguration of the Lord's passion, the most learned as it were and first of the shepherds, devoutly offered the firstlings of his flocks to the Lord.[237] *Abraham, the father* of the faith, who *rejoiced that he might see the day* of Christ, *and he saw it and was glad*,[238] is described as digging in the veins of the earth, not for mines of gold by which to procure ornaments for his way of life, but for wells of water with which to water his flocks.[239] Jacob, the father of the twelve tribes, was *parched with heat and pinched with frost*[240] for twice ten years[241] while pasturing his flocks. As a type of the true Shepherd, he improved their condition by showing the variety of their virtues in the waters of salvific teaching.[242] The law-giver Moses in prefiguration of the sevenfold Church[243] first defended seven sisters who were pasturing sheep from the wickedness of shepherds who attacked them, until they might water their own flocks,[244] and afterwards he deserved to see and speak to the Lord amid the pastures of the desert,[245] and to produce miracles with a shepherd's rod,[246] and to free the people of God. David himself, whose descendant was worthy to be called and to be our Lord, ripping his father's ram from the grasp of a bear or lion,[247] showed that Christ was going to be born from his stock and city; but David is not the equal of him who *rips the poor man from the hand of him who is stronger than he; the needy and poor man from those that strip him.*[248] /55/ And therefore the testimony

---

237 Cf. Gen. 4:2–10.
238 John 8:56.
239 Cf. Gen. 21:25–30; 26:15.
240 Gen. 31:40.
241 Cf. Gen. 31:38.
242 Cf. Gen. 30:31–43 (in reference to Jacob's trick with rods in the water to influence the colours of the lambs conceived by the drinking ewes).
243 Cf. Rev. 1:4. Bede is probably indebted for the phrase 'the sevenfold Church' (*ecclesiae septiformis*) to Primasius, *Commentarius in Apocalypsin* 1.1 (CCSL 92:9.44). For analysis of Bede's use of Primasius (and reticence about mentioning his name), see Wallis, *Bede: Commentary on Revelation*, Introduction, 16–30.
244 Cf. Exod. 2:16–17.
245 Cf. Exod. 3:1ff.
246 Cf. Exod. 4:17.
247 Cf. 1 Sam. 17:34–37.
248 Ps. 34:10 (35:10).

of the shepherds who deserved to keep vigil at that time and to hear the hymn of angelic exultation ought not to be considered of little value, when the good Shepherd leaves ninety-nine sheep in the desert in order to seek the hundredth sheep.[249] The whole flock of the faithful, longing for his coming, implores: *I have gone astray like a sheep that was lost; seek your servant, Lord.*[250]

[Luke 2:19] **But Mary kept all these words, comparing them in her heart.** What does it mean when it says, 'comparing'? It ought to have said, 'she contemplated in her heart, and she kept in her heart', but because she had read the holy Scriptures, and knew the prophets, she compared these things that were done to her by the Lord with those which she knew were written about the Lord by the prophets, and after these had been compared to one another, she recognized by the light of her countenance, like the heavenly cherubim, that these things were associated in harmony.[251] For Gabriel had said: *Behold you will conceive in your womb, and you will bring forth a son.*[252] Isaiah had prophesied: *Behold a virgin will conceive, and she will bring forth a son.*[253] Micah had prophesied that the daughters of Zion would come to the tower of the flock, and then that the supreme power would come.[254] The shepherds said that the cohorts of the celestial city had appeared to them at the tower of the flock, and that they sang that Christ was born. Mary had read: *The ox knows his owner, and the ass his master's manger.*[255] She saw the Son of God, who saves men and beasts, crying in the manger. And she compared what she had read with respect to each of these things and others of the same kind, and brought them together for comparison with those that she heard and saw.

[Luke 2:20] **And the shepherds returned, glorifying and praising God, for all the things that they had heard and seen, as they were told.** The shepherds glorify and praise God for all the things that they had heard from the angels and had seen in Bethlehem, as they were told: that is, they both glory in the fact that, on coming, they found it just has

---

249 Cf. Luke 15:4.
250 Ps. 118:176 (119:176) (not *iuxta LXX*).
251 Cf. Ps. 4:7 (4:6).
252 Luke 1:31.
253 Isa. 7:14.
254 Micah 4:8 (see above, n. 214).
255 Isa. 1:3.

they had been told, and they return glory and praises to God as they were told to do. For they were told to do this by the angels, not by a verbal command, but by the angels demonstrating their manner of devotion when they sang 'Glory to God in the highest' in harmonious exultation. For the one who says: *I bring you good news of great joy that will be to all the people*,[256] certainly gives a stimulus to glorifying and praising God. But the leaders of spiritual flocks also sometimes take the place of others who are sleeping in the contemplation of heavenly things, sometimes go around the camp of the faithful by purifying and by seeking examples of goodness, and sometimes go back to openly exercising the pastoral office through teaching, in order to *publish the memory of the abundance /56/ of the sweetness* of God by preaching to their neighbours,[257] even if they had only tasted it briefly by contemplation.

## Chapter 7

[Luke 2:21] **And after eight days were accomplished, that the child should be circumcised, his name was called Jesus, which was given by the angel before he was conceived in the womb.** The religious rite and practice of circumcision began with the blessed patriarch Abraham.[258] Since he believed perfectly in God while he still possessed a foreskin, and *it was reckoned to him as righteousness*,[259] *he received the sign of circumcision, a seal of the righteousness of the faith, which is in the foreskin.*[260] He also began the custom of selecting a suitable name for little children on the day of circumcision. He himself, when he received the covenant of circumcision from God, earlier on the same day merited the augmentation of his name, together with his wife, so that he who hitherto was called *Abram*, that is, *excellent father*,[261] from then on by reason of the merit of his faith took the name Abraham, that is, *father of many nations*,[262] and likewise Sarai would be called Sarah.[263]

---

256 Luke 2:10.
257 Ps. 144:7 (145:7).
258 Cf. Gen. 17:12.
259 Gen. 15:6; 1 Macc. 2:52; Rom. 4:3.
260 Rom. 4:11.
261 Jerome, *Hebr. nom.* (CCSL 72:61.28–29).
262 Gen. 17:4.
263 Cf. Gen. 17:15.

The type or figure of circumcision was multiform.[264] For not only was it the seal, as was said, of the righteousness of the faith of Abraham and his seed, but it was also the sign of restraint for those who belonged to this seed and this faith *from all defilement of the flesh and of the spirit*.[265] It was also a prophecy of the Saviour who was to be born from this seed, who would both cleanse us by baptism from all defilement of conduct deadly to the soul in the present, and in the future would free us forever by resurrection from the universal destruction of death itself. And especially it was a gift of forgiveness, which would release us from the sin of Adam's transgression; it was pleasing at that time to the same bearer of grace and the Law to work through circumcision. For he who now says: *Unless a man be born again of water and the Holy Spirit, he cannot enter into the kingdom of God*,[266] at that time said: *The male, whose flesh of his foreskin will not be circumcised, that soul will perish away from his people, because he has broken my covenant*.[267] Not the covenant of circumcision, certainly, which was broken not by an infant who was not yet able to make a choice, but by adults, who knew how to, and could, and should have kept it; but the covenant which God entered into with the first man, which everyone who has passed a life of even one day on earth is proven to have transgressed, and for that reason is not ignorant of having the need of some means of assistance for salvation. For those who were faithful either before the time of circumcision – or even, being from foreign nations, after the covenant of circumcision had been given, like the exemplar of patience, Job and his friends and children – saved themselves and their families from original /57/ sin either by immolating sacrificial animals or by faith alone, because *the just man lives by faith*,[268] and *without faith it is impossible to please God*.[269] Truly those who are propagated from the offshoot of sin, *conceived in iniquities*,[270] and born in transgressions need these and other similar

---

[264] For an illuminating discussion of this passage in relation to patristic tradition, and in comparison with the treatments of circumcision in Bede's homilies as well as his commentary on Genesis, see O'Brien, 'Bede's Theology of Circumcision', 594–613. The comparison with baptism is a notable example of Bede's understanding of the unity of Jews and Christians in one body of the faithful.
[265] 2 Cor. 7:1.
[266] John 3:5.
[267] Gen. 17:14.
[268] Rom. 1:17.
[269] Hebr. 11:6.
[270] Ps. 50:7 (51:5).

means of salvation. And our Redeemer, who in order to take away *the sins of the world*[271] came into the world without sin, just as he procured the means of salvation for us by his baptism – that is, he consecrated the bodies of waters which he entered in order that our sins might be washed away – so also by the circumcision which he received he did not purge his own sins which he had never committed, but taught that the decrepitude of our nature was to be renewed through him, signifying that in the present it was to be purged by him from the stain of vices, and on the last day was to be utterly restored from the plague of manifold mortality and death.

Hence it is fitting that Jesus is said to have been circumcised on the eighth day. We do not readily read in the Old Testament that this was done for anyone, although it was repeatedly ordered for all, except for Isaac alone, who, being as it were the first son of promise, is said to have received circumcision on the eighth day.[272] It is right, I say, that Jesus is circumcised on the eighth day, because as we said before, this renewal of each of us, now and in the future, in the spirit and in the flesh, is both foreshadowed in his resurrection and will be accomplished in our resurrection whenever that may be. Concerning our first resurrection, which is proclaimed by the amendment of our life and faith here on earth, the Apostle says: For *all we who were baptized in Christ Jesus, were baptized in his death, so that as Christ was raised up from the dead by the glory of the Father, so we also may walk in newness of life.*[273] And about our second, which is hoped for at the end, he says as follows: *For if we believe that Jesus died and rose again, even so, through Jesus, God will bring with him those who have slept.*[274] Nearly everyone is aware that the number eight is appropriate for the glory of the resurrection. For not only did the Lord rise again on the eighth day, that is, after the seventh of the Sabbath,[275] but, after the six ages of this world and the seventh of the Sabbath of the souls, which is now going on concurrently in another life, we ourselves will arise in an eighth era, so to speak.[276] Then we will have been truly circumcised, that is, deprived of all

---

271 John 1:29.
272 Cf. Gen. 21:4.
273 Rom. 6:3–4.
274 1 Thess. 4:14.
275 The 'seventh of the Sabbath' = the Sabbath. For this terminology, see Bede, *DTR* 8, in Wallis, *Bede: The Reckoning of Time*, 32 and n. 66.
276 This passage is the earliest appearance in Bede's *oeuvre* of his innovative 'expanded world ages' scheme, which adds to the six ages of history a seventh age of the Church Expectant and an eighth age of eternity following the general resurrection. This concept was

the vices and seductions of carnal concupiscence in which luxury chiefly reigns, and very truly cut off from the state of uncircumcision. For as the Lord says: *The children of this world marry, and are given in marriage; but those who will be accounted worthy of that world and of the resurrection of the dead are neither married /58/ nor take wives. For they cannot die any more, for they are equal to the angels, and are the children of God, since they are the children of the resurrection.*[277]

His name, Luke says, *was called Jesus, which was given by the angel before he was conceived in the womb. Jesus* means '*Saviour*'.[278] Each of his faithful and the elect in either of their states of circumcision, about which enough has been said, likewise rejoice to be sharers of his name, so that just as they take the name 'Christians' from Christ, so also, they may be called 'saved' from Saviour. They do so now from the hope of being saved by faith, but then from the reality of salvation itself through the vision of glory that is in Christ Jesus our Lord, because the name was given to them not only before they were conceived in the womb of the Church, but even before the ages of the world. Not only the etymology of this sacred name, but also the very number that it contains in its letters is redolent of the mysteries of our eternal salvation. In fact, among the Greeks it is written IHCOYC[279] with six letters, namely I and H and C and O and Y and C, the numerical values of which are ten, eight, two hundred, seventy, four hundred, and two hundred,[280] which together add up to eight hundred and eighty-eight. This number, because it delights in being a symbol of resurrection, has been sufficiently dealt with above.[281] For what eight standing alone signifies, it also signifies when multiplied by ten or a hundred.[282] And the accumulation of perfect numbers ought certainly to be regarded as a sign of strength. So we can also say that the name of the Saviour is made up of the perfect

---

destined to play an important role in his later exegesis, as well as in *DTR*, chs 68–71: Darby, *Bede and the End of Time*, ch. 3, esp. 66–67.
277 Luke 20:34–36.
278 Jerome, *Hebr. nom.* (CCSL 72:136.24; 156.11; 160.21).
279 I.e., 'Iesous' (I = the Greek iota, H = eta, C = sigma, O = omicron, Y = upsilon). Some manuscripts here and elsewhere in *On Luke* employ the Greek letters. See Introduction, 51.
280 Bede gives the numerical values of the letters of the Greek alphabet in *DTR* 1 (Wallis, *Bede: The Reckoning of Time*, 11–12).
281 See above, commentary on Luke 1:5; 1:64–65.
282 That is, Bede takes 888 as: $8 + (8 \times 10) + (8 \times 100)$. Therefore, the numbers eight, eighty, and eight hundred are all symbols of resurrection.

number eight, because he exhibited in himself the model of resurrection for mortals by rising again on the eighth day. It is made up also of eight multiplied by ten, because the Ten Commandments of the Law instructed us and likewise aided us to know how the number eight ought to be completed in a symbol of his resurrection. Just as he, *rising again from the dead, dies now no more; death will have no more dominion over him*,[283] so also do we reckon that we *are dead to sin, but alive to God in Christ Jesus*.[284] It is made up as well of eight times one hundred, because this number portends the retribution which shall be ours in the future when the glory of his resurrection is displayed. For the number one hundred, which is the first to seek the right hand after the course of so many numbers on the left hand,[285] is very aptly suited to prefiguring the joys of that age, when *the last enemy, death, will be destroyed*,[286] when *we who are alive, who are left, will be taken up together with those* who have arisen *in the clouds to meet Christ, into the air, and so we will be always with the Lord*.[287] Hence, as a lovely type of all the elect, the first son of the promise, born of and circumcised by his hundred-year-old father was called *Isaac*, which signifies '*laughter*' or '*joy*',[288] according to the Lord's prediction,[289] /59/ prefiguring felicity on the right side for all time, about which the Lord said: *But I will see you again, and your heart will rejoice, and your joy no man will take from you.*[290]

But since the text is about circumcision, we may inquire why Moses himself, who reports the law of circumcision given to the fathers by God and so often impressed upon himself, did not require anyone to be circumcised during the whole time of his authority except one only, his son,[291] whom his mother circumcised with a very sharp stone which she snatched up, lest he be slain by the Lord.[292] But all who were born

---

283 Rom. 6:9.
284 Rom. 6:11.
285 In *DTR* 1, ed. Jones (CCSL 123B:269.25–270.51); Wallis, *Bede: The Reckoning of Time*, 10, Bede explains that in Roman finger-reckoning, the signs for the numbers 1–99 are made with the left hand, while those from 100 up to, but not including, 10,000 are made with the right.
286 1 Cor. 15:26.
287 1 Thess. 4:17.
288 Jerome, *Hebr. nom.* (CCSL 72:67.15–16).
289 Cf. Augustine, *De ciuitate Dei* 18.3 (CCSL 48:595.1–2).
290 John 16:22.
291 Presumably, Gershom, the first-born son of Moses and Zipporah (cf. Exod. 2:22).
292 Cf. Exod. 4:25. According to Alter, *The Five Books of Moses*, 331: 'Traditional Jewish commentators seek to naturalize the story to a more normative monotheism by claiming that

in the desert he left to be circumcised by Joshua,²⁹³ neglecting for forty uninterrupted years a manifestly divinely ordained practice which had been observed for four hundred and six years²⁹⁴ and transmitted by ancestral succession to himself. I would certainly not believe that this was done without reason, but rather for the sake of a great mystery. Let me say briefly what I myself think about this matter, without detriment to the understanding of our forefathers. Moses proclaims circumcision, but Joshua carries it out, *for the Law was given by Moses; but grace and truth came by Jesus Christ.*²⁹⁵ And the letter profits nothing, unless saving grace comes to its aid. Uncircumcision increases while Moses is preaching, because, as the Apostle says: *By the works of the Law no flesh will be justified before him, for by the Law is the knowledge of sin.*²⁹⁶ And elsewhere: *For until the Law sin was in the world; but sin is not reckoned, when the Law is not.*²⁹⁷ And again: *Moreover, the Law entered in, that sin might abound.*²⁹⁸ *But I do not know sin, but by the Law, for I had not known what it is to covet, unless the Law had said, you shall not covet. But sin, taking occasion by the commandment, produced in me all manner of covetousness.*²⁹⁹ But, after the people were brought into the land of promise, Joshua with knives of stone put an end to uncircumcision, which had increased while Moses lived,³⁰⁰ because *where sin abounded, grace did more abound.*³⁰¹ As to why Joshua used stone knives for circumcision, anyone will understand who reads that *the rock was Christ,*³⁰² *and upon this rock, he says, I will build my Church.*³⁰³ For *what the Law could not do, in that it was weak through the flesh, God, sending his own Son in the likeness of sinful flesh, and to deal with sin, condemned sin in the flesh, that the justification of the Law might be fulfilled in us, who walk not*

---

Moses has neglected the commandment to circumcise his son (sons?), and that is why the Lord threatens his life'. Bede seems to be reaching towards a similar conclusion.
293 Cf. Jos. 5:2–7.
294 See Introduction, 47.
295 John 1:17. Bede alludes to the identity of the names Joshua and Jesus in Hebrew and Greek.
296 Rom. 3:20.
297 Rom. 5:13.
298 Rom. 5:20.
299 Rom. 7:7–8.
300 Cf. Jos. 5:2–3.
301 Rom. 5:20.
302 1 Cor. 10:4.
303 Matt. 16:18.

*according to the flesh, but according to the spirit.*[304] This grace of Christ not only justifies the faithful of the New Covenant, but all those who had been perfect in the Law were saved by faith, *not by the works of the Law,*[305] but by the same grace of Christ who was to come /60/ in the flesh. While the son of Moses signifies the former, the people circumcised by Joshua signify the latter, who, although they learned, compelled by the severity of the Law, to solicit the grace of Christ, shunned the circumcision of the rock as if it were the threatening sword of the Lord, as Peter attests who, speaking of the yoke of the Law, says: *which neither our fathers nor we have been able to bear, but by the grace of the Lord Jesus Christ, we believe that we will be saved just as they also will be.*[306] And the Psalmist, shut in by the custody as it were of the imprisoning Law, and finding no way of escape but in the grace of Christ, cries out: *When my heart was in anguish, you have exalted me on a rock. You have conducted me, for you have been my hope, a tower of strength against the face of the enemy.*[307] Let no one, when he has heard circumcision proclaimed, assert that the restraint of the one member alone is ordered, as if it suffices that one appear to be either freed from fornication, or enjoying lawful marriage in moderation, or renowned for virginity, without the addition of the other virtues, and not that the correction is ordered rather of all the senses, which we have in our heart or body. For even Moses, receiving the pure words of God, lamented that he was *uncircumcised of lips.*[308] And Stephen says to the unbelieving Jews: *Uncircumcised in heart and ears, you have always resisted the Holy Spirit.*[309] Therefore he is purified by true circumcision *who stops his ears lest he hear blood and shuts his eyes lest he see evil,*[310] who guards his ways lest he sin with his tongue,[311] and takes heed lest his heart be overcharged *with surfeiting and drunkenness,*[312] who, *as long as breath remains in* him *and the spirit of God in* his *nostrils,* does not speak iniquity with his lips,[313] who washes his *hands among the*

---

304 Rom. 8:3–4.
305 Gal. 2:16.
306 Acts 15:10–11.
307 Ps. 60:3–4 (61:2–3).
308 Exod. 6:12.
309 Acts 7:51.
310 Isa. 33:15.
311 Cf. Ps. 38:2 (39:1).
312 Luke 21:34.
313 Job 27:3–4.

innocents,[314] and has restrained his *feet from every evil way,*[315] and who above all chastises his *body, and* subjects it *to servitude,*[316] and *with all watchfulness* keeps his *heart, because life issues out from it.*[317] Surely he has been carried to Jerusalem after circumcision and offered to the Lord,[318] who in accordance with him who says: Decline *from evil and do good,*[319] afterwards desisted from sins and began to abound in good works; who can say: *My eyes are ever towards the Lord,*[320] *and I will compass your altar, Lord, that I may hear the voice of your praise;*[321] who says: *We are the good odour of Christ to God,*[322] and: *I lifted up my hands to your commandments,*[323] *and turned my feet to your* /61/ *testimonies;*[324] who, *whether* he eats *or* drinks *or whatever else* he does, does *all things for the glory of God,*[325] and says: *How sweet are your words to my palate!*[326] and finally: *My heart and my flesh have rejoiced in the living God.*[327]

But this same good conduct of one's own which is *in secret* likewise requires circumcision, so that when I fast, pray, or give *alms,* I may seek glory inwardly. For if I stand *in the corners of the streets,* disfigure my face, and sound *a trumpet before* me so that I may be seen and praised *by men,*[328] I indeed outwardly appear to be circumcised, but remain defiled in my heart. And so I incur punishment for deceitful sanctity as well, after the manner of the Shechemites, who although they seemed to imitate the

---

314 Ps. 25:6 (26:6).
315 Ps. 118:101 (119:101).
316 1 Cor. 9:27.
317 Prov. 4:23.
318 Cf. Luke 2:22.
319 Ps. 33:15 (34:14) and 1 Pet. 3:11 (blended).
320 Ps. 24:15 (25:15).
321 Ps. 25:6–7 (26:6–7).
322 2 Cor. 2:15.
323 Ps. 118:48 (119:48).
324 Ps. 118:59 (119:59).
325 1 Cor. 10:31.
326 Ps. 118:103 (119:103).
327 Ps. 83:3 (84:2). Bede's treatment of circumcision highlights the impotence of the Law and the necessity of grace. By contrast, his *Hom.* 1:11 argues that Jesus's submission to circumcision affirms the value of the Law (ed. Hurst, *Opera homiletica,* 75; trans. Martin and Hurst, *Homilies on the Gospels* 1:106). O'Brien argues that the homily's more positive reading of circumcision proves that it was written after the commentary, because Bede's view on Jewish ritual became more positive with the passage of time: 'Bede on the Jewish Church', 70; see Introduction, 64–66.
328 Matt. 6:2–5; cf. Matt. 6:16.

circumcision of the patriarchs did not do so on account of the covenant of the Lord, but for the sake of lust. Not only did they not gain any reward, but *on the third day when the pain of their wounds was most severe*, they perished among the ruins of their city.[329] For when the time of resurrection comes, such persons, having rid themselves of the virtues which they were relying upon, will be sent to everlasting death, for they have forgotten the prophetic admonition: *Be circumcised to the Lord, and take away the foreskins of your hearts*.[330] For which reason the Apostle also earnestly recommends that circumcision be secreted in the heart, *whose praise is not of men, but of God*.[331]

[Luke 2:22] **And after the days of her purification according to the Law of Moses were accomplished, they carried him to Jerusalem to present him to the Lord,** ... Indeed, the decree of the Law was that a little after the thirty-third day following the circumcision a sacrifice is brought to the temple of the Lord and given for the child,[332] and that a first-born male is sanctified to the Lord.[333] This intimates in a mystical matter, as we have said, that no one not circumcised from sins is worthy in the sight of the Lord, and that no one not freed from the bonds of mortality can fully enter into the joys of the heavenly city, since *the wicked will* not *dwell*, it says, *near you, nor will the unjust abide before your eyes*.[334] And the Apostle: *Flesh and blood will not possess the kingdom of God, nor will corruption possess incorruptibility*.[335] If you scrutinize the words of the Law itself with greater care, you will assuredly find not only that the incarnate Lord was free from the contagion of sin and from the terms of the Law, which he deigned rather to accept because he esteemed it to be holy, just, and good,[336] /62/ and because he freed us from subjection to and fear of it for the sake of grace, but also that just as the mother of God herself is free from carnal union with a man, so she is likewise free from the power of the Law. For Moses says: *If a woman having received seed bears a male child, she shall be unclean seven days, according to the days of her menstrual separation. And on the eighth day the infant shall be circumcised, but she shall remain*

---

329 Gen. 34:24; cf. Gen. 34:1–27.
330 Jer. 4:4.
331 Rom. 2:29.
332 Cf. Lev. 12:4–6.
333 Cf. Exod. 13:2.
334 Ps. 5:6 (5:4–5).
335 1 Cor. 15:50.
336 Cf. Rom. 7:12.

*thirty-three days in the blood of her purification. She shall touch no holy thing, neither shall she enter into the sanctuary, until the days of her purification be fulfilled,*³³⁷ and other things that follow pertaining to the rite of childbirth. Note, therefore, that it is not every woman giving birth that is described as unclean, but the one who gives birth having received seed, and she is taught that she must be cleansed by the rite of the Law, in contrast namely to *the virgin* who conceived and bore *a son, and* called *his name Emmanuel, which means 'God is with us'*.³³⁸ Therefore it was not the son who is 'God with man' nor the mother who gave birth with the aid of the Holy Spirit who needed to be purified by sacrificial victims, but just like Christ the Lord, so also the ever-blessed virgin Mary was voluntarily subjected to the Law so that we might be freed from the bonds of the Law.

[Luke 2:23] **As it is written in the Law of the Lord: Every male opening the womb shall be called holy to the Lord, ...** The phrase 'every male opening the womb' refers to the firstborn both of man and of beast, because each is called 'holy to the Lord', and therefore according to the commandment, belongs to the priest,³³⁹ *if only to the extent that* he receive *a price for the firstborn of man and* cause *every beast that is unclean to be redeemed.*³⁴⁰ *And the redemption of it shall be after one month, for five shekels of silver.*³⁴¹ Here, without detriment to a more thorough treatment, it should be made known briefly that all those first-born beasts were either a figure of him who, although he was the only-begotten Son of God, deigned to become the firstborn of all creation, and who was truly and uniquely holy to the Lord because *he did no sin, neither was guile found in his mouth,*³⁴² or they were a symbol of our devotion. We should attribute all the origins of the good work that we give birth to, so to speak, in our hearts to the grace of the Lord, but we must redeem the evils we have done by offering suitable fruits of penitence for each of the five senses of the body and soul. And so, the phrase 'every male opening the womb' refers to the practice of ordinary birth. Not that our Lord should be believed on his exit to have deprived the lodging of the sacred womb of its virginity /63/ which he had sanctified on his entrance, in accordance with the heretics who say

---

337 Lev. 12:2–4.
338 Isa. 7:14; Matt. 1:23.
339 Cf. Exod. 13:2; Num. 18:15.
340 Num. 18:15.
341 Num. 18:16.
342 1 Pet. 2:22.

that the blessed Virgin Mary was a virgin up the time of giving birth, but not a virgin afterwards. Rather, in accordance with the orthodox faith he should be believed to have come forth from the closed womb of the Virgin, like a bridegroom from his marriage bed. In this regard the Prophet says it beautifully: *And he brought me back to the way of the gate of the outward sanctuary, which looked towards the east, and it was shut. And the Lord said to me: This gate shall be shut, it shall not be opened, and no man shall pass through it, because the Lord, the God of Israel, has entered in by it, and it shall be shut for the Prince. The prince himself shall sit in it to eat bread before the Lord.*[343] However, it can also be mystically signified that no one except the Lord can open the womb of the Church by water and the Holy Spirit to generate children for God, and therefore that this male of incomparable worth is called holy to the Lord.

[Luke 2:24] **And to offer a sacrifice, according to what is said in the Law of the Lord, a pair of turtledoves or two young pigeons.** It is stated in the Law that for a child, if it is a male, an unspotted lamb of a year old is to be offered on the fortieth day after birth (as I said previously), as a holocaust, and a young pigeon or a turtledove for sin; if it is a female, on the eightieth day after birth.[344] *And if her hand find not sufficiency, and she is not able to offer a lamb, she shall take two turtledoves or two young pigeons, one for a holocaust and the other for sin.*[345] Therefore, *although* the Lord, Christ Jesus, *was rich, having become* poor *for* our *sakes*,[346] he willed that a pauper's offering be given for him,[347] in order by his singular poverty to make us both wealthy in faith here on earth and on the Day of Judgement, heirs of the kingdom that *God promised to those who love him.*[348]

---

343 Ezek. 44:1–3. See Introduction, 61, and Piano, 'De la porte close du temple de Salomon à la porte ouverte du Paradis', 134–39. The theme of the Virgin Mary's womb as Temple appears in Bede's *Hom.* 1.4, ed. Hurst (CCSL 122:23.77); trans. Martin and Hurst, *Homilies of the Gospels* 1:33.
344 Cf. Lev. 12:2, 4–6. Bede is characteristically precise with his figures. After the birth of a male, Leviticus speaks of two periods of uncleanliness for the mother: seven days (Lev. 12:2) + thirty-three days (Lev. 12:4); after the birth of a female, it speaks again of two periods: two weeks + sixty-six days (Lev. 12:5). Bede gives us the sums: forty days and eighty days.
345 Lev. 12:8.
346 2 Cor. 8:9.
347 Luke may have assumed that his audience would understand, what he chooses not to say, that this was the offering authorized by Jewish law for those women who were too poor to afford a lamb. Bede, following Paul, makes up for Luke's reticence.
348 James 1:12.

174    BEDE: *COMMENTARY ON THE GOSPEL OF LUKE*

But on the moral level whether anyone produces strong works or feeble ones, which are distinguished by the terms 'male' and 'female', it is necessary to offer a sheep of innocence and likewise a turtledove or pigeon of remorse in order to consecrate them in a lawful manner to the Lord. For since these birds *have groans for their song*,[349] they rightly signify the tears of the humble, which we very much stand in need of even in good works. Because even if we know that the works that we do are good, nevertheless we do not know either how the Lord will judge them, or whether we will be able to persevere in them. Truly, let the one who lacks the riches of virtue, of which the Apostle says to the Corinthians: *That in all things you are made rich in him, in all utterance, and in all knowledge*,[350] and who does not find the lamb of an innocent life in the flock of his own deeds, at least offer two turtledoves or two young pigeons, that is, let him have recourse /64/ to the aid of tears. And rightly there are *two, one for sin and the other for a holocaust*. 'Holocaust' means wholly burnt, because there are without doubt two kinds of remorse. For the soul thirsting for God is stung with remorse first by fear and afterwards by love. First it afflicts itself with tears, because when it calls to mind its evil deeds, it greatly fears to suffer eternal punishment for them. But when fear has been consumed by the long anguish of lamentation, then a certain composure is born from the assurance of forgiveness, and the spirit is roused by the love of heavenly joys. The mind contemplates what those choirs of angels might be, and what that society of blessed spirits, and the grandeur of the eternal vision of God, and it laments more because it lacks eternal goods than it wept previously when it was afraid of eternal evils. Therefore, the one who offered a turtledove for sin before, weeping lest he be brought to punishment, afterwards makes a holocaust of the other turtledove, when he begins to weep most bitterly because he is separated from the kingdom of heaven. He offers a pigeon for sin who labours in his groaning and moistens his bed every night with tears,[351] that is, he does not cease throughout the nightly gloom of troubling sin to bathe his good works, in which he ought to find repose, in tears. They carry young pigeons to the holocaust who lament the absence of the heavenly fatherland and say: *By the rivers of Babylon, there we sat and wept, when*

---

349  Gregory, *Moralia* 32.3 (CCSL 143B:1629.58–59).
350  1 Cor. 1:5.
351  Cf. Ps. 6:7.

*we remembered you Zion.*[352] Just as pigeons love to sit by the rivers so that they can see ahead of time the hawk's approach by the passage of his shadow on the waters and immediately evade him, so the souls of the poor in spirit, passing over the turbulent waters of the age in their mind, take flight more frequently towards the eternal things they desire, the more examples of the wicked enemy they see in this Babylon where they are nourished by their groans. There is a difference, of course, between the significance of the turtledove and the pigeon, because the pigeon which is accustomed to live, fly, and moan in flocks signifies the throng of the active life, about which is said: *And the multitude of believers were of one heart and one soul, neither did anyone say that any of the things which he possessed was his own, but all things were common to them.*[353] But the turtledove, which so rejoices in solitude that if its mate by chance perishes it remains single from that time on, signifies the culmination of the speculative life, because this is both the virtue of the few and is attributed to them singly. Isaiah alone sees the Lord of hosts, and contemplates the praises of the Seraphim, /65/ and because he held his peace with difficulty, he moans like a solitary turtledove.[354] Moses ascends alone to the Lord while the people far off quake in fear, and with tearful prayers he succeeds in obtaining his request that this people be not slain.[355] Daniel remains alone among the angels as his companions take flight.[356] Ezekiel when alone marvels at the chariots of the cherubim and the lofty buildings of the heavenly city.[357] Paul while alone is caught up to the pleasures of paradise and to see the secrets of the third heaven.[358] Likewise when on entering my chamber I pray to the Father with the door closed,[359] I am offering a turtledove in secret. But when I seek companions for the same purpose by singing with the Prophet: *Come let us adore and fall down and weep*

---

352  Ps. 136:1 (137:1) (not *iuxta LXX*).
353  Acts 4:32.
354  Cf. Isa. 6:1–5.
355  Cf. Exod. 19:10–25. The tearful prayers seem to be part of Bede's assumption that Moses must have begged the Lord to spare the people.
356  Cf. Dan. 10:7–12:7.
357  For the chariots of the cherubim, cf. Ezek. 1:5–21; 10:1–22. Bede may have taken the idea of allegorizing the vision of the rebuilding of the temple and the city of Jerusalem, which is the subject of Ezek. 40–48, as a foreshadowing of the heavenly city from Gregory's *Hom. in Hiezech.* 2.1.5 (CCSL 142:210–12).
358  Cf. 2 Cor. 12:2; 12:4.
359  Cf. Matt. 6:6.

*before the God that made us,*[360] I carry pigeons to the altar.[361] And because either sacrifice is equally acceptable to the Creator, Luke deliberately did not say whether turtledoves or young pigeons were offered on behalf of the Lord, in order not to give preference to one way of life over the other, but to teach that each of the two should be followed and that each of the two should be offered in divine services. Therefore, because this discourse on purification has gone on too long, what mystery might be contained in the number of days of purification itself and why the same number was ordered to be doubled for the purification of the mother of a female will be explained more suitably in Leviticus.

[Luke 2:25] **And behold there was a man in Jerusalem named Simeon, and this man was just and fearfully devout, waiting for the consolation of Israel, and the Holy Spirit was in him.** After the Lord was born in the flesh, not only angels from heaven, but every age and both sexes of mortals gave witness. Just as it was fitting that the coming in the flesh of the Saviour of all was proclaimed in advance by the speech and action of faithful people throughout history, so also it was fitting that his coming be proclaimed in the universal praise of all, fulfilling the prophecy that says: *Praise the Lord from the heavens,*[362] and so forth, up to where it says: *Young men and maidens, let the older with the younger praise the name of the Lord, for his name alone is exalted. The praise of him is above heaven and earth.*[363] Simeon was *just and fearfully devout,* Luke says, because without fear, justice is preserved with difficulty. Horror that penal law will deprive one of the good things of this world (which *perfect love* is accustomed to *cast out*[364]) is not what I term *fear*. Rather, it is the holy fear of the Lord that remains forever, by which the just man loves his God the more ardently, the more carefully he guards against offending him.

[Luke 2:26–27] **And he had received an answer from the Holy Spirit that he should not see death before he had seen the Lord's Christ. And he came by the Spirit /66/ into the temple.** Notice the phrasing of the Scriptures: it said that death was 'seen'. How or by what eyes is death seen, which by its coming closes the eyes themselves so that they see nothing?

---

360 Ps. 94:6 (95:6) (not *iuxta LXX*).
361 See Introduction, 41.
362 Ps. 148:1.
363 Ps. 148:12–14 (148:12–13).
364 1 John 4:18.

But that death is 'seen' signifies that it is experienced. And a person who is blessed will very often see the death of the flesh, in that he has exerted himself beforehand to see the Lord's Christ with the eyes of his heart, by sojourning in the heavenly Jerusalem, by frequenting the doors of the temple of God, that is, by following the pious examples of the saints in whom the Lord has his dwelling, and by sighing with the Psalmist: *One thing I have asked of the Lord, this will I seek after, that I may dwell in the house of the Lord all the days of my life, that I may see the will of the Lord.*[365] For thus he will deserve to receive the word of God in his hands and to embrace it with the arms of his faith and love. And that Luke says: *And he came by the Spirit into the temple*, signifies that by the same grace of the Spirit by which Simeon had previously foreseen that Christ would come, so now he knew that he was coming and that the Saviour was to be seen by himself at this very moment.

[Luke 2:27b–28] **And when his parents brought in the child Jesus, to do for him according to the custom of the Law, he also took him into his arms.** Indeed, the great power, but also the equally great humility of the Lord is evident in the fact that the entire being of him who is not contained by heaven and earth is borne in the arms of an aged man. But as well, Simeon takes Christ, the old man takes the child, to teach us allegorically to cast off the old man who is corrupted by his deeds, and, having been renewed in the spirit of our mind, to put on the one *who according to God is created in justice and holiness and truth*[366] – that is, putting aside falsehood, to speak truth and to accomplish other things that pertain to the state of the new man in speech, heart, and deed. The elder, just according to the Law and fearfully devout, takes the child Jesus into his arms to signify that the justice of works that was in accordance with the Law – for it is well known that works are wont to be symbolized by the hands and arms – was to be exchanged for the humble but saving grace of evangelical faith. The elder takes the infant Christ to make known that this world, now exhausted as it were by debility and old age, is going to return to the innocence and, if I may put it this way, the infancy of the Christian way of life, and that its youth is going to be renewed like the eagle's.[367]

[Luke 2:28b–29] **And he blessed God and said: Now you are dismissing your servant, Lord, according to your word in peace, ...** You

---

365 Ps. 26:4 (27:4).
366 Eph. 4:24; cf. Eph. 4:22–25.
367 Cf. Ps. 102:5 (103:5).

see that the just not only of the New Testament but also of the Old, namely those who did not doubt that they would have eternal life in the bosom of Abraham, desired to be separated from the body in hope of a future life, or rather reckoned that /67/ the way of peace was to lay aside their terrestrial burden. And Jeduthun,[368] that is, the *over-leaper of secular* desires,[369] after having contemplated for a long time in silence the many evils of the world, at length grew hot within himself in the internal meditation of his heart.[370] Finally, speaking with his tongue and declaring what he deliberated within, he says: *Lord, make me know my end, and what is the number of my days, that I may know what is wanting to me. Behold you have made my days old.*[371] With these words he certainly discloses how he hopes that he will obtain a great consolation for present misfortunes in the end which he has desired so long to reach.

[Luke 2:30–31] **Because my eyes have seen your salvation, which you have prepared before the face of all peoples, ...** Blessed are the eyes that see what Simeon saw: *Blessed are they that have not seen, and have believed.*[372] Your salvation, he says, which you have prepared for all nations, peoples, and tongues to perceive in due time by the mind and faith, and which you have foreseen is to be sought by hope and love, I myself now contemplate with the eyes of my flesh and heart.

[Luke 2:32] **A light for the revelation of the Gentiles and for the glory of the people of Israel.** The light for both peoples is the salvation of God, that is, Christ is 'prepared' by God the Father. Nevertheless it came with 'glory' more for Israel, being long expected by them and foretold from them; but it is said to be a 'revelation' for the Gentiles, whose mental vision, which was sunk in profound blindness and not raised up by any hope of the Lord's coming, it deigned to visit and likewise to unveil and illuminate.[373] Fittingly, the revelation of the Gentiles is put before the glory of Israel, because when the full measure of the Gentiles comes in, then all Israel will be saved.[374] Just as when the Psalmist said: *The Lord has made*

---

368 This name stands at the head of Psalms 38 (39), 61 (62), and 76 (77). Jeduthun was apparently a music master in the Temple.
369 Cassiodorus, *Expositio psalmorum* 61.1 (CCSL 97:542); cf. 38.1 (CCSL 97:353); Jerome, *Hebr. nom.* (CCSL 72:119.22–23).
370 Cf. Ps. 38:4–5 (39:3–4).
371 Ps. 38:5–6 (39:4–5).
372 John 20:29.
373 Cf. Rom. 11:25.
374 Cf. Rom. 11:25–26.

*known his salvation; he has revealed his justice before the sight of the Gentiles*, he added: *He has remembered his mercy to Jacob and his truth toward the house of Israel.*[375]

[Luke 2:33–34] **And his father and mother were wondering at those things which were spoken concerning him. And Simeon blessed them.** He calls Joseph the father of the Saviour, not because he truly was his father, as the Photinians would have it,[376] but because he was held by all to be his father to preserve Mary's reputation. Neither was the evangelist forgetful, since he reported that she had conceived from the Holy Spirit and had given birth as a virgin, but, *expressing the belief of the common people, which is the true law of history*,[377] he calls Joseph the father of Christ. Nevertheless, he can be said to be the latter's father in the same way as he is also rightly understood to be Mary's husband *without a mingling of flesh by the union of wedlock, far more /68/ united*, that is, *than if he had been adopted in another manner. And therefore, neither was Joseph not to be called the father of Christ because he had not fathered him by sexual intercourse, since indeed he was also rightly the father of the one, whom, not having been begotten from his wife, he had adopted in another way.*[378]

[Luke 2:34b] **And he said to Mary his mother: Behold this child is appointed for the ruin and for the resurrection of many in Israel, and for a sign which will be spoken against, ...** 'For the resurrection' is well said, because he is the light, because he is the glory of the people of Israel, and because he says: *I am the resurrection and the life. He that believes in me, although he be dead, will live, and everyone that lives and believes in me will not die forever.*[379] But how may we understand 'for the ruin', except that he is *a stone of offence and a rock of stumbling*,[380] that is, of ruin for those who offend against the Word and do not believe? Of these he himself says: *If I had not come and spoken to them, they would not have sin; but now they have no excuse for their sin.*[381] He was appointed for the ruin and resurrection of many not only in himself, but in his preachers also, as the Apostle bears witness, who says: *For we are a good odour of*

---

375 Ps. 97:2–3 (98:2–3) (not *iuxta LXX*).
376 Cf. Isidore, *Etym.* 8.5.37.
377 Jerome, *Aduersus Heluidium* (PL 23:187–88). See Introduction, 44–46.
378 Augustine, *De consensu euang.* 2.1 (CSEL 43:83.21–24; 1–4).
379 John 11:25–26.
380 Rom. 9:33.
381 John 15:22.

*Christ to God, in them that are saved and in them that perish.*[382] For as the Apostle is preaching, he who follows the word which he hears with love rises again by the good odour and is saved. He who follows with hatred falls in ruin by that same good odour and dies. But take 'the sign which will be spoken against' to mean the faith of the Lord's cross, about which the Jews say to the Apostle Paul: *For concerning this sect, we know that everywhere it is spoken against.*[383] The Apostle himself says: *But we preach Christ crucified, to the Jews indeed a stumbling block and to the Gentiles foolishness.*[384]

[Luke 2:35] **And a sword will pierce your own soul, ...** No *history records that the blessed Mary departed out of this life* by the martyrdom of the sword, especially since it is *not the soul but the body* that is usually killed by the sword.[385] Hence the only option that remains is to understand that it was that sword of which it is said: *And a sword is in their lips,*[386] that is, that the grief of the Lord's suffering had pierced her soul. Although she did not doubt that Christ, since he was the Son of God, died of his own free will, and that he was going to overcome death itself, nevertheless, as he was begotten from her flesh, she could not see him crucified without the feeling of grief. Likewise, *the sword*, which is said in song to have *pierced the soul* of Joseph, is understood to be nothing other than a severe tribulation of the mind.[387]

[Luke 2:35b] **So that, out of many hearts, thoughts may be revealed.** It was at one time uncertain which of the Jews would choose to accept the grace of Christ that /69/ they knew was assuredly going to come, and which would choose rather to reject it. But after hearing of his birth, *King Herod was troubled, and all Jerusalem with him,*[388] by the thoughts of their hearts that were soon revealed. The shepherds sing out praise to God with fear and joy; they spread a message of peace to men.[389] After Christ's teaching and virtue become widely known, some flock to him as being a teacher of truth and others flee from him as being a deceiver.[390] And after the sign

---

382 2 Cor. 2:15.
383 Acts 28:22.
384 1 Cor. 1:23.
385 Ambrose, *Expos. Lucam* 2.61 (CCSL 14:57.802–03).
386 Ps. 58:8 (59:7).
387 Ps. 104:17–19 (105:17–19).
388 Matt. 2:3.
389 Cf. Luke 2:18 & 20.
390 Cf. Matt. 7:28–29; 13:57.

of his cross is erected, the latter, blaspheming, mock him as being justly condemned to death, and the former grieve bitterly that the author, as it were, of life dies. But both until today, and to the end of the present age, the sword of severe tribulation does not cease to pierce the soul of the Church. She groans when she considers that she is opposed by the wicked with respect to the sign of the faith; for after hearing the word of God many rise up again with Christ, but more fall away from belief; and after the thoughts of many hearts have been revealed, where she sowed the best seed of the Gospel, there she sees the weeds of vices either prevail more than is right, or even, sad to say, sprout and take over entirely.

[Luke 2:36–37] **And there was Anna, a prophetess, the daughter of Phanuel, of the tribe of Asher. She was far advanced in years, and had lived with her husband seven years from her virginity. And she was a widow to the age of eighty-four years, who did not depart from the temple, serving night and day with fasting and prayers.** On the historical level it is taught that Anna lived devoutly, reached a venerable age, and was worthy in every respect to bear witness to the incarnate Lord. But on the mystical level of interpretation, she signifies the Church which at present has been widowed by the death as it were of her husband and Lord. The number of years of her widowhood signifies the time when the Church, constituted in bodily form, is on pilgrimage apart from the Lord. Keeping to the threshold of the heavenly temple with the compassion of great devotion, she awaits that daily coming of the Lord, concerning which the Lord says: *We will come, and make our home with him.*[391] For certainly seven times twelve makes eighty-four. Seven pertains to the course of this world, which stretches out over seven days; but twelve to the perfection of apostolic teaching. Therefore, either the universal Church or the individual faithful soul which has a care to give over the whole span of its life to apostolic teachings is praised for multiplying as it were seven by twelve and for serving the Lord for eighty-four figurative years. So too, the time of seven years, during which she had remained with her husband, /70/ is fittingly suited to the time of the Lord's incarnation. For as I have said, the perfection of time is customarily indicated by the number seven. But in the latter case, on account of the prerogative of the majesty of the Lord whereby he taught while dwelling in the flesh, the uncompounded number of seven years is expressed. In the former, on account of the height of Apostolic worthiness, seven years are multiplied by twelve. And it is appropriate to

[391] John 14:23.

the mysteries of the Church that Anna means 'his grace',[392] and that she is the daughter of Phanuel, which means 'the face of God',[393] repeating with the Psalm-writer: *The light of your countenance is signed upon us, Lord.*[394] She descends from the tribe of Asher, that is, 'blessed',[395] who is eighth in order of birth among the twelve patriarchs.[396] There is a rather frequent insistence upon that number, because it is sacred to the New Testament.

[Luke 2:38] **Now she, at the same hour, coming in, confessed to the Lord, and spoke of him to all that looked for the redeemer of Jerusalem.** *Simeon prophesied; Anna, having been joined in marriage, had prophesied; the virgin had prophesied. Anna had to be a widow as well, so that no sex, and no state of life, should be left out. And therefore, Anna is shown both with the duties of widowhood and with a moral character so that she may be believed to have been clearly worthy to have announced that the Redeemer of all had come.*[397]

[Luke 2:39] **And after they had performed all things according to the law of the Lord, they returned into Galilee, to their own city Nazareth.** Luke here omitted what he knew had been sufficiently expounded by Matthew, namely that after these things the Lord was brought by his parents to Egypt lest he be found in order to be killed by Herod, and that after Herod's death he returned at last into Galilee and began to dwell in his own city, Nazareth.[398] For the individual evangelists are accustomed in this way to omit certain things, which either they saw had been recounted by the others, or which in spirit they foresaw would be recounted by the others, so that with the sequence of their narrative uninterrupted they seem to have omitted nothing. By examining the text of another evangelist, a diligent reader can find those things that have been omitted in a given place.

[Luke 2:40] **And the child grew, and became strong, full of wisdom; and the grace of God was in him.** The precise distinction of the words should be noted, that the Lord Jesus Christ, in that he was a child, and had

---

392 Jerome, *Hebr. nom.* (CCSL 72:102.11).
393 Jerome, *Hebr. nom.* (CCSL 72:66.22).
394 Ps. 4:7 (4:6).
395 Jerome, *Hebr. nom.* (CCSL 72:61.7–8).
396 The twelve patriarchs that Bede refers to here are the twelve sons of Jacob. The birth order of the first eight, to different wives, can be derived only from Gen. 29:31 to Gen. 30:13. The consolidated list of his twelve sons in Gen. 35:22–26 is not presented in order of birth.
397 Ambrose, *Expos. Lucam* 2.62 (CCSL 14:57.810–14).
398 Cf. Matt. 2:13–23 (not in Mark or John).

put on the appearance of human frailty, had to grow and become strong; but in that he was also the word of God and God eternal, he neither had need to become strong nor did he have to grow. Hence, he is rightly asserted to be full of wisdom and grace – of wisdom *because /71/ in him dwells all the fullness of deity bodily*,[399] and of grace because it was given by great grace to the same *mediator of God and men, the man Jesus Christ*,[400] since he had undertaken to become man, to be made perfect and God. This is similar to what John writes, that Jesus was *full of grace and truth*,[401] himself commending the same perfection of deity and of truth that Luke does under the name of wisdom.

[Luke 2:41] **And his parents went every year to Jerusalem, at the solemn day of the Passover.** You see that it is not without reason that this Evangelist is compared to the calf among the four animals. Being as it were the animal destined for sacrifices, he dwells particularly in his narrative on the Temple and on Jerusalem. For he starts with a priest praying at the altar, and the multitude of the people in the courtyard of the temple,[402] and sends Mary to Jerusalem immediately after the Lord has been conceived, and puts her into the house of the priest.[403] He refers to the birth of the Baptist there,[404] and immediately turns his attention to the Lord and transfers him there after his nativity with a sacrifice.[405] He brings him to that place with his parents year after year,[406] and situates him at the age of twelve in the temple with a group of teachers,[407] where among other astonishing things he says to the wise men: *that I must be about my Father's business*.[408] And after other such things, he closes at the end of his Gospel with the disciples praising God in the temple.[409]

---

399 Col. 2:9.
400 1 Tim. 2:5.
401 John 1:14.
402 Cf. Luke 1:8–10.
403 Cf. Luke 1:39–40. Luke in fact says that Mary went to visit Elizabeth in 'the hill country of Judaea'. Bede's commitment to the 'Temple image' (see Introduction, 56–61) seems to have drawn him to locate this specifically in Jerusalem.
404 Cf. Luke 1:57.
405 Cf. Luke 2:22–24. On the wordplay 'refers to'/'transfers' [*refert/transfert*], see Introduction, 31.
406 Cf. Luke 2:41.
407 Cf. Luke 2:42–46.
408 Luke 2:49. Jesus's words are specifically directed to his parents, but Bede apparently wants us to understand that they are addressed in a larger sense to the doctors.
409 Cf. Luke 24:53.

## Chapter 8

[Luke 2:42–43] **And when he was twelve years old, they went up to Jerusalem, according to the custom of the feast, and having fulfilled the days, when they returned, the child Jesus remained in Jerusalem.** He, who from birth, or rather from his conception as a human being, was shown by the clear evidence of miracles to be God, also began as soon as he reached a suitable age to reveal and lay open in a reverent manner each of his two natures, both that is to say what he owes to his Father in accordance with the truth of divine majesty and what he owes to his mother in taking human frailty upon himself. At the age of twelve he showed with prescience the first elements of his faith, which was to be revealed and elucidated throughout the whole world by the ministry of the twelve apostles. We can say this, because just as the number seven can signify the complete number or perfection, either of things or of times, so also can the number twelve, which consists of the parts of seven multiplied by themselves.[410] Accordingly, the dawn which could fittingly encompass all places and times takes its beginning from the number twelve. Therefore, to state that he was forgetful of his parents is not a trivial detail, but is made in order to teach us that he exists not only before his parents themselves, but before /72/ Abraham came into being, and that he delights to remain rather in the city and temple of God under the authority, so to speak, of the Father.

[Luke 2:43b–45] **And his parents knew it not. And thinking that he was in the company, they came a day's journey, and sought him among their kinsfolk and acquaintance. And not finding him, they returned to Jerusalem, seeking him.** Someone asks how the Son of God, nurtured with such care by his parents, could be left behind by their forgetfulness when they went away. To such a one the answer must be that it was the custom for the children of Israel that at festival time, whether flocking to Jerusalem or returning home, men and women proceeded separately, forming groups, and that infants and children could go with either parent. And therefore the blessed Mary and Joseph each thought that the child Jesus, whom they did not see accompanying them, had returned with the other parent.

[Luke 2:46] **And after three days they found him in the temple, sitting in the midst of the teachers, hearing them, and asking them questions.** He sits in the midst of the teachers like a fountain of wisdom,

---

410 I.e., twelve is the product of three and four, whose sum is seven (see Introduction, 50–51).

but like a model of humility he seeks to hear and question the teachers rather than to instruct the ignorant. Let little ones not blush to learn from their elders, when God himself does not blush to listen to men when it was appropriate to his human age. *No one who is deficient should dare to teach, when that child who by the power of divinity administered the word of knowledge to these very teachers desired to be taught by asking questions.*[411]

4/2 [Luke 2:47–48] **And all that heard him were astonished at his wisdom and his answers. And seeing him, they wondered.** Note the distinction of the words, and diligently contemplate the mysteries of your salvation and faith. *They were astonished who heard him, and seeing him, they wondered.* And they were the more astonished at the wisdom of his responses because they held him in contempt, seeing he was so young. His tongue brought forth divine wisdom, but his age gave the appearance of human frailty. Truly, let the learned men of the Jews be astonished at these things as if they were new, and between the deep things that they hear and the frailty that they see, let them be agitated by doubtful wonder. But as for us, knowing that he is the one about whom the prophet once joyfully exulted: *A child is born to us, a son is given to us, and his name shall be called, Wonderful, Counsellor, the mighty God,*[412] let us not wonder at all that he who became man as a child in such a way that nevertheless he remained what he always was – God and mighty – gave signs now of his divinity, now of his humanity, to those whom he wished to instruct. Rather, /73/ let us give thanks to him with suitable faith, hope, and love, that he who was *great and exceedingly to be praised,*[413] though we did not know him, *is born a child to us,* so that by growing and advancing among children, little by little he would lead them on to comprehend the mysteries of his power and greatness.

5/10 [Luke 2:48b–49] **And his mother said to him: Son, why have you done so to us? Behold your father and I have sought you sorrowing. And he said to them: How is it that you sought me? Did you not know that I must be about my Father's business?** Not Joseph's, who was responsible for nothing in his begetting except service and sympathy (hence for his faithful service he is also called 'father' both by the evangelist and by Mary herself). Certainly, Christ himself denies that he is his father, but simply and clearly makes known to us and to them as well who is his true

---

411 Gregory, *Regula pastoralis* 3.25 (SC 382:436.138–41).
412 Isa. 9:6.
413 Ps. 47:2 (48:1).

father. He does not cast blame because they seek him as if he were their son, but rather he compels them to lift up the eyes of their mind to his duty to the one whose eternal Son he is. Because he is God and man, he exhibits now the heights of his divine nature, now the depths of his human frailty. As a man he questions the elders, as God he responds with answers which the elders and learned men wonder at. As the Son of God, he tarries in the temple of God, and as a son of man he returns with his parents to the place where they bid him.

[Luke 2:50–51] **And they did not understand the word that he spoke to them. And he went down with them, and came to Nazareth, and was subject to them.** What a great example the Lord makes of piety together with humility! His parents do not understand the word that he speaks to them about his divinity, and nevertheless, showing gratitude for their earnest human attention to him, he goes down where they direct and is subject to them. *For what would he, the teacher of virtue, do other than fulfil the duty of piety?*[414] What else would he do among us, other than what he wished to be done by us? *He paid respect to the man; he paid respect to the handmaid. For she herself says: Behold the handmaid of the Lord.*[415] *He paid respect to the one who appeared to be his father;*[416] he paid respect to God, the true Father. And certainly, the son had kept his mother a virgin and chaste; certainly, he did not distance himself from his father either in will or deed or time, so that we, instructed by his example, may learn what we owe to our parents, who suffer so much for us. The Arians are accustomed to say that the Son is imperfect, because he said, *My Father is greater than I.*[417] But what wonder if he declares that he is less than his Father in heaven because of his assumption of humanity, because of which he was subject even to his parents on earth. /74/

[Luke 2:51b] **And his mother kept all these words in her heart.** Whether it was the words of the evangelist that she understood, or the words that she could not yet understand, she laid them all up equally in her heart to be, as it were, chewed over and more diligently examined. *Therefore, let us study the purity of the holy Virgin in all things, who with a mouth as chaste as her body* kept *in her heart the proofs of the faith. And if* she *keeps silent before the Apostle gave his command, why*

---

414 Ambrose, *Expos. Lucam* 2.65 (CCSL 14:58.840–41).
415 Luke 1:38 (quoted by Ambrose).
416 Ambrose, *Expos. Lucam* 2.65 (CCSL 14:58.848–50).
417 John 14:28.

*do you prefer to teach rather than to learn after the Apostle has given his command?*[418]

[Luke 2:52] **And Jesus advanced in wisdom and age and grace with God and men.** This passage refutes the Manicheans and the Apollinarians equally, by showing that the Lord has true flesh and true spirit. *For just as it is in the nature of flesh to advance in age, so it is of the spirit* to advance *in wisdom and grace. But it would by no means advance in wisdom, if it did not have the natural intelligence that was granted to mankind for the sake of reason. It is not because God received what he lacked,* especially when the child is described above to have been *full of wisdom,*[419] but because he chose *the effects of his pious act of reception as the remedy of our salvation, so that, during the time when flesh and a rational spirit is taken on by God, he would be maintained equally by each.*[420]

## Chapter 9

6/3 [Luke 3:1] **Now in the fifteenth year of the reign of Tiberius Caesar, Pontius Pilate being governor of Judea, and Herod being tetrarch of Galilee, and Philip his brother tetrarch of Ituraea and the region of Trachonitis, and Lysanias tetrarch of Abilene, ...** Herod, Philip, and Lysanias, who ruled Judea with Pilate the Roman governor, are the sons of that Herod under whom the Lord was born. Their brother Archelaus reigned for ten years between the elder and the younger Herod. In the time of Augustus, Archelaus was blamed by the Jews for the intolerable ferocity of his disposition, and met his end in perpetual exile near Vienne.[421] But to prevent the kingdom of Judea from becoming powerful, Augustus took care to divide it into tetrarchies. Then in the twelfth year of Tiberius Caesar, Pilate was sent to Judea and undertook the administration of the nation, and carried on there for ten successive years very nearly to the end of Tiberius' rule.[422]

---

418 Ambrose, *Expos. Lucam* 2.54 (CCSL 14:54.735–40); cf. 1 Cor. 14:34.
419 Luke 2:40.
420 Fulgentius, *Ad Trasamundum* 1.8.3 (CCSL 91:105.320–27).
421 Cf. Josephus, *Antiquitates* 17.13.2.
422 In his *Chronica maiora* (*DTR* 66), Bede states, as he does here, that Tiberius sent Pilate to Judea as procurator in the 12th year of his reign (A.M. 3979). He goes on to say, on the authority of Orosius, that Pilate was driven to commit suicide by Caligula. Cf. *DTR* 66, A.M. 3979, and A.M. 3993 (Wallis, *The Reckoning of Time*, 196–97). His source for

[Luke 3:2] **Under the high priests Annas and Caiaphas, the word of the Lord came to John, the son of Zechariah, in the desert.** It is indeed the case that when John began preaching, both Annas and Caiaphas were high priests; but Annas was in charge that year, while Caiaphas was in charge the year when the Lord mounted /75/ the cross. Three others performed the duties of the pontificate in between, but notwithstanding, the evangelist especially mentioned these men, who were involved in the Lord's passion. For at that time the rule of law was suspended and ambition prevailed, and so the honour of the pontificate was bestowed not according to merit of life or family, but was offered by the supreme Roman power now to some and again to others. *Josephus has this to say* on the subject: *'After depriving Annanias of the priesthood, Valerius Gratus Anna appointed Ismael the son of Bassus high priest. But not long afterwards, casting him aside, he substituted Eleazar the son of Annanias the high priest in the priesthood in his place. But after a year he deprived even him of office and handed over the ministry of the pontificate to a certain Simon the son of Canysius. And after fulfilling this function for no more than a year, Simon received a successor whose name was Joseph Caiphas.'*[423] According to this the whole time in which our Lord is said to have taught on earth is compressed within the space of four years. In this time the four successive high priests whom Josephus mentions are said to have served for just a single year each. Therefore, *because* John *came to preach the one who was going to redeem not only some people from Judea, but also many from the Gentiles, the times of his preaching are signified by the king of the Gentiles and the high priests of the Jews. Moreover, this description of terrestrial authority also shows that the heathens had to be gathered together and the Jews scattered for the crime of faithlessness, because in the Roman republic one man is said to have been in command, but in the kingdom of Judea several ruled, each over a fourth part of the kingdom. For in the words of our Redeemer it is said: Every kingdom divided against itself will be brought to desolation.*[424] *It is clear, therefore, that the kingdom of Judea, which after being divided was subject to so many kings, had come to its end. Appropriately also, it is shown not only by which kings, but also*

---

the first of these statements was Jerome, *Chronicon* 173.4–5, and for the second, Orosius, *Historiarum aduersos paganos libri quinque* 7.5.8. Tiberius died and Caligula came to power ten years after Pilate became procurator.

423 Eusebius, *Hist. eccl.* 1.10.4–5 (GCS 9.1:75.6–13) (cf. Josephus, *Antiquitates* 18.2.2).
424 Luke 11:17.

BOOK ONE 189

*by which priests this was done, so that because John the Baptist preached the one who was at once king and priest, the evangelist Luke signified the times of his preaching by kingdom and priesthood.*[425]
7/1 [Luke 3:3] **And he came into all the country about the Jordan, preaching the baptism of repentance for the remission of sins,** ... *It is clear to everyone who reads this that John the Baptist not only preached the baptism of repentance, but also baptised some persons. Nevertheless, he could not give his baptism for the remission of sins. For the remission /76/ of sins is granted to us in the baptism of Christ alone. Therefore, let us take notice of what is said: 'preaching the baptism of repentance for the remission of sins', because he preached a baptism which takes away sins that he was not able to give, so that just as the incarnate Word of the Father surpassed the word of preaching, so the baptism of repentance by which sins are cleansed surpassed John's baptism by which they cannot be cleansed.*[426]

[Luke 3:4] **As it is written in the book of the words of Isaiah the prophet: The voice of one crying in the wilderness: 'Prepare the way of the Lord, make his paths straight'.** *In fact, this same John the Baptist, when asked who he was, replied: 'I am the voice of one crying in the wilderness'.*[427] *He is called a 'voice' by the prophet, because he preceded the Word.*[428] *Likewise, he cries in the wilderness, because he announces the relief of redemption to forsaken and abandoned Judea. And what he cried is revealed when this is followed by: 'Prepare the way of the Lord, make his paths straight'. What else does everyone who preaches the straight faith and good works prepare than the way for the Lord who comes to the hearts of his listeners in order that this power of grace may penetrate and the light of truth illuminate, and in order that he make straight paths for God, while he fashions pure thoughts in the mind by the words of good preaching?*[429]

[Luke 3:5] **Every valley will be filled, and every mountain and hill will be brought low.** *In this passage, who are signified by the name of valleys except the humble; who by the name of mountains and hills except the proud? Therefore with the coming of the Redeemer the valleys are filled, but the mountains and hills are brought low, because according to his*

425 Gregory, *Hom. in Euang.* 1.20.1 (CCSL 141:154.8–23).
426 Gregory, *Hom. in Euang.* 1.20.2 (CCSL 141:154.25–35).
427 John 1:23.
428 Gregory, *Hom. in Euang.* 1.20.3 (CCSL 141:155.40–43).
429 Gregory, *Hom. in Euang.* 1.20.3 (CCSL 141:155.43–48).

word: *'Everyone who exalts himself will be humbled, and he who humbles himself will be exalted.'*[430] *For a valley when it is filled rises, but a mountain or a hill when it is brought low falls, since certainly the heathens received a plenitude of grace in the faith of the mediator of God and men, the man Jesus Christ,*[431] *and the Jews perished through the error of faithlessness because of which they were puffed up.*[432]

[Luke 3:5b] **And the crooked will be made straight, and the rough ways plain.** *The crooked become straight when the hearts of the wicked, turned away towards injustice, are straightened out towards the straight rule of justice. And rough ways are changed into plain paths when savage and wrathful minds return to the smoothness of clemency by an infusion of divine grace. For when the word of truth is not accepted by the wrathful mind, the roughness of the way repels the steps of the one who advances. But when the wrathful mind accepts a word of correction or exhortation by receiving the grace of clemency, there the preacher finds a plain path where before he was unable to advance on account of the roughness of the path, that is, to set the steps of preaching upon the path.*[433] /77/

[Luke 3:6] **And all flesh will see the salvation of God.** *Since 'all flesh' is taken to mean all humankind, then all humankind could not see the salvation of God, namely Christ, in this life. Where then in this statement does the prophet direct the eye of prophecy, except to the Day of final Judgement? When Christ appears on the throne of his majesty,*[434] *with the heavens opened, with angels in attendance, with the apostles seated around, all will see him, the elect and the damned equally, so that the just rejoice in the gift of eternal recompense, and the unjust groan forever in the punishment of torment. And because this statement means that this will be seen at the Last Judgement by all flesh, it is rightly added:*[435]

8/5 [Luke 3:7] **He said therefore to the multitudes that went forth to be baptized by him: You brood of vipers, who has warned you to flee from the wrath to come?** *The wrath to come is the chastisement of final punishment, which the sinner who does not now resort to the lamentations of penitence cannot then flee from. And it should be noted that wicked*

---

430 Luke 14:11.
431 Cf. 1 Tim. 2:5.
432 Gregory, *Hom. in Euang.* 1.20.3 (CCSL 141:155.50–58).
433 Gregory, *Hom. in Euang.* 1.20.6 (CCSL 141:158.114–23); cf. Ps. 84:14 (85:13).
434 Cf. Matt. 19:28.
435 Gregory, *Hom. in Euang.* 1.20.7 (CCSL 141:158.124–33).

BOOK ONE 191

*offspring, imitating the actions of their wicked parents, are called a brood of vipers, because they envy the good and persecute them, render evil to some, and seek injuries for their neighbours. In all these things they follow the paths of their forefathers in the flesh, as if they are born the venomous sons of venomous parents. But since we have already sinned, since we are enveloped in the exercise of wicked custom, he makes known what we must do to be able to flee from the wrath to come.*[436]

[Luke 3:8] **Bring forth therefore fruits worthy of repentance.** *In these words, it should be noted that he warns that it is not solely fruits of repentance, but fruits worthy of repentance that must be brought forth. For it is one thing to bring forth fruit, but another to bring forth fruit worthy of repentance.*[437] *The fruit of a good deed should not be the same in the case of one who transgressed less and another who transgressed more, or of one who committed no crime and another who committed some crimes. Therefore because it is said: 'Bring forth fruits of repentance', the conscience of each individual is addressed, so that the greater the damage he has inflicted upon himself by his own fault, the greater may be the profit of good works through repentance. But the Jews, boasting of the nobility of their race, for that reason do not want to acknowledge themselves to be sinners, because they were descended from the stock of Abraham. To these it is rightly said:*[438]

[Luke 3:8b] **And do not begin to say: We have Abraham for our father. For I say to you that God is able from these stones to raise up children to Abraham.** *For what were these stones but the hearts of the Gentiles, incapable of comprehending almighty God? Just as* /78/ *it is also said to certain of the Jews: 'I will take away the stony heart out of your flesh'.*[439] *And the heathens who worshipped stones are rightly signified by the name of stones. Hence it is written: 'Let them that make them become like to them, and all who trust in them'.*[440] *Certainly from these stones the children of Abraham are raised up, since provided that the hard hearts of the Gentiles believed in the seed of Abraham, that is, in Christ, they became his children, to whose seed they were united. Hence it is also said to these same heathens by the great preacher: 'And if you are Christ's,*

---

436 Gregory, *Hom. in Euang.* 1.20.7–8 (CCSL 141:159.136–46).
437 Gregory, *Hom. in Euang.* 1.20.8 (CCSL 141:159.147–50).
438 Gregory, *Hom. in Euang.* 1.20.8–9 (CCSL 141:160.156–65).
439 Ezek. 36:26.
440 Ps. 113:16 (115:8).

then you are the seed of Abraham.'[441] *Therefore if we are now the seed of Abraham through faith in Christ, the Jews have ceased to be the children of Abraham through lack of faith.*[442]

[Luke 3:9] **For now the axe is laid to the root of the tree.** *The tree of this world is the whole human race. And assuredly the axe is our Redeemer, who is grasped as it were by handle and blade by reason of his humanity, but fells by reason of his divinity. Clearly this axe is now laid to the root of the tree, because although it waits in patience, nevertheless what it will do is plain.*[443]

[Luke 3:9b] **Every tree therefore that does not bring forth good fruit will be cut down and cast into the fire,** *because every wicked person who disdains to bring forth the fruit of good work here finds the flames of hell are prepared all the quicker. It should be noted that he says the axe is not laid next to the branches, but to the root. For when the children of the wicked are destroyed, what else could it mean except that the branches of the unfruitful tree are cut off? But when all the progeny together with the parent is destroyed, the unfruitful tree has been cut off from the root, in order that nothing remain from which a crooked offspring might again grow. In these words of John the Baptist it is well known that the hearts of his listeners were disturbed, since it is immediately added:*[444]

9/10 [Luke 3:10] **And the crowds asked him, saying: What then shall we do?** *For the multitudes that were seeking advice had been struck with fear.*[445]

[Luke 3:11] **And he answering, said to them: He who has two coats, let him give to him who has none, and he who has food, let him do in like manner.** *Because a coat is more necessary for our use than a cloak, it refers to fruit worthy of repentance, for we ought to share with our neighbours not only whatever external things are less necessary, but also those which are very necessary for us, which is to say, both the food by which we live in the flesh and the coat by which we are dressed. For since it is written in the Law: 'You shall love your neighbour as yourself',*[446] *it is clearly shown that he does not love his neighbour at all who does*

---

441 Gal. 3:29.
442 Gregory, *Hom. in Euang.* 1.20.9 (CCSL 141:160.167–79).
443 Gregory, *Hom. in Euang.* 1.20.10 (CCSL 141:161.190–94).
444 Gregory, *Hom. in Euang.* 1.20.10 (CCSL 141:161.196–204).
445 Gregory, *Hom. in Euang.* 1.20.10 (CCSL 141:162.205–06).
446 Mark 12:31 (Gregory here quotes the nearly identical phrase from Matt. 19:19).

not share with him /79/ in his need even those things that are necessary for himself. For that reason, therefore, the commandment is given about dividing two coats with a neighbour, because this could not be said about one coat, since if one is divided, no one is clothed. For indeed in half a coat both he who received and he who gave remain unclothed. From all this it may be known how very effectual are the works of mercy, since they are recommended above others as fruits worthy of repentance. Hence the Truth likewise says in his own person: *Give alms, and behold, all things are clean for you.*[447]

[Luke 3:12–13] **And the tax collectors also came to be baptized, and they said to him: Master, what shall we do? But he said to them: Do nothing more than that which is appointed you.** This shows how much power the words of the blessed Baptist had and how great an impact they had upon the minds of his listeners: it forced even the tax collectors and soldiers to seek advice about their salvation. He gives the same advice to these people as to the multitudes, that they should act mercifully in a way appropriate for themselves. Therefore, he ordered *the tax collectors not to exact more than what was legally owed.*[448] For those *who exact the public taxes, or who* are *farmers of the revenues of the treasury, or of public affairs, are called tax collectors* [*publicani*], *as their name indicates. And those who pursue the wealth of this world through business* are also called by the same name.[449] He restrains all these equally, each in his own station, from doing wrong, so that, while in the first instance the tax collectors are restrained from a desire for the property of others, in the latter case those who pursue wealth end up sharing their own things with their neighbours.

[Luke 3:14] **And the soldiers also asked him, saying: And what shall we do? And he said to them: Do violence to no man, nor make false accusation, and be content with your wages.** This excellent teacher advised an accommodation that was very just, namely that soldiers not try to plunder those they ought to benefit through their military activity by making false accusations. *For that reason, he taught that wages were appointed for the soldiery in order that they not prowl as predators when they seek their expenses.*[450] Therefore, no office, no people, is exempted from doing works of mercy, which is the perfection of virtues and alone

---

447 Gregory, *Hom. in Euang.* 1.20.11 (CCSL 141:162.208–23); Luke 11:41.
448 Ambrose, *Expos. Lucam* 2.77 (CCSL 14:64.1027).
449 Isidore, *Etym.* 9.4.32.
450 Ambrose, *Expos. Lucam* 2.77 (CCSL 14:64.1028–30).

frees us from death and confers eternal life. The Judge himself confirms this when he promised that he was going to say *Come you blessed of my Father, receive the kingdom. For I was hungry, and you gave me to eat,* and so forth.[451]

[Luke 3:15–16] **And as the people were in expectation, and all were thinking in their hearts of John, that perhaps he might be the Christ, John /80/ answered, saying to all:** ... How did he respond to those who were 'in expectation' of him and in their secret heart 'were thinking' that he was the Christ? The answer is that they were not only thinking, but also (as another evangelist declares after priests and Levites had been sent to him[452]) they were asking whether or not he was the Christ. Hence it is clear that it was very well known to the Jews at that time that in accordance with the Scriptures the time of the Lord's incarnation was at hand. But what astonishing blindness, in that they believed willingly in John, but not in this Saviour whose truth was confirmed by such great miracles and powers, and to whom even John himself bore witness!

10/1 [Luke 3:16b] **I indeed baptize you with water, but there will come one mightier than I, the thong of whose shoes I am not worthy to loosen.** John baptizes not with the spirit, but with water, because not being able to loosen sins, he washes the bodies of the baptised with water but does not wash the soul with forgiveness. Why then does he who does not loosen sins by baptism baptize? The answer is that he preserves his position as forerunner. He who was the forerunner by being born before him who was to be born, was also the forerunner by baptizing before the Lord who would baptize. And he who became the forerunner of Christ by preaching, would also become his forerunner by the imitation of the sacrament. But *among the ancients the custom was that if anyone did not want to marry a woman who was suitable for him, he who should be her bridegroom by right of kinship would undo the first man's shoe.*[453] *For what reason did Christ appear among men, except as the bridegroom of the holy Church? About this the same John also says: 'He that has the bride is the bridegroom.'*[454] *But since men thought that John was the Christ, which John himself denies, he rightly declares that he is unworthy to loosen the thong of his shoe, as if he should plainly say: I am not able to lay bare the*

---

451 Matt. 25:34; 35.
452 Cf. John 1:19.
453 Cf. Ruth 4:7–8.
454 John 3:29 (quoted by Gregory).

*Redeemer's feet, because I do not deserve to take upon myself the name of bridegroom. But this can also be understood in another way: For who doesn't know that shoes are made from dead animals? Indeed, the coming incarnate Lord, who in his divinity assumed the carcass of our corruption, appeared as though shod. But the human eye does not suffice to penetrate the mystery of his incarnation. For how the Word becomes flesh, how the highest and life-giving Spirit is brought to life in the womb of the mother, how he who has no beginning both comes into being and is conceived, can by no means be discovered. The thong of the shoe therefore is the binding of the mystery. And so, John is unable to loosen the thong of the shoe, because he who perceives the incarnation by the spirit of prophecy is not himself capable of discovering its mystery.*[455] /**81**/

[Luke 3:16c] **He will baptize you with the Holy Spirit and with fire,** ... that is, with the cleansing of sanctification and with the testing of tribulation. The Holy Spirit can be understood to be signified by the name of fire as well, because he both burns with love and illuminates with the wisdom that replenishes hearts. Hence also, they to whom it was said, *For John indeed baptized with water, but you will be baptized with the Holy Spirit,*[456] perceive the same baptism of the Spirit in the image of fire. There are those who explain that we are baptized in the present in spirit and in the future in fire, so that plainly just as we are reborn now in the remission of all sins by water and spirit, so also we may be thoroughly cleansed then of certain trifling sins that will cling to us as we go hence by the baptism of purgatorial fire before the Last Judgement. As the Apostle says: *Now if anyone builds upon this foundation, gold, silver, precious stones, wood, hay, stubble, the fire will try his work, of what sort it is. If his work abides which he has built thereupon, he will receive a reward. If his work burns, he will suffer loss, but he himself will be saved, yet so as by fire.*[457] Although this can be understood to refer to the fire of tribulation appointed for this life of ours, nevertheless if anyone understands this to refer to the fire of purgation to come, it should be carefully pondered that Paul said that it is not the one who builds upon the foundation of Christ iron, bronze, or lead, that is, the greater and harsher sins and those which by then will be irredeemable, but wood, hay, and stubble, that is, the least and most trifling sins, which fire easily consumes. But it ought to be known

---

455 Gregory, *Hom. in Euang.* 1.7.3 (CCSL 141:49.92–118).
456 Acts 1:5.
457 1 Cor. 3:12–15 (quoted from Gregory).

*that no one will obtain there any cleansing of even the least sins, unless he deserves to obtain it here by good works done when he was still placed in this life.*[458]

**11/5** [Luke 3:17] **Whose winnowing-fork is in his hand, and he will cleanse his floor.** The winnowing-fork, that is, a winnowing fan,[459] symbolizes the separation that is characteristic of a just examination; and the floor symbolizes the present Church. In this separation, unquestionably very painful, *many are called, but few are chosen.*[460] A few grains are to be taken into the heavenly mansions, in contrast with the weeds which are to be delivered up to perpetual flames. The cleansing of this floor is now done one person at a time, when each reprobate is either cast out of the Church by priestly condemnation because of manifest sin, or damned after death by divine judgement because of hidden sins. In the end it will be done to all without exception when *the Son of man will send his angels, and they will gather out of his kingdom all causes of offence.*[461] So the Lord has the winnowing-fork in his hand, that is, he has the act of judgement /82/ in his power, because *the Father* does not *judge anyone, but he has given all judgement to the Son.*[462]

[Luke 3:17b] **And he will gather the wheat into his barn, but the husks he will burn with inextinguishable fire.** The Lord himself concluded the parable of the good seed amongst which the wicked man sowed weeds, by saying: *And at the time of the harvest I will say to the reapers: Gather up first the weeds, and bind them into bundles to burn, but gather the wheat into my barn.*[463] Surely he teaches that the ungodly and the sinners are to be given over to the fires of hell, but the saints are to be crowned with heavenly glory. This distinguishes between husks and weeds, because husks like wheat come from seed, although they have degenerated from the excellence of a good root. But weeds not only differ from crops, but are also generated from a completely different source. Husks are those who are imbued with the mysteries of the same faith as the elect, but differ from the latter's true perfection either in the frivolity of their works or in the emptiness of their perfidy. But weeds are those who are not even

---

458 Gregory, *Dialogues* 4.41.5–6 (SC 265:150.36–47).
459 Cf. Isidore, *Etym.* 20.14.10.
460 Matt. 20:16.
461 Matt. 13:41.
462 John 5:22.
463 Matt. 13:30.

worthy of hearing the words of the faith, and therefore are sundered from the condition of the good both in conduct and in belief.

And so, in the field of this world, the fruit of the elect is one and the fruits of the damned is two, because not only is all that the enemy sows subject to the flames, but what is worse, much of what the good sower casts is lost either by being stolen by the birds or scorched by the sun or choked by thorns or turned to husks. Only the wheat of the elect brought forth from good earth and tried by worthy suffering is stored in the barn of heavenly life. In the same way in another parable not only do the fish that avoid the nets of apostolic faith remain unknown in the deep waters of sin, but many, after being hauled ashore among the good fish of the final separation,[464] deserve at that time to be cast *into the outer darkness* because they have offended through their wickedness.[465] He calls the fire of hell inextinguishable for two reasons: that is, because it can neither ever be extinguished, nor will it ever extinguish those whom it torments but it will embrace them with a death that is immortal (if I can put it that way). This is clearly in contrast to that most sacred fire by which he had foretold the elect of Christ would be baptized. Of this the Psalmist likewise says: *You have tried us by fire, as silver is tried by fire.*[466] And a little after: We have not remained fixed forever, but, he says, *we have passed through fire and water, and you have brought us into a refreshment. I will go into your house with burnt offerings,*[467] that is, having overcome the torments of afflictions, I will enter the courtyards of your heavenly kingdom with the thanksgiving. /83/

## Chapter 10

**12/2 [Luke 3:19–20] But Herod the tetrarch, when he was reproved by him because of Herodias, his brother's wife, and because of all the evils that Herod had done, added this also above them all, and shut up John in prison.** These matters are reported more fully by Matthew and Mark, namely that John was not only put in chains by the snares of Herodias, but was also beheaded.[468] This was not done at this time, but according to the

---

464 Cf. Matt. 13:47–50.
465 Matt. 8:12.
466 Ps. 65:10 (66:10).
467 Ps. 65:12–13 (66:12–13).
468 Cf. Matt. 14:3–11; Mark 6:17–28.

Gospel of John, after several miracles had been performed by the Lord, and it was already known far and wide that his baptism had taken place.[469] But it is reported here by the evangelist Luke by anticipation in order to amplify Herod's malice. Although the crowd flocked to John's preaching, and the soldiers believed, and the tax collectors repented, and the entire populace received baptism together, Herod on the contrary did not hesitate not only to condemn but also to kill him. Moreover, by reason of a deeper mystery, because the evangelist John undertook the work of writing about the divinity of Christ, while the other three did the same about his human nature, and because John the Baptist assuredly is the type of the Old Law, which is the forerunner of grace, the evangelist John beautifully testifies that, while the Lord's forerunner was still preaching and baptizing, the Lord himself made and baptized many disciples.[470] Thus John teaches allegorically that Christ was eternal God through the ages, and teacher of the faithful peoples through the Law. But it is also fitting that the other evangelists take up the commencement of the Lord's preaching after John was imprisoned. After the Law had been corrupted by the Jews and defiled as it were by blind ignorance and savage rendition to the darkness of prison as it were, it was their task to spread the heavenly teaching of the Lord, who came into Galilee, appearing in the flesh and working through the flesh.

**13/1** [Luke 3:21] **Now when all the people were baptized, and Jesus also had been baptized and was praying, heaven was opened.** *The Lord was baptized, not* himself wishing *to be cleansed, but* wishing *to cleanse the waters* themselves, which *washed by* his *flesh* which truly knew no sin took on *the power* of baptism,[471] and they received the power of regenerative sanctification which baptisms under the Law, innumerable as they were, were incapable of exercising against the evil of transgression. Hence, when Luke said that all the people were baptized, he rightly added nothing of importance. But *Jesus being baptized and praying, heaven*, it says, *was opened*, since when the Lord entered the waters of the Jordan with the humility of his body, he opened the gates of heaven to us by the power of his divinity. And when his innocent flesh **/84/** is bathed in frigid waters, the flaming sword set as a barrier is quenched by the water that was once so injurious.[472] If that is not the case, what is? Is it really possible

---

469 Cf. John 3:24.
470 Cf. John 3:26.
471 Ambrose, *Expos. Lucam* 2.83 (CCSL 14:67.1124–27).
472 Cf. Gen. 3:24.

that heaven was opened to him at that time, so that his eyes discerned the inner parts of the heavens? But what is shown here is the power of baptism; when anyone emerges from baptism, the gate of the heavenly kingdom is revealed. This also applies to the fact that Jesus, to whom everything belongs which belongs to the Father, is reported to have prayed after being baptized. There is no doubt that this was done to instruct us that in order for the court of heaven to be opened, we should not live idly after the washing of baptism, but rather that we must devote ourselves to fasting, prayers, and almsgiving. Although all sins are forgiven in baptism, nevertheless the flesh's weakness is still not made strong. For while we are indeed grateful that the Egyptians were killed in crossing the Red Sea, nevertheless in the desert of a worldly way of life other enemies appear who must be overcome by our labour, with the grace of Christ as our leader and collaborator, until we reach the promised fatherland of eternal life.

[Luke 3:22] **And the Holy Spirit descended upon him in a bodily shape like a dove.** It is well that the Holy Spirit was *in a bodily shape*, because he could not be seen by mortals in his natural state of divinity, just as it is well that he was *like a dove*, because [*the Spirit*] *of discipline will flee from the deceitful*,[473] *and will not dwell in a body subject to sins*,[474] and those who, following the example of Simon,[475] abide *in the gall of bitterness, and in the bond of iniquity*,[476] can in no way have their lot and destiny in him. Hence when in former times the crimes of the world were cleansed in a prefiguration of baptism by the Flood, the branch of the olive tree, brought in the mouth not of the raven, but of the dove, announced that peace was restored to the world,[477] teaching allegorically that the anointing of the Holy Spirit will come to those alone who are baptized in the simplicity of their heart. For no one should imagine that the Lord was anointed after the first baptism by the grace of the Holy Spirit, or that the Holy Spirit set out to produce a person of divine nature for the ages, but rather one should know that from the first moment of human conception the same person who is a true human being is also the true God. And by the coming of the dove, it

---

473 Wisd. 1:5.
474 Wisd. 1:4. On Bede's use of the opening poem of Wisdom in this context, see Martin, 'Bede's Originality', 197–98.
475 I.e., Simon Magus.
476 Acts 8:23.
477 Cf. Gen. 8:6–11.

is shown that it is chiefly in his body, that is, the Church, that the baptized receive the Holy Spirit.

[Luke 3:22b] **And a voice came from heaven: You are my beloved Son. In you I am well pleased.** John is deservedly second to none *among those born of women*,[478] for he is the one by whom Christ believes he ought to be baptized, the one to whom the invisible Spirit exhibits himself that he may be seen, and the one to whom the Father commends his Son from heaven. For this was a revelation not to the Son himself of what he full well knew, but either to John or to the others who were present of what they ought to know.[479] /85/ Hence it should be observed that the same John, who up to that time was proclaiming a man mightier than himself and the Christ,[480] now advised by the descent of the Spirit as well as by the testimony of the Father, would henceforth openly preach the Son of God: *This is he*, he says, *of whom I said, After me comes a man who is preferred before me, because he was before me, and I knew him not*.[481] And likewise about the dove: *And I saw, and have testified that this is the Son of God*.[482] And so the mystery of the Trinity is shown in the baptism of the Saviour to teach us that we are also to be baptized in his name. Moreover, when God says, *in you I am well pleased*, it is as if he were to say, 'I have constituted my pleasure in you', that is, it pleases me to act through you. Indeed, this explains why according to Matthew it is said *in whom I am well pleased*.[483] Because everyone who corrects his deeds by repenting, shows by the very fact that he repents that he who emends what he did was displeased with himself. And since the omnipotent Father spoke about sinners in a human manner so as to be understood by men, he said: *It displeases me that I made man on the earth*,[484] as if he were displeased with himself because he had created sinners. But he was pleased with himself in his only-begotten Jesus Christ, our Lord, because he did not repent of having created this man among men, in whom he found no sin at all, as is said of him by the Psalmist: *The Lord has sworn, and he will not repent: You are a priest forever*.[485]

478 Matt. 11:11.
479 See Introduction, 36–37.
480 Cf. Matt. 3:11.
481 John 1:30–31.
482 John 1:34.
483 Matt. 3:17.
484 Gen. 6:6 & 7 (a blend).
485 Ps. 109:4 (110:4). In his later commentary *On Genesis*, Bede explains more clearly that when Scripture attributes emotions such as repentance to God it is using language

BOOK ONE                                                        201

**14/3** [Luke 3:23] **And Jesus himself was beginning about the age of thirty years, being as was supposed the son of Joseph,** ... Jesus is baptized at the age of thirty years, and then at last begins to do miracles and to teach, clearly showing to those who think that every age is suitable whether for the priesthood or for teaching that there is a legitimate and proper time of life for these things. And furthermore, as was declared above, *when he was twelve years old he wanted to be found sitting in the temple in the midst of the learned men, not teaching, but asking questions.*[486] *For so that men would not dare to preach when they are of tender years, he who through his divinity always teaches the angels in heaven* at twelve years *questions men on earth.*[487]

*Nor ought the fact that Jeremiah and Daniel received the spirit of prophecy as children*[488] *dissuade anyone against this, since miracles must not be considered as a model of performance. For omnipotent God not only 'makes the tongues of infants eloquent',*[489] *but also 'has perfected praise out of the mouth of infants and sucklings'.*[490] *But what we learn about the practice of teaching is one thing; what we know about a miracle is another.*[491] Even the Saviour's age of thirty years when he was baptized can reveal the symbolism /**86**/ of our baptism in accordance with the faith of the holy Trinity and the workings of the Decalogue of the Law. Of course, the Decalogue is understood the more sublimely and fulfilled the more devotedly by the revelation of the grace of faith. For he who said: Go, *teach all nations, baptizing them in the name of the Father, and of the Son, and of the Holy Spirit,*[492] taught that those who are going to be baptized have as it were a certain consecrated period of three years. It is as if he ordered this same time of three years to be multiplied by ten when he added: *Teaching them to observe all things whatsoever I have commanded you.*[493]

---

adapted to the weakness of human understanding, which is not to be taken literally. See Bede, *In Genesim*, ed. Jones (CCSL 118A:101.1007–21), trans. Kendall, *Bede: On Genesis*, 171.
486   Cf. Luke 2:42 & 46.
487   Gregory, *Hom. in Hiezech.* 1.2.3 (CCSL 142:18.40–45).
488   Cf. Jer. 1:5; Dan. 13:45.
489   Wisd. 10:21.
490   Ps. 8:3 (8:2).
491   Gregory, *Hom. in Hiezech.* 1.2.4 (CCSL 142:19.78–84).
492   Matt. 28:19.
493   Matt. 28:20.

As a figure of this, we likewise hear about the bronze sea,[494] in which the priests who were about to enter the temple were washed.[495] It is said to be enclosed with a thin cord of thirty cubits on the outside,[496] and to be able to contain three thousand measures,[497] since *with the heart we believe for the sake of justice, but with the mouth confession is made for the sake of salvation.*[498] The fact that the apostles after receiving the grace of the Holy Spirit first baptize three thousand souls[499] supports this interpretation. And since the bronze sea comes to mind, it is agreeable as well to inquire how it is suited in other ways to the measure of baptism. *From brim to brim,* it says, *of ten cubits,*[500] because we must not be constricted by earthly anxiety, but expanded by the expectation of the heavenly denarius. *Its brim was like the brim of a cup or the leaf of a crisped lily,*[501] of which the cup of the Lord's passion is represented by the first, and the unveiled splendour of his resurrection by the other. For what the Apostle says: *All we who are baptized in Christ Jesus are baptized in his death,*[502] pertains to the brim of the cup; but what he adds: *as Christ is risen from the dead by the glory of the Father, so we also may walk in newness of life,*[503] looks back to the flower of the crisped lily. Its *thickness of three inches*[504] is in order that all the power of those who baptize may be strengthened by the perfection of faith, hope, and love. It was five cubits in height,[505] because whatever is offended by sight, hearing, taste, smell, or touch is washed wholly clean by the water of regeneration. The oxen that support it look by threes towards the separate quarters of the sky,[506] in order that the entire world may be baptized in the faith of the holy Trinity. And the bronze sea stood on the right side of the sanctuary of the priests *over against the*

---

494 Cf. 4 Kings 25:13. The bronze sea [*mare aeneum*] was the gigantic basin for purification situated at the entrance to the Temple, supported by twelve bronze oxen.
495 Cf. 2 Chron. 4:6.
496 Cf. 2 Chron. 4:2.
497 Cf. 2 Chron. 4:5.
498 Rom. 10:10.
499 Cf. Acts 2:41.
500 3 Kings 7:23.
501 3 Kings 7:26.
502 Rom. 6:3.
503 Rom. 6:4.
504 3 Kings 7:26.
505 Cf. 3 Kings 7:23.
506 Cf. 3 Kings 7:25.

*east southward,*[507] because when the grace of the New Testament breathed forth, it was given by *the Orient from on high, (who) has visited us.*[508] The number thirty is found in countless passages of holy Scripture, and it is appropriate to the mysteries of Christ and the Church. For Joseph, who protected the Egyptians from famine for eighty years in prefiguration of the resurrection and of the New Testament,[509] after the squalor of prison had been washed away received the governorship of the kingdom at the age of thirty. /87/ David began his reign at the same age and completed it at the age of seventy,[510] that is, at an age deserving of eternal rest. And Ezekiel merited the gift of prophecy at the age of thirty when the heavens opened to him.[511] And because misfortunes ought to be borne in patience by faith, and benefits ought to be hoped for in an uplifting way, both the height of the ark[512] and of the temple,[513] and the length of the tabernacle,[514] measure thirty cubits.

*Being as was supposed,* Luke says, *the son of Joseph.* He employed this expression on account of those who imagined that Jesus was begotten by Joseph as other men are engendered. If it troubles anyone that since Mary bore Christ from the Holy Spirit, and Joseph is called his father not truly but apparently, why it is not the genealogy of Mary that was set out rather than that of Joseph, which seemed not to pertain to Jesus at all, he should know *first, that it is not customary in the Scriptures for the line of women to be woven into the genealogies; next that Joseph and Mary came from the same tribe: hence he was constrained to take her by law as a kinswoman; and that they are taxed together in Bethlehem, clearly as having been born from one lineage,*[515] and therefore by the genealogy of Joseph the descent of Mary may also be shown. Of course, Luke, when he is about to state the

---

507 3 Kings 7:39.
508 Luke 1:78.
509 Eight is a mystical number for resurrection and the New Testament (see Introduction). It is not explicitly stated in Genesis that Joseph ruled Egypt under the Pharaoh for eighty ($8 \times 10$) years; Bede derives this number from Joseph's age (thirty) when he received the governorship (Gen. 41:46) and his age (110) at death (Gen. 50:22) ($110 - 30 = 80$).
510 Cf. 1 Sam. 5:4. Again, Bede derives the number seventy from the explicit statements (2 Sam. 5:4 & 3 Kings 2:11) that David was thirty when he became king, and that he reigned for forty years.
511 Ezek. 1:1.
512 Cf. Gen. 6:15.
513 Cf. 3 Kings 6:2.
514 Cf. Exod. 26:8.
515 Jerome, *Commentarii in Matheum* 1 (CCSL 77:10.67–71).

genealogy of Christ, very beautifully put the Father himself first, who says: *You are my beloved Son*,[516] to confirm by divine testimony that he is the same true Son of God, who is the true son of man by the lineage of human descent.

[Luke 3:23b–24] **Who was of Heli, who was of Matthat, who was of Levi**, and so forth. It is troublesome, to be sure, how Joseph could have had two fathers each coming from a different ancestral lineage, one of which Luke records, the other, Matthew. For Matthew says: *And Matthan begot Jacob. And Jacob begot Joseph the husband of Mary.*[517]

But *Africanus, writing of the harmony of the Gospels*, lucidly solves the difficulty of this question.[518] *Matthan*, he says, *and* Matthat *begat separate sons at different times from one and the same wife named Estha, because Matthan, who descended from Solomon, had first taken her to wife, and died, leaving one son named Jacob. After his death, because the Law does not forbid a widow from marrying another husband*, Matthat, *who traces his descent through Nathan, since he was from the same tribe but not from the same family, married Matthan's widow, from whom he also got a son named Heli. Because of this Jacob and Heli are brothers born of the same mother from a different paternal descent. One of them, that is, Jacob, taking the wife of his brother Heli (who died childless)* /88/ *according to the mandate of the law, begot Joseph, his son by the nature of his seed, on account of which it is also written: 'and Jacob begot Joseph'. But according to the mandate of the Law Heli had the son of Jacob, because Jacob being his brother, had taken his wife to bring forth progeny for his brother.*[519] *And by this is found a valid and complete genealogy, both that which Matthew reckons up, saying: 'And Jacob begot Joseph', and the one that Luke devises with appropriate circumspection, saying: '(Who) was supposed (to be) the son of Joseph, who was of Heli'. And Joseph himself with the same suggestive distinction was supposed the*

---

516 Luke 3:22.
517 Matt. 1:15–16; for this paragraph, cf. Jerome, *Commentarii in Matheum* 1 (CCSL 77:9.46–56).
518 Eusebius, *Hist. eccl.* 1.7.1 (GCS 9.1:55.1–2). Jerome (see note above) says that Julius Africanus and Eusebius dealt with this difficulty. The quotation that follows, which Bede attributes to Africanus, is from Rufinus' translation of Eusebius' *Historia ecclesiastica*, which in turn drew from Africanus' *Chronographies*. But Africanus also wrote a letter to Aristidis, harmonizing the genealogies of Matthew and Luke, which Bede seems to know of.
519 Bede's point is that Joseph is as much the son of Heli as of Jacob and so both the evangelists are correct.

son of Heli, who was of Matthat, *because the observant evangelist, by this information devised this succession according to the Law, which fits with a certain kind of adoption with regard to the deceased, rather than with the sufficiently obvious truth of generation, in order to be sure in successions of this kind not to declare that Joseph had begot someone or other. Because of this, by means of a fitting distinction not in order of descent, but in ascending order, he reaches back to Adam and to God himself. And these things were not invented by us or related without any authorities, but they were handed down by our Saviour's kinsmen according to the flesh, either from eagerness to depict so great a progeny or to teach what really happened.*[520] Africanus reveals these things with these very lists, except that for 'Matthat' he put 'Melchi', because possibly either his text had it so, or in the history in which he had learned these things he found that this same Matthat had a second name. Therefore, since Matthew undertook to handle the royal, and Luke, the priestly personage of the Lord – which is also why in the chariot of the cherubim, the lion, the strongest of the beasts, signifies the former, the calf of the priests, namely the sacrificial victim, signifies the latter[521] – each of the two kept to the same intention of their work in constructing the genealogy of the Saviour as well. For *it has been astutely noticed that Matthew, who had undertaken to present Christ as a royal personage, named forty men, apart from Christ himself, in the list of the generations. This number signifies that time when in this age and upon this earth we must be ruled by Christ in accordance with the stern discipline by which God, as it is written, 'scourges every son whom he receives'.*[522] The generations do not number forty-two, which is the product of three times fourteen,[523] but forty-one, because the one of Jechoniah is counted twice, if we add Christ himself, who presides as a king over our temporal and earthly life which must be governed by him, as if by the number forty. For /89/ *since this number symbolizes this toilsome time when we contend against the devil under the discipline of Christ the King, it likewise reveals that it consecrated a fast of forty days, that is, a humbling of the soul. And what else is foreshadowed by both the Law*

---

520 Eusebius, *Hist. eccl.* 1.7.7–11 (GCS 9.1:57.17–59.19).
521 For the chariot of the cherubim, cf. Ezek. 1:5–21; 10:1–22. For Bede's identification of the Matthew with the lion, see Introduction, 7–8, 56.
522 Augustine, *De consensu euang.* 2.4 (CSEL 43:88.24–89.6); Hebr. 12:6.
523 Cf. Matt. 1:17. Bede notices that Matthew apparently counted Jechoniah both as the last of the generations before the transmigration and the first of those following the transmigration.

*and the Prophets through Moses and Elijah, who fasted for forty days,*[524] *and by the Gospel through the fasting of the Lord himself, who was also tempted by the devil for forty days,*[525] *than our temptation throughout the entire duration of this world, which he deigned to assume in his flesh from our mortality?* Therefore, *this number signifies this life in time and on earth, both because the annual seasons revolve in fourfold succession, and because the world itself is marked off in four quarters. Moreover, forty consists of four tens, and ten itself is the sum of the successive numbers from one to four.*[526]

Accordingly, *because Matthew wished to signify* Christ *descending to share mortality with us, he therefore recorded at the beginning of his Gospel the generations from Abraham to Joseph right down to the birth of Christ himself in order of descent. But Luke expounds the generations of Christ not at the beginning* of his Gospel, *but after Christ's baptism, and not by descent but by ascent, as it were affirming more completely the role of the priest in the expiation of sins when the voice from heaven proclaimed him, and where John himself offered testimony, saying: 'Behold him who takes away the sins of the world'.*[527] *By ascending, he not only went back to Abraham, but also reached back to God, to whom we are reconciled after we are cleansed and have made atonement. And Luke rightly accepted the lineage through adoption, because by adoption we are made the sons of God by belief in the Son of God. Indeed, by generation in the flesh the Son of God became more precisely 'the son of man'. But Luke sufficiently demonstrated that he did not say that Joseph was the son of Heli because he was begotten by him, but because he had been adopted by him, since he also called Adam himself the son of God, although he was made by God, but by grace, which he later lost by sinning, he was established like a son in paradise.*[528]

*Thus, the acceptance of our sins by Christ the Lord is signified by the genealogy in Matthew, but the absolution of our sins by Christ our Lord is signified by the genealogy in Luke. Therefore, the former expounds them in order of descent; the latter in ascending order. For when the Apostle says: 'God sent his own Son in the likeness of sinful flesh', that is the acceptance*

---

524 Cf. Exod. 24:18; Deut. 9:9 (Moses); 3 Kings 19:4–8 (Elijah).
525 Cf. Matt. 4:1–2; Luke 4:1–2.
526 Augustine, *De consensu euang.* 2.4 (CSEL 43:90.1–10; 90.17–91.2).
527 John 1:29.
528 Augustine, *De consensu euang.* 2.4 (CSEL 43:92.11–93.8).

*of sins; but when he adds: 'in order to condemn sin in the flesh',*[529] *that is the absolution of sins. Accordingly, Matthew descends from David himself through Solomon, with whose mother David sinned.*[530] *But Luke ascends to the same David through Nathan,*[531] /90/ *since God absolved David's sin through the prophet of the same name.*[532]

[Luke 3:31–32] **Who was**, he says, **of Nathan, who was of David, who was of Jesse, ...** *This number which Luke follows most certainly also signifies the absolution of sins,*[533] which will be discussed later. *Do not be astonished if Luke set down more generations from David to Christ, and Matthew fewer – that is, the former, forty-three; the latter, twenty-eight – since you acknowledge that the line of descent has been established through different persons. For it can happen that some men led a very long life, while men of the other line of descent died at an early age, since we see that many old men live with their grandchildren, while other men die after begetting children.*[534]

[Luke 3:35–36] **Who was of Shelah, who was of Cainan, who was of Arphaxad, ...** The name and generation of Cainan according to the Hebrew truth[535] is found neither in Genesis, nor in Chronicles; but Arphaxad is said to have begotten a son Shelah, or Sale, with no one in between. For, accordingly, you have: *And Arphaxad lived thirty-five years, and begot Sale.*[536] And likewise in Chronicles: *And Arphaxad begot Sale, and Sale begot Heber.*[537] You should know, therefore, that the blessed Luke took this genealogy from the edition of the Seventy Interpreters,[538] where it is written that Arphaxad at the age of 135 years begot Cainan, and Cainan himself, when he was 130 years of age, begot Shelah. But which of these is closer to the truth, or whether both can be true, God alone knows. I am simply warning the reader that there is such a great discrepancy in the sequence of time between the two books that from the Flood to the birth of Abraham, 292

---

529 Rom. 8:3.
530 Cf. Matt. 1:6 (David seduced Bathsheba the wife of Uriah, and after Solomon was conceived had Uriah killed).
531 Cf. Luke 3:31; and for the prophet Nathan, 2 Sam. 12:1–13.
532 Augustine, *De consensu euang.* 2.4 (CSEL 43:93.9–19).
533 Augustine, *De consensu euang.* 2.4 (CSEL 43:93.20–21).
534 Ambrose, *Expos. Lucam* 3.14 (CCSL 14:83.227–33).
535 'Hebrew truth' refers to the Jewish Bible as translated by Jerome (the Vulgate).
536 Gen. 11:12.
537 1 Chron. 1:18.
538 I.e., the Septuagint.

years are found to have been reported in the Hebrew Truth, but 1077 years in the translation of the Seventy Interpreters. And now certain chronographers, stepping in as intermediaries, by removing the generation of Cainan alone, and without emending the other years according to the Hebraic exemplar, report this same age as consisting of 942 years.[539]

[Luke 3:37] **Who was of Methuselah, who was of Enoch, ...** The order of generations, ascending from the baptism of the Son of God to God the Father, beautifully places in the seventieth position Enoch, who did not die, but was translated into paradise.[540] This signifies that those who are reborn in the meantime from water and the Holy Spirit in the grace of the sons of adoption, after /91/ the cleansing of the body are going to be taken into eternal rest (indeed the number seventy on account of the seventh Sabbath is very aptly suited for signifying the rest of those who, by the saving grace of Christ, have fulfilled the Ten Commandments of the Law). It is also to show that they are to be brought together at the time of their resurrection to contemplate the wisdom of the immutable God forever.

[Luke 3:38b] **Who was of Seth, who was of Adam, who was of God.** *Since no iniquity of Christ – for he had none – was united with the iniquities of men which he took upon himself in his flesh, the number of generations in Matthew, leaving aside Christ, is forty. But since the number of his justice and of the Father joins us when we have been purified and cleansed of every sin, so that what the Apostle says may happen: 'But he who is joined to the Lord is one spirit',[541] therefore in that number which is in Luke, both Christ himself, from whom the enumeration begins, and God, to whom it reaches, are counted, and make up the number seventy-seven, by which is signified surely the remission and absolution of all sins.*[542]

*The Lord also referred to this number, when Peter asked him about forgiving the sins of his brother. For Jesus says he should be forgiven not only seven times, but seventy times seven times.[543] Hence he is rightly believed by referring to this number to have ordered that all sins be forgiven.*[544]

---

539 See Introduction, 8–10. Eusebius is the chronographer whom Bede is referring to. See Bede, *De temporibus* 18; Kendall and Wallis, trans., *On Times*, 119; Bede, *Epistola ad Pleguinam* 5–6 (Wallis, *The Reckoning of Time*, 407–08); and *DTR* 66, *sub anno* 1993 (Wallis, *The Reckoning of Time*, 163).
540 Cf. Gen. 5:24; Ecclus. 45:16; Hebr. 11:5.
541 1 Cor. 6:17.
542 Augustine, *De consensu euang.* 2.4 (CSEL 43:93.21–94.7).
543 Cf. Matt. 18:21–22.
544 Augustine, *Quaestiones euang.* 2.6.1 (CCSL 44B:48.4–8).

*Not in vain did the Lord come in the seventy-seventh generation to absolve all sins, because something lies hidden in that number that signifies all sinners. And this should be examined carefully in the numbers eleven and seven: these numbers multiplied together make this number. For eleven times seven or seven times eleven make seventy-seven. And eleven signifies the transgression*[545] *of ten. But if the perfection of blessedness is signified by ten [denarius] (for thus all those collected together in the vineyard are remunerated by a denarius,*[546] *which happens when the sevenfold creature is joined to the Trinity of the Creator), it is clear that the transgression of ten signifies the sin of desiring out of pride to have something more, and of losing innocence and perfection.*[547] *This number eleven is reckoned seven times, in order that that transgression caused by human impulse may be signified. For by the number three the incorporeal part of man is signified. Hence it is that we are commanded to love God with our whole heart, our whole soul, and our whole mind.*[548] *But the body is signified by the number four, for the body's nature is in many respects fourfold. Therefore man, consisting of body and soul joined together, is appropriately* /92/ *signified by the number seven. But impulse is not expressed in numbers when we say one, two, three, four, et cetera, but when we say once, twice, thrice, four times. Therefore, as I have said, not by seven and eleven, but by seven times eleven is transgression signified which is caused by the impulse of the sinner, that is, of one transgressing the stability of his perfection by the passionate desire of having something more.*[549]

*Appropriately*, therefore, *when eleven is added to itself seven times to make the number seventy-seven, it amounts to all sins. In this number likewise occurs the full remission of sins, with the flesh of our Priest atoning for us, from whom this number now begins, and with God restoring us, to whom this number now reaches,*[550] *through the Holy Spirit who appeared*

---

545 Two senses of 'transgressio': an untranslatable bit of meaningful wordplay. See Introduction, 31.
546 Cf. Matt. 20:9.
547 In the parable of the labourers in the vineyard (Matt. 20:1–16), the wage for a day's work is set at a denarius (originally a silver coin equivalent to ten *asses*), but when the labourers who worked all day see that the lord has paid those who worked only an hour the full day's wage, they demand more. This is 'the transgression of ten'.
548 Cf. Matt. 22:37; Mark 12:30; Luke 10:27.
549 Augustine, *Quaestiones euang.* 2.6.2 (CCSL 44B:48.23–47).
550 'This number' again refers to the seventy-seven generations in Luke's account, from Christ ('our Priest') back to God.

in the likeness of a dove in this baptism,[551] where this number is called to mind.[552]

If anyone wishes to dispute the superior truth of the aforesaid exposition by saying that Matthew set down not forty-one, but forty-two generations, because according to the authority of Chronicles Jechoniah ought to be counted as two persons,[553] that is to say, father and son,[554] let him understand that the same number forty-two nevertheless makes known the present time of the Church, during which with the help of the Lord it labours in hope of the Sabbath to come. For seven times six makes forty-two. And there is scarcely anyone who doubts that six indeed is pertinent to the signification of labours, but seven, of rest. Hence it is well that the people who are saved from the land of Egypt indeed tarry forty years in the desert,[555] but because they are zealously exercised by the hope of entering into eternal rest, they set up seven times six, that is, forty-two camps for the very difficult journey.[556] At the last of these when they take Jesus[557] as their leader,[558] with the Jordan opened up and their enemies defeated, they immediately enter the dwelling-place once promised them.[559] So likewise the Lord Jesus, coming in the flesh in the forty-second generation[560] after the world shook off the darkness of primitive blindness when Abraham became a believer, opens the gates of heaven for us by the bath of baptism. And we ourselves after we have run the course of virtue, hoping in that *which we do not see, wait in patience*[561] under the sacrament of the same number, as was said, so that led across the dry bed of the river Jordan by Christ our leader, we

---

551 I.e., the baptism of Jesus. Cf. Luke 3:22.
552 Augustine, *De consensu euang.* 2.4.12 (CSEL 43:94.19–25).
553 Cf. 1 Chron. 3:15–16.
554 Cf. Jerome, *Commentarii in Matheum* 1 (CCSL 77:39–42). Jerome would have us understand that the Jechoniah in Matt. 1:11 = the Jehoiakim in 1 Chron. 3:15–16, who was in turn the father of the Jechoniah in Matt. 1:12.
555 Cf. Num. 14:33.
556 These are the 'resting places' [*mansiones*] of the Hebrews in the Desert. Bede wrote a treatise for Acca on this subject, *De mansionibus filiorum Israel* (trans. Holder, *On the Resting-Places of the Children of Israel*). However, the allegory of the number forty-two is not fully developed there.
557 I.e., Joshua: Bede substitutes the Greek form of the name to enhance the mystical sense he is developing.
558 Cf. Deut. 34:9.
559 Cf. Jos. 3:13–14.
560 Cf. Matt. 1:17.
561 Rom. 8:25.

will joyfully reach the promised kingdom of the heavenly fatherland. That he was the one who was going to atone for the filth of the whole Church is revealed in that very baptism to which he submitted at the age of thirty by the mystical affiliation of the same numbers, because, of course, thirty reckoned *by its aliquot parts* produces twelve *more*,[562] which is /93/ the number of the patriarchs and the apostles, and makes forty-two. For the thirtieth part of thirty is one, the fifteenth part is two, the tenth part is three, the sixth part is five, the fifth part is six, the third part is ten, and the half part is fifteen, which taken together amount to forty-two.[563] By this, as I have said, it is mystically signified that the whole perfection of the Church exists in the faith and grace of Christ which was first recognized by the patriarchs, and was proclaimed more widely by the voice of the apostles, and that there is *no other name under heaven by which we must be saved*,[564] even as in forty-two there is no small part which is not contained in the aliquot parts of the number thirty. Therefore the number thirty completely fills the number forty-two with its parts, because the Lord both protects the Church now labouring in time by the sacraments of his baptism, and with its labours at an end conducts it to eternal rest.

## Chapter 11

**15/2** [Luke 4:1–2] **And Jesus being full of the Holy Spirit returned from the Jordan and was led by the Spirit into the desert for the space of forty days.** Matthew and Mark say that these events took place right after the Lord was baptized. One of them, after having described his baptism, immediately added: *Then Jesus was led by the Spirit into the desert to be tempted by the devil.*[565] The other went on thus: *And immediately the Spirit drove him out into the desert. And he was in the desert forty days and forty nights, and was tempted by Satan.*[566] But lest doubt should enter anyone's mind as to what spirit he was led or driven into the desert by, Luke expressly set down first that *Jesus being full of the Holy Spirit returned from the Jordan*, and then concluded: *and was led by*

---

562 Augustine, *De diuersis quaestionibus* 81.1 (PL 40:96).
563 That is, the sum of the aliquot parts of 30 – 1, 2, 3, 5, 6, 10, and 15 – is 42.
564 Acts 4:12.
565 Matt. 4:1.
566 Mark 1:12–13.

the Spirit into the desert. He did this in order that it not be thought that an impure spirit had any power over him, who, *being full of the Holy Spirit, willed where he would go, and did what he willed.*[567] For also below where he is plainly asserted to have been taken up or set down by the devil,[568] it is not his weakness which is made known, but the pride of the enemy, who imagines that the will of the Saviour is necessity. Therefore, Jesus is not led into the desert by the power of the evil spirit, but by the will of his good spirit he enters, certain of victory, the place of contest where he overthrows his adversary. Here Luke likewise points out the rule of right living, namely that, after the remission of sins has been received in baptism, and the grace of the Holy Spirit, we should learn to gird ourselves more tightly against new snares of the old enemy, to forsake the world in our mind, and to hunger for the joys of eternal life alone like the manna of the desert.

16/5 [Luke 4:2b] **And he ate nothing in those days, and when they were ended, he was hungry.** *Forty days of fasting has authority both from* /94/ *the books of the Old Testament from the fasting of Moses and of Elijah,*[569] *and from the Gospel, because the Lord fasted for the same number of days, showing that the Gospel does not dissent from the Law and the Prophets. The Law is understood in the person of Moses and the Prophets in the person of Elijah, between whom Christ appeared in glory on the mountain,*[570] *so that what the Apostle says of him might be more evident: 'having testimony by the Law and the Prophets'.*[571] *In which part of the year, therefore, would the observation of forty days of fasting be more fittingly constituted, other than that adjoining and bordering on the Lord's passion? Because in it is signified this wearisome life, for which restraint is needed, in order that there may be abstaining from the love of this world.*[572]

In another interpretation: *The Lord fasted before his death when he was tempted, being then without food. But he ate and drank when he was glorified after his resurrection, now not being without food.*[573] *In the former he displayed our suffering in himself; but in the latter, his consolation in regard to us, delimiting each period by forty days. By this*

---

567 Cf. Gregory, *Hom. in Euang.* 1.16.1 (CCSL 141:110).
568 Cf. Luke 4:5 & 9.
569 Cf. Exod. 34:28 (Moses) and 3 Kings 19:8 (Elijah).
570 Cf. Matt. 17:2–3.
571 Rom. 3:21.
572 Augustine, *Epistolae* 55.15.28 (CSEL 34:201.4–8).
573 Cf. Acts 1:3–4.

BOOK ONE                                    213

*number forty, he seems to signify the journey of this age by those who are called through grace to him who came not 'to destroy the law, but to fulfil'.*[574] *For the Ten Commandments of the Law have already been spread throughout the world, and ten quadrupled makes forty, since 'those who have been redeemed by the Lord, he gathered them out of the countries, from the east and the west and the north and the sea'.*[575] *Accordingly, he fasted for forty days before the death of the flesh, as if he were crying out: 'Refrain from the desires of this world';*[576] *but eating and drinking for forty days after the resurrection of the flesh, as if he were crying out: 'Behold I am with you, even to the consummation of the world'.*[577] *In the tribulation of the struggle there is fasting, because he who is in the contest abstains from everything.*[578] *But there is food in the hope of peace, which will not be achieved except when our body, whose redemption we expect, has put on immortality,*[579] *because we do not yet glory in attainment, but we are already nourished on hope. The Apostle showed that we do both together, saying: 'Rejoicing in hope, patient in tribulation',*[580] *as if the former were food, the latter fasting. For when we take the way of the Lord, we at the same time fast from the vanity of the present world, and refresh ourselves with the promise of the world to come, not setting our heart here, but nourishing our heart upwards to that place.*[581]

That the Lord was hungry at the end of his period of fasting, although the like was not written about the fasting of Moses or Elijah, happened so that the fearful enemy should not cease from tempting him, whom he saw not only /95/ heralded with so many celestial signs but also the equal of the most outstanding men in abstinence. God the humble man hungered, lest God the sublime man become known to the enemy.[582]

[Luke 4:3] **And the devil said to him: If you are the Son of God, say to this stone that it be made bread.** *The old enemy recognized that the Redeemer of the human race, his conqueror, had come into the world.*

574  Matt. 5:17.
575  Ps. 106:2–3 (107:2–3) (not *iuxta LXX*; English translations [D/R, KJV, NRSV] correct 'sea' to 'south').
576  Cf. 1 Pet. 2:11.
577  Matt. 28:20.
578  Cf. 1 Cor. 9:25.
579  1 Cor. 15:54.
580  Rom. 12:12.
581  Augustine, *Sermones* 99.4 (*Noua Patrum biblioteca* 1.206).
582  Cf. Ambrose, *Expos. Lucam* 4.16 (CCSL 14:112.211–20).

214    BEDE: COMMENTARY ON THE GOSPEL OF LUKE

*Hence, he also said through the man who was possessed: 'What have we to do with you, Son of God? Are you come hither to torment us before the time?'*[583] *Nevertheless, when he earlier discerned that this Man was capable of suffering, when he saw that he was able to endure the mortal affairs of humanity, all that he surmised about his divinity he began to doubt in the haughtiness of his pride. Comprehending nothing except what is proud, when he observes that this Man is humble, he doubted that he was God. And hence he turns to the tactics of temptation.*[584]

But unlike us, who are chaste and yet *frequently shaken by an erupting temptation, the spirit of our Redeemer is not disturbed by the constraint of temptation. For although our enemy was permitted to take him up into a high mountain, although he asserted that he would give him the kingdoms of the world, although he showed him the stones that were to be turned as it were into bread, nevertheless he could not shake the mind of the mediator of God and men with temptation. For he deigned to bear all these things externally, in such a way that his mind adhering inwardly to his divinity nevertheless remained unshaken. Although he is said to have groaned in the spirit when he was troubled,*[585] *he arranged matters divinely insofar as he was troubled in accordance with his human nature.*[586]

[Luke 4:4] **And Jesus answered him: It is written that Man lives not by bread alone, but by every word of God.** *The Lord answered thus because he intended to conquer by humility, not by power. At the same time, note that the devil would not have had an opportunity for temptation unless the Lord had begun to fast in accordance with this precept: 'Son, when you come to the service of God, prepare your soul for temptation'.*[587] *But the Saviour's very response indicates that it was a man who was tempted: 'Man lives not by bread alone, but by every word of God'. Therefore, if anyone is not fed by the word of God, that person is not alive.*[588]

In another interpretation: *Our enemy, the more he sees us rebel against him while still in the midst this life, the more he strives to overcome us. For he does not trouble to strike those whom he thinks he possesses by*

583  Matt. 8:29.
584  Gregory, *Moralia* 2.24 (CCSL 143:86.15–24).
585  Cf. John 11:33.
586  Gregory, *Moralia* 3.16 (CCSL 143:134.40–50).
587  Ecclus. 2:1.
588  Jerome, *Commentarii in Matheum* 1 (CCSL 77:20.325–33).

*secure right. But he is incited the more violently against us, because he is expelled from our heart, as if from a habitation which is his by right. The Lord signified this in himself in accordance with a certain dispensation, for he did not allow the devil to tempt him except after his baptism*[589] *to give us a sign of our future way of life,* /96/ *namely that after his followers made progress towards God, they would then be subjected to more painful assaults of temptation.*[590]

[Luke 4:5] **And the devil led him, and showed him all the kingdoms of the world in a moment of time.** *When it is reported that God the man was led by the devil, the mind recoils, and human ears are terrified to hear this. Nevertheless, we recognize that these things are not incredible in his case, if we think about him and about other facts. Certainly, the devil is the chief of all enemies, and the followers of this chief are all enemies. What wonder, therefore, if he allowed himself to be led by him onto a mountain, who even permitted himself to be crucified by the Devil's followers? It is not, therefore, unworthy of our Redeemer that he who had come to be killed desired to be tempted. Indeed, it was right that he should conquer our temptations by his temptations in this way, just as he had come to overcome our death by his death.*[591]

*It is well that worldly and temporal things are shown in a moment of time. It is not swiftness of sight that is indicated so much as the fragility of fleeting power. All these things perish in a moment, and often worldly honour has gone before it arrived. What worldly thing can be lasting, when the world itself is not lasting?*[592]

[Luke 4:6–7] **And he said to him: To you I will give all this power, and the glory of them, for to me they are delivered, and to whom I will, I give them. If therefore, prostrating yourself, you will adore before me, all will be yours.** *Arrogant and proud, he also says this in order to boast, for the devil does not have power over the whole world so that he can give all kingdoms, since we know that many holy men have been made kings by God. 'If', he says, 'prostrating yourself, you will adore before me'. Therefore, whoever is going to adore the devil has already fallen.*[593]

---

589 Cf. Matt. 3:13–4:1.
590 Gregory, *Moralia* 24.11 (CCSL 143B:1207.65–75).
591 Gregory, *Hom. in Euang.* 1.16.1 (CCSL 141:110.7–19).
592 Ambrose, *Expos. Lucam* 4.28 (CCSL 14:115.327–32).
593 Jerome, *Commentarii in Matheum* 1 (CCSL 77:22.373–77).

[Luke 4:8] **And Jesus answering said to him: It is written: You shall adore the Lord your God, and you shall serve only him.**[594] *The devil says: 'If, prostrating yourself, you will adore me': he hears that, on the contrary, he himself ought rather to adore him, his Lord and God.*[595]

Perhaps someone will ask how the fact that here the commandment is given to serve only the Lord accords with the word of the Apostle who says: *But by love serve one another.*[596] But a satisfactory explanation is provided by its origin in that Greek language from which Scripture is translated, in which service is usually expressed in two ways and with different meanings. For it is called *latria* and also *dulia*. But *dulia* means 'service in general', that is, whether it is provided to God or to man or to anything in the natural world. From it comes also the word for slave in Greek, that is, *dulos*. However, *latria* is the word for that service which is owed solely to the worship of the Divine, and which is not to be shared with any /97/ creature. Hence those who offer to idols vows, prayers, and sacrifices, which ought to have been owed to the one God, are also called 'idolaters'. Therefore we are commanded *by love to serve one another*, which is in Greek *douleuein*. We are commanded to serve the one God, which is in Greek *latreuein*. Hence it is said: *and you shall serve only him*, which is in Greek *latreuseis*. And again: *For we are the circumcision, serving the spirit of God*,[597] which is in Greek *latreuontes*.[598]

[Luke 4:9] **And he brought him to Jerusalem, and set him on a pinnacle of the temple,** *in order that he may tempt him, whom* he was unable to overcome by gluttony and avarice, *with vainglory*, or even to see if perchance he may be able to cast him down by merely boasting of his victory.[599]

[Luke 4:9b] **And he said to him: If you are the Son of God, cast yourself down from here.** *The devil does this in all the temptations to try to find out whether he is the Son of God, but the Lord tempers his response in order to leave him in doubt. 'Cast yourself down'. These are the words of the devil who always desires everyone to fall down: 'Cast yourself', he says; he can urge him, but he cannot cast him down.*[600]

---

594 Cf. Deut. 6:13 & 10:20.
595 Jerome, *Commentarii in Matheum* 1 (CCSL 77:22.386–89).
596 Gal. 5:13.
597 Phil. 3:3.
598 Much of this paragraph is closely adapted from Augustine, *De trinitate* 1.6.13 (CCSL 50:42.107–31).
599 Jerome, *Commentarii in Matheum* 1 (CCSL 77:21.340–41).
600 Jerome, *Commentarii in Matheum* 1 (CCSL 77:21.342–48).

BOOK ONE                                    217

[Luke 4:10–11] **For it is written, that he has given his angels charge over you, to keep you. And that in their hands they will bear you up, lest perhaps you dash your foot against a stone.** *We read this in the ninetieth Psalm,*[601] *but there the prophecy is not about Christ, but about a holy man. The devil, therefore, interprets the Scriptures badly. Indeed, if he knew that it was really written about the Saviour, he ought to have said what follows in the same Psalm and which is directed against himself: 'You will walk upon the asp and the basilisk, and you will trample underfoot the lion and the dragon.'*[602] *He speaks of the help of the angels as if to one who is weak; like an equivocator, he is silent about the fact that he is trampled under.*[603]

[Luke 4:12] **And Jesus answering, said to him: It is said: You shall not tempt the Lord your God.** *He dashes to pieces the false arrows of the devil with the true shield of the Scriptures. And it should be noted that he offered only the summary testimony from Deuteronomy*[604] *to show the mysteries of the Second Law.*[605]

*You shall not tempt,* he says, *the Lord your God. For it was suggested as if to a man, that by some sign he should probe how great he himself was before the face of God, that is, how much power he had. When this is done, it is done wickedly. When someone knows what he should do, it is sound teaching not to tempt the Lord God. For even the Saviour himself was not able to protect his disciples, to whom he nevertheless says: 'If they persecute you in one city, flee into another.'*[606] *He offered an earlier example of this matter: he had the power of laying down his* /98/ *life, and he would not lay it down except when he wanted to,*[607] *but as a child he fled into Egypt, carried by his parents.*[608] *And he went up to Jerusalem on the festival day not openly, but secretly,*[609] *although he spoke openly at another time to the Jews who were angry and listened with a very hostile attitude, but were unable to put their hands on him, 'because his*

---

601  Ps. 90:11–12 (91:11–12).
602  Ps. 90:13 (91:13).
603  Jerome, *Commentarii in Matheum* 1 (CCSL 77:21.351–58).
604  Deut. 6:16.
605  Jerome, *Commentarii in Matheum* 1 (CCSL 77:21.360–63). Deuteronomy means 'second law'.
606  Matt. 10:23.
607  Cf. John 10:17–18.
608  Cf. Matt. 2:13–14.
609  Cf. John 7:10.

*hour had not yet come'.*⁶¹⁰ *Therefore by openly teaching and arguing, and nevertheless by not allowing the rage of his enemies to affect him in any way, he demonstrated the power of God. But likewise, by fleeing and hiding he taught human weakness not to dare tempt God when considering what to do, in order to escape what one ought to be on guard against.*⁶¹¹

[Luke 4:13] **And all the temptation being ended, the devil receded from him for a time.** *You see that the devil himself is not constant in his purpose, that he is wont to yield to true virtue. Although he does not cease to bear malice, nevertheless he fears to press forward, because quite often he flees back to escape being conquered. And so, after hearing the name of God, he 'receded', it says, 'for a time'. For afterwards he came not to tempt, but to fight openly.*⁶¹²

*After he assails our mind with temptation, the old enemy often recedes from that struggle of his for a time, not to put an end to his ingrained malice, but so that by suddenly returning he can burst more unexpectedly upon the hearts which he renders careless by quiet.*⁶¹³ It should be observed that Luke says that all temptation ended after the exposure of only three deceptions of the tempter, because, of course, they include the beginnings and sources of all these vices, as John attests, who says that *all that is in the world is the concupiscence of the flesh, and the concupiscence of the eyes, and the pride of life.*⁶¹⁴ And in the gospel parable the reprobates are excluded from the feast of eternal life by only three matters of business. *The first,* it states, *said: I have bought a farm, and I must needs go out and see it. And another said: I have bought five yokes of oxen, and I am going to examine them. And another said: I have married a wife, and therefore I cannot come.*⁶¹⁵ The passionate longing for a wife, just like gluttony, applies to the concupiscence of the flesh. The buying of a farm, which is not free of avarice, regards the pride of life. The examination of five yokes of oxen, that is, curiosity about corporeal matters, which is vainglory, is related to the concupiscence of the eyes. For curiosity chiefly prevails through the eyes. And indeed, the Lord being as it were stronger is tempted by these things directly. But when we have received baptism through the grace of

---

610 John 7:30.
611 Augustine, *Contra Faustum* 22.36–37 (CSEL 25/1:629.27–630.16).
612 Ambrose, *Expos. Lucam* 4.36 (CCSL 14:119.441–46).
613 Gregory, *Moralia* 3.28 (CCSL 143:150.71–75).
614 1 John 2:16.
615 Luke 14:18–20.

the Spirit, and seek out the desert of virtues when we undertake the Lenten fast, that is, when we determine to refrain from worldly attractions for the whole time of our life, /99/ we are either assaulted by hidden snares or are attacked at times by something more obvious. When anyone says soothingly: 'You are a strong man, eat and drink, and stay as you are', you should be alert lest you are unaware of the old serpent, and he give you poisons to drink, and this should be said: *Man lives not by bread alone, but by every word of God.*[616] Truly, many who have overcome the concupiscence of the flesh are immediately attacked by avarice, and from time to time are even overcome, so that they do not fear to worship the devil in exchange for favours rendered. While many praise the continence of these people, and even greater persons respect it, and pay tribute to it, it happens that the vanquishers of sensual pleasures are conquered by the love of money, and as the madness increases over time, they not only curse and censure the rich, whom they realize by their open crimes are filled with an evil spirit, but also with a bow admire and defend them.

Hence the Apostle says that *avarice* is the service *of idols.*[617] And if they conquer it by following the example of the Saviour, namely by worshipping the Lord their God, and by serving him only for the sake of eternal joys, the third plague of vainglory will come, which may inflate those who overcame the preceding vices with an exaggerated view of their strength so that they assume that, having been placed at the summit of the virtues, they cannot now fall. For someone to glory in his own merits is to tempt God with the eyes of curiosity, in contrast to what he himself says to strengthen the faith of his disciples: *When you have done all these things that are commanded you, say: We are unprofitable slaves; we have done that which we ought to do.*[618] Elsewhere, when he commanded that we not do our justice in the presence of men, in defining the same he added only fasting, almsgiving, and praying, evidently opposing the same number of weapons of defence to the triple spear of the enemy, in order that concupiscence of the flesh might be overcome by fasting, avarice by almsgiving, and boasting of merits by prayers.

Let it suffice to have said these things in one book about the beginnings of the evangelical dispensation. Let us rather by beginning another book contemplate the deeds and words of the Saviour that follow, taking counsel

---

616 Luke 4:4.
617 Col. 3:5.
618 Luke 17:10.

not only for our peace, but also for the benefit of readers. *For the reader's attention,* as Augustine says, *is refreshed I know not how by the ending of a book this way, just as the fatigue of the traveller is by an inn.*[619]

Here ends Book One of the Commentary on Luke. /**100**/

---

[619] Augustine, *Contra aduers.* 1.24.53 (CCSL 49:86.43–44).

# II

[Luke 4:14–7:35]

Here begins Book Two.

Ecclesiastical history reports that the blessed apostle John preached the gospel without the supporting evidence of any Scripture until nearly the last period of his life. But, it says, when knowledge of the three Gospels reached even him, he is said to have approved the faith and truth of the sayings, but he saw that some things were missing, and especially those things that the Lord had done in the first period of his preaching. For it is true that the preceding three evangelists seem to include only events that took place in the year when John the Baptist was either shut up in prison or punished. Hence you will notice that in the first of the narratives, after Matthew tells of Jesus's forty-day fast, and of his temptation, he immediately continues, saying: *And hearing that John the Baptist was delivered up, he retired from Judea, and came into Galilee.*[1] And Mark similarly says: *After John was delivered up, Jesus came into Galilee.*[2] And Luke likewise, before he begins to relate anything about the deeds of Jesus, says that *Herod added above all the evils which he had done, and shut up John in prison.*[3] Since, I say, these things seemed to have been omitted by them, John the Apostle was asked (it is said) to write down those deeds of the Saviour that the earlier evangelists had passed over before John was placed in custody. Therefore, he says in his Gospel: *Jesus did these things at the beginning of his miracles.*[4] And again in another place he expressly indicates: *For John was not yet cast into prison.*[5] This makes it clear that he is describing those things that were done by Jesus before John was imprisoned.[6]

---

1 Matt. 4:12.
2 Mark 1:14.
3 Luke 3:19–20.
4 John 2:11.
5 John 3:24.
6 Cf. Jerome, *De uiris illustribus* 1.9.2 (ed. Ceresa-Gastaldo, 92).

At the beginning of this, that is, my second book on Luke, I have given advance warning by means of this historical record, in order that readers should not think that what is going to be explained in what follows happened immediately after the fasting of forty days; rather they should understand that the miracles performed by the Lord, whether in Judea or in Galilee, followed sometime later.

## Chapter 12

**17/1** [Luke 4:14–15] **And Jesus entered in the power of the spirit into Galilee, and the fame of him went out through the whole country. And he taught in their synagogues, and was praised highly by all.** He calls the signs of miracles 'the power of the spirit', just as elsewhere the wondering Jews say: *How came this man by his wisdom and power?*[7] – wisdom, of course, referring to his teaching, but power /101/ to his deeds. Both are joined together here, when Jesus is said to have entered in the power of the spirit and to have taught in their synagogues. Hence it is fitting that he is said both to have been praised highly by those who were present and to have been known by reputation to all those who were absent. This could certainly not happen without the supporting evidence of his prior deeds and words. But whoever seeks the time and order of these deeds will find them in the Gospel of John, as was said. Omitting others, let me offer only one testimony from John. *When he had come,* he says, *into Galilee, the Galileans received him, having seen all the things he did in Jerusalem on the festival day.*[8]

It should be noted that Luke sensibly relates that Jesus first showed the power of his spirit, and afterwards furnished the grace of his teaching; that first the fame of his powers went out, and then his teaching was praised highly. This is clearly according to the order that Luke took care to commend briefly in the Acts of the Apostles: *The things which Jesus began to do and to teach.*[9] For he put 'to do' first, and 'to teach' afterwards, lest any teacher venture to order his listeners to do what he himself has not yet accomplished by his own deeds.

**18/10** [Luke 4:16] **And he came to Nazareth, where he was brought up, and he went into the synagogue, according to his custom, on the**

---

7 Matt. 13:54.
8 John 4:45.
9 Acts 1:1.

**Sabbath day.** What is called *synagoga* in Greek is called *congregatio* in Latin, and this is the term the Jews used not only for an assembly of thronging crowds, but also for the sanctuary where they gathered for the purpose of hearing and speaking the word of God. Hence the Lord says to the high-priest Annas: *I have always taught in the synagogue, and in the temple where all the Jews gather.*[10] It is similar to the way we are accustomed to call both sacred buildings and companies of people 'churches [*ecclesiae*] of the faithful'. But there is a difference between 'synagogue', which means 'congregation', and 'church' [*ecclesia*], which means 'convocation', because the people of the Old Testament are called by either word, but the people of the New only by 'church', since, of course, both flocks of animals and inanimate things can be congregated in one place, but only flocks possessing reason can be convoked. Therefore, it seemed to apostolic writers and teachers more correct to say that the people of the new dispensation, possessed as it were of greater merit, were 'convoked' into the unity of faith, rather than 'congregated', that is, to use the word 'church', rather than 'synagogue'. But, in accordance with what the Lord commanded: *Be still and see that I am God,*[11] with the business of the world at rest, the Jews used to flock together on the Sabbath day, in order to settle down for the sake of meditating upon the admonitions of the Law with a quiet heart. The token of that obligatory devotion on that day survives to this day in the Church, which, in memory /**102**/ of the old religion, is accustomed in some places to recite the Song of Deuteronomy,[12] in which is contained the whole form of government of the old people, namely what it deserved when God was offended, and what it merited when God was appeased. Otherwise, it would be absurdly out of order to recite the Song of Moses last, after the songs of the prophets were said on the earlier days of the week. Therefore, Jesus went into the synagogue on the Sabbath day to fulfil the rite of the Mosaic Law by supplementing it with heavenly grace.

[Luke 4:16b–17] **And he rose up to read, and the book of the prophet Isaiah was delivered to him.** It is a sign of the supremely humble dispensation, whereby God came to serve humanity, and not to be served, that he does not scorn even the office of a reader. But by a higher providence Luke began to record the deeds of the Lord with

---

10 John 18:20.
11 Ps. 45:11 (46:10).
12 Cf. Deut. 32:1–43.

the reading and interpretation of the prophet, because, of course, all the prophetic writings reaching as far as the Lord himself, existed to be revealed to us by himself, and to be fulfilled in himself. Hence, Luke unfolds both quite clearly at the end of his Gospel, first in the Saviour's words: *That all things must be fulfilled, which are written about me in the Law of Moses, and in the prophets, and in the psalms.*[13] And he himself immediately added: *Then he opened their mind, that they might understand the Scriptures.*[14] Therefore, Jesus rose up to read, in order to set straight those whom he had not converted by the recent working of miracles, or by the testimony of the prophetic text.

[Luke 4:17b] **And as he unrolled the book, he found the place where it was written: ...** It gives delight to read that he received the book of the prophet closed, but read it unrolled, because first he undertook to manifest the mystery of the Incarnation foretold by the words of his prophets, and then he opened it to be understood by mortals.

[Luke 4:18–19] **The Spirit of the Lord is upon me, because he has anointed me to preach the gospel to the poor, he has sent me to preach deliverance to the captives, and sight to the blind, ...**[15] When he was speaking previously through the prophet about the calling of the nations and the establishment of the Church, the Saviour said among other things: *I the Lord will suddenly do this thing in its time,*[16] and he immediately added what is read here: *The Spirit of the Lord is upon me.*[17] It is not that the Lord God possesses the Lord God, but that he says these humble words in accordance with the dispensation of the flesh he had assumed. Already the Psalmist had said to him: *'You have loved justice and hated iniquity; therefore God, your God, has anointed you with the oil of gladness above your fellows'.*[18] For when they are called /**103**/ *'fellows',* understand the nature of the flesh, because God does not have us as fellows of his substance. And because it was a spiritual anointing, and not at all an anointing of the human body as it was among the high-priest of the Jews, he is therefore mindful that he was anointed above his fellows, that is, other saints. His anointing was completed at the time when he was baptized in

---

13 Luke 24:44.
14 Luke 24:45.
15 In Luke 4:18–19, Luke is quoting Isa. 61:1–2. The Vulgate Latin translations of the two passages are not quite identical.
16 Isa. 60:22.
17 Isa. 61:1.
18 Ps. 44:8 (45:7).

*the Jordan, and the Holy Spirit descended upon him in the form of a dove and remained in him.*[19]

He was anointed therefore *with spiritual oil and heavenly power to anoint the poverty of the human condition with the eternal treasure of resurrection, to remove the captivity of the mind, and to illuminate the blindness of souls,*[20] saying: *Blessed are you poor, for yours is the kingdom of God.*[21] And again: *If the Son will make you free, you will be truly free.*[22] And again: *He that follows me will not walk in the darkness, but will have the light of life.*[23]

[Luke 4:19b] **To release into forgiveness those who are broken, to preach the acceptable year of the Lord, and the day of reward.** *A sacrifice to God,* he says, *is an afflicted spirit; God does not spurn a broken and humbled heart.*[24] And for that reason, he says that he was sent or anointed to heal those broken or bruised of heart,[25] according to that which the Psalmist also says of him: *Who heals the broken of heart and binds up their bruises.*[26] Indeed, he came *to release into forgiveness* those who had been pressed down by the heavy and insupportable weight of the Law, and to admit them into the forgiveness of spiritual grace.

And this is what it is *to preach the acceptable year of the Lord.* For then the true year of jubilee,[27] that is, of liberty, is come, the time, namely, of the Church, when dwelling in the body, it is absent from the Lord,[28] about whom the Psalmist sings: *You will bless the crown of the year of your goodness.*[29] For that year which the Lord preached was not alone acceptable, but so is the one which the Apostle preaches, saying: *Behold, now is the acceptable time; behold, now is the day of salvation.*[30] Indeed, after the acceptable year of the Lord, he also preaches the day of final retribution, saying: *For the Son of man will come in his glory with his angels, and then he will render to*

---

19 Jerome, *Commentarii in Esaiam* 17.61 (CCSL 73A:706.16–30). For the last sentence, cf. Mark 1:9–10.
20 Ambrose, *Expos. Lucam* 4.45 (CCSL 14:122.548–51).
21 Luke 6:20.
22 John 8:36.
23 John 8:12.
24 Ps. 50:19 (51:17).
25 Cf. Isa. 61:1.
26 Ps. 146:3 (147:3).
27 Cf. Lev. 25:10.
28 Cf. 2 Cor. 5:6.
29 Ps. 64:12 (65:11).
30 2 Cor. 6:2.

*every man according to his works.*[31] Therefore he says that he is sent for the sake of preaching the gospel and doing all these things because the Spirit of the Lord is upon him.

[Luke 4:20] **And when he had folded the book, he returned it to the minister, and sat down.** The Lord /104/ read the book to all who were present and listening, but once it had been read he returned it to the officiant, because as he himself testifies elsewhere, when he was in the world, he spoke openly to the world, always teaching in the synagogue and in the temple, where all the Jews were accustomed to gather.[32] But when he was about to return to heaven, he handed over the duty of preaching the gospel to those who themselves saw from the very beginning[33] and were ministers of the word. Indeed, it is fitting that he reads standing, but having restored the book he sits down again. Standing is proper for working; sitting, for being at rest or judging,[34] because the Lord Jesus Christ deigned to work for a time in the flesh to lay open to us the path of knowledge concerning what had been written about him. But after the duty of merciful dispensation had been carried out, he chose followers of his teaching as disciples, and assumed once again his throne of heavenly rest. From there he not only governs all things in the present by hidden judgement, but also will appear openly as the Judge at the end of all time, while simultaneously offering allegorically a model for imitation, that each preacher of the word be also a doer of the same. Let him rise, read, and sit down: that is, work, preach, and so expect the reward of rest. It should be noted that he himself read the book unrolled, but he restored it folded to the minister, because when he, the Spirit of truth, was sent by the Father to his Church, he taught all truth.[35] But nevertheless he signified by his example that not all things were to be said to all people, but that the word was to be dispensed by the teacher in accordance with the capacity of the audience, when he said: *I have many things to say to you, but you cannot bear them now.*[36]

[Luke 4:20b–21] **And the eyes of all in the synagogue were fixed on him. And he began to say to them: Today this scripture is fulfilled in your ears.** It was surely fulfilled on that day, because, just as it had

---

31 Matt. 16:27.
32 Cf. John 18:20.
33 Cf. 1 John 1:1–3.
34 Cf. Gregory, *Hom. in Euang.* 2.29.7 (CCSL 141:251).
35 Cf. John 16:13.
36 John 16:12.

foretold, the Lord both did great things and preached the gospel of greater things. *What greater testimony, therefore, do we seek than that he in his own words signified that he was the one spoken of in the prophets,*[37] removing *the sacrileges of the faithless, who say there is one God of the Old Testament and another of the New, or who say that Christ's beginning is from the Virgin? For how did he begin from the Virgin, who spoke before the Virgin?*[38]

19/1 [Luke 4:22] **And all gave testimony to him, and they wondered at the words of grace that proceeded from his mouth.** They gave testimony to him by attesting that, as he had said, he was truly the one of whom the prophets sang, that he had been truly anointed by the grace of the Holy Spirit, and that they, the poor, the blind, the captives, and those who are broken, truly needed his gifts in every way.

[Luke 4:22b] **And they said: Is not this the son of Joseph?** How great is the blindness of the Nazarenes, who despise him, whom they know is Christ by his words and deeds, /105/ merely on account of their idea of his descent! Nevertheless, their *error is our salvation and the condemnation of heretics. For they discerned Jesus Christ as only a man,*[39] in that they called him the son of Joseph, and according to other evangelists a smith[40] or the son of a smith.[41] Meanwhile it ought to be observed why Christ, appearing in the flesh, wished to be called the son of a smith or indeed a smith, and it ought to be perceived by a sound understanding that even in this he taught that he was the Son before the ages of the one *who was the maker of everything: 'In the beginning God created heaven and earth'.*[42] *For although human things are not to be compared to divine, nevertheless the prefiguration is accurate, because the Father of Christ works with fire and the Spirit.*[43] Hence also his forerunner says of him as if of the son of a smith: *He will baptize you in the Holy Spirit and fire.*[44] In the great house of this world he forges vessels of different kinds, or rather by the softening fire of the spirit he turns *vessels of wrath*

---

37 Ambrose, *Expos. Lucam* 4.45 (CCSL 14:122.546–48).
38 Ambrose, *Expos. Lucam* 4.44 (CCSL 14:121.537–40).
39 Jerome, *Commentarii in Matheum* 2 (CCSL 77:115.1081–82).
40 Cf. Mark 6:3.
41 Cf. Matt. 13:55. See Introduction, 32–34, for discussion of the word we translate here as 'smith'.
42 Gen. 1:1 (Vulgate: not from Ambrose).
43 Ambrose, *Expos. Lucam* 3.1 (CCSL 14:76.19–20).
44 Matt. 3:11; Luke 3:16.

into *vessels of mercy*.[45] Hence Malachi, when he said in the voice of the Father: *Behold I send my angel, and he will prepare the way before my face, and immediately the Lord, whom you seek, will come to his temple,*[46] after a few words rightly added: *And he will sit smelting and purifying the silver, and he will purify the sons of Levi, and he will smelt them like gold and like silver.*[47] But the Jews, ignorant of this mystery, fail to see the works of divine power because of their attention to carnal lineage, and this is evident not only from what they said above, but also from the words of the Lord which follow, when it is added:

**20/10** [Luke 4:23] **And he said to them: Without doubt you are telling me this proverb, Physician, heal yourself; as great things as we have heard done in Capernaum, do also here in your own country.** The diseased faithlessness of those who call the Lord Christ 'maker' and 'physician', although ignorant of healthy faith, makes a confession of faith.[48] He is the true maker, because *all things were made by him*.[49] He is a physician, because all things in heaven and on earth were restored by him. As he testifies about himself: *They that are well have no need of a physician, but they that are sick.*[50] And because we have spoken of the kind of instruments he uses for making, let us also speak of the kind of medication he uses. *Passing by, he saw a man blind from birth,*[51] *he spat on the ground, and made clay of the spittle, and spread the clay upon his eyes, and said to him: Go and wash in the pool of Siloam, which means 'sent'. He went therefore, and washed, and he came seeing.*[52] Recognize, therefore, the method of the great art of healing and rejoice that you have deserved to be illuminated by it. The clay of the earth is the flesh of Christ. The spittle from his mouth /106/ is his divinity, because *the head of Christ is God.*[53] Spittle mixed with clay illuminates us who have been baptized in the pool of Siloam, because *the Word was made flesh, and dwelt among us, and we saw his glory,*[54] which

---

45 Rom. 9:22; 9:23.
46 Mal. 3:1.
47 Mal. 3:3.
48 The Nazarenes do not, in fact, refer to Christ either as a maker or as a physician. Bede puts these words in their mouths in the service of his exegesis.
49 John 1:3.
50 A blend of Matt. 9:12, Mark 2:17, and Luke 5:31.
51 John 9:1.
52 John 9:6–7.
53 1 Cor. 11:3.
54 John 1:14.

we being hampered by darkness could not previously perceive. Therefore, you were created by Christ, the maker, in order to exist; you were recreated by Christ, the physician, in order to be healed of your wounds. He is advised by mocking citizens to heal himself, that is, to perform miracles in his own country, but he is exonerated, and not without due consideration, by another evangelist, because *he could not do any miracles there, only that he cured a few that were sick, laying his hands upon them. And he wondered because of their unbelief*,[55] lest perchance anyone should think that love of country must make him less worthy in our eyes. And so he loved the citizens, but they deprived themselves of love and country by their ill will.

**21/1** [Luke 4:24] **And he said: Amen, I say to you, that no prophet is accepted in his own country.** Moses also bears witness that the Lord Christ is called a prophet in Scriptures, saying: *A prophet will the Lord your God raise up to you from your brothers, like me.*[56] And not only he who is the head and Lord of the prophets, but also Elijah, Jeremiah, and the other prophets were held in lower esteem in their country than in foreign cities, because *it is the way of things that citizens always envy their fellow citizens. They do not think about a man's present actions, but they remember his frail infancy, as if they themselves had not come through the same steps of life to maturity.*[57]

**22/10** [Luke 4:25–26] **In truth I say to you: There were many widows in the days of Elijah in Israel, when heaven was shut up three years and six months, when there was a great famine throughout all the earth. And to none of them was Elijah sent, except to a widow at Zarephath of Sidon.** 'The fact', he says, 'that I withhold divine favours from scornful citizens does not contradict the deeds of the prophets'. Because just as, when famine was oppressing all the earth, no one was found in Judea worthy to extend hospitality to Elijah, but a widow of a foreign nation was sought out who on account of the grace of her faith deserved to be visited by so great a prophet,[58] and just as, among the many lepers that were in that place, only Naaman the Syrian deserved to be cured by Elisha the prophet because he has asked for it with faith,[59] so also God will deprive you of a divine reward for no reason other than that of your ill will and faithlessness. And if you

---

55 Mark 6:5–6.
56 Acts 3:22 (cf. Deut. 18:15).
57 Jerome, *Commentarii in Matheum* 2 (CCSL 77:116.1087–91).
58 Cf. 3 Kings 17:9–24.
59 Cf. 4 Kings 5:1–19.

examine the deeds of these prophets allegorically, you will assuredly find that in the faithlessness of his own country, where he was not accepted, the Lord signified the pride of the Jews. Indeed, by the name Capernaum, which means *'field of consolation'*,[60] /107/ he signified the salvation of the Gentiles, where greater miracles are daily performed by the apostles and the successors of the apostles not so much in the healing of bodies as of souls. Therefore the widow to whom Elijah was sent signifies the Church of the Gentiles, which, abandoned for a long time by her founder, nourished the people ignorant of the true faith, like an impoverished son, with meager rations.[61] That is, she taught with a word lacking in profit, until *the prophetic message arrived, which was endangered by famine in Judea, when the fleece of Israel was dry,*[62] since the gate of heaven was shut; this message was nourished there[63] and at the same time provided nourishment, being, so to speak, accepted *by believers and itself* refreshing *the believers.*[64] Hence it is appropriate that this same widow is said to have stayed in Zarephath of Sidon, for *Sidon* means *'unprofitable hunting'*,[65] and *Zarephath* means *'fire'* or *'scarcity of bread'*,[66] because *where sin abounded, grace abounded all the more.*[67] There, where anxiety had been wasted in the quest to acquire useless things and where formerly the fire of terrible thirst and the scarcity of spiritual bread occurred, there *flour* and *oil is blessed* by the prophetic voice, that is, *the enjoyment and pleasure of love*, or the grace of the Lord's body and the ointment of anointing is made fertile by the unceasing gift of the heavenly word. To this very day, the oil of spiritual joy and flour of benediction *is not lacking* in her vessels, when other pagan nations that do not believe are in misery from lack of divine bread and preoccupied with unprofitable hunting. For also she herself testifies very beautifully that she wished *to gather two pieces of wood* in order to make the mystical bread

---

60 Jerome, *Hebr. nom.* (CCSL 72:139.11–12).

61 Cf. Jerome, *In Abdiam* 20/21 (CCSL 76:373.749).

62 Cf. Judg. 6:37–40. Israel is being starved by the Midianites. Gideon asks God twice for a sign: first that the dew fall on a dry fleece and not on the floor, and second that the dew not fall on the fleece but on the floor (each sign is granted). Presumably, then, the fleece is dry before either sign is carried out and symbolizes the famine of the Israelites.

63 I.e., in Zarephath/among the Gentiles.

64 Jerome, *In Abdiam* 20/21 (CCSL 76:373.735–38).

65 Jerome, *Hebr. nom.* (CCSL 72:113.18).

66 Jerome, *In Abdiam* 20/21 (CCSL 76:373.739–41); cf. *Hebr. nom.* (CCSL 72:113.17; 141:30).

67 Rom. 5:20.

BOOK TWO                                    231

*before she died*, expressing *not* only *by the name of wood, but also by the number of pieces of wood, the sign of the cross*, by which the bread of eternal life has been prepared for us.[68]

[Luke 4:27] **And there were many lepers in Israel in the time of Elisha the prophet, and none of them was cleansed but Naaman the Syrian.** Since the historical events are known, I must acquaint you with a few things about the mystery. This Naaman the Syrian, therefore, whose name *means 'comeliness'*,[69] represents the people of the Gentiles,[70] once spotted with the leprosy of faithlessness and sins, but cleansed by the sacrament of baptism from all filth of mind and body. By the counsel of the captive girl[71] – that is, by the grace of divine inspiration – whom the Gentiles carried off since the Jews were not able to protect her, and admonished to hope for salvation, Naaman is commanded to be washed seven times,[72] since, of course, only the kind of baptism that regenerates from the Holy Spirit offers eternal salvation. Hence his flesh after the washing is justly said to have appeared like the flesh of a little child,[73] either because by grace the mother gives birth to all baptized in Christ in one infancy, or because that child ought rather to be understood, of whom it is said: *A child is born to us, and a son is given to us*,[74] /108/ to whose body the whole progeny of believers is united. And in order that you might have knowledge of all the sacraments foreshadowed here, where we are commanded to renounce Satan and confess the faith, Naaman says that he will not sacrifice any longer to other gods, but that he will serve the Lord alone in every way. Also he rejoices to take away a portion of the sacred earth with him,[75] because it is proper that the baptized also be confirmed by partaking of the Lord's body. Deservedly, therefore, while his body is cleansed by water, Naaman's spirit is cleansed by faith, that is, the people of the Gentiles are given preference over the Jews who are filthy with the leprosy of stubbornness. Deservedly, the widow of Zarephath, that is, the Church, desiring to be refreshed by the wood of the cross, while the Jews

---

68 Augustine, *Contra Faustum* 12.34 (CSEL 25/1:361.20–24): with reference to 3 Kings 9–16.
69 Gregory, *Moralia* 3.22 (CCSL 143:144.65); cf. Jerome, *Hebr. nom.* (CCSL 72:117.23).
70 Cf. Ps.-Jerome, *Expositio euangeliorum* (PL 30:570C).
71 Cf. 4 Kings 5:2–3.
72 Cf. 4 Kings 5:10.
73 Cf. 4 Kings 5:14.
74 Isa. 9:6.
75 Cf. 4 Kings 5:17.

are perishing from dearth of the Word, is restored by the bread of the sacred body and by the oil of the vivifying Spirit.[76] And the Lord is shown to have denied the gifts of miracles to the citizens, not on account of his lack of power but on account of their envy, and by this final example that the whole race had been forsaken by him, not because it was not loved, but because it did not love that it was loved, with its teachers, of course, scattered from thence over the whole world for the salvation of the Gentiles. But what the Lord testifies by word about the Jews, these very Jews testify about themselves by this deed. For this follows:

[Luke 4:28–29] **And all those in the synagogue, hearing these things, were filled with anger. And they rose up and thrust him out of the city.** *Luke teaches that the sacrileges of the Jews, which the Lord had long before foretold by the prophet, saying: 'They repaid me evil for good',*[77] *were indeed fulfilled in the Gospel. For when he poured out benefits for the peoples, they inflicted injuries on him. It is no wonder that they who drove the Saviour from their borders lost their salvation. For the Lord is ethical in character: he taught his apostles by personal example to become all things to all men,*[78] *and he does not cast off the willing, nor bind the unwilling, nor does he resist those who refuse to accept him, nor does he desert those who seek. So in another passage, he left the Gerasenes who could not endure his powers as it were sick and ungrateful.*[79] *Likewise one must understand that the physical suffering of his body was not from necessity but voluntary, and that his body was not taken captive by the Jews, but offered by himself. For his body is taken captive when he wishes, it perishes when he wishes, it is hung on the cross when he wishes, and it is not held when he wishes.*[80]

[Luke 4:29b–30] **And they brought him,** Luke says, **to the brow of the hill upon which their city was built, that they might cast him down headlong. But he, passing through the midst of them, went his way.** *O the inheritance of the students is worse than the teacher!* The devil *tempts the Lord in speech;* the Jews *in deed. The former says: 'cast yourself down';*[81] *the latter undertake to* /109/ *cast him down.*[82] And indeed the Lord *went up*

76 Cf. 3 Kings 17:12–16.
77 Ps. 34:12 (35:12).
78 Cf. 1 Cor. 9:22.
79 Cf. Luke 8:37.
80 Ambrose, *Expos. Lucam* 4.55–56 (CCSL 14:126.676–91).
81 Luke 4:9.
82 Ambrose, *Expos. Lucam* 4.61 (CCSL 14:128.753–54).

*to the brow of the hill in order that he might be cast down headlong*, but *he came down through the midst of enraged people whose mind was suddenly changed or stupefied*, and whom *he still preferred to cure rather than to destroy*,[83] so that, seeing the wickedness they had started brought to naught, they ceased to call for his death thereafter. *For the hour of his Passion had not yet come*,[84] which was going to take place not on any Sabbath, but on the day of preparation for the Passover. Nor had he yet come to the place of his Passion, which was symbolized by the blood of the offerings in Jerusalem, not in Nazareth. Nor had he chosen this means of dying, who proclaimed that he was to be crucified by this generation. Therefore, he did not wish to be cast down headlong by the Nazarenes, nor to be stoned by the people of Jerusalem, not to be destroyed by Herod among the children of Bethlehem,[85] nor to die by one kind of death or another. For what sign of royal power could be raised aloft by such a death, by which the vanguard of the faithful might be armed? But they were to look for the standard of the cross alone: it can be delineated by the swiftest motion of the right hand against the temptations of the wicked enemy, and yet this same figure could be considered the symbol of a unique monarchy. As the Apostle, explaining the triumph of the cross, says: *In the name of Jesus every knee should bow, of those that are in heaven, on earth, and under the earth.*[86] This is because the upper extremity of the cross points to heaven, the lower extremity seeks hell, and the horizontal arms embrace the earth.

## Chapter 13

**23/8** [Luke 4:31] **And he went down into Capernaum, a city of Galilee, and there he taught them on the Sabbath days.** *Behold the mercy of the Lord Saviour. He leaves Judea neither stirred by indignation, nor offended by sin, nor outraged by insult; but rather, actually disregarding insult, yet mindful of mercy, now by teaching, now by freeing, now by curing, he softens the hearts of the infidel people.*[87] And because he frequently employs the gifts of his medicine and teaching especially on the Sabbath, he teaches that he, who also

---

83 Ambrose, *Expos. Lucam* 4.56 (CCSL 14:126.691–95).
84 Ambrose, *Expos. Lucam* 4.56 (CCSL 14:126.693–94); cf. John 8:20.
85 Cf. Matt. 2:13–16.
86 Phil. 2:10.
87 Ambrose, *Expos. Lucam* 4.57 (CCSL 14:126.705–09).

came not to destroy the Law, but to fulfil it, is not under the Law, but above the Law.[88] Instead, he teaches that not to choose the Jewish Sabbath, on which it is not lawful either to light a fire or to stir hand and foot, is the true Sabbath and beloved rest to the Lord, if, busying ourselves for the salvation of souls, we restrain ourselves from manual labour, that is, from all illicit works.[89]

**24/2** [Luke 4:32] **And they were astonished at his teaching, because his speech was with power.** The speech of a teacher is with power, when he carries out what he teaches. For he who undermines his words by his deeds is despised. The Apostle, giving instructions against such a teacher,[90] says: *Let no man despise your youth.*[91] And *the Lord in particular and from the outset spoke solely good things out of power, because* /110/ *he did nothing bad out of weakness. Indeed, he had from the power of divinity that which he ministered to us through the innocence of his humanity.*[92]

In another interpretation: *his speech was with power*, or as another evangelist says, *he was teaching them as one having power, and not as the scribes*,[93] because the scribes gave the people commands that they had learned from the Law, but he, being as it were the author and fulfiller of the Law, by his action freely supplied what seemed lacking, whether by changing the Law or by enlarging it.

**25/8** [Luke 4:33] **And in the synagogue there was a man who had an unclean demon,** ... *It is fitting that there was a man who had an unclean spirit in the synagogue, because the Jews had lost the Holy Spirit. For the devil had entered in when Christ had gone out*,[94] just as even now some *say they are Jews and are not, but are the synagogue of Satan.*[95]

[Luke 4:33b–34] **And he cried out with a loud voice, saying: Let us alone, what have we to do with you, Jesus of Nazareth?** Cease for a bit, he says, from vexing me, you who have no connection with our wrongdoing. And it is true: *For what participation has light with darkness? What community has Christ with Belial?*[96]

---

88 Cf. Matt. 5:17.
89 Cf. Ambrose, *Expos. Lucam* 4.58 (CCSL 14:127.713–17).
90 Cf., perhaps, 1 Tim.1:7, where Paul refers to 'teachers of the law, understanding neither the things they say, nor whereof they affirm'.
91 1 Tim. 4:12.
92 Gregory, *Moralia* 23.13 (CCSL 143B:1162.39–42).
93 Matt. 7:29.
94 Ambrose, *Expos. Lucam* 4.61 (CCSL 14:128.745–48).
95 Rev. 2:9.
96 2 Cor. 6:14–15.

[Luke 4:34b] **Have you come to destroy us? I know you, that you are the holy one of God.** *This is not the profession of faith of free will which earns the confessor's reward, but an extortion of necessity which forces the unwilling. If fugitive slaves see their lord after a long time, they pray for nothing worse than a whipping. So also, demons seeing the Lord unexpectedly dwelling on earth believed that they had come to be judged. The presence of the Saviour is the torment of demons.*[97]

[Luke 4:35] **And Jesus rebuked him, saying: Hold your peace, and go out of him.** Since *by the envy of the devil, death came into the world,*[98] the medicine of salvation first had to operate against the author of death: first the serpent's tongue had to be silenced, lest its poison spread beyond. But then the woman who first was seduced had to be cured of the fever of carnal concupiscence. Thirdly, the man who heard the words of his wife wickedly tempting him had to be cured of the leprosy of his error, so that for this evangelist the order of restoration might follow that of the Fall.

[Luke 4:35b] **And when the demon had thrown him into the midst, he went out of him, and he did not hurt him at all.** It is by divine leave that the man is thrown by the demon into the midst in order to be freed, so that the visible power of the Saviour may attract many to the faith and the way of salvation. But what is said, *and he did not hurt him at all*, seems to be inconsistent with Mark, who says: /111/ *And the unclean spirit tearing him, and crying out with a loud voice, went out of him,*[99] unless we understand that Mark said this, *tearing him*, because Luke said: *'And when the demon had thrown him into the midst'*, so that what he then said: *'and he did not hurt him at all'*, may be understood to mean that this throwing out and shaking of the limbs did not cripple him, just as demons are also accustomed to go out when certain limbs are amputated or torn off.[100] Hence, those who were present, fearing although not yet believing, but quite correctly in view of such a complete restoration of sanity, said among themselves:[101]

[Luke 4:36] **For with authority and power he commands the unclean spirits, and they go out.** For holy men also are able to drive out demons, but in the Word of God; but the Word himself works miracles with his own authority.

---

97 Jerome, *Commentarii in Matheum* 1 (CCSL 77:53.1195–1201).
98 Wisd. 2:24.
99 Mark 1:26.
100 Augustine, *De consensu euang.* 4.2 (CSEL 43:395.11; 18–22).
101 The second half of this sentence paraphrases the first two cola of Luke 4:36.

## Chapter 14

**26/2** [Luke 4:38] **And rising up out of the synagogue, he went into Simon's house. And Simon's wife's mother was taken with a great fever.** If we say that a man freed from a demon signifies on the moral level the soul cleansed of impure thought, it follows that a woman possessed by fever but healed at the Lord's command reveals the flesh restrained from the heat of its concupiscence by the precepts of continence. For *all bitterness and anger and indignation and clamour and blasphemy*[102] is the rage of the unclean spirit. And understand that *fornication, uncleanness, lust, evil concupiscence, and covetousness, which is the service of idols*,[103] is the fever of the seductive body.

[Luke 4:38b–39] **And they solicited him on her behalf. And standing over her, he commanded the fever, and it left her.** On one occasion the Saviour is solicited, on another he cures the sick on his own accord, showing that he grants prayers directed against the suffering even of sinners and always against the suffering of the faithful, and those things that they do not understand at all on their own, he either grants that they may be understood, or else leaves them not understood. This accords with what the Psalmist asserts: *Who can understand sins? From my secret ones cleanse me, O Lord.*[104]

[Luke 4:39b] **And immediately rising, she ministered to them.** It is natural for those having a fever, when their health begins to return, still to be exhausted and to feel the discomfort of illness, *but health that is conferred* by order of the Lord *returns immediately and completely.*[105] Not only does it return, but so much strength accompanies it that it immediately is capable of ministering to those who had aided it and that, in accordance with the laws of tropology, limbs, which had been slaves to impurity to the point of iniquity that would end in death, might be slaves to justice for the sake of eternal life.[106] /112/

[Luke 4:40] **And when the sun had set, all those who had any sick with various diseases brought them to him. But he, laying his hands on each of them, healed them.** The setting of the sun signifies the passion

---

102 Eph. 4:31.
103 Col. 3:5.
104 Ps. 18:13 (19:12).
105 Jerome, *Commentarii in Matheum* 1 (CCSL 77:50.1131–32).
106 Cf. Rom. 6:16–22.

and death of the one who said: *As long as I am in the world, I am the light of the world.*[107] And as the sun sets, more demoniacs than before and more who were sick are cured, because he who taught a few of the Jews when he lived temporarily in the flesh, sent the gifts of faith and salvation to all nations throughout the world when the kingdom of death was conquered. Concerning his ministers, the heralds as it were of life and light, the Psalmist sings: *Make a way for him who ascends above the west.*[108] The Lord indeed *ascends above the west, because from the place where he lay in the passion, from that place he manifested greater glory by rising again.*[109]

**27/8** [Luke 4:41] **And the demons went out from many, crying out and saying: You are the Son of God. And rebuking them he did not allow them to speak, for they knew that he was Christ.** The demons confessed the Son of God, and as the evangelist attests, *they knew that he was Christ.* The devil knew that the one who had been wearied by the fast of forty days was a man, but he could not discover by tempting whether he was also the Son of God. But now, he either understood from the power of the miracles, or at least guessed that he was the Son of God.[110] Therefore he did not persuade the Jews to crucify him because he thought that he was not Christ or the Son of God, but because he did not foresee that he would be damned by his death. Concerning this mystery hidden from the world the Apostle says: *none of the princes of this world knew; for if they had known it, they would never have crucified the Lord of glory.*[111] Moreover, the Psalmist makes it clear why the Lord prevents the demons from speaking of himself when he says: *But God said to the sinner: Why do you declare my justices?*[112] and so forth, *lest anyone should follow an errant preacher. For the devil is a wicked teacher, who often mingles false things with true to cover evidence of deceit with the appearance of truth.*[113] And elsewhere not only demons who unwillingly confessed are ordered to keep silent about Christ, but also those who having been cured by him and who wished to confess willingly. Moreover, even the apostles themselves, who after the resurrection were to preach him to the whole world, are ordered to be entirely silent about him before his passion, lest, of course, by preaching his divine majesty, the

---

107 John 9:5.
108 Ps. 67:5 (68:4).
109 Gregory, *Hom. in Euang.* 1.17.2 (CCSL 141:117.20–23).
110 Cf. Jerome, *Commentarii in Matheum* 1 (CCSL 77:53.1205–06).
111 1 Cor. 2:8.
112 Ps. 49:16 (50:16).
113 Ambrose, *Expos. Lucam* 6.102 (CCSL 14:211.1109–12).

dispensation of his passion be abandoned, and with his passion abandoned, the salvation of the world, which was to take place by its means, come to nought.

**28/8** [Luke 4:42] **And when it was day, going out he went into a desert place, and the crowds /113/ sought him, and came to him**, and so forth. If the death of the Lord is expressed by the setting of the sun, why will not his resurrection be proclaimed by the returning day? In its bright light he is sought by the crowds of believers, and when he is found in the desert of the Gentiles he is detained there lest he depart, particularly the going out, the seeking and the finding fell on the first day of the week, when the Resurrection is celebrated.[114]

## Chapter 15

**29/10** [Luke 5:1] **And it happened that, when the crowds pressed upon him to hear the word of God, he was standing by the lake [*stagnum*] of Gennesaret.** They say that the lake of Gennesaret is the same as what they call the sea of Galilee, or the sea of Tiberias.[115] But it was called the sea of Galilee after the adjacent province, and the sea of Tiberias after the nearest city, which was once called Chinnereth,[116] but after it was restored by the tetrarch Herod, it was named Tiberias in honour of Tiberius Caesar.[117] Moreover, *it is called by the Greek word Gennesar,*[118] *as if generating [**generans**] a breeze [**auram**] for itself,* from the nature of the lake itself, whereby it is said to stir up *for itself a breeze from itself by its curling waters.* For its water is not spread out flat like a pool, but is stirred *by frequent breezes, sweet* to taste *and good for drinking.*[119] But in the usage of the Hebrew language, every body of water, whether sweet or salt, is called a 'sea'. This lake, which the Jordan flows through, is a hundred and forty stades in length and forty stades in width.[120] Therefore,

---

114 Cf. Luke 4:42.
115 For the 'sea of Tiberias', cf. John 21:1.
116 Cf. Num. 34:11 (the lake); Jos. 19:35 (the city).
117 Cf. Jerome, *De situ et nom.* (*Onomastica sacra* 112.28–31).
118 Cf. 1 Macc. 11:67.
119 Isidore, *Etym.* 13.19.6.
120 Cf. Isidore, *Etym.* 13.19.6. A 'stade' [*stadium*] = 600 Roman feet, or about an eighth of a mile.

because 'lake' [*stagnum*] or 'sea' signifies the present age, the Lord stands by the sea when, after overcoming the mortality of fleeting life in that flesh in которой he suffered, he entered upon the stability of eternal rest.[121] The assemblage of crowds is an allegorical figure of the nations rushing together to him in faith. Of them Isaiah says: *And all nations shall flow to it, and many people shall go, and say: Come and let us go up to the mountain of the Lord.*[122]

[Luke 5:2] **And he saw two ships standing by the lake.** The two ships placed by the lake symbolize circumcision and lack of circumcision.[123] Jesus is well said to have seen them, because among both peoples *the Lord knows who are his*,[124] and he conveys their heart from the billows of this age to the calm of future life, by seeing them as it were coming towards the firmness of the shore, that is, by seeing them with the mercy of his heart.

[Luke 5:2b] **But the fishermen were gone out of them, and were washing their nets.** The fishermen are the doctors of the Church, who convey us who are caught in the net of faith, and brought up from the deep to the light, like fish to the shore, and so to the land /114/ of the living. For like the nets of the fishermen, certain sayings of the preachers are complex in order not to lose those whom they have caught in faith. Hence, nets [*retia*] are so-called from 'retaining' [*retinentia*].[125] But these nets are now opened for a catch, and now folded up after being washed, because not every occasion is suitable for teaching, but at one time the tongue ought to be used by the teacher, and at another it ought to be governed by care for itself.

[Luke 5:3] **And going into one of the ships that was Simon's, he desired him to draw back a little from the land. And sitting he taught the crowds from the ship.** Simon's ship is the primitive Church, of which Paul says: *For he who worked through Peter to the apostleship of the circumcision, worked through me also among the Gentiles.*[126] 'One' is the right word in this: *The multitude of believers had but one heart and*

---

121 Bede echoes these words in the closing paragraph of *DTR* 71, ed. Jones (CCSL 123B:544.91–93), trans. Wallis, *The Reckoning of Time*, 249.
122 Isa. 2:2–3.
123 Ps.-Jerome, *Expositio euangeliorum* (PL 30:570C–D): '*duae naves, id est, duas Ecclesias*'.
124 2 Tim. 2:19.
125 Cf. Isidore, *Etym.* 19.5.
126 Gal. 2:8.

*one soul.*[127] He taught the crowds from that ship, because *he teaches the Gentiles right to the present from the authority of the Church.*[128]

**30/9 [Luke 5:4] Now when he had ceased to speak, he said to Simon: Launch out into the deep, and let down your nets for a catch.** That he first asked Simon to draw back his ship a little from the land *signifies either that he should speak to the crowds in a measured fashion, so as to avoid both teaching them earthly things, and withdrawing from earthly matters into the depths of the mysteries, so that they fail to understand thoroughly. Or it could mean that he should preach first to the Gentiles in the neighbouring districts, so that what he also says to Peter: 'Launch out into the deep, and let down your nets for a catch', may apply.*[129]

[Luke 5:5] **And Simon answering said to him: Master, we have laboured all the night, and have taken nothing. But at your word I will let down the net.** *Unless the Lord build the house, they labour in vain that build it.*[130] Unless the Lord illuminates the heart of the pupils, the teacher labours in the night. Unless the tools of disputation are let down at the word of divine grace, the preacher hurls the javelin of his word in vain, because the faith of the people springs not from the wisdom of logical terminology, but from the gift of a divine calling.

[Luke 5:6] **And when they had done this, they enclosed a very great multitude of fish, and their net broke.** *The net broke on account of the multitude of fish, because now along with the elect so many damned also enter upon the confession of faith, and these people split apart the Church itself with heresies.*[131] The net breaks, but the fish does not slip away, because the Lord saves his own, even as he traps the persecutors.

[Luke 5:7] **And they beckoned to their partners who were in the other ship to come and help them.** The other ship, as we said above, is the Church of the Gentiles, which, since the one ship was not sufficient, is filled with the elect fish, because *the Lord knows who are his,*[132] and with /115/ him the number of his elect is fixed. As long as he does not find in Judea as many future believers as he knows have been predestined to faith and eternal life, he fills up the hearts of the Gentiles as well with the grace of faith as it were

---

127 Acts 4:32.
128 Augustine, *Quaestiones euang.* 2.2 (CCSL 44B:42.2–3).
129 Augustine, *Quaestiones euang.* 2.2 (CCSL 44B:42.5–11).
130 Ps. 126:1 (127:1).
131 Gregory, *Hom. in Euang.* 2.24.3 (CCSL 141:199.56–58).
132 2 Tim. 2:19.

seeking a container for his fish in another ship. And the accompanying ship is rightly summoned after the net was broken, seeing that before this Judas the betrayer and Simon Magus, both very wicked fish, were caught; seeing that before this Ananias and Sapphira were deceitfully trying to enter the net of faith;[133] and seeing that before this, as John witnesses, *many of his disciples went back, and walked no more with him*.[134] But after that Barnabas and Paul were set apart for the apostleship of the Gentiles.[135]

[Luke 5:7b] **And they came, and filled both the ships, so that they began to sink.** The filling of these ships increases up to the end of the world. But when they are filled, they begin to sink, that is, they are threatened by submersion, for while they are not submerged, nevertheless they are put at risk. The Apostle explains, saying: *In the last days there will be dangerous times, and men will be lovers of themselves*,[136] and so forth. For the sinking ships represent those who had been lifted up from this age by faith, but who have relapsed by the depravity of their character. Peter himself, still mired in weakness, demonstrates this here. Hence there follows:

31/10 [Luke 5:8] **When Simon Peter saw this, he fell down at Jesus's knees, saying: Depart from me, for I am a sinful man, O Lord**, because all carnal men in the Church *cast off from themselves, so to speak, the governance of the spiritual members, and particularly of the person of Christ. For they do not ask those good servants of God aloud in so many words to cast them off, but they encourage them to do so by the language of their character and deeds, lest they be governed by the good men. They honour them ever more vehemently, yet by their own deeds they admonish them to depart from them, just as Peter, in falling to the feet of the Lord, signified that he honoured those feet, but signified his character by what he says: 'Depart from me, for I am a sinful man, O Lord'. Nevertheless, the Lord did not do it, for he did not depart from them, but, guided the ships to land on the shore. This signifies that good and spiritual men, when disturbed by the sins of the crowds, must shun the urge to abandon the Church's gift in order to live in greater safety and tranquillity.*[137]

[Luke 5:10b] **And Jesus says to Simon: Fear not; ...** The Lord comforts the fear of carnal men and fortifies the minds of weak ones. By consoling

---
133 Cf. Acts 5:1–10.
134 John 6:67.
135 Cf. Acts 13:2.
136 2 Tim. 3:1–2.
137 Augustine, *Quaestiones euang.* 2.2 (CCSL 44B:43.19–32).

he gives encouragement, in order that no one, whether trembling from knowledge of his own guilt, or dumbfounded by the innocence of others, should fear to approach the path of holiness. And what follows: /116/

32/2 [Luke 5:10c] **From henceforth you will be catching men,** pertains specifically to Peter himself. For the Lord explains to him what this catching of fish signifies: namely that just as now he catches fish with nets, so in the future he will catch men with words. And the Lord also explains that the whole order of this action shows what is done daily in the Church, of which Peter is the type. And then is added:

[Luke 5:11] **And having brought their ships to land, leaving all things, they followed him.** *This can signify the end of time, when those who have clung tightly to Christ will depart from the deep sea of this world.*[138] But it should be known that this is not the same text in which Matthew and Mark tell how fishermen were called two at a time from their ships by the Lord – first Peter and Andrew, and then the sons of Zebedee.[139] For Luke does not declare that they *were called* at this time *by the Lord, but only that it was foretold to Peter that he was going to catch men. This was not said as if he was from now on never going to catch fish, for we read that they fished even after the resurrection of the Lord.*[140] *Hence it is understood that they came back according to their custom to catch fish, as later happened in accordance with what Matthew and Mark tell when he called them two at a time. For then, they did not bring their ships to land, as if preparing to go out again, but followed him as if he were calling and commanding them to follow him.*[141]

## Chapter 16

33/2 [Luke 5:12] **And when he was in a certain city, behold there was a man full of leprosy, who, seeing Jesus and falling on his face, beseeched him, saying: Lord, if you will, you can make me clean.** *It is good that the place where the leper is cleansed is not specified, in order to show that not one people in one particular city were cleansed, but people everywhere.*[142]

---

138 Augustine, *Quaestiones euang.* 2.2 (CCSL 44B:43.33–35).
139 Cf. Matt. 4:19–22; Mark 1:17–20. Bede is here implicitly offering a correction to Luke Canon Table section number 32/2, which directs the reader to these passages in Matthew and Mark.
140 Cf. John 21:3.
141 Augustine, *De consensu euang.* 2.17 (CSEL 43:141.6–18).
142 Ambrose, *Expos. Lucam* 5.1 (CCSL 14:135.4–6).

And *because the Lord says: 'I have not come to destroy the Law, but to fulfil it',*[143] *this man who was excluded from the Law, taking it to be the case that he was cleansed by the power of the Lord, judged that the grace which could wash away the stain of a leper was not from the Law but above it. Truly, just as the authority of power in the Lord is made plain, so too is the leper's steadiness of faith. He fell on his face because he is a man of humility and possessed a sense of shame, in order that each person may blush for the stains of his own life, but he did not hold back his confession out of shame. He showed his wound; he asked for a cure. And his confession itself is full of religion and faith. 'If you will', he says, 'you can make me clean'. He ascribed power to the will of the Lord. But he was not uncertain of the will of the Lord as if he doubted the Lord's goodness; rather, being conscious as it were of his own filthiness, he did not presume upon it.*[144] /117/

[Luke 5:13] **And stretching forth his hand, he touched him, saying: I will. Be cleansed. And immediately the leprosy departed from him.** *There is no interval between God's deed and his command, because the deed is in the command. Indeed: 'He spoke, and they were made.'*[145] *You see,*[146] *therefore, that it cannot be doubted that God's will is power. If, therefore, his will is power, those who affirm [a Trinity] of a single will, certainly affirm [a Trinity] of a single power.*[147] *And so, having, as it were, the power of healing, and the authority of commanding, he does not shrink from proving it by taking action. For he says, 'I will', on account of Photinus; he commands, on account of Arius; he touches, on account of Mani.*[148] And indeed *the Law forbids lepers to be touched, but he who is the Law's Lord does not submit to the Law, but makes it.* Accordingly, *he touched therefore, not because he could not cure without touching, but in order to prove that he was not subject to the Law. And he did not fear contagion as men do, but because he who freed others could not be*

---

143 Cf. Matt. 5:17.
144 Ambrose, *Expos. Lucam* 5.1–2 (CCSL 14:135.12–24).
145 Ps. 32:9 (33:9).
146 Here, as elsewhere, Bede changes a second-person plural verb to a singular.
147 Ambrose, *Expos. Lucam* 5.3 (CCSL 14:136.26–29). Ambrose is speaking of the single will and power of the Trinity. Bede's omission of the word 'Trinity', for whatever reason, obscures the meaning.
148 Ambrose, *Expos. Lucam* 5.4 (CCSL 14:136.37–40). Ambrose (and therefore Bede) takes Christ's several actions as refuting some essential aspect of each of these heresies (the Photinian, the Arian, the Manichean).

contaminated, *leprosy, which usually contaminated the one touching, was driven out by the touch of the Lord.*[149] And *likewise it is wonderful that he cured in the same manner as he had been begged: 'if you will, you can make me clean'. 'I will'*, he says. *'Be cleansed'. You have the will, and you have also the power of benevolence.*[150]

[Luke 5:14] **And he charged him that he should tell no man, ...** *Why is he charged to tell no one, unless it is to teach that our blessings are not to be noised abroad, but kept hidden, in order that we abstain not only from the reward of money, but also from the reward of favour?*[151]

[Luke 5:14b] **But: Go, show yourself to the priest, and make an offering for your cleansing as Moses commanded,**[152] **for a testimony to them.** *He is commanded to show himself to the priest, in order that the priest might understand that* he *had been cured not in the regular course of the Law, but by the grace of God which is above the Law. And he is commanded to offer a sacrifice, in order that the Lord might show that he did not cancel the Law, but fulfilled it – the Lord who, proceeding according to the law, cured above the Law those whom the remedies of the Law had not cured. And he appropriately added: 'for a testimony to them', that is, to see if they believe in God, or if the leprosy of unbelief is departed.*[153] Because if anyone is bothered that the Lord's way seems *to approve the* Mosaic *sacrifice, although the Church will not accept it*, he should remember *that the holiest of holy sacrifices, which is his body, had not yet come into being. For he had not yet offered himself as a holocaust in the Passion. And it was not fitting for the symbolic sacrifices to be abolished before that which was symbolised had been confirmed by the testimony of the apostles' preaching and by the faith of the believing peoples.*[154] Indeed, because this man signifies allegorically the human race enfeebled by sins, /118/ he is described as being not only leprous, but as full of leprosy. *For all have sinned, and need the glory of God.*[155] They need it, of course, so that, by the Saviour's outstretched hand, that is, by the Word of God made flesh and touching human nature, they may be cleansed of the vicissitudes of ancient error, and may be able to hear with the apostles: *Now you are*

---

149 Ambrose, *Expos. Lucam* 5.7 (CCSL 14:137.61–67).
150 Ambrose, *Expos. Lucam* 5.7 (CCSL 14:137.57–60).
151 Ambrose, *Expos. Lucam* 5.5 (CCSL 14:136.46–48).
152 The Mosaic ritual for the cleansing of leprosy is the subject of Leviticus, chs 13 and14.
153 Ambrose, *Expos. Lucam* 5.8–9 (CCSL 14:137.67–77).
154 Augustine, *Quaestiones euang.* 2.3 (CCSL 44B:44.4–8; 11–13).
155 Rom. 3:23.

*clean by the reason of the Word, which I have spoken to you.*[156] And those who were despised and long cut off from the stronghold of the people of God, now at last may be able to return to the temple and to be offered to the priest, namely to him to whom it is truly said: *You are a priest forever,*[157] and to hear from the Apostle: *For the temple of God is holy, which you are.*[158] And they may make an offering for their cleansing as Moses commanded, that is, that they present their *bodies a living sacrifice, holy, pleasing to God.*[159]

**34/1** [Luke 5:15] **But the fame of him went abroad the more, and great multitudes came together to hear, and to be healed of their infirmities.** The salvation accomplished in one man drives great multitudes to the Lord. For in order to teach that he has been cured without and within, the former leper is not at all silent about the blessing he received, even though he is ordered to do so by him from whom he received it. But rather, as Mark relates, performing the duty of an evangelist, he immediately *went out and began to publish and to blaze abroad the word, so that Jesus could not openly go into the city, but was out in the country in desert places, and they flocked to him from all sides.*[160] Hence it is appropriate to ask why it should be that the Lord ordered some things that he did to be concealed, and yet they could not be concealed even for a moment. For *could it be that in this matter the only-begotten Son, coeternal with the Father and the Holy Spirit, had a wish that he was unable to fulfil?*[161] But it must be observed that *our Redeemer offered everything that he did in his mortal body as an example of action for us. For instance, performing a miracle, he ordered it to be passed over in silence, and yet it could not be passed over in silence. This is surely in order that his elect also, following the examples of his teaching, should want to remain incognito when they do great things. But in order to do good to others, they may be revealed against their will, since it is both a matter of great humility that they seek that their works be passed over in silence, and a matter of great sublimity that their works cannot be passed over in silence. Therefore, it is not that the Lord willed something*

---

156 John 15:3.
157 Ps. 109:4 (110:4).
158 1 Cor. 3:17.
159 Rom. 12:1. On Bede's understanding of the Christian priesthood as both continuing and superseding the Jewish priesthood as expressed in this passage, see O'Brien, *Bede's Temple*, 53–54.
160 Mark 1:45.
161 Gregory, *Dialogues* 1.9.6 (SC 260:80.61–63).

*to be done and couldn't do it; but by the authority of his teaching, he gave an example of what his members ought to will, or else of what may happen when they are still unwilling.*[162]

**35/2** [Luke 5:16] **And he retired into the desert and prayed.** Do not attribute the fact that he retired into the desert to that nature which says, *'I will. Be cleansed'*, and cured a man of his infirmities, but to the one which, stretching forth his hand, touched the leper. Not that the person of the Son is doubled as Nestorius would have it, /119/ but that just as there are two natures of the same person, so there are also two operations.[163]

In another interpretation: The fact that he does *miracles in the city, but that he spends the night praying* in the desert *or on the mountain*, as we read below,[164] shows us examples of both the active and the contemplative life, *lest* anyone neglect *the care of neighbours from zeal for contemplation, or, being excessively engaged in the care of neighbours,* abandon *the zeal for contemplation. The fact is that love of neighbour does not hinder love of God, nor does love of God cast aside love of neighbour because it surpasses it.*[165] Indeed, to leave behind the preoccupations of disabling thoughts and to pray on the mountain with one's whole heart, is to hasten to the eternal joys of divine contemplation. To retire into the desert and pray is to repress the turmoil, surging up from within, of earthly desires, and to seek for oneself something hidden with the Lord, where one may speak with him silently about one's inner longings, with all external uproar hushed.

**Chapter 17**

**36/2** [Luke 5:17] **And it happened on a certain day, as he sat teaching, that there were also Pharisees sitting by**, and so forth. For the sake of brevity, Luke does not say where it was that the Lord taught while sitting, when he cured the paralytic with the scribes and the Pharisees sitting by, but Matthew and Mark, who relate the same story,[166] seem to raise a

---

162 Gregory, *Dialogues* 1.9.7 (SC 260:80.66–79).
163 The two natures of Christ are the divine and the human. The Council of Ephesus (431) declared that the two natures coexisted in the one person of Christ; it condemned as heretical the doctrine of Nestorius, which held that there were two persons in Christ. Cf. Isidore, *Etym.* 6.16.8.
164 Luke 6:12.
165 Gregory, *Moralia* 28.13 (CCSL 143B:1420.10–11; 14–21).
166 Cf. Matt. 9:1–8; Mark 2:1–12.

difficulty, since indeed Matthew testifies that he did this in his own city, but *Mark, in Capernaum. This is rather difficult to resolve, even had Matthew named the place as Nazareth*. Either Galilee itself, *in* which *Nazareth was*,[167] must be understood to have been called the city of Christ, in distinction to the country of the Gerasenes across the sea, from which Jesus (as Matthew writes) had passed over to come to Galilee;[168] or else Capernaum itself was called the city of Christ, a city which he had made his own, not from his birth but from making it famous by his miracles.

37/1 [Luke 5:18] **And behold, men brought a man in a bed, who was a paralytic, and they sought means to bring him in, and to lay him before him.** The cure of this paralytic signifies the salvation of the soul who sighs out to Christ, after the long stagnation of carnal pleasure. First of all, it has need of servants, who may lift it up and bring it to Christ, that is, of good teachers, who may furnish hope of healing and the means of intercession. These are properly found to have been four, as Mark relates,[169] whether because the whole power and message of preaching is fortified by the four books of the Gospel, or because there are four virtues by which the faith of the soul is raised up to deserve redemption. Of these virtues it is said in praise of eternal wisdom: *For she teaches moderation, and wisdom, and justice, and courage,* /120/ *which are such things as men can have nothing more profitable in life.*[170] Some call these by the alternative names of prudence, fortitude, temperance, and justice.

[Luke 5:19] **And when they could not find by what way they might bring him in because of the multitude, they went up onto the roof through the roof-tiles.** They want to bring the paralytic to Christ, but every way was cut off by the intervening multitude, because often the soul who comes in repentance to God and desires to be healed by divine grace after languishing in shameful torpor is held back by the obstacle of its old habits. Often amid these very prayers of secret sweetness and as it were pleasant colloquy with the Lord, a multitude of intervening thoughts blocks the keen vision of the soul from seeing Christ. And what is to be done amid these distractions? Certainly, there should be no staying outside down below, but the roof of the house in which Christ teaches must be ascended, that is, the sublimity of holy Scripture must be sought after, and the Law of

---

167 Augustine, *De consensu euang.* 2.25 (CSEL 43:161.5–8).
168 Cf. Matt. 8:28.
169 Cf. Mark 2:3: Mark specifies that the paralytic was brought in by four men.
170 Wisd. 8:7.

the Lord must be pondered with the Psalmist day and night. For: *By what does a young man correct his way? By observing your words*, he says.[171]

[Luke 5:19b] **And they let him down with his bed into the midst before Jesus.** The roof was laid open, and the sick man is let down before Jesus, because, after the mysteries of the Scriptures have been revealed, he is brought *to a knowledge of Christ, that is,* he is lowered *to his humility by the piety of faith.* The house of Jesus is well described as being covered with roof-tiles, because the divine virtue of spiritual grace will be found under the contemptible clothing of letters, if there is a teacher present who will reveal it. *And the fact that he is set down with a bed signifies that Christ ought to be recognized by man while he is still constituted in this flesh.*[172]

[Luke 5:20] **When he saw their faith, he said: Man, your sins are forgiven you.** The Lord, who was about to cure a man from paralysis, first loosened the chains of his sins to show that he is doomed to the weakness of his limbs because of the chains of his faults, and that he is not able to be healed with the recovery of his limbs unless those bonds have been loosened. And so the Lord says to that paralytic who waited so long by the sheep pond in vain for the moving of the water and whom he cured:[173] *Behold you are made whole, sin no more, lest something worse happen to you.*[174] It is proper that he whose *sins were forgiven* is called a man, *who because he was a man by this very fact was unable to say, I have not sinned, and likewise in order that the one who forgave the man might be understood to be God.*[175] It is well worth noting how much each person's personal faith may be efficacious with God, when the faith of unknown others was so efficacious that the whole man suddenly, that is, outwardly and inwardly, arose already saved. Deservedly, the errors of some were undone by others. /121/

[Luke 5:21] **And the scribes and Pharisees began to think, saying: Who is this who speaks blasphemies? Who can forgive sins, but God alone?** The scribes speak the truth, because no one can forgive sins but God alone, who also forgives through those to whom he gives the power of forgiveness. And for that reason, Christ is proved to be truly God, since he can forgive sins like God. They give true testimony to God, but they err

---

171 Ps. 118:9 (119:9).
172 Augustine, *Quaestiones euang.* 2.4 (CCSL 44B:45.5–6; 8–9).
173 Cf. John 5:1–9.
174 John 5:14.
175 Augustine, *De consensu euang.* 2.25.57 (CSEL 43:159.18–20).

in denying the person of Christ. And likewise, the Jews err, who although they believe that Christ is also God and can forgive sins, nevertheless do not believe that Jesus is Christ. But the Arians err far more foolishly, who although they dare not deny that Jesus is also Christ and, overcome by the words of the Gospel, that he can forgive sins, nevertheless recklessly deny that he is God. But desiring to save the faithless both by his knowledge of mysteries and by the power of his works, Jesus makes clear that he is God.

[Luke 5:22b] **For, answering, he said to them: What do you think in your hearts?** For to the same God who says: *I am, I am he who blots out your iniquities*,[176] the wisest of speakers says: *For you alone know the heart of all the children of men.*[177] Therefore, God says, *By the same majesty and power with which I contemplate your thoughts, I am also able to forgive men's sins; understand from within yourselves what the paralytic gains.*[178]

[Luke 5:23] **Which is easier, to say, 'Your sins are forgiven you', or to say, 'Arise and walk'?** *He alone who did the forgiving, knew whether the sins of the paralytic were forgiven. But 'arise and walk' – he who arose as well as those who saw him arising could affirm that. Therefore, a physical miracle is performed to prove a spiritual one.*[179]

[Luke 5:24] **But that you may know that the Son of man has power on earth to forgive sins, ...** And if, according to that memorable testimony of Isaiah, it is God who *blots out* our *iniquities*,[180] and *the Son of God has power on earth of forgiving sins*,[181] therefore both God himself and the Son of man is the same, so that not only the man Christ can forgive sins by the power of his divine nature, but also the same God Christ can die for sinners by virtue of the fragility of his human nature.

[Luke 5:24b] **He says to the paralytic, I say to you, Arise, take up your bed and go into your house.** Spiritually, to arise from the bed is for the soul to withdraw itself from carnal desires in which it found respite when it was sick. But to take up the bed is for the flesh, having been caught by the bridle of continence, to free itself from earthly delights by the hope of divine rewards. /122/ For this is the bed that is washed *every night* by David,[182] that is, is chastised for the stains of every fault by a river of

---

176 Isa. 43:25.
177 3 Kings 8:39: the speaker is Solomon.
178 Jerome, *Commentarii in Matheum* 1 (CCSL 77:54.1245–48).
179 Jerome, *Commentarii in Matheum* 1 (CCSL 77:54.1251–55).
180 Ps. 50:11 (51:9).
181 Matt. 9:6; Mark 2:10.
182 Ps. 6:7 (6:6).

penitence well deserved. But to go home, carrying the bed, is to return to paradise. For that is the true house, which received man in the beginning. It was lost not rightly, but by deceit, and at length was restored by him who owed nothing to the deceitful enemy. Or in another interpretation: A healthy man who once languished carries a bed back to his house, when the soul, after receiving the forgiveness of sins, takes care to guard himself internally, and his body as well, lest after forgiveness it admit anything from which it might be justly punished again.

[Luke 5:25] **And immediately rising up before them, he took up the bed on which he lay, and he went away to his own house, glorifying God,** and so forth. The marvellous effect of divine power is that rapid healing follows the Saviour's command without the slightest delay intervening. Rightly, those who were present with their cursed spears of blasphemy turned their astonished hearts to the praise of such great majesty.[183]

## Chapter 18

**38/2** [Luke 5:27] **And after these things he went forth, and saw a tax collector named Levi, sitting at the custom-house, and he said to him: Follow me.** This Levi is the same person as Matthew, but Luke and Mark *out of respect and honour did not want* to give the evangelist his common name. *But he is the Matthew according to that which is written, 'The just is the accuser of himself.'*[184] *In the beginning of his text he calls himself Matthew and a tax collector,*[185] *to show to his readers that no* convert ought to despair of salvation, *seeing that he himself was suddenly changed from tax collector to apostle,* from customs collector to evangelist.[186]

[Luke 5:28] **And leaving all things, he rose up and followed him.** Matthew, understanding what it is truly to follow the Lord, leaves everything and follows. For to follow is to imitate. And therefore, in order that he might be able to emulate the poor man, Christ, *not so much in gait* as *in state of mind,* he who was accustomed to seize *what belonged to another* left *what was his own.*[187] Showing us the perfect pattern of the

---

183 This sentence interprets Luke 5:26, which Bede does not quote.
184 Prov. 18:17.
185 Cf. Matt. 9:9.
186 Jerome, *Commentarii in Matheum* 1 (CCSL 77:55.1266–74).
187 Ambrose, *Expos. Lucam* 5.16 (CCSL 14:140.157–60).

renunciation of the world, he not only left the profits of taxes, but also scorned the danger that could come upon him from the rulers of the world, because he left the computation of the taxes unfinished and in disorder. He was led by so great a desire to follow the Lord that he set at nought all consideration for his life and thought for himself. On account of this, when he zealously abandoned human affairs, he deserved to be the faithful treasurer of the Lord's talents.

39/2 [Luke 5:29] **And Levi made him a great feast in his own house.** *The one who receives Christ in his inner dwelling is fed by the greatest delights /123/ of abundant pleasures. And so the Lord willingly enters and reclines in the affection of him who believed.*[188] And *this is the spiritual banquet of good works, where rich people are needy and the poor feast.*[189]

[Luke 5:29b] **And there was a great company of tax collectors and others who were at table with them.** They had seen that the tax collector who had been converted from sins to better things had found room for repentance, and on account of this they also do not despair of salvation.[190]

[Luke 5:30] **But the Pharisees and their scribes murmured, saying to his disciples: Why do you eat and drink with tax collectors and sinners?** When the tax collectors feast with the Lord, the Pharisees, murmuring, boast of their fasting. This is where it is made clear first how great is the distance *between the Law and grace*, since *those who follow the Law suffer the eternal fast of a starving mind, but those who have accepted the Word of divine nourishment in the innermost parts of their soul, and have been refreshed by the abundance of the fountain, cannot hunger and thirst.*[191] Then, *the particular nature of their future* punishment *is prefigured* when, while the elect *feast* with Christ, *the perfidy* of the proud *will be tormented with fasting.*[192] To these it is said: *Harlots and tax collectors go before you into the kingdom of God.*[193] Because if the faith of the Gentiles is signified by the choice of Matthew, who formerly longed for the wealth of the world, but now refreshes the body of Christ with zealous devotion, certainly the arrogance of the Pharisees hints at the envy of the Jews which turns them away from the salvation of the Gentiles.

---

188 Ambrose, *Expos. Lucam* 5.16 (CCSL 14:140.162–65).
189 Ambrose, *Expos. Lucam* 5.19 (CCSL 14:141.193–94).
190 Jerome, *Commentarii in Matheum* 1 (CCSL 77:56.1288–90).
191 Ambrose, *Expos. Lucam* 5.17 (CCSL 14:140.168–72).
192 Ambrose, *Expos. Lucam* 5.17 (CCSL 14:140.166–68).
193 Matt. 21:31.

40/2 [Luke 5:31–32] **And Jesus answering, said to them: Those who are whole need not the physician, but those who are sick. I have come not to call the just, but sinners to repentance.** *He reproaches the scribes and the Pharisees, who, thinking themselves just, shunned the company of sinners and tax collectors.*[194] He who, by a wonderful kind of healing, *was wounded for our iniquities, and by his bruises we are healed*[195] calls himself a physician. Moreover, he calls those people 'whole' and 'just' who, *not knowing the righteousness of God, and seeking to establish their own righteousness, have not submitted themselves to the justice of God.*[196] *They do not seek the grace of the Gospel,*[197] but mistakenly count [on being justified] *by the Law*. But he calls 'sick' and 'sinners' those who are overcome by awareness of their own fragility, and seeing that they cannot be justified by the Law, submit /124/ themselves to the grace of Christ by repenting. It also shows that, *while the Pharisees and scribes were murmuring*, the tax collectors abandoned their former vices and came penitent *to Jesus*,[198] and that Jesus himself also deigned to go *to the feast of the sinners to have the opportunity to teach and to offer spiritual food to his hosts. Finally, although Jesus is said to go frequently to feasts, only what he did there, and what he taught, is recorded in order to show both the Lord's humility in going to sinners and the power of his teaching in converting penitents.*[199]

[Luke 5:33] **And they said to him: Why do the disciples of John fast often and make prayers, and the disciples of the Pharisees in like manner; but yours eat and drink?** Matthew reports that the disciples of John themselves said this to the Saviour.[200] Hence it is clear that both groups troubled him with this question. Here the disciples of John are particularly to be censured not only for boasting of their fasting, but also because they were unjustly criticizing the one whom they knew had been foretold by their teacher, and because they were joined by the Pharisees whom they knew had been condemned by him. The fact that the disciples of John and of the Pharisees fast, but the disciples of Christ eat and drink, means on a spiritual level that whether one follows the works of the Law

---

194 Jerome, *Commentarii in Matheum* 1 (CCSL 77:56.1304–05).
195 Isa. 53:5.
196 Rom. 10:3.
197 Ambrose, *Expos. Lucam* 5.21 (CCSL 14:141.206–07).
198 Jerome, *Commentarii in Matheum* 1 (CCSL 77:56.1290–91).
199 Jerome, *Commentarii in Matheum* 1 (CCSL 77:56.1296–1301).
200 Cf. Matt. 9:14.

or the traditions of men, or receives Christ's preaching only through the ear of the body, one wastes away with a hungry heart if one abstains from spiritual goods. But he who is incorporated with the limbs of Christ in faithful love cannot fast, because he feasts upon Christ's flesh and blood.

In another interpretation: *John does not drink wine and strong drink*,[201] but the Lord *eats and drinks with tax collectors and sinners*, because *the former, whose power does not come from his nature, increases his merit by abstinence, but why would* the Lord *who forgave sins by virtue of his very nature shun those whom he* could render purer *than those who were abstaining? But Christ also fasted, in order that you not shun his bidding, and ate with sinners, so that you might discern grace, and acknowledge his power.*[202]

[Luke 5:34–35] **To whom he said: Can you make the children of the bridegroom fast, while the bridegroom is with them? But the days will come, when the bridegroom will be taken away from them. Then they will fast in those days.** *Christ is the bridegroom; the Church is the bride. From this holy and spiritual marriage, the apostles are born.*[203] Hence, Mark the evangelist properly calls them the children of the marriage,[204] not only of the bridegroom, but also of the bride, wishing it to be understood that they have been taken up /125/ into the dignity of the divine family by the regeneration of baptism. *They are unable* to fast and *mourn as long as they see the bridegroom in the bedchamber and know that he is with his bride. But when the wedding is over and the time of the passion and resurrection is come, then the children of the bridegroom will fast.*[205] However, Luke does not say, as the others do: Can the children of the bridegroom or of the marriage fast or mourn?[206] But: *Can you make the children of the bridegroom fast?* He fittingly makes known that those very people who spoke were going to make the children of the bridegroom fast and mourn, since they were going to kill the bridegroom. But it should be noted that this mourning for the absence of the bridegroom does not only take place now, after the death and resurrection of this same bridegroom, but also took place throughout history before his incarnation. Certainly,

---

201 Cf. Luke 1:15.
202 Ambrose, *Expos. Lucam* 2.10–11 (CCSL 14:34.139–43; 35.147–49).
203 Jerome, *Commentarii in Matheum* 1 (CCSL 77:57.1319–20).
204 Cf. Mark 2:19.
205 Jerome, *Commentarii in Matheum* 1 (CCSL 77:57.1320–24).
206 Cf. Matt. 9:15; Mark 2:19.

the first age of the Church had saints who longed for the advent of the incarnation of Christ before the Virgin bore her child. But this present age, since he ascended into heaven, has saints who long for his appearance to judge the living and the dead. This ardent mourning of the Church knew no respite, except while he dwelt here in the flesh with his disciples. *And in accordance with the laws of tropology it should be known that as long as the bridegroom is with us, and we are in joy, we can neither fast nor mourn. But when he withdraws and flees from us on account of our sins, then fasting must be imposed and mourning brought back again.*[207]

[Luke 5:36] **And he spoke also a parable to them: That no man puts a piece from a new garment upon an old garment. Otherwise he both rends the new, and the piece taken from the new does not agree with the old.** *When the Lord was asked why his disciples did not fast,*[208] he replied that they were all still carnal, and not yet confirmed in the faith of his passion and resurrection, and so could not bear the precepts of stricter fasting and continence, lest by extreme austerity they lose even the faith that they seemed to have.[209] Therefore *he speaks* of the disciples up to this time *as if they were old garments to which it is not suitable to sew new cloth, that is, any bit of teaching that pertains to the sobriety of the new life; because, if this is done, and the teaching itself is torn off in some way, the bit that applies to fasting from food is lost in an untimely fashion, since that bit teaches fasting in a general sense, not only from the eager desire for food, but from all the pleasures of temporal delights. He says that this cloth, that is, any part that pertains to food,* /126/ *ought not to be shared with men who are still devoted to the old custom, both because the tear seems to be from that direction, so to speak, and also because it is not suitable for that decrepit age.*[210]

[Luke 5:37–38] **And no man puts new wine into old bottles; otherwise the new wine breaks the bottles, and it spills, and the bottles will be lost. But new wine must be put into new bottles, and both are preserved.** He also compares those same men to *old bottles, which he says are more readily broken by new wine, that is, by spiritual precepts, than able to contain it. And they will become new bottles, when they are renewed after the Lord's ascension with longing for his consolation by prayer and hope.*

---

207 Jerome, *Commentarii in Matheum* 1 (CCSL 77:57.1332–36).
208 Augustine, *Quaestiones euang.* 2.18 (CCSL 44B:60.4–6).
209 Cf. Jerome, *Commentarii in Matheum* 1 (CCSL 77:58.1343–47).
210 Augustine, *Quaestiones euang.* 2.18 (CCSL 44B:61.13–23).

*For then they received the Holy Spirit, and filled with the Spirit they spoke in every language; then the Jews, knowing nothing and yet witnessing correctly, said 'that these men are full of new wine'.*[211] *For now new wine had come in new bottles*,[212] that is, the ardour of the Holy Spirit had refilled the hearts of spiritual men. In another interpretation: Let the teacher take care, lest he entrust the secrets of the new mysteries to a soul who is not yet renewed, but still persists in the senescence of wickedness.

[Luke 5:39] **And no man drinking old wine has immediately a desire for new; for he says, 'The old is better.'** This signifies the Jews, tainted by the spittle of the old life, who deemed the precepts of the new grace unworthy; besmirched by the traditions of their elders, they were entirely unable to perceive the sweet taste of spiritual words.

## Chapter 19

41/2 [Luke 6:1] **And it happened on the second-first Sabbath**[213] **as they went through the grain fields that his disciples plucked the ears and ate, rubbing them in their hands.** Mark says[214] that the disciples, *on account of the excessive importunity* of those who were coming to be healed, *had not even time to eat, and therefore they hungered like men. But the fact that they rub the ears of grain in their hands, and thus allay their hunger points to the stricter life of those who seek simple fare and not banquets laid out for them.* And *note that the first apostles of the Saviour destroy the letter of the Sabbath; this is contrary to the position of the Ebionites*,[215] *who reject Paul as a transgressor of the Law, although they accept the other apostles.*[216]

Hence Luke rightly calls the day on which the letter of the Sabbath began to be destroyed '*deuteroproton*', that is, second-first, wishing to make known that the observance of the Sabbath of the Law ought to cease from that time on, and the freedom of the natural Sabbath, /127/ which was the same as other days up to the time of Moses, ought to be restored.

211  Acts 2:13.
212  Augustine, *Quaestiones euang.* 2.18 (CCSL 44B:61.24–30).
213  Authorities differ as to what this means. Bede's explanation is what he has drawn from Ambrose.
214  Cf. Mark 6:31.
215  Cf. Isidore, *Etym.* 8.5.36.
216  Jerome, *Commentarii in Matheum* 2 (CCSL 77:87.286–90; 293–95).

And this is so that, just as Abraham's faith, by which he was justified in uncircumcision, working through love, maintains the Church, and not circumcision or the ceremonies of the Law, so the spiritual Sabbath, whereby Abraham himself always was free from servile, that is, culpable deeds, may commend the Church to God through the sevenfold grace of the Holy Spirit. So Luke calls 'second-first' the Sabbath of this age, on which it is permitted to do all useful things just as on other days – this in contrast to the Sabbath of the Jews, on which it was not permitted to take a journey, or to gather wood, or to do any necessary things whatever. To be sure, this first Sabbath came before the second, whether one speaks of temporal order, because through uncounted ages before the Law it was spent by the patriarchs just as it is spent now, or whether it indeed signifies by the gift of grace that you should understand the second-first Sabbath to be none other than the superior in comparison to the lesser. For also: *The first man was of the earth, earthly, the second man, from heaven, heavenly.*[217] Nevertheless no one errs, if he wishes to call the Lord Jesus Christ the second-first Adam, who preceded the first Adam in merit and grace, though not by order of human birth, according to what his forerunner says: *He who comes after me, is preferred before me, because he was before me.*[218] And the expression 'the second-first Sabbath' can be understood so that one and the same Sabbath of the New Testament is both second and first. Second, because it is observed by us after the Sabbath of the Law; first, because it was also observed by the just men of old before the decrees of the Law.[219]

But in a mystical sense, the disciples go through the grain fields, namely those people of whom the Lord says: *Lift up your eyes, and see the fields, for they are white already for harvest, and he who reaps receives wages,*[220] and therefore they are understood to hunger for nothing better than the salvation of men. Once when the first of these reapers was praying, he hungered for this when the feast he longed for was immediately spread out, and he heard: *Arise, Peter, kill and eat.*[221] And that animals are ordered to be killed and eaten in that passage,[222] and ears of grain are said to be rubbed and nevertheless eaten in this one, illustrates the marvellous

---

217  1 Cor. 15:47.
218  John 1:15. John the Baptist is the forerunner who says this.
219  Bede draws upon Ambrose, *Expos. Lucam* 5.31 (CCSL 14:146.350–71) for this paragraph without quoting him directly.
220  John 4:35–36.
221  Acts 10:13.
222  Cf. Acts 10:12.

harmony of a mystery. For it is said: *Mortify your members which are upon the earth* and strip *yourselves of the old man with his deeds,*[223] because no one passes into the body of Christ otherwise, and not otherwise does progress nourish the preacher with its fruits. So, to pluck ears is to pluck men from earthly purposes on which they had fixed the foundation of their mind like a root. And to rub /**128**/ with the hands, is to release purity of mind with examples of virtues even from the eager desire of the flesh, like the husks and coverings of the ears of grain. But to eat grain is for everyone who has been cleansed *from all defilement of the flesh and of the spirit*[224] to be incorporated through the mouths of preachers with the members of the Church. And it is well said, according to Mark, that the disciples did this as they went out ahead of the Lord,[225] because it is necessary that the discourse of the teacher come first, and thus the heart of the pupil will light up with the grace of divine visitation.

[Luke 6:2] **And some of the Pharisees said to them: Why do you do what is not lawful on the Sabbath days?** Other evangelists relate that these objections were made instead to the Lord himself.[226] But whether they were said to him, or to his disciples, or to both by several accusers in different places (for it was impossible for any evangelist to write a falsehood), nevertheless since whatever is done by the disciples refers to the one whose spiritual authority they follow in their actions, he immediately overcomes false defenders of the Law with true examples of the saints, in accordance with what Isaiah says: *And he will reprove with equity for the meek of the earth.*[227] For Jesus said:

[Luke 6:3b–4] **Have you not read so much as this, what David did, when he himself was hungry, and they that were with him; how he went into the house of God, and took and ate the bread of proposition, and gave to them that were with him, which it is not lawful to eat but only for the priests?** The history of the Kings[228] tells how the blessed David escaping the snares of Saul came to Ahimelech the priest in Nob and begged for food for himself and his servants. But not having any ordinary bread, the priest first ascertained that the young men were free

---

223 Col. 3:5 & 9.
224 2 Cor. 7:1.
225 Cf. Mark 2:23.
226 Cf. Matt. 12:2; Mark 2:24.
227 Isa. 11:4.
228 Cf. 1 Sam. 21:1–6.

from impurity with women for the previous three days, and then he did not hesitate to give him consecrated bread, judging it better, even as the prophet says: *'I want mercy and not sacrifice'*,[229] *to free men from the danger of hunger than to offer sacrifice to God. For the salvation of men is a sacrifice acceptable to God. Therefore, the Lord objects* to the false accusations *of the Pharisees and says: If David is holy and the chief priest Ahimelech is not faulted by you, even though both have transgressed the commandment of the Law with an acceptable excuse and hunger is the reason, why do you not approve of the same hunger in the apostles that you approve in the others? Although there may also be a great difference in this: these are rubbing the ears in their hand on the Sabbath, while those ate the Levitical bread, and the ceremony of the Sabbath was in the offing.*[230] *For* the loaves of the bread of proposition used to be *baked before the* /129/ *Sabbath, and the offerings were placed on the sacred table early in the morning on the Sabbath,* facing one another in two stacks of six loaves each, *with two golden bowls filled with frankincense set above them. The bowls remained until the next Sabbath, and then other loaves* were fetched in in place of these loaves, and these *were given to the priests. And after the frankincense was burned in the sacred fire in which all the burnt offerings used to be made, other frankincense was heaped upon another twelve loaves.*[231] David, appearing at this hour, and receiving the consecrated loaves, makes known figuratively *that the priestly food is to be given over to the use of the people, whether because we all ought to imitate the priestly life, or because all the children of the Church are priests. For we are anointed into the holy priesthood, offering ourselves up as spiritual sacrifices to God.*[232]

[Luke 6:5] **And he said to them: The Son of man is also Lord of the Sabbath.** If, he says, King David may be excused for having fed on priestly food, and according to the assurance of another Gospel the priests who violate the Sabbath through their ministry of the temple are blameless,[233]

---

229 Matt. 9:13, quoting Hosea 6:6.
230 Jerome, *Commentarii in Matheum* 2 (CCSL 77:88.300–17).
231 Josephus, *The Latin Josephus: The Antiquities* 3.10.7 (*Acta Jutlandica* 30:251.11–16); cf. Lev. 24:1–9. In his commentary on 1 Samuel Bede mentions that he had cited this passage in his commentary on Luke: see DeGregorio and Love, *Bede: On First Samuel*, Introduction, 4.
232 Ambrose, *Expos. Lucam* 5.33 (CCSL 14:147.384–88): the last sentence draws on 1 Pet. 2:5.
233 Cf. Matt. 12:5.

how much more is the Son of man not held responsible for the offence of having plucked out ears of grain on the Sabbath, he *who is the true King and the true Priest, and therefore is the Lord of the Sabbath.*[234]

## Chapter 20

42/2 [Luke 6:6] **And on another Sabbath he entered into the synagogue and taught, and there was a man there whose right hand was withered.** The Lord teaches in the synagogue and works miracles chiefly on Sabbath days, not only to introduce the spiritual Sabbath, but also because there was a more numerous assembly of people on that day. At that time it was the custom, following the ancient institutions of the patriarchs, for those who were commanded by the Law to abstain from work to attend to reading and listening to the Scriptures, just as James says in the Acts of the Apostles: *For Moses from olden days has those who preach him in the synagogues, where he is read every Sabbath.*[235] For just as those who practise the art of hunting spread their nets where they have learned that wild animals, fish, and birds are more abundant, so likewise the Lord *always taught in the synagogue and in the temple where all the Jews congregated,*[236] because he wished *everyone to be saved and to come to knowledge of the truth.*[237] Clearly, the man who had a withered hand signifies the human race, withered up by the fruitlessness of good work, but cured by the mercy of the Lord. Its right hand, which had withered in the first parent as he plucked the fruits of the forbidden tree,[238] has been restored to health by the sap of good works through the grace of the Redeemer as he stretched out his innocent hands on the tree of the cross. And it is well that in the synagogue the hand was withered, because where there is the greater gift of knowledge, there is there the graver danger of unforgivable sin.[239] /130/

[Luke 6:7] **And the scribes and the Pharisees watched if he would heal on the Sabbath, so that they might find an accusation against him.** Since the teacher *had excused with a credible example the violation of the*

---

234 Augustine, *Quaestiones xvii in Matt.* 10 (CCSL 44B:124.6–7).
235 Acts 15:21.
236 John 18:20.
237 1 Tim. 2:4.
238 Cf. Gen. 3:6: in Genesis Eve does the plucking, but Ambrose, whose commentary Bede is following, says it was Adam.
239 Cf. Ambrose, *Expos. Lucam* 5.39 (CCSL 14:149.421–24).

Sabbath, which the Pharisees had blamed in the disciples, now *they want to trick* the teacher *himself* by watching him, *so that if* he should heal on the Sabbath, they may blame him *for his transgression, and if he should not, for his cruelty or powerlessness.*[240]

[Luke 6:8] **But he knew their thoughts**, and so forth. That is, because we read: *The Lord knows the thoughts of men, that they are vain.*[241] And what follows: *Blessed is the man whom you will instruct, Lord, and you will teach him out of your Law*,[242] was said of those who learned that the Law was fulfilled by Christ, and that what it commanded was not a carnal, but a spiritual Sabbath.

[Luke 6:9] **Then Jesus said to them: I ask you, if it is lawful on the Sabbath to do good or evil,** ... Anticipating the trickery which the Jews had perfidiously prepared for him, the Lord reproved them for violating *the commandments of the Law* with a perverse interpretation by judging that there ought to be a respite *on the Sabbath even from good works. For the Law* orders an abstention from evil works, saying: *You shall do no servile work on that day*,[243] that is, sin: for *whoever commits sin is the slave of sin.*[244] He also foreshadows *in the present*, by the same command at the same time, *the nature* of the world to come when those who have done good works throughout the six ages of this world will in the seventh age enjoy rest only from evil works, not from good ones. *For although worldly works entirely cease, to repose in the praise of God is an active deed of good work.*[245]

[Luke 6:9b] **To save life or to destroy?** That is, to heal a man or not? It is the same as what he had said just before: *To do good or evil?* Of course, God, who is supremely good, could not be the author of our evil or our destruction; rather, it is customary for Scripture to say that he destroys, not saves. For example, he is said to have hardened the heart of Pharaoh,[246] not because he hardened a heart that was soft, but because he would not soften in pity one that was hardened by earlier deeds. And when we pray that he not lead *us into temptation*, we immediately add *but free us from evil*,[247] because

---

240 Jerome, *Commentarii in Matheum* 2 (CCSL 77:89.351–55).
241 Ps. 93:11 (94:11) (*iuxta LXX* blended with *iuxta Hebr.*).
242 Ps. 93:12 (94:12).
243 Lev. 23:3 ('servile' [Lat. *seruile*] does not appear in the Vulgate text, but is common among patristic fathers when they cite the verse).
244 John 8:34.
245 Ambrose, *Expos. Lucam* 5.39 (CCSL 14:149.424–30).
246 Cf. Exod. 7:3.
247 Matt. 6:13.

BOOK TWO                                                              261

we are clearly being taught that to lead a man's soul into temptation is none other than not to free his soul from evil; and that to destroy his soul is not to make his soul safe from destruction.[248] But if it bothers anyone that when the Lord was about to heal the body, he would ask about the salvation of the soul, one should understand either that, as is customary in the Scriptures, 'soul' has been used /131/ in place of 'man' (as for example when it is said: These are *the souls that went out from Jacob's thigh*[249]), *or that he did those miracles for the sake of the salvation of the soul, or that healing of the hand in itself signified the salvation of the soul, which, in ceasing from good works, as I said above, seemed in some way to have a withered right hand.*[250]

[Luke 6:10] **And looking round about on them all, he said to the man: Stretch forth your hand. And he stretched it forth, and his hand was restored.** He orders the withered hand to be stretched out to be healed, because the infirmity of the unfruitful soul is cured in no better way than by generous alms. To the multitudes who asked what they should do that they not be cast like withered trees into the fire,[251] John the Baptist commanded only this: *He who has two coats, let him give to him who has none; and he who has food, let him do in like manner.*[252] And in Ecclesiasticus it is said: *Son, let not your hand be stretched out to receive, and shut when you should give.*[253] For he, who would not extend his hands to offer a kindness to a begging widow, spreads them out in vain to God to beg forgiveness for his sins.

[Luke 6:11] **And they were filled with madness, and they discussed with one another what they might do to Jesus.** It was great madness indeed, that those who especially stood in need of salvation took counsel about killing the Saviour. It shows how devoted they are to wickedness that they consider it an offence that at Jesus's word, the sick man stretched out his right hand, as if each of them had not done greater things on Sabbath days by carrying food, by offering a cup, and by carrying out other things that are necessary for nourishment. For he who *spoke, and they were made,*[254] could not be found guilty of labouring on the Sabbath.

---

248 Cf. Gregory, *Hom. in Hiezech.* 1.11.25 (CCSL 142:181); *Moralia* 31.14 (CCSL 143B:1569).
249 Gen. 46:26; Exod. 1:5.
250 Augustine, *Quaestiones euang.* 2.7 (CCSL 44B:51.6–9).
251 Cf. Luke 3:8–10.
252 Luke 3:11.
253 Ecclus. 4:1 & 36.
254 Ps. 32:9 (33:9).

## Chapter 21

**43/2** [Luke 6:12] **And in those days he went out onto a mountain to pray.** *Not everyone who prays [orat] ascends onto a mountain. For it is speech [oratio] that causes sin. But the one who prays well, who seeks God here on earth through prayer, ascends to the summit of sublime solicitude, advancing from earthly to heavenly things.* But the one *who anxiously prays for wealth and for worldly preferment,*[255] or indeed for the death of an enemy, lying in the depths, sends worthless prayers to God. But *the Lord does not pray to pray for himself, but to intercede for me. For although the Father put everything in the power of the Son,*[256] *nevertheless the Son, to fulfil the nature of man, deems that the Father ought to be prayed to on our behalf, because he is our advocate. For, it says, 'we have an advocate with the Father, Jesus Christ'.*[257] *If he is my advocate, he ought to intercede for my sins. Therefore, he prays not as one who is frail, but like one who is benevolent. You want to know how he can do everything that he wishes? He is both advocate and judge. In the former is the duty of benevolence, in the latter is the badge of office of power.*[258] /132/

[Luke 6:12b] **And he passed the whole night in the prayer of God.** *The pattern which you should emulate is prescribed for you. For what must you do for your salvation, when Christ passes the whole night for you in prayer? What is it fitting for you to do, when you wish to undertake some duty of devotion, when Christ, who was about to send forth his apostles, first* took care first to pray? *You want to know how he prayed for me, not for himself?*[259]

**44/2** [Luke 6:13] **And when day came**, it says, **he called his disciples and he chose twelve of them,** ... It should be observed here that evangelical and apostolic Scripture[260] not only calls these men the twelve disciples of Christ, but also all those who, believing in him, were instructed for the kingdom of heaven by his teaching. Indeed, disciples [*discipuli*] are so called from 'learning' [*discendo*],[261] and it is from the multitude of these that he chose whom he wished.

---

255 Ambrose, *Expos. Lucam* 5.41 (CCSL 14:149.441–45).
256 Cf. John 17:2.
257 1 John 2:1.
258 Ambrose, *Expos. Lucam* 5.42 (CCSL 14:150.455–66).
259 Ambrose, *Expos. Lucam* 5.43 (CCSL 14:150.467–72; 475–76).
260 I.e., the Gospels and the Epistles.
261 Cf. Isidore, *Etym.* 1.1.1.

[Luke 6:13b] **Whom he also named apostles:** ... They are called 'apostles' [*apostoli*] in Greek, but 'messengers' [*missi*] in Latin. The evangelist Mark explains the mystery of this term, saying: *And he brought it about that twelve should be with him, and that he might send* [*mitteret*] *them to preach the Gospel.*[262] And the Lord himself says: *As the Father has sent* [*misit*] *me, I also send* [*mitto*] *you.*[263] It is appropriate that twelve were chosen, in order that the salvation of the world which they preach by their word might be commended allegorically in their number. For *three times four is twelve.*[264] As I said earlier,[265] it is for this reason that when Solomon built the temple for the Lord he also made the bronze 'sea' in which the priests were washed as a token of the Church, and he placed it on the haunches of twelve oxen, three of which faced north, three west, three south, and three east,[266] thus allegorically making known that the apostles and the successors of the apostles were going to cleanse from sins all the regions of the quadripartite world with the faith and confession of the holy Trinity.

[Luke 6:14] **Simon, whom he surnamed Peter, and Andrew his brother,** ... This was not the first time he gave the surname Peter to Simon, but long before, when he looked upon him after he was brought to him by his brother Andrew, he said: *You are Simon, the son of Jona; you will be called Cephas, which is interpreted Peter.*[267] But when Luke, wishing to recall the names of the twelve apostles, had to refer to 'Peter', he wished briefly to intimate that he was not called this before, but that the Lord surnamed him thus, although not at that time, but when John set down those very words of the Lord, making his listeners attentive. For if he had been called 'Peter' before, you would not see the mystery of the stone because you would think that he was called so by chance, and not by the providence of God. For this reason, Luke wished /133/ him to be called something else first, so that from this very change of name the living force of the mystery might be entrusted. Therefore, Peter in Latin is the same as

---

262 Mark 3:14.
263 John 20:21.
264 Literally: 'three times four is ten-plus-two' (*ter etiam quaterni decus dipondius*): Primasius, *Commentarius in Apocalypsin* 2.7.55–56 (CCSL 92:108.55–56), quoted by Bede in *Exp. Apoc.*, 313 (trans. Wallis, 150).
265 Cf. above, in commentary on Luke 3:23a, 202.
266 Cf. 3 Kings 7:23–25; 2 Chron. 4:2–4. Bede takes up this allegory in greater detail in *De templo* 18.13 & 19.1–3.
267 John 1:42.

264    BEDE: *COMMENTARY ON THE GOSPEL OF LUKE*

Cephas in Syriac, and in both languages the name is derived from 'rock', which is without doubt the one of which Paul says: *And the rock was Christ.*[268] For just as the true light, Christ,[269] granted to the apostles that they be called *the light of the world*,[270] so also he bestowed the name of Peter upon Simon, who believed in Christ the rock. On another occasion playing upon its etymology, he said: *You are Peter, and upon this rock I will build my Church.*[271] But some people, incautiously seeking a Hebrew etymology for a Latin or a Greek word, say that Peter means 'destroying', or 'removing the shoe', or 'recognizing',[272] although both the exposition of John the evangelist which I recalled earlier, and the Hebrew language itself, which completely lacks the sound of the letter P,[273] proves that this is not a Hebrew word. For by improperly writing 'Feter' for Peter, just like 'Faul' and 'Filate' for Paul and Pilate, they are incautiously binding a false meaning to a made-up word. And Simon means 'obedient'.[274] Next, Andrew is a Greek word, and *apo tou andros, that is, he is called 'manly', from 'man'.*[275] The first of the apostles, who immediately recognized the Lamb of God thanks to John, and took care to see and hear him, are rightly graced by these names. The fact that Simon means 'laying down grief' or 'hearing sorrow' is suited to that time, when he saw the Lord after the resurrection, and laid down the grief of the latter's death and of his own denial, but heard immediately the sorrow of his own death, when the Lord says: *But when you will be old, you will stretch forth your hands, and another will gird you and lead you where you would not go.*[276]

[Luke 6:14b–15] **James and John, Philip and Bartholomew, Matthew and Thomas, ...** In the list of apostles, Luke beautifully and reverently calls Matthew by his usual name, but in his first mention of the custom-house

---

268  1 Cor. 10:4. Bede is correct about the meaning of these two names, although it is not clear how he learned about the latter. Neither Jerome nor Isidore explicitly declares that Cephas means 'rock' in Syriac, although it might be inferred from Isidore's *Etym.* 7.9.2–3 (where it is also confusingly stated that Cephas is related to the Greek word for head, because Peter was 'the head of the apostles').
269  Cf. John 8:12.
270  Matt. 5:14.
271  Matt. 16:18.
272  Jerome is one of these persons. Cf. his *Hebr. nom.* (CCSL 72:141.18 ['recognizing']; 147. 16 ['destroying']; 155.21 ['removing the shoe']).
273  Cf. Jerome, *Hebr. nom.* (CCSL 72:141.19–21).
274  Cf. Jerome, *Hebr. nom.* (CCSL 72:148.4).
275  Jerome, *Hebr. nom.* (CCSL 72:142.26–27).
276  John 21:18.

BOOK TWO 265

he preferred to call him Levi, as I pointed out above.[277] In accordance with what was written: *Tell your iniquities to justify yourself,*[278] Matthew not only clearly called himself Matthew the tax collector when he was summoned from the custom-house[279] and in the list of the apostles,[280] but also he placed himself after his companion Thomas in the list, although he was placed before by the other /134/ evangelists.[281] Of course, James and John, who on account of their extraordinary eminence of virtue and soul, are named by the Lord 'the sons of thunder', that is, Boanerges, or as it is more correctly written, Banereem.[282] And not without reason! One of them, thundering from the heavens that theological pronouncement which no one before knew how to bring forth, burst out: *In the beginning was the Word, and the Word was with God, and the Word was God,* and so forth.[283] He left these words, which are filled with such great power that, if he had wished to thunder much more, the world itself *would not be able to contain* them.[284] But both James and John were also often privileged to be led into a mountain apart[285] and once to hear a terrifying sound *from a cloud: This is my beloved Son.*[286] They also bore ancient names that were very appropriate to their merits. For *James* is called *the supplanter,*[287] and John means *'in whom is grace'* or *'the grace of the Lord'*.[288] For the former rejoiced to supplant the care of the flesh at the Lord's summons, and to despise the flesh itself when Herod slew him;[289] the latter on account of the extraordinary grace, which he had acquired by his virginal glory, reclined on the breast of his Redeemer at the supper.[290]

277 See above, in commentary on Luke 5:27.
278 Isa. 43:26.
279 Cf. Matt. 9:9–11.
280 Cf. Matt. 10:3.
281 Cf. Matt. 10:3; Mark 3:18; Luke 6:15. Bede assumes, as many modern scholars do not, that the apostle Matthew and the evangelist were one and the same person.
282 Cf. Mark 3:17; Jerome, *Commentarii in Danielem* 1.1.7 (CCSL 75A:780.76–79); *Hebr. nom.* (CCSL 72:142.9–10).
283 John 1:1.
284 John 21:25.
285 Cf. Matt. 17:1.
286 Matt. 17:5.
287 Jerome, *Hebr. nom.* (CCSL 72:67.19); cf. Gen. 27:36. The Hebrew name 'Jacob' (as in the story of Jacob and Esau), which is Latinized in the Vulgate New Testament as *Iacobus* (and hence in Bede), is rendered in English versions of the New Testament as 'James'.
288 Jerome, *Hebr. nom.* (CCSL 72:146.16–17).
289 Cf. Acts 12:2.
290 Cf. John 13:23.

*Philip* means *mouth of the lamp*,[291] and rightly so, because he was also called by the Lord, and immediately after, finding Nathanael, he preached the light which he had recognized, saying: *We have found him of whom Moses in the Law, and the prophets wrote, Jesus the son of Joseph of Nazareth.*[292] And afterwards, because he felt that he knew too little about the light, he humbly asked, saying: *Lord, show us the Father, and it is enough for us.*[293]

*Bartholomew is Syriac, not Hebrew*, and means *son of one supporting the waters*,[294] that is, the Son of God, who supports the minds of his preachers so that they may contemplate divine matters, and so that the more freely they fly through the heights, the more fruitfully they inebriate their hearts with the drops of his earthly sayings. Hence Moses, speaking allegorically of the Church, well says: *For the land, which you go to possess, is not like the land of Egypt, from whence you came out, where, when the seed is sown, waters are brought in to water it after the manner of gardens, but it is a land expecting rain from heaven, which its God always visits.*[295] For worldly wisdom slithers through the soil like a serpent, but divine wisdom thunders from the heavens.

*Matthew* means *given*,[296] surely because by a great gift of the Lord he was transferred from being a collector of public revenue to the office of apostle and evangelist.[297]

*Thomas* means *the abyss or twin*; hence he is also called *Didymus* in Greek,[298] because insofar as he doubted longer than the others, to that extent he learned the truth /135/ of the Lord's resurrection the more deeply.[299] The priest Paulinus of Nola sang beautifully about this:

Here lies doubting Thomas with the twin name Didymus;
Christ permitted him to doubt with the hesitation of a fearful mind
For the benefit of our faith, so that we too,
Strengthened by this leader, and trembling before the Lord and God,

---

291 Jerome, *Hebr. nom.* (CCSL 72:140.22–23).
292 John 1:45.
293 John 14:8.
294 Jerome, *Hebr. nom.* (CCSL 72:135.20–21).
295 Deut. 11:10–12.
296 Jerome, *Hebr. nom.* (CCSL 72:137.20).
297 Cf. Matt. 9:9.
298 Jerome, *Hebr. nom.* (CCSL 72:138.10–11).
299 Cf. John 20:24–28.

BOOK TWO  267

May confess that Jesus truly lives after death,
Showing on his body the living wounds of his flesh.[300]
[Luke 6:15b] **James son of Alphaeus, and Simon who is called Zelotes,** ... He set down these names with an additional indication to distinguish them from James son of Zebedee and Simon Peter, and even from Judas the traitor. For John pointed out that the latter was also called Simon, saying: *And when he had dipped the bread, he gave it to Judas Simon [the son] of Iscariot.*[301] And indeed James the son of Alphaeus himself is the one who is called in the Gospel the brother of the Lord,[302] since Mary, the wife of Alphaeus, was the sister of Mary, the mother of the Lord. She was the one whom the evangelist John surnamed Mary of Cleophas,[303] perhaps either because this same Alphaeus was also called Cleophas, or because Mary herself, when Alphaeus died after James was born, was married to Cleophas. Ecclesiastical history relates that she bore him a son, Simeon, and that this Simeon (or else the apostle Simon, or some other Simeon) being the cousin of the Lord, because Cleophas was the brother of Joseph, ruled the Church at Jerusalem after James. But that James was rightly surnamed 'son of Alphaeus', that is, of the learned one,[304] the apostles themselves testify, who ranked him as bishop of Jerusalem immediately after the Lord's passion. And that before he shed his blood James was likewise the true supplanter of carnal desire the historian *Hegesippus, who lived at the time of the apostles,* testifies, saying: *James, the brother of*

---

300 Paulinus of Nola, *Carmen* 27.415–20 (CSEL 30:280).
301 John 13:26. In Bede's rendering of John's verse, Judas is identified as *Iudae Simoni Scariotis,* where *Iudae* and *Simoni* must be datives and *Scariothis* looks to be a genitive. The phrase appears in the Weber/Gryson edition of the Vulgate as *Iudae Simonis Scariotis,* with *Simoni* and *Iscariotae* recorded as variants. 'Iscariot', which appears eleven times in the Vulgate, gave scribes a headache. They sometimes opted for the invariable form *Scarioth. Schariothen,* acc., and *Iscariotae,* gen., occur; but more commonly scribes followed the pattern of third declension Greek names like 'Pericles'. So: *Scariotes/Iscariotes,* nom., *Iscariotem,* acc. In this pattern *Scariot(h)is* would be the expected form of the genitive; but some scribes apparently treated *Scariotis* as invariable, like *Scarioth.* Douay/Rheims and KJV translate the phrase as 'Judas Iscariot, *the son* of Simon'; NRSV as 'Judas son of Simon Iscariot' (NRSV, 1905, note e, adds: 'Other ancient authorities read *Judas Iscariot son of Simon*; others, *Judas son of Simon from Karyot'.* In short, we cannot be sure whether Bede understood the phrase to mean 'Judas Simon [the son] of Iscariot', or simply 'Judas Simon Iscariot'.
302 Cf. Matt. 13:55.
303 Cf. John 19:25.
304 Cf. Isidore, *Etym.* 7.9.15.

the Lord, surnamed the Just, received the church of Jerusalem after the apostles. Many indeed are called James; this one was called Holy from the womb of his mother, drank neither wine and liquor, ate no flesh, was never shaved, and was neither anointed with perfume nor used the baths. It was his custom to enter the Holy of Holies. Since he did not use woollen clothing, but linen, and he used to enter alone into the temple and pray for the people on bended knees so much, that his knees were believed to have become as hard as those of camels.[305] This Simon Zelotes is the same as Simon the Cananaean[306] from the village of Cana /136/ in Galilee, where the Lord turned water into wine.[307] *For indeed Cana means 'zeal',*[308] *and Cananaean means 'zealot'.*

[Luke 6:16] **Jude brother of James, and Judas Iscariot, who was the traitor.** In order to distinguish them,[309] he composed their names with two elements. One of them, as Jude himself writes in his Catholic Epistle, is the brother of James,[310] who is also called Thaddeus.[311] The other *acquired an appellation, either from the village in which he was born, or from the tribe of Issachar, that presaged his damnation. For indeed Issachar, because it means 'fee', reveals the price of treason,*[312] and Iscariot, because it means *'remembrance of death',*[313] reveals that he was not suddenly induced, but intended for a very long time to secretly commit the sin of betraying the Lord. *He is chosen* among the apostles *not through want of foresight, but by Providence. For how great is the truth, which a hostile servant does not damage? How great is the moral rectitude of the Lord, who preferred when among us to endanger his exercise of judgement, rather than his love? For he had taken upon himself the frailty of a man, and therefore he did not reject these elements of human weakness. He willed to be abandoned; he willed to be betrayed; he willed to be handed over by his own apostle, in order that, abandoned by your companion, betrayed by your companion, you may bear quietly that your virtue went astray, and that your favour perished.*[314]

---

305 Jerome, *De uiris illustribus* 2 (ed. Cerasa-Gastaldo, 74–76).
306 Cf. Matt. 10:4; Mark 3:18.
307 Cf. John 2:1–10.
308 Jerome, *Commentarii in Matheum* 1 (CCSL 77:64.1520).
309 Jude and Judas are different English renderings of the same name (*Iudas*).
310 Cf. Jude 1:1.
311 Cf. Matt. 10:3; Mark 3:18.
312 Jerome, *Commentarii in Matheum* 1 (CCSL 77:64.1526–29).
313 Jerome, *Hebr. nom.* (CCSL 72:137.9).
314 Ambrose, *Expos. Lucam* 5.45 (CCSL 14:151.484–91).

**45/1** [Luke 6:17] **And coming down with them, he stood in a level place, and the company of his disciples, and a great multitude of people.** When he was about to choose his apostles, the Lord went into the hill country, but when he is about to teach the multitudes, he returns to the plains, because the multitudes are not capable of seeing Christ except in a low place.[315] For this is the precept which the Apostle, having obeyed it, prescribes: *I could not speak to you as spiritual people, but as people of the flesh, as little ones in Christ. I gave you milk to drink, not meat, for you were not able as yet, but neither indeed are you now able.*[316] And the apostles themselves, according to Matthew, being as it were more perfect, are reported to have been taught both on a mountain and from the Saviour's open mouth.[317] Where, if anyone should wish to investigate each evangelist more thoroughly, it *can be understood, when he chose on the mountain twelve disciples from many, 'whom he also named apostles',*[318] *which Matthew omitted, that he gave then the sermon, which Matthew included and Luke passed over in silence, that is, on the mountain. But then, after he had descended in a level place, it can be understood that he gave another similar sermon about which Matthew is silent, but Luke is not, and that each sermon was ended in the same way.*[319]

[Luke 6:17b] **From all Judea and Jerusalem and the maritime region, both of Tyre and of Sidon,** and so forth. I think the multitude from the 'maritime region' was so-called, not from the nearby sea [*mare*] of Galilee (for he did not specify this as the site of the miracle), but from the Great Sea, which would include Tyre and Sidon as well. Because the cities of the Gentiles were actually allotted to the Jews,[320] but not occupied by them /137/ because they were unable to expel their enemies, they are deliberately set down by name to make known how great is the renown and power of the Saviour, which invites even foreign cities to grasp his salvation and his teaching. Here it should be noted that the Lord is not known to have entered their cities,[321] even though he took pity on the Gentiles coming to him, which is why, after confirming the faith of the petitioners, he healed the centurion's

---

315 Cf. Ambrose, *Expos. Lucam* 5.46 (CCSL 14:151.493–95).
316 1 Cor. 3:1–2.
317 Cf. Matt. 5:1–2; Ambrose, *Expos. Lucam* 5.47–48 (CCSL 14:151.504–14).
318 Luke 6:13.
319 Augustine, *De consensu euang.* 2.19.25 (CSEL 43:146.20–147.4).
320 Cf. Jos. 19:28–29. Tyre and Sidon were among the cities given by lot to Asher.
321 That is, the cities of the Gentiles, like Tyre and Sidon.

servant[322] and the daughter of the Canaanite woman.[323] Evidently this was done so as not to furnish an occasion for complaint to the calumniating Jews. Instead, he kept back the full salvation of the Gentiles until the time of his passion and resurrection. When that time was drawing near, he says to the Gentiles seeking to see him: *Unless the grain of wheat falling to the ground dies, it remains alone. But if it dies, it brings forth much fruit.*[324]

[Luke 6:19] **And all the multitude sought to touch him, for power went out from him and healed all.** Just as earlier on the leper is cured when the Lord touches him,[325] so here all the multitude that were able to touch him are healed. The Saviour's touch, therefore, is necessary for salvation. To touch him is faithfully to believe in him. To be touched by him is to be confirmed by his grace. But each one abounds in his own understanding. The multitudes, which flow together from afar, are healed by the touch of the Lord as he descends into the plain. The disciples, who have already been instructed in lesser things, are conveyed to the top of the mountain for instruction in greater ones. From them are likewise chosen those who will witness in private his transfiguration on the mountain.[326] One who surpassed the others, drunk so to speak from a fountain of higher wisdom, reclines on the Master's breast.[327] Rarely will you find anywhere either multitudes following the Lord to higher things or a cripple being healed on a mountain, but, when the fever of wanton desire has been extinguished and the light of knowledge kindled, you will find the person who experiences this approaching step by step the summit of virtues. Even in the Old Testament Moses, when he ascended the mountain of God alone with Joshua, appointed Aaron and Hur to rule the people on the plain until they should return.[328] *Aaron* indeed, which means *mountain of fortitude*,[329] signifies the unique loftiness of the Lord's incarnation. But *Hur*, which means *fire*,[330] signifies

---

322 Cf. Matt. 8:5–13. The healing of the centurion's servant took place in Capernaum, a city on the west coast of the Sea of Galilee that was a residence of Christ and his disciples and the site of many of his miracles.
323 Cf. Matt. 15:21–28. The Canaanite woman is said to come from the shores of Tyre and Sidon.
324 John 12:24.
325 Cf. Luke 5:12–13.
326 Cf. Matt. 17:1–2; Mark 9:1; Luke 9:28–29.
327 Cf. John 13:23.
328 Cf. Exod. 24:13–14.
329 Jerome, *Hebr. nom.* (CCSL 72:73.6).
330 Jerome, *Hebr. nom.* (CCSL 72:77.5).

the gift of the Holy Spirit, because many little ones in the Church, although they are unable to accompany their teachers as they enter into the mysteries of the supreme godhead, can nevertheless be redeemed by the sacraments of the incarnation, and be sealed by the heat of the Holy Spirit.

## Chapter 22

**46**/5 [Luke 6:20] **And he, lifting up his eyes on his disciples, said: Blessed are you who are poor, for yours is the kingdom of God.** Although he is speaking to all in general, nevertheless the Saviour lifts up his eyes on the disciples in particular, /138/ to open more widely to them, who perceive the Word with the attentive ear of the heart, spiritual illumination of the deepest savour. This is similar to what Matthew says: *And after he sat, his disciples came to him, and opening his mouth, he taught them, saying: Blessed are the poor in spirit.*[331] For sitting on the mountain, he opens his mouth to them, so that they may hear great things on high; standing on the plain, he directs his eyes on them, so that they may clearly understand what they have heard. Therefore, the poor are blessed. Not, certainly, all of them, but only those who set the whole summit of the present age at nought even if it seems high. These are deservedly said to be worthy of the gift of the heavenly kingdom, because they are proved to be stripped of the desire for human pleasure. King David, declaring that he himself had undergone such poverty, says: *But I am needy and poor.*[332] And because for the Lord's sake he cared little not only for earthly things but even for supercelestial ones, he said in another place: *For what have I in heaven, and besides you, what do I desire on earth?*[333] and then immediately made it clear where he had fixed the anchor of his hope by adding: *But it is good for me to adhere to God, to put my hope in the Lord God.*[334] On the other hand, some who live in a most wretched condition of poverty lack joys both in this world because they are poor in possessions and in the kingdom of God because their merits are worthless.

**47**/5 [Luke 6:21] **Blessed are you who hunger now, for you will be filled.** Matthew explains what the blessed should hunger and thirst for,

---

331 Matt. 5:1–3.
332 Ps. 69:6 (70:5).
333 Ps. 72:25 (73:25).
334 Ps. 72:28 (73:28).

namely justice,³³⁵ instructing us very plainly that we should never consider ourselves sufficiently just, but always love, or rather have a burning passion for, the daily progress of justice. The Psalmist ardently shows that it cannot be perfectly fulfilled in this age, but in the future, through desire of heavenly things, when he says: *But as for me, I will appear before your sight with justice, I will be filled sufficiently when your glory will be manifest.*³³⁶ *Blessed are you who hunger now,* can also be interpreted simply as, 'you who chastise your body and subject it to servitude',³³⁷ and 'you who in hunger and thirst give heed to the Word',³³⁸ because then you have the fullness of heavenly joys to enjoy.

**48/5** [Luke 6:21b] **Blessed are you who weep now, for you will laugh.** Those who weep not for the loss of temporal goods, but for the loss of spiritual virtues, will be consoled with eternal blessedness. In this we are commanded to lament not only our offences, but also the offences of our neighbour; for if we love our neighbour as ourselves, we must both rejoice in his success, and be afflicted by his failure – and not only be afflicted, but be inflamed to the point of tears. For thus Samuel and David mourn the sin and destruction of Saul.³³⁹ Thus the Lord himself wept over the sinful city,³⁴⁰ and having compassion for the sorrowful sisters, he first wept with human pity for Lazarus, /139/ whom he was going to bring back to life by his divine majesty.³⁴¹ Thus he showed allegorically that sinners who are laid to rest in death should be lamented by their neighbours so that that they may rise again. And the fact that he promises that those weeping now are going to laugh, ought not to be taken in a childish sense, but as is customary in Scripture we should understand that the word 'laughter' signifies an exultation of the spirit and a certain more joyful state of mind, as when for example Sarah says: *God has made a laughter for me;*³⁴² and in Job it is said: *And the mouth of those that speak the truth will be filled with laughter.*³⁴³ By these words, as I have said, the inner joy of the soul is represented.

---

335 Cf. Matt. 5:6.
336 Ps. 16:15 (17:15).
337 Cf. 1 Cor. 9:27.
338 Cf. 2 Cor. 11:27.
339 Cf. 1 Sam. 15:35; 2 Sam. 1:12.
340 Cf. Luke 19:41.
341 Cf. John 11:1–44.
342 Gen. 21:6.
343 Job 8:21.

BOOK TWO                                   273

49/5  [Luke 6:22] **Blessed will you be when men will hate you, and when they will separate you, and will reproach you.** He is blessed who having wept wishes to suffer hunger and poverty for the sake of the wealth of the inheritance of Christ in the saints, for the sake of the bread of eternal life, and for the sake of the hope for heavenly joys. But he is far more blessed, who is not afraid to observe the virtues in the midst of calamity, because although men hate with a wicked heart, they cannot injure a heart dear to Christ. Let them separate and drive you from the congregation: Christ finds and strengthens you. Let them reproach the name of the crucified one: *he raises us up together*, we who are dead with him, *and makes us sit together in the heavenly places.*[344]

[Luke 6:22b] **And they will cast out your name as evil on account of the Son of man.** 'Your name' signifies the name of 'Christians', which was very often erased from memory by Gentiles and Jews as far as they were able, and was cast out by men. Now there is no reason to hate it, except on account of the Son of man, since, of course, believers wished to give themselves the name of Christ. Therefore, persecutors of the supreme name are indicated not undeservedly by the name of men. *Blessed*, he says, *will you be when men will hate you*, teaching them that they are going to be persecuted by men, but blessed beyond men.

[Luke 6:23] **Be glad in that day and rejoice, for behold, your reward is great in heaven.** This precept cannot be fulfilled by anyone and everyone who suffers, but only by him who suffers for the sake of a divine reward, so that amid the hatreds of hearts, amid the insults of tongues, amid the very hands of persecutors, he may carry on with a soul which does not waver, but rather is even more joyful. They do not avail in this like us, but like those who *went from the presence of the council, rejoicing that they were accounted worthy to suffer reproach for the name of Jesus.*[345] Those, therefore, who endure many misfortunes, will receive many gifts in heaven from Christ. But on the other hand, false prophets endured countless verbal javelins from Elijah. Laughing them to scorn, he said: *Cry with a louder voice; for he is the god* /**140**/ *Baal, and perhaps he is talking, or is in an inn, or on a journey, or perhaps he is asleep, and must be awaked.*[346] How much bloodshed did they bring upon themselves when all eight hundred and fifty of them were

---

344 Eph. 2:6 (with tenses altered).
345 Acts 5:41.
346 3 Kings 18:27.

killed!³⁴⁷ But because Baal and not Christ was in dispute, they did not rejoice when they were mocked, nor did they deserve a reward when they were killed, but eternal punishment.

[Luke 6:23b] **For their fathers did to the prophets accordingly.** *He rightly gave encouragement with an example, because those telling the truth usually suffer persecution, and yet the prophets of old did not for that reason cease from the preaching of the truth from fear of persecution.*³⁴⁸ It should be noted that just as Matthew, by the eight beatitudes that he set down, implied the eighth perfection of our hope, which is affirmed by the glory of the resurrection, so Luke by four beatitudes comprehends the cardinal virtues.³⁴⁹

Blessed are the poor who are restrained from the allurements of the world through moderation.³⁵⁰ Blessed are the hungry who, having been reminded by their hunger that the hungry are to be pitied, are themselves shown pity through justice in whatever way they can be. The Psalmist testifies that it is right to call alms 'justice', in that we do not give what we have to Christ but restore to him what is his own, saying: *He has distributed, he has given to the poor; his justice remains forever and ever.*³⁵¹ For it is justice insofar as we bestow what we have on another, owing nothing to anyone, except that we love each other. Blessed are those who, prudently distinguishing good from evil, know how to weep for perishable things and to aspire to eternal things. Blessed are those who, through fortitude of faith are able to endure every kind of trouble.³⁵²

Therefore, those who are not yet able to climb into the citadel of perfected virtue, must be encouraged in the meantime by the blessedness of a shared perfection, so that when they have progressed little by little from good things to better, and as long as they gladly give heed to the Lord standing on the plain, they may ascend to him whenever he is sitting high up on the mountain. For he, while standing, strives with the hearts of

---

347 Cf. 3 Kings 18:19 & 40.
348 Augustine, *De sermone Domini* 1.5.15 (CCSL 35:15.325–28).
349 Cf. Ambrose, *Expos. Lucam* 5.49 (CCSL 14:152.524–31). 'Eighth perfection' [*octauam ... perfectionem*] alludes to Bede's identification of the number eight as the symbol of eternity and resurrection after the end of the seven world ages (e.g., in *De temporum ratione*, ch. 71).
350 Cf. Ambrose, *Expos. Lucam* 5.64 (CCSL 14:157.686–88).
351 Ps. 111:9 (112:9).
352 This paragraph is loosely based on Ambrose, *Expos. Lucam* 5.64–68 (CCSL 14:157.686–711).

the former, which must still be subdued and instructed; while seated, he addresses as though he were standing the latter who are struggling. But to those whom he finds already prepared and easily taught by long exercise of spiritual study the Saviour, sitting at rest as it were, makes known all the mysteries of heaven with the freedom and authority of a teacher. These different stages of spiritual advancement are expressed by lovely symbols in the dress of the people of Israel. All the common people, wearing any kind of clothing whatsoever, were commanded to make for themselves blue fringes in the four corners of their garments;[353] the priests were to have four vestments distinguished with wondrous variety by the same number of mystical colours; and the chief priests were to wear both those that /141/ the priests have and four kinds of garment of the same colours but, for the sake of their more sublime worthiness, both shimmering with glittering gold and girded with the name of the patriarchs and of the Lord himself.[354] Luke expects that the diligence of his own work will either expound these things one at a time, or at least put them on display.

**50**/10 [Luke 6:24] **But woe to you that are rich, for you have your consolation.** That woe will come to the rich is better understood from the contrary, where it is said that the kingdom of God belongs to the poor.[355] Those who seek to be consoled here alienate themselves from that kingdom, and are about to hear from the just Judge: *Sons, remember that you received good things in your life.*[356] Here it should be noted that it is not so much riches as love of riches that is at fault. For not everyone who has riches, but, as Ecclesiastes says, everyone *who loves riches will reap no fruit from them.*[357] This is because he who does not know how to despise in his mind temporal possessions, or how to pay them out to a poor man, takes delight in the use of these things in the present, but in the future will lack the fruit that he could have acquired by giving. And elsewhere we read: *Blessed is the rich man that is found without blemish, and who has not gone after gold, nor put his trust in money nor in treasures.*[358]

[Luke 6:25] **Woe to you who are filled, for you will hunger.** That wealthy man clothed in purple took his fill when he feasted sumptuously

---

353 Cf. Num. 15:38.
354 Cf. Exod. 39:1–30.
355 Cf. Luke 6:20.
356 Luke 16:25.
357 Eccles. 5:9.
358 Ecclus. 31:8.

every day, but he was hungry when he endured dire woe, and when he sought a drop of water from the finger of Lazarus, whom he had looked down upon.[359] And another interpretation: If the blessed are those who always hunger for works of justice, those who satisfy themselves in their desires, and experience no hunger for truth and the unwavering good, thinking themselves blessed enough, if they are not deprived of their pleasure for the moment, must be considered unfortunate.

[Luke 6:25b] **Woe to you that now laugh, for you will mourn and weep.** And Solomon says: *Laughter will be mingled with sorrow, and mourning takes hold of the end of joy.*[360] And again: *The heart of the wise is where there is mourning, and the heart of fools where there is mirth.*[361] He clearly teaches that foolishness is always to be imputed to those who laugh and wisdom to those who weep, as we have taught above.

51/10 [Luke 6:26] **Woe to you when all men will speak well of you.** This is what the Psalmist deplores: *For the sinner is praised in the desires of his soul, and the one who does unjust things is blessed.*[362] It is not the least part of his punishment that his sins are not only not censured, but are even praised as if they were well done. Hence the Lord is careful not to say: 'Woe because men speak well of you', as if at some distant time the punishment might belatedly follow the fault. Instead he says: *Woe to you when all men will speak well of you.* Flattery is the very nurse of sin – like oil to flames, so flattery is accustomed /142/ to furnish kindling to those burning with blame – and for this reason it is certainly the greatest punishment of sinners. For just as it is fitting that the poor who hunger and weep should be tested by the depravity of the wicked, so they who lack wealth, feasts, and laughter are comforted by the wrath of the strict Judge when they see that the punishment of the wickedly indulgent is greater than their privileged status.

[Luke 6:26b] **For according to these things did their fathers to the prophets.** He means the false prophets who often in holy Scripture are also themselves accustomed to be called prophets, because in order to curry favour with the people they attempt to predict, that is, to foretell the future. Hence Ezekiel says: *Woe to the foolish prophets that follow their own spirit, and see nothing. Your prophets, O Israel, were like foxes in the*

---

359 Cf. Luke 16:19–24.
360 Prov. 14:13.
361 Eccles. 7:5.
362 Ps. 9:24 (10:3).

BOOK TWO 277

*desert.*³⁶³ And so on the mountain the Lord only describes the beatitudes of the good, but on the plain he also describes the woes of the wicked, because it is necessary for pupils who are still ignorant to be summoned with threats, but only rewards are necessary to attract the perfect.

**52**/5 [Luke 6:27] **But I say to you that hear: Love your enemies, do good to them that hate you.** Because he had said previously what they could suffer from their enemies, now he shows how they ought to behave towards these very enemies. However, *many think that not to hate their enemies is all our powers can accomplish, but that to be commanded to love them is more than human nature permits,* not seeing that Moses,³⁶⁴ Samuel,³⁶⁵ and Stephen³⁶⁶ also prayed for their enemies, and that David³⁶⁷ bewailed his dead enemies. For the Lord would not command *impossibilities, but perfection.*³⁶⁸ *Not failing, therefore, while there is time, let us work good to all men, but especially to those who are of the household of the faith.*³⁶⁹

[Luke 6:28] **Bless them that curse you, and pray for them that calumniate you.** And the Apostle testifies that he and those like him did these things when he says: *We are reviled, and we bless; we are blasphemed, and we entreat.*³⁷⁰ But someone might well wonder why it is not contrary to this commandment of the Lord that *many imprecations against enemies are also found in the prophets, which are considered to be curses, as is this for example: 'Let their table become as a snare before them',*³⁷¹ *and others that are uttered there.*³⁷² And *the apostle John says: 'He that knows his brother to sin a sin which is not to death, let him ask, and life shall be given to him, who sins not to death. There is a sin to death: for that I do not say that any man ask'.*³⁷³ First, it should be seen that *the prophets uttered imprecations about what was to come with the spirit of one who saw the future, and not with the prayer of one who desired harm. They are especially accustomed to*

---

363 Ezek. 13:3–4.
364 Cf. Num. 12:13; 14:13–19.
365 Cf. 1 Sam. 8:6; 15:11.
366 Cf. Acts 7:59.
367 Cf. 2 Sam. 1:11–12; 18:33.
368 Jerome, *Commentarii in Matheum* 1 (CCSL 77:34.696–701).
369 Gal. 6:9–10.
370 1 Cor. 4:12–13.
371 Ps. 68:23 (69:22).
372 Augustine, *De sermone Domini* 1.21.71 (CCSL 35:79.1736–38).
373 Augustine, *De sermone Domini* 1.21.73 (CCSL 35:81.1774–77); 1 John 5:16.

foretell /143/ *future events using the imagery of invoking those events, just as they often sang of things that were going to happen using the imagery of past events.*[374] Then, it should be understood from the words of the apostle *that there are some brothers for whom we are not commanded to pray, although the Lord orders us to pray even for our persecutors.* This *question cannot be resolved, unless we grant that there are some sins in brothers that are graver than the persecution of enemies. And that 'brothers' signify Christians can be proved by many instances in the Sacred Scriptures.*[375]

*Therefore, I think that a sin of a brother is 'to death', when someone attacks the brotherhood after he has been accepted by God through the grace of our Lord Jesus Christ, and is stirred up by the flames of envy against that very grace by which he was reconciled to God. But sin is not 'to death', if anyone fails through some infirmity of the soul to manifest the obligatory duties of brotherhood, but does not renounce brotherly love. This is why on the cross the Lord also says: 'Father, forgive them, for they know not what they do'.*[376] *For the participants of the deed had not yet entered the community of the holy brotherhood by the grace of the Holy Spirit. And the blessed Stephen prays for those who stone him, because they had not yet put their faith in Christ, and thus they were not contending against that universal grace.*[377] *And therefore the apostle Paul, I believe, does not pray for Alexander, because he was already a brother, and he had sinned to death, that is, by envy, by attacking the brotherhood. But for those who had not severed love, but had succumbed from fear, he prays that they might be forgiven. For he says as follows: 'Alexander the coppersmith has done me much evil; the Lord will reward him according to his works. Avoid him also, for he has greatly opposed our words'.*[378] *Then he adds for whom he prays, saying thus: 'At my first answer, no one stood with me, but all forsook me. May it not be laid to their charge'.*[379] *This distinction between the sins distinguishes the betrayal of Judas from the denial of Peter.*[380]

**53/5** [Luke 6:29] **To him who strikes you on the cheek, offer also the other.** *He does not say: 'Don't strike him who strikes you', although this is likewise a great commandment, but* he says: *'Prepare yourself* to be

---

374 Augustine, *De sermone Domini* 1.22.72 (CCSL 35:80.1748–50; 1760–62).
375 Augustine, *De sermone Domini* 1.22.73 (CCSL 35:81.1777–83).
376 Luke 23:34.
377 Cf. Acts 7:59.
378 2 Tim. 4:14–15.
379 2 Tim. 4:16.
380 Augustine, *De sermone Domini* 1.22.73–74 (CCSL 35:82.1791–1814).

struck yet again'. *They especially feel that this pertains to mercy, who care for those whom they love much, like their own children or any of their dearly beloved ones that are sick, or for little ones or the insane, from whom they often suffer a great deal. And if their salvation demands it, they resign themselves also to suffering more, until the infirmity of age or illness passes. What else could the Lord, the physician of souls, teach those whom he instructed in the cure of the neighbours, except that they should calmly endure the weaknesses of those whose salvation* /144/ *they wish to provide for? For every depravity comes from the weakness of the soul, because nothing is more innocent than one who is perfected in virtue.*[381]

Many, however, know they should offer the other cheek, but do not know they should love him by whom they are struck. Indeed, the Lord himself, who certainly first fulfilled the precepts that he taught, did not offer the other cheek to the servant of the priest striking him on the cheek, but in addition he said: *'If I have spoken evil, give testimony of the evil; but if well, why do you strike me?'*[382] Nevertheless, he was not for that reason unprepared in his heart not only to be struck on the other cheek for the salvation of all, but even for his whole body to be crucified.[383]

[Luke 6:29b] **And do not withhold from him, who will take away from you your cloak, your tunic also.** *What is said about the cloak and the tunic applies not only to these things, but to everything which can with some justification be said to be our property, at least for the time being. For if this is commanded with respect to necessities, how much more appropriate is it to despise superfluities.*[384]

[Luke 6:30] **Give to everyone who asks you.** *He says, 'everyone who asks', not 'to one who asks for everything', in order that you give what you decently and rightly are able to give. For what if one were to ask for money with which to attempt to destroy an innocent person? What if in the end he sought debauchery? But not to pursue countless such cases, I would simply say that what harms neither you nor another, as far as it can be known or believed by a man, surely ought to be given. And to him, to whom you have rightly denied what he asks for, this same righteousness should be made known, so that you do not dismiss him empty-handed. Thus, you will give to everyone who asks you, although you will not always give what he asks*

---

381 Augustine, *De sermone Domini* 1.19.57 (CCSL 35:65.1415–28).
382 John 18:23.
383 Augustine, *De sermone Domini* 1.19.58 (CCSL 35:68.1481–88).
384 Augustine, *De sermone Domini* 1.19.59 (CCSL 35:69.1492–96).

*for. And sometimes you will give something better, after you have corrected the person asking for things that are not right.*³⁸⁵

[Luke 6:30b] **And if anyone takes away things that are yours, do not ask for them again.** He says this about *clothing, house, land, cattle, and about all money in general. But whether this must be accepted about slaves is the great question. For it is not proper for a Christian to possess a slave in the same way as he possesses a horse or silver, although it can happen that a horse is worth more than a slave, and something made of gold or silver much more. But that slave, if he is brought up by you, his master, and guided to worship God more correctly, decently and fitly than he can be by the one who wishes to take him away, I don't know whether anyone would dare to say that he ought to be as little valued as a cloak. For a man should love another as himself, who is even commanded by the Lord of all to love his enemies.*³⁸⁶

## Chapter 23(a)³⁸⁷

54/5 [Luke 6:31] **And as you would that men would do to you, do you also to them likewise.** Because *love is patient, is kind,*³⁸⁸ it not only stoutly endures the injuries of an enemy, but also kindly forestalls /145/ the favour of a friend. For nature has taught all men to return love to the one who loves them. But he teaches the perfect to compel the lover to the love of Christ through teaching alone, and not rewards. When he ordered us first to do to others as we would wish to be done to us, he immediately supported this same interpretation in a broader sense by adding:

55/5 [Luke 6:32] **And if you love those who love you, what thanks are owed to you? For sinners also love those who love them,** and so forth. *If even sinners, tax collectors, and pagans under the guidance of nature know how to be generous to those who love them,* how much the more *ought you,* he says, also *to embrace those who do not love you with a love that is more capacious? For as the state of your faith is more excellent, so should your cultivation of virtue be more productive.*³⁸⁹ Since the Lord testifies that

---

385 Augustine, *De sermone Domini* 1.20.67 (CCSL 35:76.1671–80).
386 Augustine, *De sermone Domini* 1.19.59 (CCSL 35:69.1502–15).
387 See Introduction, 19.
388 1 Cor. 13:4.
389 Ps. Augustine, *Sermones* 62.6 (PL 39:1862).

those who only love those who love them, only do good to those who do good to them, and only lend to their friends, not only do not have perfect love, but are equivalent to sinners, it seems worth investigating how John who reclined upon the Lord's chest, at the culmination of his Epistle about the love of God and neighbour, reminded us that enemies ought to be loved not to this or that extent, but absolutely, saying: *If we love one another, God abides in us, and his love is perfected in us.*[390] Anyone whom this bothers should know that John was not silent about the love of enemies, but that he included them under the name of brothers, and taught that they were to be loved for the sake of brotherly love, and that we were to pray for them that they not always remain enemies, but *that they recover themselves from the snares of the devil,*[391] and that they join with us in a brotherly covenant. Nor should it seem difficult if we say that those who do not yet believe can be called brothers because there is hope that they will believe. For the same John frequently called them the children of God as well. He says: *that Jesus would die for the nation, and not only for the nation, but to gather together in one the children of God, who were dispersed.*[392] For as long as they are dispersed, they are not yet the children of God, but they become so now by coming together in one.

[Luke 6:35] **But love your enemies, do good and lend, hoping for nothing thereby.** Because he has proved that loving, benefiting, and lending to sinners is not unfruitful, he now shows how these things ought to be done fruitfully by the faithful. *Everyone who receives, borrows, even if he himself is not going to repay. For since God restores many things to the merciful, everyone who gives a benefit to another, lends with interest. Or if it does not seem acceptable to deal with a borrower, except one who will take it upon himself to repay, it should be understood that the Lord embraced precisely these two kinds of giving. And so, either we give what we give as a present with good will or we lend to one who will repay.*[393] **/146/**

Because, as it has been written, *many have looked upon a thing lent as a thing found, and have given trouble to those who helped them,*[394] many have refused to lend, not out of wickedness, but because they were afraid

---

390 1 John 4:12.
391 2 Tim. 2:26.
392 John 11:51–52.
393 Augustine, *De sermone Domini* 1.20.68 (CCSL 35:77.1683–89).
394 Ecclus. 29:4.

to be defrauded without cause.³⁹⁵ Divine authority also remedies this infirmity, saying: *and lend, hoping for nothing thereby*, that is, not fixing your hope of reward on a human being. If he repays what you lent, God will also repay what you did at his behest, and if he does not repay, your inheritance will be everlasting. For *the sinner will borrow, and not pay again, but the just shows mercy and will give. For such as bless him will inherit the land.*³⁹⁶ And elsewhere when he said: *Acceptable is the man who shows mercy and lends*,³⁹⁷ he added immediately: *The just will be in everlasting remembrance.*³⁹⁸

[Luke 6:35b] **And your reward will be great, and you will be the sons of the Highest.** There can be no greater reward for earth-born sons of men than to become the sons of the Highest in heaven. Therefore, what he says: *and you will be the sons of the Highest*, should be understood in the sense that John gives it when he says: *He gave them power to be made the sons of God.*³⁹⁹ For there is one Son who is unable by nature to sin at all. But after having received power, we are made sons to the extent that we fulfil those things that are commanded by him. Hence apostolic doctrine calls it 'adoption',⁴⁰⁰ whereby we are called to an eternal inheritance, so that we can be co-heirs.⁴⁰¹ Therefore he does not say: Do these things because you are the sons, but: Do these things 'and you will be the sons'. But when he calls us to this by the Only-begotten himself, he calls us to his own image,⁴⁰² saying:

[Luke 6:35c] **For he is kind to the ungrateful and to the evil**, and so forth. God is kind to the ungrateful and to the evil, whether by bestowing temporal goods out of his mercy, which is of course manifold, for he even saves cattle, or by inspiring us toward heavenly gifts by the special grace whereby he glorifies only the elect. *But whether you understand it this way, or that way, or in both senses, it happens by the great goodness of God, which we are ordered to imitate, if we wish to be the sons of God.*⁴⁰³

---

395 Ecclus. 29:10.
396 Ps. 36:21–22 (37:21–22) (not *iuxta LXX*).
397 Ps. 111:5 (112:5).
398 Ps. 111:7 (112:6).
399 John 1:12.
400 Cf. Rom. 8:15; Gal. 4:5.
401 Cf. Rom. 8:17.
402 Augustine, *De sermone Domini* 1.23.78–79 (CCSL 35:87.1907–13; 88.1919–22).
403 Augustine, *De sermone Domini* 1.23.79 (CCSL 35:89.1940–42).

BOOK TWO 283

Chapter 23(b)

56/2 [Luke 6:37] **Judge not, and you will not be judged. Condemn not, and you will not be condemned.** *I think that the only thing this passage commands us is that we put the best construction upon dubious deeds done by another soul. For what is written: 'By their fruits you will know them',*[404] *is said about deeds which are obviously evil, and which cannot be done by a good soul, as for instance acts of debauchery, blasphemy, theft or drunkenness, although to the extent that such things do occur, we are allowed to pass judgement upon them. But when it comes to different kinds of foods, because any human foods whatever can be consumed indiscriminately by a good soul and a simple heart without the vice of concupiscence, the Apostle forbids that those /147/ who were accustomed to eat flesh and drink wine be judged by those who were accustomed to abstain from nourishment of this kind. 'Let him who eats, he says, not despise him who does not eat, and he who does not eat, let him not judge him who eats.'*[405]

*Likewise, what he says elsewhere pertains to this: 'Judge not before the time, until the Lord comes who will both bring to light the hidden things of darkness, and will make manifest the thoughts of the heart.'*[406] *Some deeds are ambiguous: we do not know in what spirit they are done, and a person can do them either in a good spirit or in a bad spirit. It is rash to judge these, and particularly so if we condemn them. But the time will come for them to be judged, when the Lord 'will bring to light the hidden things of darkness, and will make manifest the thoughts of the heart'. There are, however, two circumstances in which we ought to avoid a rash judgement: when it is uncertain with what spirit something was done, or when it is uncertain how something which now appears either bad or good will turn out in the future.*[407]

[Luke 6:37b-38] **Forgive, and you will be forgiven. Give, and it will be given to you.** He commands us to forgive injuries and to give benefits, in order that our sins be forgiven and eternal life be given us. With this brief but extraordinary statement, he concludes by expressing everything

---

404 Matt. 7:20.
405 Augustine, *De sermone Domini* 2.18.59 (CCSL 35:154.1352–58; 155.1360–66); Rom. 14:3.
406 1 Cor. 4:5.
407 Augustine, *De sermone Domini* 2.18.60–61 (CCSL 35:155.1372–80; 157.1393–96).

that he had mandated at length about how we should conduct ourselves with our enemies.

[Luke 6:38b] **Good measure, pressed down and shaken together, and running over, will they give into your bosom.** This is similar to what he says elsewhere: *That they themselves may also receive you into everlasting dwellings.*[408] For it is not the poor themselves but Christ who is going to reward those who gave alms. Nevertheless, the poor are said to give it into the bosom, because they gave the opportunity to deserve a reward when, whether in desperate need or wrongfully venting their rage against those stronger than they, they were not only supported by patience and bounty, but also sustained by kindness, and sometimes summoned by sweet grace to faith itself.

[Luke 6:38c] **For indeed with the same measure by which you will measure, it will be measured to you again.** And the Apostle, urging the Corinthians to give alms, says among other things: *The point is this: He who sows sparingly, will also reap sparingly, and he who sows in blessings, will also reap blessings.*[409] And this can also apply to all the things we do with mind, hand, or tongue, *for you will render to individuals*, it says, *according to their works.*[410]

57/5 [Luke 6:39] **And he spoke to them also a parable: Can the blind lead the blind? Do they not both fall into the ditch?** The meaning of this passage depends upon the previous ones, which gave commandments concerning the need for giving alms and forgiving wrongs. If, it says, anger has blinded /148/ you against someone who has committed violence and avarice against someone who asks, will you be able to tend to his defect, when your mind is defective? Or is only he who did the wrong to be considered guilty, and not you also who were unable to bear it? But if his wickedness finds you mild and of a peaceful spirit, not only will he be stirred to repentance, but you will be presented with the reward of patience, because with a seeing eye, that is, with a serene heart, you took care to lead one who was blind to the light.

58/3 [Luke 6:40] **The disciple is not above his master. But everyone will be perfect, if he is as his master.** If the master, who like God was certainly able to avenge his wrongs, preferred not to do so, but rather to render his persecutors milder, it is necessary for the disciples, who are pure men, to follow the same rule of perfection.

---

408 Luke 16:9.
409 2 Cor. 9:6.
410 Ps. 61:13 (62:12) (not *iuxta LXX*).

BOOK TWO 285

**59**/5 [Luke 6:41] **And why do you see the mote in your brother's eye, but do not consider the beam in your own eye?** This looks back to the preceding passages where he warned that the blind cannot be led by the blind, that is, the one who is sinning cannot by chastised by a sinner. For many who are led on by pride, or hate, by avarice or greed, or by any fault whatever, judge these things as unimportant or insignificant, and yet they caustically reproach those whom they see are agitated by sudden anger for having shifted the eye of the mind, bothered by a mote, from its usual state of purity. Such people forget the Lord's commandment, where he says: '*Condemn not, and you will not be condemned*',[411] *and they love to censure and condemn more than to amend and correct.*[412]

[Luke 6:42] **And how can you say to your brother: Brother, let me pull the mote out of your eye, when you yourself do not see the beam in your own eye?** You do these things to your brother, *if, for example, you rebuke him out of hatred* because *he sinned out of anger. But there is as much difference between a mote and a beam, as there is between anger and hatred. For hatred is a longstanding anger which has grown so great over a long lifetime, so to speak, that it is rightly called a beam. It can be the case that if you are angry with a man, you want him to be corrected. But if you hate a man, you cannot want to correct him.*[413] And therefore it is said to be impossible for one who has a beam in his own eye to take away a mote from the eye of his brother.

[Luke 6:42b] **Hypocrite, cast first the beam out of your own eye, and then you will see clearly to take out the mote from your brother's eye.** *That is, first expel hatred from yourself, and only then will you be able to correct him whom you love. We should be on our guard against the vexatious race* of hypocrites, that is, *pretenders, a kind of men who, although they receive any accusation of vice with hatred and spite, yet they wish themselves to be seen as dispensers of sound advice. And for that reason, we must be devoutly and cautiously alert, so that, when necessity forces us to reprove or chide anyone, we first consider* /**149**/ *whether the fault be of a kind that we have never had, or that we have now been freed from. And if we have never had it, let us consider likewise that we are men and could have had it. But if we had it and do not have it now, let the universal infirmity stir our memory, so that mercy, not hatred,*

---

411  Luke 6:37.
412  Augustine, *De sermone Domini* 2.19.63 (CCSL 35:159.1443–44).
413  Augustine, *De sermone Domini* 2.19.63 (CCSL 35:159.1447–53).

*may precede reproof or chiding, so that whether it leads to the correction of the one concerned or the opposite (for the result is uncertain) we may nevertheless be reassured that our eye is innocent. But if we find ourselves thinking that we are suffering from the same fault as the person we are preparing to reprove, let us not reprove or chide, but nevertheless let us groan; and let us entreat him not to submit to us, but to struggle together with us.*[414]

*Reproaches, therefore, ought to be employed rarely and from great necessity, so that even in doing this, we nevertheless insist that we serve not ourselves but God. For this is the object: that we do nothing with a double heart, by taking out from our eye the beam of envy or malice or hypocrisy, in order that we may see to remove the mote from the eye of a brother.*[415]

60/5 [Luke 6:43] **For there is no good tree that brings forth evil fruit, nor an evil tree that brings forth good fruit.** He follows up on what he had begun to say against the hypocrite. If, he says, you want to have true as opposed to false justice, take care to match what you say by deeds, so that, the tree being good, you are furnished with good fruits as well. Because even if the hypocrite feigns goodness, he is not good, if he does evil deeds. And if he reproves an innocent person, he is not for that reason bad, if he does good deeds.

[Luke 6:44] **For every tree is known by its fruit.** The Apostle reveals what the fruit is by which the bad or good tree ought to be distinguished, saying: *Now the works of the flesh are manifest, which are fornication, uncleanness, immodesty, luxury, idolatry, witchcrafts, enmities, contentions, emulations, wraths, quarrels, dissensions, sects, envies, murders, drunkenness, feastings, and such like. I warn you of these, as I have warned you, that those who do such things will not obtain the kingdom of God. But the fruit of the Spirit is love, joy, peace, patience, benignity, goodness, forbearance, mildness, faith, modesty, continency, chastity.*[416] On the other hand, almsgiving or prayer or fasting is indeed the fruit of good men in particular, but sometimes the fruit is feignedly acquired also by evil men, and the Lord says about them: *They have received their reward.*[417]

---

414 Augustine, *De sermone Domini* 2.19.64 (CCSL 35:160.1457–59; 1464–81).
415 Augustine, *De sermone Domini* 2.19.66 (CCSL 35:162.1502–07).
416 Gal. 5:19–23.
417 Matt. 6:5.

And elsewhere he says: *Beware of false prophets, who come to you in the clothing of sheep, but inwardly they are ravening wolves.*[418] *But sheep should not hate their clothing, just because wolves often hide themselves within it, and while they flaunt one for the sake of deception, they use another to ravage or /150/ kill those who are unable to see the wolves under this sheepskin garment. This, therefore, is not the fruit by which he teaches that the tree is to be known,* but that which has been shown above.[419]

**61/5** [Luke 6:44b] **For men do not gather figs from thorns, nor from a bramble bush do they gather the grape.** I believe that the thorns and bramble bush are the cares of the world and the pricking of vices, concerning which it was said to the man who sinned: Your *earth will bring thorns and thistles forth to you.*[420] But I believe that the figs and the grape are the sweetness of the new way of life, which the Lord hungers for in us, and the fervour of love, which gladdens the heart of a man, concerning which, in the gleaming light of the Gospel, *the voice of the turtle-dove* resounded far and wide *in the land, the fig-tree has put forth her green figs, the vines in flower yield their sweet smell.*[421] But figs are not gathered from thorns, nor the grape from a bramble bush, because the mind, when it is still weighed down by the customary behaviour of the old man, can imitate the fruits of the new man, but cannot bear them. Someone might want to object and say that not only did Moses gather the grape from the bramble bush when he took useful counsel from a Gentile kinsman,[422] but also that those to whom it was said concerning the Pharisees: *Do what they say, not what they do,*[423] gathered figs from thorns. But let that person know that just as a true vine-shoot sometimes sprawls out and becomes entangled with the fence, bearing its fruit on a thorn, and so does not preserve it for human use, so if the words or deeds of the wicked ever benefit the good, it is not the wicked themselves that do this, but rather, the benefit to the good happens in accordance with the wisdom of the divine plan.

**62/5** [Luke 6:45] **A good man out of the good treasure of his heart brings forth that which is good, and an evil man out of the evil treasure brings forth that which is evil.** The treasure of the heart is the same as the root of

---

418 Matt. 7:15.
419 Augustine, *De sermone Domini* 2.24.80 (CCSL 35:180.1861–62; 1855–59).
420 Gen. 3:17–18 (God is addressing Adam).
421 Song 2:12–13.
422 Jethro; cf. Exod. 18:1–27.
423 Matt. 23:3.

the tree, and what is brought forth from the heart is the same as the fruit of the tree. He, therefore, who has the treasure of patience and of perfect love in his heart, bringing forth without doubt the best fruits, loves his enemy, does good to the one who hates him, blesses the one who curses him, prays for the one who bears false witness, does not resist the one who strikes and robs him, gives to everyone who asks, does not seek to recover things taken from him, desires neither to judge nor to condemn, corrects the one going astray with patience and love, and does other things that the Saviour taught above. But the one who keeps a vile treasure in his heart hates his friend, curses the one who loves him, curses the one who blesses him, and does other things that the Lord's sermon condemned, things contrary to the good treasure. Lest he flatter himself in vain, Jesus goes on to say:

[Luke 6:45b] **For out of the abundance of the heart the mouth speaks.** As if not the fruits of the tree but its leaves are sought after – that is words only, and not deeds, be these of a true Christian or of a hypocrite – the Lord in consequence adds: /151/

63/3 [Luke 6:46] **And why do you call me, 'Lord, Lord', and do not do the things that I say?** It is as if he were to say: Why do you brandish the leaves of true confession to put out your shoots, you who display no fruits of good work? Hence the Apostle, when he is preparing to separate what is precious from what is worthless, that is, when he is going to set the good treasure apart from the bad, the good tree from the bad, the perfected disciple of the good teacher from the hypocrite, the sighted leader from the blind, says: *But I will come to you, if the Lord wills, and will know not the talk of them that are puffed up, but the power. For the kingdom of God is not in talk, but in power.*[424] By the speech of his mouth the Lord makes known everything which we bring forth from the heart, whether in deed or word or thought, which *are naked and open to his eyes* more than words are to men.[425] For Scripture often uses 'words' when what is meant is 'things'. Hence the Psalmist says: *Say to my soul, you are my salvation.*[426] And Hezekiah: *There was no word that I did not show to them.*[427] He certainly revealed the secrets of things, not words, to the Chaldeans. And likewise, the Apostle says: *And no man says that Jesus is the Lord, but by the Holy Spirit,*[428] which is as if

---

424 1 Cor. 4:19–20.
425 Hebr. 4:13.
426 Ps. 34:3 (35:3).
427 Isa. 39:2.
428 1 Cor. 12:3.

he said, no man understands that Jesus is the Lord by the intellect, no man understands it by the will, except by the grace of the Holy Spirit.

**64/5** [Luke 6:47–48] **Every one that comes to me, and hears my words, and does them, I will show you to whom he is like. He is like a man building a house,** ... The Lord, preaching many things above about men who are obviously good or bad, and many things about men who are good, but whose goodness is pretence, concludes his whole sermon with a parable at once beautiful and terrible, in which he compares some hearers of the word to the devil and others to Christ, each of whom does not cease to build his house for the submission of men throughout the whole time of this world. And so he who hears the words of Christ, and acts on them, will be compared to Christ, because just as Christ constructs, teaches, and governs one universal Church for himself from the various types of men, in order to consecrate them some day to eternal life, so also, the one who hears in a profitable manner, advancing to heavenly things as much as he is able by a many-sided zeal for the virtues, builds himself a habitation in an eternal dwelling, whose construction he can pursue in the present with stones that are to be squared, polished, and joined with the mortar of love, but which in the future he may delight in dedicating to Christ.

[Luke 6:48b] **Who dug deep, and laid foundations upon a rock.** In the mystery of the Church, when 'foundations' (in the plural) are laid, they signify teachers, of whom it is said: *Its foundations are in /152/ the holy mountains.*[429] But when 'a foundation' (in the singular) is laid, the teacher of teachers and the foundation of foundations, Christ himself, is meant, of whom it is said: *For other foundation no man can lay, but that which is laid, which is Christ Jesus.*[430] The wise architect[431] laid these foundations not upon the earth, but upon a rock, because he established the minds of upright men not on earthly desires, but with his own unconquerable faith, hope, and love. *And the rock was Christ*, he says.[432] *Who dug deep*, because with the precepts of humility he roots out all earthly things from the hearts of the faithful, lest they serve God for the sake of some trivial or temporal advantage. Morally, the foundations of that same house are exertions in the good way of life. These the perfected hearer of the word, when the rubble of unnecessary and unstable thoughts has been removed

---

429 Ps. 86:1 (87:1).
430 1 Cor. 3:11.
431 The wise architect is Paul (1 Cor. 3:10).
432 1 Cor. 10:4.

by Christian humility, firmly lays down to fulfil the mandates of Christ. What Christ does generally in the universal Church, he does particularly in himself, Christ working with him, and he rejoices with the Psalmist that: *He brought me out of the pit of misery and the mire of dregs, and he set my feet upon a rock,* and so forth.[433]

[Luke 6:48c] **And when a flood came, the stream beat vehemently upon that house, and could not shake it. For it was founded upon a rock.** The flood of the stream, which elsewhere he calls the gates of hell, saying: *That you are Peter, and upon this rock I will build my church, and the gates of hell will not prevail against it,*[434] is what he mentions above, saying: *Blessed will you be when men will hate you, and when they will separate you, and will reproach you. And they will cast out your name as evil.*[435] Although the stream could rush upon the firm cornerstones of the Church, it could not destroy them, because they were rejoicing on that day and exulting, exhorting one another against the raging of the waters thus: *Behold, we account them blessed who have endured. You have heard of the patience of Job, and you have seen the end of the Lord.*[436] And again: *The stream of the river makes the city of God joyful, the Most High has sanctified his own tabernacle. God is in the midst thereof, it will not be moved.*[437] But also in accordance with the laws of tropology our individual 'houses' are daily disturbed by the restlessness either of impure spirits, or of wicked men, or of their own mind or flesh. Insofar as they trust in their own strength they are bent, but insofar as they adhere to that completely invincible rock they cannot be overthrown.

[Luke 6:49] **But he who hears, and does not do, is like a man building /153/ his house upon the earth without a foundation,** ... *'The world',* which *'is seated in wickedness',*[438] is called *'the house'* of the devil, *not because of the excellence of the Creator, but because of the magnitude of the offender.*[439] He builds it on the earth, because he drags down those who submitted to him from heaven to the earthly realm. He builds without a foundation, because *all sin lacks a foundation, because it does not from its own nature remain standing. In fact, evil is without*

---

433 Ps. 39:3 (40:2).
434 Matt. 16:18.
435 Luke 6:22.
436 James 5:11.
437 Ps. 45:5–6 (46:4–5).
438 1 John 5:19.
439 Jerome, *Commentarii in Matheum* 2 (CCSL 77:94.470–71).

substance, because in order to exist at all it must be united with the nature of the good. And since *'foundation'* [*fundamentum*] derives from *'bottom'* [*fundo*], we can also take *'foundation'* not unsuitably as meaning *'bottom'*, just as *'hearing'* [*auditus*] derives from *'ear'* [*auris*], and yet the ear itself is frequently designated by the word *'hearing'*. Therefore, just as whoever is plunged in a well is checked by the bottom of the well, so the sinking soul would come to a halt, as it were, on a certain place at the bottom, if once it had fallen it could check itself by some limitation on sin. But when it cannot be held with the sin by which it falls, while it is cast daily down to worse things, it does not find the bottom where it may be held in place in the well into which it fell, as it were. Hence it is said elsewhere: *'The sinner when he comes into the depth of evils contemns.'*[440] For he neglects to return, because he despairs of mercy for himself, but when he sins more by despairing, he lowers the bottom of his well, so that he does not find a place where he can be checked.[441] Therefore, whoever hears the words of Christ and does not do them, whether he is initiated into the mysteries of Christ, or is a complete stranger to Christ, because he builds himself badly, is like the foolish man of whom it is said: *An enemy has done this.*[442]

[Luke 6:49b] **Against which the stream beat vehemently, and immediately it fell, and the ruin of that house was great.** When trials of any kind rush in, it is clear that both the truly bad and the feignedly good immediately become worse, until they sink down at last into eternal torment. Then it must be said on the moral level that *every man is tempted by his own concupiscence, being drawn away and allured. Then when concupiscence has conceived, it brings forth sin. But sin, when it is completed, begets death.*[443] Likewise the decisive moment of Last Judgement can be understood by the violent impulse of the stream, when, with both houses completed, *everyone who exalts himself will be humbled, and he who humbles himself will be exalted,*[444] and not only wicked men, but also angels who attached themselves to the house of the devil, *will go into eternal punishment, but the just into eternal life.*[445]

---

440 Prov. 18:3.
441 Gregory, *Moralia* 26.37 (CCSL 143B:1317.2–38 [with gaps]).
442 Matt. 13:28.
443 James 1:14–15.
444 Luke 14:11.
445 Matt. 25:46.

## Chapter 24

**65/3 [Luke 7:1] And when he had finished all his words in the hearing of the people, he entered into Capernaum.** *Here it should be understood that, when he had finished all his words in the hearing of the people, Christ entered Capernaum,* /154/ *that is, that he did not enter before he had finished speaking these words. But how long after he had ended these sermons he entered Capernaum is not expressed. Certainly, it was during that interval that the leper was cleansed. Matthew introduced him in his proper place,*[446] but Luke took him up earlier.[447]

**[Luke 7:2] And the slave of a certain centurion, who was dear to him, being sick, was going to die.** Perchance some pious person seeks to discover, or some wicked person to censure, why the evangelist said that the slave was going to die, when it says later that he did not die. The short answer to this, is that in fact he was going to die, if he had not been returned to life by the faith of his master praying for him and by the compassion of the merciful Christ. So too King Hezekiah, when he heard in the words of the truth-speaking prophet: *Set your house in order, for you will die, and not live,*[448] was going to die, in accordance with a certain measure of human nature. But by the secret judgement of divine providence, which has *ordered all things in measure and number and weight,*[449] he was still going to obtain fifteen years of life by his tears and prayers.[450]

**[Luke 7:3] And when he had heard of Jesus, he sent to him the elders of the Jews, entreating him to come and heal his slave.** It happened by divine dispensation that the elders of the Jews were sent to the Lord, and he who was ill was cured with these people standing by, so that it would be inexcusable for them not to believe, when a Gentile was a believer. Even so the question arises why it happens that Luke says that the centurion sent messengers to the Lord, but Matthew says that he approached him himself.[451] But to those asking piously it is easily explained, that Matthew for the sake of brevity said that the centurion himself approached, whose desire and will truly were conveyed to the Lord, even if they were conveyed by

---

446 Augustine, *De consensu euang.* 2.20.48 (CSEL 43:149.8–15); cf. Matt. 8:1–3.
447 Cf. Luke 5:12–13.
448 Isa. 38:1.
449 Wisd. 11:21.
450 Cf. Isa. 38:1–5.
451 Cf. Matt. 8:5.

others, thus allegorically commending to us that which is written: *Come to him and be enlightened.*⁴⁵² Accordingly, *because he himself praised the faith of the centurion, in that he truly approaches Jesus, so that he said: 'I have not found so great a faith in Israel',*⁴⁵³ *the sagacious evangelist wanted to say that the centurion himself approached Christ, rather than those by whom he had sent his words. But then Luke disclosed how the whole thing was done, in order that we might be compelled to understand from this how the other evangelist, who could not lie, had said that the centurion had approached. Just as that woman, who suffered a flowing of blood, although she held the hem of his garment, nevertheless, because she believed, touched the Lord, rather than those multitudes by whom he was thronged,*⁴⁵⁴ *so also the more the centurion believed, the more he approached the Lord.*⁴⁵⁵ /155/

[Luke 7:5] **For he loves our nation, and he has built a synagogue for us.** Those who say that a synagogue was built for them by the centurion plainly show that just as we do with 'church', so likewise they were accustomed to call not only the assembly of the faithful, but also the place where they gathered, 'synagogue', in accordance with what I said above.⁴⁵⁶

[Luke 7:6] **And Jesus went with them.** Great is the loftiness of the Lord, who was able to cure by his word alone, but not less so is his humility, who deigned to visit an infirm slave. For he set forth to save as one who was powerful, kind, and who had been entreated, and when he was entreated in the middle of the journey, he saved with a word. Surely he did this so that his powers would not be thought impotent because he travelled physically,⁴⁵⁷ but rather, for the sake of an example of humility. On another occasion he did not wish to come to cure the son of the ruler, lest he seem to honour wealth.⁴⁵⁸ Here, he consented to go immediately to the slave of the centurion, lest he seem to despise the servile condition.

[Luke 7:6b] **And when he was now not far from the house, the centurion sent his friends to him, saying: Lord, do not trouble yourself, for I am not worthy that you should enter under my roof.** Because he

---

452   Ps. 33:6 (34:5).
453   Matt. 8:10.
454   Cf. Luke 8:43–48.
455   Augustine, *De consensu euang.* 2.20 (CSEL 43:151.11–22).
456   See above, on Luke 4:16.
457   I.e., Christ could have healed at a distance, with a word; his powers did not depend on him physically travelling to the sick slave (see Introduction, 36–37).
458   Cf. John 4:46–50.

was conscious of the fact that he was a Gentile, the centurion thought he would be more burdened than helped by the good will of the Lord, and that he could not have Christ as a guest, for though he was endowed with faith in him, nevertheless he had not yet been anointed by the sacraments. But what our infirmity does not take for granted, divine grace knows how to give. For another centurion, who, just like this one, prefigures the believing people of the Gentiles, deservedly received the Holy Spirit's gift of great faith and justice, before he was baptized,[459] and this one, not yet instructed, deserved not only to have his faith praised by the Lord, but also that his slave be saved. On this point it is beautifully said by way of allegory that he did not keep Jesus far from his house, although he did not dare invite him under his roof, because *his salvation is near to them that fear him.*[460] And the more one who practises natural law rightly does the good things he knows how to do, the more he approaches the one who is truly good. But what the Lord says elsewhere to the multitudes flocking to him: *For some of them came from afar off,*[461] can be applied to those who added sin to the error of paganism.

[Luke 7:7] **Therefore I did not think myself worthy to come to you.** We also, who are believers from among the Gentiles, cannot come to the Lord, whom now we can never see in the flesh. But those of us who have acknowledged the sufferings of our servitude must first approach him who resides at the right hand of the Father by faith, and then send the elders of the Jews, that is, /156/ the best men of the Church, who came before us, to the Lord, to acquire by humble prayer advocates who will testify on our behalf that we love the Church, and that we endeavour as much as we can to build it, and intercede for us and for our sins before the Lord.

[Luke 7:7b] **But say the word, and my servant will be healed.** The great faith of the centurion, whereby he confesses the power of the word in Christ, provides an allegory of our healing, who, *even though we have known Christ according to the flesh, now know him so no longer.*[462]

[Luke 7:8] **For I also am a man subject to authority, having under me soldiers.** He says he is a man subject to the power of the tribune or the governor, but able to command his inferiors, so that it may be understood by how much more he is God who holds sway over all things, and who has an unlimited army of angelic power which obeys his commands.

---

459 The 'other' centurion is Cornelius (Acts 10); cf. verse 7:8b below.
460 Ps. 84:10 (85:9).
461 Mark 8:3.
462 2 Cor. 5:16.

[Luke 7:8b] **And I say to one: 'Go', and he goes, and to another: 'Come', and he comes, and to my slave: 'Do this', and he does it.** He wants *to show also that the Lord is able to carry out what he wishes, not only by the presence of his body, but by the services of his angels. For either the weaknesses of the body or the hostile powers by which man is often consigned to debility, were to be repelled both by the word of the Lord and by the services of the angels.*[463] And in another interpretation: The soldiers and slaves who obey the centurion are the natural virtues, and many who come to the Lord have no small share of these. Of these it is said in praise of the centurion Cornelius, that *he was a just man, and fearing God with all his house, giving many alms to the people, and always praying to God.*[464]

[Luke 7:9] **When Jesus heard this, he marvelled.** *He marvelled because he saw that the centurion understood his majesty.*[465] But who had created this same faith or understanding in him, except the very one who marvelled at it? But if someone else had done this, what would he who is all-knowing marvel at? It should be noted, then, that the fact that *the Lord marvels signifies that we should marvel, who still need to be warned in this way.* For *all such sentiments*, when ascribed to God, *are signs not of a confused mind, but of a teacher teaching.*[466]

[Luke 7:9b] **And turning about to the multitude that followed him, he said: Amen I say to you, I have not found so great a faith, not even in Israel.** *He is speaking, not about all the patriarchs and prophets of times past, but of men of the present* age.[467] Therefore the faith of the centurion is superior to theirs, because they were taught by the counsels of the Law /157/ and the prophets, but he, without anyone teaching him, believed without any external influence.

66/5 [Luke 7:10] **And they who were sent, having returned to the house, found the slave whole who had been sick.** *The faith of the Lord is proved, and the health of the slave is confirmed. The Lord's merit can also advocate for his servants not only when it comes to the merit of faith, but also to zeal in correction.*[468] Matthew explains these things more fully,

---

463 Jerome, *Commentarii in Matheum* 1 (CCSL 77:49.1096–98; 1100–03).
464 Acts 10:1–2 & 22.
465 Jerome, *Commentarii in Matheum* 1 (CCSL 77:49.1099–100).
466 Augustine, *De Genesi contra Manichaeos* 1.8.14 (CSEL 91:80).
467 Jerome, *Commentarii in Matheum* 1 (CCSL 77:49.1105–06).
468 Ambrose, *Expos. Lucam* 5.88 (CCSL 14:163.913–16).

because when the Lord says to the centurion: *Go, and as you have believed, so let it be done to you*,⁴⁶⁹ the servant was cured from that hour. But it is the custom of the blessed Luke to abridge things that he saw were fully expounded by the other evangelists, or even deliberately to omit them. On the other hand, things that he knew were omitted by them, or touched on briefly, he usually elucidates very skilfully.

Allegorically, as I have said, the **cent**urion, whose faith is superior to that of Israel, surely represents those who are chosen from among the Gentiles. These people, backed as it were by a hundredfold company of troops, are raised up by the perfecting of their spiritual virtues, and seek nothing earthly from the Lord, but only the joys of eternal salvation for themselves and their people. For the number one hundred [*numerus centenarius*], which is transferred from the left hand to the right, was customarily used to signify heavenly life.⁴⁷⁰ Hence it is that Noah's ark is built in a hundred years;⁴⁷¹ that the **centen**arian Abraham received the child of promise;⁴⁷² that *Isaac sowed, and he found in that same year a hundredfold*;⁴⁷³ that the atrium of the tabernacle is a hundred cubits long;⁴⁷⁴ that in the One-hundredth Psalm mercy and judgement is sung to the Lord;⁴⁷⁵ and other examples of this kind. Therefore, it is necessary that men of such merit kneel down to the Lord on behalf of those who are still weighed down *in fear* by *the spirit of bondage*,⁴⁷⁶ for as they are little by little carried to higher things, *perfect love casts out fear*.⁴⁷⁷

---

469 Matt. 8:13.
470 Cf. Jerome, *Aduersus Iouinianum* (PL 23:213–14). See Book 1 n. 245, Book 3 n. 92, for discussion of this number symbolism.
471 It is not explicitly stated in Genesis that Noah built the ark sometime within a period of a hundred years, but Bede, who was adept at bringing to light unexpressed numerical symbolism (as he saw it) in the Bible, based this inference on the facts that (a) Noah was 500 years old when he fathered Shem, Ham, and Japheth (Gen. 5:31), and (b) that, sometime after their births and the multiplication of people on earth, God determined to destroy mankind for its wickedness (Gen. 6:1–7), and (c) that Noah was 600 years old when the flood came (Gen. 7:6). Bede takes up this numerical symbolism again in *In Genesim* (CCSL 118A:102.1060–1003.1081); trans. Kendall, *Bede: On Genesis*, 172–73.
472 Cf. Gen. 21:5. For Isaac as a 'child of promise', cf. Gal. 4:28.
473 Gen. 26:12.
474 Cf. Exod. 27:9.
475 Cf. Ps. 100:1 (101:1).
476 Rom. 8:15.
477 1 John 4:18.

BOOK TWO                                             297

Chapter 25

67/10 [Luke 7:11] **And afterwards he went into a city that is called Nain.** *Nain is a city in Galilee, at the second milestone from Mount Tabor facing south and close to Endor,* which *is a large village at the fourth milestone* from the same mountain *to the south.*[478]

[Luke 7:11b–12] **And his disciples and a great crowd went with him. And when he approached the gate of the city, behold, a dead man was carried out, the only son of his mother.** This dead man, who was carried out of the gate of the city in the sight of many, signifies that man is rendered senseless by the deadly destruction of his offences, and in addition that he is not hiding the death of his spirit upon the bed of the heart, but disclosing it by word and deed to the sight of many, as it were through the gates of his own city. He is well said to have been the only son of his mother, /158/ because, although formed from many persons, mother Church is one perfect and immaculate virgin, and yet all the faithful very properly confess themselves to be sons of the universal Church. For any of the elect, when instructed in the faith, is a son; when he instructs others, he is a mother. Did he not act with maternal affection towards little children, who said: *My little children, for whom I am in labour again until Christ be formed in you?*[479] I think that the gate of the city, where the dead man was carried out, stands for any one of corporeal senses. For he who sows discord among brothers, who speaks injustice on high, is carried dead through the gate of the mouth. *Whoever will look at a woman to lust after her,*[480] reveals the signs of his death through the gate of his eyes. Whoever willingly opens his ear to idle tales and lewd songs or slanders, makes this gate of the soul the gate of his death, and whoever does not guard his other senses, himself surrenders the gates of death to himself. I pray, Lord Jesus, that you make all the gates of my city *gates of justice,* that *I may go in to them and give praise* to your name,[481] and that the stench of the corpse carried in not reach your majesty, who frequently visits it with your celestial ministers, but that salvation may take possession of its walls, and praise, its gates.[482]

---

478 Jerome, *De situ et nom.* (*Onomastica sacra* 96.32–97.2; 143.22–24).
479 Gal. 4:19.
480 Matt. 5:19.
481 Ps. 117:19 (118:19).
482 Cf. Is. 60:18. Bede's prayer for his community sounds like the peroration of a sermon.

[Luke 7:12b] **And she was a widow, and a great multitude of the city was with her.** Every soul who bears in mind that it was redeemed by the death of its bridegroom and Lord, knows that the widow is the Church. And by divine command, a great multitude accompanied the Lord, and a great crowd, the widow, so that at the sight of so great a miracle, many witnesses might become many eulogists of God.

[Luke 7:13] **When the Lord had seen her, being moved with pity towards her, he said to her: Weep not.** Cease weeping for him, he says, as if he were dead, whom you will soon see rise again alive. Here, in allegorical form, is a refutation of the teaching of Novatus who, boasting proudly of his cleanliness, attempts to nullify the humble cleansing of penitents, and denies that the true mother Church, who weeps over the spiritual extinction of her children, should be consoled by the hope that life might be restored.[483] And the evangelist testifies beautifully that the Lord first was moved with pity towards the mother, and then raised up her son, in order that in his first action he might offer an example of piety worthy of being imitated and in the second he might affirm faith in a power worthy of wonder.

[Luke 7:14] **And he came near and touched the bier. And they that carried it stood still.** The bier on which the dead man is borne is the desperate sinner's /159/ wickedly careless conscience. Those who carry someone to be buried are either unclean desires which snatch a man to destruction, or the poisonous enticements of flattering companions. By cheering on sins, these people pile them high, and then they bury sinners with contempt as with a mound of earth. Of these it is said elsewhere: *Let the dead bury their dead.*[484] Indeed, the dead bury the dead, when sinners lure others like them with noxious applause, and submerge them in a heap of the worst adulation, cutting off any hope of rising again at some time or other. Therefore, when the Lord touched the bier, the bearers of the body stood still, because conscience, touched by fear of divine judgement, returns to its senses, and swiftly responds to the Saviour who summons it to life by restraining both the abundance of pleasures, often carnal, and the multitude of those who praise unjustly. Hence it rightly follows:

[Luke 7:14b–15] **And he said: Young man, I say to you, arise. And he that was dead sat up, and began to speak. And he gave him to his mother.** He that was dead indeed sits up, when the sinner is restored to life by inner remorse. He begins to speak, when he displays the marks of

---

483 On the heresy of Novatus, cf., e.g., Isidore, *Etym.* 8.5.34.
484 Matt. 8:22.

restored life to all who had caused him to indulge in sin. He is returned to his mother, when he is joined to the communion of the Church by the ordinances of priestly judgement.

[Luke 7:16] **And there came a fear on them all, and they glorified God, saying: A great prophet has risen up among us.** The more hopeless the death of the soul who is recalled to life, the more people are corrected by that example. Witness the prophet David;[485] witness the apostle Peter.[486] The higher their station, the heavier their fall. But the heavier the fall, the more pleasing the devotion of the one who rises up. Truly the more pleasing the compassion of the Lord appeared in them, the more certain the hope of salvation appeared to all penitents, so that all who hear may justly say:

[Luke 7:16b] **God has visited his people**, not only by once making his word flesh, but also by always sending it into our hearts, in order that we should be raised up.

69/5 [Luke 7:18] **And John's disciples told him of all these things.** John's disciples tell him of Christ's powers and miracles, not, as I think, with a heart that is sincere, but with one goaded on by envy. For elsewhere they are said to have complained about him in this way: *Rabbi, he that was with you beyond the Jordan, to whom you gave testimony, behold he baptizes, and all men come to him.*[487] John then replies to them: *A man cannot receive anything, unless it be given him /160/ from heaven,*[488] and so forth. He manifestly declares to them that Jesus is both a spotless man and Christ, the son of God. But because envy remained, and malice could not be expelled, notice what the excellent teacher did now to correct them:

## Chapter 26

[Luke 7:19] **And John called to him two of his disciples, and sent them to Jesus, saying: Are you he that is to come, or are we looking for another?** Plainly, John did so, *in order that on this occasion at least, seeing the miracles* that Jesus performed, *they might believe in him, and by means of their teacher's questioning, they might learn this for themselves.*[489]

---

485 Cf. 2 Sam. 12:13.
486 Cf. Matt. 26:75.
487 John 3:26.
488 John 3:27.
489 Jerome, *Commentarii in Matheum* 2 (CCSL 77:77.11–13).

Therefore, *he does not say: 'Are you he that has come', but: 'Are you he that is to come'. And the sense is: Command me, because I* am about to be killed by Herod and *to descend to hell, whether I, who announced you to those here on earth, should announce you also in hell, or whether it is not fitting for the son of God to taste death, and you are going to send another to carry out these mysteries?*[490]

[Luke 7:21] **And in that same hour, he cured many of their diseases, and hurts, and evil spirits, and to many that were blind he gave sight.** *John had asked through his disciples: 'Are you he that is to come, or do we await another?' Christ sets out miracles, not as a reply to these questions, but as a stumbling block to the messengers.*[491]

[Luke 7:22] **Go,** *Jesus says,* **and relate to John what you have heard and seen: The blind see, the lame walk, the lepers are made clean, the deaf hear, the dead rise again, to the poor the gospel is preached.** *Whether it be the poor in spirit, or the poor in wealth, the consequence is that when it comes to preaching there is no difference between the high-born and the base-born, between the rich and the needy. These demonstrate the teacher's strictness, and the instructor's truth, since everyone who can be saved is equal in his sight. And for this reason, he says:*[492]

[Luke 7:23] **And blessed is whoever will not be caused to stumble in me.** And he reproves the messengers of John, who had not believed that he was Christ because of the stumbling block of lack of faith, and he explains to John what he sought to know, that *He is the God of salvation, and the way out of death is from the Lord.*[493] *For, having seen so many miracles and such great powers, no one could be caused to stumble, but could only be astonished. But the mind of the infidels encountered a grave stumbling block in him, when they saw him dying after so many miracles.*[494]

*What is it, therefore, to say: 'Blessed is he who will not be caused to stumble in me',*[495] *except to signify aloud the abjectness and humility of his death? It is as if he should openly say: Indeed, I do wonders, but I do not scorn to endure what is abject; because by dying I follow you, so therefore men must take great care, lest those who revere my miracles despise my death.*[496]

---

490 Jerome, *Commentarii in Matheum* 2 (CCSL 77:77.22–27).
491 Jerome, *Commentarii in Matheum* 2 (CCSL 77:78.33–34).
492 Jerome, *Commentarii in Matheum* 2 (CCSL 77:78.37–41).
493 Ps. 67:21 (68:20).
494 Gregory, *Hom. in Euang.* 1.6.1 (CCSL 141:39.26–29).
495 Matt. 11:6.
496 Gregory, *Hom. in Euang.* 1.6.1 (CCSL 141:40.35–40).

[Luke 7:24] **And when the messengers of John were departed, he began to speak to the multitudes /161/ concerning John.** *Because the multitude standing around did not know the spiritual significance of his question, and thought that John harboured doubts about Christ, whom he himself had pointed out,* Christ heaps worthy praises upon John *so that they might understand that John had not asked on his own behalf, but for the sake of his disciples.*[497]

[Luke 7:24b] **What did you go out into the desert to see? A reed shaken by the wind?** *He starts not with an assertion, but a denial. Indeed, as soon as a breeze touches a reed, it bends in its direction. And what is signified by a reed but a carnal spirit, which leans in any direction the moment it is touched by approval or disparagement. For if the breeze of approval blows from a human mouth, it grows cheerful, is lifted up, and bends itself entirely to indulgence as it were. But if the wind of disparagement bursts forth from the place where the breeze of praise used to come, it immediately bends it in another direction as it were towards the violence of anger. But John was not a reed shaken by the wind, because indulgence did not make him ingratiating, nor did any anger make him harsh, and prosperity could not lift him up, nor could adversity bend him down.*[498]

[Luke 7:25] **But what did you go out to see? A man clothed in soft garments? Behold, they that are in costly apparel and live delicately are in the houses of kings.** *For indeed it is written that John was clothed with camel's hair.*[499] *Therefore, he says, people who flee from undergoing adversity for God, and seek the wantonness and pleasure of this present life, do not serve the heavenly kingdom, but an earthly one. Let no one, therefore, deem that there is no sin in the abundance of and care for clothing, because, if this were not a fault, the Lord would certainly not have praised John for the roughness of his garment.*[500]

*Although it is a fact that John is said not to have been clothed in soft clothing, this can also be understood allegorically in another way. For he was not clothed in soft clothing, because he did not encourage the life of sinners with flattery, but reproached it with the force of harsh invective, saying: 'You brood of vipers, who has warned you to flee from the wrath to come?'*[501]

---

497 Jerome, *Commentarii in Matheum* 2 (CCSL 77:78.51–54).
498 Gregory, *Hom. in Euang.* 1.6.2 (CCSL 141:40.43–54).
499 Cf. Mark 1:6.
500 Gregory, *Hom. in Euang.* 1.6.3 (CCSL 141:41.67–72).
501 Gregory, *Hom. in Euang.* 1.6.4 (CCSL 141:41.77–81): Luke 3:7; cf. Matt. 3:7.

[Luke 7:26] **But what did you go out to see? A prophet? Yes, I say to you, and more than a prophet.** *The office of a prophet, certainly, is to say what is to come, not actually to show it. John, therefore, is more than a prophet, because the one whom he had prophesied by being the precursor, he also announced by pointing him out.*[502]

70/2 [Luke 7:27] **This is he of whom it is written: Behold, I send my angel before your face, who will prepare your way before you.**[503] *What is called 'angel' [angelus] in Greek, is called 'messenger' [nuntius] in Latin. Rightly, therefore, he who is sent* /162/ *to announce the divine judgement is called an angel so that he might maintain in name the grandeur which he fulfils in the work. Indeed, the name is elevated, but the life is not inferior to the name.*[504]

But also *all who are enrolled under the name of the priesthood are called 'angels', as witnesses the prophet, who says: 'The lips of the priest will keep knowledge, and they will seek the law at his mouth, because he is the angel of the Lord of hosts.'*[505] *And likewise each one* of the faithful *receives the grace of divine inspiration if he recalls his neighbour from wrongdoing, if he takes care to encourage good works, if he proclaims the eternal kingdom and punishment to the one straying; then he distributes words of holy prophecy, then truly an angel appears.*[506]

71/5 [Luke 7:28] **For I say to you: Among those who are born of women, there is not a greater prophet than John the Baptist.** *Among those, he says, who are born of women. He is preferred, therefore, to those men who were born of women, and from copulation with a man, and not to him, who was born from a virgin and the Holy Spirit. Nevertheless,* in this statement *he did not prefer John to the other prophets and patriarchs and to all other men, but he made the others equal to John. For it does not immediately follow that, if others are not greater than him, he is greater than the rest, but that he has equality with other saints.*[507]

[Luke 7:28b] **But he that is lesser in the kingdom of God is greater than he.** This statement can *be understood in two ways. Either he called the kingdom* of God *what we have not yet received, and which we are not*

---

502 Gregory, *Hom. in Euang.* 1.6.5 (CCSL 141:42.87–90): cf. John 1:29.
503 Cf. Mal. 3:1.
504 Gregory, *Hom. in Euang.* 1.6.5 (CCSL 141:42.95–99).
505 Mal. 2:7.
506 Gregory, *Hom. in Euang.* 1.6.6 (CCSL 141:42.101–09). See Introduction, 30.
507 Jerome, *Commentarii in Matheum* 2 (CCSL 77:80.81–90).

*yet in, for which reason he is going to say at the end: 'Come, you blessed of my Father, possess the kingdom',*[508] *and the least of the holy angels, however many there are, is surely greater than any holy and just man bearing 'a body that is corruptible' and that 'weighs upon the soul';*[509] *or, he wanted the kingdom* of God *to be understood* as the Church of this age, *whose children – those, however many they are, who can be called just and holy – are everyone from the creation of the human race up to the end, and if this is the case, truly the Lord signified himself, because in the timing of his birth he was lesser than John, but greater in the eternity of divinity and lordly power. Consequently, in accordance with the first interpretation, the distinction is drawn in this way: 'But he that is lesser in the kingdom of God', but then it is added: 'is greater than he'. According to the second, in this way: 'But he that is lesser', but then it is added: 'in the kingdom of God is greater than he'.*[510]

**72/10** [Luke 7:29] **And all the people hearing, and the tax collectors, justified God, being baptized with John's baptism.** *God himself is justified by baptism, when men justify themselves by confessing their own sins, just as* /163/ *it is written: 'Tell your iniquities in order that you be justified.'*[511] *And he is justified in* this sense, *because the gift of God is not opposed by stubbornness, but recognized by justice. For 'The Lord is just, and has loved justice.'*[512] *The justification of God, therefore, consists in this: he is seen to have bestowed his gifts not on the unworthy and the guilty, but on those who are made innocent and righteous by the cleansing of baptism.*[513]

*Likewise, David says: 'To you only have I sinned, and have done evil before you, that you may be shown to be just in your words, and may overcome when you are judged.'*[514] *Therefore, he who sins and confesses his sin to God justifies God, yielding to him as the conqueror, and hoping for grace from him. In baptism, therefore, God is shown to be just, in whom is both the confession and the forgiveness of sins.*[515]

[Luke 7:30] **But the Pharisees and the lawyers despised the counsel of God to themselves, being not baptized by him.** The phrase that he

---

508 Matt. 25:34.
509 Wisd. 9:15.
510 Augustine, *Contra aduers.* 2.5.20 (CCSL 49:106.604–19).
511 Isa. 43:26.
512 Ps. 10:8 (11:8).
513 Ambrose, *Expos. Lucam* 6.2 (CCSL 14:175.14–22).
514 Ps. 50:6 (51:4).
515 Ambrose, *Expos. Lucam* 6.3 (CCSL 14:175.26–31).

uses, 'to themselves', either signifies 'against themselves', because he who rejects the grace of God, does so against himself, or being foolish and ungrateful they are censured because they did not want to receive the counsel of God sent 'towards themselves'. The counsel of God, therefore, is that by which he decided to save the world by the passion and death of Jesus the Lord. But the Pharisees and the lawyers despised it, rejecting the secret and salvific mystery, the divine tokens of which came before in the preaching and baptism of John. Nevertheless, they were subject to the same counsel through their ignorance and lack of willingness, in accordance with what the apostle Peter, speaking of the Lord, says to them: *Him, being delivered up, by the determinate counsel and foreknowledge of God, you by the hands of wicked men have crucified and slain.*[516]

**73/5** [Luke 7:31–32] **To what then will I liken the men of this generation, and what are they like? They are like children sitting in the marketplace, and speaking to one another, saying: We have sung to you with flutes, and you have not danced; we have mourned, and you have not wept.** The generation of the Jews is compared to children sitting in the marketplace, because they received the teachers, and after them, the prophets, of whom it is said: *Out of the mouths of infants and of sucklings, you have perfected praise*;[517] and elsewhere: *The declaration of your words gives me light, and gives understanding to little ones*,[518] that is, to the humble in spirit. And the Lord's marketplace is either the Synagogue or Jerusalem itself, in which the laws of heavenly precepts were stored up, where these children were speaking to one another, or according to Matthew, to their companions.[519] For day by day it was their custom to reprove in fatherly tones the peoples of their race and nation for the fact that they would nod their assent, despite having neither been attracted at first by the Psalms of David, nor aroused later by prophetic lamentations. How often was either a future victory over the enemy prophesied, /164/ or a past victory recalled, and yet they did not resolve to rise to deeds of virtue. For the word 'dancing' signifies not the twirling of a body bent with an actor's motions, but the devotion of a diligent heart and the religious agility of the limbs. How often either destruction wrought by an enemy or lamentations of prophets of coming destruction resounded, and yet those

---

516 Acts 2:23.
517 Ps. 8:3 (8:2).
518 Ps. 118:130 (119:130).
519 Cf. Matt. 11:16.

who heard did not accordingly endeavour to take refuge in the remedies of penitence. The Psalmist sings: *Rejoice to God our helper, sing aloud to the God of Jacob. Take a psalm, and bring here the timbrel*, and so forth.[520] But what follows? *But my people heard not my voice, and Israel harkened not to me.*[521] The prophet cries out: *The Lord says these things: Be converted to me with all your heart, in fasting, and in weeping, and in mourning. And rend your hearts, and not your garments.*[522] And again: *My bowels, my bowels are in pain, the senses of my heart are troubled within me, I will not hold my peace, for my soul has heard the sound of the trumpet, the cry of battle.*[523] And a little after: *For my foolish people have not known me, they are foolish and senseless children.*[524]

[Luke 7:33-34] **For John the Baptist came neither eating bread nor drinking wine, and you say: He has a demon. The Son of man has come eating and drinking, and you say: Behold a man that is a glutton and a drinker of wine, and friend of tax collectors and sinners.** Just as then, he says, so also now you reject both paths of salvation. *For when he says, 'we have mourned, and you have not wept', this pertains to John, whose abstinence from food and drink signified the lamentation of penitence. And when he says, 'We have sung with flutes, and you have not danced' this pertains to the Lord himself, who, by taking food and drink with others, prefigured the joy of the kingdom. But they wished neither to be humble with John nor to rejoice with Christ, saying that he has a demon, this glutton and drunkard and friend of tax collectors and sinners. And what he adds:*[525]

[Luke 7:35] **And wisdom is justified by all her children**, *shows that the children of wisdom understand that justice lies neither in abstaining nor in eating, but in enduring poverty with patience, and practising moderation by not corrupting ourselves with excess, but taking food and drink in a suitable manner, and not taking those things of which there is no need. But eager desire must be condemned. 'For the kingdom of God is not meat and drink, but justice and peace and joy', and since men are accustomed to take much joy in carnal feasting, he added: 'in the Holy Spirit'.*[526]

---

520 Ps. 80:2-3 (81:1-2).
521 Ps. 80:12 (81:11).
522 Joel 2:12-13.
523 Jer. 4:19.
524 Jer. 4:22.
525 Augustine, *Quaestiones euang.* 2.11 (CCSL 44B:53.3-11).
526 Augustine, *Quaestiones euang.* 2.11 (CCSL 44B:54.12-16; 55.34-36); Rom. 14:17.

In another interpretation: *Wisdom is justified by all her children*, that is, the faithful confirm that the dispensation and teaching of God, which *resists the proud* /165/ *and gives grace to the humble*,[527] is just. Counted amongst them were those of whom it is said above: *And all the people hearing, and the tax collectors, justified God.*[528] Amen.

Here ends Book Two of the Commentary on Luke. /166/

---

527 James 4:6; 1 Pet. 5:5.
528 Luke 7:29.

# III

[Luke 7:36–11:13]

Here begins Book Three.

Although for the sake of lessening the work of readers the sacred history of Mary the penitent, which comes first in our third book on Luke, begins from a new starting point, nevertheless the thread of the action looks back on the end of the second book. For there, either out of the mouth of the evangelist, or, as was the opinion of some, of the Lord Saviour, came the statement: *And all the people hearing, and the tax collectors, justified God, being baptized with John's baptism.*[1] Because if you conclude that the Lord said this, it is understood that it is the people hearing John that are meant. But if it were interposed by the evangelist, the people are understood as hearing the Lord himself discussing the greatness of John. *But the Pharisees and the lawyers despised the counsel of God to themselves, being not baptized by him.*[2] The same evangelist goes on to add to the words as well as deeds that he had propounded, that *wisdom* is certainly *justified by all her children,*[3] that is, both by the just, and after injustice, by the penitents, proving this by a very fitting example:

## Chapter 27

74/1 [Luke 7:36–37] **And one of the Pharisees, he says, desired him to eat with him. And he went into the house of the Pharisee, and took his place at the table. And behold, a woman who was in the city, a sinner, when she knew that he took his place at the table in the Pharisee's house, brought an alabaster box of ointment.** Alabaster is a kind of white

---

1 Luke 7:29.
2 Luke 7:30.
3 Luke 7:33.

marble intermixed with various colours, which people are accustomed *to hollow out for ointment vessels, because it is said to be best for preserving ointments from spoiling. The whitest kind of all is found around Egyptian Thebes and Damascus in Syria, but the most excellent is found in India.*[4]

Some say that this is not the same woman who, when the Lord's passion was at hand, moistened his head and feet with ointment,[5] because this woman washed his feet with her tears, and dried them with her hair, and is clearly called a sinner;[6] but nothing like this is written about the other one, nor could a harlot be made immediately worthy of the head of the Lord. But those who investigate more thoroughly find that the same woman, namely Mary Magdalene the sister of Lazarus, as John says, had performed the same service twice. One occasion was in this passage, when she approached for the first time with humility and tears, and merited the remission of her sins. For John, although he did not, like Luke, tell how it happened, nevertheless also spoke of this, commending Mary herself, when he began to speak about the resurrection of her brother, saying: *Now a certain man was sick, named Lazarus, of Bethany, of the town of Mary and Martha her sister. And* /167/ *Mary was the one who anointed the Lord with ointment, and wiped his feet with her hair.*[7] On the second occasion, however, in Bethany (for the first happened in Galilee), the woman, no longer a sinner, but chaste, holy, and devoted to Christ, is found to have anointed not only his feet, but also his head.[8] This is beautifully suited to the rules of allegory, because every faithful soul is likewise first bent down at the feet of the Lord, humbled and about to be absolved of sins; and then, with its merits increasing over time, with the ardour of joyful faith, it bathes the head, as it were, of the Lord with the odour of spices. And the universal Church of Christ herself, by celebrating the mysteries in the present age of his incarnation, which is signified by the word 'feet', offers services devoted to her Redeemer. But in the future, she glorifies as if with pure spikenard, at the same time gazing with perpetual praises of confessions, both the glory of his human nature and the eternity of his divine nature, because *the head of Christ is God.*[9] And therefore, it says, 'she brought an alabaster box of ointment'.

---

4 Pliny, *Naturalis historia* 36.12.60–61.
5 Cf. Matt. 26:7–13; Mark 14:3–9; John 12:3.
6 Cf. Luke 7:38–39.
7 John 11:1–2.
8 Cf. John 12:1–3.
9 1 Cor. 11:3.

[Luke 7:38] **And standing behind at his feet, she began to wash his feet with tears, and wiped them with the hair of her head, and kissed his feet, and anointed them with the ointment.** *It is clear to all that the woman in time past, when intent upon illicit deeds, applied the ointment to herself for the perfuming of her own flesh. That which, therefore, she had used shamefully for herself, she now offered in a praiseworthy manner to God. She had longed for earthly things with her eyes, but now she wept, rubbing them in penitence. She had exhibited her hair for the stylish arrangement of her face, but now she wiped her tears with her hair. She had spoken proud things with her mouth, but kissing the feet of the Lord, she fixed it on the footsteps of her Redeemer. She discovered as many sacrifices from herself as she had found pleasures in herself. She converted the number of her sins to the number of her virtues, so that everything which had once defied God through sin might serve God through penitence.*[10]

[Luke 7:39] **And the Pharisee, who had invited him, seeing it, spoke within himself, saying: This man, if he were a prophet, would certainly know who and what kind of woman this is who touches him, that she is a sinner.** *Behold, the Pharisee, truly proud of himself and falsely just, rebuked the sick woman for her sickness, and the doctor for his aid, though he was himself suffering from the wound of pride and didn't know it. Hence, it is always necessary that when we take notice of certain sinners, we lament for ourselves in their ruin, because perhaps we have lapsed ourselves in similar ways, or we can lapse, if we haven't already. And if the severe judgement of the magisterium ought always to pursue vices with the virtue of discipline, nevertheless it is necessary that we exercise great discernment, because we owe correction to vices, /168/ but compassion to nature.*[11]

*But now let us hear by what wisdom this proud and arrogant man may be overcome:*[12]

[Luke 7:41–43] **A certain creditor**, he says, **had two debtors, the one owed five hundred denarii, and the other fifty. And when they had not the wherewithal to repay, he forgave them both. Which of them therefore loves him most? Simon, answering, said: I suppose the one to whom he forgave the most.** *In this case it should be observed that when the Pharisee is overcome by Christ's wisdom, like a madman he carries*

---

10 Gregory, *Hom. in Euang.* 2.33.2 (CCSL 141:289.25–35).
11 Gregory, *Hom. in Euang.* 2.33.3 (CCSL 141:290. 40–42; 57–62).
12 Gregory, *Hom. in Euang.* 2.33.4 (CCSL 141:290.67–68).

the rope by which he is tied. *The good deeds of the sinning woman are recounted, and the wicked deeds of the man who pretends to be just are recounted, when it is said:*[13]

[Luke 7:44b] **I entered into your house, and you did not give me water for my feet. But she has watered my feet with tears, and has wiped them with her hair,** and so forth. *But after recounting this, he added this statement:*[14]

[Luke 7:47] **Therefore I say to you: Many sins will be forgiven her, because she has loved much.** *What do we believe love to be, but fire? And what is sin, but rust? Hence it is now said: 'Many sins will be forgiven her, because she has loved much.' As if it were said in plain words: She burns away completely the rust of sin, because she blazes fiercely with the fire of love. The more the heart of the sinner is burned up by the great fire of love, the more fully the rust of sin is consumed. Behold, she who had come sick to the physician is healed, but after her healing the others are still sick.*[15] For it goes on:

[Luke 7:49] **And those who took their place at the table with him began to say within themselves: Who is this who also forgives sins?** *But the heavenly physician is not concerned for those sick persons whom he sees are even made worse from his medicine. He strengthens her whom he had cured with the wisdom of his compassion, saying:*[16]

[Luke 7:50b] **Your faith has made you safe, go in peace.** *Faith made her safe, because she did not doubt that she could receive what she asked for. But she had also already received the certitude of hope from him from whom she was seeking salvation likewise through hope. And she is commanded to go in peace, in order not to be drawn again from the path of truth to the highway of temptation.*[17]

Granted that *these statements are a historical account,* let us now view the secrets of *allegorical signification. For whom does the Pharisee who deceives himself about false justice signify, but the Jewish people? Whom does the woman signify – a sinner, but one who comes and weeps at the feet of the Lord – but the converted Gentiles?*[18] The Pharisee asked the Lord to

---

13 Gregory, *Hom. in Euang.* 2.33.4 (CCSL 141:290.72–75).
14 Gregory, *Hom. in Euang.* 2.33.4 (CCSL 141:291.79–80).
15 Gregory, *Hom. in Euang.* 2.33.4 (CCSL 141:291.81–89).
16 Gregory, *Hom. in Euang.* 2.33.4 (CCSL 141:291.91–93).
17 Gregory, *Hom. in Euang.* 2.33.4 (CCSL 141:291.94–98).
18 Gregory, *Hom. in Euang.* 2.33.5 (CCSL 141:292.102–06).

eat with him, because the same Jewish people did not cease to hope that he whom they did not want to believe was come was going to come, nay, they did not cease to desire that he come with prayers of entreaty, saying: *Stir up your might, and come to save us.*[19] Certainly for the Lord to eat with the Pharisee /169/ is to receive joy of mind from the devotion of a believing people. Hence elsewhere, when Samaria is about to believe, he says to his disciples: *I have food to eat that you do not know.*[20] And when they are uncertain about what he said, he explains: *My food is to do the will of him who sent me, that I may perfect his work.*[21] *And he went*, it says, *into the house of the Pharisee, and took his place at the table.*[22] This same house of the Pharisee is the guardianship of the Law and the prophets, in which the Jewish people boasted that they had a habitation in which they dwell without ceasing. The Lord entered this habitation, because when he appeared in time in the flesh, he did not come to destroy the Law or the prophets, but to fulfil them.[23] He took his place at the table, because he, who could not be comprehended in the loftiness of his majesty, put on the humility of a servile shape by which he could be seen. And so, 'a woman who was in the city, a sinner, knew that he took his place at the table in the Pharisee's house',[24] because the Gentiles, bound previously by their wicked deeds in their way of life in the world, learned from the report of the Apostle's speech that *God sent his Son, made of a woman, made under the Law, that he might redeem them who were under the Law.*[25] And in the Pharisee's house, she, and not the Pharisee, is justified, when the people of the Jews follow only the letter of the Law, but we follow also the grace of the Spirit in the Law. They judge that Jesus is not a prophet, because he receives sinners, but we recognize that he who can justify sinners is the true God.

And *'the woman brought an alabaster box of ointment'*.[26] What is meant by the ointment, but the good odour of belief? Hence Paul likewise says: *'We are the good odour of Christ to God in every place.'*[27] Therefore, if we do righteous deeds, by which we besprinkle the Church with the good

---

19 Ps. 79:3 (80:2).
20 John 4:32; cf. John 4:39–42.
21 John 4:34.
22 Luke 7:36.
23 Cf. Matt. 5:17.
24 Luke 7:37.
25 Gal. 4:4–5.
26 Luke 7:37.
27 2 Cor. 2:14–15.

odour of belief, what do we pour on the body of the Lord but ointment? *But the woman stood at his feet.*[28] *For we stood opposite the feet of the Lord, when, fixed in our sins, we were kept from his paths. But if we are converted to true penitence after our sins, we now stand once again at his feet, because we are following his footsteps which we used to oppose. The woman washes his feet with tears. We also do this rightly, if we may be bent down by compassion to any of the Lord's lowliest members, if we sympathize with his saints in their troubles, if we consider their sorrow as ours. The woman wiped his feet, which she had washed, with her hair.*[29] *Indeed, hair is a bodily superfluity. And what is an abundant earthly substance, save a kind of hair, which flows out of the body naturally, and does not even feel that it has been cut off?*[30] *We wipe the feet of the Lord, therefore, with our hair, when we feel pity for his saints, for whom we have compassion out of love, even from these things which we have an abundance of, since the mind grieves through compassion, just as* /170/ *likewise a liberal hand displays the effect of grief. The woman kisses the feet which she wipes.*[31] *We do this fully, if we eagerly love those whom we preserve out of our liberality, so that we do not consider our neighbour's need as a burden, so that his indigence, which we relieve, not come to be seen as onerous, and the soul grow weary of love when the hand bestows necessities.*[32]

*The mystery of Christ's incarnation itself can be understood by his feet, whereby divinity touched the earth, because it took on flesh. 'For the Word was made flesh and dwelt among us.'*[33] *We kiss the feet of the Redeemer, therefore, when we love the mystery of his incarnation with all our heart. We anoint his feet with oil, when we preach that power of his humanity with the good repute of sacred eloquence. But the Pharisee sees and envies this, because when the Jewish people see that the Gentiles are preaching God, they are eaten up from inside by their own wickedness. But our Redeemer recounts to him the Pharisee the good deeds of the woman, as if of the Gentiles, so that he may learn in what evil he lies.*[34]

---

28 Cf. Luke 7:38.
29 Cf. Luke 7:38.
30 Gregory is alluding to the physiological theory that hair is a waste product of digestion 'excreted' or 'exhaled' from the body: see Aristotle, *Generation of Animals* 5.3–5 (781b–785b), and pseudo-Aristotle, *Problemata* 10.23 (893a–b).
31 Cf. Luke 7:38.
32 Gregory, *Hom. in Euang.* 2.33.5 (CCSL 141:292.111–40).
33 John 1:14.
34 Gregory, *Hom. in Euang.* 2.33.6 (CCSL 141:293.141–50).

*'I entered into your house, and you did not give me water for my feet. But she has watered my feet with tears.'*[35] *Indeed, water is outside us, and the moisture of tears is within us, because that faithless people never offered those things that were outside themselves for the Lord; but the Gentiles when they were converted not only poured out material things for him, but also their blood.* '*You did not give me a kiss, but she, since she came in, has not ceased to kiss my feet.*'[36] *A kiss is certainly a sign of love. And that faithless people did not give God a kiss, because they did not want to love him out of affection, whom they served out of fear. The Gentiles, having been called, do not cease to kiss the footsteps of their Saviour, because they sigh with a continuous love of him.*[37]

*'You did not anoint my head with oil.'*[38] *If we take the Lord's feet as an allegorical symbol of the incarnation, divinity itself is fittingly signified by his head. Hence it is also said by* the Apostle: *'The head of Christ is God.'*[39] *The Jewish people acknowledged that they believed in God, certainly, and not in his capacity as man. But to the Pharisee it is said: 'You did not anoint my head with oil', because he also neglected to preach with worthy praise that very power of divinity, in which the Jewish people promised that they believed. 'But she has anointed my feet with ointment',*[40] *because when the Gentiles believed the allegorical symbol of his incarnation, they preached the lowest parts of him with the highest praise.*[41]

Likewise, the two debtors, about whom the parable is set forth to Simon, signify both peoples, namely the people of the Jews and the people of the Gentiles, who owed to one creditor, that is, to their Creator, not material money, but the coin of their own salvation.[42] For indeed our Creator created them in his /171/ own image and likeness, as if he promoted them with a denarius lent for their salvation. For a denarius is usually fashioned with the image and name of a king. *And from everyone to whom much is given, much will be required, and from him to whom they have committed much, they demand more.*[43] And indeed the debt of each of the two peoples is

---

35 Luke 7:44.
36 Luke 7:45.
37 Gregory, *Hom. in Euang.* 2.33.6 (CCSL 141:293.153–64).
38 Luke 7:46.
39 1 Cor. 11:3.
40 Luke 7:46.
41 Gregory, *Hom. in Euang.* 2.33.6 (CCSL 141:294.168–77).
42 Cf. Luke 7:40–43.
43 Luke 12:48.

multiplied by the number five, because, of course, there are five senses, and when we make use of them in this life, we ought to honour the image that we received of our Creator. But the people to whom the Ten Commandments of the Law were given by the servant owe less.[44] And the people to whom the grace of eternal life was entrusted by the Son owe more. Therefore, the interest of the former is heaped up by the number ten, and of the latter by the number one hundred, which no one doubts serves to signify the heavenly kingdom, which will be given by the right hand. For it is not for nothing that this is done by the same bending of the fingers by which the number ten is signified in the left hand and the number one hundred in the right,[45] except that not only does faith now accomplish the works of the Ten Commandments, which the letter could not, and also in the future *'will render to each according to his works', to those indeed who, according to the patience in good work, seek glory and honour and incorruption, eternal life.*[46]

But because neither of us, Jew or Gentile, is saved by our efforts, but by his grace through faith,[47] it is rightly said: *And when they had not the wherewithal to repay, he forgave them both,*[48] and he loves more the one to whom more is forgiven, *but to whom less is given, he loves less.*[49] Because whether you take this to mean the advantages of perfecting the knowledge which we have received or of avoiding the folly which we have incurred, surely much more is given to the Church than to the Synagogue. The Church was also once corrupted by the fouler filth of idolatry, seeing that no teacher forbade it, but *where sin abounded, grace abounded more,*[50] and now it is uplifted by the greater proclamation of the perfection of the Gospel. With respect to this, it is said: *Many prophets and just men have desired to see the things that you see, and to hear the things that you hear and have not heard them.*[51] It certainly accords with this passage that the account in the book of Numbers relates that those who came from the battle after the spoils of the slaughtered Midianites had been divided

---

44 The servant is Moses. See below, nn. 54 and 55.
45 See above, Book 1, n. 285.
46 Rom. 2:6–7.
47 Cf. Eph. 2:8.
48 Luke 7:42.
49 Luke 7:47.
50 Rom. 5:20.
51 Matt. 13:17.

BOOK THREE 315

equally, gave the five-hundredth head[52] of their portion to the Lord, but the others the fiftieth.[53] This is because he who keeps himself whole within the encampment from hostile assault by the practice of virtues offers great things, but certainly he who overthrows the unnumbered forces of the opposing army by brandishing the sword of the word offers greater.

Chapter 28

75/10 [Luke 8:1] **And afterwards he travelled through the cities and towns, preaching and evangelizing the kingdom of God, and the /172/ twelve with him.** We see fulfilled in the disciples of Christ what we read was said about that ancient people of the Jews. And it is no wonder, because the one God of both Testaments who gave the Law himself through his servant,[54] will give blessing through his Son. *Just like,* he says, *the eagle enticing his chicks to fly, and hovering over them, he spread his wings, and has taken him and carried him on his shoulders.*[55] For just as chicks recently hatched cannot conquer the air by flying until they are fledged, so each and every one of the faithful, in order to be capable of flying to heaven, must first clothe themselves with the plumage of the virtues in the nest of faith. So the apostles, the teachers of the faithful, inasmuch as they can also be set over others to instruct them, themselves ascend step by step to the heights. Indeed, the Lord at first teaches in synagogues, performs miracles, spreads his fame everywhere, receives the multitudes coming together to him, heals, and instructs. After this he appoints disciples, provides for them in the wedding of the bridegroom, leads them through the crops, and defends them from the false accusations of the Pharisees, as the eagle defends her tender chicks from snakebites by introducing [into the nest] a precious eagle-stone.[56] From these he chooses twelve, whom he names apostles, but likewise he also

---

52 I.e., one out of every 500.
53 Cf. Num. 31:27–30.
54 Cf. Ps. 83:8; the servant is the lawgiver, Moses.
55 Deut. 32:11. Deut. 32:1–43 is what is known as the 'Song of Moses'. The speaker is God's servant, Moses (see above Book 3 n. 44). The fledgling ('him') whom the eagle (= God) carries are the people of Israel.
56 Both Pliny and Isidore mention the eagle-stone (*aetitis*), but neither seems to be the source of Bede's comment. The eagle-stone or 'pregnant stone' (sometimes identified as a geode) was allegedly placed in the nest by a parent eagle to protect the chicks from predators: see Barb, 'The Eagle Stone', 316–18, esp. 317, n. 8.

teaches these people at first in the presence of the multitude, and with the multitude following along with them, he gives his customary gifts to those in dire need. But afterwards, as we read in the present verse, *preaching through the cities and towns*, he keeps with him only those who attend him more intimately, to whom alone he expounds the mysteries of the kingdom of God, of which he had spoken allegorically to the others. And thus finally, after they have been strengthened by the manifestation of his miracles as if by the protection of his wings, he also gives them the power of healing and sends them to preach the kingdom of God.

[Luke 8:2] **And certain women who had been healed of evil spirits and infirmities, Mary who is called Magdalene, from whom seven demons had gone forth, ...** Mary Magdalene is she whose penitence the previous passage narrates, but without naming her.[57] The evangelist, when he records that she travelled with the Lord, and ministered to him from her substance, reveals her clearly with this well-known name, in a manner both lovely and reverent. But when he describes the sinner, but one who repents, he generally says 'woman', in order, surely, not to blacken by the disgrace of her former error so famous a name, by which she is venerated today by all the churches. Seven demons are said to have gone forth from her, to show that she had been burdened with innumerable vices, or rather, with all of them. For since the ages [of the world] run in seven 'days',[58] Scripture often represents an entirety by the number seven. Hence also the prophet expresses the grace of the Holy Spirit by distinguishing between the seven virtues.[59] /173/

[Luke 8:3] **And Joanna the wife of Chuza, Herod's steward, ...** If Mary stands for the Church of the Gentiles which is cleansed from the filth of vices, why does Joanna not signify the same Church, once indeed subjected to the adoration of idols, but now redeemed by the true faith of Christ? For any malign spirit which is inclined to the deception of the human race, as long as it does so on behalf of the kingdom of the devil, is as it were a steward of an utterly godless Herod.

[Luke 8:3b] **And Susanna and many others who ministered to him from their substance.** *It was a Jewish practice and not considered a*

---

57 Cf. Luke 7:37–50. This identification is made by Ps.-Jerome, *Expositio euangeliorum* (PL 30:572A).

58 For Bede's analogy between the seven days of creation and the seven ages of the world, see esp. *DTR* 10 (trans. Wallis, *The Reckoning of Time*, 39–41).

59 Cf. Isa. 11:2–3.

BOOK THREE                                              317

*fault by the ancient custom of the people for women to minister food and clothing from their substance to preachers. But since this could create a stumbling block among the Gentiles, Paul mentions that he had humbled himself. For he himself says: 'Have we not power of leading about women, sisters, as the rest of the apostles do?'*[60] *The women ministered to the Lord from their substance, in order that he whose spiritual goods they reaped, might reap their carnal things.*[61] *Not because the Lord of created things lacked food, but in order that he might display a symbolic image of teachers, that they ought to have been content with food and clothing from the disciples.*[62] *Susanna is interpreted as 'lily' or 'his grace', but it is better, I believe, if a woman's name is figured by a lily,*[63] on account of the pure fragrant whiteness of heavenly life and the golden ardour of inward love. *Joanna means 'Lord his grace', or 'merciful Lord',*[64] namely because his grace is all that we live for. Mary is interpreted as *'bitter sea' [Maria amarum mare],*[65] surely on account of the ingrained howling of penitence, with which either Mary herself, or each of us individually, laments our former sins, in order to deserve to attain to grace and eternal splendour. *Magdalene means 'tower': but better, just as* [the personal name] *'Montanus' derives from 'mountain [mons]', so 'Turrensis' derives from 'tower [turris]',*[66] plainly her name derives from that tower to whom the Psalmist sings: *You have conducted me; for you have been my hope, a tower of strength against the face of the enemy.*[67]

76/2    [Luke 8:4-5] **And when a very great multitude gathered together, and hastened to him out of the cities, he spoke by a parable: A sower went out to sow his seed.** *The Lord deigned to expound this parable himself* to make known *that he spoke figuratively*, and to teach that *the allegorical meanings of things* are to be sought *even in those things which he did not wish to explain himself.*[68] But because the Lord himself explained that the

---

60   1 Cor. 9:5.
61   Cf. 1 Cor. 9:11.
62   Jerome, *Commentarii in Matheum* 4 (CCSL 77:277.1847–56).
63   Jerome, *Hebr. nom.* (CCSL 72:141.2–3).
64   Jerome, *Hebr. nom.* (CCSL 72:140.1–2).
65   Jerome, *Hebr. nom.* (CCSL 72:137.19).
66   Jerome, *Hebr. nom.* (CCSL 72:137.21–22). What Jerome left unsaid, but probably intended, was that in his view 'Magdalene' derived from the Hebrew *migdal*, 'tower'. Whether Bede understood Jerome's intention is unclear.
67   Ps. 60:3–4 (61:2–3).
68   Gregory, *Hom. in Euang.* 1.15.1 (CCSL 141:104.8–11).

seed is the word of God,[69] and the varied terrain signifies the diverse heart of the auditors,[70] he left the sower to be interpreted by us. We cannot do better than to understand him as the Son of God, who *went out to sow his seed*, because in going out from the bosom of the Father to which /174/ there was no means of access for a created being, he came into the world to give testimony to the truth.[71] Hence it is well said (according to the other evangelists) that when he was about to tell this parable, he went out of the house, approached the sea, and got into a boat,[72] and so made the tenor of his sermon clear by the location of his body.

[Luke 8:5b] **And as he sowed, some fell by the roadside, and it was trodden down, and the birds of the air devoured it.** Those things that the Lord explained are to be received with pious faith. But we should briefly consider what he left unexplained, for us to discern. The seed that fell by the roadside perished in two ways, that is to say, not only was it trodden down by travellers, but it was also snatched up by birds. The road therefore is the heart, worn down and dried up by the constant passage of wicked thoughts, so that it does not avail to receive and germinate the seed of the Word. And for that reason, whatever of the good seed happens to land in the vicinity of such a road, trodden down by the passage of evil thinking, is snatched up by demons. The demons are called 'birds of the sky', because they are of a heavenly and spiritual nature,[73] or because they fly through the air.

[Luke 8:6] **And some other fell on a rock, and as soon as it was sprung up, it withered away because it had no moisture.** He calls a hard and ungovernable heart, and one penetrated by no ploughshare of the true faith, a 'rock'. But moisture for the root of the seed is love and constancy of virtue, which according to another parable is oil for feeding the lamps of the virgins.[74]

[Luke 8:8] **And some other fell on good ground, and being sprung up, yielded fruit a hundredfold.** He calls perfect fruit 'fruit a hundredfold'. For *the number ten is always interpreted as perfection, because the protection of the Law is contained in ten precepts. The active and the contemplative*

---

69 Cf. Luke 8:11.
70 Cf. Luke 8:12–15.
71 Cf. John 18:37.
72 Cf. Matt. 13:1–2; Mark 4:1.
73 The demons are fallen angels.
74 Cf. Matt. 25:1–4.

BOOK THREE 319

*life are united together in the commandments of the Decalogue, because it commands us to observe both love of God and love of one's neighbour. Love of God certainly pertains to the contemplative, but love of one's neighbour to the active life.*[75] The number ten multiplied by itself amounts to the number one hundred. Hence great perfection is properly signified by the number one hundred, just as it is said of the one who leaves his earthly possessions for the Lord's sake: *He will receive a hundredfold and will possess life everlasting.*[76] For whoever despises temporal and earthly possessions for the sake of God's name, not only receives perfection of mind here, so that he does not now desire those things that he despises, but also in the next age arrives at the eternal glory of life. Therefore, good ground is made fertile with fruit a hundredfold, /175/ when the docile heart is endowed with the perfection of spiritual virtues.

[Luke 8:8b] **Saying these things, he cried out: He who has ears to hear, let him hear.** Whenever this reminder is inserted both in the Gospel and in the Apocalypse of John,[77] it indicates that what is said is allegorical, and ought to be inquired into the more intently by us.

[Luke 8:9] **And his disciples asked him what this parable might be.** Let no one think that the disciples asked the Saviour about this as soon as the parable was ended, but as Mark says: *And when he was alone, the twelve that were with him asked him about the parable. He said to them: To you it is given to know the mystery of the kingdom of God*, and so forth.[78]

77/1 [Luke 8:10b] **But to the rest in parables, that seeing they may not see, and hearing may not understand.** Mark says it this way: *But to them who are without, all things are done in parables.*[79] And therefore let us enter into the sanctuary of God that we may understand the ultimate mysteries of the kingdom of God.[80] For those who draw near to his feet may receive some of his teaching, saying with the Psalmist: *Open our eyes, and we will consider the wondrous things of your Law.*[81] Those people are rightly said to hear in parables and riddles when the senses of

---

75  Gregory, *Hom. in Hiezech.* 2.6.5 (CCSL 142:297.86–91).
76  Matt. 19:29.
77  Cf. Matt. 13:9; Mark 4:9; Rev. 2:7; etc.
78  Mark 4:10–11.
79  Mark 4:11.
80  Cf. Ps. 72:17 (73:17) and above, Luke 1:24–25.
81  Ps. 118:18 (119:18) (altered from 1st sg. to 1st pl. for sake of context).

their hearts are closed and they do not bestir themselves to enter into or to know the truth, and so forget the Lord's precept: *He who has ears to hear, let him hear.*[82]

**78/2** [Luke 8:12] **And they by the roadside are they who hear. Then the devil comes, and takes the word out of their heart, lest believing they should be saved.** Mark puts it this way: *And these are they by the roadside, where the word is sown, and as soon as they have heard, immediately Satan comes and takes it away.*[83] Matthew puts it this way: *When anyone hears the word of the kingdom, and does not understand it, the wicked one comes and catches it away.*[84] This teaches plainly that those sown by the roadside are those who see fit to take in the word that they hear with no faith, no understanding, and no opportunity to test its usefulness. Next, as the Lord declares, those that *are sown on stony ground* and *on thorns*,[85] are those who both esteem the usefulness of the word which they heard and experience a desire for it, and yet are held back from gaining what they esteem either because they are frightened by the adversities of this life, or seduced by its favours. On the other hand, he took care to guard the seed which he had received against both threats, when he said: *By the armour of justice on the right hand and on the left, by honour and dishonour, by evil report and by good report, as deceivers and yet true.*[86] You should know, therefore, that these three kinds of earth signify all who do not act on the word /176/ they have heard. He who protects the seed he has received from all these is the good earth. Of course, the Jews and Gentiles who do not deserve even to hear are excluded.

[Luke 8:14] **And that which fell among the thorns are they who have heard, and going their way, are choked with the cares and riches and pleasures of this life, and yield no fruit.** It is marvellous how the Lord interpreted the thorns as riches, *since the former sting and the latter attract. And yet they are thorns, because they lacerate the soul with the pricking of their desires, and when they lead to sin, they stain with blood as if inflicting a wound. According to the testimony of another evangelist, the Lord in this passage rightly calls these not 'riches' at all, but 'deceitful riches'.*[87] *For*

82 Luke 8:8.
83 Mark 4:15.
84 Matt. 13:19.
85 Mark 4:16 & 18.
86 2 Cor. 6:7–8.
87 Cf. Matt. 13:22.

*riches are deceitful that cannot remain with us long; riches are deceitful that do not expel the poverty of our mind. True riches, however, are those alone that make us wealthy in virtues.*[88]

But it should be noted that the Lord says that cares and pleasures and riches 'choke'. *For they choke because they strangle the soul's throat with savage desires, and as long as they do not permit good longing to enter the heart, they block the access, as it were, of the living spirit. It should be noted also that there are two things that he yokes together with riches, namely cares and pleasures, because assuredly not only do they oppress the soul with worry, but also they enervate it with affluence. By their contrasting nature, they make their possessors both miserable and deceitful. But because pleasure cannot consort with affliction, sometimes they cast us down by worry about protecting them, and at other times they weaken us toward pleasures by their abundance.*[89]

[Luke 8:15] **But that on the good ground are they who in a good and perfect heart, hearing the word, keep it, and bring forth fruit in patience.** The good ground, as I said above, stands in contrast to all three worthless varieties of earth by both willingly receiving the seed of the word, and by patiently protecting what it takes amid adversities and good fortune right up to the season of fruit.

In another interpretation: *And the good ground returns fruit through patience, because the good things that we do are evidently of no value, if we do not also endure the evil deeds of our neighbours with equanimity. For the higher one progresses, the harsher one finds what one endures in this world, because when the love of our soul withdraws from the present age, the hostility of the same age grows. Hence it is that we perceive that many people do good deeds* /**177**/ *and nevertheless sweat under a heavy burden of tribulations. But according to the word of the Lord, they render fruit through patience, because when they bear misfortune humbly, after misfortune they are taken on high to rest.*[90]

But according to Matthew it is phrased: *And it bears fruit, and one yields a hundredfold, and another sixty, and another thirty.*[91] Thirty refers to marriage. *For this union of the fingers, embracing each other and joining together as it were with a gentle kiss, depicts husband and wife.* Sixty

---

88 Gregory, *Hom. in Euang.* 1.15.1 (CCSL 141:104.14–21).
89 Gregory, *Hom. in Euang.* 1.15.3 (CCSL 141:106.65–75).
90 Gregory, *Hom. in Euang.* 1.15.4 (CCSL 141:106.76–86).
91 Matt. 13:23.

refers to widows because they are situated in straitened circumstances and tribulation. Hence, they are depressed against the upper finger; and the greater is the difficulty of abstaining from the allurements of passion that one has once experienced, the greater also is the reward. Finally, the number one hundred (attend carefully, reader, I beg!) is transferred from the left hand to the right, and by the same fingers indeed, but not by the same hand, making a circle, by which marriage and widows are signified on the left hand, it expresses the crown of virginity.[92]

In another interpretation: The word brings forth thirtyfold [*tricesimum*] fruit, which builds the faith of the holy Trinity. It brings forth sixtyfold fruit, which teaches the perfecting of work, because there are six days in which it is necessary to work. It brings forth hundredfold fruit, which foretells life everlasting on the right hand of the kingdom.

## Chapter 29

**79/2** [Luke 8:16] **Now no man lighting a lamp covers it with a vessel, or puts it under a bed, but sets it on a lampstand, that they who come in may see the light.** Because he had previously said to the apostles: *To you it is given to know the mystery of the kingdom of God, but to the rest in parables*,[93] he now shows that the same mystery is to be revealed at last by them even to the rest, and that the heart of all who are going to enter into the house of God would be illuminated by the flames of faith. By these words he also teaches by means of allegory that one should be bold in preaching, lest anyone conceal the light of knowledge that he knows *from fear of fleshly inconveniences*. For he signifies the flesh *by the appellation 'vessel' and 'bed'*, but the word by the appellation 'lamp'.[94] As I have said, the one who hides the word on account of fear of fleshly inconveniences surely prefers the flesh itself to displaying the truth, and the flesh covers, as it were, the word that he trembles to preach. He *who subjects his flesh to the service of God in order that the preaching of the truth be above, and the servitude of the body below* sets a lamp on a lampstand; *so that by that very servitude of the body, Christian doctrine, which is conveyed to disciples in*

---

92 Jerome, *Aduersus Iouinianum* 1 (PL 23:213–14); cf. Bede, *DTR* 1 (trans. Wallis, *Bede: The Reckoning of Time*, 9–10). For explanation, see above Book 1, n. 285.
93 Luke 8:10.
94 Augustine, *Quaestiones euang.* 2.12 (CCSL 44B:55.5–8).

*good works by the body's ministrations (that is, by the voice and tongue, and other movements of the body) may notwithstanding* /178/ *shine higher. Therefore, he sets a lamp on a lampstand when the Apostle says: 'I so fight, not as one beating the air, but I chastise my body, and bring it into subjection, lest perhaps, while preaching to others, I myself should become a castaway.'*[95]

80/2 [Luke 8:17] **For there is not anything secret that will not be made manifest, nor hidden, that will not be known and come into the open.** Do not, he says, be ashamed of the Gospel of God, but amid the darkness of persecutors, raise the light of the word on the lampstand of your body, keeping firmly in mind that day of final retribution, when God *will bring to light the hidden things of darkness, and will make manifest the thoughts of the hearts.*[96] For then praise from God awaits you, and eternal punishment enemies of the truth.

81/5 [Luke 8:18] **Take heed therefore how you hear.** He urgently teaches us to listen intently to the word, to the extent that we are capable of ruminating continuously over it in our heart, and of regurgitating it into another's ears.[97]

[Luke 8:18b] **For whoever has, to him will be given, and whoever has not, that also which he thinks he has, will be taken away from him.** Give heed, he says, with your full attention to the word that you hear, because whoever has love of the word will also be given the ability to understand what he loves. But whoever does not love to hear the word, even if he thinks that he understands either by his natural abilities or by literary training, will not enjoy any pleasure of true wisdom. Even if this seems to have been said specifically about the Apostles, to whom since they have obtained love and faith *it is given to know the mystery of the kingdom of God,*[98] and about the faithless Jews who, seeing in the parables, did not see,

---

95 Augustine, *De sermone Domini* 1.6.17 (CCSL 35:17.374–82); 1 Cor. 9:26–27.
96 1 Cor. 4:5.
97 Here is an early expression of the image that Bede will later use in his memorable account of the oral poet Caedmon, who 'learned all he could by listening to them and then, memorizing it and ruminating over it, like some clean animal chewing the cud, he turned it into the most melodious verse: and it sounded so sweet as he recited it that his teachers became in turn his audience' (*Historia ecclesiastica* 4.24; trans. Colgrave and Mynors, 419). For a comprehensive survey of Bede's use of the rumination image across his writings, see Crépin, 'Bede and the Vernacular', 187–88, n. 6. On Caedmon, see West, 'Rumination in Bede's Account of Caedmon', 217–36, and Wieland, 'Caedmon, the Clean Animal', 194–203.
98 Luke 8:10.

## 324  BEDE: COMMENTARY ON THE GOSPEL OF LUKE

and hearing did not understand[99] (because, of course, they were about to lose the letter of the Law in which they boasted), nevertheless it can also be taken generally, that the clever reader by neglect often deprives himself of wisdom, which an ingenuous, but studious, reader learns by taking pains.[100] *For that reason also an indolent man often receives cleverness so that he may more justly be punished for neglect, because he scorns to know what he could come to understand without effort. For that reason a studious man is sometimes prodded by the sluggishness of his intellect to find greater rewards in return for the greater pains he takes by zealously applying his capacity for discovery.*[101]

**82/2** [Luke 8:19] **And his mother and his brothers came to him, and they could not come at him for the crowd.** The brothers of the Lord must not be considered (following Helvidius) to be the sons of the blessed Mary ever virgin, nor (according to others) the sons of Joseph by another wife, but rather they must be understood to be their kinsmen, as I have argued above.[102] Plainly the fact that the Lord, /179/ when asked to come to his mother and brothers, seemingly departs from the obligation of the word, *does not refute the duty of maternal devotion, the commandment* of which *is: 'Honour your father and your mother'*.[103] But he shows *that he is under greater obligation to paternal mysteries than to maternal love*,[104] manifesting the same thing to us by example as he does by the word: *He who loves father and mother more than me, is not worthy of me.*[105] He does not regard his brothers with contempt *unjustly, but* preferring spiritual work to the kindred of the body, he teaches that the *ties of souls are more sacred than the ties of bodies.*[106]

Allegorically this text harmonizes with the one above, where it is said of the Jews who attend only to the letter of the Law: *And whoever has not, that also which he thinks he has, will be taken away from him.*[107] For the Synagogue from whose flesh he was begot is the mother and brothers

---

99 Cf. Luke 8:10.
100 Cf. Gregory, *Moralia* 6.10 (CCSL 143:291–92).
101 Gregory, *Moralia* 6.10 (CCSL 143:293.1–6).
102 Cf. Jerome, *Commentarii in Matheum* 2 (CCSL 77:101.653–61). See above, Bede's commentary on Luke 2:6–7 and Book 1, n. 197.
103 Exod. 20:12.
104 Ambrose, *Expos. Lucam* 6.36 (CCSL 14:187.385–88).
105 Matt. 10:37.
106 Ambrose, *Expos. Lucam* 6.36 (CCSL 14:187.389–90).
107 Luke 8:18.

of Jesus and the Jewish people. Because the Saviour is teaching inside they are unable to enter in, even though they come, since they neglect to understand his sayings spiritually. The crowd in anticipation enters his house,[108] because, with Judea abandoning him, the Gentiles flocked to Christ, and being more mentally receptive the nearer they were in faith, they drank in the inward mysteries of life, in accordance with what the Psalmist says: *Come to him and be enlightened.*[109]

[Luke 8:20] **And it was told him: Your mother and your brothers stand outside, desiring to see you.** *The word is inside, the light is inside.*[110] Hence he says above: *That they who come in may see the light.*[111] Therefore *if his own relatives standing outside are not acknowledged, and for the sake of furnishing an example let us suppose they are not acknowledged, how will we be acknowledged, if we stand outside?*[112] For those who, not seeking the spiritual sense in the Law, attached themselves to the preservation of the letter on the outside, wish to see the Lord standing outside. And they try as it were to avoid Christ for the sake of teaching carnal things, rather than fit themselves to enter for the sake of learning spiritual things.

[Luke 8:21] **He answering, said to them: My mother and my brothers are they who hear the word of God, and do it.** The whole perfection of heavenly life is comprehended by these two things, namely to hear and do the word of God. Hence when the Lord explains above the parable of the seed, he says that those who only received the word by hearing it are the sterile ground;[113] but those who *keep the word* that they hear *in a good and most virtuous soul, and bring forth fruit in patience,* are the good ground.[114] They are called the mother of the Lord, because they give birth as it were to him daily in the soul of their neighbours either through example or words. They are also his brothers, when they do the will of his Father who is in heaven.[115] **/180/**

---

108 In the three Gospel accounts of this episode, only Mark mentions a house (Mark 3:20) that Jesus and the crowd are inside, although one must be assumed in the narratives of Matthew and Luke.
109 Ps. 33:6 (34:5).
110 Ambrose, *Expos. Lucam* 6.37 (CCSL 14:187.392–93).
111 Luke 8:16.
112 Ambrose, *Expos. Lucam* 6.37 (CCSL 14:187.394–96).
113 Cf. Luke 8:12–14.
114 Gregory, *Hom. in Euang.* 1.15 (CCSL 141:103.21–22). Cf. Luke 8:15.
115 Cf. Matt. 12:50.

## Chapter 30

**83/2** [Luke 8:22] **And on a certain day he went on a little ship with his disciples, and he said to them: Let us go over to the other side of the lake. And they launched forth.** In this sailing voyage the Lord deigned to display both natures of his one, identical person – while as man he sleeps in the ship, as God he commands with a word the rage of the sea. Furthermore, on the allegorical level, the sea or lake that he wishes to cross with his disciples is understood to be the dark and bitter commotion of the present age. And the little ship which they went on is understood to be none other than the tree of the Lord's passion. With its help, each of the faithful, having traversed the turbulence of the world, arrives at the dwelling-place of the heavenly kingdom, the stability as it were of the safe shore.[116] And what the fact that the Saviour himself goes on a little ship with his disciples signifies, he reveals elsewhere, when in foreshadowing the mystery of his passion and resurrection *he said to all* shortly afterwards: *If any man will come after me, let him deny himself, and take up his cross daily, and follow me.*[117]

[Luke 8:23] **And when they were sailing, he slept.** Christ slept when the disciples were sailing, because when the faithful were scorning the present age and meditating in their soul on the repose of the kingdom to come, and were eagerly tossing the faithless pride of the world behind them either by the favouring breeze of the Holy Spirit or by rowing with their own effort, suddenly the time of the Lord's passion was at hand. Hence Mark rightly declares that this was done as night approached,[118] so that not only the sleeping of the Lord, but also the very hour of the fading light, should signify the setting of the true Sun.

[Luke 8:23b] **And there came down a storm of wind on the lake, and they were swamped, and were in danger.** As the Lord goes on the ship of the cross, where he took the sleep of death, the waves of the blaspheming persecutors aroused by the demonic storm surged up. Nevertheless, his patience is not disturbed by this, but the helplessness of the disciples is stirred up, trembles, is in danger.

---

116 Compare Bede's image and choice of words (*fluctus, stabilitas*) in the final chapter of *DTR*: 'And so our little book concerning the fleeting and wave-tossed course of time comes to a fitting end in eternal stability and stable eternity' (trans. Wallis, *The Reckoning of Time*, 249); see also above, Book 2 n. 121.
117 Luke 9:23.
118 Cf. Mark 4:35.

[Luke 8:24] **And they came and awoke him, saying: Master, we perish.** The disciples awake the Lord, lest they perish from the savagery of the waves while he sleeps, because they were seeking with the most earnest prayers the resurrection of the one whose death they had seen, lest, if he were to sleep in the death of the flesh any longer, their soul would perish forever in spiritual death. Hence it rightly follows:

[Luke 8:24b] **But he arising, rebuked the wind and the rage of the water; and it ceased, and there was a calm.** In arising, indeed, he rebuked the wind, because, with the proclamation of his resurrection, he overthrew the pride of the devil, /181/ while by his death he destroyed the one who had the empire of death. Also, arising, he made the rage of the water cease, because, by arising from the tomb, he overthrew the mad rage of the Jews, which, tossing its head, had cried out: *If he is the Son of God, let him now come down from the cross, and we will believe him.*[119]

Here, on the literal level, it should be noted *that all created things perceive their Creator. For those things which are rebuked and commanded perceive the commander, not in accordance with the error of the heretics who think all things are alive, but by the majesty of the Creator, things which are insensitive in our experience are sensitive to him.*[120]

[Luke 8:25] **And he said to them: Where is your faith?** Those who were afraid when Christ was present are justly rebuked, since certainly anyone who clings to him cannot perish. Similar to this is the fact that when he appeared to his disciples after the sleep of death, *he upbraided them with their incredulity and hardness of heart, because they did not believe them who had seen him after he had risen.*[121] And likewise *he said to them: O foolish, and slow of heart to believe in all things which the prophets have spoken. Ought not Christ to have suffered these things, and so to enter into his glory,*[122] as if he had said using a metaphor of sailing: Ought not Christ to lie still while the waves sweep the ship in which he is resting hither and thither, and so reveal to all the power of his divinity when the swelling heaps immediately quiet down?

[Luke 8:25b] **They, being afraid, wondered, saying to one another: Who do you suppose is this, that he commands both the winds and the sea, and they obey him?** Matthew writes thus: *But the men wondered,*

---

119 Matt. 27:40 & 42.
120 Jerome, *Commentarii in Matheum* 1 (CCSL 77:52.1183–87).
121 Mark 16:14.
122 Luke 24:25–26.

saying: *What manner of man is this*, and so forth.[123] *Not the disciples, therefore, but the sailors and others who were in the ship wondered.* But if anyone obstinately will have it that those who wondered were the disciples, we will reply that they are rightly called men, because they did not yet know the power of the Saviour.[124] And also we, individually impressed with the sign of the Lord's cross, arrange to leave the world; we truly board the ship with Jesus; and we attempt to go over the lake. But while he who always *keeps Israel will not slumber nor sleep*,[125] nevertheless during the time when we are sailing, he often sleeps as it were amid the thunder of the waves, when with the increasing assault either of unclean spirits, or of vicious men, or with the very assault of our own thoughts as we strive for virtue, the splendour of the faith grows dark, the lofty height of hope wastes away, and the flame of love grows cold. But amid storms of this kind, it is necessary for us to hasten to that helmsman, and diligently arouse him who does not serve the winds, but commands them. /182/ Soon he will calm the tempest, he will bring back tranquillity, and he will grant access to the harbour of salvation.

After having briefly examined the diverse accounts of the apostles' ship, it is worthwhile to observe how seclusion aids good men, or how mixing with wicked men stirs up a storm. For behold, in order for us to begin from the more perfect examples, after the solemnities of the Lord's resurrection had been celebrated, seven chosen disciples go on a ship to fish,[126] and because they were not far from the land of eternal rest, but some two hundred cubits distant (that is, they had applied as much attention to the world as twofold love demanded, because Peter had stripped himself for worldly business)[127] they deserve now to see the Lord standing on the shore of immortality, now to feast with him, now in the favouring morning of eternal light to take their nets filled with the mystical number of great fish[128] and yet not torn, and to drag them out from the deepest billows of the age.

---

123 Matt. 8:27.
124 Jerome, *Commentarii in Matheum* 1 (CCSL 77:52.1189–93).
125 Ps. 120:4 (121:4).
126 Cf. John 21:1–14. It is Bede who points out that the disciples mentioned by John total seven. As always, Bede is alert to the possibility of concealed number symbolism in biblical texts.
127 Cf. John 21:7.
128 I.e., 153: cf. John 21:11. This is a much discussed number, especially by Augustine: cf. *In Iohannis euang.* 122.8; *Enarrationes in Psalmos* 49.9; *Sermones* 248.3–4; 270.7; *De diuersis*

Elsewhere Peter, as is written above,[129] at the Lord's command, lets down his nets for a catch, and takes a great multitude of fish. But since he was still possessed of a fragile soul, so that trembling he said to Christ: *Depart from me, for I am a sinful man, O Lord*,[130] not only were their nets broken at that moment, but if his partners had not helped, even the ships would have sunk to the bottom.

Likewise, in this passage the disciples board the ship with the Lord, and they put to sea. But because Judas was present, the Lord is said to have slept in the poop, where the helm was located, and the wind and the sea to have raged outside. For although the many merits of the disciples sailed there, nevertheless the treachery of the traitor still tossed the ship, and those who were firm in their own merits were thrown into disorder by the crimes of others. And again, Paul, sailing with the brothers to Jerusalem, and hastening to celebrate there the day of Pentecost and the joys of the Holy Spirit, travels on a straight course through all the cities.[131] Then he goes fettered from Jerusalem to Rome, because he makes the journey with infidels. The sea rages, the winds oppose, a rainstorm threatens, cold vexes, the stars darken, land is denied, the wheat is cast into the sea, the ship's tackle is raised, the ship itself having been dashed to pieces on the shore is destroyed, and the sailors seek the land which they do not recognize by swimming.[132] And those who had entered the waves burdened by the desires of the world, scarcely escaped naked when that same world turned against them, in accordance with what the same Apostle says: *But he himself will be saved, yet so as by fire.*[133]

Chapter 31

[Luke 8:26] **And they sailed to the country of the Gerasenes, which is opposite Galilee.** Gerasa is *a famous city of Arabia across the Jordan,* /183/ *near Mount Galaad, which the tribe of Manasseh held*,[134] not far from

---

*quaestionibus* 1.57. It is the sum of the first seventeen numbers $(1 + 2 + 3 \ldots + 17 = 153)$, and mystically, $153 = (3 \; [= \text{the number of the Trinity}] \times 50) + 3$.
129 Cf. Luke 5:4–8.
130 Luke 5:8.
131 Cf. Acts 20:16; 21:1–15.
132 Cf. Acts 27:1–44.
133 1 Cor. 3:15.
134 Jerome, *De situ et nom.* (*Onomastica sacra* 125.27–29).

Lake Tiberias into which the swine were cast.[135] It signifies the people of the Gentiles, whom the Saviour deigned to visit with divine grace after the sleep of his passion and the glory of his resurrection by sending preachers. Hence Gerasa, or Gergesenes as some read,[136] is rightly interpreted as *'casting out a peasant'* or *'a stranger is approaching'*,[137] meaning, of course, that the people of the Gentiles had cast him – the enemy by whom they were wickedly inhabited – out from their hearts, and they *who* were *far off* were *made near in the blood of Christ.*[138]

[Luke 8:27] **And when he had come forth to the land, a certain man met him who had a demon now for a very long time.** This man becomes the symbol of the Gentile people[139] who were tormented by raving madness for a very long time, that is, from almost the beginning of the new-born world.

[Luke 8:27b] **And he wore no clothes**, because he lost the covering of his nature and virtue. For after they had sinned our first parents are found to have been deprived of this garment of faith and love.[140] The prodigal son, after he returned penitently to his father, is clothed with this best robe.[141]

[Luke 8:27c] **Nor did he abide in a house, but in the sepulchres**, because *he was not resting in his own good conscience*, but *in dead deeds, that is, he took pleasure in sins.*[142] *For what are the bodies of infidels, except a kind of sepulchre of the dead in which* the word *of God does* not dwell,[143] *but in which the dead soul is shut up with its sins?*

[Luke 8:28] **And when he saw Jesus, he fell down before him; and crying out in a loud voice, he said: What have I to do with you, Jesus, Son of the most high God?** How great was the madness of Arius to believe Jesus a created being and not God, whom the demons believe to be the Son of the most high God, and tremble! What sacrilege of the Jews to say that he cast out *demons by the prince of the demons*,[144] whom the demons

---

135 Jerome, *De situ et nom.* (*Onomastica sacra* 130.20–21); cf. Matt. 8:28–32; Mark 5:1–13; Luke 8:26–33.
136 Cf. Jerome, *De situ et nom.* (*Onomastica sacra* 125.27–29).
137 Jerome, *Hebr. nom.* (CCSL 72:66.24–25); cf. Eph. 2:12.
138 Eph. 2:13.
139 Cf. Ps.-Jerome, *Expositio euangeliorum* (PL 30:572A).
140 Cf. Gen. 3:7–11.
141 Cf. Luke 15:22.
142 Augustine, *Quaestiones euang.* 2.13 (CCSL 44B:56.5–7).
143 Ambrose, *Expos. Lucam* 6.45 (CCSL 14:190.462–63).
144 Matt. 9:34.

themselves claim to have nothing in common with! They do not cease to say and confess this very fact, which they cried out then through the madness of the man possessed by demons, and afterwards in the temples of the idols, namely that Jesus is Christ, the Son of the most high God, and that they do not have any peace or fellowship with him.

[Luke 8:28b–29] **I beseech you, do not torment Me. For he commanded the unclean spirit to go out of the man. For many times it seized /184/ him.** The enemy of human salvation does not consider it to be an insignificant torment to have to cease from injuring the man; also, the longer he is accustomed to possess him, the more difficult it is for him to agree to release him. Hence it is very important to study how we ought to strive immediately to avoid his snares, even if, as men, we were overcome by the devil, lest if we are slow to resist his power, his expulsion later on will be more painful.

[Luke 8:29b] **And he was bound in chains, and kept in fetters.** By chains and *fetters* are signified *the severe and harsh laws in their commonwealth by which sins are likewise restrained.*[145]

[Luke 8:29c] **And breaking the bonds, he was driven by the demon into the desert,** because *even after transgressing these laws, he was led by cupidity to those wicked deeds which now went beyond ordinary custom.*[146]

[Luke 8:30] **And Jesus asked him, saying: What is your name? But he said: Legion, because many demons had entered into him.** He doesn't ask his name as though he were ignorant of it, but in order that the power of the healer might be more appreciated when it is displayed in the presence of the acknowledged curse which the madman endured. But even the priests of our time, who know how to drive out demons by the grace of exorcism, are accustomed to say that sufferers cannot be healed unless they reveal openly by confession, as far as they can know, all that they suffered, waking or sleeping, from the unclean spirits through sight, hearing, taste, touch, or whatever other sense of body or soul. And especially when, appearing either to men in the shape of a woman or to women in the guise of a man, by an abominable miracle, incorporeal spirits, *demons whom the Gauls call Dusii,*[147] pretend that they desire and perform sexual intercourse with the human body. And the priests order that the name of the demon by

---

145 Augustine, *Quaestiones euang.* 2.13 (CCSL 44B:56.8–9).
146 Augustine, *Quaestiones euang.* 2.13 (CCSL 44B:56.11–13).
147 Augustine, *De ciuitate Dei* 15.23 (CCSL 48:489.18–19) (= Isidore, *Etym.* 8.11.103).

which he said he was called be made known as well as the terms of the oath by which they concluded either contract of love.

An affair very like a fable, but still true, and which is very well known by the testimony of many, is that a certain priest close to me reported that he began to heal a nun from a demon, but that as long as the matter was concealed, he was able to make no progress with her. However, he said that once she had acknowledged the apparition by which she was molested, he immediately put it to flight with the necessary prayers and other kinds of purifications, and that he had healed the body of the same woman of the ulcers she had contracted from the touch of the demon by means of blessed medicinal salt which he applied with care. But he said that when he could not by any means close one of the ulcers which he found had pierced the upper part of her side without it immediately opening, he received the advice by which she was healed from the very woman /185/ that he wanted to heal. 'If', she said, 'you sprinkle the holy oil for the sick as the same remedy, and so anoint me, I will immediately be restored. For in the spirit, I once saw a girl in a certain faraway city, which I never saw with my own eyes, labouring under the same adversity, and she was healed in this way by a priest.' He did as she had suggested, and immediately the ulcer consented to accept the remedy, which it had before rejected.[148]

I have taken care to explain these things briefly in opposition to the deceits of the demons, in order for you to understand how purposefully the Lord asked the name of the spirit he was going to expel. But the fact that many demons are reported to have entered the man signifies that the people of the Gentiles had been subjected not to any one idolatrous cult in particular, but to innumerable and various ones. In contrast to which, it is written that *the multitude of believers had but one heart and one soul*.[149] Hence the unity of languages was rightly broken in Babylon,[150] while in Jerusalem the variety of languages was unified.[151] The former means '*confusion*', while the latter means '*vision of peace*',[152] because, of course, one faith and religion strengthens the elect of many tongues and nations by making peace, but when there are more sects than tongues the damned are confounded by disunion.

---

148 On this unusual passage, see Introduction, 69–71.
149 Acts 4:32.
150 I.e. Babel; cf. Gen. 11:1–9.
151 Cf. Acts 2:4–11.
152 Jerome, *Hebr. nom.* (CCSL 72:62.18; 121.9–10).

BOOK THREE                                    333

[Luke 8:31] **And they begged him not to command them to go into the abyss.** The demons knew that it would someday happen that they would be sent into the abyss by the coming of the Lord; they did not themselves divine what would come to pass, but they recalled what the prophets said about them,[153] and so they lamented that the glory of the Lord's coming, which they marvelled at, led to their own destruction.

[Luke 8:32] **And there was there a herd of many swine feeding on the mountain; and they begged him to permit them to enter into them. And he permitted them.** He permitted the demons what they asked, *so that the killing of the swine might provide an opportunity for salvation to men. For the shepherds, seeing these things, immediately report them to the city. Let the Manichaean blush. If the souls of men and of beasts are of the same substance and from the same ancestor, how are two thousand swine destroyed for the sake of the salvation of one man?*[154] But their destruction allegorically signifies impure men, devoid of speech and reason, who, feeding on the mountain of pride, take delight in filthy actions. *Demons can rule over such men through the worship of idols.*[155] For unless someone lives like a pig, the devil will never get power over him, or will only get to test him, but not to destroy him. /186/

[Luke 8:33] **The demons therefore went out of the man, and entered into the swine; and the herd ran violently down a steep place into the lake, and were stifled.** *This signifies that now that the Church has become illustrious, and the people of the Gentiles have been freed from the dominion of the demons, those who would not believe in Christ perform their sacrilegious rites in secret places, overwhelmed by blind and deep superstition.*[156] It should be noted that *impure spirits could not go into the swine, unless the merciful Saviour himself granted this to those who begged him and whom indeed he could have banished into the abyss. But he wished to teach us something essential, namely that those who could not harm the swine in any way, can even less harm human beings by their own power. The good God can give us this power with secret justice, but he cannot give those things which are unjust.*[157]

---

153  Cf. Ambrose, *Expos. Lucam* 6.46 (CCSL 14:190.475–78).
154  Jerome, *Commentarii in Matheum* 1 (CCSL 77:53.1210–15). Jerome is alluding to the Manichean teaching on metempsychosis.
155  Augustine, *Quaestiones euang.* 2.13 (CCSL 44B:57.15).
156  Augustine, *Quaestiones euang.* 2.13 (CCSL 44B:57.16–19).
157  Augustine, *Contra aduers.* 2.12.39 (CCSL 49:128.1248–54).

[Luke 8:34] **When they that fed them saw what was done, they fled, and told it in the city and in the villages.** *The fact that the fleeing swineherds told these things signifies that some leaders of the impious, although they flee from the Christian law, nevertheless preach its power over the Gentiles by being astonished and amazed.*[158]

[Luke 8:35] **And they went out to see what was done; and they came to Jesus, and found the man, out of whom the demons were departed, sitting at his feet, clothed, and in his right mind; and they were afraid,** and so forth. *This signifies that the multitude, delighted by their old way of life, indeed respects the Christian law, but does not wish to submit to it, claiming that they cannot fulfil it; nevertheless, they marvel that the faithful people have been healed of their original corrupt way of life.*[159] For to sit at the feet of the Lord is for someone to contemplate the footsteps of the Saviour which he should follow, relying on reasoned mental consideration. For someone to put on clothing again is to be adorned with a zeal for the virtues which he had lost when he was ensnared.

[Luke 8:37] **And all the multitude of the country of the Gerasenes begged him to depart from them, for they were taken with great fear.** The Gerasenes, conscious of their own weakness, concluded that they were unworthy of the presence of the Lord, as they could not grasp the word of God, or sustain the weight of wisdom with a mind still infirm. We read that this happened even to Peter himself, when he saw the miracle of the fish.[160] And the widow from Sarephta, even though she perceived that she was blessed by the hospitality of the blessed Elijah, nevertheless thought she was threatened by his presence.[161] *What have I to do with you*, she says, *O man of God? Have you come to me that my iniquities should be remembered, and that you should kill my son?*[162] /187/

84/8 [Luke 8:37b] **And he, going up into the ship, returned back again.** Luke said above that, having left his parents, the Lord went up into the ship and, after calming the waves along with the wind, that he came forth and cured the man possessed by the demon who ran to meet him. Therefore, we have taught that it signifies that having left the peoples of Judea, from which he derived his fleshly origin, and after the tempest of his passion

---

158 Augustine, *Quaestiones euang.* 2.13 (CCSL 44B:57.19–23).
159 Augustine, *Quaestiones euang.* 2.13 (CCSL 44B:57.26–30).
160 Cf. Luke 5:8.
161 Cf. 3 Kings 17:8–17.
162 3 Kings 17:18.

had been accomplished, he procured the salvation of the Gentiles. After these deeds took place in this way, he returns to his native land, *because blindness in part has happened in Israel, until the fullness of the Gentiles will have come in, and so all Israel will be saved.*[163] He goes up into the ship, but he is neither gripped by sleep nor is the ship beaten by a storm, because *Christ, rising again from the dead, now dies no more; death will no more have dominion over him.*[164] But the victory of his passion and the glory of his resurrection will be announced to the tribes of Judea who are destined to believe, and after the banner of his death,[165] by which he conquered death, has been displayed to the world, when he begins to be believed by the Jews, he will return to his native land, regaining, as it were, the ship in which he had slept.[166]

[Luke 8:38–39] **Now the man, out of whom the demons had departed, begged him that he might be with him. But Jesus sent him away, saying: Return to your house, and tell what great things God has done for you.** These things can *rightly be understood in the light of that statement of the Apostle, when he says: 'To be dissolved and to be with Christ, a thing by far the best; to remain in the flesh is necessary for you'.*[167] *In this way everyone can understand that after his sins are forgiven he must be returned to himself in good conscience, and be subject to the Gospel, even for the salvation of others, in order that he may then rest with Christ; otherwise, when he wishes to be with Christ too hastily, he may neglect the ministry of preaching suitable for fraternal redemption.*[168]

*But as to the fact that Matthew says that two* were cured of the legion of demons, *but Mark and Luke speak of one, you may understand that one of them was a personage of more distinction and reputation; that district especially grieved for him, and made a great to-do about his health. The other two evangelists, wishing to signify this, determined only to report about the one whose fame had blazed more widely and more brightly.*[169] But the main point of the allegory is in agreement that just as one man

---

163 Rom. 11:25–26.
164 Rom. 6:9.
165 I.e., the Cross.
166 The future conversion of the Jews *en masse*, which will usher in Christ's Second Coming, is an important element in Bede's 'preconditions narrative' for the End Times: see Wallis, *Bede: Commentary on Revelation*, Introduction, 77–80.
167 Phil. 1:23–24.
168 Augustine, *Quaestiones euang.* 2.13 (CCSL 44B:58.32–39).
169 Augustine, *De consensu euang.* 2.24 (CSEL 43:158.11–18).

possessed by a demon is a suitable symbol of the Gentile people, so also are two.¹⁷⁰ For *since Noah begot three sons, the family* of one only *was received into the possession of God;* /188/ *from the* other *two were engendered the peoples of the various nations* which were given over to idols.¹⁷¹

## Chapter 32

85/2 [Luke 8:40] **And when Jesus returned, the multitude received him. For they were all waiting for him.** I said above that at the end of the world the Lord is going to return in a merciful fashion to the Jews, and will be willingly received by them through their confession of faith. For that 'all were waiting for him' is undoubtedly what he says to that same Synagogue through the prophet: *You will wait for me many days; you will not play the harlot, and you will be no man's.*¹⁷² For now she has neither been subjected to Christ the man, nor has she been playing the harlot with idols during the very long wait for her former husband, that is, the Lord Christ, inasmuch as she awaits the embrace of him who is to come by grace.

[Luke 8:41] **And behold there came a man whose name was Jairus, and he was a ruler of the synagogue.** The preceding text, which we explained as being about the rejection of the Synagogue and the faith of the Church, and about the eventual renewal of the Synagogue, is suitably followed by the account of the chief ruler's dying daughter; as the Lord hastens to revive her, the haemorrhaging woman took a position ahead of her and seized her healing first, and so it came to pass that the one who arrived first is the first to obtain health. For: *Ethiopia will soon stretch out her hands to God,*¹⁷³ and: *When the fullness of the Gentiles has entered in, then all Israel will be saved.*¹⁷⁴

And so, 'the ruler of the synagogue' is understood to be no one more fitting than Moses himself. Hence, he is rightly called Jairus, that is, '*illuminating*' or '*illuminated*',¹⁷⁵ because he who receives the words of life in order to give them to us, not only illuminates others with them, but is

---

170 Cf. Ambrose, *Expos. Lucam* 6.44 (CCSL 14:189.446–49).
171 Ambrose, *Expos. Lucam* 6.44 (CCSL 14:189.450–52).
172 Hosea 3:3.
173 Ps. 67:32 (68:31).
174 For this paragraph, cf. Jerome, *Commentarii in Matheum* 1 (CCSL 77:59.1364–70); Rom. 11:25–26.
175 Jerome, *Hebr. nom.* (CCSL 72:140.2–3).

himself illuminated by the Holy Spirit, by whom he is enabled to write and teach vital counsels.

[Luke 8:41b] **And he fell down at the feet of Jesus, begging him that he would come into his house.** If *the head of Christ is God*,[176] the feet are appropriately to be taken as the incarnation, whereby he touched the earth of our mortality. The ruler of the synagogue, therefore, fell down at the feet of Jesus, because the law-giver, together with the whole progeny of the fathers, knew that Christ appearing in the flesh was to be preferred by far to himself in the glory of his worthiness, and proclaims with the zealous devotion of the Apostle that *the weakness of God is stronger than men*.[177] He begged him to enter into his house, because he wished to witness his coming with uninterrupted prayers of joy. *But my soul*, he says, *rejoiced in the Lord, and will be delighted* in his Jesus. *All my bones will say: Lord, who is like to you?*[178] And this is to fall at the feet of Jesus, to confess with pious faith his unique greatness above all others.

[Luke 8:42] **For he had an only daughter, almost twelve years old, and she was /189/ dying.** The Synagogue itself, which was organized by the sole institution of the Law, was as it were the only daughter of Moses. She was almost in the twelfth year of her age, that is, she was dying as the time of puberty neared, because, having been excellently brought up by the prophets, after she had reached the years of understanding, after she ought to bear spiritual fruits for God, in a sudden state of shock because of the disease of errors, she neglected in despair to enter the paths of spiritual life. And if she had not been succoured by Christ, she would have collapsed into a dreadful death under the weight of these things.

[Luke 8:42b] **And it happened as he went, that he was thronged by the multitude.** On his way to heal the girl, the Lord is thronged by the multitude, because while he offered the salvation that had been foretold to the Jewish nation he aroused a troubled consciousness of their sins, and so he was harassed by the noxious way of life of the carnal peoples.

[Luke 8:43] **And there was a certain woman having an issue of blood for twelve years, ...** The woman issuing with blood is the Church[179] gathered together from the Gentiles, which had been rendered unclean by the innate issue of carnal delights, and had now been separated from the assembly

---

176 1 Cor. 11:3.
177 1 Cor. 1:25.
178 Ps. 34:9–10 (35:9–10).
179 Cf. Ps.-Jerome, *Expositio euangeliorum* (PL 30:572B).

of the faithful. But until such time as the Word of God determined to save Judea, it anticipated the salvation already prepared and promised to others with a fixed hope. And it should be noted both that daughter of the ruler of the synagogue is twelve years old, and that this woman had experienced an issue of blood from twelve years back, that is, the woman became sick at the same time as the daughter of Jairus was born.[180] For at nearly one and the same age of this world the Synagogue was born among the patriarchs, and the nation of the Gentiles was defiled throughout the world by the bloody matter of idolatry.[181] For the issue of blood can be understood in two ways, that is, both in regard to the prostitution of idolatry, and in regard to those things that are brought about by delight in flesh and blood. Hence Sacred History, at the time when David while still a child felled the giant Goliath, beautifully relates that the Philistines had pitched camp in the borders of Dommim,[182] that is, *'of blood'*,[183] because, of course, the Lord, appearing in humble guise for the sake of overcoming the prince of the world, found the peoples of the Gentiles given over not only to fruitless works, but also to a most foul religion. Therefore, as long as the Synagogue flourished, the Church suffered. The inadequacy of the former is the power of the latter, because their fault is salvation for the Gentiles.

[Luke 8:43b] **Who had bestowed all her substance on physicians, and could not be healed by any.** The word 'physicians' signifies either false theologians, or philosophers /**190**/ and doctors of secular laws, who would discuss many things about the virtues and vices with great subtlety, and who used to promise to give mortals useful things instituted for living and believing. Or indeed it signifies the impure spirits themselves, who, by pretending to care for humans, kept insisting that now they ought to be worshipped as God. By hearing these things over and over, the more the Gentiles expended their powers of natural zeal, the less they were able to be healed of the filth of their iniquity. Hence Mark, writing about this woman, says it well: *And she had suffered many things from many physicians, and had spent all that she had, and was nothing the better, but rather worse.*[184] But when she knew that the people of the Jews were sick, and that the true

---

180 Cf. Jerome, *Commentarii in Matheum* 1 (CCSL 77:59.1373–76).
181 Cf. Ps.-Jerome, *Expositio euangeliorum* (PL 30:572B), who interprets the twelve years as 'two ages' (*duae aetates*).
182 Cf. 1 Sam. 17:1 & 4 & 50.
183 Jerome, *Hebr. nom.* (CCSL 72:103.11).
184 Mark 5:26.

physician had come from heaven, she herself began not only to hope but likewise to seek out a cure for her weakness.

[Luke 8:44] **She came behind him, and touched the hem of his garment, and immediately the issue of her blood stopped.** The Church, which approaches the Lord through the truth of faith, comes and touches him. But she comes from behind, either in accordance with what Jesus himself says: *If any man minister to me, let him follow me*,[185] and elsewhere it is taught: *You will walk after the Lord your God*,[186] or because, not seeing the Lord present in the flesh, but having fulfilled the obligations of temporal dispensation, she now begins to follow his footsteps through faith. She touches the hem of his garment, and stops the flow of blood, because one who touches even the outermost part of the Word with the hand of faith is blessed and will be cleansed. For those who deserve either to recline on his breast[187] or to anoint his head with pure spikenard,[188] are exceedingly rare, since even the one who was great[189] said that he was not worthy to carry his shoes.[190] And she was also great who anointed his feet, and merited wiping them with her hair.[191]

[Luke 8:45] **And Jesus said: Who is it that touched me?** He asks, not that he may be taught what he does not know, but that the power of faith, which he knew, or rather had given, may be proclaimed in the woman.[192]

[Luke 8:45b] **And when all denied it, Peter and they that were with him said: Master, the crowds throng and afflict you, and do you say: Who touched me?** One believing woman touches the Lord, whom the crowds following everywhere thronged, because he who is afflicted by the various heresies of those who crowd together inordinately is earnestly and faithfully questioned by the single heart of the universal Church. For just as some *seeing see not, and hearing hear not*,[193] so also those who do not touch Christ faithfully, touching, touch not. Hence /**191**/ to a certain one who loved him indeed, but did not yet fully believe, he says: *Do not touch*

---

185 John 12:26.
186 Deut. 13:4.
187 Cf. John 13:23.
188 Cf. Matt. 26:7; Mark 14:3; John 11:2; 12:3.
189 I.e., John the Baptist.
190 Cf. Matt. 3:11.
191 Cf. Luke 7:37–38.
192 This is substantially the interpretation of Ps.-Jerome, *Expositio euangeliorum* (PL 30:572B).
193 Matt. 13:13.

*me, for I have not yet ascended to my Father*,[194] openly teaching what it is to touch him truly, namely to believe him to be equal to the Father.

[Luke 8:46] **And Jesus said: Somebody has touched me, for I know that the power has gone out from me**, and so forth. If that is what he wants, let Pelagius say that he is saved by his own effort. But let us say that *vain is the salvation of man; through God we will enact power*.[195] For indeed Christ knows that the power, which *forgives all* our *iniquities*, and *heals all* our *weaknesses*,[196] goes out not from us, but from himself. Therefore, the one who touches his hem is not unknown to him: that is, one who perfectly believes the mysteries of the incarnation out of love, until she or he reaches the point of comprehending greater things.

[Luke 8:48] **But he said to her: Daughter, your faith has made you whole; go in peace.** *He calls her 'daughter', because, 'your faith has made you whole'. And he did not say, 'your faith is going to make you whole', but 'it made you whole, for because you believed in him you were already made whole'.*[197]

[Luke 8:49] **While he was still speaking, someone came to the ruler of the synagogue, saying to him: Your daughter is dead, trouble him not.** After the woman was rescued from the flux of blood, it is immediately reported that the daughter of the ruler is dead, because when the Church is cleansed of the stain of sins and is called 'daughter' on account of the merit of faith, the Synagogue is immediately freed from the Law of faithlessness and envy – of faithlessness indeed, because she would not believe in Christ, and of envy, because she lamented that the Church had believed. For it is written in the Acts of the Apostles: *But on the next Sabbath, almost the whole city came together, to hear the word of the Lord. And the Jews, seeing the crowds, were filled with envy, and contradicted those things which were said by Paul*,[198] *speaking evil of the way* [of the Lord] *in the presence of the multitude.*[199] *Trouble him not* is said still today by those who see the state of the Synagogue so very destitute that they do not believe that she can be renewed, and therefore they do not deem that any prayer can be

---

194 John 20:17. The person referred to here is Mary Magdalene.
195 Ps. 59:13–14 (60:11–12).
196 Ps. 102:3 (103:3).
197 Jerome, *Commentarii in Matheum* 1 (CCSL 77:60.1389–92).
198 Acts 13:44–45.
199 Acts 19:9.

BOOK THREE 341

offered which would raise her again from the dead. But *the things that are impossible with men are possible with God.*[200] Hence there follows:

[Luke 8:50] **And Jesus, hearing this word, answered the father of the girl: Fear not; only believe, and she will be safe.** The father of the girl is interpreted as the assembly of doctors of the Law, about which the Lord says: *The scribes and the Pharisees sat on the chair of Moses.*[201] If they themselves want to believe, the Synagogue, which is subject to them, will be saved.

[Luke 8:51] **And when he had come to the house, he did not permit anyone to go in with him except Peter and James and John, and the father and mother of the girl.** *Earlier, the widow's son was resurrected in public.*[202] *Here many* /192/ *witnesses are excluded. I think, therefore, that in the first case also the compassion of the Lord is made clear, because the widowed mother of the only child could not tolerate delay, and for that reason, lest she be affected further, promptness is added. Also, it is a form of wisdom: in the case of the widow's son, it is the Church who will quickly believe; with the ruler of a synagogue's daughter, it is the Jews who will believe, but very few out of many.*[203]

[Luke 8:52] **And all wept and mourned for her.** *Can the children of the bridegroom mourn,* Jesus says, *as long as the bridegroom is with them? But the days will come, when the bridegroom will be taken away from them, and then they will fast.*[204] Therefore the Synagogue, because she has lost the joy of the bridegroom, by which she could live, as if mourning prostrate amongst the dead, does not even understand what she is mourning about.

[Luke 8:52b] **But he said: Do not weep; the girl is not dead, but sleeps.** Dead to men, who had been unable to revive her, she was sleeping with God, and her soul that had been taken under his authority was alive, and her flesh was resting in order to be resurrected. Hence it became the Christian custom to say that the dead, who without question are going to be resurrected, are sleeping, just as the Apostle says: *We will not have you ignorant about those who are asleep, so that you do not sorrow, as others do who have no hope.*[205] But also in respect of allegory, although the soul

---

200 Luke 18:27.
201 Matt. 23:2.
202 Cf. Luke 7:11–15.
203 Ambrose, *Expos. Lucam* 6.64 (CCSL 14:196.639–45).
204 Matt. 9:15.
205 1 Thess. 4:13.

itself which has sinned dies, nevertheless someone which has deserved to be resurrected by Christ can be said to have been dead indeed to us, but to have fallen asleep to him.

[Luke 8:53] **And they laughed at him, knowing that she was dead.** Since they preferred to laugh at rather than to believe the word of the one doing the resuscitating, they are rightly kept outside, unworthy of seeing the miracle of the girl being resurrected.[206]

[Luke 8:54] **But holding her hand, he cried out, saying: Child, arise.** In Mark it is written: *He said to her: 'Talitha cumi', which means: 'Child', I say to you, 'arise', and immediately she arose.*[207] Here the observant reader may wonder why the veracious evangelist, expounding the words of the Saviour, should have interjected a phrase of his own, 'I say to you', when in the Syrian language which he set down no more is said than 'Child, arise',[208] [unless perhaps he thought that these words ought to be augmented for the sake of expressing the force of the Lord's command, taking care to make known to his readers the sense of the words rather than the words themselves. For it is well known to be customary for the evangelists and the apostles, when they take up the testimonies of the Old Testament, to take care to put down the prophetic sense rather than the words].[209] Therefore, holding the child's hand, Jesus healed her, because *unless the hands of the Jews, which are full of blood, have first been cleansed, their dead Synagogue does not arise.*[210]

[Luke 8:55] **And her spirit returned, and she arose immediately.** Mark puts it this way: *And immediately the child arose and walked,*[211] spiritually revealing that whoever recovers from the death of the soul when Christ strengthens his hand ought not only to arise from the squalor of sins, but also to advance immediately in good works. /193/

---

206 Cf. Jerome, *Commentarii in Matheum* 1 (CCSL 77:60.1402–03).
207 Mark 5:41–42.
208 Cf. Jerome, *Hebr. nom.* (CCSL 72:139.29–30).
209 Bede, *In Marci Euangelium expositio* 2, ed. Hurst (CCSL 120:500.440–45). In *On Mark*, which he wrote some years after *On Luke*, Bede repeats this query verbatim and adds the explanation for the interjection 'I say to you' that seems to be called for. We have ventured to insert this explanation in square brackets, on the assumption that an early copyist of *On Luke* inadvertently omitted the bracketed material. The copyist's eye might have skipped in a kind of haplography from the first word in the bracketed material, 'unless' [*nisi*], down to the first word of Jerome's comment, 'unless' [*nisi*], and then backtracked to pick up Bede's lead-in to Jerome.
210 Jerome, *Commentarii in Matheum* 1 (CCSL 77:60.1404–06).
211 Mark 5:42.

BOOK THREE   343

[Luke 8:55b] **And he bid them give her something to eat.** After she had been raised up again to life, he ordered her to eat as testimony that this was not a phantasm, but a credible truth. But even if someone has arisen from spiritual death, it is necessary that he be immediately filled with heavenly bread, and made a sharer, certainly, of the divine word and of the sacred altar. For according to the moral sense, those three dead people whom the Saviour raised up in their bodies signify three kinds of resurrection of souls. For some by giving consent to wicked delight but concealing the thought of sin inflict death upon themselves. But the Saviour shows that he restores such people to life by reviving the daughter of the ruler of the synagogue, who had not yet been carried outside, but was dead inside the house, hiding vice as it were in her secret heart. Others, not only by consenting to wicked delight, but also by performing the evil they took delight in, bring on their own death outside the gates. And showing that he brings these to life again if they repent, he raises up the young son of the widow who had been brought outside the gates, and restored him to his mother,[212] because he restored the soul recovering from the darkness of sin to the unity of the Church, as we have previously taught. But some, not only by thinking or doing illicit things, but also by the very habit of sinning, corrupt themselves by burying themselves as it were.[213] And truly the power and grace of the Saviour is not diminished in raising these people up, even though anxious thoughts are present, which keep watch over their salvation like sisters devoted to Christ. For to proclaim this, he raised Lazarus from the dead, who *had been four days already in the grave*,[214] and whose sister attested that he was already stinking,[215] because the worst infamy is accustomed to accompany wicked deeds.

But it should be noted that the more severely death has assaulted the soul, the more zealously is it necessary for the fervour of the penitent to persist in order to deserve to rise again. Wishing to show this in private, the Lord brings the girl lying dead in the room back to life again, saying in a calm and gentle voice: *Child, arise.* Because it was so easy to bring her back to life again, he had just now denied that she was dead. But he gives the young man carried outside the city strength to revive, when he says

---

212 Cf. Luke 7:11–15.
213 Cf. Ps.-Jerome, *Expositio euangeliorum* (PL 30:571C); see Introduction, 39.
214 John 11:17.
215 Cf. John 11:39.

using more words: *Young man, I say to you, arise.*[216] But in order that the man who was dead for four days might be able to put aside the long bars of the oppressing grave, Jesus *groaned in spirit, troubled himself,*[217] shed tears,[218] groaned again,[219] and *cried with a loud voice: Lazarus, come forth.*[220] And thus, at length, he who had been despaired of, when the weight of darkness is dispelled, is restored to life and light. But it also should be noted that because a public offence needs a public remedy, but light /194/ sins are able to be wiped out by a lighter and hidden penitence, the girl lying in the house arises with few witnesses, and it is enjoined upon the same that they not divulge the miracle.

[Luke 8:56] **And her parents**, he says, **were astonished, whom he charged to tell no man what was done.** The young man is aroused outside the gate, accompanied and watched by a great crowd. Lazarus, called from the tomb, became so well known among the peoples that, because of the testimony of those who saw, huge crowds ran to meet the Lord with palm-branches,[221] and *many of the Jews, because of him*, went away, *and believed in Jesus.*[222] Certainly the Lord acknowledges a fourth dead man, whom the disciple reports.[223] But because there were no living people present to beg the Lord for his deliverance, he says: *Let the dead bury their dead,*[224] that is, let the wicked burden the wicked with damaging praises, and because *the just man* is not present to correct *in mercy*, let *the oil of the sinner anoint* their *head.*[225]

## Chapter 33

**86/2** [Luke 9:1–2] **Then calling together the twelve apostles, he gave them power and authority over all demons, and to cure diseases. And he sent them to preach the kingdom of God, and to heal the sick.**

---

216 Luke 7:14.
217 John 11:33.
218 Cf. John 11:35.
219 Cf. John 11:38.
220 John 11:43.
221 Cf. John 12:13.
222 John 12:11.
223 Cf. Matt. 8:21; Luke 9:59.
224 Matt. 8:22; Luke 9:60 (a blend).
225 Ps. 140:5 (141:5).

After granting them the power to perform miracles, he immediately sent them to preach the kingdom of God in order that the greatness of their deeds might likewise attest to the greatness of the promises, and *that power displayed might produce faith in the words, and that those who preached new things might do new things.*[226] *Hence now also, when the number of the faithful have increased, there are many within the holy Church who maintain a life of virtue, and do not have the miraculous signs of virtues, because a miracle is vainly displayed outwardly, if what should be worked inwardly is lacking. For according to the word of the teacher of the Gentiles: 'Tongues are a sign, not for believers, but for unbelievers.'*[227]

87/2 [Luke 9:3] **And he said to them: Take nothing for your journey, not a staff, nor a bag, nor bread, nor money; and do not have two coats.** *It is often asked why Matthew and Luke recounted that the Lord said to his disciples that they should not take a staff,*[228] *when Mark says: 'And he commanded them that they should take nothing for the way, but a staff only'.*[229] *This problem is resolved in such a way that we may understand the aforesaid staff which according to Mark ought to be carried, in one sense, and that staff which according to Matthew and Luke must not be carried, in another, just as the temptation of which it was said: 'God tempts no one',*[230] *is understood in one sense, and in another that of which it was said:* /**195**/ *'The Lord your God tempts you, to know if you love him'.*[231] *The former is a matter of seduction; the latter, of testing.*[232]

*Therefore, both statements by the Lord to the apostles must be accepted, both that they should not carry a staff, and that they should carry nothing but a staff. For although according to Matthew he said to them: 'Do not possess gold, nor silver',*[233] *and so forth, he immediately added: 'For the workman is worthy of his food'.*[234] *Hence it is sufficiently shown why he did not wish them to possess and carry these things. Not because they are not necessary to sustain this life, but because he sent them in this way to*

---

226 Gregory, *Hom. in Euang.* 1.4.3 (CCSL 141:28.55–56).
227 Gregory, *Hom. in Euang.* 1.4.3 (CCSL 141:29.67–74); 1 Cor. 14:22.
228 Cf. Matt. 10:10.
229 Mark 6:8.
230 James 1:13.
231 Deut. 13:3.
232 Augustine, *De consensu euang.* 2.30 (CSEL 43:175.8–176.1).
233 Matt. 10:9.
234 Matt. 10:10.

show that these things are owed to them by those believers to whom they announced the Gospel.[235]

But let it be clear *that the Lord did not order these things, as if the evangelists ought not to live anywhere other than the places which those to whom they are preaching the Gospel provide for them. Moreover, the Apostle, who sustained himself with the labours of his own hands, acted contrary to this teaching in order not to be a burden to anyone.*[236] *But the Lord gave the power by which they knew that these things were owed to them. When anything is commanded by the Lord, unless it is done, it is the sin of disobedience. But when power is given, one is allowed not use it, and to withdraw, as it were, from its jurisdiction.*[237]

*Ordaining what the Apostle says he ordained to those who preach the Gospel – namely, to live according to the Gospel – the Lord said these things to the apostles so that they would not carelessly possess or carry about the necessities of life, great or small. For that reason, he declared: 'not a staff', showing that his faithful owe everything to his ministers, who require nothing superfluous. But by adding this: 'For the workman is worthy of his food', he absolutely revealed and made clear why he spoke all these things. Therefore, he signified this power by the word 'staff', when he said, 'that they should take nothing for the way, but a staff only', so that it may be understood that through the power received from the Lord, which is signified by the word 'staff', even the things that are not carried are not lacking.*[238]

*This must be understood about the two coats as well, so that none of them might think that another coat ought to be carried besides that which he had put on, as if he were afraid that he might come to be in want, while he could get [what he needed] from that power [he had received from the Lord].*[239] According to Mark, *he did not prohibit two coats from being carried or possessed, but expressly prohibited putting two coats on, saying: 'and that they should not put on two coats';*[240] *what admonition does this deliver, except not to walk duplicitously but in simple honesty?*[241]

And in another interpretation: *By two coats, Mark seems to me to mean a garment folded double. It is not that anyone ought to be content with one*

---

235 Augustine, *De consensu euang.* 2.30 (CSEL 43:177.12–22).
236 Cf. 1 Thess. 2:9.
237 Augustine, *De consensu euang.* 2.30 (CSEL 43:178.7–15).
238 Augustine, *De consensu euang.* 2.30 (CSEL 43:179.8–23).
239 Augustine, *De consensu euang.* 2.30 (CSEL 43:180.5–8).
240 Mark 6:9.
241 Augustine, *De consensu euang.* 2.30 (CSEL 43:180.12–14).

*coat in the region of Scythia, stiffening with icy snow, but that by 'coat' we should understand a garment of any kind, in order that, having been clothed in one, we not keep another for ourselves from fear of the future.*[242] /196/
[Luke 9:4] **And whatever house you enter into, abide there, and do not**[243] **depart from there.** *He gives a general commandment of constancy, that they should keep the laws of hospitable relationship, adding that it ill becomes a preacher of the heavenly kingdom to run back and forth from house to house and impair the laws of inviolable hospitality.*[244] *And according to Matthew,*[245] *the house that the apostles enter, it is decreed, ought not to be chosen casually, in order that there should be no cause for impairing hospitality and violating this relationship.*[246]

88/2 [Luke 9:5] **And whoever will not receive you, when you go out of that city, shake off even the dust from your feet, for a testimony against them.** *Dust is shaken off from their feet, in testimony of their own work, because they entered the city, and the apostolic preaching had reached them. Or dust is shaken off, in order that they receive nothing from those who had scorned the Gospel, not even for necessary sustenance.*[247] Allegorically, those who direct their attention humbly to the word, if as men they are blinded by these blemishes of earthly inconstancy, are immediately cleansed by these footsteps of evangelical preaching. But *it is declared that communion* with those who condemn out of perfidy or negligence or even from zeal, *must be avoided, their assembly shunned, the dust of their feet shaken off, lest the footstep of the* pure *mind be soiled* by *deeds that are vain and comparable to dust.*[248]

89/8 [Luke 9:6] **And going out, they went about through the towns, preaching the gospel, and healing everywhere.** Mark explains more fully what the apostles preached and how they healed. *They preached*, he says, *that men should do penance, and they anointed with oil many that were sick, and healed them.*[249] And James says: *Is any man sick among you? Let him bring in the priests of the church, and let them pray over him, anointing him with oil in the name of the Lord. And if he be in sins,*

---

242 Jerome, *Commentarii in Matheum* 1 (CCSL 77:66.1571-75).
243 KJ & NRSV both omit 'not'.
244 Ambrose, *Expos. Lucam* 6.66 (CCSL 14:197.658-61).
245 Cf. Matt. 10:11.
246 Ambrose, *Expos. Lucam* 6.66 (CCSL 14:197.667-70).
247 Jerome, *Commentarii in Matheum* 1 (CCSL 77:68.1626-30).
248 Ambrose, *Expos. Lucam* 6.68 (CCSL 14:198.690-95).
249 Mark 6:12-13.

*they shall be forgiven him.*²⁵⁰ Hence it is plain that this practice of the holy Church, that the sick be anointed with consecrated oil with an episcopal blessing, was handed down by these very apostles. For *they preached that men should do penance*; and above he says: *he sent them to preach the kingdom of God,*²⁵¹ because, of course, they preached both according to the example of John the Baptist and of the Saviour himself: *Do penance, for the kingdom of heaven draws nigh.*²⁵² For to draw nigh to the gates of the kingdom of heaven is for each one to repent of those things for the sake of which he had moved away from it.

## Chapter 34

90/2 [Luke 9:7–8] **Now Herod, the tetrarch, heard of all the things that were done by him; and /197/ he was in doubt, because it was said by some that John was risen from the dead.** Almost every passage in the Gospel teaches us how great was the envy of the Jews, and why the fury of malice arose. For behold they believed without evidence that John, of whom it was said *that he made no sign,*²⁵³ was able to rise from the dead. But they preferred to believe that *Jesus, a man approved of God by miracles and signs*²⁵⁴ – the elements quaked at his death,²⁵⁵ angels, apostles, men, and women earnestly foretold his resurrection and indeed ascension – was not raised from the dead, but had been furtively carried away.²⁵⁶ And it should not be thought contradictory that Luke says that Herod was in doubt, *because it was said by some that John was risen from the dead,* when Matthew and Mark report that this same Herod, having heard the fame of Jesus, said *to his servants, 'This is John the Baptist; he has risen from the dead, and therefore mighty works show forth in him.'*²⁵⁷ Rather *it must be understood that in the wake of this doubt, what was said by others confirmed* him *in his mind.*²⁵⁸

---

250 James 5:14–15.
251 Luke 9:2.
252 Matt. 3:2 (the words of John the Baptist); 4:17 (the words of Jesus).
253 John 10:41.
254 Acts 2:22.
255 Cf. Matt. 28:2.
256 Cf. Matt. 28:13.
257 Matt. 14:2.
258 Augustine, *De consensu euang.* 2.43 (CSEL 43:196.2–3; 15–16; 12–14).

[Luke 9:9] **And Herod said: I have beheaded John. But who is this of whom I hear such things? And he sought to see him.** These are the words of the doubting Herod, which were discussed above. He also wishes to see the one whose greatness he had learned from report, to see if perchance he can discern whether or not he is this John. Since the other evangelists fully describe the sequence and cause of his beheading, Luke according to his custom has taken care to narrate for the sake of revealing the situation of the time, rather than to repeat things that he saw had been copiously recorded. But since the beheading of John is mentioned, it should be noted that the same John and the Lord each declared his situation both by means of the time of his nativity and by the sequence of his passion. For John was decreased by the loss of his head; the Lord was raised up on the cross. John was born when the days began to decrease; the Lord, when they began to increase. As likewise what the reality is appeared in these words: *He must increase, but I must decrease*,[259] that is, he who was considered a prophet must be recognized as Christ, and I who was held to be Christ must be understood to be his forerunner.

91/8 [Luke 9:10] **And the apostles, when they returned, told him all they had done.** The apostles not only told the Lord what they themselves had done and taught, but also either his own or John's disciples reported what John suffered while they were engaged in teaching, as Matthew makes known.[260] Hence what follows:

92/3 [Luke 9:10b] **And taking them, he went aside into a desert place, apart, which /198/ belongs to Bethsaida.** He did not do this, *as some think, from fear of death, but to spare his enemies, in order that they not add homicide to homicide*,[261] and also to await the suitable time for his passion. For anyone who reads the Gospels carefully will find that the passions of John and the Lord are separated by more than a year's time. According to the three harmonizing evangelists, the Lord performed the miracle of the loaves after the beheading of John.[262] When the evangelist John was about to describe this miracle,[263] he first declared that *the Passover, the festival day of the Jews, was near at hand*,[264] and afterwards,

---

259 John 3:30. On the connection to the timing of John's and Jesus's births, see above, 130.
260 Cf. Matt. 14:12.
261 Jerome, *Commentarii in Matheum* 2 (CCSL 77:119.1188–90).
262 Cf. Matt. 14:10–21; Mark 6:28–42; Luke 9:9–17.
263 Cf. John 6:9.
264 John 6:4 (syntax adjusted).

he says that Jesus went up to their festival day of Tabernacles,[265] where, he says, as he was *teaching in the temple*,[266] *they sought to apprehend him; and no man laid hands on him, because his hour was not yet come*,[267] and then that the victory of the cross was consummated at the time of the next Passover.[268] After John was killed, and awaiting this time, *Jesus went aside into a desert place, apart, which belongs to Bethsaida*, teaching allegorically that, having abandoned Judea, which had cut off its head by not believing the prophecy concerning himself, he was going to distribute the nourishment of the Word in the desert to the Church, which did not have a husband.[269] Hence Bethsaida beautifully expresses 'the house of fruits'.[270] For it is the same about which Isaiah says: *The land that was desolate and impassable will be glad, and the wilderness will rejoice, and will flourish like the lily.*[271] And a little further on: *They will see the glory of the Lord, and the beauty of our God.*[272] Moreover *Bethsaida is the city in Galilee of the apostles Andrew, Peter, and Philip, near the lake of Gennesaret*, as we find in the Book of Places.[273]

[Luke 9:11] **Which when the people knew, they followed him; and he received them, and spoke to them of the kingdom of God and healed them who had need of healing.** The Lord puts the people's faith to the test, and having found it good, he repays them with a fitting reward. For by seeking solitude, he ascertains whether they would take the trouble to follow. And by following *not on beasts of burden, not in vehicles of various kinds, but*, as other evangelists report, by taking the route of the desert *by their own foot-power*,[274] they show how great a care for their own salvation they have. In turn he makes known by supporting the weary, by teaching the ignorant, by refreshing the hungry how much he, as a Saviour and physician at once powerful and gentle, is pleased by the believers' devotion. In accordance with the laws of allegory, the many crowds of the faithful,

---

265  Cf. John 7:2 & 10.
266  John 7:28 (syntax adjusted).
267  John 7:30.
268  Cf. John 13:1.
269  Cf. Jerome, *Commentarii in Matheum* 2 (CCSL 77:120.1199–1203).
270  Cf. Jerome, *Hebr. nom.* (CCSL 72:135.21).
271  Isa. 35:1.
272  Isa. 35:2.
273  Jerome, *De situ et nom.* (*Onomastica sacra* 107.31–32).
274  Jerome, *Commentarii in Matheum* 2 (CCSL 77:120.1208–09); cf. Matt. 14:13; Mark 6:33.

abandoning the customs of their former way of life, and without the confirmation of various teachings, follow Christ seeking the desert places /199/ of the Gentiles. And he who says in former times: *God is known in Judea*,[275] says in after times: *the teeth of the Jews are weapons and arrows, and their tongue is become a sharp sword* against him. *Be exalted, O God, above the heavens, and your glory above all the earth.*[276]

Chapter 35

93/1 [Luke 9:12] **Now the day began to decline. And the twelve came and said to him: Send away the multitude, so that going into the towns and villages round about they may lodge and get victuals.** With the decline of the day the Saviour refreshes the multitude, because either with the end of times approaching, or when the Sun of justice has set for us, we are saved from the prolonged wasting away of spiritual fasting.[277]

[Luke 9:13] **But he said to them: Give them something to eat.** *He calls upon the apostles to break bread, in order that the magnitude of the miracle be more known to those who could see that they did not have any*,[278] *revealing at the same time that our hungry hearts are to be fed by them daily. For what does Peter do, when he speaks through the Epistles, except satisfy our exceedingly hungry hearts with the food of the Word? What does Paul, what does John accomplish, speaking through the Epistles, unless our minds perceive the heavenly nourishment, and overcome the lack of appetite brought on by fasting, from which they were dying?*[279]

[Luke 9:13b] **And they said: We have no more than five loaves and two fish.** The apostles did not yet have more than the five loaves of the Law of Moses, and the two fish of each Testament, the secrets of which were covered and nourished for a long time by the concealment of the hidden mysteries, as if by the waters of the abyss.[280] And the loaves that signify the Law are well said, according to the Gospel of John, to have

---

275 Ps. 75:2 (76:1).
276 Ps. 56:5–6 (57:4–5).
277 Cf. Jerome, *Commentarii in Matheum* 2 (CCSL 77:121.1227–32).
278 Jerome, *Commentarii in Matheum* 2 (CCSL 77:121.1236–38).
279 Gregory, *Moralia* 27.12 (CCSL 143B:1347.25–29).
280 In his commentary *On Mark* (cf. CCSL 120:513.936–43), Bede interprets the five loaves and two fish as the whole of the Old Testament: the five loaves being the five books of the Pentateuch, and the two fish the Psalms and the Prophets.

been of barley,[281] which is chiefly the food of pack-animals and of country slaves, because the Law's rather bitter and, as it were, somewhat coarse precepts must be entrusted to catechumens who are just beginning and are not yet perfected. For *the sensual man does not perceive these things that are of the Spirit of God.*[282] And for that reason the Lord, bestowing his gifts to each according to his strength, and always calling upon each for greater perfections, first refreshes five thousand men with five loaves, and secondly four thousand with seven loaves.[283] Thirdly, he confides the mystery of his flesh and blood to his disciples.[284] And last he gives as a great gift to the elect that they may eat and drink at his table in his kingdom.[285]

[Luke 9:14] **Now there were about five thousand men**. Since there are five senses of the external man, the five thousand men following the Lord /200/ signify those who, still placed in a worldly condition, know how to use properly the external things that they possess. They are rightly fed by five loaves, because it is necessary that such people still be instructed by the precepts of the Law. For there are also four thousand men who, for the sake of withdrawing entirely from the world, are both refreshed by seven loaves, that is, uplifted by the refreshment of the gospel, and instructed by spiritual grace. I think for the sake of signifying mystically the difference that five gilded columns indeed were ordered in the entrance of the tabernacle, but four were ordered before the sanctuary, that is, the holy of holies.[286] Because, of course, beginners are restrained from sinning by the Law, but the perfected are admonished by grace to live more devoutly in God.

[Luke 9:14b–15] **And he said to his disciples: Make them sit down by fifties in a company. And they did so.** The various seats of those feasting signify the various assemblies of the churches throughout the world, *which make up one catholic Church.*[287] And not only did the fifties sit down, but also, as Mark attests, the hundreds.[288] For since the fiftieth Psalm is the Psalm of penitence,[289] and the number one hundred passes from the left

---

281 Cf. John 6:9.
282 1 Cor. 2:14.
283 Cf. Mark 8:5–9.
284 Cf. Luke 22:19–20; 1 Cor. 11:24–25.
285 Cf. Luke 22:30.
286 Cf. Exod. 26:32–37.
287 Gregory, *Moralia* 16.55.68 (CCSL 143A:838.4).
288 Cf. Mark 6:40.
289 Ps 50 (D/R); Ps. 51 (KJV; NRSV).

to the right hand,²⁹⁰ the fifties sit down to the Lord's feast, who, still doing penitence for transgressions, receive the auditory instruction of the Word. But the hundreds are those who already confident in the hope of forgiveness sigh out of longing for eternal life alone.

[Luke 9:16] **And taking the five loaves and the two fish, he looked up to heaven and blessed them; and he broke them, and distributed them to his disciples to set before the multitude.** The Saviour does not create new foods for the hungry multitude, but taking those that the disciples had he blesses them, because, coming in the flesh, he may foretell nothing other than what was foretold. But he shows that the sayings of the prophetic texts are filled with the mysteries of grace. He looks up to heaven to teach that the power of the mind must be directed there where the light of knowledge is to be sought. He breaks the loaves and distributes them to his disciples to set before the multitude, because he lays open the hidden sacraments of the Law and the prophetic books to those who will preach them throughout the world.

[Luke 9:17] **And what remained to them – twelve baskets of fragments – was taken up.** What remains to the multitude is taken up by the disciples, because the more sacred mysteries that cannot be grasped by the ignorant must not be heedlessly abandoned, but are to be searched into by the spiritually initiated. For by the baskets are allegorically signified the twelve apostles, and by the apostles, all the multitudes of teachers to come, despised by men outside the Church, but perfected within by the remains of the salvific food for nourishing the hearts of the humble. For it is well known that servile work is accustomed to be done with baskets, /201/ but he who chose the weak things of this world to confound the strong,²⁹¹ filled the baskets with fragments of the loaves.

## Chapter 36

94/1 [Luke 9:18] **And it happened, when he was alone praying, that his disciples were also with him.** The disciples were with the Lord; they followed him on the way, as Mark points out,²⁹² but he alone prayed to the Father. This is because the saints can be joined to the Lord in a fellowship

---

290 See Book 2 n. 92 for explanation of this allusion to finger-reckoning.
291 Cf. 1 Cor. 1:27.
292 Cf. Mark 8:27.

of faith and love; they can observe that he has been separated from other mortals by the glory of divine majesty; and they can follow with the steps of humility the way which he taught when he dwelt in the flesh; but the Son alone knows how to penetrate the inconceivable mysteries of the Father's providence. For nowhere, unless I am mistaken, is he found to have prayed with the disciples; everywhere he prays alone, because human prayers do not determine God's plan, nor can anyone be a sharer with Christ of his inner life.

[Luke 9:18b–19] **And he asked them, saying: Who does the crowd say that I am? But they answered and said: John the Baptist, but some say Elijah, and others say that one of the former prophets has risen again.** It is fitting that the Lord, who is going to put the faith of the disciples to the test, first asks about the opinions of the crowd, lest indeed their belief seem formed by the fancies of the common people, rather than proved by the perception of the truth, and that they be thought not to believe with informed faith, but like Herod to be in doubt about what they had heard.[293] And hence, according to Matthew, he says to Peter who acknowledges that he is Christ:[294] *Because flesh and blood has not revealed it to you*,[295] that is, human instruction did not teach you the truth of faith. Aptly also, those who offer diverse opinions about the Lord are denoted by the word 'crowd', which is always a dubious, unstable, and inconstant expression and concept. In order to distinguish the disciples from them, he immediately adds:

[Luke 9:20] **But who do you say I am?** For the disciples of Christ are not of the crowd, nor are they who go alone with the Lord and are privileged to see him praying apart part of the crowd; but also, if anyone of the crowd believes in Christ, he will immediately indeed cease to be of the crowd.

[Luke 9:20b] **Simon Peter answering, said: The Christ of God.** *Although the other apostles knew this, nevertheless Peter answered before the rest. And so he encompassed everything, who described both Christ's nature and name, in which is the sum total of virtues. Do we still raise questions about how God was begotten, although Paul judged that he knew nothing 'but Jesus Christ and him crucified',*[296] *and Peter reckoned that nothing more than the Son of God should be confessed? Do we find out*

---

293 Cf. Luke 9:7.
294 Cf. Matt. 16:16.
295 Matt. 16:17.
296 1 Cor. 2:2.

*when and how he was born and how great he is with the eyes of human weakness?* Therefore, *the outer limit of my faith is Christ, the end term of my faith is the Son of God.* /202/ *I am not permitted to know the sequence of his begetting; I am nevertheless not permitted to be ignorant of faith in his begetting.*[297]

95/2 [Luke 9:21–22] **But he strictly charging them, commanded they should tell this to no man, saying: The Son of man must suffer many things**, and so forth. *He did not wish to be proclaimed before his passion and resurrection, so that afterwards, when the sacrament of his blood was accomplished, he might at that more opportune moment say to the apostles: 'Go, teach all nations, baptizing them in the name of the Father, and of the Son, and of the Holy Spirit'*,[298] *because there was no use in him being proclaimed publicly, and his majesty being bruited about among the people, when shortly thereafter they would see him whipped and crucified, and suffering many things from the elders and scribes and chiefs of the priests.*[299] And it should be noted that he calls the one who must suffer many things and be killed and rise again the Son of man, because although Christ suffered in the flesh, his divinity remained incapable of suffering. It should also be noted that he himself confesses that he is the Son of man, but Peter avows that he is Christ the Son of God, so that from these both together he is proved to be true God and man.

## Chapter 37

96/2 [Luke 9:23] **And he said to all: If anyone will come after me, let him deny himself**. Fittingly, Luke specified *to all*, because Jesus dealt separately with the higher things that pertain to faith in the Lord's nativity and passion with his disciples alone. But *we deny our very selves when we shun what we were in time gone by, and strive toward what we are called to be in this new state.*[300] *Therefore let Truth declare, let him declare: 'If anyone will come after me, let him deny himself', because unless someone breaks loose from himself, he does not approach him who is above himself; and he is unable to apprehend what is beyond himself, if he is unwilling to*

---

297 Ambrose, *Expos. Lucam* 6.93 (CCSL 14:207.997–1005; 1010–12).
298 Matt. 28:19.
299 Jerome, *Commentarii in Matheum* 3 (CCSL 77:142.106–09; 143.118–20).
300 Gregory, *Hom. in Euang.* 2.32.2 (CCSL 141:279.46–48).

*destroy what he is.*³⁰¹ *But now he who withholds himself from vices, has to seek the virtues in which he may prosper, for immediately* it is added:³⁰²

[Luke 9:23b] **And let him take up his cross daily, and follow me.** *The cross is taken up in two ways, both when the body is affected by abstinence, and when the soul is afflicted by sympathy for a neighbour. Let us consider how Paul bore his cross in both ways, who said: 'I chastise my body, and bring it into subjection: lest perhaps, preaching to others, I myself should become a castaway.'*³⁰³ *Lo, we have heard in the affliction of the body the cross of the flesh; let us now hear the cross of the spirit in sympathy for a neighbour. He says: 'Who is weak, and am I not weak? Who is caused to stumble, and am I not on fire?'*³⁰⁴ *But it should be noted that in either way we carry the cross, we are commanded both to take it up daily and after taking it up to follow the Lord.* /203/

[Luke 9:24] **For whoever wants to save his life, will lose it; but he who will lose his life for my sake, will save it.** *Thus, it is said to a believer: 'For whoever wants to save his life, will lose it; but he who will lose his life for my sake, will save it', as if it were said to the farmer: If you save your grain, you lose it; if you sow it, you gain it anew. For is there anyone who does not know that grain is lost to sight when it is broadcast as seed, and disappears in the earth? But from the place where it moulders in the soil it greens up in renewal. But since the holy Church now experiences a time of persecution, and now a time of peace, our Redeemer distinguished these times in his commandments. For the soul must be subdued in a time of persecution, but those earthly desires that can be mastered further must be subdued in a time of peace. And hence it is now said:*³⁰⁵

[Luke 9:25] **For what does it profit a man, if he should gain the whole world, but lose himself and cast himself away?** *In the absence of persecution from adversaries, the heart must watch over itself much more vigilantly. For in a time of peace, since it is at liberty to live, it likes to wander as well.*³⁰⁶ *And commonly we despise all failings, but nevertheless we are still hindered by the habit of human shame, so that we are still*

---

301 Gregory, *Hom. in Euang.* 2.32.2 (CCSL 141:279.56–59).
302 Gregory, *Hom. in Euang.* 2.32.3 (CCSL 141:280.65–67).
303 1 Cor. 9:27.
304 Gregory, *Hom. in Euang.* 2.32.3 (CCSL 141:280.73–76); 2 Cor. 11:29.
305 Gregory, *Hom. in Euang.* 2.32.4 (CCSL 141:281.107–17).
306 Gregory, *Hom. in Euang.* 2.32.4 (CCSL 141:282.119–21).

*unable to express in our speech the rectitude that we preserve in our soul. But the appropriate remedy is also added to this fault, when the Lord says:*[307]

**97/2 [Luke 9:26] For he who is ashamed of me and of my words, of him the Son of man will be ashamed, when he will come in his majesty, and that of his Father, and of the holy angels.** *But lo, now men say among themselves: Now we are not ashamed of the Lord and of his words, because we acknowledge him in open speech. To which I reply that in this Christian populace there are many who acknowledge Christ because they perceive that all are Christians. Therefore, a verbal declaration is not sufficient as a proof of faith, when the declaration of the multitude shields one from shame. But it is when each one examines himself, that he fully tests himself in the faith of Christ. For certainly in time of persecution the faithful could be shamed, stripped of possessions, cast out of offices, and afflicted with scourges. But in time of peace, because our 'persecutions' do not entail these things, it is another thing when we are displayed to ourselves. We are often in fear of being despised by our neighbours, and we refuse to endure verbal insults. If a quarrel breaks out perchance with a neighbour, we are ashamed to be the first to make amends. Indeed, as long as the carnal heart seeks the glory of this life, it scorns humility.*[308]

**98/2 [Luke 9:27] But I tell you truly: There are some standing here who will not taste death, till they see the kingdom of God.** *In this passage, the present Church is called the kingdom of God.*[309] *And because some of the disciples were going to triumph in the body to so great an extent, that they would see the Church of God built and raised up in opposition to the glory of this world, it is now* /204/ *said with a consolatory promise: 'There are some of them standing here, who will not taste death, till they see the kingdom of God'.*[310] *But when the Lord gave such strong commandments about submitting to death, why was it necessary that he should suddenly arrive at this promise, unless because he was likewise going to promise something to his ignorant disciples about the present life, in order that they might be more firmly strengthened in the future life?*[311] *To these he promises that the kingdom of God will be seen on earth, so that it may with greater*

---

307 Gregory, *Hom. in Euang.* 2.32.4 (CCSL 141:282.127–35).
308 Gregory, *Hom. in Euang.* 2.32.5 (CCSL 141:282.138–55).
309 Gregory, *Hom. in Euang.* 2.32.6 (CCSL 141:283.170–72).
310 Mark 8:39 (9:1).
311 Gregory, *Hom. in Euang.* 2.32.6 (CCSL 141:284.177–86).

*confidence be taken to be so in heaven.*³¹² But if we would understand by this statement that the kingdom of God will be blessedness in heaven, some of those standing there also saw it on the mountain not many days later, evidently in order that through the contemplation of enduring joy, although it was speedily removed, they might with greater discipline bear misfortune in the press of the passing age. Certainly, by this very fitting word it is shown that the saints taste death, for the death of the body is tasted when it is poured out, while the life of the soul is retained having it in their control.

[Luke 9:28] **And it happened about eight days after these words that he took Peter and James and John.** On the eighth day the Lord shows clearly to the disciples the promised glory of the blessedness to come, in order both to refresh the hearts of all who can hear these things by displaying the sweetness of heavenly life, and by the number eight in reference to the days, to teach that true joy will come at the time of the resurrection. For not only did he himself rise from the dead on the eighth day, that is, after the sixth day of the Sabbath on which he ascended the cross, and after the seventh day of the Sabbath on which he rested in the tomb, but also, we ourselves, after the six ages of this world, in which we rejoice to suffer and toil for the Lord, and after the seventh age of the repose of souls, which is passed for a time in another life, will rise again in as it were the eighth age.³¹³ For the fact that Matthew and Mark say that the Lord was transfigured after six days³¹⁴ results neither from the order of time nor because there is a symbolic meaning, because they only count the intervening days, and hence they say accurately that it happened after six days. Luke adds the first and the last day, and therefore reports more correctly *about eight days.* And Matthew and Mark signify that after the six ages of the world the saints are going to rest from labour, while Luke signifies that in the eighth age they will rise again. Hence the sixth Psalm is aptly inscribed 'for the octave', the beginning of which is: *O Lord, do not rebuke me in your anger,*³¹⁵ because certainly throughout the six ages during which it is permitted to do good work, we must beseech this in our prayers, lest we be reproached in the eighth age of retribution by the angry Judge. And the Lord himself wanted in this passage to teach us this by the clear example of his prayer, about which is added: /205/

---

312 Gregory, *Hom. in Euang.* 2.32.6 (CCSL 141:284.198–99).
313 See above, Book 1, n. 276.
314 Cf. Matt. 17:1; Mark 9:1.
315 Ps. 6:2 (6:1); Bede cites this Psalm in *DTR* c. 71 in his discussion of the 8th Age.

[Luke 9:28b] **And he went up onto a mountain to pray.** For he goes up onto a mountain to pray and so to be transfigured to show that those who *await the fruit of the resurrection*,[316] and who desire to see *the king in his beauty*,[317] must live with their souls on high, and devote themselves to continuous prayers. He only takes three disciples with him, because *many are called, but few are chosen*.[318] And those who have kept the faith of the holy Trinity with which they are imbued here, with untarnished souls, deserve to delight there in beholding it forever.[319]

[Luke 9:29] **And while he prayed, the appearance of his face was altered, and his clothing became white and glittering.** When the Saviour was transfigured, he did not lose the substance of his flesh, but he displayed the glory both of his future resurrection and of ours. He appeared to the apostles then, just as he will appear to all the elect after the Judgement. For at the very moment when the good must be judged together with the wicked, he will be seen in the form of a slave, to declare that they will be able to recognize the Judge whom the wicked scorned, the Jews denied, the soldiers crucified, and Pilate and Herod judged. But the Lord's clothing is understood to be the company of his saints, which the Apostle glorifies, when he says: *Therefore, as many of you as have been baptized in Christ have put on Christ.*[320] While the Lord remains on the plain his appearance seemed contemptible and like that of others, but when he seeks the mountain he glitters with a new whiteness, because *We are now the sons of God, and it has not yet appeared what we will be. We know that when he appears, we will be like to him, because we will see him just as he is.*[321] Hence Mark, describing these garments, fittingly says: they are *such as no fuller on earth can make white.*[322] For, since in this passage one should understand that Fuller whom the penitent Psalmist entreats: *Wash me yet more from my iniquity, and cleanse me from my sin*,[323] he cannot give to his faithful on earth the splendour which remains preserved for them in heaven.

---

316 Ambrose, *Expos. Lucam* 7.7 (CCSL 14:217.92).
317 Isa. 33:17; cf. Cuthbert's letter on the death of Bede, where Bede quotes this passage. See above, Prologue n. 12.
318 Matt. 22:14.
319 Cf. Ambrose, *Expos. Lucam* 7.9 (CCSL 14:218.109–11).
320 Gal. 3:27.
321 1 John 3:2.
322 Mark 9:2 (9:3).
323 Ps. 50:4 (51:2) (not *iuxta LXX*).

# 360 BEDE: COMMENTARY ON THE GOSPEL OF LUKE

[Luke 9:30–31] **And behold two men were talking with him. And they were Moses and Elijah, appearing in majesty.** Moses and Elijah, one of whom we read was dead and the other taken up into heaven,[324] *appearing in majesty* with the Lord signify the future of all the saints, who at the time of Judgement, whether they are to be found alive in the flesh or to be revived from death tasted in the past, will reign equally with him. For the Apostle testifies: *The dead who are in Christ will rise first. Then we who are alive, who are left, will be taken up together with them in the clouds to meet Christ, into the air, and so we will be always with the Lord.*[325]

In a different interpretation: Moses and Elijah, that is, the lawgiver and the greatest of the prophets, appear and speak with the Lord to show that he is the very one whom all the writings of the Law /206/ and the prophets promised. But they appear not down below, but on the mountain with him, because they alone, who searched with divine understanding, perceive the majesty of holy Scripture that was fulfilled in the Lord. And finally, the Jews deserve to see Moses, but not to follow him as he draws near to God in the mountains.[326] Also when he returns to them, they do not see him without a veil.[327] They know Elijah, but only Elisha with the sons of the prophets observes the triumph of his ascent,[328] because many of us read the words of Scripture here and there, but very few of us understand how exaltedly it gleams with the mysteries of Christ.[329]

[Luke 9:31b] **And they spoke of his decease which he was about to accomplish in Jerusalem.** And up to the present, the Law and the prophets teach everyone they find at the summit of the true faith the mystery of the Lord's dispensation in matching terms.

[Luke 9:32] **But Peter and those who were with him were heavy with sleep. And waking, they saw his majesty, and the two men who stood with him.** The disciples were heavy with sleep not by chance, but for a symbolic reason, namely that *they should see the appearance of the resurrection after* the body's *rest.* The saints, when they are raised up in

---

324 Cf. Deut. 34:5; 4 Kings 2:11.
325 1 Thess. 4:16–17.
326 Cf. Exod. 24:1–2.
327 Cf. Exod. 34:33.
328 Cf. 4 Kings 2:5–15.
329 Intertextual exegesis, since the time of Origen, rested upon the principle that all scripture was 'about' Christ. Bede is articulating this patristic concept of the unified 'mind of Scripture' that alone can reveal true interpretation: see Introduction, 29–35, and Young, *Biblical Exegesis and the Formation of Christian Culture*, esp. ch. 2.

glory, will *see the majesty* of the Lord the more truly, because they will also rejoice in the immortality of his flesh through which they had conquered death.[330] Then they will contemplate Moses and Elijah in glory, because they will better understand how not one jot or one tittle will have passed from the Law,[331] and how the Lord will come not to destroy the Law and the prophets, but to fulfil them.[332]

[Luke 9:33] **And it happened that, as they were departing from him, Peter said to Jesus: Master, it is good for us to be here; and let us make three tabernacles, one for you, and one for Moses, and one for Elijah; not knowing what he said.** How great will be the happiness to be present amid the chorus of angels with a perpetual vision of the Deity, if the transfigured human nature of Christ and the company of the two saints seen for a moment gives so much delight that Peter even wishes them to pause for a celebration so as not to depart! And if he does not know what he says on account of human nature, he nevertheless gives proof of the love innate in himself. For he did not know what he said, for he forgot that the kingdom promised by the Lord to the saints was not in some place on earth, but in heaven, and that he and his fellow apostles, while still burdened with mortal flesh, could not enter the state of immortal life, and that in that age there was no need for a house to be built. But it is a sign of ignorance even to this day; everyone longs to make three tabernacles, for the Law, for the prophets, and for the Gospel, although these cannot at all be separated from one another, having one tabernacle, that is, the Church of God. /207/

[Luke 9:34] **And as he spoke these things, there came a cloud, and overshadowed them.** He who *sought* a material *tabernacle* received a *canopy* in the form of a *cloud*,[333] to teach that the saints are going to be protected in the resurrection not by the shade of houses, but by the glory of the Holy Spirit. About this the Psalmist declares: *But the children of men will put their trust in the protection of your wings.*[334] And in his Apocalypse John says: *And I saw no temple therein. For the Lord Almighty is the temple thereof, and the Lamb.*[335]

[Luke 9:34b–35] **And they were afraid, when they entered into the**

---

330 Ambrose, *Expos. Lucam* 7.17 (CCSL 14:220.194–96).
331 Cf. Matt. 5:18.
332 Cf. Matt. 5:17.
333 Jerome, *Commentarii in Matheum* 3 (CCSL 77:149.284–85).
334 Ps. 35:8 (36:7).
335 Rev. 21:22.

cloud. *And a voice came out of the cloud, saying: This is my beloved Son. Hear him.* *Human weakness cannot endure to bear the sight of greater glory, but shaking all over in soul and body, falls to the earth. The more anyone seeks greater things, the more he falls to lesser things, if he is ignorant of his own capacity.*[336]

Certainly, *the voice of the Father speaking from heaven is heard, which also gives testimony of the Son,*[337] *and teaches Peter – or rather, the other disciples in Peter – the truth, after bearing with their error. 'This is', he says, 'my beloved Son', a tabernacle must be made for him, and he must be obeyed. He is the Son; they are the servants. Moses and Elijah together with you must prepare a tabernacle for the Lord in the innermost part of their heart.*[338]

And take note, just as when the Lord was baptized in the Jordan, so when the Lord was glorified in the mountain, that the mystery of the entire Trinity is made clear, because we will see in the resurrection his glory which we confess in baptism. And not without reason does the Holy Spirit appear here in a shining cloud, and there in a dove,[339] because he who now serves the faith that he perceives with a simple heart, will then contemplate with the light of clear vision what he had believed, and he will be sheltered forever by that very grace by which he will be illuminated.

[Luke 9:36] **And while the voice was uttered, Jesus was found alone.** When the Son started to be proclaimed, his servants immediately departed, lest one think that the Father's voice was directed to them.

In another interpretation: When the voice was uttered in regard to the Son, he himself was found alone, because when he manifests himself to the elect, *God* will be *all in all,*[340] or rather he himself with his followers will be one Christ through all, that is, the head will shine with the body. On account of this unity he said elsewhere: *And no man has ascended into heaven, but he who descended from heaven, the Son of man who is in heaven.*[341]

[Luke 9:36b] **And they held their peace, and told no one in those days any of the things which they had seen.** *A preview of the kingdom to come and the glory of the triumphant one had been* displayed *on the*

---

336 Jerome, *Commentarii in Matheum* 3 (CCSL 77:149.295–99).
337 Cf. John 5:37 & 8:18.
338 Jerome, *Commentarii in Matheum* 3 (CCSL 77:149.285–91).
339 At the Baptism; cf. Matt. 3:16.
340 1 Cor. 15:28.
341 John 3:13.

BOOK THREE 363

*mountain.* Therefore, the disciples hold their peace, /208/ and at the Lord's command they tell no one of the vision until the Son of man shall rise again from the dead, *lest it not* be *believed on account of the greatness of the event, and lest following after such great glory the cross* become *a stumbling block for ignorant souls.*[342]

Chapter 38

99/2 [Luke 9:37–38] **And it happened the day following, when they came down from the mountain, a great multitude met him. And behold a man among the crowd cried out, saying: Master, I beg you, look upon my son, because he is my only one.** The places are suited to the actions: the Lord prays on the mountain, he is transfigured, he reveals the secrets of his majesty to the disciples; descending to the plain, he is intercepted by the rush of the crowd and assailed by the lamentation of miserable people. On high he discloses mysteries to the disciples; below he reproves the multitudes for sins of infidelity. On high he unfolds the voice of the Father to those who were able to follow him; below he drives out evil spirits from those who were being tormented. Even now in accordance with the nature of their merits he does not cease to ascend for some, and descend for others. For as if seeking the depths, he strengthens, teaches, and chastises those who are still earth-bound and beginners, but he glorifies those who are perfected, whose way of life is in heaven, by exalting them more highly, and he informs them more freely about eternal things, and often he teaches those things which cannot even be heard by the multitudes.

[Luke 9:39] **And behold, a spirit seizes him, and he suddenly cries out, and it throws him down and convulses him with foam at the mouth, and bruising him it scarcely departs.** This demoniac, whom the Lord cured when he descended from the mountain, is described by Matthew as a lunatic,[343] while Mark describes him as deaf and dumb.[344] And this signifies those of whom it is written: *A fool is changed as the moon,*[345] who, never remaining in the same state, having been converted now to these faults, and

---
342 Jerome, *Commentarii in Matheum* 3 (CCSL 77:150.316–20).
343 Cf. Matt. 17:14.
344 Cf. Mark 9:24.
345 Ecclus. 27:12.

now to those, wax and wane, the dumb by not confessing the faith, and the deaf by not hearing the word of faith itself to any extent.

[Luke 9:40] **And I begged your disciples to cast it out, and they could not.** With this statement, *he indirectly accuses the apostles, although the impossibility of curing is sometimes blamed not on the weakness of those doing the curing, but on the faith of those who are to be cured, as the Lord says: 'According to your faith, let it be done to you.'*[346]

[Luke 9:41] **And Jesus answering, said: O faithless and perverse generation, how long will I be with you, and suffer you?** *Not that he who was mild and gentle, who 'did not open his mouth, like a lamb before his shearer',*[347] *was overcome by annoyance nor burst out in words of fury; but rather that, like a physician, if he should see a patient acting contrary to his orders, he says: How long should I come to your house, how /209/ long should I waste the skill of my art, with me prescribing one thing, and you doing something else? But he was not so much angry with the man as with the fault, and through one man he accused the Jews of infidelity, so that he immediately added:*[348]

[Luke 9:41b–42] **Bring your son here. And as he was coming to him, the devil threw him down, and convulsed him.** As the boy approaches Jesus, the devil throws him down, and convulses him, because often, having been converted to God after sinning, we are disturbed by new and greater snares of the old enemy, who is acting, of course, either to incite a hatred of virtue, or to avenge the affront of his expulsion. Hence it is, to pass from the specific to the general, that he inflicted so very many serious struggles on the first beginnings of the Church, because he mourned the losses to his kingdom that were suddenly incurred.

[Luke 9:43] **And Jesus rebuked the unclean spirit, and cured the boy, and restored him to his father.** He does not rebuke the boy who suffered the violence, but the devil who inflicted it, because he wishes to correct the sinner by denouncing the vice in particular, and to drive it out by hating it, but he must reinvigorate the man by loving him, until he can restore him cured to the spiritual fathers of the Church.

---

346 Jerome, *Commentarii in Matheum* 3 (CCSL 77:152.363–66); Matt. 9:29.
347 Isa. 53:7.
348 Jerome, *Commentarii in Matheum* 3 (CCSL 77:152.369–76).

BOOK THREE 365

Chapter 39

101/2 [Luke 9:44b] **But while all wondered at all the things that he did, he said to his disciples: Lay up in your hearts these words,** [Luke 9:44c] **for it will happen that the Son of man will be delivered into the hands of men.** Amid the mighty works of divine power, he very frequently insists upon and repeats the squalid deeds of human passion, in order that these deeds not fill men with terror by approaching suddenly, but rather be endured by well-prepared minds. Of course, what he says, 'Lay up', ought to be read more distinctly and with more vigorous force to imply, 'you, who adhere more intimately to my discipleship, to whom I have revealed more openly *the unknowable and hidden things of* my *wisdom*,[349] while others are wondering only at my divine deeds, store away in your minds also the spilling out [*euentum*][350] of my precious blood, by which the world is to be redeemed.'

[Luke 9:45] **But they did not understand this word.** This lack of understanding on the part of the disciples originates not so much from dullness as from love. Still carnal and ignorant of the mystery of the cross, they were unable to believe that the one whom they knew to be the true God was going to die. And because they were accustomed to hear him speaking often in allegories, they thought that what he was saying about his betrayal signified something else allegorically.

102/2 [Luke 9:46] **And the disputation entered into them, which of them should be greater.** Because they had seen that Peter, James, and John were led up onto the mountain, and that something secret was entrusted to them there, but also that the keys of the kingdom of heaven had been promised to Peter earlier, and that the Church was going to be built upon him, they supposed either that these same three were preferred to the others, or that /210/ Peter was preferred to all the apostles. There are those who imagine that this disputation was disturbing to the disciples, because the Lord, according to Matthew, gave the coin taken from the mouth of a fish to those who demanded tribute for himself and for Peter,[351] as if Peter were more eminent that the others, seeing that he was paired with the Lord himself in rendering the tribute. But the careful reader will find

---

349 Ps. 50:8 (51:6).
350 See Introduction, 30–31.
351 Cf. Matt. 17:24–27; Jerome, *Commentarii in Matheum* 3 (CCSL 77:155.450–55).

that this question had been pondered among them, and before the tribute was returned. In fact, Matthew recounts that this happened in Capernaum.[352] And Mark says: *And they came to Capernaum. And when they were in the house, he asked them: What did you treat of on the way? But they held their peace, for on the way they had disputed among themselves, which of them should be greater.*[353] But whether they were disturbed on this occasion, or on that, or on both, *Jesus seeing their disputations, and understanding the causes of their errors, wished to heal the desire for glory with the struggle for humility.*[354]

[Luke 9:47–48] **Taking a child, he says, he set him by him, and he said to them: Whoever receives this child in my name, receives me.** Not only does he plainly teach that the poor of Christ are to be received for his sake by those who wish to be greater, but he also certainly urges them to be infants in evil,[355] and to preserve simplicity without arrogance, love without envy, and devotion without rage, following the pattern of childlike innocence. Hence after he said in a fitting manner: *Whoever receives this child*, he added: *in my name*, evidently so that they themselves should follow the ideal of virtue which a child naturally observes with the active help of reason for the sake of the name of Christ. But because he taught that he is received in the child, obviously because he himself was also born for us as a child,[356] lest it be thought that this was all, he added on and said:

[Luke 9:48b] **And whoever receives me, receives him who sent me**, desiring, of course, that he himself be believed to be like the Father, and as great as he. For the difference, he says, between him and me is insignificant, so that he who receives me may receive him who sent me.

103/8  [Luke 9:49] **And John, answering, said: Master, we saw a certain man casting out devils in your name, and we forbade him, because he does not follow with us.** John, who loved the Lord with special devotion, and for that reason was worthy of being loved in return, thought that the one who did not offer allegiance ought to be excluded from favour. But he is taught that no one should be blocked from the good which he has in part, but should be encouraged towards that which he does not yet have.

---

352  Cf. Matt. 18:1.
353  Mark 9:32–33.
354  Jerome, *Commentarii in Matheum* 3 (CCSL 77:156.483–85).
355  Cf. 1 Cor. 14:20.
356  Cf. Isa. 9:6.

BOOK THREE 367

[Luke 9:50] **And Jesus, he says, said to him: Don't forbid him; for he /211/ that is not against you, is for you.** The Apostle, having learned from this statement, says: But *whether opportunely, or truly, Christ will be preached, and in this also I rejoice, yes, and I will rejoice.*[357] But although he rejoices even in those who do not preach Christ sincerely, and people of this kind who perform miracles in the name of Christ at any time are judged not to be prohibited from saving others, nevertheless their own conscience is not restored to themselves untroubled by such miracles. But rather in that day when they say: *Lord, Lord, have we not prophesied in your name, and cast out devils in your name, and done many miracles in your name?* they will receive the answer, *I never knew you, depart from me, you who do evil.*[358] And so, with regard to heretics and sinful Catholics, we should not renounce and prohibit communal sacraments by which they are with us and not against us, but we should renounce and prohibit dissension contrary to peace and truth, by which they are against us and do not follow the Lord with us.

**Chapter 40**

104/10 [Luke 9:51] **And it happened, when the days of his assumption were being fulfilled, that he steadfastly set his face to go to Jerusalem.** Luke calls the time of the passion, the day of assumption. This time being near at hand, Jesus makes his way slowly to Jerusalem. Let the pagans therefore cease to mock the crucified one as if he were a man. Not only is it certain that he foresaw the time of his crucifixion as if he were God, but also that with steadfast face, that is, with a steady and undaunted spirit, he sought the place where he was about to be crucified like one who was going to be crucified of his own free will.

[Luke 9:53] **And they did not receive him, because his face was of one going to Jerusalem.** Because the Samaritans see that he is going to Jerusalem, they do not receive the Lord.[359] *For the Jews do not have dealings with the Samaritans,* as the evangelist John indicates.[360]

---

357 Phil. 1:18.
358 Matt. 7:22–23.
359 In the omitted verse (Luke 9:52) emissaries of Jesus go into a Samaritan city to make arrangements for him.
360 John 4:9.

[Luke 9:54-55] **And when his disciples James and John had seen this, they said: Lord, do you want us to command fire to come down from heaven and consume them? And turning, he rebuked them, saying: You know not of what spirit you are.** *Great and holy men, who already knew very well that this death that separated the soul from the body was not to be feared, yet, in accordance with the views of those who might fear it, punished some sins with death. In this way they struck useful fear into the living, while at the same time it was not death that harmed those who were punished by death, but sin, which could be increased, if they lived. Those to whom God had given such power of judging did not judge rashly. Hence it is that Elijah*[361] *struck many men with death both by his own hand and by fire brought down from heaven.*[362]

In this example, /212/ although the apostles wanted to seek *fire from heaven to consume those who did not offer hospitality to them, the Lord did not reprehend in them the example set by the holy prophet, but the fact that they were punishing ignorance that was still in the uninstructed. He pointed out to them that they desired not correction with love, but punishment with hate. So after that he taught them what it was to love one's neighbour as one's self.*[363] *Even after the Holy Spirit was poured out,*[364] *such punishments were not completely absent, although they were much more rare than in the Old Testament. For then people in servitude were restrained mainly by fear, but now, free men were sustained chiefly by love. For Ananias and his wife*[365] *also fell lifeless at the words of the apostle Peter, and they were not restored to life, but buried.*[366]

And Paul says *of a certain sinner: 'I have delivered him to Satan for the destruction of the flesh, that his soul may be saved'.*[367]

[Luke 9:56] **The Son of man came not to destroy souls, but to save.** And therefore, he says, you have been signed by his spirit, and you not only imitate his deeds now in deliberating compassionately, but will do so in the future in judging justly.

**105/5** [Luke 9:57] **And it happened, as they walked on the way, that a certain man said to him: I will follow you wherever you go**, and so forth.

---

361 Elijah (NRSV): cf. 3 Kings 18:40; 4 Kings 1:10.
362 Augustine, *De sermone Domini* 1.20.64 (CCSL 35:73.1595-1603).
363 Cf. Matt. 19:19.
364 Cf. Acts 2:4.
365 Cf. Acts 5:1-10.
366 Augustine, *De sermone Domini* 1.20.64 (CCSL 35:74.1607-20).
367 Augustine, *De sermone Domini* 1.20.65 (CCSL 35:74.1623-24); 1 Cor. 5:5.

BOOK THREE 369

The secret dispensation of righteous judgements is wonderful and fearful at the same time. The Samaritans are asked to receive the Lord, and when they were unwilling to do so, Christ forbade that they should be struck down. This man vows to follow, and then he disappears from the scene. Another wishes first to bury his father, and he is urged to preach. Another person who is ready to follow the Lord, desires to give notice of this very thing at home, and he is not permitted to do so. A certain man not following Christ works miracles in the name of Christ, and he is not ordered to be forbidden to do so. But in each of these instances we should say as the Apostle did: *O the depth and the riches of the wisdom and knowledge of God! How incomprehensible are his judgements, and how unsearchable his ways!*;[368] and with Samuel: *Man sees those things that appear, but the Lord beholds the heart.*[369]

[Luke 9:58] **And Jesus said to him: The foxes have holes, and the birds of the air nests; but the Son of man has nowhere to lay his head.** By the words of the Lord *it is shown* that this man who promises obedience *is rejected because when he saw the greatness of the miracles, he wanted to follow the Saviour to seek profit from the miracles of his works, desiring the same thing that Simon Magus wanted to purchase from Peter.*[370] *Such faith is therefore justly condemned by the words of the Lord, and it is said to him: Why do you desire to follow me for the wealth and the profits of the world, when I am so poor that I have not even a little dwelling place, and I do not* /213/ *possess a shelter for myself.*[371]

In another interpretation: *The meaning of this, is that this man was excited by the Lord's miracles. He wanted to follow him so that he could make empty boasts, which is symbolized by the birds, and feign the obedience of a disciple, which is signified by the term 'foxes'. But when he refers to laying down his head, Jesus signified his humility, which had no place in that proud hypocrite.*[372]

[Luke 9:59] **But he said to another: Follow Me. And he said: Allow me first to go, and to bury my father.** He does not refuse discipleship, but

---

368 Rom. 11:33.
369 1 Sam. 16:7.
370 Cf. Acts 8:18–19.
371 Jerome, *Commentarii in Matheum* 1 (CCSL 77:51.1150–57).
372 Augustine, *Quaestiones xui in Matt.* 5 (CCSL 44B:121.4–9). In a phrase that Bede does not quote, Augustine makes clear that the man to whom Jesus addresses the words 'The foxes have holes', etc., is a scribe (Matt. 8:19). Luke merely refers to this person as 'a certain man'.

he desires to follow him in greater freedom after first fulfilling the duty of a father's burial; he is worthy in every respect, on whom the Son of man lays his head, that is, in whose humble breast the divine essence may find a dwelling in which to rest.

[Luke 9:60] **And Jesus said to him: Let the dead bury the dead; but go and preach the kingdom of God.** In this statement, it should be observed *that sometimes in our actions lesser things must be passed over for the benefit of greater things. For who does not know that to bury the dead has the merit of a good deed? Nevertheless, to him who had asked to be released to bury his father it was said: 'Let the dead bury the dead; but go and preach the kingdom of God'. For indeed obedience to this service had to be set aside in favour of the duty of preaching, because by the former he would bury the dead in the earth carnally, but by the latter he would resurrect the dead to life spiritually.*[373]

*And how* can *the dead bury the dead, unless you understand the double death, the one of nature, the other of sin;*[374] the one by which the soul is separated from the flesh, the other by which God is separated from the soul. And *he does not say 'dead believers', but 'their dead', who nonetheless departed the body without faith.*[375]

106/10 [Luke 9:61] **And another said: I will follow you, Lord; but first let me take my leave of those who are at home.** If a disciple who is going to follow the Lord is blamed because he wishes to take his leave even from this worldly home, what will be done to those who, not for some useful end, not for the sake of building the faith, too often do not fear to return to the homes of those whom they have left in the world?

[Luke 9:62] **And Jesus said to him: No man putting his hand to the plough and looking back is fit for the kingdom of God.** For anyone *to put his hand to the plough is* to break up *as it were* the hardness of his heart *with a kind of instrument of remorse* – the wood and iron of the Lord's passion – and *to open* it *to bringing forth the fruits* of good works.[376] If anyone beginning to plough up this hardness of heart is enticed to look back with Lot's wife at those vices which he had left, he is already deprived of the gift of the kingdom to come.

---

373 Gregory, *Moralia* 19.25 (CCSL 143B:990.10–19).
374 Ambrose, *Expos. Lucam* 7.35 (CCSL 14:226.376–78).
375 Augustine, *Quaestiones xui in Matt.* 6 (CCSL 44B:121.2–4).
376 Gregory, *Hom. in Hiezech.* 1.3.16 (CCSL 142:43.319–21).

## Chapter 41

107/10 [Luke 10:1] **And after these things the Lord appointed also seventy-two others.** Just as no one doubts that the twelve apostles exhibit and at the same time /214/ presage the nature of bishops, so also it should be known that these seventy-two manifested the nature of presbyters, that is, of the second order of priests. Yet in the early days of the Church, as apostolic Scripture testifies, they are all called priests, and they are all called bishops; one of these signifies the perfection of wisdom, and the other the activity of pastoral care. It is fitting that seventy-two are sent. Either this was because the Gospel was to be preached to this identical total number of the nations of the world – just as the apostles were appointed for the sake of the twelve tribes of Israel, so also these were appointed for the sake of instructing the foreign nations – or else it was so because *the whole world* which was to be illuminated *by the Gospel of the* supreme and indivisible *Trinity* was made known by this very number of preachers,[377] for it is well known that the sun is accustomed to bring a three-day circuit of its light to the world in a period of seventy-two hours. For likewise the Lord himself calls himself the day, but his apostles the hours, saying: *Are there not twelve hours of the day? If a man walks in the day, he does not stumble.*[378] And in the Psalms it is ordered: *Show forth fittingly his salvation from day to day,*[379] that is, *light from light, true God from true God.*[380] But in many passages of the holy Scriptures as well, the mystery of the Trinity is expressed by three days, especially because the Lord rose again from the dead on the third day. Also, in the Old Testament the people coming to the mount Sinai on the third day received the Law.[381] The same people crossed over the river Jordan, where the grace of baptism was made manifest, on the third day after they reached it.[382]

[Luke 10:1b] **And he sent them two by two before his face into every city and place where he himself was to come.** *Since there are two commandments of love, namely, love of God and of neighbour, and love cannot exist if there are fewer than two people (for no one is properly*

---

377 Augustine, *Quaestiones euang.* 2.14 (CCSL 44B:58.2–3).
378 John 11:9.
379 Ps. 95:2 (96:2).
380 Nicene Creed.
381 Cf. Exod. 19:11 & 16.
382 Cf. Jos. 3:1 & 14.

*said to possess love toward himself, but through affection he reaches out toward another so that love becomes possible), the Lord sends the disciples two by two to preach, in order to signify to us without words that whoever does not have love toward another must by no means undertake the duty of preaching. And it is fittingly said that he sent them 'before his face into every city and place where he himself was to come'. For the Lord follows his preachers, because preaching comes first, and then the Lord comes to the dwelling-place of our soul. Words of exhortation precede, and through them the truth is received in our soul.*[383]

**108/5** [Luke 10:2] **And he said to them: The harvest indeed is great, but the labourers are few. Pray therefore the Lord of the harvest, that he send labourers into his harvest.** *The great harvest signifies the multitude of people, and the few labourers, the scarcity of teachers. These are the workers of whom the Psalmist /215/ speaks: 'Those who sow in tears will reap in joy. Going they went and wept, casting their seeds. But coming they will come with joyfulness, carrying their sheaves'.*[384] *And to speak more plainly, the great harvest is the whole multitude of believers, and the few labourers, the apostles and those who imitate them, who are sent to the harvest.*[385]

**109/5** [Luke 10:3] **Go: Behold I send you as lambs among wolves.** *The scribes and Pharisees, who are the clergy of the Jews, he calls wolves.*[386]

**110/2** [Luke 10:4] **Carry neither purse, nor bag, nor shoes, and salute no man on the road.** *The preacher's trust in God must be so great that although he does not provide for the expenses of the present life, nevertheless he knows with absolute certainty that they will not be lacking for him, lest, while his soul is occupied with temporal things, he does not provide eternal things for others. Likewise, he is forbidden to salute anyone on the road, in order to show with how much haste he ought to proceed on the road of preaching. If anyone should wish these words to be understood as well through allegory, money is enclosed in the purse. But the enclosed money is hidden wisdom. Whoever, therefore, has a word of wisdom, but neglects to spend it on his neighbour, keeps as if it were his money tied up in his purse. And it is written: 'Wisdom that is hid, and a treasure that is*

---

383 Gregory, *Hom. in Euang.* 1.17.1–2 (CCSL 141:117.5–18).
384 Ps. 125:5–6 (126:5–6).
385 Jerome, *Commentarii in Matheum* 1 (CCSL 77:63.1476–85).
386 Cf. Ps.-Jerome, *Expositio euangeliorum* (PL 30:572D).

*not seen, what profit is there in them both?'*[387] *What is meant by the bag save the burdens of the world? And what is meant by shoes in this passage unless they signify examples of dead works that we are warned against? So when anyone undertakes the duty of preaching, it is not fitting that he bear the burden of the affairs of this world, lest while this bends down his neck, he not rise up to preaching the affairs of heaven. And he ought not to admire the examples of the works of fools, lest he believe that his own works, like dead hides, offer protection.*[388] *And everyone who salutes on the road, salutes from the chance occasion of the journey, not from the desire of obtaining the same salute. Whoever therefore preaches not from the love of the eternal fatherland, but preaches salvation to his auditors from a desire for reward, salutes as it were on the road, because he desires salvation for his auditors opportunistically, not intentionally.*[389]

**111/5** [Luke 10:5–6] **Into whatever house you enter, first say: Peace be to this house. And if a son of peace is there, your peace will rest on him; but if not, it will return to you.** *The peace that is offered from the mouth of the preacher either rests in the house, if a son of peace is in it, or returns to the same preacher. For either there will be someone who has been predestined to life, and follows the heavenly word that he hears, or if no one wishes to hear, the preacher himself will not be* /216/ *without fruit, because peace returns to him, since it will be repaid to him by the Lord for the labour of his work. And behold, he who prohibited the bag and the purse from being carried allowed resources and food from the same preaching, for he goes on:*[390]

**112/2** [Luke 10:7] **And in the same house, remain, eating and drinking such things as they have.** *If our peace is received, it is fitting that we remain in the same house, eating and drinking such things as they have, in order to obtain earthly wages from those to whom we are offering the rewards of the heavenly fatherland. Hence Paul likewise, taking these very things to be of no importance, says: 'If we have sown spiritual things among you, is it a great matter if we reap your carnal things?'*[391] *And what is added should be noted:*[392]

---

387 Ecclus. 41:17.
388 Gregory, *Hom. in Euang.* 1.17.5 (CCSL 141:119.76–93).
389 Gregory, *Hom. in Euang.* 1.17.5 (CCSL 141:120.97–101).
390 Gregory, *Hom. in Euang.* 1.17.6–7 (CCSL 141:120.104–12).
391 1 Cor. 9:11.
392 Gregory, *Hom. in Euang.* 1.17.7 (CCSL 141:121.114–20).

[Luke 10:7b] **For the labourer is worthy of his wages**, *because he already receives these same foods of sustenance from the wages of his work, so the wages from the work of preaching begin here, which are achieved there from the vision of the truth. In this matter, it should be considered that two wages are owed for our one work – one on the road, the other in the fatherland: the one that sustains in our work; the other that repays us in the resurrection.*[393]

113/10 [Luke 10:8] **And into whatever city you enter, and they receive you, eat such things as are set before you**, and so forth. In describing the hospitality of diverse households, he at the same time teaches what they ought to do in the cities, namely to share with all the pious people, but to be separated from the society of the impious in every way.

114/2 [Luke 10:10–11] **But into whatever city you enter, and they receive you not, going forth into its streets, say: Even the dust of the city that clings to us, we wipe off against you**, *either for testimony of the earthly labour that they had undertaken in vain on their behalf, or to show to what extent they sought nothing earthly from them, in that they do not even permit the dust from their land to cling to them.*[394]

In another interpretation: The feet of the disciples signify the work of preaching itself and how it is carried out. But the dust with which they are bestrewn is the levity of earthly thought, from which even the most learned teachers are not exempt, although they exert themselves with great concern and incessantly on behalf of their pupils with salutary attention, and as it were on the highways of the world, they hardly ever gather the dust of the land with their heel. Those, therefore, who have received the word turn the afflictions and cares of the teachers, which they endured on their behalf, into evidence of their own humility. But those who have scorned teaching turn the labours and perils of their teachers and the weariness of their cares into a testimony of their damnation. And this is that same dust which is commanded to be wiped off against those who despise the Gospel, and from which their feet are to be washed by good hearers of the evangelists, or rather they are said to have been washed by the Saviour himself. /217/

[Luke 10:12] **And I say to you, it will be more tolerable on that day for Sodom, than for that city.** The Sodomites indeed, among so many shameful acts of the flesh and of the spirit with which they were insatiably

---

393 Gregory, *Hom. in Euang.* 1.17.7 (CCSL 141:121.120–26).
394 Augustine, *Quaestiones xvii in Matt.* 7 (CCSL 44B:122.2–5).

BOOK THREE 375

enflamed, also lacked hospitality, as Ezekiel attests,[395] but no guests were found among them like the Jewish prophets, and like the apostles. And Lot indeed was just to all appearances, and according to what we have heard, but he is not reported to have taught anything or to have done any miracles there. And therefore, *to whom much is given, of him much will be required,*[396] and *the mighty will be mightily tormented.*[397]
115/5 [Luke 10:13] **Woe to you, Chorazin, woe to you, Bethsaida.** Chorazin, Bethsaida, and Capernaum, and Tiberias, which John names,[398] are cities of Galilee located on the shore of Lake Gennesaret, which is fed by the river Jordan, and is also called by the evangelists the Sea of Galilee, or the Sea of Tiberias. Therefore the Lord laments over the cities that after such great miracles and deeds of power did not repent. And worse than the Gentiles, who only violated natural law, these cities did not fear, after scorning the written Law, to despise even the Son of God and being ungrateful, to scorn grace.
[Luke 10:13b] **For if in Tyre or Sidon the deeds of power had been done that have been done in you, they would have repented long ago, sitting in sackcloth and ashes.** We see today that the saying of the Saviour has been fulfilled, because, of course, Chorazin and Bethsaida would not believe when the Lord was present. But Tyre and Sidon not only were friendly once to David and Solomon,[399] but also believed after hearing the disciples of Christ proclaim the Gospel. And they received the faith with such great devotion, that all the citizens *with their wives and children* accompanied the Apostle Paul as he was departing *outside the city*,[400] so that in a very beautiful spectacle a great crowd of people escorted the strangers, who were exceedingly few but most dear on account of the faith of Christ, to the ships to say farewell.[401] But why the Gospel was not preached long ago to these, who were able to believe, but rather to the Jews, who would not believe, is for him to know, *all* of whose *ways are mercy and truth.*[402] Truly it is as the Lord says: *they would have repented, sitting in sackcloth and ashes.* 'In sackcloth', which is woven from the hair of she-goats, signifies

395 Cf. Ezek. 16:49.
396 Luke 12:48.
397 Wisd. 6:7.
398 Cf. John 6:1 & 23.
399 Cf. 2 Sam. 5:11; 3 Kings 5:1.
400 Acts 21:5.
401 Cf. Acts 21:6.
402 Ps. 24:10 (25:10).

the bitter memory of pricking sin, in which on the Day of Judgement those on the Lord's left side are to be clothed. And 'in ashes' demonstrates the contemplation of death, by which the whole mass of the human race must be returned to dust. Finally, 'sitting' signifies the humbling of one's own conscience, of which the Psalmist says: *Rise after you have sat*,[403] which is to say: *Be /218/ humbled therefore under the mighty hand of God, so that he may exalt you in the time of visitation.*[404]

[Luke 10:15] **And you, Capernaum, who were exalted to heaven, you will be thrust down to hell.** There is a *double* meaning in this sentence. *Either you will be* thrust down *to hell, because you most insolently offered resistance against my preaching, or because you were exalted to heaven by my hospitality, and were privileged by my miracles and acts of power, you will be punished with greater torments, because you did not want to believe them.*[405] And lest anyone think this chiding applies only to the cities or persons who despised the Lord when they saw him in the flesh, and not to all who still today disdain the words of the Gospel, he fittingly went on, saying:

116/1 [Luke 10:16] **He who hears you, hears me, and he who despises you, despises me**, so that anyone in hearing or despising a preacher of the Gospel might learn that he does not despise or hear some ordinary person, but the Lord Saviour, or rather the Father himself. For he goes on:

[Luke 10:16b] **And he who despises me, despises him who sent me**, because beyond doubt the teacher is heard in the disciple, and the father is honoured in the son. *He who despises you, despises me*, can also be understood in this way: He who does not show mercy to *one of the least of these my brothers*,[406] does not show it to me, because I myself also took the form of a slave and the appearance of a poor man for their sake. *And he who despises me*, not willing to believe God and treating the Son of God with contempt, *despises him who sent me*, because *I and the Father are one.*[407]

117/10 [Luke 10:17] **And the seventy-two returned with joy, saying: Lord, the devils also are subject to us in your name.** Indeed, they fittingly make a profession of faith, deferring the honour to the name of

---

403 Ps. 126:2 (127:2).
404 1 Peter 5:6.
405 Jerome, *Commentarii in Matheum* 2 (CCSL 77:84.206–11).
406 Matt. 25:40.
407 John 10:30.

Christ, but since they rejoice in their powers while their faith is still weak, see what they hear:

[Luke 10:18] **And he said to them: I saw Satan like lightning falling from heaven**, that is: 'Not only do I see him, but I saw him formerly when he fell.' And the fact that he said: *like lightning*, signifies either that he fell headlong from heaven to the depths, or that after being cast down he still *transforms himself into an angel of light*.[408] Therefore because he saw the disciples puffed up by the working of miracles, he frightens them with a warning example, and summons them back to the humiliation of the one who first fell because of pride, so that those who keep in mind that Satan was ejected from heaven on account of pride, may recognize how much more those brought forth from earth deserve to be humbled if they are given to pride.

[Luke 10:19] **Behold, I have given you power to tread upon serpents and scorpions, and upon all the power of the enemy, and nothing will hurt you**, that is, to eject the whole race of impure spirits from possessed bodies, /219/ although it can also very correctly be taken literally. Indeed, not only does Paul, when he is attacked by a viper, suffer no harm,[409] but also John, as history reports, is not harmed when he drinks poison.[410] I think there is a difference between serpents which inflict injury by their teeth and scorpions by their tail, because on the one hand serpents raging openly signify human beings, and on the other, scorpions lying secretly in ambush signify devils. Serpents cast the poisons of perverted beliefs against virtues that are just forming; scorpions strive to corrupt accomplished virtues at the end.

[Luke 10:20] **But yet do not rejoice in this, that spirits are subject to you**. They are forbidden to rejoice over the subjection of spirits when they are flesh, because *to cast out* spirits, just as *also to do other miracles, sometimes is not due to the merit of the one who does it, but the invocation of the name of Christ does it, to the condemnation of those who invoke it; or it is granted in the interest of those who see and hear, so that although they despise the men doing the miracles, nevertheless they honour God, at the invocation of whom so many miracles are performed. For also in the*

---

408 2 Cor. 11:14.
409 Cf. Acts 28:3–5.
410 We have been unable to trace Bede's source for this story, which goes back to the apocryphal Acts of John (s. ii¹) and can be found in *The Golden Legend*. See Elliot, *A Collection of Apocryphal Christian Literature*, 343–45.

378 BEDE: *COMMENTARY ON THE GOSPEL OF LUKE*

*Acts of the Apostles the sons of Sceva were seen to cast out devils,*[411] *and the apostle Judas with the soul of a traitor is said to have performed many miracles among the other apostles.*[412]

[Luke 10:20b] **But rejoice in this, that your names are written in heaven.** If Satan, he says, lost his seat in heaven with his companions through pride, it is not proper for you to rejoice in their humiliation, but in your elevation, seeing that you who are humble, being raised up, ascend to where they fell. And one should not think in a childish fashion that God writes the good in heaven, the bad in the earth, (as Jeremiah says: *Let all who forsake you be confounded, let all departing be written in the earth)*[413] so that he will not forget. Rather it is to be understood in a salutary manner that whoever has performed works whether heavenly or earthly is noted down by these as if in writing, fixed eternally in the memory of God.

## Chapter 42

**118/5** [Luke 10:21] **In that same hour, he rejoiced in the Holy Spirit, and said: I confess to you, Father, Lord of heaven and earth, ...** *Confession does not always signify repentance, but also giving thanks, as we frequently read in the Psalms. Let those who falsely declare that the Saviour was not born but created,*[414] *hear that he calls the Lord of heaven and earth his Father. For if he is himself a creature, and a creature can call his maker Father, it was foolish not to call him likewise the Lord or Father both of himself and of heaven and earth.*[415]

[Luke 10:21b] **Because you have hidden these things from the wise and the prudent, and have /220/ revealed them to little ones.** He gives thanks and rejoices in the Father, because his advent revealed mysteries to the apostles, which the scribes and the Pharisees, who seemed to themselves wise and prudent in their sight, had no knowledge of. *'Wisdom is justified by her children.'*[416] In this he beautifully opposed not the foolish and the stupid, but little ones, that is, the humble, to the wise and the prudent,

---

411 Cf. Acts 19:13–16.
412 Jerome, *Commentarii in Matheum* 1 (CCSL 77:45.996–1006).
413 Jer. 17:13; cf. Augustine, *Contra aduers.* 1.20.44 (CCSL 49:76–77).
414 I.e., the Arians.
415 Jerome, *Commentarii in Matheum* 2 (CCSL 77:85.232–38).
416 Jerome, *Commentarii in Matheum* 2 (CCSL 77:85.240–44); Luke 7:35.

to show that he condemned pride, not acumen, because this humility is the key, about which he elsewhere says: *You have taken away the key of knowledge,*[417] that is, the humility of the faith of Christ, by which you could have arrived at the acknowledgement of his divinity, but which you despised and preferred to cast it away.

[Luke 10:21c] **Yes, Father, for so it was pleasing in your sight.** *In these words of the Lord, we receive examples of humility, in order that we not presume rashly to discuss heaven's purpose in calling some and rejecting others. For after he had introduced both, he did not launch into an explanation, but said, 'so it was pleasing to God', showing certainly that what was pleasing to the just one cannot be unjust. Hence also, when, paying wages to the labourers in the vineyard, he gave equal pay to some workers who were unequal in labour, and when one who had sweated more at work asked for more in pay, he said: 'Did you not agree with me for a denarius? I will also give to this last the same as to you. Or, is it not lawful for me to do what I will?'*[418] *In all these things that are arranged externally, the clear reason for the account is the justice of the hidden will.*[419]

**119/3** [Luke 10:22] **All things have been handed over to me by my Father.** *When you read 'all things', you recognize Christ as the omnipotent, immaculate, not base-born son of the Father. When you read 'handed over', you confess the Son, to whom all things belong by nature, by right of his being of one substance [with the Father], not conferred as a gift by grace.*[420] But 'all things' that he says were handed over to him must be understood not as elements of the world, which he himself created, but those things by which the Father revealed the mysteries of the Son by the Spirit to little ones, over whose salvation the Son rejoices in the Holy Spirit when he said these things. Concerning all these things he says elsewhere: *All that the Father gives to me will come to me.*[421]

[Luke 10:22b] **And no one knows who the Son is, but the Father, and who the Father is, but the Son, and to whom the Son will reveal him.** *This must not be understood to mean that the Son can be* known *by no one but the Father alone, and the Father not only by the Son, but also by those to whom the Son will reveal him.* But what he says, *'and to whom the Son*

---

417 Luke 11:52.
418 Matt. 20:13–15.
419 Gregory, *Moralia* 25.14 (CCSL 143B:1258.17–28).
420 Ambrose, *Expos. Lucam* 7.67 (CCSL 14:237.690–93).
421 John 6:37.

*will reveal him'*, must be referred to both, *so that we may understand both the Father and the Son himself to be revealed by the Son.*[422] /221/

**120/5** [Luke 10:23] **And turning to his disciples, he said: Blessed are the eyes that see the things which you see.** Not the eyes of the scribes and the Pharisees, which can see only the body of the Lord, but those blessed eyes which can recognize the mysteries, concerning which it is said: *and you have revealed them to little ones.*[423] Blessed are the eyes of the little ones to whom the Son deigns to reveal both himself and his Father.

[Luke 10:24] **For I say to you, that many prophets and kings have desired to see the things that you see, and have not seen them, and to hear the things that you hear, and have not heard them.** *Abraham rejoiced that he might see the day* of Christ, *and he saw and was glad.*[424] Likewise Isaiah and Micah[425] and many other prophets saw the glory of the Lord, who for that reason were also called 'seers'. But all these, beholding and greeting from afar, saw *in a mirror and darkly.*[426] However, the apostles, having the Lord in their presence, and eating with him, and learning whatever they wished by asking him, did not have any need at all to be taught by angels or by various kinds of visions. Indeed, those whom Luke calls 'many prophets and kings', Matthew more plainly calls 'prophets and just men'.[427] For these just men are great kings, because they know how not to succumb to the disturbances of their temptations by obeying them, but to take command by ruling them.

## Chapter 43

**121/2** [Luke 10:25] **And behold a certain lawyer stood up, tempting him, and saying: Master, what must I do to possess eternal life?** The lawyer who, tempting Christ, asks about eternal life, took the opportunity, as I think, to tempt the Lord about his own words, when he said: *But rejoice in this, that your names are written in heaven.*[428] But Christ makes clear by this very temptation directed against him what is that true confession of the

---

422 Augustine, *Quaestiones euang.* 1.1 (CCSL 44B:7.6–9).
423 Luke 10:21.
424 John 8:56.
425 Cf. Isa. 6:1; Micah 1:1.
426 1 Cor. 13:12.
427 Cf. Matt. 13:17.
428 Luke 10:20.

Lord that he spoke of to the Father: *Because you have hidden these things from the wise and the prudent, and have revealed them to little ones.*[429]

[Luke 10:26–27] **But he said to him: What is written in the Law? How do you read it? He answering, said: You shall love the Lord your God with your whole heart, and your whole soul, and with all your strength, and with all your mind; and your neighbour as yourself.** When he responds to the lawyer, the Saviour shows us the perfect path of heavenly life. First, he says to him when the latter sets forth the words of the Law about the love of God and neighbour:

[Luke 10:28] **You have answered right; do this, and you will live.** Then, after setting forth a parable, he adds by way of reply to the lawyer, who says that the *one who showed mercy to him* was the neighbour of the wounded man: *Go, and do likewise*,[430] that is, remember to love and sustain your neighbour in need /222/ with the devotion of such mercy, openly declaring that this alone is the love that leads to eternal life – not what is vaunted in speech, but what is carried out in deed.

**122**/10 [Luke 10:29] **But he, willing to justify himself, said to Jesus: And who is my neighbour?** What madness of vainglory! The lawyer for the sake of gaining the favour of the crowd, in order to boast that he had replied wisely, acknowledges, in response to what the Saviour wise and prudent in the Law says, that he is ignorant of the first commandment of the Law.[431] For he does not desire to be humble with the little ones of Christ, but to justify himself, refusing to receive the blessed eyes of the doves washed with the milk of innocence[432] with which he could see the mysteries of Christ. Indeed, the Lord tempered his response to him in order to teach that everyone is a neighbour who shows mercy to anyone whomsoever, and yet to signify these things by this parable, specifically to signify the Son of God himself, who deigned to become our neighbour by his assumption of humanity. We must not interpret the neighbour, whom we are commanded to love as ourselves, to be above Christ, in such a way as to weaken and set aside the moral teachings of mutual brotherhood which are taught under the rules of allegory.

[Luke 10:30] **And Jesus looking up, said: A certain man went down from Jerusalem to Jericho.** This man *is understood as Adam in the human*

---

429 Luke 10:21.
430 Luke 10:37.
431 Cf. Luke 10:21.
432 Cf. Song 5:12.

*race, and Jerusalem, that city of heavenly peace. Adam, having fallen from its blessedness, came into this mortal and miserable life. Jericho, which means 'moon', aptly signifies* by its fluctuating and unpredictable eclipses this life, which is always uncertain.[433]

[Luke 10:30b] **And he fell among robbers, ...** Take the *robbers as the devil and his angels,* among whom he fell, because he 'went down'.[434] For unless he first swelled up within, he would not so easily have fallen when tempted from without. For the proverb is very true which says: For *the spirit is lifted up before a fall.*[435]

[Luke 10:30c] **Who also stripped him, ...** That is to say, they stripped him of the glory of immortality and the clothing of innocence. For this is the first robe, with which, according to another parable, the prodigal son is adorned through his repentance on his return,[436] and by the loss of which those first humans knew *that they were naked,* and clothed themselves in tunics made of the skins of mortal nature.[437]

[Luke 10:30d] **And having inflicted him with wounds, they went away, leaving him half-dead.** The wounds are the sins[438] with which, by violating the integrity of human nature, they planted in weary flesh as a kind of seedbed, as I might call it, in which death would grow. And they 'went away', not by ceasing in any measure from their plots, /223/ but by concealing the deceptions of their plots. They left him half-dead, because they had the power to deprive him of the blessedness of immortal life, but not to destroy his sense of reason. For *in the part where he can* know *and recognize God, the man is alive, but in the part where he wastes away from sins,*[439] and grows faint from misery, the same man is dead, and disfigured by the deadly wound.

[Luke 10:31–32] **And it chanced, that a priest went down by the same way, and seeing him, passed by. In like manner also a Levite, when he was near the place and saw him, passed by.** *The priest and the Levite, who after seeing the wounded man, passed by,* is *the priesthood and ministry of the Old Testament,*[440] where the wounds of the feeble world

---

433 Augustine, *Quaestiones euang.* 2.19 (CCSL 44B:62.3–5).
434 Augustine, *Quaestiones euang.* 2.19 (CCSL 44B:62.6–7).
435 Prov. 16:18.
436 Cf. Luke 15:22.
437 Cf. Gen. 3:7.
438 Cf. Ps.-Jerome, *Expositio euangeliorum* (PL 30:573A).
439 Augustine, *Quaestiones euang.* 2.19 (CCSL 44B:62.8–10).
440 Augustine, *Quaestiones euang.* 2.19 (CCSL 44B:62.11–12).

could only be shown by the commandments of the Law, but not treated, because *it is impossible*, as the Apostle says, *for sins to be taken away with the blood* of calves and sheep *and goats.*[441]

[Luke 10:33] **But a Samaritan, being on his journey, came near him, and seeing him, was moved with compassion.** The Samaritan, which means 'preserver', signifies the Lord,[442] and it is to him that the Prophet prays that these robbers not be able to attack, saying: *Keep me from the snare, which they have laid for me, and from the stumbling blocks of those who work iniquity.*[443] *For us men and for our salvation descending from heaven,*[444] he took the journey of the present life, and came near him who languished under the wounds inflicted on him, that is, *being made in the likeness of men, and in habit found as a man,*[445] he became *a fellow by taking on our suffering, and a neighbour by the consolation of his mercy.*[446]

[Luke 10:34] **And going up to him, bound up his wounds, pouring on oil and wine.** He restrained the sins that he found in men by setting himself against them, arousing hope of forgiveness in penitents, and fear of punishment in sinners. For he binds up wounds when he orders: *Do penance*; he pours on oil when he adds: *For the kingdom of heaven is at hand.*[447] And he pours on wine when he says: *Every tree that does not yield good fruit will be cut down and cast into the fire.*[448]

[Luke 10:34b] **And setting him on his own beast, he brought him to an inn, and took care of him.** *His beast is the flesh in which he deigned to come to us.*[449] He set the wounded man on it, because *he bore our sins in his body on the tree,*[450] and in accordance with another parable, having found the sheep that had wandered off, having set it on his shoulders, he bore it back to the flock.[451] And so *to be set on a beast is to believe in the*

---

441 Hebr. 10:4.
442 Cf. Augustine, *Quaestiones euang.* 2.19 (CCSL 44B:62.13–14); Ambrose, *Expos. Lucam* 7.24.
443 Ps. 140:9 (141:9).
444 Nicene Creed.
445 Phil. 2:7.
446 Ambrose, *Expos. Lucam* 7.74 (CCSL 14:239.764–66).
447 Matt. 3:2. This interpretation of the binding of the wounds as penance is found in Ps.-Jerome, *Expositio euangeliorum* (PL 30:573A).
448 Matt. 3:10.
449 Augustine, *Quaestiones euang.* 2.19 (CCSL 44B:63.17–18).
450 1 Pet. 2:24.
451 Cf. Luke 15:4–5.

incarnation /224/ *of Christ itself*,⁴⁵² and to be initiated into his mysteries as well as to be protected from the assault of the enemy. The inn *is the present*⁴⁵³ *Church, where travellers returning from* this *pilgrimage to the heavenly kingdom are refreshed.*⁴⁵⁴ And fittingly, having set him on a beast, he brought him to an inn, because no one, unless he is baptized, unless he is united to the body of Christ, will enter the Church.

[Luke 10:35] **And the next day he took out two denarii, and gave them to the innkeeper, and said: Take care of him.** *The 'next day' is after the resurrection of the Lord.*⁴⁵⁵ Prior to that he had given light through the grace of his Gospel to those who were seated in the dark and in the shadow of death, but the splendour of the eternal light shone forth stronger after the resurrection was proclaimed. The two denarii are the two Testaments, in which the name and image of the eternal King is contained.⁴⁵⁶ *For the end of the Law is Christ.*⁴⁵⁷ On the next day, after they were taken out, the denarii are given to the innkeeper, because *then he opened their understanding, that they might understand the Scriptures.*⁴⁵⁸ On the next day the innkeeper took the denarii, for the price of which he would take care of the wounded man, because when the Holy Spirit came, he taught the apostles the whole truth,⁴⁵⁹ by which they were able to instruct the Gentiles and to preach the Gospel.⁴⁶⁰

[Luke 10:35b] **And whatever you spend over and above, when I return, I will repay you.** The innkeeper spends 'over and above', what he did not receive in the two denarii, when the Apostle says: *Now concerning virgins, I have no commandment of the Lord, but I give counsel,*⁴⁶¹ and likewise: *The Lord also ordained that they who preach*

---

452 Augustine, *Quaestiones euang.* 2.19 (CCSL 44B:63.18–19).
453 The phrase 'present Church' is characteristic of Bede: as O'Brien explains (*Bede's Temple*, 68–70) in connection with this passage, Bede echoes Gregory the Great's use of the term to denote the 'institution where good and bad were all mixed together, only to be separated when the elect enter the kingdom of heaven' (68), but avoids the Augustinian sense of a 'mixed Church' of both damned and elect.
454 Augustine, *Quaestiones euang.* 2.19 (CCSL 44B:63.19–21).
455 Augustine, *Quaestiones euang.* 2.19 (CCSL 44B:63.21).
456 Cf. Ambrose, *Expos. Lucam* 7.80 (CCSL 14:240).
457 Rom. 10:4.
458 Luke 24:45.
459 Cf. John 16:13.
460 The innkeeper as teacher: cf. Ps.-Jerome, *Expositio euangeliorum* (PL 30:573B).
461 1 Cor. 7:25; cf. Augustine, *Quaestiones euang.* 2.19 (CCSL 44B:63.27–28).

the Gospel should live by the Gospel,[462] but we have not used this power,[463] lest we should be a burden to any of you.[464] Returning to him, the debtor repays what he had promised, because the Lord, coming in judgement, says: *Because you have been faithful over a few things, I will place you over many things; enter into the joy of your Lord.*[465]

[Luke 10:36-37] **Which of these three, in your opinion, was neighbour to him who fell among the robbers? But he said: He who showed mercy to him**. On the literal level the Lord's meaning is clear, that no one is more a neighbour to us than he who shows mercy, if one who was neither a priest nor a Levite from the same nation and moreover born and bred in the same city, but the inhabitant of a foreign nation, became a neighbour to a citizen of Jerusalem, because he showed more mercy. But in a more mystical sense, since no one is more a neighbour than he who cares for our wounds, let us love him as our Lord God, let us love him as our neighbour. For nothing is as much a neighbour as the head is to the limbs. Likewise let us love him who is an imitator of Christ. For this is what follows: /225/

[Luke 10:37b] **And Jesus said to him: Go, and do likewise**. That is, to show clearly that you truly love your neighbour as yourself, do whatever you are able to do devoutly for the relief of either his bodily or his spiritual need.

## Chapter 44

[Luke 10:38-39] **Now it happened as they went that he entered into a certain town, and a certain woman named Martha received him into her house. And she had a sister called Mary,** ... This passage is connected to the above one in a very beautiful way, because the former signifies the love of God and neighbour by words and parables, but this one, by the facts themselves and in truth. Indeed, these two sisters, beloved by the Lord, reveal the two spiritual lives by which in the present age the holy Church conducts itself: Martha, of course, the active life, by which we are joined to our neighbour in love; and Mary the contemplative life,

---

462  1 Cor. 9:14.
463  1 Cor. 9:12.
464  1 Thess. 2:9.
465  Matt. 25:21.

by which we sigh for the love of God. *For the active life is to give bread to the hungry, to teach the ignorant with the eloquence of wisdom, to correct the erring, to recall the haughty neighbour to the path of humility, to care for the sick, to distribute to everyone individually what they need, and, for those entrusted to us, to foresee how they may be able to subsist. But the contemplative life is to maintain the love of God and neighbour with the whole heart, but to refrain from action on the outside, to cling to an ardent desire for the Creator alone, so that it is now pleasing to do nothing save, spurning all cares, to burn to see the face of its Creator, so that now it will know how to carry the weight of corruptible flesh with lamentation, and to seek with all its desires to attend those choirs of angels singing hymns, to mingle with the heavenly citizens, and to rejoice over eternal incorruptibility in the sight of God.*[466]

[Luke 10:39b–40] **Who sitting also at the Lord's feet, heard his word. But Martha was busy with frequent service, ...** There is no one who doubts that these correspond to each way of life. The uniform perfection of the contemplative life is indeed to have a soul divested from all earthly matters, and to unite it to Christ, as much as human weakness permits. But the teacher of the Gentiles, who relates his labours and perils on land and sea for Christ in the abundant words of his epistles, reveals how constant the service of the active life is. In them he recorded visions and revelations he had received from the Lord, and thus showed that he was no less perfect in contemplative power, which very few can imitate. Hence, he says: *For if we depart from our mind, it is for God; if we are reasonable, it is for you.*[467]

[Luke 10:40b] **Who stood and said: Lord, have you no care that my sister has left me alone to serve? Tell her therefore to help me.** /226/ She speaks in the character of those who are still ignorant of divine contemplation, and consider only the work of brotherly love, which they have learned is pleasing to God, and therefore they believe that all who wish to be devoted to Christ should be consigned to that. And it is well said that Martha stood, and Mary sat at the feet of the Lord, because the active life sweats mightily in the laborious struggle, but the contemplative life, when the disturbances of vices have been subdued, enjoys to the full the long-desired peace of mind in Christ.

[Luke 10:41–42] **And the Lord answering, said to her: Martha, Martha, you are anxious, and are troubled about many things; but one**

---

466 Gregory, *Hom. in Hiezech.* 2.2.8 (CCSL 142:230.187–99).
467 2 Cor. 5:13.

thing is necessary. The blessed David, defining the one thing necessary for man, desires to cling perpetually to God, saying: *But it is good for me to adhere to my God, to put my hope in the Lord God.*[468] And elsewhere: *One thing I have asked of the Lord, this will I seek after: that I may dwell in the house of the Lord all the days of my life, that I may see the delight of the Lord, and may visit his holy temple.*[469] *Therefore there is one and only one 'theoria', that is, contemplation, of God, to which all the merits of good works, and the universal application to the virtues, are rightly subordinated.*[470]

[Luke 10:42b] **Mary has chosen the best part, which will not be taken away from her.** *Notice that the part of Martha is not censured, but that of Mary is praised. For he does not say that Mary chose the good part, but the 'best part', in order that the part of Martha might also be shown to be good. And why the part of Mary is best is implied when it is said: 'which will not be taken away from her', because the active life ends with the body. For who in the eternal home offers bread to the hungry, where no one is hungry? Who gives drink to the thirsty, where no one thirsts? Who buries the dead, where no one is dead? Therefore, the active life is taken away with the present age. But the contemplative life begins here, to be perfected in the heavenly home, because the fire of love which begins to burn here, when it sees the very one whom it loves, burns more fiercely in love. Therefore, the contemplative life is not taken away at all, because it is perfected when the light of the present age is removed.*[471]

## Chapter 45

123/5 [Luke 11:1] **And it happened, when he was in a certain place praying, that when he ceased, one of his disciples said to him: Lord, teach us to pray, as John taught his disciples.** After the story of the sisters, who signified the two lives of the Church, the Lord is purposely said to have prayed himself, and to have taught his disciples how to pray, because not only does the prayer that he taught contain in itself the hidden meaning of both ways of life, but also the fulfilment of these lives must be

---

468 Ps. 72:28 (73:28).
469 Ps. 26:4 (27:4).
470 Cassian, *Collationes* 23.3 (CSEL 13:642:11–13).
471 Gregory, *Hom. in Hiezech.* 2.2.9 (CCSL 142:231.219–32).

obtained by us not by our exertions but by prayers. And because Luke had frequently described the Saviour praying, he implies what he achieved by praying, who certainly never entreated for himself, but for us, /227/ when at the end of the prayer, he reports that the disciples ask how they ought to pray.

[Luke 11:2–4] **And he said to them: When you pray, say: Father, hallowed be your name. Your kingdom come. Give us today our daily bread. And forgive us our sins, for we ourselves also forgive everyone indebted to us. And lead us not into temptation.** *In the evangelist Matthew the Lord's prayer is seen to contain seven petitions, in three of which eternal things are asked for, and in the remaining four, temporal things, which are nevertheless necessary for the sake of obtaining eternal things. For what we say: 'Hallowed be your name. Your kingdom come. Your will be done on earth as it is in heaven',*[472] *some persons have understood as 'in spirit and body', and this is not absurd. These things must be retained in every respect everlastingly. They are begun here, and to the extent that we advance, they are increased in us. But the perfect things, because we must hope for them in the other life, will always be possessed. But what we say: 'Give us today our daily bread. And forgive us our debts, as we also forgive our debtors. And lead us not into temptation. But deliver us from evil',*[473] *who does not see that this pertains to the needs of the present life? Therefore, in that eternal life, where we hope always to be, not only the sanctification of the name of God, but also his kingdom and his will, will remain perfectly and immortally in our spirit and body. But the bread is called 'daily', because it is necessary here, as much as must be allotted to spirit and flesh, whether it be understood spiritually or carnally or both ways. The forgiveness that we ask for is here, where there is the commission of the sins. Here, there are the temptations that either attract us or drive us to sin. Here finally is the evil from which we desire to be freed. But there, there are none of these things.*[474]

*The evangelist Luke included in the Lord's prayer not seven petitions, but five. He certainly did not differ from that other evangelist, but he indicates how those seven ought to be understood by his very conciseness. Of course, the name of God is sanctified in spirit, but the kingdom of God is going to come in the resurrection of the flesh. Therefore Luke, showing that*

---

472 Matt. 6:9–10.
473 Matt. 6:11–13.
474 Augustine, *Enchiridion* 115 (CCSL 46:110.12–35).

*the third petition*[475] *is in a certain way the repetition of the two previous ones, caused it to be understood more thoroughly by omitting it. Then he added those three about daily bread, about forgiveness of sins, and about avoiding temptation. But indeed, he did not put at the end what Matthew did, 'But deliver us from evil', so that we might understand that what was previously said about temptation applies to it. For that reason, Matthew certainly says, 'But deliver'; he does not say, 'And deliver', as if showing that it is one petition* /228/ *(don't do this, but this), so that everyone may know that they are delivered from evil, because they are not led into temptation.*[476]

## Chapter 46

124/10 [Luke 11:5-6] **And he said to them: Which of you will have a friend, and will go to him at midnight, and will say to him: Friend, lend me three loaves of bread, because a friend of mine has come from his journey to me, and I have nothing to set before him.** The Saviour not only teaches the form of the prayer when asked by the disciple, but also the urgency and frequency of praying. Therefore, *the friend to whom we come at midnight* is understood to be God himself, to whom we must kneel down *in the midst of tribulation*, and we must urgently beg for three loaves of bread, that is, *an understanding of the Trinity, whereby the labours of the present life are lightened.*[477] The friend who has come from his journey is our spirit, which withdraws from us as often as it wanders outside in search of earthly and temporal things. But it returns, and desires to be refreshed with heavenly nourishment, whenever it returns to itself and begins to meditate divine and spiritual things. Concerning this, he who begged added (and it is lovely that he did) that he had nothing to set before him, since after the darkness of the world, nothing pleases the soul sighing for God except to think about him, to speak about him, to contemplate him. It has enough to do just to contemplate the joy of the most high Trinity and for that purpose to arrive at contemplation more fully.

[Luke 11:7] **And he from within would say: Do not trouble me, the door is now shut, and my children are with me in bed; I cannot rise and**

---

475 'Your will be done on earth as it is in heaven' (Matt. 6:10).
476 Augustine, *Enchiridion* 116 (CCSL 46:111.36–50).
477 Augustine, *Quaestiones euang.* 2.21 (CCSL 44B:64.1–5).

give you anything. The door of the heavenly friend is an understanding of speech, which the Apostle prays to be opened to him for the sake of speaking of the mystery of Christ.[478] And it is shut by a time *of hunger for the word, when understanding* is not given. *And those who preached evangelical wisdom, dispensing as it were bread through the whole world, are the children of the father of the family already in secret rest with the Lord. Nevertheless, through prayer it happens that one desiring understanding may receive it from God himself, even if there is no man by whom wisdom may be preached.*[479]

[Luke 11:8] **Yet if he should continue knocking, I say to you, although he will not rise and give him anything because he is his friend; yet, because of his importunity, he will rise, and give him as much as he needs.**

125/5 [Luke 11:9] **And I say to you, Ask, and it will be given you, seek, and you will find, knock, and it will be opened to you.** *The comparison is from the lesser.*[480] *For if a friendly man rises up from his bed, and gives, compelled not by friendship, but by weariness, how much more does God give, who gives lavishly without weariness what is sought for? But he wishes to be asked for this purpose, in order that those who seek become fit for his gifts.*[481]

And, accordingly, lest the friend coming from his journey perish from fasting, that is, lest /229/ the spirit, newly recovering from the falsity of its error, waste away any longer from the lack of spiritual desire, let us ask for a feast of the word, by which it may be nourished, let us seek a friend who may give, and let us knock at the door by which hidden things are kept safe. For he, who does not deceive with his promises, gave and gives great hope.[482]

[Luke 11:10] **For everyone**, he says, **who asks, receives, and he who seeks, finds; and for him who knocks, it will be opened.** *Therefore, according to the aforesaid parable of the importunate friend, we must needs be steadfast to receive what we ask for, and to find what we seek, and for what we knock at to be opened.*[483] For *if it is given to the one who asks, and he finds by seeking, and it is opened to the one who knocks, it is therefore*

---

478  Cf. Eph. 6:19.
479  Augustine, *Quaestiones euang.* 2.21 (CCSL 44B:65.24–29).
480  Sc. 'to the greater'. Augustine explains the comparison in the following sentence.
481  Augustine, *Quaestiones euang.* 2.21 (CCSL 44B:65.6–9).
482  Augustine, *De sermone Domini* (CCSL 35:170.1665–66).
483  Augustine, *De sermone Domini* (CCSL 35:170.1667–69).

*evident that the one to whom it is not given, and he who does not find, and to whom it is not opened, did not properly ask, seek, and knock.*[484]

[Luke 11:11] **And which of you, if he asks his father for bread, will he give him a stone?** *Bread is understood to be love, because we have such an appetite for it and because it is so necessary that without it other things are nothing, just as without bread a meal is impoverished. The opposite of this is hardness of heart, which he compared to a stone.*[485]

[Luke 11:11b] **Or if a fish, will he for a fish give him a serpent?** *A fish is faith in unseen things, whether on account of the water of baptism, or because it is taken from unseen places. Also, because faith is not broken by the waves of the world roaring about, it is rightly compared to a fish. He contrasted a serpent to it, on account of the poison of deceit which the serpent sowed in the first man in advance, to lead him astray.*[486]

[Luke 11:12] **Or if he asks for an egg, will he offer him a scorpion?** *Hope is displayed in an egg. For an egg is an offspring not yet perfected, but hoped for by being kept warm. He contrasted to it the scorpion, whose envenomed sting from behind must be feared, just as the opposite of hope is to look back, when hope of things to come stretches forth to those things which are in front.*[487]

[Luke 11:13] **If you then, being evil, know how to give good gifts to your children, how much more will your Father from heaven give the good Spirit to them that ask him?** *How do evil people give good gifts? But he called those who are still lovers of this world and sinners evil. Certainly, the good gifts that they give should be called good according to their intention, because these things have that quality for good people. And although these things are good in the overall nature of things, they are also temporal things pertaining to this feeble life. And any wicked person who gives them does not give them from himself, for 'the earth is the Lord's and the fullness thereof',*[488] *'who made the heaven and the earth and the sea, and* /230/ *all things that are in them'.*[489] *How greatly therefore is it to be hoped that God will give good gifts to us who ask him, and that we cannot be deceived with the result that we receive one thing in place of another*

---

484 Jerome, *Commentarii in Matheum* 1 (CCSL 77:42.916–19).
485 Augustine, *Quaestiones euang.* 2.22 (CCSL 44B:66.3–6).
486 Augustine, *Quaestiones euang.* 2.22 (CCSL 44B:66.6–11).
487 Augustine, *Quaestiones euang.* 2.22 (CCSL 44B:66.11–15).
488 Ps. 23:1 (24:1).
489 Acts 14:14.

## 392  BEDE: COMMENTARY ON THE GOSPEL OF LUKE

*when we ask from God himself, when we also know how to give that which we are asked for, although we are evil! For we do not deceive our children, and whatever kind of good gifts we give, we give not from ourselves, but from God himself.*[490]

In another interpretation: *The apostles, who by the merit of election had exceeded in many ways the goodness of the human race, are said to be evil in comparison to* divine goodness, *because nothing is stable in itself, nothing is immutable, nothing is good, except the Deity alone. Indeed, all created things, in order to obtain the blessedness of eternity and immutability, attain this not by their own nature, but by the incarnation and grace of their Creator.*[491] Truly what is said: *how much more will your Father from heaven give the good Spirit to them that ask him*, in place of which Matthew set down: *he will give good things to them that ask him*,[492] shows that the Holy Spirit is the fullness of the good things of God, and that those things that are divinely supplied cannot stand firm without it because all benefits which are received from the grace of the gifts of God flow from that same source.

Here ends Book Three of the Commentary on Luke. /231/

---

490 Augustine, *De sermone Domini* 2.21.73 (CCSL 35:171.1677–90).
491 Ps.-Augustine, *Sermones* 102.4 (PL 39:1943).
492 Matt. 7:11. If this parallel were not already present in his mind, Bede would have been guided to it by the Eusebian number (125/5) above, which effectively informs users with access to Gospel books marked with Eusebian numbers that Luke 11:9–13 is to be compared to Matt. 7:7–11.

# IV

[Luke 11:14–15:32]

Here begins Book Four.

As we read above, the Lord, rejoicing in the Holy Spirit, says: *I confess to you, Father, Lord of heaven and earth, because you have hidden these things from the wise and the prudent, and have revealed them to little ones.*[1] This statement, always privy to a hidden judgement, does not cease to renew the effect of its power. For it never ceases to be revealed according to the varying nature of its meaning, whether it refers generally to the casting out of the Jews and the raising up of the Gentiles, or specifically to individuals. In conclusion, to touch briefly upon previous matters, the lawyer, who wished to justify himself approached the Lord to tempt him, but went away perplexed,[2] but Mary, sitting humbly at his feet, chose the best part of heavenly philosophy.[3] Likewise, the little ones of Christ, who had learned to trust not in the Redeemer's justice, but in his grace, ask by what kinds of prayers they ought to invoke his grace, and they immediately hear both in what words to pray, and with what urgency to persevere, and for what things especially it is proper to beg humbly, namely faith, hope, and love, and that, asking in a perfect way the one who bestows these things, they may receive the good Spirit from the Father. Conversely, the wise and the prudent pay the unpardonable penalty of their obstinacy both now and in the future, because they not only do not trouble themselves to ask, seek, and knock for the Spirit of grace, but they go about blaspheming. And he who will read as far as the end of the Gospel, or rather he who will contemplate wisely all the way to the end of the world, will understand that *God resists the proud, but to the humble he gives grace.*[4]

---

1 Luke 10:21.
2 Cf. Luke 10:25–37.
3 Cf. Luke 10:39–42.
4 1 Pet. 5:5.

Therefore, beginning the fourth book of gospel commentary from a passage in which the spirit of pride is *cast out by the finger of God,*[5] I myself humbly beg for your mercy, Christ, that *your good Spirit* may *lead me onto the right* path,[6] and may the Lord *remove the northern army far from me,*[7] so that when *the malignant ones* have been cast out *from me I* may *search the commandments of my God,*[8] and so that I, a faithful reader, with the eyes of the mind unveiled, may undertake a contemplation of the wondrous things of your sacred Law.[9]

## Chapter 47

**126/5** [Luke 11:14] **And he was casting out a devil, and the same was dumb. And when he had cast out the devil, the dumb man spoke, and the multitudes were astonished.** In Matthew the man possessed by the demon is reported to have been not only dumb, but also blind, and he is said to have been healed by the Lord, *so that he spoke and saw.*[10] *Three miracles, therefore, were accomplished in one man: blind, he sees; dumb, he speaks; possessed by a devil; he is freed. And not only did it certainly happen then in the flesh, but also* /232/ *it is accomplished daily in the conversion of believers, so that after the devil has been driven out, they first see the light of faith, and then their mouths, previously silent, are opened for the praises of God.*[11]

**127/2** [Luke 11:15] **But some of them said: He casts out devils by Beelzebub, the prince of devils.** Not some of the crowd, but some of the Pharisees and scribes were putting these things in a false light, as the other evangelists testify.[12] Indeed, although the multitudes, who were seemingly less educated, always marvelled at the deeds of the Lord, the Pharisees and scribes on the contrary laboured either to deny these things, or to pervert the things they were unable to deny with a false interpretation, as if they were works not of divinity, but of an impure spirit, that is, *Beelzebub,*

---

5 Luke 11:20.
6 Ps. 142:10 (143:10).
7 Joel 2:20.
8 Ps. 118:115 (119:115).
9 Cf. Ps. 118:18 (119:18).
10 Matt. 12:22.
11 Jerome, *Commentarii in Matheum* 2 (CCSL 77:91.410–15).
12 Cf. Matt. 12:24; Mark 3:22.

who was the god *of Accaron.*[13] For *Beel is* certainly *Baal himself, and zebub* means *'fly'.*[14] And the letter *l* or *d* should not, in accordance with some faulty copies, be read at the end of the word instead of *b.* Beelzebub therefore means 'Baal of the flies', that is, *a man of flies* or *having flies,*[15] on account of the filth of sacrificial blood. That is to say, they called the prince of demons after a hideously foul ritual or name.

**128/5** [Luke 11:16] **And others tempting, asked of him a sign from heaven.** *Either in the manner of Elijah they wished fire to come from on high,*[16] *or like Samuel at harvest time they desired thunder to roar, lightning to flash, and the rains to fall,*[17] *as if they could not both put these things in a bad light, and say that they had come about from hidden and varied disturbances of the air.* But you *who put in a bad light these things that you see with your eyes and hold in your hand, and whose usefulness you recognize, what will you make of those things that come from heaven? Surely, you will reply that magicians in Egypt did many miracles from heaven.*[18]

**129/2** [Luke 11:17] **But when he saw their thoughts, he said to them: Every kingdom divided against itself is forsaken, and house falls on house.** He replied not to what they said, but to what they thought, so that they might thus be compelled to trust in the power of him who saw what was hidden in their heart. And if every kingdom divided against itself is forsaken, accordingly the kingdom of the Father and of the Son and of the Holy Spirit is not divided, which without the slightest doubt is not to be forsaken by any shock, but will abide in eternal stability. But if the kingdom of the holy and undivided Trinity is undivided, or rather because it remains undivided, the Arians should cease from saying that the Son is less than the Father, the Holy Spirit, less than the Son; because theirs is one kingdom, theirs is also one majesty.

[Luke 11:18] **And if Satan is also divided against himself, how will his kingdom /233/ stand? – for you say that I cast out devils by Beelzebub?** *By saying this, he wanted it to be understood from their acknowledgement that by not believing in him they chose to be in the devil's kingdom, which certainly could not stand against him. The Pharisees therefore should*

---

13 Cf. 4 Kings 1:2.
14 Jerome, *Commentarii in Matheum* 1 (CCSL 77:70.1680–83).
15 Jerome, *Hebr. nom.* (CCSL 72:142.11–12).
16 Cf. 3 Kings 28:38.
17 Cf. 1 Sam. 12:18.
18 Jerome, *Commentarii in Matheum* 2 (CCSL 77:96.548–55). On the Egyptian magicians, see comment on Luke 11:20 below.

choose what they want. *If Satan cannot cast out Satan, they could find nothing to say against the Lord. But if he can, they should look out much more for themselves and withdraw from his kingdom, which cannot stand divided against itself. As to the question of by whom Christ the Lord casts out devils, lest they suppose him to be the prince of devils, they should give heed to what follows.*[19]

[Luke 11:19] **Now if I cast out devils by Beelzebub, by whom do your children cast them out? Therefore they themselves will be your judges.** *Without doubt, he said this about his disciples, the children of that people, since the disciples of the Lord Jesus Christ were certainly aware that they had learned no wicked arts from their good teacher in order to cast out devils by the prince of the devils. 'Therefore', he says, 'they themselves will be your judges.' 'They themselves', he says, 'they being the low and despised things of this world,*[20] *in whom there appears, not artful malignity, but the holy simplicity of my virtue, they themselves will be my witnesses, and your judges.'*[21]

In another interpretation: *He means the children of the Jews, exorcists according to custom of that people, who after an invocation used to cast out devils. And he compels* them *by skilled questioning to acknowledge that it is the work of the Holy Spirit. He says, 'If the expulsion of devils by your children is imputed to God rather than to devils, why does the same work not have the same cause in me? Therefore they themselves will be your judges, not through power, but by comparison, as long as they assign the expulsion of devils to God, and you to Beelzebub the prince of devils.'*[22]

[Luke 11:20] **But if I by the finger of God cast out devils, doubtless the kingdom of God has come to you.** *This is the finger which the magicians who did miracles in competition with Moses and Aaron also acknowledge, saying: 'This is the finger of God',*[23] *by which also the stone tablets were written on Mount Sinai.*[24] *If therefore the hand and the arm of God is the Son, and his finger is the Holy Spirit, the substance of the Father and the Son and the Holy Spirit is one. Do not let the inequality of the limbs bother you, since the unity of the body edifies.*[25]

19 Augustine, *Sermones* 71.1.1–2 (CCSL 41Ab:15.18–28).
20 Cf. 1 Cor. 1:28.
21 Augustine, *Sermones* 71.1.2 (CCSL 41Ab:15–16.16–36).
22 Jerome, *Commentarii in Matheum* 2 (CCSL 77:92.438–46).
23 Exod. 8:19 (cf. Exod. 8:16–19).
24 Cf. Exod. 31:18.
25 Jerome, *Commentarii in Matheum* 2 (CCSL 77:93.453–59).

In another interpretation: *The Holy Spirit* is called *the finger of God on account of the division of the gifts that are given by it, suitable for each, whether they be men or angels. For in none of our limbs does division appear more than in our fingers.*[26] Because he said: *the kingdom of God has come to you*, he now says the kingdom of God where the wicked are damned, /234/ and are separated from the faithful who are now doing penance for their sins.

[Luke 11:21] **When a strong man armed keeps his court, all those things are in peace which he possesses.** He calls the devil 'a strong man', and he calls the world, which *is seated in wickedness*,[27] his 'court', in which until the coming of the Saviour he ruled over the empire he had pacified wickedly, because he rested in the hearts of the infidels without any opposition. Hence, he is elsewhere also called 'the prince of the world', when the Lord says: *For the prince of this world comes, and in me he will find nothing.*[28] And again: *Now will the prince of this world be cast out.*[29] About this casting out it is also added here:

[Luke 11:22] **But if one stronger than he comes upon him, he will take away all his armour in which he trusted, and will distribute his spoils.** Indeed, he is speaking about himself, because it was not a liar who freed men from the devil by collaborating with him, as these people accused him of doing, but one who was victorious through superior power. The armour in which that strong man incompetently trusted is the cunning and deceit of spiritual wickedness. His spoils are those men deceived by him, which Christ the victor distributed, because it is the badge of him who triumphs, that leading captivity captive, he gave gifts to men, ordaining some indeed as apostles, some as evangelists, the latter as prophets, and the former as pastors and doctors.[30]

[Luke 11:23] **He who is not with me is against me, and he who does not gather with me scatters.** *Let no one think that this was said about heretics and schematics, although it can also be understood by extension in that way, but logically and from the tenor of the speech it refers to the devil, and the fact that the works of the Saviour cannot be compared to the works of Beelzebub. He wishes to hold the souls of men captive; the Lord,*

---

26 Augustine, *Quaestiones euang.* 2.17 (CCSL 44B:60.2–5).
27 1 John 5:19.
28 John 14:30.
29 John 12:31.
30 Cf. Ps. 67:19 (68:18); Eph. 4:8 & 11.

to free them. He preaches false gods; the Lord, knowledge of the one God. He leads to vices; the Lord summons to virtue. How therefore can they have concord between them, whose works are divided?[31]

**130/5** [Luke 11:24] **When the unclean spirit has gone out of a man, he walks through places without water,** ... Although the fact that the Lord added these things can be understood simply to mean that he distinguishes between his and Satan's works – because, of course, he always hastens to clean polluted things, but Satan hastens to contaminate cleansed things with graver sins – nevertheless it can suitably be taken to refer to any heretic, or schismatic, or even a bad Catholic. From the moment of baptism, the unclean spirit which had lived in him before may be cast out on confession **/235/** of the catholic faith and renunciation of the worldly way of life, and may wander over places without water – that is, the cunning traitor may search the hearts of the faithful that have been cleansed of the weakness of dissolute thought, to see if perchance he can find any entryway for his wickedness there. But it is well said:

[Luke 11:24b] **Seeking rest and not finding it,** because fleeing from chaste souls, the devil can find a resting place pleasing to himself only in the heart of the wicked. Hence the Lord says of him: *He sleeps under the shadow, in the covert of the reed, and in moist places,*[32] by 'shadow', implying dark consciences, by 'the reed', which is glossy on the outside, but empty within, dissimulating women, by 'moist places', lascivious and pliant souls.

[Luke 11:24c] **He says: I will return into my house from which I came out.** This verse should be feared, not explained, lest the fault that we believed was wiped out in us overwhelm us through carelessness when we are empty.

[Luke 11:25] **And when he comes, he finds it swept with brooms,** that is, set right from the stain of sins by the grace of baptism, but not yet perfected by diligently practising good works. Hence Matthew says this house was found empty, swept with brooms, and adorned:[33] 'swept' that is to say from former sins by baptism, but 'empty' of good deeds through negligence, and 'adorned' with feigned virtues through hypocrisy.[34]

[Luke 11:26] **Then he goes and takes with him seven other spirits more wicked than himself, and entering in they dwell there.** By seven

---
31 Jerome, *Commentarii in Matheum* 2 (CCSL 77:94.476–84).
32 Job 40:16.
33 Cf. Matt. 12:44.
34 Cf. Augustine, *Quaestiones euang.* 1.8 (CCSL 44B:12.6–14).

evil spirits he signifies all sins. For if heretical wickedness or worldly cupidity seizes someone after baptism, it will immediately cast him down into the depths of all sins. Hence the spirits entering in are rightly said to be more wicked than the first one, because *not only will he have those seven sins that are contrary to the seven spiritual virtues, but also he will feign through hypocrisy to have those same virtues himself.*[35]

[Luke 11:26b] **And the last state of that man becomes worse than the first.** Indeed, *it had been better for him not to have known the way of truth, than after knowing it to turn back.*[36] We read that this was fulfilled specifically in the case of Judas the traitor and Simon Magus, and others like them. But what this parable points to generally, the Saviour himself expounded according to Matthew, when at its conclusion he immediately added the words: *So will it be also to this wicked generation,*[37] that is, what I said normally happens to particular individuals, does not fail to happen collectively in the case of the whole nation of this people. Indeed, *the unclean spirit came out from the Jews, when they received the Law, and he walked through dry* /236/ *places, seeking rest for himself. That is to say, having been driven out by the Jews, he walked through the deserted places of the Gentiles. When the Gentiles later on believed in the Lord, he, not having found a place among the nations, said: 'I will return to my former house from which I came out.'*[38] *I will have the Jews, whom I had abandoned before. 'And coming he finds it empty, swept with brooms.'*[39] *For the temple of the Jews fell vacant, and did not have Christ as a guest, who said: 'Your house will be abandoned to you, desolate.'*[40] *Therefore because they did not have the protection of God and his angels, and they were adorned with the superfluous observances of the Pharisees, the devil returns to* them, *and bringing seven devils with him, he dwells in his former house, and the later state of that people becomes worse than the earlier.* For now they who blaspheme Jesus Christ in their synagogues are possessed by a much greater number of devils than they had been possessed by in Egypt before their knowledge of the Law. Because it is one thing not to believe that he is going to come, and another not to have received him who did come. And

---

35 Augustine, *Quaestiones euang.* 1.8 (CCSL 44B:12.11–14).
36 2 Pet. 2:21.
37 Matt. 12:45.
38 Matt. 12:44.
39 Matt. 12:44.
40 Matt. 23:38; Luke 13:35.

you should understand that the number seven was added to the devil either on account of the Sabbath, or on account of the number of the Holy Spirit. Just as in Isaiah, the seven spirits of the virtues are said to have descended upon the rod of the root of Jesse, and upon the flower which ascended from the root,[41] so also, contrariwise, the same number of vices was dedicated in the devil.[42]

## Chapter 48

131/10 [Luke 11:27] **And as he spoke these things, a certain woman from the crowd, lifting up her voice, said to him: Blessed is the womb that bore you, and the breasts that you have sucked.** This woman is shown to be of great devotion and faith; as the scribes and Pharisees are at once tempting and blaspheming the Lord, in the presence of them all, she recognizes his incarnation with such integrity and confesses it with such trust that she not only confounds the falsehood of the leading men who are present, but also the faithlessness of heretics to come. For just as the Jews, by blaspheming the works of the Holy Spirit, denied that the Son of God was the true God and consubstantial with the Father at that time, so in after times heretics, by denying that Mary, ever virgin, had furnished the material of her own flesh for the only-begotten God who was to be born from human limbs by the operative power of the Holy Spirit, said that the Son of man ought not to claim to be both the true God and consubstantial with his mother. But if the flesh of the Word of God born according to the flesh is declared to be unrelated to the flesh of the Virgin mother, the womb that bore it and the breasts that gave it milk are blessed without good reason. For by what logic is he believed to have been nurtured by her milk, when it is denied that he was conceived by seminal fluid, since, according to the natural philosophers, both fluids[43] are shown to emanate from the source of one and the same spring? Unless perhaps one should think that by a greater and more extraordinary miracle the Virgin was able to supply the procreative material of her flesh /237/ to the Son of God by suckling in the flesh, but not to have been able to do so by making flesh. But the Apostle stands opposed to this opinion, saying that *God sent his Son, made of a*

---

41 Cf. Is. 11:1–3.
42 Jerome, *Commentarii in Matheum* 2 (CCSL 77:99.608–33).
43 That is, menstrual blood and milk. See Introduction, 53–55.

*woman, made under the Law.*[44] They must not be listened to, who suppose that it should be read, *born of a woman, made under the Law*. But he was *made of a woman*, because having been conceived from a virgin womb, he drew his flesh not from nothing, not from somewhere else, but from his mother's flesh. Otherwise, he would not be truly called the Son of man, who did not have his beginning from man. And therefore, let us lift up our voice with the universal Church, of which this woman was the type, with these words against Eutyches;[45] and let us lift up our mind from the midst of the multitudes, and let us say to the Saviour: *Blessed is the womb that bore you, and the breasts that you have sucked*. For truly blessed is the parent, who, as someone[46] says:

In childbirth brought forth the King,
Who rules heaven and earth forever, and whose
Name, embracing all things in an eternal circle,
Is dominion without end. She with her blessed womb,
Having a mother's joys with the honour of virginity,
Is known to have neither a predecessor nor a follower.[47]

[Luke 11:28] **But he said: Blessed rather are they who hear the Word of God, and guard it**. The Saviour beautifully agrees with the woman's testimony, asserting not only that Mary, who had been worthy of bringing forth the Word of God bodily, is blessed, but that all those who strove to conceive the same Word spiritually by hearing about the faith, and by maintaining good works, to give birth to it either in their own heart or in that of their neighbours, and to nourish it are blessed as well. This is because Mary, the mother of God, was not only blessed, because she was made the temporal handmaid for incarnating the Word, but far more blessed, because she remains the eternal guardian of the same Word for the sake of loving it always. By this statement Christ covertly smites the Jewish sages who sought not to hear and guard the Word of God but to deny and blaspheme it.

---

44 Gal. 4:4.
45 The Eutychian heresy denied the human nature of Christ; cf., e.g., Isidore, *Etym.* 6.16.9 and 8.5.65.
46 Sedulius was one of Bede's favorite Christian-Latin poets, whom he frequently cites by name in *De arte metrica*, ed. Kendall (CCSL 123A); trans. Kendall, 'The Art of Poetry': e.g., chs. 3, 10, 11, 14, 15, 21. Bede's reticence here might suggest that he harboured a doubt about the propriety of including poets among the named authorities of his scriptural commentary, but elsewhere in the text he names both Sedulius and Paulinus of Nola.
47 Sedulius, *Paschale carmen* 2.63–68 (CSEL 10:48).

132/5 [Luke 11:29] **And as the crowds gathered, he began to say: This generation is a wicked generation; it asks for a sign, and a sign will not be given it, but the sign of Jonah the prophet.** He had been assailed by a two-fold question. For some persons were accusing him falsely of having cast out devils by Beelzebub, and up to this point he has responded to them. Others, tempting him, were asking for a sign from heaven from him, and from this point on, he starts to respond to them, not granting them a sign from heaven, which they were unworthy to see, but a sign from the infernal deep, just as Jonah the prophet, when shipwrecked and devoured by being swallowed by a whale, but freed from the abyss and the gullet /**238**/ of death, both received and gave a sign of the incarnation, though not of the divine nature, nor of the passion, and not of the glorification. But to his disciples Jesus gave a sign from heaven, for to them he shows the glory of eternal blessedness both before this, when he was figuratively transformed on the mountain,[48] and afterwards when he was actually raised up into heaven.[49]

[Luke 11:30] **For as Jonah was to the Ninevites, so will the Son of man also be to this generation.** He shows that like the Ninevites, the Jews are overwhelmed with grave sins, and are very near to shipwreck if they will not repent. Truly just as *not only is the torment made known, and the remedy displayed* to the Ninevites, so *likewise the Jews ought not to despair of forgiveness, if they will practise penitence.*[50] But see what follows:

[Luke 11:31] **The queen of the south will rise at the judgement with the men of this generation, and will condemn them, ...** Of course, she will condemn not by the power of judgement, but by the counter-example of a better deed. But if the queen of the south, who is certainly saved, will rise at the Judgement with the damned, then the resurrection of all mortals, that is, the good and the bad, is shown to be at one and the same time, and this resurrection is going to take place, not in accordance with the stories of the Jews in the thousand years before the Judgement,[51] but at the Judgement itself.

---

48 Cf. Matt. 17:1–2.
49 Cf. Mark 16:19.
50 Ambrose, *Expos. Lucam* 7.97 (CCSL 14:247.1012–14).
51 Bede, following Tyconius, Augustine, and others, rejected the notion that the millennium or thousand-year reign of the resurrected saints prophesied in Rev. 20:4–6 was a literal span of time in which Christ would rule on earth, preferring to interpret it as a symbol of the Church: see Wallis, *Bede: Commentary on Revelation*, Introduction, 6–11, 15–16, 39–40.

[Luke 11:31b] **Because she came from the ends of the earth to hear the wisdom of Solomon; and see, one more than Solomon is here.** In this passage, the Latin word *'hic'* is meant *not as a pronoun, but as an adverb of place* ('here'), *that is,* one lives *among you now,*[52] who is incomparably greater than Solomon. Scripture relates how *Queen Sheba through such great difficulties, leaving her people and empire behind, came to Judea to hear the wisdom of Solomon, and* bringing *him many gifts,* she received more gifts from him.[53] Therefore she will condemn the Jews at the Judgement, because from the farthest ends of the earth, she sought the one whom she knew was renowned for the gift of wisdom that he had received. But they, having among them the one who did not receive wisdom from another, but is himself the wisdom and power of God,[54] preferred not only not to hear, but to blaspheme and attack him insidiously.

[Luke 11:32] **The men of Nineveh will rise at the judgement with this generation, and will condemn it, because they did penance at the preaching of Jonah; and see, one more than Jonah is here.** *Jonah preached* for a few days; *I for a long time. He to the Assyrians, a people without faith; I to the Jews, the people of God. He to foreigners; I to citizens. He, speaking in simple language and making no use of signs,* was accepted; *I, doing such great signs,* /239/ *endure the false accusation of allegiance to Beelzebub. Therefore, one who is greater than Jonah is here,*[55] that is, preaching in the midst of you. And therefore in the same way as the queen of the south the men of Nineveh will likewise condemn the generation of the Jews, that is, they will accuse them of infidelity.

In another interpretation: *For* in the men of Nineveh *and the queen* of the south *the faith* of the Church *is preferred to Israel.*[56] This faith is reconciled to the Lord through penitence for folly that has been committed, no less than through zeal for learning wisdom. Indeed, the unity of the Church is assembled from two parts, namely those who are unwilling to sin, and those who cease to sin. *For penance wipes out the wrong; wisdom guards against it.*[57]

---

52 Jerome, *Commentarii in Matheum* 2 (CCSL 77:97.573–74; 579).
53 Jerome, *Commentarii in Matheum* 2 (CCSL 77:98.586–88); cf. 3 Kings 10:1–13.
54 Cf. 1 Cor. 1:24.
55 Jerome, *Commentarii in Matheum* 2 (CCSL 77:98.574–79).
56 Jerome, *Commentarii in Matheum* 2 (CCSL 77:98.588–89).
57 Ambrose, *Expos. Lucam* 7.96 (CCSL 14:247.1007–08).

## Chapter 49

**133**/2 [Luke 11:33] **No man lights a lamp, and puts it in a hidden place, nor under a bushel, ...** The Lord says these things about himself, showing that, although he said above that no sign would be given to a wicked generation except the sign of Jonah,[58] the splendour of his light will nonetheless not be entirely hidden from the faithful. Indeed, he himself lit the lamp, who filled the clay lamp of human nature with the flame of his own divinity. He certainly wanted neither to hide the lamp from believers, nor to put it under a bushel, that is, to confine it under the jurisdiction of the Law, or to restrict it within the boundaries of a single people, the Jews.

[Luke 11:33b] **But upon a lampstand**, he says, so **that those who enter may see the light**. He calls the Church a lampstand, upon which he placed the lamp, because he imprinted faith in his incarnation on our foreheads, so that those who wish to enter the Church faithfully are able to see the light of the truth clearly. With this verse he also condemns the leaders of the Jews who, seeking for signs from without, do not want to enter the open door of the light by believing. Finally, he commands that they remember to cleanse and correct not only their deeds, but also their thoughts and even the very intentions of their hearts, for he goes on:

**134**/5 [Luke 11:34] **The lamp of your body is your eye**. He calls the deeds which appear openly to all 'the body', but that very intention of the mind by which it works he calls 'the eye', and identical deeds are judged to be deeds of light or deeds of darkness according to their merit, as he himself subsequently explained, saying:

[Luke 11:34b] **If your eye is single, your whole body will be light; but if it is evil, your body will also be dark**. If, he says, you endeavour with a pure and upright purpose to do those good things that you are able to do, surely the deeds that you do are deeds of light, even if they seem to have some imperfection in the eyes of men, *since for those who love God, all things work together for good, for such as, according to his purpose, are called to be saints*.[59] But if the purpose that preceded is evil, the whole work that follows is wicked, even if it seems to be correct. /240/

[Luke 11:35] **Take heed therefore that the light that is in you be not darkness**, that is, in order that the intention of the heart, which is the light of the soul, be not darkened by a fog of evils, examine with careful

---

58 Cf. Luke 11:29.
59 Rom. 8:28.

discernment, in accordance with what is commanded elsewhere: *With all watchfulness, keep your heart, because life issues out from it.*[60]

[Luke 11:36] **If then your whole body be light, not having any part of darkness, the whole will be light, and as a lamp of splendour will enlighten you.** He calls our deeds our 'whole body', *since the Apostle also calls certain deeds, which he condemns, our limbs, and commands them to be mortified, saying: 'Mortify therefore your limbs which are on the earth, fornication, impurity, lust',*[61] *and others like them.*[62] If then you yourself do good with good intention, not having in your consciousness any element of dark thought, even if it happens that some one of your neighbours is injured by your good action, for example, or does or suffers any evil as a result of the money which he needed, sought, and received from you, or perhaps errs more perniciously as a result of the word of exhortation with which you wished to correct him, nevertheless you will be forgiven both now and in the future for the sake of your simple and luminous heart on account of the light. May these things, spoken specifically against the hypocrisy of the Pharisees who craftily seek signs, teach us all in accordance with the moral level of interpretation.

### Chapter 50

**135/5** [Luke 11:37] **And while he was speaking, a certain Pharisee asked him to dine with him. And going in, he sat down to eat.** Luke deliberately does not say, 'And when he said these things', but *while he was speaking*, to show that Jesus was asked to dine with the Pharisee not at the moment when he had finished what he was saying, but in a brief interruption. And Matthew explains what these things he was saying were, who at the end of this speech of the Lord, which Luke reports sometimes more concisely and sometimes at greater length, immediately added: *While he was still speaking to the multitude, behold, his mother and his brothers stood outside, seeking to speak to him.*[63] He says, *while he was still speaking*, so that you may understand *that he was speaking those things that he recorded above.* But *Mark as well, after he* had *reported what*

---

60 Prov. 4:23.
61 Col. 3:5.
62 Augustine, *De sermone Domini* 2.13.45 (CCSL 35:136.1000–03).
63 Matt. 12:46.

the Lord said – that bit about blasphemy against the Holy Spirit[64] – says: *'And his mother and his brothers came.'*[65] However, Luke did not keep the order of this event, but moved it up, and narrated the remembered event earlier. Finally, he inserted it so that it appears free from entanglement with what comes before and after.[66] And so, when he is told that his mother and brothers are outside, after he says: *For whoever will do the will of God, he is my brother and my sister and my mother,*[67] he was, we are given to understand, asked to enter the Pharisee's feast. /241/

[Luke 11:38] **And the Pharisee began to say, thinking within himself, why he was not washed before dinner.** The evangelist Mark revealed the reason for the Pharisee's thought, saying: *For the Pharisees and all the Jews do not eat without often washing their hands, keeping the tradition of the elders. And when they come from the market, unless they are washed, they do not eat.*[68]

[Luke 11:39] **And the Lord said to him: Now you Pharisees make clean the outside of the cup and of the platter. But your inside is full of plundering and wickedness.** And indeed, Mark relates that they were accustomed to observe the cleansing of cups and pitchers and of beds and bronze vessels, but more than this, by the term 'vessels' they are shown to be vessels *of falsehood* and *hypocrisy, because they display one thing to people outside, they do another at home,*[69] maintaining the appearance of piety outwardly, but inwardly being deformed by the filth of sins. For the Lord wishes to explain at greater length what he had mentioned briefly above about cleansing the eye of the heart.[70]

[Luke 11:40] **Fools, did not he who made that which is without, make also that which is within?** – he who, he says, made each of the two natures of man, and desires each to be made clean. This is said against the Manicheans, who think that only the soul is created by God, but that the flesh is created by the devil. This is said against those, who denounce the corporal sins, namely *fornication, impurity, lust,*[71] theft, plundering, and other such, as if they were the most serious, but disdain as trifling the

---

64 Cf. Mark 3:29.
65 Mark 3:31.
66 Augustine, *De consensu euang.* 2.40 (CSEL 43:190.1–3; 6–9).
67 Mark 3:35.
68 Mark 7:3–4.
69 Jerome, *Commentarii in Matheum* 4 (CCSL 77:216.221–23).
70 Cf. Luke 11:34–35.
71 Col. 3:5.

spiritual sins, which the Apostle condemns more, that is, *bitterness, wrath, indignation, clamour, blasphemy,*[72] pride, *and avarice, which is the service of idols.*[73]

[Luke 11:41] **But rather, what remains, give alms, and behold, all things are clean to you.** Give to the poor what remains of needful food and clothing, in accordance with what John likewise commands: *He who has two coats, let him give to him who has none.*[74] For alms are commanded, not so that you destroy yourself by want, but so that, with the management of your body taken care of, you may sustain a destitute person as much as you can. Or *what remains* should be understood in such a way that, to those who are beset by so much wickedness, to *give alms* remains the sole remedy. This speech *applies to all things that are done with proper compassion.* For he *gives alms* who *not only gives food to the hungry, drink to the thirsty, clothing to the naked, lodging to the wanderer,* and other acts of this kind, *but also gives forgiveness to the sinner. And he gives alms who, being endowed with the power to do so, corrects with a rod, or restrains with some discipline, and nevertheless forgives from his heart the sin of him whereby he was injured or offended,* /242/ *or prays that it be forgiven him, not only because he forgives and prays, but also because he corrects and punishes with some corrective penalty, and because he shows mercy. And so there are many kinds of alms, and when we perform them, we are aided so that our sins may be forgiven us, but nothing is greater than the alms by means of which we forgive from our heart the sin which someone has committed against us.*[75]

But *are we to understand* what he says: *'give alms, and behold, all things are clean to you'*, to mean that, to the Pharisees who do not have the faith of Christ, all things are clean, even if they do not believe in him, and are not reborn *'of water and the* Holy Spirit*'*,[76] *just because they give alms as* some *think they ought to be given, although all are unclean whom the faith of Christ does not cleanse, of which it is written: 'Cleansing their hearts by faith'?*[77] *And nevertheless what they had heard is true: 'give alms, and behold, all things are clean to you'.*[78]

72 Eph. 4:31.
73 Eph. 5:5.
74 Luke 3:11.
75 Augustine, *Enchiridion* 19.72–73 (CCSL 46:88.20–42).
76 John 3:5.
77 Acts 15:9.
78 Augustine, *Enchiridion* 20.75 (CCSL 46:90.15–26).

*He who wishes to give alms in an orderly way ought to begin with himself, and give them to himself first. For almsgiving is a deed of compassion, and it is very truly said: 'Have pity on your own soul, pleasing God'.[79] On account of this we are born again in order to please God, who is deservedly displeased with that which we contracted in being born.[80] This is the first alms, which we gave to ourselves, because we looked after our wretched selves by the compassion of God, who is compassionate.[81]*

*On account of this order of love it is written: 'You shall love your neighbour as yourself'.[82] Therefore, after he had rebuked them because they washed themselves on the outside, but within were full of plundering and iniquity, warning that there are some alms which a man ought to give to himself first and to cleanse the inner parts, he says: 'But rather, what remains, give alms, and behold, all things are clean to you'. Then, to show what he admonished, but what they themselves could not take the trouble to do, and lest they think that he was ignorant of their alms,[83]* he says:

**136/5** [Luke 11:42] **But woe to you, Pharisees, ...** *as if he should say: I indeed impressed upon you that alms ought to be given by which all things are clean to you, but woe to you,[84]*

[Luke 11:42b] **Because you tithe mint and rue and every herb, ...** *For I know these alms of yours, and so do not think that I admonished you about them.[85]*

[Luke 11:42c] **And you pass over judgement and the love of God, ...** *By alms of this kind, you could be cleansed of all inner filth, so that even the bodies that you wash could be clean to you – for that is what 'all things' means, namely things both inner and outer; just as elsewhere it is written: 'Clean the things that are inside, and those that are outside will be clean'.[86] But lest it seem that those /243/ alms that are made from the fruits of the earth were rejected, he says,[87]*

---

79 Ecclus. 30:24.
80 Augustine is referring to 'original sin': that is, the congenital sinfulness inherited physically by all humans through their descent from Adam and Eve.
81 Augustine, *Enchiridion* 20.76 (CCSL 46:90.27–33).
82 Mark 12:31.
83 Augustine, *Enchiridion* 20.76 (CCSL 46:91.45–53).
84 Augustine, *Enchiridion* 20.76 (CCSL 46:91.53–55).
85 Augustine, *Enchiridion* 20.76 (CCSL 46:91.55–58).
86 Matt. 23:26.
87 Augustine, *Enchiridion* 20.76 (CCSL 46:91.58–64).

BOOK FOUR 409

[Luke 11:42d] **And these things it was necessary to do,** *that is, judgement and the love of God,*[88] *so that we may live piously and righteously, judging our wretched condition accurately, and loving the love of God which he himself gave,*[89] *confessing his just judgement, by which we were afflicted, concerning which the Apostle says:* 'Indeed *judgment was by one to condemnation',*[90] *giving thanks for his great love, concerning which the very same herald of grace says:* 'But God commends his love towards us, because when as yet we were sinners, Christ died for us'.[91]

[Luke 11:42e] **And these things it was necessary to do, and not to omit those,** that is, the alms of the fruits of the earth. *Let them not, therefore, deceive themselves, who reckon that they buy impunity by alms, however generous, of their own fruits or of riches to persist in the enormity of their outrages and the wickedness of their shameful deeds.*[92]

137/2 [Luke 11:43] **Woe to you, Pharisees, because you love the best seats in the synagogues, and salutations in the marketplace.** *Woe to us wretches, to whom the sins of the Pharisees are transferred,*[93] we who did not fear to burden further with sins the course of our brief and uncertain life by contending proudly with one another for precedence, when we ought to have bewailed our sins humbly.

138/5 [Luke 11:44] **Woe to you, because you are like graves that are not visible, and men who walk over them are not aware.** This verse refutes the foolish behaviour of the Pharisees, who outwardly simulate the appearance of proper teaching, but inwardly conceal whatever filth they bear, like graves that, although they display a surface of ordinary earth, are within full of the stench of worm-eaten bodies. Of these, when the Psalmist said: *Their throat is an open grave,* he immediately clarified what he had said by adding: *They dealt deceitfully with their tongues.*[94]

139/5 [Luke 11:45] **And one of the lawyers answering, said to him: Master, in saying these things, you also reproach us.** How pitiful is the conscience, which, having heard the word of God, thinks a reproach is directed toward itself, and recalling the punishment of the faithless, knows that it is to be damned forever. Hence for me and for those like me there

---

88 Augustine, *Enchiridion* 20.76 (CCSL 46:91.64–65).
89 Augustine, *Enchiridion* 20.76 (CCSL 46:90.39–41).
90 Rom. 5:16.
91 Augustine, *Enchiridion* 20.76 (CCSL 46:90.33–39); Rom. 5:8.
92 Augustine, *Enchiridion* 20.76–77 (CCSL 46:91.64–70).
93 Jerome, *Commentarii in Matheum* 4 (CCSL 77:211.70–71).
94 Ps. 5:11 (5:9).

remains a single refuge, to kneel with the Prophet before the Lord: *O that my ways may be directed to keep your justifications! Then I will not be confounded, when I look on all your commandments.*[95]

[Luke 11:46] **But he said: Woe to you lawyers also, because you load men with burdens that cannot be borne, and you yourselves do not touch the burdens /244/ with one of your fingers.** The burdens of the Law cannot be borne in the way such lawyers laid them on men. Hence, they hear correctly that they did not touch its burdens with one of their fingers: that is, in order that they might not have to carry out the Law even in the most trifling matters. Contrary to the custom of the patriarchs, the Pharisees believed they both preserved these, and handed them down to be preserved, without the faith and grace of Jesus Christ. And therefore, they tried to cast away and extirpate the sweet yoke of Christ and his light burden,[96] where there is rest of souls,[97] even though it is written: *The just man lives by faith,*[98] and although the apostle Peter bears witness against these men who taught that believers from the Gentiles were to be circumcised[99] and says: *And now, why do you tempt God to put a yoke on the neck of the disciples, which neither our fathers nor we have been able to bear? But we believe to be saved by the grace of the Lord Jesus, just as they also.*[100]

140/5 [Luke 11:47] **Woe to you who build the monuments of the prophets, and your fathers killed them.** It is not a kind of crime to decorate the monuments of the prophets, but to imitate the killers of the prophets. Therefore, by building the monuments of the prophets, the Jews censured the deeds of their fathers who had killed them, but by emulating their fathers' outrage, in pursuing Christ and his apostles, they cast the judgement back upon themselves, namely by doing the same things that they condemned in their parents.

[Luke 11:48] **Truly you bear witness that you consent to the deeds of your fathers. For they indeed killed them, and you build their tombs.** In order to gain the favour of the people, they pretended that they trembled at the faithlessness of their fathers by magnificently adorning the memorials of the prophets who were killed by them, but they testify by that very deed

---

95 Ps. 118:5–6 (119:5–6).
96 Cf. Matt. 11:30.
97 Cf. Matt. 11:29.
98 Rom. 1:17.
99 Cf. Acts 15:1–5.
100 Acts 15:10–11.

how much they consent to their fathers' iniquity, by inflicting injuries upon the Lord, who was foretold by these same prophets. In this they reveal that they sin, knowing both that they are the sons of murderers and that they are adding to their own condemnation. Hence it is rightly added:

**141/5** [Luke 11:49] **Therefore also the wisdom of God said: I will send to them prophets and apostles, and some of them they will kill and persecute, ...** He calls himself the wisdom of God, for he himself is the power of God and the wisdom of God, as the Apostle teaches.[101] And then in Matthew you find this: *Therefore, behold I send to you prophets and wise men and scribes.*[102] And if the same wisdom of God sent the prophets which sent the apostles, let the heretics cease to attribute Christ's origins to the Virgin,[103] let them leave off preaching that there is one God of the Law and the prophets, and another God of the New Testament,[104] /245/ although even apostolic Scripture often calls 'prophets' not only those who foretell that the incarnation of Christ will be, but also those who foretell the joys of the heavenly kingdom. *Let the prophets speak*, he says, *two or three, and let the rest judge.*[105] But I would definitely not believe that the prophets should be preferred to the apostles in precedence.

[Luke 11:50] **So that the blood of all the prophets, which was shed from the foundation of the world, may be required of this generation, ...** It is asked how the blood of all the prophets and the just may be required of one generation of the Jews, since not only were many of the saints killed by other peoples either before the incarnation or after the death and resurrection of the Saviour, but also the Lord himself was crucified by a Roman governor and by Roman soldiers, albeit with the approval of the Jews. But it is customary in the Scriptures in numerous instances to reckon two generations of men, of the good and of the wicked, that is, of those, *Who are born, not of the blood, nor of the will of the flesh, nor of the will of man, but of God,*[106] and of those to whom it is said: *You are of your father the devil,*[107] and elsewhere: *Serpents, generation of vipers.*[108]

---

101 Cf. 1 Cor. 1:24.
102 Matt. 23:34.
103 Cf. Ambrose, *Expos. Lucam* 1.25 (CCSL 14:19.391–92).
104 Cf. Ambrose, *Expos. Lucam* 1.2 (CCSL 14:7.30–31). See Bede's comment on Luke 1:16–17, above.
105 1 Cor. 14:29.
106 John 1:13.
107 John 8:44.
108 Matt. 23:33.

[Luke 11:51] **From the blood of Abel up to the blood of Zechariah, who was slain between the altar and the temple.** Why 'from the blood of Abel', who first suffered martyrdom, is not to be wondered at, but it must be asked, why 'up to the blood of Zechariah', when not only are there many who were killed after him up to the birth of Christ, but also immediately after Christ's birth the innocent children in Bethlehem were killed by this generation.[109] Perhaps because Abel was a shepherd of sheep, and Zechariah a priest, and the one was slain in the field, and the other in the courtyard of the temple, he wanted to make known under their name martyrs of both kinds, that is to say, both the laity and those dedicated to the office of the altar.

**142/5** [Luke 11:52] **Woe to you lawyers, for you have taken away the key of knowledge. You yourselves have not entered in, and those who were entering in, you have hindered.** The key of knowledge is *the humility of Christ*, which the lawyers *wished neither to understand themselves* in the Law and the prophets, *nor to be understood by others*.[110] For to enter in, is not to be content with the surface of the letter, but to penetrate to the mysteries of a more spiritual understanding. In another interpretation: every teacher, who causes his pupils, whom he edifies with his word, to stumble by his example, neither enters the kingdom of God, nor allows those who could to enter.

**143/10** [Luke 11:53] **And as he was saying these things to them, the Pharisees and the lawyers began violently to urge him**, and so forth. The same people who endeavour with such a great thundering storm not to recover their own senses, but to assault the teacher of truth with ambushes, bear witness that they heard the true crimes of their own faithlessness, hypocrisy, and impiety.

## Chapter 51[111]

**144/2** [Luke 12:1b] **Beware of the leaven of the Pharisees, which is hypocrisy.** Everything which Jesus had discussed earlier when he was

---

109 Cf. Matt. 2:16.
110 Augustine, *Quaestiones euang.* 2.23 (CCSL 44B:67.4–5).
111 The Codex Amiatinus and Gorman, 'Source Marks', Appendix 3, place the beginning of chap. 51 at Luke 11:45. We follow the logic of chapter summaries 50 & 51. See Introduction, 20.

dining with /246/ the Pharisee pertains to this leaven. The Apostle likewise gives direction about this: *Therefore let us feast, not with the old leaven, nor with the leaven of malice and wickedness, but with the unleavened bread of sincerity and truth.*[112] For just as *a little leaven spoils the whole lump* of flour into which it is thrown,[113] and immediately pollutes all the dough with its taste, so without doubt once hypocrisy has stained anyone's soul, it will defraud it of all integrity of virtues, and of truth.

**145**/5   [Luke 12:2] **For there is nothing covered that will not be revealed, nor hidden that will not be known.** How long the hypocrisy of many people lies concealed in this present age! Therefore, this verse ought to be understood to refer to the time to come, when the Lord will pass judgement on the secrets of men. For as one of the friends of the blessed Job very truly said: *The praise of the wicked is short, and the joy of the hypocrite but for a moment. If his pride mounts up to heaven, and his head touches the clouds, in the end he will be destroyed like a dunghill.*[114] In the end, he says, he who seemed to flourish in the beginning will be destroyed. Therefore, this is the sense: Beware not to emulate the hypocrites, because the time will certainly come when both your virtue and their hypocrisy will be revealed to all. But what follows:

[Luke 12:3] **For whatever things you have spoken in darkness will be spoken in the light, and that which you have spoken in the ear in the chambers will be preached on the housetops,** can be taken to apply not only in the future, when all that is hidden in the heart will be brought to light, but also in the present age, and aptly. For whatever in times past the apostles either said or suffered amid the dark shadows of afflictions and prisons are now, when the Church's renown has spread throughout the world, preached openly, since their deeds have been read about. Doubtless what he says, *it will be preached on the housetops*, he says after the custom of the province of Palestine, where people are used to living on the housetops. For they don't make peaked roofs after our fashion, but level ones with a flat design. Hence the Law ordered that whoever built a new house should put a wall for the roof around the entire edge, lest innocent blood be shed there by anyone slipping and falling headlong.[115] And in the construction of the temple we read: *And he covered the house*

---

112  1 Cor. 5:8.
113  Cf. Gal. 5:9.
114  Job 20:5–7.
115  Cf. Deut. 22:8.

414  BEDE: *COMMENTARY ON THE GOSPEL OF LUKE*

*with roofs of cedar. And he built a floor over all the house five cubits in height.*[116] There *it will be preached on the housetops*; it will be said openly to all who listen.

[Luke 12:4] **And I say to you, my friends: Be not afraid of those who kill the body, and after that have no more that they can do.** When those who persecute the saints have killed their bodies, there is nothing more that they can do against them, and so they rage with useless madness who cast the dead limbs of the martyrs to wild beasts and birds /247/ to be torn apart; and whether they cause them to be desiccated in the air, or to be dissolved in the water, or to be reduced to ashes by flames, they are completely unable to block the omnipotence of God from restoring them to life by raising them up again.

[Luke 12:5] **Fear him, who after he has killed has power to cast into hell.** Since there are two kinds of persecutors, one of men who openly rage, the other of men who flatter feignedly and fraudulently, the Saviour, wishing to guard and instruct us against each, admonishes us both above to beware of the hypocrisy of the Pharisees, and here not to be fearful of the slaughter of executioners, because neither the cruelty of the latter nor the hypocrisy of the former can last after death. Instead, it is the Lord who always sees who must be appeased, and the Lord who is able to punish or set free who must be feared.

[Luke 12:6] **Are not five sparrows sold for tuppence, and not one of them is forgotten in God's sight?** If God cannot forget the tiniest animals, he says, and the birds that are borne through the air wherever they please, you who were made in the image of the Creator ought not to be frightened of those who kill the body, because he who governs creatures lacking reason, does not cease to care for rational beings. The tuppence [*dipondius*] for which five sparrows are sold [*ueneunt*] (that is, are vended [*uenduntur*]), is a kind of very lightweight [*ponderis leuissimi*] coin made up of two pennies [*assibus*].[117]

*Perhaps someone* asks: *Why does the Apostle say, 'Does God have a care for oxen',*[118] *since surely an ox is more valuable than a sparrow? But*

---

116  3 Kings 6:9–10.
117  The active verb, *ueneo, uenire*, 'to be sold', was used in the classical period as the passive of *uendo, uendere*, 'to sell'. Coins were described in terms of 'weight' (*pondo/pondus*), the *dupondius/dipondius* being the weight of two *asses*, or copper coins. Bede the teacher sounds in these words.
118  1 Cor. 9:9.

BOOK FOUR 415

*care is one thing, knowledge is* truly *another. And then the number of hairs about which he says next:*[119]

[Luke 12:7] **But even the hairs of your head are all numbered,** *is understood not as an act of computation, but as* the capacity *to know. For God does not keep an anxious eye on the business of numbering, but all things are known to him as though they were all numbered. Nevertheless they are properly said to be numbered, because we number those things that we want to preserve.*[120]

In these words, *he shows the boundless providence of God toward men, and signifies his inexpressible love, because nothing of ours is hidden from God, and even small and inconsequential remarks do not escape his knowledge. Those who deny the resurrection of the flesh deride the Church's reading of this passage. They think we are saying that*[121] *the very earthly matter itself which at the departure of the soul becomes a corpse,* must be restored *by the resurrection in such a way that those things that are lost and turned into different kinds and forms of different things, even though they go back to the body from which they were lost, must necessarily go back as well to the same parts of the body where they had been. Otherwise, to suppose that the hair so often clipped off returns to the head, and the nails so often removed,* /248/ *would strike the mind as a disfigurement both excessive and repellent, and for that reason, people would not believe in the resurrection. But just as, if a statue of whatever kind of destructible material either melted in fire, or was worn away into dust, or was jumbled into a heap, and the maker wished to restore it again from a quantity of that stuff, it would make no difference to its integrity what particle of the stuff was returned to what part of the statue, as long as it recovered all the material of which it had been made, so God, a Craftsman wondrous and ineffable in power, will restore it with wondrous and ineffable swiftness from everything of which our flesh had ever existed; and nothing will affect its restoration in any way, whether hair return to hair and nails to nails, or whether that portion of these things which had been lost change into flesh and be summoned back into other parts of the body, with the wisdom of the Maker taking care that nothing unseemly occur.*[122]

---

119 Ambrose, *Expos. Lucam* 7.112 (CCSL 14:251.1134–37).
120 Ambrose, *Expos. Lucam* 7.112 (CCSL 14:251.1137–41).
121 Jerome, *Commentarii in Matheum* 1 (CCSL 77:73.1759–63). Note the unusual blending of this quotation from Jerome with the following one from Augustine.
122 Augustine, *Enchiridion* 23.89 (CCSL 46:97.58–77).

[Luke 12:7b] **Fear not therefore; you are of more value than many sparrows.** This text should not read, 'you are more than' [*plures estis*], which refers to numerical comparison, but 'you are of more value than' [*pluris estis*], that is, you are reckoned of greater merit, dignity, and worth, than the countless bodies and species of sparrows.[123]

[Luke 12:8] **And I say to you: Whoever confesses me before men, the Son of God will also confess him before the angels of God.**

146/2 [Luke 12:9] **But he who denies me before men will be denied before the angels of God.** He looks back to what was said above, that whatever things are covered and hidden are going to be revealed, concluding that this revelation is not going to occur in some base conventicle, but in the presence of the heavenly city and of the eternal King and Judge.[124] And lest one think that because he says that those who deny him will be denied, a single category will include both those who deny intentionally and those who deny from weakness or ignorance, he immediately added:

147/2 [Luke 12:10] **And whoever speaks a word against the Son of man, it will be forgiven him; but to him who blasphemes against the Holy Spirit, it will not be forgiven.** He who is scandalized *by my flesh, thinking that I am only a man, because I am the son of a carpenter and have brothers, James, and Joseph, and Jude,*[125] *and am a man who eats and is a drinker of wine*[126] – *such supposition and blasphemy, although not innocent of error, nevertheless is forgivable on account of the baseness of the body. But someone who clearly understands God's works and cannot deny their power, and who goaded with envy brings a false accusation, and says that Christ and the Word of God and the works of the Holy Spirit are Beelzebub, 'it will not be forgiven him, neither in* /249/ *the present world nor in the world to come'.*[127] We do not deny that if he is able to repent, he can be forgiven by him *who wishes all men to be saved, and to come to the knowledge of the truth.*[128] Rather, we trust in that same Judge and Dispenser of pardon, and even though he says that he will always accept penance and that this blasphemy can never be forgiven, we may believe that just as this blasphemer will never attain forgiveness on the basis of compelling merit,

---

123 The Codex Amiatinus is one of the manuscripts of the Vulgate that reads *pluris*.
124 Cf. Luke 12:2–3.
125 Cf. Matt. 13:55.
126 Cf. Matt. 11:19.
127 Jerome, *Commentarii in Matheum* 2 (CCSL 77:95.500–08); Matt. 12:32.
128 1 Tim. 2:4.

so also he will not achieve the fruits of a worthy penance. This accords with what the evangelist John wrote with great accuracy about certain persons deservedly blinded to their own blasphemy: *Therefore they could not believe, because Isaiah also said: He has blinded their eyes, and hardened their heart, so that they might not see with their eyes, and understand with their heart, and be converted, and I heal them.*[129]

Of course, some people[130] suppose that he speaks a word, or blasphemes, against the Holy Spirit, who resists with an impenitent heart the unity of the Church, where the forgiveness of sins is made by the Holy Spirit.[131] They say that *the Church is the sole refuge; and that the impenitent heart should be warned lest blasphemy be unforgivable.*[132] Their opinion does not seem at all convincing to many, seeing that whoever resists with an impenitent heart the unity of the Church, whether he be a Jew or a Gentile, or even a heretic, can certainly have forgiveness of sins by the Holy Spirit, if he flees for shelter to the unity of the Church with a penitent heart. But they say as long as anyone resists with an impenitent heart the Spirit of grace, he will not have forgiveness. But the latter object that this condition applies to all crimes. For as long as anyone in any way commits fornication, idolatry, adultery, intercourse between males, theft, and other outrages, *he will not have inheritance in the kingdom of Christ and of God.*[133] But when these crimes have been rejected, he can be washed, sanctified, and justified in the name of our Lord, Jesus Christ, and by the Spirit of our God. So, they say, even the impenitent, as long as he has an impenitent heart, cannot have forgiveness, but as soon as he repents, he will also obtain forgiveness. And by no distinction is impenitence found to be more binding or more irremediable than other sins. Like other sins, it persists until repentance; it will immediately be wiped out when penance has been done. Only blasphemy against the Holy Spirit whereby, like the devil and his angels, someone knowingly does not hesitate to oppose the majesty of the Deity, *will never have forgiveness, but will be guilty of an everlasting sin,*[134] as the evangelist Mark clearly explains, who, after having reported this testimony of the

---

129 John 12:39–40 (cf. Isa. 6:10).
130 It is Augustine who supposes these things. Is Bede unaware of his authorship, or is he dubious about the supposition?
131 Cf. Augustine, *Sermones* 71.23 (CCSL 41Ab:45.585–87).
132 Augustine, *Sermones* 71.37 (CCSL 41Ab:70.1019).
133 Eph. 5:5.
134 Mark 3:29.

Lord, went on and said: *Because they used to say: he has an unclean spirit.*[135] For neither those who believe and confess /250/ that the Holy Spirit does not exist, nor those who believe that he does exist, but that he is not God, nor those who believe that he is indeed God but lesser than the Father and the Son, are bound by this crime of unforgivable blasphemy when they are led by human ignorance, and not by diabolical envy. Insofar as the Jews' own rulers and any like them who are corrupted by the curse of envy blaspheme the divine, they will perish eternally. Read the first book of the blessed Augustine on the Sermon on the Mount.[136]

148/2 [Luke 12:11] **And when they bring you into the synagogues, and to the magistrates and powers,** ... For above he had said: *I will send to them prophets and apostles, and some of them they will kill and persecute.*[137]

[Luke 12:11b–12] **Be not solicitous how or what you will answer, or what you will say, for the Holy Spirit will teach you in the same hour what you must say.** *Therefore, when we are brought before judges on account of Christ, we ought to offer only our will to Christ. For the rest, Christ himself, who lives in us, will speak on his own behalf, and he will be directed in answering by the grace of the Holy Spirit.*[138]

## Chapter 52

149/10 [Luke 12:13–14] **And one of the multitude said to him: Teacher, tell my brother to divide the inheritance with me. But he said to him: Man, who has appointed me a judge or a divider over you?** Deservedly is this brother rebuked for wanting to burden a teacher who is commending the joys of divine peace and unity with the vexation of earthly division. Deservedly is he censured by the word 'man'. *For whereas there is among you*, he says, *envying and contention, are you not carnal, and walk according to man?*[139] And the Lord says that he is not 'a divider over men', to whom he had come both by himself and with angels in order to bring peace. He is not the God of dissension but of peace. And *the multitude of believers had but one heart and one soul, nor did anyone say that any of*

---

135 Mark 3:30.
136 Cf. Augustine, *De sermone Domini* 1.22.75 (CCSL 35:84–85).
137 Luke 11:49.
138 Jerome, *Commentarii in Matheum* 1 (CCSL 77:69.1653–56).
139 1 Cor. 3:3.

the things that they possessed was his own, but all things were common to them.[140] And the only divider of brotherhood and author of dissension is the one of whom it is said above: *and he who does not gather with me scatters;*[141] and of his members: *Every kingdom divided against itself is forsaken, and house falls on house.*[142]

[Luke 12:15] **And he said to them: Take heed, and beware of all avarice, for one's life does not consist in the abundance of things that he possesses.** Just as the Lord had said many things above against blasphemers and hypocrites, so here when the opportunity of this foolish petitioner presents itself, he makes an effort by precept and example to protect both the multitude and his disciples against the plague of avarice, for the sake of which a great many mortals /251/ labour more than enough. It should be observed that he did not say, 'beware of avarice', but inserted, 'of all avarice', because some things seem to people to be carried out innocently, but the inward Judge, because he discerns the intention by which they are done, passes judgement. For who would consider an inheritance to be divided with a brother, or fruits grown in one's own field to be stored in barns to be a crime? But the Lord is the witness and the judge, as it is written.[143]

[Luke 12:16–18] **The land of a certain rich man brought forth plenty of fruits. And he thought within himself, saying: What should I do, because I have nowhere to store my fruits? And he said: This I will do: I will pull down my barns and build greater ones; and there I will store all things that are grown to me and my goods.** This rich man is not reproached because he cultivated the earth, or stored the fruits grown from it in barns, but because he trusted his life entirely to this abundance of things, and the fruits that the earth habitually produced very plentifully. Reckoning the fruits and good things his own, he was keen not to bestow them on the poor, according to the command of the Lord, who says: *what remains, give alms,*[144] but, having enlarged his storage space, to preserve them for the future for his own riotous living, saying:

[Luke 12:19] **Soul, you have many things laid up for many years. Take your rest, eat, drink, be merry.** We read something similar to this

---

140 Acts 4:32.
141 Luke 11:23.
142 Luke 11:17.
143 Cf. Jer. 29:23.
144 Luke 11:41.

in Ecclesiasticus: *There is one who is enriched by living sparingly, and this is the portion of his reward: that he says: I have found rest for myself, and now I will eat my goods alone. And he does not know what time will pass, and that he must leave all to others.*[145]

[Luke 12:20] **But God said to him: You fool, this night they require of you your soul. And whose will be those things that you have provided?** You, who foolishly promised yourself a lengthy period of delights in life, will be snatched away by death this coming night, and will leave the things you stored to others. For God to say these things to the man is to curb his perverse stratagems with a sudden reproach.

In another interpretation: *At night* the soul *was taken away, which was lost in the darkness of the heart. At night* the soul *was taken away, which did not want to have the light of contemplation, so that it might foresee what it would endure. Hence the apostle Paul properly says to his disciples, who are thinking of things to come: 'But you, brothers, are not in darkness, that that day should overtake you like a thief. For you all are the children of light, and children of the day. We are not of the night, nor of darkness'.*[146] *For the day of death overtakes like a thief in the night, when it casts out the souls of fools who are not thinking ahead about the future.*[147] /252/

[Luke 12:21] **So is he who lays up treasure for himself and is not rich toward God.** If the one who lays up treasure for himself and is not rich toward God is a fool and is going to be seized in the night, it follows that he who wishes to be rich toward God must not lay up treasure for himself, but distribute what he possesses to the poor. For in this way the wise man will also deserve to be a child of light. Hence the Psalmist, right after saying about the avaricious rich man: *But he is disquieted in vain. He lays up treasure, and he does not know for whom he will store these things,*[148] immediately and correctly revealed where he had placed the treasure of his own heart, saying: *And now what is my hope? Is it not the Lord? And my substance is with you.*[149]

150/5 [Luke 12:22] **And he said to his disciples: Therefore I say to you, be not solicitous for your life, what you will eat, nor for your body, what you will put on.** When he says, *Therefore I say*, he looks

---

145 Ecclus. 11:18–20.
146 1 Thess. 5:4–5.
147 Gregory, *Moralia* 25.3 (CCSL 143B:1231.13–21).
148 Ps. 38:7 (39:6).
149 Ps. 38:8 (39:7).

back to what was said above, that is, 'Therefore I forbid solicitude for temporal things, lest you be convinced to lay up treasure for yourselves with the rich of the world'. *Therefore, what nature gives to all, to pack animals and wild beasts alike, is likewise common to men, and so we are completely free from anxiety about it; but it is enjoined upon us that we be not solicitous for what we eat.* And *because we prepare bread for ourselves by the sweat of our face,*[150] *work must be done, but solicitude eliminated.*[151]

[Luke 12:23] **The soul is more than food, and the body is more than the garment.** The Lord *admonishes us to remember that God gave us much more than food and a garment, because he made and fashioned us with a soul and body, so that you may understand that he who gave the soul will give food much more readily, and likewise he who gave the body will give a garment much more readily. In this passage it is usual to ask whether this food pertains to the soul, since the soul is incorporeal, but this food is corporeal. But we should know that in this passage the soul stands for this life, and that same corporeal food is its mooring cable. The same meaning is conveyed by this saying: 'He who loves his soul will lose it'.*[152] *For this precept will contradict that sentence where it is said: 'What does it profit a man, if he gains the whole world, but causes the loss of his own soul?' unless we take it to mean that it refers to this life which one must lose for the sake of the kingdom of God, which clearly the martyrs were able to do.*[153]

[Luke 12:24] **Consider the ravens, for they neither sow nor reap; they have neither storehouse nor barn; and God feeds them.** *Because if birds – which live today and will be gone tomorrow, whose spirit is mortal, and when they cease to be, are annihilated –* /253/ *are nourished by God's providence without care and hardship, how much more are men, to whom eternity is promised, ruled by God's* authority.[154]

[Luke 12:24b] **How much more valuable are you than they!** *That is, how much more dearly are you valued, because certainly a rational animal such as man is ranked more highly in the nature of things than irrational ones such as birds.*[155]

---

150 Cf. Gen. 3:19.
151 Jerome, *Commentarii in Matheum* 1 (CCSL 77:39.838–42).
152 John 12:25.
153 Augustine, *De sermone Domini* 2.15.49–50 (CCSL 35:140.1075–77; 1079–82; 141.1083–92); Matt. 16:26.
154 Jerome, *Commentarii in Matheum* 1 (CCSL 77:40.861–65).
155 Augustine, *De sermone Domini* 2.15.51 (CCSL 35:141.1095–98).

[Luke 12:25-26] **And which of you, by taking thought, can add one cubit to his stature? If then you are unable to do what is the least thing, why are you anxious about the rest?** *That is: That your body extends to your stature is due to God's power and sovereignty, by whose providence it can also be clothed. And from this it can be understood that it was not by your effort that your body came to this stature of yours, because if you try to and wish to add one cubit to this stature, you cannot. Leave likewise to him, therefore, the care of covering your body, by whose care you see that it came to pass that you have a body of this stature.*[156] *'If then you are unable to do what is the least thing'*, he says. *For this is the least thing, but for God the least thing is to create bodies.*[157] *And a lesson was also going to be given about clothing, just as had been given about food. Accordingly, it follows, and he says:*[158]

[Luke 12:27] **Consider the lilies, how they grow, they do not labour, nor do they spin.** *But these lessons must not be discussed as if they were allegorical, so that we inquire what the ravens or the lilies signify. For they were set forth in order that greater things might be established from lesser ones.*[159]

[Luke 12:27b] **But I say to you: Not even Solomon in all his glory was clothed like one of these.** *And in fact, what silk, what purple garment of kings, what weavers' embroidery, can be compared to flowers? What is so red as a rose? What is so white as a lily? But that the purple of the violet is not surpassed by any purple dye is a verdict of the eyes more than a matter of disputation.*[160]

[Luke 12:28] **Now if God clothe in this manner the grass that is today in the field, and tomorrow is cast into the oven, how much more you, O you of little faith?** *In Scripture, 'tomorrow' is understood as the future, as when Jacob says: 'And my justice will give heed to me tomorrow';*[161] *and through the apparition of Samuel the sorceress says to Saul: 'Tomorrow you will be with me'.*[162]

[Luke 12:29] **And do not seek what you will eat or what you will drink.** It should be noted that he does not say, 'do not seek or be anxious

---

156 Augustine, *De sermone Domini* 2.15.51 (CCSL 35:141.1101-08).
157 Augustine, *Quaestiones euang.* 2.28 (CCSL 44B:69.3-4).
158 Augustine, *De sermone Domini* 2.15.52 (CCSL 35:142.1109-11).
159 Augustine, *De sermone Domini* 2.15.52 (CCSL 35:142.1116-19).
160 Jerome, *Commentarii in Matheum* 1 (CCSL 77:41.872-75).
161 Gen. 30:33.
162 Jerome, *Commentarii in Matheum* 1 (CCSL 77:41.879-82); 1 Sam. 28:19.

about food or drink or clothing', but he says more precisely, *what you will eat or what you will drink*; and above, *nor for your body, what you will put on.*[163] It seems to me that those people are censured who scorn common nourishment or clothing, /254/ and seek food or clothing which is either more sumptuous or more austere than that of the people they live with.[164]

[Luke 12:29b] **And do not be lifted up on high.** Having forbidden anxiety over food, he next warned them not to be puffed up. *For people first seek these things to fill a need; but when they become abundant, they begin to take pride in such things as well. It is as if a wounded person should boast that he has many bandages in his house in contrast to another who was fortunate not to have wounds and did not need even one bandage.*[165]

[Luke 12:30–31] **For the nations of the world seek all these things, and your Father knows that you need these things. But yet seek the kingdom of God and his justice, and all these things will be added to you.** *Here he shows very clearly that these things ought not to be striven for as if they were our goods, so that on account of them we ought to do well, if we do anything, but nevertheless that they are necessary. For what the difference is between the good that ought to be striven for and the necessity that must be acquired, he declared in this statement, when he says: 'But yet seek the kingdom of God and his justice, and all these things will be added to you'. The kingdom of God, therefore, is our good, and it ought to be striven for, and there the end must be fixed for the sake of which we do all that we do. But since to attain that kingdom we soldier on in this life, which cannot be carried on without these necessities, he says: 'These things will be added to you, but seek the kingdom of God.'*[166]

*And the fact that he did not say 'will be given' but 'will be added' certainly indicates that what is given originally is one thing, and what is added to it is another. For eternity must be in our purposes, but time has to be in our practices, and the former is given, and the latter without doubt is superabundantly added to.*[167]

---

163 Luke 12:22.
164 On the echoes of this passage in Bede's account of the sins of Coldingham abbey (*Ecclesiastical History* 4.25), see Barrow, 'Bede's Wise and Foolish Virgins', 296–97.
165 Augustine, *Quaestiones euang.* 2.29A (CCSL 44B:69.3–8).
166 Augustine, *De sermone Domini* 2.16.53 (CCSL 35:143.1133–45).
167 Gregory, *Moralia* 15.47 (CCSL 143A:781.9–13).

## Chapter 53

**151**/10 [Luke 12:32] **Fear not, little flock, for it has pleased your Father to give you a kingdom.** He calls the flock of the elect 'little', either on account of the greater number of the damned, or (which is preferable) on account of their zeal for humility, because he nevertheless wishes his Church, now spread out in such great numbers, to expand to the end of the world, and to attain the promised kingdom through humility. And for that reason, having gently encouraged the labours of the Church, which he orders to seek only the kingdom of God, he promises out of his kindness, so well disposed, that the Father will give the kingdom to that flock.

**152**/2 [Luke 12:33] **Sell what you possess and give alms.** Fear not, he says, that those who soldier on for the sake of the kingdom of God will lack the necessities of life, but sell even the things you possess for the sake of giving alms. For when one has scorned all possessions for the Lord's sake, /255/ it is appropriate that one nevertheless afterwards labour with the work of one's hands so as to be able both to support oneself and to give alms. Hence the Apostle boasts, saying: *I have not coveted any man's silver, or gold, or apparel, as you yourselves know. For such things as were needful for me and those who are with me, these hands have furnished. I have showed you all things, how that so labouring you ought to support the weak.*[168]

**153**/5 [Luke 12:33b] **Make for yourselves purses which do not grow old**, namely by giving alms, the reward of which remains forever. One must not think that this is a commandment that the saints not save up money, whether for their own use, or for that of the poor, since we read that even the Lord himself, to whom the angels ministered,[169] nevertheless had a purse in order to teach his Church to keep the offerings of the people and to distribute them for their own needs and those of others,[170] but also so that fear of poverty should not deter one from entering God's service or abandoning righteousness.

[Luke 12:33c] **A treasure in heaven which does not fail, where no thief approaches and no worm corrupts.** This can be taken in the straightforward sense to mean that money which is saved, or that wealth stolen from a treasury by a thief, or corrupted in a treasury due to its fragility, fails, but that which is donated for the sake of Christ confers the eternal

---

168 Acts 20:33–35.
169 Cf. Matt. 4:11.
170 Cf. John 12:6.

BOOK FOUR 425

fruit of mercy in heaven. Or it should be taken to mean that the treasure of good work, if produced for earthly reward, has been corrupted, and may easily perish, but if it is heaped up with a heavenly intention alone, it is not able to be defiled externally by the applause of men, or inwardly by the blemish of vainglory. For the thief steals from without, and the worm destroys internally. The thief carried away the wealth of those of whom the Lord says: *They have received their reward;*[171] the moth corrupts the clothing of those whom the Psalmist rebukes, saying: *For the Lord scatters the bones of men pleasing themselves.*[172] For he calls bones the strength of virtues.

[Luke 12:34] **For where your treasure is, there your heart will be also.** *This should be understood to apply not only to money, but also to all the passions. The god of a glutton is the belly;*[173] *therefore he has his heart there, where his treasure is also. The treasures of the voluptuary are luxurious banquets; of the frivolous, entertainments; of the lover, concupiscence. 'Anyone is a slave to him by whom he is overcome'.*[174]

154/10 [Luke 12:35] **Let your loins be girded, and lamps burning.** Because he had showed that many people were either completely subjected to the world, or in service to the Lord in consideration of worldly reward, he beautifully and concisely teaches his own people /256/ both to gird their loins *for the sake of abstaining from the love of worldly things,* and to keep their *lamps burning so as to do this with a true aim and proper purpose.*[175]

In another interpretation: *We gird our loins when we restrain the wantonness of the flesh by abstinence. And we hold burning lamps in our hands, when we show our neighbours examples of light by good works. Indeed, the one cannot please our Redeemer at all without the other – whether he who does good things still does not abandon the filth of wantonness, or whether he who is preeminent in chastity still does not busy himself with good works. But if both are present, it remains for everyone aiming for the heavenly fatherland with hope by no means to restrain himself from vices for the sake of the honour of this world, but to build his whole hope on the coming of his Redeemer. Hence also he immediately adds:*[176]

---

171 Matt. 6:2.
172 Ps. 52:6 (53:5) (not *iuxta LXX*).
173 Cf. Phil. 3:19.
174 Jerome, *Commentarii in Matheum* 1 (CCSL 77:38.813–17); 2 Peter 2:19.
175 Augustine, *Quaestiones euang.* 2.25 (CCSL 44B:67.2–4).
176 Gregory, *Hom. in Euang.* 1.13.1–2 (CCSL 141:90.9–31). Bede's preference for a tropological approach to this passage contrasts with his later view that 'loins girded and

[Luke 12:36] **And be you yourselves like men who wait for their lord, when he will return from the wedding,** ... *Indeed, the Lord went away to the wedding, because arising from the dead, ascending into heaven, the new man coupled to himself the heavenly multitude of angels. He then returns, when he is made manifest to us now in judgement. And it is properly added about the servants who wait:*[177]

[Luke 12:36b] **So that when he comes and knocks, they may open to him immediately.** *He comes indeed, when he hastens to judgement, but he knocks when he signals through the vexations of illness that death is already near. We 'open to him immediately', if we receive him with love. No one who trembles to leave his body wants to open the door to a judge when he knocks, for when he remembers that he despised the judge, he is afraid to see him. But he who is untroubled about his hope and love immediately opens to him when he knocks, because he receives the judge joyfully, and when he recognizes the time of his approaching death, he rejoices in the glory of his recompense. Hence also it is immediately added:*[178]

155/5 [Luke 12:37] **Blessed are those servants, whom the Lord when he comes will find watching.** *He watches, who keeps the eyes of his mind open to the sight of the true light; he watches, who serves by performing what he believes; he watches, who repels from himself the darkness of sluggishness and heedlessness. Hence Paul says: 'Awake, you just, and sin not.'*[179] *Hence he says again: 'It is now the hour for us to rise from sleep'.*[180] *But let us hear what the Lord, when he comes, will do for his servants who are watching.*[181]

[Luke 12:37b] **Truly I say to you that he will gird himself, and make them sit down to eat, and coming by will minister to them.** *He girds himself, that is, he prepares to repay them; he will make them sit down to eat, that is, to be refreshed* /257/ *in eternal rest. Indeed, to sit down to eat is to rest in the kingdom. Hence again the Lord says: 'They will come and sit down with Abraham and Isaac and Jacob'.*[182] *The Lord will*

---

lamps burning' represents the correct attitude of watchful expectation of the Second Coming, e.g., *Reckoning of Time* 67 (trans. Wallis, 240): Darby, *Bede and the End of Time*, 197–98.
177 Gregory, *Hom. in Euang.* 1.13.2–3 (CCSL 141:91.32–36).
178 Gregory, *Hom. in Euang.* 1.13.3 (CCSL 141:91.37–45).
179 1 Cor. 15:34.
180 Rom. 13:11.
181 Gregory, *Hom. in Euang.* 1.13.3–4 (CCSL 141:91.46–53).
182 Matt. 8:11. Neither Gregory nor Bede quotes the rest of this verse, 'in the kingdom of heaven', which makes it more apposite to the exegesis they propose.

*come and minister, because he satisfies us with the splendour of his light. But 'he comes by' means he returns from judgement to his kingdom. Or indeed the Lord comes to us after judgement, because he lifts us up from his human appearance by the contemplation of his divinity. And his 'to come by', is to lead us to the contemplation of his splendour, when we see him in divine form after the judgement, whom we perceive in human form in the judgement.*[183]

[Luke 12:38] **And if he comes in the second watch, or comes in the third watch, and finds them so, blessed are those servants.** *The first watch is certainly the time of the first period of life, that is, childhood. The second, youth or young manhood, which on the authority of sacred Scripture, which says: 'Rejoice, young man, in your youth',*[184] *are the same. And the third is taken as old age. Therefore, he who would not keep watch in the first watch may yet stand guard in the second, so that he who neglected to be converted from his depravities in his childhood may at least be watchful for the paths of life in the time of his youth. And he who would not keep watch in the second watch may not lose the remedies of the third watch, so that he who is also not watchful for the paths of life in young manhood may at least come to his senses in old age.*[185] *But to shake off the slothfulness of our soul, Christ brings out external injuries by way of comparison, so that it may be aroused by this to a care for itself. For it is said:*[186]

**156/2** [Luke 12:39] **But know this, that if the householder knew at what hour the thief would come, he would surely watch, and would not let his house be broken into.** *Likewise, he adds an exhortation after the preceding comparison, saying:*[187]

[Luke 12:40] **And be ready, for the Son of man is coming at an hour which you do not suspect.** *Indeed, the thief breaks into the house when the householder is unaware, because as long as the spirit sleeps without showing concern for itself, death comes unexpectedly and bursts into the dwelling-place of our flesh; and he kills the lord of the house whom he finds sleeping, because when the spirit least foresees approaching harm, death*

---

183 Gregory, *Hom. in Euang.* 1.13.4 (CCSL 141:91.54–64). Bede's conviction that the blessed would enjoy face to face contact with God appears throughout his commentaries and sermons: see Darby, *Bede and the End of Time*, 138.
184 Eccles. 11:9.
185 Gregory, *Hom. in Euang.* 1.13.5 (CCSL 141:92.69–82).
186 Gregory, *Hom. in Euang.* 1.13.5 (CCSL 141:93.102–05).
187 Gregory, *Hom. in Euang.* 1.13.5 (CCSL 141:94.107–08).

snatches it unawares to punishment. *If it were keeping watch, it could resist the thief because to guard against the coming of the judge who snatches the soul secretly, it would meet him by being penitent, in order not to perish impenitent. But our Lord wanted the last hour to be unknown to us, so that it would always be uncertain and so that while we cannot foresee it, we may be constantly prepared for it.*[188]

**157/5** [Luke 12:41] **And Peter said to him: Lord, do you speak this parable to us, or likewise to all?** Indeed, the Lord had warned of two things with the afore-mentioned parable, /258/ namely, that he would not only come suddenly, but also that people ought to await him in a state of preparedness. But it is not readily apparent which of these Peter asked about, or whether both, or whom he connected with himself and his companions, when he said, 'do you speak to us, or likewise to all'. And indeed, in that he said, 'us', and 'all', he must be supposed to signify either the apostles and those like them, and the rest of the faithful, or those who die as individuals every day and willingly or unwillingly receive the coming of their judge, and those who are alive and must be judged in the flesh with the universal judgement coming. But it would be astonishing if the blessed Peter doubted that there was going to be a judgement, either for all who would live *soberly and justly and piously*, looking for *the blessed hope and coming of the glory of the great God,*[189] *who wills all men to be saved,*[190] or, that a judgement of one and all, of the great and the small, of the faithful and the infidels, would be unforeseen.

Given that these things are now well known, it remains to be understood that Peter thought these things, which perhaps he did not know, deserved further investigation – namely whether those sublime teachings about heavenly life, for the sake of which the Lord had ordered his disciples to sell their possessions, to make purses that do not grow old, to store up a treasure in heaven,[191] to keep watch with loins girded and lamps burning, and to wait for the Lord,[192] pertain to the apostles alone and those like them, or to all who are going to be saved. What the one who posed this question meant is made clear, unless I am mistaken, by this response of the Lord:

---

188 Gregory, *Hom. in Euang.* 1.13.5–6 (CCSL 141:94.109–20).
189 Titus 2:12–13.
190 1 Tim. 2:4.
191 Cf. Luke 12:33.
192 Cf. Luke 12:35–36.

[Luke 12:42] **And the Lord said: Who do you think is the faithful and wise steward, whom his lord sets over his household, ...** Responding to these questions, the Saviour first teaches that judgement will come to all, and that individuals will receive rewards or punishments in accordance with what their works deserve, and the capacity of their understanding. Then, what he had chiefly asked,[193] he showed, namely that the grace of virtues which he brought to the world should be pursued by individuals as much as they could. *I have come*, he says, *to cast fire on the earth, and what do I want, but that it be kindled?*[194] Of course, because he says, *Who do you think is*, he implies the difficulty of achieving virtue, not the impossibility, just as the Psalmist, who says: *Who is wise, and will keep these things?*[195] does not mean that no one will, but that an exceptional person will. Elsewhere, on the other hand, he used the same phrasing to refer not to what is difficult, but to what is impossible: *O God, who will be like to you?*[196] that is, no one: *For you alone are the Most High over all the earth.*[197]

[Luke 12:42b] **To give them their measure of wheat in due season?** *The proper quantity of exposition is expressed by the measure of wheat. And indeed, everything of an exalted nature ought to be hidden from a large audience, and opened to a bare few, so that when /259/ something incomprehensible is bestowed on a narrow mind it is not rejected. Hence Moses, departing from the secret place of God, veils his gleaming face in the presence of the people,*[198] *because certainly he does not disclose the mysteries of innermost glory to the multitudes.*[199] *Therefore the speech of teachers ought to be adapted to the condition of the audience so that it is appropriate for the needs of individuals, and nonetheless does not depart from the art of general instruction.*[200]

[Luke 12:43–44] **Blessed is that servant, whom his lord will find doing so, when he comes. Truly I say to you, he will set him over all he possesses.** The difference between the rewards given to good pupils and those given to good teachers is as great as the difference of their

---

193 I.e., *Who do you think is the faithful and wise steward?*
194 Luke 12:49.
195 Ps. 106:43 (107:43).
196 Ps. 82:2 (83:1).
197 Ps. 82:19 (83:18).
198 Cf. Exod. 34:29–35; 2 Cor. 3:13.
199 Gregory, *Regula pastoralis* 3.39 (SC 382:528.10–11; 5–7; 11–12).
200 Gregory, *Regula pastoralis* 3 prol. (SC 382:258.10–13); also, *Moralia* 30.3 (CCSL 143B:1499.97–100).

merits. For when the Lord at his coming finds the former keeping watch, he will make them sit down to eat, and 'coming by' will minister to them. But when the Lord finds the latter faithfully and wisely dispensing the nourishment of Scripture to a household devoted to himself, he will set them over all he possesses, that is, over all the joys of the heavenly kingdom, not, of course, in order that they may have sole possession of them, but so that they may enjoy eternal possession of them more abundantly than other holy people. *For those who are learned will shine like the brightness of the firmament, and those who instruct many to justice, like stars for all eternity.*[201] And the Apostle says: *Let the priests who rule well be esteemed worthy of double honour, especially those who labour in word and doctrine.*[202]

**158/5** [Luke 12:45] **But if that servant says in his heart: My lord delays coming, and if he begins to strike the menservants and maids, and to eat and drink and get drunk, ...** Just as the whole order of good teachers is taught how to live and be rewarded through the example of one faithful steward, so also the damnable action and the eternal damnation of all wicked prelates is exhibited in this good-for-nothing servant – prelates who not only give themselves up to licentiousness, but who also vex their underlings with acts of injustice. However, he can also be understood to strike the menservants and maids allegorically, that is, to corrupt the hearts of the weak, not yet strengthened by faith, hope, and love, by displaying an example of perverse deeds and speech. And to eat, drink, and get drunk, is to be occupied with all the sins and enticements of the world that madden the mind and cause it to go astray.

Note that it was reckoned among the faults of the wicked servant that he thought that the return of his lord was delayed; it was not numbered among the virtues of the good steward that he hoped for his master's swift return, but only that at the lord's command he gave to his fellow servants their measure of wheat in due season no matter when he came. That is, he displayed a basic principle both of the divine word and of his own example. Indeed we read that /260/ certain good servants were chastised by the Apostle, because, fearing and anxious, they believed the day of the Lord was at hand,[203] which the Lord himself promised would come unexpectedly.[204]

---

201 Dan. 12:3.
202 1 Tim. 5:17.
203 Cf. 2 Thess. 2:2.
204 Cf. 1 Thess. 5:2.

BOOK FOUR 431

Hence although we earnestly desire to know, if it is permitted, when the Desired of all nations will come,[205] it is nevertheless considered best if we are serenely ignorant of what it is not permitted for us to know, and are just prepared to await and to long for his coming, following the example of the good servant.[206]

[Luke 12:46] **The lord of that servant will come in a day that he does not expect, and at an hour that he does not know, and will divide him, and will assign him his portion with the unbelievers.** He will divide him not by cutting him apart with a sword, but by separating him from the community of the faithful, and by joining him to those who had never even had anything to do with the faith,[207] because, as the Apostle says, he who *does not care for his own people and especially for his household servants has denied the faith, and is worse than an infidel.*[208]

159/10 [Luke 12:47] **And that servant who knew the will of his lord, and did not prepare, and did not do according to his will, was beaten with many stripes.** Many people, badly misunderstanding this statement, *do not wish to know what they should do, and think that they will be beaten less, as it were, if they do not know what they should have done. But it is one thing not to have known, and another not to have wished to know. For he who wishes to learn and is not able is ignorant; but he who averts his ear from the voice of truth in order not to know, that person is adjudged to be not ignorant but a despiser of knowledge.*[209]

[Luke 12:48] **But he who did not know, and did things worthy of stripes, was beaten with few stripes. And to whomever much is given, of him much will be required; and to whom they have committed much, of him they demand the more.** Why, after he said, *to whom much is given*, did he add, *and to whom they have committed much* (you understand 'divine judgements'), unless perhaps he wished thereby to make known both orders of the faithful, the clergy and the laity, because often much is given even to lay persons whomever they may be, to whom is entrusted not only knowledge of the Lord's will, but also the ability to carry out what they know. But much is committed to him to whom is also entrusted, along

---

205 Cf. Hagg. 2:8 (2:7 NRSV).
206 For Bede's aversion to speculation about the time of the Second Coming, see Introduction, 3–4, 10.
207 Cf. Jerome, *Commentarii in Matheum* 4 (CCSL 77:235.688–89).
208 1 Tim. 5:8.
209 Gregory, *Moralia* 15.45 (CCSL 143A:780.6–11).

with his own salvation, the care of feeding the Lord's flock. And therefore, *the powerful are powerfully tormented*,[210] and *a mightier punishment is ready for the mightier*,[211] that is, a greater punishment will follow those endowed with greater grace, if they do wrong.

But *the mildest punishment of all will be for those who, aside from the original sin which they inherited, added nothing further; and as for the others who have added sins, /261/ each one will have a punishment there which will be more bearable in proportion as his iniquity here was less grave.*[212]

## Chapter 54

**160**/5 [Luke 12:49] **I have come to cast fire on the earth, and what do I want, except that it be kindled?** This statement specifically responds to the question of the blessed Peter, who wants to know whether a stricter mode of life should be sought by all. Indeed, Christ calls the love of the Holy Spirit 'fire',[213] which, illuminating the secret places of the heart, stirs it up to heavenly things by its continuous motion, burns up the vices of carnal concupiscence like thorns and thistles, refines the golden vessels of the Lord's house by trying them in fire, *consumes wood, hay, and stubble*,[214] and which, having been sent to earth, immediately makes fertile by the inmost scattering of its light those one hundred and twenty lamps which it found in the citadel of Zion.[215] He spoke of this above: *Let your loins be girded*, he added: *and lamps burning.*[216] You seek to know, he says, whether I warn everyone to await the coming of the Lord with girded loins and burning lamps. But I who have gone forth from the bosom of the Father for this alone, and have come into the world to kindle men from earthly desires into heavenly longings, what else do I want, do you suppose, than that the splendour of this fire may illuminate all the regions of the world, that the flame of this devotion may always increase in the heart of the

---

210 Wisd. 6:7.
211 Wisd. 6:9.
212 Augustine, *Enchiridion* 23.93 (CCSL 46:99.133–37).
213 Cf. Ps.-Jerome, *Expositio euangeliorum* (PL 30:573C), where fire is *caritas*.
214 Jerome, *Commentarii in Esaiam* 18.66.15/16 (CCSL 73A:782.25–26).
215 Cf. Acts 1:15; 2:1–4.
216 Luke 12:35. See also Barrow, 'Bede's Wise and Foolish Virgins', 297, for echoes in the *Ecclesiastical History*'s account of the destruction by fire of Coldingham.

faithful until the end of the world, and that it may never be extinguished by any assault either of waves or of winds?

[Luke 12:50] **But I have a baptism with which to be baptized.** First I have to be steeped in the baptism of my own blood, he says, and thus kindle the hearts of believers with the fire of the Spirit, whereby they are able to despise, or rather, to hate all earthly things as well as their own soul. *For as yet the Spirit was not given, because Jesus was not yet glorified,*[217] that is, by the victory of the passion. About this he says: *Can you drink of the chalice that I drink of, or be baptized with the baptism whereby I am baptized?*[218]

[Luke 12:50b] **And how I am constrained until it is accomplished!** Some codices read, *'And how I am tormented'. The Lord's graciousness is so great that he declares that there is in him zeal for instilling devotion in us, and for achieving perfection in us, and of hastening his passion for our sakes. He who had nothing in himself to be sorry for, nevertheless was tormented* or constrained *by our tribulations, and displayed sorrow at the time of the passion, which he took on not because he was afraid of his own death, but because our redemption was delayed, in connection with which,* he says: *'And how I am tormented, until it is accomplished.' Certainly, he who is tormented until something is accomplished is sure that it will be accomplished.*[219]

[Luke 12:51] **Do you think that I have come to give peace on earth? I tell you, no, but division.** He declares how, after the baptism of his passion, /262/ after the advent of the fire of the Spirit, the earth is going to burn. Since *in consequence of the faith of Christ, the whole world was divided against itself, each household had both infidels and believers, and therefore a good war was sent to break a bad peace.*[220] Isaiah also prophetically foretold this using the symbol of Egypt, saying: *Behold the Lord will ascend upon a swift cloud, and will enter into Egypt, and the idols of Egypt will be moved at his presence, and the heart of Egypt will melt in the midst of it. And I will set the Egyptians to fight against the Egyptians,*[221] with the latter, of course, fighting against the faith, and the former for the faith.

---

217 John 7:39.
218 Mark 10:38.
219 Ambrose, *Expos. Lucam* 7.133 (CCSL 14:259.1417–25).
220 Jerome, *Commentarii in Matheum* 1 (CCSL 77:73.1227–29).
221 Isa. 19:1–2.

[Luke 12:52] **For henceforth five in one house will be divided, three in two, and two in three, ...** 'In two' and 'in three' signifies against two and against three. It should be observed how he says the five were divided, since the words *for six persons are seen* to have been appended below: namely, *father and son, mother and daughter, and mother-in-law and daughter-in-law*. It should be understood that the same person was designated by the name of mother-in-law as by the name of mother, because *whoever is the mother of the son* is herself *the mother-in-law of his wife*,[222] and for that same reason the latter person herself is said to have been divided between daughter and daughter-in-law. If anyone should seek likewise to interpret these divisions allegorically, three are divided in two and two in three, because the good suffer enmity at the hands of the bad, and show enmity towards them, and the bad likewise from and towards the good. For there is no one who doubts that three pertains to those who keep the faith of the supreme Trinity, and also that two is suited to those who dissent from the unity of the faith; and it is proved in many passages of the Scriptures, and there especially, that not only are the unclean animals held in the ark under this number,[223] but also in Genesis of the second day only is it not said that the works seen by God are good.[224]

[Luke 12:53] **The father against the son, and the son against his father, ...** This father is the devil, whose sons we once were, not because he created us, but because we imitated him, just as the Lord says: *You are of your father the devil.*[225] But after we heard the voice warning us: *Forget your people and the house of your father*,[226] that fire came, that is, the grace of the Spirit divided us against each other, and it revealed another father, to whom we would say: *Our Father, you who are in heaven.*[227]

[Luke 12:53b] **The mother against the daughter, and the daughter against the mother, ...** The mother is the Synagogue. The daughter is the primitive Church, which both withstood the Synagogue, the persecutor of the faith, from whom she led the people, and also refuted that same Synagogue with the truth of the faith.

[Luke 12:53c] **The mother-in-law against her daughter-in-law, and**

---

222 Ambrose, *Expos. Lucam* 7.137 (CCSL 14:261.1477–80).
223 Cf. Gen. 7:3.
224 Cf. Gen. 1:8. Bede discusses this omission at greater length in *In Genesim* 1, ed. Jones (CCSL 118A:11.291–306); trans. Kendall, *On Genesis*, 77.
225 John 8:44.
226 Ps. 44:11 (45:10).
227 Matt. 6:9.

the daughter-in-law against her mother-in-law. The mother-in-law is the Synagogue, and the daughter-in-law is the Church of the Gentiles, because the bridegroom of the Church, Christ, is the son of the Synagogue, as the Apostle says: *To which belong the fathers, /263/ and from which comes Christ, according to the flesh.*[228] Therefore the mother-in-law, that is, the mother of the bridegroom, is divided both against her daughter-in-law, as we said above, and against her daughter, because the carnal Synagogue does not cease to persecute believers both circumcised and uncircumcised. But the daughter and daughter-in-law themselves also are divided against the mother-in-law and the mother, not wanting to accept fleshly circumcision, as the Acts of the Apostles teach.[229]

**161/5** [Luke 12:54–55] **And he said also to the multitudes: When you see a cloud rising from the west, you immediately say: A shower is coming, and so it happens. And when you see a south wind blowing, you say: There will be heat, and it happens.** *A cloud rising from the west signifies the Lord's flesh rising from death. For from it the shower of gospel preaching is poured over the whole earth. A south wind blowing before heat signifies the less severe tribulations that precede the judgement.*[230]

[Luke 12:56] **You hypocrites, you know how to discern the face of the earth and the sky; but how is it that you do not discern this time?** What is allegorically signified by the cloud and south wind, we have touched upon by way of anticipation. But the literal sense is also clear, because those who could very easily know in advance the direction of the winds from the alteration of the elements when they wanted to, could also, if they wished, understand this time, that is, the time either of the first or the second coming of the Lord (for he had foretold many things about each), from the sayings of the prophets, who prefigured both times by evident signs in the form of events, and by the courses of the years.[231] And lest any of the crowd should perchance have deluded themselves concerning their ignorance and pled that they, being uneducated and ignorant of the prophetic texts, were not able to discern the course of times, he being alert to this argument adds:

---

228 Rom. 9:5.
229 Cf. Acts 15:1–11; 21:21.
230 Augustine, *Quaestiones euang.* 2.27 (CCSL 44B:68.2–6).
231 This is a striking statement, given that Bede, in the letter to Plegwine, was adamant that the first coming of Christ did not correspond to the beginning of the sixth millennium, nor could the second coming of Christ be 'scheduled' for any particular time in the future – a position he would repeat in his exposition of Luke 17:21–23. It is not clear which prophetic statements he is referring to.

[Luke 12:57] **And why do you not even judge for yourselves what is right?** He shows that these people, as rational creatures, even if they are unlettered, nevertheless can by their innate intellect discern not only that he who did miracles by himself, which no one else did, must be understood to be above mankind, and therefore must be believed to be God, but also that after so many injustices of this world, the righteous judgement of the Creator is going to come. Therefore no one should presume upon the benefit of ignorance while continuing to sin just because of what was said above, that a servant not knowing the will of the Lord is beaten with few stripes.[232] To say the least, by the very fact that he is a man, he cannot ignore either the evils that he guards against, or the good things that he strives for.

**162**/5 [Luke 12:58] **And when you go with your adversary to the magistrate, on the way endeavour to be delivered from him, lest perhaps he hand you over to the judge, and the judge hand you over to the officer, and the officer cast you into prison.** These words like those above teach that the allurements of the world ought to be trampled underfoot /264/ and the coming of the fearful Judge should be awaited with constant expectation. *Indeed, our adversary on the way is the word of God, which is opposed to our carnal desires in the present life. One who is subject in humility to its commands is delivered from it. Otherwise, the adversary will hand him over to the judge, and the judge to the officer, because the accused will be held liable as a sinner in the scales of the judge for having despised the word of the Lord. The judge will hand him over to the officer, because he will permit the officer to drag him to the evil spirit for chastisement, in order himself to demand that the soul be compelled out of the body for punishment, which was its willing accomplice in crime. The officer will cast him into prison, because he is thrust back into hell by the evil spirit until the day of judgement comes, and therefore he himself will in its company likewise be tormented in the fires of hell.*[233]

[Luke 12:59] **I say to you: You will not go out from there, until you pay the very last penny**, that is, until you atone for your least sins. Because you can always serve your sentence by suffering the penalty, but never atone by seeking forgiveness (for there will be no room for forgiveness there), you will never go out from that place where you will undergo the eternal penalty of your deeds.

---

232 Cf. Luke 12:48.
233 Gregory, *Hom. in Euang.* 2.39.5 (CCSL 141:385.145–55).

## Chapter 55

163/10 [Luke 13:1] **And there were some present at that very time who told him of the Galileans, whose blood Pilate had mingled with their sacrifices.** These Galileans, who were killed by an impious governor amidst their own sacrifices, indeed pay the penalty of their sins by an impious and sinful death. Nevertheless, it was not death itself that injured them – for the glory of the blessed martyrs makes clear that the good could also die this way – but a wicked life, for which they were sent to the second death. In truth they were punished by such a death for the correction of the living, so that a fool might become wiser by the whipping of a wicked man, or else as an example of people who are not willing to be corrected and accordingly are going to perish in the worst way. And finally, there follows:

[Luke 13:2–3] **And answering, he said to them: Do you think that these Galileans were sinners above all the Galileans, because they suffered such things? No, I say to you, but unless you do penance, you will all perish likewise.** For in fact those who had not done penance perished likewise, because in the fortieth year of the Lord's passion, the Romans, whom Pilate represented, inasmuch as he belonged to their nation and realm, appeared on the scene, and beginning from Galilee, where the Lord's preaching had also begun, utterly destroyed the impious people, even defiling with human blood not only the forecourts of the temple, where sacrifices were customarily offered, but also the interior of the building to which the Galileans did not have access.[234] Because Pilate, which means 'mouth of the hammerer',[235] actually allegorically signifies the devil, /265/ who is always prepared to kill, while blood signifies sin, and sacrifices, good deeds, Pilate mingles the blood of the Galileans with their sacrifices when the devil defiles the alms, prayers, fasting, and other good deeds of the faithful, either with the fatal delight of flesh and blood, or with the practice of hatred, the madness of envy, the desire for human praise, or any other abominable wickedness, so that however much they seem to have been offered to the Lord, nevertheless the cunning traitor brings it about that those making the offerings do not profit from them. Would that we did not know that this is happening among us daily.

---

234 This refers to the overthrow of Judea and the destruction of the Temple by Titus in 70, which by Bede's reckoning took place forty years after the crucifixion of Christ (cf. Bede, *The Reckoning of Time* 66; trans. Wallis, 199).
235 Cf. Jerome, *Hebr. nom.* (CCSL 72:141.18–19).

[Luke 13:4–5] **Or those eighteen upon whom the tower fell in Siloam, and killed them. Do you think that they also were debtors above all the men dwelling in Jerusalem? No, I say to you; but unless you do penance, you will all perish likewise.** These Jerusalemites just like those Galileans were not the only sinners, but were punished to put fear in the rest. Those who were crushed by the fall of the tower foretell that all the Jews who do not repent are going to perish with these very walls of theirs. The number eighteen [in Latin 'ten and eight'] is not an accident. Among the Greeks the number is expressed by I [iota = 10] and H [eta = 8], that is, by the same letters with which the name Jesus begins.[236] They indicate that the Jews especially deserved to be damned, because, having heard the name of the Saviour, they preferred to reject it rather than to accept it. Allegorically the tower of Siloam is him to whom the Psalmist sings: *You have conducted me, for you have been my hope, a tower of strength against the face of my enemy.*[237] And when the man blind from birth received the light, the name of Siloam itself, *which means Sent,*[238] surely signified the one who said: *I have come a light into the world.*[239] And again: *And he who sent me is with me.*[240] About the tower's fall it is elsewhere said under the metaphor of a stone: *Whoever falls upon that stone, will be shattered, and upon whomever it falls, it will break him to pieces.*[241]

In another interpretation: *Each of us ought to build a tower* of virtues, *having first counted the costs, lest, when he is unable* to finish it, *he be ridiculed* by passers-by.[242] This tower, having been well constructed, remains. But if on the contrary a tower erected out of pride does not have firm foundations, it will fall upon him by whom it was built.[243]

**164/10** [Luke 13:6] **He spoke also this parable: A certain man had a fig tree planted in his vineyard.** Certainly, this fig tree can signify the nature of the human race, which was well planted, that is, was created in the likeness of its Creator. But for three years it refused to give its fruit

---

236 See above, Luke 2:21. In medieval inscriptions, the word 'Jesus' is frequently written IHSVS/IHSVM/IHSV/IHS, or even IHESVS, etc.
237 Ps. 60:3–4 (61:2–3).
238 John 9:7.
239 John 12:46.
240 John 8:29.
241 Luke 20:18.
242 Cf. Luke 14:28–29.
243 Jerome, *Commentarii in Esaiam* 1.2.15 (CCSL 73:36.15–19).

to God when he sought it,[244] because it disdained /266/ to obey before the Law, under the Law, and under Grace.[245] But if you glance back at the above, you will notice that although the fig tree generally bears the figure of all three periods of history, it nevertheless specifically symbolizes the Synagogue. For when he immediately adds to that fearful and terrible sentence pronounced above: *unless you do penance, you will all perish likewise*,[246] the parable of the barren tree which is doomed to be eradicated, he very clearly teaches that those to whom he spoke were going to be cut down like the unfruitful fig tree if they did not repent. Therefore, *the vineyard of the Lord of hosts is the house of Israel*,[247] as we are taught by the Song of Isaiah. And the fig tree in the vineyard is the Synagogue founded in the same house. But he who permitted his vineyard to be plundered by wayfarers, also ordered the fig tree to be cut down.

[Luke 13:6b] **And he came seeking fruit on it, and found none.** The Lord himself, who instituted the Synagogue through Moses, appeared, and was born in the flesh, and teaching frequently in the synagogue sought the fruit of the faith; but in the soul of the Pharisees he did not find it.

[Luke 13:7] **And he said to the planter of the vineyard: Look! For three years I come seeking fruit on this fig tree, and I find none.** The order of the apostles and teachers, by whose prayers and admonitions God provides constant care for his people, is symbolized by the planter of the vineyard. And indeed, the Lord very frequently complained of the fruitless nation of the Jews, because through the three years when he visited it, that is, in the commandments of the Law, in the proofs of the prophets, and in the very grace of the glittering Gospel, it paid no heed.

[Luke 13:7b] **Cut it down therefore. Why does it encumber the ground?** The Jewish nation was cut down by the Romans, not by the apostles, and was ejected from the land of promise. But *Cut it down*, he says; expose the calamity of the felling that is about to happen to it by urging penitence. The nation, which lost its land together with its kingdom by a just judgement, did not fear to persecute the citizens of heaven because they loved heaven, and to kill the very king of heaven and earth, saying

---

244 Cf. Luke 13:7.
245 Bede's commentary on Luke 13:6–11 is loosely based on Gregory, *Hom. in Euang.* 2.31.2–6 (CCSL 141:270–74). Before the Law, under the Law, and under Grace refers to three periods of sacred history, namely the age of the patriarchs before Moses, the time from Moses to Christ, and the age inaugurated by the Incarnation.
246 Luke 13:5.
247 Isa. 5:7.

through its high-priests and Pharisees: *If we let him alone thus, all will believe in him; and the Romans will come, and take away both our place and nation.*[248] Also the multitude of the Jewish people can be symbolized by the land encumbered by a sterile fig tree, for they were hidden by the noxious shade of their rulers so that they could not receive the light of the truth, and hindered by the example of their rulers' depravity, so that they were not warmed by the sun of heavenly love. This accords with what the Saviour says to these same rulers elsewhere: *Woe to you scribes and Pharisees, hypocrites, who shut the kingdom of heaven against men. For you yourselves do not enter in, and those who are going in, you do not allow to enter.*[249]

[Luke 13:8] **But he answering, said to him: Lord, let it alone this year also, until I dig about it,** ... This is the voice of the apostles, who, after /267/ the passion of the Lord, prayed very hard for the Jews that vengeance for the Lord's suffering on the cross not be sought from them even though they were impenitent. *Until I dig about it*, he says, that is, striking the deep root of the unfruitful heart with the hoe of bitter invective in two ways, with the horror both of present afflictions and of eternal damnation. *Certainly, every ditch is in the lowest part, and doubtless a rebuke when it shows the heart to itself humbles it.*[250]

[Luke 13:8b] **And until I put dung on it**, that is, until I make it remember the abomination of the evils which it did, and arouse the grace of remorse[251] as it were from the rottenness of dung.

[Luke 13:9] **And if happily it bears fruit. But if not, then after that you will cut it down.** Although he said, *And if happily it bears fruit*, he did not add anything to it, but left the sentence hanging. And when he went on, *But if not*, he immediately connected it with the judgement of the damnation to come, saying: *then after that you will cut it down*, because, of course, he saw that the Synagogue was far more inclined to deny than to confess God. Elsewhere, using the same figure in things as here in words, he condemned the unfruitful fig tree with a curse of eternal sterility,[252] thus showing that even

---

248 John 11:48.
249 Matt. 23:13.
250 Gregory, *Hom. in Euang.* 2.31.5 (CCSL 141:272.67–69).
251 Cf. Ps.-Jerome, *Expositio euangeliorum* (PL 30:573D), where fertilizing with dung is confession of sins.
252 Cf. Matt. 21:19; Mark 11:13–14. The parable of the fig tree in Luke falls into the category of 'verbal allegory', as opposed to the fig trees that Christ puts the curse of eternal sterility upon in Matthew and Mark, which fall into the category of 'historical allegory', as

if the apostles not only dig by chiding, but also carry in dung by upbraiding sins, that it nevertheless will not be laden with any fruits of penitence, but will be destroyed by the severity of the outstretched two-edged sword.

[Luke 13:10–11] **And he was teaching in their synagogue on the Sabbath. And behold there was a woman, who had a spirit of infirmity for eighteen years.** After he spoke the parable of the fig tree, the Lord is reported to have taught in the synagogue, in order to make it clear that the parable applies not to some other topic, but that to seek fruit on the fig tree and not find it is to bestow the word upon the Synagogue, and not to be accepted. Nevertheless, in order that you may not think that this entire tree must be completely rooted out because it is sterile, but know that a remnant is going to be saved by the election of grace, the healing of the primitive Church immediately follows under the guise of the bent-over woman. It is fitting that she had been bent over for eighteen years, a number which is formed by three multiplied by six, because it shows that she was faint through infirm works in the testimony of the Law, in the prediction of prophecy, and in the revelation of grace.[253] For the number six, in which the creation of the world was accomplished, signifies the perfection of works. Indeed, there are three times of the Lord's visitation,[254] during which Judea, because it knew how to work earthly rather than heavenly things, was as it were bent from the rectitude of its soul for eighteen years.

[Luke 13:11b] **And she was bent over, neither could she look upwards at all**, because earthly wisdom, seeking infirm things, did not yet know how to ponder heavenly ones, /268/ hearing through the prophet: *If you are willing, and will hear me, you will eat the good things of the land.*[255] Against which the Apostle says to members of the Church: *Mind the things that are above, not the things that are upon the earth.*[256]

[Luke 13:12–13] **When Jesus saw her, he called her to him, and said to her: Woman, you are delivered from your infirmity. And he laid his hands on her, and immediately she was made straight, and glorified**

---

these terms are defined and discussed by Bede under the heading of 'Allegory' in Bede, *De schematibus et tropis* 2.12, ed. Kendall (CCSL 123A:164.218–166.235); trans. Kendall, *The Figures of Rhetoric*, 201–03, and see *The Art of Poetry and Rhetoric*, Introduction, 26–27).

253 Cf. Ps.-Jerome, *Expositio euangeliorum* (PL 30:573D), 'per tres senos, ostendit, quod infirma fuit ante legem, sub lege, sub gratia'.

254 I.e., the three ages: before the Law, under the Law, and under Grace (see note 245 above).

255 Isa. 1:19.

256 Col. 3:2.

God. By predestining with grace, he saw; by illuminating with teaching, he called; by supporting with spiritual gifts, he laid hands; and by exalting through good works to a firm end, he straightened for the sake of glorifying God. Those, the Apostle says, *whom he predestined, he also called. And those whom he called, he also justified. And those whom he justified, he also glorified.*[257]

**165/5** [Luke 13:14] **And the ruler of the synagogue, being angry that Jesus had healed on the Sabbath, answering, said to the multitude: Six days there are on which you ought to work. On them therefore come and be healed, and not on the Sabbath day.** Jesus healed on the Sabbath, showing that now was the time, according to the prophecy of the Canticle of Canticles, that day would break, and the shadows be removed.[258] But the ruler of the synagogue did not know either this mystery or one more excellent by far, which the Lord revealed by healing on the Sabbath, because after the six ages of this world, he was going to give the eternal joys of life everlasting. As a symbol of this, Moses commanded that there should be a holiday on the Sabbath, not from good deeds, but from servile, that is, harmful action, thus certainly prefiguring that time when our worldly works, but not our religious ones, that is, the acts of praising God, would cease.[259] The ruler of the synagogue, therefore, is deceived and deceives, because the Law did not forbid a man to heal on the Sabbath, but it forbade him to bear burdens, that is, to be weighed down by sins.

[Luke 13:15] **And the Lord answering him, said: You hypocrites, does not everyone of you on the Sabbath day, loose his ox or his ass from the manger, and lead them to water?** He charges the rulers of the synagogue with infidelity, and he deservedly reproaches them with the name of hypocrites, that is, of pretenders, for although they wanted to be taken for teachers of the common people, they were not ashamed to neglect the healing of a person for the sake of caring for cattle. But in a deeper sense by the appellation 'ox' and 'ass' he signifies Jew and Greek, of whose calling it is written: *The ox knows his owner and the ass his lord's manger.*[260]

---

257 Rom. 8:30.
258 Cf. Song 2:17. In his commentary on this verse in *On the Song of Songs* 2, ed. Hurst (CCSL 119B:228.673–710; trans. Holder, 86–87), Bede does not remark on Jesus's healing on the Sabbath, but he does expand on the themes of the two forms of spiritual life, the active and the contemplative, and the twin joys of the light of revelation in the present and the light of the life of blessedness in the future.
259 Cf. Lev. 23:3.
260 Isa. 1:3.

Both of them, loosed from the bondage of sin, laid aside the thirst and heat of this world by drinking from the lord's fountain.

[Luke 13:16] **And ought not this daughter of Abraham, whom Satan has bound, lo, for eighteen years, be loosed from this bondage on the Sabbath day?** The daughter of Abraham is every faithful soul. The daughter of Abraham is the Church gathered from both peoples in the unity of faith which when the time of the Law and the Lord's resurrection was accomplished burst the bonds /269/ of long captivity by the sevenfold grace of the Holy Spirit. For in this way also perhaps the mystery of the Sabbath and of the eighteen years can appropriately be understood. Therefore, that the ox and the ass loosed from the manger are driven to water, is the same allegorically as that the daughter of Abraham was made straight from the bondage of her injurious bent-over condition, namely that the Church, gathered from the Jews and the Gentiles, is loosed from the snares of sins by the water of baptism, and is raised up to the hope of heavenly things.

It certainly should be noted that, because the Lord says that the woman was bound by Satan, an exceedingly shocking heresy attempts to add *that the defects of human bodies belong not to the creator, God, but rather to the devil, as if* the devil, *although he always has the desire of doing harm, can harm anyone unless he has received the power to do so from the Omnipotent. For what else is revealed, not only in the book of the blessed Job,*[261] which the aforesaid heresy scornfully rejects, together with the other books of the Old Testament, along with God himself, who as if he were in a state of frenzy gave to the wicked prince of the world [the power?],[262] *but also in the Gospel,*[263] *where* the demons *would not have run into the swine, unless he himself yielded this to them,*[264] just as I taught above?

**166/10** [Luke 13:17] **And when he said these things, all his adversaries were ashamed and all the people rejoiced for all the things that were gloriously done by him.** Those who are ashamed by what the Saviour says show that they should rightly be compared to the sterile fig tree. Those who rejoice over his miracles make clear that they belong to the daughter of Abraham who glorified God for being made straight, that is, that they belonged to the Church by the devoutness of their faith.

---

261 Cf. Job 2:6.
262 Bede's parenthetical remark appears to have become garbled in transmission.
263 Cf. Luke 8:32.
264 Augustine, *Contra aduers.* 2.12.39 (CCSL 49:128.1240–42; 1244–50).

## Chapter 56

167/2 [Luke 13:18–19] **He said therefore: What is the kingdom of God like, and what will I judge it to be like? It is like to a grain of mustard seed, ...** *The preaching of the Gospel is the kingdom of God and the knowledge of the Scriptures which leads to life.* Concerning this the Jews are told: *'The kingdom of God will be taken from you, and will be given to a nation yielding the fruits thereof'*.[265] *Therefore the kingdom is like a grain of mustard seed,*[266] *on account of the fervent heat of faith, or because it is said to expel poisons.*[267] Hence also we read elsewhere that perfect faith was compared to a mustard seed,[268] because certainly it overcomes all doctrines of depravity by its own simplicity and humility.

[Luke 13:19b] **Which a man received and cast into his garden.** The man is Christ; the garden is the Church, which must both be cultivated by learning and endowed with gifts. He is rightly said to have received the same seed which he sowed, because the gifts from his divine nature which he gave to us along with the Father, he received with us from his human nature. Hence it is said: He *received gifts in men.*[269] And elsewhere Peter says: *And having received of the Father the promise of the Holy Spirit, he has poured forth this which you see and hear.*[270] /270/

[Luke 13:19c] **And it grew and became a tree.** The preaching of the Gospel grew and spread throughout the whole world, and it grows in the soul of each believer, because no one suddenly becomes perfect, but *he who has determined*, the Psalmist says, *in his heart assents in the valley of tears,*[271] and a little below: *They will go from strength to strength; the God of gods will be seen in Zion.*[272] Indeed, there is an ascent step by step from the valley of tears, so that the God of gods may be seen on the mountain of heavenly joys. And by growing, the seed of mustard shoots up, not like crops which quickly wither, but like a tree rejoicing in its longevity and rich fertility. And note that while the fig tree in the old vineyard is condemned, a new mustard tree is brought forth afterwards in the garden of the Gospel.

---

265 Matt. 21:43.
266 Jerome, *Commentarii in Matheum* 2 (CCSL 77:107.843–46).
267 Augustine, *Quaestiones euang.* 1.11 (CCSL 44B:14.2–3).
268 Cf. Luke 17:6.
269 Ps. 67:19 (68:18).
270 Acts 2:33.
271 Ps. 83:6–7 (84:5–6) (not *iuxta LXX*).
272 Ps. 83:8 (84:7) (not *iuxta LXX*).

BOOK FOUR 445

[Luke 13:19d] **And the birds of the heavens rested in its branches.** The branches of this tree are the diverse teachings in which chaste souls that know how to direct their course with the wings of virtues to heavenly things rejoice to build nests and rest.[273] *Who will give me,* the Psalmist says, *wings like a dove, and I will fly and be at rest?*[274] In the mustard seed, *which a man received and cast into his garden,*[275] can be understood the very humility of the Lord's incarnation, because after Joseph received the body of the crucified Saviour, he buried it in the garden.[276] It grew and became a tree, because he rose again and ascended into heaven. It spread branches in which the birds of the heavens rested, because he dispersed preachers throughout the world, by whose sayings and consolations all the faithful find refreshment from the weariness of this life.

**168/5** [Luke 13:20–21] **And again he said: What will I judge the kingdom of heaven to be like, and what is it like? It is like yeast, which a woman took and hid in three satums of flour, until the whole was leavened.** *A satum is a kind of measure, according to the usage of the province of Palestine, containing a peck and a half.*[277] Therefore he calls *love, which ferments and lifts up* the soul, *yeast.*[278] But he calls that woman, on whom in the preceding passage he laid his hands, and immediately she was made straight and glorified God, the daughter of Abraham,[279] that is, the Church, whose flour we are. We are all ground by the practice of fear and hope, as if by the upper and lower millstone, in order that, according to the Apostle, we being many may be one bread, one body.[280] Therefore the woman hides the yeast of love in three measures of flour, because the Church commands us to love the Lord with our whole heart, our whole soul, and our whole strength.[281] To the Church symbolized by Sarah Abraham said: *Hasten, knead three measures of fine flour, and make bread baked under the ashes.*[282] In the three measures of flour can be understood /271/ likewise the three fruits of the Lord's seed, namely the thirtyfold, the

---

273 Cf. Jerome, *Commentarii in Matheum* 2 (CCSL 77:108.867–71).
274 Ps. 54:7 (55:6).
275 Luke 13:19.
276 Cf. John 19:38–42 (Joseph is Joseph of Arimathea).
277 Jerome, *Commentarii in Matheum* 2 (CCSL 77:110.920–21).
278 Augustine, *Quaestiones euang.* 1.12 (CCSL 44B:14.3–4).
279 Cf. Luke 13:13 & 16.
280 Cf. 1 Cor. 10:17.
281 Cf. Mark 12:33.
282 Gen. 18:6.

sixtyfold, and the hundredfold,[283] that is, the married, the chaste, and the virgins.[284] And he beautifully says that the yeast was hidden in the flour until the whole was leavened, because love hidden in our heart ought to grow until it changes the whole heart into the perfection of itself, so that the soul can certainly love, act, and recollect nothing except the very love of its Creator. Because it has to begin here, but be perfected there, where since *God is all in all*,[285] he warms all with one and same fire of his love.

170/5 [Luke 13:23–24] **And a certain man said to him: Lord, are they few that are saved? But he said to them: Strive to enter by the narrow gate.** The hall of salvation is entered by a narrow gate, because it is necessary that the allurements of the deceptive world be overcome by works and fasting. And well did he say: *'Strive to enter', because unless there is a fervent striving of the heart, the waters of the world by which the soul is always recalled to the depths are not overcome.*[286]

[Luke 13:24b] **For many, I say to you, seek to enter, and they will not be able.** Stirred by the love of salvation, they seek to enter, and discouraged by the roughness of the journey, they will not be able. They seek this from a desire for rewards, and immediately they flee out of fear of hardship, not because the yoke of the Lord is rough or his burden heavy, but because they do not wish to learn from him, for he is meek and humble of heart, that they may find rest for their souls.[287] Therefore the gate by which to enter life becomes narrow.

171/5 [Luke 13:25] **But when the master of the house goes in and shuts the door, you will begin to stand outside and knock at the door, saying: Lord, open to us.** The master of the house is certainly Christ, who, although entirely everywhere in his divine nature, is indeed 'inside' to those whom he gladdens by the vision of him, while he is present in the heavenly fatherland. But he is as it were still 'outside' to those who struggle in this pilgrimage, and whom he, the hidden comforter, aids, according to what he himself promised: *Behold I am with you always to the consummation of the world.*[288] But he will go in and shut the door, when after conveying his whole body, which is the Church made bright by the glory

---

283 Cf. Matt. 13:23.
284 Cf. Jerome, *Commentarii in Matheum* 2 (CCSL 77:106.805–11).
285 1 Cor. 15:28.
286 Gregory, *Moralia* 11.50 (CCSL 143A:625.51–52).
287 Cf. Matt. 11:29–30.
288 Matt. 28:20.

of the resurrection, to the joy of contemplation of himself, he will take away from the wicked the opportunity to repent, which now he opens to all who devoutly knock. For to stand outside to knock at the door, separated from the destiny of the blessed, is to beg in vain for mercy, which they had neglected to beg from God.[289]

[Luke 13:25b] **And he answering will say to you: I do not know you where you are from**. How is it that he does not know where they are from, when the Psalm says: *The Lord knows the thoughts /272/ of men, that they are vain*,[290] and elsewhere it is written: *He knows the deceiver, and him who is deceived*,[291] unless *God is said to know, sometimes in the sense of 'to know thoroughly', and sometimes in the sense of 'to approve'*.[292] *For the Lord knows the way of the just*,[293] but he who *does not know will not be known*.[294] And therefore he knows the reprobates whom he judges by knowing them thoroughly, for he would not have judged those whom he did not know thoroughly at all, and nevertheless in a certain way he does not know where they are from, in the sense that he does not approve the character of their faith and love for himself.[295]

[Luke 13:26] **Then you will begin to say: We have eaten and drunk in your presence, and you have taught in our streets**. On a literal reading it should be understood that the Jews, rejecting the mysteries of the faith, believe that they are acceptable to the Lord if only they bring sacrificial victims to the temple, eat in the presence of the Lord, and give ear to the reading of the prophets, not knowing that passage of the Apostle: *The kingdom of God is not food and drink, but justice and peace and joy in the Holy Spirit*,[296] and elsewhere: *Whose god is their belly, and whose glory is in their shame*,[297] that is, in carnal circumcision. On an allegorical level it should be perceived that those who take the nourishment of the word with worthy eagerness eat and drink in the presence of the Lord. Hence those

---

289 This passage is pertinent to Bede's conception of purgatory, for which see Moreira, *Heaven's Purge*, 147–76.
290 Ps. 93:11 (94:11).
291 Job 12:16.
292 Gregory, *Moralia* 11.12 (CCSL 143A:596.6–7).
293 Ps. 1:6.
294 1 Cor. 14:38.
295 A concentrated example of Bede's intertextual exegesis, on which see Introduction, 29–35.
296 Rom. 14:17.
297 Phil. 3:19.

same persons who say these things add as if by way of exposition: *And you have taught in our streets. For holy Scripture is sometimes our food and sometimes our drink. In more obscure passages it is food, because it is broken by exposition as it were and swallowed by chewing. But it is drink in more open passages, because it is swallowed down just as it is found.*[298] And therefore *they testify that they have understood both the hidden and open commands of sacred Scripture*, who complain *to the judge reproving them, that they ate and drank in his presence.*[299] But they ought to be exceedingly fearful of what is added:

[Luke 13:27] **And he will say to you: I do not know you whence you are. Depart from me, all you workers of iniquity.** Feasting on the prescribed festivals, he says, is no help to someone whom faith does not commend; a knowledge of the Scriptures does not make one known to God, when wicked deeds show one to be unworthy in his eyes.

[Luke 13:28] **There will be weeping and gnashing of teeth.** Weeping is usually stimulated by heat and gnashing of teeth by cold. Here is where the double nature of hell is shown: that is, that it is a place of exceeding cold and of unbearable heat. The statement of the blessed Job confirms this: *They will pass from the waters of snow to exceeding heat.*[300] Or indeed: *Gnashing of teeth betrays the state of mind of someone who is indignant, because he repents too late, groans too late, is angry with himself too late, that he transgressed with such wilful depravity.*[301] /273/

173/2 [Luke 13:30] **And behold, they are last who will be first, and they are first who will be last.** The principal meaning of this statement is evident from the passages above, because the peoples of the Gentiles, living for a long time without faith, were to be called to the faith, and the Jews, occupying first place in faith and righteousness for so many ages, were going to be at the tail. But it can also be understood in such a way that some who are despised in the world are going to have great glory in the future, and others who are glorified among men must be damned by the strict Judge. It can also be understood in such a way that many who come late to the service of God are distinguished by the great merits of their life, but others who are inflamed with spiritual zeal from youth, in the end grow weary with sluggish laziness.

---

298 Gregory, *Moralia* 1.21 (CCSL 143:40.7–10).
299 Gregory, *Moralia* 1.21 (CCSL 143:41.29–31).
300 Job 24:19.
301 Ambrose, *Expos. Lucam* 7.206 (CCSL 14:286.2284–86).

BOOK FOUR 449

Chapter 57

174/10 [Luke 13:31–32] **On that same day, there came some of the Pharisees, saying to him: Depart, and go hence, for Herod wants to kill you. And he said to them: Go and tell that fox,** ... On account of his deceits and snares he calls Herod a fox, because a fox is an animal full of tricks, who always wants to lie concealed in his den, stinking with a foul odour, *and never runs on straight paths, but on tortuous circuitous routes*.[302] All these traits are applicable to heretics, of whom Herod is the prototype, who contrive to kill Christ, that is, to steal the humility of Christian faith from believers.

[Luke 13:32b] **'Behold I cast out devils, and I perfect cures today and tomorrow, and on the third day I am consummated'.** *These statements by the Lord are understood allegorically and figuratively, for he did not suffer on the third day after this day, since he immediately says:*[303]

[Luke 13:33] **'Nevertheless I must walk today and tomorrow and the day following, because it is not possible for a prophet to perish outside of Jerusalem.'** *Therefore, what he says, 'I cast out devils, and I accomplish cures today and tomorrow, and on the third day I am consummated', must refer to his body, which is the Church. Devils are expelled, when the Gentiles believe after having abandoned their ancestral superstitions, and cures are accomplished when life is lived according to his commandments from the time the devil and this world are renounced up to the time of the resurrection, which will be consummated as it were on the third day, that is, his Church will likewise be perfected to angelic plenitude by the immortality of the body.*[304]

175/5 [Luke 13:34] **Jerusalem, Jerusalem, you that kill the prophets, and stone them that are sent to you, how often would I have gathered your children as the bird does her nest under her wings, and you would not!** *He calls Jerusalem, not the stones and buildings of the city, but its inhabitants, which he bewails with a father's compassion, just as we also read in another passage that when he saw Jerusalem /274/ he wept.*[305] *But in this passage, he testifies that all the prophets were sent by him, for he says: 'How often would I have gathered your children.' Also we read in*

---

302 Isidore, *Etym.* 12.2.29.
303 Augustine, *De consensu euang.* 2.75.145 (CSEL 43:249.22–250.2).
304 Augustine, *De consensu euang.* 2.75.145 (CSEL 43:250.7–15).
305 Cf. Luke 19:41.

*the Song of Deuteronomy an analogous image* of a bird *gathering her nest under her wings*: *Just as an eagle will desire to protect her nest and be above her children, spreading her wings she took them up and bore them above her wings.*[306] And he who had called Herod, who was thinking about killing him, a fox, beautifully compares himself to a bird. For the deceitful fox never ceases to lie in ambush for birds.

[Luke 13:35] **Behold your house is left to you.** He now calls that city, which he had called his nest, the 'house' of the Jews. Stripped of the aid of the Lord and deservedly so, it is left to their rule, because not only did it scorn to be protected by the wings of that omnipotent bird, which Matthew calls a hen,[307] but it also handed over the same bird, which was willing to protect it, to the foxes to be devoured – that is, it handed over Christ to Herod and Pilate to be crucified. And without delay it is itself given over to be pillaged by those same wolves, that is, of the kings of the earth. For after the Lord was slain the Romans came, and, tearing apart an empty nest so to speak, they took their territory, their people, and their kingdom.

[Luke 13:35b] **And I say to you, that you will not see me until the time comes when you will say: Blessed is he who comes in the name of the Lord.** The multitudes indeed said these words as the Lord entered Jerusalem.[308] *But because* Luke *does not say* where the Lord *withdrew to* from here *so as not to come to Jerusalem until the time when those words be said* (*indeed he continues on his travels until he comes to Jerusalem*), *he certainly compels this to be understood allegorically*, that is, *about* his *advent, when he is going to come in splendour*,[309] especially since Matthew testifies that the Lord said these things after these praises had been sung to him by the crowd.[310]

In another interpretation, what he says is this: '*Unless you do penance*',[311] *and have confessed that the one about whom the prophets sang is me, the Son of the almighty Father, you will not see my face. The Jews have a time for repentance given to them; let them confess that he is blessed who comes in the name of the Lord, and let them look upon the face of Christ.*[312]

---

306 Jerome, *Commentarii in Matheum* 4 (CCSL 77:221.341–49); Deut. 32:11.
307 Cf. Matt. 23:37.
308 Cf. Matt. 21:9–10.
309 Augustine, *De consensu euang.* 2.75 (CSEL 43:249.17–20; 250.5–6).
310 Cf. Matt. 21:15–16; 23:37–39.
311 Luke 13:3.
312 Jerome, *Commentarii in Matheum* 4 (CCSL 77:222.365–69).

BOOK FOUR                                    451

## Chapter 58

176/10  [Luke 14:1–2] **And it happened, when Jesus went into the house of a certain chief of the Pharisees on the Sabbath to eat bread, that they were watching him. And behold, there was a certain man before him who had dropsy.** The disease *dropsy* [*hydropis*] takes its name *from the watery fluid,* for in Greek *water* is called *ydor. It is a fluid beneath the skin* originating in a defect /275/ of the bladder, *accompanied by turgid swelling and a foul breath.*[313] And it is characteristic of a dropsical person that *the more he abounds in an inordinate amount of fluid, the more he thirsts.* For that reason, he is rightly compared to someone weighed down by the excessive flow of carnal pleasures. He is compared *to the avaricious rich man,* who, *the more he abounds in wealth, which he does not use well, the more ardently he desires such things.*[314]

177/5  [Luke 14:3–4] **And Jesus answering, said to the lawyers and Pharisees: Is it lawful to heal on the Sabbath? But they were silent.** That Jesus is said to have answered refers back to what was said above: *That they were watching him.* For *the Lord knows the thoughts of men.*[315] But when they are asked, they are justly silent, who see that whatever they said was said against themselves. For if it is lawful to heal on the Sabbath, why are they watching the Saviour to see whether he heals? If it is not lawful, why do they themselves care for their domestic animals on the Sabbath?

[Luke 14:4b] **But he taking him, healed him, and sent him away.** With prudent governance the Lord heals the dropsical man in the presence of the lawyers and Pharisees, and he immediately preaches against avarice, in order that by the sickness of his body the sickness of their soul might be made explicit. Finally, after the many exhortations of his preaching, it is added: *And the Pharisees, who were avaricious, heard all these things, and they derided him.*[316] Indeed, the more the dropsical man drinks, the more he thirsts. And every avaricious man increases his thirst, who, when he has obtained the things that he strives for, pants more heavily to demand other things.

[Luke 14:5] **And answering them, he said: Which of you will have an ass or an ox fall into a well, and will not immediately draw it out**

---

313  Isidore, *Etym.* 4.7.23.
314  Augustine, *Quaestiones euang.* 2.29B (CCSL 44B:70.6–9).
315  Ps. 93:11 (94:11) (not *iuxta LXX*).
316  Luke 16:14.

on the Sabbath day? Thus, he clearly shows those who are watching him, the Pharisees, that they should also judge themselves guilty of avarice. *He says, if you hasten on the Sabbath to snatch up an ass or an ox, or any other animal that has fallen into a well, having regard not for the animal, but for your avarice, how much the more ought I to free the man, who is much better than the beast?*[317]

And *he fittingly compared the dropsical man to an animal that fell into a well; for he was struggling with water. In the same way, he compared that woman, who he said had been bound for eighteen years, and he loosed her from that same bondage, to a pack animal that is loosed to be led to water.*[318] And he appropriately set an ox and an ass in both places,[319] either because we feel that they signify every wise and stupid person, or, as was said above, they signify both peoples:[320] the people, that is to say, whose neck the yoke of the Law wore down, and the people whom any deceiver could come upon, seize and lead away into any error he pleased, like an animal brutish and devoid of reason. When he came, the Saviour found them all bound together by Satan's chains, all submerged in the bottom of the well of lust. *For there is no distinction.* /276/ *For all have sinned, and need the glory of God. Being justified freely by his grace, through the redemption that is in Christ Jesus.*[321]

**178/10** [Luke 14:7–8] **And he spoke a parable also to those who were invited, marking how they chose the first seats at table, saying to them: When you are invited to a wedding, do not sit down at table in the first place, ...** This admonition of the Saviour is clear on the literal level, teaching that humility is praiseworthy not only before God, but also before men. But since the evangelist does not call it a parable without a reason, it ought briefly to be considered what its hidden meaning is. It is evident that the union of Christ and the Church is called in many passages of Scripture a marriage. One of these is: *Can the children of the marriage fast, as long as the bridegroom is with them?*[322] Another is: *The kingdom of heaven is likened to a king, who made a marriage for his son. And he sent his servants to call those who were invited to the marriage.*[323] Whoever,

---

317 Jerome, *Commentarii in Matheum* 2 (CCSL 77:90.361–64).
318 Augustine, *Quaestiones euang.* 2.29B (CCSL 44B:69.2–6); cf. Luke 13:15–16.
319 I.e., in Luke 13:15 and here.
320 I.e., Jews and Gentiles.
321 Rom. 3:22–24.
322 Mark 2:19.
323 Matt. 22:2–3.

having been invited, comes to this wedding – that is, unites himself with the members of the Church for the sake of the faith – does not sit down in the first place, that is, does not exalt himself by boasting of his merits as if he were higher than the others. And indeed, let him take pains to appear clothed in a wedding garment in accordance with the parable found in another passage,[324] that is, flashing with the splendour of virtues, but let him adorn the attire of these virtues for a place of devout humility.

[Luke 14:8b–9] **Lest perhaps one more honourable than you be invited by him, and he who invited you and him, come and say to you: Give this man your place. And then you begin with shame to take the lowest place.** He who is overly complacent because of his confidence in his long practice of a moral way of life, gives up his place to someone more honourable who was invited later, when he is preceded by the quick agility of those who followed him to Christ. And he takes the lowest place with shame, when, learning better things of others, he admits the inferiority of all the works that he thought so well of, saying with the Prophet: *I am poor, and in labours from my youth, and being exalted have been humbled and troubled.*[325]

[Luke 14:10] **But when you are invited, go, sit down in the lowest place,** ... *To the extent you are great,* he says, *humble yourself in all things.*[326] And the Psalmist boasts: *I have been humbled, Lord, exceedingly, restore me to life according to your word,*[327] manifestly signifying in this way that he can be restored to life, if he himself experienced humble thoughts about his virtues.

[Luke 14:10b] **So that when he who invited you comes, he may say to you: Friend, go up higher.** When the Lord comes and blesses with the name of friend the one whom he finds humble, he will order him to go up higher. *Whoever therefore will humble himself as a little child, he is the greater in the kingdom of heaven.*[328]

[Luke 14:10c] **Then you will have glory in the presence of those sitting down at table together.** It is beautifully said, *Then you will have glory,* lest you now begin to ask what may save you in the end, because as Solomon says: *The inheritance got* /277/ *hastily in the beginning, in the end*

---

324 Cf. Matt. 22:11–12.
325 Ps. 87:16 (88:15) (not *iuxta LXX*).
326 Ecclus. 3:20.
327 Ps. 118:107 (119:107).
328 Matt. 18:4.

will be without a blessing.³²⁹ But the person who sits down in the lowest place and is found raised up at the coming of the Lord can also refer to this life, because the Lord enters his marriage daily, daily judges the character, the seating, the dress of the guests, and disdaining the proud often offers to the humble such great gifts of his spirit, that he deservedly glorifies that company of those sitting down at table together, that is, the company of those resting in the faith, who with unanimous admiration leap up in praise of its Creator, saying: *But to me your friends, O God, are made exceedingly honourable, their principality is exceedingly strengthened.*³³⁰

**179/5** [Luke 14:11] **Because everyone who exalts himself will be humbled, and he who humbles himself will be exalted.** And from this conclusion it is manifestly clear that the Lord's preceding discourse should be understood allegorically. For everyone who exalts himself in the presence of men will not immediately be humbled, nor will he who humbles himself in the sight of men be exalted by them, but on the contrary sometimes he who raises himself to the peak of official dignity or to any acquired glory does not cease to be exalted right to the end. Similarly, some humble and modest men persevere in their insignificance in which they are content up to the end of their life. And therefore, because in accordance with the statement of the Truth everyone who raises himself up rashly with respect to his merits will be humbled by the Lord, and he who humbles himself prudently with regard to his good deeds will be exalted by him, the previous statement of the Redeemer, by which he forbids the first seats at table in the wedding to be sought, agrees in the same sense without a doubt.

**180/10** [Luke 14:12] **And he said to him also who had invited him: When you make a dinner or a supper, do not call your friends or your brothers or kinsmen or rich neighbours, ...** He does not forbid reciprocal feasts to honour brothers, friends, and rich men as if this were a crime, but like other transactions involving human obligation in which *sinners also lend to sinners to receive things of equal value,*³³¹ he shows that this does not avail to earn the rewards of heavenly life. And then he adds:

[Luke 14:12b] **Lest perhaps they also invite you again, and a repayment be made to you.** He does not say, 'and a sin be done to you', but *and a repayment be made to you.* What he says elsewhere is similar: *And if you do good to those who do good to you, what thanks are to you?*

329 Prov. 20:21.
330 Ps. 138:17 (139:17).
331 Augustine, *Speculum* 27 (CSEL 12:181).

And here he does not say, 'a sin is to you', but *what thanks are to you? For sinners also do this.*[332] And still there are some reciprocal feasts of brothers, friends, kinsmen, and rich neighbours, which not only receive repayment in the present, but also damnation in the future. And then the Apostle includes them among the works of darkness. *Let us walk honestly,* he says, *as in the day, not in rioting and drunkenness.*[333] *Wanton feasts are* indeed *riots, which are either celebrated by a general gathering of everyone, or are customarily hosted in turn by comrades, so that* /278/ *no one is ashamed to say or do anything disgraceful, because an abundance of wine is especially suited for doing shameful things, and for arousing the varied pleasure of lust.*[334]

[Luke 14:13–14] **But when you make a feast, call the poor, the maimed, the lame, and the blind, and you will be blessed, because they do not have the wherewithal to repay you. For repayment will be made to you at the resurrection of the just.** He says 'the resurrection of the just' because although all rise again, nevertheless the resurrection of those who do not doubt they will be blessed in it is rightly named as if it were their own. Therefore, he who calls the poor to a feast will gather his reward in the future. He who calls friends, brothers, and the rich has received his reward.[335] But even though he does this for God following the example of the sons of the blessed Job,[336] just like other offices of fraternal love, he himself who ordered it repays. He who invites gluttons and lechers for the sake of lewdness, will be punished with eternal suffering in the future.

[Luke 14:15] **When one of those who sat at table with him had heard these things, he said to him: Blessed is he who has eaten bread in the kingdom of God.** Bread which is eaten in the kingdom of God must not be understood as food for the body as Cerinthus teaches,[337] but without doubt it is the one who says: *I am the living bread which came down from heaven. If any man eat of this bread, he will live forever.*[338] That is, 'if any man perfectly marked by the sacrament of my incarnation deserves to enjoy

---

332 Luke 6:33.
333 Rom. 13:13.
334 Ambrosiaster, *Commentaria in epistolam ad Romanos* 13 (PL 17:166).
335 Cf. Matt. 6:2.
336 Cf. Job 1:4.
337 According to Isidore, *Etym.* 8.5.8, the Cerinthian heretics 'say that there will be one thousand years of enjoyment of the flesh after resurrection' (*The Etymologies*, trans. Barney *et al.*, 175). See also below, Book 5, n. 210.
338 John 6:51–52.

the vision of my divine majesty, he will rejoice in the eternal blessedness of immortal life.' But because some men take this bread by faith alone, by smelling as it were, but scorn to attain its sweetness by truly tasting, the Lord shows by his next parable that the sluggishness of such men is not worthy of heavenly feasts. For this follows:

## Chapter 59

**181/5** [Luke 14:16] **But he said to him: A certain man made a great supper and invited many.** *Who is this man but the one of whom the prophet says: 'And he is a man, and who knows him?'*[339] *He gave a great supper, because he prepared an abundance of interior sweetness for us; he invites many, but few come, because sometimes those who are subjected to him by faith oppose his eternal feast by living badly.*[340]

[Luke 14:17] **And he sent his servant at the hour of supper to say to those who were invited, that they should come, for all things are now ready.** *What is the hour of supper, unless it is the end of the world? This is surely the time we are now living in, just as Paul testified long ago, saying: 'we, on whom the ends of the world have come'.*[341] *If, therefore, the hour of supper is now, when we are invited, we have all the less reason to dispense with the feast of God, the more we perceive that the end of the world is already approaching.*[342] *Accordingly, this feast of God is not called a dinner,* /279/ *but a supper, because after a dinner a supper is left, but after a supper no feast is left. And because an eternal feast will be prepared for us at the end, it was right that this was not called a dinner, but a supper. But what is signified by this servant who is sent by the head of the household to issue the invitations, unless it is the order of preachers? But to dispel* our *lack of appetite, 'all things are now ready', because* to wipe

---

339 Jer. 17:9.
340 Gregory, *Hom. in Euang.* 2.36.2 (CCSL 141:333.33–38).
341 1 Cor. 10:11.
342 At this point in his transcription of Gregory's homily Bede omits a sentence: 'As we reflect that there is no time remaining, we must dread to lose the time at hand' (Gregory, *Hom. in Euang.* 2.36.2 [CCSL 141:333.44–46], trans. Hurst, *Gregory the Great: Forty Gospel Homilies*, 314). Darby presents this as an example of how Bede mutes Gregory's sense of the immediacy of the end-times, while preserving his conviction of their approach: *Bede and the End of Time*, 163–64; see Markus, 'Gregory and Bede: The Making of the Western Apocalyptic Tradition', 247–55.

BOOK FOUR                                                        457

*away our souls' half-heartedness, in the Lord's supper that matchless lamb was killed,*[343] *who* took away *the sins of the world.*[344]
[Luke 14:18] **And they began all at once to make excuse.** *God offers what he ought to have been asked for. Not having been asked, he wishes to give what could scarcely be hoped for. Because he deigned to give bountifully the things asked for, he is despised. Surely, he proclaims the delights of eternal refreshment, and nevertheless they all at once make excuses. But some say: We do not want to make excuses; for we are thankful both to be invited and to come to that feast of divine refreshment. Certainly, they say the truth, provided they do not love earthly more than heavenly things, and provided they are not occupied more by bodily than by spiritual things. So the reason they are making excuses is included, when it is immediately added:*[345]

[Luke 14:18b] **The first said to him: I have bought a farm, and I must needs go out and see it. I beg you, hold me excused.** *What is signified by a farm, if not earthly substance? Therefore, someone who thinks only of outward things on account of their substance goes out to see a farm.*[346]

[Luke 14:19] **And another said: I have bought five yokes of oxen, and I am going to try them out. I beg you, hold me excused.** *What do we understand in five yokes of oxen, if not the five senses of the body? They are also rightly called yokes, because they are paired in either sex. That is to say, because the bodily senses do not know how to comprehend inward things, but know outward things alone, and forsaking the deepest, innermost things, touch those things that are without, they aptly signify inquisitiveness. For the vice of inquisitiveness is grave, for while it leads a person's mind to probe into his neighbour's way of life outwardly, it always conceals his own deepest, innermost condition from him. For indeed on account of this it is also said of the same five yokes of oxen: 'I am going to try them out', because sometimes someone who tries out is liable to be led into inquisitiveness. But it should be noted that both the one who excuses himself from the invitation to supper because of a farm, and the one who does so for the sake of trying out his yokes of oxen, mix in expressions of humility, saying: 'I beg you, hold me excused'. For as long as he says, 'I beg', and nevertheless disdains to come, humility resounds in his voice, but*

---

343 Gregory, *Hom. in Euang.* 2.36.2 (CCSL 141:333.40–73 with gap).
344 John 1:29.
345 Gregory, *Hom. in Euang.* 2.36.3–4. (CCSL 141:334.75–93).
346 Gregory, *Hom. in Euang.* 2.36.4 (CCSL 141:335.95–97).

pride in his action. And behold, this is what every wicked man condemns when he hears it, and nevertheless he does not cease doing the things that he condemns. For when /280/ we say to anyone acting wickedly: 'Reform, follow God, abandon the world', to what place are we calling him, if not to the Lord's supper? But when he answers: 'Pray for me, because I am a sinner, I cannot do this', what else is he doing except begging and excusing himself? For indeed saying: 'I am a sinner', insinuates humility, but adding: 'I cannot be reformed', shows pride.[347]

[Luke 14:20] **And another said: I have married a wife, and therefore I cannot come.** What is meant by a wife, but the pleasure of the flesh? For although marriage is good and instituted by divine Providence for the propagation of the race, nevertheless some do not seek abundance of offspring by it, but the desires of pleasure. And therefore, something unrighteous can fittingly be signified by something righteous. The supreme Master of the house invites us therefore to the supper of the eternal feast, but as long as earthly care occupies this one, and clever thinking about someone else's actions ravages another, and carnal pleasure likewise stains the soul of another, no one who is hard to please hastens to the banquet of eternal life.[348]

[Luke 14:21] **And the servant returning, told these things to his lord. Then the master of the house, being angry, said to his servant: Go out quickly into the streets and lanes of the city, and bring in here the poor, and the feeble, and the blind, and the lame.** Behold, those who are attached to their worldly wealth more than is right refuse to come to the Lord's supper; those who sweat at the work of inquisitiveness turn up their nose at the nourishment of life that has been provided; those who cling to carnal desires scorn the spiritual banquet of the feast. Therefore, because the proud refuse, the poor are chosen. Why is this? Because according to the words of Paul, 'God has chosen the weak things of the world, so that he may confound the strong.'[349] But they are called the poor and the feeble, who in their own judgement are weak. For there are also the poor and strong so to speak, who are proud even when is a state of poverty. The blind are those who have no light of natural ability. Likewise, the lame are those who do not have a straight gait when they go about their work. But when faults of character are signified by the lameness of the limbs, it is certainly

---

347 Gregory, *Hom. in Euang.* 2.36.4 (CCSL 141:335.99–126).
348 Gregory, *Hom. in Euang.* 2.36.5 (CCSL 141:336.129–39).
349 1 Cor. 1:27.

clear that, just as those who were invited and did not come are sinners, so these who are invited and come are also sinners. But the proud sinners are scorned, and the humble sinners are chosen. Accordingly, he has chosen those whom the world despises, because often being despised calls a man back to himself. The poor and the feeble, the blind and the lame are invited, and they come, because the weak and those who are despised in this world often hear the words of God the more readily, the less they have in this world with which to be led astray. But, after the poor have been brought in to the supper, let us hear what the servant adds:[350]

[Luke 14:22] **Lord, it is done as you have commanded, and there is still room.** *Many such were gathered from Judea to the Lord's supper, but the multitude* /281/ *from the people of Israel who believed did not fill all the places of the celestial feast. A throng of Jews had already entered, but still there is unoccupied room in the kingdom, where a great number of Gentiles ought to be taken in. Hence it is also said to the same servant:*[351]

[Luke 14:23] **Go out into the highways and hedges, and compel them to come in, so that my house may be filled.** *When the Lord invites people from the lanes and the streets to his supper, he signifies, to be sure, those people who knew how to maintain the Law in an urban setting. But when he orders his guests to be gathered from the highways and hedges, he doubtless seeks to gather country folk, that is, Gentiles. It should be noted that in this third invitation, it is not said, 'Invite them', but 'compel them to come in'. For there are some who understand that good things ought to be done, but refrain from doing them. As we said above, it often happens that the adversity of this world strikes these people through their carnal desires. For indeed they often either waste away from a long illness, or perish, afflicted with injuries, or stung by heavy losses are struck down, and rebuking themselves for their desires they turn their hearts to the Lord. So what does it mean that those who are broken by the adversities of this world return to the love of God, and they are restored from the desires of the present life, except that they are compelled to come in? But exceedingly fearful is the statement that immediately follows. For he says:*[352]

[Luke 14:24] **But I say to you, that none of those men who were invited will taste my supper.** *Behold, he invites through himself, he invites through the angels, he invites through the patriarchs, he invites through*

---

350 Gregory, *Hom. in Euang.* 2.36.6–8 (CCSL 141:337.142–96).
351 Gregory, *Hom. in Euang.* 2.36.8 (CCSL 141:339.196–201).
352 Gregory, *Hom. in Euang.* 2.36.8–10 (CCSL 141:339.202–77).

*the prophets, he invites through the shepherds, he invites often through miracles, he invites often through scourges, sometimes he invites through the favourable things of this world, sometimes through the adverse things. Let no one take lightly the fact that as long as he makes excuses after being invited he may not be able to enter when he wishes.*[353]

## Chapter 60

**182/5** [Luke 14:25-26] **And great crowds were going with him. And turning, he said to them: If anyone comes to me, and does not hate his father, and mother, and wife, and children, and brothers, and sisters, yes and even his own life, he cannot be my disciple.** *It is useful to inquire how it is that we are commanded to hate our parents and blood relations, when we are at the same time ordered to love our enemies. Indeed, the Truth says of the wife: 'What God has joined together, let no man put asunder.'*[354] *And Paul says: 'Husbands love your wives, as Christ also loved the Church.'*[355] *Behold, the disciple* commands *that the wife be loved, although the Master says of anyone who does not hate his wife: 'he cannot be my disciple'. Does the judge declare one thing, and the herald another? Or are we able to hate and to love at the same time? But if we weigh carefully the force of the commandment, we can do both by making a distinction,* /282/ *so that we love those who are joined to us by kinship of the flesh as neighbours, and that we must not know them, but hate and avoid them, when they are adversaries on the path to God. But in order for the Lord to show that this hate towards neighbours proceeds not from lack of affection, but from love, he immediately went on, saying: 'yes and even his own life'. And then indeed we hate our own life in the right way, when we do not acquiesce in its carnal desires, when we crush its appetites, and when we resist sensual pleasures. When therefore we despise our life, it is led to the better, as if we loved it by hating it. Thus, doubtless we ought to make a distinction in hating our neighbours, in that we at the same time love them because they exist, and regard them with hate because they obstruct us on the path of God.*[356]

---

353 Gregory, *Hom. in Euang.* 2.36.10 (CCSL 141:342.278-83).
354 Matt. 19:6.
355 Eph. 5:25.
356 Gregory, *Hom. in Euang.* 2.37.2 (CCSL 141:348.21-44).

BOOK FOUR  461

*But how this same hate of life ought to be exhibited, the Truth shows subsequently by saying:*[357]
[Luke 14:27] **And whoever does not bear his cross and come after me cannot be my disciple.** *Cross [crux] clearly is so-called from torture [cruciatu]. And we bear the cross of the Lord in two ways: either when we vex the flesh by abstinence, or when by compassion we consider our neighbour's need to be our own. For he who displays sorrow in another's need bears the cross in his soul. But it must be known that there are some who display abstinence of the flesh not for God, but for vainglory. And there are many more who expend compassion on their neighbour not spiritually but carnally, so that they incline him not toward virtue, but as it were by taking pity incline him toward sin. Accordingly, these people seem to bear the cross, but they are not following the Lord. Hence this same Truth rightly says: 'whoever does not bear his cross and come after me cannot be my disciple.' And indeed, to bear the cross and to go after the Lord is to display either abstinence of the flesh or compassion for one's neighbour by zeal prompted by eternal motivation. For anyone who displays these things out of temporal motivation bears the cross indeed, but refuses to go after the Lord. But because lofty commandments are given, a comparison to building something lofty is immediately added, when it is said:*[358]
**183**/10 [Luke 14:28] **For which of you, wishing to build a tower, does not first sit down and reckon the costs that are necessary, whether he has the wherewithal to finish it?** *We should prepare for everything we do by an effort of reflection. For look, according to the word of the Truth, whoever builds a tower provides the costs of the building first. Therefore, if we desire to construct a tower of humility, we ought first to prepare ourselves for the adversities of this world. For there is this difference between an earthly and a heavenly building, that the earthly building is constructed by gathering in money, but the heavenly building by dispersing it. For the former we meet the costs, if we gather in the money we do not have, for the latter we meet the costs, if we also let go of the money we have. But what is said should be considered:*[359] /283/
[Luke 14:29-30] **Lest, after he has laid the foundation and is not able to finish, all who see it begin to mock him, saying: This man began to build and was not able to finish.** *Because, according to the word*

357 Gregory, *Hom. in Euang.* 2.37.5 (CCSL 141:351.88-89).
358 Gregory, *Hom. in Euang.* 2.37.5-6 (CCSL 141:351.91-108).
359 Gregory, *Hom. in Euang.* 2.37.6 (CCSL 141:352.113-29).

*of Paul, 'we are made a spectacle to the world, to angels and to men'.*[360] *And in all that we do, we ought to consider our secret adversaries, who always attend to our works, and always rejoice in our failure. When he sees them, the Prophet says: 'In you, my God, I put my trust; let me not be ashamed. Let my enemies not laugh at me'.*[361] *For, having attended to our good works, unless we are anxiously vigilant against the wicked spirits, we suffer derision from those who instigate us to evil. But because a simile of constructing a building was given, now a comparison is furnished from lesser to greater, so that from little things greater things may be pondered. For it goes on:*[362]

[Luke 14:31–32] **Or what king about to go to war against another king, does not first sit down, and think whether he is able, with ten thousand, to meet the one who comes against him with twenty thousand? Otherwise, while the other is still far off, sending an embassy, he desires conditions of peace.** *A king comes to do battle against another king who is his equal, and nevertheless if he judges that he cannot prevail, he sends an embassy and asks for conditions of peace. With what kind of tears, therefore, ought we to look for mercy, we who are not coming to judgement in that fearful examination with our king on equal terms, we whom condition, infirmity, and situation indisputably display as inferiors? But perhaps we have already shed the faults of wicked deeds and have already outwardly shunned every wickedness. Are we able to offer an accounting for our thoughts? He comes therefore with an army twice the size of ours, who examines us simultaneously about our works and thoughts, we who are scarcely prepared in works alone.* And for that reason, *while he is still far off, let us send an embassy and ask for conditions of peace. For he is said to be far off because he is not yet seen at hand for judgement. Let us send our tears as an embassy, let us send works of mercy, let us offer on his altar sacrificial victims of appeasement. This is our embassy which appeases the king who is coming.*[363]

184/5 [Luke 14:33] **So therefore every one of you who does not renounce all that he possesses cannot be my disciple.** With this conclusion the Lord very plainly teaches what it is to build a tower, or to make peace with a stronger king – namely, that this is what it is to be his disciple. To provide

---

360 1 Cor. 4:9.
361 Ps. 24:2–3 (25:2–3).
362 Gregory, *Hom. in Euang.* 2.37.6 (CCSL 141:352.130–40).
363 Gregory, *Hom. in Euang.* 2.37.6–7 (CCSL 141:353.144–70).

the costs to complete the tower, and to send an embassy to obtain peace, is nothing other than to renounce all that we possess. *Among all these things, both the love of our neighbours, which has already been mentioned, and our soul itself, which some think was mentioned in place of this temporal life, must be understood as* [this temporal life] *which we should possess in the proper way for the time being so that it does not impede us from eternal things, if anyone should threaten to take it away.*[364] There is a difference, of course, between renouncing all things and abandoning them. For /284/ it is the part of the poor and the perfect to abandon all things, to neglect the cares of the world, and to gaze longingly at eternal desires alone. But it is the part of all the faithful to renounce all that they possess, that is, to possess the things that are of the world, so that nevertheless they are not possessed by them in the world; to keep what is temporal in use, and what is eternal in longing; to carry on with earthly matters, so that nevertheless they aim with their whole soul at heavenly things.

185/2 [Luke 14:34] **Salt is good. But if the salt loses it savour, with what will it be seasoned?** After commanding that the tower of the virtues not only be begun but completed, he looks to higher things. Indeed, it is good to hear the word of God, to season frequently the mysteries of the soul with the salt of spiritual wisdom, or rather to become with the apostles the very salt of the earth, that is, to meet as well the need of imbuing with salt the souls of those who still savour earthly things. But if anyone, having once been enlightened with the seasoning of the Truth, returns to apostasy, what other teacher can correct him, when he has cast away that sweetness of wisdom that he tasted, either because he was terrified by the adversities of the age, or attracted by its allurements, just as a certain wise man says: *Who will cure an enchanter struck by a serpent?*[365] This saying is credibly believed to signify the companions of Judas Iscariot and Judas himself, who, overcome by avarice, did not hesitate both to abandon the office of the apostleship and to betray the Lord.

[Luke 14:35] **It is useful neither for the land nor for the dunghill, but it will be cast out.** Just as salt deprived of taste, when it ceases to be able to season foods and to cure meats, will not be fit for any use[366] – for it is neither useful for the land, for land strewn with salt will be prevented from producing crops, nor will it be profitable for the agricultural dunghill,

---

364 Augustine, *Quaestiones euang.* 2.31 (CCSL 44B:71.8–11).
365 Ecclus. 12:13.
366 Cf. Jerome, *Commentarii in Matheum* 1 (CCSL 77:26.487–88).

because even if mixed with fertile soils, it is not accustomed to fructify, but to destroy the seeds of plants – so everyone who turns *back after knowledge of the Truth*,[367] is able neither himself to bear the fruit of good work nor to improve others, but will be cast out, that is, will be separated from the unity of the Church, so that, in accordance with the previous parable, his enemies will mock him, and say: *This man began to build and was not able to finish.*[368] And for that reason a very useful exhortation is added, when it is said:

[Luke 14:35b] **He who has ears to hear, let him hear.** That is, he who has ears of understanding, with which he is able to comprehend the word of God, let him not disdain, but hear, namely by obeying and by doing what he has learned. For *not a forgetful hearer, but a doer of the work, this man will be blessed in his deed.*[369]

## Chapter 61

**186/2** [Luke 15:1–2] **Now the tax collectors and sinners drew near to him to /285/ hear him. And the Pharisees and the scribes murmured, saying: This man receives sinners, and eats with them.** Since not only can the just sin by feebleness, but also the sinner can recover his taste by diligence, after it is said that salt deprived of taste must be cast out, Luke immediately describes a throng of penitents that has been given admittance. Drawing near to hear the word of God, they are received *not only for the sake of talking together but even for eating together. Seeing this, the Pharisees are scornful, because true justice has compassion, but false justice has scorn, although even the just are rightly accustomed to scorn sinners. But it is one thing to be agitated by the vanity of pride, and another by the zeal for discipline.*[370]

*But as for those who suffered in such a way that they did not know they were sick, so that they might recognize how sick they were, the physician heals them with divine soothing lotions; he offers a gentle parable, and he suppresses the swelling of the wound in their soul. For he says:*[371]

---

367 2 Pet. 2:21.
368 Luke 14:30.
369 James 1:25.
370 Gregory, *Hom. in Euang.* 2.34.2 (CCSL 141:300.14–19).
371 Gregory, *Hom. in Euang.* 2.34.3 (CCSL 141:301.33–36).

187/5 [Luke 15:4] **Which one of you who has a hundred sheep, and if he loses one of them, does he not leave the ninety-nine in the desert, and go after that which was lost, until he finds it?** *Look, in a wonderful dispensation, Truth provided an example of devotion which a man might recognize in himself, and yet it pertained specifically to the Author of mankind himself. For because the number one hundred is perfect, he himself had a hundred sheep when he created the substance of angels and men. But then one sheep was lost, when man abandoned the pastures of life by sinning. And he left ninety-nine sheep in the desert, because he abandoned those highest choirs of angels in heaven. And why is heaven called a desert, unless it is because we call what is abandoned a desert? Man deserted heaven when he sinned. But ninety-nine sheep remained in the desert, when the Lord was seeking one on earth, because the number of rational creatures, that is to say, of angels and of men, which had been created to see God, was diminished by the loss of man, and in order that the perfect sum of sheep be made whole in heaven, the man who was lost was sought on earth.*[372]

[Luke 15:5] **And when he has found it, he lays it on his shoulders, rejoicing, ...** *He laid the sheep on his shoulders, because in taking on human nature he himself carried our sins.*[373]

[Luke 15:6] **And coming home, he calls together his friends and neighbours, saying to them: Rejoice with me, because I have found my sheep that was lost.** *After the sheep was found, he returned home, because our Shepherd returned to the heavenly kingdom after humanity had been restored. There he found his friends and neighbours, that is to say, those choirs of angels. They are his friends, because they support his will without interruption in their steadfastness. They are* /286/ *also his neighbours, because by their constant presence they fully enjoy the splendour of his vision. And it should be noted that he does not say: 'Rejoice with the sheep that was found', but 'with me', because, of course, his joy is our life, and when we are led back to heaven, we fulfil the festival of his joy.*[374]

[Luke 15:7] **I say to you that even so there will be joy in heaven over one sinner who does penance, more than over ninety-nine just who do not need penance.** There will be *more joy in heaven over repentant*

---

372 Gregory, *Hom. in Euang.* 2.34.3 (CCSL 141:301.38–53).
373 Gregory, *Hom. in Euang.* 2.34.3 (CCSL 141:301.57–58); cf. Isa. 53:11; 1 Pet. 2:24.
374 Gregory, *Hom. in Euang.* 2.34.3 (CCSL 141:302.60–68).

sinners than over the righteous who have been steadfast, because very often the latter know that they have not been oppressed by a heavy burden of sins; they abide in the path of justice, they commit no illicit actions, but nevertheless they do not ardently desire the heavenly kingdom. They allow themselves to use what is lawful to the extent that they do not remember that they have done anything forbidden. Frequently they are slow to carry out deeds of exceptional worth, since they are exceedingly carefree because they have committed no very grave sins. But on the other hand sometimes those who remember that they have done some unlawful things, filled with remorse out of their very sorrow, are kindled toward the love of God, and occupy themselves with great deeds of virtue. Therefore, there is greater joy in heaven over a reformed sinner than a steadfast just man, because even a general in battle loves that soldier who returns after fleeing and presses the enemy bravely, more than the one who never turned his back, but never did anything bravely.[375]

Despite all this, it should be known that there are many righteous people in whose lives there is so much joy, that no penance for sins can be imposed on them at all. For there are many who are unconscious of any sins in themselves, and yet they give themselves over with great eagerness to suffering as if they are bound by every sin. They even disapprove of everything which is permitted, they are sublimely girded for contempt of the world, they rejoice in lamentations, they humble themselves in everything, and just as some lament the sins of their deeds, so these lament the sins of their thoughts. Hence, therefore, one can imagine how great the joy the just man who humbly repents gives God, if the wicked causes joy in heaven, when he condemns by penance that which he did wickedly.[376]

188/10 [Luke 15:8] **Or what woman, having ten silver coins, if she loses one coin, does not light a lamp, and turn the house upside down, and seek diligently until she finds it?** *He who is signified by the shepherd is also signified by the woman. For the one is God, and the other is the wisdom of God. And because an image is stamped on the coin, the woman lost the coin when man, who was created in the image of God, receded from the likeness of his Creator by sinning. But the woman lights a lamp, because the wisdom of God appeared in humanity. Indeed, the lamp is light in the head; and truly light in the head is divinity in the flesh. But when the lamp is lit, she turns the house upside down, because*

---

375 Gregory, *Hom. in Euang.* 2.34.4 (CCSL 141:302.72–91).
376 Gregory, *Hom. in Euang.* 2.34.5 (CCSL 141:303.95–109).

*as soon as its divinity became visible in the flesh, our whole conscience was smitten. For indeed a house is turned upside down, when the human conscience is troubled by the contemplation of its own guilt.* But *when the house is turned upside down, the coin is found, because when the conscience of man is troubled, the likeness of the Creator is restored in man.*[377] /287/

[Luke 15:9] **And when she has found it, she calls together her friends and neighbours, saying: Rejoice with me, because I have found the coin that I had lost.** *Who are these friends and neighbours but those heavenly powers spoken of already above? As they are near to divine wisdom, so they approach it by the grace of uninterrupted vision.* But it should be observed *why this woman is said to have had ten coins. Certainly, the Lord created the nature of angels and men so that they might know him, and when he wished it to endure forever, he created it without doubt in his own likeness. Truly, the woman had ten coins, because there are nine orders of angels. But in order to complete the number of the elect, man was created as the tenth, who was not undone by his Creator after his fault, because the eternal Wisdom, gleaming with miracles through the flesh, renewed him by the light of the head.*[378]

**189/5** [Luke 15:10] **So I say to you, there will be joy in the presence of the angels of God over one sinner doing penance.** *To do penance is both to lament wicked deeds done, and not to do things that must be lamented. For anyone who bewails some deeds of this nature in this way, in order nevertheless to commit other deeds of this nature, either still does not know how to do penance, or feigns doing it. For what benefit is it, if someone laments the sins of luxury, and yet still pants with the feverish passion of avarice? Or what benefit is it, if he now laments the faults of wrath, and yet still is consumed in the fires of envy? But it is still less beneficial to say that he who deplores sins should not commit sins to be deplored at all. For it ought above all to be considered that anyone who remembers that he has committed wicked deeds should strive to abstain even from certain lawful ones, in order by this to make amends to his Creator, and that anyone who has committed forbidden deeds ought to cut himself off even from allowable ones.*[379]

---

377 Gregory, *Hom. in Euang.* 2.34.6 (CCSL 141:303.113–31).
378 Gregory, *Hom. in Euang.* 2.34.6 (CCSL 141:304.133–47).
379 Gregory, *Hom. in Euang.* 2.34.15–16 (CCSL 141:314.418–30).

## Chapter 62

190/10 [Luke 15:11–12] **And he said: A certain man had two sons, and the younger of them said to his father: Give me the portion of the substance that falls to me. And he divided his substance between them.** In response to the grumbling of the scribes and the Pharisees about the reception of sinners, the Saviour delivered three parables in turn. In the first two of these, the disputation reveals how much he rejoices with his angels over the salvation of penitents. But in the third, he not only shows his own joy and that of his angels, but he also rebukes the envious for grumbling.

And so, the man who is said to have had two sons is understood to signify God the Father, the begetter, that is to say, of the two peoples, and as it were the author and creator of the two branches of the human race. For the elder son signifies those who remained in the worship of the one God; the younger, those who abandoned God for the sake of worshipping idols.[380] The portion of the substance that fell to the younger son, is the /288/ human sense of reason. For to live, to understand, to remember, to excel with quick intelligence, is the substance of the divine gift. The younger son covets this from his father when man, delighted with his power, sought to rule himself by his free will and to cast himself off from the rule of the Creator.[381] And the father divided his substance between the sons by granting the protection of his grace to the faithful, which they desired, but granting to the unbelievers only the gift of natural intelligence, with which they were contented.

[Luke 15:13] **And not many days after, the younger son, gathering all together, went abroad into a far country, and there wasted his substance, living riotously.** He went far off, not by changing his place, but by changing his mind. And indeed, the more anyone transgresses through wicked deeds, the farther he recedes from the grace of God. *Luke said it happened not many days after that, gathering all together, he went abroad into a far country, because not long after the creation of the human race the soul determined through free will to bear with itself a certain*

---

380 The two sons as Jews and Gentiles: cf. Ps.-Jerome, *Expositio euangeliorum* (PL 30:574C).

381 Cf. Augustine, *Quaestiones euang.* 2.33 (CCSL 44B:73.2–15). Most of the remainder of Bede's book 4 alternates between more or less close paraphrase and verbatim transcription of this chapter (2.33) of Augustine's *Quaestiones euangeliorum*.

*faculty, so to speak, of its own nature, and to forsake him by whom it was created, managing by its own strength. The more it forsakes him by whom it was given, the more rapidly it squanders this strength. And so, Luke calls 'prodigal' a life which loves to pour itself out lavishly and to roam around with outward ostentation, while becoming empty inwardly, and this happens when anyone pursues the things that result from the prodigal life, and abandons the inner man.*³⁸²

[Luke 15:14] **And after he had wasted all, there came a mighty famine in that country.** *'All that he wasted' signifies the ornaments of nature that he squandered. The 'famine in that far country' is the lack of the word of truth,*³⁸³ *when one forgets the Creator. The prophets said concerning this that the Lord will send* a famine into the land, not a famine of bread, nor a thirst for water, but of hearing the word of the Lord.³⁸⁴

[Luke 15:14b–15] **And he began to be in want. And he went and attached himself to one of the citizens of that country.** *He who forsook the treasures of the wisdom of God and the exalted heights of spiritual wealth is accurately said to 'be in want'.*³⁸⁵ *The citizen of that country to whom he attached himself when he was in want is surely the one whom the Lord calls the prince of this world, who thanks to his own depravity has authority over worldly desires.*³⁸⁶ *And the Apostle says of him:* The god of this world has blinded the minds of unbelievers.³⁸⁷

[Luke 15:15b] **And he sent him to his farm to feed the pigs.** *To be sent to a farm is to be subjugated by the desire for worldly substance. In another parable a certain man, disdaining the spiritual feasts to which he was invited, referred to this when he said:* I have bought a farm, and I must needs go out and see /289/ it.³⁸⁸ *Truly, to feed the pigs is to do those things over which the unclean spirits rejoice.*³⁸⁹

[Luke 15:16] **And he desired to fill his belly with the husks that the pigs were eating.** *The husks that the pigs were eating are* worldly teachings that resound with sterile *sweetness. Among these, the praises of idols and fables about the gods of the Gentiles in which evil spirits*

---

382 Augustine, *Quaestiones euang.* 2.33 (CCSL 44B:74.15–24).
383 Augustine, *Quaestiones euang.* 2.33 (CCSL 44B:74.24–26).
384 Amos 8:11.
385 Ambrose, *Expos. Lucam* 7.215 (CCSL 14:289.2385–87); cf. Rom. 11:33.
386 Cf. Augustine, *Quaestiones euang.* 2.33 (CCSL 44B:74.26–27).
387 2 Cor. 4:4.
388 Luke 14:18.
389 Cf. Augustine, *Quaestiones euang.* 2.33 (CCSL 44B:74.28–29).

*delight are noised abroad in diverse tales and songs. Hence when this man desired to be filled, he wished to find in such things something solid and correct that would pertain to the blessed life. But he could not. For this is what he says:*[390]

[Luke 15:16b–17] **And no one gave to him. And coming back to himself,** ... *Having now come back to the inner truths of conscience from those outward things that had led him astray for no reason and seduced him, he formed this resolution:*[391]

[Luke 15:17b] **He said: How many of my father's hired hands abound with bread, and I am perishing here with hunger.** *How could he know this, he who like all idolators was so oblivious of God, unless this is the reflection of one already coming to himself again, when the Gospel was being preached?*[392] The hired hands of the father, therefore, abound with bread, because those who busy themselves with doing worthy deeds with a view to future reward, are refreshed with the daily nourishment of divine grace. But they truly perish with hunger, who, placed outside of the house of the Father, desire to fill their belly with husks. That is, those who, living without faith, search for the blessed life by studying empty philosophy.[393] For just as *bread*, which *strengthens the heart of man*,[394] is like the word of God, by which he refreshes the soul, so the husk, which is itself empty within and soft without, and does not refresh the body, but fills it so that it is more a burden than a benefit, is rightly compared to worldly wisdom, whose discourse resounds with applause for its eloquence, but which is devoid of any power to be of use.

[Luke 15:18] **I will arise and go to my father, and I will say to him: Father, I have sinned against heaven, and before you.** He knew how merciful and kind was the father, who, vexed by his son, does not even scorn to hear the word 'father'. *'I will arise'* therefore, he says, because I know that I am cast down, *'and go'*, because I have gone far off, *'to my father'*, because I am wasting away in miserable poverty *under the prince of the pigs*.[395] *'I have sinned against heaven'* means I have sinned *before* the angelic spirits *and the holy souls among whom is the throne of God. But*

---

390 Augustine, *Quaestiones euang.* 2.33 (CCSL 44B:74.29–35).
391 Augustine, *Quaestiones euang.* 2.33 (CCSL 44B:75.36–38).
392 Augustine, *Quaestiones euang.* 2.33 (CCSL 44B:75.39–41).
393 Interestingly, Ps.-Jerome, *Expositio euangeliorum* (PL 30:574C), interprets the citizen to whom the younger son hired himself out as a philosopher.
394 Ps. 103:15 (104:15).
395 Augustine, *Quaestiones euang.* 2.33 (CCSL 44B:75.53–54).

'before you' signifies in that very chamber of the inner conscience, where the eyes of God alone were able to penetrate.[396]

[Luke 15:19] **And now I am not worthy to be called your son. Treat me as one of your hired hands.** With regard to the state of mind of the son, who does not dispute that everything of his father's is his own, he does not presume to aspire to it, but desires the status of a hired hand in order now to serve for pay. But he testifies that he cannot deserve even this /290/ unless his father grants it. Where does this leave the Pelagians, who are confident that they are able to be saved by their own virtue, in the face of the very clear statement of the Truth, which says: *Without me you can do nothing*?[397]

[Luke 15:20] **And rising up he came to his father.** *To come to the father is to be established by faith in the Church, where there can now be a proper and fruitful confession of sins.*[398]

[Luke 15:20b] **And when he was still far off**, and *before he understood God, but nevertheless when he already sought him devoutly,*[399]

[Luke 15:20c] **His father saw him,** ... *For he is justly said not to see, not to have before the eyes, as it were, the wicked and the proud. For only those who are loved are customarily said to be 'before the eyes'.*[400]

[Luke 15:20d] **And was moved with compassion and running to him fell on his neck,** ... *For the Father did not forsake his only-begotten Son, through whom he ran right up to our long exile and descended, because 'God in Christ was reconciling the world to himself'.*[401] *And the Lord himself says: 'The Father who abides in me does his works'.*[402] *And what is it to fall on his neck, except to bend and humble his arm in his embrace? 'And to whom is the arm of the Lord revealed?'*[403] *That arm is certainly our Lord, Jesus Christ.*[404]

[Luke 15:20e] **And kissed him.** *To be comforted by the word of the grace of God in the hope of remission of sins – this is what is meant by returning after distant journeys to merit the kiss of love from the father.*[405]

---

396 Augustine, *Quaestiones euang.* 2.33 (CCSL 44B:76.65–67).
397 John 15:5.
398 Augustine, *Quaestiones euang.* 2.33 (CCSL 44B:76.57–59).
399 Augustine, *Quaestiones euang.* 2.33 (CCSL 44B:76.69–70).
400 Augustine, *Quaestiones euang.* 2.33 (CCSL 44B:76.70–72).
401 2 Cor. 5:19.
402 John 14:10.
403 John 12:38 (Isa. 53:1).
404 Augustine, *Quaestiones euang.* 2.33 (CCSL 44B:77.74–80).
405 Augustine, *Quaestiones euang.* 2.33 (CCSL 44B:77.81–83).

[Luke 15:21] **And the son said to him: Father, I have sinned against heaven and before you. Now I am not worthy to be called your son.** *Having been established in the Church, he now begins to confess his sins. He does not say everything that he had promised that he was going to say, but he goes as far as this: 'I am not worthy to be called your son'. He wished to become a son by grace, because he says that he is unworthy by his merits. He did not add what he had said in that earlier meditation: 'Treat me as one of your hired hands'. For when he did not have bread, he even wished to be a hired hand. This he now very honourably disdains after his father's kiss.*[406]

Indeed, he understands that there is a great difference between a son, a hired hand, and a servant[407] — the servant is the one who still abstains from vices from fear of hell or of the laws in force; the hired hand is the one who abstains from vices from the hope and desire of the kingdom of heaven; the son is the one who abstains from vices from devotion to the good itself and from love of the virtues.[408] In his *summation of* these *three virtues, the blessed Apostle, concluding the whole sum of salvation, says: 'Now there remain faith, hope, and love, these three, but the greatest of these is love.'*[409] *And indeed it is faith that leads from fear of the future judgement and torments* /291/ *to shunning the contagion of sins; hope that, calling our soul away from present circumstances, disdains all the pleasures of the body in expectation of heavenly rewards; and love that, kindling us with the ardent desire of our soul toward the love of Christ and the fruit of spiritual virtues, leads us to abominate with total hatred whatever is contrary to them.*[410] Hence, this prodigal after *returning to his own home feared the torments of cruel hunger as if he had already become a servant, yet he desired the condition of a hired hand when he thought of the wages.*[411] But his father running to him, *not being content to grant him lesser things, he passed over both conditions without hesitation, and restored him to the pristine dignity of sons,*[412] and made him think now not of the wages of a hireling, but of inheritance from a father.

---

406 Augustine, *Quaestiones euang.* 2.33 (CCSL 44B:77.83–90).
407 Cf. Ambrose, *Expos. Lucam* 7.228 (CCSL 14:293.2500–01).
408 Cf. Cassian, *Collationes* 11.6 (CSEL 13:317.18–20).
409 1 Cor. 13:13.
410 Cassian, *Collationes* 11.6 (CSEL 13:317.26–318.8).
411 Cassian, *Collationes* 11.7 (CSEL 13:319.6–10).
412 Cassian, *Collationes* 11.7 (CSEL 13:319.17–19).

[Luke 15:22] **And the father said to his servants: Bring forth quickly the first robe, and put it on him.** *The first robe is the garb of innocence, which man who was rightly created received but being wickedly led astray lost.*[413] When, after the guilt of his transgression, he knew that he was naked and had lost the glory of immortality, he put on a garment made of skins, that is, a mortal garment.[414] *The servants who bring it forth are those who preach reconciliation with God.*[415] They bring forth the first robe when they affirm that mortal and terrestrial men are going to be raised up, so that they will be not only fellow-citizens of the angels, but also *the heirs of God and joint heirs with Christ.*[416]

[Luke15:22b] **And put a ring on his hand, and shoes on his feet.** The ring is either the sign of sincere faith, whereby all things promised in the hearts of believers are sealed by a true impression,[417] or *the pledge of that marriage to which the Church is betrothed.*[418] And the ring is rightly put on the hand, in order that faith become visible in works, and that works may be strengthened by faith. And shoes on the feet proclaim the duty of preaching the Gospel, so that the course of the soul that leads to heavenly things may be preserved inviolate and pure from the contagion of earthly things, and protected by the examples of those who have gone before, may advance free of worry about serpents and scorpions. Hands and feet are adorned – that is, the work and the way: the work, that we may live aright; the way so that we may hasten to eternal joys. *For we do not have here a lasting city, but we seek one that is to come.*[419]

[Luke 15:23] **And bring the fatted calf, and kill it.** *The fatted calf is the same Lord himself, but according to the flesh.*[420] And rightly is it 'fatted', because his flesh is so very rich with spiritual virtue *that it suffices for the salvation of the whole world through the odour of sweetness, which*

---

413 Gregory, *Moralia* 12.6 (CCSL 143A:633.10–11).
414 Cf. Gen. 3:21.
415 Augustine, *Quaestiones euang.* 2.33 (CCSL 44B:77.91).
416 Rom. 8:17.
417 Ps.-Jerome, *Expositio euangeliorum* (PL 30:574D), interprets the ring as the cross on the forehead made at baptism, which is possibly what Bede is alluding to here.
418 A verbatim quotation from *De patre et duobus filiis (Homilia de duobus filiis)*, one of the homilies contained in the collection of thirty-eight homilies ascribed to John Chrysostom referred to above (Book 1, n. 64). This work is included in the pseudepigrapha of Jerome as *Epistula 35* (PL 30:256–62), and noted by Wenk, *Zur Sammlung der 38 Homilien*, 93; Love, 'Bede and John Chrysostom', 81.
419 Hebr. 13:14.
420 Augustine, *Quaestiones euang.* 2.33 (CCSL 44B:78.94–95).

is to say, to send to God the smell of sacrifice and to pray for all.[421] To bring the calf and kill it is to preach Christ and /292/ to make known his death. And then indeed when we believe that he was slain, it is as if he were newly slain for each of us. His flesh is eaten then, when the sacrament of his passion is both taken by mouth for cleansing and is pondered in the heart for imitation.

[Luke 15:23b–24] **And let us eat and feast; because this my son was dead and has come to life again; he was lost and is found.** Not only does the son feast, who has come to life again and is found, but also the father and his servants, renewed by the flesh of the most sacred calf which was killed for the sake of the son. For the father's food is our salvation, and the father's joy is the forgiveness of our sins. And not only the joy of the Father, but also of the Son, and of the Holy Spirit, because just as in divinity will and accomplishment are one, so also the love of the holy and indivisible Trinity is one. Hence, we read that the blessed Abraham, receiving the three angels with a hospitable reception, killed a very tender and very good calf, and offered it to them as a feast with milk, bread, and butter.[422] Because whoever desires to refresh, that is, to delight the blessed Trinity with the offices of righteous devotion, ought likewise to celebrate the death of the only-begotten Son of God in the flesh, which is one person in the same Trinity, with the purity of a pious profession of faith.

And it should be noted that the first robe, the ring, and the shoes are presented before, and then finally the calf is sacrificed, because unless each one has clothed himself with the hope of our first immortality, unless he has fortified his works with the ring of faith, unless he has preached that same faith by a pious avowal, he cannot take part in the heavenly sacraments.

[Luke 15:24b] **And they began to feast.** *Now that the Church is spread out and diffused, this feast and festivity is celebrated through the whole world. For in the Lord's body and blood, that calf is both offered to the Father and feeds the whole house.*[423]

[Luke 15:25] **Now his elder son was in the field.** *The* elder *son is the people of Israel,* who although they did not go away *into far off* places are *nevertheless* said to have remained not at *home,* but *in the field.* For this same people did not forsake the Creator to the point of worshipping

---

421 Anon., *Homilia de duobus filiis* 11 (PL 30:253); see n. 417.
422 Cf. Gen. 18:2–8.
423 Augustine, *Quaestiones euang.* 2.33 (CCSL 44B:78.102–05).

idols, but neither did they penetrate the inner spirit of the Law that they had received. Content solely with the observing the letter, they were accustomed rather to do outward and earthly deeds, and to hope for them as well,[424] hearing from the Prophet: *If you are willing and will listen to me, you will eat the good things of the earth.*[425]

[Luke 15:25b] **And when he came and approached the house, he heard harmonious music and a choir.** The son approaches the house, when the Jewish people *in Israelite meditations of whatever kind, for many such were and often are found among them, condemn the labour of servile work and contemplate the freedom of the Church in these same Scriptures. /293/ He hears harmonious music and a choir, evidently meaning that men full of the spirit preach with voices in harmony, to whom it was said: 'I beseech you, brothers, that you all speak the same thing',*[426] and he hears *the soul and single heart of those living harmoniously together in the praises of God.*[427]

[Luke 15:26–27] **And he called one of the servants, and asked what these things meant. And he said to him:** ... *He calls one of the servants, when he takes one of the prophets to read, and inquiring from him, asks, so to speak, for what reason these same festivities are celebrated in the Church, in which he does not see that he is included. Let the servant of the father, the prophet, respond:*[428]

[Luke 15:27b] **Your brother has come, and your father has killed the fatted calf, because he has received him safe.** *Your brother was at the ends of the earth, but from there came a very great rejoicing of those singing 'to the Lord a new song', because 'his praise is from the ends of the earth'.*[429] *And for the sake of him who was absent* that calf *was killed*[430] to which it was said: *May your whole burnt offering be made fat.*[431]

[Luke 15:28] **And he was angry and would not go in. His father therefore coming out began to entreat him.** *He is angry even now, and still does not want to go in. Therefore 'when the full number of Gentiles has gone in', his father will come out at a suitable time, in order that 'all Israel'*

---

424 Augustine, *Quaestiones euang.* 2.33 (CCSL 44B:78.106–09).
425 Isa. 1:19.
426 1 Cor. 1:10.
427 Augustine, *Quaestiones euang.* 2.33 (CCSL 44B:78.109–17).
428 Augustine, *Quaestiones euang.* 2.33 (CCSL 44B:79.117–21).
429 Isa. 42:10.
430 Augustine, *Quaestiones euang.* 2.33 (CCSL 44B:79.122–26).
431 Ps. 19:4 (20:3).

may be 'saved' as well. Its 'blindness' happened 'in part',[432] just like his absence in the field, when the full number of the younger son, that is, of the Gentiles, who dwelt far off in idol worship, having returned, went in to feast on the calf. For at some time there will be a clear summoning of the Jews in the salvation of the Gospel. The text refers to the father's coming out to entreat his older son as the manifestation of the summons.[433]

[Luke 15:29] **And he answering, said to his father: Behold, for so many years I am serving you, and I have never transgressed your commandment,** ... The question arises how it can be said *that those people never transgressed the commandment of God. But the answer is easy: this was not said of every commandment, but particularly of the indispensable one, whereby they were ordered to worship no other god.*[434] *And this son may be understood to represent not all Israelites, but those who were never converted from the one God to idols. For although this son, set as it were in a field, desired earthly things, nevertheless he desired those good things from the one God. This is also established by the testimony of the father himself, when he says: 'You are always with me'. For he does not refute him as if he were lying, but approving his steadfast abiding with him, invites him to the full enjoyment of a better and more pleasing rejoicing.*[435]

[Luke 15:29b] **And you have never given me a young goat to feast with my friends.** *Indeed, a sinner is customarily signified by the name of a young goat. But God forbid that I understand the Antichrist to be the goat. For it is absurd that the one to whom* /294/ *it is said, 'You are always with me', demanded that his father believe in the Antichrist. And it is not at all right that this son be understood to be one of the Jews who are going to trust in the Antichrist. And how would he who does not trust in it feast from that young goat, if it is itself the Antichrist? Or if this is to feast from the killing of a young goat, because it is to rejoice over the perdition of the Antichrist, how is it that the son, whom the father receives, says that this had not been granted to him, when all the sons of God are going to rejoice over the damnation of that adversary? Doubtless then he is complaining that the Lord himself is denied to him for the sake of feasting, as long as he thinks him a sinner. For as long as he is a young goat to that people,*

---

432 Rom. 11:25–27.
433 Augustine, *Quaestiones euang.* 2.33.4–5 (CCSL 44B:79.128–37). Bede also takes up the eventual conversion of the Jews in his *Commentary on Revelation*: see above, Book 3, n. 166.
434 Cf. Exod. 20:2–3.
435 Augustine, *Quaestiones euang.* 2.33.5 (CCSL 44B:80.138–54).

*that is, as long as they judge him to be a violator of the Sabbath and a profaner of the Law,*[436] *he did not deserve to take pleasure in his feast. The result is that what he says: 'you have never given me a young goat to feast with my friends', is much as if he had said, 'you have never given me one that seemed to me a young goat to feast upon, not granting that very one to me, because it seemed to me a young goat'. And what he says: 'with my friends', is understood to be said either in the character of the leaders with the common people, or in the character of the people of Jerusalem with the other peoples of Judah.*[437]

[Luke 15:30] **But as soon as this your son has come, who has devoured his substance with prostitutes, you have killed the fatted calf for him.** *The prostitutes* are *the false religious practices* of the Gentiles, *with whom to squander his substance* is *to fornicate with a multitude of devils in the most shameful lust, having abandoned the single marriage of the word of God.*[438]

[Luke 15:31–32] **But he said to him: Son, you are always with me, and all my things are yours. But it was fit that we should feast and rejoice, for this your brother was dead and has come to life again; he was lost and is found.** The fact that he says: *'And all my things are yours'*, should not be thought *to have been said, as though they are not also the brother's, so that it is as if you suffer diminution of your earthly inheritance. How can all his things be the elder's, if the younger also has his portion there? All things are possessed by the sons who are perfected and thoroughly cleansed and now immortal in such a way that individual things are the possession of all, and all things the possession of each. For just as cupidity possesses nothing without distress, so love possesses nothing with distress. Therefore, when we obtain that blessedness, higher things will be ours for the sake of eternal life, equal things will be ours for the sake of living together, lesser things will be ours for the sake of ruling over them.*[439]

But if it bothers anyone that when the Truth beseeches the Father and says: *And all my things are yours, and all your things are mine,*[440] which seems to sound very similar to what is said to this son: *And all my things are yours,* he should know that all the things that are the Father's are the

---

436 Cf. Matt. 12:2.
437 Augustine, *Quaestiones euang.* 2.33 (CCSL 44B:81.156–77).
438 Augustine, *Quaestiones euang.* 2.33 (CCSL 44B:82.177–80).
439 Augustine, *Quaestiones euang.* 2.33 (CCSL 44B:82.183–89; 207–09).
440 John 17:10.

only-begotten Son's, because he is likewise God, and being born from the Father, is equal to the Father. For what /295/ he said when speaking of the Holy Spirit: *All the things that the Father has are mine. Therefore, I said that he will receive what is mine and show it to you*,[441] he said of those things that belong to the very divinity of the Father, in which things the Spirit is equal, by having all the things that the Father has. For the Holy Spirit was not going to receive what is from the creation that is subject to the Father and the Son, when he says *he will receive what is mine*, but surely what is the Father's, from whom the Spirit proceeded, and from whom the Son was born. Whether you wish these two sons to refer to both peoples, or as some believe to any two individuals, namely one who is penitent and righteous, or one who seems righteous in his own eyes, *may the elder brother join in rejoicing, because the younger brother was dead and has come to life again; he was lost and is found.*[442]

Here ends Book Four of the Commentary on Luke. /296/

---

441 John 16:15.
442 Augustine, *Quaestiones euang.* 2.33 (CCSL 44B:83.210–11).

# V

[Luke 16:1–21:4]

Here begins Book Five.

After the Saviour refuted in three consecutive parables, which we discussed above, those who seemed righteous in their own eyes and who grumbled about receiving sinners, teaching that the salvation of those who come to their senses is very pleasing indeed to God and the angels, but very grievous to envious men, he immediately adds a fourth and fifth parable about giving alms and pursuing moderation,[1] and shows that those who distribute earthly goods and give to the poor with devout and righteous discernment are destined to be received by them *into everlasting dwellings*.[2] But those who wish only to luxuriate in these goods will be buried in hell, and will not receive the smallest drop of water to cool the eternal fires of the torments even for a moment. The order of his preaching is certainly very fitting, in that almsgiving, that is, the work of mercy, is urged after repentance. For the penitent who is not slow to take pity on his neighbour who is in want justly obtains God's mercy for himself. But *he who turns away his ears from hearing the poor man, his prayer will be an abomination.*[3] Hence also John the Baptist, when he exhorted the multitudes that they not to be sent into the fire in punishment of their own fruitlessness, and that they bring forth worthy fruits of penitence, immediately added and said to those seeking counsel for their own salvation: *He who has two coats, let him give to him who has none, and he who has food, let him do in like manner.*[4] And likewise the Pharisees and scribes, weakened by the plague of avarice no less than by pride, refused to give money to the needy just as they refused forgiveness to the penitent. But he *who wishes all men to be saved, and to*

---

1 Cf. Luke 16.
2 Luke 16:9.
3 Prov. 28:9; cf. Prov. 21:13.
4 Luke 3:11.

*come to the knowledge of the truth*,⁵ in his kindness does not cease to proffer his gifts by speaking with his wonted gentleness now to these people, and now to those who listen to his disciples. But let us come to the text.

## Chapter 63

[Luke 16:1–4] **And he said also to his disciples: There was a certain rich man who had a steward, and this man was accused before him of having wasted his goods. And he called him and said to him: What is this that I hear about you? Give an account of your stewardship, for now you can be steward no longer. And the steward said to himself: What shall I do, because my lord takes away from me the stewardship? I am not able to dig, I am ashamed to beg. I know what I will do, so that when I am removed from the stewardship, they may receive me into their houses.** *We should not take everything we read about* this *steward, whom the lord cast out from the stewardship, and yet praised because he looked out for himself for the future*,⁶ *as something we should imitate. Our Lord is neither* /297/ *going to deceive anyone in order for us to give alms from that deceit, nor it is proper that those by whom we wish to be received into everlasting dwellings be understood as debtors of God and of our Lord, since this passage signifies just and holy men who lead into everlasting dwellings those who share earthly goods when they are in need themselves. He also says about these people that if anyone 'will give a cup of cold water to any of these only in the name of a disciple, he will not lose his reward'.*⁷ *But also in the opposite sense these parables aim to make us understand that if a deceitful person could be praised by his lord, how much more do those who act according to his commandments please the Lord God. In the same way, he drew a comparison between the unjust judge importuned by the widow*⁸ *and to God the judge, to whom an unjust judge ought in no way to be compared.*⁹

Of course, we say that those who have the title of steward and who have riches ought to be thought of as no longer lords of their own, but rather as

---

5  1 Tim. 2:4.
6  Cf. Luke 16:8.
7  Matt. 10:42.
8  Cf. Luke 18:2–8.
9  Augustine, *Quaestiones euang.* 2.34 (CCSL 44B:84.2–17).

dispensers of another's property. If according to the example of this servant they foresee an opportunity to prudently end their stewardship, after being abruptly stripped of the enjoyment as well as the love of all earthly things, they will take care to provide for themselves by searching for friends in the future life more than by gathering them in the present life. A person in this situation goes over many things with himself with great anxiety, and says: *What shall I do? I am not able to dig, I am ashamed to beg.* Indeed, with the stewardship taken away, we cannot dig, because after this life, in which alone it is possible to work, we cannot seek the fruit of the good way of life with the hoe of devout remorse any more. To beg is a kind of disgrace, and this is certainly true with respect to that worst kind of begging such as the foolish virgins are reported to have begged, who, when the time of the wedding drew near, lacking the oil of the virtues, said to the wise virgins: *Give us some of your oil, for our lamps are gone out.*[10] And about which Solomon says: *Because of the cold the sluggard would not plough; he will beg therefore in the summer, and it will not be given to him.*[11]

[Luke 16:5–7] **Therefore, calling together every one of his lord's debtors, he said to the first: How much do you owe my lord? But he said: A hundred jugs of olive oil. And he said to him: Take your bill and sit down quickly, and write fifty. Then he said to another: And how much do you owe? He said: A hundred containers of wheat. He said to him: Take your bill, and write eighty.** *A jug is a Greek amphora containing three urns,* and *a container* is made up *of thirty pecks.*[12]

*The fact that of the hundred /298/ jugs of olive oil he made the debtor write fifty, and of the hundred containers of wheat, eighty, I think means nothing else than whatever the priests among the Jewish Levites do, is likewise done by priests in the Church of Christ, so that their justice exceeds those of the scribes and Pharisees – where they give tenths, Christian priests give halves. This is just what Zacchaeus did, not from fruits, but from his own goods, or indeed he may double the tenths,*[13] *in order to surpass the outlays of the Jews by giving two tenths.*[14] Or one could perhaps think that this parable should be simply accepted to mean that every one of the saints who alleviates the needs of any poor man whatever,

---

10 Matt. 25:8.
11 Prov. 20:4.
12 Isidore, *Etym.* 16.26.13 & 17.
13 Cf. Luke 19:8.
14 Augustine, *Quaestiones euang.* 2.34 (CCSL 44B:85.18–25).

whether with a half or indeed with a fifth part, which are the equivalents of twenty to a hundred, or fifty to a hundred, ought to be given a sure reward for his mercy.

[Luke 16:8] **And the lord commended the unjust steward, because he had acted prudently. For the children of this world are more prudent in their generation than the children of light.** Let the wise men of this world hear, so that they may abandon foolish wisdom and learn the wise foolishness of God – how highly divine Justice will value their wisdom, whom he relates are not truly prudent, but prudent in their generation. This is in accord with what is said elsewhere: *Woe to you who are wise in your own eyes, and prudent in your own sight.*[15] In fact, by calling lovers of eternal life the children of light, he shows that those who are wise in doing evil, and do not know how to do well, are nothing but the children of darkness. The 'children of light' and the 'children of this world' are called thus in the same way as the 'children of the kingdom' and the 'children of perdition'. For each one carries on the works of the one whose son he is also called.

[Luke 16:9] **And I say to you: Make friends for yourselves from the mammon of iniquity, so that when you depart, they may receive you into everlasting dwellings.** The property *that we possess for the time being* he calls the mammon *of iniquity, because by mammon riches are meant. And these are not riches except for the unjust, who place their hope and enjoyment of happiness in them. But when they are possessed by the just, this is indeed* property, *but for them there are no riches save divine and spiritual ones. They supply their wants in a spiritual fashion with these things, and when the poverty of misfortune is removed, they are enriched by an abundance of blessedness.*[16] But if those who offer alms from unjust mammon make friends for themselves by which they may be received into everlasting dwellings, how much more should those who lavish spiritual feasts, who give common fare to their fellow servants in their own time, be lifted up by a sure hope of the highest reward? /299/

[Luke 16:10] **He who is faithful in that which is least is faithful also in that which is greater, and he who is unjust in that which is little is unjust also in that which is greater.** There are those who know nothing of the innermost feelings of compassion and the works of mercy which are owed to their neighbours, and yet nevertheless consider themselves truly faithful because of their chastity, vigils, prolonged prayer, full faith,

---

15 Isa. 5:21.
16 Augustine, *Quaestiones euang.* 2.34.2 (CCSL 44B:85.25–32).

fasting, and other virtues that the love of God is accustomed to engender. But, as the Judge himself attests, *he who is faithful in that which is least,* that is, in the riches that ought to be shared with the poor man, *is faithful also in that which is greater,* namely in that impulse by which he desires specially to cling to the Creator and to become one spirit with him. But he who neglects to dispense the temporal things that he possesses in the right way, deprives himself of the glory of eternal things about which he boasts. *For he who does not love his brother, whom he sees, how can he love God, whom he does not see?*[17] And as the same one says: *He who has the substance of the world and sees his brother in need and shuts up his innermost feelings from him, how does the love of God abide in him?*[18]

[Luke 16:11] **If then you have not been faithful with the unjust mammon, who will trust you with that which is the true mammon?** An explanation of the unjust mammon, which signifies the wealth of the wicked, was given above. Elsewhere, the Saviour, referring to this, says that *the deceitfulness of wealth chokes the word.*[19] But mammon signifies true wealth, or the very joys of eternal life, of which it is written: *what the wealth is of his inheritance in the saints,*[20] or the abundance of the spiritual virtues by which life is attained, of which Isaiah says: *the wealth of salvation, wisdom, and knowledge. The fear of the Lord is his treasure.*[21]

[Luke 16:12] **And if you have not been faithful in that which is another's, who will give you that which is your own?** The riches of this world do not belong to us, that is, they are situated outside our human nature. *For we brought nothing into this world, and certainly we can carry nothing out.*[22] But the kingdom of heaven is our possession; Christ is our life; the fruits of spiritual works are our riches, of which Solomon says: *The ransom of a man's life is his own wealth.*[23] Therefore he accuses the Pharisees of deceit and avarice: because they were not faithful with their own riches, and preferred to possess the common goods of the Creator in private, they did not deserve to receive Christ, whom that tax collector, Zacchaeus, of whom I spoke a little earlier, offered half of his goods to be able to gain.[24]

17  1 John 4:20.
18  1 John 3:17.
19  Matt. 13:22.
20  Eph. 1:18.
21  Isa. 33:6.
22  1 Tim. 6:7.
23  Prov. 13:8.
24  Cf. Luke 19:8.

## Chapter 64

**191/5** [Luke 16:13] **No servant can serve two lords,** *because he is not able /300/ to love transitory things and eternal things at the same time. If we love eternity, we possess all temporal things for use, not love.*[25]

[Luke 16:13b] **For either he will hate the one and love the other, or he will hold to the one and despise the other.** These words must be carefully considered, for he subsequently explains who the two lords are, saying:

[Luke 16:13c] **You cannot serve God and mammon.** *Let the covetous man hear this, let the man who is called by the name of Christian hear that he cannot serve* **Mammon,** *that is,* **wealth,** *and Christ at the same time. And yet he did not say, 'who has wealth', but 'who serves wealth'. For he who is the servant of wealth guards wealth like a servant. But he who has shaken off the yoke of servitude distributes it like a master.*[26] *But he who serves mammon certainly serves the one who, having been set in command of these earthly things by the fault of his own perversity, is called the prince of this world by the Lord.*[27] *Therefore 'either he will hate the one and love the other', as ought to be done, that is to say, he will hate the devil and love God, or 'he will hold to the one and despise the other', that is to say, he will hold to the devil, when he pursues as it were his temporal rewards, but he will despise God. He did not say, 'he will hate', but as they flatter themselves that they are immune to punishment because God is good, they are wont to downplay his threats to their desires. To these Solomon says: 'Son, do not add sin on sin, and say: The mercy of God is great'.*[28]

**192/10** [Luke 16:14] **And the Pharisees, who were avaricious, heard all these things, and they derided him.** Indeed, the Lord warned the scribes and the Pharisees not to think proudly, not to be confident of their own justice, but to accept both penitent sinners and tax collectors, and to redeem with alms their own sins, which perchance had befallen them. But they derided the teacher of mercy, humility, and moderation chiefly for two reasons: namely that he either injuriously commanded things that are not at all useful and that should never be done, or that he unnecessarily insisted upon things that are indeed useful, but which they had already done.

---

25 Gregory, *Hom. in Hiezech.* 2.7.17 (CCSL 142:331.542–44).
26 Jerome, *Commentarii in Matheum* 1 (CCSL 77:39.830–35).
27 Augustine, *De sermone Domini* 2.14.47 (CCSL 35:138.1038–41).
28 Augustine, *Quaestiones euang.* 2.36 (CCSL 44B:86.7–14); Ecclus. 5:5–6.

[Luke 16:15] **And he said to them: You are those who justify yourselves before men. But God knows your hearts. For that which is highly esteemed to men is an abomination before God.** They justify themselves before men, who despise sinners as weak and irremediable, yet believe themselves to be perfect in all things and free from all weakness, and so to have no need of the remedy of alms-giving. But he, *who will bring to light the hidden things of darkness, and will make manifest the counsels of the hearts*,[29] sees the height of this noxious arrogance, and that it should justly be condemned.

**193**/5 [Luke 16:16] **The Law and the prophets were until John. From that time the kingdom of God is preached, /301/ and everyone uses violence to gain it.** The Pharisees derided the Saviour who contended against the love of money, as if he were teaching things contrary to the Law and the prophets, when we read that the legislators and prophets were numerous and very wealthy and yet pleasing to God. Moreover, Moses himself foretold that if the people whom he ruled followed the Law, they would abound in all the good things which the earth bears, but if they disregarded it, they would be struck with pestilence, famine, want, and every evil. Jesus, answering them, shows that there must not be any distinction at all between the Law and the Gospel when it comes to their promises as well as to their commandments, and indeed that greater things are commanded for the sake of the kingdom of heaven and lesser ones for the kingdom of earth by one and the same God who created heaven and earth. Accordingly, it is written there [in the Old Testament]: *If you are willing and will listen to me, you will eat the good things of the earth.*[30] And here [in the New Testament]: *Blessed are the poor in spirit, for theirs is the kingdom of heaven.*[31] Therefore when he said that the kingdom of God was preached, he rightly added: *and everyone uses violence to gain it.* Great is the power and grand is the violence, that we, born from the earth, use to seek the throne of heaven, and wish to possess by virtue what we could not hold by nature, not only to despise earthly things, but also to despise the tongues of those who laugh at us when we despise such things. For he added this, when, having spoken of scorning wealth, he was derided by the Pharisees.

**194**/5 [Luke 16:17] **And it is easier for heaven and earth to pass away, than for one tip of a letter to fall out from the Law.** So that they might

---

29 1 Cor. 4:5.
30 Isa. 1:19.
31 Matt. 5:3.

not think that the destruction of the Law and the prophets was proclaimed by him because he said: *The Law and the prophets were until John*, he plainly bears witness that the greatest elements of the world pass away more easily than the least sayings of the Law. And this is a fact: *For the fashion of this world passes away.*[32] *And elsewhere: But we look for new heavens and a new earth according to his promises, in which justice dwells.*[33] But in the Law, nothing is void of spiritual mysteries, even the *smallest* matters that seem unimportant and *superstitious*, because *all these things are recapitulated in the Gospel.*[34] Nevertheless *the Law and the prophets were until John*, because nothing could be prophesied save what was to come; John's proclamation, however, made it clear that he had already come.

**195/2** [Luke 16:18] **Everyone who puts away his wife and marries another commits adultery, and he who marries her who is put away from her husband commits adultery.** What he preached about the Law's perpetual inviolability, he confirms for the sake of an example by one testimony taken from it, so that they might learn from this case, as in others, that he had not come to destroy the commandments of the Law but /302/ to fulfil them.[35] If anyone wishes to find out more about the exposition of this testimony, he should examine not my writings, but those of our elders. Indeed, the blessed Fathers, first of all Augustine in his book of the Lord's Sermon on the Mount, Jerome and Ambrose in their commentaries on the evangelists Matthew and Luke, but also how very many others, have each said enough and more about it in their works.

## Chapter 65

**196/10** [Luke 16:19] **There was a rich man who was clothed in purple and byssum and feasted sumptuously every day.** Everyone knows that purple is *the colour* of royal attire, dyed *from marine shellfish. For shellfish cut around with a blade emit drops of a purple colour* with which wool is dyed.[36] But *byssum is a kind of linen cloth, exceedingly white and very soft,*

---

32 1 Cor. 7:31.
33 2 Pet. 3:13.
34 Jerome, *Commentarii in Matheum* 1 (CCSL 77:27.512–15).
35 Cf. Matt. 5:17.
36 Isidore, *Etym.* 19.28.2 & 4.

that the Greeks call 'papaten'.³⁷ The Lord had admonished above that with the mammon of iniquity we should make friends who may receive us into everlasting dwellings when we depart from this life. The Pharisees, hearing this, derided him. So, demonstrating what he taught by examples, he shows that the rich man clothed in purple was tormented irremediably among the damned, because he had neglected to make the poor man, Lazarus, his friend, by whom he could have been received into the dwellings of life. And *some think that the commandments of the Old Testament are stricter than those of the New, but without doubt they are deceived by careless thinking. For in the Old Testament, not avarice, but robbery is punished; taking something wrongfully is punished by fourfold restitution.*³⁸ *But in the New Testament, this rich man is blamed, not for having carried off someone else's property, but for not having given his own. And it is not said that he overpowered anyone by force, but that he prided himself in the things he had received. So from this one should infer with the greatest seriousness what the penalty will be for someone who steals someone else's property, if he who does not share his own is struck with infernal damnation. There are some who think that adornment with splendid and very costly clothing is not a sin. But if, of course, it were not a sin, the word of God would by no means express with such precision that the rich man who was tormented among the damned had been clothed in byssum and purple. Indeed, no one seeks exceptional clothing except for vainglory, namely to seem more distinguished than others. We can better consider this sin from the opposite point of view, because if the humility of vile clothing were not a virtue, the evangelist would not state precisely about John: 'He was clothed with camels' hair.'*³⁹ *But we should particularly note how important the order of the narrative of the proud rich man and the humble pauper is* /**303**/ *in the speech of the Truth. For look, it is said: 'There was a certain rich man', and immediately after it is added:*⁴⁰

[Luke 16:20] **And there was a beggar, named Lazarus,** ... *Certainly, the names of the rich are usually better known among the people than the names of the poor. Why is it, therefore, that the Lord, speaking of the rich man and the pauper, tells us the name of the pauper and not of the rich man, unless it is that God knows and approves of the humble and ignores*

---

37 Isidore, *Etym.* 19.27.4.
38 Cf. Exod. 22:1; 2 Sam. 12:6.
39 Matt. 3:4.
40 Gregory, *Hom. in Euang.* 2.40.3 (CCSL 141:398.117–47).

*the proud? Hence to those who boast of their power to work miracles he will say in the end: 'I do not know you whence you are. Depart from me, all you workers of iniquity.'*[41] *But on the contrary it is said to Moses: 'I know you by name.'*[42] *Therefore he speaks of the rich man as 'a man', and he speaks of the pauper as 'an indigent named Lazarus', as if he would say plainly: 'I know the humble pauper; I don't know the proud rich man; I hold the former to be known by my approval; I ignore the latter by my judgement of reproof.'*[43]

[Luke 16:20b–21] **Who lay at his gate, full of sores, desiring to be filled with the crumbs that fell from the rich man's table; moreover the dogs came and licked his sores.** *The beggar, Lazarus, full of sores, lies before the doors of the rich man. From this one event, the Lord makes two points. The rich man would possibly have had some excuse, if Lazarus, a poor man and full of sores, had not lain at his gate, if he had been far off, or if his poverty had not been distressing to the eyes. On the other hand, if the rich man were at a distance from the eyes of the pauper full of sores, the pauper would have suffered a lesser trial to his spirit. But when he placed him needy and full of sores at the gate of a man who was rich and abounding in luxury, in one and the same incident he indicated the overwhelming condemnation that awaited the merciless rich man because he saw the pauper, and on the other hand his approval of the pauper who was tested daily by seeing the rich man. Certainly, poverty would be sufficiently painful for the pauper, even if he had been healthy, and in turn illness would have sufficed, even if help were at hand. But in order for the pauper to be tested more thoroughly, both poverty and illness wasted him at the same time. Moreover, he saw that the rich man when he came out was flanked by an obsequious crowd, and that he himself was attended by no one in his illness and poverty. That no one was there to attend to him is shown by the dogs that willingly licked his sores. From one incident therefore the almighty God exhibited two judgements, when he permitted the poor man, Lazarus, to lie at the gate of the rich man, so that not only did the wicked rich man increase the pains of his own damnation, but the poor man, having been tested, gained a recompense.*[44]

---

41 Luke 13:27.
42 Exod. 33:12.
43 Gregory, *Hom. in Euang.* 2.40.3 (CCSL 141:399.148–59).
44 Gregory, *Hom. in Euang.* 2.40.4 (CCSL 141:400.162–89).

[Luke 16:22] **And the beggar died and was carried by the angels into Abraham's bosom. And the rich man also died, and he was buried in hell.** *The bosom of Abraham is the rest of the blessed poor, to whom belongs the kingdom of heaven where they are received after this life.* /304/ *The tomb of hell is the immensity of punishments which swallows up the proud and the merciless after this life.*[45]

[Luke 16:23-24] **And lifting up his eyes when he was in torments, he saw Abraham afar off, and Lazarus in his bosom. And he cried and said: Father Abraham, have mercy on me and send Lazarus, that he may dip the tip of his finger in water to cool my tongue, for I am tormented in this flame.** *O how great is the subtlety of the judgements of God! O how strictly does he repay good and evil deeds! Indeed, it was said above that in this life Lazarus sought the crumbs that fell from the table of the rich man, and no one gave any to him. Now it is said of the punishment of the rich man that he longs for water to be trickled into his mouth from Lazarus' fingertip. He, therefore, who would not give even the least little something from his table, placed in hell, reaches the point of seeking a little something. But it should be closely observed why the rich man, placed in the fire, entreats that his tongue be cooled. In fact, it is the way of sacred Scripture sometimes to say one thing, but to signify another with the same expression. The Lord had mentioned above this proud rich man did not have any time for conversation, but feasted to excess; and he said that he had sinned not from talkativeness, but from gluttony with avarice and obstinacy. But because talkativeness usually abounds in feasts, he who is said to have feasted wickedly here is said to burn more grievously on his tongue among the damned. But what follows ought to be pondered with exceedingly grievous fear.*[46]

[Luke 16:25] **And Abraham said to him: Son, remember that you received good things in your life, and likewise Lazarus evil things, but now he is comforted, and you are tormented.** *For, behold, when it is said: 'You received good things in your life', this same rich man is shown to have also had some goodness, from which he received good things in this life. And on the contrary, when it is said of Lazarus that he received evil things, Lazarus is certainly shown to have had some evil that was purged. But the fire of indigence purged Lazarus' evil, and the felicity of this transient life repaid the goodness of the rich man.*[47]

---

45 Augustine, *Quaestiones euang.* 2.38 (CCSL 44B:89.28–31).
46 Gregory, *Hom. in Euang.* 2.40.5–6 (CCSL 141:401.201–27).
47 Gregory, *Hom. in Euang.* 2.40.6 (CCSL 141:402.237–42).

[Luke 16:26] **And besides all this, between you and us, there is fixed a great gulf, so that those who wish to pass from here to you cannot, nor from there can you come here.** *In this matter, it should be carefully investigated why it is said: 'those who wish to pass from here to you cannot, nor from there can you come here.' For there is no doubt that those who are in hell wish to come to the condition of the blessed. But how can it said that those who have already been taken up in the condition of blessedness wish to pass over to those who are tormented in hell? But just as the damned wish to pass to the elect, that is, to depart from the affliction of their punishments, so the righteous are minded out of pity to pass over to those who are afflicted and placed in torments, and to wish to free them. But those who wish to pass from the seat of the blessed to those afflicted and placed in torments cannot, because although the souls of the just have pity out of the goodness of their* /305/ *nature, already they are constrained by the great rectitude of their Creator with which their own righteousness is united, so that they are not moved by any compassion towards the damned.*[48]

*But after the hope of the rich man in flames is taken from him, his mind turns to the relations whom he had left, because their punishment directs the heart of the damned toward love, though it is of no use to them, so that even now they love their relatives spiritually, who on earth, when they loved sins, did not love themselves. Hence it now* follows:[49]

[Luke 16:27–28] **And he said: Then, father, I beseech you that you send him to my father's house, for I have five brothers, that he may testify to them, lest they also come into this place of torments.** *In this matter, it should be observed how many things are heaped upon the burning rich man for punishment. For he recognizes Lazarus whom he scorned, and he also remembers his brothers whom he left. Certainly his punishment with respect to the poor man would not have been complete, if he did not recognize him in his state of reward. And his punishment in the fire would not have been complete, if he did not fear that his relatives would suffer what he is suffering. Therefore, in order that sinners be punished more in torments, they not only see the glory of those whom they had despised, but they are even tormented with respect to the punishment of those whom they loved to no avail. But it must be believed that before*

---

48 Gregory, *Hom. in Euang.* 2.40.7 (CCSL 141:403.255–67).
49 Gregory, *Hom. in Euang.* 2.40.8 (CCSL 141:404.275–79).

*the recompense of last judgement, the unjust see some of the just in rest, so that seeing them in joy, they are tormented not only with respect to their own punishment, but also with respect to the good of those just men. But the just always witness the unjust in torments, so that their joy may increase from this, because they see the evil that they mercifully escaped, and so that they may return so much the greater thanks to their Saviour, the more plainly they see in others what they themselves could have suffered, if they had been* heedless, *because nothing is done in creation which those who see the splendour of their Creator cannot see.*[50]

[Luke 16:29] **And Abraham said to him: They have Moses and the prophets; let them hear them.** *But the rich man who had scorned the words of God judged that those who came after him would not be able to hear them. And hence the rich man responded:*[51]

[Luke 16:30b] **No, father Abraham, but if someone went to them from the dead, they will do penance.** *A true answer was given to him straight away:*[52]

[Luke 16:31b] **If they do not hear Moses and the prophets, neither will they believe if someone rises again from the dead.** *Because certainly those who scorn the words of the Law will find it more difficult to carry out the commandments of the Redeemer, who rose again from the dead, because they are more exacting. And certainly, it is clear that they refused to believe the one whose words they refuse to fulfil.*[53]

But, allegorically, *whom does this rich man, who 'was clothed in purple and byssum and feasted sumptuously every day', signify, if not the Jewish people, who cultivated a very outward way of life, and who employed the adornments of the Law which they had received for splendour rather than for benefit?* And *whom does Lazarus, 'full of sores', represent figuratively, except the Gentile people? When, having turned to God, he did not blush to confess his sins, the sore was in his skin. Indeed, in a sore of the skin, poison* /306/ *is drawn from the innards and bursts out. Therefore, what is a confession of sins but a kind of bursting of sores? Because the poison of the sin that hid noxiously in the soul is opened wholesomely in confession.*[54]

---

50 Gregory, *Hom. in Euang.* 2.40.8 (CCSL 141:404.282–307).
51 Gregory, *Hom. in Euang.* 2.40.9 (CCSL 141:405.311–13).
52 Gregory, *Hom. in Euang.* 2.40.9 (CCSL 141:406.314–15).
53 Gregory, *Hom. in Euang.* 2.40.9 (CCSL 141:406.316–27).
54 Gregory, *Hom. in Euang.* 2.40.2 (CCSL 141:394.16–26).

But Lazarus, covered with sores, wished 'to be filled with the crumbs that fell from the rich man's table, and no one gave any to him', because that proud people disdained to admit any Gentile people to knowledge of the Law. As long as they made use of the teaching of the Law not for love, but for pride, they were puffed up as it were with the wealth they obtained. And the reason is that words of knowledge fell on them like crumbs falling from the table.[55]

But on the other hand dogs licked the sores of the poor man as he lay there. Sometimes in sacred Scripture, preachers are signified by dogs. And indeed, when a dog licks a sore with his tongue, he cures it, because not only do holy teachers when they instruct us in the confession of our sin, touch as it were our soul's sore with their tongue, but also because they liberate us from sins by speaking, as if they lead us back to health by touching our sores.[56]

Hence, also, Lazarus is properly translated as 'help', because they themselves help him to liberation, who cure his sores by the liberating admonition of the tongue.[57]

But it happened that each of them died. The rich man, who was clothed in purple and byssum, was buried in hell, but Lazarus was brought by angels into the bosom of Abraham. What does the bosom of Abraham signify but the secret resting place of the Father? Of this the Truth says: 'Many will come from the east and the west and will sit down with Abraham and Isaac and Jacob in the kingdom of heaven. But the children of this kingdom will be cast out into the outer darkness.'[58] For he who is said to be clothed in purple is rightly called a child of the kingdom. He lifts his eyes from afar to see Lazarus, because, when the infidels are in hell through the torments of their damnation, each of the faithful waits above them in a place of rest before the day of the Last Judgement, and what their joys will be after that they cannot see at all. But what they see is far off, because they do not arrive at that place by their deserts.[59]

The rich man shows the great burning in his tongue, when he says: 'Send Lazarus, that he may dip the tip of his finger in water to cool my

---

55 Gregory, *Hom. in Euang.* 2.40.2 (CCSL 141:395.29–34).
56 Gregory, *Hom. in Euang.* 2.40.2 (CCSL 141:395.35–40).
57 Gregory, *Hom. in Euang.* 2.40.2 (CCSL 141:395.52–54).
58 Matt. 8:11–12.
59 Gregory, *Hom. in Euang.* 2.40.2 (CCSL 141:396.58–69).

*tongue, for I am tormented in this flame.'*[60] *The faithless people had the words of the Law in their mouth, which they scorned to observe in deed. Therefore, he will burn more severely, since he shows that he knows what he was not willing to do. He desires to be touched by the tip of Lazarus' finger, because, having been handed over to eternal torments, he wishes by the work of the just to share even in the least things which they enjoy. He gets the answer that he received good things in this life, because he thought that all his joy lay in transitory happiness. And indeed, the just can also have good things here, and nevertheless they do not receive these things in recompense, because as long as they seek better, that is, eternal things, whatever good things in their judgement are present do not seem good at all, when they are aflame with holy desires.*[61]

*But amongst this it should be noted what is said to him: Remember, Son. For, behold, Abraham calls him 'son', whom nevertheless he does not free from torment,* /307/ *since the faithful forefathers of this faithless people, because they observe that many have deviated from their faith, do not deliver them from torments with any compassion, whom nevertheless they recognize as sons in the flesh. And the rich man set in torments asserts that he has five brothers, because that same proud Jewish people, who have now in large part been damned, know that their followers whom they left on earth are given over to the five senses of the body. Accordingly, he represents the brothers whom he had left by the number five, because he laments that those placed in hell did not rise up to spiritual understanding. He, to whom it is said that they have Moses and the prophets, begs that Lazarus be sent to them. But he says that they do not believe unless someone will have risen again from the dead. He is immediately answered: 'If they do not hear Moses and the prophets, neither will they believe if someone rises again from the dead.' Indeed, the Truth says of Moses: 'For if you did believe Moses, you would certainly believe me also. For he wrote of me.'*[62] *Therefore, what is said in Abraham's response is fulfilled. For the Lord rose again from the dead, but because they would not believe Moses, the Jewish people likewise scorned to believe the one who rose again from the dead. And when they refused to understand the words of Moses spiritually, they did not come to him of whom Moses had spoken.*[63]

60  Luke 16:24.
61  Gregory, *Hom. in Euang.* 2.40.2 (CCSL 141:396.70–86).
62  John 5:46.
63  Gregory, *Hom. in Euang.* 2.40.2 (CCSL 141:397.90–111).

## Chapter 66

197/2 [Luke 17:1] **And he said to his disciples: It is impossible that stumbling blocks should not come. But woe to him though whom they come.** And the Apostle says: But *there must also be heresies, so that they who are approved may be made manifest among you.*[64] In this world full of errors and tribulations, it is impossible for stumbling blocks not to come very often, but woe to him who makes what cannot be avoided happen by his own fault, so that it comes about through himself. Although in a general sense this can be interpreted either as some false brother or as Judas himself who was preparing his soul for betrayal, nevertheless according to the sequence of this discourse this passage refers back to what was said above, when the Lord is laughed at by the Pharisees for what he said about giving alms.[65] For he who censures anyone who speaks the truth certainly offers a stumbling block, that is, an obstacle, and ruin to weak listeners, especially if he also seems like the Pharisees to have knowledge of the law. Rebuking them, the Apostle says: *And through your knowledge will the weak brother perish, for whom Christ died?*[66]

[Luke 17:2] **It is better for him that a millstone be hung about his neck and he be cast into the sea than that he cause one of these little ones to stumble.** This is said according to the custom *of this territory, for among the old Jewish people the punishment for greater crimes was to be drowned in the depths tied with a rock.*[67] Indeed, it is better finally that an innocent man end his bodily life with a temporal, although very dreadful punishment /308/ than that a man who wrongs his brother incur the eternal death of his soul. He who can be caused to stumble is rightly called a little one. For he who does not turn aside from the faith, whatever he sees and whatever he suffers, is great. But he who is little and small in soul seeks pretexts to stumble. For that reason, finally, we must counsel those who are little in the faith, lest our people be offended by an occasion for sin and depart from the faith and fall away from salvation.

Of course, it should be observed that *in our good work, sometimes a neighbour's stumbling block must be guarded against, but sometimes it must be disregarded.* For *insofar as we are able without sin, we ought to*

---

64 1 Cor. 11:19.
65 Cf. Luke 16:14.
66 1 Cor. 8:11.
67 Jerome, *Commentarii in Matheum* 3 (CCSL 77:158.528-30).

*shun the neighbours' stumbling block. But if the stumbling block is taken from the truth, it is better that the stumbling block is allowed to arise than that the truth be abandoned.*⁶⁸

**198/5** [Luke 17:3] **Give heed to yourselves. If your brother sin against you, rebuke him, and if he do penance, forgive him.** Such is what we also read in Deuteronomy: *You shall not hate your brother in your heart, but reprove him openly, lest you incur sin through him.*⁶⁹ He therefore makes known in what way we can overturn stumbling blocks and avoid eternal woe, if, that is to say, we give heed to ourselves, lest we harm anyone; if we reprove the one sinning with a zeal for justice; if we lay open from the heart the bowels of mercy and compassion to the penitent. In which case it should be carefully considered that we are not commanded to forgive the sinner indiscriminately, but to forgive the one doing penance, and indeed first to rebuke the sinner compassionately, so that he may be one whom we afterwards are able to forgive justly. Therefore, he who sees that a brother sins and keeps silent, is no less a transgressor of the Lord's commandment than the one who will not forgive the same penitent, because he who said: *If he do penance, forgive,* first said: *If he sins, rebuke.* Accordingly, forgiveness should be granted to a brother after rebuke, but, of course, to one who converts from error by doing penance, let forgiveness not be difficult nor gentleness abated.

**199/5** [Luke 17:4] **And if he sins against you seven times a day, and seven times a day turns back to you, saying: I repent, forgive him.** Forgiveness is not to end with the number seven, but it is ordered both that all sins be forgiven and that forgiveness always be given to the penitent. For the number seven usually represents the totality of anything whatever or of time. Hence, what is sung in the Psalm: *Seven times a day I have given you praise,*⁷⁰ is nothing other than: *His praise will always be in my mouth.*⁷¹ For in another passage the Lord replies to Peter, who asks how many times he should forgive *a brother sinning against him,* whether up to seven times: I say to you *not up to seven times, but up to seventy times seven times, that is, four hundred* /309/ *and ninety times, so that his sinning brother could not sin as many times as he forgave him in a day.*⁷² Therefore,

---

68 Gregory, *Hom. in Hiezech.* 1.7.4–5 (CCSL 142:85.66–67; 87–90).
69 Lev. 19:17.
70 Ps. 118:64 (119:64).
71 Ps. 33:2 (34:1).
72 Jerome, *Commentarii in Matheum* 3 (CCSL 77:163.666–71).

you *have the power, or rather the necessity, of forgiving* the brother sinning against you,[73] if he does penance, in order that the Father who is in heaven may likewise pardon you when you are penitent and asking for mercy. But if, having been rebuked, someone does not trouble to be converted and do penance, consider what the word of the Truth judges about this: *But if your brother offends against you, go and rebuke him*, and so forth as far as where it says: *But if he will not hear the Church, let him be to you as a heathen and a tax collector.*[74] And deservedly so, because he has done the deeds of infidels in the name of a person of faith. We are commanded to show mercy to a brother seeking it in one way, and to show it to an enemy who strives to obtain it in another. Namely, to the latter, so that, after he has received forgiveness of his sin whereby he injured us who were innocent, he may share with us in mutual love; but to the former, so that when he wishes us evil and, if he can, does it, we always wish him good and do what we can. David, although mourning them compassionately, was not able to offer the same kind of forgiveness to his persecutors when they stood deprived of the remedy of penance that Joseph showed to his brothers who had been chastised by salutary remorse in order to be recognized with kindness.[75]

## Chapter 67

**200/5** [Luke 17:5] **And the apostles said to the Lord: Increase our faith.** The Lord had said above: *He who is faithful in that which is least is faithful also in that which is greater;*[76] *and if you have not been faithful in that which is another's, who will give you that which is your own?*[77] And therefore the apostles, who were already faithful in that which was another's and in the least, that is, in contempt for earthly things, ask that their faith be increased in that which was their own and in that which is greater. For no one suddenly becomes best, but everyone begins in a good way of life from least things, in order to attain to great ones. Indeed the starting points for virtue are one thing, advancing thither is another, attaining it yet another. Seeking above all this last, they say to the Lord: *Increase our faith.*

---

73 Jerome, *Commentarii in Matheum* 3 (CCSL 77:161.607–08).
74 Matt. 18:15–17.
75 Cf. 2 Sam. 1:12; 18:33; Gen. 45:5.
76 Luke 16:10.
77 Luke 16:12.

[Luke 17:6] **And the Lord said: If you had faith like a grain of mustard seed, you might say to this mulberry tree: Be uprooted and transplanted in the sea; and it would obey you.** He compares perfect faith to a grain of mustard seed, which is both humble in appearance and burning in the stomach, worthless indeed to those viewing it casually, seemingly of no strength, but when it is crushed under pressure, displaying something of the perfection it carries within. But also, it should be noted that a grain of mustard seed is very wholesome and effective for purging of the head. For if you mix it well, rubbed and sifted, with thick warm honey, and gargle it, fasting, facing the hot sun or in the baths, it purges every noxious humour even if it were very thick, and /310/ causes the perils of threatening infirmity to be avoided.[78] Thus certainly faith which is put to the test by the pestle of temptations, skimmed by the sieve of discretion from all superficiality of trivial thoughts, and sweetened with the honey of perfect love, not only empties all the filthy waters of sins from the heart, which is the head of our inner man, in the present, but also prevents them from being able to congregate together again in the future.

The mulberry tree being uprooted and transplanted or simply placed in the sea can be understood to mean that it is a mark of perfect faith to rule over the elements with the word, so that what is said in particular about one thing is believed to be experienced in general by all things. Elsewhere the Lord says to the disciples marvelling at the fig tree withered by the word: *If you have faith and are not uncertain, not only will you do this with a fig tree, but also if you say to this mountain, 'Lift yourself up and cast yourself into the sea', it will be done.*[79] Or indeed by the mulberry, the fruits and cuttings of which are reddened [*rubent*] with a bloody colour, whence it is also called *rubus* by speakers of Latin,[80] the Gospel of the cross is expressed.[81] This was uprooted from the people of the Jews, among whom it was held as it were in the stock of its lineage through the faith of the apostles and was transferred and planted in the sea of the Gentiles by the words they preached.[82] This sense agrees with the sense of the next parable,

---

78 Cf. Marcellus, *De medicamentis* 1.5.9 and 15 (ed. Niedermann, 92, 94). On Bede's interest in medicine, see Introduction, 53.
79 Matt. 21:21.
80 Cf. Isidore, *Etym.* 17.7.19.
81 Cf. Ps.-Jerome, *Expositio euangeliorum* (PL 30:575B): the mulberry is 'the Gospel, which announces the ruddy Cross of Christ'.
82 Cf. Ps.-Jerome, *Expositio euangeliorum* (PL 30:575B–C).

which deals with ministers of the word.[83] And the fact that mulberry leaves cast over a snake cause death[84] also supports this, because the word of the cross, just as it confers all things salvific, destroys all noxious things.

**201/10 [Luke 17:7] But which of you having a servant ploughing or feeding cattle,** ... This parable teaches that the more faith excels outwardly in virtues, the humbler it becomes inwardly in its own conscience. The servant ploughing or feeding cattle, of course, is understood as any teacher of the Church, about whom the Lord says: *No man putting his hand to the plough and looking back is fit for the kingdom of God.*[85] And he replies for the third time to the one testifying for the second time that he loves him: *Feed my sheep.*[86]

[Luke 17:7b–8] **When he has returned from the field will say to him: Go immediately and sit down at the table; and will not rather say to him: Prepare my supper,** ... The servant returns from the field when the teacher, leaving off the work of preaching for a time, reverts to his conscience, and, coming back from public discourse to the tribunal of his heart by withdrawing within himself, he re-examines his own words and deeds. The Lord does not say to him, *Go immediately and sit down at the table*, that is, go from this mortal life and be restored in the blessed seat of eternal life. For he is going to say these things afterwards. In the meantime, after the servant has cared for the cattle and fields, the master orders him to prepare supper at home for himself, that is, after the work of open speaking, to show also the humility of self-reflection. /311/ And indeed, the Lord deigns to enter the temple of such awareness; he desires to be fed very willingly with such a supper. *Behold*, he says, *I stand at the gate and knock. If any man arises and opens to me, I will come in to him, and I will sup with him, and he with me.*[87]

[Luke 17:8b] **And gird yourself and minister to me while I eat and drink,** ... To be girded is to restrain the humbled soul from the whole domain of wavering thoughts which normally interfere with the course of good works. For whoever girds his clothing certainly does it in order not to

---

83 Cf. Luke 17:7–10.
84 Cf. Isidore, *Etym.* 17.7.19.
85 Luke 9:62.
86 John 21:17.
87 Rev. 3:20. de Margerie, *Introduction à l'histoire de l'exégèse*, 197, notes that this passage is much more fully developed here than in Bede's Commentary on Revelation, ed. Gryson (CCSL 121A:275); trans. Wallis, 130), but what is actually at play here is an example of 'exegesis by concordance' (see Introduction, 29–30).

be tangled up in error while proceeding on foot. But to minister to God is to acknowledge oneself least [*minimum*] in everything and lacking any power without the help of his grace. For the word **min**ister took its name from its lesser [*minori*] status, that is, servitude, just as the word **ma**ster from its greater [*maiori*] status.[88] Whoever thinks upon the Creator's nature and fears his judgements, humbling himself with respect to his own virtues, ministers to the Creator.

[Luke 17:8c] **And afterwards you will eat and drink?** After, he says, I myself have been delighted by the work of your preaching, and refreshed by the banquet of your remorse, then finally you will go and sit down at the table, and you will be refreshed forever by the feast of my eternal wisdom.

[Luke 17:9–10] **Does he thank that servant because he did the things which he commanded him to do? I think not. So you also, when you have done all the things you were ordered to do, say: We are unprofitable servants.** If a man, he says, demands from his serving man not a simple but a manifold service, and yet does not thank him, how much more should you, who *without me can do nothing*,[89] not weigh the reward of your labours by how long they take, but augment the rewards you have already earned by love and voluntary servitude with ever new efforts. And so *say: We are unprofitable servants*. Indeed, you are servants, because *you were bought with a price*,[90] and unprofitable, because the Lord has no need of your good works.[91] But if he is unprofitable who did everything, what must it be said of the one who either was not able to complete the things he was ordered to do out of weakness, or, what is worse, disdained to do them out of pride?

In another interpretation: *We are unprofitable servants*, because *the sufferings of this time are not worthy to be compared with the glory to come that will be revealed in us*.[92] And elsewhere: *Who crowns you with compassion and mercy*.[93] He does not say 'with merits and good works', because mercy goes before us to that we may serve God humbly, and we are crowned by his gift, in order that we reign with him on high.

---

88 Cf. Isidore, *Etym.* 10.170.
89 John 15:5.
90 1 Cor. 7:23.
91 Cf. Ps. 15:2 (16:2).
92 Rom. 8:18.
93 Ps. 102:4 (103:4).

[Luke 17:10b] **We have done what we ought to have done.** Truly, we ought to have done it, because he who *did not come to be ministered to, but to minister*[94] made us his debtors, so that, not trusting in our good works, but being always terrified of his judgement, we may say with the prophet David: *What will* we *render to the Lord, for all the things that he has rendered to* us?[95] David spoke prophetically /312/ in order to show that he had faith like a grain of mustard seed, that is to say, humble and fervent, saying: *I have believed, therefore have I spoken, but I have been humbled exceedingly.*[96] In order to show that he had no trust in his own powers, he added, speaking in amazement: *Every man is a liar.*[97] In order to signify that even after receiving the chalice of a precious death he was an unprofitable servant, he exclaims: *O Lord, I am your servant, I am your servant, and the son of your handmaid. You have broken my bonds.*[98] He does not say, 'I myself have broken, I myself am sufficient for saving myself', but: *You have broken my bonds, I will sacrifice to you the sacrifice of praise.*[99] This is the sole perfection of faith among men: to know that they are imperfect even if they have accomplished everything which they were ordered to do, and, as long as they wander from the Lord, always to remember that the evils which they lament are present in them, and that the good things towards which they advance with the aid of his grace are lacking.

## Chapter 68

[Luke 17:11–12] **And it happened, as he was going to Jerusalem, that he passed through the midst of Samaria and Galilee. And as he entered into a certain town, ten men who were lepers met him,** ... *The lepers can reasonably be understood as those who lacking knowledge of the true faith, profess various heretical teachings. For assuredly they do not hide their ignorance, but bring it forth into the light as if it were the highest knowledge, and make a show of boasting of their speech. But there is no false teaching which is not mingled with some true teaching. Therefore,*

---

94 Matt. 20:28.
95 Ps. 115:12 (116:12).
96 Ps. 115:10 (116:10).
97 Ps. 115:11 (116:11).
98 Ps. 115:16 (116:16).
99 Ps. 115:16–17 (116:16–17).

BOOK FIVE 501

*true things that are mixed in a disorderly fashion with false ones in a man's argument or narration, as if appearing in the colour of a single body, suggest leprosy, in the same way as leprosy dapples and spots human bodies with true and false patches of colour. But these lepers of the Church must be avoided, so that, when they are removed farther off, they may if this be possible call upon Christ with a great clamour.*[100] Hence it is fittingly added:

[Luke 17:12b–13] **Who stood far off, and lifted up their voice, saying: Jesus, teacher, have mercy on us.** *Well do* they call Jesus, 'teacher', *in order to be saved. Since they indicate by these words that they have gone astray, they humbly call him teacher in order to be saved, and when they come to recognize the teacher, they immediately have recourse to that form of salutation.*[101] For it goes on:

[Luke 17:14] **When he saw them, he said: Go, show yourselves to the priests. And it happened as they went that they were made clean.** The Lord *is never found to have sent to the priests any of those to whom he gave bodily help except the lepers,*[102] because, of course, *the priesthood of the Jews* was *a figure of the royal priesthood to come, which is in the Church, whereby are consecrated all those belonging to the body of Christ, the highest and true chief of the priests.*[103] And whoever through the Lord's grace is free either from heretical perversity, or from pagan superstition, or from Jewish perfidy, or even from fraternal schism – from mottled colour /313/ as it were – must come to the Church and display the true colour of the faith that he has received.

But *the Lord heals and corrects inwardly by himself other (so to speak) diseases of the body's health and of the limbs of the spirit and the senses through conscience and the intellect. And Paul, after hearing the Lord's voice: 'Why do you persecute me?' and: 'I am Jesus whom you persecute',*[104] *was nevertheless sent to Ananias to receive the sacrament of the teaching of the faith by that priesthood which was constituted in the Church and to test his true colour.*[105] *Not that the Lord cannot do all things by himself, for who else does these things even in the Church, but so that this fellowship*

---

100 Augustine, *Quaestiones euang.* 2.40 (CCSL 44B:98.21–31).
101 Gregory, *Moralia* 5.11 (CCSL 143:237.286–90).
102 Augustine, *Quaestiones euang.* 2.40 (CCSL 44B:97.9–10).
103 Augustine, *Quaestiones euang.* 2.40 (CCSL 44B:98.37–40).
104 Acts 9:4–5.
105 Cf. Acts 9:4–19.

*of faithful congregants, by continually affirming and communicating the teaching of the true faith in all the words which are spoken or are signified by the sacraments, may bring forward as it were a single form of its true colour.*[106]

*Cornelius as well, although an angel announces to him both that his almsgiving has been accepted and that his prayers have been heard, is nevertheless commanded for the sake of the integrity of teaching and the sacraments to send for Peter, as if it were said to him and his people: 'Go, show yourselves to the priests'. For in the same way when they went, they were made clean. For Peter had already come to them, but nevertheless, since they had not yet received the sacrament of baptism, they had not yet spiritually reached the priests. Nonetheless their cleansing is shown by the infusion of the Holy Spirit and their wonderment at the speaking with tongues.*[107]

[Luke 17:15–16] **And one of them, when he saw that he was made clean, went back with a loud voice praising God. And he fell on his face at his feet, giving thanks.** This one, who went back praising God, signifies the devout humility of the one Church. He fittingly gave thanks, falling at the Lord's feet. For he truly gives thanks to God *who, having repressed the notions of his own assumptions, humbly sees how weak he is in himself,* does not ascribe any virtue to himself, *and realizes that the good things that he does are from the mercy of the Creator.*[108] Hence it is rightly added:

[Luke 17:16b] **And he was a Samaritan.** *Samaritan in fact means 'guardian'. This name very appropriately signifies those who give thanks to him from whom they received, and attribute everything to him that they have received, singing as it were that verse of the Psalm: 'I will guard my strength to you, for you, God, are my protector. My God, his mercy will precede me'.*[109] He falls on his face, because he blushes at the evils he remembers committing. For man falls when he is ashamed. *And hence, to certain persons falling as it were on their face,* Paul /314/ *said: 'What fruit therefore had you then in those things of which you are now ashamed?'*[110] But it is said in the opposite sense *of the horse's rider, that is, of the one who is carried away by the glory of this world: 'that his rider may fall*

---

106 Augustine, *Quaestiones euang.* 2.40.3 (CCSL 44B:99.44–46; 51–60).
107 Augustine, *Quaestiones euang.* 2.40.3 (CCSL 44B:100.71–79); cf. Acts 10.
108 Gregory, *Moralia* 2.52 (CCSL 143:110.57–59).
109 Augustine, *Quaestiones euang.* 2.40.4 (CCSL 44B:101.102–04); Ps. 58:10–11 (59:9–10).
110 Gregory, *Hom. in Hiezech.* 1.8.32 (CCSL 142:121.705–07); Rom. 6:21.

backward'.¹¹¹ *And again it is written of the persecutors of the Lord: 'They went backward and fell to the ground'.*¹¹² *Why is it that the elect fall on their face and the damned fall backward, except that everyone who falls backward, without doubt falls when he does not see, but he who fell forward, fell when he does see? The unrighteous, therefore, because they fall by things unseen, are said to fall backward, because they fall when they cannot even see what is following them. But the righteous, because they willingly cast themselves down before these visible things, in order to be raised up by invisible things, fall as it were on their face, because when they see they are goaded by fear and humbled.*¹¹³

[Luke 17:17] **And Jesus answering, said: Were not ten made clean? And where are the nine?** *If one is added to nine, a certain likeness of unity comes about, in which there is so great a combination that numeration may not go on, unless it returns again to one, and this rule of number is kept through infinity. Accordingly, nine needs one, in order to be filled out with a certain kind of unity and become ten, but one does not need nine in order to keep its unity. Therefore, as the one who gave thanks is approved and praised by being a symbol of the one Church, so those nine who did not give thanks, having been damned, are excluded from the fellowship of unity. And for that reason, such persons, lacking perfection as it were, will remain in the ninth number.*¹¹⁴ Well does the Saviour ask for them as if he doesn't know where they are. For as concerns God, to know is to elect, and not to know is to damn.

[Luke 17:18] **There is no one found to return and give glory to God, but this stranger.** Certainly, it is easy to be able to see that a man does not have leprosy in body and yet that he is not of good spirit, but following the significance of this miracle, it is disturbing to consider how a clean person could be called ungrateful. But *now it is also easy to see that someone in the fellowship of the Church may succeed in understanding the whole and true teaching, and treat all things according to the rule of the Catholic faith, and distinguish the creation from the Creator, and so can evidently be free from a variety of falsehoods, as if from leprosy. Yet that same person may be ungrateful to God and the Lord who purified him, because, puffed up with pride, he is not prostrated by the pious humility of giving*

---

111 Gen. 49:17.
112 John 18:6.
113 Gregory, *Hom. in Hiezech.* 1.9.5 (CCSL 142:125.100–11).
114 Augustine, *Quaestiones euang.* 2.40 (CCSL 44B:101.90–100).

thanks, and becomes like those of whom the Apostle says: 'When they knew God, they did not glorify him as God or give /315/ thanks'.[115] The fact that he says that they knew God certainly shows that they had been cleansed from leprosy, but nevertheless he immediately reproaches them for being ungrateful.[116]

[Luke 17:19] **And he said to him: Arise, go your way, for your faith has made you whole.** He who devoutly fell before the Lord is ordered to arise and go on his way, because whoever keenly recognizes his own weakness and lies humbly prostrate, is commanded by the consolation of the divine word to rise up to courageous deeds, and with his merits increasing day by day, to proceed step by step to more perfect works. And if faith made the man who bowed down to thank his Saviour and purifier whole, then faithlessness destroyed those who failed to give glory to God for the blessings they received. Therefore, this text is also linked to the one above by this reasoning, because it is decreed by the parable given there that faith must be augmented by humility, and here it is shown more openly by these facts that it is not just understanding the rationale of faith, but carrying out the work of faith that makes the believer whole and gives glory to the Father who is in heaven.

## Chapter 69

202/5 [Luke 17:20] **And being asked by the Pharisees, when the kingdom of God was coming, he answered them and said: The kingdom of God is coming unlooked for.** They ask about the time of the kingdom of God, because, as Luke revealed below, they thought that, when the Lord came to Jerusalem, *the kingdom of God would immediately be made manifest,*[117] just as the apostles themselves, led astray by this opinion, questioned him after his resurrection, and said: *Lord, will you at this time restore again the kingdom to Israel?*[118] And elsewhere Cleophas said: *But we hoped that it was he who was going to redeem Israel.*[119] But *the kingdom of God is coming unlooked for.*

---

115 Rom. 1:21.
116 Augustine, *Quaestiones euang.* 2.40 (CCSL 44B:100.80–90).
117 Luke 19:11.
118 Acts 1:6.
119 Luke 24:21.

BOOK FIVE 505

[Luke 17:21] **Nor will they say: Look here.** Because when it comes can be observed neither by angels nor by men in the way that the time of the Lord's incarnation was both set in advance by the very definite prophecies of the prophets and made manifest by the proclamations of the angels, so much so that his being conceived, born, and baptized, his preaching, and now his dying and rising again, and returning to heaven, were incessantly revealed by accompanying signs both of angels and of men, and indeed of miracles.[120]

[Luke 17:21b] **For lo, the kingdom of God is within you.** He says the kingdom of God itself is placed within them, that is, in their hearts, where they believed him to be reigning. Hence it is written: *The word is near you, even in your mouth and in your heart. This is the word of faith, which we preach.*[121]

203/10 [Luke 17:22] **And he said to his disciples: The days will come when you will desire to see one day of the Son of man, and you will not see it.** To see the day of Christ is in fact to see the kingdom of God which we hope will come. And well is it said to be 'one day', because there is no interval of darkness in that glory of blessedness, of which the Prophet /316/ said longingly: *For better is one day in your courtyards above thousands.*[122] Not even the memory of misery and sorrow, the first things to depart, darkens the light of eternal peace. Therefore, it is good to long for this day to appear, and yet not through the magnitude of our desire to indulge in dreams, *as if the day of the Lord were at hand.*[123] And hence the Lord fittingly, by foretelling things to come, added:

204/2 [Luke 17:23] **And they will say to you: Look here, look there. Do not go or pursue.** Although this statement can be understood not only with respect to time, but also to person, it can also be understood with respect to time, because there were some who, computing the courses of the ages, claimed that they had found a fixed year, day, and hour of the end of the world, contrary to the authority of the Lord, who says: *It is not for you to know the times or the moments.*[124] And certainly it can be understood with

---

120 Bede is contrasting the second coming with the first and underscoring his hostility to any attempt to predict the time of the second coming. See note on Luke 12:56 and Bede's exegesis on Luke 17:22–23.
121 Rom. 10:8.
122 Ps. 83:11 (84:10).
123 2 Thess. 2:2.
124 Acts 1:7. On Bede's hostility to any attempt to calculate the second coming, see Introduction, 3–4, 10.

respect to person, because many have come who oppose the Church, and many heretics are going to come to proclaim that they are Christs,[125] chief among them, Simon Magus.[126] And the last, greater than the rest, is the Antichrist. If, therefore, they say: *Look here, look there*, that is, in respect to this or that person, or to the hour that the kingdom of God comes or is going to come, they are not to be followed, who do not fear that they seek things that are above them and declare things that cannot be uttered.

**205/5** [Luke 17:24] **For as the lightning gleaming from under heaven shines on the parts that are under heaven, so will the Son of man be in his day.** This is what a psalm says: *God will come manifestly, our God, and will not keep silence,*[127] because, of course, *the second coming of the Saviour is going to be manifested not in humility as before, but in glory,*[128] and he will be in majesty. And well he says: *gleaming from under heaven*, because the separation of the Judgement will take place beneath the heaven, that is, in the midst of the air, as the Apostle testifies, who says: *We will be taken up together with them in the clouds to meet the Lord in the air.*[129] Moreover, since the Lord will appear in judgement like lightning, no one at that time is permitted to hide in his mind, because even that will be penetrated by that lightning of the Judge. Therefore, mortals cannot observe the time or place of the one who will come like lightning, that is, gleaming on all, and without warning. The Lord's reply can without inconsistency refer as well to that advent by which he daily comes to the Church. Certainly, the kingdom of God is within us, because he who will come someday as the Judge of all reigns even now, being present in the heart of the faithful. But the heretics, who all say /317/ that the faith of Christ is maintained only in their own teaching, have often thrown the Church into so much confusion that all the faithful of those times desired that the Lord return to the earth even for a single day if possible, and reveal in person how the truth of faith should sustain itself. *And you will not see it*, he says, because there is no need for the Lord to exhibit with a bodily vision what he once exhibited spiritually by the lightning of his Gospel dispersed throughout the whole

---

125 Cf. Matt. 24:23–24; Mark 13:21–22.
126 Cf. Acts 8:9–11. Bede's comparison of Simon Magus to Antichrist is strikingly absent in his own commentary on Acts: see Darby, *Bede and the End of Time*, 191, who sees the commentary on Luke as marking a point where Bede becomes more attuned to eschatological imminence (194–95).
127 Ps. 49:3 (50:3).
128 Jerome, *Commentarii in Matheum* 4 (CCSL 77:229.527–28).
129 1 Thess. 4:17.

world, and strengthened by the indivisible light of his love against all the idle talk of apocryphal authors.[130]

**206/2** [Luke 17:25] **But first he must suffer many things and be rejected by this generation.** While saying many things about the glory of his coming, the Lord took care to add a few words about the terror of his passion as well, so that, when his followers saw him dying, whom they had heard was to be glorified, they might mitigate the sorrow of the passion with the hope of the promised glorification, and at the same time prepare themselves not to tremble at the danger of death if they loved the glory of the kingdom. And he addresses the progeny not only of the Jews, but of all the damned, from whom even now the Son of man suffers many things in his body, that is, in the Church, and is rejected. For *although Christ, the head of this body, which, of course, we are, now freely lifts himself above all creation, nevertheless he still feels the wounds of the damned in its body, which he keeps below.*[131]

**207/5** [Luke 17:26] **And as it happened in the days of Noah, so it will be also in the day of the Son of man.** He affirms with many examples that the day of his coming will be sudden. For the same day which he had compared to lightning speedily flashing over everything he compares to the days of Noah or Lot, when sudden destruction overcame mortals.

[Luke 17:27] **They ate and drank, they married wives and were given in marriage,** ... Here *marriages* and *food are not condemned* in accordance with the mad teaching of Marcion and the Manicheans and Tatian, the leader of the Encratites,[132] *since they are* employed *in* the latter case *to support procreation* and *in the former, nature,*[133] but, it is immoderate use, not the use of lawful things, which is censured in accordance with what the Apostle says: *All things are lawful to me, but all things are not expedient.*[134] For they did not perish by water and fire because they were doing these things, but because by giving themselves entirely over to these things, they held the judgements of God in contempt.

[Luke 17:27b] **Until the day that Noah entered into the ark, and the flood came and destroyed them all.** Noah builds the ark, when the Lord

---

130 See above, 115–17, where Bede emphasizes that Luke was moved to compose his Gospel to refute apocryphal and heretical pseudo-gospels.
131 Gregory, *Moralia* 3.19 (CCSL 143:137.29–32).
132 Cf. 1 Tim. 4:1–4; Isidore, *Etym.* 8.5.21 (Marcion); 25 (Tatian); 31 (Manicheans).
133 Ambrose, *Expos. Lucam* 8.37 (CCSL 14:310.401–02).
134 1 Cor. 6:12.

constructs the Church from men of faith, as if by joining it with well-planed timber. He enters it perfectly completed, when the eternal Dweller glorifies the Church on the Day of Judgement by the presence of a vision of himself. When the ark is being built, the unjust give themselves over to debauchery, but when he enters, /318/ they perish, because those who revile the saints struggling here will be punished there, after they have been crowned, with eternal damnation.

**208**/10 [Luke 17:28] **Likewise as it happened in the days of Lot, they ate and drank, they bought and sold, they planted and built.** Passing over that great and unspeakable sin of Sodom, the Lord only mentions those offences that could be considered light or not offences at all, so that you may understand the kind of punishment that will strike unlawful deeds, if lawful actions and those without which this life is spent more temperately are punished with fire and brimstone. Rightly, therefore, the blessed Augustine, after viewing the allurements of wicked custom, and moved by righteous sorrow, cries out: *Woe to the sins of men. We tremble only at the extraordinary ones; but we are often obliged to tolerate the sight of the ordinary sins, which the Son of God shed his blood to wash away although they are so great that they cause the kingdom of God to be completely closed against them, and often by tolerance, to commit many of them as well!*[135]

[Luke 17:29] **And on the day that Lot went out of Sodom, it rained fire and brimstone from heaven and destroyed them all.** Up to this point, Lot in Sodom, that is, the people of the elect among the damned, remains as a stranger, himself righteous both in sight and hearing, and, in accordance with the interpretation of the name of Lot, 'avoiding' as much as he can their shameful acts.[136] When Lot goes out, Sodom will perish, because at the end of the world the angels will go out, and they will separate the wicked from the midst of the just, and they will send them into the fiery furnace. Here it should be noted that fire and brimstone, which he records rained from heaven, signify not the flame itself of eternal punishment, but the sudden coming of that day. For that continuous fire that falls upon the wicked will not punish them; instead, having been cast out from the sight of the Judge, they will be sent into the eternal fire, although we should not doubt that brimstone is in that same fire, as John testifies, who, describing both fires, namely that of sudden reproach and that of everlasting conflagration,

---

135 Augustine, *Enchiridion* 21.80 (CCSL 46:94.78–83).
136 Cf. Jerome, *Hebr. nom.* (CCSL 72:68.5–6).

BOOK FIVE 509

says: *And fire came down from God out of heaven and devoured them. And the devil who seduced them was cast into the lake of fire and brimstone, where both the beast and the false prophets will be tormented day and night forever and ever.*[137]

[Luke 17:30] **It will be like that on the day when the Son of man will be revealed.** *It will be revealed* is excellently said, because he who sees all things without appearing will judge all things when he appears. And he will appear in order to judge particularly when he will perceive that all men have forgotten his judgements and have been delivered over to this world. For although the end of the world is going to come hereafter at a predetermined time, nevertheless with the love /319/ of many growing cold near the end, such great iniquity of the human race will increase, that it deserves to be destroyed with the very world that it inhabits.[138] For even now we see that countless men engage in feasting and drinking, buying and selling, and other affairs of the world, so that it is obvious that they openly provoke the wrath of the strict Judge, but nevertheless, because even the wise can scarcely think about it without heavy sorrow, we fear worse things about to come upon us at this very moment. For what was said about a certain sinful people when they were about to be destroyed: *for as yet the sins of the Amorites are not yet complete,*[139] should without doubt be believed about the whole mass of the depraved who are to be damned.

**209/2** [Luke 17:31] **In that hour, he who will be on the housetop and his goods in the house, let him not go down to take them away.** Up to this point the text speaks of the fact that the kingdom of God, that is, Christ, comes not with watching, but unlooked for; now it is shown by what kind of people the same coming ought to be awaited. *He is on the housetop,* therefore, *who, leaving behind carnal things, lives spiritually as it were in the open air.*[140] His goods in the house are carnal desires, which he had loved excessively, but had abandoned, seeking divine things in this world, and now that Judgement threatens he must by no means take them up again. For when Christ says 'in that hour', he means not the hour in which the Judge comes, but in which he is going to come, not in which the fire descends on Sodom, but in which Lot is forced to go out, or rather, as he

---

137 Rev. 20:9–10.
138 Cf. Matt. 24:12.
139 Gen. 15:16.
140 Augustine, *Quaestiones euang.* 2.41 (CCSL 44B:102.3–4).

was lingering, he was taken hold of by the angels, and dragged out.[141] For when the Judge has already come and appeared in the world no one will wish to go down to take anything away from there. But this hour happens now, while we wait for the Judge to come with anxious watching, uncertain when he may come. John says of it: *Little children, it is the last hour.*[142]

[Luke 17:31b] **And he who is in the field, let him likewise not return back.** *He who works in the Church, like Paul and Apollo, plants and waters, let him not look upon worldly hope, which he has renounced.*[143]

210/10 [Luke 17:32] **Remember Lot's wife.** *Lot's wife signifies those who in tribulation look back, and turn away from the hope of the divine promise. And for that reason, she is made a statue of salt,*[144] *so that, by warning men not to do this, she may season their heart so to speak in order that they not be insipid.*[145]

211/3 [Luke 17:33] **Whoever seeks to save his life will lose it.** This statement can be correctly understood in two ways, but both interpretations refer only to one end, namely that /320/ we not fear to meet adversities for Christ, not even death itself. For when a persecutor threatens death unless one denies Christ, whoever chooses instead to save his life for the time by denying him, prepares it beyond a doubt for eternal damnation. Likewise, whoever seeks eternal salvation for his life does not hesitate to lose it at the hands of persecutors, that is, to give it over to death. And what follows fittingly suits both meanings:

[Luke 17:33b] **And whoever loses it will restore it to life.** That is, whoever loses it here will restore it to life there; whoever surrenders it to death for the sake of Christ the whole day long, counting it as a sheep for slaughter,[146] when Christ rises up and brings him help, will find it liberated for the sake of Christ's name.

212/5 [Luke 17:34] **I say to you: In that night there will be two men in one bed.** The Lord had said above that the one who is in the field ought not to return back. But in order that you not think this was said only about those who are plainly going to return back from the field, that is, who are going to openly deny the Lord, he goes on to show some who, although

---

141 Cf. Gen. 19:16.
142 1 John 2:18.
143 Augustine, *Quaestiones euang.* 2.42 (CCSL 44B:103.3–4).
144 Cf. Gen. 19:26.
145 Augustine, *Quaestiones euang.* 2.43 (CCSL 44B:103).
146 Cf. Rom. 8:36 (also Ps. 43:22 (44:22)).

they seem to keep their face fixed forward, nevertheless look back with their soul and mind. He said, therefore, that in that night, in tribulation so dark *as to lead into error, if possible, even the elect*,[147] there will be two men in bed, namely, those *who choose leisure and quiet, and are not taken up either with worldly or with ecclesiastical affairs. This quiet of theirs is signified by the word 'bed'.*[148]

[Luke 17:34b] **The one will be taken, and the other will be left.** *This is said, not as if of two men, but of two kinds of dispositions.*[149] He who applies himself to abstinence for the sake of God, so that living without solicitude he may think on the things of God,[150] will be taken by God. But he, who either from the love of human praise, or from any other corruption of vice, troubles the condition of the monastic life in which he has been instructed, is going to be left in the situation implied by the Lamentations of Jeremiah, when, describing the fall of any idle and sinful soul under the allegory of Judaea, it says: *The enemies have seen her, and have mocked at her Sabbaths.*[151]

[Luke 17:35] **Two women will be grinding as one with millstones.** He describes as 'grinding with millstones', *the common folk who are guided by teachers, doing those things that pertain to this world, and he applies to them the name of 'women', because, as I have said, it is advantageous for them to be guided by the counsels of experts. And he said 'grinding with millstones', on account of the circle and circuit of temporal business. But he said 'grinding together with millstones' inasmuch as they provide from these things and their business for the needs of the Church.*[152] For any action of this /321/ world is a millstone, which while it heaps up many cares, turns human minds around as if in a circle, and grinds out, as it were, flour from itself, because it always bears the most trifling cogitations to the restless soul.

[Luke 17:35b] **One will be taken and the other will be left.** That part will be taken that engages in marriage for the sake of offspring alone, and distributes its earthly substance to gain heavenly things. And the other part that is devoted to marriage for the sake of the pleasures of the flesh will

---

147 Matt. 24:24.
148 Augustine, *Quaestiones euang.* 2.44 (CCSL 44B:104.5–7).
149 Augustine, *Quaestiones euang.* 2.44 (CCSL 44B:105.22–23).
150 Cf. 1 Cor. 7:32 & 34.
151 Lam. 1:7.
152 Augustine, *Quaestiones euang.* 2.44 (CCSL 44B:104.7–13).

be left; indeed, if it offers any earthly things to the Church or the poor, it does so, because, having as it were bought off the Lord, it may abound even more in these things.

[Luke 17:35c] **Two men will be in the field; one will be taken and the other will be left.** Just as above he wrote 'in *one* bed' and 'grinding as *one* with millstones', so here I think 'in *one* field' ought to be understood. It signifies those who carry out the ministry of the Church in God's field as it were, of which ministry his tiller of the field said: *You are God's field cultivation.*[153] And that one will be taken, who speaks, not adulterating *the word of God, but as from God, before God, in Christ.*[154] But he who preaches Christ not devoutly, but from false motives,[155] will be left by him. *And I do not think that the Church consists of other than these three, which each have two distinct outcomes as far as being taken up and being left are concerned, although as individuals they can show many differences of effort and inclination, these nevertheless come together in harmony and unity.*[156]

Hence, the prophet Ezekiel *saw three saved men, Noah, Daniel, and Job,*[157] *in which three surely are signified preachers, the continent, and married men. For Noah governed the ark on the waters,*[158] *and therefore he embodied the figure of those who govern. And Daniel was dedicated to abstinence while in the royal hall,*[159] *and therefore he signified the life of continence. But Job, settled in marriage and taking care of his own household, was acceptable to God; by him the station of good married couples is worthily symbolized.*[160]

**213/5** [Luke 17:36–37] **They answering, say to him: Where, Lord? He said to them: Wherever the body is, there the eagles will be gathered together.** The Saviour, having been asked two questions, namely, where the good are to be taken, and where the wicked are to be left, answered one, and left the other to be inferred. For by asserting that the saints will be with him, he makes known without doubt that the wicked are going to

---

153 1 Cor. 3:9.
154 2 Cor. 2:17.
155 Cf. Phil. 1:18.
156 Augustine, *Quaestiones euang.* 2.44 (CCSL 44B:106.37–41).
157 Cf. Ezek. 14:14.
158 Cf. Gen. 7:7.
159 Cf. Dan. 1:8–16.
160 Gregory, *Hom. in Hiezech.* 2.4.5 (CCSL 142:261.168–75). On Bede's recurring use of this theme of the three 'orders' of Christians, see O'Brien, *Bede's Temple*, 147.

BOOK FIVE 513

be separated from his sight, and accordingly are to be damned nowhere other than with the devil. Wherever, therefore, the Lord is, the chosen will be gathered together with that body. By imitating his passion and humility, they are filled as it were by his flesh, whose *youth will be renewed like the eagle's*.[161] It accords likewise /322/ with the efforts of those who thirst to contemplate the glory of the heavenly majesty with their whole heart, because the eagle, surpassing other birds in flight, enjoys fixing its eyes on the very rays of the sun.[162] And it suits it, because it is accustomed to bring to its nest the eagle-stone that resists poisons, lest perchance a serpent venture to attack its chicks or take away its eggs.[163] Because, of course, it is necessary that each wise man, in order to be able to protect his deeds and thoughts from the assault of the old serpent, preserve that stone, which, cut *out of a mountain without hands*, overthrew the kingdom of the devil,[164] that is, always preserve the faith and love of Christ in his heart.

Chapter 70

214/10 [Luke 18:1] **And he also spoke a parable to them, that we ought always to pray, and not to fail.** And the Apostle says: *Always rejoice, pray without ceasing*.[165] But who can always pray thus, and devote himself to prayers without failing or ceasing, so that he lacks time for taking nourishment or sleeping? Therefore, either it ought to be said that he always prays and does not fail who does not cease to praise and entreat the Lord daily at the canonical hours according to the rite of ecclesiastical tradition with the singing of psalms and with the customary prayers, and that this is what the Psalmist said: *I will bless the Lord at all times, his praise will always be in my mouth*;[166] or else it should be said that everything that a righteous man does and says according to the will of God ought to be reckoned as prayer, for because the righteous man does what is righteous

---

161 Ps. 102:5 (103:5). Bede interprets the Lord's answer as a reference to the chosen – the eagle's annual moulting is a sign of renewal and resurrection. Most commentators take the eagles as gathering to feed on a dead body. NRSV translates: 'Where the corpse is, there the vultures will gather'.
162 Cf. Isidore, *Etym*. 12.7.11.
163 Cf. Pliny, *Naturalis historia* 10.3–5.
164 Dan. 2:34.
165 1 Thess. 5:16–17.
166 Ps. 33:2 (34:1).

# 514 BEDE: COMMENTARY ON THE GOSPEL OF LUKE

without ceasing, the righteous man will by the same token pray without ceasing, and will never cease from prayer unless he ceases to be righteous.

[Luke 18:2–5] **There was a judge in a certain city, who neither feared God nor respected man. And there was a widow in that city, and she came to him, saying: Give me justice from my adversary. And he would not for a long time. But later he said to himself: Although I neither fear God nor respect man, yet because this widow is troublesome to me, I will give her justice, so that by continually coming she may not weary me.** *The Lord either presents parables in accordance with some likeness, as of the man who had two sons, the elder staying with him on his domain, but the younger luxuriating in a distant land, or he demonstrates something by its very unlikeness, such as this*: 'That if God so clothes the grass of the field, which is today, and tomorrow is cast into the oven, how much the more will he clothe you, O you of little faith?'[167] Therefore, the first type can be followed by these words: 'As this, so also that'. But the latter type can be followed by these words: 'If this, how much the more that?' or 'If this, how much the less that?' But these things are set forth in one place obscurely, in another plainly. Here therefore the unjust judge is invoked not from likeness, but from unlikeness. /323/ *For in no way does that unjust judge allegorically represent the character of God, but nevertheless the Lord wished to be inferred from this how much God, who is good and just, cares for those who pray to him, because the unjust man cannot refuse those who importune him with incessant prayers if only to avoid irksomeness.*[168] *For that is what he says*: 'So that by coming she may not weary me.' *But the widow herself can have a likeness to the Church, because she seems forsaken until the Lord comes, who even now secretly tends to her.*[169]

[Luke 18:6–8] **And the Lord said: Hear what the unjust judge says. And will not God avenge his elect who cry to him day and night, and will he have patience in their regard? I say to you, that he will quickly avenge them.** *If it troubles* anyone *why God's chosen ones pray to be avenged, which is likewise said of the martyrs in the Apocalypse of John,*[170] *although we are admonished unambiguously that we should pray for our enemies and persecutors,*[171] *it must be understood that the vengeance of*

---

167 Augustine, *Quaestiones euang.* 2.45 (CCSL 44B:106.7–8; 11–13; 15–18); Matt. 6:30.
168 Augustine, *De sermone Domini* 2.15.52 (CCSL 35:142.1123–27).
169 Augustine, *Quaestiones euang.* 2.45 (CCSL 44B:108.40–42).
170 Cf. Rev. 6:9–10.
171 Cf. Matt. 5:44.

*the righteous is that all the wicked perish. But they perish in two ways, either by conversion to righteousness, or by losing their power through punishment – that power which they exert in some measure against the good for as long as this is to the advantage of the good. When the just desire this end, even though they pray for their enemies, nevertheless it is not absurd to say that they desire vengeance.*[172]

[Luke 18:8b] **But yet when the Son of man comes, will he find faith on earth, do you think?** Although the omnipotent Creator is always prepared to avenge his chosen who cry out to him, nevertheless when the Creator appears in the form of the Son of Man on the Day of Judgement (which should be remembered with trembling heart), the chosen will be so few in number that the destruction of the whole world is going to be hastened not so much on account of the outcry of the faithful who are unjustly condemned, as on account of the sluggishness of those who are justly condemned. And as to the fact that the Lord says: *Will he find faith on earth, do you think?* as if he had doubts, know that he does not doubt, but rebukes. Christ's divinity is not made suspect by an expression of doubt, but rather infidelity is chided. And indeed, we sometimes utter a word of doubt chidingly about things that we consider certain, although we do not doubt at heart. *It is as if you are angry at your servant and say: 'You defy me: perhaps consider that I am your lord'. And the Apostle says to certain of his despisers: 'And I think that I also have the spirit of God'.*[173] *Anyone who says, 'I think', seems to doubt, but he was chiding, not doubting.*[174] Accordingly, therefore, the Lord, by whom all things were made, not only knows everything, but nonetheless chides the hearts of the unfaithful by doubting.

## Chapter 71

[Luke 18:9] **And to some who trusted in themselves as just, and despised others, /324/ he spoke also this parable.** The Lord concluded his parable by which he taught us to pray and not to fail, by saying that faith would be hard to find on earth when the Judge comes. But lest perchance anyone delude himself by thinking that faith or even confession is useless, another related parable immediately shows more pointedly that not the words but the works

---

172 Augustine, *Quaestiones euang.* 2.45 (CCSL 44B:108.42–50; 53–55).
173 1 Cor. 7:40.
174 Augustine, *In Iohannis euang.* 37.3 (CCSL 36:333).

of faith are going to be examined by God. Among these works without a doubt humility reigns supreme. And hence above, when he compared faith to a grain of mustard seed that is tiny, but burning with contrition, he added by way of explanation as it were: *When you have done all the things you were ordered to do, say: We are unprofitable servants.*[175] In contrast to this the proud, when they do not do all they are ordered to do, but only a few things, not only directly presume upon his justice, but despise all the weak, and for that reason, when they pray with empty faith as it were, they are not heard.

[Luke 18:10] **Two men went up into the temple to pray, the one a Pharisee and the other a tax collector.** The tax collector who prays humbly belongs to those members of the widow, that is, the Church, of whom it is said above: *And will not God avenge his elect who cry to him?*[176] But the Pharisee boasting of his merits belongs to those members about whom a fearful statement is added in conclusion: *But yet when the Son of man comes, will he find faith on earth, do you think?*[177]

[Luke 18:11] **The Pharisee standing, prayed thus with himself: God, I give you thanks that I am not like other men, robbers, unjust, adulterers, as also is this tax collector.** *There are four ways in which every conceit of the arrogant is demonstrated: either they judge that they possess the good in their own right; or if they believe it was given to them from above, they think they received it on account of their own merits; or indeed when they boast that they have what they do not have: or when, despising others, they seek to be seen to be the only ones to have what they have.*[178] Afflicted with this plague of boasting that *Pharisee went down from the temple without justification,* and he is understood to have erred, *because, attributing the merits of good works to himself as if he were unique, he set himself above the tax collector who was praying.*[179]

[Luke 18:12] **I fast twice a week; I give tithes of all that I possess.** The prophet Ezekiel writes of the animals of heaven that were displayed to him: *And the whole body was full of eyes round about all the four.*[180] Surely

---

175 Luke 17:10.
176 Luke 18:7.
177 Luke 18:8.
178 Gregory, *Moralia* 23.6 (CCSL 143B:1153.7–11).
179 Gregory, *Moralia* 23.6 (CCSL 143B:1154.50–53); cf. Luke 18:14.
180 Ezek. 1:18. The reference is to the four animals pulling the throne-chariot of God: the man, lion, ox, and eagle. These reappear as the supporters of God's throne in Rev. 4:6–7, and came to symbolize the four evangelists: see Introduction, 7–8, 56. Gregory here furnishes a moral reading, focusing on the creatures' many eyes.

BOOK FIVE 517

*the bodies of the animals are described as full of eyes, because the action of saints is worthy of respect on every side, foreseeing good things with ardent desire, skilfully avoiding evil things.*[181]

But *often, while we are intent on some things, it happens that we neglect others, and where we are neglectful, there without doubt we do not have our eye. For, look, the Pharisee had his eye* /325/ *on displaying abstinence, on doling out pity, on giving thanks to God, but he did not have his eye on observing humility. And what use is it that nearly the whole city is cautiously guarded against the snares of the enemy, if one hole is left open, through which the enemy may enter it?*[182]

[Luke 18:13–14] **And the tax collector, standing far off, would not so much as lift up his eyes towards heaven, but struck his breast, saying: God, be merciful to me, a sinner. I say to you, this man went down into his house justified rather than the other,** ... How much assurance of forgiveness he rightfully offers to penitents, in that the tax collector, who perfectly recognized the guilt of his wickedness, wept and confessed, and if he came to the temple an unjust man, he returned from the temple justified. Allegorically, the Pharisee stands for the people of the Jews, who extoll their own merits from the justifications of the Law. But the tax collector is the people of the Gentiles, who standing at a distance from God, confess their sins. Of these, the first drew away from God, humbled by pride; the second, exalted by lamentation, deserved to draw near him.

**215/5** [Luke 18:14b] **Because everyone who exalts himself will be humbled, and he who humbles himself will be exalted.** This can rightly be understood of each of the aforesaid peoples, and of every person proud or humble, just as we read elsewhere: *The spirit is exalted before destruction, and is humbled before glory.*[183] And therefore from the words of the haughty Pharisee for which he deserved to be humbled, we can in the opposing sense grasp the kind of humility by which we may be raised up. Just as he was lifted up to destruction by contemplating both the vices of those who were worse and his own virtues, so we may be humbled to glory by contemplating not only our own sluggishness, but also the virtues of those who are better. For each of us entreats this for himself submissively on his knees: Almighty God, have mercy on your supplicant, because I am not like your countless servants who are uplifted by contempt for the world,

---

181 Gregory, *Hom. in Hiezech.* 1.7.2 (CCSL 142:83.19–22).
182 Gregory, *Hom. in Hiezech.* 1.7.6 (CCSL 142:85.93–95; 86.101–06).
183 Prov. 16:18; 18:12.

renowned for the merit of righteousness, angelic by the praise of chastity, but just like those many folk who after public disgrace deserved to be devoted to you through penance. Yet I am one who, if I do any good with the benefit of your grace, does not know for what purpose I do these things, or with what rigour you will weigh them.

## Chapter 72

**216/2** [Luke 18:15] **And they also brought to him infants that he might touch them. When the disciples saw this, they rebuked them.** This rich reading glows with the teaching of humility, and shows that the innocent and simple can attain the grace of God. But the disciples rebuked those bringing them forward, *not because they did not wish* for the children *to be blessed by the hand and voice of the Saviour, but because, not yet having complete faith, they thought that he was tired out, as men would be, by the importunity of those who brought them forward*.[184]

[Luke 18:16] **But Jesus, calling them together, said: Let the children come to /326/ me, and do not forbid them; for of such is the kingdom of God.** *Significantly he said 'of such', not 'of these', in order to show that not age but character rules, and that the reward is promised in turn to those who have a similar innocence and simplicity. The Apostle likewise shares in this same view: 'Brothers, do not become children in sense, but in malice be infants, and in sense be perfect'.*[185]

**217/2** [Luke 18:17] **Amen, I say to you: Whoever will not receive the kingdom of God as a child, will not enter into it.** *Just as* a child *does not persist in anger, forgets having been offended, is not allured from the right path when he sees a beautiful woman, and does not think one thing and say another, so likewise, unless you have such innocence and purity of mind, you will not be able to enter the kingdom of heaven.*[186]

In another interpretation: We are commanded to receive the kingdom of heaven, that is, the teaching of the Gospel, like a child, because a child while learning does not contradict his teachers, nor does he concoct arguments and words to oppose them, but faithfully accepts what he is taught, and anxiously submits and is quiet.

---

184 Jerome, *Commentarii in Matheum* 3 (CCSL 77:169.825–27).
185 Jerome, *Commentarii in Matheum* 3 (CCSL 77:169.829–35); 1 Cor. 14:20.
186 Jerome, *Commentarii in Matheum* 3 (CCSL 77:157.500–05).

BOOK FIVE 519

Chapter 73

218/2 [Luke 18:18] **And a certain ruler asked him, saying: Good Teacher, what shall I do to possess everlasting life?** I believe this ruler had heard from the Lord that only those who wanted to be children would enter the kingdom of heaven. Anxious for clarification, he asks that it be explained to him, not in parables but openly, by what meritorious works he should attain eternal life.

[Luke 18:19] **And Jesus said to him: Why do you call me good? No one is good but God alone.** *Because he had called the Teacher good, and had not praised him as God or the Son of God, he learns that a man however holy is not good in comparison with God, of whom it is said: 'Praise God, because he is good'.*[187] But the fact that God alone is good is not to be understood to mean the Father alone, but also the Son, who says: *I am the good Shepherd,*[188] and the Holy Spirit as well, because *The Father from heaven will give the good Spirit to them that ask him.*[189] That is, the Trinity itself, one and undivided, Father, Son, and Holy Spirit, is the sole and one good God. The Lord, therefore, does not deny that he is good, but he signifies that he is God. He gives witness not that he is not a good teacher, but that no teacher is good apart from God.

[Luke 18:20] **You know the commandments: You shall not kill; you shall not commit adultery; you shall not steal; you shall not bear false witness; honour your father and mother.** It is the purity of childlike innocence that is put forth for us to imitate, if we wish to enter the kingdom of God. Of course, it should be noted, since the righteousness of the Law was observed in his time, that he offers not only the good things of earth but also eternal life.

[Luke 18:21] **He said: All these things I have kept from my youth.**
219/2 [Luke 18:22] **When Jesus /327/ heard this, he said to him: You still lack one thing.** One should not imagine that his ruler lied when he said that he had kept the commandments of the Law, but rather that he acknowledged that he lived simply, because if he were guilty of falsehood, the evangelist Mark, when writing of him, would not have added: *And Jesus looking on him, loved him, and said to him: You lack one thing: Go, and*

---

187 Jerome, *Commentarii in Matheum* 3 (CCSL 77:169.842–44); Ps. 117:1 (118:1).
188 John 10:11.
189 Luke 11:13.

*sell whatever you have*, and so forth.[190] For the Lord loves those who keep the commandments of the Law, although the commandments are lesser, but nevertheless he shows what was not in the Law to those who wish to be perfect.

[Luke 18:22b] **Sell all whatever you have, and give to the poor, and you will have treasure in heaven; and come, follow me.** *Whoever wishes to be perfect must sell what he has, and not sell in part, as Anaias and Sapphira did,*[191] *but sell the whole, and when he sells, give all to the poor, and in this way prepare a treasure for himself in the kingdom of heaven. And this is not sufficient for perfection, unless after disdaining wealth he follows the Saviour, that is, unless he does good after abandoning evil. For it is easier to spurn treasure than pleasure. Many, abandoning wealth, do not follow the Lord. He follows the Lord, who imitates him and walks in his footsteps. 'And he who says he believes in Christ ought himself also to walk as he walked.'*[192]

220/2 [Luke 18:23] **When he heard these things, he became sorrowful, for he was very rich.** *This is the sorrow* of temporal life, *which* brings about *death*; this is the deceitful wealth, *which* like thorns *choked the lord's crops.*[193]

[Luke 18:24] **And Jesus, seeing him become sorrowful, said: With what difficulty will those who have riches enter into the kingdom of God.** Indeed, it is clear that those who apply themselves here to amassing wealth disdain to seek the joys of the other life. But there is a considerable difference between having riches and loving riches. Many people having wealth do not love it, and many who do not have it, love it. Likewise, some both have it and love it. Others rejoice that they neither have nor love the riches of the world. Their condition is more secure who can say with the Apostle: *The world is crucified to* us, *and we to the world.*[194] Hence Solomon did not say: 'He who has', but: *He who loves riches will reap no fruit from them.*[195] And according to Mark, the Lord himself, when his disciples were astonished at the words of this very assertion, added by way

---

190 Mark 10:21.
191 Cf. Acts 5:1–2.
192 Jerome, *Commentarii in Matheum* 3 (CCSL 77:170.868–78); 1 John 2:6.
193 Jerome, *Commentarii in Matheum* 3 (CCSL 77:171.880–82). Cf. Luke 8:7: it should be noted that Bede omits Luke 8:7 from its proper place in the *Commentary*.
194 Gal. 6:14.
195 Eccles. 5:9.

BOOK FIVE 521

of explanation: *Children, how hard it is for those who trust in riches to enter the kingdom of God.*[196] And it should be noted that he did not say that it is impossible, but difficult, that is, it demands the greatest effort for those who have riches or trust in them to enter the palace of the heavenly kingdom after casting off the bonds of avarice.[197] /328/

[Luke 18:25] **For it is easier for a camel to pass through the eye of a needle, than for a rich man to enter into the kingdom of God.** If it is easier for a huge camel with its enormous limbs to penetrate the narrow eye of a needle, than for a rich man to enter into the kingdom of God, then no rich man will enter into the kingdom of God. And how in the Gospel did Mathew, Zacchaeus,[198] and Joseph of Arimathea enter the kingdom of God, and how in the Old Testament did so many rich men do so, unless perchance they learned through the Lord's inspiration either to consider riches of no account or to give them up completely?[199] Did David trust in the riches of his kingdom, when he sang of himself: *For I am alone and poor,*[200] and urges others: *If riches abound, do not set your heart upon them,*[201] not having dared to say, I suppose, 'Do not receive them'? Is it credible that Abraham preferred his substance to the Lord, for whom he did not hesitate to kill his only heir?

*But* in another sense it is *easier for Christ to suffer for the lovers of the world, than for lovers of the world to be converted to Christ.* For *by the word 'camel' he wanted himself to be understood, because, having* willingly[202] *been humbled, he bore the burden* of our infirmity. *In this image one gets a clearer understanding of what is written: 'To the degree that you are great, humble yourself in all things'.*[203] *And by 'needle' he signifies prickings, and by prickings, the sorrows received in suffering. He calls the anguish of suffering, therefore, the eye of the needle.*[204] Inasmuch

---

196 Mark 10:24.
197 Cf. Jerome, *Commentarii in Matheum* 3 (CCSL 77:171.890–93).
198 Cf. Luke 19:2–9.
199 Cf. Jerome, *Commentarii in Matheum* 3 (CCSL 77:171.885–90).
200 Ps. 24:16 (25:16).
201 Ps. 61:11 (62:10).
202 *Sponte* ['willingly'] is Bede's insertion into Augustine's text. Meyvaert, 'Bede's *Capitula Lectionum*', 370, remarks that Bede 'is fond of this adverb and uses it to underline the gratuitousness of God's action towards mankind'.
203 Ecclus. 3:20.
204 Augustine, *Quaestiones euang.* 2.47 (CCSL 44B:112.13–19).

as he deigned to mend in some fashion the torn garments as it were of our nature, that is, to restore us, so that we might better be reformed after the fall, let us rejoice in the testimony of the Apostle, who says: *For as many of you as have been baptized in Christ have clothed yourselves in Christ.*[205]

[Luke 18:26] **And those who heard it said: Who then can be saved?** What does this response pertain to, *since the multitude of the poor is incomparably greater*, who because they are deprived of riches could be saved, unless those who heard it understood that all those who love riches, even if they are unable to acquire them, are counted in the number of the wealthy?[206]

[Luke 18:27] **He said to them: The things that are impossible with men are possible with God.** *This should not be taken to mean that the covetous and the proud, who are signified by the name of that rich man, are going to enter into the kingdom of heaven with their cupidity and pride; but with God it is possible that they may be converted by his word from cupidity for temporal things to love of eternal things, and from pernicious pride to the most salubrious humility, as we see has already happened, and still happens every day.*[207] /329/

[Luke 18:28] **Then Peter said: Behold, we have left all things, and we have followed you.** *Great trust! Peter was a fisherman, he was not a rich man, he sought his food with his hand and skill; and nevertheless he speaks confidently: 'We have left all things'. And since merely leaving is not sufficient, he adds what is perfect: 'And we have followed you'. We have done what you commanded; what reward will you give us accordingly?*[208]

221/2 [Luke 18:29–30] **He said to them: Truly, I say to you, there is no man who has left house or parents or brothers or wife or children, for the sake of the kingdom of God, who will not receive much more in this present time, and in the world to come life everlasting.** *On the basis of this statement, some people* fabricate a Jewish tale of a thousand years *after the resurrection* of the just, when everything that we have left for the sake of God will be restored to us with great profit, and eternal life will be given to us besides.[209] These foolish people do not see that,

---

205 Gal. 3:27.
206 Augustine, *Quaestiones euang.* 2.47 (CCSL 44B:112.9–10).
207 Augustine, *Quaestiones euang.* 2.47 (CCSL 44B:112.21–26).
208 Jerome, *Commentarii in Matheum* 3 (CCSL 77:172.913–17).
209 Rev. 20:2–5 refers to the thousand-year 'reign of the just' after the devil is bound as 'the first resurrection'. Bede rejected the notion that this indicated a literal millennium and an earthly reign of the saints in his commentary on Revelation, ed. Gryson (CCSL

BOOK FIVE 523

*although the promise is proper when it comes to other things,* nevertheless 'a hundredfold', in the words of the other evangelists, would be offensive if it applied to 'wives'; especially when the Lord testifies that there will be no marriage in the resurrection and, according to the evangelist Mark, also confirms that those things that had been left will be received in this time along with persecutions.[210] Those chiliasts proclaim as dogma that these persecutions certainly will be entirely absent from their thousand years. So, *the sense is this: Whoever* disdains all affections for the sake of gaining the kingdom of God and scorns all the delights and luxuries of the world will receive much more in the present,[211] because he will *receive love more pleasing* by far *even in this life from those who are his brothers and share his way of life, who are tied to him by a spiritual bond. Since this love, which either the union of the marriage tie or the affinity of blood relationship binds together between parents and children, and cousins, wives, or relations, is known to be brief and fragile, at times it is ruptured for entirely legitimate reasons. Only those*[212] *who believe that everything of theirs is their brothers', and everything of their brothers' is theirs, maintain the bond of eternal union and possess all things without discrimination.*[213] Read the Acts of the Apostles, which says: *The multitude of believers had but one heart and one soul,* and *all things were common to them,* and no one *was needy among them,* because they had left their things for the Lord's sake.[214] And Paul said of them: *As having nothing, and possessing all things.*[215]

*Likewise* far *greater delight will surely be received from conjugal abstinence than what the joining of the sexes offers to each. Before, I possessed a wife* /330/ *in the lustful passion of desire; now I possess this same wife in the honour of sanctification and the true love of Christ. The*

---

121A:504–09); trans. Wallis, 252–54; see also Wallis's Introduction, 6–11, 15–16 and references cited there. See also Bede's comments on the Cerinthian heresy above, Book 4, n. 336.
210 Cf. Matt. 19:29; Mark 10:30. Matthew and Mark both say such a man will receive 'a hundredfold', and Matthew, like Luke, specifically speaks of a man who has left his 'wife'. However, only Mark adds that these rewards will be accompanied by persecutions.
211 Jerome, *Commentarii in Matheum* 3 (CCSL 77:173.938–52).
212 Cassian says specifically 'monks alone'; Bede universalizes the proposition.
213 Cassian, *Collationes* 24.26 (CSEL 13:705.12–25).
214 Acts 4:32 & 34.
215 2 Cor. 6:10.

woman is the same, but the merit of chastity increased a hundredfold.²¹⁶ For what is said, according to Mark: *He will receive a hundred times as much, now in this time; houses, and brothers, and sisters, and mothers, and children, and lands, with persecutions,*²¹⁷ can be taken at a higher level. Indeed, the number one hundred transferred from the left hand to the right, although it seems to maintain the same shape in the bending of the fingers, nevertheless greatly increases with respect to quantity,²¹⁸ because certainly all those who scorn temporal things for the sake of the kingdom of God even in this life which is so filled with persecutions taste joys that are secure by means of their faith, and in expectation of the heavenly fatherland they delight as well in the pure love of all the chosen ones.

## Chapter 74

222/2 [Luke 18:31–33] **Then Jesus took the twelve to him, and said to them: Behold, we go up to Jerusalem, and all things will be accomplished which were written by the prophets concerning the Son of man. For he will be delivered to the Gentiles, and he will be mocked and flogged and spat upon. And after they have flogged him, they will put him to death, and on the third day he will rise again.** The Saviour, *foreseeing that the disciples' spirits would be disturbed by his passion, tells them far in advance about both the suffering of his passion and the glory of his resurrection, so that when they saw him dying as foretold, they would not doubt that he would be resurrected as well.*²¹⁹ Foreseeing also that there were going to be certain heretics in the Church who would say that Christ taught things contrary to the Law and the prophets, and that we should believe one thing about the God of the Old Testament and another of the New, he shows that what the prophets foresaw pertained to nothing more than to the mystery of his divine plan. This he undertook for a time for our sake, so that the fulfilment of the prophecy is the solemn accomplishment of his passion and subsequent glory. Also, he very clearly confutes the madness of the pagans, who ridicule his cross, when he not only shows the time of his approaching passion as if foreknowing the

---

216 Cassian, *Collationes* 24.26 (CSEL 13:705.27–706.2; 22–25).
217 Mark 10:30.
218 See Book 2 n. 92.
219 Gregory, *Hom. in Euang.* 1.2.1 (CCSL 141:12.1–5).

future, but he also goes to the place of his passion as if undaunted by death.

**223**/10 [Luke 18:34] **And they understood none of these things, and this word was hidden from them, and they did not understand the things that were said.** We read in the Gospel according to John that, when the Lord said: *If I am lifted up from the earth, I will draw all things to myself,* the crowd answered and said: *We have heard from the Law that Christ abides forever. And how is it that you say: The Son of man must be lifted up?*[220] Why is it, therefore, that the disciples are unable to understand the mystery of the Lord's passion so often unfolded to them, while the Jews immediately understood /331/ from a single statement that the exaltation of the cross was meant, and why was that statement so obscurely phrased that the evangelist thought it worthy of explanation: *Now this he said, signifying what death he would die*[221] – unless it meant that the disciples desired above all to see his life and could not bear to hear of his death? They could not imagine that the one whom they knew was not only without sin, but also true God, could even die. And because they were accustomed to hear him speak in parables, they did not understand what they heard, however often he would say something about his passion; compelled by love they believed that it must refer allegorically to something else. But the Jews, because they had conspired in his killing, understood whatever he said about his passion or the cross; for he said that which they themselves with the utmost effort both wished to happen and strove to achieve. And so, in a wonderful and extraordinary way, envy revealed to the infidels the very mystery of the Cross that he was about to undergo that love hid from the faithful.

## Chapter 75

**224**/2 [Luke 18:35-37] **And it happened, when he drew near to Jericho, that a certain blind man sat by the wayside, begging. And when he heard the crowd passing by, he asked what this meant. And they told him that Jesus of Nazareth was passing by.** This *blind man* signifies allegorically *the human race, which, having been expelled from the joys of paradise through its first parent, does not know the brilliance of the divine*

---

220  John 12:32 & 34.
221  John 12:33.

light, but endures the darkness of its damnation. But *when Jesus is said to draw near to Jericho, the blind man is illuminated.*²²²

In fact, Jericho means 'moon'.²²³ And 'moon' in sacred Scripture is used for the body's shortcomings,²²⁴ because when it decreases in the course of its monthly movement, it signifies the shortcomings of our mortality. Therefore, when our Creator draws near to Jericho, the blind man returns to the light, because when Divinity takes on the shortcomings of our flesh, the human race receives the light that it had lost. The blind man is rightly described both as sitting by the wayside and as begging. For the Truth himself said: 'I am the way.'²²⁵ Therefore he who does not know the brilliance of the eternal light is blind. But if he already believes in the Redeemer, he is sitting by the wayside. And if he already believes, but pretends to ask for eternal light, if he ceases from prayers, the blind man is indeed sitting by the wayside, but not begging at all. But if he both believes and implores, *the blind man both sits by the wayside and begs.*²²⁶

[Luke 18:38–39] **And he cried out, saying: Jesus, son of David, have mercy on me. And those who were passing by thundered at him to hold his peace. But he cried out much more: Son of David, have mercy on me.** *What do the people who were passing by* /332/ *as Jesus approached symbolize but the crowds of carnal desires and tumults of sins, which, before Jesus comes to our heart, scatter our meditation with their temptations and crowd in upon the voices of our heart in prayer? For often, when we wish to turn to God after committing sins, when we try to entreat him against these same sins that we have committed, spectres of the sins we have done rush into our heart, strike against the battle line of our mind, confound the soul, and repress the voice of our prayer.*²²⁷ *But he whom the crowd clamours at to hold his peace cries out more and more, because the more severe the tumult of carnal thoughts by which we are oppressed, the more ardently we must press on with prayer.*

[Luke 18:40] **And Jesus, standing still, commanded him to be brought to him.** *Behold, he stands still, who before was passing by, because as long as*

---

222 Gregory, *Hom. in Euang.* 1.2.1–2 (CCSL 141:13.14–16; 20–21).
223 Cf. Jerome, *Hebr. nom.* (CCSL 72:127.2).
224 Gregory's word is *defectum*, which refers either to a physical or a moral fault or defect; it can also mean 'eclipse', an ambiguity that is doubtless deliberate here. See Introduction, 30–32.
225 John 14:6.
226 Gregory, *Hom. in Euang.* 1.2.2 (CCSL 141:13.21–35).
227 Gregory, *Hom. in Euang.* 1.2.3 (CCSL 141:14.40–49).

we still allow crowds of fantasies in our prayer, we feel as if Jesus is passing by. But when we vehemently persist in prayer, Jesus stands still and restores the light, because God is fixed in our heart, and the lost light is recovered.[228]

[Luke 18:40b–41] **And when he came near, he asked him, saying: What do you want me to do for you? But he said: Lord, let me see.** *Was he who could restore the light ignorant of what the blind man wanted? But he wants to be asked for what he knows in advance we will ask for, and he will grant. For indeed he directs our attention to pray in and out of season, and nevertheless says: 'For your heavenly Father knows what you need, before you ask him'.*[229] *For this reason, therefore, he demands to be asked; for this reason, he demands that the heart be aroused to prayer. And hence the blind man immediately added: 'Lord, let me see'. Behold, the blind man does not seek gold, but light. He scorns to seek anything but light, because even if a blind man can have anything whatsoever, he cannot see what he has without light. Let us, therefore, imitate him whom we have heard was saved both in body and in spirit.*[230] *Let us seek from the Lord not deceitful wealth, not earthly gifts, not fugitive honours, but light,* namely that *light that we can see with the angels alone, which neither has a beginning, nor is diminished by an ending. Faith is truly the way to this light. And hence to enlighten the blind man it is immediately* added:[231]

[Luke 18:42–43] **And Jesus said to him: Receive your sight. Your faith has made you whole. And immediately he saw, and followed him, glorifying God.** *He who does good because he understands sees and follows. And he who indeed understands the good, but disdains to do good things, sees, but does not follow. For he who imitates Jesus follows him.*[232] *And hence he says:* /333/ *'If any man serves me, let him follow me'.*[233] *Let us therefore ponder where he goes, so that we may be worthy to follow him. And in consequence not only is our life useful to God, but our way of life in itself stimulates others also to the praise of God. Hence it is appended there:*[234]

[Luke 18:43b] **And all the people, when they saw it, gave praise to God.** Indeed, the people gave praise to God, not only for the gift of light

---

228 Gregory, *Hom. in Euang.* 1.2.5 (CCSL 141:15.71–75).
229 Matt. 6:8.
230 Gregory addresses this exhortation to his 'dearest brothers', which words Bede omits.
231 Gregory, *Hom. in Euang.* 1.2.7 (CCSL 141:16.91–111).
232 Between this sentence and the previous, Bede omits another passage in which Gregory addresses his 'dearest brothers'. See note 231 above.
233 John 12:26.
234 Gregory, *Hom. in Euang.* 1.2.8 (CCSL 141:17.123–66).

that had been obtained by the blind man, but also for the merit of faith which obtains it. They gave praise to God, both because they saw that Jesus mercifully and effectually restored light to the one who asked for it, and because they recognized that the renown of a steadfast faith, which they justly sought, could be attained immediately. Hence it should be noted that the Lord when he appeared in the flesh, confirmed by example everything that he taught in words. For he taught us: *Let your light shine before men, so that they may see your good works and glorify your Father who is in heaven*,[235] and he himself, in all the things *which he began to do and to teach*,[236] sought not his own glory from men, but the glory of the Father.[237]

## Chapter 76

225/10 [Luke 19:1-4] **And entering in, he walked through Jericho. And behold, there was a man named Zacchaeus, who was the chief of the tax collectors, and he was rich. And he sought to see who Jesus was, and he could not on account of the crowd, because he was short of stature. And running ahead, he climbed up into a sycamore tree to see him, for he was to pass that way.** *The things that are impossible with men are possible with God.*[238] For, behold, a camel passes through the eye of a needle when it lays down the burden of its hump,[239] that is, the rich tax collector, having abandoned the burden of wealth and scorning the riches gained by deceit, climbs up to the narrow gate and the strait way that leads to life.[240] By climbing the tree to see the Saviour, he supplies what he lacked by nature with the wonderful devotion of faith, and therefore justly received, although he dares not ask for it, the blessing he hoped for, to welcome the Lord.

Allegorically, Zacchaeus, whose name means 'justified',[241] signifies Gentile believers. The more he was taken up with worldly cares, the humbler he became as his disgraceful acts weighed him down. But he is

---

235 Matt. 5:16.
236 Acts 1:1.
237 Cf. John 8:50.
238 Luke 18:27.
239 Cf. Matt. 19:24.
240 Cf. Matt. 7:14.
241 Cf. Jerome, *Hebr. nom.* (CCSL 72:138.16–17).

BOOK FIVE 529

washed clean, sanctified, justified, in the name of our Lord Jesus Christ,[242] and in the spirit of our God. He kept trying to see the Saviour as he entered into Jericho, but he could not on account of the crowd, for he desired to share the grace of faith which the Saviour brought to the world, but the ingrained habit of sin had blocked him from achieving his wish. For the same crowd of noxious habits that rebuked the clamouring blind man for seeking light, likewise hinders the expectant tax collector from seeing Jesus. But just as the blind man overcame the shouts of the crowds by crying /334/ out more and more, so the short man must overcome the obstacle of the obstructing crowd, abandon earthly things, and climb the tree of the cross.[243] And indeed, *the sycamore [sycamorus]*, which is a tree *similar to a mulberry [**morus**]* with respect to its leaves, but very tall, is for this reason also called by Latin speakers a *celsa*.[244] The sycamore *is called a foolish (i.e., false) fig-tree*,[245] and the same cross of the Lord which unbelievers deride as foolish nourishes believers like a fig-tree. *But we preach Christ crucified, to the Jews indeed a stumbling block and to the Gentiles foolishness, but to those who are called, both Jews and Gentiles, Christ the power of God and the wisdom of God.*[246] Zacchaeus, who is short of stature, climbs this tree to get higher up so that he can be raised up, when any person, humble and properly aware of his weakness, trusting in the Lord, cries out: *But God forbid that I should glory, save in the cross of our Lord Jesus Christ.*[247] And after climbing the sycamore he sees the Lord passing close by, *because by this praiseworthy foolishness* he directs his attention to the light of heavenly wisdom, *so that it is now perceived, although not yet completely, yet* hurriedly and *as it were in passing.*[248]

[Luke 19:5] **And when Jesus had come to the place, looking up, he saw him.** Walking through Jericho, the Saviour came to the place where Zacchaeus, running ahead, had climbed the sycamore, because after the heralds of his word through whom he himself truly both spoke and went forth had been sent into the world, he came to the Gentiles. Uplifted by

---

242 Cf. Rom. 8:30.
243 Both the interpretation of the crowd as sins and the tree as the cross are found in Ps.-Jerome, *Expositio euangeliorum* (PL 30:575D).
244 Isidore, *Etym.* 17.7.20; *celsa* is from the Latin word for 'high', 'lofty'.
245 Gregory, *Moralia* 27.46 (CCSL 143B:1392.118).
246 1 Cor. 1:23–24.
247 Gal. 6:14.
248 Gregory, *Moralia* 27.46 (CCSL 143B:1392.112; 1393.132–34).

faith in his passion, they ardently desired to be blessed with the vision of his divinity. *Looking up, he saw him,* because he chose the one who was lifted up from earthly desires by the grace of faith and stood out above the faithless multitudes. For God, to see is to choose or to love. Hence is this saying: *The eyes of the Lord are upon the just.*[249] And we also hasten to see the things we love, and to avert our sight from those things we detest. Therefore, Jesus saw the one who saw him, because he chose the one who chose him, and loved the one who loved him. The distinguished teacher displays this same process of attaining knowledge of Divinity through faith in the Lord's incarnation, of observing the sycamore as if catching sight of the face of Jesus, when he says: *For I judged not myself to know anything among you, but Jesus Christ, and him crucified.*[250] And again, reproaching others, he says: *You are become such as have need of milk, and not of solid food,*[251] calling trivial matters of the temporal dispensation 'milk' and lofty matters of eternal grandeur 'solid food'.

[Luke 19:5b–6] **And he said to him: Zacchaeus, make haste and come down, for today I must abide in your house. And making haste, he came down and received him with joy.** Earlier the Lord stayed in the house of the chief of the Pharisees, that is, he taught in the synagogue of the Jews. But /335/ because they rebuked him in envenomed language for not having washed before dinner,[252] for healing on the Sabbath, for receiving tax collectors and sinners, for contending against avarice, and for doing other things worthy of God, having patiently put up with their outrages, he departed and fled away, saying: *Your house will be left to you, desolate.*[253] But today it is fitting for him to abide in the house of little Zacchaeus, that is, to rest with the grace of the new light gleaming in the humble heart of Gentile believers. And as to the fact that Zacchaeus is ordered to climb down from the sycamore, and thus to prepare a room for Christ in his own house, this is what the Apostle says: *Although we have known Christ according to the flesh, yet now we know him so no longer.*[254] For although he died because of human weakness, yet he lives by the strength of God.

---

249 Ps. 33:16 (34:15).
250 1 Cor. 2:2.
251 Hebr. 5:12.
252 Cf. Luke 11:38.
253 Matt. 23:38.
254 2 Cor. 5:16.

## BOOK FIVE

[Luke 19:7] **And when all saw it, they murmured, saying that he had gone to be a guest with a man who was a sinner.** It is clear that the Jews always hated the salvation of the Gentiles. For it is written: *But the next Sabbath almost the whole city came together to hear the word of God. But the Jews seeing the crowds were filled with envy and contradicted those things that were said by Paul.*[255] And elsewhere: Even the faithful brothers *contended* with the prince of the apostles, *saying: Why did you go in to uncircumcised men and eat with them?*[256]

[Luke 19:8] **But Zacchaeus, standing, said to the Lord: Behold, Lord, the half of my goods I give to the poor, and if I have cheated anyone of anything, I repay him fourfold.** While others are falsely reproaching him for being a sinful man, Zacchaeus himself, standing, that is, remaining steadfast in that truth of faith which he had taken up, demonstrates not only that he has himself been converted from being a sinner, but also that he is in the company of the perfect. However, when the Lord says: *If you will be perfect, go, sell all that you have and give to the poor,*[257] whoever has lived blamelessly before conversion can give all to the poor after being converted. But he who has profited by any deceit, must first repay it according to the law, and then give what remains to the poor. So also in the case of this man – because he keeps nothing for himself, disperses all his goods, and gives to the poor, *his justice remains forever and ever.*[258] This is that wise foolishness, which the tax collector had plucked as if it were the fruit of life from the sycamore – namely, to repay what was stolen, to give up his own things, to scorn the visible world, to wish even to die for the sake of the invisible world, to deny himself, and to desire to follow the footsteps of that Lord who is not yet seen.

[Luke 19:9] **Jesus said to him: Today is salvation come to this house, because he too is a son of Abraham.** Zacchaeus is called the son of Abraham, not because he was born from his stock, but because he imitated his faith. Just as Abraham, at the Lord's command, deserted his land, his kindred, and his /336/ paternal house in hope of future inheritance,[259] so Zacchaeus, in order to gain treasure in heaven, abandoned his goods to be shared among the poor. And Jesus says, beautifully: *he too*, in order

---

255 Acts 13:44–45.
256 Acts 11:2–3.
257 Matt. 19:21.
258 Ps. 111:9 (112:9).
259 Cf. Gen. 12:1–4.

to declare not only that those who are steadfastly just, but also those who come to their senses from injustice, belong to the children of promise.[260]

In another interpretation: Salvation, which once filled the house of the Jews, today has begun to shine upon the Gentiles, because these people too are the children of Abraham, believing in him of whom the Apostle says: *And if you are Christ's, then you are the seed of Abraham.*[261] And, as he says elsewhere, Abraham himself *is the father of circumcision, not to them only, that are of the circumcision, but to them also that follow the steps of the faith that is in the uncircumcision of our father Abraham.*[262]

**226**/5 [Luke 19:10] **For the Son of man has come to seek and save what was lost.** This is what he says elsewhere: *I have not come to call the just, but sinners.*[263] He is indeed a merciful Teacher who does not refuse to expound his mysteries to the murmuring crowds, so true is it that the repentance of sinners must not be rejected, and that the Son of God himself was destined for earth chiefly for the sake of seeking this repentance. He frequently calls himself the Son of Man in order to emphasize the dispensation of his compassion for us, earnestly commending to us what he mercifully became for our sake.

## Chapter 77

**227**/10 [Luke 19:11] **As they were hearing these things, he added and spoke a parable, because he was near Jerusalem, and because they thought that the kingdom of God was to be immediately manifested.** It was the Lord's custom to reinforce what he had previously said by adding parables. Therefore, after he had accepted and approved the rich tax collector's repentance, he added a parable. He teaches that the repentance of sinners pleases him more than the righteousness of the proud, and that he is going to reign more extensively over the Gentiles, who are humbled by their ignorance of the Law, than over the Jews, who are puffed up with their righteousness which derives from the Law. And because the disciples, although they just heard that the Lord's passion and resurrection was about to be accomplished in Jerusalem,[264] did not understand what was being

---

260 Cf. Gal. 3:29.
261 Gal. 3:29.
262 Rom. 4:12.
263 Matt. 9:13.
264 Cf. Luke 9:22; 18:31.

said, and imagined that the kingdom of God was going to come at once, the Lord, shining a light on their ignorance, shows that he is first going to spread the faith of his kingdom throughout the whole world, and then at the end of the world the Judge and King of all the ages is going to come.

**228/2** [Luke 19:12] **He said therefore: A certain nobleman went into a far country to receive a kingdom for himself and to return.** The nobleman is the one to whom the blind man cried out above: *Son of David, have mercy on me.*[265] And he is the one coming to Jerusalem to whom they cried out: *Hosanna to the son of David, blessed is he who comes in the name of the Lord, the king of Israel.*[266] The far country is the Church of the Gentiles, concerning which the Father replies to the same nobleman who says: *But /337/ I am appointed king by him:*[267] *Ask of me, and I will give you the Gentiles for your inheritance, and the ends of the earth for your possession.*[268] This inheritance and possession is surely called a far country for a twofold reason, both because the Psalmist cries out to the Lord from the ends of the earth,[269] and because *salvation is far from sinners.*[270] And although God is present everywhere, nevertheless the true God is far away from the perception of those who worship idols. But those who were *far off, are made near in the blood of Christ.*[271]

**229/5** [Luke 19:13] **And calling his ten servants, he gave them ten pounds.** The number ten pertains to the Law on account of the Ten Commandments.[272] Accordingly, the master calls ten servants, because the Lord chose disciples who were brought up on the letter of the Law. He gives them ten pounds, because he reveals that the sayings of the Law must be understood spiritually. Indeed, after his passion and resurrection, *he opened their understanding, so that they might understand the Scriptures.*[273] For *the pound*, which the Greeks call a *mna*, *weighs a hundred drachmas.*[274] And every discourse of Scripture, because it calls to mind the perfection of heavenly life, gleams as it were with the weight of the number one hundred.

265 Luke 18:38.
266 Matt. 21:9; John 12:13 (a blend).
267 Ps. 2:6.
268 Ps. 2:8.
269 Cf. Ps. 60:3 (61:2).
270 Ps. 118:155 (119:155).
271 Eph. 2:13.
272 Cf. Augustine, *Quaestiones euang.* 2.46 (CCSL 44B:109.6–8).
273 Luke 24:45.
274 Isidore, *Etym.* 16.25.21.

## 534   BEDE: COMMENTARY ON THE GOSPEL OF LUKE

[Luke 19:13b] **And he said to them: Trade until I come.** Offer to the people, he says, the words of the Law and the prophets after their allegorical interpretation has been discussed, and accept from them their confession of faith and the probity of their morals, in accordance with what the Psalmist enjoins upon his auditors: *Take a psalm, and sound the drum.*[275] That is, take the praise of preaching by the fervour [*intentione*] of the heart, and take back the curse of work by chastising the flesh. A drum, of course, is a skin stretched [*extenta*] on wood. Truly, a skin stretched on wood is our flesh afflicted according to the example of the Lord's cross.

[Luke 19:14] **But his citizens hated him, and they sent a delegation after him, saying: We do not want this man to rule over us.** He calls impious Jews 'citizens', about whom he elsewhere testifies: *But now they have both seen and hated both me and my Father.*[276] They not only hated him in person up to his death on the cross, but also after his resurrection they inflicted persecution on his apostles and scorned the preaching of the heavenly kingdom.[277]

[Luke 19:15] **And he returned after receiving the kingdom.** He signifies the time when *he is going to return in the most conspicuous and lofty splendour, he who appeared humbly to them, when he said: 'My kingdom is not of this world'.*[278]

[Luke 19:15b] **And he commanded his servants, to whom he had given the money, to be called so that he might know how much every man had gained by trading.** He says: *So that he might know*, not because /338/ anything is unknown to him, to whom it was very truly said: *Lord, you know all things*,[279] but rather to let everyone know. For then everyone's deeds and thoughts are openly displayed to all, just as Moses says in Deuteronomy: *The Lord your God tests you, so that he may know whether you love him*,[280] that is, he lets everyone know. Of course, no one should suppose that only those to whom the grace of preaching was given are going to be called to judgement at that time, and not those to whom preaching is directed as well. For the latter are the money that the good servants gained by trading. Of course, he also knows that those destined

---

275  Ps. 80:3 (81:2).
276  John 15:24.
277  Cf. Augustine, *Quaestiones euang.* 2.46 (CCSL 44B:109.12–13).
278  Augustine, *Quaestiones euang.* 2.46 (CCSL 44B:109.14–16); John 18:36.
279  John 21:17.
280  Deut. 13:3.

for damnation and who were never preached to are there. Of these, we will speak below.[281]

[Luke 19:16] **And the first came, saying: Lord, your pound has gained ten pounds.** The first servant is the order of teachers sent among the circumcised, who in order to trade received one pound, because he was commanded to preach one Lord, one faith, one baptism, and one God.[282] But this same pound gained ten pounds, because by teaching he associated with himself the people established under the Law.

[Luke 19:17] **And he said to him: Well done, good servant! Because you have been faithful in a little, you will have power over ten cities.** The servant is faithful in a little, who does not falsify the word of God, but speaks *as from God, before God, in Christ*.[283] For any gifts we receive in the present are exceedingly few and small in comparison to those we will receive in the future, because *we know in part, and we prophesy in part. But when what is perfect comes, what is in part will be done away with*.[284] The ten cities are souls who come through the word of the Law to the grace of the Gospel. He, who is rightly to be glorified gives them the money of a word worthy of God, and is then set over them. Hence a certain distinguished trader, addressing the cities which he was in charge of, that is, the souls which he had received to be guided, says: *What is our hope, or joy, or crown of glory? Are you not in the presence of the Lord Jesus?*[285]

[Luke 19:18] **And the second came, saying: Lord, your pound has gained five pounds.** This servant is the company of those who were sent to evangelize the uncircumcised, to whom as they set out to preach the Lord had furnished one pound, that is, one and the same faith which he also lent to the circumcised. But he gained these five pounds, because he converted the Gentiles, who were formerly subjected to the senses of the body, to the grace of gospel faith. /339/

[Luke 19:19] **And he said to him: You shall be also over five cities.** That is, you will shine great and exalted because of the faith and conversion of those souls which you have instructed. About these Isaiah allegorically says: *In that day there will be five cities in the land of Egypt, speaking the*

---

281 See Bede's commentary on Luke 19:27.
282 Cf. Eph. 4:5–6.
283 2 Cor. 2:17.
284 1 Cor. 13:9–10.
285 1 Thess. 2:19.

*language of Canaan.*²⁸⁶ The five cities in the land of Egypt are the five senses of the body which we use in this world, namely, sight, hearing, taste, smell, and touch. And, *whoever looks at a woman to lust after her;*²⁸⁷ whoever averts his ears so as not to hear the poor man;²⁸⁸ whoever is drunk *with wine, in which is debauchery;*²⁸⁹ whoever rejoices to crown himself *with roses before they wither;*²⁹⁰ whose hands are filled with blood, and whose *right hand is filled with gifts,*²⁹¹ his five cities speak the language of Egypt, that is, all his senses do the deeds of darkness. For Egypt means 'darkness'.²⁹² But he *who stops his ears from hearing of blood, and shuts his eyes from seeing evil,*²⁹³ he who chastises his body, and brings it into subjection,²⁹⁴ he who can say with the Apostle: *We are the good odour of Christ to God,*²⁹⁵ his cities speak a language that is different, which is what Canaan means.²⁹⁶ And he who had transformed these people from darkness by his teaching is rightly said to be set over the five cities, because he is honoured not only for his own moral progress, but also for that of his listeners, whom he called to the light.

[Luke 19:20–21] **And another came, saying: Lord, behold, here is your pound, which I have kept laid up in a handkerchief; for I feared you, because you are an austere man; you take up what you did not lay down, and you reap what you did not sow.** The servant, who had been commanded to trade, but who laid up in a handkerchief the Lord's money which he received, represents those who are capable of preaching, but when the Lord prescribes the duty of preaching by the Church, they either refuse to undertake it, or if they do undertake it, fail to do so in a worthy fashion. Indeed, to wrap up money in a handkerchief is to hide the gifts one has received beneath the idleness of sluggish inactivity. *For there are men deluding themselves with this perversity, so that they say: It is enough*

---

286 Isa. 19:18.
287 Matt. 5:28.
288 Cf. Prov. 21:13.
289 Eph. 5:18.
290 Wisd. 2:8.
291 Ps. 25:10 (26:10).
292 Cf. Jerome, *Hebr. nom.* CCSL 72:143.28–29.
293 Isa. 33:15.
294 Cf. 1 Cor. 9:27.
295 2 Cor. 2:15.
296 Cf. Jerome, *Hebr. nom.* CCSL 72:63.14–15; 80.11–12; Isidore, *Etym.* 7.6.19. Bede's word for 'different' is *mutata*, something 'changed' or 'moved'. Jerome and Isidore interpret Canaan as having to do with motion.

*that each one render an account of himself.* What need is there to preach to others, so as to try to render an account of them, since those to whom the Law was not given, and yet slept in their sins and did not learn about the Gospel, are even now inexcusable before the Lord, because they could have known the Creator through his creation?[297] *For this is as it were to reap where one did not sow; that is, to hold guilty of impiety even those to whom the word of the Law and the Gospel was not given. But, by avoiding this danger of judgement, /340/ they take a rest from the ministration of the word with lazy lassitude, and this is, so to speak, to wrap what they received in a handkerchief.*[298]

[Luke 19:22] **He says to him: Out of your own mouth I judge you, you wicked servant.** He is called a wicked servant, because he is both lazy and idle in carrying out trade and insolent and proud in complaining of the Lord's judgement.

[Luke 19:22b–23] **You knew that I was an austere man, taking up what I did not lay down, and reaping what I did not sow. And why then did you not give my money into a bank?** *What the servant thought he had said by way of excuse is turned into his particular fault. If, the lord says, you knew that I was harsh and severe, and that I frequented foreign parts, and that I reaped where I did not sow, why did this thought not strike fear in you, so that you would know that I was going to seek diligently what was my own, and give my money and silver* into a bank? *For the Greek word 'argurion' signifies both.*[299] *'The words of the Lord', he says, 'are pure words, as silver tried by fire.'*[300] *Therefore money and silver is the preaching of the Gospel and the divine word, which ought to be given* into the bank,[301] that is, ought to be made known to the hearts of the faithful, which are ready and waiting. Into this bank, that is, the mind of the hearers, nothing other than the Lord's money should be given, in order that every word of the teacher might follow the sense of the scripture. The Apostle explains why the Lord says here that not that any money, but his own money should be given on interest to the money lenders, saying: *If any man speaks, let him do so as speaking the words of God.*[302]

---

297 Cf. Rom. 1:19–20.
298 Augustine, *Quaestiones euang.* 2.46 (CCSL 44B:110.22–33).
299 I.e., both 'money' and 'silver coin'.
300 Ps. 11:7 (12:6).
301 Jerome, *Commentarii in Matheum* 4 (CCSL 77:241.1766–73).
302 1 Pet. 4:11.

[Luke 19:23b] **Then at my coming, I might have exacted it with interest.** He who receives the money of the word from a teacher, and puts it out by believing, must pay it back with interest by working, in order to carry out also by deed what he learned by hearing. Or yet indeed he pays back the interest from the profit of the word he received when he exerts himself to understand as well things which he has not yet learned from the mouth of a preacher.

[Luke 19:24–25] **And he said to those who stood by: Take the pound away from him and give it to him who has ten pounds. And they said to him: Lord, he has ten pounds.** It is right that he should lose the grace he received which he failed to communicate to others by preaching, and that consequently there should be more for him who worked, in accordance with what is said *to the angel of the church of Ephesus: And I will move your candlestick out of its place, unless you do penance*;[303] and when David gained the royal anointing by obedience, which Saul lost out of pride: *The spirit of the Lord*, it says, *departed from Saul, and came upon David from that day forward.*[304] But the fact that the pound taken from the wicked servant was ordered to be given to the one who had ten pounds shows allegorically, as I believe, that when the fullness of the Gentiles comes in all Israel /341/ is going to be saved,[305] and then that an abundance of spiritual grace, which now we employ tepidly, will be conferred upon the teachers of that people.

230/2 [Luke 19:26] **But I say to you that to everyone who has will be given. And from him who has not, even what he has will be taken from him.** This statement looks back to the ones above, teaching *both that someone who has a gift from God but who does not have it in the sense that he does not use it, can lose it, and that someone who has a gift, and has it in the sense that he uses it well, can find it augmented.*[306] Because this transfer of gifts usually occurs in this life, it should be noted that the examination which the Lord will conduct on his return is conducted in part even now, but then it will be carried out universally. For after receiving the kingdom from the Father, he returns every day because he sees the condition of the Church which is always on pilgrimage on earth. In the case of a great number of faithful servants, he lends money daily to it for trade; in the case of another

---

303 Rev. 2:1 & 5.
304 1 Sam. 16:13–14.
305 Cf. Rom. 11:25–26.
306 Augustine, *Quaestiones euang.* 2.46 (CCSL 44B:111.47–49).

number, he examines how much it has accomplished. To the first group, who have worked faithfully and wisely, he presents the gift of more ample grace; the latter, who pursue pleasant idleness and languid leisure with luxury, he deprives even of what he had given. But though it is terrible to say it, when the universal Judgement has been made clear, many who seemed to have the right qualities to receive instruction will be reckoned among the ignorant on account of their negligence. But those brothers who are more sincere and yet completely unaware of the rudiments will nevertheless receive the highest distinction among the apostolic teachers because of the devotion of their exceptional conduct. For *he who receives a prophet in the name of a prophet will receive the reward of a prophet.*[307]

**231/5** [Luke 19:27] **But as for my enemies who did not want me to reign over them, bring them here and kill them before me.** This signifies that the impiety of the Jews or of all the wicked who are unwilling to be converted to Christ must be punished on the Day of Judgement; just as the teachers of both these groups may be signified by the two faithful servants and the same believing peoples by the five and ten pounds, and evil Catholics by the wicked servant; the impiety of those who preferred either never to hear the word of faith or to corrupt it by interpreting it badly is symbolized by the enemies who did not want him to reign over them; and the examination of those who did not happen to hear the word of God by the reaping of the fields which had not been sown. These five sets of people represent the whole human race as it will be on the Day of Judgement.

**232/2** [Luke 19:28] **And having said these things, he went before, going up to Jerusalem.** Having finished the parable, he goes up to Jerusalem to show that the parable had been first pronounced chiefly about the fate of that same city, which shortly thereafter would both slay Christ and perish at the hands of the enemy for hating Christ's kingdom. /342/

## Chapter 78

[Luke 19:29–30] **And it happened, when he had come near to Bethphage and Bethany to the mountain which is called Olivet, he sent two of his disciples, saying: Go into the town which is over against you, ...** *Bethphage was a little village of priests on the mountain of Olivet.*[308]

---

307 Matt. 10:41.
308 Jerome, *Commentarii in Matheum* 3 (CCSL 77:182.1175–77).

# 540   BEDE: COMMENTARY ON THE GOSPEL OF LUKE

Bethany likewise was the village or city *on the side of the* same *mountain*[309] *about fifteen stades* from Jerusalem,[310] as indeed the evangelist John shows clearly, where Lazarus was raised from the dead,[311] *and whose sepulchre the church now erected in the same place marks.*[312] Moreover, *Bethphage* means *the house of the puffed-out cheeks, and Bethany, the house of obedience.*[313] On his way to Jerusalem, the Saviour elevated these villages by the dignity of his presence, because, by teaching many persons before his passion, he filled them with the gifts of devout confession and spiritual obedience. These villages are beautifully reported to have been situated on the mountain of Olivet, that is, on the Lord himself, who restores us with the oil of spiritual gifts and the light of knowledge and piety. Hence, when he elsewhere said: *A city seated on a mountain cannot be hid,* he immediately added: *Nor do men light a candle and put it under a bushel,*[314] because the same mountain of Olivet, that is, the supreme distributor of spiritual graces, who exalts his city to make it prominent, likewise sets it aflame with the oil of rejoicing in order that it can shine brightly. And because he did not want the same light to be put under a bushel, he sent his disciples into the village which was over against them, that is, he took care to appoint teachers to penetrate the untaught and barbarous shores of the whole world, the ramparts as it were of the walled town set over against them, by preaching the Gospel. And it is appropriate that two are sent, either on account of the knowledge of the truth and the purity of the work, or on account of preaching to the whole world the mystery of two-fold love, that is to say, love of God and of one's neighbour.

[Luke 19:30b–31] **At your entering into which, you will find the colt of an ass tied, on which no man has ever sat. Untie it and bring it here. And if any man asks you: Why do you untie it? say thus to him: Because the Lord has need of his service.** Entering into the world, preachers found the people of the Gentiles entangled in the chains of faithlessness. For each people, not only of the Gentiles, but also of the Jews, had been tied up with the cords of their own sins. *For all have sinned and are in need of the glory of God.*[315] Hence it is well that in Matthew an ass is also found tied, with a

---

309  Jerome, *De situ et nom.* (*Onomastica sacra* 108.3–4).
310  John 11:18.
311  Cf. John 12:1.
312  Jerome, *De situ et nom.* (*Onomastica sacra* 108.4–5).
313  Jerome, *Hebr. nom.* (CCSL 72:135.24–27).
314  Matt. 5:14–15.
315  Rom. 3:23.

colt.³¹⁶ Surely, *the ass which was accustomed to the yoke and, completely tamed, had taken on the yoke of the Law* signifies *the Synagogue*; *the colt, frisky and free*, represents *the people of the Gentiles.*³¹⁷ *On which no man has ever sat*, that is, none /343/ of the philosophers had employed the bridle of reproach to force the Gentiles to repress the tongue from evil or to go into the strait way of life; none, by urging useful actions, had put on them the garments of salvation by which they might be spiritually warmed. For indeed a man might have sat on this colt, if anyone using reason had corrected their follies by repression. Hence the two disciples appointed to procure the animals for the Lord, according to the example of the above parable, can deservedly be understood as the two orders of preachers, one directed to the Gentiles, the other to the circumcised.³¹⁸ And it should be noted that the three evangelists who wrote in Greek mention only the colt;³¹⁹ but Matthew alone, who wrote his Gospel for the Hebrews in the Hebrew language, relates that the ass was also untied and led to the Lord, to show that even the salvation of that same Hebrew race, if they repented, was not to be despaired of. *Untie them*, he says, *and bring them.*³²⁰ *And whatever you untie on earth will be untied also in heaven.*³²¹

233/2 [Luke 19:32] **And those who were sent went their way and found the colt standing, as he had said to them.** Mark writes that the colt was found *before a door outside in a place where two ways meet.*³²² This is the same door that says: *I am the door of the sheep. By me, if any man enter in, he will be saved; and he will go in and go out, and will find pastures.*³²³ This colt, that is, the people of the Gentiles, was deprived of the pastures of life as long it stood tied outside this door in a place where two ways meet. And rightly in a place where two ways meet, because the Gentiles did not keep resolutely to the single way of life and faith, but wandered about and followed many and dubious footpaths of heresies. About these it is aptly added:

[Luke 19:33] **And as they were untying the colt, its owners said to them: Why are you untying the colt?** Indeed, that people, who were

316  Cf. Matt. 21:2.
317  Jerome, *Commentarii in Matheum* 3 (CCSL 77:183.1203–05).
318  Cf. Jerome, *Commentarii in Matheum* 3 (CCSL 77:183.1206).
319  Cf. Mark 11:2; John 12:14.
320  Matt. 21:2.
321  Matt. 18:18.
322  Mark 11:4.
323  John 10:7 & 9.

not given up *to one doctrine* and superstition, *had many owners*;[324] they were in a wretched state, carried off by the caprice of unclean spirits into various and diverse errors, going *to dumb idols, according as* they were *led*.[325] Finally, by a custom peculiar to Scripture, what is unclean is called common, just as a voice from heaven says to Peter: *What God has made clean, do not call common*,[326] because he who is holy belongs to the one God, and is common to no one. But he who is a sinner and unclean belongs to the many, for many devils possess him, and therefore he is called common.

[Luke 19:34–35] **But they said: Because the Lord has need of it. And they brought it to Jesus.** Those who had objected to the colt being untied fell silent on hearing the name of the Lord, because the leaders of false religions who opposed the teachers who come to save the Gentiles defended their spiritual darkness up to the time when, as miracles offered proof, /344/ the power of the true Owner and Lord shone forth. But after the power of the Lord's faith appeared, and the complaints of his adversaries everywhere subsided, the assembly of believers which carries God in its heart is brought forth, released from its confinement.

[Luke 19:35b] **And casting their garments on the colt, they set Jesus on it.** *The garments of the apostles* can be understood *as either the teaching of the virtues, or the exposition of the Scriptures*, or indeed *the diversity of church doctrines*,[327] with which the apostles cover the hearts of men, formerly bare and cold, in order to make them worthy of Christ the rider.

[Luke 19:36] **And as he went, they spread their garments underneath on the way.** As the ass is carrying the Lord, the disciples spread their own garments on the way, because in stripping themselves of the cloak of their own body, they prepare the way with their own blood for the simpler servants of God, so that they may go so to speak with their mental progress unimpeded to Jerusalem where Jesus leads them. For Jesus *goes to Jerusalem sitting on an ass*, either *when governing the soul of each of the faithful, he leads his pack animal so to speak to a vision of inward peace*, or *indeed when he watches over the holy Church everywhere, and kindles it to a desire for heavenly peace*.[328] But according to the other

---

324 Jerome, *Commentarii in Matheum* 3 (CCSL 77:182.1186–88).
325 1 Cor. 12:2.
326 Acts 11:9.
327 Jerome, *Commentarii in Matheum* 3 (CCSL 77:183.1215–17).
328 Gregory, *Hom. in Hiezech.* 2.5.2 (CCSL 142:275.33–37).

BOOK FIVE 543

evangelists, not only the disciples, but also many of the crowd spread their garments on the way, and they signify those who, having followed the examples of the martyrs, *subdue their bodies through abstinence to prepare the way* for the Lord *to the soul, or to offer good examples to those following after.*[329]

**234/1 [Luke 19:37] And when he was now coming near the descent of mount Olivet, the whole multitude of those descending,**[330] **rejoicing, began to praise God with a loud voice, ...** As the Lord descends from the Mount of Olives, that same rejoicing and praising multitude also descends, because after the author of mercy was humbled of his own free will, it is necessary that those who stand in dire need of mercy follow in the footsteps of his humility as far as they are able. It is necessary, I say, that we ourselves, contemplating how Jesus descended from mount Olivet, that is, *although he was in the form of God, he humbled himself, becoming obedient to death, even to the death of the cross,*[331] likewise be humbled under his mighty hand, so that we may deserve to be exalted at the time of his visitation.[332]

[Luke 19:37b–38] **For all the mighty works they had seen, saying: Blessed be the king who comes in the name of the Lord, ...** Indeed, they had seen many works, but chiefly they were astounded /345/ at the resurrection of Lazarus, which had happened recently, as the crowd that was with him bore witness, when he summoned Lazarus from the sepulchre and raised him up from the dead.[333] So the crowd came to meet him, because they heard that he had done this miracle. For it should be noted that the Saviour was not going from Galilee for the first time now, that is, five days before Passover, but in the previous year, in the seventh month, he came there for the feast day of Tabernacles, as John relates, and after that for the next six months, that is, up to the day of Passover on which he suffered, he on one occasion did miracles in Jerusalem, on another ascended the mount of Olives, on another went across the Jordan when he was driven from Judea, and then stayed with his disciples in a

---

329 Gregory, *Hom. in Hiezech.* 2.5.2 (CCSL 142:276.38–40).
330 Bede's copy text of the Vulgate read *descendentium*, 'of descenders' (so, Amiatinus), which is one of several variants in the manuscript tradition for the received reading *discentium*, 'of disciples'. Bede's exegesis then builds on the related notions of descent, abasement, humility.
331 Phil. 2:6 & 8.
332 Cf. 1 Pet. 5:6.
333 Cf. John 11:43–44; 12:9.

city of the desert, which is called Ephrem, but never did he return back to Galilee in that time.[334] Therefore, for all the mighty works they had seen him do in so much time, the multitude praises God, saying: *Blessed be the king who comes in the name of the Lord.*

[Luke 19:38b] **Peace in heaven and glory on high.** But *'Blessed be the king who comes in the name of the Lord'* ought rather to be taken in such a way that 'in the name of the Lord' is understood as 'in the name of the Father', although it can even be understood as 'in his own name', because Christ himself is also the Lord. Hence elsewhere it is written: 'The Lord rained from the Lord'.[335] But his words better direct our understanding when he says: 'I have come in the name of my Father, and you have not received me; if another will come in his own name, you will receive him'.[336] For the teacher of humility is Christ, who 'humbled himself, becoming obedient to death'.[337] Accordingly, he does not lose his divine nature when he teaches us humility. But *Christ is not the king of Israel for the sake of exacting tribute, or of equipping an army with weapons, or of openly conquering an enemy, but he is the king of Israel because he rules souls, because he counsels forever, and because he guides those who believe, hope, and love into the kingdom of heaven. The fact, therefore, that the Son of God, who was equal to the Father, the Word by which all things were made,*[338] *willed to be the king of Israel is a matter of honour, not promotion; it is a mark of compassion, not an augmentation of power. For he who on earth was called the king of the Jews is in heaven the Lord of the angels.*[339] Truly, because Christ, the atonement of the whole world, both of men, of course, and of the angels, appeared clearly in the flesh, heaven as well as earth sing beautifully together in harmony in praise of his dispensation. For as at his birth the troops of the heavenly powers, praising God, sing: *Glory to God in the highest, and on earth peace to men of good will,*[340] so as he is about to triumph over the prince of the world, and immediately return /346/ to heaven, mortals renew the office of praise: *Peace in heaven and glory on high.*

---

334 Cf. John 7:1–12:18.
335 Gen. 19:24.
336 John 5:43.
337 Phil. 2:8.
338 Cf. John 1:1 & 3.
339 Augustine, *In Iohannis euang.* 51.3 (CCSL 36:440–41).
340 Luke 2:14.

BOOK FIVE                                                                 545

235/5 [Luke 19:39] **And some of the Pharisees from among the multitude said to him: Teacher, rebuke your disciples.** With the astounding mindlessness of the envious, they do not doubt that he ought to be called 'Teacher' because they knew that he was teaching the truth. Yet, as if they were better instructed, these people think that his disciples must be rebuked, and they urge that he, whom they see revealed as God by proven miracles, correct those whom he taught.

[Luke 19:40] **To them he said: I say to you that, if these hold their peace, the stones will cry out.** At the crucifixion of the Lord, *all his acquaintances stood far off.*[341] They feared to confess God, whom they saw fastened to a tree, but, while these were silent, the stones and rocks sang of the King who came in the name of the Lord with a mighty noise. For *he yielded up the spirit, and behold, the earth quaked, and the rocks were rent, and the graves were opened,*[342] and even the hardest elements proclaim with open mouth that the one whom men trembled out of fear or treachery to confess is God and Lord of the world. But in a profounder allegory he reveals shows under the word 'stones' the Gentiles,[343] who once were without faith and hard of heart, and to whom, after taking away their stony heart, he gave a heart of flesh,[344] that is, a feeling and human one, with which they can believe, praise, and know their God and Creator. Therefore, although the multitude of men hold their peace, the stones will cry out *that blindness in part has happened in Israel, until the fullness of the Gentiles comes in, and so all Israel will be saved.*[345]

Chapter 79

236/10 [Luke 19:41–42] **And when he drew near, seeing the city, he wept over it, saying: If you had known, you also, ...** No one who has read the story of the destruction of Jerusalem carried out by the Roman emperors Vespasian and Titus is ignorant of the fact that this is what the Lord's weeping represented. But first it should be asked why it is that it is said: 'seeing the city, he wept over it, saying: If you had known, you

---

341 Luke 23:49.
342 Matt. 27:50–52.
343 Cf. Ps.-Jerome, *Expositio euangeliorum* (PL 30:576A).
344 Cf. Ezek. 11:19.
345 Rom. 11:25–26.

*also'. For indeed, the kind Redeemer wept for the ruin of the faithless city, which the city itself was unaware was going to come upon it. You should understand what the weeping Lord rightly said: 'If you had known, you also', to mean: 'would have wept over what now you exult in, because you do not know what is imminent'. Hence also it is added:*[346]

[Luke 19:42b] **And indeed, in this your day, the things that are to your peace.** *For when Jerusalem gave itself up the pleasures of the flesh and did not foresee the evils to come, it had in its day the things that could be for its peace. But why it held that present goods would make for its peace is made clear, when it is added:*[347] /347/

[Luke 19:42c] **But now they are hidden from your eyes.** *For if the imminent evils were not hidden from the eyes of its heart, it would not have rejoiced in its present prosperity. And the impending punishment from the Roman emperors, as I have already said, is immediately added,* when it is said:[348]

[Luke 19:43–44] **For the days will come upon you, and your enemies will surround you with a rampart and surround you, and confine you on every side, and they will throw you down to the ground, and your children who are in you.** And what follows:

237/2 [Luke 19:44b] **And they will not leave in you a stone upon a stone,** ... Likewise, this very transmigration of the same city is proof that while now it is built on the location where the Lord was crucified outside the gate, the previous city of Jerusalem was completely destroyed.[349] To which is added the fault for which the punishment of its destruction was inflicted:

[Luke 19:44c] **Because you did not know the time of your visitation.** Indeed, the Creator of all things deigned to visit Jerusalem by the mystery of the incarnation, but it was not mindful of the fear and love it owed him. Hence the prophet calls the birds of the air to witness his rebuke of the human heart, when he says: *The kite in the air has known its time; the turtledove, and the swallow, and the stork have observed the time of their coming; but my people have not known the judgement of the Lord.*[350]

---

346 Gregory, *Hom. in Euang.* 2.39.1 (CCSL 141:379.3–6; 380.22–27).
347 Gregory, *Hom. in Euang.* 2.39.1 (CCSL 141:380.28–31).
348 Gregory, *Hom. in Euang.* 2.39.1 (CCSL 141:381.32–35).
349 Cf. Bede, *De locis sanctis* 1.1, ed. Fraipont (CCSL 175:252). Bede notes that this is why the sites of the Lord's passion are now inside the city walls.
350 Jer. 8:7.

238/1 [Luke 19:45–46] **And entering into the temple, he began to cast out those selling in it, and those buying, saying to them: It is written: My house is a house of prayer.** *He who told of the evils to come and immediately entered the temple to cast out from it those who sold and bought, assuredly made known that the ruin of the people was chiefly the fault of the priests. Indeed, describing the destruction [of Jerusalem], but smiting the sellers and buyers in the temple, he shows by the very effect of his deed whence the root of the destruction proceeded.*[351]

[Luke 19:46b] **But you have made it a den of thieves.** *Those who resided in the temple to take offerings undoubtedly sought to do harm to any who would not give an offering. Therefore, the house of prayer had been made a den of thieves, because it was known that those who were present in the temple were there in order either to physically harm those who did not give offerings, or to slay spiritually those who did. But because our Redeemer does not take away the words of his preaching from the unworthy and ungrateful, after he upheld the force of his teaching by casting out the wicked, he immediately displayed the gift of grace. For it goes on:*[352]

239/1 [Luke 19:47] **And he was teaching daily in the temple.** *I have gone over these things by treating them briefly on the literal level.* Now let me begin again by discussing these same matters on the moral level. 'Seeing the city, he wept over it, saying: /348/ If you had known, you also'.[353] He did this once when he announced that the city was going to be destroyed. Our Redeemer by no means ceases to do this daily through his elect, when he sees that some have left the good life for wicked habits. For he weeps over those who do not know why they are wept over, because according to the words of Solomon: 'They are glad when they have done evil, and rejoice in most wicked things'.[354] If they had known of their impending condemnation, they would weep over themselves with tears for their transgressions.[355]

'And indeed, in this your day, the things that are to your peace'.[356] The wicked soul, which rejoices in transitory time, has its day here. The things

---

351 Gregory, *Hom. in Euang.* 2.39.2 (CCSL 141:381.39–44).
352 Gregory, *Hom. in Euang.* 2.39.2 (CCSL 141:381.51–59).
353 Luke 19:41–42.
354 Prov. 2:14.
355 Gregory, *Hom. in Euang.* 2.39.2–3 (CCSL 141:382.60–61; 66–74).
356 Luke 19:42.

which are present are its peace, because as long as it rejoices in temporal things, as long as it is exalted by honours, as long as it is enervated by the pleasure of the flesh, as long as it does not dread the punishment to come, it has peace in its day, and this will be a grave obstacle leading to its damnation on another day. For there where the just will rejoice it must be afflicted.[357]

'But now they are hidden from your eyes'.[358] The wicked soul, given over to things of the present, enfeebled by earthly pleasures, hides the evils to follow from itself, because it refuses to foresee what is coming, which might disturb present pleasure. And as long as it abandons itself in the delights of the present life, what is it doing other than marching into the fire with its eyes shut?[359]

'For the days will come upon you, and your enemies will surround you with a rampart'.[360] What greater enemies does the human soul have than the evil spirits who besiege it when it leaves the body, for when the soul is occupied in the love of the flesh, they nourish it with deceitful delights? They surround it with a rampart, because, when the iniquities that the soul performed have been brought back before the eyes of the mind, the evil spirits drag it away and force it to join the company of their own damnation.[361]

'And surround you, and confine you on every side'.[362] Evil spirits confine the soul on every side, when they display to it its iniquities not only of deed, but also of word, and especially of thought, so that the soul which earlier spread itself out in wickedness through many things, at the last is locked away from everything in retribution.[363]

'And they will throw you down to the ground, and your children who are in you'.[364] Then the soul is thrown to the ground by the recognition of its guilt, when the flesh, which the soul believed was its life, is forced to return to dust. Then its children fall in death, when the forbidden thoughts, which now come forth from it, are destroyed in the last judgement of life,

---

357 Gregory, *Hom. in Euang.* 2.39.3 (CCSL 141:382.76–83).
358 Luke 19:42.
359 Gregory, *Hom. in Euang.* 2.39.3 (CCSL 141:383.88–93).
360 Luke 19:43.
361 Gregory, *Hom. in Euang.* 2.39.4 (CCSL 141:383.104–10).
362 Luke 19:43.
363 Gregory, *Hom. in Euang.* 2.39.4 (CCSL 141:384.114–19).
364 Luke 19:44.

BOOK FIVE 549

*just as it is written: 'In that day all their thoughts will perish'.*[365] *Indeed, these hard thoughts can likewise be understood through the symbolism of stones. For this follows:*[366]

*'And they will not leave in you a stone upon a stone'.*[367] *For when a wicked mind adds to a wicked thought one still more wicked, what else is it but to place a stone upon a stone? But in a ruined /349/ city a stone is not left upon a stone, because when the soul is brought to its judgement, the whole edifice of its thoughts is destroyed.*[368]

*'Because you did not know the time of your visitation'.*[369] *Almighty God is also accustomed to visit the* wicked *soul in many ways. For he visits it continually with commands, and sometimes with a whip, and sometimes with a miracle, so that it may hear true things that it did not know, and if it is still proud and disdainful, so that it may either recover, stung by sorrow, or blush for the evil that it did, overcome by God's kindness. But because it does not know the time of its visitation, at the end of its life it is handed over to those enemies, to be gathered in company with them in the eternal Judgement of its damnation.*[370]

*'And entering into the temple, he began to cast out those selling in it, and those buying'.*[371] *Just as the temple of God is in the city, so the life of the clergy is in the faithful laity. And often many people put on the attire of religion, but while they assume the place of the sacred orders, they give over the duty of sacred religion to transacting earthly business. Indeed, those who sell in the temple are those who take a bribe for what people should have as a right. For to sell justice is to reserve it in exchange for the taking of a bribe. Those who buy in the temple are those who purchase sin when they refuse a neighbour his rights, or disdain to carry out what is justly owed, if a patron pays them not to. To these it is well said:*[372]

*'My house is a house of prayer. But you have made it a den of thieves',*[373] *because, when sometimes wicked men hold religious office, they slay with*

365 Ps. 145:4 (146:4).
366 Gregory, *Hom. in Euang.* 2.39.4 (CCSL 141:384.120–27).
367 Luke 19:44.
368 Gregory, *Hom. in Euang.* 2.39.4 (CCSL 141:384.127–32).
369 Luke 19:44.
370 Gregory, *Hom. in Euang.* 2.39.5 (CCSL 141:385.133–42).
371 Luke 19:45.
372 Gregory, *Hom. in Euang.* 2.39.6 (CCSL 141:386.157–68).
373 Luke 19:46.

the swords of their malice in that place, where they ought to have restored their neighbours to life with the intercession of their prayer.[374]

The soul and conscience of the faithful is also the temple and house of God. If ever it brings forth wicked thoughts that injure a neighbour, it is as if thieves reside in a den and kill those going about their business blamelessly, when they plunge swords of injury into the guiltless. For the soul of the faithful is no longer a house of prayer, but the den of a thief, when, after it gives up the innocence and simplicity of holiness, it attempts to do what it can to harm its neighbours. But because we are instructed unceasingly by the words of our Redeemer in the holy pages against all these things, what is said to have been done then is done up to now, when it is said: 'And he was teaching daily in the temple.' For when he carefully instructs the soul of the faithful to avoid evils, Truth teaches daily in the temple.[375]

[Luke 19:47b–48] **And the chief priests and the scribes and the rulers of the people sought to destroy him, and they did not find anything to do to him,** ... The envious leaders sought to destroy him either because he was teaching daily in the temple, or because he had cast out the thieves /350/ from the temple, or because coming to it as King and Lord he received the praise of a heavenly hymn from so great a crowd of believers.[376]

[Luke 19:48b] **For all the people were very attentive to hear him.** This can be understood in two ways, either because, fearing the tumult of the people, they did not find anything to do to Jesus, whom they determined to destroy; or they sought to destroy Jesus, because, after their own teachings were neglected, they realized that many flocked to hear him. Meanwhile I should like to notice briefly how beautifully the shadow of the Paschal feast of the Law agrees with our true Paschal feast in which Christ

---

374 Gregory, *Hom. in Euang.* 2.39.6 (CCSL 141:386.168–72). Bede paraphrases these sentiments in *Hom.* 2.1, ed. Hurst (CCSL 122:187.124–188.150; trans. Lawrence and Hurst, *Homilies of the Gospels* 2:6); see O'Brien, *Bede's Temple*, 135.

375 Gregory, *Hom. in Euang.* 2.39.7 (CCSL 141:386.173–85). In his later commentary on Mark, Bede would reiterate Gregory's interpretation of the casting out of the money-changers, but add ideas of his own about how inappropriate behaviour in church might defile the sacred space: see O'Brien, 'The Cleansing of the Temple in Early Medieval Northumbria', 201–20. On the impact in the Carolingian period and later of Bede's reading of this episode as relating to reverence for ecclesiastical space, see Bien, 'Les marchands chassés du temple', 56–59.

376 Cf. Luke 19:37–38 & 45.

BOOK FIVE 551

is sacrificed,[377] not only by reason of the mystery, but also of time. *On the tenth day of the first month*, it says, *let every man take a lamb by the families of his house. According to which rite also you will take a goat, and you will keep it until the fourteenth day of the same month.*[378] On the tenth day of the first month, that is, five days before the Paschal feast, as the evangelist John testifies,[379] all the people, going out to the Mount of Olives, took the Lord there. He is the lamb, because he came to take away sins,[380] and there is no sin in him;[381] he is the goat, because he was falsely accused of sin. Those who rejoicing sang: *Blessed be the king who comes in the name of the Lord*,[382] brought the lamb to the house; those who said against those filled with zeal: *Teacher, rebuke your disciples*,[383] brought the goat. *All the people who were very attentive to hear him* brought the lamb; the chiefs who wished to destroy him brought the goat.[384] And five days before the Paschal feast, that is, from the tenth day of the moon to the fourteenth day, they kept the lamb or goat they were going to sacrifice, because although even then they thirsted for his blood, nevertheless *no man laid hands on him, because his hour had not yet come.*[385] Those who gladly gave ear to his words kept the lamb. Those who *lying in wait* sought *to catch something from his mouth, that they might accuse him*,[386] kept the goat. But at the end of the fourteenth day, that is, when the day had declined into evening, after he delivered to his disciples the sacraments to be celebrated of his body and blood, with those coming to bind him after he had been seized,[387] what follows began to be fulfilled: *And the whole multitude of the children of Israel will sacrifice it in the evening.*[388] For not only the impious who mocked his death, but also the saints who mourned, stood by the cross of Jesus.[389] I wanted to go over these

---

377 Cf. 1 Cor. 5:7. What follows is a sketch of the allegorical reading of the computistical parameters of the Easter feast that Bede will develop in ch. 60 of *DTR* (ed. Jones, 456–59; trans. Wallis, 151–55).
378 Exod. 12:3; 5–6.
379 Cf. John 12:1 & 12.
380 Cf. John 1:29.
381 Cf. Isa. 53:9.
382 Luke 19:38.
383 Luke 19:39.
384 Cf. Luke 19:48.
385 John 7:30; 8:20 (a blend).
386 Luke 11:54 (Bede omits this verse from its regular place above).
387 Cf. Matt. 27:2.
388 Exod. 12:6.
389 Cf. Luke 23:35; John 19:25.

matters briefly, in order to teach the reader that everything which follows in succession up to the passion of the Lord /351/ relates to the figure of the lamb kept in the house and prepared for slaughter.

## Chapter 80

240/2 [Luke 20:1–2] **And it happened that on one of the days, as he was teaching the people in the temple and preaching the gospel, the chief priests and the scribes, with the elders, met together, and spoke to him saying: Tell us, by what authority do you do these things?** *In different ways they spread the same falsehood as above when they said: 'He casts out devils by Beelzebub, the prince of devils'.*[390] *For when they say: 'By what authority do you do these things?' they doubt that it is the authority of God, and want it to be understood that what he does is by the devil's authority. And going on, they add:*[391]

[Luke 20:2b] **Or: Who is he who has given you this authority?** *Very plainly they deny that he is the Son of God, whom they suppose does miracles not by his own, but by another's power.*[392]

[Luke 20:3–4] **And answering, he said to them: I will also ask you one thing. Answer me: The baptism of John was it from heaven, or of men?** *The Lord could refute the falsehood of the tempters by a direct response, but he wisely asks a question to condemn them either by their silence or by what they say.*[393]

[Luke 20:5] **But they pondered among themselves, saying: If we say, 'From heaven', he will say: Why then did you not believe him?** *'He, whom you confess had the power of prophecy from heaven, gave witness for me, and you have heard therefore by what authority I do these things'.*[394]

[Luke 20:6] **But if we say, 'Of men', all the people will stone us, for they are persuaded that John was a prophet.** *They saw, therefore, that whichever reply they gave, they were going to fall into a trap,*[395] fearing stoning, but fearing more a confession of the truth.

---

390 Luke 11:15.
391 Jerome, *Commentarii in Matheum* 3 (CCSL 77:192.1468–73).
392 Jerome, *Commentarii in Matheum* 3 (CCSL 77:192.1473–75).
393 Jerome, *Commentarii in Matheum* 3 (CCSL 77:193.1481–83).
394 Augustine, *In Iohannis euang.* 35.2 (CCSL 36:318).
395 Augustine, *In Iohannis euang.* 35.2 (CCSL 36:318).

BOOK FIVE 553

[Luke 20:7–8] **And they answered that they did not know whence it was. And Jesus said to them: Neither do I tell you by what authority I do these things.** *'I do not tell you what I know, because you do not want to confess what you know'.* Very justly repulsed and confounded on every point they went away, and what God the Father says in the psalm through the prophet is fulfilled: *'I have prepared a lamp for my Christ'*, that is, John himself, *'His enemies I will clothe with confusion'*.[396]

It should be noted that knowledge of the truth should be hidden from those who seek it chiefly for two reasons: namely when the seeker is either incapable of understanding what he seeks, or because he who seeks the truth, and to whom it could be revealed, is unworthy of it because he hates it and is contemptuous of it. On account of one of these the Lord says: *I still have many things to say to you, but you cannot bear them now.*[397] And on account of the other he orders his disciples: *Do not give what is holy to dogs, and do not cast your pearls before swine.*[398]

## Chapter 81

**241/2** [Luke 20:9] **And he began to tell the people this parable: A certain man planted /352/ a vineyard, and leased it to tenant farmers, and he was abroad for a long time.** While the Lord was teaching the people and preaching the gospel, the chief priests and the scribes, with the elders, met together, and as a way to test him, asked by what authority he performed miracles.[399] After overcoming them by his skill, the Lord carries on with what he had begun. And while the chief priest and scribes listen, he addresses the people instead, because they hear his words more willingly. And he introduces a parable which will accuse them of impiety, and teach that the kingdom of God was to be transferred to the Gentiles. The man who planted the vineyard, then, is the same one who, according to another parable, *hired labourers for his vineyard.*[400] *For the vineyard of the Lord of hosts is the house of Israel.*[401] The tenant farmers are the same labourers

---

396 Augustine, *In Iohannis euang.* 35.2 (CCSL 36:318); Ps. 131:17–18 (132:17–18).
397 John 16:12.
398 Matt. 6:7.
399 Cf. Luke 20:1–2.
400 Matt. 20:1.
401 Isa. 5:7.

who are said to have been hired to cultivate the vineyard at the first, third, sixth, and ninth hour.[402] But *'he was abroad for a long time'*, not by a change of place, for where can God not be present, who says: *'I fill heaven and earth'*,[403] and elsewhere: *'I am a God at hand, and not far off, says the Lord'*? But he is said *to be away from the vineyard to leave full freedom of action to the vineyard workers*.[404] This is similar to what he says through Isaiah with respect to the vineyard leased to the tenant farmers: *I expected that it would bring forth grapes*.[405]

[Luke 20:10] **And at the season he sent a servant to the farmers, so that they might give him some fruit of the vineyard. They, beating him, sent him away empty.** He spoke with good reason of the season of fruits, not the produce. For *no fruit of the Jews sprang forth, no produce of this vineyard* was found,[406] even though it was sought repeatedly and carefully. Therefore, the servant who was sent first is understood to be the Law-giver Moses himself, who for forty continuous years kept seeking from the farmers some fruit of the Law which he had given, but they beat him, and sent him away empty. For *they provoked Moses in the camp and Aaron the holy one of the Lord*.[407] *And Moses was afflicted for their sakes, because they exasperated his spirit*.[408] And he is the very servant who openly declares in song what he sees of the fruit of the vineyard, saying: *Their vines are of the vineyard of Sodom, and of the offspring of Gomorrah; their grapes are grapes of gall, a cluster of bitterness to them. Their wine is the rage of dragons, and the rage of asps, which is incurable*.[409]

[Luke 20:11] **And again, he sent a second servant. But they beat him also, and treating him shamefully, sent him away empty.** The second servant signifies David, the prophet and king. He was sent after Moses to arouse the tenant farmers of the vineyard after the proclamations of the Law to the exercise of good work with the melody of psalm-singing and the charm of the harp. /353/ For indeed David himself, in order to lift the heart of the people to heavenly things, instituted among the rituals of carnal sacrifices continuous praises of the Lord to be repeated with delightful

---

402 Cf. Matt. 20:2–5.
403 Jer. 23:24.
404 Jerome, *Commentarii in Matheum* 3 (CCSL 77:196.1560–66); Jer. 23:23.
405 Isa. 5:4.
406 Ambrose, *Expos. Lucam* 9.25 (CCSL 14:340.227–29).
407 Ps. 105:16 (106:16).
408 Ps. 105:32–33 (106:32–33).
409 Deut. 32:32–33.

melody. But they also sent him away empty after treating him shamefully, saying in effect: *What portion do we have in David? Or what inheritance in the son of Jesse?*[410] They exchanged David's kingdom for an ignoble stock and his religion for impiety. But David still prays for this vineyard, which, brought out of Egypt, covered the hills of Palestine under its shadow,[411] lest it be completely destroyed: *Lord God of hosts, return now, look down from heaven, and see, and visit this vineyard, and arrange it, which your right hand planted.*[412] Here he explains at the same time who planted this vineyard, namely the Lord God of hosts.

[Luke 20:12] **And again, he sent a third, and wounding him also, they cast him out.** You should understand the third servant to be the multitude of prophets who addressed the people with constant testimonies, and prophesied the evils to come which threatened this vineyard. But *which of the prophets have they not persecuted? And they have slain those who foretold of the coming of the Just One.*[413] These prophets also said much about the barrenness of this vineyard, but it may suffice to give a lament of Jeremiah alone. *Yet I planted you as a chosen vineyard*, he says, *all true seed; how then did you turn into perversity, you strange vineyard?*[414] We read that Naboth the Jezreelite was not only wounded, but killed because he protected this vineyard, lest fragile and weak plants whose taste rapidly deteriorates be produced in it or for it.[415] Although we do not accept any word of his as prophetic, nevertheless we accept the deed as prophetic, because he prophesied by his own blood that many persons were going to be martyrs on account of this vineyard. The Lord elsewhere clearly makes known that the three missions of the servants symbolize all the teachers under the law, saying: *That all things must be fulfilled, which were written about me in the Law of Moses, and in the prophets, and in the psalms.*[416]

[Luke 20:13] **Then the lord of the vineyard said: What shall I do? I will send my beloved son. It may be, when they see him, they will respect him.** The fact that the lord of the vineyard is said to speak doubtfully and in a deliberative way *does not come from ignorance. For what does* the lord of the vineyard *not know, who in this place is understood as God*

---

410 3 Kings 12:16.
411 Cf. Ps. 79:9 & 11 (80:8 & 10).
412 Ps. 79:15–16 (80:14–15) (not *iuxta LXX*).
413 Acts 7:52.
414 Jer. 2:21.
415 Cf. 3 Kings 21:13.
416 Luke 24:44.

the Father? For when God is said to be in doubt, it is always to preserve human free will.[417]

[Luke 20:14] **When the tenant farmers saw him, they thought it over among themselves, saying: This is the heir, let us kill him so that the inheritance may be ours.** /354/ The Lord plainly demonstrates that the leaders of the Jews crucified the Son of God not from ignorance but from envy. They understood that this was the one to whom it was said: *Ask of me, and I will give you the Gentiles for your inheritance*,[418] and for that reason, consulting among themselves, they said: *Behold, the whole world has gone after him*,[419] and: *If we let him alone so, all will believe in him.*[420] Therefore, the inheritance the Son received is the Church of all the Gentiles, which the Father did not leave to him by dying, but which he himself gained miraculously by his own death, because he took possession of it by rising again. But the wicked tenant farmers tried to snatch it away by killing him, when the Jews, by crucifying him, attempted to extinguish the faith which is through him, and to promote their own justice which derives instead from the Law, and to implant that for the instruction of the Gentiles.

[Luke 20:15] **So, casting him out of the vineyard, they killed him.** The heir of the vineyard is slain outside the vineyard, because *Jesus, in order that he might sanctify the people by his own blood, suffered outside the gate.*[421] Or he was cast out of the vineyard and killed, because he was first expelled from the heart of the unbelievers, and then delivered over to the cross. In a prefiguration of this Moses put the altar of holocaust on which the blood of victims was poured out, not within the tabernacle, but at its entry,[422] teaching allegorically not only that the altar of the Lord's cross should be placed outside the gate of Jerusalem, but also that Christ himself, the true sacrifice of the Father, would not be received by the inmost heart of the house of the Jews, which he had approached in order to sanctify it, but that he would be bathed in his own blood out of doors. But the fact that, according to Mark, it is said with the order reversed: *And laying hold of him, they killed him, and cast him out of the vineyard*,[423] charges with obstinacy those who, after the Lord had been crucified and had risen again

---

417 Jerome, *Commentarii in Matheum* 3 (CCSL 77:197.1584–86).
418 Ps. 2:8.
419 John 12:19.
420 John 11:48.
421 Hebr. 13:12.
422 Cf. Exod. 40:27.
423 Mark 12:8.

from the dead, would not believe the preaching of the apostles, but cast it out like a common corpse, because, excluding it from their territory as much as they were able, they gave it for the Gentiles to take.

[Luke 20:15b–16] **What then will the lord of the vineyard do to them? He will come and destroy these tenant farmers, and will give the vineyard to others. When they heard this, they said: God forbid!** They objected to the Lord's statement, because they knew that it was spoken against their own faithlessness. For they understood the parable, not because by the merits of sanctity they were now prepared to receive the message of the allegory, but because they were kindled by the fires of malice to do the things that were said in the parable. For that reason they were prepared to recognize what they had in mind as if they had been pondering it for a long time, even though it was spoken of in parables.

Notice therefore what the Saviour replies to the Jews, who were denying that it would be right for knowledge of the divine Law, which they themselves rejected, to be transferred to the Gentiles:

[Luke 20:17] **But he looking on them said: What is this then that is written: 'The stone, which the builders rejected, the same has become the cornerstone'?**[424] How, he asks, will this prophecy be fulfilled, /355/ which says that the stone, rejected by the builders, must be placed as the cornerstone, unless Christ, rejected and killed by you, is going to be preached to the Gentiles who will believe, so that the cornerstone, joining as it were the two into itself,[425] builds from each people one city and one temple of the faithful for itself? For those same teachers of the Synagogue, whom he had called tenant farmers above, he now calls builders,[426] because those who as it were tended the vineyard to bring forth the fruits of life, with the common people subject to them, were themselves ordered to construct and adorn this house, so to speak, to be worthy of its inhabitant, God. Hence, the Apostle, writing to the faithful, likewise says: *You are God's husbandry; you are God's building.*[427] But those who like wicked farmers denied the fruit of God's vineyard, these same like wicked masons took away the precious stone chosen for the house of God, which was going to be placed either in the foundations or in the corner,[428] that is, they were trying to snatch away the

---

424 Ps. 117:22 (118:22).
425 Cf. Eph. 2:15.
426 Cf. Jerome, *Commentarii in Matheum* 3 (CCSL 77:198.1607–08).
427 1 Cor. 3:9.
428 Cf. Jerome, *Commentarii in Matheum* 3 (CCSL 77:198.1609–12).

faith of Christ from their audience. But although they were unwilling, the same stone was established as the cornerstone, because from both peoples he united by his faith as many as he himself wished.

[Luke 20:18] **Everyone who falls on that stone will be shattered, and on anyone it falls, it will crush him.** *It is one thing to offend Christ by wicked deeds; another to deny him* by impiety. *He who is a sinner and yet believes in him, falls indeed on the stone and is shattered, but is not entirely crushed. For by his suffering he is preserved for salvation. But anyone on whom that stone falls, that is, whom the stone itself smashes, and who completely denies Christ, the stone will crush* him, *so that not even a shard remains with which a drop of water may be scooped up.*[429]

Or: *he speaks about these people because they fall on him, who despise him now or do him injuries. For that reason, they are not yet completely destroyed, but nevertheless* are shattered, *so that they may not walk upright. But as for those on whom he falls, he will come on them in the Judgement with the punishment of damnation. Therefore, he said* he will crush *them, insofar as they are impious, 'like the dust, which the wind drives from the face of the earth'.*[430]

## Chapter 82

242/1 [Luke 20:19] **And the chief priests and the scribes sought to lay hands on him the same hour, but they feared the people, for they knew that he spoke this parable against themselves.** The chief priests and the scribes sought to kill the Lord as if he were speaking falsely against them, but by seeking this, they taught that what he said was true. Certainly, he is the heir, whose unjust slaughter he said should be avenged; they are the wicked tenant farmers, who were able to be held back a bit from killing the Son of God by human fear until his hour came, but could never be restrained by divine love. /356/ Indeed, on the moral level of understanding, when the mystery of baptism which should be put into action in doing works is entrusted to each of the faithful, it is leased like a vineyard which he may cultivate. One servant is sent, and a second, and a third, to take some fruit, when the Law, the psalmody, and the book of the prophets is read, for each of them admonishes what one should

---

429 Jerome, *Commentarii in Matheum* 3 (CCSL 77:199.1628–35).
430 Augustine, *Quaestiones euang.* 1.30 (CCSL 44B:24.3–9); Ps. 1:4.

BOOK FIVE                                                        559

follow in doing well. But the servant who was sent is treated shamefully or wounded, and cast out, when he is either scorned or, what is worse, even blasphemed after his message has been heard. Whoever not only treats the Son of God with contempt, but also offers insults to the Spirit of grace by whom he was sanctified, also kills, as far as he himself is concerned, the heir who was sent. After the wicked farmer has been destroyed, the vineyard will be given to another, when each humble person will be enriched with the gift of grace which the proud rejected. But also, the fact that the chief priests and the scribes, seeking to lay a hand on Jesus, are restrained by fear of the people is manifested daily in the Church, when anyone who is a brother in name alone either blushes or fears, on account of the multitude of good brothers dwelling together, to impugn that unity of ecclesiastical faith and peace which he does not love. Nevertheless, as the Lord says about the ostrich, the most foolish of birds: *When time will be, she spreads her wings on high*,[431] the fact is that this false brother, by persecuting the Church, will rejoice as it were to bring the Lord to the cross and to make him a mockery.[432]

**243/2** [Luke 20:20] **And watching him, they sent spies, who would pretend to be just, in order to take hold of him by his words, that they might deliver him up to the authority and power of the governor.** The chief priests and the scribes, seeking to catch hold of the Lord, feared the people, and for that reason what they could not to do by themselves, they tried to accomplish at the hands of the governor, so that they themselves would seem blameless for his death. For *recently under Caesar Augustus, Judea, having been subjected to the Romans, had been made a tributary province when the census was carried out throughout the whole world.*[433] *And there was violent discord among the people, with some saying that for the sake of security and quiet, in so far as the Romans performed military service for all, tribute ought to be paid, but with the Pharisees, who boasted of their righteousness, contending on the contrary that the people of God, who paid tithes, and gave first-fruits, and other things which are written in the Law, ought not to be subject to human laws.*[434] The heat of discord grew so great that after the Lord's passion, as the Romans were repressing them, the Jews preferred to lose country, nation, and kingdom, that famous

---

431  Job 39:18.
432  Cf. Hebr. 6:6.
433  Cf. Luke 2:1–2.
434  Jerome, *Commentarii in Matheum* 3 (CCSL 77:202.1742–49).

temple with their religion, and moreover even the light itself, rather than to pay tribute.

[Luke 20:21–22] **And they asked him, saying: Teacher, we know that you speak and teach rightly, and you do not respect any person, but teach the way of God in truth. Is it lawful for us to give tribute to Caesar, or no?** *The flattering and /357/ deceitful question invites him to reply that he fears God more than Caesar, and to say that tribute ought not to be paid, so that* the officers of the governor, who we learn according to the other evangelists were present,[435] *hearing this might immediately seize him as a leader of a faction against the Romans.*[436]

[Luke 20:23–24] **But he, considering their guile, said to them: Why do you tempt me? Show me a denarius. Whose image and inscription does it have?** *Wisdom always acts wisely, so that he very ably refutes the tempters with their own words. 'Show me', he says, 'a denarius'. This is a kind of coin which is reckoned as ten pennies, and has the image of Caesar. But those who think the query of the Saviour is ignorance and not forethought, let them learn from the present passage that Jesus was certainly capable of knowing whose image was on the coin. But he asks in order to respond suitably to their words.*[437]

[Luke 20:24b–25] **Answering, they said: Caesar's. And he said to them: Render therefore to Caesar the things that are Caesar's, and to God the things that are God's.** *Let us not suppose that Caesar Augustus is signified, but Tiberius, his step-son, who had succeeded in place of his step-father, and under whom the Lord suffered. But all the Roman kings are called Caesars, after the first Gaius Caesar who had seized the supreme power. Furthermore, what he says: 'Render to Caesar the things that are Caesar's', let us understand as coin, tribute, and money, and 'the things that are God's to God', as tithes, first-fruits, offerings, and sacrifices, just as he rendered tribute on behalf of himself and Peter,*[438] *and rendered to God the things that are God's, doing the will of the Father.*[439]

In another interpretation: *'Render to Caesar the things that are Caesar's, and to God the things that are God's'. Just as Caesar demands from you the stamping of his image, so also does God; so that just as the*

---

435 Cf. Matt. 22:16; Mark 12:13.
436 Jerome, *Commentarii in Matheum* 3 (CCSL 77:203.1762–65).
437 Jerome, *Commentarii in Matheum* 3 (CCSL 77:203.1773–81).
438 Cf. Matt. 17:26 (17:27).
439 Jerome, *Commentarii in Matheum* 3 (CCSL 77:204.1784–92); cf. John 6:38.

coin is rendered to him, so the soul is embellished and stamped by God through the light of his countenance.[440] Hence the Psalmist says: 'The light of your countenance, Lord, is stamped on us'.[441] Certainly this light, which is seen not by the eyes, but by the soul, is the whole and true good of man. But he said, 'stamped on us', just as the denarius is stamped with the image of the king. For man was made in the image and likeness of God,[442] which he corrupted by sinning. Therefore, his good is true and eternal, if he is stamped by being born again.[443]

[Luke 20:26] **And they could not reprehend his word before the people, and marvelling at his answer, they held their peace.** *Those who ought to have believed, marvelled at his great wisdom, and that their cunning had not found an opportunity for ensnaring him.*[444] /358/

## Chapter 83

[Luke 20:27] **And there came to him some of the Sadducees, who deny that there is any resurrection.** *There were two heresies among the Jews: one of the Pharisees, and the other of the Sadducees. The Pharisees prefer the righteousness of traditions and observances, which they call 'supplementary tradition [deuterosis]'. Hence, they were also called 'set apart from the people'. But the Sadducees, which means 'the righteous', also claimed to be righteous, which they were not. The former believed in the resurrection both of the body and the soul, and confessed the existence of angels and spirits; the latter, according to the Acts of the Apostles, denied all these.*[445]

[Luke 20:27b–28] **And they asked him, saying: Teacher, Moses wrote to us that, if any man's brother dies, having a wife, and he leaves no children, his brother should take her to wife, and raise up offspring for his brother.** Notice the difference between letter and spirit. According to the letter, the brother of the dead man is compelled in life to marry to raise up offspring; but the spirit is the teacher of chastity.

---

440 Augustine, *Enarrationes in Psalmos* 4.8 (CCSL 38:17.29–32).
441 Ps. 4:7 (4:6).
442 Cf. Gen. 1:26.
443 Augustine, *Enarrationes in Psalmos* 4.8 (CCSL 38:17.20–26).
444 Jerome, *Commentarii in Matheum* 3 (CCSL 77:204.1793–95).
445 Jerome, *Commentarii in Matheum* 3 (CCSL 77:204.1799–1806); cf. Acts 23:8.

[Luke 20:29–32] **There were therefore seven brothers, and the first took a wife, and died without children. And the next took her to wife, and he also died childless. And the third took her. And in like manner all the seven, and they left no offspring, and died. Last of all the woman died also.** *Those who did not believe in the resurrection of bodies,* concluding *that souls die with the bodies, logically make up a story of this kind, which accuses those who maintain the resurrection of the dead of absurdity. But it is possible that this really happened once in their nation.*[446]

[Luke 20:33] **In the resurrection therefore, the wife of which of them will she be? For the seven had her to wife.** *They adduce the obscenity of the story to deny the truth of the resurrection.*[447] But allegorically, these seven brothers, who died without children, correspond to the wicked, who pass through the whole life of this world, which extends over seven days, barren of good works.[448] After these men have been snatched away one at a time by a miserable death, finally that worldly way of life itself, which they had carried on without life-giving work, will pass away like the unfruitful wife.

[Luke 20:34] **And Jesus said to them: The children of this world marry, and are given in marriage.** Although the Lord says: *Do not give what is holy to dogs, nor cast your pearls before swine,*[449] he should not be thought to have himself given what is holy to dogs or cast pearls before swine *because* he *is found to have said certain things* here about the glory of the resurrection, or elsewhere about the mystery of the dispensation or even of his divinity, *which many who were present did not comprehend, and either resisted or disdained. For he did not give to those who were unable to comprehend, but to those who were able and at the same time present. It was not fitting* /359/ *for them to be neglected on account of the impurity of others. And when the tempters kept asking, and he replied to them in such a way that they did not have anything to contradict, although they were consumed by their own poisons rather than satisfied with his food, nevertheless others, who were able to comprehend, heard many things profitably as they had opportunity.*[450]

---

446 Jerome, *Commentarii in Matheum* 3 (CCSL 77:205.1813–18).
447 Jerome, *Commentarii in Matheum* 3 (CCSL 77:205.1820–21).
448 To understand this buried allusion to the seven days of creation as type of the seven ages of the world, see Bede's *The Reckoning of Time*, ch. 10 ('The Week of the World-Ages'), trans. Wallis, 39–41.
449 Matt. 7:6.
450 Augustine, *De sermone Domini* 2.20.70 (CCSL 35:166.1580–90).

BOOK FIVE 563

[Luke 20:35] **But those who will be accounted worthy of that world and of the resurrection of the dead are neither married nor take wives.** This should not be understood to mean that only the worthy or the unwed are going to rise again, or that the unworthy, that is, sinners, are either not going to rise again, or are going to rise again to be married. Rather, it should be understood that all are both going to be resurrected and will remain unmarried in that age. The Lord Saviour, however, in order to arouse souls to seek the glory of the resurrection wanted to speak only of the chosen ones. But *if in the resurrection they are neither married nor take wives, it follows that bodies rise again which can be married* and take wives, that is, distinct members with the regular appearances of women and men, but freed from any pleasure in or necessity for sexual intercourse. *No one says of a stone and tree, and of those things which lack genital members, that they do not marry nor take wives, but of these persons who, although they can marry, nevertheless do not marry for another reason.*[451]

[Luke 20:36] **For they cannot die any more.** *Since marriages are for the sake of children, children for the sake of heirs, and heirs for the sake of death, therefore when there is no death, neither are there marriages.*[452]

[Luke 20:36b] **For they are equal to the angels, and are the children of God, since they are the children of the resurrection.** They are equal to the angels and the children of God, who, renewed by the glory of the resurrection, enjoy the vision of God without any fear of death, without any blemish of corruption, without any impulse of earthly status. Whoever desires to ascend then to that equality of angelic worthiness must now descend to the level of the least of the brothers.

[Luke 20:37] **And the fact that the dead rise again Moses also showed at the bush, when he called the Lord the God of Abraham, and the God of Isaac, and the God of Jacob.** *To prove the truth of the resurrection he could have used other far clearer examples, among which is this: 'The dead will live, and they will rise again, who are in their graves'.*[453] *So the question arises why the Lord wanted to offer this testimony which seems ambiguous and does not sufficiently pertain to the truth of the resurrection.*[454] But the Sadducees *accepted only the five books of Moses,*

---

451 Jerome, *Commentarii in Matheum* 3 (CCSL 77:206.1831–36).
452 Augustine, *Quaestiones euang.* 2.49 (CCSL 44B:115.2–4).
453 Isa. 26:19.
454 Jerome, *Commentarii in Matheum* 3 (CCSL 77:206.1842–49).

rejecting the predictions of the prophets. It was foolish, therefore, to offer /360/ testimonies from those sources whose authority they did not accept. Then, to prove the eternity of souls, he gives the example from Moses: 'I am the God of Abraham, and the God of Isaac, and the God of Jacob',[455] and immediately adds:[456]

[Luke 20:38] **For he is not the God of the dead, but of the living,** ... So that after he proved that souls endure after death, which among other things the Sadducees denied, *for it could not have been that he was the God of those who had no continuing existence at all, the resurrection of the bodies which carried out good or evil deeds with souls was introduced as a logical consequence.*[457]

[Luke 20:38b] **For to him all are alive.** That is to say, all those whose Lord is God.[458] They are alive to him with a true life indeed, whereby the just live even when they die in body. Of this the Lord says elsewhere: *He who believes in me, although he is dead, will live.*[459] Believe, therefore, and even if you are dead, you will live. But if you do not believe, you are also dead even when you are alive. For the widow *who lives in pleasures, is dead while she is living.*[460]

[Luke 20:39] **And some of the scribes answering, said to him: Teacher, you have said well.**

244/2 [Luke 20:40] **And after that they did not dare to ask him any more questions.** The chief priests, *the Sadducees*, and the scribes *who sought an opportunity to trick him, and to find any word which would ensnare him, were silenced by his discourses, and did not question him anymore. But having comprehended him very clearly, they hand him over to the Roman authority. From this we understand that the poison of envy can indeed be overcome, but is hard to bring under control.*[461]

---

455 Exod. 3:6.
456 Jerome, *Commentarii in Matheum* 3 (CCSL 77:207.1856–62).
457 Jerome, *Commentarii in Matheum* 3 (CCSL 77:207.1862–66).
458 Cf. Ps. 143:15 (144:15).
459 John 11:25.
460 1 Tim. 5:6.
461 Jerome, *Commentarii in Matheum* 4 (CCSL 77:210.37–42).

BOOK FIVE                                                              565

Chapter 84

245/2 [Luke 20:41–44] **But he said to them: How can they say that Christ is the son of David? And David himself says in the book of Psalms: The Lord said to my Lord: Sit at my right hand, until I make your enemies your footstool. David therefore calls him Lord; and how can he be his son?** *Even today, the questioning of Jesus is useful to us in confronting the Jews. For these people, who believe that the Christ is about to come, assert that he is a human being pure and simple and a holy man of the race of David. Let us, therefore, instructed by the Lord, ask them this: if he is a simple human being and merely the son of David, how can David call him his Lord?*[462] They are not rebuked because they say that he is the son of David, but because they do not believe that he is the Son of God. Since indeed not only is he David's Lord in that he exists as God before the ages, but he also appeared as the son of David by being born as a man at the end of the ages. And the fact that his enemies are subjected by the Father signifies not the weakness of the Son, but the unity of their nature whereby the one works in the other. For the Son likewise subjects enemies to the Father, because he glorifies the Father on earth.

246/2 [Luke 20:45–46] **And in the hearing of all the people, he said to his disciples: Beware of the scribes, who desire to walk in long robes, and love salutations in the marketplace, and the first chairs in the synagogues, and the best places at /361/ feasts.** To walk in long robes means that they went about in public clothed in elegant garments. Among other things that *rich man* who *feasted sumptuously every day* is described to have sinned in this way.[463] But it should be noted that he does not prohibit those to whom it is proper from the rank of their office from being saluted in the marketplace and from sitting in the best seats or from dining well. Rather, he teaches that those who love these things for no good reason, whether they are available or not, should be avoided like the damned by all of the faithful. He impugns the soul, not the rank, by a just rigour, although even the rank does not lack blame, if the same people who wish to be called teachers in the seat of the Synagogue of Moses take part in disputes in the marketplace. Certainly, we are commanded to beware of persons longing for vain glory for two reasons, namely lest we be either led astray by their

---

462 Jerome, *Commentarii in Matheum* 4 (CCSL 77:209.10–15).
463 Luke 16:19.

hypocrisy, judging that the things they do are good, or inflamed by envy, in vain delighting to be praised for the good things which they feign to do. **247/8** [Luke 20:47] **They devour the houses of widows, feigning long prayer. These will receive greater damnation.** Not only did he say, '*They will receive damnation*', but he added '*greater*', to make known not only that those who pray *standing in corners, so that they may be seen by men*,[464] deserve damnation, but that those who, by doing these things at greater length, as if they are more pious, seek not only praises from men, but also money, are going to be punished with a more extensive damnation. For there are those who, feigning that they are just and of great merit in the presence of God, do not hesitate to receive money from any persons whatever who are weak and troubled by awareness of their own sins, as if they will be their patrons at the Judgement. And although the hand stretched out to the pauper customarily promotes prayers, those persons pass the night in prayers chiefly in order to steal the pauper's coin. The curse directed at Judas deservedly suits these people: *When he is judged, may he go out condemned, and may his prayer to turned to sin.*[465] He goes out condemned indeed when he is judged, and brings back his prayer to sin, who, held in great esteem among men now, in the divine Judgement not only finds that he is not able to intervene for others, but that his own merits cannot suffice for himself. On the contrary among his offences he pays the penalty of those very prayers by which he deceived human judgement.

[Luke 21:1] **And looking about, he saw that those who were casting their gifts into the gazophilacium were rich men.** *Since in the Greek language 'phylaxe' means 'to keep safe', and 'gaza' in the Persian tongue means 'wealth', a place where wealth is kept safe is customarily called a gazophilacium.*[466] It was a box, having an opening above, placed next to the altar on the right of those entering the house of the Lord, into which the priests who guarded the doors cast all the money which was brought to /362/ the temple of the Lord, and it was kept safe for the restoration of the temple. Read Chronicles.[467] And even now anyone who scrutinizes those praying in the house of the Lord also keeps an eye out for those bearing

---

464 Matt. 6:5.
465 Ps. 108:7 (109:7). The typological association of this verse with Judas, which Bishop Challoner accepted in his eighteenth-century notes to the Douay-Rheims translation of the Vulgate, must have already been a commonplace in Bede's day.
466 Gregory, *Hom. in Hiezech.* 2.6.2 (CCSL 142:295.15–17).
467 Cf. 4 Kings 12:9–12; 2 Chron. 24:8–12.

gifts, and praises any whom he sees to be worthy, and condemns any whom he sees to be wicked.[468]

[Luke 21:2–3] **And he saw also a certain poor widow casting in two little brass coins. And he said: Truly I say to you that this poor widow has cast in more than all of them.** On a moral level, this passage shows us how anything is acceptable which we offer in good spirit to God, who without a doubt judges the heart and not the substance, and weighs carefully not how much is offered in one's offering, but from how much. Furthermore, in accordance with the laws of allegory, the rich men who were casting their gifts into the gazophilacium signify the Jews puffed up by the righteousness of the Law, while the poor widow on the other hand signifies the simple purity of the Church. She is rightly called poor, because she cast aside both the spirit of pride and sins just like the wealth of the world. She is truly a widow, because her husband endured death for her sake, and lives now in the sanctuary of heaven, hidden from her eyes, as if in another land. She casts these two little brass coins into the gazophilacium, because in the sight of divine Majesty, whereby the offerings of our work are kept safe like coins signed and sealed and in a specific number, she brings either the love of God and neighbour, or the gifts of her faith and prayer. These are small in respect of their own weakness, but received by the worth of pious devotion, and surpass all the works of the proud Jews.

[Luke 21:4] **For all of these have out of their abundance cast into the offerings of God, but she out of her want has cast in all her living that she had.** Out of his abundance the Jew casts into the offerings of God, who trusting in his righteousness prays *thus with himself: God, I give you thanks that I am not like other men, robbers, unjust,* and so forth.[469] But the Church casts into the offerings of God all her living, who understands that all that sustains life is not of her own deserving, but the gifts of God, saying: *God, be merciful to me, a sinner.*[470] And elsewhere: *I will keep my strength to you, for you, God, are my protector. My God, his mercy will prevent me.*[471]

Here ends Book Five of the Commentary on Luke. /363/

---

468 On Bede's understanding of Christian clergy as the successors of the temple's priestly hierarchy, see O'Brien, *Bede's Temple*, 115–20.
469 Luke 18:11.
470 Luke 18:13.
471 Ps. 58:10–11 (59:9–10).

# VI

[Luke 21:5-24:53]

Here begins Book Six.

When Solomon, the wisest of kings, built a temple to the Lord as an image of Christ and the Church, he also warned in advance with seemly symbolic examples, among other things, that all that symbolic foreshadowing and so to say allegory of types would be utterly destroyed when the truth and light behind all that was signified in a shadowy manner drew nigh and appeared.[1] For indeed after the house of incomparable work of stone, wood, and gold was made, *he sent, and, as a symbol of the Gentiles who were destined to believe, brought Hiram from Tyre, the son of a widow woman* (no doubt, of that woman who, above, by casting two coins into the gazophilacium, is praised for having cast more than all the others) *of the tribe of Naphtali, whose father was a Tyrian, an artificer in brass, and full of wisdom and understanding, and skill.*[2] And *all the vessels that Hiram made for King Solomon for the house of the Lord were of fine brass. In the plains of the Jordan the king cast them in clay earth.*[3] For he who made all his vessels not with beaten, but with cast work, evidently first fashioned an image from potter's clay in the likeness of each vessel. This was indeed necessary, until the work on the vessel was completed, but afterwards it was not only not fit for any use, but in order for the perfection of the vessel to appear, it doubtless had to be smashed. Therefore, it is as though the sacred rites of the Law come first like a clay mould, so that the gifts of gospel truth may follow like vessels of fine brass. Let the common earthenware pot fashioned for the occasion wear away, so that the splendour of the permanent ornamental vessel which lay hidden may be exposed to view. Let the ashes of a heifer,

---

1 On this prologue as a 'miniature' *De Templo*, see O'Brien, *Bede's Temple*, 183-84; Introduction, 60.
2 3 Kings 7:13-14.
3 3 Kings 7:45-46.

which sanctified the impure,[4] be removed, and let the cross of Christ, which may redeem the world, be proclaimed. With the passage of time, when the sea of brass[5] in whose vivifying wave all those about to enter the Church would be baptized, and when the twin columns of the Law bearing lilies on their capitals[6] would strengthen on this side and that the gate of the sheep devoted to Christ, and when the twice-five hand-basins of our works were prepared for the cleansing of the sacrificial victims,[7] the earthenware which concealed these things for a long time in the plains is broken apart so that thereafter countless thousands of vessels of election might be brought to the Temple mount. That is, with the impending proclamation of the Lord's passion, by which the sacraments of the Church were revealed which were formerly hidden by the covering of the letter, the clay earth little by little is loosened, /364/ and that shadow that concealed heavenly secrets now begins to be destroyed. Hence it is proper that after the offering of the poor widow, that is, after the faith of the Church had been praised by the mouth of the Lord, the evangelist goes on to add:

### Chapter 85

**248/2** [Luke 21:5-6] **And when some were saying about the temple, that it was adorned with goodly stones and gifts, he said: These things which you see, the days will come in which a stone will not be left upon a stone that will not be thrown down.** For *Jerusalem was at first that great royal city, where the famous temple had been erected to God. But afterwards, he who was the true temple of God came,* and *began to reveal the mysteries of the heavenly Jerusalem; the earthly city was destroyed when the heavenly one appeared, and in that temple there did not remain a stone upon a stone. At first there was a high-priest purifying the people with the blood of bulls and goats; but from him came the true High-Priest, who* would purify *believers with his own blood. That first high-priest is no more, nor is any place left for him. At first there was an altar, and sacrifices were celebrated; but the true Lamb came, who offered himself*

---

4 Cf. Hebr. 9:13.
5 Cf. 4 Kings 25:13 ('sea of brass'); 3 Kings 7:23 ('molten sea'). See above, Book 1, n. 274.
6 Cf. 3 Kings 7:19.
7 Cf. 3 Kings 7:38–39.

*as the sacrificial victim to God,*[8] *all those things, established as it were temporarily, ceased. For that reason,* certainly, *the divine dispensation took care that both the city itself, and the temple, and all those things were overthrown at one and the same time, lest perchance anyone still a suckling infant in the faith, if he saw those things enduring, should be snatched away by the very sight of the various forms while dazzled in amazement at the ritual of sacrifice and at the arrangement of the services. But God, foreseeing our weakness and wishing his Church to be multiplied, caused all those things to be overthrown and completely removed, so that when those things had beyond any doubt ceased to exist, we might believe these things to which those types had pointed the way to be true.*[9]

**249/2** [Luke 21:7] **And they asked him, saying: Teacher, when will these things be, and what will be the sign when they will begin to come to pass?** Since the Lord had replied openly to those who praised the buildings of the temple that all these things were going to be destroyed, the disciples, when he is sitting on mount Olivet, as Matthew and Mark testify,[10] privately ask the time and the signs of the predicted destruction.

[Luke 21:8] **He said: Take care that you are not led astray; for many will come in my name, saying, I am he, and, The time is at hand. Do not therefore go after them.** At the impending ruin of Jerusalem many leaders appeared, who announced that they were Christ and that the time of liberation was now approaching. Many heretical leaders in the Church came forth even in the times of the apostles, who, among many other things contrary to the truth, preached that the day of the Lord was at hand. The Apostle condemned these people in his letters to the Thessalonians.[11] /365/ Many antichrists came in the name of Christ, the first of whom was Simon Magus, *to whom,* as we read in the Acts of the Apostles, *they all,* who were in Samaria, *gave ear from the least to the greatest, saying: This man is the power of God, which is called great,* because *for a long time he had bewitched them with his magical practices.*[12]

[Luke 21:9] **And when you hear of wars and insurrections, do not be terrified. These things must first come to pass, but the end is not yet at hand.** Wars pertain to enemies; insurrections, to citizens. It is a fact

---

8 Cf. Hebr. 9:11–14.
9 Origen, *In Leviticum Homiliae* (GCS 29:441.16–442.9). See Introduction, 27–28.
10 Cf. Matt. 24:3; Mark 13:3–4.
11 Cf. 2 Thess. 2:2.
12 Acts 8:10–11; cf. Jerome, *Commentarii in Matheum* 4 (CCSL 77:223.389–94).

that both of these abounded enough and more than enough in the time of the Lord's passion among the people of the Jews, who chose in place of the Saviour a seditious robber.[13] But the apostles are warned not to be terrified by these precursory events, nor to abandon Jerusalem and Judea, because, of course, the end was not at hand, which would be put off rather to the fortieth year,[14] that is, the desolation of the country and the final destruction of the city and the temple would follow.

[Luke 21:10–11] **Then he said to them: Nation will rise against nation, and kingdom against kingdom. And there will be great earthquakes in various places, and plagues, and famines,** ... It is a fact that these things happened word for word before the end of the devastation of the temple, that is, at the time of the Jewish insurrection.[15] But *kingdom against kingdom, and a plague of those whose speech spreads like a cancer,*[16] *and a famine of hearing the word of God,*[17] *and an upheaval of the whole world, and a separation from the true faith,* can *be understood* likewise *among the heretics, who, continually fighting among themselves, give victory to the Church.*[18]

[Luke 21:11b] **And terrors from heaven, and there will be great signs.** Anyone who reads the history of Josephus will find that these things were fulfilled at the same time. For not only did a star like a sword, as he asserts, hang for a whole year over Jerusalem and terrify the anxious citizens with an unlucky omen, and in like manner for forty days chariots and armed horsemen were seen to rush about through the air and imitate the behaviour of warriors, but also a calf, brought to the sacrifice, brought forth a lamb at the hands of those who slew it.[19] Why these things deservedly happened is immediately added, when it is said:

250/1   [Luke 21:12] **But before all these things, they will lay their hands on you and persecute you, delivering you up to the synagogues and into prisons, handing you over to kings and governors, for my name's sake.** This indeed was either the sole or the chief cause of destruction for the

---

13 Cf. Luke 23:18–19; John 18:40.
14 See above, Bede's commentary on Luke 13:2–3, and note.
15 Ps.-Jerome, *Expositio euangeliorum* (PL 30:576B) interprets 'nation against nation' as 'the [Jewish] nation against the Romans'.
16 Cf. 1 Tim. 2:17.
17 Cf. Amos 8:11.
18 Jerome, *Commentarii in Matheum* 4 (CCSL 77:224.409–13).
19 Cf. Josephus, *Bellum Iudaicum* 6.5 & 3. Ps.-Jerome, *Expostio euangeliorum* PL30.576B mentions the chariots and the 'star like a sword'.

BOOK SIX                                                                 573

Jewish people, because after the killing of the Lord Saviour, they tormented both the heralds and the confessors of his name with wicked cruelty. /366/

[Luke 21:13] **And it will happen to you for a testimony.** *Whose testimony, unless it be of those who either inflict death by persecution or who do not imitate what they see? Indeed, the death of the righteous sustains the good and serves as a testimony to the wicked, so that in consequence the wicked may perish without excuse, while the elect take hold of a model for living. But after hearing about so many terrors, the hearts of the weak could be disturbed, and therefore a consolation is immediately added:*[20]

251/2 [Luke 21:14–15] **Lay it up therefore in your hearts, not to premeditate how you will answer; for I will give you a mouth and wisdom, which all your adversaries will not be able to resist and contradict.** *It is as if he openly says to his weak members: Do not be afraid, do not be overly frightened. You are advancing to the struggle, but I am doing the fighting. You are uttering the words, but I am the one who is speaking.*[21]

[Luke 21:16–17] **And you will be betrayed by your parents and brothers and relatives and friends, and some of you they will put to death. And you will be hated by all men for my name's sake.** *Evils brought upon by strangers inflict lesser grief; but those torments rage more in us which we suffer from those whose hearts we trusted, because along with bodily injuries we are tormented by the evils of lost love. But because the things foretold about the affliction of death are hard to bear, the consolation of the joy of resurrection is immediately added, when it is said:*[22]

[Luke 21:18] **But not a hair of your head will perish.** *We know that when the flesh is cut it feels pain, but when hair is cut it does not feel pain. Therefore, he says to his martyrs: 'Not a hair of your head will perish', meaning: Why do you fear that what feels pain when it is cut may perish, when that part in you that does not feel pain when it is cut cannot perish?*[23]

In another interpretation: Not a hair of the head of the disciples of the Lord will perish, because not only are all of the deeds and words of the saints, of whom it is said: *The Lord keeps all their bones*,[24] strong, but

---

20 Gregory, *Hom. in Euang.* 2.35.2–3 (CCSL 141:323.65–71).
21 Gregory, *Hom. in Euang.* 2.35.3 (CCSL 141:323.74–77).
22 Gregory, *Hom. in Euang.* 2.35.3–4 (CCSL 141:323.79–83; 324.98–100).
23 Gregory, *Hom. in Euang.* 2.35.4 (CCSL 141:324.100–04).
24 Ps. 33:21 (34:20).

also the fleeting, if I may call it so, and most insignificant thoughts of the faithful, which come forth from the hidden root of the heart, like the hair of the head from the brain, will be preserved, and in the presence of the just Judge will be presented with a worthy reward. Hence the Prophet, in order to show how acceptable likewise to the Lord are the merits of good thoughts, rightly says: *And the remainders of the thoughts will take a holiday from you.*[25] Hence also the Nazarites under the Law at the time of consecration are commanded to grow their hair,[26] and it is said that no razor came over the head of Samuel.[27] But on the contrary a captive woman in order to be able to marry an Israelite husband[28] and a man cleansed of leprosy in order to deserve communion with the Church[29] are instructed /367/ to shave all the hairs of their body, because certainly all the thoughts of the wise that are good, pleasing, and perfect, are preserved eternally, and are their reward from the Lord. But the thought of the deeds of the foolish and the wicked, like a root unworthy of the eyes of God, ought to be cut off by penance.

[Luke 21:19] **And you will possess your souls in patience**. *The possession of the soul by the virtue of patience is laid down for this reason, because patience is the root and guardian of all the virtues. Indeed, we possess our souls through patience, because when we learn to govern ourselves, we begin to possess that very thing that we are.* For we were created marvellously, so that reason may possess the soul, and the soul may possess the body. But the right of the soul to possess the body is removed if the soul is not first possessed by reason. Therefore, the Lord showed that patience is the guardian of our condition, who taught that by it we possess ourselves. But *true patience is to bear the evils inflicted by others with equanimity, and also not to be stirred by vexation against the one who inflicts evils. For he who bears the evils inflicted by his neighbour, so that he suffers silently, but seeks a time of suitable retribution, does not exercise patience, but makes a show of it.*[30]

---

25 Ps. 75:11 (76:10).
26 Cf. Num. 6:5.
27 Cf. 1 Sam. 1:11.
28 Cf. Deut. 21:10–13.
29 Lev. 14:8.
30 Gregory, *Hom. in Euang.* 2.35.4 (CCSL 141:324.106–09; 109–13).

## Chapter 86

**252**/10 [Luke 21:20] **And when you see Jerusalem surrounded by an army, then know that its desolation is at hand.** Hitherto the words of the Lord tell of the things that were going to be for [the next] forty years, with the end not yet at hand; now they tell of the end itself of desolation carried out by the Roman army.

**253**/2 [Luke 21:21] **Then let those who are in Judea flee to the mountains.** The *Ecclesiastical History* relates that all those in Judea who were Christians, forewarned by the Lord, withdrew from there and took up residence in a certain town by the name of Pella, until the desolation of Judea was completed.[31]

[Luke 21:21b–22] **And let those who are in its midst depart, and do not let those who are in the lands enter into it. For these are the days of vengeance, that all things may be fulfilled that are written.** It seems to be a suitable admonition, that those who are outside Jerusalem not enter, but how may those who are in the midst depart, when the city is already surrounded by an army? Unless perhaps we say that what he prefixed, *'Then'*, that is, *Then, let those who are in Judea flee*, pertains not to the time of the siege itself, but to the time just before the siege, when the Roman soldiery first began to spread itself through the land of Galilee and Samaria, so that 'then' everyone might hasten to flee, while there was still time for flight. And *these are the days of vengeance*, seeking, that is to say, vengeance for the Lord's blood. /368/

**254**/2 [Luke 21:23] **But woe to those who are pregnant and to those who are nursing in those days.** In the face of captivity, woe to those who are pregnant and to those who are nursing, or suckling, as some translate it. Either their wombs or their hands, encumbered with the burden of children, greatly impede the need for flight.[32] Read the narrative of Kings, where the wife of Jonathan, while seeking to escape the evil of captivity by a hasty flight, caught up her son, who had fallen from her bosom, thus leaving him permanently lamed.[33]

**255**/2 [Luke 21:23b] **For there will be great distress in the land and wrath against this people.** This distress and wrath clings to that people

---

31 Cf. Eusebius, *Hist. eccl.* 3.5 (GCS 9.1:197.10–15).
32 Cf. Jerome, *Commentarii in Matheum* 4 (CCSL 77:227.478–81).
33 Cf. 2 Sam. 4:4 (Bede assumes that the 'nurse' who dropped the boy in the OT narrative was Jonathan's wife).

who are scattered right up to the present day throughout all the nations like an inseparable companion, yet it must not be believed that it is going to cling forever. For afterwards the Lord shows the sequence of this same distress or wrath, saying:

**256**/10 [Luke 21:24] **And they will fall by the edge of the sword and be led away as captives among all nations, and Jerusalem will be trampled on by the Gentiles,** ... In accordance with the prophetic text that proclaims: *In your anger, you will remember mercy*,[34] he immediately went on to say:

[Luke 21:24b] **Until the times of the nations are fulfilled.** The times of the nations are certainly those which the Apostle recalls when he says: *That blindness in part has happened in Israel, until the fullness of the Gentiles comes in, and so all Israel will be saved.*[35] When Israel obtains its promised salvation, it is hoped, perhaps not rashly, that it will also return to its native soil and rejoice in the possession and habitation of its former chief city, because it is said that it was not going to be distressed in this way forever, but until the times of the nations are fulfilled. What follows, after the times of the nations have been fulfilled and Israel has thus been saved, the Lord reveals in sequence. For according to Matthew, the disciples kept asking about this, seeking to know not only the time of overturning the temple, but also the sign of his coming, and of the consummation of the world.[36]

**257**/2 [Luke 21:25] **And there will be signs in the sun, and in the moon, and in the stars; and upon the earth distress of nations, by reason of the confusion of the roaring of the sea and the waves,** ... Because as the Lord makes known in the following verses, with the coming of the universal Judgement, heaven and earth will pass away. As we read in the Apocalypse of John, by the same impending Judgement the sea will rightly be no more,[37] the roaring of the sea and the waves is confounded, the whole world is corrupted by the inhabitants distressing each other, and the chief lights of heaven, with their rays shocked by the new horror, veil their troubled faces. Just as trees impelled to fall customarily send ahead of time signs that they are breaking and moving, so as the end approaches, the elements quaking as it were /369/ with fear stagger and tremble. Therefore, what Matthew

---

34 Hab. 3:2.
35 Rom. 11:25–26.
36 Cf. Matt. 24:3.
37 Cf. Rev. 21:1.

says: *The sun will be darkened and the moon will not give her light, and the stars will fall from heaven*,[38] signifies that the Judgement is really at hand when at the appearance of the true light of glory, all the lights of the world are comparable to darkness and shadows. But what Luke says: *There will be signs in the sun, and in the moon, and in the stars*, indicates forerunners of approaching Judgement, messengers as it were. One of these is that statement of the Prophet: *The sun will be turned into darkness, and the moon into blood, before the great and manifest day of the Lord comes*.[39] Likewise what Luke says: *And upon the earth distress of nations*, I believe is the same as what Matthew says, describing the times of the Antichrist: *For there will be then great tribulation, such as has not been from the beginning of the world until now, nor will there be*.[40] And what Luke adds: *By reason of the confusion of the roaring of the sea and the waves*, heralds, among other mutable things of the world, what John understood, namely the fact that the sea was going to go away.

[Luke 21:26] **With men withering away from fear and expectation of what will come upon the whole world. For the powers of heaven will be moved.** I believe that this statement points to the advent itself of the Judge, when, according to the parable found in another passage, all the virgins, both the wise and the foolish, are aroused by an unexpected cry and trim their lamps, that is, they inwardly count up their deeds, for because of them they await with the greatest fear the outcome impending at that very moment of the eternal Judgement.[41] For up to this point nearly the whole world is going to act without any fear of the Judge, as the Apostle witnesses, who says: *For when they say, peace and security, then sudden destruction will come upon them*.[42] So then, with the fear and expectation of the strict Judgement coming upon the whole world, many who seemed to flourish in this world will wither away when they realize that they are without good fruit. Then the faith that had bloomed without works, probed by the fire of the just Judge, will shrivel up. It is no wonder that human beings, who are earthbound either by nature or by understanding, are disturbed at his judgement, at the prospect of which the very powers of heaven themselves, that is, the angelic powers, tremble, as the blessed Job also attests, who

---

38 Matt. 24:29.
39 Joel 2:31 blended with Acts 2:20.
40 Matt. 24:21.
41 Cf. Matt. 25:6–7.
42 1 Thess. 5:3.

578   BEDE: COMMENTARY ON THE GOSPEL OF LUKE

says: *The pillars of heaven tremble and are struck with fear at his rebuke.*[43] What do wooden boards do, therefore, when pillars tremble? What does a twig of the desert suffer, when a cedar of paradise is shaken to its roots? **258/2** [Luke 21:27] **And then they will see the Son of man coming in a cloud with great power and majesty.** *They are going to see in power and majesty the one whom they did not want to hear when he was in a condition of humility, so that then they will feel his power all the more severely, as now they do not bend the neck of their /370/ heart to his suffering. But because these things are said against the damned, his words are immediately turned to the consolation of the elect. For this is added:*[44]


Chapter 87

[Luke 21:28] **But when these things begin to happen, look up, and lift up your heads, because your redemption is at hand.** *When,* he says, *the blows of the world become more frequent, when the outraged powers announce the terror of the Judgement, lift up your heads, that is, cheer your hearts, because when the world which is not your friend is ended, the redemption that you sought is at hand. Indeed, in Sacred Scripture 'head' often means 'mind', because just as the limbs are governed by the head, so thoughts are ordered by the mind. Accordingly, to lift up our heads is to raise up our minds to the joys of the heavenly fatherland.*[45]

The Lord *makes clear by an insightful comparison that the world ought to be trampled upon and despised.*[46] For this follows:

[Luke 21:29-31] **And he told them a parable. See the fig tree and all the trees. At the time when they produce their fruit, you know that summer is near. So, when you see these things taking place, know also that the kingdom of God is at hand.** Therefore, he teaches *openly that just as we know how close summer is by the fruit of the trees, so we know how close the kingdom of God is from the destruction of the world. These words surely show that the fruit of the world is destruction. For it increases only to fall; it sprouts only so that whatever it puts forth may be annihilated by*

---

43  Job 26:11.
44  Gregory, *Hom. in Euang.* 1.1.2–3 (CCSL 141:7.42–46).
45  Gregory, *Hom. in Euang.* 1.1.3 (CCSL 141:7.49–55).
46  Gregory, *Hom. in Euang.* 1.1.3 (CCSL 141:8.76–77).

BOOK SIX 579

*disasters. And the kingdom of God is aptly compared to summer, because then the clouds of our sorrow pass, and the eternal days of life gleam with the brightness of the sun. All these things are confirmed with great certitude, when the statement is added which says:*[47]

[Luke 21:32] **Amen, I say to you, this generation will not pass away until all things have happened.** *Indeed, the Lord summons us to pay particular attention to what he proclaims in this way. In a certain manner, 'Amen, I say to you', is so to speak his oath. For Amen means 'true', and yet it is not translated, although it could have been said, I tell you a truth. But neither the Greek nor the Latin translator dared to do this. Thus, 'Amen' has remained and is not translated, in order to have the honour of cloaking a mystery, not that it might be disavowed, but so that it not be cheapened by being disrobed.* Therefore, *the Truth says, I say to you what is true, which certainly even if he did not say it, he could not lie at all. Nevertheless, he calls us to attention, he is emphatic, he arouses those who are as it were asleep, he makes them intent, he does not want them to be condemned,*[48] saying: *Amen, I say to you, this generation will not pass away until all things have happened.* And by 'generation' he means either the whole human race or the people of the Jews in particular.

[Luke 21:33] **Heaven and earth will pass away, but my words will not pass away.** /371/ We must understand that the heaven that will pass away is not the celestial or starry heaven, but the airy sky, which gives its name to the 'birds of the sky' and the 'clouds of the sky'.[49] Peter is a witness, who says: *That the heavens were before, and the earth out of water, and through water, consisting by the word of God, whereby the world that then was, perished. But the heavens and the earth which are now, by the same word are kept in store, reserved for fire, until the Day of Judgement and perdition of the ungodly men.*[50] He plainly teaches that there are no other heavens that are going to perish by fire than those that were once destroyed by water, that is, these empty and cloudy spaces of windy air. For the water of the flood that rose as much as fifteen cubits above the summits of the

---

47 Gregory, *Hom. in Euang.* 1.1.3–4 (CCSL 141:8.80–89).
48 Augustine, *In Iohannis euang.* 41.3–4 (CCSL 36:359.10–15; 1–4).
49 Cf. Gregory, *Hom. in Euang.* 2.29.5 (CCSL 141:249); cf. also Bede's discussion of this point in *DTR* 70 (trans. Wallis, *The Reckoning of Time*, 243–44) and his commentary on Rev. 21:1 (ed. Gryson, 518–9; trans. Wallis, 259–260). Similar views are expressed by Primasius, *Commentarius in Apocalypsin* 21.2–9, 11–19 (Bede's direct source in his Revelation commentary) and by Augustine, *De civitate Dei* 20.16 (726.7–727.34).
50 2 Pet. 3:5–7.

mountains must be believed to have reached beyond the confines of air and ether.[51] And wherever it was able to reach, the fire of Judgement without doubt will also reach there in accordance with the aforesaid statement of Peter's.

If *heaven and earth will pass away*, let Ecclesiastes tell how it can be moved: *One generation passes away, and another generation comes, but the earth stands forever.*[52] Clearly heaven and earth *pass away with respect to what we now see, but nevertheless they remain standing in their essence forever. For the fashion of this world passes away.*[53] And the angel says *to John: 'There will be a new heaven and a new earth'.*[54] *These, of course, are not different things that are going to be created, but are the same things renewed. Therefore, heaven and earth will both pass away and continue to exist, because they are cleansed by fire from their present appearance, and yet they are always preserved in their own nature. Hence it is said by the Psalmist: You will change them, and they will be changed.*[55] *Indeed, they announce that ultimate change to us even now by means of the changes which alternate incessantly for our benefit. For the earth departs from its appearance during winter's aridity, and turns green with vernal moisture. Heaven is daily obscured by the darkness of night, and is renewed by the day's splendour. Therefore, in both cases let the faithful consider that these things perish, and nevertheless are restored by renewal, things which it is well known are continually remade now, as for example in an eclipse.*[56]

**259**/10 [Luke 21:34–35] **And take heed to yourselves, lest perhaps your hearts be overcharged with surfeiting and drunkenness, and the cares of this life and that day come upon you suddenly. For as a snare will it come upon all that sit upon the face of the whole earth.** O foolish obstinacy of the human heart, which foresees the lamentable end of cupidity, drunkenness, and surfeiting, while the Judge himself takes no action, but like a wicked servant scorns /372/ the edict of the eternal King after he had learned it. Certainly, if any skilled and learned physician gave orders to us, saying: Take heed to yourselves, that none of you partake too

---

51 Cf. Gen. 7:20.
52 Eccles. 1:4.
53 1 Cor. 7:31.
54 Cf. Rev. 21:1.
55 Cf. Ps. 101:27 (102:26).
56 Gregory, *Moralia* 17.9 (CCSL 143A:858.21–33).

BOOK SIX 581

greedily of a potion of (for instance) this or that herb, because if he does so, sudden destruction will come upon him, everyone would follow the orders of the physician who forewarned them with great care, lest by tasting the forbidden potion they perish. But now the Saviour and Lord of souls as well as bodies orders that the herb of drunkenness and surfeiting be avoided, and that lethal potions of worldly cures[57] (so to speak) be avoided. And yet how many of us do not fear not only being hurt but even being destroyed by these things? I believe this is simply because they disdain to grant to the words of the Lord the faith that they grant to the words of the physician. For if they believed, they would surely fear by believing, and by fearing would guard against the impending danger. But on the contrary by being dull they prove what was rightly said: *When the Son of man comes, will he find faith on earth, do you think?*[58]

[Luke 21:36] **Watch, therefore, praying at all times that you may be accounted worthy to escape all these things that are to come and to stand before the Son of man.** He who desires to stand before the Son of man and to serve him day and night in his temple in accordance with the Apocalypse of John,[59] and not to be cast off from his sight, cursed, into the eternal fire, ought not only to refrain from worldly allurements, but also to pray and to watch: and he should do this not on certain fixed days, but at all times, according to what the Psalm says: *I will bless the Lord at all times, his praise will always be in my mouth.*[60] For truly in this way he will deserve to dwell in the house of the Lord and praise him eternally.

[Luke 21:37–38] **And in the daytime, he was teaching in the temple, but at night, going out, he stayed in the mount that is called Olivet. And all the people came early in the morning to him in the temple to hear him.** The things that the Lord orders by his words he confirms by his examples. For he urges us, before the sudden coming of the universal Judgement, before our unforeseeable death, to disregard both the pleasures and cares of this life, and to keep watch and pray. And he himself, as the time of his passion approaches, devotes himself to teaching through vigils and prayers as well as by example; and he

---

57 *curarum saecularium*: Bede is exploiting the double meaning of *cura* as 'care, concern, worry' and 'medical treatment'. The poison of 'worldly cares' is set against Christ's medicine as 'worldly cures'.
58 Luke 18:8.
59 Cf. Rev. 7:15.
60 Ps. 33:2 (34:1).

shows to those who are near him, by word and deed, that the way of truth is to worthily keep vigil for God, stimulating the faith of those for whom he would suffer by this works, and entrusting them to the Father by prayer. When we live *soberly, and justly, and godly*[61] in prosperity, but in adversity /373/ never despair of the loftiness of divine mercy, we assuredly teach every day in the temple, because we display the ideal image of good works to the faithful. But we stay in the mount of Olivet, because in the darkness of distress we are refreshed with the consolation of spiritual joy, in accordance with the one who said: *But I, as a fruitful olive tree in the house of God, have hoped in the mercy of my God*;[62] that is, as one who distributes the fruit of mercy to those whom he can, I do not doubt that mercy will be shown to me by the Lord. And likewise, all the people come early in the morning to hear us, when the children of light imitate us either by casting away *the works of darkness* or with the clouds of afflictions by the grace of God overcome, by walking *honestly, as in the day, not in rioting and drunkenness*.[63]

**260/1** [Luke 22:1] **Now the festival day of unleavened bread, which is called the Passover, was at hand.** Passover [*pascha*], which is called *'phase'* in Hebrew, is not named after the passion, as many think, but from *'passing over'*, for the destroyer, seeing blood on the doors of the Israelites, passed over and did not strike them, or else the Lord himself, offering help to his people, strode down from on high.[64] The evangelist John, seeking the divine mystery of this word, says more sublimely: *Jesus knowing that his hour had come that he should pass over from this world to the Father.*[65] By this he plainly declares that the day of this festival is called allegorically 'passing over' in the Law, because on that day either the Lamb of God, who took away the sins of the world,[66] was going to pass over himself from this world, or he was going to lead us by a salvific passing over from Egyptian servitude, as it were. Certainly, according to the letter of the Old Testament there is this difference between the Passover and the feast of unleavened bread that only the day on which the lamb was sacrificed in the evening

---

61 Titus 2:12.
62 Ps. 51:10 (52:8).
63 Rom. 13:12–13.
64 Jerome, *Commentarii in Matheum* 4 (CCSL 77:245.976–81); cf. Exod. 12:23 & 27.
65 John 13:1: Bede perhaps assumes that his auditors know that this clause in John 13:1 is immediately preceded by the phrase: 'Before the festival day of the Passover'.
66 Cf. John 1:29.

is called the Passover, that is, the fourteenth day of the moon of the first month.[67] But on the fifteenth day of the moon, when the Exodus from Egypt took place, the festival of unleavened bread succeeded. Its celebration was decreed for seven days, that is, up to the twenty-first day of the same month, in the evening.[68] But in the Gospel, Scripture is accustomed to use the day of unleavened bread for the Passover and the Passover for the day of unleavened bread. For Luke says: *The festival day of unleavened bread, which is called the Passover.* Likewise, John, when it was a matter of the first day of the feast of unleavened bread, that is, the fifteenth day of the moon, says: *And they did not go into the hall, so that they might not be defiled, but in order that they might eat the Passover.*[69] Because surely both the day of the Passover was commanded to be celebrated with unleavened bread, and we are commanded always to pass over from this world, making us, as it were, /374/ the eternal Passover. Indeed, after the sacrifice of the lamb in the evening on the first day, the seven days of the feast of unleavened bread follow in order. Because Jesus Christ suffered for us in the flesh once in the fullness of times, he commands that we have to live for the whole time of this world, which is accomplished in seven days, *with the unleavened bread of sincerity and truth.*[70] And he admonishes us always to flee with all our strength the pleasures of the world as if the bonds of Egypt, and from a worldly way of life to enter, as it were, a secret solitude, a path of virtues.

**261**/1 [Luke 22:2] **And the chief priests and the scribes sought how they might put Jesus to death, but they feared the people.** Matthew testifies that these things took place two days before the Passover, when the chief priests and the elders of the people and the scribes were gathered together in the courtyard of Caiaphas.[71] But they feared the people, *not fearing sedition, but taking care that he not be snatched from their hands by the help of the people.*[72]

---

67 Cf. Exod. 12:6. Bede devotes the entirety of chapter 63 to this question in *DTR* (trans. Wallis, *The Reckoning of Time*, 149–51.
68 Cf. Exod. 12:18–19.
69 John 18:28.
70 1 Cor. 5:8.
71 Cf. Matt. 26:2–3.
72 Jerome, *Commentarii in Matheum* 4 (CCSL 77:245.992–94).

## Chapter 88

**262/9 [Luke 22:3] And Satan entered into Judas, who was called Iscariot, one of the twelve.** John writes in his Gospel that *when the Lord had dipped the bread, he gave it to Judas Iscariot, the son of Simon. And after the morsel, Satan entered into him.*[73] But this does not contradict Luke, who relates that Satan had already entered Judas before the morsel, because Satan entered him now in order to ensnare him, whom afterwards he entered to possess him more fully who had already been handed over to him. Satan entered him now to tempt one who was as it were still averse, but then to drag him, who belonged to him as it were, to whatever wicked deeds he wished to be done.

**263/2 [Luke 22:4–5] And he went away and spoke with the chief priests and the magistrates about how he might betray him to them. And they were glad.** The fact that Luke said, *he went away and spoke*, shows that he formed the plan by the volition of his own wicked soul, not summoned by the chief priests, nor bound by any necessity.

**[Luke 22:5b–6] And they agreed to give him money. And he promised. And he sought an opportunity to betray him in the absence of the multitude.** Many people today shudder at Judas' crime – the fact that he betrayed his Lord and Teacher and God for money – as if it were monstrous and abominable, and yet they do not guard against it. For when they give false witness against anyone for a reward, they certainly deny the truth for money, they betray for money. For he himself said: *I am the truth.*[74] When they foul the fellowship of brotherhood with any plague of discord, they betray the Lord, because *God is love.*[75] Even if no one gives them money, they sell the Lord for pieces of silver, because they take on the image of the prince of the world, that is, portraits[76] of the old enemy, neglecting the image of the Creator in which they were created. For /375/ just as John the Baptist, who died not for confessing Christ, but for defending truth, nevertheless underwent martyrdom for Christ, because he did so for the truth, so on the other hand he who spurns the laws of love and truth certainly betrays Christ, who is the truth and love. This is especially

---

73  John 13:26–27.
74  John 14:6.
75  1 John 4:16.
76  'Portraits' here translates *exempla*, i.e., copies (of a pattern or matrix). Bede is alluding to the portrait head of the ruler stamped with a matrix onto a coin; to accept the pieces of silver was to take (on) this secular and hostile 'image'.

the case when he does not sin from weakness or deceiving ignorance, but like Judas seeks the opportunity in the absence of witnesses to exchange truth for falsehood, and virtue for crime.

[Luke 22:7–8] **And the day of unleavened bread came, on which it was necessary that the Passover should be killed. And he sent Peter and John, saying: Go and prepare the Passover for us that we may eat.** He calls the fourteenth day of the first month the day of unleavened bread of the Passover, when after the leaven had been set aside, the Passover, that is, the lamb, was killed in the evening according to custom, as was stated above.[77] Explaining this, the Apostle says: *For Christ who is our Passover has been sacrificed.*[78] For it was necessary for this Passover to be killed at that time, that is, consecrated by the Father's counsel and determination. Although he was crucified on the following day, that is, on the fifteenth day of the moon, nevertheless on this night on which the lamb was sacrificed, he entrusted his disciples with the mysteries of his flesh and blood that were to be celebrated, and, held and tied by the Jews, he sanctified the beginning of this very sacrifice, that is, of his passion.

[Luke 22:9] **But they said: Where do you want us to prepare?** *'We do not have a dwelling; we do not have a tent'. Let those who are preoccupied with building houses hear – those who plan encircling galleries and delight in the display of precious marbles and ceiling panels adorned with gold – let them recognize Christ, the Lord of all, who did not have a place where he might lay his head.*[79] *And therefore the disciples ask him: 'Where do you want us to prepare the Passover for you to eat?'*[80]

[Luke 22:10] **And he said to them: Behold, as you go into the city, a man will meet you there carrying a pitcher of water; follow him into the house where he enters.** It is a sign indeed of prescient divinity that,

---

77 Cf. Jerome, *Commentarii in Matheum* 4 (CCSL 77:248.1072–74); Exod. 12:6 & 18–19.
78 1 Cor. 5:7.
79 Cf. Matt. 8:20; Luke 9:58. O'Brien (*Bede's Temple*, 174–75) suggests that Bede is reproaching Wilfrid for his lavish taste in church architecture. Both the Wilfridians and Bede thought that Christian church should reflect the image of the biblical temple, but Bede seems to have had reservations about Wilfrid's materialistic reading of that image.
80 John Chrysostom, *De proditione Judae*: this is one of the genuine homilies of Chrysostom included in the collection of thirty-eight homilies used by Bede elsewhere (see Introduction n. 64 and Book 4, n. 417). This reference is provided by Love, 'Bede and John Chrysostom', 83–84, who cites the third edition of Erasmus's edition of *Opera d. Iohannis Chrysostomi ... quotquot per Graecorum exemplarium in Latinam linguam hactenus traduci potuerunt* (Basel: Froben, 1539), v. 3, 535–41.

speaking with his disciples, he knows what will happen elsewhere. And as the disciples are about to prepare the Passover, a man meets them carrying a pitcher of water, in order to show in a lovely way that the mystery of this Passover is going to be celebrated for the sake of the perfect cleansing of the whole world. Indeed, water signifies the bath of grace; the pitcher, the perfect measure. Therefore, they prepare the Passover, when the pitcher of water is carried in, because certainly the time is at hand for the worshippers of the true Passover, when the figurative blood is removed from the doorposts, and the baptism of the life-giving fountain is consecrated to the bearing away of sins.

[Luke 22:11] **And you will say to the owner of the house: The Teacher says to you, Where is the guest chamber, where I may eat the Passover with my disciples?** The names of both the man carrying the water and the owner of the house are deliberately /376/ omitted, to signify that an opportunity ought to be given to all who wish to celebrate the Passover, that is, to be instructed in the sacraments of Christ, and who seek to receive Christ in the guest chamber of their mind.

[Luke 22:12–13] **And he will show you a large upper room, furnished; and there prepare. And going, they found as he had said to them. And they prepared the Passover.** The large upper room is *the spiritual law that, emerging from the narrowness of the letter, receives the Saviour in a lofty place.*[81] For anyone who still serves the letter which kills,[82] who does not understand the lamb as anything other than a sheep, certainly celebrates the Passover at the lowest level, because he does not yet know how to comprehend the majesty of the Spirit. But anyone who follows the man carrying the pitcher of water, that is, the herald of grace, into the house of the Church, by climbing above the roof of the letter with the aid of the vivifying Spirit, prepares a room for Christ in the upper room of the mind, because he understands all the mysteries both of the Passover and of the other decrees of the Law that were written about him.

[Luke 22:14] **And when the hour had come, he sat down, and the twelve apostles with him.** He refers to the hour of eating the Passover, which, as has often been pointed out, in accordance with the edicts of the Law came to pass on the evening of the fourteenth day of the first month,[83] when the fifteenth day of the moon was already appearing over the earth.

---

81 Jerome, *Commentarii in Matheum* 4 (CCSL 77:249.1088–90).
82 Cf. 2 Cor. 3:6.
83 Cf. Exod. 12:18.

264/10 [Luke 22:15] **And he said to them: With desire, I have desired to eat this Passover with you before I suffer.** To begin with, he desires to eat the figurative Passover with his disciples, and thus to reveal the mysteries of his passion to the world, since he both shows his approval of the Passover of the old Law, and by teaching that it pertained to the symbolism of his dispensation, forbids it to be employed carnally any longer. Rather, with the shadow passing away, he shows that the light of the true Passover has already arrived. This is beautifully prefigured in the timing and sequence by which manna ceased in the time of Joshua, where it is written: *And they kept the Passover on the fourteenth day of the month in the evening in the plains of Jericho. And they ate on the next day of the produce of the land, unleavened bread, and barley meal, of the same year. And the manna ceased after they ate of the produce of the land, and the children of Israel did not use that food any more.*[84] Indeed, Joshua refreshed the people, whom he took over leading after the death of Moses, with the usual food of manna on the other side of the Jordan. He himself is refreshed with it, even though he knew and sometimes tasted the produce of the land of promise. Then he crosses the Jordan, carries out circumcisions with stone knives, and for three and a half months right up to the full day of the Passover God does not take away the accustomed manna.[85] Indeed, Joshua was appointed leader after the death of Moses, because Christ was made flesh when the Law was corrupted /377/ by the teachings of the Pharisees. Joshua feeds on manna on the far side of the Jordan and is fed, because up to the time of his baptism the Lord himself keeps the ceremonies of the Law himself and desires them to be kept by all. Joshua circumcises the people who have been led across the Jordan with stone, because after the celebration of the grace of baptism the Saviour cuts off likewise the allurements of thoughts by the rigour of the faith since the Law was not able to do this. And for three and a half years Christ did not cease from being nourished so to speak by the customary manna, or from observing the sacraments of the Law, although little by little appealing to heavenly promises, until having eaten the desired Passover at the prescribed time with his disciples, finally at daybreak he bestows the purest mysteries of his body and blood, consecrated on the altar of the cross[86] for the instruction of the faithful – the unleavened bread of the promised land, as it were. And then there follows:

84  Jos. 5:10–12.
85  Cf. Jos. 5:2–10.
86  See Introduction, 61.

**265/2** [Luke 22:16] **For I say to you that from this time I will not eat it, until it is fulfilled in the kingdom of God.** How well this harmonizes with the words of Joshua, who says: *And the children of Israel did not use that food any more, but they ate of the produce of the land of Canaan.*[87] Therefore he says: *I will not eat it, until it is fulfilled in the kingdom of God*, that is, I will by no means celebrate the Mosaic Passover any longer, until it is fulfilled by being spiritually understood by the Church. For the Church itself is the kingdom of God. Elsewhere he says of it to the disciples: *The kingdom of God is within you.*[88] In this kingdom the Lord even today eats the old Passover that has been fulfilled, when he performs spiritually in his members – that is, in the Church itself – those things that Moses ordered the ignorant people to observe in the flesh.

[Luke 22:17] **And having taken the cup, he gave thanks, and said: Take, and divide it among you.** And this cup pertains to that old Passover, to which he desired to put an end. Having taken it, he doubtless gave thanks because old things were going to pass away and all things were going to come new.[89]

[Luke 22:18] **For I say to you that I will not drink of the fruit of the vine until the kingdom of God comes.** This short phrase can certainly be taken in a straightforward sense, because he was not going to drink wine from this hour of the supper until the time of the resurrection when he was about to enter into the kingdom of God. For the apostle Peter testifies that he took food and drink afterwards, who says: *We who ate and drank with him after he arose again from the dead.*[90] But much more appropriately, just as he says above that he will not taste the figurative food of the lamb, so he says that he will not taste the figurative drink of the Passover any more until, after the glory of his resurrection has been revealed and made manifest, the faith of the kingdom of God reaches the world. This is so that, when you are spiritually transformed by the two greatest edicts of the Law, namely the paschal food and drink, you might learn that all the sacraments of the Law, or /378/ the commands that seemed to signify carnally, were now already going to be transferred to a spiritual observance.

**266/1** [Luke 22:19] **And taking bread, he gave thanks, and broke it and gave it to them, saying: This is my body, which is given for you. Do this**

---

87 Jos. 5:12.
88 Luke 17:21.
89 Cf. Isa. 42:9; 2 Cor. 5:17; Rev. 21:5.
90 Acts 10:41.

in remembrance of me. With the ending of the rites of the old Passover, which were done in remembrance of the ancient liberation from Egypt, he passed to the new Passover, which the Church desires to celebrate in remembrance of her redemption, so that, substituting the sacrament of his flesh and blood in the figure of the bread and wine for the flesh and blood of the lamb, he might show that he was the one to whom *The Lord has sworn and will not repent: You are a priest forever according to the order of Melchizedek.*[91] And he himself breaks the bread which he offers to show that the breaking of his body was not going to happen without his free will, but, as he elsewhere says, that he has the power of laying down his life, and of taking it up again.[92] And just as he had done concerning the old rites that were to end, so he gives thanks concerning the new ones that are to begin, bestowing on us at the same time an example for beginning and completing every good work by which the Father in heaven is glorified.[93] And the Apostle Paul explains the fact that he says: *Do this in remembrance of me.* After he recorded that he said: *this is my body which is broken for you, do this in remembrance of me*, and again: *This cup is the new testament in my blood, do this as often as you will in remembrance of me*, he says in addition by way of explanation: *For as often as you will eat this bread and drink the cup, declare the death of the Lord until he comes.*[94]

**267/2** [Luke 22:20] **In like manner the cup also, after he had supped, saying: This is the cup, the new testament in my blood, which will be shed for you.** The phrase, '*In like manner the cup also*', is understood *apo koinou* with 'he gave to them', so that the full meaning is: 'In like manner, after he had supped, he gave the cup to them'. Therefore, *because the bread affirms the body*, but *the wine realizes the blood in the flesh*, the former is referred mystically to the body of Christ, while the latter *is referred to the blood.*[95]

But because it is necessary both for us to remain in Christ and for Christ to remain in us, the wine of the Lord's cup is mixed with water. For as John attests: *The waters are peoples.*[96] It is not permitted to offer anyone either water alone, or wine alone, just as it is not permitted to offer a grain of wheat

---

91 Ps. 109:4 (110:4).
92 Cf. John 10:18.
93 Cf. Matt. 5:16.
94 1 Cor. 11:24–26.
95 Isidore, *De ecclesiasticis officiis* 1.18 (CCSL 113:20.30–33).
96 Rev. 17:15.

alone without mixing it with water and making it into bread, lest such an offering signify /379/ that the head is as it were to be separated from the limbs, and either that Christ could suffer without love of our redemption, or that we could be saved and presented to the Father without Christ's suffering. If it bothers anyone why we are taught to receive the sacrament fasting, according to the custom of the universal Church, when the Saviour gave his body and blood to his apostles after they dined, let him hear briefly that the apostles at that time took communion after dining, because it was necessary that that figurative Passover be taken earlier, and thus be transformed to the sacraments of the true Passover. Now, in honour of so great and so fearful a sacrament, the teachers of the Church determined that we first be strengthened by sharing in the Lord's passion, and that we first be consecrated inwardly and outwardly by the spiritual feast, and afterwards that our body be restored by an earthly feast and common food. The fact that he says: *This is the cup, the new testament in my blood*, points to a difference from the Old Testament, because the Old Testament was consecrated by the blood of goats and calves,[97] while the Lawgiver sprinkled it, saying: *This is the blood of the testament, which God has ordained for you.*[98] For it is indeed necessary that the exemplars of heavenly things be cleansed by these, and that the heavenly things themselves be cleansed by better victims than these, according to what the Apostle declares with exquisite exposition and full reasoning throughout the whole of his Epistle to the Hebrews when he distinguishes between the Law and the Gospel.

**268/2** [Luke 22:21–22] **But yet behold, the hand of him who betrays me is with me on the table. And the Son of man indeed goes, according to what was determined; but yet, woe to that man by whom he will be betrayed.** *He who had told of the passion, also tells of the betrayer, giving him an opportunity of penitence, so that when he had understood that his thoughts and secret counsels were known, he might repent of his deed. And yet he does not point him out specifically, lest, being openly accused, he become more shameless. He assigns the crime to a number*[99] *so that the conspirator may do penance.*[100] He also foretells the punishment, in order that the stipulated torments may reform the one whom shame had not conquered. But both today and likewise in eternity, woe to that man who

---

97 Cf. Hebr. 10:4.
98 Hebr. 9:20. The Lawgiver is Moses.
99 I.e., to 'one of the twelve' disciples, without naming the one. Cf. Mark 14:18–20.
100 Jerome, *Commentarii in Matheum* 4 (CCSL 77:249.1097–102).

wickedly approaches the table, who with snares hidden in his mind, and who with his heart defiled by some enormity, does not fear to share in the secrets of the mysteries of Christ. For that man following Judas' example also betrays the Son of man, not indeed to Jewish sinners, but nevertheless to sinners, namely to his own limbs, with which he dares to profane that inestimable and inviolable body of the Lord.[101] That man sells the Lord, who, neglectful of love and fear of him, is shown to love and care more for earthly and transitory things, or rather criminal things. Woe, I say, to that man, about whom Jesus, who no one doubts is present at the sacred altars during the sacrifice, since he is about to consecrate his intentions, /380/ is compelled to lament to the heavenly ministers standing by him, saying: *behold, the hand of him who betrays me is with me on the table.*

**269/1** [Luke 22:23] **And they began to inquire among themselves, which of them it was who was going to do this thing.** *And certainly, eleven apostles knew that they had plotted no such thing against the Lord, but they believe the Teacher more than themselves, and fearing their own frailty they sadly* ask *about the sin of which they had no knowledge.*[102] And Judas shamelessly asks, as Matthew and Mark relate, in order boldly to feign a good conscience.[103]

## Chapter 89

**270/2** [Luke 22:24] **And there was also a strife among them, which of them would seem to be the greater.** Just as good men usually always seek in the Scriptures for the exemplary models of the Fathers through which they may advance to better things, and by which, once they know about them, they may be humbled concerning their own deeds, so on the contrary wicked men, if they find by chance anything reprehensible in the elect, are accustomed to grab hold of it eagerly, as if they would thereby be able to conceal their own wickedness or defend it as just. And for that reason, they read much more eagerly that there was a strife among the disciples of Christ, *which of them would seem to be greater,* than that *the multitude of believers had but one heart and one soul.*[104] They recall much more

---

101 Cf. Eph. 5:30.
102 Jerome, *Commentarii in Matheum* 4 (CCSL 77:249.1104–08).
103 Cf. Matt. 26:25; Mark 14:19.
104 Acts 4:32.

tenaciously that dissension arose between Barnabas and Paul, *so that they departed from one another*,[105] than that the same Paul says: *For while there is among you envying and strife, are you not carnal? Are you not men?*[106] as if the frailty of holy men is proposed to us for imitation, and not rather that *they recovered strength from weakness, became mighty in war.*[107] This is particularly the case in this passage, where even the very cause of their strife is unknown to us. For it is not unbelievable that they might contend by outdoing one another in honour,[108] in accordance with what is elsewhere commanded: *Strive to enter by the narrow gate.*[109] But for whatever reason they strove, let us rather see not what the disciples, who were still carnal, did, but what the spiritual Teacher ordered.

[Luke 22:25–26] **And he said to them: The kings of the Gentiles lord it over them; and those who have power over them are called benefactors. But you not so; but he who is the elder among you, let him become like the younger, and he who is the leader, like a servant.** While the disciples contend over precedence, the good Teacher does not reproach them for initiating strife, but instead he describes the form of the humility that they should seek in a restrained way. The elders and leaders, that is, the teachers of the Church, have need of great discernment when it comes to this form of humility that should be obtained, particularly lest, like the kings of the Gentiles, they rejoice in lording over those who are subject to them, /381/ and in being extolled by them with empty praises. But, following the example of the eternal King, let them become as it were subordinates and servants of those whom they are in charge of ruling. Because without doubt it is necessary that there be companions *to those doing good through humility*, so that they be *raised up by a zeal for justice against the vices of those doing wrong*, so that not only do they in no way set themselves above the good, but also, when the fault of the wicked demands it, that they *directly recognize the power of their own precedence*. For lest the soul of the leader be carried away to pride by delight in its own power, it is rightly said by a certain wise man: '*Have they made you ruler? Do not be lifted up; be among them as one of them*'.[110]

---

105 Acts 15:39.
106 1 Cor. 3:3–4.
107 Hebr. 11:34.
108 Cf. Rom. 12:10.
109 Luke 13:24.
110 Ecclus. 32:1.

Hence Peter likewise says: *'Not lording it over the clergy, but being made a pattern for the flock'.*[111] *Nevertheless, when dealing with the wicked it is always a more serious fault, if more equality than discipline is maintained. For since Eli overcome by false kindness did not want to punish his sons when they sinned in the presence of the strict Judge, he smote himself with his sons in a severe act of condemnation.*[112] *Hence it is necessary that a leader show towards those beneath him both the tenderness of a mother and the discipline of a father. And in these things, one should be anxiously cautious that neither strict rigour nor tenderness should be surrendered.*[113]

**271**/10 [Luke 22:27] **For who is greater, he who sits at table or he who serves? Is it not he who sits at table? But I am in the midst of you as he who serves.** To the words of his own exhortation he adds examples. Recording these more fully, John the evangelist among other things writes: *If then I, your Lord and Teacher, have washed your feet, you ought also to wash one another's feet.*[114] However, even by the word 'serving', everything that God performed in the flesh can be understood. And he signifies that the sacrament of his blood should be served to us, when he says: *Just as the Son of man came not to be served, but to serve, and to give his life as a ransom for many,*[115] and by this he also shows the elders of the Church the particular kind of serving that ought to be imitated, so that we not only furnish the services of mercy, alms, salvific teaching, and spiritual example to our brothers, but also that we learn to give our lives for one another, just as he gave his life for us.[116]

[Luke 22:28–29] **And you are those who have stood by me in my temptations, and I confer on you, as my Father has conferred on me, a kingdom,** ... Not beginning, but persevering in endurance is given by the glory of the heavenly kingdom, because without doubt perseverance, which is a synonym for constancy, is strength and fortitude of mind, and the pillar, if I might put it so, of all the virtues. When /382/ this pillar stands very erect and firm, nothing is more certain, nothing is more secure for good morals. But if, struck by some whirlwind, it is cast down, it does not fall alone; for all the good things of the soul fall headlong together.

---

111 1 Peter 5:3.
112 Cf. 1 Sam. 4:17–18.
113 Gregory, *Regula pastoralis* 2.6 (SC 381:202.3–6; 212.143–47; 214.163–67; 214.178; 216.183–86).
114 John 13:14.
115 Matt. 20:28.
116 Cf. 1 John 3:16.

Therefore, just as the Father conferred a kingdom on his Son, who became *obedient to death, even to the death of the cross, and the Father exalted him and gave him a name above every name*,[117] so also the same Son will lead those who stand by him in his trials to the eternal kingdom. *For if we have been planted together in the likeness of his death, we will be also in the likeness of his resurrection.*[118] The accursed Judas is excluded from the sublimity of this promise. Indeed, before the Lord said these things, Judas must be supposed to have gone out. He not only scorned to stand by him in his trials, but he assisted the very authors of those trials. And they are excluded who, having heard the words of the incomprehensible mystery, *went back and walked no more with him.*[119] For those who withdrew from the Lord could not be saved, save only those, however many, who returned by doing penance.

[Luke 22:30] **So that you may eat and drink at my table in my kingdom.** This table, offered for the enjoyment of all the saints, is the glory of heavenly life. That is the food and drink of which it is elsewhere said: '*Blessed are those who hunger and thirst for justice, for they will be filled*',[120] by delighting, of course, in the joy *of the true and unchanging good*,[121] which they had desired and loved from of old.

**272**/5 [Luke 22:30b] **And you may sit on thrones judging the twelve tribes of Israel.** This is that *change of the right hand of the Most High* that the Psalm sings of,[122] that those who now humbly serve their fellow servants may then be nourished at the Lord's table on high with the feast of eternal life; that those who are condemned unjustly here when they stand by the Lord in his trials may come there with him as just judges over those who perpetrated his trials, and inasmuch as they are despised by this world for their great humility, they may then increase when they take their seats at the pinnacle of power.

**273**/10 [Luke 22:31–32] **And the Lord said: Simon, Simon, behold Satan has sought after you all to sift you like wheat, but I have prayed for you that your faith may not fail.** Lest the eleven apostles boast or attribute to their own power that they were almost the only ones amongst so many

---

117 Phil. 2:8–9.
118 Rom. 6:5.
119 John 6:67.
120 Matt. 5:6.
121 Augustine, *De sermone Domini* 1.2.6 (CCSL 35:5.93–95).
122 Ps. 76:11 (77:10).

BOOK SIX 595

thousand Jews who were said to have stood by the Lord in his trials, he also shows them, that if they had not been protected by the succouring aid of the Lord they could have been destroyed by the same tempest with the others. But when Satan seeks to test them, and to shake them, like one who cleans wheat by winnowing, the Lord teaches that no one's faith is tested by the devil unless God allows it. Of course, it is Satan's part to seek to sift the good, /383/ *to pant after their affliction with surges of malice. For where he in his jealousy longs to try them, there he seeks, as if craving their assent.*[123] But when the Saviour, praying for Peter, entreats not that he not be tempted, but that his faith not fail – that is, that after his fault of denial he rise again to his former condition by doing penance – he recommends that it is useful for the saints to be tested by the flames of trials, so that either they may be seen to be tempted because they were strong, or, having recognized their frailty through their temptations, that they may learn to become stronger, and so, after they have been tested, that they themselves may also receive *the crown of life, which God has promised to those who love him.*[124]

**274/9** [Luke 22:32b] **And you, when once you have turned back, strengthen your brothers.** Just as I myself, he says, protected your faith by praying, lest it fail when Satan puts you to the test, so remember also to raise up and strengthen any weaker brothers by the example of your penance, lest they perchance despair of forgiveness. He exhorted the same thing after the resurrection when Simon Peter declared for the third time that he loved him (for it was fitting that the love of a third confession wash clean the fear of a third denial), and likewise on that third occasion Christ entrusted to him the feeding of his sheep.[125]

## Chapter 90

**275/1** [Luke 22:33–34] **And he said to him: Lord, I am ready to go with you both to prison and to death. And he said: I say to you, Peter, the cock will not crow this day, until you thrice deny that you know me.** Because the Lord had said that he prayed for Peter's faith, the latter, knowing his present love and fervent faith, but unaware of his future fall, does not believe that he can forsake him in any way. But lest any of the faithful

---

123 Gregory, *Moralia* 2.7 (CCSL 143:68.152–54).
124 James 1:12.
125 Cf. John 21:15–17.

either recklessly rely on his own state or even more recklessly despair when he falls, Christ, who alone knows what is in a man, both foretells like God the mode, time, and number of Peter's denial, and promises like a merciful man the help of his own protection.

**276**/10   [Luke 22:35–36] **And he said to them: When I sent you without a purse and bag and shoes, did you lack anything? But they said: Nothing. Then he said to them: But now he who has a purse, let him take it, and likewise a bag; and he who does not have a sword, let him sell his coat, and buy one.** How rightly does a maxim of the Fathers define discretion as the mother and nurse of all the virtues, and the Lord's speech proves this, for he does not instruct the disciples to love the same way in time of persecution as in time of peace. For indeed there are virtues that must be maintained always and with all one's strength, and there are those that must be altered because of time and place by provident discretion. Who does not know that *the bowels of mercy, benignity, humility, patience, modesty*,[126] chastity, faith, hope, love, and others similar to these, must be observed /384/ by the faithful without any interruption because of the times? But truly when it comes to hunger, thirst, vigils, exposure, reading, psalmody, prayer, the toil of working, teaching, silence, and others of this kind, if anyone thinks they should always be observed, not only will he deprive himself of their benefit, but he will incur also the disgrace of indiscriminate stubbornness, or rather of wilful foolishness. And so, in order to recommend the way of discretion, after the disciples have been sent to preach, the Teacher and Lord of virtues *commanded them not to take anything for the way*,[127] ordaining, that is to say, that *those who proclaim the Gospel, live by the Gospel.*[128] But when the danger of death is pressing, and the whole nation at once is persecuting the shepherd and his flock, he decrees a suitable rule for the time, namely, by allowing them to take the money needed for food, until, when the madness of the persecutors has been laid to rest, the time for evangelizing returns. Also, he gives us an illustration that when from time to time there is just cause to do so, then we can omit without guilt some elements of the rigour we have intended. For example, when we travel through distant inhospitable lands we are allowed to carry more for the sake of the journey than we had at home. He either orders them to take a sword and a coat, or he directs

---

126 Col. 3:12.
127 Mark 6:8.
128 1 Cor. 9:14.

them not to buy a coat [but rather, a sword], so that readers may know that the disciples did not lack the power of putting up resistance, but rather that they suffered for love of the Teacher. That is why if there were no other reason to draw a sword, that one sufficed, so that the servant's ear that had been cut off would be healed by the Lord's touch,[129] and so that the Saviour's beneficent virtue could warn even his murderers that when they are struck they should prefer not to cling to anger but to accept the faith of the one who rises again.

**277/8** [Luke 22:37] **For I say to you, that this that was written must yet be fulfilled in me: 'And he was reckoned with the wicked.'**[130] **For the things concerning me have an end.** Behold the reason why the disciples are admonished to take a purse, bag, and sword, namely because the Lord had been reckoned with the wicked. This is what Isaiah states when he describes Christ's passion, referring either to the robbers, between whom he was destined to be crucified, or to the dead to whom he was going to descend by his death. For indeed he was reckoned with the wicked, when he descended to the dead, and summoned those of his own whom he found there to heaven. In this regard another prophet proclaims: *You also by the blood of your Testament have sent forth your prisoners out of the pit, where there is no water.*[131]

**278/10** [Luke 22:38] **But they said: Lord, behold, here are two swords. And he said to them: It is enough.** Two swords suffice as testimony that the Saviour suffered willingly. One of these taught that the audacity of fighting for the Lord was present in the apostles, and when its blow struck off an ear, that kindness and the power to heal was present /385/ in the Lord who was also going to die. The other, which was not removed from its sheath at all, showed that the disciples were not permitted to do all that they could to protect him.

**279/1** [Luke 22:39] **And going out, he went according to his custom to the Mount of Olives; and his disciples also followed him.** The Lord, who is about to be betrayed by a disciple, goes to a place of accustomed solitude where he could very easily be found. Where are those, therefore, who contend that he feared death and was crucified against his will? And it is pleasing that he leads his disciples, imbued with the mysteries of his body and blood, to the Mount of Olives, to signify that all those baptized

---

129 Cf. Luke 22:50–51.
130 Isa. 53:12.
131 Zech. 9:11.

by his death are to be confirmed by the supreme unction of the Holy Spirit, and can say with the Psalmist: *The light of your countenance is signed on us, O Lord; you have given gladness in my heart.* Concerning which, it is fittingly added: *By the season of their grain, their wine and oil, they are multiplied.*[132]

**280/2** [Luke 22:40] **And when he had come to the place, he said to them: Pray that you not enter into temptation.** *It is impossible for the human soul not to be tempted. And hence in the Lord's Prayer we say: 'Lead us not into temptation',*[133] *not refusing temptation completely, but praying for strength to withstand temptations. Therefore, in the present circumstances, he does not say: 'Pray that you not be tempted', but: 'Pray that you not enter into temptation', that is, that* extreme *temptation not conquer you, and hold you within its net. For example: the martyr, who poured out his blood for professing faith in the Lord, was certainly tempted, but he was not entangled in a net of temptation. But he who denies [the Lord] runs into temptation's snares.*[134]

**281/1** [Luke 22:41–42] **And he withdrew from them about a stone's throw; and kneeling down, he prayed, saying,** ... *After having given the apostles direction* about praying, and having himself withdrawn, he prays alone for all, who alone was going to suffer for all, signifying that his prayer is as different from ours as is his suffering. And he prays kneeling down *to show the humility of his soul by the posture of his body.*[135]

And *'he withdrew from them about a stone's throw':* by this he admonished them allegorically, *as it were, to aim the stone at him, that is, to direct the purpose of the Law, which was written in stone,*[136] *to him. For that stone can reach him, because Christ is the 'end of the Law, for justice for everyone who believes'.*[137]

**282/1** [Luke 22:42b] **Father, if you will, remove this cup from me; yet, not my will but yours be done.** *He asks that the cup be removed from him, not indeed from fear of suffering, but from pity for the first people,*[138] *so as not to drink the cup offered by them. And hence it is significant that he did not say:* /386/ *'Remove the cup from me', but, 'this cup', that is:*

---

132 Ps. 4:7–8 (4:6–7).
133 Matt. 6:13.
134 Jerome, *Commentarii in Matheum* 4 (CCSL 77:255.1265–74).
135 Jerome, *Commentarii in Matheum* 4 (CCSL 77:254.1244–46).
136 Cf. Exod. 31:18.
137 Augustine, *Quaestiones euang.* 2.50 (CCSL 44B:116.3–8); Rom. 10:4.
138 I.e., the Jews.

BOOK SIX 599

*'Remove the cup of the people of the Jews, who, having the Law and the prophets who prophesy me daily, cannot have the excuse of ignorance if they kill me'. And nevertheless, reverting to himself, what he had refused with trepidation in the person of a man, he confirms in* the power of the Son of God: *'yet, not my will but yours be done'. Let what I say in my human state of mind not be done, he says, but rather that for the sake of which I descended to earth according to your will.*[139] *Therefore, he says, if it can come to pass, that the multitude of nations may believe without the destruction of the Jews, I refuse the passion. But if they must be blinded in order that all nations may see,*[140] *not my will,* Father, *but yours be done.*

In another interpretation: *Approaching the passion,* the Saviour *assumed the voice of the weak, saying: 'Father, if you will, remove this cup from me', and took on their fear in order to remove it. And again displaying* the fortitude of his soul *through obedience, he says: 'yet, not my will but yours be done', so that when what we do not will to be done is at hand, we may beg through weakness that it not be done, since we are prepared through fortitude for the will of our Creator to be done even against our will.*[141]

**283**/10 [Luke 22:43] **And there appeared to him an angel from heaven, strengthening him.** Elsewhere we read that *'Angels came and ministered to him'.*[142] *As a testimony to both his natures it is written not only that angels ministered to him, but also that an angel strengthened him, since he who was God before the ages became a man at the end of the ages.*[143] *And he is the one who, before he was exalted by the glory of the resurrection, was above the angels in his divine nature, but nevertheless, as it is written, he was less than the angels in his human nature,*[144] *and because of that he was subject to death. But after he trampled upon death by rising again, he placed his human nature even above the majesty of the archangels.*[145]

*Certainly, if any heresy deludes itself so far as to claim that he who needed the help of a strengthening angel was weak, it should remember that the Creator of the angels had no need of the aid of his creation.*[146]

---

139 Jerome, *Commentarii in Matheum* 4 (CCSL 77:255.1249–58).
140 Jerome, *Commentarii in Esaiam* 3.9.3/5 (CCSL 73:124.27–30).
141 Gregory, *Moralia* 12.12 (CCSL 143A:638.9–17).
142 Matt. 4:11.
143 Gregory, *Hom. in Hiezech.* 1.8.24 (CCSL 142:115.508–11).
144 Cf. Ps. 8:6 (8:5).
145 Gregory, *Hom. in Hiezech.* 1.8 (CCSL 142:114.490–93).
146 Hilary, *De trinitate* 10.41 (CCSL 62A:494.6–9).

Indeed, *he is the one who, if he wished, might bring down twelve thousand legions of angels from heaven.*[147] *Then it necessarily follows that he is 'strengthened' in the same way that he is 'sad'. For if he is sad for us, that is, if he is sad for our sake, it is necessary that he be strengthened both for our sake and for us.*[148]

[Luke 22:43b] **And being in agony, he prayed the longer.** *Why would he pray in agony for himself, who, placed on earth, bestowed heavenly things with authority? But, as death drew near, he expressed in himself the struggle of our soul, we who suffer particularly from the power of fear and terror, when through the dissolution of the flesh we are approaching eternal Judgement.* /387/ *For then every soul is deservedly terrified, when shortly thereafter it learns that it cannot change for eternity.*[149]

[Luke 22:44] **And his sweat became like drops of blood, falling down on the ground.** Let *no one impute this* sweat *to weakness, because it is also contrary to nature to sweat blood. It does not support the heresy of weakness, but the sweat of blood establishes the reality of Christ's body against the heresy which claims that it was only an apparent body.*[150] But rather, by the earth watered and sanctified by Christ's blood, one may understand that it was declared – not to Christ, who knew it, but openly to us – that he already achieved the purpose of his prayer, namely that he should cleanse by his blood the faith of the disciples that earthly weakness still accused; and whatever stumbling block that weakness endured because of his death, he himself destroyed it all by dying. On the contrary, by his innocent death he restored to heavenly life the whole world that was dead far and wide from sins.

**284/2** [Luke 22:45–46] **And when he rose up from prayer and came to his disciples, he found them sleeping for sorrow. And he said to them: Why do you sleep? Arise and pray, lest you enter into temptation.** That is, *lest the cup of* my *suffering weigh upon* you.[151] Here he clearly shows that because he also prayed for those whom he earnestly warns, they share in his prayers by staying awake and praying.

**285/1** [Luke 22:47] **And as he was still speaking, behold, a multitude; and he who was called Judas, one of the twelve, went before them, and**

---

147 Hilary, *De trinitate* 10.42 (CCSL 62A:495.10–11); cf. Matt. 26:53.
148 Hilary, *De trinitate* 10.41 (CCSL 62A:494.9–12).
149 Gregory, *Moralia* 24.11 (CCSL 143B:1212.252–59).
150 Hilary, *De trinitate* 10.41 (CCSL 62A:494.14–19). The heresy is Docetism.
151 Hilary, *De trinitate* 10.37 (CCSL 62A:491.42–43).

approached Jesus to kiss him. The other evangelists reveal that the reason he kissed him was so that the multitude could recognize by this sign the one whom he betrayed.[152] But the Lord received the kiss of the betrayer, not to teach us by this to deceive, but so as not to seem to flee the betrayal, fulfilling at the same time that Psalm of David's: *With those who hate peace I was peaceable.*[153]

**286/2** [Luke 22:48] **And Jesus said to him: Judas, do you betray the Son of man with a kiss?** He says: 'Do you betray *the Son of man'*, *because flesh was arrested, not divinity. Yet that is yet another reproach against the ungrateful disciple that he betrayed him, who, although he was the Son of God, nevertheless for our sake willed to be the Son of man, and he says as it were: For your sake I have accepted, ungrateful one, that you betray me. I think that* doubtless *it should be spoken in the form of a question, as if he reproaches the betrayer with the affection of a lover: 'Judas, do you betray the Son of man with a kiss?' That is, do you inflict a wound with a pledge of love, and do you shed blood with a ceremony of charity, and do you inflict death with the means of peace? Do you, the servant, betray the Lord; do you, the disciple, betray the Teacher; do you, the chosen one, betray the Creator?*[154]

**287/1** [Luke 22:49–50] **And those who were around him, seeing what would follow, /388/ said to him: Lord, shall we strike with the sword? And one of them struck the servant of the high priest, and cut off his right ear.** Peter did *this*, as John the evangelist teaches,[155] *with the same ardour of spirit* doubtless *with which* he had done *other things.*[156] For he knew how Phinehas received the reward of righteousness and priesthood forever for punishing the impious.[157] But in fact it goes on:

[Luke 22:51] **But Jesus answering, said: Permit it thus far.** It should not be perceived *as though what was carried out thus far was acceptable to him, but he did not wish it to go any further.* Since in the words of Matthew it is known that *the Lord said: 'Put up your sword in its place, for all who take the sword will perish with the sword',*[158] *it is understood rather that the whole act for which Peter used the sword was displeasing to the Lord.*

152 Cf. Matt. 26:48; Mark 14:44.
153 Ps. 119:7 (120:6–7).
154 Ambrose, *Expos. Lucam* 10.63 (CCSL 14:364.621–31).
155 Cf. John 18:10.
156 Jerome, *Commentarii in Matheum* 4 (CCSL 77:257.1324–25).
157 Cf. Num. 25:7–13.
158 Matt. 26:52 (not quoted by Augustine).

For it is more precisely the case that when they questioned him, saying: *'Shall we strike with the sword?'*, then he answers: *'Permit it thus far'*. That is, do not let what is going to happen disturb you; they must be allowed to advance thus far, that is, to seize me and fulfil what has been written about me. But in the delay between the questioning of the Lord and his response, Peter struck out of an eagerness to defend the Lord and in great agitation. But those things that could be done at once could not be said at once. For he would not have said: *'But Jesus answering'*, unless he was replying to their questioning. And indeed, Matthew alone says what he had condemned about Peter's deed. Even Matthew did not say there: *'Jesus replied to Peter: Put up your sword'*. Instead, he said: *'Then Jesus says to him: Put up your sword'*, which it appears that the Lord said after the deed.[159]

**288**/10 [Luke 22:51b] **And when he had touched his ear, he healed him.** The Lord is never forgetful of his goodness and does not allow even his enemies to be wounded. They inflict death on a just man; he heals the wounds of his persecutors, teaching allegorically that even those wounded by conspiring his death can be healed, if they convert. Allegorically, this servant is the people of the Jews, wrongly subject to the service of the chief priests, to such an extent that at their request they sought that Barabbas be released, but for Jesus to be crucified,[160] whom a little before, singing hosanna, they were proclaiming the son of David and the king.[161]

The servant lost his right ear during the Lord's passion, that is, the spiritual understanding of the Law, for he was content with his left ear only, that is, with the trifling value of the letter.[162] The ear is cut off by Peter's sword, not indeed that that takes away the listeners' sense of understanding, but that it makes known to the negligent that this sense is lost by divine judgement. But truly /389/ in those from among that same people who chose to believe, that same right ear was restored to its former duty by the condescension of divine goodness.

In another interpretation: *The ear cut off for the sake of the Lord and healed by the Lord* signifies that the sense of hearing has been renewed with its old condition taken away, so that it is *'in the newness of spirit and not in the oldness of the letter'*.[163] Because he who is appointed by Christ

---

159 Augustine, *De consensu euang.* 3.5 (CSEL 43:288.5–23).
160 Cf. Luke 23:18–21.
161 Cf. Matt. 21:9; Mark 11:9–10.
162 Cf. Jerome, *Commentarii in Matheum* 4 (CCSL 77:257.1327–32).
163 Rom. 7:6.

will also be *appointed* to reign *with Christ*. Hence it is fitting also that *Malchus*, the name by which the servant was called, *means* 'king' or *'going to reign'*. *But the fact that he was found to be a servant likewise pertains to that antiquity which gives 'birth to bondage, which is Agar'*.[164] *But when health arrived, freedom was also prefigured.*[165]

**289**/1 [Luke 22:52] **And Jesus said to the chief priests and magistrates of the temple and the elders who had come to him:** ... The question arises how Jesus is said to address the chief priests and magistrates of the temple and the elders who came to him, for according to the other evangelists they are said not to have come themselves, but to have sent their servants, while they waited in the court of Caiaphas.[166] This is because the priests, Pharisees, and elders were agitating for the murder of the Lord in such a way that they themselves might seem as it were innocent of his blood. *He is not betrayed by us, but by his disciple*;[167] he is not seized by us, but by a tribune and the multitude; Barabbas is not chosen in his place by us, but by the people; he is not condemned to death by us, but by the governor; he is not nailed to the cross by our hands, but by the Roman military. The evangelist, desiring to show that those by whose counsel everything was done were especially guilty of his blood, says that the chief priests and magistrates of the temple and the elders came to seize the Saviour, so that it could be inferred from this that *just as* they *came to seize Christ not by themselves, but by those whom they sent, what else is it but that they themselves came by the authority of their own command? Thus, all who clamoured with wicked words for him to be crucified killed him, not by themselves, but nevertheless by the one who was forced to this crime by their outcry.*[168]

[Luke 22:52b–53] **Have you come out, as if against a thief, with swords and clubs? When I was with you daily in the temple, you did not stretch forth your hands against me. But this is your hour, and the power of darkness.** *It is foolish, he says, to seek him with swords and clubs, who of his own accord gives himself into your hands, and to search after him as if he were lying hidden in the night and avoiding your eyes as a traitor, who teaches daily in the temple. But you are gathered against me in*

---

164 Gal. 4:24.
165 Augustine, *In Iohannis euang.* 112.5 (CCSL 36:635.7–13).
166 Matt. 26:57–58; Mark 14:53–54.
167 Augustine, *Enarrationes in Psalmos* 63.11 (CCSL 39:813.3).
168 Augustine, *In Iohannis euang.* 114.4 (CCSL 36:642.33–39).

*darkness, because your power,* with which you are armed against the light of the world, *is in darkness.*[169] /390/

**290/1 [Luke 22:54] And seizing him, they led him to the chief priest's house.** He means the chief priest Caiaphas, who was the high priest of that year, as the evangelist John testifies.[170]

**291/1 [Luke 22:54b] But Peter followed at a distance.** It is appropriate that he who was about to deny Christ and who just now was very close to him should follow him at a distance. *For he would not have been able to deny Christ, if he had remained very close to him.* But *he ought to be revered by us with the greatest admiration, because he did not abandon the Lord even when he was afraid. It is natural* for him to be afraid; *that he follows is a matter of fealty; that he denies is a matter of being taken by surprise; that he repents is a matter of faith.*[171]

In another interpretation: *That Peter followed at a distance the Lord as he was going to his passion signified that the Church was indeed going to follow, that is to imitate, the sufferings of the Lord, but far differently. For the Church suffers for herself, but Christ suffered for the Church.*[172]

**[Luke 22:55] And when they had kindled a fire in the middle of the hall, and were sitting around it, Peter was in the midst of them.** Fire is a symbol of love, and also of cupidity. Of the former it is said: *I have come to cast fire on the earth, and what do I want, except that it be kindled?*;[173] and of the latter: *Behold, all you who kindle a fire, encompassed with flames; walk in the light of your fire, and in the flames which you have kindled.*[174] The former fire, descending from heaven upon the believers in the upper room of Zion, taught them to praise God in various tongues.[175] The latter fire, sustained by the earthly matter in the hall of Caiaphas, kindled the crowds with the flames of denying the Lord. With the former fire Moses destroyed the golden head of the idol;[176] with the latter fire Zedekiah destroyed the writings of the prophet Jeremiah.[177] Whoever extinguishes a wicked and

---

169 Jerome, *Commentarii in Matheum* 4 (CCSL 77:258.1356–61).
170 Cf. John 18:13.
171 Ambrose, *Expos. Lucam* 10.72 (CCSL 14:367.703–09).
172 Augustine, *Quaestiones euang.* 1.46 (CCSL 44B:35.2–6).
173 Luke 12:49.
174 Isa. 50:11.
175 Cf. Acts 2:3–4.
176 Cf. Exod. 32:20.
177 Cf. Jer. 36:23 & 27. In Jeremiah 36, the king who burns the writings is Jehoiakim; Zedekiah was the successor of the son of Jehoiakim (Jer. 37:1).

BOOK SIX                                                              605

noxious fire in himself can sing to the Lord: *For I have become like a bottle in the frost; I have not forgotten your justifications.*[178] But he who has lost the flame of virtues hears from the Lord: *Because iniquity has abounded, the love of many grows old.*[179] Being numb with this cold at this hour, the apostle Peter desired to be warmed by the persecutors' hot coals, since he sought the solace of temporary advantage in the company of the faithless. But immediately, having been glanced at by the Lord, when he abandoned their fire with his body, then he abandoned infidelity with his heart.[180]

[Luke 22:56] **When a servant-girl saw him sitting in the firelight and earnestly beheld him, she said: This man also was with him.** *Why does he want a servant-girl to be the first to reveal him, when the men were certainly better able to recognise him, except in order that that sex might be seen both to have sinned in the killing of the Lord, and to have been redeemed by the Lord's passion? And therefore* /391/ *a woman is the first to receive the mystery of the resurrection and to keep the Lord's commands, in order to abolish the old fault of the transgression.*[181]

[Luke 22:57] **But he denied him, saying: Woman, I do not know him.** Some persons *out of pious sympathy towards the apostle Peter* interpret *this passage thus:*[182] he properly said that he did not know him, whom the human mind is unable to comprehend, because no one knows the Son but the Father.[183] Asked a second time he also said: *Man, I am not,*[184] preferring to deny himself rather than Christ. But asked again a third time, when he says: *Man, I do not know what you are saying,*[185] he signified that he did not know how to condemn their sacrileges, that is, by rejecting and cursing them. But how frivolous this explanation is, is revealed both by the Lord, who by conclusive testimony had prophesied that he would be denied three times by Peter, and by Peter himself, who clearly shows by his ensuing tears that he said these things not out of zeal, but in order to deceive.

292/1  [Luke 22:58] **And after a little while, another seeing him, said: You are also one of them. But Peter said: Man, I am not.** In this *denial of* the blessed *Peter, we learn not only that Christ is denied by anyone who*

178 Ps. 118:83 (119:83).
179 Matt. 24:12.
180 Cf. Luke 22:61–62.
181 Ambrose, *Expos. Lucam* 10.73 (CCSL 14:367.712–17); cf. John 20:14–17.
182 Jerome, *Commentarii in Matheum* 4 (CCSL 77:262.1442–43).
183 Cf. Matt. 11:27.
184 Luke 22:58.
185 Luke 22:60.

606    BEDE: COMMENTARY ON THE GOSPEL OF LUKE

says that he [i.e. Jesus] is not Christ, but also by anyone who denies that he [himself] is a Christian, even though he is. For the Lord did not say to Peter: You will deny that you are my disciple, but 'you will deny me'.[186] Therefore he denied Christ himself, when he denied that he was his disciple.[187]

[Luke 22:59] **And after the space of about one hour, another man affirmed, saying: Truly, this man was also with him; for he is also a Galilean.** Not that Galileans spoke one language and Jerusalemites another, for both were *Hebrews, but that each province and region, has its own peculiarities in speaking the native language which cannot be ignored.*[188] Hence, in the Acts of the Apostles, when those on whom the Holy Spirit had settled spoke in the languages of all the nations, even those who lived in Judea (among the others who had come together from the various parts of the world) said in astonishment: *Behold, are not all these who speak Galileans? And how have we heard, each of us, in our own language in which we were born?*[189]

[Luke 22:60] **And Peter said: Man, I do not know what you are saying. And immediately, while he was still speaking, the cock crowed.** Holy Scripture often signifies the salience of things by the state of the time. Hence Peter, who uttered his denial in the middle of the night, repented at the crowing of the cock. Also, after the resurrection, in the light of day, he professed for the third time that he loved the Lord,[190] whom he had denied three times, because without doubt he wandered in the darkness of oblivion, and so he made amends by recalling /392/ the light he already desired. Having acquired the protection of that same true light, he completely set right everything he had made worse.[191] I think this cock should be understood as one of the teachers who, arousing us from our indolence and chiding us in our sleep, says: *Awake, just ones, and do not sin.*[192]

293/2  [Luke 22:61–62] **And the Lord turning, looked at Peter. And Peter remembered the word of the Lord, how he had said: Before the cock crows, you will deny me thrice. And Peter going out, wept bitterly.** When the Lord looks at Peter, Peter turning to his heart cleanses the stain of denial with tears of penitence, for God's mercy is required not only when

---

186  Matt. 26:34.
187  Augustine, *In Iohannis euang.* 113.20–25 (CCSL 36:637).
188  Jerome, *Commentarii in Matheum* 4 (CCSL 77:262.1453–56).
189  Acts 2:7–8.
190  Cf. John 21:17.
191  Cf. Jerome, *Commentarii in Matheum* 4 (CCSL 77:253.1204–07).
192  1 Cor. 15:34.

we repent, but in order for us to repent. For Christ to look at Peter is for him to have mercy on him. Hence the Psalmist says: *How long will my enemy be exalted over me? Look and hear me, O Lord, my God,*[193] that is, have mercy and help. How hurtful, indeed, are the exhortations of the faithless! When he was among the Jews he denied that he knew the man, whom among his fellow disciples he had confessed to be the Son of God. But could he not do penance when he was retained in the hall of Caiaphas? He goes out so that, separated from the council of the wicked, he may cleanse the filth of his cowardly denial with open tears.

**294/1** [Luke 22:63–64] **And the men who held him, mocked him and struck him. And they blindfolded him and struck his face.** In this passage the prophecy was fulfilled that said: *With a rod they will strike the cheek of the judge of Israel.*[194] But he who was struck then with the blows of the Jews, is struck even now by the blasphemies of false Christians. They blindfolded him, not so that he might not see their wicked deeds, but so that they might hide his face from themselves, just as they once did to Moses.[195] For if they believed Moses, they would perhaps believe the Lord also.[196] The fact is that the veil remains not unveiled up to the present over their hearts, but has been removed from us who are believers in Christ. Nor is it without significance that as he was dying, *the veil of the temple was torn in the middle.*[197]

[Luke 22:64b–65] **And they asked him, saying: Prophesy, who is it that struck you? And blaspheming, they kept saying many other things against him.** They kept doing these things as if reproaching someone who wished to be considered a prophet by the people. But all things are done for our sakes in accordance with the dispensation of the one who suffers, so that just as Peter urges after Christ suffered in the flesh, we may arm ourselves with the same thought.[198] Both heretics and Jews, who deny that Jesus is God even today, and wicked Catholics, who afflict him with evil actions, and do not believe that their thoughts and deeds of darkness are seen by him, say to him as if in jest: *Prophesy, who is it that struck you.*

**295/2** [Luke 22:66] **And as soon as it was day, the elders of the people, and the chief priests and scribes, came together; and they brought**

---

193 Ps. 12:3–4 (13:2–3).
194 Micah 5:1.
195 Cf. Exod. 34:33; 2 Cor. 3:13.
196 Cf. John 5:46.
197 Luke 23:45.
198 Cf. 1 Peter 4:1.

him into their council, saying: /393/ **If you are the Christ, tell us.** They were not seeking the truth, but preparing a trap. Since they expected that Christ would come in human form only from the stock of David, just as they themselves on another occasion replied to him when he asked,[199] *they were seeking this above all from him: that if he said, I am the Christ, since they knew that Christ could come only from the seed of David, they could falsely charge that he claimed the royal power for himself.*[200]

**296**/10 [Luke 22:67–68] **And he said to them: If I tell you, you will not believe me. And if I also ask you, you will not answer me, nor let me go.** He had often told them that he was Christ, for example, when he said: *I and the Father are one;*[201] and again: *The works that I do in the name of my Father, they give testimony of me, but you do not believe;*[202] and other examples of this kind. Also, he had asked how they could say that Christ was the son of David, when David himself in spirit called him his Lord, so that, challenged by such a question, they might learn not only that he was truly human, because he was the son of David, but also that he was the true God, because he was the Lord of David.[203] They wished neither to believe that he was speaking the truth by following his guidance, nor to reply to his questions by inquiry, nor to dismiss him as guiltless, who was proved innocent. But those who sought to accuse falsely the seed of David go beyond what they hear.

**297**/1 [Luke 22:69] **But hereafter the Son of man will be sitting at the right hand of the power of God.** Therefore, O Jew, Gentile, and heretic, if scorn, weakness, and the cross, is an affront to you, see that by these things the Son of man will sit at the right hand of God the Father, and he who was born a man from the Virgin's giving birth will come in his majesty with the clouds of the heavens. Hence, after he had described the lowly things of the cross, the Apostle went on to say: *For which cause God also has exalted him, and has given him a name which is above every name, so that in the name of Jesus every knee should bow, of those that are in heaven and on earth and under the earth, and that every tongue should confess that Jesus Christ is in the glory of God the Father.*[204]

---

199 Cf. John 10:32–33.
200 Augustine, *In Iohannis euang.* 48.4 (CCSL 36:414.1–4).
201 John 10:30.
202 John 10:25–26.
203 Cf. Matt. 22:41–45.
204 Phil. 2:9–11.

**298**/10 [Luke 22:70] **Then they all said: Are you then the Son of God? And he said: You say that I am.** He tempers his response so that not only does he speak the truth but also so that his words do not lead to a trap. He preferred to show that he was Christ, the Son of God, rather than to say it, in order that the pretext for condemnation might be removed from those who profess what they themselves object to.

**299**/2 [Luke 22:71] **And they said: What further testimony do we need? For we ourselves have heard it from his own mouth.** They received the testimony of the Lord, that he himself said that he was Christ and the Son of God, when he said: *The Son of man will be sitting at the right hand of the power of God.* And to those /394/ asking: *Are you then the Son of God?* he replies: *You say that I am.*[205] Those who hand over to death the one whom they recognise to be God by the testimony of their own words and deeds, condemn themselves, therefore, by their own statement. They condemn also the Arians, who will not understand the words that bring tidings of divine Majesty when the Lord came into glory after his death, words which, while he was still bound and scourged and scorned, the executioners themselves who were about to crucify him understood.[206]

**300**/1 [Luke 23:1] **And the whole multitude of them rising up, led him to Pilate**, so that the words of Jesus might be fulfilled, which he had foretold about his death: *For he will be delivered to the Gentiles, and he will be mocked and flogged and spat upon. And after they have flogged him, they will put him to death.*[207] By the Gentiles he surely means the Romans. For Pilate was a Roman, and the Romans had sent him as governor to Judea. The Lord is handed over to him to be crucified by the Jews, who by this means wish to dissociate themselves so to speak from killing him, so that not their innocence but their madness is shown.

**301**/10 [Luke 23:2] **And they began to accuse him, saying: We found this man perverting our nation, and forbidding us to give tribute to Caesar, and saying that he himself is Christ the king.** The Jews are charged with impiety, because accusing the Saviour they find that they cannot even falsely reproach him with anything having the appearance of truth. And for that reason, as Mark says: *Their testimonies were not in agreement.*[208]

---

205  Luke 22:69–70.
206  Cf. Matt. 27:54; Mark 15:39; Luke 23:47; John 19:33–35.
207  Luke 18:32–33.
208  Mark 14:56.

But he himself, to offer us a model of patience, remains silent and refuses to answer, just as he did before when he was scourged and likewise now when he is accused.

**302/1** [Luke 23:3] **And Pilate asked him, saying: Are you the king of the Jews? But he answering, said: You say it.** He replies with the same words to the governor as to the chief priests, in order that they be condemned by their own judgement. And it should be noted that with respect to the two accusations against the Lord, namely that he forbade giving tribute to Caesar, and that he said that he was Christ the king, Pilate thought that he should be questioned only about the statement regarding kingship. For it could be that Pilate had also heard the judgement of the Lord, which said: *Render to Caesar the things that are Caesar's, and to God the things that are God's,*[209] and for that reason he conducted this case as if the manifest falsehood of hostile people was worthless, and only what he did not know was worthy of investigation.

**303/9** [Luke 23:4] **And Pilate said to the chief priests and the multitudes: I find no case against this man.** This is what Christ himself said among other things to the disciples on the day before he suffered: *For the prince of this world is coming, and he has nothing against me.*[210] But because the prince of the world, that is, Pilate, declared him innocent, in that he found no cause /395/ to condemn him, see what the Jews do, who bustle about not to investigate the truth from love of justice, but goaded by envy, to condemn a just man.

**304/10** [Luke 23:5] **But they insisted, saying: He stirs up the people, teaching throughout all Judea, beginning from Galilee to this place.** This talk of the accusers teaches instead that the one who is accused is innocent, and that those who accuse are evil. To have taught the people, and by teaching to have stirred them up from the ignorance of the former age, and by such action to have passed through from Galilee as far as Judea, that is, the whole land of promise from end to end, is certainly a sign not of a crime, but of virtue. Indeed any lover of the Lord could offer the same message as praise, just as Peter did, saying to good listeners: *You know the word which has been published through all Judea, for it began from Galilee, after the baptism which John preached, Jesus of Nazareth,*[211] and so forth. Finally, Pilate, believing that the Saviour ought not to be questioned about

---

209 Luke 20:25.
210 John 14:30.
211 Acts 10:37–38.

BOOK SIX 611

this, seizing an opportunity, desires instead to free himself from judging him. For it goes on:

[Luke 23:6-7] **But Pilate, hearing Galilee, asked if the man were from Galilee. And when he understood that he was of Herod's jurisdiction, he sent him away to Herod, who was also himself in Jerusalem in those days.** Pilate, in order not to be forced to give a sentence against him, whom he knew to be innocent and to have been betrayed out of jealousy, sent him to Herod for judgement, so that preferably the tetrarch of his country would either absolve or punish him. But by divine providence, so that there might remain to the Jews no excuse, whereby it might seem as if not themselves but the Romans crucified Christ, Herod also, who was a Jew by birth and religion, was permitted along with his army to reveal what he thought of him. And at the same time this shows the impiety of both provinces in plotting his death, namely Judea where he was born, and Galilee, where he was brought up and lived.

[Luke 23:8-9] **And Herod, seeing Jesus, was very glad; for he was desirous for a long time to see him, because he had heard many things about him; and he hoped to see some sign done by him. And he questioned him with many words. But he said nothing to him in reply.** *He was silent and said nothing, because the other's cruelty did not deserve to see divine things, and the Lord avoided boasting. And perhaps by Herod all the wicked are signified, who if they did not believe in the Law and the prophets, also could not see the wondrous works of Christ in the Gospel.*[212]

305/2 [Luke 23:10] **And the chief priests and the scribes stood by, steadily /396/ accusing him.** As the chief priests and the scribes were accusing him, the Lord replied a few words in the presence of Pilate, and none at all in the presence of Herod, *lest he should be dismissed by the governor and the crime be washed away, and the benefit of the cross be put off.*[213] For it was certainly right that he should reply in some measure to Pilate, who conducted the legal proceeding unwillingly, but that he should consider Herod and the other aristocrats of the Jews, who act against the decrees of their own law in condemning an innocent man, unworthy of any words. *On account of those things*, therefore, since *he did not want to reply to this, the prophetic type of the lamb was given*,[214] so that by his

---

212 Ambrose, *Expos. Lucam* 10.99 (CCSL 14:374.944-48).
213 Jerome, *Commentarii in Matheum* 4 (CCSL 77:265.1546-47).
214 Cf. Isa. 53:7.

silence he would not be considered guilty, but innocent.[215] For when he was silent, like a lamb about to be sacrificed, he was offering his suffering for the sake of the whole flock; but when he replied, like a good shepherd, he was fighting against the snares of the wolves and the thieves on behalf of the sheep trusting in him.

**306/10** [Luke 23:11] **And Herod with his army scorned him and mocked him, putting on him a white garment, and sent him back to Pilate.** *The fact that he is clothed in a white garment* gives *proof of the unstained passion*, because the unstained *lamb of God* is going to carry away *the sins* of the whole *world*.[216] For he, who was scorned and mocked in a white garment, suffered and was buried in spotless flesh.

In another interpretation: The fact that here he is mocked in a white garment, but according to the other evangelists in a purple or scarlet garment,[217] expresses the twofold nature of the martyrdom by which he is adorned through the sufferings of holy Church. She marvels at the innocent death of this same Lord and also of her spouse: *My beloved*, she says, *is white and ruddy*,[218] white, namely, from the act; ruddy from the blood. And he himself, flourishing with the varied flowers of his members, bears *lilies in peace and roses in war.*[219]

[Luke 23:12] **And Herod and Pilate became friends that same day; for before they were enemies to one another.** This most unspeakable pact of Herod and Pilate which they struck in order to kill Christ, their successors preserve as if by hereditary right, when Gentiles and Jews, who disagree so much in race, religion and mind, nevertheless agree in persecuting Christians, and in destroying in them the faith of Christ.

**307/9** [Luke 23:13–14] **And Pilate, calling together the chief priests and the magistrates and the people, said to them.** Notice how great an effort Pilate makes to release Jesus. First, he says to the chief priests who are accusing him, that he has found no case against him. Then, as they persist in their undertaking, he sends him to Herod to learn whether the latter can find any crime in him, or whether perhaps he wishes to decide that he should be released. And finally, after discerning Herod's will, and since no crime had been found in Jesus, he seeks the sentence of the people,

---

215 Augustine, *In Iohannis euang.* 116.4 (CCSL 36:648).
216 Ambrose, *Expos. Lucam* 10.103 (CCSL 14:374.967–70).
217 Cf. Matt. 27:28; Mark 15:17; John 19:2.
218 Song 5:10.
219 Gregory, *Hom. in Euang.* 2.35.8 (CCSL 141:329.230).

BOOK SIX 613

to whom he had been accustomed to release one person on Passover. And again, desiring /397/ to release him, he asks for a third time. But the more diligently he seeks someone to help him release Jesus, and does not find him, the more culpable he proves those who unanimously desire his death to be.

[Luke 23:14b] **You have brought this man to me, as one perverting the people; behold, I, having examined him before you, find no case against this man in those things of which you accuse him.** By saying these things, Pilate indeed absolved Jesus, whom he proved innocent, but in order that the Scriptures might be fulfilled, the one whom *he absolved by judicial investigation, he crucified for the sake of a divine mystery.*[220]

308/10 [Luke 23:15] **And neither has Herod. For I sent you to him, and behold, nothing worthy of death has been done by him.** Listen, blind Jew; listen hard-hearted Gentile! Pilate himself acknowledges that neither he nor Herod found anything worthy of death in Christ, but only complied with those clamouring with insane cruelty in killing and mocking an innocent man. May the writings perish, therefore, that, composed so much later against Christ, fail to prove that he was accused of magic before Pilate, but prove rather that you should be accused of infidelity and falsehood before the Lord.

309/2 [Luke 23:16] **I will chastise him therefore, and release him.** I will afflict him with whips and derision as much as you yourselves demand, provided that you are not thirsting for innocent blood.

[Luke 23:17] **Now he necessarily had to release someone to them on the feast day.** He necessarily had to, not by an imperial decree of law, but obligated by the yearly custom of the nation, which he took pleasure in gratifying by such means.

310/1 [Luke 23:18–19] **But the whole multitude together cried out, saying: Away with this man, and release Barabbas to us; who for a certain sedition made in the city, and for murder, was cast into prison.** Their petition, which they obtained with such great effort, clings to the Jews right up to the present. For when given the choice, because they chose a robber instead of Jesus, a murderer instead of the Saviour, one who took life instead of the Giver of life,[221] they deservedly lost salvation and life, and sank themselves so deeply with villainies and seditions that they have lost their fatherland and kingdom, which they loved more than Christ. And

---

220 Ambrose, *Expos. Lucam* 10.97 (CCSL 14:374.935–36).
221 Cf. Augustine, *In Iohannis euang.* 116.1 (CCSL 36:647).

up to now they have not deserved to receive what they betrayed for money, namely freedom either of the soul or of the body.

**311/1  [Luke 23:20–21] And Pilate again spoke to them, desiring to release Jesus. But they kept shouting, saying: Crucify, crucify him.** How great the cruelty of the faithless, which desires not only to kill one who is innocent but also to kill him by the worst kind of death, that is, to crucify him! *For those crucified, hanging on the wood, fastened with nails through the feet and hands to the wood, were killed by a prolonged death, /398/ and lived for a long time on the cross, not because they chose to live longer, but because death itself was stretched out, so that their suffering was not easily ended.*[222] But *he himself from the worst death killed all death. It was the worst, not in the understanding of the Jews, but because it had been chosen by the Lord. He was going to have his cross itself as his sign, the very cross on which the devil was defeated. He was going to place it as a token of victory on the foreheads of the faithful, as the Apostle said: 'But God forbid that I should glory, except in the cross of our Lord Jesus Christ, by whom the world has been crucified to me, and I to the world.'*[223]

**312/9  [Luke 23:22] And he said to them a third time: Why, what evil has he done? I find no case for death in him. I will chastise him therefore, and let him go.** He particularly chose chastisement in order to satisfy the people, so that they not vent their rage against the Saviour to the point of crucifixion. Both the words of the evangelist John,[224] and the very column to which he is bound testify not only that Pilate brought him in for interrogation, but also that he delivered him up at the wish of the impious to be mocked and scourged. He who was accustomed to set free the shackled handed over the limbs that were full of God to be scourged. This column, placed in the church of Mount Zion, shows proven traces of the Lord's blood to observers up to the present day.[225] But although Pilate does these things, notice what the insatiable fury of the sacrilegious crowd does!

**313/1  [Luke 23:23] But they kept urging with loud voices, demanding that he should be crucified; and their voices prevailed.** Because they saw that Pilate's repeated and careful questioning obviated the entire complaint which they had brought against the Lord, these shameless people in the end resort to a single entreaty, in order that what they had

---

222 Augustine, *In Iohannis euang.* 36.4 (CCSL 36:326.42–46).
223 Augustine, *In Iohannis euang.* 36.4 (CCSL 36:326.49–55); Gal. 6:14.
224 Cf. John 18:33; 19:1–3.
225 Cf. Bede, *De locis sanctis* 2.5, ed. Fraipont (CCSL 175:258).

BOOK SIX 615

been unable to accomplish by accusations and so-called reasoning they might achieve now by demands and shouting. The history of the Church sufficiently demonstrates as well what excessive madness the persecutors of the blessed martyrs possessed.

**314/1** [Luke 23:24–25] **And Pilate gave sentence that their demand should be granted. And he released to them him who had been cast into prison for murder and sedition, whom they had desired; but Jesus he delivered up to their will.** *The seditious robber* and *author of murders was released to the people of the Jews, that is, the devil,* who once before had been expelled from the fatherland of light for the sin of pride, and cast into the prison of darkness. And for that reason the Jews *cannot have peace*, because they preferred to choose the prince of seditions rather than the Lord.[226] But because Barabbas means '*son of the father*',[227] or '*son of their teacher*',[228] /399/ he can act as the type of the Antichrist, whom those to whom it is said: *You are from your father, the devil*,[229] are going to prefer to the Son of God. But the Antichrist is called the son of the devil, not by his birth itself, but by imitating him as other sinners do.[230]

**315/1** [Luke 23:26] **And as they led him away, they laid hold of a certain Simon of Cyrene, coming from the country; and they laid the cross on him to carry after Jesus.** The evangelist John reports that the Lord bore the cross himself.[231] Hence it is understood that the cross was carried first by the Lord, and then was placed on Simon, whom they had met by chance as they were going out, by a quite fitting arrangement of the divine mystery.[232] *Because* he himself *suffered for us, leaving us an example, so that* we *should follow his steps.*[233] Simon is rightly described as having carried the cross after Jesus, in accordance with what he himself commanded: *And let him take up his cross and follow me.*[234] And because Simon himself is

---

226 Jerome, *Commentarii in Matheum* 4 (CCSL 77:267.1603–06).
227 Jerome, *Hebr. nom.* (CCSL 72:142.13).
228 Jerome, *Commentarii in Matheum* 4 (CCSL 77:265.1550).
229 John 8:44.
230 Bede is concerned to distinguish Antichrist from the Devil, as Antichrist will be a human being. In his commentary on Revelation, Bede reproduced the view of Primasius and Irenaeus of Lyon that Antichrist would come from the Hebrew tribe of Dan, but he seems to have quietly abandoned this idea, as it appears neither here nor in any subsequent exegesis: Darby, *Bede and the End of Time*, 119.
231 Cf. John 19:17.
232 Cf. Jerome, *Commentarii in Matheum* 4 (CCSL 77:269.1661–64).
233 1 Peter 2:21.
234 Matt. 16:24.

said not to be from Jerusalem, but from Cyrene, and because Cyrene is a city of Libya, as we read in the Acts of the Apostles,[235] he rightly signifies the peoples of the Gentiles. They, who were once foreigners and strangers, are now by being obedient to the faith citizens and household servants of God,[236] and, as is said elsewhere: *Heirs indeed of God and joint heirs with Christ.*[237] Hence it is beautifully fitting that Simon means 'being obedient' and Cyrene 'heirs'.[238] Nor should it be overlooked that Simon is said to have come from the country. For country is called 'pagos' in Greek, from which they derive the word 'pagans', because they are aliens from the city of God and ignorant as it were of the urban manner of life. But Simon, going out from the country, carries the cross after Jesus, when the people of the Gentiles, after discarding their pagan rituals, obediently embrace the steps of the Lord's passion.

**316/10**  [Luke 23:27–28] **And a great crowd of people followed him, and of women, who bewailed and lamented him. But Jesus, turning to them, said: ...** A great crowd followed the cross of the Lord together, but not with one and the same mind. For the people who brought about his death happily followed to see him die; but the women followed to weep for him whom they wanted to live as he was about to die, as he was dying, and when he was dead. It was not that the women's lamentation alone followed him, because a small crowd of believing men was also very sorrowful about his passion; rather it is that the lamentation of the female, as it were the more despised sex, was able more freely to display to the chief priests and rulers who were present what it felt toward them. But because *the Lord knows who are his,*[239] ignoring the crowd of raging people, he turns his eyes and mouth to the loving and lamenting women, saying: /400/

[Luke 23:28b] **Daughters of Jerusalem, do not weep for me, but weep for yourselves and for your children.** Do not lament, he says, that I am about to die, whose swift resurrection can dissolve death, whose death is going to destroy both all death and the very author of death. Rather, cleanse yourselves and your offspring in worthy fountains of tears, so as not to condemn yourselves to eternal death with the faithless in the avenging of my cross.

---

235  Cf. Acts 2:10.
236  Cf. Eph. 2:19.
237  Rom. 8:17.
238  Cf. Jerome, *Hebr. nom.* (CCSL 72:148.4 & 144.29–30).
239  2 Tim. 2:19.

BOOK SIX 617

It should be noted, when he addresses the daughters of Jerusalem, that not only the women who had come with him from Galilee, but also citizens of that same city adhered to him. And now as well, a double-minded crowd accompanies Jesus who is about to be, as it were, sacrificed; for some read, hear, and reflect upon the narrative of his passion as if it were a tale worthy of laughter, and others, as is fitting, with eyes shedding tears. The former see the mysteries of his flesh and blood as if they were cheap and common fare; the latter perceive them with feelings worthy of so great a matter. But when he sees a contrite and humble heart, and in addition the grace of salvific remorse, the Lord, the diligent teacher and agreeable comforter, bestows the means by which the heart should weep more willingly, sweetly, and fully.

[Luke 23:29-30] **For behold, the days will come when they will say: Blessed are the barren, and the wombs that have not borne, and the breasts that have not given suck. Then they will begin to say to the mountains: Fall on us, and to the hills: Cover us.** He signifies the days of siege and captivity by the Romans that are going to come. About these he said earlier among other things to his disciples: *Then they who are in Judea, let them flee to the mountains,* and a little after: *And woe to those who are pregnant and to those who give suck in those days.*[240] For when captivity threatens, and the enemy's destruction rages through fields and cities, it is natural that all who are able to escape seek out whatever high or hidden refuges in which they may be concealed. And specifically Josephus reports that as the Romans were pressing upon them, the Jews eagerly sought the caves of the mountains and hills. Thus, he testifies that he himself with forty companions was betrayed, found, and captured by the enemy in a certain particularly secure cave of the destroyed city of Jotapata.[241] Because Jesus says that sterile and not pregnant women should be blessed, it can also, by extension, be understood about those of either sex *who have made themselves eunuchs for the kingdom of heaven.*[242] It can be said to the mountains and hills: *Fall on us* and *cover us,* when any persons whatever, mindful of their own weakness, when the critical moment of any lofty temptation threatens, seek to be defended either by virginity itself, or by martyrdom, or by whatever other human virtue with examples, warnings, and prayers.

240 Matt. 24:16 & 19.
241 Cf. Josephus, *Bellum Iudaicum* 3, 7, 35–38, 8.
242 Matt. 19:12.

[Luke 23:31] **For if in the green wood they do these things, what will be done in the dry?** Green wood signifies himself and his chosen ones, but dry wood, the unfaithful /401/ and sinners. Therefore, if I myself, he says – I, who did not make sin, and who, deservedly called the wood of life, bring the fruits of grace throughout each of the twelve months[243] – if I do not leave the world without the fire of suffering, what kind of torment do you think awaits those, who being without fruits themselves, do not fear to give the wood of life himself to the flames as well? If now is the time that the judgement of the house of God begins, *and all who want to live godly in Christ suffer persecution*,[244] what is the end of those who do not believe in the Gospel of God?

317/1 [Luke 23:32] **And there were also two other malefactors led with him to be put to death**, in order that it might be fulfilled, which says: *And he was reckoned with the wicked.*[245] But he was reckoned with the wicked in death, in order to justify the wicked in resurrection, *who, when he was in the form of God*,[246] became a man for the sake of men, in order to give to men *the power to be made the sons of God.*[247]

318/1 [Luke 23:33] **And when they came to the place which is called Calvary, they crucified him there, ...** *There was an area outside the city of Jerusalem and beyond the gate where the heads of the condemned were cut off, and it took the name of Calvary, that is, the 'skulls' of the beheaded. But on account of the fact that the Lord was crucified there, where before was a place of the damned, the banners of martyrdom were erected. And as for us he was made a curse of the cross,*[248] *and scourged and crucified, so for the salvation of all he is crucified as if a criminal among criminals,* so that *where sin abounded, grace may more abound.*[249]

How the Lord was actually placed on the cross, or what this placement of the most sacred body contains as a symbol, Sedulius in his Paschal Song said beautifully in these verses:

---

243 A reference to the tree in the midst of the Heavenly Jerusalem that bears fruit through all twelve months of the year (Rev. 22:2).
244 2 Tim. 3:12.
245 Mark 15:28; Luke 22:37 (a blend); cf. Isa. 53:12.
246 Phil. 2:6.
247 John 1:12.
248 Cf. Gal. 3:13.
249 Jerome, *Commentarii in Matheum* 4 (CCSL 77:270.1672–78; 1683–84), quoting Rom. 5:20.

## BOOK SIX

Or lest anyone be ignorant that the form of the cross must be worshipped,
Which carried the Lord, triumphing with powerful reason,
Thereafter it gathers the four quarters of the four-part world.
The splendid morning-star gleams from the head of the Maker,
The sacred feet are licked by the western star.
It holds the Bear on the right, it lifts the middle axis on the left,
And all nature has its life from the limbs of the Creator,
And Christ rules the world represented by the cross everywhere.[250]

The Apostle describes the moral allegory of the holy cross, when he says: *That being rooted and founded in love, you may be able to comprehend, /402/ with all the saints, what is the breadth and length, the height and depth, and to know the love of Christ that surpasses knowledge.*[251] Certainly he signifies *by breadth, the good works of love; by length, the constancy* of the holy way of life *right to the end; by height, the hope of heavenly rewards; by depth, the inscrutable judgements of God, from whence this very grace comes to men. And these things correspond to the mystery of the Cross, so that by breadth is understood the transverse wooden beam by which the hands are extended, by reason of the signification of the works; by length, from that beam right into the ground, where the whole crucified body seems to stand, which signifies persistence, that is, endurance with long-suffering; by height, from that transverse beam upwards towards the part that projects above the head, by reason of the expectation of celestial things, in order that we might believe that those good works and constancy in them are not for the sake of the earthly and temporal benefits of God, but rather for that which* 'faith that works by love' *hopes for above, and which is eternal;*[252] *and by depth, that part of the wood which lies fixed in the secrecy of the earth, but from whence all that which projects arises, just as from the hidden will of God man is called to the sharing of such great grace,* 'one after this manner and another after that':[253] *truly the love of Christ that surpasses knowledge, assuredly that where is that* 'peace which surpasses all understanding'.[254]

**319/1** [Luke 23:33b] **And the robbers, one on the right hand and the other on the left.** The robbers who are crucified with the Lord on either

---

250 Sedulius, *Paschale carmen* 5.188–95 (CSEL 10:128).
251 Eph. 3:17–19.
252 Gal. 5:6.
253 1 Cor. 7:7.
254 Augustine, *Epistolae* 147.34 (CSEL 44:307.16–308.13); Phil. 4:7.

side signify those who in the faith and confession of Christ suffer either the struggle of martyrdom or the practice of stricter abstinence. But they, however many they are, who do these things for the sake of eternal and heavenly glory alone, are certainly designated by the merit and faith of the robber on the right. But those who renounce the world either out of consideration for human praise, or for whatever less worthy intention, rightly imitate the mind and deeds of the blaspheming robber on the left. Of such the Apostle says: *If I deliver my body to be burned, if I give all my goods to feed the poor,* if I do many other things, *and have not love, it profits me nothing.*[255] But truly: *Blessed are those who suffer persecution of the sake of justice, for theirs is the kingdom of heaven.*[256]

## Chapter 91

320/10 [Luke 23:34] **And Jesus said: Father, forgive them; for they do not know what they do.** Since Luke who is represented allegorically as a calf determined to write of the sacerdotal office of Christ, it is right that in his account the Lord not only intercedes for his persecutors in accordance with a priest's privilege, but also by the same office opens /403/ the gate of paradise to the confessing robber. For it must not be thought that he prayed to the Father for these things in vain, but that without doubt he obtained what he prayed for, namely for those who after his passion believed. Indeed, it should be noted that he offered prayers to the Father not for those who, incited by the goads of envy and pride, preferred to crucify rather than confess the one whom they believed to be the Son of God, but rather for those who, possessing a zeal *for God, but not according to knowledge,*[257] did not know what they did. But the apostle John also says: *There is a sin to death; I do not say that anyone should pray for it.*[258] Therefore, imitate your Lord, intercede for your enemies, and if you are not yet able to do so, at least beware, lest you dare to pray against them. Thus indeed, strengthened by daily progress and with the help of the Lord, at some time or other you will reach the point that you can even intercede for them.

---

255 1 Cor. 13:3.
256 Matt. 5:10.
257 Rom. 10:2.
258 1 John 5:16.

BOOK SIX 621

**321/1 [Luke 23:34b–35] But they, dividing his garments, cast lots. And the people stood by, watching.** The evangelist John expounds these matters more fully, in particular that the soldiers divided the rest into four parts in accordance with their number, and cast a lot for the coat which *was without a seam, woven from the top throughout.*[259] And *the Lord's clothing divided into four parts allegorically represents his four-part Church, spread that is to say over the whole world, which consists of four parts, and equally (that is, harmoniously) distributed in all these same parts. But that coat obtained by lot signifies the unity of all the parts, which is held together by the bond of love.* For *if love*, according to the Apostle, *not only possesses a more surpassing way,*[260] *and also surpasses all knowledge,*[261] *and is enjoined above all things, the coat by which it is signified is rightly said to be woven from the top. And what is commended to our attention by 'lot' save the grace of God? Thus, indeed grace comes to all by a single lot, when the lot was agreeable to all, because the grace of God comes to all in unity, and although the lot is cast, it is granted not by the merits of any person, but by the hidden judgement of God.*[262]

**322/2 [Luke 23:35b] And the leaders with them derided him, saying: He saved others; let him save himself, if he is Christ, the chosen of God.** Likewise the leaders and the people of the Jews confess against their will that he saved others. And so, your words condemn you. For he who saved others, surely, if he wished, could save himself.[263] Let him save himself, they say, *if he is Christ, the chosen of God.* On the contrary, he did not wish to save himself by descending from the cross, because he is Christ, the chosen of God. For he who came in order to be crucified for us, disdained to save himself by descending from the cross, /404/ because by dying he desired to save, along with other sinners, even those who crucified him.

**323/2 [Luke 23:36–37] And the soldiers also mocked him, coming to him and offering him vinegar, and saying: If you are the king of the Jews, save yourself.** *The Jews themselves, deteriorating from the wine of the patriarchs and the prophets, were the vinegar.*[264] This means that the soldiers gave this vinegar to drink to the Lord whom they delivered to

---

259 John 19:23.
260 Cf. 1 Cor. 12:31.
261 Cf. Eph. 3:19.
262 Augustine, *In Iohannis euang.* 118.4 (CCSL 36:656.2–6; 9–17; 657.30–34).
263 Jerome, *Commentarii in Matheum* 4 (CCSL 77:272.1724–27).
264 Augustine, *In Iohannis euang.* 119.4 (CCSL 36:659.18–20).

death at the urging of the Jews. And it should be noted that the blaspheming Jews mock the appellation of 'Christ' and of 'the Son of God' entrusted to them by the authority of Scripture. But the soldiers, since they are ignorant of the Scriptures, scoff, not at Christ, the chosen of God, but at the King of the Jews.

**324/1** [Luke 23:38] **And there was also an inscription written over him in letters of Greek and Latin and Hebrew: This is the King of the Jews.** The inscription that asserts Christ to be king is appropriately placed not below but above the cross, because although he suffered for us on the cross with the weakness of a man,[265] nevertheless he shone above the cross with the majesty of a king. Because he is at once king and priest, when he offered the extraordinary sacrifice of his own flesh to the Father on the altar of the cross,[266] he fittingly laid claim also to the dignity of a king as he possessed that title, so that it may become clear to all willing to read (that is, to hear and believe) that he did not destroy his sovereignty by the cross, but confirmed it and strengthened it instead. Hence, after the Apostle described the disgrace of the cross, he added: *Therefore God also has exalted him and given him a name which is above every name*, and so forth.[267] The fact that this name was written in Hebrew, Greek, and Latin is because the same Apostle, going on, added: *And that every tongue should confess that Jesus Christ is <Lord> in the glory of God the Father.*[268] As for the inscription, *these three tongues stood out at that time above the rest: Hebrew on account of the Jews glorying in the Law; Greek on account of the wise men of the Gentiles; Latin on account of the Romans ruling over many, and at that time nearly all of the Gentile nations.*[269] Whether they will or no, therefore, the Jews bear witness to the whole realm of the world, to all worldly wisdom, to all the sacraments of divine Law, that Jesus is the king of the Jews, that is, the ruler of those who believe and confess God.

**325/2** [Luke 23:39] **And one of those robbers who were hanged, blasphemed him, saying: If you are Christ, save yourself and us.** Perhaps it bothers some people why the other evangelists say that the robbers /405/

---

265 Cf. Ambrose, *Expos. Lucam* 10.112 & 113 (CCSL 14:377.1055–57; 1061–64).
266 See Introduction, 56. For Bede, Luke ('the calf') particularly stresses Christ's role as both sacrificing priest and sacrificial victim: O'Brien, *Bede's Temple*, 101.
267 Phil. 2:9.
268 Phil. 2:11. The Vulgate reads '*quia Dominus Iesus Christus in gloria est Dei patris*'. The omission of *dominus* is inexplicable, and alters the meaning, particularly as Bede is discussing Christ's rulership.
269 Augustine, *In Iohannis euang.* 117.4 (CCSL 36:653.6–10).

who were crucified with him reviled him, *seeing that, according to Luke's testimony, one of them reviled him and the other restrained himself and believed in God.* But *let us understand that* the other evangelists, *treating this passage briefly, used the plural number for the singular; just as in the Epistle to the Hebrews we read it said in the plural: 'they stopped the mouths of lions',*[270] *when Daniel alone is understood to be meant; and it is said in the plural: 'they were cut asunder',*[271] *when it refers to Isaiah alone. And likewise what is said in the Psalm: 'The kings of the earth set themselves, and the rulers take counsel together',*[272] *puts the plural number for the singular, and this is explained in the Acts of the Apostles: for the apostles, who made use of the authority of that same psalm, understood the kings to refer to Herod, and the rulers to refer to Pilate.*[273] *And what is more common, for example, than that someone may say: And the peasants abuse me insolently, although it is only one doing the abusing?*[274]

**326/10   [Luke 23:40–42]. But the other answering, rebuked him, saying: Do you not fear God, seeing you are under the same condemnation? And we indeed justly, for we receive the due reward of our deeds; but this man has done no evil. And he said to Jesus: Lord, remember me when you come into your kingdom.** Who does not marvel at the spirit of this robber? Or rather who does not marvel at the grace of the Lord which aids him? Who does not worship with a fitting act of gratitude? *On the cross nails fixed his hands and feet, and nothing had been left free except his heart and tongue; at the inspiration of God he offered to him all that he found free in himself, so that, according to what is written: 'With the heart* he believed *in justice; with the mouth* he made confession *to salvation'.*[275] *And the Apostle testifies that three virtues above all remain in the heart of the faithful, saying: 'And now there remain faith, hope, and love'.*[276] *Filled with sudden grace the robber both received and retained all these three on the cross. He who believed that the Lord would reign, whom he saw dying alongside himself, had faith. He had hope, who asked for admission to his kingdom. And he maintained a lively charity even as he was dying, denouncing his brother*

---

270  Hebr. 11:33.
271  Hebr. 11:37.
272  Ps. 2:2.
273  Cf. Acts 4:26–27.
274  Augustine, *De consensu euang.* 3.16 (CSEL 43:340.5–17; 19–21).
275  Rom. 10:10.
276  1 Cor. 13:13.

and fellow robber who was dying for the same crime for his wickedness, and proclaiming to him the life which he had come to know. A person like this comes to the cross because of guilt, and behold, he departs from the cross because of grace. He confessed the Lord whom he saw dying with him in his human weakness, when the apostles denied him whom they had seen doing miracles with divine power.[277]

[Luke 23:43] **And Jesus said to him: Amen I say to you: Today you will be with me in /406/ paradise.** *This is a magnificent example of the way of life one should strive for, that mercy is so quickly opened to the robber, and grace is more fruitful than prayer. For the Lord always gives more than he is asked for. The robber asked that the Lord remember him when he came into his kingdom. But the Lord says: 'Amen I say to you: Today you will be with me in paradise.' For it is life to be with Christ, because where Christ is, there is the kingdom.*[278]

Some persons associate the two robbers crucified with the Lord with two kinds of baptized persons. For *all of us, who have been baptized in Christ Jesus, were baptized in his death.*[279] Indeed both were crucified alike, but one became a worse blasphemer on the cross; the other became a martyr by confession. For some are crowned by the baptism with which we as sinners are cleansed, when they praise with faith, hope, and love the God who suffered in the flesh; others, as long as they refuse to have either faith or the works of baptism, are deprived of the gift that they received.

**327/2** [Luke 23:44–45] **And it was about the sixth hour; and there was darkness over all the earth until the ninth hour. And the sun was darkened.** *The brightest light of the world* withdrew *its beams, either in order that it might not see the Lord hanging, or that the wicked blasphemers might not enjoy its light.*[280] It should be noted that the Lord was crucified at the sixth hour, that is, when the sun is about to recede from the zenith, but that he solemnized the mysteries of his resurrection at dawn, that is, when the sun was rising. For by the circumstances of time he signified what he brought about in accomplishing his work, because *he died for our sins and rose again for our justification.*[281] Indeed, when Adam was sinning, it is written that he heard *the voice of the Lord God walking in paradise in*

---

277 Gregory, *Moralia* 18.40 (CCSL 143A:929.96–117).
278 Ambrose, *Expos. Lucam* 10.121 (CCSL 14:379.1123–29).
279 Rom. 6:3.
280 Jerome, *Commentarii in Matheum* 4 (CCSL 77:274.1763–65).
281 Rom. 4:24.

*the breeze after noon.*²⁸² It is truly 'after noon', when the light of faith has sunk down, and 'in the breeze', as the heat of love grows cold. And God was heard walking, because he had withdrawn from the man who sinned. Right reason, therefore, demands that at the time of day when God shut the gate of paradise on Adam who sinned, he now opened it to the robber who repented.

**328/2** [Luke 23:45b] **And the curtain of the temple was torn in half.** This happened as the Lord was expiring, as Matthew and Mark attest, but Luke related it by prolepsis.²⁸³ For wishing to join miracle to miracle, after he said, *the sun was darkened,* he immediately thought it necessary to add, *And the curtain of the temple was torn in half.* The curtain of the temple is torn, in order for the ark of the Covenant *and all the sacraments of the Law, which were formerly hidden,* to appear and to pass *to /407/* the Gentiles.²⁸⁴ Previously it had been said: *In Judea God is known, his name is great in Israel;*²⁸⁵ but now he says: *Be exalted, O God, above the heavens, and your glory above all the earth.*²⁸⁶ And in the Gospel he earlier said: *Do not go into the way of the Gentiles;*²⁸⁷ but after the passion he says: *Going therefore, teach all nations.*²⁸⁸

**329/1** [Luke 23:46] **And Jesus crying with a loud voice, said: Father, into your hands I commend my spirit. And saying this, he breathed his last.** By calling upon the Father, he declares that he is the Son of God. But by commending his spirit, he reveals not a defect of his own power, but his confidence in the Father's power. For he loves to give glory to the Father, in order to instruct us to give glory to the Creator. And so, he commends his spirit to the Father, in accordance with what is said with a glad heart and joyful lips in another psalm: *Because you will not leave my soul in hell; nor will you allow your holy one to see corruption.*²⁸⁹

**330/2** [Luke 23:47] **Now the centurion, seeing what was done, glorified God, saying: Truly this was a just man.** Not only did the centurion

---

282 Gen. 3:8.
283 Prolepsis, or anticipation, is the first rhetorical figure (or 'scheme') that Bede takes up in *De schematibus et tropis,* ed. Kendall (CCSL 123A:143–44); trans. Kendall, *The Figures of Rhetoric,* 171.
284 Jerome, *Commentarii in Matheum* 4 (CCSL 77:275.1799–801).
285 Ps. 75:2 (76:1).
286 Ps. 56:6 (57:5).
287 Matt. 10:5.
288 Matt. 28:19.
289 Ps. 15:10 (16:10).

glorify God, but also the soldiers *who were with him, keeping watch over Jesus*, as Matthew writes, *having seen the earthquake, and the things that were done, were sore afraid, saying: Truly this was the Son of God.*[290] How great, therefore, was the blindness of the Jews who after so many miracles performed by the Lord, and with such great signs appearing at his death, refused to believe, and in company with the more unfeeling Gentiles disdained to glorify or fear God. Hence the centurion[291] rightly signifies the faith of the Church, which immediately, after the curtain of the heavenly mysteries is opened by the death of the Lord, confirms that Jesus is not only truly a just man, but also truly the Son of God, while the Synagoge keeps silent. Likewise, the number one hundred, which by the bending of the fingers, as I mentioned above,[292] passes from the left to the right hand, corresponds very aptly to the sacraments of the Church and to the faith, which believes in the Gospel in place of the Law and promises the kingdom of heaven in place of the wealth of the earth.

**331/10** [Luke 23:48] **And all the crowd of those who had gathered for that sight and had seen the things that were done returned, beating their breasts.** Beating their breasts is sign of penitence and of mourning, and it can be understood in two ways. Either they were grieving for him who was killed unjustly, and whose life they loved, or they were trembling with fear at him who had been further glorified by death and whose death they remembered that they had brought about. But whether diverse and differing persons in the crowd were driven to beat the breast for the first reason or the second or both, the difference between nation and nation should be noted. The Gentiles, fearing God, glorify Christ as he is dying with words of express confession; the Jews, merely beating their breasts, return home in silence. /408/

[Luke 23:49] **And all his acquaintances, and the women who had followed him from Galilee, stood far off, beholding these things.** This is what the Lord himself in the Psalm complains to the Father, laying out the sequence of his passion, saying: *You have put far from me friend and neighbour, and my acquaintances, because of misery.*[293]

---

290 Matt. 27:54.
291 A centurion commanded a century, a company of 100 men; hence Bede invokes the symbolism of the number 100.
292 For this allusion to finger-reckoning, see Bede's commentary on Luke 9:14b–15, as well as Book 1 n. 285, Book 2 n. 92, and Book 3 n. 290.
293 Ps. 87:19 (88:18).

332/1 [Luke 23:50–51] **And behold, there was a man named Joseph, who was a decurion, a good and just man. He had not consented to their counsel and doings.** A decurion is so called, because he is *of the curial order* and holds *office in the curia*; he is also called a *curialis*, because he has charge of [*procurando*] *civil duties*.²⁹⁴

[Luke 23:51b] **He was of Arimathea, a city of Judea, who also himself was waiting for the kingdom of God.** Arimathea itself is Ramathaim, *the city of Elkanah and Samuel in the district of Thamnitica, near Diospolis*.²⁹⁵

[Luke 23:52] **This man gained access to Pilate and asked for the body of Jesus.** This Joseph is esteemed to have been of great worthiness in the world, but to have been more meritorious in the eyes of God, so that by the righteousness of his merits he was worthy to bury the Lord's body, and by the nobility of his worldly power he was able to take possession of the same body. *For no* base-born person could *gain access to a ruler and obtain the body of a crucified man*.²⁹⁶

333/1 [Luke 23:53] **And taking him down, he wrapped him in fine linen, and laid him in a tomb that was hewn in stone in which no one had ever yet been laid.** *The humble burial of the Lord condemns the vanity of the wealthy who cannot forgo their wealth even in their tombs. But we can also understand this in a spiritual sense, because Joseph, who took him with a pure mind, wraps Jesus in 'clean linen'*.²⁹⁷ And *he is placed 'in a new tomb'*,²⁹⁸ *so that after the resurrection another person might not be supposed to have arisen, other bodies being present there. Because it is well recalled that the tomb had been* hewn out of rock, *lest if it had been constructed from many stones it could be said that Jesus had been removed by theft after the foundations of the tomb had been undermined*.²⁹⁹

In another interpretation: The Lord is enclosed alone in the tomb, in order for his burial, as well as his resurrection, to be signified as special, that is, unlike ours, just as also other mysteries of his dispensation differ from the weakness of our nature. For he also appeared as a true man, but he was conceived and born from a virgin mother. And he was tempted in every respect, but to indicate his resemblance to us and without sin. And he

---

294 Isidore, *Etym.* 9.4.23–24; trans. Barney *et al.*, 204.
295 Jerome, *De situ et nom.* (*Onomastica sacra* 96.17–19); cf. 1 Sam. 1:1–20.
296 Jerome, *Commentarii in Matheum* 4 (CCSL 77:277.1867–69).
297 Matt. 27:59.
298 Matt. 27:60.
299 Jerome, *Commentarii in Matheum* 4 (CCSL 77:278.1874–80; 278.1883–85; 279.1902–04).

died, but in the way he himself wanted. And he was buried, but for as long as he wanted. And he was raised from the dead, but when he wanted. This is therefore what he says: *I am alone until I pass.*[300] And /409/ elsewhere, about his being buried alone: *In peace in the same I will sleep, and I will rest, for you, O Lord, have settled me alone in hope,*[301] that is, although resurrection has been reserved for other mortals at the end of time, you have promised by a gift unique in its kind that I will rise again from the dead on the third day.

**334**/10 [Luke 23:54] **And it was the day of Parasceve and the Sabbath was dawning.** Parasceve means preparation [*praeparatio*], and it is by this term that the Jews who lived among the Greeks used to call the sixth day of the Sabbath, which we now call the sixth day of the week, because on that day they prepared the things that would be necessary on the Sabbath. This accords with what was once commanded about manna: 'But on the sixth day you will gather double', and so forth.[302] But *the Jews* who live among the Romans *more usually* call it *in Latin 'cena pura'.*[303] Therefore, because man was made and the whole creation of the world was completed on the sixth day, and on the seventh day the Creator rested from his work,[304] he also commanded this day to be called the Sabbath, that is, rest. The Lord, who was crucified on that same sixth day, rightly fulfilled on that day the mystery of the redemption [*reparatio*] of mankind. Hence, *when he had taken the vinegar, he said: It is finished,*[305] that is, 'all the work of the sixth day, which I undertook to restore the world, has been completed'. On the Sabbath, resting in the sepulchre, he awaited the resurrection which was to come on the eighth day. At the same time a figural model of our devotion shines brightly there. It is necessary that the faithful suffer in this sixth age of the world for the Lord and be, as it were, crucified to the world;[306] but in the seventh age, that is, when all have settled the debt of death, the bodies remain in the tombs, but the souls remain in a peace reserved for them with the Lord. And after good works it is proper to rest, until when the eighth age comes at last even the bodies glorified by that resurrection, together with the souls, receive the incorruptibility of their eternal inheritance.

300 Ps. 140:10 (141:10).
301 Ps. 4:9–10 (4:8).
302 Cf. Exod. 16:5.
303 Augustine, *In Iohannis euang.* 120.5 (CCSL 36:663).
304 Cf. Gen. 1:27; 2:1–2.
305 John 19:30.
306 Cf. Gal. 6:14.

Hence, the seventh day in Genesis is well said not to have had an evening, because the rest of the souls, which is in that seventh age now, must not be consumed by any sorrow, but must be increased by the more abundant joy of the resurrection to come.[307]

[Luke 23:55] **And the women who had come with him from Galilee, following after, saw the tomb and how his body was laid.** We read above that *all his acquaintances, and the women who had followed him, stood far off.*[308] When these acquaintances, therefore, returned to their homes after his dead body was laid down, only the women who loved him more deeply, having followed the funeral procession, desired to see how it was laid, so that at a suitable time they might offer the gift of their /410/ devotion to him. But even now holy women carry out Parasceve on the same day, when these souls, humble and conscious of their greater weakness, but burning with a greater love of the Saviour, diligently give themselves up to retracing his passion in this age in which the rest to come must be prepared for, and if perchance they are able to imitate, they ponder with a careful diligence how that passion was accomplished.

**335**/8 [Luke 23:56] **And returning, they prepared spices and ointments, and on the Sabbath they rested, according to the commandment.** The commandment was that silence should be observed from nightfall to nightfall on the Sabbath, and for that reason, after the Lord was buried, the devout women were occupied with the preparation of the ointments as long as work was permitted, that is, up to sunset. For they worked not only on the day of Parasceve, but at the end of the Sabbath, that is, at sunset. As soon as licence to work was restored, they purchased spices, so that coming in the morning, they might anoint his body, as the evangelist Mark testifies.[309] Nor could they approach the tomb on the evening of the Sabbath, from the time of nightfall. But after witnessing the burial of the Lord, they returned home and prepared spices and ointments. After observing, hearing, and storing in their heart the passion of the Lord, they immediately turn to carrying out the virtuous deeds with which Christ is pleased, and, having prepared the spices, they rest on the Sabbath. They will come after the

---

307 Cf. Gen. 2:1–3. Bede revisits and elaborates on this interpretation at the end of his excursion on the six ages of the world. See *In Genesim* 1, ed. Jones (CCSL 118A:39.1203–24; trans. Kendall, *On Genesis*, 104–05). On the Seventh and Eighth Ages (Bede's 'expanded world ages' scheme), see Book 1, n. 276.
308 Luke 23:49.
309 Cf. Mark 16:1–2.

Sabbath with offerings to the Lord, when, with the Parasceve of the present life at an end, they wait rejoicing in blessed rest, and when with the time of the resurrection appearing, they run to meet Christ with the sweet-smelling spices (so to speak) of spiritual deeds.

## Chapter 92

336/1 [Luke 24:1] **And on the first of the Sabbath, very early in the morning, they came to the tomb, bringing the spices which they had prepared.** The 'first of the Sabbath' is the first day after the Sabbath, which Christian custom calls the Lord's day because of the resurrection of the Lord. As for the fact that the women came to the tomb very early in the morning, it shows on the literal level the great fervour of their love in seeking and finding the Lord, but on the allegorical level we are given a mystical example to approach the sacred body of the Lord with our outward form suffused with spiritual light and with the darkness of sins shaken off. Indeed, that tomb so worthy of veneration contains a symbol of the Lord's altar, on which the mysteries of his flesh and blood are wont to be celebrated. Hence the ecclesiastical rule affirms that the same mysteries ought to be celebrated, not upon silk, not upon dyed cloth, but upon a pure linen cloth like the linen with which /411/ Joseph wrapped him, so that just as he offered the true substance of his earthly and mortal nature to death for us, so also in memory of this same sacrament, so awesome and worthy of veneration, we should lay on the altar from the fruit of the earth linen pure and white, and chastised as it were by many kinds of deadly blows.[310] The spices that the women brought signify the sweetness and odour of virtues and prayers with which we ought to approach the altar. Hence John in his Apocalypse, after he had described *the golden vials full of odours* in the hands of the angels, that is, the pure consciences in the hearts of the chosen ones, added in explanation: *which are the prayers of saints*.[311]

[Luke 24:2-3] **And they found the stone rolled back from the tomb. And going in, they did not find the body of the Lord Jesus.** Matthew explained in a satisfactory manner how the stone was rolled back by an angel. But allegorically the rolling back of the stone makes known the

---

310 Bede refers here to the process by which linen is prepared from flax by a lengthy and strenuous process of 'breaking'.
311 Rev. 5:8.

BOOK SIX 631

exposure of the mysteries that were hidden by the veil of the letter. For the Law was written in stone and when its covering is removed the dead body of the Lord is not found, but his living body is proclaimed, because *although we have known Christ according to the flesh, but now we know him so no longer.*[312]

[Luke 24:4] **And it happened, while they were perplexed in their mind at this, behold, two men stood by them in shining apparel.** They were perplexed in their mind, because not only were they astonished that a stone of such immense size was rolled back, but also they were grieved that the body worthy of such extraordinary veneration was not found. Just as when the Lord is tempted in the solitude [of the desert], angels come and minister to him as soon as he achieves victory,[313] so when the same Saviour suffers in the flesh, after overcoming the struggles of death, angels come who proclaim the glory of the victor not only with consoling words, but also in shining apparel. We read that just as the angels stood in attendance after the Saviour's body was placed in the tomb, so they may likewise be believed to assist with the mysteries of that same most sacred body that are to be celebrated at the time of consecration [of the Eucharist]. The Apostle warns women to wear a veil in church because of the angels.[314]

337/2 [Luke 24:5–6] **And as they were afraid and bowed their face to the ground, they said to them: Why do you seek the living with the dead? He is not here, but has risen.** Do not seek him, they say, with the dead, that is, in the tomb which is properly the place of the dead, who has now risen to life from the dead. And we too, following the example of the women in their devotion to God, whenever we enter the church ought to enter with all humility and fear, /412/ either because angelic powers are present or out of veneration for the sacred offering, for we are close to the heavenly mysteries. We bow our face indeed to the ground at the presence of angels, when, as we contemplate what the eternal joys of the citizens of heaven are, we humbly reflect that we are ashes and dirt. As the blessed Abraham says: *I will speak to my Lord, although I am dust and ashes.*[315] It should be noted that the holy women are not said to have fallen to the ground before the angels who stood by them, but to have bowed their faces to the ground. Nor do we read that

---

312  2 Cor. 5:16.
313  Cf. Matt. 4:11.
314  Cf. 1 Cor. 11:10.
315  Gen. 18:27.

any of the saints at the time of the Lord's resurrection adored either the Lord himself, or the angels seen by them, prostrate on the ground. Hence, the custom of the Church obtained that, whether in remembrance of the Lord's resurrection, or in the hope of our resurrection, we pray not on bended knee but with faces to the ground every Sunday, and during the whole time of Quinquagesima.[316]

[Luke 24:6b–7] **Remember how he spoke to you, when he was still in Galilee, saying: The Son of man must be delivered into the hands of sinful men, and be crucified, and on the third day rise again.** On the third day the Lord celebrated the triumph of his resurrection, and as we learn from this passage, he foretold this even to the women who were following him among the men, his disciples. For indeed, yielding up his spirit on the day of Parasceve at the ninth hour, and having been buried in the evening, he rose in the morning, on the first day of the week, as the evangelist Mark clearly describes.[317] *Rightly, therefore, he lay one day and two nights in the tomb, because evidently he added the light of his own single death to the darkness of our double death. He came certainly to us, we who were being held in the death of the spirit and the flesh; he delivered his own single death, that is, of the flesh, to us, and he released our two deaths, which he received. For if he himself took both, he would free us from neither; but he accepted one out of pity, and rightly condemned both. He conferred his single death upon our double death, and dying conquered our double death.*[318]

[Luke 24:8] **And they remembered his words.** May the women standing in the Lord's tomb, who remember the words that he said before about his dispensation, be our model – that, amidst the rites of the Lord's passion which we are to celebrate, we should remember with the veneration

---

316 Evidently for Bede, 'to bow the face to the ground' [*vultum in terram declinasse*] means to stand with head lowered; not to kneel, and not to prostrate oneself [*uisis terrae prostratum adorare*], though *prostrare* can mean 'to bow low to the ground' and *prostratio* can mean 'kneeling, genuflection' (*DMLBS s.v. prostrare* 2 and *prostratio* 2). Bede points out in his commentary on Rev. 19:10 (ed. Gryson, 494; trans. Wallis, 246) that there is ample Old Testament precedent for 'falling at the feet' of angels. In the thirteenth century the liturgist William Durandus (ca. 1220–1296) stipulated that at the Easter liturgy the congregation should worship standing, in imitation of the women at the Sepulchre (*Rationale divinorum officiorum* 6.86.17 (450) and cites Ambrose's commentary on Luke as his source: however, Ambrose does not mention this, and Durandus's source was probably Bede.
317 Mark 16:2.
318 Gregory, *Moralia* 4.16 (CCSL 143:183.45–53).

due to it not only this blessed passion, but also the resurrection from hell, and the glory of the ascension to heaven.

**338/2** [Luke 24:9] **And coming out from the tomb, they told all these things to the eleven and to all the rest.** *For as in the beginning woman was the cause of sin /413/ for man, and man was the performer of the fault, so now she who had tasted death first, saw the resurrection first, and so that she might not bear the disgrace of eternal guilt among men, she who had spread sin to man, also spread grace.*[319]

**339/10** [Luke 24:10] **And it was Mary Magdalen, and Joanna, and Mary of James, and the other women who were with them, who told these things to the apostles.** This Mary Magdalen is the sister of Lazarus who anointed the Lord with oil.[320] *Joanna is the wife of Chuza, Herod's steward*, about whom we read above.[321] Mary of James is the mother of James the Less and Joseph, as the evangelist Mark says,[322] the sister of the mother of the Lord. Hence this James also deserved to be called the brother of the Lord.[323]

[Luke 24:11] **And these words seemed to them like nonsense; and they did not believe them.** *The fact that the disciples were slow to believe the resurrection of the Lord was not so much because of their weakness as for the sake of our future strength, if I may put it so. For that resurrection was made known to those doubters by many pieces of evidence. When we come to know these things through reading, what else is it than that we are strengthened by their doubt?*[324]

[Luke 24:12] **But Peter rising up, ran to the tomb, and stooping down, he saw the linen cloths laid by themselves; and he went away wondering within himself at what had happened.** Luke refers to Peter's running briefly; but John describes more fully how it happened, saying also that the disciple whom Jesus loved ran with Peter, implying, of course, that it was himself.[325] Hence it is asked why Luke says of Peter: *and stooping down, he saw the linen cloths laid by themselves*, when John indicates instead that he himself had done this, but that Peter entering *into the tomb* had seen not only *the linen cloths*, but *also the napkin that had been about*

---

319  Ambrose, *Expos. Lucam* 10.156 (CCSL 14:390.1472–77).
320  Cf. John 12:3.
321  Luke 8:3.
322  Cf. Mark 15:40.
323  Cf. Mark 6:3.
324  Gregory, *Hom. in Euang.* 2.29.1 (CCSL 141:244.1–45).
325  Cf. John 20:2–6.

*his head.*³²⁶ But it must be understood that Peter, stooping down, was the first to have seen these, which Luke remarks upon, while John is silent, and that he entered afterwards, in order to distinguish the things inside more carefully, and that he entered nevertheless before John entered.³²⁷

## Chapter 93

[Luke 24:13–14] **And behold, two of them went that same day to a village which was sixty stades from Jerusalem, named Emmaus. And they talked together of all these things which had happened.** A stade, by which the Greeks, on the authority they say of Hercules,³²⁸ measure the lengths of roads, is an eighth of a mile, and therefore sixty stades signifies seven thousand five hundred paces. The length of that journey is very appropriate to those who made their way, certain of the death and burial /414/ of the Saviour, but doubtful of his resurrection. For who will doubt that the resurrection, which happened after 'the seventh day of the Sabbath' [i.e., the Sabbath], is consonant with the number eight? Therefore the disciples, who walked along talking of the Lord, first completed six miles of the journey they had begun, because they were grieving that he, living without reproach, had arrived at death, which he underwent on the sixth day of the Sabbath [i.e., Friday], and then they completed the seventh mile, because they were not in doubt that he had rested in the tomb. But they finished only half of the eighth mile, because they did not yet completely believe in the glory of the resurrection that was already celebrated. *Emmaus* itself *is the distinguished city of Nicopolis in Palestine,*³²⁹ which was restored under the emperor Marcus Aurelius Antoninus after the campaign in Judea, and changed its name with its status.

[Luke 24:15] **And it happened that while they talked and reasoned with themselves, Jesus himself also drawing near, went with them.** As they are talking of him, the Lord, drawing near, accompanies them, in order both to kindle in their mind faith in his resurrection and to signify by the presence of his hidden majesty that he would always carry out what he

---

326 John 20:6–7.
327 Cf. Augustine, *De consensu euang.* 3.25 (CSEL 43:369.16–26).
328 Cf. Isidore, *Etym.* 15.16.3. A Roman pace was a double step (i.e., from left foot to left foot), or about five feet. Hence, 1000 paces = a mile, and 7500 paces = seven and a half miles.
329 Jerome, *De situ et nom.* (*Onomastica sacra* 121.6–8).

BOOK SIX 635

promised: *For where two or three are gathered together in my name, there am I in the midst of them.*[330]

[Luke 24:16–17] **But their eyes were held in check, in order that they not know him. And he said to them: What are these conversations that you hold with one another as you walk, and you are sad?** Indeed, *the Lord appeared to the disciples, but he did not appear to them in a form that they could recognize. The Lord, therefore, did outwardly to the eyes of the body what was done among them inwardly to the eyes of the heart. For among themselves they inwardly both loved and doubted; and the Lord was both present to them outwardly, and did not show who he was. Therefore, he exhibited his presence to them as they were speaking of him, but he hid the form by which he could be recognized because of their doubts.*[331]

[Luke 24:18] **And one of them, whose name was Cleophas, answering, said to him: Are you only a stranger in Jerusalem, and do you not know the things that have been done there in these days?** They supposed that he, whose face they did not recognize, was a stranger. But truly he was a stranger to them, for he was far removed from the weakness of their nature now that he had received the glory of the resurrection. He was a stranger to them, because he remained a stranger from their faith, seeing that they were unaware of his resurrection.

[Luke 24:19] **To whom he said: What things? And they said to him: Concerning Jesus of Nazareth, who was a prophet mighty in work and word before God and all the people.** They speak of him as a great prophet, and say nothing of him as the Son of God, either because they did not completely believe or because they were anxious not to fall into the hands of the persecuting Jews, and so they hid the truth which they believed, because they did not know who /415/ he was with whom they were speaking.

[Luke 24:20–21] **And how our chief priests and rulers delivered him to be condemned to death and crucified him. But we hoped that it was he who was to redeem Israel.** It was proper that they walked sadly, for in a way they blamed themselves because they had hoped for redemption by him, whom they had already seen dead, and they did not believe that he would rise again. And they especially grieved that he had been killed without committing any fault, because they knew he was innocent.

---

330 Matt. 18:20.
331 Gregory, *Hom. in Euang.* 2.23.1 (CCSL 141:193.6–14).

[Luke 24:21b–23] **And now besides all this, today is the third day since these things were done. And yet certain women of our company frightened us, who before it was light, were at the tomb. And not finding his body, they came, saying that they had indeed seen a vision of angels, who say that he is alive.** The women are rightly said to have frightened them, because they were able to add more sorrow to their minds concerning their failure to find the Lord's body than to instil joy at the angels' proclamation of his resurrection, by which their spirits might be cheered.

[Luke 24:24] **And some of our people went to the tomb and found it just as the women said, but they did not find him.** *When Luke himself said above that Peter ran to the tomb, and now reported that Cleophas said that some of them went to the tomb, he is understood to attest that two went to the tomb, but he first mentioned only Peter, because Mary originally announced these things to him.*[332]

[Luke 24:25–27] **Then he said to them: O foolish, and slow of heart to believe in all things which the prophets have spoken. Was it not necessary for Christ to suffer these things and so to enter into his glory? And beginning with Moses and all the prophets, he interpreted to them in all the Scriptures the things that were about himself.** In this passage it is not the need to interpret Scripture that weighs upon us, but the two-fold need to humble ourselves, seeing that we are neither educated in the Scriptures as much as is necessary, nor intent as much as is fitting upon fulfilling the things which we have been able perchance to learn from them. For if Moses and all the prophets spoke of Christ, and said that he was going to enter into his glory by the straits of the passion, why do they boast that they are Christians, who neither desire to investigate the Scriptures as they pertain to Christ (as much as their capacity allows), nor to attain to the glory that they wish to have with Christ by suffering tribulations?

[Luke 24:28–29] **And they drew near to the village to which they were going; and he made as though he would go farther. But they constrained him, saying: Stay with us, because /416/ it is almost evening and the day is now far spent. And he went in with them.** *The simple Truth does nothing by duplicity, but,* because it is said: 'he made as though he would go farther', *the way he showed himself to the disciples in body was congruent with the way that he was with them in spirit. They were going to be tested, to see whether, even if they did not yet cherish*

---

332 Augustine, *De consensu euang.* 3.25 (CSEL 43:369.12–16).

*him as God, they were able at least to love him as a stranger. But because those with whom Truth walked could not be estranged from love, they invite him as a stranger to the inn. But why do I say 'they invite', when it is written there: 'but they constrained him'? It is inferred, doubtless, from this example, that strangers are not only to be invited, but even to be drawn to an inn.*³³³

[Luke 24:30-31] **And it happened, when he was at table with them, he took bread, and blessed and broke it, and gave it to them. And their eyes were opened, and they knew him.** *In the narrative of holy Scripture, they recognize him whom they had not known, in the breaking of the bread. They are illuminated not by hearing the commands of God, but by action, since it is written: 'For the hearers of the Law are not just before God, but the doers of the Law will be justified.'*³³⁴ *Whoever, therefore, wishes to understand what is heard, should hasten to fulfil the things which he could already understand by deeds.*³³⁵

[Luke 24:31b-32] **And he vanished out of their sight. And they said to one another: Was not our heart burning within us, while he was speaking to us on the road and opening the Scriptures to us?** *I have come,* he says, *to cast fire on the earth, and what do I want, except that it be kindled?*³³⁶ Indeed, *the Lord cast fire on the earth, when he inflamed the heart of carnal people with the breath of the Holy Spirit. And the earth burns, when the cold heart* of carnal people *abandons eager desires of the present world for its former pleasures and is inflamed with the love of God.*³³⁷

*'Was not our heart,'* they say, *'burning within us, while he was speaking to us on the road and opening the Scriptures to us?' Indeed, when words are heard, the soul burns, the cold of sluggishness recedes, the mind, solicitous for divine pleasure, becomes averse to earthly desires. The true love, which replenished it, torments it with weeping, but while it is tormented with such ardent desire, it is nourished by its own torments. It pleases it to hear heavenly precepts, and by as many commandments as it is instructed it is inflamed as if by so many torches.*³³⁸

---

333 Gregory, *Hom. in Euang.* 2.23.1 (CCSL 141:194.19–27).
334 Rom. 2:13.
335 Gregory, *Hom. in Euang.* 2.23.1–2 (CCSL 141:194.28–34).
336 Luke 12:49.
337 Gregory, *Hom. in Euang.* 2.30.5 (CCSL 141:260.118–19; 121–24).
338 Gregory, *Hom. in Euang.* 2.30.5 (CCSL 141:261.140–46).

[Luke 24:33-34] **And rising up at the same hour, they returned to Jerusalem; and they found the eleven and those who were with them gathered together, saying: The Lord has risen indeed, and he has appeared to Simon.** *Already the report that Jesus had risen again had been made by those women, and by Simon Peter to whom he had now appeared. For these two men found those to whom they came in Jerusalem saying this. So it may be that out of fear they were unwilling to say previously that they had heard that he had risen again, when they said that only angels* /417/ *were seen by the women. Not knowing with whom they spoke, they could rightly have been anxious, lest, boasting about Christ's resurrection in public, they might fall into the hands of the Jews.*[339] Therefore the Lord is understood to have appeared first to Peter of all men, of all those at least whom the four evangelists and the apostle Paul mentioned. For Paul says to the Corinthians about the Lord: *That he was buried, and that he rose again on the third day, according to the Scriptures; and that he appeared to Cephas, and after that to the eleven.*[340]

[Luke 24:35] **And they told what things were done on the road, and how they knew him in the breaking of the bread.** *Because their spirit, which still did not know that it was necessary for Christ to die and to rise again, deserved this, their eyes suffered something similar, not because the truth led them astray, but because they were unable to perceive the truth and because they believed something other than what is the fact.* In addition to this, *for the sake of the preordained mystery he showed them another symbol, and so they did not know him except by the breaking of the bread, lest anyone should suppose that he might recognize Christ without being a sharer of his body, that is, of the Church, whose unity the Apostle commends in the sacrament of the bread, saying: 'We, being many, are one bread, one body',*[341] *so that when he gave the blessed bread to them, their eyes were opened, and they knew him when the impediment that stopped them from knowing him was removed. But let us understand as is fitting that this impediment in their eyes came from Satan in order that Jesus not be known. But nevertheless, permission was given by Christ for the sake of the sacrament of the bread, so that, after the unity of his body has been shared, the impediment of the enemy is understood to be removed, so that Christ can be known.*[342]

---

339 Augustine, *De consensu euang.* 3.25.73 (CSEL 43:373.7-15).
340 1 Cor. 15:4-5.
341 1 Cor. 10:17.
342 Augustine, *De consensu euang.* 3.25 (CSEL 43:371.25-372.2; 371.22-24; 372.3-24).

BOOK SIX 639

Chapter 94

340/9 [Luke 24:36] **Now while they were speaking these things, Jesus stood in the midst of them, and says to them: Peace be to you; it is I, fear not.** It is a fact that John also records this appearance of the Lord after the resurrection, when he says: *Now when it was late that same day, the first of the Sabbath, and the doors were shut where the disciples were gathered together for fear of the Jews, Jesus came and stood in the midst, and says to them: Peace be with you*, and so forth. But given that John says that the apostle Thomas was not with them,[343] when, according to Luke, the two disciples, one of whom was Cleophas, on returning to Jerusalem, *found the eleven and those who were with them gathered together*,[344] it doubtless ought to be understood that Thomas had left that place before the Lord appeared to them, when the two disciples were saying these things.[345] /418/

[Luke 24:37] **But they, being troubled and terrified, supposed that they saw a spirit.** What the heretical Manicheans admire and believe about Christ, namely that he was not true flesh, but a spirit, is a speculation that rose up first in the hearts of the apostles. What is more, those Manicheans believe that Jesus never was a man. But the disciples knew that he with whom they had lived so long was a man. But after he died, which they knew had happened, when would they believe that he who was able to die would come to life again? He appeared, therefore, to their eyes such as they knew him. And not believing that true flesh could rise again from the tomb on the third day, they thought that they saw a spirit. This mistake of the apostles is the doctrine of the Manicheans. But when these things are brought up against them, they are accustomed to reply in this fashion: 'Seeing that we believe that Christ is God, why is it evil to believe that he was a spirit, and not flesh? Spirit is better than flesh. We believe what is better; we do not want to believe what is worse'. If there were no evil in this talk, Jesus may as well leave his disciples in this error. And what evil did the disciples believe? They believed that Christ was a spirit. But they did

---

343 Cf. John 20:24.
344 Luke 24:33.
345 In the corresponding *Hom.* 2.9 (ed. Hurst [CCSL 122:240]; trans. Martin and Hurst, *Homilies on the Gospels* 2:79–81) Bede avoids mentioning this issue, probably because he was addressing a more mixed audience, not just 'teachers and preachers': see Del Giacco, 'Exegesis and Sermon', 16, and Introduction, 41–43.

not believe he was nothing but spirit. You think that you are risking a slight disease; listen to the opinion of the physician.

[Luke 24:38] **And he said to them: Why are you troubled, and why do thoughts ascend into your hearts?** What kind of thoughts, surely, but false, sickly, and ruinous ones? For Christ would have lost the fruit of his passion, if that fruit were not the truth of the resurrection. *Why are you troubled, and why do thoughts ascend into your hearts?* As a good farmer would say: Because I planted there, I will not find thorns that I did not plant. Faith has descended into your heart, because it is from above. But these thoughts have not descended from above, but have ascended in that heart like bad weeds.

[Luke 24:39] **See my hands and feet, that it is I myself; handle and see, for a spirit does not have flesh and bones, as you see that I have.** *He deigned to convince them that his resurrection was certain and true by many and varied proofs, for the sake of building faith and putting falsehood to flight and overthrowing all doubt in his resurrection. It was not enough for him to offer to be seen by eyes, if he did not offer as well to be touched by hands.*[346] While he directs his disciples to handle his bones and flesh, he openly signifies the nature of the true resurrection that he had undergone and that we shall undergo. *Because, in that glory of resurrection our body will not be impalpable, more subtle than the winds and the air, as Eutychius, the bishop of the city of Constantinople has written. For in that glory of resurrection our body will be subtle indeed /419/ by the effect of spiritual power, but palpable by the truth of nature.*[347] And let it not be thought that this assertion is contradicted by the words of the Apostle: *That flesh and blood will not possess the kingdom of God.*[348] For in this passage the Apostle signifies by the term 'flesh and blood' not the substance of a true body, but the corruption of mortality, as he himself explains immediately afterwards, saying: *Nor will corruption possess incorruptibility.*[349] For indeed *in one place in holy* Scripture *flesh* is invoked *in connection with nature*, in another, *in connection with sin*, in another in connection *with the corruption* of mortality that came about from sin.[350] In

---

346 Augustine, *Sermo* 229.1 (Morin Guelf App. 7), *Miscellanea Agostiniana* (Rome, 1930) 1:581.13.
347 Gregory, *Moralia* 14.56 (CCSL 143A:743.3–8).
348 1 Cor. 15:50.
349 1 Cor. 15:50.
350 Gregory, *Moralia* 14.56 (CCSL 143A:744.33–35).

connection with nature when it was said: *This now is bone of my bones, and flesh of my flesh;*[351] *and the Word was made flesh, and dwelt among us.*[352] But in connection with sin when it is said: *The flesh lusts against the spirit, and the spirit against the flesh.*[353] And in connection with corruptibility, when it was written: *And he remembered that they are flesh,*[354] that is, fragile and mortal, for the Psalmist himself makes clear that he meant this by the word 'flesh', since he immediately adds: *A wind [spiritus] passing and not returning.*[355] Therefore, flesh will not possess the kingdom of God, that is, flesh in accordance with sin or mortality, and yet flesh – that is, flesh in accordance with nature – will possess the kingdom of God. After the resurrection the Lord also offered his flesh to the disciples to be seen and touched. And concerning this, the blessed Job, when he described the glory of the resurrection, says: *And I will be clothed again with my skin, and in my flesh I will see my God.*[356] Read the letter of Saint Augustine to Consentius about the body of the Lord after the resurrection.[357]

[Luke 24:40] **And when he had said this, he showed them his hands and feet.** He showed not only his hands and feet, on which the implanted marks of the nails were visible, but, as John attests, also his side, which the lance had pierced,[358] in order to cure the wound of their doubt and faithlessness by displaying the gashes of his own wounds. But just as after the resurrection, he deigned to strengthen the faith and hope of the disciples by exposing the places pierced by the nails and lance, so on the Day of Judgement, by showing both the same marks of his passion, and also the cross itself, he is going to come to confound the wickedness and infidelity of the proud, and to show openly to all angels and men that it is he himself who died by the wicked and for the wicked, and so that they may, as it is written, look upon him whom *they pierced, and all the tribes of the earth* may bewail *themselves because of him.*[359] Certainly it should be noted that the pagans are accustomed to fabricate a false accusation in this place, and to ridicule with foolish babbling the faith of the resurrection

---

351 Gen. 2:23.
352 John 1:14.
353 Gal. 5:17.
354 Ps. 77:39 (78:39).
355 Ps. 77:39 (78:39).
356 Job 19:26.
357 Cf. Augustine, *Epistolae* 120 (CSEL 44:712.5–16; 717.10–15).
358 Cf. John 20:27.
359 Rev. 1:7.

that we long for. If your God himself, they say, did not /420/ have power to heal the wounds inflicted on him by the Jews, but brought the marks of his wounds to heaven with him, as you say, by what foolhardiness do you think that he is going to restore your limbs to wholeness from dust? To these it should be replied that our God, who was able to raise up his own flesh, now glorified by eternal immortality, from the tomb when he wished and in the way he wished, also raised his flesh in the state he wished. For it does not make sense that he who is proved to have done greater things, will not be able to do lesser things. But certainly, he who did more for the sake of a firm dispensation, refrained from doing less, that is, he who destroyed the realms of death, did not wish to erase the signs of death. This was done in the first place to affirm the disciples' faith in his resurrection; then, by praying to the Father on our behalf, to show what kind of death he endured for the sake of the life of mortals; third, to proclaim to those redeemed by his death how mercifully they were aided, with the marks of that same death always on display, and that for that reason they not cease singing *the mercies of the Lord forever*,[360] but *let them say so who have been redeemed by the Lord, for he is good, for his mercy endures forever*;[361] and finally, to make known likewise to the wicked how justly they are condemned in the judgement, by displaying among other shameful things the scars of the wounds he received from them. Some people are like this: an exceptionally valiant man, at the command of his king, exerts himself in single battle for the salvation of the whole nation, and after receiving many wounds, nevertheless kills the enemy, tears away his spoils, and carries back the victory to his people. And when asked by the physician to whom he is entrusted to be healed, if he does not wish to be healed in such a way that no traces at all of his wounds remain, or rather that the scars remain, but all deformity and ugliness be gone, he replies that he would rather be healed in such a way that, after regaining the whole former state of his health and looks, he may carry around with him the permanent signs of so great a triumph. In this way the Lord chose not to efface the wounds of the passion received for our sakes as a sign of eternal victory, but to carry the scars of those very wounds to heaven. Nevertheless, this does not prejudice in any way the faith of our resurrection, of which true promise it is foretold: *But not a hair of your head will perish.*[362]

360 Ps. 88:2 (89:1).
361 Ps. 106:2 & 1 (107:2 & 1).
362 Luke 21:18.

341/9 [Luke 24:41] **But while they still did not believe and wondered for joy, he said: Have you anything here to eat?** To reveal the truth of his resurrection, he deigns not only to be touched by the disciples, but also to eat together with them. He did this not because he needed food after the resurrection, nor to signify that we will need food in the resurrection that we look forward to, but to affirm in this way /421/ the nature of the body that rises again, *in order that they might not think it was not a body, but a spirit, and that it appeared to them not in the flesh, but figuratively.*[363] *He ate because he could, not because he needed to.*[364] *For the earth, thirsting, absorbs water in one way and the sun's dazzling ray in another. The former is need, the latter, power.*[365]

[Luke 24:42–43] **And they offered him a piece of broiled fish and a honeycomb. And when he had eaten in their presence, taking the remains, he gave them to them.** *What do we believe the broiled fish signifies except that the Mediator between God and men himself suffered as a man? For he, having deigned to lie concealed in the waters of the human race, wished to be taken by the snare of our death, and was broiled as it were at the time of his passion. But he who deigned to be broiled in the passion is a honeycomb to us in the resurrection. Or perhaps he wished that the tribulations of his passion be symbolized in the broiled fish, but to express the double nature of his person in the honeycomb? Indeed, a honeycomb is in wax, and honey in wax is the divine in human nature.*[366]

And *thus, the Redeemer declares by his own nature that he paves a path for us to imitate by following him.* For *in the food he ate, he wanted to join honeycomb to broiled fish, because he takes to eternal rest in his body those who do not withdraw from the love of inner sweetness when they feel tribulations here for the sake of God. The honeycomb is taken with the broiled fish, because those who receive affliction here for the sake of the truth are furnished abundantly there with true sweetness.*[367]

342/10 [Luke 24:44] **And he said to them: These are the words which I spoke to you, while I was still with you, ...** That is, 'while I was still with you in the mortal flesh in which you are also'. For then he was going to be revived in the same flesh, but he was not with them in the same

---

363 Augustine, *Epistolae* 102.7 (CSEL 34:549.18–19).
364 Augustine, *Sermones* 116.3 (PL 38:659.1).
365 Augustine, *Epistolae* 102.6 (CSEL 34:549.16–17).
366 Gregory, *Hom. in Euang.* 2.24.5 (CCSL 141:201.116–24).
367 Gregory, *Hom. in Euang.* 2.24.5 (CCSL 141:201.133–38).

mortality. And *indeed, after he rose again, he was with them for forty days, as we read, in a display of his bodily presence,*[368] *but not in a fellowship of human weakness.*[369]

[Luke 24:44b] **That all things must be fulfilled, which were written about me in the Law of Moses, and in the prophets, and in the psalms.** *See how he dealt with all obscurities. He was seen, he was touched, he ate, he was certainly himself. But so as not to seem to deceive the human senses in some way, he took hold of the Scriptures. Let the pagans say whatever they want, 'he was a magician, he could show himself thus'. Was a magician able to prophesy about himself before he was born? Offer the Scriptures, because what you see was foreseen before, what you discern was foretold before. 'Hear, O daughter, and see';*[370] *hear things foretold, see things fulfilled.*[371]

[Luke 24:45–46] **Then he opened their mind to understand the Scriptures. And he said to them: Thus it is written, and thus it was necessary for Christ to suffer /422/ and to rise again from the dead on the third day,** ... He allows himself to be seen by eyes; he allows himself to be touched by hands. It is not enough; read – he cites the Scriptures. And that is too little; he opens the mind so that you may understand what you read. Then after the truth of his body has been made known, he commends the unity of the Church.

[Luke 24:47] **And for repentance and remission of sins to be preached in his name to all nations, beginning at Jerusalem.** The madness of the heretics does not lie hidden in a corner, the Church is diffused throughout the whole world, all nations have the Church, no one deceives us; it is true, it is universal, it begins at Jerusalem, it reaches us, and it is there and here. For in order for it to come here, it did not leave from there. It grew; it did not migrate. This was rightly written among other mysteries of the Lord's goodness, and thus it was necessary for the ministers of the word who were about to preach repentance and remission of sins in the name of Christ, crucified and revived from the dead, to all nations, to begin at Jerusalem. This is not only because the words of God were believed there, but because *the adoption as of children, and the*

---

368 Cf. Acts 1:3.
369 Augustine, *In Iohannis euang.* 64.1 (CCSL 36:489.28–30).
370 Ps. 44:11 (45:10).
371 Augustine, *Sermo* 229J (Morin Guelf App. 7), *Miscellanea Agostiniana* (Rome, 1930), 1. 583.30.

BOOK SIX 645

*glory, and the testament, and the giving of the Law, and the service, and the promises belong to Jerusalem and*, because to it belong *the fathers, and Christ according to the flesh, who is over all things, God blessed forever.*[372] And furthermore, this was particularly so, for this mark of divine righteousness summoned the nations entangled in various errors and crimes to the hope of obtaining forgiveness, because they saw that both the forgiveness of sin and the joy of eternal life had been given even to those who crucified the Son of God.

[Luke 24:48–49] **And you are witnesses of these things. And I send to you the promise of my Father.** That the grace of the Holy Spirit is called the promise of the Father is made clear more fully in the gospel of John,[373] but also briefly here, when he goes on:

[Luke 24:49b] **But stay in the city until you are clothed with power from on high.** About this power, that is, the Holy Spirit, the angel also says to Mary: *And the power of the Most High will overshadow you.*[374] And elsewhere the Lord himself says: *For I know that the power has gone out from me.*[375] But also Luke himself mentions this promised power from on high and the command to remain place more openly in the Acts of the Apostles: *He commanded them*, he says, *not to depart from Jerusalem, but to wait for the promise of the Father, which you have heard from my mouth. For John indeed baptized with water, but you will be baptized with the Holy Spirit not many days from now.*[376] And a little farther on: *But you will receive /423/ the power of the Holy Spirit coming upon you, and you will be witnesses to me.*[377] It should be noted that *there are those whom either imperfection or age prohibits from the office of preaching, and nevertheless headlong haste impels them to preach. These people must be warned that they should consider that Truth itself, who could have confirmed right away those whom he wanted to, nonetheless after fully instructing his disciples about the power of preaching, immediately added in order to give an example to his followers that the imperfect should not presume to preach*: '*But stay in the city until you are clothed with power from on high*'. We will indeed stay in the city, if within the

---

372 Rom. 9:4–5. Whereas Paul says these things of the Jews, Bede says them of the city of Jerusalem.
373 Cf. John 14:26; 16:13.
374 Luke 1:35.
375 Luke 8:46.
376 Acts 1:4–5.
377 Acts 1:8.

cloister of our minds we restrain ourselves in order not to stray by speaking on the outside, so that when we are perfectly clothed with divine power, we may then go outside from ourselves, as it were, and teach others also.[378]

[Luke 24:50–51] **And he led them out as far as Bethany, and, lifting up his hands, he blessed them. And it happened that, while he was blessing them, he withdrew from them, and was carried up to heaven.** By omitting all the things which Jesus was able to do in the forty days with his disciples, Luke tacitly joins the last day when he ascends to heaven to the first day of the resurrection. And it is beautifully appropriate that, being about to ascend to heaven, he leads the disciples whom he blesses out as far as Bethany. This is first of all on account of the name of the city, which means *house of obedience*,[379] because he who descended on account of the disobedience of the wicked, without doubt ascended on account of the obedience of the converted, for he died, as the Apostle says: *for our sins, and he rose again for our justification*.[380] Second, Bethany was chosen because of the site of that same town or small city which is said to have been located on the side of the Mount of Olives, because the house of the obedient Church, worthy of apostolic hospitality, set the foundations of its faith, hope, and love nowhere else than on the side of that very high mountain, that is, on the side of Christ, from whose side laid open by the lance, it rejoices that the sacraments of blood and water sprang forth for its sake, by which it is born and at the same time nourished. And from the fertile summit of that mountain that is, from the highest point of divinity, it desires the reward of spiritual anointing, and eagerly awaits the promises of eternal light and peace. And thirdly, it is because, as John writes: *Now Bethany was near Jerusalem, about fifteen stades away*.[381] This number, composed of seven and eight, is suitable to the mysteries of the Scriptures, whether it expresses by its content the life which is now and to come, or the Old and New Testament, or the Sabbath of souls in the future and the resurrection of the flesh, or indeed anything else of an ever heavenly and spiritual /424/ mystery. For that reason, he rightly revealed knowledge of both Testaments to those whom he taught the whole rule of living and hoping. And he led them out fifteen stades to the place where he

---

378 Gregory, *Regula pastoralis* 3.25 (SC 382:436.113–22).
379 Jerome, *Hebr. nom.* (CCSL 72:135.27).
380 Rom. 4:25.
381 John 11:18.

blessed them and gave them the command to teach. Rightly, he separated the place of his glorious ascension by fifteen stades from the place of his most victorious passion, in order to strengthen all those wishing either to live or to die for his sake with the desire together with the love, first to rest after death and in the end to rise again from the dead.

[Luke 24:52–53] **And worshipping, they went back to Jerusalem with great joy. And they were always in the temple, praising and blessing God.** As the Lord ascends into heaven, the disciples, worshipping *in the place where his feet* last *stood*,[382] immediately return to Jerusalem, because they were commanded to wait there for the promise of the Father that they heard from the Lord's mouth. They return 'with great joy' because they rejoice that their God and their Lord entered heaven after the triumph of the resurrection. They always remain in the temple, praising and blessing God, in order to await in a place of prayer and amid the devotions of praises the promised coming of the Holy Spirit with hearts ready and prepared for everything.

And, following the example of the disciples, after the ceremonies of the Lord's passion and resurrection have been celebrated in Jerusalem, that is, in the vision of peace, let us immediately seek the fields of Bethany with Christ as our guide, so that, with a mind now quiet and soothed from every tumult of dissension, we may be imbued with the sacraments of his flesh and blood. And let us take care to be these very 'houses of obedience', following the footsteps of him who, to give us the model for living, *became obedient to death*.[383] For thus we ourselves likewise deserve to be lifted up by his daily blessing, if, mindful daily of his triumphant ascension to heaven, we remain praising and blessing God in Jerusalem, that is, in the vision of heavenly peace, at this very moment hoped for and desired, *like men who wait for their lord, when he will return from the wedding*.[384] Among the four heavenly animals, the evangelist Luke is understood as symbolized by the calf, by the sacrifice of which those who were chosen for the priesthood were ordered to be consecrated, because more than the others, he undertook to expound the priesthood of Christ. In a beautiful manner he began his gospel with the service of the temple by the priesthood /**425**/ of Zechariah, and he completed it with the consecration of the temple, when he showed that

---

382 Ps. 131:7 (132:7).
383 Phil. 2:8.
384 Luke 12:36.

in that place the apostles were going to be the ministers, so to speak, of the new priesthood, not with the blood of sacrificial victims, but with the praise and blessing of God. Amen.

Here ends Book Six of the Commentary on Luke.

# APPENDIX 1

## Emendations to text of CCSL 120

A = ANGERS, Bibliothèque municipale 63 (Hurst)
B = PARIS, BN 11681 (online)
C = CAMBRAI, Médiathèque municipale 295 (Hurst)
D = PARIS, BN 12281 (online)
E = PARIS, BN 17451 (online)
G = ST GALL, Stiftsbibliothek 85 (online)
J = OXFORD, Bodleian Library, Bodl. 218 (Hurst)
K = KARLSRUHE, Landesbibliothek 64 (online)
W = WOLFENBÜTTEL, Herzogliche Bibliothek, Guelf. 20-Weiss. (online)
Am = Codex Amiatinus (online)
Bede on Mark = Bede, *In Marci Euangelium expositio*. CCSL 120
Vg = Vulgate, ed. Weber/Gryson

| Page/Line | CCSL 120 | Reading adopted |
|---|---|---|
| 11.1 | *praefatio* | *praefatione*, G, K, W, Am |
| 16.1 | *et* | *ex*, B¹, G, K, W, Am |
| 16.41 | *mendicanti* | *caeco mendicanti*, G, W, Am; *caeco medicanti*, K |
| 22.111 | *quod* | *quo*, B², C, D, K, W |
| 22.123 | *genus* | *genere*, B² |
| 25.231 | *gratia* | *gratiam*, D, E, G, K, W |
| 25.232 | *donatum* | *donatam*, E, G, K |
| 27.303 | *aedem* | *eadem*, D, E, G, K, W |
| 47.1119 | *cubili* | *cubiculis*, D, G, K, W, Vg; *cubilis*, E |
| 54.1384 | *fugare* | *fucare*, G, K, W |
| 56.1472 | *ministrari* | *ministrare*, D, G |

650  BEDE: *COMMENTARY ON THE GOSPEL OF LUKE*

| Page/Line | CCSL 120 | Reading adopted |
|---|---|---|
| 59.1580 | *maiore* | *maiorum*, **A, B², E, G, J, K, W** |
| 77.2294 | *alius* | *aliud*, **B, D, E, G, K, W**, Gregory |
| 77.2308 | *intellegendum* | *intellectum*, **D, G, K, W**, Gregory |
| 82.2480 | *boni* | *bonae*, **K2** |
| 84.2579 | *aduentum* | *aduentu*, **D, G, K, W** |
| 89.2752 | *praefigurans* | *praefigurant*, **B²** |
| 99.3151 | *quas* | *quos*, **B, D, E, G, K, W** |
| 100.27 | *praemonere* | *praemunire*, **G, K**; *praemunere*, **D¹, W** |
| 103.143 | *benedicis* | *benedices*, **G, K, W** |
| 104.174 | *audiendum* | *audientium*, **D, W**; *audientum*, **G, K** |
| 107.306 | *apte* | *captae*, **D, E, G, K, W** |
| 121.830 | *quia* | *qui*, **B, D, E, G, W**, Bede on Mark |
| 140.1587 | *laborantis* | *laborantes*, **E** |
| 145.1776 | *orari* | *orare*, **B², G²** |
| 145.1794 | *commendamus* | *commodamus* Augustine |
| 151.2009 | *factu* | *fatu*, **G, K, W** |
| 154.2153 | *maius* | *magis*, **D, G, K, W**, Augustine |
| 155.2157 | *quia* | *qui*, **A, D, G, K, W** |
| 157.2247 | *centurio* | *centenario*, **G, W** |
| 164.2533 | *temperantiam* | *temperantia*, **G, W**, Augustine |
| 179.512 | *exempla* | *exemplo*, **B, D, E, G, K, W** |
| 186.787 | *religare* | *relegare*, Augustine |
| 188.875 | *accepit* | *accipit*, **G, K** |
| 209.1698 | *intentione* | *intentiore*, **G, K** |
| 212.1797 | *correptionem* | *correctionem*, **D, W**, Augustine |
| 219.2074 | *uipera* | *a uipera*, **B, D, E, G, K, W** |
| 249.741 | *quando* | *quomodo*, **D, G, K, W** |
| 251.829 | *ac misera* | *amissa*, **D, K2, W**, Gregory |
| 251.834 | *simus* | *sumus*, **B²**, Gregory, Vg |

# APPENDIX 1

| Page/Line | CCSL 120 | Reading adopted |
|---|---|---|
| 264.1309–1310 | contemptor eius | contempto reus, **D**, **G**, **K**, **W**, Gregory |
| 272.1639 | sperantes | spernentes, **G**, **K**, **W** |
| 272.1667 | quid | qui, **B**, **E** |
| 275.1748 | sitire | sitit, **W2**, Augustine |
| 279.1926 | paratus | paratas, **D**, **G**$^2$, **K2**, **W**, Gregory |
| 289.2347 | resipientis | resipiscentis, **D**$^2$, **G**$^2$, Augustine |
| 291.2415 | mortem | amorem, **D**, **G**$^2$, **K2**, **W**, Cassian |
| 306.434 | terrenis | aeternis, **D**, **G**, **K**, **W**, Gregory |
| 321.1013 | fuerat | fuerit, **D**$^2$, **G**, **K**, **W** |
| 322.1073 | adiungit | adiungi, **D**, **G**, **K**, **W** |
| 338.1685 | scire | sciri, **G**, **K** |
| 354.2331 | additus | addictus, **G**, **K**; adductus, **W** |
| 373.396 | his | is, **G**, **K** |
| 384.846 | nos | nobis, **A**, **B**, **C**, **D**, **E**, **G**, **K**, **W** |
| 387.991 | prodit | prodis, **G**, **K**, **W**, Ambrose |
| 397.1390 | clauibus | clauis, Augustine |
| 405.1682 | digne [2] | digna, **D**, **G**, **K**, **W** |
| 418.2220 | aerique | aereque, Gregory |
| 424.2439–2440 | et hoc | hoc est, **B**, **G**, **K** |

# APPENDIX 2

## Chapter numbers and Eusebian canon section numbers

B = PARIS, BN 11681, s. viii$^2$, Corbie
D = PARIS, BN 12281, s. ix$^1$, Burgundy
E = PARIS, BN 17451, s. ix$^1$, Corbie (E breaks off just before Luke 23:53)
G = ST GALL, Stiftsbibliothek 85, ca. 820/840, St Gall
K = KARLSRUHE, BL 64, s. ix$^{1/3}$, St-Denis
W = WOLFENBÜTTEL, Guelf. 20 Weiss., s. ix$^1$, Weissenburg
Am = Codex Amiatinus
Go = Gorman, 'Source Marks', Appendix 3

N.B.: Chapter and canon section numbers in this appendix are followed in brackets by the verses in Luke which begin the respective chapters and canon sections. Canon section numbers are based on the edition of the Vulgate edited by Weber/Gryson.

| Chapter Number/Mss | Canon Section Number/Mss |
|---|---|
| **BOOK 1** | |
| 1 [1:1]/K, Am, Go | 1 [1:1]/Am |
| 2 [1:5]/Am, Go | |
| 3 [1:26]/E, G, K, W, Am, Go | 2 [1:35]/Am [1:19], K [1:19] |
| | 3 [1:36]/Am [1:20] |
| 4 [1:57]/D, E, G, K, W, Am, Go | |
| 5 [2:1]/D, G, K, Am, Go | |
| 6 [2:15]/G, K, Am, Go | |
| 7 [2:21]/B, E, G, K, W, Am, Go | |
| 8 [2:42]/B, E, G, K, Am, Go | 4 [2:47]/Am, D |
| | 5 [2:48b]/Am, G, K, W |

| Chapter Number/Mss | Canon Section Number/Mss |
|---|---|
| 9 [3:1]/**D, W,** Am, Go | 6 [3:1]/Am, **D, G. K** |
| | 7 [3:3]/Am, **G, K** |
| | 8 [3:7]/Am, **G, K** |
| | 9 [3:10]/Am, **D** |
| | 10 [3:16b]/Am, **G, K** |
| | 11 [3:17]/Am |
| 10 [3:19]/**K, W,** Am, Go | 12 [3:19]/Am, **D, K** |
| | 13 [3:21]/Am |
| | 14 [3:23]/Am, **G, K** |
| 11 [4:1]/**B** [10], **D, E, G, K, W,** Am, Go | 15 [4:1]/Am, **B, D, E, G, K** |
| | 16 [4:2b]/Am, **G, K** |
| **BOOK 2** | |
| 12 [4:14]/**B, D, E, G, K, W,** Am, Go | 17 [4:14]/Am, **B, D, E** [14], **G, K** |
| | 18 [4:16]/Am, **D, G, K** |
| | 19 [4:22]/Am, **D, G** [21], **K** [21] |
| | 20 [4:23]/Am, **G, K** |
| | 21 [4:24]/Am, **G, K** |
| | 22 [4:25]/Am, **G, K** |
| 13 [4:31]/**B, D, E, G, K, W** [4:33], Am, Go | 23 [4:31]/Am, **B, D, E, G, K** |
| | 24 [4:32]/Am, **D** |
| | 25 [4:33]/Am, **E, G, K** |
| 14 [4:38]/**B, D, E, G, K, W,** Am [13], Go | 26 [4:38]/Am, **B, D, E** |
| | 27 [4:41]/Am, **B, D, E, G, K** |
| | 28 [4:42]/Am, **B, E, G, K** |
| 15 [5:1]/**B, E, G, K, W,** Am, Go | 29 [5:1]/Am, **B, E, G, K** |
| | 30 [5:4]/Am, **B, D, E, G, K** |
| | 31 [5:8]/Am, **B, D, E, G, K** |
| | 32 [5:10b]/Am, **B, D, E** [5:10], **G, K** |

# APPENDIX 2

| Chapter Number/Mss | Canon Section Number/Mss |
|---|---|
| 16 [5:12]/**B, D, E, G, K, W**, Am, Go | 33 [5:12]/Am, **B, D, E, G, K** |
| | 34 [5:15]/Am, **B, D, E, G, K** |
| | 35 [5:16]/Am, **B, D, E, G, K** |
| 17 [5:17]/**B, D, E, G, K, W**, Am, Go | 36 [5:17]/Am, **B, D, E, G, K** |
| | 37 [5:18]/Am, **B, D, E, G, K** |
| 18 [5:27]/**B, D, E, G, K, W**, Am, Go | 38 [5:27]/Am, **B, D, E, G, K** |
| | 39 [5:29]/Am, **B, D, E, G, K** |
| | 40 [5:31]/Am, **D, G, K** |
| 19 [6:1]/**B, D, G, K, W**, Am, Go | 41 [6:1]/Am, **B, D, E, G, K** |
| 20 [6:6]/**B, D, E, G, K, W**, Am, Go | 42 [6:6]/Am, **B, D, E, G, K** |
| 21 [6:12]/**B, D, E, G, K, W**, Go | 43 [6:12]/Am, **B, D, E, G, K** |
| | 44 [6:13]/Am, **B, D, E, G, K** |
| | 45 [6:17]/Am, **D** [43], **K** |
| 22 [6:20]/**D, G, K, W**, Am [21], Go | 46 [6:20]/Am, **B, D, E, G, K** |
| | 47 [6:21]/Am, **D, E** |
| | 48 [6:21b]/Am, **D, E, G, K** |
| | 49 [6:22]/Am, **D, E, G, K** |
| | 50 [6:24]/Am, **B, D, E** |
| | 51 [6:26]/Am, **B, D, E** |
| | 52 [6:27]/Am, **B, D, E** |
| | 53 [6:29]/Am, **B, D, E** |
| 23(a) [6:31]/**D** [22], **E** [22], **G, K**, Am [22], Go | 54 [6:31]/Am, **B, D, E, G, K** |
| | 55 [6:32]/Am, **B, D, E** |
| 23(b) [6:37]/**D, G** [24], **K** [24], **W** [6:41], Am, Go [24] | 56 [6:37]/Am, **B, D, E, G, K** |
| | 57 [6:39]/Am, **B, D, E, K** |
| | 58 [6:40]/Am, **B, D, E, K** |
| | 59 [6:41]/Am, **B, D, E, K** |
| | 60 [6:43]/Am, **B, E, K** |

656　BEDE: *COMMENTARY ON THE GOSPEL OF LUKE*

| Chapter Number/Mss | Canon Section Number/Mss |
|---|---|
| | 61 [6:44b]/Am, **B, D** [60], **E, K** |
| | 62 [6:45]/Am, **B, D, E, K** |
| | 63 [6:46]/Am, **B, D, E, K** |
| | 64 [6:47]/Am, **B, D, E, K** |
| 24 [7:1]/**W** [7:2], Am | 65 [7:1]/Am, **B, D, E, K** |
| | 66 [7:10]/Am, **D** [7:2], **E** [7:2], **K, W** [64] |
| 25 [7:11]/**D, E, G, K, W**, Am, Go | 67 [7:11]/Am, **B** [66], **D** [7:10; 68(7:11)], **E** [66], **K** |
| | (68 [7:17]/Am; Bede omits 7:17) |
| | 69 [7:18]/Am, **B, D, E, G** [49], **K, W** [70] |
| 26 [7:19]/**D, E, G, K, W** [7:19; 7:24], Am, Go | 70 [7:27]/Am, **B, D, E, K** |
| | 71 [7:28]/Am, **B, D, E, G, K** |
| | 72 [7:29]/Am, **B, D, E, K** |
| | 73 [7:31]/Am, **B, D, E** |
| **BOOK 3** | |
| 27 [7:36]/**B, D, E, G, K, W**, Am, Go | 74 [7:36]/Am, **B, D** [77], **E** |
| 28 [8:1]/**B, D, E, G, K, W**, Am, Go | 75 [8:1]/Am, **B, D, E, G, K** |
| | 76 [8:4]/Am, **D, G, K** |
| | 77 [8:10b]/Am, **B, E** |
| | (78 [8:11]/Am; Bede omits 8:11) |
| 29 [8:16]/**B, D** [30], **E, G, K, W**, Am, Go | 79 [8:16]/Am, **B, D, E, G, K** |
| | 80 [8:17]/Am, **B, D, E** |
| | 81 [8:18]/Am, **B** [8:18b], **D** [8:18b], **E** [8:18b], **W** [8:18b] |
| | 82 [8:19]/Am, **B, D, E, G, K** |
| 30 [8:22]/**D, G, K, W**, Am, Go | 83 [8:22]/Am, **D, G, K** |
| 31 [8:26]/**B, D, E, G, K, W**, Am, Go | 84 [8:37b]/Am, **B, D, E, G, K** |

APPENDIX 2 657

| Chapter Number/Mss | Canon Section Number/Mss |
|---|---|
| 32 [8:40]/**D, G, K, W** [8:41], Am, Go | 85 [8:40]/Am, **B, D, E, G, K** |
| 33 [9:1]/**B, D, G, K, W**, Am, Go | 86 [9:1]/Am, **B, D, E, G, K** |
| | 87 [9:3]/Am, **B, D, E, G, K** |
| | 88 [9:5]/Am, **B, D, E, G, K, W** |
| | 89 [9:6]/Am, **B, D, E** [88], **G, K, W** |
| 34 [9:7]/**G, K, W**, Am, Go | 90 [9:7]/Am, **B, E, G, K** |
| | 91 [9:10]/Am, **B, D, E, W** |
| | 92 [9:10b]/Am, **B, D, E, W** |
| 35 [9:12]/**D, G, K, W**, Am, Go | 93 [9:12]/Am, **B, D, E, G, K, W** |
| 36 [9:18]/**D, G, K, W** [9:18b], Am, Go | 94 [9:18]/Am, **B, D, E, G, K** |
| | 95 [9:21]/Am, **B, D, E, G, K** |
| 37 [9:23]/**D, K, W**, Am [9:27], Go | 96 [9:23]/Am, **B, D, E, G, K** |
| | 97 [9:26]/Am, **B** [9:27], **D** [9:27], **E** [9:28], **G** [9:27], **K** [9:27] |
| | 98 [9:27]/Am, **B** [9:28] |
| 38 [9:37]/**D, G, K, W**, Am, Go | 99 [9:37]/Am, **B, D** [119], **E, G, K** |
| | (100 [9:44a]/Am; Bede omits 9:44a) |
| 39 [9:44b]/**D, G, K, W**, Am [9:44c], Go | 101 [9:44b]/Am, **B** [9:44c], **D, E** [9:44c], **G, K** |
| | 102 [9:46]/Am, **D** |
| | 103 [9:49]/Am, **B, E, G, K** |
| 40 [9:51]/**D, G, K, W**, Am [9:51b], Go | 104 [9:51]/Am, **B, D, E, G, K** |
| | 105 [9:57]/Am, **B, E** [104] |
| | 106 [9:61]/Am, **B, D, E, G, K** |
| 41 [10:1]/**D, E, G, K, W**, Am, Go | 107 [10:1]/Am, **B, D, E, G, K** |
| | 108 [10:2]/Am, **B, D, E** |
| | 109 [10:3]/Am, **B, D, E, G, K** |
| | 110 [10:4]/Am, **B, D, E, G, K** |
| | 111 [10:5]/Am, **B, D, E, W** |
| | 112 [10:7]/Am, **B, D, E, W** |

| Chapter Number/Mss | Canon Section Number/Mss |
|---|---|
| | 113 [10:8]/Am, **B, D, E, G, K, W** |
| | 114 [10:10]/Am, **B, D, E, W** |
| | 115 [10:13]/Am, **B, D, E, W** |
| | 116 [10:16]/Am, **B, D, E, W** |
| | 117 [10:17]/Am, **B, D, E, G, K, W** |
| 42 [10:21]/**B, D [41], E, G, K**, Am, Go | 118 [10:21]/Am, **B, D, E, G, K, W** |
| | 119 [10:22]/Am, **B, D, E, G, K, W** |
| | 120 [10:23]/Am, **B, D, E, G, K** |
| 43 [10:25]/**B, D, E, G, K**, Am, Go | 121 [10:25]/Am, **B, D, E, G, K, W** [**120**] |
| | 122 [10:29]/Am, **B, D, E, W** [**121**] |
| 44 [10:38]/**B [45], D, E [45], G, K, W**, Am, Go | |
| 45 [11:1]/Am, Go | 123 [11:1]/Am, **B, D [124], E, G** [11:2], **K, W** |
| 46 [11:5]/**B, D [45], E, G, K**, Am, Go | 124 [11:5]/Am, **B, D, E, G, K, W** |
| | 125 [11:9]/Am, **B, D, E, G, K** |
| **BOOK 4** | |
| 47 [11:14]/**B, D, G, K, W**, Am, Go | 126 [11:14]/Am, **B, D, E, G, K** |
| | 127 [11:15]/Am, **B, D, E** |
| | 128 [11:16]/Am, **B, D, E** |
| | 129 [11:17]/Am, **B, D, E, G, K** |
| | 130 [11:24]/Am, **B, D [140], E, G, K** |
| 48 [11:27]/**B, D, E, G, K, W**, Am, Go | 131 [11:27]/Am, **B, D, E, G, K** |
| | 132 [11:29]/Am, **B, D, E, G, K, W** |
| 49 [11:33]/**B [149], D [46], G, K, W**, Am, Go | 133 [11:33]/Am, **B, D [132], E, G, K** |
| | 134 [11:34]/Am, **B, D, E, G, K** |
| 50 [11:37]/**B, D, G, K, W**, Am, Go | 135 [11:37]/Am, **B, D, E, G, K** |
| | 136 [11:42]/Am, **B, D, E, G, K, W** [**133**] |

APPENDIX 2                    659

| Chapter Number/Mss | Canon Section Number/Mss |
|---|---|
|  | 137 [11:43]/Am, **B, D, E, G [138], K [138], W** |
|  | 138 [11:44]/Am, **B, D, E, W** |
|  | 139 [11:45]/Am, **B, D, E, G, K, W** |
|  | 140 [11:47]/Am, **D, G, K, W** |
|  | 141 [11:49]/Am, **B, D, E, G, K, W** |
|  | 142 [11:52]/Am, **B, D, E, G, K, W** |
|  | 143 [11:53]/Am, **B, D, E, G, K, W** |
| 51 [12:1b]/Am [11:45], Go [11:45] | 144 [12:1b]/Am, **B, D, G [145], K [145], W** |
|  | 145 [12:2]/Am, **B, D, E, G, K, W** |
|  | 146 [12:9]/Am, **B** [12:3], **D, E** [12:3], **G** [12:3; 12:9], **K** [12:3; 12:9], **W** [12:3] |
|  | 147 [12:10]/Am, **D, G, K, W** [12:8; W**148**] |
|  | 148 [12:11]/Am, **D, W [149]** |
| 52 [12:13]/**G, K**, Am, Go | 149 [12:13]/Am, **B, D, E, G, K, W [150]** |
|  | 150 [12:22]/Am, **D** |
| 53 [12:32]/**G, K**, Am, Go | 151 [12:32]/Am, **B, D, E, G, K, W** |
|  | 152 [12:33]/Am, **B, D, E, G, K** |
|  | 153 [12:33b]/Am, **B, D, E** |
|  | 154 [12:35]/Am, **B, D, E, G, K** |
|  | 155 [12:37]/Am, **B, E, G, K** |
|  | 156 [12:39]/Am, **B, E, G, K** |
|  | 157 [12:41]/Am, **B, D** [12:41; 12:43], **E, G** [12:41; 12:43], **K** [12:41; 12:43] |
|  | 158 [12:45]/Am, **B** [12:43], **D, E [159], G, K** |
|  | 159 [12:47]/Am, **B** [12:45], **D [150], E [160], G, K** |

| Chapter Number/Mss | Canon Section Number/Mss |
|---|---|
| 54 [12:49]/**B, E, G, K**, Am, Go | 160 [12:49]/Am, **B** [12:47], **D, E** [**161**], **G, K, W** [**152**] |
| | 161 [12:54]/Am, **B** [12:49], **D, E** [**162**], **G, K** |
| | 162 [12:58]/Am, **B** [12:54], **D, E** [**163**], **G** [cxlxii], **K** [cxlxii] |
| 55 [13:1]/**B, G, K**, Am, Go | 163 [13:1]/Am, **B** [12:58], **D, E, G, K** |
| | 164 [13:6]/Am, **B** [13:1] |
| | 165 [13:14]/Am, **B, E, G** [**164**], **K** [**164**] |
| | 166 [13:17]/Am, **B, D** [**162**], **E, G** [**165**], **K** [**165**] |
| 56 [13:18]/**B, G, K**, Am [13:6], Go | 167 [13:18]/Am, **B, E, G** [**165**], **K** [**165; 166**] |
| | 168 [13:20]/Am, **B, E** |
| | (**169** [13:22]/Am; Bede omits13:22) |
| | 170 [13:23]/Am, **B** [**169**], **E** [**169**] |
| | 171 [13:25]/Am, **B** [**170**], **E** [**170**], **G** [**169**], **K** [**169**] |
| | (**172** [13:28b]/Am; Bede omits 13:28b–29) |
| | 173 [13:30]/Am, **B** [**171**], **D** [**180**], **G** [**183**], **K** [**183**] |
| 57 [13:31]/**G, K**, Am, Go | 174 [13:31]/Am, **B** [**172**], **D** [**181**], **E** [**172**], **G** [**184**], **K** [**184**] |
| | 175 [13:34]/Am, **D** [**182**], **G, K** |
| 58 [14:1]/**G, K**, Am, Go | 176 [14:1]/Am, **B** [**174**], **E** [**174**], **G, K** [**175**] |
| | 177 [14:3]/Am |
| | 178 [14:7]/Am, **B** [**175**], **E** [**175**], **G** [**176**], **K** [**176**] |
| | 179 [14:11]/Am, **K** [**177**] |

# APPENDIX 2

| Chapter Number/Mss | Canon Section Number/Mss |
|---|---|
| | 180 [14:12]/Am, **B** [177], **E** [177] |
| 59 [14:16]/**B, E, G, K** [*bis*], Am, Go | 181 [14:16]/Am |
| 60 [14:25]/**E, G, K**, Am, Go | 182 [14:25]/Am, **G, K, W** [177] |
| | 183 [14:28]/Am, **B** [178], **E** [179], **G, K** |
| | 184 [14:33]/Am, **E** [180] |
| | 185 [14:34]/Am, **B** [181], **E** [181], **G, K** |
| 61 [15:1]/**B, E, G, K, W**, Am, Go | 186 [15:1]/Am, **G, K** |
| | 187 [15:3]/Am, **G** [15:4], **K** [15:4] (Bede omits 15:3) |
| | 188 [15:8]/Am, **B** [184], **D** [183], **E** [184], **G, K** |
| | 189 [15:10]/Am, **B** [185], **D** [184], **E** [185], **K** |
| 62 [15:11]/**B, E, G, K, W**, Am, Go | 190 [15:11]/Am, **B** [186], **D** [185], **E** [186], **G, K** |
| **BOOK 5** | |
| 63 [16:1]/**B, E, K** [62], **W**, Am, Go | |
| 64 [16:13]/**G, K, W**, Am, Go | 191 [16:13]/Am, **B** [190], **E** [190], **G, K** |
| | 192 [16:14]/Am, **B, E, G, K** |
| | 193 [16:16]/Am, **B, E, G, K** |
| | 194 [16:17]/Am, **B, E, G, K, W** [192] |
| | 195 [16:18]/Am, **B, E** |
| 65 [16:19]/**B, E, G, K, W**, Am, Go | 196 [16:19]/Am, **B, E, G, K** |
| 66 [17:1]/**B, E, G, K, W**, Am, Go | 197 [17:1]/Am, **B, E, G, K** |
| | 198 [17:3]/Am, **B, E, G, K** |
| | 199 [17:4]/Am, **B, E, G, K** |
| 67 [17:5]/**G, K, W**, Am, Go | 200 [17:5]/Am, **B, D, E, G, K** |
| | 201 [17:7]/Am, **B, E, G** [202], **K** |

| Chapter Number/Mss | Canon Section Number/Mss |
|---|---|
| 68 [17:11]/**E, G, K, W**, Am, Go | |
| 69 [17:20]/**G, K, W**, Am, Go | 202 [17:20]/Am, **B** [17:11], **G** [203], **K** |
| | 203 [17:22]/Am, **G, K** |
| | 204 [17:23]/Am |
| | 205 [17:24]/Am, **B, D, E, G, K** |
| | 206 [17:25]/Am, **B, E, G, K** |
| | 207 [17:26]/Am, **B, E, G, K** |
| | 208 [17:28]/Am, **B, E** |
| | 209 [17:31]/Am, **B, E, G, K** |
| | 210 [17:32]/Am, **B, E, G, K** |
| | 211 [17:33]/Am, **B, E, G, K** |
| | 212 [17:34]/Am, **B, E, G, K** |
| | 213 [17:36]/Am, **B, E** |
| 70 [18:1]/**B, G, K, W**, Am, Go | 214 [18:1]/Am, **B, E, G, K** |
| 71 [18:9]/**B, E, G, K, W**, Am, Go | 215 [18:14b]/Am, **B, E, G, K** |
| 72 [18:15]/**G, K, W**, Am, Go | 216 [18:15]/Am, **B, E, G, K** |
| | 217 [18:17]/Am |
| 73 [18:18]/**B, E, G, K**, Am, Go | 218 [18:18]/Am |
| | 219 [18:22]/Am, **B, E, G** [18:21], **K** |
| | 220 [18:23]/Am, **B, E, G, K** |
| | 221 [18:29]/Am, **B, E, G, K** |
| 74 [18:31]/**B, G, K, W**, Am, Go | 222 [18:31]/Am, **B, E, G, K** |
| | 223 [18:34]/Am, **B, E, G, K** |
| 75 [18:35]/**B, G, K, W**, Am, Go | 224 [18:35]/Am, **B, E, G, K** |
| 76 [19:1]/**B, E, G, K, W**, Am, Go | 225 [19:1]/Am, **B, E, G, K** |
| | 226 [19:10]/Am, **B** [223], **E** [223], **G, K** |
| 77 [19:11]/**B, E** [19:12], **G, W** [19:12], Am, Go | 227 [19:11]/Am, **B** [224], **E** [224], **G, K** |
| | 228 [19:12]/Am, **B, E, G, K** |

| Chapter Number/Mss | Canon Section Number/Mss |
|---|---|
| | 229 [19:13]/Am [19:13b], **B, E, G, K** |
| | 230 [19:26]/Am, **B, D, E** |
| | 231 [19:27]/Am, **B, E, K** |
| | 232 [19:28]/Am [19:29], **B, E, K** |
| 78 [19:29]/**E, G, K** [*bis*], **W**, Am, Go | 233 [19:32]/Am, **B** [19:29; 19:32], **D, E** [19:29; 19:32], **G** [**223**], **K** |
| | 234 [19:37]/Am, **B** [**235**], **D, E** [**235**], **G** [**233**], **K** [**233**] |
| | 235 [19:39]/Am, **B** [**236**], **E, G, K** |
| 79 [19:41]/**B, E** [19:47], **G, K, W**, Am, Go | 236 [19:41]/Am, **B, E** |
| | 237 [19:44b]/Am, **B** [**239**], **E, G, K** |
| | 238 [19:45]/Am, **B** [**239**], **E** [**239**], **G, K** |
| | 239 [19:47]/Am, **B, G, K** |
| 80 [20:1]/**B, E, G, K, W**, Am, Go | 240 [20:1]/Am, **B, E, G, K** |
| 81 [20:9]/**B, E, G, K, W**, Go | 241 [20:9]/Am, **B, E, G, K** |
| 82 [20:19]/**B, E** [20:19; 20:20], **G, K, W** [20:20], Am [20:20], Go | 242 [20:19]/Am, **G, K** |
| | 243 [20:20]/Am, **G, K** |
| 83 [20:27]/**D** [**86**], **E, G, K, W**, Am, Go | 244 [20:40]/Am, **D, G, K** |
| 84 [20:41]/**E, G, K, W**, Am, Go | 245 [20:41]/Am, **D, G, K** |
| | 246 [20:45]/Am, **D, G** [**256**], **K** [**256**] |
| | 247 [20:47]/Am, **D, G, K** |
| **BOOK 6** | |
| 85 [21:5]/**B, D** [**55**], **E, G, K, W**, Am, Go | 248 [21:5]/Am, **D, G, K** |
| | 249 [21:7]/Am, **D, G, K** |
| | 250 [21:12]/Am, **D, G, K** |
| | 251 [21:14]/Am, **D** |

664    BEDE: *COMMENTARY ON THE GOSPEL OF LUKE*

| Chapter Number/Mss | Canon Section Number/Mss |
|---|---|
| **86** [21:20]/**B, E, G, K, W**, Am, Go | **252** [21:20]/Am, **B, D, E, G, K, W** [**256**] |
| | **253** [21:21]/Am, **B, D, E, G, K** |
| | **254** [21:23]/Am, **B, D, E, G, K** |
| | **255** [21:23b]/Am, **B, D, E, G, K** |
| | **256** [21:24]/Am, **B, D, E** |
| | **257** [21:25]/Am, **B, D, E** |
| | **258** [21:27]/Am, **B, D, E, G, K** |
| **87** [21:28]/**B** [86], **E, G, K** [86], **W**, Am, Go | **259** [21:34]/Am, **B, D, E, G, K** |
| | **260** [22:1]/Am, **B, D** [**261**], **E, G, K** |
| | **261** [22:2]/Am, **B, D, E** |
| **88** [22:3]/**B, E, G, K, W**, Am, Go | **262** [22:3]/Am, **B, E, G** [**263**], **K** [**263**] |
| | **263** [22:4]/Am, **B, D** [**262**], **E** |
| | **264** [22:15]/Am, **B, D, E, G, K** |
| | **265** [22:16]/Am, **B** [**255**], **D, E, G, K** |
| | **266** [22:19]/Am, **B, D, E, G, K** |
| | **267** [22:20]/Am, **B, D, E, G, K** |
| | **268** [22:21]/Am, **B, D, E, G, K** |
| | **269** [22:23]/Am, **B, D, E, G, K** |
| **89** [22:24]/**B** [84], **E, G, K, W**, Am, Go | **270** [22:24]/Am, **B, D, E, G, K** |
| | **271** [22:27]/Am, **B, D, E, G, K** |
| | **272** [22:30b]/Am, **B, D, E, G, K** |
| | **273** [22:31]/Am, **B, D, E, G, K** |
| | **274** [22:32b]/Am, **B, D, G, K** |
| **90** [22:33]/**G, K, W** [22:35], Am, Go | **275** [22:33]/Am, **B, D, G, K** |
| | **276** [22:35]/Am, **G, K** |
| | **277** [22:37]/Am, **B, D, G, K** |
| | **278** [22:38]/Am, **B, D, G, K** |

APPENDIX 2 665

| Chapter Number/Mss | Canon Section Number/Mss |
|---|---|
| | 279 [22:39]/Am, **B, D, G, K** |
| | 280 [22:40]/Am, **B, D, G, K** |
| | 281 [22:41]/Am, **B, D, G, K** |
| | 282 [22:42b]/Am, **B, D, G, K** |
| | 283 [22:43]/Am, **B, D, G, K** |
| | 284 [22:45]/Am, **B, D, G, K, W** |
| | 285 [22:47]/Am, **B, D, G, K, W** |
| | 286 [22:47b]/Am [22:48], **B** [22:48], **D** [22:48], **G** [22:48], **K** [22:48] |
| | 287 [22:49]/Am, **B, D, G** [277], **K** [277], **W** |
| | 288 [22:51b]/Am [22:51], **B, D, G, K, W** |
| | 289 [22:52]/Am, **B, D, G** [ccxxxxl], **K** [ccxxxxl], **W** [280] |
| | 290 [22:54]/Am, **B, D, G, K** |
| | 291 [22:54b]/Am, **B, D, G, K** |
| | 292 [22:58]/Am, **B, D, G, K** |
| | 293 [22:61]/Am, **B, D, G, K** |
| | 294 [22:63]/Am, **B, D, G, K** |
| | 295 [22:66]/Am, **B, D, G, K** |
| | 296 [22:67]/Am, **B, D, G, K** |
| | 297 [22:69]/Am, **B, D, G, K** |
| | 298 [22:70]/Am, **B, D, G, K** |
| | 299 [22:71]/Am, **B, D, G, K** |
| | 300 [23:1]/Am, **B, D, G, K** |
| | 301 [23:2]/Am, **B, D, G, K** |
| | 302 [23:3]/Am, **B, D, G, K** |
| | 303 [23:4]/Am, **B, D, G, K** |
| | 304 [23:5]/Am, **B, D, G, K** |
| | 305 [23:10]/Am, **B, G, K** |

666    BEDE: *COMMENTARY ON THE GOSPEL OF LUKE*

| Chapter Number/Mss | Canon Section Number/Mss |
|---|---|
| | 306 [23:11]/Am, **B, G, K** |
| | 307 [23:13]/Am, **B, G, K** |
| | 308 [23:15]/Am, **B [309], G [310], K [310]** |
| | 309 [23:16]/Am, **B** [23:17], **G** [311(23:17), **K** [311(23:17)] |
| | 310 [23:18]/Am, **B, D, G [311], K [311]** |
| | 311 [23:20]/Am, **B, D, G, K** |
| | 312 [23:22]/Am, **B, D, G, K** |
| | 313 [23:23]/Am, **D, G, K** |
| | 314 [23:24]/Am, **B [304], D, G, K** |
| | 315 [23:26]/Am, **B, D, G, K** |
| | 316 [23:27]/Am, **D, G, K** |
| | 317 [23:32]/Am, **B, D** |
| | 318 [23:33]/Am, **B, D** |
| | 319 [23:33b]/Am, **B [318], D [320], E** |
| 91 [23:34]/**G, K, W**, Am, Go | 320 [23:34]/Am, **B, D** |
| | 321 [23:34b]/Am, **B [310], D** |
| | 322 [23:35b]/Am, **B, D, G [323], K [323]** |
| | 323 [23:36]/Am, **B, D, G, K** |
| | 324 [23:38]/Am, **B, D, E, G, K** |
| | 325 [23:39]/Am, **B, D, E, G, K** |
| | 326 [23:40]/Am, **B, D, G, K** |
| | 327 [23:44]/Am, **B, D, G, K** |
| | 328 [23:45b]/Am, **B, D, G, K** |
| | 329 [23:46]/Am, **B, D, G [324], K** |
| | 330 [23:47]/Am, **B, D, G, K** |
| | 331 [23:48]/Am, **B, G, K** |

## APPENDIX 2

| Chapter Number/Mss | Canon Section Number/Mss |
|---|---|
|  | 332 [23:50]/Am, **B** |
|  | 333 [23:53]/Am, **B** [**332**], **D, G, K** |
|  | 334 [23:54]/Am, **B, D, G, K** |
|  | 335 [23:56]/Am, **B, D, G, K** |
| 92 [24:1]/**D, G** [**112**], **K, W**, Am, Go | 336 [24:1]/Am, **B, D, G, K** |
|  | 337 [24:5]/Am, **B, D, G, K** |
|  | 338 [24:9]/Am, **B, D, G, K** |
|  | 339 [24:10]/Am, **B, D, G, K** |
| 93 [24:13]/**D, G** [**113**], **K**, Am, Go |  |
| 94 [24:36]/**D, G, K, W**, Am, Go | 340 [24:36]/Am, **B** [24:13; 24:36], **D, G, K** |
|  | 341 [24:41]/Am, **B** [**351**], **G, K** |
|  | 342 [24:44]/Am, **B, D, G, K** |

# APPENDIX 3

## Luke canon section and table numbers with equivalent canon section numbers and modern chapter/verse parallels in Matthew [Mt], Mark [Mk], and John [Jo]

Each of the 342 Luke section numbers is paired with its table number. There are ten tables in all. Table number 1 (=/1) identifies textual parallels to Luke that are found in Matthew, Mark, and John; table number 2 (=/2), parallels that are found in Matthew and Mark; table number 3 (=/3), parallels that are found in Matthew and John; table number 5 (=/5), a parallel that is found in Matthew; table number 8 (=/8), a parallel that is found in Mark; table number 9 (=/9), a parallel that is found in John; and table number 10 (=/10), a passage in Luke that is unique to that Gospel. (Tables 4, 6, and 7 do not involve Luke.) It should be understood that each section number refers to the portion of gospel text between it and the next section number.

| | | |
|---|---|---|
| 1/10 | – | |
| 2/5 | Mt 3 [= Mt 1:18] | |
| 3/10 | – | |
| 4/2 | Mt 62; Mk 13 [= Mt 7:28; Mk 1:22] | |
| 5/10 | – | |
| 6/3 | Mt 7; Jo 2; 25 [= Mt 3:1; Jo 1:6; 3:23] | |
| 7/1 | Mt 8; Mk 2; Jo 10 [= Mt 3:3; Mk 1:3; Jo 1:23] | |
| 8/5 | Mt 10 [= Mt 3:7] | |
| 9/10 | – | |
| 10/1 | Mt 11; Mk 4; Jo 6; 12; 14; 28 [= Mt 3:11; Mk 1:7; Jo 1:15; 1:26; 1:30; 3:28] | |
| 11/5 | Mt 12 [= Mt 3:12] | |
| 12/2 | Mt 144; Mk 59 [= Mt 14:3; Mk 6:17] | |

| 13/1 | Mt 14; Mk 5; Jo 15 [= Mt 3:16; Mk 1:9; Jo 1:32] |
| 14/3 | Mt 1; Jo 1; 3; 5 [Mt 1:1; Jo 1:1; 1:9; 1:14] |
| 15/2 | Mt 15; Mk 6 [= Mt 4:1; Mk 1:12] |
| 16/5 | Mt 16 [= Mt 4:2] |
| 17/1 | Mt 23; Mk 27; Jo 46 [= Mt 4:23; Mk 3:7; Jo 6:1] |
| 18/10 | – |
| 19/1 | Mt 141; Mk 50; Jo 59 [= Mt 13:54; Mk 6:1; Jo 6:41] |
| 20/10 | – |
| 21/1 | Mt 142; Mk 51; Jo 35 [= Mt 13:57; Mk 6:4; Jo 4:44] |
| 22/10 | – |
| 23/8 | Mk 12 [= Mk 1:21] |
| 24/2 | Mt 62; Mk 13 [= Mt 7:28; Mk 1:22] |
| 25/8 | Mk 14 [= Mk 1:23] |
| 26/2 | Mt 67; Mk 15 [= Mt 8:14; Mk 1:29] |
| 27/8 | Mk 16; 28 [= Mk 1:34; 3:11] |
| 28/8 | Mk 17 [= Mk 1:35] |
| 29/10 | – |
| 30/9 | Jo 219 [= Jo 21:1] |
| 31/10 | – |
| 32/2 | Mt 21; Mk 10 [= Mt 4:19; Mk 1:17] |
| 33/2 | Mt 63; Mk 18 [= Mt 8:1; Mk 1:40] |
| 34/1 | Mt 23; Mk 27; Jo 46 [= Mt 4:23; Mk 3:7; Jo 6:1] |
| 35/2 | Mt 149; Mk 66 [= Mt 14:23; Mk 6:46] |
| 36/2 | Mt 153; Mk 69 [= Mt 14:35; Mk 6:54] |
| 37/1 | Mt 70; Mk 20; Jo 38 [= Mt 9:1; Mk 2:1; Jo 5:1] |
| 38/2 | Mt 71; Mk 21 [= Mt 9:9; Mk 2:13] |
| 39/2 | Mt 72; Mk 22 [= Mt 9:10; Mk 2:15] |
| 40/2 | Mt 73; Mk 23 [= Mt 9:12; Mk 2:17] |
| 41/2 | Mt 114; Mk 24 [= Mt 12:1; Mk 2:23] |
| 42/2 | Mt 116; Mk 25 [= Mt 12:9; Mk 2:27] |
| 43/2 | Mt 149; Mk 66 [= Mt 14:23; Mk 6:46] |

APPENDIX 3                                    671

44/2   Mt 80; Mk 30 [= Mt 10:2; Mk 3:16]
45/1   Mt 23; Mk 27; Jo 46 [= Mt 4:23; Mk 3:7]
46/5   Mt 25 [= Mt 5:2]
47/5   Mt 28 [= Mt 5:6]
48/5   Mt 27 [= Mt 5:5]
49/5   Mt 30 [= Mt 5:11]
50/10  –
51/10  –
52/5   Mt 40 [= Mt 5:44]
53/5   Mt 38 [= Mt 5:39]
54/5   Mt 54 [= Mt 7:12]
55/5   Mt 41 [= Mt 5:46]
56/2   Mt 50; Mk 41 [= Mt 7:1; Mk 4:24]
57/5   Mt 156 [= Mt 15:14]
58/3   Mt 90; Jo 118; 139 [= Mt 10:24; Jo 13:16; 15:20]
59/5   Mt 51 [= Mt 7:3]
60/5   Mt 58 [= Mt 7:17]
61/5   Mt 57 [= Mt 7:16]
62/5   Mt 125 [= Mt 12:35]
63/3   Mt 59; Jo 116 [= Mt 7:21; Jo 13:13]
64/5   Mt 61 [= Mt 7:24]
65/3   Mt 64; Jo 37 [= Mt 8:5; Jo 4:46]
66/5   Mt 66 [= Mt 8:13]
67/10  –
[68/10 omitted]
69/5   Mt 102 [= Mt 11:2]
70/2   Mt 103; Mk 1 [= Mt 11:10; Mk 1:1]
71/5   Mt 104 [= Mt 11:11]
72/10  –
73/5   Mt 107 [= Mt 11:16]
74/1   Mt 276; Mk 158; Jo 98 [= Mt 26:6; Mk 14:3; Jo 12:2]

| | |
|---|---|
| 75/10 | – |
| 76/2 | Mt 131; Mk 36 [= Mt 13:1; Mk 4:1] |
| 77/1 | Mt 133; Mk 37; Jo 109 [= Mt 13:13; Mk 4:11b] |
| 78/2 | Mt 135; Mk 38 [= Mt 13:18; Mk 4:14] |
| 79/2 | Mt 32; Mk 39 [= Mt 5:14; Mk 4:21] |
| 80/2 | Mt 92; Mk 40 [= Mt 10:26; Mk 4:22] |
| 81/5 | Mt 132 [= Mt 13:12] |
| 82/2 | Mt 130; Mk 35 [= Mt 12:46; Mk 3:31] |
| 83/2 | Mt 69; Mk 47 [= Mt 8:23; Mk 4:35] |
| 84/8 | Mk 48 [= Mk 5:18] |
| 85/2 | Mt 74; Mk 49 [= Mt 9:18; Mk 5:21] |
| 86/2 | Mt 79; Mk 29 [= Mt 10:1; Mk 3:13] |
| 87/2 | Mt 82; 83; Mk 53; 54 [= Mt 10:7; 10:11; Mk 6:7b; 6:10] |
| 88/2 | Mt 85; Mk 55 [= Mt 10:14; Mk 6:11] |
| 89/8 | Mk 56 [= Mk 6:12] |
| 90/2 | Mt 143; Mk 57 [= Mt 14:1; Mk 6:14] |
| 91/8 | Mk 61 [= Mk 6:30] |
| 92/3 | Mt 146; Jo 47 [= Mt 14:13; Jo 6:3] |
| 93/1 | Mt 147; Mk 64; Jo 49 [= Mt 14:15; Mk 6:35; Jo 6:5] |
| 94/1 | Mt 166; Mk 82; Jo 74; 17 [= Mt 16:13; Mk 8:27; Jo 6:69; 1:41] |
| 95/2 | Mt 168; Mk 83 [= Mt 16:20; Mk 8:30] |
| 96/2 | Mt 170; Mk 85 [= Mt 16:24; Mk 8:34] |
| 97/2 | Mt 94; Mk 86 [= Mt 10:33; Mk 8:38] |
| 98/2 | Mt 172; Mk 87 [= Mt 16:28; Mk 8:39] |
| 99/2 | Mt 174; Mk 91 [= Mt 17:14; Mk 9:16] |
| [100/8 omitted] | |
| 101/2 | Mt 176; Mk 93 [= Mt 17:21; Mk 9:29] |
| 102/2 | Mt 178; Mk 95 [= Mt 18:1; Mk 9:33] |
| 103/8 | Mk 97 [= Mk 9:37] |
| 104/10 | – |
| 105/5 | Mt 68 [= Mt 8:19] |

APPENDIX 3 673

106/10 –
107/10 –
108/5 Mt 78 [= Mt 9:37]
109/5 Mt 86 [= Mt 10:16]
110/2 Mt 82; Mk 53 [= Mt 10:7; Mk 6:7b]
111/5 Mt 84 [= Mt 10:12]
112/2 Mt 83; Mk 54 [= Mt 10:11; Mk 6:10]
113/10 –
114/2 Mt 85; Mk 55 [= Mt 10:14; Mk 6:11]
115/5 Mt 108 [= Mt 11:20]
116/1 Mt 98; Mk 96; Jo 120; 111; 40; 144; 129; 131 [= Mt 10:40; Mk 9:36b; Jo 13:20; 12:44; 5:23b; 15:23; 14:21b; 14:24b]
117/10 –
118/5 Mt 110 [= Mt 11:25]
119/3 Mt 111; Jo 148; 30; 114; Mt 112; Jo 87; 44; 61; 8; 76; 90; 154; 142 [= Mt 11:27; Jo 16:15; 3:35; 13:3; Mt 11:27b; Jo 8:19b; 5:37b; 6:46; 1:18; 7:28; 10:15; 17:25; 15:21b]
120/5 Mt 134 [= Mt 13:16]
121/2 Mt 193; Mk 107 [= Mt 19:16; Mk 10:17]
122/10 –
123/5 Mt 43 [= Mt 6:7]
124/10 –
125/5 Mt 53 [= Mt 7:7]
126/5 Mt 119 [= Mt 12:22]
127/2 Mt 121; Mk 32 [= Mt 12:24; Mk 3:22]
128/5 Mt 127 [= Mt 12:38]
129/2 Mt 122; Mk 33 [= Mt 12:25; Mk 3:23]
130/5 Mt 129 [= Mt 12:43]
131/10 –
132/5 Mt 128 [= Mt 12:39]
133/2 Mt 32; Mk 39 [= Mt 5:14; Mk 4:21]
134/5 Mt 47 [= Mt 6:22]

135/5   Mt 236 [= Mt 23:25]
136/5   Mt 234 [= Mt 23:23]
137/2   Mt 229; Mk 135 [= Mt 23:5; Mk 12:38]
138/5   Mt 237 [= Mt 23:27]
139/5   Mt 228 [= Mt 23:4]
140/5   Mt 238 [= Mt 23:29]
141/5   Mt 240 [= Mt 23:34]
142/5   Mt 232 [= Mt 23:13]
143/10  –
144/2   Mt 164; Mk 79 [= Mt 16:6; Mk 8:15]
145/5   Mt 93 [= Mt 10:27]
146/2   Mt 94; Mk 86 [= Mt 10:33; Mk 8:38]
147/2   Mt 123; Mk 34 [= Mt 12:31; Mk 3:28]
148/2   Mt 88; Mk 141 [= Mt 10:19; Mk 13:11]
149/10  –
150/5   Mt 49 [= Mt 6:25]
151/10  –
152/2   Mt 194; Mk 108 [= Mt 19:21; Mk 10:21]
153/5   Mt 46 [= Mt 6:20]
154/10  –
155/5   Mt 266 [= Mt 24:46]
156/2   Mt 264; Mk 155 [= Mt 24:43; Mk 13:35]
157/5   Mt 265; 266 [= Mt 24:45; 24:46]
158/5   Mt 267 [= Mt 24:48]
159/10  –
160/5   Mt 95 [= Mt 10:34]
161/5   Mt 162 [= Mt 16:2]
162/5   Mt 36 [= Mt 5:25]
163/10  –
164/10  –
165/5   Mt 116 [= Mt 12:9]

APPENDIX 3 675

166/10 –
167/2 Mt 137; Mk 44 [= Mt 13:31; Mk 4:30]
168/5 Mt 138 [= Mt 13:33]
[169/2 omitted]
170/5 Mt 55 [= Mt 7:13]
171/5 Mt 60 [= Mt 7:22]
[172/5 omitted]
173/2 Mt 199; Mk 111 [= Mt 19:30; Mk 10:31]
174/10 –
175/5 Mt 241 [= Mt 23:37]
176/10 –
177/5 Mt 116 [= Mt 12:9]
178/10 –
179/5 Mt 231 [= Mt 23:12]
180/10 –
181/5 Mt 221 [= Mt 22:1]
182/5 Mt 96 [= Mt 10:37]
183/10 –
184/5 Mt 96 [= Mt 10:37]
185/2 Mt 31; Mk 102 [= Mt 5:13; Mk 9:49]
186/2 Mt 72; Mk 22 [= Mt 9:10; Mk 2:15]
187/5 Mt 182 [= Mt 18:12]
188/10 –
189/5 Mt 182 [= Mt 18:12]
190/10 –
191/5 Mt 48 [= Mt 6:24]
192/10 –
193/5 Mt 105 [= Mt 11:12]
194/5 Mt 34 [= Mt 5:18]
195/2 Mt 190; Mk 105 [= Mt 19:9; Mk 10:11]
196/10 –

676  BEDE: *COMMENTARY ON THE GOSPEL OF LUKE*

197/2    Mt 179; Mk 99 [= Mt 18:6; Mk 9:41]
198/5    Mt 183 [= Mt 18:15]
199/5    Mt 187 [= Mt 18:21]
200/5    Mt 175 [= Mt 17:18]
201/10   –
202/5    Mt 255 [= Mt 24:26]
203/10   –
204/2    Mt 253; Mk 148 [= Mt 24:23; Mk 13:21]
205/5    Mt 256 [= Mt 24:27]
206/2    Mt 168; Mk 83 [= Mt 16:20; Mk 8:30]
207/5    Mt 261 [= Mt 24:37]
208/10   –
209/2    Mt 248; Mk 143 [= Mt 24:29; Mk 13:17]
210/10   –
211/3    Mt 97; Jo 105 [= Mt 10:39; Jo 12:25b]
212/5    Mt 262 [= Mt 24:40]
213/5    Mt 257 [= Mt 24:28]
214/10   –
215/5    Mt 231 [= Mt 23:12]
216/2    Mt 192; Mk 106 [= Mt 19:13; Mk 10:13]
217/2    Mt 178; Mk 95 [= Mt 18:1; Mk 9:33]
218/2    Mt 193; Mk 107 [= Mt 19:16; Mk 10:17]
219/2    Mt 194; Mk 108 [= Mt 19:21; Mk 10:21]
220/2    Mt 195; Mk 109 [= Mt 19:22; Mk 10:22]
221/2    Mt 198; Mk 110 [= Mt 19:29; Mk 10:29]
222/2    Mt 201; Mk 112 [= Mt 20:17; Mk 10:32]
223/10   –
224/2    Mt 205; Mk 116 [= Mt 20:29; Mk 10:46]
225/10   –
226/5    Mt 158 [= Mt 15:24]
227/10   –

APPENDIX 3    677

228/2  Mt 269; Mk 154 [= Mt 25:14; Mk 13:34]
229/5  Mt 270 [= Mt 25:15]
230/2  Mt 271; Mk 42 [= Mt 25:29; Mk 4:25]
231/5  Mt 272 [= Mt 25:30]
232/2  Mt 206; Mk 117 [= Mt 21:1; Mk 11:1]
233/2  Mt 208; Mk 118 [= Mt 21:6; Mk 11:4]
234/1  Mt 209; Mk 119; Jo 100 [= Mt 21:9; Mk 11:9; Jo 12:12]
235/5  Mt 213 [= Mt 21:15]
236/10  –
237/2  Mt 242; Mk 137 [= Mt 24:1; Mk 13:1]
238/1  Mt 211; Mk 121; Jo 21 [= Mt 21:12; Mk 11:15; Jo 2:14]
239/1  Mt 220; Mk 122; Jo 85 [= Mt 21:45; Mk 11:18; Jo 7:44]
240/2  Mt 217; Mk 127 [= Mt 21:23; Mk 11:27]
241/2  Mt 219; Mk 128 [= Mt 21:33; Mk 12:1]
242/1  Mt 220; Mk 129; Jo 88 [= Mt 21:45; Mk 12:12; Jo 8:20]
243/2  Mt 223; Mk 130 [= Mt 22:15; Mk 12:13]
244/2  Mt 226; Mk 133 [= Mt 22:46; Mk 12:34b]
245/2  Mt 225; Mk 134 [= Mt 22:41; Mk 12:35]
246/2  Mt 229; Mk 135 [= Mt 23:5; Mk 12:38]
247/8  Mk 136 [= Mk 12:40]
248/2  Mt 242; Mk 137 [= Mt 24:1; Mk 13:1]
249/2  Mt 226; Mk 133 [= Mt 22:46; Mk 12:35]
250/1  Mt 244; Mk 139; Jo 146; 141 [= Mt 24:9; Mk 13:9; Jo 16:2b; 15:21]
251/2  Mt 88; Mk 141 [= Mt 10:19; Mk 13:11]
252/10  –
253/2  Mt 248; Mk 143 [= Mt 24:16; Mk 13:14b]
254/2  Mt 249; Mk 144 [= Mt 24:19; Mk 13:34]
255/2  Mt 251; Mk 146 [= Mt 24:21; Mk 13:19]
256/10  –
257/2  Mt 258; Mk 150 [= Mt 24:29; Mk 13:24]
258/2  Mt 259; Mk 151 [= Mt 24:30b; Mk 13:26]

| | |
|---|---|
| 259/10 | – |
| 260/1 | Mt 274; Mk 156; Jo 20; 48; 96 [= Mt 26:2; Mk 14:1; Jo 2:13; 6:4; 11:55] |
| 261/1 | Mt 220; Mk 122; Jo 77 [= Mt 21:45; Mk 11:18; Jo 7:30] |
| 262/9 | Jo 124 [= Jo 13:26b] |
| 263/2 | Mt 278; Mk 160 [= Mt 26:14; Mk 14:10] |
| 264/10 | – |
| 265/2 | Mt 285; Mk 166 [= Mt 26:27; Mk 14:21] |
| 266/1 | Mt 284; Mk 165; Jo 55; 63; 65; 67 [= Mt 26:26; Mk 14:22; Jo 6:35; 6:48; 6:51; 6:56] |
| 267/2 | Mt 285; Mk 166 [= Mt 26:27; Mk 14:23] |
| 268/2 | Mt 281; Mk 163 [= Mt 26:23; Mk 14:20] |
| 269/1 | Mt 280; Mk 162; Jo 122 [= Mt 26:22; Mk 14:19; Jo 13:22] |
| 270/2 | Mt 203; Mk 114 [= Mt 20:24; Mk 10:41] |
| 271/10 | – |
| 272/5 | Mt 197 [= Mt 19:28b] |
| 273/10 | – |
| 274/9 | Jo 229; 227; 231 [= Jo 21:16b; 21:15b; 21:17b] |
| 275/1 | Mt 289; Mk 170; Jo 126 [= Mt 26:33; Mk 14:29; Jo 13:36] |
| 276/10 | – |
| 277/8 | Mk 216 [= Mk 15:28] |
| 278/10 | – |
| 279/1 | Mt 291; Mk 172; Jo 156 [= Mt 26:36; Mk 14:32; Jo 18:1] |
| 280/2 | Mt 296; Mk 177 [= Mt 26:40; Mk 14:37] |
| 281/1 | Mt 294; Mk 175; Jo 161 [= Mt 26:39; Mk 14:35; Jo 18:11b] |
| 282/1 | Mt 295; Mk 176; Jo 57; 42 [= Mt 26:39b; Mk 14:36b; Jo 6:38; 5:30b] |
| 283/10 | – |
| 284/2 | Mt 296; Mk 177 [= Mt 26:40; Mk 14:37] |
| 285/1 | Mt 300; Mk 181; Jo 158; 79 [= Mt 26:47; Mk 14:43; Jo 18:3; 7:32b] |
| 286/2 | Mt 301; Mk 182 [= Mt 26:48; Mk 14:44] |
| 287/1 | Mt 302; Mk 183; Jo 160 [= Mt 26:51; Mk 14:47; Jo 18:10] |

APPENDIX 3 679

288/10 –
289/1 Mt 304; Mk 184; Jo 170 [= Mt 26:55; Mk 14:48; Jo 18:20]
290/1 Mt 306; Mk 187; Jo 162; 174 [= Mt 26 57; Mk 14 53; Jo 18 12; 18 24]
291/1 Mt 314; Mk 195; Jo 168; 166 [= Mt 26:69; Mk 14:66; Jo 18:17; 18:16]
292/1 Mt 315; Mk 196; Jo 175 [= Mt 26:71; Mk 14:68b; Jo 18:25]
293/2 Mt 316; Mk 197 [= Mt 26:75; Mk 14:72b]
294/1 Mt 313; Mk 194; Jo 172 [= Mt 26:67; Mk 14:65; Jo 18:22]
295/2 Mt 317; Mk 198 [= Mt 27:1; Mk 15:1]
296/10 –
297/1 Mt 310; Mk 191; Jo 69 [= Mt 26:64b; Mk 14:62; Jo 6:63]
298/10 –
299/2 Mt 312; Mk 193 [= Mt 26:65b; Mk 14:63b]
300/1 Mt 318; Mk 199; Jo 176 [= Mt 27:2; Mk 15:1b; Jo 18:28]
301/10 –
302/1 Mt 320; Mk 200; Jo 178 [= Mt 27:11; Mk 15:2; Jo 18:33]
303/9 Jo 186 [= Jo 19:4]
304/10 –
305/2 Mt 308; Mk 189 [= Mt 26:59; Mk 14:55]
306/10 –
307/9 Jo 186 [= Jo 19:4]
308/10 –
309/2 Mt 322; Mk 202 [= Mt 27:15; Mk 15:6]
310/1 Mt 325; Mk 204; Jo 184 [= Mt 27:20; Mk 15:11; Jo 18:40]
311/1 Mt 326; Mk 205; Jo 188 [= Mt 27:22; Mk 15:12; Jo 19:6]
312/9 Jo 182 [= Jo 18:38b]
313/1 Mt 326; Mk 205; Jo 194 [= Mt 27:22; Mk 15:12; Jo 19:15]
314/1 Mt 328; Mk 206; Jo 196 [= Mt 27:26; Mk 15:15; Jo 19:16]
315/1 Mt 331; Mk 209; Jo 197 [= Mt 27:31b; Mk 15:20b; Jo 19:16b]
316/10 –
317/1 Mt 336; Mk 215; Jo 198 [= Mt 27:38; Mk 15:27; Jo 19:18b]
318/1 Mt 332; Mk 210; Jo 197 [= Mt 27:33; Mk 15:22; Jo 19:16b]

319/1   Mt 336; Mk 215; Jo 198 [= Mt 27:38; Mk 15:27; Jo 19:18b]
320/10  –
321/1   Mt 334; Mk 212; Jo 201 [= Mt 27:35; Mk 15:24; Jo 19:23]
322/2   Mt 338; Mk 218 [= Mt 27:41; Mk 15:31]
323/2   Mt 342; Mk 222 [= Mt 27:48; Mk 15:36]
324/1   Mt 335; Mk 214; Jo 199 [= Mt 27:37; Mk 15:26; Jo 19:19]
325/2   Mt 339; Mk 219 [= Mt 27:44; Mk 15:32b]
326/10  –
327/2   Mt 340; Mk 220 [= Mt 27:35; Mk 15:24]
328/2   Mt 344; Mk 224 [= Mt 27:51; Mk 15:38]
329/1   Mt 343; Mk 223; Jo 204 [= Mt 27:50; Mk 15:37; Jo 19:30]
330/2   Mt 346; Mk 225 [= Mt 27:54; Mk 15:39]
331/10  –
332/1   Mt 348; Mk 227; Jo 206 [= Mt 27:57; Mk 15:42; Jo 19:38]
333/1   Mt 349; Mk 228; Jo 208 [= Mt 27:59; Mk 15:46; Jo 19:40]
334/10  –
335/8   Mk 230 [= Mk 16:1]
336/1   Mt 352; Mk 231; Jo 209; 211 [= Mt 28:1; Mk 16:2; Jo 20:1; 20:11]
337/2   Mt 353; Mk 232 [= Mt 28:4; Mk 16:6]
338/2   Mt 354; Mk 233 [= Mt 28:8; Mk 16:8]
339/10  –
340/9   Jo 213; 217 [= Jo 20:19; 20:26]
341/9   Jo 221; 223; 225 [= Jo 21:9; 21:12; 21:13]
342/10  –

# BIBLIOGRAPHY

**Primary Works**

Adomnán. *De locis sanctis*. Ed. Ludwig Bieler. CCSL 175. Turnhout: Brepols, 1965.
Ambrose. *Expositio Euangelii secundum Lucam* [A/M]. Ed. Marcus Adriaen. CCSL 14. Turnhout: Brepols, 1957.
Ambrosiaster. *Commentaria in epistolam ad Romanos*. PL 17.
Anon. *De solstitia et aequinoctialia* [sic] *conceptionis et nativitatis Domini nostri Jesu Christi et Iohannis Baptistae*. PL Supplementum 1: 557–67.
—. *Historia Abbatum auctore Anonymo*. In *BOH* 1. Ed. and trans. Christopher Grocock and I.N. Wood. *Abbots of Wearmouth and Jarrow*. Oxford: Clarendon Press, 2013.
—. *Homilia de duobus filiis, frugi et luxurioso*. PL 30.
Augustine. *Contra aduersarium legis et prophetarum* [A/V]. Ed. Klaus-D. Daur. CCSL 49. Turnhout: Brepols, 1985.
—. *Contra Faustum* [A/V]. Ed. Joseph Zycha. CSEL 25/1. Vienna: Tempsky, 1891.
—. *De ciuitate Dei*. Ed. Bernhard Dombart and Alphonse Kalb. CCSL 47–48. Turnhout: Brepols, 1955.
—. *De consensu euangelistarum* [A/V]. Ed. Franciscus Weihrich. CSEL 43. Vienna: Tempsky, 1904.
—. *De diuersis quaestionibus*. PL 40.
—. *De Genesi contra Manichaeos*. Ed. Dorothea Weber. CSEL 91. Vienna: Österreichischen Akademie der Wissenschaften, 1998.
—. *De sermone Domini in monte* [A/V]. Ed. Almut Mutzenbecher. CCSL 35. Turnhout: Brepols, 1967.
—. *De trinitate*. Ed. W.J. Mountain and Fr. Glorie. CCSL 50–50A. Turnhout: Brepols, 1968.
—. *Enarrationes in Psalmos* [A/V]. Ed. Eligius Dekkers and Johannes Fraipont. CCSL 38–40. Turnhout: Brepols, 1956 (2nd edn, 1990).
—. *Enchiridion ad Laurentium* [A/V]. Ed. E. Evans. CCSL 46. Turnhout: Brepols, 1969.

—. *Epistolae* [A/V]. Ed. Al. Goldbacher. CSEL 34/1, 34/2, 44. Vienna: Tempsky, 1895–1904.
—. *In Iohannis euangelium tractatus CXXIV* [A/V]. Ed. Radbodus Willems. CCSL 36. Turnhout: Brepols, 1954.
—. *Quaestiones euangeliorum* [A/V]. Ed. Almut Mutzenbecher. CCSL 44B. Turnhout: Brepols, 1980.
—. *Quaestiones xui in Matthaeum* [A/V]. Ed. Almut Mutzenbecher. CCSL 44B. Turnhout: Brepols, 1980.
—. *Sermones* [A/V]. Ed. A. Mai. *Noua Patrum biblioteca* 1. Rome, 1852. *Sermones* 1–50, ed. Cyrillus Lambot. CCSL 41. Turnhout: Brepols, 1961. PL 38.
—. *Speculum*. Ed. Franciscus Weihrich. CSEL 12. Vienna, 1887.
Ps.-Augustine. *Sermones suppositii de Scripturis*. PL 39.
Bede. *Baedae opera historica* [*BOH*]. Ed. Charles Plummer. 2 vols. Oxford: Clarendon Press, 1896.
—. *Bede: A Biblical Miscellany*. Trans. with Notes and Introduction, W. Trent Foley and Arthur G. Holder. TTH 28. Liverpool: Liverpool University Press, 1999.
—. *Bede's Latin Poetry*. Ed. Michael Lapidge. Oxford: Clarendon Press, 2019.
—. *De arte metrica*. Ed. Calvin B. Kendall. CCSL 123A. Turnhout: Brepols, 1975.
Ed. and trans. Kendall. *The Art of Poetry*. In *Bede: The Art of Poetry and Rhetoric*. Bibliotheca Germanica, series nova 2. AQ-Verlag: Saarbrücken, 1991.
—. *De locis sanctis*. Ed. J. Fraipont. CCSL 175. Turnhout: Brepols, 1965.
Trans. W. Trent Foley. *On the Holy Places*. In Foley and Holder, trans., *Bede: A Biblical Miscellany*.
—. *De mansionibus filiorum Israel*. PL 94.
Trans. Arthur G. Holder. *On the Resting-Places of the Children of Israel*. In Foley and Holder, trans., *Bede: A Biblical Miscellany*.
—. *De schematibus et tropis*. Ed. Calvin B. Kendall. CCSL 123A. Turnhout: Brepols, 1975.
Ed. and trans. Kendall. *The Figures of Rhetoric*. In *Bede: The Art of Poetry and Rhetoric*. Bibliotheca Germanica, series nova 2. AQ-Verlag: Saarbrücken, 1991.
—. *De templo*. Ed. D. Hurst. CCSL 119A. Turnhout: Brepols, 1969.
Trans. Seán Connolly. *Bede: On the Temple*. TTH 21. Liverpool: Liverpool University Press, 1995.
—. *De temporibus liber*. Ed. Charles W. Jones. *Bedae Opera De Temporibus* [*BOT*]. Cambridge, MA: The Mediaeval Academy of America, 1943.
Ed. Jones (with the addition of chs 17–22 = *Chronica minora*). CCSL 123C. Turnhout: Brepols, 1980.

# BIBLIOGRAPHY 683

Trans. Calvin B. Kendall and Faith Wallis. *Bede: On Times.* In *Bede: On the Nature of Things and On Times.* TTH 56. Liverpool: Liverpool University Press, 2010.

—. *De temporum ratione.* Ed. Charles W. Jones. *BOT.*
Ed. Jones (with the addition of chs. 66–71 = *Chronica maiora*). CCSL 123B. Turnhout: Brepols, 1977.
Trans. Faith Wallis. *Bede: The Reckoning of Time.* TTH 29. Liverpool: Liverpool University Press, 1999.

—. *Epistola ad Pleguinam.* Ed. Charles W. Jones. *BOT.*
Trans. Faith Wallis. *Bede: The Reckoning of Time.* TTH 29. Liverpool: Liverpool University Press, 1999.

—. *Expositio Actuum Apostolorum et Retractatio.* Ed. M.L.W. Laistner. Cambridge, MA: Mediaeval Academy of America, 1939.
Ed. Laistner. CCSL 121. Turnhout: Brepols, 1983.
Trans. Lawrence T. Martin, *The Venerable Bede: Commentary on the Acts of the Apostles.* CSS 117. Kalamazoo: Cistercian Publications, 1989.

—. *Expositio Apocalypseos.* Ed. Roger Gryson. CCSL 121A. Turnhout: Brepols, 2001.
Trans. Faith Wallis. *Bede: Commentary on Revelation.* TTH 58. Liverpool: Liverpool University Press, 2013.

—. *Historia Abbatum auctore Baeda.* In *BOH* 1. Ed. and trans. Christopher Grocock and I.N. Wood. *Abbots of Wearmouth and Jarrow.* Oxford: Clarendon Press, 2013.
Ed. and trans. Bertram Colgrave and R.A.B. Mynors. *Bede's Ecclesiastical History of the English People.* Oxford: Clarendon Press, 1969.
Trans. Leo Sherley-Price and R.E. Latham. *Ecclesiastical History of the English People.* London: Penguin Books, rev. 1990.

—. *In Cantica canticorum.* Ed. David Hurst. CCSL 119B. Turnhout: Brepols, 1983.
Trans. Arthur Holder. *The Venerable Bede:* On the Song of Songs *and Selected Writings.* The Classics of Western Spirituality. New York: Paulist Press, 2011.

—. *In Epistolas VII catholicas.* Ed. David Hurst. CCSL 121. Turnhout: Brepols, 1983.
Trans. Hurst. *The Venerable Bede: Commentary on the Seven Catholic Epistles.* CSS 82. Kalamazoo: Cistercian Publications, 1985.

—. *In Genesim.* Ed. Charles W. Jones. CCSL 118A. Turnhout: Brepols, 1969.
Trans. Calvin B. Kendall. *Bede: On Genesis.* TTH 48. Liverpool: Liverpool University Press, 2008.

—. *In Lucae Euangelium expositio.* Ed. David Hurst. CCSL 120. Turnhout: Brepols, 1960.

—. *In Marci Euangelium expositio*. Ed. David Hurst. CCSL 120. Turnhout: Brepols, 1960.
—. *In primam partem Samuhelis*. Ed. David Hurst. CCSL 119. Turnhout: Brepols, 1962.
Trans. Scott DeGregorio and Rosalind Love. *Bede: On First Samuel*. TTH 70. Liverpool: Liverpool University Press, 2019.
—. *Opera homiletica*. Ed. David Hurst. CCSL 122. Turnhout: Brepols, 1955.
Trans. Lawrence T. Martin and David Hurst. *Bede the Venerable: Homilies on the Gospels*. CSS 110–11. 2 vols. Kalamazoo: Cistercian Publications, 1991.
The Bible. *Biblia Sacra Vulgata*. Ed. Robert Weber, 4th edn, rev. Roger Gryson. Stuttgart: Deutsche Bibelgesellschaft, 1994.
—. *The Five Books of Moses: A Translation with Commentary*. Trans. Robert Alter. New York and London: W.W. Norton, 2004.
—. *The Holy Bible: Douay Rheims Version*. Ed. Richard Challoner. Repr. Rockford, IL: Tan Books and Publishers, 1971.
—. *The King James Study Bible*. Ed. C.I. Scofield. Uhrichsville, OH: Barbour, n.d.
—. *The New Oxford Annotated Bible: New Revised Standard Version*. 4th edn. New York: Oxford University Press, 2010.
—. Vulgate. *Codex Amiatinus*. Florence, Biblioteca Medicea Laurenziana, MS Amiatino 1. Digital facsimile. https://www.loc.gov/item/2021668243/
Cassian. *Collationes*. 2nd edn. Ed. Michael Petschenig, with Gottfried Kreuz. CSEL 13. Vienna: Österreichischen Akademie der Wissenschaften, 2004.
Cassiodorus. *Expositio Psalmorum I–LXX*. Ed. Marcus Adriaen. CCSL 97. Turnhout: Brepols, 1958.
—. *Institutiones*. Ed. R.A.B. Mynors. Oxford: Clarendon Press, 1937.
Trans. James W. Halporn, with an introduction by Mark Vessey. *Institutions of Divine and Secular Learning*. TTH 42. Liverpool: Liverpool University Press, 2004.
Chrysostom, John. *Opera D. Iohannis Chrysostomi ... quotquot per Graecorum exemplarium in Latinam linguam hactenus traduci potuerunt*. Basel: Froben, 1539.
Corpus Christianorum series latina. Turnhout: Brepols, 1953–.
Corpus Scriptorum Ecclesiasticorum Latinorum. Vienna, Prague, Leipzig: Tempsky, etc., 1866–.
Dionysius Exiguus. *Epistula ad Petronium episcopum*. Ed. Bruno Krusch. *Studien zur christlich-mittelalterichen Chronologie: Die Entstehung unserer heutigen Zeitrechnung*. 63–68. Berlin: Akademie der Wissenschaften, 1930.
Eusebius. *Historia ecclesiastica*. See Rufinus of Aquileia.
Fulgentius of Ruspe. *Ad Trasamundum libri III*. Ed. Johannes Fraipont. CCSL 91. Turnhout: Brepols, 1968.
Gregory. *Dialogues* [G/R]. Ed. Adalbert de Vogüé. SC 251, 260, 265. Paris: Éd. du Cerf, 1978–1980.

# BIBLIOGRAPHY 685

—. *Homeliae in Euangelia* [G/R]. Ed. Raymond Étaix. CCSL 141. Turnhout: Brepols, 1999. Trans. David Hurst. *Gregory the Great: Forty Gospel Homilies*. CSS 123. Kalamazoo: Cistercian Publications, 1990.
—. *Homeliae in Hiezechielem prophetam* [G/R]. Ed. Marcus Adriaen. CCSL 142. Turnhout: Brepols, 1971.
—. *Moralia in Iob* [G/R]. Ed. Marcus Adriaen. CCSL 143, 143A, 143B. Turnhout: Brepols, 1979.
—. *Regula pastoralis* [G/R]. *Règle pastorale*. Ed. Bruno Judic, Floribert Rommel, and Charles Morel. SC 381–82. Paris: Éd. du Cerf, 1992.
Guillelmus (William) Durandus. *Rationale divinorum officium*. Ed. A Davril and T.M. Thibodeau. CCSL 140A–B. Turnhout: Brepols, 1995–2000.
Hilary of Poitiers. *De trinitate* VIII–XII. Ed. P. Smulders. CCSL 62A. Turnhout: Brepols, 1980.
Isidore. *De ecclesiasticis officiis*. Ed. Christopher Lawson. CCSL 113. Turnhout: Brepols, 1989.
—. *Etymologiae*. Ed. W.M. Lindsay. *Isidori Hispalensis Episcopi Etymologiarum sive Originum libri XX*. 2 vols. Oxford: Clarendon Press, 1911 (unpaginated). Trans. Stephen A. Barney, W.J. Lewis, J.A. Beach, and Oliver Berghof. *The Etymologies of Isidore of Seville*. Cambridge: Cambridge University Press, 2006.
—. *Regula monachorum*. PL 83.
Jerome. *Aduersus Heluidium de Mariae uirginitate perpetua*. PL 23.
—. *Aduersus Iouinianum* [H/R]. PL 23.
—. *Commentarii in Danielem*. Ed. Franciscus Glorie. CCSL 75A. Turnhout: Brepols, 1964.
—. *Commentarii in Esaiam* [H/R]. Ed. Marcus Adriaen. CCSL 73–73A. Turnhout: Brepols, 1963.
—. *Commentarii in Matheum* [H/R]. Ed. David Hurst and Marcus Adriaen. CCSL 77. Turnhout: Brepols, 1969.
—. *Commentarius in Abdiam*. Ed. Marcus Adriaen. CCSL 76. Turnhout: Brepols, 1969.
—. *Commentarius in Ecclesiasten*. Ed. Marcus Adriaen. CCSL 72. Turnhout: Brepols, 1959.
—. *De situ et nominibus locorum Hebraicorum*. Ed. Paul de Lagarde. *Onomastica sacra*. Göttingen, 1870.
—. *De uiris illustribus*. Ed. A. Ceresa-Gastaldo, *Gli uomini illustri. De viris illustribus*. Florence: Nardini, 1988.
—. *Dialogus contra Pelagianos*. PL 23.
—. *Liber interpretationis Hebraicorum nominum*. Ed. Paul de Lagarde. CCSL 72. Turnhout: Brepols, 1959.
Ps.-Jerome. *Expositio euangeliorum*. PL 30:531–88.

# 686 BEDE: COMMENTARY ON THE GOSPEL OF LUKE

Josephus. *Antiquitates Judaicae.* Ed. and trans. H. St. J. Thackeray. LCL, 6 vols. Cambridge, MA: Harvard University Press, 1926.
Franz Blatt, ed. *The Latin Josephus I. Introduction and Text. The Antiquities: Books I–V.* Acta Jutlandica XXX. Copenhagen: Ejnar Munksgaard, 1958.
—. *Bellum Iudaicum.* https://sites.google.com/site/latinjosephus/.
Marcellus Empiricus. *De medicamentis liber. Über Heilmittel.* Ed. Max Niedermann. 2nd edn. Rev. Eduard Liechtenhan, trans. Jutta Kollesch and Diethard Nickel. Berlin, 1968 (= Corpus Medicorum Latinorum 5).
Origen. *In Leviticum Homiliae.* See Rufinus of Aquileia.
Patrologia cursus completus series latina. Ed. J.-P. Migne. 221 vols. Paris: J.-P. Migne and Garnier Frères, 1841–1880, with volumes reissued by Garnier to 1905.
Paulinus of Nola. *Carmina.* Ed. Wilhelm de Hartel. CSEL 30. Vienna: Tempsky, 1894.
Pliny. *Naturalis historia.* Ed. H. Rackham, W.E.S. Jones, and D.E. Eichholz. *Natural History* LCL, 10 vols. Cambridge, MA: Harvard University Press/ London: Heinemann, 1938 (repr. 1961).
Primasius. *Primasius episcopus Hadrumentinus Commentarius in Apocalypsin.* Ed. A.W. Adams. CCSL 92. Turnhout: Brepols, 1985.
Rufinus of Aquileia. Trans. of Eusebius, *Historia ecclesiastica.* Ed. Th. Mommsen, *Eusebius Werke* 2.1. GCS 9.1. Leipzig: J.C. Hinrichs, 1903.
—. Trans. of Origen, *In Leviticum Homiliae.* Ed. W.A. Baehrens, *Origenes Werke* 6. GCS 29. Leipzig: J.C. Hinrichs, 1920.
Sedulius. *Paschale carmen.* Ed. Iohannes Huemer. CSEL 10: Vienna, 1885.
Translated Texts for Historians. Liverpool: Liverpool University Press, 1988–.

## Secondary Works

Alter, Robert. *The Five Books of Moses* (see above, under *The Bible*).
Babcock, Robert G. 'The "proverbium antiquum" in Acca's Letter to Bede', *Mittellateinisches Jahrbuch* 22 (1987): 53–55.
Bankert, Dabney Anderson, Jessica Wegmann, and Charles D. Wright, *Ambrose in Anglo-Saxon England with Pseudo-Ambrose and Ambrosiaster*, Old English Newsletter Subsidia 25. Kalamazoo: Medieval Institute, Western Michigan University, 1997.
Barb, A.A. 'The Eagle Stone', *Journal of the Warburg and Courtauld Institutes* 13.3–4 (1950): 316–18.
Barrow, Julia. 'Bede's Wise and Foolish Virgins: *Streanæshalch* and Coldingham', in DeGregorio and Kershaw, eds. *Cities, Saints and Communities*, 287–308.
Beer, Rudolf. *Handschriftenschätze Spaniens.* Vienna: Tempsky, 1894.
Bieler, Ludwig. 'Corpus Christianorum', *Scriptorium* 16.2 (1962): 324–33.

Bien, Emmanuel. 'Les marchands chassés du temple, entre commentaires et usages sociaux', *Médiévales* 55 (2008): 53–74.
Bischoff, Bernhard. *Die südostdeutschen Schreibschulen und Bibliotheken in der Karolingerzeit.* Leipzig, 1940.
—. *Katalog der festländischen Handschriften des neunten Jahrhunderts (mit Ausnahme der wisigotischen):* I Aachen–Lambach. Wiesbaden: Harrassowitz, 1998; II Laon–Paderborn. Wiesbaden: Harrassowitz, 2004; III (Bischoff and Birgit Ebersperger) Padua–Zwickau. Wiesbaden: Harrassowitz, 2014.
—. *Manuscripts and Libraries in the Age of Charlemagne.* Trans. Michael M. Gorman. Cambridge: Cambridge University Press, 1994.
—. 'Turning-Points in the History of Latin Exegesis in the Early Irish Church: AD 650–800', in McNamara, Martin, ed. *Biblical Studies: The Medieval Irish Contribution.* Dublin: Dominican Publications, 1976, cat. 11A, 108–09. Translation of 'Wendepunkte in der Geschichte der lateinischen Exegese im Frühmittelalter', *Sacris Erudiri* 6.2 (1954): 189–281.
Bonner, Gerald, ed. *Famulus Christi: Essays in Commemoration of the Thirteenth Centenary of the Birth of the Venerable Bede.* London: S.P.C.K., 1976.
Brown, George Hardin. *A Companion to Bede.* Anglo-Saxon Studies 12. Woodbridge: The Boydell Press, 2009.
—, and Frederick M. Biggs. *Bede.* Sources of Anglo-Saxon Literary Culture. 2 vols. Amsterdam: Amsterdam University Press, 2018.
Brown, Michelle. 'Bede's Life in Context', in DeGregorio, ed. *The Cambridge Companion to Bede,* 3–24.
Bruce-Mitford, R.L.S. 'The Art of the Codex Amiatinus', in Lapidge, Michael, ed. *Bede and His World: The Jarrow Lectures 1958–1993.* 2 vols. Variorum: Ashgate Publishing; Aldershot, 1994, 1: 187–234.
*A Catalogue of the Manuscripts Preserved in the Library of the University of Cambridge.* Vol. 1. Cambridge: University Press, 1856.
Chazelle, Celia. *The Codex Amiatinus and its 'Sister' Bibles: Scripture, Liturgy, and Art in the Milieu of the Venerable Bede.* Leiden: Brill, 2019.
—. 'Debating the End Times with Bede', *Irish Theological Quarterly* 80.3 (2–15): 212–32.
Cilliers, Louise. 'Vindicianus's *Gynaecia*: Text and Translation of the Codex Monacensis (Clm4633)', *Journal of Medieval Latin* 15 (2005): 153–236.
Corradini, Richard, ed. *Ego Trouble: Authors and their Identities in the Early Middle Ages.* Vienna: Österreichische Akademie der Wissenschaften, 2010.
Crawford, Matthew. *The Eusebian Canon Tables: Ordering Textual Knowledge in Late Antiquity.* Oxford: Oxford University Press, 2019.
Crépin, André. 'Bede and the Vernacular', in Bonner, ed. *Famulus Christi,* 170–92.
Darby, Peter. 'Apocalypse and Reform in Bede's *De die iudicii*', in Matthew Gabriele and James T. Palmer, eds. *Apocalypse and Reform from Late Antiquity to the Middle Ages.* London and New York: Routledge, 2019, 77–100.

—. *Bede and the End of Time*. Farnham: Ashgate, 2012.
—. 'Heresy and Authority in Bede's *Letter to Plegwine*'. In DeGregorio and Kershaw, eds. *Cities, Saints and Communities*, 145–70.
—, and Faith Wallis, eds. *Bede and the Future*. Farnham: Ashgate, 2014.
DeGregorio, Scott, ed. *The Cambridge Companion to Bede*. Cambridge: Cambridge University Press, 2010.
—, ed. *Innovation and Tradition in the Writings of the Venerable Bede*. Medieval European Studies VII. Morgantown: West Virginia University Press, 2006.
—. '*Interpretatio monastica*: Biblical Commentary and the Forging of Monastic Identity in the Early Middle Ages', in Stephenson, Rebecca, and Emily V. Thornbury, eds. *Latinity and Identity in Anglo-Saxon Literature*. Toronto: University of Toronto Press, 2016, 38–53.
—. '"Nostrorum socordiam temporum": The Reforming Impulse of Bede's Later Exegesis', *Early Medieval Europe* 11 (2002): 107–22.
—. 'The Venerable Bede and Gregory the Great: Exegetical Connections, Spiritual Departures', *Early Medieval Europe* 18 (2010): 43–60.
—, and Paul Kershaw, eds. *Cities, Saints and Communities in Early Medieval Europe: Essays in Honour of Alan Thacker*. Turnhout: Brepols, 2020.
Del Giacco, Eric Jay. 'Exegesis and Sermon: A Comparison of Bede's Commentary and Homilies on Luke', *Medieval Sermon Studies* 50 (2006): 9–29.
de Margerie, Bertrand. 'Bède le Vénérable, commentateur original du Nouveau Testament', in *Introduction à l'histoire de l'exégèse*. Vol. 4: *L'Occident latin de Léon le Grand à Bernard de Clairvaux* (Paris: Éd. du Cerf, 1990), 187–228.
*Dictionary of Medieval Latin from British Sources*. London: Printed for the British Academy by Oxford University Press, 1975–2013. Accessed electronically via Brepolis.
Elliot, J.K., ed. *A Collection of Apocryphal Christian Literature in an English Translation Based on M.R. James*. New York: Oxford University Press, 1993/2005.
Flanders, Judith. *A Place for Everything: The Curious History of Alphabetical Order*. New York: Basic Books, 2020.
Gameson, Richard, *Codex Amiatinus: Making and Meaning*. Jarrow Lecture, 2017.
Goffart, Walter. 'Bede's *uera lex historiae* Explained', *Anglo-Saxon England* 34 (2005): 111–16.
Gorman, Michael M. 'Source Marks and Chapter Divisions in Bede's Commentary on Luke', *Revue Bénédictine* 112 (2002): 246–90.
Halporn, James. 'Methods of Reference in Cassiodorus', *Library History* 16.1 (1981): 71–91.
Hart-Hasler, J.N. 'Bede's Use of Patristic Sources: The Transfiguration', *Studia Patristica* 28 (1993): 197–204.

# BIBLIOGRAPHY 689

Hauke, Hermann. *Katalog der lateinischen Fragmente der Bayerischen Staatsbibliothek München*. Vol. 2: *Clm 29315-29520*. Wiesbaden: Otto Harrassowitz, 2001.
Higham, N.J. *(Re-)Reading Bede: The Ecclesiastical History in Context*. London: Routledge, 2006.
Hill, Joyce. 'Carolingian Perspectives on the Authority of Bede', in DeGregorio, ed. *Innovation and Tradition*, 227-49.
Hilliard, Paul. 'Acca of Hexham through the Eyes of the Venerable Bede'. *Early Medieval Europe* 26 (2018): 440-61.
—. 'The Venerable Bede as Scholar, Gentile and Preacher', in Corradini, Richard, ed. *Ego Trouble: Authors and their Identities in the Early Middle Ages*. Vienna: Österreichische Akademie der Wissenschaften, 2010, 101-09.
Holder, Arthur G. 'The Anti-Pelagian Character of Bede's Commentary on the Song of Songs', in Leonardi, Claudio, and Giovanni Orlandi, eds. *Biblical Studies in the Early Middle Ages*. Florence: SISMEL – Edizione del Galluzzo, 2005, 91-103.
—. 'Bede and the New Testament', in DeGregorio, ed. *The Cambridge Companion to Bede*, 142-55.
—. 'Bede and the Tradition of Patristic Exegesis', *Anglican Theological Review* 72 (1990): 399-411.
—. 'Hunting Snakes in the Grass: Bede as Heresiologist', in Mullins, Elizabeth, and Diarmuid Scully, eds. *Listen, O Isles, unto Me: Studies in Medieval Word and Image in Honour of Jennifer O'Reilly*. Cork: Cork University Press, 2011, 104-14.
*Inventario General de Manuscritos de la Biblioteca Nacional*. Vol. 2: *(501 a 896)*. Madrid: Ministerio de Educacion Nacional, 1956.
James, Montague Rhodes. *The Western Manuscripts in the Library of Trinity College, Cambridge: A Descriptive Catalogue*. Vol. 1: *Containing an Account of the Manuscripts Standing in Class B*. Cambridge: Cambridge University Press, 1900.
Jenkins, Claude. 'Bede as Exegete and Theologian', in Thompson, ed. *Bede: His Life, Times, and Writings*, 152-200.
Jones, Charles W. *Saints' Lives and Chronicles in Early England*. Ithaca, NY: Cornell University Press, 1947.
Kaczynski, Bernice. 'Bede's Commentaries on Luke and Mark and the Formation of a Patristic Canon', in Echard, Siân, and Gernot R. Wieland. *Anglo-Latin and Its Heritage: Essays in Honour of A.G. Rigg on his 64th Birthday*. Publications of the Journal of Medieval Latin 4. Turnhout: Brepols, 2001, 17-26.
Kelly, Joseph F. 'Bede's Exegesis of Luke's Infancy Narrative', *Mediaevalia* 15 (1993 for 1989): 59-70.

Kendall, Calvin B. 'Bede and Education', in DeGregorio, ed. *The Cambridge Companion to Bede*, 99–112.

—. 'Bede and Islam', in Darby and Wallis, eds. *Bede and the Future*, 93–114.

—. 'Bede's *Historia ecclesiastica*: The Rhetoric of Faith', in Murphy, James J., ed. *Medieval Eloquence: Studies in the Theory and Practice of Medieval Rhetoric*. Berkeley and Los Angeles: University of California Press, 1978, 145–72.

—. 'Imitation and the Venerable Bede's *Historia Ecclesiastica*', in King, Margot H., and Wesley M. Stevens, eds. *Saints, Scholars, and Heroes: Studies in Medieval Culture in Honour of Charles W. Jones*. 2 vols. Collegeville, MN: Hill Monastic Manuscript Library, Saint John's Abbey and University, 1979, 1: 161–90.

—. 'Let Us Now Praise a Famous City: Wordplay in the OE *Durham* and the Cult of St. Cuthbert', *Journal of English and Germanic Philology* 87 (1988): 507–21.

—. 'The Responsibility of *Auctoritas*: Method and Meaning in Bede's Commentary on Genesis', in DeGregorio, ed. *Innovation and Tradition*, 101–19.

Laistner, M.L.W. 'The Library of the Venerable Bede', in Thompson, ed. *Bede: His Life, Times, and Writings*, 237–66. Reprinted in Starr, Chester G., ed., *Intellectual Heritage of the Early Middle Ages: Selected Essays by M.L.W. Laistner*. New York: Octagon Books, 1983, 117–49.

—. 'Source-Marks in Bede Manuscripts', *The Journal of Theological Studies* 34 (1933): 350–54.

Laistner, M.L.W. and H.H. King. *A Hand-List of Bede Manuscripts*. Ithaca: Cornell University Press, 1943.

Lapidge, Michael. *The Anglo-Saxon Library*. Oxford: Oxford University Press, 2006.

—. 'Some Remnants of Bede's Lost *Liber Epigrammatum*', *English Historical Review* 90 (1975): 798–820.

Levison, Wilhelm. *England and the Continent in the Eighth Century*. London: Oxford University Press, 1946.

Lindsay, W.M. *Notae Latinae: An Account of Abbreviation in Latin MSS. of the Early Minuscule Period (c. 700–850)*. Cambridge: Cambridge University Press, 1915.

Love, Rosalind. 'Bede and John Chrysostom', *Journal of Medieval Latin* 17 (2007): 72–86.

—. 'The Library of the Venerable Bede', in Gameson, Richard, ed. *The Cambridge History of the Book in Britain*. Vol. 1: *ca. 400–1100*. Cambridge: Cambridge University Press, 2012, 606–32.

Lowe, E.A. *Codices Latini Antiquiores*. 11 vols + Supplement. Oxford: Clarendon Press, 1934–1972.

MacCarron, Máirín. *Bede and Time: Computus, Theology and History in the Early Medieval World*. London and New York: Routledge, 2020.

McCarthy, Daniel. 'Bede's Primary Source for the Vulgate Chronology in His Chronicles in *De temporibus* and *De temporum ratione*', in Warntjes, Immo, and Dáibhí Ó Cróinín, eds. *Computus and Its Cultural Context in the Latin West, AD 300–1200*. Turnhout: Brepols, 2010, 159–89.

McClure, Judith. 'Bede's *Notes on Genesis* and the Training of Anglo-Saxon Clergy', in Walsh, Katherine, and Diana Wood, eds. *The Bible in the Medieval World: Essays in Memory of Beryl Smalley*. Oxford: Oxford University Press, 1985, 17–30.

Madan, Falconer, and H.H.E. Craster. *A Summary Catalogue of Western Manuscripts in the Bodleian Library at Oxford*. Vol. 2, part 1. Oxford: Clarendon Press, 1922.

Major, Tristan. 'Words, Wit, and Wordplay in the Latin Works of the Venerable Bede', *The Journal of Medieval Latin* 22 (2012): 185–219.

Markus, R.A. 'Gregory and Bede: The Making of the Western Apocalyptic Tradition', in *Gregorio Magno nel XIV centenario della morte*. Rome: Accademia nazionale dei Lincei, 2004, 249–55.

Marsden, Richard. '*Manus Bedae*: Bede's Contribution to Ceolfrith's Bibles', *ASE* 27 (1998): 65–85.

Martin, Lawrence T. 'Bede and Preaching', in DeGregorio, ed. *The Cambridge Companion to Bede*, 156–69.

—. 'Bede's Originality in His Use of the Book of Wisdom in His *Homilies on the Gospels*', in DeGregorio, ed. *Innovation and Tradition*, 189–202.

Meyvaert, Paul. 'Bede, Cassiodorus, and the Codex Amiatinus', *Speculum* 71 (1996): 827–83.

—. 'Bede's *Capitula Lectionum* for the Old and New Testaments', *Revue Bénédictine* 105 (1995): 348–80.

Moreia, Isabel. *Heaven's Purge: Purgatory in Late Antiquity*. New York: Oxford University Press, 2010.

Murray, Alexander. 'Bede and the Unchosen Race', in Pryce, H., and J. Watts, eds. *Power and Identity in the Middle Ages: Essays in Memory of Rees Davies*. Oxford: Oxford University Press, 2007, 52–67.

Nelson, Jinty. 'Hincmar of Reims meets Bede', in DeGregorio and Kershaw, eds. *Cities, Saints and Communities*, 334–36.

Neuman de Vegvar, Carol. 'Remembering Jerusalem: Architecture and Meaning in Insular Canon Table Arcades', in Moss, Rachel, ed. *Making and Meaning in Insular Art*. Dublin: Four Courts, 2007, 242–56.

O'Brien, Conor. 'Bede on the Jewish Church', in Clarke, Peter D., and Charlotte Methuen, eds. *The Church on Its Past*. Woodbridge: Boydell, 2013, 63–73.

—. *Bede's Temple: An Image and Its Interpretation*. Oxford: Oxford University Press, 2015.

—. 'Bede's Theology of Circumcision, Its Sources and Significance', *The Journal of Theological Studies* NS 67.2 (2016): 594–613.

—. 'The Cleansing of the Temple in Early Medieval Northumbria', *ASE* 43 (2015): 201–20.

—. 'A Quotation from Origen's *Homilies on Leviticus* in Bede's Commentary on Luke's Gospel', *Notes and Queries* 60 (2013): 185.

O'Reilly, Jennifer. 'Bede and Monotheletism', in DeGregorio and Kershaw, eds. *Cities, Saints and Communities*, 105–28.

—. 'Bede on Seeing the God of Gods in Zion', in Minnis, Alastair, and Jane Roberts, eds. *Text, Image, Interpretation: Studies in Anglo-Saxon Literature and Its Insular Context in Honour of Éamonn Ó Carragían*. Turnhout: Brepols, 2007, 3–29.

—. 'Patristic and Insular Traditions of the Evangelists: Exegesis and Iconography', in Luiselli Fadda, A.M., and É. Ó Carragáin, eds. *Le Isole Britanniche e Roma in età romanobarbarica*. Rome: Herder, 1998, 49–94.

Palmer, James. *The Apocalypse in the Middle Ages*. Cambridge: Cambridge University Press, 2014.

Piano, Natacha. 'De la porte close du temple de Salomon à la porte ouverte du Paradis', *Studi medievali* 50 (2009): 133–57.

Plummer, Charles. 'Bede's Life and Works', in *BOH* 1: ix–lxxix.

Ray, Roger. 'Bede and Cicero', *ASE* 16: 1–15.

—. 'Bede, the Exegete, as Historian', in Bonner, ed. *Famulus Christi*, 125–40.

—. 'Bede's *Vera Lex Historiae*', *Speculum* 55 (1980): 1–21.

—. 'What Do We Know about Bede's Commentaries?', *Recherches de théologie ancienne et médiévale* 49 (1982): 1–20.

—. 'Who Did Bede Think He Was?', in DeGregorio, ed. *Innovation and Tradition*, 11–14.

Scheil, Andrew P. *The Footsteps of Israel: Understanding Jews in Anglo-Saxon England*. Ann Arbor: University of Michigan Press, 2004.

Seimens, James. 'Another Book for Jarrow's Library? Coincidences in Exegesis between Bede and the *Laterculus Malalianus*', *Downside Review* 132 (2013): 15–34.

Shailor, Barbara A. 'Beinecke MS 441': Yale University/Beinecke Rare Book and Manuscript Library/General Collection of Rare Books and Manuscripts/ Medieval and Renaissance Manuscripts. https://pre1600ms.beinecke.library. yale.edu/docs/pre1600.ms441.htm.

Sharpe, Richard. 'The Varieties of Bede's Prose', in Reinhardt, Tobias, Michael Lapidge, and J.N. Adams, eds. *Aspects of the Language of Latin Prose*. Proceedings of the British Academy 129. Oxford: Oxford University Press for the British Academy, 2005, 339–55.

Smetana, Cyril L. 'Paul the Deacon's Patristic Anthology', in Szarmach, Paul, and Bernard F. Huppé, eds. *The Old English Homily and Its Backgrounds*. Albany: SUNY Press, 1978, 75–97.

Smith, Lesley. *The Glossa Ordinaria: The Making of a Medieval Bible Commentary*. Leiden: Brill, 2009.
Spilling, Herrad. *Die Handschriftenkataloge der Staats- und Stadtbibliothek Augsburg*. Vol. 3: *2° Cod 101–250*. Wiesbaden: Otto Harrassowitz, 1984.
Stancliffe, Clare. 'Bede and Bishop Acca', in DeGregorio and Kershaw, eds. *Cities, Saints and Communities*, 171–94.
—. 'Dating Wilfrid's Death and Stephen's *Life*', in N.J. Higham, ed. *Wilfrid: Abbot, Bishop, Saint: Papers from the 1300th Anniversary Conferences*. Donington: Shaun Tyas, 2013, 17–26.
—. 'Disputed Episcopacy: Bede, Acca, and the Relationship between Stephen's *Life of St Wilfrid* and the Early Prose Lives of St Cuthbert', *ASE* 41 (2012): 7–29.
Stansbury, Mark. 'Early-Medieval Biblical Commentaries, Their Writers and Readers'. *Frühmittelalterliche Studien* 33.1 (1999): 49–82.
—. 'Source Marks in Bede's Biblical Commentaries', in Hawkes, Jane, and Susan Mills, eds. *Northumbria's Golden Age*. Stroud: Sutton Publishing, 1999, 383–89.
Thacker, Alan. 'Bede and History', in DeGregorio, ed. *The Cambridge Companion to Bede*, 170–89.
—. 'Bede and the Ordering of Understanding', in DeGregorio, ed. *Innovation and Tradition*, 37–63.
—. 'Bede, the Britons and the Book of Samuel', in Baxter, Stephen, ed. *Early Medieval Studies in Memory of Patrick Wormald*. Farnham and Burlington, VT: Ashgate, 2009, 129–47.
—. 'Why Did Heresy Matter to Bede? Present and Future Contexts', in Darby and Wallis, eds. *Bede and the Future*, 47–66.
Thompson, A. Hamilton, ed. *Bede: His Life, Times, and Writings: Essays in Commemoration of the Twelfth Centenary of His Death*. New York: Russell & Russell, 1966.
Thompson, E. Maunde. *Index to the Catalogue of Additions to the Manuscripts in the British Museum in the Years MDCCCLIV–MDCCCLXXV*. London: British Museum, 1880.
Vezin, J. 'Observations sur l'origine des manuscrits légués par Dungal à Bobbio', *Paläeographie 1981* (Munich, 1982), 125–44.
Wallis, Faith. 'Bede and Science', in DeGregorio, ed. *The Cambridge Companion to Bede*, 113–26.
—. 'Caedmon's Created World and the Monastic Encyclopedia', in Frantzen, Allen, and John Hines, eds. *Caedmon's Hymn and Material Culture in the Anglo-Saxon World*. Morgantown: West Virginia University Press, 2007, 80–111.
—. *Communis et universalis: The Catholicon of Giovanni Balbi of Genoa, o.p.* Memoire, Licentiate in Mediaeval Studies, Pontifical Institute of Mediaeval Studies, Toronto, 1981.

—. 'The Experience of the Book: Manuscripts, Texts, and the Role of Epistemology in Early Medieval Medicine', in Bates, Don G., ed. *Knowledge and the Scholarly Medical Traditions*. Cambridge: Cambridge University Press, 1995, 101–26.

—. *Medieval Medicine: A Reader*. Toronto: University of Toronto Press, 2010.

—. '"Number Mystique" in Early Medieval Computus Texts', in Koetsier, Tuen, and L. Bergmans, eds. *Mathematics and the Divine: A Historical Study*. Amsterdam: Elsevier, 2005, 181–99.

—. '*Rectores* at Risk: Erudition and Heresy in Bede's *Commentary on Proverbs*', in DeGregorio and Kershaw, eds. *Cities, Saints and Communities*, 129–44.

—. '*Si Naturam Quaeras*: Reframing Bede's "Science"', in DeGregorio, ed. *Innovation and Tradition*, 61–94.

—. 'Why Did Bede Write a Commentary on Revelation?', in Darby and Wallis, eds. *Bede and the Future*, 23–45.

Walther, Hans. *Proverbia sententiaeque medii aevi*. Göttingen: Vandenhoek & Ruprecht, 1963–1969.

Wenk, Wolfgang. *Zur Sammlung der 38 Homilien des Chrysostomus Latinus: Mit der Edition der Nr 6, 8, 27, 32 und 33*. Vienna: Verlag des Österreichischen Akademie der Wissenschaften, 1988.

West, P. 'Rumination in Bede's Account of Caedmon', *Monastic Studies* 12 (1976): 217–36.

Westgard, Joshua A. 'Bede and the Continent in the Carolingian Age and Beyond', in DeGregorio, ed. *The Cambridge Companion to Bede*, 201–15.

Wieland, Gernot. 'Caedmon, the Clean Animal', *American Benedictine Review* 35 (1984): 194–203.

Wright, C.D. 'Hiberno-Latin and Irish-Influenced Biblical Commentaries', in Biggs, F.M., T.D. Hill, and P.E. Szarmach, eds. *The Sources of Anglo-Saxon Literary Culture: A Trial Version*. Binghamton, NY: SUNY Press, 1990, cat. 18, 100–01.

Young, Frances M. *Biblical Exegesis and the Formation of Christian Culture*. Cambridge: Cambridge University Press, 1997.

## Digitized Manuscript Repositories and Catalogues

BAV: Biblioteca Apostolica Vaticana. Manuscripts Catalogue. www.mss.vatlib.

Beinecke Medieval MSS: Yale University. Beinecke Rare Book and Manuscript Library. General Collection of Rare Books and Manuscripts. Medieval and Renaissance Manuscripts. http://brbl-net.library.yale.edu.

# BIBLIOGRAPHY 695

*Biblioteca Firenze*: Biblioteca Medicea Laurenziana. *Biblioteca Firenze. Teca digitale*. http://teca.bmlonline.it/TecaRicerca/index.jsp.
BLB: Badische Landesbibliothek. https://digital.blb-karlsruhe.de.
BNP: Biblioteca Nacional de Portugal. *Biblioteca digital*. http://purl.pt/index/geral/PT/index.html.
Bodley Checklist: Bodleian Library, Checklist of Medieval Manuscripts Acquired since 1916: MSS. Lat.th. www.bodley.ox.ac.uk/dept/scwmss/online/medieval/chklst/chklatth.htm.
The British Library MS Viewer. www.bl.uk. Digitised Manuscripts Home.
BVMM: Bibliothèque virtuelle des manuscrits médiévaux. http://bvmm.irht.cnrs.fr/.
DVL: digi.vatlib.it.
*e-codices*: Virtual Manuscript Library of Switzerland. www.e-codices.unifr.ch/en.
Gallica. *Bibliothèque numérique*. http://gallica.bnf.fr/.
Manuscripta.at. Mittelalterliche Handschriften in Österreich. http://manuscripta.at/.
MDZ: Münchener Digitalisierungszentrum. *Digitale Bibliothek*. www.digitale-sammlungen.de/.
Mirabile. Archivio digitale della cultura medievale. http://mirabileweb.it/.
Orbis. Yale University Library Catalog <orbis.library.yale.edu.
Schoenberg Database. Schoenberg Database of Manuscripts. www.sdbm.library.upenn.edu.
UB-Graz – Handschriftenkatalog. http://manuscripta.at/.
*Virtual Monastic Library of Lorsch*: Bibliotheca Laureshamensis digital. *Virtual Monastic Library of Lorsch*. http://bibliothecva-laureshamensis-digital.de/.
WDB: Wolfenbütteler Digitale Bibliothek. http://www.hab.de/en/home/library/wolfenbuettel-digital-library.html.

# INDEX OF SOURCES

All references are to the chapter and verse of Luke on which Bede is commenting, except for Bede and Acca's Prologue and the prefaces to each of the six books of his commentary. The Index does not include allusions or parallels.

## 1. BIBLICAL CITATIONS

**Genesis**
1:1   Luke 4:22b
2:23   Luke 24:39
3:8   Luke 23:44–45
3:17–18   Luke 6:44b
6:6   Luke 3:22b
6:7   Luke 3:22b
11:12   Luke 3:35–36
12:3   Luke 1:72–74
15:6   Luke 1:55; 2:21
15:16   Luke 17:30
17:4   Luke 2:21
17:5   Luke 1:13b
17:14   Luke 2:21
18:6   Luke 13:20–21
18:27   Luke 24:5–6
19:24   Luke 19:38b
26:1   Luke 6:21b
26:12   Luke 7:10
30:33   Luke 12:28
31:40   Luke 2:18
34:24   Luke 2:21
35:29   Luke 1:57
46:26   Luke 6:9b
49:10   Luke 1:5
49:17   Luke 17:16b

**Exodus**
1:5   Luke 6:9b
3:6   Luke 20:37
6:12   Luke 2:21
6:23   Luke 1:36–37
8:19   Luke 11:20
12:2   Luke 1:9b–10
12:3   Luke 1:9b–10; 19:48b
12:5–6   Luke 19:48b
12:6   Luke 19:48b
13:2   Luke 2:6–7
20:12   Luke 8:19
33:12   Luke 16:20

**Leviticus**
11:44   Luke 1:49
12:2–4   Luke 2:22
12:8   Luke 2:24
14:8   Luke 21:18
19:17   Luke 17:3
23:3   Luke 6:9

**Numbers**
18:15   Luke 2:23
18:16   Luke 2:23

# 698 BEDE: COMMENTARY ON THE GOSPEL OF LUKE

**Deuteronomy**
6:16    Luke 4:12
11:10–12    Luke 6:14b–15
13:3    Luke 9:3; 19:15b
13:4    Luke 8:44
32:11    Luke 8:1; 13:34
32:32–33    Luke 20:10

**Joshua**
5:10–12    Luke 22:15
5:12    Luke 22:16

**1 Samuel**
16:7    Luke 9:57
16:12    Luke 2:4–5
16:13–14    Luke 19:24–25

**3 Kings**
6:9–10    Luke 12:3
7:13–14    Book 6, preface
7:23    Luke 3:23
7:26 (x2)    Luke 3:23
7:39    Luke 3:23
7:45–46    Book 6, preface
8:39    Luke 5:22b
12:16    Luke 20:11
17:18    Luke 8:37
18:27    Luke 6:23

**1 Chronicles**
1:18    Luke 3:35–36
17:11–13    Luke 1:72–74
24:5    Luke 1:5
24:5    Luke 1:5
24:19    Luke 1:5
24:6    Luke 1:5

**2 Chronicles**
3:1    Luke 1:57

**Job**
8:21    Luke 6:21b
12:16    Luke 13:25b

19:26    Luke 24:39
20:5–7    Luke 12:2
24:19    Luke 13:28
26:11    Luke 21:26
27:3–4    Luke 2:21
39:18    Luke 20:19
40:16    Luke 11:24b

**Psalms**
1:4    Luke 20:18
1:6    Luke 13:25b
2:2    Luke 23:39
2:6    Luke 19:12
2:8    Luke 19:12; 20:14
4:7(4:6)    Luke 2:36–37; 20:24b–25
4:7(4:6–7)    Luke 2:2–3
4:7–8(4:6–7)    Luke 22:39
4:9–10(4:8)    Luke 23:53
5:6(5:4–5)    Luke 2:22
5:11(5:9)    Luke 11:44
6:2(6:1)    Luke 9:28
6:7(6:6)    Luke 5:24b
8:3(8:2)    Luke 3:23; 7:31–32
9:24(10:3)    Luke 6:26
10:8(11:8)    Luke 7:29
11:7(12:6)    Luke 19:22b–23
12:3–4(13:2–3)    Luke 22:61–62
15:10(16:10)    Luke 23:46
16:15(17:15)    Luke 6:21
18:6(19:5)    Luke 1:35
18:7(19:6)    Luke 1:9b–10
18:13(19:12)    Luke 4:38b–39
19:4(20:3)    Luke 15:27b
21:24(22:23)    Luke 1:32b–33
22:1–2(23:1–2)    Luke 2:16–17
22:5(23:5)    Luke 2:16–17
23:1(24:1)    Luke 11:13
23:8(24:8)    Luke 2:13–14
23:8(24:8)    Luke 1:26
23:10(24:10)    Luke 1:26
24:2–3(25:2–3)    Luke 14:29–30
24:10(25:10)    Luke 10:13b
24:15(25:15)    Luke 2:21

# INDEX OF SOURCES 699

24:16(25:16)   Luke 18:25
25:6(26:6)   Luke 2:21
25:6–7(26:6–7)   Luke 2:21
25:10(26:10)   Luke 19:19
26:4(27:4)   Luke 2:26–27; 10:41–42
32:9(33:9)   Luke 5:13; 6:11
33:2(34:1)   Luke 17:4; 18:1; 21:36
33:3(34:2)   Luke 1:76
33:4(34:3)   Luke 1:49
33:6(34:5)   Luke 7:3; 8:19
33:15(34:14)   Luke 1:79; 2:21
33:16(34:15)   Luke 19:5
33:21(34:20)   Luke 21:18
34:3(35:3)   Luke 6:46
34:9(35:9)   Luke 1:46–47
34:9–10(35:9–10)   Luke 8:41b
34:10(35:10)   Luke 2:18
34:12(35:12)   Luke 4:28–29
35:8(36:7)   Luke 9:34
36:21–22(37:21–22)   Luke 6:35
38:5–6(39:4–5)   Luke 2:28b–29
38:7(39:6)   Luke 12:21
38:8(39:7)   Luke 12:21
39:3(40:2)   Luke 6:48b
44:3(45:2)   Luke 2:4–5
44:8(45:7)   Luke 4:18–19
44:11(45:10)   Luke 12:53; 24:44b
45:5–6(46:4–5)   Luke 6:48c
45:11(46:10)   Luke 4:16
47:2(48:1)   Luke 2:47–48
49:3(50:3)   Luke 17:24
49:16(50:16)   Luke 4:41
50:4(51:2)   Luke 9:29
50:6(51:4)   Luke 7:29
50:7(51:5)   Luke 1:35b; 2:21
50:8(51:6)   Luke 9:44b
50:19(51:17)   Luke 4:19b
51:10(52:8)   Luke 21:37–38
52:6(53:5)   Luke 12:33c
53:6(54:4)   Luke 1:54
54:7(55:6)   Luke 13:19d
54:24(55:23)   Luke 1:57
56:5–6(57:4–5)   Luke 9:11

56:6(57:5)   Luke 23:45b
58:8(59:7)   Luke 2:35
58:10–11(59:9–10)   Luke 17:16b; 21:4
59:13–14(60:11–12)   Luke 8:46
60:3–4(61:2–3)   Luke 2:21; 8:3b; 13:4–5
61:11(62:10)   Luke 18:25
61:13(62:12)   Luke 6:38c
64:12(65:11)   Luke 4:19b
65:10(66:10)   Luke 3:17b
65:12–13(66:12–13)   Luke 3:17b
67:5(68:4)   Luke 1:26; 4:40
67:19(68:18)   Luke 13:19b
67:21(68:20)   Luke 7:23
67:32(68:31)   Luke 8:41
68:23(69:22)   Luke 6:28
69:6(70:5)   Luke 6:20
72:25(73:25)   Luke 6:20
72:28(73:28)   Luke 6:20; 10:41–42
75:2(76:1)   Luke 9:11; 23:45b
75:11(76:10)   Luke 21:18
76:11(77:10)   Luke 22:30b
77:39(78:39)   Luke 24:39
79:3(80:2)   Luke 7:50b
79:15–16(80:14–15)   Luke 20:11
80:2–3(81:1–2)   Luke 7:31–32
80:3(81:2)   Luke 19:13b
80:12(81:11)   Luke 7:31–32
82:2(83:1)   Luke 12:42
82:19(83:18)   Luke 12:42
83:3(84:2)   Luke 2:21
83:8(84:7)   Luke 13:19c
83:8(84:7)   Luke 13:19c
83:11(84:10)   Luke 17:22
84:10(85:9)   Luke 7:6b
86:1(87:1)   Luke 6:48b
86:5(87:5)   Luke 1:76
87:16(66:15)   Luke 14:8b–9
87:19(88:18)   Luke 23:49
88:2(89:1)   Luke 24:40
90:11–12(91:11–12)   Luke 4:10–11
90:13(91:13)   Luke 4:10–11
93:11(94:11)   Luke 6:8; 13:25b; 14:3–4

# 700  BEDE: COMMENTARY ON THE GOSPEL OF LUKE

93:12(94:12)   Luke 6:8
94:6(95:6)   Luke 2:24
95:2(96:2)   Luke 10:1
97:2–3(98:2–3)   Luke 2:32
102:3(103:3)   Luke 8:46
102:4(103:4)   Luke 17:9–10
102:5(103:5)   Luke 17:36–37
103:15(104:15)   Luke 15:17b
104:17–19(105:17–19)   Luke 2:35
105:16(106:16)   Luke 20:10
105:32–33(106:32–33)   Luke 20:10
106:1(107:1)   Luke 24:40
106:2(107:2)   Luke 24:40
106:2–3(107:2–3)   Luke 4:2b
106:43(107:43)   Luke 12:42
108:7(109:7)   Luke 20:47
109:4(110:4)   Luke 3:22b; 5:14b; 22:19
110:2(111:2)   Luke 1:65b–66
111:5(112:5)   Luke 6:35
111:7(112:6)   Luke 6:35
111:9(112:9)   Luke 6:23b; 19:8
113:16(115:8)   Luke 3:8b
115:10(116:10)   Luke 17:10b
115:11(116:11)   Luke 17:10b
115:12(116:12)   Luke 2:7b; 17:10b
115:16(116:16)   Luke 17:10b
115:16–17(116:16–17)   Luke 17:10b
117:1(118:1)   Luke 18:19
117:19(118:19)   Luke 7:11b–12
118:5–6(119:5–6)   Luke 11:45
118:9(119:9)   Luke 5:19
118:18(119:18)   Luke 8:10b
118:48(119:48)   Luke 2:21
118:59(119:59)   Luke 2:21
118:64(119:64)   Luke 17:4
118:83(119:83)   Luke 22:55
118:101(119:101)   Luke 2:21
118:103(119:103)   Luke 2:21
118:107(119:107)   Luke 14:10
118:115(119:115)   Book 4, preface
118:130(119:130)   Luke 7:31–32
118:155(119:155)   Luke 19:12
118:165(119:165)   Luke 2:13–14

118:166(119:166)   Luke 2:13–14
118:176(119:176)   Luke 2:18
119:7(120:7)   Luke 22:47b
120:4(121:4)   Luke 8:25b
125:5–6(126:5–6)   Luke 10:2
126:1(127:1)   Luke 5:5
126:2(127:2)   Luke 10:13b
131:7(132:7)   Luke 24:52–53
131:11(132:11)   Luke 1:42
131:17–18(132:17–18)   Luke 20:7–8
133:1(134:1)   Luke 1:5
133:3(134:3)   Luke 1:5
136:1(137:1)   Luke 2:24
138:17(139:17)   Luke 14:10c
140:5(141:5)   Luke 8:56
140:9(141:9)   Luke 10:33
140:10(141:10)   Luke 23:53
142:10(143:10)   Book 4, preface
144:7(145:7)   Luke 2:20
145:4(146:4)   Luke 19:47
146:3(147:3)   Luke 4:19b
148:1   Luke 2:25
148:12–14(148:12–13)   Luke 2:25

**Proverbs**
2:4   Luke 19:47
3:16   Luke 1:11
4:23   Luke 2:21; 11:35
13:8   Luke 16:12
14:13   Luke 6:25b
16:18   Luke 10:30b; 18:14b
18:3   Luke 6:49
18:12   Luke 18:14b
18:17   Luke 5:27
20:4   Luke 16:1–4
20:21   Luke 14:10c
28:9   Book 5, preface
31:10   Luke 1:67–68

**Ecclesiastes**
1:4   Luke 21:33
5:9   Luke 6:24; 18:24
7:5   Luke 6:25b

# INDEX OF SOURCES

7:17   Luke 1:6
11:9   Luke 12:38

**Song of Solomon**
2:12–13   Luke 6:44b
5:10   Luke 23:11

**Wisdom of Solomon**
1:4   Luke 3:22
1:5   Luke 3:22
2:8   Luke 19:19
2:24   Luke 4:35
6:7   Luke 10:12; 12:48
6:9   Luke 12:48
8:7   Luke 5:18
9:15   Luke 7:28b
10:21   Luke 3:23
11:21   Luke 7:2

**Ecclesiasticus**
2:1   Luke 4:4
3:20   Luke 14:10; 18:25
4:1   Luke 6:10
4:36   Luke 6:10
5:5–6   Luke 16:13c
11:41   Luke 12:19
12:13   Luke 14:34
27:12   Luke 9:39
29:4   Luke 6:35
29:10   Luke 6:35
30:24   Luke 11:41
31:8   Luke 6:24
32:1   Luke 22:25–26
41:17   Luke 10:4

**Isaiah**
1:3   Luke 2:19; 13:15
1:19   Luke 13:11b; 15:25; 16:16
2:2   Luke 2:1
2:2–3   Luke 5:1
2:4–5   Luke 2:1
5:4   Luke 20:9
5:7   Luke 13:6; 20:9
5:21   Luke 16:8
7:14   Luke 1:34; 2:19; 2:22
9:5   Luke 2:7b
9:6   Luke 2:47–48; 4:27
9:7   Luke 1:32b–33
11:4   Luke 6:2
19:1   Luke 1:35
19:1–2   Luke 12:51
19:18   Luke 19:19
26:19   Luke 20:37
33:6   Luke 16:11
33:15   Luke 2:21; 19:19
33:17   Prologue (Acca); 9:28b
35:1   Luke 9:10b
35:2   Luke 9:10b
38:1   Luke 7:2
39:2   Luke 6:46
42:10   Luke 15:27b
43:25   Luke 5:22b
43:26   Luke 6:14b–15; 7:29
48:22   Luke 2:13–14
50:11   Luke 22:55
53:5   Luke 2:12; 5:31–32
53:7   Luke 9:41
60:22   Luke 4:18–19
61:1   Luke 4:18–19

**Jeremiah**
2:21   Luke 20:12
4:4   Luke 2:21
4:19   Luke 7:31–32
4:22   Luke 7:31–32
8:7   Luke 19:44c
17:9   Luke 14:16
17:13   Luke 10:20b
23:23   Luke 20:9
23:24   Luke 20:9

**Lamentations**
1:7   Luke 17:34b

**Ezekiel**
1:1   Luke 3:23

1:18   Luke 18:12
13:3–4   Luke 6:26b
34:11–12   Luke 2:8–9
34:23   Luke 2:8–9
34:25   Luke 2:8–9
36:26   Luke 3:8b
44:1–3   Luke 2:23

**Daniel**
2:34   Luke 17:36–37
12:3   Luke 12:43–44

**Hosea**
3:3   Luke 8:40
11:1   Luke 1:54

**Joel**
2:12–13   Luke 7:31–32
2:20   Book 4, preface
2:31   Luke 21:25

**Amos**
8:11   Luke 15:14

**Micah**
4:8   Luke 2:8–9; 2:19
5:1   Luke 22:63–64

**Habakkuk**
3:2   Luke 21:24

**Zechariah**
6:12   Luke 1:78
9:11   Luke 22:37

**Malachi**
2:7   Luke 7:27
3:1   Luke 4:22b
3:3   Luke 4:22b

**1 Maccabees**
2:52   Luke 2:21

**Matthew**
1:1   Luke 1:72–74
1:12–13   Luke 4:1–2
1:15–16   Luke 3:23b–24
1:21   Luke 1:31
1:23   Luke 2:24
2:3   Luke 35b
3:2   Luke 9:6; 10:34
3:4   Luke 16:19
3:10   Luke 10:34
3:11   Luke 4:22b
3:17   Luke 3:22b
4:1   Luke 4:1–2
4:11   Luke 22:43
4:12   Book 2, preface
4:17   Luke 9:6
5:1–3   Luke 6:20
5:3   Luke 16:16
5:6   Luke 22:30
5:10   Luke 23:33b
5:14   Luke 6:14
5:14–15   Luke 19:29–30
5:16   Luke 18:43b
5:17   Luke 4:2b
5:19   Luke 1:49; 7:11b–12
5:28   Luke 19:19
6:2   Luke 12:33c
6:2–5   Luke 2:21
6:5   Luke 6:44; 20:47
6:7   Luke 20:7–8
6:8   Luke 18:40b–41
6:9   Luke 12:53
6:9–10   Luke 11:2–4
6:11–13   Luke 11:2–4
6:13   Luke 6:9b; 22:40
6:30   Luke 18:2–5
7:6   Luke 20:34
7:11   Luke 11:13
7:15   Luke 6:44
7:20   Luke 6:37
7:22–23   Luke 9:50
7:29   Luke 4:32
8:10   Luke 7:3

# INDEX OF SOURCES

8:11  Luke 12:37b
8:11–12  Luke 16:31b
8:12  Luke 3:17b
8:13  Luke 7:10
8:22  Luke 7:14; 8:56
8:27  Luke 8:25b
8:29  Luke 4:3
9:6  Luke 5:24
9:12  Luke 4:23
9:13  Luke 6:3b–4; 19:10
9:15  Luke 8:52
9:29  Luke 9:40
9:34  Luke 8:28
10:5  Luke 23:45b
10:10  Luke 9:3
10:23  Luke 4:12
10:37  Luke 8:19
10:41  Luke 19:26
10:42  Luke 16:1–4
11:6  Luke 7:23
11:11  Luke 3:22b
12:22  Luke 11:14
12:32  Luke 12:10
12:44  Luke 11:26b
12:45  Luke 11:26b
12:46  Luke 11:37
13:13  Luke 8:45b
13:17  Luke 7:50b
13:19  Luke 8:12
13:22  Luke 16:11
13:23  Luke 8:15
13:28  Luke 6:49
13:30  Luke 3:17b
13:41  Luke 3:17
13:54  Luke 4:14–15
14:2  Luke 9:7–8
16:17  Luke 9:18
16:18  Luke 2:21; 6:14; 6:48b
16:24  Luke 23:26
16:26  Luke 12:23
16:27  Luke 4:19b
17:5  Luke 6:14b–15
18:4  Luke 1:54; 14:10b

18:15–17  Luke 17:4
18:18  Luke 19:30b–31
18:20  Luke 2:1; 24:15
19:6  Luke 14:25–26
19:12  Luke 23:29–30
19:21  Luke 19:8
19:29  Luke 8:8
20:1  Luke 20:9
20:13–15  Luke 10:21c
20:16  Luke 3:17
20:28  Luke 17:10b; 22:27
21:2  Luke 19:30b–31
21:9  Luke 19:12
21:21  Luke 17:6
21:31  Luke 5:30
21:43  Luke 13:18–19
22:2–3  Luke 14:7–8
22:14  Luke 9:28b
22:19–21  Luke 2:2–3
23:2  Luke 8:50
23:3  Luke 6:44b
23:13  Luke 13:7b
23:26  Luke 11:42c
23:33  Luke 11:50
23:34  Luke 11:49
23:38  Luke 11:26b; 19:5b–6
24:12  Luke 22:55
24:16  Luke 23:29–30
24:19  Luke 23:29–30
24:21  Luke 21:25
24:24  Luke 17:34
24:29  Luke 21:25
25:8  Luke 16:1–4
25:21  Luke 10:35b
25:34  Luke 3:14; 7:28b
25:35  Luke 3:14
25:40  Luke 10:16b
25:46  Luke 6:49b
26:31  Luke 2:11
26:34  Luke 22:58
26:52  Luke 22:51
26:57–58  Luke 22:52
27:40  Luke 8:24b

27:42  Luke 8:24b
27:50–52  Luke 19:40
27:54  Luke 23:47
27:59  Luke 23:53
27:60  Luke 23:53
28:19  Luke 3:23; 9:21–22; 23:45b
28:20  Luke 3:23; 4:2b; 13:25

**Mark**
1:14  Book 2, preface
1:26  Luke 4:35b
1:45  Luke 5:15
2:10  Luke 5:24
2:17  Luke 4:23
2:19  Luke 14:7–8
3:14  Luke 6:13b
3:29  Luke 12:10
3:30  Luke 12:10
3:31  Luke 11:37
3:35  Luke 11:37
4:10–11  Luke 8:9
4:11  Luke 8:10b
4:15  Luke 8:12
4:16  Luke 8:12
4:18  Luke 8:12
5:26  Luke 8:43b
5:41–42  Luke 8:54
5:42  Luke 8:55
6:5–6  Luke 4:23
6:8  Luke 9:3; 22:35–36
6:9  Luke 9:3
6:12–13  Luke 9:6
7:3–4  Luke 11:38
8:3  Luke 7:6b
8:39(9:1)  Luke 9:27
9:2(9:3)  Luke 9:29
9:32–33  Luke 9:46
10:9  Luke 9:3
10:21  Luke 18:22
10:24  Luke 18:24
10:30  Luke 18:29–30
10:38  Luke 12:50
11:4  Luke 19:32

12:8  Luke 20:15
12:31  Luke 3:11; 11:41
14:30  Luke 2:11
14:53–54  Luke 22:52
14:56  Luke 23:2
15:28  Luke 23:32
16:2  Luke 24:6b–7
16:14  Luke 8:25
16:15–16  Luke 2:1
16:18  Book 1, preface

**Luke**
1:7  Luke 1:24b–25
1:8  Luke 1:34
1:15  Luke 1:32
1:31  Luke 2:19
1:32  Prologue (Bede)
1:33  Prologue (Bede)
1:35  Luke 24:49b
1:38  Luke 2:50–51
1:40–41  Luke 1:15
1:66  Luke 1:7
1:78  Luke 3:23
1:79  Luke 2:7b
2:6  Luke 1:57
2:10  Luke 1:14; 2:20
2:14  Luke 19:38b
2:23  Luke 2:6–7
2:40  Luke 2:52
2:49  Luke 2:41
3:7  Luke 7:25
3:11  Luke 6:10; 11:41; Book 5, preface
3:16  Luke 4:22b
3:19–20  Book 2, preface
3:22  Luke 3:23
4:4  Luke 4:13
4:9  Luke 4:29b–30
5:8  Luke 8:25b
5:31  Luke 4:23
6:1  Luke 1:24b–25
6:12  Luke 5:16
6:13  Luke 6:17

# INDEX OF SOURCES

| | | | |
|---|---|---|---|
| 6:20 | Luke 4:18–19 | 12:36 | Luke 24:52–53 |
| 6:22 | Luke 6:48c | 12:48 | Luke 7:50b; 10:12 |
| 6:33 | Luke 14:12b | 12:49 | Luke 12:42; 22:55; 24:31b–32 |
| 6:37 | Luke 6:41 | 13:3 | Luke 13:35b |
| 7:14 | Luke 8:55b | 13:5 | Luke 13:6 |
| 7:28 | Luke 1:15 | 13:19 | Luke 13:19d |
| 7:29 | Luke 7:35; Book 3, preface | 13:24 | Luke 22:24 |
| 7:30 | Book 3, preface | 13:27 | Luke 16:20 |
| 7:33 | Book 3, preface | 13:35 | Luke 11:26b |
| 7:35 | Luke 10:21b | 14:11 | Luke 3:5; 6:49b |
| 7:36 | Luke 7:50b | 14:18 | Luke 15:15b |
| 7:37 | Luke 7:50b(x2) | 14:18–20 | Luke 4:13 |
| 7:42 | Luke 7:50b | 14:30 | Luke 14:35 |
| 7:44 | Luke 7:50b | 16:9 | Luke 6:38b; Book 5, preface |
| 7:45 | Luke 7:50b | 16:10 | Luke 17:5 |
| 7:46 | Luke 7:50b(x2) | 16:12 | Luke 17:5 |
| 7:47 | Luke 7:50b | 16:14 | Luke 14:4b |
| 8:3 | Luke 24:10 | 16:19 | Luke 20:45–46 |
| 8:8 | Luke 8:10b | 16:24 | Luke 16:31b |
| 8:10 | Luke 8:16; 8:18b | 16:25 | Luke 6:24 |
| 8:16 | Luke 8:20 | 17:10 | Luke 4:13; 18:9 |
| 8:18 | Luke 8:19 | 17:21 | Luke 22:16 |
| 8:46 | Luke 24:49b | 18:7 | Luke 18:10 |
| 9:2 | Luke 9:6 | 18:8 | Luke 18:10; 21:34–35 |
| 9:23 | Luke 8:22 | 18:11 | Luke 21:4 |
| 9:60 | Luke 8:56 | 18:13 | Luke 21:4 |
| 9:62 | Luke 17:7 | 18:27 | Luke 8:49; 19:1–4 |
| 10:20 | Luke 10:25 | 18:32–33 | Luke 23:1 |
| 10:21 | Luke 10:23; 10:25; Book 4, preface | 18:38 | Luke 19:12 |
| 10:37 | Luke 10:28 | 19:11 | Luke 17:20 |
| 11:13 | Luke 18:19 | 19:38 | Luke 19:48b |
| 11:15 | Luke 20:1–2 | 19:39 | Luke 19:48b |
| 11:17 | Luke 3:2; 12:13–14 | 19:41–42 | Luke 19:47 |
| 11:20 | Book 4, preface | 19:42 | Luke 19:47 |
| 11:23 | Luke 12:13–14 | 19:42b | Luke 19:47 |
| 11:41 | Luke 3:11; 12:16–18 | 19:43 | Luke 19:47 |
| 11:49 | Luke 12:11 | 19:43b | Luke 19:47 |
| 11:52 | Luke 10:21b | 19:44 | Luke 19:47 |
| 11:54 | Luke 19:48b | 19:44b | Luke 19:47 |
| 12:3 | Luke 2:2–3 | 19:44c | Luke 19:47 |
| 12:22 | Luke 12:29 | 19:45 | Luke 19:47 |
| 12:35 | Luke 12:49 | 19:46 | Luke 19:47 |
| | | 20:18 | Luke 13:4–5 |

20:25   Luke 23:3
20:34–36   Luke 2:21
21:18   Luke 24:40
21:34   Luke 2:21
22:37   Luke 23:32
22:58   Luke 22:57
22:60   Luke 22:57
22:69–70   Luke 22:71
23:34   Luke 6:28
23:45   Luke 22:63–64
23:49   Luke 19:40; 23:55
24:21   Luke 17:20
24:25–26   Luke 8:25
24:33   Luke 24:36
24:44   Luke 4:16b–17; 20:12
24:45   Luke 4:16b–17; 10:35; 19:13

**John**

1:1   Luke 2:15; 6:14b–15
1:3   Luke 1:51; 2:7b; 4:23
1:9   Luke 1:26
1:12   Luke 6:35b; 23:32
1:13   Luke 11:50
1:14   Prologue (Bede); Luke 2:6–7; 2:15; 2:40; 4:23; 7:50b; 24:39
1:15   Luke 6:1
1:17   Luke 2:21
1:23   Luke 1:64–65; 3:4
1:29   Luke 2:21; 3:23b–24; 14:17
1:30–31   Luke 3:22b
1:34   Luke 3:22b
1:42   Luke 6:14
1:45   Luke 6:14b–15
1:47   Luke 1:6
2:11   Book 2, preface
3:5   Luke 2:21; 11:41
3:13   Luke 9:36
3:24   Book 2, preface
3:26   Luke 7:18
3:27   Luke 7:18
3:29   Luke 3:16b
3:30   Luke 1:24; 1:26; 9:9
4:9   Luke 9:53

4:32   Luke 7:50b
4:34   Luke 7:50b
4:35–36   Luke 6:1
4:45   Luke 4:14–15
5:14   Luke 5:20
5:22   Luke 3:17
5:43   Luke 19:38b
5:46   Luke 1:70; 16:31b
6:4   Luke 9:10b
6:37   Luke 10:22
6:51   Luke 2:6–7
6:51–52   Luke 14:15
6:67   Luke 5:7; 22:28–29
7:28   Luke 9:10b
7:30   Luke 4:12; 9:10b; 19:48b
7:39   Luke 12:50
8:12   Luke 4:18–19
8:20   Luke 19:48b
8:29   Luke 13:4–5
8:34   Luke 6:9
8:36   Luke 4:18–19
8:44   Luke 11:50; 12:53; 23:24–25
8:56   Luke 2:18; 10:24
9:1   Luke 4:23
9:5   Luke 4:40
9:6–7   Luke 4:23
9:7   Luke 13:4–5
10:7   Luke 19:32
10:9   Luke 19:32
10:11   Luke 18:19
10:16   Luke 1:31
10:25–26   Luke 22:67–68
10:30   Luke 10:16b; 22:67–68
10:41   Luke 9:7–8
11:1–2   Luke 7:36–37
11:9   Luke 10:1
11:17   Luke 8:55b
11:18   Luke 19:29–30; 24:50–51
11:25   Luke 20:38b
11:25–26   Luke 2:34b
11:33   Luke 8:55b
11:43   Luke 8:55b
11:48   Luke 13:7b; 20:14

11:51–52   Luke 6:32
12:11   Luke 8:56
12:13   Luke 19:12
12:19   Luke 20:14
12:24   Luke 6:17b
12:25   Luke 12:23
12:26   Luke 8:44; 18:42–43
12:31   Luke 11:21
12:32   Luke 18:34
12:33   Luke 18:34
12:34   Luke 18:34
12:38   Luke 15:20d
12:39–40   Luke 12:10
12:46   Luke 13:4–5
13:1   Luke 22:1
13:14   Luke 22:27
13:26   Luke 6:15b
13:26–27   Luke 22:3
14:2   Luke 2:7b
14:6   Luke 2:7b; 18:35–37; 22:5b–6
14:8   Luke 6:14b–15
14:10   Luke 15:20d
14:23   Luke 2:36–37
14:28   Luke 2:50–51
14:30   Luke 11:21; 23:4
15:3   Luke 5:14b
15:5   Luke 15:19; 17:9–10
15:22   Luke 2:34b
15:24   Luke 19:14
16:12   Luke 4:20; Luke 20:7–8
16:15   Luke 15:31–32
16:22   Luke 2:21
17:10   Luke 15:31–32
18:6   Luke 17:16b
18:20   Luke 4:16; 6:6
18:28   Luke 22:1
18:36   Luke 19:15
19:23   Luke 23:34b–35
19:30   Luke 23:54
20:6–7   Luke 24:12
20:17   Luke 8:45b
20:21   Luke 6:13b
20:29   Luke 2:30–31

20:33–35   Luke 12:33
21:17   Luke 17:7; 19:15b
21:18   Luke 6:14
21:25   Luke 1:1–4; 6:14b–15

**Acts**
1:1   Luke 4:14–15; 18:43b
1:1–2   Book 1, preface
1:4–5   Luke 24:49b
1:5   Luke 3:16c
1:6   Luke 17:20
1:7   Luke 17:23
1:8   Luke 24:49b
2:7–8   Luke 22:59
2:13   Luke 5:37–38
2:20   Luke 21:25
2:22   Luke 9:7–8
2:23   Luke 7:30
2:33   Luke 13:19b
3:22   Luke 4:24
4:12   Luke 3:38b
4:32   Luke 2:24; 5:3; 8:30; 12:13–14; 18:29–30; 22:24
4:34   Luke 18:29–30
5:41   Luke 6:23
7:51   Luke 2:21
7:52   Luke 20:12
8:10–11   Luke 21:8
8:23   Luke 3:22
9:4–5   Luke 17:14
10:1–2   Luke 7:8b
10:22   Luke 7:8b
10:13   Luke 6:1
10:35   Luke 1:50
10:37–38   Luke 23:5
10:41   Luke 22:18
11:2–3   Luke 19:7
11:9   Luke 19:33
13:24   Luke 1:26
13:44–45   Luke 8:49; 19:7
14:14   Luke 11:13
15:9   Luke 11:41
15:10–11   Luke 1:17b; 2:21; 11:46

15:21  Luke 6:6
15:28  Luke 1:1–4
15:39  Luke 22:24
19:9  Luke 8:49
21:5  Luke 10:13b
28:22  Luke 2:34b

**Romans**
1:17  Luke 1:17b; 2:21; 11:46
1:21  Luke 17:18
2:6–7  Luke 7:50b
2:13  Luke 24:30–31
2:29  Luke 2:21
3:20  Luke 2:21
3:21  Luke 4:2b
3:22–23  Luke 14:5
3:23  Luke 5:14b; 19:30b–31
4:3  Luke 2:21
4:11  Luke 2:21
4:12  Luke 19:9
4:24  Luke 23:44–45
4:25  Luke 24:50–51
5:8  Luke 11:42d
5:13  Luke 2:21
5:16  Luke 11:42d
5:20  Luke 2:21 (x2); 4:25–26; 7:50b
6:3  Luke 3:23; 23:43
6:3–4  Luke 2:21
6:4  Luke 3:23
6:5  Luke 22:28–29
6:9  Luke 2:21; 8:37b
6:11  Luke 2:21
6:21  Luke 17:16b
7:6  Luke 22:51b
7:7–8  Luke 2:21
7:12  Luke 1:24b–25
8:3  Luke 3:23b–24
8:3–4  Luke 2:21
8:15  Luke 7:10
8:17  Luke 15:22; 23:26
8:18  Luke 17:9–10
8:24  Luke 1:71
8:25  Luke 3:38b

8:28  Luke 11:34b
8:29  Luke 2:6–7
8:30  Luke 13:12–13
8:34  Prologue (Bede)
9:4–5  Luke 24:47
9:5  Luke 12:53c
9:22  Luke 4:22b
9:23  Luke 4:22b
9:33  Luke 2:34b
10:2  Luke 23:34
10:3  Luke 5:31–32
10:4  Luke 10:35; 22:41–42
10:8  Luke 17:21b
10:10  Luke 3:23; 23:40–42
11:24  Luke 1:32b–33
11:25–26  Luke 8:37b; 8:41; 19:40; 21:24b
11:25–27  Luke 15:28
11:33  Luke 9:57
12:1  Luke 5:14b
12:12  Luke 4:2b
12:17  Luke 1:6
13:7–8  Luke 2:4–5
13:11  Luke 12:37
13:12–13  Luke 2:11; 21:37–38
13:13  Luke 14:12b
14:3  Luke 6:37
14:17  Luke 7:35; 13:26

**1 Corinthians**
1:5  Luke 2:24
1:10  Luke 15:25b
1:23  Luke 2:34b
1:23–24  Luke 19:1–4
1:25  Luke 8:41b
1:27  Luke 14:21
2:2  Luke 9:20b; 19:5
2:8  Luke 4:41
2:14  Luke 9:13b
3:1–2  Luke 6:17
3:3  Luke 12:13–14
3:3–4  Luke 22:24
3:9  Luke 17:35c; 20:17

# INDEX OF SOURCES

3:11   Luke 6:48b
3:12–15   Luke 3:16c
3:15   Luke 8:25b
3:17   Luke 5:14b
4:5   Luke 6:37; 8:16; 16:15
4:9   Luke 14:29–30
4:12–13   Luke 6:28
4:13   Luke 6:46
5:5   Luke 9:54–55
5:8   Luke 12:1b; 22:1
6:12   Luke 17:27
6:17   Luke 3:38b
7:7   Luke 23:33
7:23   Luke 17:9–10
7:25   Luke 10:35b
7:31   Luke 16:17; 21:33
7:40   Luke 18:8b
8:11   Luke 17:1
9:5   Luke 8:3b
9:9   Luke 12:6
9:11   Luke 10:7
9:12   Luke 10:35b
9:14   Luke 10:35b; 22:35–36
9:26–27   Luke 8:16
9:27   Luke 2:21; 9:23b
10:4   Luke 2:21; 6:14; 6:48b
10:11   Luke 14:17
10:17   Luke 24:35
10:31   Luke 2:21
11:3   Luke 4:23; 7:36–37; 7:50b; 8:41b
11:19   Luke 17:1
11:24–26   Luke 22:19
12:2   Luke 19:33
12:3   Luke 6:46
13:3   Luke 23:33b
13:4   Luke 6:31
13:4   Prologue (Acca); Prologue (Bede)
13:7   Prologue (Acca); Prologue (Bede)
13:9–10   Luke 19:17
13:12   Luke 10:24
13:13   Luke 1:56; 15:21; 23:40–42

14:20   Luke 18:16
14:22   Luke 9:1–2
14:29   Luke 11:49
14:38   Luke 13:25b
15:4–5   Luke 24:33–34
15:26   Luke 2:21
15:28   Luke 9:36; 13:20–21
15:34   Luke 12:37; 22:60
15:47   Luke 6:1
15:50   Luke 2:22; 24:39
15:54   Luke 4:2b

**2 Corinthians**
2:14–15   Luke 7:50b
2:15   Luke 2:21; 2:34b; 19:19
2:17   Luke 17:35c; 19:17
4:4   Luke 15:14b–15
5:13   Luke 10:39b–40
5:16   Luke 7:7b; 19:5b–6; 24:2–3
5:19   Luke 15:20d
6:2   Luke 4:19b
6:7–8   Luke 8:12
6:10   Luke 18:29–30
6:14–15   Luke 4:33b–34
7:1   Luke 2:2–3; 2:21; 6:1
8:9   Luke 2:12; 2:24
9:6   Luke 6:38c
11:14   Luke 10:18
13:11   Prologue (Acca)

**Galatians**
2:8   Luke 5:3
2:16   Luke 2:21
3:19   Luke 1:24b–25
3:27   Luke 9:29; 18:25
3:29   Luke 1:55; 3:8b; 19:9
4:4   Luke 1:57; 11:27
4:4–5   Luke 7:50b
4:19   Luke 7:11b–12
4:24   Luke 22:51b
5:6   Luke 23:33
5:13   Luke 4:8
5:17   Luke 24:39

# 710  BEDE: COMMENTARY ON THE GOSPEL OF LUKE

5:19–23  Luke 6:44
6:14  Luke 18:24; 19:1–4; 23:20–21

**Ephesians**
1:18  Luke 16:11
2:6  Luke 6:22
2:13  Luke 8:26; 19:12
3:17–19  Luke 23:33
4:10  Luke 1:9b–10
4:24  Luke 2:27b–28
4:31  Luke 4:38; 11:40
5:5  Luke 11:40; 12:10
5:8  Luke 1:79
5:18  Luke 1:15
5:25  Luke 14:25–26
5:28  Luke 19:19
6:9–10  Luke 6:27

**Philippians**
1:18  Luke 9:50
1:23–24  Luke 8:38–39
2:6  Luke 19:37; 23:32
2:7  Luke 10:33
2:8  Luke 19:37; 19:38b; 24:52–53
2:8–9  Luke 22:28–29
2.9  Luke 23:38
2:9–11  Luke 22:69
2.11  Luke 23:38
2:10  Luke 4:29b–30
3:3  Luke 4:8
3:19  Luke 13:26
4:7  Luke 23:33

**Colossians**
2:3  Prologue (Acca)
2:9  Luke 1:35; 2:40
3:5  Luke 4:13; 4:38; 6:1; 11:36; 11:40
3:9  Luke 6:1
3:12  Luke 22:35–36

**1 Thessalonians**
2:9  Luke 10:35b
2:19  Luke 19:17

3:2  Luke 13:11b
4:13  Luke 8:52b
4:14  Luke 2:21
4:16–17  Luke 9:30–31
4:17  Luke 2:21; 17:24
5:3  Luke 21:26
5:4–5  Luke 12:20
5:16–17  Luke 18:1

**2 Thessalonians**
2:2  Luke 17:22

**1 Timothy**
2:4  Luke 6:6; 12:10; 12:41; Book 5, preface
2:5  Prologue (Bede); Luke 2:16–17; 2:40
4:12  Luke 4:32
5:6  Luke 20:38b
5:8  Luke 12:46
5:17  Luke 12:43–44
6:7  Luke 16:12

**2 Timothy**
2:19  Luke 5:2; 5:7; 23:27–28
2:26  Luke 6:32
3:1–2  Luke 5:7b
3:12  Luke 23:31
4:14–15  Luke 6:28
4:16  Luke 6:28

**Titus**
2:12  Luke 21:37–38
2:12–13  Luke 12:41

**Hebrews**
4:13  Luke 6:46
5:12  Luke 19:5
7:19  Luke 1:24b–25
7:25  Prologue (Bede)
9:6–7  Luke 1:9b–10
9:20  Luke 22:20
10:4  Luke 10:31–32

… INDEX OF SOURCES

| | | | |
|---|---|---|---|
| 11:6 | Luke 2:21 | 3:13 | Luke 16:17 |
| 11:33 | Luke 23:39 | | |
| 11:34 | Luke 22:24 | **1 John** | |
| 11:37 | Luke 23:39 | 1:1–2 | Luke 2:15 |
| 13:12 | Luke 20:15 | 2:1 | Luke 6:12 |
| 13:14 | Luke 15:22b | 2:6 | Luke 18:22b |
| | | 2:16 | Luke 4:13 |
| **James** | | 2.18 | Luke 17:31 |
| 1:12 | Luke 2:24; 22:31–32 | 2:19 | Luke 12:34 |
| 1:13 | Luke 9:3 | 3:2 | Luke 9:29 |
| 1:14–15 | Luke 6:49b | 3:17 | Luke 16:10 |
| 1:25 | Luke 14:35b | 4:12 | Luke 6:32 |
| 4:6 | Luke 7:35 | 4:16 | Luke 22:5b–6 |
| 5:11 | Luke 6:48c | 4:18 | Luke 2:25; 7:10 |
| 5:14–15 | Luke 9:6 | 4:20 | Luke 16:10 |
| | | 5:16 | Luke 6:28; 23:34 |
| **1 Peter** | | 5:19 | Luke 6:49; 11:21 |
| 2:13–14 | Luke 2:4–5 | | |
| 2:21 | Luke 23:26 | **Revelation** | |
| 2:22 | Luke 2:23 | 1:7 | Luke 24:40 |
| 2:24 | Luke 10:34b | 2:1 | Luke 19:24–25 |
| 3:11 | Luke 2:21 | 2:5 | Luke 19:24–25 |
| 4:11 | Luke 19:22b–23 | 2:9 | Luke 4:33 |
| 5:2 | Luke 2:8–9 | 3:20 | Luke 17:7b–8 |
| 5:3 | Luke 22:25–26 | 4:6–7 | Prologue (Bede) |
| 5:5 | Luke 7:35; Book 4, preface | 5:5 | Prologue (Bede) |
| 5:6 | Luke 10:13b | 5:8 | Luke 24:1 |
| | | 17:15 | Luke 22:20 |
| **2 Peter** | | 20:9–10 | Luke 17:29 |
| 2:21 | Luke 11:26b; 14:35 | 21:22 | Luke 9:34 |
| 3:5–7 | Luke 21:33 | | |

## 2. CLASSICAL, PATRISTIC, AND MEDIEVAL AUTHORS

**Ambrose**
*Expositio Euangelii secundam Lucam*
 (CCSL 14:)
12.186–88 (1.11)  Luke 1:1–4
12.191–94 (1.11)  Luke 1:1–4
15.286–98 (1.18)  Luke 1:6
16.327–35 (1.20–21)  Luke 1:6

16.325 (1.19)  Luke 1:6
24.546–48 (1.36)  Luke 1:16–17
29.703–12 (1.45–46)  Luke 1:44
30.15–16 (2.1)  Luke 1:27
33.103–08 (2.7)  Luke 2:6–7
33.111–22 (2.9)  Luke 1:28
34.123–25 (2.9)  Luke 1:28

**Ambrose** *Expositio Euangelii secundam Lucam* (CCSL 14:) continued
34.139–43 (2.10–11) Luke 5:33
35.147–49 (2.10–11) Luke 5:33
39.288–90 (2.19) Luke 1:38b–39
40.305–09 (2.22) Luke 1:40
40.312–13 (2.22) Luke 1:40
40.318–27 (2.23) Luke 1:41
41.336–37 (2.24) Luke 1:42
42.359–60 (2.26) Luke 1:44
43.410–14 (2.29) Luke 1:58
44.429–35 (2.31) Luke 1:59–60
44.435–38 (2.31–32) Luke 1:61–63
44.445–50 (2.31–32) Luke 1:61–63
45.472–74 (2.34) Luke 1:76
45.477–80 (2.34) Luke 1:76
53.704 (2.51) Luke 2:8–9
54.725–27 (2.53) Luke 2:18
54.735–40 (2.54) Luke 2:51b
57.802–03 (2.61) Luke 2:35
57.810–14 (2.62) Luke 2:38
58.840–41 (2.65) Luke 2:50–51
58.848–50 (2.65) Luke 2:50–51
64.1027 (2.77) Luke 3:12–13
64.1028–30 (2.77) Luke 3:14
67.1124–27 (2.83) Luke 3:21
76.19–20 (3.1) Luke 4:22b
83.227–33 (3.14) Luke 3:31–32
115.327–32 (4.28) Luke 4:5
119.441–46 (4.36) Luke 4:13
121.537–40 (4.44) Luke 4:20b–21
122.546–48 (4.45) Luke 4:20b–21
122.548–51 (4.45) Luke 4:18–19
126.676–91 (4.55–56) Luke 4:28–29
126.691–95 (4.56) Luke 4:29b–30
126.693–94 (4.56) Luke 4:29b–30
126.705–09 (4.57) Luke 4:31
128.745–48 (4.61) Luke 4:33
128.753–54 (4.61) Luke 4:29b–30
135.4–6 (5.1) Luke 5:12
135.12–24 (5.1–2) Luke 5:12

136.26–29 (5.3) Luke 5:13
136.37–40 (5.4) Luke 5:13
136.46–48 (5.5) Luke 5:14
137.57–60 (5.7) Luke 5:13
137.61–67 (5.7) Luke 5:13
137.67–77 (5.8–9) Luke 5:14b
140.157–60 (5.16) Luke 5:28
140.162–65 (5.16) Luke 5:29
140.166–68 (5.17) Luke 5:30
140.168–72 (5.17) Luke 5:30
141.193–94 (5.19) Luke 5:29
141.206–07 (5.21) Luke 5:31–32
147.384–88 (5.33) Luke 6:3b–4
149.424–30 (5.39) Luke 6:9
149.441–45 (5.41) Luke 6:12
150.455–66 (5.42) Luke 6:12
150.467–72 (5.43) Luke 6:12b
150.475–76 (5.43) Luke 6:12b
151.504–14 (5.45) Luke 6:16
163.913–16 (5.88) Luke 7:10
175.14–22 (6.2) Luke 7:29
175.26–31 (6.3) Luke 7:29
187.385–88 (6.36) Luke 8:19
187.389–90 (6.36) Luke 8:19
187.392–93 (6.37) Luke 8:20
187.394–96 (6.37) Luke 8:20
189.450–52 (6.44) Luke 8:38–39
190.462–63 (6.45) Luke 8:27c
196.639–45 (6.64) Luke 8:51
197.658–61 (6.66) Luke 9:4
197.667–70 (6.66) Luke 9:4
198.690–95 (6.68) Luke 9:5
207.997–1005 (6.93) Luke 9:20b
207.1010–12 (6.93) Luke 9:20b
211.1109–12 (6.102) Luke 4:41
217.92 (7.7) Luke 9:28b
220.194–96 (7.17) Luke 9:33
226.376–78 (7.35) Luke 9:60
237.690–93 (7.67) Luke 10:22
239.764–66 (7.74) Luke 10:33
247.1007–08 (7.96) Luke 11:32
247.1012–14 (7.97) Luke 11:30
251.1134–37 (7.112) Luke 12:6

# INDEX OF SOURCES 713

251.1137–41 (7.112) Luke 12:7
259.1417–25 (7.133) Luke 12:50b
261.1477–80 (7.137) Luke 12:52
286.2284–86 (7.206) Luke 13:28
289.2385–87 (7.215) Luke 15:14b–15
310.401–02 (8.37) Luke 17:27
340.227–29 (9.25) Luke 20:10
364.621–31 (10.63) Luke 22:48
367.703–09 (10.72) Luke 22:54b
367.712–17 10.73) Luke 22:56
374.935–36 (10.97) Luke 23:14b
374.944–48 (10.99) Luke 23:8–9
374.967–70 (10.103) Luke 23:11
379.1123–29 (10.121) Luke 23:43
390.1472–77 (10.156) Luke 24:9

**Ambrosiaster**
*Commentaria in epistolam ad Romanos* (PL 17:)
166 (13) Luke 14:12b

**Anonymous**
*De solstitia et aequinocialia* [sic] *conceptionis et nativitatis Domini nostri Jesu Christi et Iohannis Baptistae. Homilia de duobus filiis, frugi et luxurioso* (PL 30:) Luke 1:24
253 (11) Luke 15:2
Proverb
Untraced Prologue (Acca)

**Augustine**
*Contra aduersarium legis et prophetarum* (CCSL 49:)
86.43–44 (1.24.53) Luke 4:13
106.604–19 (2.5.20) Luke 7:28b
128.1240–42 (2.12.39) Luke 13:16
128.1248–54 (2.12.39) Luke 8:33
128.1244–50 (2.12.39) Luke 13:16
*Contra Faustum* (CSEL 25/1:)
361.20–24 (12.34) Luke 4:25–26
629.27–630.16 (22.36) Luke 4:12

*De ciuitate Dei* (CCSL 48:)
489.18–19 (15.23) Luke 8:30
*De consensu euangelistarum* (CSEL 43:)
4.4–23 (1.2) Prologue (Bede)
4.25–5.3 (1.3) Prologue (Bede)
6.3–15 (1.3) Prologue (Bede)
6.16–7.3 (1.4) Prologue (Bede)
9.3–10.14 (1.6) Prologue (Bede)
83.1–4 (2.1) Luke 2:33–34
83.21–24 (2.1) Luke 2:33–34
88.24–89.6 (2.4) Luke 3:23b–24
90.1–10 (2.4) Luke 3:23b–24
90.17–91.2 (2.4) Luke 3:23b–24
92.11–93.8 (2.4) Luke 3:23b–24
93.9–19 (2.4) Luke 3:23b–24
93.20–21 (2.4) Luke 3:31–32
93.21–94.7 (2.4) Luke 3:38b
94.19–25 (2.4.12) Luke 3:38b
141.6–18 (2.17) Luke 5:11
146.20–147.4 (2.19) Luke 6:17
149.8–15 (2.20) Luke 7:1
151.11–22 (2.20) Luke 7:3
158.11–18 (2.24) Luke 8:38–39
159.18–20 (2.25) Luke 5:20
161.5–8 (2.25) Luke 5:17
175.8–176.1 (2.30) Luke 9:3
177.12–22 (2.30) Luke 9:3
178.7–15 (2.30) Luke 9:3
179.8–23 (2.30) Luke 9:3
180.5–8 (2.30) Luke 9:3
180.12–13 (2.30) Luke 9:3
190.1–3 (2.40) Luke 11:37
190.6–9 (2.40) Luke 11:37
196.2–3 (2.43) Luke 9:7–8
196.12–14 (2.43) Luke 9:7–8
196.15–16 (2.43) Luke 9:7–8
249.17–20 (2.75) Luke 13:35b
249.22–250.2 (2.75) Luke 13:32b
250.5–6 (2.75) Luke 13:35b
250.7–15 (2.75) Luke 13:33
288.5–23 (3.5) Luke 22:51
340.5–17 (3.16) Luke 23:39

# 714 BEDE: COMMENTARY ON THE GOSPEL OF LUKE

**Augustine** *De consensu euangelistarum* (CSEL 43:) continued
340.19–21 (3.16)  Luke 23:39
369.12–16 (3.25)  Luke 24:24
371.22–24 (3.25)  Luke 24:35
371.25–372.2 (3.25)  Luke 24:35
372.3–24 (3.25)  Luke 24:35
373.7–15 (3.25)  Luke 24:33–34
395.11 (4.2)  Luke 4:35b
395.18–22 (4.2)  Luke 4:35b
*De diuersis quaestionibus* (PL 40:)
96 (81.1)  Luke 3:38b
*De Genesi contra Manichaeos* (CSEL 91:)
80 (1.8.14)  Luke 7:9
*De sermone Domini in monte* (CCSL 35:)
5.93–95 (1.2.6)  Luke 22:30
15.325–28 (1.5.15)  Luke 6:23b
17.374–82 (1.6.17)  Luke 8:16
65.1415–28 (1.19.57)  Luke 6:29
68.1481–88 (1.19.58)  Luke 6:29
69.1492–96 (1.19.59)  Luke 6:29b
69.1502–15 (1.19.59)  Luke 6:30b
73.1595–1603 (1.20.64)  Luke 9:54–55
74.1607–20 (1.20.64)  Luke 9:54–55
74.1623–24 (1.20.65)  Luke 9:54–55
76.1671–80 (1.20.67)  Luke 6:30
77.1683–89 (1.20.68)  Luke 6:35
79.1736–38 (1.21.71)  Luke 6:28
80.1748–50 (1.21.72)  Luke 6:28
80.1760–62 (1.22.72)  Luke 6:28
81.1774–77 (1.21.73)  Luke 6:28
81.1777–83 (1.22.73)  Luke 6:28
82.1791–1814 (1.22.73–74)  Luke 6:28
87.1907–13 (1.23.78)  Luke 6:35b
88.1919–22 (1.23.78–79)  Luke 6:35b
89.1940–42 (1.23.79)  Luke 6:35c
136.1000–03 (2.13.45)  Luke 11:36
138.1038–41 (2.14.47)  Luke 16:13c
140.1075–77 (2.15.49)  Luke 12:23
140.1079–82 (2.15.49)  Luke 12:23
141.1083–92 (2.15.50)  Luke 12:23
141.1095–98 (2.15.51)  Luke 12:24
141.1101–08 (2.15.51)  Luke 12:25–26
142.1109–11 (2.15.52)  Luke 12:25–26
142.1116–19 (2.15.52)  Luke 12:27
142.1123–27 (2.15.52)  Luke 18:2–5
143.1133–45 (2.16.53)  Luke 12:30–31
154.1352–58 (2.18.59)  Luke 6:37
155.1360–66 (2.18.59)  Luke 6:37
155.1372–80 (2.18.60)  Luke 6:37
157.1393–96 (2.18.61)  Luke 6:37
159.1443–44 (2.19.63)  Luke 6:41
159.1447–53 (2.19.63)  Luke 6:42
160.1457–59 (2.19.64)  Luke 6:42b
160.1464–81 (2.19.64)  Luke 6:42b
162.1502–07 (2.19.66)  Luke 6:42b
166.1580–90 (2.20.70)  Luke 20:34
170.1665–66 (2.21.73)  Luke 11:8–9
170.1667–69 (2.21.73)  Luke 11:10
171.1677–90 (2.21.73)  Luke 11:13
180.1855–59 (2.24.80)  Luke 6:44
180.1861–62 (2.24.80)  Luke 6:44
*De trinitate* I–XII (CCSL 50:)
33.25–26 (1.3)  Prologue (Acca)
*Enarrationes in Psalmos I–L* (CCSL 38:)
17.20–26 (4.8)  Luke 20:24b–25
17.29–32 (4.8)  Luke 20:24b–25
*Enarrationes in Psalmos LI–C* (CCSL 39:)
813.3 (63.11)  Luke 22:52
*Enchiridion ad Laurentium* (CCSL 46:)
88.20–42 (19.72–73)  Luke 11:41
90.15–26 (20.75)  Luke 11:41
90.27–33 (20.76)  Luke 11:41
90.33–39 (20.76)  Luke 11:42d
90.39–41 (20.76)  Luke 11:42d
91.45–53 (20.76)  Luke 11:41
91.53–55 (20.76)  Luke 11:42

INDEX OF SOURCES 715

91.55–58 (20.76)  Luke 11:42b
91.58–64 (20.76)  Luke 11:42c
91.64–65 (20.76)  Luke 11:42d
91.64–70 (20.76–77)  Luke 11:42e
94.78–83 (21.80)  Luke 17:28
97.58–77 (23.89)  Luke 12:7
99.133–37 (23.93)  Luke 12:48
110.12–35 (30.115)  Luke 11:2–4
111.36–50 (30.116)  Luke 11:2–4
*Epistolae* (CSEL 34/2:)
201.4–68(55.15.28)  Luke 4:2b
549.16–17 (102.6)  Luke 24:41
549.18–19 (102.7)  Luke 24:41
*Epistolae* (CSEL 44:)
307.16–308.13 (147.34)  Luke 23:33
*In Iohannis Euangelium tractatus CXXIV* (CCSL 36:)
318 (35.2)  Luke 20:5
318 (35.2)  Luke 20:6
318 (35.2)  Luke 20:7–8
326.42–46 (36.4)  Luke 23:20–21
326.49–55 (36.4)  Luke 23:20–21
333 (37.3)  Luke 18:8b
359 (41.3–4)  Luke 21:32
414.1–4 (48.4)  Luke 22:66
440–41 (51.3)  Luke 19:38b
452 (53.2)  Luke 1:51
489.28–30 (64.1)  Luke 24:44
635.7–13 (112.5)  Luke 22:51b
637 (113.20–25)  Luke 22:58
642.33–39 (114.4)  Luke 22:52
648 (116.4)  Luke 23:10
653.6–10 (117.4)  Luke 23:38
656.2–6 (118.4)  Luke 23:34b–35
656.9–17 (118.4)  Luke 23:34b–35
657.30–34 (118.4)  Luke 23:34b–35
659.18–20 (119.4)  Luke 23:36–37
663 (120.5)  Luke 23:54
*Quaestiones Euangeliorum* (CCSL 44B:)
7.6–9 (1.1)  Luke 10:22b
12.11–14 (1.8)  Luke 11:26
14.2–3 (1.11)  Luke 13:18–19

14.3–4 (1.12)  Luke 13:20–21
24.3–9 (1.30)  Luke 20:18
35.2–5 (1.46)  Luke 22:54b
41.8–11 (2.1)  Luke 1:13b
41.13 (2.1)  Luke 1:13b
42.2–3 (2.2)  Luke 5:3
42.5–11 (2.2)  Luke 5:4
43.19–32 (2.2)  Luke 5:8
43.33–35 (2.2)  Luke 5:11
44.4–8 (2.3)  Luke 5:14b
44.11–13 (2.3)  Luke 5:14b
45.5–6 (2.4)  Luke 5:19b
45.8–9 (2.4)  Luke 5:19b
48.4–8 (2.6.1)  Luke 3:38b
48.23–47 (2.6.2)  Luke 3:38b
53.3–11 (2.11)  Luke 7:33–34
54.12–16 (2.11)  Luke 7:35
55.34–36 (2.11)  Luke 7:35
55.5–8 (2.12)  Luke 8:16
56.5–7 (2.13)  Luke 8:27c
56.8–9 (2.13)  Luke 8:29b
56.11–13 (2.13)  Luke 8:29c
57.15 (2.13)  Luke 8:32
57.16–19 (2.13)  Luke 8:33
57.19–23 (2.13)  Luke 8:34
57.26–30 (2.13)  Luke 8:35
58.32–39 (2.13)  Luke 8:38–39
60.2–5 (2.17)  Luke 11:20
60.4–6 (2.18)  Luke 5:36
61.24–30 (2.18)  Luke 5:37–38
62.3–5 (2.19)  Luke 10:30
62.6–7 (2.19)  Luke 10:30b
62.8–10 (2.19)  Luke 10:30d
62.11–12 (2.19)  Luke 10:31–32
63.17–18 (2.19)  Luke 10:34b
63.18–19 (2.19)  Luke 10:34b
63.19–21 (2.19)  Luke 10:34b
63.21 (2.19)  Luke 10:35
64.1–5 (2.21)  Luke 11:5–6
65.6–9 (2.21)  Luke 11:9
65.24–29 (2.21)  Luke 11:7
66.3–6 (2.22)  Luke 11:11
66.6–11 (2.22)  Luke 11:11b

# 716  BEDE: COMMENTARY ON THE GOSPEL OF LUKE

**Augustine** *Quaestiones*
*Euangeliorum* (CCSL 44B:) *continued*
66.11–15 (2.22)   Luke 11:12
67.4–5 (2.23)   Luke 11:52
67.2–4 (2.25)   Luke 12:35
68.2–6 (2.27)   Luke 12:54–55
69.3–4 (2.28)   Luke 12:25–26
69.3–8 (2.29A)   Luke 12:29b
69.2–6 (2.29B)   Luke 14:5
70.6–9 (2.29B)   Luke 14:1–2
71.8–11 (2.31)   Luke 14:33
74.15–24 (2.33)   Luke 15:13
74.24–26 (2.33)   Luke 15:14
74.29–35 (2.33)   Luke 15:16
75.36–38 (2.33)   Luke 15:16b–17
75.39–41 (2.33)   Luke 15:17b
75.53–54 (2.33)   Luke 15:18
76.57–59 (2.33)   Luke 15:20
76.65–67 (2.33)   Luke 15:18
76.69–70 (2.33)   Luke 15:20b
76.70–72 (2.33)   Luke 15:20c
77.74–80 (2.33)   Luke 15:20d
77.81–83 (2.33)   Luke 15:20e
77.83–90 (2.33)   Luke 15:21
77.91 (2.33)   Luke 15:22
78.94–95 (2.33)   Luke 15:23
78.102–05 (2.33)   Luke 15:24b
78.106–09 (2.33)   Luke 15:25
78.109–17 (2.33)   Luke 15:25b
78.117–21 (2.33)   Luke 15:26–27
79.122–26 (2.33)   Luke 15:27b
79.128–37 (2.33)   Luke 15:28
80.138–54 (2.33)   Luke 15:29
81.156–77 (2.33)   Luke 15:29b
82.177–80 (2.33)   Luke 15:30
82.183–89 (2.33)   Luke 15:31–32
82.207–09 (2.33)   Luke 15:31–32
83.210–11 (2.33)   Luke 15:31–32
84.2–17 (2.34)   Luke 16:1–4
85.18–25 (2.34)   Luke 16:5–7
85.25–32 (2.34)   Luke 16:9
86.7–14 (2.36)   Luke 16:13c
89.28–31 (2.38)   Luke 16:22

97.9–10 (2.40)   Luke 17:14
98.21–31 (2.40)   Luke 17:11–12
98.37–40 (2.40)   Luke 17:14
99.44–46 (2.40)   Luke 17:14
99.51–60 (2.40)   Luke 17:14
100.71–79 (2.40)   Luke 17:14
100.80–90 (2.40)   Luke 17:18
101.90–100 (2.40)   Luke 17:17
101.102–04 (2.40)   Luke 17:16b
102.3–4 (2.41)   Luke 17:31
103.3–4 (2.42)   Luke 17:31b
103 (2.43)   Luke 17:31b
104.5–7 (2.44)   Luke 17:34
104.7–13 (2.44)   Luke 17:35
105.22–23 (2.44)   Luke 17:34b
106.7–8 (2.45)   Luke 18:2–5
106.11–13 (2.45)   Luke 18:2–5
106.15–18 (2.45)   Luke 18:2–5
106.37–41 (2.44)   Luke 17:35c
108.40–42 (2.45)   Luke 18:2–5
108.42–50 (2.45)   Luke 18:6–8
108.53–55 (2.45)   Luke 18:6–8
109.14–16 (2.46)   Luke 19:15
110.22–33 (2.46)   Luke 19:20–21
111.47–49 (2.46)   Luke 19:26
112.9–10 (2.47)   Luke 18:26
112.13–19 (2.47)   Luke 18:25
112.21–26 (2.47)   Luke 18:27
115.2–4 (2.49)   Luke 20:36
116.3–8 (2.50)   Luke 22:41–42
*Quaestiones xui in Matthaeum*
   (CCSL 44B:)
121.4–9 (5)   Luke 9:58
121.2–4 (6)   Luke 9:60
122.2–5 (7)   Luke 10:10–11
124.6–7 (10)   Luke 6:5
*Sermones* (CCSL 41Ab:)
15.18–28 (71.1.1–2)   Luke 11:18
15–16.16–36 (71.1.2)   Luke 11:19
45.585.87 (71.23)   Luke 12:10
70.1019 (71.37)   Luke 12:10
*Sermones* PL 38
659.1 (116.3)   Luke 24:41

# INDEX OF SOURCES 717

*Sermones* (Morin Guelf App.
   Miscellanea Agostiniana)
1.51.13 (229.1)   Luke 24:39
1.583.30 (229J)   Luke 24:44b
*Sermones* (*Noua Patrum biblioteca*)
1.206 (99.4)   Luke 4:2b
*Speculum* (CSEL 12:)
181 (27)   Luke 14:12

**Ps. Augustine**
*Sermones suppositii de Scripturis*
   (PL 39:)
1862 (62.6)   Luke 6:32
1943 (102.4)   Luke 11:13

**Cassian**
*Collationes* (CSEL 13:)
317.26–318.8 (11.6)   Luke 15:21
319.6–10 (11.7)   Luke 15:21
319.17–19 (11.7)   Luke 15:21
642:11–13 (23.3)   Luke 10:41–42
705.12–25 (24.26)   Luke 18:29–30
705.27–706.2 (24.26)   Luke 18:29–30
706.22–25 (24.26)   Luke 18:29–30

**Cassiodorus**
*Expositio psalmorum* (CCSL 97:)
542 (61.1)   Luke 2:28b–29

**Eusebius**
*Historia ecclesiastica* (GCS 9.1:)
47.6–9 (1.5)   Luke 2:2–3
55.1–2 (1.7)   Luke 3:23b–24
57.17–59.19 (1.7)   Luke 3:23b–24
75.6–13 (1.10)   Luke 3:2

**Fulgentius**
*Ad Trasamundum* (CCSL 91:)
105.320–27 (1.8.3)   Luke 2:52

**Gregory**
*Dialogues* 1–3 (SC 260:)
80.61–63 (1.9.6)   Luke 5:15

80.66–79 (1.9.7)   Luke 5:15
*Dialogues* 4 (SC 265:)
150.36–47 (4.41.5–6)   Luke 3:16c
*Homeliae in Euangelia* (CCSL 141:)
7.42–46 (1.1.2–3)   Luke 21:27
7.49–55 (1.1.3)   Luke 21:28
8.76–77 (1.1.3)   Luke 21:28
8.80–89 (1.1.3–4)   Luke 21:29–31
12.1–5 (1.2.1)   Luke 18:31–33
13.14–16 (1.2.1)   Luke 18:35–37
13.20–21 (1.2.2)   Luke 18:35–37
13.21–35 (1.2.2)   Luke 18:35–37
14.40–49 (1.2.3)   Luke 18:38–39
15.71–75 (1.2.5)   Luke 18:40
16.91–111 (1.2.7)   Luke 18:40b–41
17.123–66 (1.2.8)   Luke 18:42–43
28.55–56 (1.4.3)   Luke 9:1–2
29.67–74 (1.4.3)   Luke 9:1–2
39.26–29 (1.6.1)   Luke 7:23
40.35–40 (1.6.1)   Luke 7:23
40.43–54 (1.6.2)   Luke 7:24b
41.67–72 (1.6.3)   Luke 7:25
41.77–81 (1.6.4)   Luke 7:25
42.87–90 (1.6.5)   Luke 7:26
42.95–99 (1.6.5)   Luke 7:27
42.101–09 (1.6.6)   Luke 7:27
49.92–118 (1.7.3)   Luke 3:16b
54.8–13 (1.8.1)   Luke 2:6–7
55.26–30 (1.8.1)   Luke 2:8–9
90.9–31 (1.13.1–2)   Luke 12:35
91.32–36 (1.13.2–3)   Luke 12:36
91.37–45 (1.13.3)   Luke 12:36b
91.46–53 (1.13.3–4)   Luke 12:37
91.54–64 (1.13.4)   Luke 12:37b
92.69–82 (1.13.5)   Luke 12:38
93.102–05 (1.13.5)   Luke 12:38
94.107–08 (1.13.5)   Luke 12:39
94.109–20 (1.13.5–6)   Luke 12:40
103.21–22 (1.15)   Luke 8:21
104.8–11 (1.15.1)   Luke 8:4–5
104.14–21 (1.15.1)   Luke 8:14
106.65–75 (1.15.3)   Luke 8:14
106.76–86 (1.15.4)   Luke 8:15

**Gregory**  *Homeliae in Euangelia*
(CCSL 141:) *continued*
110.7–19 (1.16.1)  Luke 4:5
117.5–18 (1.17.1–2)  Luke 10:1b
117.20–23 (1.17.2)  Luke 4:40
119.76–93 (1.17.5)  Luke 10:4
120.97–101 (1.17.5)  Luke 10:4
120.104–12 (1.17.6–7)  Luke 10:5–6
121.114–20 (1.17.7)  Luke 10:7
121.120–26 (1.17.7)  Luke 10:7b
154.8–23 (1.20.1)  Luke 3:2
154.25–35 (1.20.2)  Luke 3:3
155.40–48 (1.20.3)  Luke 3:4
155.43–43 (1.20.3)  Luke 3:4
155.50–58 (1.20.3)  Luke 3:5
158.114–23 (1.20.6)  Luke 3:5b
158.124–33 (1.20.7)  Luke 3:6
159.136–46 (1.20.7–8)  Luke 3:7
159.147–50 (1.20.8)  Luke 3:8
160.156–65 (1.20.8–9)  Luke 3:8
160.167–79 (1.20.9)  Luke 3:8b
161.190–94 (1.20.10)  Luke 3:9
161.196–204 (1.20.10)  Luke 3:9b
162.205–06 (1.20.10)  Luke 3:10
162.208–23 (1.20.11)  Luke 3:11
193.6–14 (2.21.1)  Luke 24:16–17
194.19–27 (2.23.1)  Luke 24:28–29
194.28–34 (2.23.1–2)  Luke 24:30–31
199.56–58 (2.24.3)  Luke 5:6
201.116–24 (2.24.5)  Luke 24:42–43
201.133–38 (2.24.5)  Luke 24:42–43
244.1–45 (2.29.1)  Luke 24:11
260.118–19 (2.30.5)  Luke 24:31b–32
260.121–24 (2.30.5)  Luke 24:31b–32
261.140–46 (2.30.5)  Luke 24:31b–32
272.67–69 (2.31.5)  Luke 13:8
279.46–48 (2.32.2)  Luke 9:23
279.56–59 (2.32.2)  Luke 9:23

280.65–67 (2.32.3)  Luke 9:23
280.73–76 (2.32.3)  Luke 9:23b
281.107–17 (2.32.4)  Luke 9:24
282.119–21 (2.32.4)  Luke 9:25
282.127–35 (2.32.4)  Luke 9:25
282.138–55 (2.32.5)  Luke 9:26
283.170–72 (2.32.6)  Luke 9:27
284.177–86 (2.32.6)  Luke 9:27
284.198–99 (2.32.6)  Luke 9:27
289.25–35 (2.33.2)  Luke 7:38
290.40–42 (2.33.3)  Luke 7:39
290.57–62 (2.33.3)  Luke 7:39
290.67–68 (2.33.4)  Luke 7:39
290.72–75 (2.33.4)  Luke 7:41–43
291.79–80 (2.33.4)  Luke 7:44b
291.81–89 (2.33.4)  Luke 7:47
291.91–93 (2.33.4)  Luke 7:49
291.94–98 (2.33.4)  Luke 7:50b
292.102–06 (2.33.5)  Luke 7:50b
292.111–40 (2.33.5)  Luke 7:50b
293.141–50 (2.33.6)  Luke 7:50b
293.153–64 (2.33.6)  Luke 7:50b
294.168–77 (2.33.6)  Luke 7:50b
300.14–19 (2.34.2)  Luke 15:1–2
301.33–36 (2.34.3)  Luke 15:1–2
301.38–53 (2.34.3)  Luke 15:4
301.57–58 (2.34.3)  Luke 15:5
302.60–68 (2.34.3)  Luke 15:6
302.72–91 (2.34.4)  Luke 15:7
303.95–109 (2.34.5)  Luke 15:7
303.113–31 (2.34.6)  Luke 15:8
304.133–47 (2.34.6)  Luke 15:9
306.192–98 (2.34.8)  Luke 1:26
307.213–21 (2.34.9)  Luke 1:26
307.214–15 (2.34.9)  Luke 2:13–14
313.369–75 (2.34.13)  Luke 1:19–20
314.418–30 (2.34.15–16)  Luke 15:10
323.65–71 (2.35.2–3)  Luke 21:13
323.74–77 (2.35.3)  Luke 21:14–15
323.79–83 (2.35.3)  Luke 21:16–17
324.98–100 (2.35.4)  Luke 21:16–17
324.100–04 (2.35.4)  Luke 21:18

INDEX OF SOURCES 719

324.106–13 (2.35.4)  Luke 21:19
329.230 (2.35.8)  Luke 23:11
333.33–38 (2.36.2)  Luke 14:16
333.40–73 (2.36.2)  Luke 14:17
334.75–93 (2.36.3–4)  Luke 14:18
335.95–97 (2.36.4)  Luke 14:18b
335.99–126 (2.36.4)  Luke 14:19
336.129–39 (2.36.5)  Luke 14:20
337.142–96 (2.36.6–8)  Luke 14:21
339.196–201 (2.36.8)  Luke 14:22
339.202–77 (2.36.8–10)  Luke 14:23
342.278–83 (2.36.10)  Luke 14:24
348.21–44 (2.37.2)  Luke 14:25–26
351.88–89 (2.37.5)  Luke 14:25–26
351.91–108 (2.37.5–6)  Luke 14:27
352.113–29 (2.37.6)  Luke 14:28
352.130–40 (2.37.6)  Luke 14:29–30
353.144–70 (2.37.6–7)  Luke 14:31–32
379.3–6 (2.39.1)  Luke 19:41–42
380.22–27 (2.39.1)  Luke 19:41–42
380.28–31 (2.39,1)  Luke 19:42b
381.32–35 (2.39.1)  Luke 19:42c
381.39–44 (2.39.2)  Luke 19:45–46
381.51–59 (2.39.2)  Luke 19:46b
382.60–61 (2.39.2)  Luke 19:47
382.66–74 (2.39.3)  Luke 19:47
382.76–83 (2.39.3)  Luke 19:47
383.88–93 (2.39.3)  Luke 19:47
383.104–110 (2.39.4)  Luke 19:47
384.114–19 (2.39.4)  Luke 19:47
384.120–27 (2.39.4)  Luke 19:47
384.127–32 (2.39.4)  Luke 19:47
385.133–42 (2.39.5)  Luke 19:47
385.145–55 (2.39.5)  Luke 12:58
386.157–68 (2.39.6)  Luke 19:47
386.168–72 (2.39.6)  Luke 19:47
386.173–85 (2.39.7)  Luke 19:47
394.16–26 (2.40.2)  Luke 16:31b
395.29–34 (2.40.2)  Luke 16:31b
395.35–40 (2.40.2)  Luke 16:31b
395.52–54 (2.40.2)  Luke 16:31b
396.58–69 (2.40.2)  Luke 16:31b
396.70–86 (2.40.2)  Luke 16:31b
397.90–111 (2.40.2)  Luke 16:31b
398.117–47 (2.40.3)  Luke 16:19
399.148–59 (2.40.3)  Luke 16:20
400.162–89 (2.40.4)  Luke 16:20b–21
401.201–27 (2.40.5–6)  Luke 16:23–24
402.237–42 (2.40.6)  Luke 16:25
403.255–67 (2.40.7)  Luke 16:26
404.275–79 (2.40.8)  Luke 16:26 2.40.8
404.282–307 (2.40.8)  Luke 16:27–28
405.311–13 (2.40.9)  Luke 16:29
406.314–15 (2.40.9)  Luke 16:30b
406.316–27 (2.40.9)  Luke 16:31b

*Homeliae in Hiezechielem prophetam* (CCSL 142:)
9.154–62 (1.1.8)  Luke 1:45
18.40–45 (1.2.3)  Luke 3:23
19.78–84 (1.2.4)  Luke 3:23
43.319–21 (1.3.16)  Luke 9:62
83.19–22 (1.7.2)  Luke 18:12
85.66–67 (1.7.4)  Luke 17:2
85. 87–90 (1.7.5)  Luke 17:2
85.93–95 (1.7.6)  Luke 18:12
86.101–06 (1.7.6)  Luke 18:12
114.490–93 (1.8.23)  Luke 22:43
115.508–11 (1.8.24)  Luke 22:43
121.705–07 (1.8.32)  Luke 17:16b
125.100–111 (1.9.5)  Luke 17:16b
230.187–99 (2.2.8)  Luke 10:38–39
231.219–32 (2.2.9)  Luke 10:42b
261.168–75 (2.4.5)  Luke 17:35c
275.33–37 (2.5.2)  Luke 19:36
276.38–40 (2.5.2)  Luke 19:36
295.15–17 (2.6.2)  Luke 21:1
297.86–91 (2.6.5)  Luke 8:8
331.542–44 (2.7.17)  Luke 16:13

*Moralia in Iob* I–X (CCSL 143:)
40.7–10 (1.21)  Luke 13:26
41.29–31 (1.21)  Luke 13:26

# 720  BEDE: COMMENTARY ON THE GOSPEL OF LUKE

**Gregory**  Moralia in Iob I–X (CCSL 143:) continued
68.152–54 (2.7)   Luke 22:31–32
86.15–24 (2.24)   Luke 4:3
110.57–59 (2.52)   Luke 17:15–16
134.40–50 (3.16)   Luke 4:3
137.29–32 (3.19)   Luke 17:25
144.65 (3.22)   Luke 4:27
150.71–75 (3.28)   Luke 4:13
183.45–53 (4.16)   Luke 24:6b–7
237.286–90 (5.11)   Luke 17:12b–13
293.1–6 (6.10)   Luke 8:18b
Moralia in Iob XI–XXII (CCSL 143A:)
596.6–7 (11.12)   Luke 13:25b
625.51–52 (11.50)   Luke 13:23–24
633.10–11 (12.6)   Luke 15:22
638.9–17 (12.12)   Luke 22:42b
743.3–8 (14.56)   Luke 24:39
744.33–35 (14.56)   Luke 24:39
780.6–11 (15.45)   Luke 12:47
781.9–13 (15.47)   Luke 12:30–31
838.4 (16.55.68)   Luke 9:14b–15
858.21–33 (17.9)   Luke 21:33
929.96–117 (18.40)   Luke 23:40–42
948.25–31 (18.52)   Luke 1:35b
990.10–19 (19.25)   Luke 9:60
Moralia in Iob XXIII–XXXV (CCSL 143B:)
1153.7–11 (23.6)   Luke 18:11
1154.50–53 (23.6)   Luke 18:11
1162.39–42 (23.13)   Luke 4:32
1207.65–75 (24.11)   Luke 4:4
1212.252–59 (24.11)   Luke 22:43b
1231.13–21 (25.3)   Luke 12:20
1258.17–28 (25.14)   Luke 10:21c
1317.2–38 (26.37 [with gaps])   Luke 6:49
1347.25–29 (27.12)   Luke 9:13
1392.112 (27.46)   Luke 19:1–4
1392.118 (27.46)   Luke 19:1–4
1393.132–34 (27.46)   Luke 19:1–4
1420.10–11 (28.13)   Luke 5:16
1420.14–21 (28.13)   Luke 5:16

1499.97–100 (30.3)   Luke 12:42b
1629.58–59 (32.3)   Luke 2:24
Regula pastoralis 1–2 (SC 381:)
202.3–6 (2.6)   Luke 22:25–26
212.143–47 (2.6)   Luke 22:25–26
214.163–67 (2.6)   Luke 22:25–26
214.178 (2.6)   Luke 22:25–26
216.183–86   Luke 22:25–26
Regula pastoralis 3–4 (SC 382:)
258.10–13 (3.prol.)   Luke 12:42b
436.113–22 (3.25)   Luke 24:49b
436.138–41 (3.25)   Luke 2:46
528.5–7 (3.39)   Luke 12:42b
528.10–12 (3.39)   Luke 12:42b

**Hilary**
De trinitate VIII–XII (CCSL 62A:)
491.42–43 (10.37)   Luke 22:45–46
494.6–9 (10.41)   Luke 22:43
494.9–12 (10.41)   Luke 22:43
494.14–19 (10.41)   Luke 22:44
495.10–11 (10.42)   Luke 22:43

**Isidore**
De ecclesiasticis officiis (CCSL 113:)
20.30–33) (1.18)   Luke 22:20
Etymologiae:
4.7.23   Luke 14:1–2
7.2.7   Luke 1:31
7.10.1   Luke 1:27
8.11.103   Luke 8:30
9.4.23–24   Luke 23:50–51
9.4.32   Luke 3:12–13
12.2.29   Luke 13:31–32
13.19.6   Luke 5:1
16.25.21   Luke 19:13
16.26.13   Luke 16:5–7
16.26.17   Luke 16:5–7
17.7.20   Luke 19:1–4
19.27.4   Luke 16:19
19.28.2   Luke 16:19
19.28.4   Luke 16:19

# INDEX OF SOURCES 721

**Jerome**
*Aduersus Heluidium* (PL 23:)
187–88   Luke 2:33–34
*Aduersus Iouinianum* (PL 23:)
213–14   Luke 8:15
*Commentarii in Esaiam I–XI* (CCSL 73:)
36.15–19 (1.2.15)   Luke 13:4–5
124.27–30 (3.9.3/5)   Luke 22:42b
*Commentarii in Esaiam XII–XVIII* (CCSL 73A:)
706.16–30 (17.61)   Luke 4:18–19
PL 24:663 (18.812)   Luke 12:49
*Commentarii in Matheum* (CCSL 77:)
10.67–71 (1)   Luke 3:23
20.325–33 (1)   Luke 4:4
21.340–41 (1)   Luke 4:9
21.342–48 (1)   Luke 4:9b
21.351–58 (1)   Luke 4:10–11
21.360–63 (1)   Luke 4:12
22.373–77 (1)   Luke 4:6–7
22.386–89 (1)   Luke 4:8
27.512–15 (1)   Luke 16:17
34.696–701 (1)   Luke 6:27
38.813–17 (1)   Luke 12:34
39.830–35 (1)   Luke 16:13c
39.838–42 (1)   Luke 12:22
40.861–65 (1)   Luke 12:24
41.872–75 (1)   Luke 12:27b
41.879–82 (1)   Luke 12:28
42.916–19 (1)   Luke 11:10
45.996–1006 (1)   Luke 10:20
49.1096–98 (1)   Luke 7:8b
49.1099–1100 (1)   Luke 7:9
49.1100–03 (1)   Luke 7:8b
49.1105–06 (1)   Luke 7:9b
50.1131–32 (1)   Luke 4:39b
51.1150–57 (1)   Luke 9:58
52.1183–87 (1)   Luke 8:24b
52.1189–93 (1)   Luke 8:25b
53.1195–1201 (1)   Luke 4:34b
53.1210–15 (1)   Luke 8:32
54.1245–48 (1)   Luke 5:22b
54.1251–55 (1)   Luke 5:23
55.1266–74 (1)   Luke 5:27
56.1288–90 (1)   Luke 5:29b
56.1290–91 (1)   Luke 5:31–32
56.1296–1301 (1)   Luke 5:31–32
56.1304–05 (1)   Luke 5:31–32
57.1319–20 (1)   Luke 5:34–35
57.1320–24 (1)   Luke 5:34–35
57.1332–36 (1)   Luke 5:34–35
60.1389–92 (1)   Luke 8:48
60.1404–06 (1)   Luke 8:54
63.1476–85 (1)   Luke 10:2
64.1520 (1)   Luke 6:15b
64.1526–29 (1)   Luke 6:15b
66.1571–75 (1)   Luke 9:3
68.1626–30 (1)   Luke 9:5
69.1653–56 (1)   Luke 12:11b–12
70.1680–83 (1)   Luke 11:15
73.1227–29 (1)   Luke 12:51
73.1759–63 (1)   Luke 12:7
77.11–13 (2)   Luke 7:19
77.22–27 (2)   Luke 7:19
78.33–34 (2)   Luke 7:21
78.37–41 (2)   Luke 7:22
78.51–54 (2)   Luke 7:24
80.81–90 (2)   Luke 7:28
84.206–11 (2)   Luke 10:15
85.240–44 (2)   Luke 10:21b
87.286–90 (2)   Luke 6:1
87.293–95 (2)   Luke 6:1
88.300–17 (2)   Luke 6:3b–4
89.351–55 (2)   Luke 6:7
90.361–64 (2)   Luke 14:5
91.410–15 (2)   Luke 11:14
92.438–46 (2)   Luke 11:19
93.453–59 (2)   Luke 11:20
94.470–71 (2)   Luke 6:49
94.476–84 (2)   Luke 11:23
95.500–08 (2)   Luke 12:10
96.548–55 (2)   Luke 11:16
97.573–74 (2)   Luke 11:31b
97.579 (2)   Luke 11:31b
98.586–88 (2)   Luke 11:31b

# 722   BEDE: COMMENTARY ON THE GOSPEL OF LUKE

**Jerome**   Commentarii in Matheum
(CCSL 77:) continued
98.574–79 (2)   Luke 11:32
98.588–89 (2)   Luke 11:32
99.608–33 (2)   Luke 11:26b
107.843–46 (2)   Luke 13:18–19
110.920–21 (2)   Luke 13:20–21
115.1081–82 (2)   Luke 4:22b
116.1087–91 (2)   Luke 4:24
119.1188–90 (2)   Luke 9:10b
120.1208–09 (2)   Luke 9:11
121.1236–38 (2)   Luke 9:13
142.106–09 (3)   Luke 9:21–22
143.118–20 (3)   Luke 9:21–22
149.284–85 (3)   Luke 9:34
149.285–91 (3)   Luke 9:34b–35
149.295–99 (3)   Luke 9:34b–35
150.316–20 (3)   Luke 9:36b
152.363–66 (3)   Luke 9:40
152.369–76 (3)   Luke 9:41
156.483–85 (3)   Luke 9:46
157.500–05 (3)   Luke 18:17
158.528–30 (3)   Luke 17:2
161.607–08 (3)   Luke 17:4
163.666–71 (3)   Luke 17:4
169.825–27 (3)   Luke 18:15
169.829–35 (3)   Luke 18:16
169.842–44 (3)   Luke 18:19
170.868–78 (3)   Luke 18:22b
171.880–82 (3)   Luke 18:23
172.913–17 (3)   Luke 18:28
173.938–52 (3)   Luke 18:29–30
182.1175–77 (3)   Luke 19:29–30
182.1186–88 (3)   Luke 19:33
183.1203–05 (3)   Luke 19:30b–31
183.1215–17 (3)   Luke 19:35b
192.1468–73 (3)   Luke 20:1–2
192.1473–75 (3)   Luke 20:2b
193.1481–83 (3)   Luke 20:3–4
196.1560–66 (3)   Luke 20:9
197.1584–86 (3)   Luke 20:13
199.1628–35 (3)   Luke 20:18

202.1742–49 (3)   Luke 20:20
203.1762–65 (3)   Luke 20:21–22
203.1773–81 (3)   Luke 20:23–24
204.1793–95 (3)   Luke 20:26
204.1799–1806 (3)   Luke 20:27
204.1784–92 (3)   Luke 20:24b–25
205.1813–18 (3)   Luke 20:29–32
205.1820–21 (3)   Luke 20:33
206.1831–36 (3)   Luke 20:35
206.1842–49 (3)   Luke 20:37
207.1856–62 (3)   Luke 20:37
207.1862–66 (3)   Luke 20:38
209.10–15 (4)   Luke 20:41–44
210.37–42 (4)   Luke 20:40
211.70–71 (4)   Luke 11:43
216.221–23 (4)   Luke 11:39
221.341–49 (4)   Luke 13:34
222.365–69 (4)   Luke 13:35b
224.409–13 (4)   Luke 21:10–11
229.527–28 (4)   Luke 17:24
241.1766–73 (4)   Luke 19:22b–23
245.976–81 (4)   Luke 22:1
245.992–94 (4)   Luke 22:2
249.1088–90 (4)   Luke 22:12–13
249.1097–1102 (4)   Luke 22:21–22
249.1104–08 (4)   Luke 22:23
254.1244–46 (4)   Luke 22:41–42
255.1249–58 (4)   Luke 22:42b
255.1265–74 (4)   Luke 22:40
257.1324–25 (4)   Luke 22:49–50
258.1356–61 (4)   Luke 22:52b–53
262.1442–43 (4)   Luke 22:57
262.1453–56 (4)   Luke 22:59
265.1546–47 (4)   Luke 23:10
265.1550 (4)   Luke 23:24–25
267.1603–06 (4)   Luke 23:24–25
270.1672–78 (4)   Luke 23:33
270.1683–84 (4)   Luke 23:33
272.1724–27 (4)   Luke 23:35b
274.1763–65 (4)   Luke 23:44–45
275.1799–1801 (4)   Luke 23:45b
277.1847–56 (4)   Luke 8:3b

### INDEX OF SOURCES

277.1867–69 (4)  Luke 23:52
278.1874–80 (4)  Luke 23:53
278.1883–85 (4)  Luke 23:53
279.1902–04 (4)  Luke 23:53
*Commentarius in Abdiam* (CCSL 76:)
373.735–38 (20/21)  Luke 4:25–26
373.739–41 (20/21)  Luke 4:25–26
*Commentarius in Ecclesiasten* (CCSL 72:)
257.230–32  Prologue (Acca)
*De situ et nominibus locorum Hebraicorum* (*Onomastica sacra:*)
96.17–19  Luke 23:51b
96.32–97.2  Luke 7:11
107.31–32  Luke 9:10b
108.3–4  Luke 19:29–30
108.4–5  Luke 19:29–30
112.28–31  Luke 5:1
121.6–8  Luke 24:13–14
125.27–29  Luke 8:26
130.20–21  Luke 8:26
143.22–24  Luke 7:11
*De uiris illustribus* (PL 23:)
609 (2)  Luke 6:15b
*Liber interpretationis Hebraicorum nominum* (CCSL 72:)
61.7–8  Luke 2:36–37
61.28–29  Luke 2:21
62.18  Luke 8:30
66.22  Luke 2:36–37
66.24–25  Luke 8:26
67.15–16  Luke 2:21
67.19  Luke 2:6–7; 6:14b–15
73.6  Luke 6:19
77.5  Luke 6:19
102.11  Luke 2:36–37
103.11  Luke 2:4–5; 8:43
113.18  Luke 4:25–26
121.9–10  Luke 8:30
135.20–21  Luke 6:14b–15
135.24–27  Luke 19:29–30

135.27  Luke 24:50–51
136.24  Luke 2:21
137.9  Luke 6:16
137.16–20  Luke 1:27
137.19  Luke 8:3b
137.20  Luke 6:14b–15
137.21–22  Luke 8:3b
138.10–11  Luke 6:14b–15
139.11–12  Luke 4:25–26
140.1–2  Luke 8:3b
140.2–3  Luke 8:41
140.22–23  Luke 6:14b–15
141.2–3  Luke 8:3b
141.24–25  Luke 1:15
142.11–12  Luke 11:15
142.13  Luke 23:24–25
142.26–27  Luke 6:14
146.16–17  Luke 1:13b; 6:14b–15
146.17  Luke 2:6–7
156.11  Luke 2:21
160.21  Luke 2:21

**Josephus**
*The Antiquities* (*Acta Jutlandica* 30:)
251.11–16 (3.10.7)  Luke 6:3b–4

**Origen**
*In Leviticum Homiliae* (GCS 29:)
441.16–442.9  Luke 21:5–6

**Paulinus of Nola**
*Carmina* (CSEL 30:)
280.27.415–20  Luke 6:14b–15

**Pliny**
*Naturalis historia* (LCL:)
36.12.60–61  Luke 7:36–37

**Primasius**
*Commentarius in Apocalypsin* (CCSL 92:)
7.55–56  Luke 6:13b

**Sedulius**
*Paschale carmen* (CSEL 10:)
48 (2.63–68)   Luke 11:27
128 (5.188–95)   Luke 23:33

**Terence**
*Eunuchus*:
  prologue 41 (cited by
    Jerome)   Prologue (Acca)

# GENERAL INDEX

Aaron 118, 135
Abel 145, 161, 412
Abijah 117–18
Abraham 47, 122, 141–42, 145–46, 161, 163–64, 191–92, 210, 296, 380, 445, 474, 489–91, 493, 521, 531–32, 632
Acca (bishop of Hexham) 2–8, 11–12, 22, 56, 71, 95–98
active life/contemplative life 42, 175, 246–47, 318–19, 385–87
Adam 145, 164, 206, 382, 624–25
Adomnán 156n214
Ælfric of Eynsham 73
ages of the world *see* World Ages
Aidan (bishop of Lindisfarne) 7
Africanus, Julius 9, 204–05
Ahimelech 257–58
alabaster 52, 307–08
Alexander the coppersmith 278
allegory, 'law(s) of allegory' 29–33, 38, 308, 317, 319, 322, 326, 350, 365, 372, 381, 447, 569–60
almsgiving 284, 407–08, 424
Alphaeus 267
altar, Christ's tomb as symbol of 630
Ambrose (bishop of Milan) 7, 14, 22–27, 41, 43, 61, 65, 95–97, 99, 486
Ananias and Sapphira 241, 368, 520
Andrew (apostle) 263–64, 350
angel(s) 114, 122–26, 129–36, 156–59,
163, 217, 295, 302, 465, 599–600, 631–32
names of 129–130
nature of 122, 126, 158
*see also* Gabriel
Anna (prophetess) 50, 106, 181–82
Annas (high priest) 188, 223
anointing 224–25
of sick 332, 348
Antichrist(s) 147, 158, 476, 506, 571, 577, 615
Apelles 116
apostles 114, 323, 353–55, 367–68, 591–94, 639
calling of the Twelve 107, 262–68
mission of the Seventy-Two 371–378
mission of the Twelve 14, 108, 109, 269, 344–48
teaching of Christ to 108, 111, 271–91, 319, 387–92, 496–500
Archelaus (son of Herod the Great) 187
Arianism *see* heresy
Arimathea 627
Aristotle 54
Ark of the Covenant 203, 625
Asher 180–81
Atonement, day of 121, 127
Augustine of Hippo 5, 7–9, 12, 22–25, 27, 37, 40, 43, 46, 49–50, 52, 56, 69, 96, 99–103, 486
Augustus (emperor) 105, 119, 148–50, 559

Baal 273–74
Babylon 332
Balbi, Giovanni 12
baptism 189, 194–95, 199, 202, 212, 231, 303–04
Barabbas 602–03, 613, 615
Barnabas 241, 592
Bartholomew (apostle) 116, 266
Basilides 116
Beelzebub 109, 394–96, 402–03, 552
Bede
  accusation of heresy against 3–5
  and the Britons 64–65
  Irish influence on 3, 28, 49–50
  works:
    *On the Acts of the Apostles* 2, 5–6, 11, 45n116, 95
    *On the Day of Judgement* 2
    *Ecclesiastical History* 1, 7, 43–45, 62, 71, 423n164
    *On Ezra and Nehemiah* 2, 57
    *On First Samuel* 1–2, 67
    *On Genesis* 1–2, 63, 67
    *Homilies* 40–43, 156n214
    *Letter to Plegwine* 3–5, 9–10, 435n231
    *On Luke*
      audience 41–43
      chapter numbers and summaries (*capitula*) 16–20
      Codex Amiatinus 12, 15–21, 72
      composition, circumstances surrounding 1–10
      composition of, date 1
      composition of, material conditions 11–13, 99
      composition of, method 8, 11–13, 23–29, 99–100
      edition by David Hurst 92
      exegetical methods 29–37
      exorcism episode in 69–71
      Eusebian canon section and numbers 20–22
      heresy in 61–63
      Jews in 63–67, 170n327
      manuscripts and editions 19, 21, 72–92, Appendix 2
      preachers and teachers in 67–68
      relationship to historical writings 43–46
      relationship to homilies 40–43
      relationship to scientific interests 47–55
      source marks 8, 13, 22–24, 100
      sources 23–29
      structure and divisions 13–23
      style and vocabulary 71–72
      'Temple image' 56–61
      'true law of history' 44–46, 179
    *On Mark* 22–23, 67
    *On the Nature of Things* 48
    *On Proverbs* 63
    *On the Reckoning of Time* 9, 47–49, 55, 62, 326n116, 550–51
    *On the Resting Places of the Children of Israel* 2
    *On Revelation* 1–2, 5, 7–8, 10, 51, 56, 97–98
    *On the Seven Catholic Epistles* 2, 6
    *On the Song of Songs* 12–13, 62, 67
    *On the Tabernacle* 57, 66
    *On the Temple* 2, 43, 57, 60, 66
    *On Times* 3, 9, 47–48
    *On What Isaiah Says* 2
    *Retractations on the Acts of the Apostles* 67
Benedict Biscop 7, 15
Bethany 539–40, 646–47
Bethlehem 151–53, 156, 160, 162, 203, 233
Bethphage 539–40
Bethsaida 349, 375
Byrhtferth of Ramsey 73

Caiaphas (high priest) 188, 583, 603–04, 607

Cainan 4, 6, 9, 207–08
Calvary 618
Cana 268
Capernaum 230, 233, 247, 292, 366, 375–76
Cassiodorus 8n31
'Catholic(s), bad' 68, 367, 398, 539, 607
centurion (at the Crucifixion) 625–66
Ceolfrith (abbot of Wearmouth-Jarrow) 1, 5n21, 15
Chaldeans 288
Chinnereth 238
Chorazin 375
Christ Jesus
　ascension of 646
　baptism of 51–52, 106, 198–201, 211, 215
　Beatitudes 271–77
　birth of 3, 48, 105, 148–163, 349, 644
　as Bridegroom 194, 253, 341, 452, 454
　circumcision of 105, 163–66
　child(ren), teaching about 366, 518
　conception of 48, 129–36
　crucifixion *see* Passion
　entry into Jerusalem 112, 539–45
　Eucharist, institution of 588–89
　genealogy of 4, 6–9, 50, 101, 106, 203–11
　as Judge 254, 413, 533
　as King 101–03, 135, 149, 151, 205, 259, 533, 544, 550, 602, 621–22
　as Lamb 570, 582, 611–12
　Lord's Prayer 109, 387–89
　mission of 201
　name of 51, 132, 147, 166–67
　'not peace but division' 433–35
　Passion 14, 49, 113–14, 233, 367, 524–25, 545, 597–626
　as Passover 585
　Pharisees, interactions with 246–49, 251–55, 257–61, 307–15, 394–400, 405–13, 451–52

　as Physician 228–29, 233–35, 252, 279, 309–10, 338–39, 350, 364, 581
　poverty of 173, 369
　prayer of 353–54, 598–600
　Presentation in the Temple 171–82
　as Priest 56, 101, 103, 121–22, 135, 205, 259, 570, 620, 622
　as Prophet 229
　resurrection and post-resurrection appearances 114, 632, 634–47
　Sabbath, disputes about 107, 110, 233, 257–61, 441–43, 451–52
　Sadducees, dispute with 561–65
　as second Adam 256
　Sermon on the Mount (Luke's parallel version) 107, 269, 271–91
　as Shepherd 155, 161, 465, 612
　son of a smith (*faber*) 33–34, 227–29
　in the synagoge 106–07, 222–35, 259–61, 441
　as Teacher 68, 233, 295, 501, 519, 532, 545
　as Temple 61
　in the Temple 51, 112, 113, 171–86, 547–50, 581–82, 603
　temptation by the lawyer 380–85
　temptation in the wilderness 14, 106, 206, 211–18, 631
　tomb of 627–33
　transfiguration 26–27, 108, 265, 270, 358–63, 365
　tribute money 113, 150–51, 365, 560–61, 610
　trilingual inscription on Cross 622
　two natures of 53–55, 132, 134, 154, 184, 186, 199, 246, 249, 299, 326, 355, 400, 596, 599, 643
　as Victim 103
　as Wisdom/and wisdom 184–85, 187, 222, 411
　as Word 159

wounds of 641–42
see also miracles, parables 36–37, 106
Christian, name of 273
chronology 3–5, 9–10, 46–47
circumcision 164–71, 410, 587
  see also Christ, circumcision of
Cleophas 114, 267, 504, 635–36, 639
clothing, symbolism of 157, 194–95, 275, 301, 330, 334, 359, 375–76, 382, 473, 487, 621
Coldingham abbey 423n164
Colgrave, Bertram 71
column of the Flagellation 614
*computus* 47–49, 52, 550–51
conception *see* reproduction, human
concordance, exegesis by 29
contemplative life *see* active life
Cornelius, centurion 294–95, 502
cross 231–33, 614, 618–19
  as altar 61
Cuthbert (bishop of Lindisfarne) 5
Cyrene 616

Damasus (pope) 6, 8
Daniel (prophet) 145, 175, 201, 512, 623
Darby, Peter 3n12, 95n1
David (king) 113, 118, 120, 130, 132–33, 135–36, 145–46, 151–52, 161, 203, 207, 249, 257–58, 271–72, 277, 299, 338, 375, 387, 496, 500, 521, 538, 554–55, 565, 608
  Psalms of 304
Decalogue 51–52, 151, 201, 208
DeGregorio, Scott 68n165
Del Giacco, Eric Jay 40–42
demons and devils 69–71, 234–35, 237, 330–33
  nature of 122, 398–99
  *see also* Beelzebub, Satan
Deuteronomy 217, 223

Devil *see* Satan
disciples *see* apostles
Dommim 338
Durandus, William 632n316

eagle(s) 52–53, 315, 450, 513
eagle-stone 52–53, 315, 513
Easter controversy 62–63
Egypt 217
Eleazar 118, 135
Eli 593
Elijah 124–25, 206, 213, 229–30, 273–74, 334, 360–62, 368, 395
Elisha 229, 360
Elizabeth (mother of John the Baptist) 103, 105, 117, 119–20, 122, 126–29, 135–38, 141–42
Elkanah 627
Emmaus 114, 634
end times *see* eschaton
Enoch 145, 208
Ephrem 544
equinox(es) 48–49, 127, 130
eschaton, eschatology 242, 336, 426–32, 456n341, 571
  Last Judgement 190, 195–96, 225–26, 291, 359, 402–03, 413, 436, 492, 506, 515, 539, 558, 565, 579–80, 641
  signs of 65, 435, 576–81
  time of unknowable and unexpected 4, 10, 112, 431, 504–13
  *see also* millennium, World Ages
etymology 30–31, 35
eucharist 588–91, 638, 647
Eusebius (bishop of Caesarea) 3–4, 9, 20–22, 208n539
Evangelists 99–103, 257
  animal symbols 7–8, 56, 97–98, 100–03, 205, 620, 647
  differences and alternative readings among 8–9, 40, 198, 204–06, 208–11, 221, 235, 242, 246–47,

250, 252, 274, 292–93, 304, 327–28, 335–36, 345–47, 349, 358, 363–64, 366, 387–88, 450, 543, 584, 612, 615, 623, 625, 639
'harmony' of 39–40, 44, 100–02, 116, 205–06, 221
other evangelists supplement Luke's narrative 39–40, 182, 197, 255, 338, 348, 351, 365, 380, 394, 405–06, 411, 519–20, 541, 571, 577, 591, 600–02, 604, 609, 621, 626, 629, 630, 632, 633, 641, 645
see also Matthew, Mark, Luke, John the Evangelist
Eve 139
exorcism 69–71, 331–32, 396
Ezekiel 57, 61, 176, 203

feast, fast 251–53
finger-reckoning 50, 167, 296, 314, 321–22, 352–53, 524, 626
fishermen 239
flesh and spirit 640–41
Flood (in Genesis) 199, 507–08, 579–80
forgiveness 283–84, 416–18

Gabriel (angel) 125, 129–30, 137, 162
see also angel(s)
Galaad, Mount 329
Galileans 437–38, 606
Galilee 129, 182, 198, 233, 247, 297, 375, 543–44, 575, 610–11
sea of 52, 238, 269, 329, 375
gematria 51, 166, 438
Gennesaret, sea of see Galilee, sea of
Gentiles (see also Jews) 178, 188, 230–32, 238, 240, 269–70, 294, 320, 330, 332, 338, 351, 410, 529–30, 541–42, 545, 608, 625
Gerasa, Gerasenes 247, 329–30
Goffart, Walter 45
Goliath 338

grace
and nature 468
see also Law, contrasted with
Greek (terms, numbers) 51, 139–40, 174, 216, 238, 255, 263–64, 266, 387, 451, 487, 533, 537, 566, 634
Gregory the Great (pope) 7, 12–13, 22–25, 27, 32, 35, 37, 41–41, 43, 65, 96, 99

hair, symbolism of 573–74
Hart-Hasler, Joan 25–27
Haymo of Auxerre 73
Hebrew (language, names, terms) 52, 123, 131, 155, 238, 264–65
'Hebrew truth' see Vulgate
Hegesippus 267–68
hell 448, 490
Helvidius see heresy – Helvidian
heresy, heretics 61–63, 116, 133, 172–72, 227, 240, 326, 339–40, 367, 398–01, 411, 443, 449, 494, 500–01, 506, 524, 541, 571, 599–600, 607–08, 644
Apollinarian 62, 187
Arian 62–63, 124, 147, 186, 243, 249, 330, 378n414, 609
Cerinthian 62, 455, 522–23n210
Docetism 600n150
Ebionite 61, 255
Encratite 62
Eutychian 401, 640
Helvidian 62, 153, 324
Manichean 61–62, 124, 187, 243, 333, 406, 639
Marcionite 62
Nestorian 132, 135, 246
Novatian 62, 298
Pelagian 62, 340, 471
Photinian 124, 179, 243
Herod the Great 46, 103, 117, 119, 152, 158, 180, 182, 187, 233
Herod (tetrarch of Galilee) 106, 108,

110, 187, 197–98, 238, 265, 300, 348–49, 354, 450, 611–12, 623
Herodias 197
Hezekiah 288, 292
High-Priest *see* priests and priesthood, Jewish, *and names of individuals, e.g.,* Annas, Caiphas
Hilliard, Paul 8, 66
Hincmar (archbishop of Reims) 70–71
Hippocrates 54
Hiram of Tyre 569
Holder, Arthur G. 29, 62
Holy Spirit 199–200, 211–12, 393, 432–33, 645, 647
 blasphemy against 416–18
Hrabanus Maurus 73
Hur 270–72
Hwætberht ('Eusebius') 2, 5
hypocrisy *see* sin
Hyrcanus 119

intertextual exegesis 29–35
Iona 62
Isaac 47, 63, 165, 167, 296
Isaiah 145, 175, 623
Ishmael 63
Isidore (bishop of Seville) 52, 54–55
Issachar 268
Ithamar 118, 135

Jacob (patriarch) 122, 161
 'house of' 133
Jairus 336–37
James (apostle, 'the Just', son of Alphaeus) 259, 267–68
James (apostle, son of Zebedee) 265
Jechoniah 205, 210
Jeduthun 178
Jehoiakim 604n177
Jeremiah 123–24, 145, 201
Jericho 112, 382, 525–26, 528–29
Jerome 3–6, 8, 22–27, 44–45, 52, 61, 99, 116, 486

(ps.-) Jerome, *Expositio euangeliorum* 28
Jerusalem 14, 57, 61, 110, 112, 183–84, 216–17, 233, 304, 329, 332, 367, 382, 449–50, 504, 539–40, 556, 639, 644, 647
 destruction by Romans 113, 437, 450, 539, 545–47, 548–49, 559–60, 570–76, 617–18
 inhabitants of 438
Jews 63–66, 294, 320, 326, 351, 375, 403, 438, 438, 440, 447, 475–76, 525, 534, 554, 565, 598–99, 602, 607–09, 613, 615, 621–22, 635
 conflated with heretics 63–64, 400
 conversion of 66, 178, 335–36, 476n432, 538, 541, 575
 faults of 63–65, 107, 145, 147, 169, 189, 194, 198, 218, 228, 230–32, 234, 249, 255, 260, 270, 304–05, 312, 323–25, 330, 348, 401–02, 404, 439, 491–93, 501, 539, 556, 567
 and Gentiles complementary 57, 59, 65–67, 164n264, 239, 314, 315, 340, 442–43, 459, 468, 540, 557–58, 612–13, 626
 and Gentiles contrasted 65, 157, 178, 191–92, 251, 292, 310, 313, 314, 399, 517, 530–31, 532, 541, 626
 'supercession' by Gentiles 66, 191–92, 240–41, 325, 334–35, 393, 403, 448, 532, 553, 556
 *see also* circumcision, Law, synagogue
Joanna (wife of Chuza) 316–17, 633
Job 512
John Chrysostom 126–27
John the Baptist 105, 107, 111, 113, 132, 137, 141–148, 146–147, 188–89, 197–98, 221, 252–53, 299–304, 307, 348, 485–87, 552–53, 584

birth of 48, 57, 193, 349
death of 197–98
conception of 14, 48–49, 117–129
name 123, 142–43
preaching of 106, 189–97, 261, 479
John the Evangelist 46, 102–103, 198, 221–22, 265, 281, 351, 366, 377
Jonah 109, 402–04
Jonathan (wife of) 575
Jordan (river) 210–22, 238, 375, 597
Joseph of Arimathea 445n275, 521, 627, 630
Joseph (father of Jesus) 9, 130, 132, 153, 159, 179–80, 184–85, 201, 203–06, 227, 324
Joseph (patriarch) 203, 496
Josephus 5, 188, 572, 617
Joshua 168–69, 210, 270, 587–88
Josiah 122–23
Jotapata 617
jubilee 225
Judaea, (city of, land of) Judah 46, 153, 187–89, 233, 559, 572, 575, 606, 610–11, 617, 634
Judas Iscariot 241, 268, 278, 329, 378, 463, 494, 566, 584–85, 590–91, 594, 600–01
Jude (apostle, also known as Thaddeus) 268
Judgement, Last *see* eschatology
Julian of Eclano 92
Julius Caesar 560

Laistner, M.L.W. 7
Law 217, 234, 258–60, 324, 325, 337, 491, 519–20, 588, 598, 25
and Gospel 485, 569, 590
and Grace 168–69, 177, 198, 208, 223, 244–45, 251–52, 410
and prophets 224, 311, 360–61, 485–86, 524, 599, 611
summary of 381
*see also* Moses, Decalogue

Lazarus 272, 308, 540, 543
Lent 219
leprosy 231, 244
*see also* miracles
Levi *see* Matthew
Lindisfarne 7, 7n30
Lindisfarne Gospels 17
Lot 375, 507–08
Lot's wife 510
Lothar II (king of Lotharingia) 70–71
love 280–82
Luke (evangelist) 6, 44, 101–03
*Acts of the Apostles* 222
purpose in writing 61, 115–17
symbolized by calf/ox 56
Lysanias (tetrarch of Abilene) 187

Magi 102
Malchus 603
Manasseh 329
Manicheans *see* heresy
manna 587, 628
Marcellus Empiricus 53
Marcus Aurelius 634
Mark (evangelist) 101–03
Martha (sister of Lazarus) 109, 385–87
Mary of Cleophas/Mary wife of Alphaeus 267
Mary Magdalene 107, 109, 307–13, 316–17, 385–87, 393, 633
Mary (mother of James and Joseph) 633
Mary (mother of Jesus Christ) 34–35, 48, 54–55, 103, 142, 153–55, 159–60, 162, 179–80, 184–87, 203, 324, 400–01
annunciation to 48, 105, 129–36, 645
Magnificat 138–41
Purification of 105, 171–72
reader of Scripture 162
as Temple 61
virginity, perpetual 172–73
Visitation 57, 105, 136–42

Mary (sister of Lazarus and Martha)
  see Mary Magdalene
Matthew (evangelist) 64, 101–103, 107,
  205–07, 250–52, 264–66, 521
  see also Evangelists
Matthias (apostle) 116
Meyvaert, Paul 16–17
Midianites 314
millennium 402, 522–23
  see also eschaton
miracles 70, 345, 378
miracles of Jesus 36–39, 64, 222,
  228–29, 232, 245, 300, 343
  blind beggar of Jericho 112,
    525–28
  boy from evil spirit 108
  Canaanite woman's daughter 270
  centurion's slave 107, 269–70,
    292–96
  demoniac boy 363–64
  demoniac in the synagogue of
    Capernaum 234–35
  draught of fish 106, 197, 240–41, 329
  dropsical man 110, 451
  dumb demoniac 394
  feeding of the five thousand 108,
    351–53
  fig tree withered 497
  Gerasene/Gadarene demoniac 63,
    69, 108, 232, 329–36, 443
  Jairus' daughter 108, 336–44
  Lazarus, raising of 344
  leper(s) 106, 111, 242–45, 500–04
  man with withered hand 259–61
  mute man 109
  paralytic by the Sheep Gate 248
  paralytic let down through roof 106,
    246–50
  Peter's mother-in-law 106, 236
  stilling of the storm 108, 326–29
  widow of Nain's son 107, 297–99,
    344
  woman bent over 110, 441–43

woman with the issue of blood 108,
  293, 336–40, 645
moral interpretation of Scripture see
  tropology
Moses 61, 113, 161, 167–69, 175, 205,
  213, 223, 229, 259, 266, 270,
  277, 287, 336–37, 341, 360–62,
  429, 442, 488, 493, 554, 556,
  563–64, 587–88, 590, 604, 607,
  636
mountain (symbolism of)
  and plain 270–71, 277, 363–64

Naaman the Syrian 106, 229, 231
Naboth the Jezreelite 555
Nain 297
Naphtali 569
Nathan 207
Nathanael 266
Nazarenes 123–24
Nazareth 64, 153, 182, 186, 222, 233
Nazarites 573
Ninevites 402–03
Noah 296, 507–08, 512
  ark 434
  sons of 63, 336
  see also Flood
number symbolism 25, 49
  one 503
  two 351, 371, 434, 540
  three 50, 57–58, 201–02, 209, 263,
    359, 371, 434, 441, 445–46
  four 50, 206, 209, 247, 263, 274, 354
  five 58, 129, 202, 314, 351–52, 457,
    493, 535
  six 129, 210, 358, 441, 624
  seven 50–51, 118, 181, 184, 208–10,
    352, 358, 400, 495, 634, 646
  eight 51, 118, 143–44, 165–67,
    181–82, 274, 358, 646
  ten 51, 58, 166, 201, 206, 314,
    318–19, 467, 503, 535–36
  eleven 50, 209

## GENERAL INDEX

twelve 50, 58, 184, 211, 263, 353
thirty 50–51, 201, 203, 211, 321–22, 445–46
forty 205–06
forty-two 50, 210–12
fifty 352–53
sixty 321–22, 446, 634
seventy 208
seventy-two 371
seventy-seven 50, 208–09
eighty-four 50–51, 181
one hundred 166–67, 296, 314, 318–19, 321–22, 352–53, 446, 465, 533, 626
three thousand 202

O'Brien, Conor 41, 56–57, 59, 66
Olivet (Olives), mount of 539–40, 543, 581–82, 597–98, 646
Origen 5, 27–28, 58–59
original sin 164, 408n80, 432
*see also* sin
Othlo of St Emmeram 72

parables of Jesus 319
  blind leading the blind 284–85
  bridegroom 107
  building a tower 111, 461–64
  camel and eye of needle 521–22, 528
  candle 108
  debtors 65, 107, 309–10, 313–15
  fig tree 65, 110, 438–41, 443, 578–79
  garment 107, 254
  good Samaritan 109, 381–85
  guests invited to a feast 111, 218, 452–54, 454–60, 469
  houses built on sand and rock 107, 289–91
  importunate friend 109, 389–90
  king going to war 110, 462–63
  knocking on the locked door 446–48
  labourers in the vineyard 379, 553
  lamp 404–05

leaven 110
lost coin 111, 466–67
lost sheep 111, 162, 383, 465
mote and beam 107, 285–86
mustard seed 111, 444–45, 497, 516
old wine in new bottles 107, 254–55
Pharisee and tax collector 112, 515–18
prodigal son 111, 382, 468–78
rich man 110, 419–20
rich man and Lazarus 111, 275–76, 486–93
servant returning from the field 498–99
servants waiting for their lord 426–27
sower 108, 196–97, 317–22, 325
stewards, faithful and unfaithful 429–32
strong man 397
talents 68, 112, 533–39
trees good and evil 107, 286–88
unjust judge 112, 480, 513–15
unjust steward 14, 111, 480–93
vineyard 61
vineyard, tenants in 113, 553–58
wise and foolish virgins 481, 577
yeast 445–46
Parasceve, day of 628–30, 632
Passover 49, 585–90
  timing of 121, 550–51
  Unleavened Bread, feast of 49, 582–82
Paul (apostle) 175, 241, 255, 278, 329, 351, 375, 377, 531, 592
Paul the Deacon 73–74
Pentecost 329
persecution 357
Persian language 566
Peter, Simon (apostle) 106, 108, 113–14, 208, 239–42, 256, 263–64, 278, 299, 329, 334, 350–51, 354–55, 358–62, 369, 410, 428, 432, 502, 522, 560,

594–96, 601–02, 604–07, 610, 633–34, 636, 638
Phanuel 181–82
Pharaoh 260
Pharisees 65, 107, 109, 111, 128–29, 158, 287, 303–04, 341, 378, 449, 479, 483–85, 487, 545, 559
Phineas 601
Philip (apostle) 266, 350
Philip (tetrarch of Ituraea) 187
Philistines 338
pigeon, symbolism of 174–75
Pilate, Pontius 110, 187, 437, 450, 609–15, 623, 627
plain *see* mountain
Pliny the Elder 52–53
prayer 262, 387–93, 513–15
preachers and preaching *see rectores*
priests and priesthood 258, 302, 481, 549–50, 648
   Christian 69–70, 126, 159, 201, 371
   Jewish 65, 118–122, 126, 128–29, 143–44, 244–45, 382, 501–02
   Jewish priests opposed to Christ 158, 550–53, 558–61, 583, 603, 611–12
Primasius (bishop of Hadrumentum) 51, 161n243
prophets and prophecy 145, 224, 230, 274, 277, 302, 304, 311, 380, 410–11, 524, 555, 636
   false prophets 273–74, 276–77, 287
   *see also* Law and prophets
purgatory, purgatorial fire 195, 447n288

Queen of Sheba 109, 402–03
Quirinius 46, 149–50

Ray, Roger 45
readers, reading 223–24, 226, 324

*rectores* ('rulers', i.e. teacher, preachers, 'doctors', pastors) 42, 67–68, 163, 201, 226, 234, 239, 247, 255, 372–74, 429–30, 492, 498–99, 511, 534–38, 541, 592–93, 645–46
reform 67–68
reproduction, human 53–55
resurrection 113, 561–64
   arguments against deniers 415
riches *see* wealth
robbers crucified with Christ 114, 619–20, 622–24
Roman Empire, Romans, Rome 46, 188, 329, 437, 439–40, 450, 545–47, 559–60, 564, 575, 609, 611, 617
   peace of Roman Empire 148–49
roofs 413–14

Sabbath 107, 118, 234, 255–56, 628–30
   *see also* Christ – Sabbath, disputes over
Sadducees 113, 561–64
Samaria, Samaritans 146, 311, 367, 502, 571, 575
Samson 123–24
Samuel 119, 271, 277, 369, 395, 574, 627
Saracens 63
Sarah (wife of Abraham) 163, 272, 445
Satan 212–17, 232, 235, 237, 326, 377, 396–98, 584, 594–95
Saul (king) 272, 538
Sceva, sons of 378
Scheil, Andrew 66
scribes 565–66
   *see also* Pharisees, priests – Jewish
   Jewish
Scripture 160, 217, 247–48, 259, 448, 636, 644

usages and expressions in 259–60, 288, 422, 489, 542, 640–61
Septuagint translation ('Seventy Translators') of Old Testament 3–5, 9, 207–08
Shechemites 170–71
shepherds witnesses of Nativity 105, 155–163
Sidon 375–76
Siloam 228, 438
Simeon 106, 176–81
Simon of Cyrene 615–16
Simon Magus 199, 369, 506, 571
Simon the Pharisee 307–15
Simon Zelotes (apostle) 267–68
sin 278
  avarice 219, 419, 451–52, 483–84, 487
  curiosity 219
  hypocrisy 406–07, 412–13, 442
  unforgivable 416–18
  vainglory 219, 409, 423, 565
  see also original sin
slavery 280
Smaragdus of St Mihiel 73
smith (*faber*) 33–34
Sodom 374–75, 508–09
soldiers 193–94
Solomon 15, 118, 145, 207, 263, 276, 375, 403, 483–84, 520, 547, 569
solstice(s) 48, 130
Stancliffe, Clare 3n9, 7
Stephen (protomartyr) 169, 277–78
Susanna 316–17
synagogue 293
  compared to/contrasted with Church 434–35
  meaning of 'synagogue' 223
  symbol of Jews 65, 304, 322, 336–38, 340–41
  see also Christ in synagogue
Syriac (names, terms etc.) 131, 264, 266, 342

tabernacle 361–62
Tabernacle, Mosaic 61, 203, 352, 556
Tabernacles, feast of 123–24, 543
Tabor, Mount 297
tax collector(s) 193, 251
teachers and teaching see *rectores*
Temple at Jerusalem 14–15, 46, 56–61, 66, 106, 113, 119, 121–22, 128, 176–77, 183, 203, 216, 245, 258–59, 413–14, 569–70, 625, 647, 647
  Ark of the Covenant 625
  bronze 'sea' 57–58, 60, 202–03, 263, 570
  destruction of 113, 437, 559–60, 570–74
  Holy of Holies 121, 268, 352
Thacker, Alan 62–63, 67n164
Theophilus 105, 115, 117
Theutberga (queen of Lotharingia) 70–71
Thomas (apostle) 116, 265–67, 639
Tiberias, sea of see Galilee, sea of
Tiberius (emperor) 106, 187, 238, 560
Titus (emperor) 545
'Tower of the Flock' 155–56
Trinity 200
tropology, 'laws of tropology' 35, 236, 254, 405
typology 34
Tyre 375–76

Unleavened Bread, feast of see Passover

Vespasian (emperor) 545
*Vetus latina* translation of Bible 15
Vindicianus Afer 55
virgins and virginity 131, 148
Vulgate translation of Bible 3–4, 6, 9–10, 15, 207–08

wealth 111–12, 275–76, 319–20, 424–25, 482–84, 520–22, 528
  *see also* sin – avarice
widow of Zarephath 106, 229–31, 334
widow's mite 113, 567
Wilfred (bishop) 3, 5, 7
wisdom 147, 305–06, 372, 378–79, 403
  *see also* Christ as Wisdom
woman, women (as symbol, characteristics of) 54–55, 69–71, 141, 203, 236, 316, 400–01, 511, 605, 631, 633
  with alabaster jar *see* Mary Magdalene
  of Jerusalem 616–17
  ministering to Christ and disciples 108, 316–17, 617, 629, 632
  'mother Church' 297–98
  Valiant Woman (of Proverbs) 144
  witnesses of resurrection 114, 630–33, 636
World Ages 3–4, 129, 165, 260, 316, 358, 442, 562
  Second Age 9, 207–08
  Sixth Age 628
  Seventh Age 260, 628–29, 646
  Eighth Age 628, 646

Zacchaeus 112, 481, 483, 521, 528–32
Zechariah (father of John the Baptist) 103, 105, 117–29, 142–48, 647
Zechariah (prophet) 412
Zedekiah 604

Printed in the USA
CPSIA information can be obtained
at www.ICGtesting.com
CBHW052143220424
7385CB00003B/65